THE NEW MAKERS OF
MODERN STRATEGY

THE NEW MAKERS OF MODERN STRATEGY

FROM THE ANCIENT WORLD
TO THE DIGITAL AGE

EDITED BY HAL BRANDS

PRINCETON UNIVERSITY PRESS

PRINCETON AND OXFORD

Copyright © 2023 by Princeton University Press

Princeton University Press is committed to the protection of copyright and the intellectual property our authors entrust to us. Copyright promotes the progress and integrity of knowledge. Thank you for supporting free speech and the global exchange of ideas by purchasing an authorized edition of this book. If you wish to reproduce or distribute any part of it in any form, please obtain permission.

Requests for permission to reproduce material from this work should be sent to permissions@press.princeton.edu

Published by Princeton University Press
41 William Street, Princeton, New Jersey 08540
99 Banbury Road, Oxford OX2 6JX

press.princeton.edu

All Rights Reserved

ISBN 9780691204383
ISBN (e-book) 9780691226729

British Library Cataloging-in-Publication Data is available

Editorial: Eric Crahan and Barbara Shi
Production Editorial: Karen Carter
Text and Jacket/Cover Design: Karl Spurzem
Production: Danielle Amatucci
Publicity: Kate Farquhar-Thomson and Kate Hensley
Copyeditor: Michelle Garceau Hawkins

This book has been composed in Arno Pro

Printed on acid-free paper. ∞

Printed in the United States of America

10 9 8 7 6 5 4 3

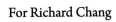

For Richard Chang

CONTENTS

ACKNOWLEDGMENTS

The heroes of this volume are the contributors, who put aside important projects to focus on this one, and then put up with the editor's incessant hectoring along the way. Second only to the contributors themselves are the countless authors whose scholarship has created the intellectual foundation on which this volume rests.

I am grateful also to a number of individuals whose advice and counsel more directly informed the project at various stages of its development: Lawrence Freedman, Michael Horowitz, Will Inboden, Andrew May, Aaron MacLean, Thomas Mahnken, Sally Payne, Erin Simpson, and Hew Strachan, among others. Eliot Cohen deserves a special thanks: he helped conceive this project before other obligations pulled him away from it. Eric Crahan at Princeton University Press first proposed a third edition of *Makers* and then saw it through to completion, aided by many others at the press. Several research assistants, namely Lucy Bales, Steven Honig, Jacob Paikin, and Jurek Wille helped prepare and format the chapters, as part of a process that Nathaniel Wong oversaw. Chris Crosbie lent invaluable support, as well.

I owe a special debt to a few key institutions. The Johns Hopkins School for Advanced International Studies and the American Enterprise Institute both provided a wonderful intellectual climate. The America in the World Consortium provided valuable financial support. Most importantly, this project simply would not have been possible without the Henry Kissinger Center for Global Affairs and its director, Frank Gavin. Frank helped formulate this project from the beginning; he and the Kissinger Center staff helped sustain the endeavor in ways too many to count. Under his leadership, the Kissinger Center has become a unique place, one that is committed to the same values that inform this volume, and one that will surely produce pathbreaking work on history and strategy for many years to come.

CONTRIBUTORS

DMITRY ADAMSKY

Dmitry (Dima) Adamsky is a Professor at the School of Government, Diplomacy, and Strategy at Reichman University, Israel. He is the author of *The Culture of Military Innovation* and of *Russian Nuclear Orthodoxy*.

JOHN BEW

John Bew is Professor of History and Foreign Policy at the War Studies Department at King's College London. He became the Prime Minister's Foreign Policy Advisor in 2019. Bew is the author of five books, the former Kissinger Chair at the Library of Congress, and a winner of the Orwell Prize as well as the Philip Leverhulme Award.

TAMI DAVIS BIDDLE

Tami Davis Biddle retired from the US Army War College as the Elihu Root Chair of Military Studies. She is the author of *Rhetoric and Reality in Air Warfare*, as well as many articles about the Second World War. She is currently writing *Taking Command: The United States at War, 1941–1945*.

HAL BRANDS

Hal Brands is the Henry Kissinger Distinguished Professor of Global Affairs at Johns Hopkins University's School of Advanced International Studies and a senior fellow at the American Enterprise Institute.

ANTULIO J. ECHEVARRIA II

Professor Antulio J. Echevarria II, US Army War College, holds a doctorate from Princeton University and has published extensively on strategic thinking, including *War's Logic: Strategic Thought and the American Way of War* (Cambridge 2021).

ELIZABETH ECONOMY

Elizabeth Economy is a Senior Fellow at the Hoover Institution, Stanford University. She is currently on leave to serve as Senior Advisor for China at the Commerce Department. Her most recent book is *The World According to China* (Polity 2021).

CHARLES EDEL

Charles Edel is the Australia Chair and a Senior Adviser at the Center for Strategic and International Studies. Previously, Dr. Edel served on the US Secretary of State's Policy Planning Staff. He is the author of *Nation Builder: John Quincy Adams and the Grand Strategy of the Republic*.

ERIC S. EDELMAN

Eric S. Edelman is Counselor at the Center for Strategic and Budgetary Assessments and a Distinguished Practitioner-in-Residence at Johns Hopkins University's School of Advanced International Studies.

ANDREW EHRHARDT

Andrew Ehrhardt is a post-doctoral fellow at the Henry Kissinger Center for Global Affairs at the Johns Hopkins University School of Advanced International Studies.

LAWRENCE FREEDMAN

Lawrence Freedman is Emeritus Professor of War Studies, King's College London. He was appointed Official Historian of the Falklands Campaign in 1997 and served as a member of the official inquiry into Britain and the 2003 Iraq War. He has written on international history, strategic theory, and nuclear weapons issues.

JOHN LEWIS GADDIS

John Lewis Gaddis is Robert A. Lovett Professor of Military and Naval History at Yale University, where he currently teaches courses on grand strategy, biography, and historical methods. His most recent books are *George F. Kennan: An American Life* (2011) and *On Grand Strategy* (2018).

FRANCIS J. GAVIN

Francis J. Gavin is the director of the Henry A. Kissinger Center for Global Affairs at the School of Advanced International Studies–The Johns

Hopkins University. His writings include *Gold, Dollars, and Power; Nuclear Statecraft: History and Strategy in America's Atomic Age;* and *Nuclear Weapons and American Grand Strategy,* a Choice 2020 Outstanding Academic Title.

CHRISTOPHER J. GRIFFIN

Christopher J. Griffin is a senior program officer at the Smith Richardson Foundation. He previously served as executive director of the Foreign Policy Initiative and on the staff of Senator Joseph I. Lieberman. Griffin is a graduate of Austin College and The Johns Hopkins University School of Advanced International Studies.

AHMED S. HASHIM

Ahmed S. Hashim is Associate Professor of Strategic Studies at Deakin University, School of Humanities and Social Sciences at the Australian Defence College. He specializes in military history and strategic studies with a focus on insurgency and counterinsurgency, conventional wars in the Global South, and Asian defense issues.

ERIC HELLEINER

Eric Helleiner is a Professor in the Department of Political Science at the University of Waterloo. His books include *The Neomercantilists: A Global Intellectual History* and *States and the Reemergence of Global Finance.*

WAYNE WEI-SIANG HSIEH

Wayne Wei-siang Hsieh is an Associate Professor of History at the US Naval Academy. He is the author of *West Pointers and the Civil War: The Old Army in War and Peace* and co-author of *A Savage War: A Military History of the Civil War.*

SETH G. JONES

Seth G. Jones is senior vice president and Harold Brown Chair at the Center for Strategic and International Studies. He is the author of *Three Dangerous Men: Russia, Iran, China, and the Rise of Irregular Warfare* and other books. He received his Ph.D. from the University of Chicago.

ROBERT KAGAN

Robert Kagan is a senior fellow at the Brookings Institution. He served in the Department of State and is the author of numerous books and essays on foreign policy and world affairs. He is currently at work on the *Dangerous Nation Trilogy*, a three-volume history of American foreign policy.

JONATHAN KIRSHNER

Jonathan Kirshner is Professor of Political Science and International Studies at Boston College. His books include *An Unwritten Future: Realism and Uncertainty in World Politics* and *American Power after the Financial Crisis.*

MATTHEW KROENIG

Matthew Kroenig is a professor of government at Georgetown University and the Director of the Atlantic Council's Scowcroft Strategy Initiative. He is fluent in Italian and has taught an annual course on Machiavelli in Florence, Italy, since 2013. His latest book is *The Return of Great Power Rivalry.*

JAMES LACEY

Dr. James Lacey is the Mathew C. Horner Chair of War studies at Marine Corps University and a professor of Strategic Studies at the Marine Corps War College. He is the author of *The Washington War, Gods of War,* and *Rome: A Strategy for Empire.*

GUY LARON

Guy Laron is senior lecturer in international relations, the Hebrew University of Jerusalem, and has been a visiting scholar at the University of Maryland, Northwestern University, and the University of Oxford. He is the author of *Origins of the Suez Crisis* and *The Six Day War.*

MICHAEL V. LEGGIERE

Dr. Michael V. Leggiere is Professor of History and Deputy Director of the Military History Center at the University of North Texas. He is the author of several award-winning works on Napoleon's military campaigns.

MARGARET MACMILLAN

Margaret MacMillan is professor of History at the University of Toronto and emeritus professor of International History at Oxford University. She specializes in the international history of the nineteenth and twentieth centuries and her publications include *The War That Ended Peace: The Road to 1914* and *War: How Conflict Shaped Us.*

TANVI MADAN

Tanvi Madan is a senior fellow and directs the India Project at the Brookings Institution. She is the author of *Fateful Triangle: How China Shaped US-India Relations during the Cold War* (2020).

THOMAS G. MAHNKEN

Thomas G. Mahnken is a Senior Research Professor at the Philip Merrill Center for Strategic Studies at The Johns Hopkins University School of Advanced International Studies and President and Chief Executive Officer of the Center for Strategic and Budgetary Assessments. He previously taught strategy at the US Naval War College.

CARTER MALKASIAN

Dr. Carter Malkasian is the author of *The American War in Afghanistan: A History*. Other books include *War Comes to Garmser: Thirty Years of Conflict on the Afghan Frontier* and *Illusions of Victory: The Anbar Awakening and the Islamic State*. He is a professor at the Naval Postgraduate School.

DANIEL MARSTON

Daniel Marston is a historian and award-winning author focusing on war and society from the eighteenth to the twenty-first centuries. He is currently Director of the Strategic Thinkers Program at The Johns Hopkins School of Advanced International Studies.

JOHN H. MAURER

John H. Maurer is the Alfred Thayer Mahan Distinguished Professor of Sea Power and Grand Strategy and served as Chairman of the Strategy and Policy Department at the Naval War College.

WALTER RUSSELL MEAD

Walter Russell Mead is the Ravenel B. Curry III Distinguished Fellow in Strategy and Statesmanship at Hudson Institute, the Global View Columnist at the *Wall Street Journal*, and the James Clarke Chace Professor of Foreign Affairs and Humanities at Bard College in New York.

MICHAEL COTEY MORGAN

Michael Cotey Morgan is associate professor of history at the University of North Carolina at Chapel Hill, and author of *The Final Act: The Helsinki Accords and the Transformation of the Cold War.*

MARK MOYAR

Mark Moyar holds the William P. Harris Chair in Military History at Hillsdale College. He is the author of seven books, most recently, *Triumph Regained: The Vietnam War, 1965–1968*, and he is currently writing the final volume of a Vietnam War trilogy. He received a B.A. *summa cum laude* from Harvard University and a Ph.D. from the University of Cambridge.

WILLIAMSON MURRAY

Williamson Murray received his BA and PhD in history from Yale University. He served five years in the United States Air Force. He has written and edited numerous books and is currently professor emeritus at the Ohio State University and the Marshall Professor at Marine Corps University.

S.C.M. PAINE

S.C.M. Paine, the William S. Sims University Professor of History and Grand Strategy, Strategy & Policy Department, US Naval War College, has published *Wars for Asia, 1911–1949, Japanese Empire*, and, with Bruce A. Elleman, *Modern China: Continuity and Change 1644 to the Present*, as well as co-editing five books on naval operations.

SERGEY RADCHENKO

Sergey Radchenko is a historian of the Cold War and the Wilson E. Schmidt Distinguished Professor at The Johns Hopkins School of Advanced International Studies.

ISKANDER REHMAN

Iskander Rehman is the Senior Fellow for Strategic Studies at the American Foreign Policy Council, in Washington, DC, where he leads a research effort on applied history and grand strategy. He holds a PhD from the Institute of Political Studies (Sciences Po), in Paris.

THOMAS RID

Thomas Rid is Professor of Strategic Studies at The Johns Hopkins School of Advanced International Studies. He is best known for his work on the history and risks of information technology in conflict. Rid is the author of *Active Measures, Rise of the Machines, Cyber Will Not Take Place,* and other works.

JOSHUA ROVNER

Joshua Rovner is an associate professor at American University, where he teaches and writes on intelligence and strategy. Rovner is also managing editor of H-Diplo's *International Security Studies Forum,* and deputy editor of the *Journal of Strategic Studies.*

PRIYA SATIA

Priya Satia is the Raymond A. Spruance Professor of International History at Stanford University and the award-winning author of *Spies in Arabia: The Great War and the Cultural Foundations of Britain's Covert Empire in the Middle East; Empire of Guns: The Violent Making of the Industrial Revolution;* and *Time's Monster: How History Makes History.*

KORI SCHAKE

Kori Schake leads the foreign and defense policy studies team at the American Enterprise Institute. She is the author of *Safe Passage: The Transition from British to American Hegemony* and has worked in the National Security Council, State Department, and Department of Defense.

MATT J. SCHUMANN

Matt J. Schumann (Ph.D., University of Exeter, 2005) teaches at Eastern Michigan University and Bowling Green State University. He has published on the trans-Atlantic Seven Years' War and both continental and Atlantic dimensions of the Anglo-French strategic rivalry. He is currently pursuing a global history of the 1748 Peace of Aix-la-Chapelle.

BRENDAN SIMMS

Brendan Simms is Professor of the History of European International Relations and Director of the Forum on Geopolitics at the University of Cambridge. His publications include *Europe, the Struggle for Supremacy, 1453 to the Present Day, Britain's Europe: A Thousand Years of Conflict and Cooperation,* and *Hitler: Only the World was Enough.*

JASON K. STEARNS

Jason K. Stearns is Assistant Professor of International Studies at Simon Fraser University and is director of the Congo Research Group at New York University. He is author of *The War That Does Not Say Its Name: The Unending Conflict in the Congo.*

HEW STRACHAN

Sir Hew Strachan is the Wardlaw Professor of International Relations at the University of St. Andrews and an Emeritus Fellow of All Souls College, Oxford, where he was the Chichele Professor of the History of War, 2002–15. His books include *The First World War, Clausewitz's On War,* and *The Direction of War.*

SUE MI TERRY

Sue Mi Terry is the Director of the Wilson Center's Hyundai Motor-Korea Foundation Center for Korean History and Public Policy. A former CIA analyst, she served on the National Intelligence Council in 2009–10 and the National Security Council in 2008–9.

TOSHI YOSHIHARA

Toshi Yoshihara is a Senior Fellow at the Center for Strategic and Budgetary Assessments. He was previously the John A. van Beuren Chair of Asia-Pacific Studies at the US Naval War College. He is co-author of *Red Star over the Pacific: China's Rise and the Challenge to U.S. Maritime Strategy.*

THE NEW MAKERS OF
MODERN STRATEGY

Introduction

THE INDISPENSABLE ART: THREE GENERATIONS OF *MAKERS OF MODERN STRATEGY*

Hal Brands

There's no substitute for strategy. Strategy is what allows us to act with purpose in a disordered world; it is vital to out-thinking and out-playing our foes. Without strategy, action is random and devoid of direction; power and advantage are squandered rather than deployed to good effect. The mightiest empires may survive for a while if they lack good strategy, but no one can thrive for long without it.

Strategy is very complex, and strategy is also very simple. The concept of strategy—what it is, what it encompasses, how it is best pursued—is subject to unending debate, confusion, and redefinition. Even the most talented leaders have struggled to conquer strategy's dilemmas. Yet the essence of strategy is straightforward: it is the craft of summoning and using power to achieve our central purposes, amid the friction of global affairs and the resistance of rivals and enemies. Strategy is the indispensable art of getting what we want, with what we have, in a world that seems set on denying us.

In this sense, strategy is intimately related to the use of force, because the specter of violence hangs over any contested relationship. If the world was harmonious and everyone could achieve their dreams, there would be no need for a discipline focused on mastering competitive interactions. Indeed, this book was completed as Russia's invasion of Ukraine gave Europe its largest interstate land war since World War II, thereby reminding all of us—tragically—that hard power has hardly gone out of style. Yet strategy encompasses the use of *all* forms of power to prosper in an unruly world. It is, in fact, a fundamentally optimistic endeavor, premised on the idea that coercive means can serve constructive ends, that leaders can impose control on events rather than being dominated by them.[1]

Strategy, then, is timeless, but our understanding of it is not. The basic challenges of strategy would have been familiar to Thucydides, Machiavelli, or Clausewitz, which is why their works are still required reading today. The field of strategic studies is rooted in the belief that there is a basic logic of strategy that transcends time and space. But the basic meaning of the term "strategy" has never been fixed, and we forever reinterpret even the most enduring texts through the lens of our own preoccupations. If strategy seems to be such an elusive, protean creature, it's because every era teaches us something about the concept and the requirements of doing it well.

It is essential to renew our understanding of strategy today. Serious people can no longer believe, as was sometimes argued a generation ago, that war—and perhaps strategy itself—have become passé in an era of post-Cold War peace. Fierce competition, punctuated by the threat of catastrophic conflict, is the grim reality of our time. The democratic world faces sharper challenges to its geopolitical supremacy and basic security than at any point in decades. Strategy is most valuable when the stakes are high and the consequences of failure are severe. This means that the premium on good strategy, and on the deep understanding of the history that informs it, is becoming high indeed.

I

"When war comes, it dominates our lives," wrote Edward Mead Earle in his introduction to the first edition of *Makers of Modern Strategy*.[2] That volume was conceived during some of the worst moments of history's worst war; it was

---

1. There is a robust literature on the meaning and nature of strategy. As examples, see Lawrence Freedman, *Strategy: A History* (New York, NY: Oxford University Press, 2014); Hal Brands, *What Good is Grand Strategy? Power and Purpose in American Statecraft from Harry S. Truman to George W. Bush* (Ithaca, NY: Cornell University Press, 2014); John Lewis Gaddis, *On Grand Strategy* (New York, NY: Penguin, 2018); Paul Kennedy, *Grand Strategies in War and Peace* (New Haven, CT: Yale University Press, 1992); Edward Luttwak, *Strategy: The Logic of War and Peace* (Cambridge, MA: Harvard University Press, 2002); Hew Strachan, *The Direction of War: Contemporary Strategy in Historical Perspective* (New York, NY: Cambridge University Press, 2013); Beatrice Heuser, *The Evolution of Strategy: Thinking War from Antiquity to the Present* (Cambridge: Cambridge University Press, 2012).

2. Edward Mead Earle, "Introduction," in *Makers of Modern Strategy: Military Thought from Machiavelli to Hitler*, Earle, ed. (Princeton, NJ: Princeton University Press, 1943 [republished New York, NY: Atheneum, 1966]), vii.

published in 1943, as that conflict raged across oceans and continents. This setting lent the book extraordinary urgency by underscoring that the study of strategy had become, for the world's few remaining democracies, a matter of life and death.

The contributors, a collection of American and European scholars, sought to promote a better understanding of strategy by tracing the evolution of military thought through key individuals from Machiavelli to Hitler.[3] Yet the volume emphasized another reality made inescapable by World War II—that a country's fate depended on far more than its excellence in combat. "In the present-day world," Earle wrote, "strategy is the art of controlling and utilizing the resources of a nation—or a coalition of nations—including its armed forces, to the end that its vital interests shall be effectively promoted and secured against enemies, actual, potential, or merely presumed."[4] It was a discipline that involved multiple dimensions of statecraft and operated in peace as well as war.

Makers of Modern Strategy drove home the point, made during the interwar period by British thinkers such as J.F.C. Fuller and Basil Liddell Hart, that strategy was not simply the preserve of great military commanders. It was the province, also, of economists, revolutionaries, politicians, historians, and all the concerned citizens of democracies.[5] The book showed how an immersion in history could produce a richer, more rigorous engagement with the intricacies of strategy and the dynamics of war and peace. The first *Makers* thereby helped establish strategic studies as a modern academic field, one that used the past as a primary source of insight on present problems.

If strategic studies was a child of hot war, it matured during the Cold War. The United States became a superpower, with vast intellectual needs to match its sprawling global commitments. The nuclear revolution raised fundamental questions about the purpose of war and the relationship between force and diplomacy. A new generation of scholars studied and, in many cases, revised the body of historical knowledge upon which the discipline drew. Scholars and statesmen reinterpreted old works, such as the writings of Carl von Clausewitz, through the prism of Cold War challenges.[6]

---

3. Many of the Europeans were refugees from Hitler's Germany. See Anson Rabinach, "The Making of *Makers of Modern Strategy*: German Refugee Historians Go to War," *Princeton University Library Chronicle* 75:1 (2013): 97–108.

4. Earle, "Introduction," viii.

5. See Lawrence Freedman's essay "Strategy: The History of an Idea," Chapter 1 in this volume; also, Brands, *What Good is Grand Strategy?*

6. See Hew Strachan's essay "The Elusive Meaning and Enduring Relevance of Clausewitz," Chapter 5 in this volume; also, Michael Desch, *Cult of the Irrelevant: The Waning Influence of*

This was the context that eventually led, after more than one false start, to a second edition of *Makers of Modern Strategy* in 1986.[7] That volume, edited by Peter Paret with the assistance of Gordon Craig and Felix Gilbert, dipped into issues, such as nuclear strategy and violent insurgency, that had come to the forefront of Cold War politics.[8] It considered World War I and World War II as part of a discrete historical era rather than more-or-less current events. The second edition paid increased attention to the historical development of American strategy, while also bringing the interpretation of key issues and individuals up to date. Yet interestingly, the Paret volume took a somewhat narrower view of strategy, defining it as "the development, intellectual mastery, and utilization of all of the state's resources for the purpose of implementing its policy *in war*."[9] The overall thrust of the book was that the incalculably high stakes of modern war made an understanding of military strategy essential.

Both volumes were—and remain—classics, which can still be read profitably for the insights of individual essays as well as the window they provide into the evolution of strategic analysis in the Western world. Both were models of how to employ academic knowledge for the purpose of educating democratic publics so that they could better defend their interests and values. But both volumes have aged, unavoidably, since publication, and so both remind us that the state of the art does shift over time.

II

Since 1986, the world has changed dramatically. The Cold War ended and America won a degree of primacy unrivaled in modern history, only to face problems old and new. Nuclear proliferation, terrorism and insurgency, gray-zone conflict and irregular warfare, and cybersecurity all joined—or re-joined—a growing list of strategic concerns. New technologies and modes of warfare challenged accepted patterns of strategy and conflict. For a time,

---

Social Science on National Security (Princeton, NJ: Princeton University Press, 1943); Fred Kaplan, *The Wizards of Armageddon* (Stanford, CA: Stanford University Press, 1991).

7. On the evolution of the franchise, see Michael Finch, *Making Makers: The Past, The Present, and the Study of War* (New York, NY: Cambridge University Press, forthcoming 2023).

8. Perhaps because the Cold War still qualified as "current events" in 1986, the book contained only three substantive essays, along with a brief conclusion, that considered strategy in the post-1945 era.

9. Peter Paret, "Introduction," in *Makers of Modern Strategy: From Machiavelli to the Nuclear Age*, Paret, ed. (Princeton, NJ: Princeton University Press, 1986), 3, emphasis added.

America enjoyed a respite from great-power geopolitical competition. But that holiday is now unmistakably over, as China challenges for hegemony, Russia seeks dramatic revisions to the European balance, and an array of revisionist actors test Washington and the international order it leads.

Today, the global status quo is sharply and unceasingly contested; the prospect of war between nuclear-armed states is frighteningly real. There is no guarantee that the democracies will prevail, geopolitically or ideologically, in the twenty-first century as they eventually did in the twentieth. After a period of unprecedented dominance that cushioned the effects of strategic lassitude, America and its allies find themselves in an era that will demand strategic discipline and insight.

As the future has grown foreboding, our understanding of the past has changed. In the last forty years, scholarship on international politics, war, and peace has become increasingly internationalized, with the opening of new archives and the incorporation of new viewpoints. Scholars have brought fresh insights to the study of seemingly familiar subjects, from the meaning of classic texts to the causes and course of the world wars and the Cold War.[10] It may be a challenging time to do strategy, but it is also a good time to update our understanding of it.

There is, first, the question of who and what counts as a "maker." Theorists and practitioners of war remain fundamentally important. Many of the great men of strategy whose ideas and exploits filled earlier volumes—Machiavelli and Clausewitz, Napoleon and Jomini, Hamilton and Mahan, Hitler and Churchill—reappear in this one.[11] Individual makers still receive top billing, because it is people who formulate and execute strategy, and it is through their ideas and experiences that we can best comprehend the unrelenting demands of those tasks.

Yet individuals do not make strategy in a vacuum; it is molded, as well, by technological change and organizational culture, social forces and intellectual movements, ideologies and regime types, generational mindsets and professional cohorts.[12] It is debatable, for instance, whether America's Cold War

---

10. See, as surveys, Thomas W. Zeiler, "The Diplomatic History Bandwagon: A State of the Field," *Journal of American History* 95:4 (2009): 1053–73; Hal Brands, "The Triumph and Tragedy of Diplomatic History," *Texas National Security Review* 1:1 (2017); Mark Moyar, "The Current State of Military History," *Historical Journal* 50:1 (2007): 225–40; as well as many of the contributions to this volume.

11. The essays on them, however, are entirely original to this volume.

12. A point that the second volume of *Makers* also stressed. See Paret, "Introduction," 3–7.

nuclear strategy flowed primarily from elegant analysis by the Wizards of Armageddon or from opaque, unglamorous, and often-impersonal bureaucratic processes.[13] Perhaps more importantly, strategic thought and actions by non-Western makers—Sun Zi and Mohammed, Tecumseh and Nehru, Kim Jong-Un and Mao Zedong, among others, individuals largely absent from earlier volumes—have powerfully shaped our world and must inform our comprehension of the art. This isn't a matter of faddishness or political correctness: looking for strategy in unfamiliar places is what prevents the intellectual stagnation that can come from merely playing the greatest hits again and again.

What counts as "modern" has also shifted. New domains of warfare have emerged; the digital age has transformed intelligence, covert action, and other long-standing tools of strategy. The list of issues that will preoccupy policymakers in the coming decades—and influence what is seen as relevant history—is not the same as it was in 1986 or 1943. Today, moreover, a bloody, tumultuous twentieth century can be studied in its entirety; both the Cold War and the post-Cold War era represent discrete historical periods that have a great deal to teach us about issues ranging from nuclear strategy to counter-terrorism and to the survival mechanisms of rogue states. Consequently, roughly half of the essays in this volume deal with events in the twentieth century and later.

Finally, what counts as "strategy?" The term originally connoted tricks or subterfuges that generals used to outwit their opponents. In the nineteenth century, it came to be associated with the art of military leadership. Later, amid the world wars and the Cold War, a larger concept of strategy became more common, even as the concept was still associated primarily with military conflict.[14] Here, too, a certain revision is warranted.

Some of the greatest American strategists, such as John Quincy Adams and Franklin Roosevelt, have been diplomats and politicians rather than soldiers. Strategies of peacetime competition can be as consequential as strategies of military conflict, not least because the former often determine whether, and on what terms, the latter occurs. Geopolitical rivalry plays out in international organizations, cyberspace, and the global economy; tools as varied as finance and covert action, and as intangible as morality, can be potent weapons of statecraft. Even strategies of non-violent resistance have profoundly influenced international order.

---

13. See the essays by Francis Gavin ("The Elusive Nature of Nuclear Strategy," Chapter 28) and Eric Edelman ("Nuclear Strategy in Theory and Practice," Chapter 27) in this volume.

14. See Earle, "Introduction," viii; Paret, "Introduction"; as well as Lawrence Freedman's contribution ("Strategy: The History of an Idea," Chapter 1) to this volume.

To be clear, the study of war and preparations for war remains utterly central to the study of strategy, if only because violent conflict is the final arbiter of the disputes that strategy is meant to address. When war comes, it does indeed dominate our lives; the history of military coercion and organized violence could hardly be more relevant given the many contemporary threats to international peace. But if Napoleon, who mastered the use of violence, led his country to ruin, while Gandhi, who mostly abhorred violence, helped lead his country to freedom, then surely that tells us something about what qualifies as strategy after all.

III

This book represents an effort to grasp the enduring realities of strategy, while taking new insights and perspectives into account. Its essays are essays organized into five sections.

Section I examines "Foundations and Founders." These essays grapple anew with the classics of the genre, exploring their contested meanings and continued relevance. They examine ongoing debates in our understanding of strategy, while also discussing how foundational issues such as finance, economics, ideology, and geography shape its practice. And they show how modern strategy is still heavily influenced, for better or worse, by the thoughts and actions of individuals who have been dead for centuries or even longer.

Section II investigates "Strategy in an Age of Great-Power Rivalry," stretching from the rise of the modern international state system in the sixteenth and seventeenth centuries to the eve of the great tumults of the twentieth. This section explores patterns of war and competition in an earlier, multipolar world, against the backdrop of momentous developments—intellectual, ideological, technological, and geopolitical—that encouraged equally remarkable innovations in strategy. It traces the rise of concepts, such as the balance of power and the laws of war, meant to simultaneously harness and regulate the antagonisms within the international system. Finally, it examines the strategies of those who resisted the established and emerging great powers of the era— whether a confederation of Native American tribes in North America, or theorists and practitioners of anti-colonial activism in British India and beyond.

Section III covers "Strategy in an Age of Global War," focusing on the development of the ideas, doctrines, and practices that featured in World War I and World War II. These cataclysms were unlike anything humanity had seen before. They had the potential to destroy civilization; they pitted advanced industrial societies against each other in desperate, prolonged struggles for survival; they broke the existing world order in irreparable ways. Leaders crafted strategies to address the novel challenges and opportunities inherent in conducting modern warfare on a global scale; they advanced visions for the reconstruction of global affairs. In their achievements and their shortcomings, the strategies that emerged from these conflicts molded international politics through the end of the twentieth century and beyond.

Section IV addresses "Strategy in a Bipolar Era." After World War II, America and the Soviet Union emerged as rival superpowers atop a divided international system. European empires dissolved, generating new states and widespread disorder. Nuclear weapons forced statesmen to reconsider the role of force in global affairs and to consider how tools of war might be used to prevail in peacetime competition. Leaders everywhere, not just in Moscow and Washington, had to devise strategies for securing their interests amid a global Cold War. This section covers the issues—nuclear strategy, alignment and nonalignment, conventional and proxy wars, the strategies of small states and revolutionary regimes, the question of how to blend rivalry and diplomacy—that marked the late twentieth century and remain salient today.

Finally, Section V considers "Strategy in the Post-Cold War World," an era characterized mainly by America's primacy and the reactions that primacy generated. A preponderant America sought to make the most of its advantages. Yet power provided no exit from perpetual dilemmas of strategy, such as balancing costs and risks or reconciling means and ends. Nor did it permit an escape from the actions of rivals pursuing their own strategies for undermining or overturning the US-led international order. By the early twenty-first century, the prevailing understandings of strategy were being tested by technological changes that carried competition and warfare into new arenas and accelerated the speed of global interactions. This section thus analyzes the strategic problems that marked America's hegemonic moment and the rise of the threats that mark the contemporary landscape.

In each section, the authors consider the time-bound and the timeless—the particular historical circumstances that produced a given body of thought or action, as well as strategic insights or ideas whose purchase is not limited to any particular setting. Across the various sections, this volume offers a number of thematic and comparative essays, meant to highlight issues and debates that are larger than any single historical figure.[15]

---

15. The chronological breakdown of the sections is, necessarily, somewhat imprecise. For example, certain themes that figured in the world wars—the concept of total war, to name

Taken collectively, the essays in the book contain examples of both failed and successful strategies. There are strategies designed to win wars decisively and strategies meant to limit or even prolong them. There are strategies informed by religion and ideology, and there are examples of actors who believed that struggle itself was a strategy—that resistance, whether effective or not, could be a form of liberation. There are maritime and continental strategies, strategies of attrition and strategies of annihilation, strategies of democracies and strategies of tyrannies, strategies of transformation and strategies of equilibrium. The conclusions that emerge are rich and complex; the authors don't always agree about key issues, episodes, or individuals. Nonetheless, six key themes cut across the volume and the history it relates.

IV

First, the church of strategy must be a broad one. Even in 1943, amid a global war, it was clear to Edward Mead Earle that strategy was too important and complex to be left entirely to the generals. That insight looms even larger today. One has only to look at Vladimir Putin's violent revisionism, or at China's awesome naval buildup and threats to forcibly reorder the Western Pacific, in order to understand that war and the threat of war remain central to human affairs. Yet one has only to look at the expansiveness of Beijing's bid for global primacy—which also involves seizing the initiative in international organizations, weaving webs of economic dependence around foreign countries, striving for dominance in key technologies of the twenty-first century, using information operations to divide and demoralize democratic societies, and promoting Chinese ideological influence worldwide—to understand that strategy is something far more multifaceted than war or the threat thereof.[16]

The apotheosis of strategy is synergy: combining multiple tools, whether arms, money, diplomacy, or even ideas to achieve one's highest objectives. Its essence lies in fusing power with creativity to prevail in competitive situations, whatever the precise form of that power may be. This means that expanding the database of cases we consider is vital to making our knowledge of strategy as rich and varied as strategy itself.

---

one—had their roots in earlier eras. And some figures, such as Stalin, straddled the divide between eras.

16. The same point could be made about the strategies being pursued by other US rivals today. See Seth Jones, *Three Dangerous Men: Russia, China, Iran, and the Rise of Irregular Warfare* (New York, NY: W. W. Norton, 2021); Elizabeth Economy, *The World According to China* (London: Polity, 2022).

Second, grappling with strategy requires recognizing the primacy and pervasiveness of politics. This isn't simply an affirmation of Clausewitz's much-misunderstood dictum that war is the continuation of politics by other means. The point, rather, is that while the challenges of strategy may be universal, the content of strategy can hardly be divorced from the political system that produces it.

The strategies of Athens and Sparta in the Great Peloponnesian War were rooted in these powers' domestic institutions, proclivities, and fissures. Napoleon's innovations in military strategy were products of the epochal political and social changes wrought by the French Revolution. The strategy that John Quincy Adams fashioned for nineteenth-century America was meant to ensure the success of the democratic experiment, in part by harnessing the ideological force it exerted abroad. And the strategies of geopolitical revolution pursued by the great tyrants of the twentieth century were intimately related to the strategies of political and social revolution that they pursued in their own countries. All strategy is suffused by politics, which is why political and social change—the rise of democracy, the rise of totalitarianism, or the onset of decolonization—so often drives the evolution of strategy.

This is also why strategic competition is as much a test of political systems as it is a test of individual leaders. The debate over whether liberal societies can outperform their illiberal enemies reaches back to Thucydides and Machiavelli. It is a fundamental question of America's ongoing rivalries with China and Russia. A prominent, though not undisputed, theme of this volume is that democracies may well do strategy better. The concentration of authority can produce dexterity and brilliance in the short term, but the diffusion of authority makes for stronger societies and wiser decisions in the end.[17]

Third, strategy is most valuable when it reveals power in unexpected places. Even the strongest countries need strategies; the application of overwhelming might can be a winning approach. Yet reliance on brute strength isn't the most interesting form of strategy, and the outcome of competitive interactions is not always determined by the material balance of power. The most impressive strategies are those that shift the balance of forces by creating new advantages.[18]

17. On this debate, see the essays in this volume by (among others) Walter Russell Mead ("Thucydides, Polybius, and the Legacies of the Ancient World," Chapter 2), Tami Biddle Davis ("Democratic Leaders and Strategies of Coalition Warfare: Churchill and Roosevelt in World War II," Chapter 23), and Matthew Kroenig ("Machiavelli and the Naissance of Modern Strategy," Chapter 4).

18. The point is also made in Richard Betts, "Is Strategy an Illusion?" *International Security* 25:2 (2000): 5–50; Freedman, *Strategy*.

Those advantages can come from an ideological commitment that unlocks new and deadly ways of warfare, as the Prophet Mohammed demonstrated in the Arabian Peninsula. They can emerge from the superior orchestration of coalitions, as the Grand Alliance managed in World War II, or from the deft application of multiple tools of statecraft, as Tecumseh revealed in his war against westward US expansion. Advantage can come from pressing in areas where the enemy is vulnerable or sensitive, as Russian and Iranian strategies of irregular warfare have proven. Strength can even come, paradoxically, from weakness, as the Cold War's lesser powers showed by exploiting their vulnerability in order to coerce superpower concessions. Or it can come from a unique insight about the nature of a contest: Mao ultimately triumphed in the Chinese civil war because he manipulated regional and global conflicts to win a local one. Indeed, though strategy may be manifested in action, it is a deeply intellectual discipline. It involves skillfully sizing up complex situations and relationships, thereby finding within them some crucial source of leverage.

Admittedly, creativity can't always negate the cruel arithmetic of power: having big battalions and lots of money never hurts. But "be stronger" isn't useful counsel. What is useful, perhaps, is to understand just how diverse the sources of advantage can be, and how good strategy can make the ledger more favorable than it might otherwise be.

What, then, is the key to making effective strategy? Thinkers and practitioners have long sought a universal formula for success. The principles of war and strategy were "as true as the multiplication table, the law of gravitation, or of virtual velocities, or any other invariable rule of natural philosophy," claimed William Tecumseh Sherman.[19] A fourth theme of this work, however, is that strategy will always remain an imprecise art, no matter how much we might like it to be a science instead.

To be sure, the essays in this volume suggest plenty of general guidelines and helpful advice. Skilled strategists find ways of applying their strengths against an adversary's weaknesses; they never lose sight of the need to keep means and ends in equilibrium. Knowing when to stop is critical, because overreach can be fatal; understanding oneself and one's enemy is a cliché, but vital nonetheless. If strategic failures are often failures of imagination, then strategists need ways of ensuring that their assumptions are probed and

---

19. Lawrence Freedman, "The Meaning of Strategy, Part II: The Objectives," *Texas National Security Review* 1:2 (2018): 45.

checked.[20] Yet the quest for fixed maxims of strategy—as opposed to insights about good process—has invariably gone wanting, because the enemy also gets a say. Strategy is an incessantly interactive endeavor, one in which a thinking adversary is poised to spoil even the most elegant design.[21]

If anything, the following essays underscore the ubiquity of surprise and the perishability of strategic advantage. Hitler's strategies of expansion produced brilliant results, until they didn't. In the post–Cold War era, the very fact of American dominance led adversaries to devise asymmetric responses. The emergence of new domains of warfare usually leads strategists to dream of capturing enduring advantage, only for reality to set back in as others catch up. In almost every era, eminent leaders have gone to war expecting short, victorious conflicts, only to get long, grinding ones instead.

All this ensures that strategy is a never-ending process, one in which adaptation, flexibility, and that most intangible quality—sound judgment—are as important as the brilliance of any initial scheme. This may be why democracies, on balance, fare better: not because they are immune to errors of strategic judgment, but because they demand an accountability, and provide built-in course correction opportunities, that aid in recovering from them. It also reminds us why history is so important to good strategy: not because it reveals checklists for achieving strategic excellence, but because history offers examples of leaders who managed to thrive amid all the risk, uncertainty, and failure that the world invariably threw their way.

This leads to a fifth theme—that the cost of strategic and historical illiteracy can be catastrophically high. If tactical and operational mastery mattered most, Germany might have won not one but two world wars. In reality, what twice doomed Germany—and the losers of nearly every great-power showdown in the modern era—were critical strategic miscalculations that eventually left them in hopeless straits. Good strategic choices provide an opportunity to recover from tactical shortcomings; serial strategic errors are far less forgiving.[22] From ancient times to the present, the quality—or lack thereof—of strategy has determined the rise and fall of nations and the contours of international order.

---

20. On strategic failures as failures of imagination, see Kori Schake's "Strategic Excellence: Tecumseh and the Shawnee Confederacy," Chapter 15 in this volume.

21. Hal Brands, "The Lost Art of Long-Term Competition," *The Washington Quarterly* 41:4 (2018): 31–51.

22. This point runs throughout Alan Millett and Williamson Murray, *Military Effectiveness*, Volumes 1–3 (New York, NY: Cambridge University Press, 2010).

Herein lies the value of history. There is always a need for humility in drawing on lessons from the past. It is easy to forget that the most "timeless" texts were products of particular eras, places, and agendas not exactly analogous to our own. "History," wrote Henry Kissinger, "is not . . . a cookbook offering pretested recipes." It cannot yield universal "maxims" or "take from our shoulders the burden of difficult choices."[23]

Yet if history is an imperfect teacher, it's still the best we have. History is the only place we can go to study what virtues have made for good strategies and what vices have produced bad ones. The study of history lets us expand our knowledge beyond what we have personally experienced, thereby making even the most unprecedented problems feel a bit less foreign.[24] Indeed, the fact that strategy cannot be reduced to mathematical formulas makes such vicarious experience all the more essential. History, then, is the least costly way of sharpening the judgment and fostering the intellectual balance that successful statecraft demands. Above all, studying the past reminds us of the stakes—that the fate of the world can hinge on getting strategy right.

This is history's greatest lesson. The first *Makers of Modern Strategy* was produced when horrible tyrannies ruled much of the earth and the survival of democracy was in doubt. The second was published near the end of a long, demanding struggle that put the free world to the test. The third comes as the shadows cast by competition and conflict are growing longer and it often seems that authoritarian darkness is drawing near. The better we understand the history of strategy, the more likely we are, in the exacting future that awaits us, to get it right.

Thus, a final theme: the contents of *Makers of Modern Strategy* may change over time, but the vital purpose never does. The study of strategy is a deeply instrumental pursuit. And because it concerns the well-being of nations in a competitive world, it can never be value-free.

The editors of the first two editions of *Makers* were unembarrassed about this fact: they explicitly aimed to help the citizens of America and other democratic societies better understand strategy so that they might be more effective in practicing it against deadly rivals. This was engaged scholarship in its most enlightened form—and it is the model this new edition of *Makers* aspires to emulate today.

---

23. Henry Kissinger, *White House Years* (Boston, MA: Little, Brown, 1959), esp. 54.

24. Hal Brands, *The Twilight Struggle: What the Cold War Can Teach Us About Great-Power Rivalry Today* (New Haven, CT: Yale University Press, 2022).

PART I

Foundations and Founders

CHAPTER 1

Strategy

THE HISTORY OF AN IDEA

Lawrence Freedman

"I hardly bother with scientific words," Napoleon remarked when discussing strategy in exile on the island of Saint-Helena, "and cannot care less about them." He was wary about theory. "I beat the enemy without so much intellect and without using Greek words." None of the variety of definitions of strategy on offer met with his satisfaction, though when pushed, Napoleon offered his own: "strategy is the art of plans of campaign and tactics the art of battles."[1] This was in line with other definitions around at the time. Strategy was purely military and required a contrast with tactics. It is telling that some five decades after the word had entered the French language, and some two decades after Napoleon had revolutionized the practice of war, there was still no consensus on how strategy was best understood. Napoleon's definition, if well known, might have gained currency by virtue of his authority. But it was not.

With the passage of another 200 years there is still no consensus on definition, although contemporary usage has moved well beyond the narrow confines of military operations, covering all aspects of human affairs. There is no longer a purely military definition of strategy. It is now expected to relate operations to political objectives. This chapter tells the story of how this came about. It will show that there has never been an agreed upon definition, and this has regularly been lamented, especially by those offering their own for consideration, yet the broad shifts in meaning have been recognized and

---

1. Bruno Colson, *Napoleon on War* (Oxford: Oxford University Press, 2015), 84.

generally understood. Shifts in definitions have been linked to changing views about war. When the word first entered the vernacular in 1771, it expressed a view of generalship that admired ruses and maneuvers to avoid pitched battles, but then developed over the nineteenth century with pitched battles very much in mind. During the twentieth century the focus shifted to the interaction of military means with political ends, and from there, on to how ends might be achieved by a variety of means, of which the military was but one.

The reasons why these issues of definition and scope mattered also changed. At least until the First World War, these were largely issues for military textbooks written to instruct officers in the essentials of their profession. After this war, strategy became bound up with national discussions about how best to prepare for and fight the next war. After the Second World War and into the nuclear age, strategy began to be seen as a specialist discipline in itself, with its own concepts and theories. Not least because of the importance of deterrence, strategy became detached from the actual practice of war. The more it was studied in universities and think-tanks, the more it became an area for academic inquiry, although still without an agreed upon definition.

Strategy remains hard to pin down. People are described as having acted strategically without ever having known the term, and those that have used the term knowingly have not always meant the same thing. It is a term employed to understand the actions of others, in ways they might not recognize, and also one which individuals employ to explain their own actions, in ways others might not accept. Strategies have been found making fleeting appearances in leaders' minds as they took critical decisions or in detailed documents distributed around organizations to ensure that everyone knew what was expected of them. Those sufficiently confident in their theories of causation have described strategy as a science, while those who doubted the certainty, but relished the opportunities for creativity, have insisted it is an art. But then the terms "science" and "art" have also not had settled and consistent meanings. The conclusion of this chapter is that it is too late to expect consensus on these matters. Nonetheless, as a permissive "umbrella" concept, strategy still has a core meaning sufficient to sustain a range of diverse discourses.[2]

---

2. I have drawn extensively from Lawrence Freedman, "The Meaning of Strategy, Part I: The Origins," *Texas National Security Review* 1:1 (2017): 90–105; and "The Meaning of Strategy, Part 2: The Objectives," *Texas National Security Review* 1:2 (2018): 34–57. These provide more details and full references on many of this chapter's themes. Two books by Beatrice Heuser provide valuable accounts of developments in strategic thinking—*The Evolution of Strategy: Thinking War from Antiquity to the Present* (Cambridge: Cambridge University Press, 2010) and *The*

I

Until the late eighteenth century what we now called strategy would have been discussed under the headings of the "art of the general" or the "art of war." By the middle of that century these were considered matters for serious inquiry, reflecting the spirit of the Enlightenment. Military practice was changing. Innovations in cartography allowed generals to work out how they might advance from their home base to confront an enemy, with an eye to logistics, and then to plot the conduct of battle. As armies grew larger, requiring generals to coordinate their infantry, cavalry, and artillery, command became more demanding and general staffs began to be formed. Frederick the Great's Prussia was the first to introduce a general staff. His tactical innovations during the War of the Austrian Succession and then the Seven Years' War encouraged an interest in military theory while France's unimpressive performances led to an introspective debate about the failings of their military system and the need for reform. It was in the context of this debate that the word "strategy" first made its appearance in France in 1771.

It was not a true neologism. Writers on military affairs in the eighteenth century regularly turned back to the classics for their inspiration. The original Greek words, *strategos* and *strategía*, referring to generals and the things generals did, made regular appearances in these works, along with *taktiké*, or *tactics*. The Roman Senator Frontinus (c. 40 to 103 CE) wrote a wide-ranging work on strategy, which was lost, but an extract covering stratagems survived. His writings, including possibly his lost work, influenced Flavius Vegetius Rematus in the late fourth century. Vegetius's *De Re Militari* ("The Military Institutions of the Romans") never lost its popularity and by the eighteenth century was studied as a vital guide to the military art.

Strategía tended to be translated as the art of the general or of command, but variants of the Greek word were already in use, with the dichotomous relationship between the derivatives of *strategía* and *taktiké* well established.

Strategy Makers: Thoughts on War and Society from Machiavelli to Clausewitz (Santa Barbara, CA: Praeger Security International, 2010). Azar Gat's trilogy provides a fine history of military thought—*The Origins of Military Thought: From the Enlightenment to Clausewitz*, *The Development of Military Thought: The Nineteenth Century*, and *Fascists and Liberal Visions of War* (Oxford: The Clarendon Press, 1899, 1992, and 1998, respectively). Edward Luttwak discusses definitions in his *Strategy: The Logic of War and Peace* (Cambridge, MA: Harvard University Press, 2002) while Hew Strachan provides a critical account of tendencies in strategic thinking in *The Direction of War: Contemporary Strategy in Historical Perspective* (Cambridge: Cambridge University Press, 2014). On grand strategy see Lukas Milevski, *The Evolution of Modern Grand Strategic Thought* (Oxford: Oxford University Press, 2016).

For example, an early seventeenth-century translation of Herodian of Alexandria's *History of the Roman Empire* observed, concerning a discussion of captains and soldiers "expert in Marshalling of Armies and Military Exploits," that this referred to "both the parts of war: viz, *tactick* and *Strategmatick*."[3] The best-known derivation from *strategía* was "stratagem," referring to any cunning ploy or ruse. It was in use as early as the fifteenth century. The *Oxford English Dictionary* has identified other related words in use from the sixteenth century—stratagematic, stratagematical, strategematist, and stratagemical. *Stratarithmetrie* (made up of the Greek words for army, number, and measure) was a form of military arithmetic, popularized by the mathematician John Dee in his introduction to a translation of Euclid in 1570, distinguishing it from "tacticie." Stratarithmetrie was a forerunner of contemporary operational analysis, urging the use of geometrical analogies in the organization of armies.

A guide to the available lexicon of the first part of the eighteenth century is Ephraim Chambers's *Cyclopædia*, the first edition of which was published in 1728. It contained a reference to stratagem (a "military wile"), *stratarithmetry* ("the art of drawing up an Army or any part of it, in any given Geometric figure") and, lest the origins of the word be forgotten, *strategus* (as one of the two appointed Athenians who would "command the troops of the state").[4] As dictionaries of this time tended to copy each other's entries, these became the standard definitions. They found their way, for example, into the *Encyclopaedia Britannica*, which was reproduced in its entirety as *Dobson's Encyclopædia*, published in the United States from 1799. In France, the great *Encyclopédie*, compiled by Denis Diderot, first published in 1765 and originally intended as a French translation of Chambers, included entries for "stratagem" and "stratarithmetry," noting that the latter was not used in France. There was also a discussion of the role of the strategos. In 1771, the French officer Paul Gédéon Joly de Maizeroy published his translation of the Byzantine emperor Leo VI's *Taktiká*. That he did not translate *strategía* as the science of the general, which might have been done before, but simply transliterated it as *stratégie*, would not necessarily have seemed remarkable. His readers would have had little difficulty in making sense of the word; it should not have posed great difficulties for the more educated students of warfare in the late eighteenth century.

---

3. Herodian of Alexandria, *History of Twenty Roman Caesars and Emperors (of his Time)*, trans. James Maxwell (London: Printed for Hugh Perry, 1629).

4. Ephraim Chambers, *Cyclopædia, or, An Universal Dictionary of Arts and Sciences* (London: J. and J. Knapton, 1728), 135.

Because the term slipped into the vernacular in this way, without an agreed upon definition, what would Maizeroy and his contemporaries have assumed that strategy was about? There was a link with stratagem that was more than etymological. The importance of ruses was a theme evident in Polybius, while Frontinus described strategy (*strategikon*) as "everything achieved by a commander, be it characterized by foresight, advantage, enterprise, and resolution."[5] Stratagem (*strategematon*) was not just about trickery. It was about achieving success through "skills and cleverness." The theme of avoiding unnecessary battles was to the fore in Vegetius and also in Byzantine writings of war. The *Strategikon* of the Byzantine Emperor Maurice (582 to 602 CE), for example, described warfare to be like hunting. "Wild animals are taken by scouting, by nets, by lying in wait, by stalking, by circling around, and by other such stratagems rather than by sheer force." He cautioned against pitched battles, "unless a truly exceptional opportunity or advantage presents itself.[6]

These ideas influenced Emperor Leo VI, whose book was completed in the tenth century. He considered the art of the general to be bound up with stratagem and that was probably how his translator, Maizeroy, also understood the word. In a later work Leo VI identified the rules of strategy, with a clear link to stratagem. These included not doing "what one's enemy appears to desire" and identifying "the enemy's principal objective in order not to be misled by his diversions" and "always to be ready to disrupt his initiatives without being dominated by them."[7]

The other influence on Maizeroy's work was Marshal Maurice de Saxe, under whom Maizeroy had served as a captain in the French army. In *My Reveries Upon the Art of War*, published posthumously in 1756, Saxe referred to neither strategy nor tactics, but did distinguish between the "higher" and "lesser" parts of war. The lesser parts were fundamental, covering methods of fighting and discipline, but they were also elemental and mechanical. The most challenging, intellectually demanding parts were the higher ones, thereby putting warfare among the "sublime arts." Maizeroy picked this up, describing the higher parts of war in 1767 as "military dialectics," and including "the art of forming the plans of a campaign, and directing its operations." Following his translation of Leo VI, Maizeroy described strategy ("quite sublime") as residing

5. Freedman, "The Meaning of Strategy: Part I."

6. Emperor Maurice, *Strategikon: Handbook of Byzantine Military Strategy*, trans. George T. Dennis (Philadelphia, PA: University of Pennsylvania Press, 1984).

7. Freedman, "The Meaning of Strategy: Part I."

"solely in the head of the general." He distinguished between tactics and strategy, as the lesser and higher:

> Tactics is easily reduced to firm rules because it is entirely geometrical like fortifications. Strategy appears to be much less susceptible to this, since it is dependent upon innumerable circumstances—physical, political, and moral—which are never the same and which are entirely the domain of genius.[8]

Although Maizeroy was not alone in France in following these themes, he was not the most influential theorist in France at this time. Jacques-Antoine-Hippolyte, Comte de Guibert published his *Essai Général de Tactique* in 1773, in which he distinguished between the lesser and higher solely on the basis of tactics, "the one elementary and limited, the other composite and sublime." The higher level, which Guibert described as "grand tactics," to which all other parts were "secondary," contained "every great occurrence of war" and was "properly speaking . . . the science of the generals."[9] In a later, 1779 book, Guibert referred to *la stratégique*, but it was "grand tactics" that stuck. This was the formulation adopted by Napoleon Bonaparte, whose deeds as a general provided the greatest stimulus to thinking about war. In one of his maxims, Napoleon distinguished between what an "engineer or artillery officer" might need to know, which could "be learned in treatises," and the "grand tactics" that required experience and the study of "the campaigns of all the great captains."[10] Another important French text during this period, approved by the emperor, was Gay de Vernon's *Traité élémentaire d'art militaire et de fortification*, published in 1805. This did not contain a discussion of strategy or even of grand tactics but rather of "*la tactique générale*."[11]

II

A German debate started at more or less the same time in the same way, with a translation of Leo VI's *Taktika* in 1777 by the Austrian Johann W. von Bourscheid who also referred to "strategie." The individual who did most to establish strategy

8. Paul Gédéon Joly De Maizeroy, *Théorie de la guerre* [Theory of War] (Lausanne: Aux dépens de la Société, 1777).

9. Jacques Antoine Hippolyte Comte de Guibert, *Essai général de Tactique* [General Essay on Tactics] (Liege: C. Plomteaux, 1773).

10. Jacques Antoine Hippolyte Comte de Guibert, *Maximes de Guerre de Napoleon* [Military Maxims of Napoleon] (Paris: Chez Anselin, 1830).

11. Freedman, "The Meaning of Strategy, Part II."

as a distinctive realm of analysis, however, was Heinrich von Bülow, the son of a minor nobleman and a former officer in the Prussian army. His *Spirit of the Modern System of War*, published in 1799, was more in the "Stratarithmetrie" tradition than in that of the "stratagem," involving, as it did, the application of geometrical and mathematical principles. Bülow was famously disparaged by Clausewitz who considered him a charlatan. No enthusiast for fighting battles, Bülow's approach was also at odds with the developing Napoleonic method.

Bülow's starting point was that the French concept of *la stratégique* was too limited, dealing as it did only with "the science of the stratagems of war." Because of his belief in mathematical models, which did not necessitate any military genius, Bülow did not see himself as exploring the sublime. He appreciated that "the General's Art" stayed close to the original meaning. The problem was that this art involved both tactics and strategy and he wanted a definition that distinguished one from the other. After trying to do this on the basis of objectives, Bülow eventually opted to distinguish strategy and tactics on the basis of proximity. What he called "strategics" was "the science of the movements in war of two armies, out of the visual circle of each other, or, if better liked, out of cannon reach." By contrast, tactics were "the science of the movements made within sight of the enemy, and within reach of his artillery." Strategics was about marching and encamping; tactics about attacking and defending in battle.[12] These definitions lasted because they were more descriptive than prescriptive. Moreover, they could be employed without adopting his whole theory of war.

This distinction between strategy and tactics was picked up by the Swiss Baron Antoine-Henri de Jomini, a veteran of the Napoleonic Wars and the most influential writer on war for much of the nineteenth century. Following Guibert, Jomini's first book was entitled *Traité de Grande Tactique*, published in 1805. His most complete book was *Precis de l'Art de la Guerre*, published in 1838. Jomini did not quite follow Bülow, but he did accept the Prussian's sequence by defining strategy in terms of the preparation for battle, while tactics were bound up with the actual conduct of battle. In Jomini's most concise formulation: "Strategy decides where to act; logistics brings the troops to this point; grand tactics decides the manner of execution and the employment of the troops."[13]

12. Dietrich Heinrich von Bülow, *The Spirit of the Modern System of War*, trans. Malorti de Martemont (Cambridge: Cambridge University Press, 2013).

13. Antoine Henri de Jomini, *The Art of War* [*Traité de Grande Tactique*], trans. G.H. Mendell and W.P. Craighill (El Paso, TX: El Paso Norte Press, 2005 [1838]), 79–100.

For Jomini, strategy was geared toward a campaign's overall concept rather than its execution, and it was not a substitute for grand tactics. Jomini accepted that strategy did not depend solely on a general's genius but could benefit through the application of timeless principles. In the *Précis*, he suggested that strategy "may be regulated by fixed laws resembling those of the positive sciences."[14] Jomini's principles, however, were quite different from Bülow's. Influenced by Napoleon's example, Jomini saw war in terms of decisive battles that would leave the enemy's army destroyed, requiring them to seek a political settlement on the victor's terms. This sharp focus on battle helped contain the concepts of tactics and strategy by relating them both to a climactic event.

The Prussian Carl von Clausewitz is now considered to be more important and profound than Jomini. Clausewitz's unfinished work *On War* was published posthumously (1832–35) and was generally considered more difficult to follow and so less suitable for instructional purposes. Although Clausewitz stressed the importance of political ends for the conduct of war, strategy remained a largely military concept, focused on battle. In notes written in 1804 Clausewitz distinguished between elementary and higher tactics, the first appropriate to small units and the second to larger formations. The next year, in an anonymous, scathing review of Bülow, Clausewitz developed the formulation with which he stayed thereafter—"Tactics constitute the theory of the use of armed forces in battle; strategy forms the theory of using battle for the purposes of the war."[15] In the discussion in Book 2 of *On War*, Clausewitz described tactics as being about individual engagements, and strategy about using a number of engagements to support the overall objective of the campaign. In terms of command, strategy was superior to tactics. Nonetheless, the plan the strategist wrote for a war could only be a draft. Tactics would still determine outcomes, which would take shape "when the fragmented results have combined into a single, independent whole."[16]

Without any challenge to the assumption that wars between the major powers would be decided through battle, there would be no need to challenge the prevailing definitions of strategy as being largely about getting in position for battle and tactics as largely about how battles should be fought. Moreover,

14. Jomini, *The Art of War*.

15. Peter Paret, *Essays on Clausewitz and the History of Military Power* (Princeton, NJ: Princeton University Press, 1992), 100.

16. Carl von Clausewitz, *On War*, trans. Michael Howard and Peter Paret (Princeton, NJ: Princeton University Press, 1989), 128–32, 206–8.

while strategy might be considered the higher calling—in that it was a senior commander's responsibility—in terms of officer training and drills, the emphasis was on tactics. The opportunities created by strategy would be wasted without effective and well-executed tactics. It was also the area most subject to innovation. At a time when symmetry in the composition and capabilities of armies was assumed, as was the convention that the decision of battle would be accepted, tactical competence could—and did—make all the difference. The study of strategy required paying attention to moving troops and keeping them supplied, looking after their health and encampments, as well as seeking out the best spots for battle, and getting forces in order for the coming fight. The claim, not unique to Jomini, that the main principles of strategy could be understood by studying the great battles of the past, encouraged a conservative approach to strategy. There were no incentives to consider the implications of changing political context or of technological innovations. Another Swiss general, Guillame-Henri Dufour, explained in a moderately influential book in the mid-nineteenth century that, while strategy looked back, tactics looked forward. Strategy was subject to timeless principles, while tactics was changing all the time and so varied with the "arms in use at different periods":

> Much valuable instruction in *strategy* may therefore be derived from the study of history: but very grave errors would result if we attempt to apply to the present days the *tactics* of the ancients.[17]

III

The influence of these ideas can be seen in the United Kingdom and the United States. At first, the British were largely consumers of military writing from France and Prussia, with publications such as the regularly updated *New Military Dictionary* progressively including references to foreign ideas, defining strategy in 1805, for example, as "the art or science of military command," with an observation that the term did "not exist in any of our English lexicographers," and that there was no agreed upon view of the term.[18] Bülow was the first in the field by virtue of a relatively early translation. Neither Jomini's *Precis* nor Clausewitz's *On War* were published in English translations until much later, though their work was known and had some influence over the British

---

17. Guillame-Henri Dufour, *Strategy and Tactics* (New York, NY: Van Nostrand, 1864), 8.
18. Charles James, *New and Enlarged Military Dictionary* (London: T Egerton, 1805).

debate and included significant commentators such as the former major-
generals, William Napier and John Mitchell. Napier, an accomplished military
historian, opined in 1821 that strategy was the area in which "the great qualities
with which a general may be endowed will have ample room to display themselves: fine perception, unerring judgement, rapid decision, and unwearied
activity both of mind and body, are here all requisite."[19]

From 1846 to 1851, a committee of officers produced three volumes of an
Aide-mémoire to the Military Sciences in order "to supply, as far as practicable,
the many and common wants of Officers in the Field, in the Colonies, and
remote Stations, where books of reference are seldom to be found." In the
first volume, Lt. Col. C. Hamilton Smith provided a "Sketch of the Art and
Science of War." This contained an early reference to "great operations" (the
French concept of *grande tactique*) and then a reference to strategics, "a term
to which it has been vainly endeavored to affix a strict definition from Folard
to Klausewitz [*sic*], Dufour, and Jomini." A "dialectician," noted Smith, "might
hint that a distinction might be pointed out between Strategics and Strategy,
or Strategique and Strategie; but no inconvenience seems to have arisen from
the promiscuous use of both." Jomini making war upon a map was Strategics,
while activities that were strategical in direction, and tactical in execution—
landings, march maneuvers, passage of rivers, retreats, winter-quarters, am-
buscades, and convoys, among others—might take the denomination of
strategy, so long as they were executed without the presence of an enemy
prepared for resistance. If the enemy was present then those same activities
became tactics. Smith also insisted that the principles of war, largely as identified by Jomimi, explained not only success and failure in past wars but also
those of the future.[20]

There was no imperative to bring clarity to the concept. The debate in the
mid-nineteenth century was largely about where to draw the line between
strategy and tactics and there it stayed for some time. In 1856, the superintendent of studies at the Royal Military College observed that the distinction
between the two was arbitrary, as they must both follow the same principles;
he stuck with Bülow's rule that the best guide was whether one was in the
"actual presence or eyesight of an enemy, however great or small the distances

19. William Napier, "Review of *Traité des grandes opérations militaires*," *Edinburgh Review*
XXXV (1821): 377–409.

20. Committee of the Corps of Royal Engineers, eds., *Aide-memoire to the Military Sciences*,
3 Volumes (London: John Weale, High Holbern, 1846–52), 5–7.

which separate them."[21] By the end of the century, the official army distinction was still between strategy as "the art of bringing the enemy to battle, while tactics are the methods by which a commander seeks to overwhelm him when battle is joined."[22] The qualities that made for excellence in strategy were discussed within a narrow framework—considering how commanders might avoid routine approaches to battle and how they could see the possibilities in new circumstances.

The Operations of War published first in 1866 by Col. Edward Hamley of the Staff College at Camberley, with its pronounced Jominian influence, was the core British Army text throughout this period and beyond.[23] Hamley saw mastery of strategy as a source of initiative in battle. Col. G. F. R. Henderson, an able military historian and teacher at the Staff College who wrote at the turn of the century, also emphasized strategy as the highest form of generalship. The strategist must look beyond the principles of warfare—"which to a certain extent are mechanical, dealing with the manipulation of armed bodies"—to the "spirit of warfare." This involved the moral element that could inspire troops, as well as the elements of "surprise, mystery, [and] strategem." Nonetheless, the end of strategy was "the pitched battle," and the aim was to gain every "possible advantage of numbers, ground, supplies, and moral" to ensure the "enemy's annihilation."[24] The prospect of battle thus continued to limit the development of the concept of strategy and to push it towards approaching standard problems with flair and imagination.

The American experience was similar. While Jomini may not have been used extensively in the teaching of cadets, his influence can be seen in the writings of Dennis Mahan, chair of civil and military engineering at West Point from 1832–71, and particularly in the writings of his most famous protégé, General Henry Halleck. Little time, however, was spent studying strategy. Americans looked for inspired and resolute leadership rather than learned professionals. Nor did Jomini play much of a role in the debates on how the Civil

21. Lt. Col. P. L. McDougall, The Theory of War: Illustrated by Numerous Examples from Military History (London: Longmans, 1856), 2–3.

22. As cited in Beatrice Heuser, "Clausewitz, Die Politik, and the Political Purpose of Strategy," in The Oxford Handbook of Grand Strategy, Thierry Balzacq and Ronald Krebs, eds. (New York, NY: Oxford University Press, 2021), 69.

23. Edward Bruce Hamley, The Operations of War: Explained and Illustrated (London: William Blackwood, 1866).

24. Col. G. F. R. Henderson, Science of War: A Collection of Essays and Lectures 1891–1903 (London: Longmans, Green & Co.: 1906), in Freedman, "The Meaning of Strategy, Part II," 42.

War should best be fought. Yet, after it was over, he was still considered the leading authority on the conduct of war, as could be seen with Mahan's successor at West Point, Cornelius J. Wheeler. James Mercur, who briefly followed Wheeler at the academy in 1884, considered the importance of the wider political context in his book *The Art of War*, but his approach was still orthodox and the book was soon forgotten.

General William Tecumseh Sherman's Georgia campaign did not follow any orthodoxy. His target was the morale of the adversary population. Yet, in his short memoir entitled "The Grand Strategy of the Wars of the Rebellion," Sherman stressed that the principles of war were fixed and unchanging, "as true as the multiplication table, the law of gravitation, or of virtual velocities, or any other invariable rule of natural philosophy." Sherman pointed his readers to a treatise by France J. Soady on *Lessons of War*, a compilation of thoughts extracted from major texts, which referred to Sherman as a "man of genius."[25] Capt. Bigelow's *Principles of Strategy: Illustrated Mainly from American Campaigns*, published in 1894, was the most substantial effort to draw broader lessons. Though his starting definition was entirely conventional, Bigelow saw the need for officers at all levels to have a grasp of strategy and, most importantly, he appreciated that there was a political dimension to strategy— "undermining the political support of the opposing army, or at effecting recall from the war."[26] Yet still the focus remained on defeating the enemy army, so no new framework for thinking about strategy emerged. Even though there were regular laments in the years before the First World War, there was still no agreement on what the topic involved.

IV

Perhaps most surprising was the limited impact of the 1870–71 Franco-Prussian War on thinking about strategy, not least because of the importance of French civilian resistance and the Prussian debate about how such resistance could be best overcome. In France, shocked by defeat, there was an effort to reform the army, and to develop a professional general staff. The debate, however, was more backward- than forward-looking, with a continuing commitment to the

---

25. Gen. W. T. Sherman, "The Grand Strategy of the Wars of the Rebellion," *The Century Magazine*, February 1888, 582–97.

26. John Bigelow Jr., *Principles of Strategy: Illustrated Mainly from American Campaigns* (Philadelphia, PA: J. B. Lippincott, 1894).

Napoleonic system. The most important claim was that offensive *élan* would allow a weaker force to overcome a stronger. Ferdinand Foch, who went on to command Allied forces in the First World War, was far from alone in insisting that tactics were more important than strategy. The conclusion of the French debate was to emphasize the importance of the offensive in seeking to destroy the enemy army in battle.

The German debate was more substantial, though the focus was still more on tactics than strategy. Field Marshal Moltke, who had been in charge through the wars of German unification, believed that tactical successes drove strategic outcomes, which is why strategy was a "system of expedients," requiring responses to developments in the campaign. One of his subordinates, Wilhelm von Blume, warned against disregarding "the nature of strategy to seek to transform it into a learned system exactly determined," and stressed the importance of tactics as dealing with the "proper ordering" of the action of troops "towards the object of fighting." Strategy was more residual—all that did not come under the heading of tactics—including the "decision as to when and for what object battle shall be joined, the assembly of the necessary forces, and the reaping of the proper result."[27] The question, raised by the France's resistance after its defeat at the battle at Sedan, was whether it was possible to stop future wars dragging on, and only being decided through the exhaustion of one of the belligerents rather than by battle. The determination to avoid a long war led to an emphasis on quick victories, exemplified by Moltke's successor, Count Alfred von Schlieffen's plan to ensure the early "annihilation" of the French army should the two countries fight again. The most substantial challenge to this approach came from the historian Hans Delbrück who argued that it was possible to win wars by exhausting enemies as well as through great battles, and, in so doing, challenged the view that there was a uniquely correct form of strategy.

Separate from but related to this debate was the issue of civil-military relations. When the sovereign led both the government and the armed forces, any tension between the two was resolved in one person's head. Once these became two distinct functions, the interface was going to be problematic and so it proved. The logic was for the military to be subordinate to the political, at least in terms of setting the objectives for a war and sorting out the aftermath, but the natural military inclination was to insist on controlling the conduct of war. This was not straightforward. The political context of a war could change,

---

27. Wilhelm von Blume, *Strategie* (Berlin: E.S. Mittler und Sohn, 1882).

for example by new allies joining the hitherto weaker side. This is what Chancellor Otto von Bismarck feared could happen if Paris held out for too long when it was put under siege in 1870, which led to arguments with Moltke about how French resistance could be broken quickly, something the Field Marshal felt was a matter for him to decide. Moltke turned this into a principle. Policy set the goals "in its action, strategy is independent of policy as much as possible. Policy must not be allowed to interfere in operations."[28] Bismarck insisted that politics must still influence operations and not just objectives. The German General Staff, and their counterparts elsewhere in Europe, resisted such views. Politicians meddling in operational decisions were bound to jeopardize military success.

This was a difficult objection to sustain. President Abraham Lincoln had hired and fired generals during the Civil War until he found those prepared to fight the war as he wanted to fight it. Bismarck's intervention was successful in 1870. Moreover, the military still needed governments to understand their requirements. Thus, Colonel Henderson, who saw political interference in military decision-making as being fraught with danger, also argued that the "soldier must often be the adviser of the statesman," and that strategy should be "concerned as much with preparation for war as with war itself." Such preparations he described as the "Peace Strategy" (as in what should be done at a time of peace as opposed to achieving peace when at war).[29] But even with a greater appreciation of prewar factors such as alliances, bases, and budgets, the generals were determined to maintain a strict division of labor between themselves and statesmen, and so long as they did that, strategy was contained within the established boundaries.

The challenge to this view came from the maritime side. The literature on war at sea was small compared with that concerning war on land. Those who did write on the former topic stuck with definitions derived from land warfare. Thus, when writing on the principles of naval warfare in 1891, Rear Adm. Philip Columb remarked in passing that strategy determined where a battle would be fought and tactics, its conduct.[30] His famous American contemporary, Alfred Thayer Mahan, son of Dennis, was largely a historian of sea power, urging the US to follow Britain's example as a sea power. The younger Mahan's view of

---

28. Moltke as quoted in Daniel Hughes, *Moltke on the Art of War: Selected Writings* (Novato, CA: Presidio Press, 1995), 35.

29. Lt. Col. G. F. R. Henderson, "Strategy and its Teaching," *Journal of the Royal United Services Institution* 42:1 (1898): 761.

30. On Columb's contributions, see Freedman, "The Meaning of Strategy, Part II."

strategy was essentially Jominian, with general principles to be discerned from historical studies. The "dividing line between tactics and strategy" was identified as the point of contact between armies or fleets. Tactics were more interesting as they were subject to the "unresting progress of mankind."[31] Mahan, however, did identify one important difference between land and sea warfare. In sea warfare, there were positions that could be occupied at times of peace that would be of value at times of war. Mahan defined the goals of naval strategy: "to found, support, and increase, as well in peace as in war, the sea power of a country."[32]

Mahan's stress on the wider political and economic consequences of sea operations, and the importance of peacetime dispositions, pointed to a more expansive definition of strategy. This was realized by the British maritime theorist Sir Julian Corbett, an influential civilian who had studied Clausewitz. Corbett's view was that naval and military strategy should be considered in relation to each other, and that both needed to be released from the fallacy "that war consists entirely of battles between armies and fleets." The destruction of the enemy armed forces was, at most, a means to an end, which was normally territory. He defined strategy as "the art of directing forces to the ends in view." In 1906, Corbett published his lectures as a pamphlet in which he divided strategy into "major" (or "grand" and dealing with ulterior objects, or war plans) and "minor" (dealing with "primary objects," or operational plans). For Corbett, the vital feature of major/grand strategy was that it involved the "whole resources of the nation for war" and not just armed forces. In 1911, when he revised these notes, Corbett left the distinction between major and minor. The ends of major or grand strategy were a matter for the statesman while minor strategy was the responsibility of the army and navy. He urged officers to accept the "deflection of strategy by politics"; it was part of the inevitable "friction of war."[33]

V

Corbett opened the way for a new approach to strategy in Britain after the First World War. The idea that the conduct of war must be protected from civilian interference was subject to increasing challenge. In 1927, the diplomat and

31. Alfred Thayer Mahan, *The Influence of Sea Power Upon History, 1660–1783* (Boston, MA: Little, Brown, and Company, 1890), 8.

32. Alfred Thayer Mahan, *Mahan on Naval Strategy: Selections from the Writings of Rear Admiral Alfred Thayer Mahan* (Annapolis, MD: Naval Institute Press, 1991), 22.

33. Julian Corbett, *Some Principles of Maritime Strategy* (London: Longmans, Green & Co., 1911). The "Green Pamphlet" of 1909 appears as an appendix.

military historian, Sir William Oman, urged "the directing classes in any nation" to "have a certain general knowledge of the history of the Art of War" and not to feel "bound to accept blindfold[ed] the orders of their military mentors."[34] In 1923, Col. John "Boney" Fuller, picking up on Corbett, argued that a focus on military victory was inadequate and that the conduct of war must also depend on a grasp of much broader economic, political, and cultural factors. In his 1926 book, *The Foundations of the Science of War*, Fuller developed his arguments further, with a core theme being that the aim of military operations was to cause the enemy a form of nervous breakdown.[35] His arguments, however, while innovative, were hard to follow.

In contrast, though Basil Liddell Hart was not as original a thinker, his style was sharper and more lucid. Moreover, with his growing reputation as a historian and commentator on military affairs, Liddell Hart had the platforms with which to spread his ideas. His starting point, also following Corbett, was that the objective of war was a good peace. The destruction of the enemy army was not an end in itself. Pitched battles were best avoided if there was a better way to achieve the objective. In 1929, Liddell Hart published *The Decisive Wars of History*, a book which he reworked several times, appearing in 1967 in its final version as *Strategy: The Indirect Approach*. At first, he defined strategy as the "art of distributing and transmitting military means to fulfill the ends of policy."[36] Later, Liddell Hart substituted "employing" for "transmitting." He limited tactics to matters concerned with "the fighting." Grand strategy was about the coordination and direction of all the resources of the nation to the attainment of the political object of the war. Although Liddell Hart's definitions were geared to promoting his "indirect approach," their advantage was that they could be adopted without accepting the whole package.

Liddell Hart's approach elevated the importance of policy. To military practitioners this risked relegating the importance of tactics. Field Marshall Lord Wavell held that "tactics, the art of handling troops on the battlefield, is and always will be a more difficult and more important part of the general's task than strategy, the art of bringing forces to the battlefield in a favorable position." Strategy, the Field Marshall averred, was "simpler and easier to grasp."[37]

34. Sir Charles Oman, "A Defence of Military History," in *The Study of War for Statesmen and Citizens* (London: Longmans, Green & Co., 1927), 40–41.

35. J. F. C. Fuller, *The Foundations of the Science of War* (London: Hutchinson, 1926).

36. Basil Liddell Hart, *Strategy: The Indirect Approach* (London: Faber, 1967).

37. Lord Wavell, *Soldiers and Soldiering* (London: Jonathan Cape, 1953), 47.

Here Wavell was harking back to the distinction favored in the British army from when he was learning his trade. Liddell Hart's seemed more appropriate for the post-1945 age of deterrence and limited war. In a volume published in 1970 entitled *Problems of Modern Strategy*, Michael Howard opened his essay by observing that Liddell Hart's definition was "as good as any, and better than most."[38] Liddell Hart is still regularly cited whenever strategy is being defined. The 1989 article by US Army Colonel Arthur Lykke, which introduced the definition of strategy currently popular in military circles, opened with a quotation from Liddell Hart about how military means must serve political ends. Lykke's innovation was to introduce "ways" as the course of action that brings means and ends together: "Strategy equals ends (objectives toward which one strives) plus ways (courses of action) plus means (instruments by which some end can be achieved)."[39] The advantage of this was that it is theoretically neutral and so could be used by those working with a variety of perspectives.

There were other competing definitions. The former French General André Beaufre referred to strategy as "the art of the dialectic of two opposing wills using force to resolve their dispute."[40] The former American Admiral Joseph Wylie wrote that strategy was "a plan of action designed in order to achieve some end; a purpose together with a system of measures for its accomplishment."[41] The first definition captured the centrality of conflict but not much else; the second assumed fixed objectives and that a strategy could be synonymous with a plan, playing down the problems of implementation caused by conflicts. Other definitions tended towards superfluous specificity or else were aspirationally normative. A 2018 Pentagon document, for example, defined a strategy only as something positive—"a prudent idea or set of ideas for employing the instruments of national power in a synchronized and integrated fashion to achieve theater or multinational objectives."[42] Other definitions are more theoretically loaded. The idea of strategy they all encompass, however, is that it is about the interaction of military means with political ends.

38. Michael Howard, "The Classic Strategists," in *Problems of Modern Strategy*, Alastair Buchan, ed. (London: Chatto & Windus for the Institute for Strategic Studies, 1970), 47.

39. Col. Arthur Lykke Jr., "Strategy = E + W + M," *Military Review* LXIX:5 (1989): 2–8.

40. André Beaufre, *Introduction to Strategy* (New York, NY: Praeger, 1965)

41. J. C. Wylie, *Military Strategy: A General Theory of Power Control* (Annapolis, MD: Naval Institute Press, 1989)

42. Joint Staff, Joint Doctrine Note 1–18, *Strategy*, April 25, 2018.

VI

One of the consequences of this shift in the understanding of strategy was that it moved attention away from the relationship between tactics and strategy, in which strategy was in some way superior, to the relationship between strategy and policy, in which strategy was subordinate.

As Corbett, Fuller, and Liddell Hart had discerned, the link between strategy and policy raised a further question. If military means had to be linked to political objectives, where did non-military means fit? The original idea of grand strategy was that, to win a war, it was necessary to draw on all the instruments of national power, not just the military instrument. That kept a link to the conduct of war. But by the late nineteenth century peacetime issues of policy had been identified as having to do with managing budgets and armaments, negotiating bases, forming alliances, or calming areas of tension, issues that determined preparedness for war or possibly made war avoidable. But at times governments might see only a comparatively minor role for the military instrument in their overall policy. Other instruments, for example those to do with commerce and finance, might be more important. Grand strategy, therefore, came to include not only how governments sought to win wars using all available means, but also the most effective combination of means—non-military as well as military—to achieve the objectives of national security and prosperity at times of peace.

The start of this shift can be seen in the first landmark edition of *Makers of Modern Strategy*, published in 1943. In his introduction, Edward Mead Earle remarked that, narrowly defined, strategy was "the art of military command, of projecting and directing a campaign," where tactics was "the art of handling forces in battle." But, he observed, strategy had "of necessity required increasing consideration of nonmilitary factors, economic, psychological, moral, political, and technological." Strategy, therefore, was "an inherent element of statecraft at all times." Earle defined strategy as:

> the art of controlling and utilizing the resources of a nation—or a coalition of nations—including its armed forces, to the end that its vital interests shall be effectively promoted and secured against enemies, actual, potential, or merely presumed.

Earle saw grand strategy as the highest form; it was here that the policies and armaments of the nation could be integrated. Earle went beyond Liddell Hart.

Through grand strategy, "the resort to war is either rendered unnecessary or is undertaken with the maximum chance of victory."[43]

After the Second World War and through the Cold War, the big questions of grand strategy appeared settled because of the bipolar conflict between one bloc led by the United States and another by the Soviet Union. The term was used as much as a historical construct—as in Edward Luttwak's *Grand Strategy of the Roman Empire*—as in discussions of contemporary security policies. In the late-1980s there was a revival of interest, presaging the end of the Cold War. Available definitions of strategy were still close to Liddell Hart's. At Yale, Professor Paul Kennedy, who had known Liddell Hart while a graduate student, introduced an edited book on the topic with quotations from Liddell Hart and Earle, noting how the term "strategy" was concerned with peace as much as war and the "balancing of ends and means." Kennedy concluded that:

> The crux of grand strategy lies therefore in policy, that is, in the capacity of the nation's leaders to bring together all of the elements, both military and nonmilitary [*sic*], for the preservation and enhancement of the nation's long-term (that is, wartime and peacetime) best interests.[44]

Over the next three decades, the amount of attention given to grand strategy expanded, and so did the concept. The risk was when a country was not at war, or was not preparing for one, and did not have some sort of grand project to improve its security and enhance its status for an extended period of time, grand strategy merged into general discussions of foreign policy. This was especially so once the Cold War threat had evaporated and there was uncertainty about whether there were strategic objectives that had to be pursued. Much of the (largely American) literature on grand strategy was concerned with advocacy, explaining why a grand strategy was needed and describing its appropriate content. Compared with military strategy, which tended to be about solving a particular and often urgent problem, grand strategy inclined towards the aspirational, setting out how to act in a constantly changing international environment, and providing an overarching framework to accommodate a range of foreign policy concerns. The historian Williamson Murray warned that, as resources and interests would always be out of balance, attempts

43. Edward Meade Earle, ed. *Makers of Modern Strategy* (Princeton, NJ: Princeton University Press, 1943), vi–viii.

44. Paul Kennedy, ed., *Grand Strategy in War and Peace* (New Haven, CT: Yale University Press, 1991), 1–5.

to provide clarity would struggle in an "environment of constant change, where chance and the unexpected are inherent." Murray likened grand strategy to French peasant soup, with whatever happened to be available thrown into a pot. "In thinking about the soup of grand strategy, recipes and theoretical principles are equally useless."[45]

Many definitions of grand strategy were essentially broader definitions of strategy. Thus, the political scientist Barry Posen described grand strategy as a "a chain of political ends and military means," while the historian John Gaddis described it as "the alignment of potentially unlimited aspirations with necessarily limited capabilities." Similarly, Peter Feaver, after discussing grand strategy as "the collection of plans and policies that comprise the state's deliberate effort to harness political, military, diplomatic, and economic tools together to advance that state's national interest," added that this was "the art of reconciling ends and means."[46] Thus, just as strategy lost its specificity when it became unhinged from battle, so too did grand strategy lose its specificity as it became detached from war. Instead of discussions on strategy staying close to those on tactics, they moved to a much higher plane.

VII

An even broader definition of strategy emerged during the first decades of the nuclear age. The demands of nuclear deterrence prompted big innovations in strategic thinking from the 1940s to the 1960s. These demands challenged the conservative bias in strategic thinking, which had long depended on studies of the great battles of history to help elucidate the principles of war. Amongst practitioners, the conservative bias did not go away. The officers in charge of nuclear arsenals showed little interest in new ways of thinking to accommodate the new weapons and did not let such issues or ideas influence their plans. Away from the military staffs, civilians—at universities and think-tanks such as RAND—took the view that they could and should address the special dilemmas posed by the new weaponry, including intercontinental missiles and nuclear weapons. A number of these civilians came from the humanities and

45. Williamson Murray, Richard Hart Sinnreich, and James Lacey, eds., *The Shaping of Grand Strategy* (New York, NY: Cambridge University Press, 2011), 9.

46. Barry R. Posen, *The Sources of Military Doctrine: France, Britain, and Germany between the World Wars* (Ithaca, NY: Cornell University Press, 1984), esp. 13; John Gaddis, *On Grand Strategy* (New York, NY: Penguin Press, 2018), 21; Peter Feaver, "What Is Grand Strategy and Why Do We Need It?" *Foreign Policy*, April 8, 2009.

understood the history of strategic thought. Bernard Brodie's *Strategy in the Missile Age* was exemplary in this regard, pointing to the military inclination to focus on tactics and their over-regard for offensives. Brodie also noted the "intellectual no-man's land where military and political problems meet," which was the realm of strategy. His complaint was about insufficient attention being paid to strategy and not about any need for a fundamental reappraisal.[47]

Others with backgrounds in economics, and often an interest in game theory, adopted new analytical methodologies to suggest how deterrence could be made to work and what to do should it fail. The origins of game theory were in mathematician John von Neumann's exploration in the 1920s of how probability theory could be applied to poker. He later teamed up with Oskar Morgenstern to produce the classic text, *The Theory of Games and Economic Behavior*, published in 1944.[48] By presenting potential outcomes using a two-by-two matrix, the work showed how one set of strategic moves depended on expectations about the moves of others. This insight could be used to design better moves. It pointed to the importance of imperfect information about opponents, and of thinking in terms of minimizing losses as well as maximizing gains.

By framing confrontations in abstract terms, game theory provided a way to grapple with the complexities of nuclear deterrence in a bipolar world without constant reference to the daunting humanitarian implications of these weapons being employed on any scale. The thing about a game of strategy, compared with games of chance or skill, Schelling observed, is that "each player's best choice depends on the action he expects the other to take, which he knows depends, in turn, on the other's expectation of his own." Strategy was defined in terms of this interdependence: "the conditioning of one's own behavior on the behavior of others."[49] This could apply to partnerships as well as conflicts, and so encouraged explorations of arms control. A distinct advantage of this approach was that it pointed to ways in which antagonists might cooperate and partners compete. Nuclear strategy remained an area in which civilians felt that they had as much competence as military officers. They assessed possible strategic moves in speculative, and even fantastical, scenarios, though their theories tended to work better when considering reinforcing deterrence than working out optimum moves should deterrence break

47. Bernard Brodie, *Strategy in the Missile Age* (Princeton, NJ: Princeton University Press, 1959), esp. 7.

48. John von Neumann and Oskar Morgenstern, *The Theory of Games and Economic Behavior* (Princeton, NJ: Princeton University Press, 1944).

49. Thomas Schelling, *The Strategy of Conflict* (Cambridge, MA: Harvard University Press, 1960).

down. These endeavors introduced many sub-concepts into strategic discourse, such as escalation, damage limitation, and crisis stability.

It was not necessary to adopt the full methodological apparatus to appreciate the importance of the interdependence of decision-making and the possibility of cooperation at times of conflict. Nor was the methodology only appropriate to a specific and extreme type of strategic problem. Its employment soon gravitated away from nuclear issues and towards economics and business strategy. This both encouraged and reflected the tendency for an increasing proportion of the literature on strategy to become geared to business and other non-military audiences, with its own definitions and formulations. While this literature would occasionally pick up on Sun Zi, Clausewitz, and Liddell Hart, there was little evidence of influence in the other direction.

By the 1970s the concept of strategy had moved far from the original, narrow military concept and was trending towards a general concept relevant to a range of situations, not all of which involved armed force. Debates were underway about the boundary lines between strategy and grand strategy, and between grand strategy and policy. Yet the boundary line between tactics and strategy, left over from earlier times, was still unresolved. Should the line be between preparations for fighting and actual fighting? Or between the higher and lower levels of command? These questions were most relevant to regular warfare. In the more irregular warfare of colonial times, the boundary line had already proved harder to draw because of the large importance of small engagements. This issue returned with counterinsurgency warfare in Vietnam.

In the aftermath of the frustrations of Vietnam, which provided more opportunities for civilians to get involved in operational decisions, and against the backdrop of the nuclear bias of the Cold War, there was a resurgence of interest in conventional warfare. In part, this became a debate about strategy, in particular about the comparative merits of attritional versus maneuver warfare, animated by a conviction that the American military needed to relearn the operational art. Just as the domain of tactics had shrunk, the generals had forgotten how to command; they had become inclined to assess the political implications of every move. An operational level of war was defined between strategy and tactics. This was defined in the 1982 *Field Manual 100* as a level which involved "planning and conducting campaigns."[50] Here senior commanders could think once again about how best to defeat enemies with forces similar in composition

---

50. For a discussion, see Justin Kelly and Mike Brennan, *Alien: How Operational Art Devoured Strategy* (Carlisle, PA: Strategic Studies Institute, 2009).

to their own ("peer competitors") and in an arena that left little room for the intrusion of politicians. The higher level of strategy was left for the highest level of command, those who would be charged with managing the interface with the political leadership. Edward Luttwak's book *Strategy: The Logic of War and Peace* was the most substantial attempt to consider strategy in terms of distinct levels (technical, tactical, and operational).[51] The alternative, set out in an influential article by Sir Michael Howard in *Foreign Affairs*, was to think not in terms of levels but rather in terms of dimensions—the operational, the logistical, the social, and the technological—which had to be accounted for in any successful strategy although the respective weighting might vary.[52]

The basic problem was that warfare had burst out of its boundaries, pushing out into societies with the possibility of destroying not only whole cities but also civilizations, or else requiring constant engagement with local populations to gain their support or to monitor their hostility. Once warfare could not be contained within manageable limits, it was unlikely that classical operations—geared as they were towards decisive battles—would suffice or that nations would dare to commit the totality of their resources to an epic struggle. The incentives shifted to limiting wars or avoiding them altogether, and strategy had to adjust accordingly.

VIII

This account has largely followed debates in the West. The content of a Russian, Chinese, or Indian strategy will be different from one adopted by the United States or France. Differences in culture and situations will make a significant difference in both their concepts of what strategy is and how it relates to tactics. Their concepts have different roots—whether Sun Zi in China or Kautilya in India. Yet the differences can be overdone. Sun Zi, for example, was a major influence on Liddell Hart, while those seeking support for the existence of an "operational level" found it in Soviet publications. The focus of this chapter has not been so much on content but rather on what can be discussed under the heading of strategy. Over the past 250 years "strategy" has become an umbrella term of potential relevance to all human affairs. Because it lacks specificity, it can include many national strategies, so long as they are about relating means to ends. It has

---

51. Edward Luttwak, *Strategy: The Art of War and Peace* (Cambridge, MA: Harvard University Press, 1987).

52. Michael Howard, "The Forgotten Dimensions of Strategy," *Foreign Affairs* 57: 5 (1979): 975–86.

become one of those words, along with politics and power, that are generally understood, even though they can be interpreted with great variation.

The use of "strategy" was never fully settled, even when employed as a more specific military term. Even then, there was a distinct set of practical activities associated with being strategic, largely connected with preparing forces for battle, working out where and how a battle would be fought, and then getting the forces into position. At that point tactics would take over. Strategy was also a matter for senior commanders. All this began to change once battle was recognized to be a means to an end and not an end in itself. Strategy could be approached from either a political or a military perspective because it was focused on the relationship between these two distinct spheres. But holding together these two distinct types of activities was always challenging, and so strategy was always apt to drift off in one direction at the expense of the other. Within the political sphere, strategy soon became detached from questions of war and peace, and came to be invoked whenever means must be aligned with ends. Eventually even the elements of conflict and competition diminished, so that strategy merely became a synonym for plan. There was still an association with a higher form of thinking, focused on the important, long-term, and essential, but the word could also be used to endow more mundane decisions with those properties. Strategy has come to represent a way of thinking, a habit of mind, an ability to assess vulnerabilities and possibilities in situations, an appreciation of causes and effects, and a capacity to link disparate activities in pursuit of a shared purpose.

Despite the promiscuous use of the term, there is still a close association of strategy with generalship. Discussions about strategy are still a vital part of any discourse about the use of armed force. There are very special issues raised when contemplating purposive violence. But whereas the complaint in the early twentieth century was that strategy was focused too much on operational issues and had neglected policy, later the concern became one of a focus on the political sphere, leading to a neglect of operational issues. In practice, the operational dimension is vital, not only when discussing whether desired objectives are at all realistic but also when it comes to execution. It may be important for even the most junior officers to have an understanding of the political context and the commander's intent when deciding on their tactics, but they also need to have a professional understanding of what can be expected of their subordinates and their equipment. When strategy is seen to be a higher calling, to be developed by specialist staffs, there is a risk that the practicalities of implementation will be neglected in favor of the elegance of the design.

CHAPTER 2

Thucydides, Polybius, and the Legacies of the Ancient World

Walter Russell Mead

The five centuries between the start of the Peloponnesian War and the death of Nero exercise a unique fascination on our world. The first half of the period saw the defeat of Athens, the meteoric career of Alexander the Great, the rise of the Roman Republic, and the defeat of Hannibal in the Second Punic War. The second half saw the development of the political crisis that ultimately destroyed the Roman Empire and the life and death of Jesus of Nazareth—two events that, respectively, shaped the political and religious imagination of the Western world. The art, the poetry and drama, the philosophy, the mathematics, the political thought, and the religious culture of the contemporary West still bear the imprint of this time.

The contribution of the ancient historians to Western culture is not as widely understood or appreciated as it ought to be. Thucydides and Polybius, in particular, not only provide the best available narratives of many of the critical events of the era and lay out the basic methods and ideas that still guide historians today. They were also shrewd and insightful political thinkers and their observations and conclusions have reverberated down through the millennia, guiding the thoughts of political philosophers and the actions of generals, politicians, and state-builders.

The magnitude of their accomplishments can make the true importance of the ancient historians difficult to appreciate. To demarcate the various and shifting roles that natural endowments, sheer chance, human psychology, national culture, and individual leadership played in politics and war, and to employ a consistent and responsible methodology to weave that analysis into a coherent narrative reconstruction of events was an immense intellectual accomplishment that continues to influence our perceptions of contemporary events as well as our construction of historical narratives. That these historians pulled it off with such elegance and sophistication that we still find these narratives instructive and intelligible today is an achievement on a par with the philosophical and mathematical triumphs of their era. And the vision of human society and history emerging from their work—complex, varied, and above all, political—has done as much to form the consciousness of the West as any other product of the Greek spirit.

Thucydides and Polybius are the most insightful and reliable of the great historians. While neither was infallible or wrote in the easy and luminous prose of the most gifted stylists of antiquity, and while both suffered the handicaps of writing history in a time without public archives, printed sources, or digital media, both produced extraordinary works that have stood the test of millennia.

Both men were well placed to understand political events. Thucydides fought in the Peloponnesian War.[1] Polybius lived on intimate terms with the Scipio family, fought in the Third Punic War, and was present at the sack of Carthage in 146 BCE.[2] Both Thucydides and Polybius held public office and had practical as well as academic knowledge of both military and civil affairs. Through family connections, both were thoroughly integrated into the international elite of their times, with many opportunities to take the measure of rulers and senior officials and to familiarize themselves with the details of political and military leadership. That perspective led them to a vision of international politics that is as unfashionable in the academy as it is necessary in the real world: that regime type matters enormously in foreign policy, but that democracies are not necessarily wiser, more peaceful, or more just than other regime types.

Like many of their modern successors, both Thucydides and Polybius embraced ideals of accuracy and objectivity which in practice they did not always uphold. Thucydides's narrative reflects a deep, and not always justified, criticism of Athenian democracy and its political partisans. That bias, which presumably

1. Thucydides, *The Peloponnesian War* (Boston, MA: E. P. Dutton, 1910), Book 4, Section 104. Unless otherwise noted, citations of this source are given as Thucydides, *The Peloponnesian War*, followed by book and section number.

2. Polybius, *Histories* (Bloomington, IN: Indiana University Press, 1962), Book 39, Section 4. Unless otherwise noted, citations of this source are given as Polybius, *Histories*, followed by book and section number.

was not unaffected by the Athenian vote to ostracize Thucydides following the defeat of their forces under his command in the northeastern theater, led him to hold the conservative Nicias, the person most responsible for the decisive defeat of the Sicilian Expedition, in higher regard than Cleon, the democratic leader responsible for Athens's dramatic victory at Pylos.[3] Similarly, Polybius's profound lack of curiosity about Carthaginian institutions and culture both reflects his sympathy for the Roman side and limits his ability to provide his readers with a truly comprehensive history of the war. And both historians uncritically share many attitudes of their time about slavery, pedophilia, the intellectual and moral capacity of women, and the superiority of their own cultures to "barbarian" peoples around them that modern readers find repugnant or incomprehensible. Their achievement is not to avoid such lapses, but to have described complex events so clearly and to have provided such a wealth of information that later readers can engage with the stories they tell— and even dispute their interpretations of events.

The legacy of the great historians of the most importance to our times, and the subject of this chapter, is the way they integrated strategy, the art of winning wars, and statecraft, the art of building and leading states. As they analyzed the wars and revolutions of their times, the ancient historians concluded that the success of states in international competition is, within the limits set by fate and chance on all human calculations, determined by the strength of their political culture as expressed and embodied in state institutions and the capacity of leaders to enlist their society's forces in the service of a viable international strategy. The interplay of statecraft and strategy, seen against the background of factors that human beings can do little to affect or control, is the topic the two men sought to illuminate, and to understand their treatment of this topic is to engage in a mode of historical analysis that still can serve policymakers well.

In the histories of Thucydides and Polybius we are given two contests between two states. In both conflicts, the successes and the failures of the principal antagonists (Athens and Sparta in the Peloponnesian War, Carthage and Rome in the Second Punic War) owed at least as much to their qualities as states and societies as to the specific decisions made by generals and admirals in the field. Effective leadership in these societies required a dual mastery of the political and the strategic domains. Pericles had to understand the world of Athenian politics clearly enough to defend his power and his policies against

3. Thucydides, *The Peloponnesian War*, 4.28.

internal opponents. He also had to develop an understanding of the nature of the contest with Sparta and to develop what was necessarily an unconventional strategy to offset Sparta's decisive advantages in land warfare—and he then had to build a bridge between the requirements of his war strategy and the realities of Athenian politics. After Pericles, no Athenian leader appeared who could reconcile the realms of internal politics and external war. Rome, as Polybius saw it, ultimately triumphed over Carthage because its robust domestic institutions staggered, but did not fall, under Hannibal's blows.

I

Neither statecraft nor strategy existed in a vacuum for these historians. The arena in which states competed was shaped in the first instance by natural forces which human beings did not control and to a very large extent did not and could not understand. Beyond that, humans themselves were shaped by psychological realities, some communal and cultural, some individual, that human beings did not choose and could only overcome by great efforts. The third factor that shaped the arena of conflict was the arc of historical development, both of individual states and of human civilization overall. Between them, nature, human nature, and history set the boundaries within which states competed, and before turning to their analyses of the Peloponnesian and Punic conflicts, I will briefly look at their analysis of the "givens" that shaped the two wars and did much to determine their outcomes.

While their subject was warfare, Thucydides and Polybius emphasized the influence of the non-human world on human affairs. Nature, as we may call this force, acts in politics through two avenues. The first is the influence of geography and, more generally, of the physical world on human polities and their interactions. Athens's hinterland in Attica had relatively poor soil but was situated next to a good harbor.[4] As a result, Athens looked to the sea. Rome, by contrast, was blessed with more fertile soil, but then so were its closest neighbors and rivals. The poor soil and mountainous terrain of much of Greece limited the size and power of most Greek city states, but it also reduced the dangers of conquest by over-mighty neighbors. Rome enjoyed an easy prosperity that many Greeks would envy, but from early times faced a regional environment in which security could only be obtained through winning bitter contests with one powerful and prosperous rival after another.

4. Thucydides, *The Peloponnesian War*, 1.2.

Nature did not restrict itself to setting the stage and defining the strategic priorities of rival states. It also intervened actively in the form of chance. Plagues, good and bad harvests, storms at sea, eclipses, fog, and other variables frequently upset the most carefully laid plans. Luck mattered. Neither historian was superstitious, but both saw the hand of fate in the role that natural events beyond any human knowledge or control regularly played in international politics. Augurs might struggle to interpret the auspices, angry deities could be propitiated, and the oracles could be consulted, but the reality that neither individuals nor states controlled their own destinies was central to the political understanding of these historical pioneers.

In opposition to the default assumptions of many people in our more technocratic world today, both Thucydides and Polybius believed that, while exceptionally gifted individuals might divine something of future events, policymakers in general had little understanding of the forces around them. This was partly, of course, due to the scientific and technical limits of their era. At sea, fleet commanders often did not know where their opponents might be, and the best battle plans could be easily disrupted by a change in the unpredictable winds. More broadly, political leaders did not know whether the next harvest would bring feast or famine, how their far-flung forces in the field were faring on any given day, or what was happening in the politics of allied and enemy cities.

Psychology, whether of humanity (human nature), of a particular community or place (culture), or of individuals (character) was another critical factor influencing the fortunes of war. Thucydides and Polybius's understandings of the psychological dimension of history began with the belief that there were drives and perceptions that were common to all human beings when placed in certain situations. The inhabitants of a besieged or threatened city knew fear. The poor were jealous of the rich, the rich suspicious of the poor. Virtuous actions were widely admired, cowardice and other vicious actions universally condemned.

Beyond the universal realities of human psychology, different groups of human beings were seen to have specific characteristics reflecting their history, their geographic location, their culture, and what somewhat anachronistically we can call their level of technological and social development. Barbarian troops were seen as often more courageous and more inured to hardship than troops from civilized states, but they generally lacked discipline and, if the ferocity of their initial attack failed to achieve an objective, they could be routed and scattered. The Greeks and the Romans saw differences between themselves and the peoples of "the East" and of "Egypt." Athenians saw themselves, and were seen by others, as an excitable and changeable people, quick to see new possibilities but not always steadfast in pursuing their goals. Spartans by contrast were seen as sluggish and conservative and slow to move, though when set on a course they were seen as difficult to deflect or deter. A similar polarity appears in the Punic Wars. The Carthaginians were seen as more enterprising but less grounded than the stolid Romans.[5]

The art of war required a knowledge of these psychological and cultural factors. Armies were often made up of troops from different cities, barbarian kingdoms, and tribes. The successful general would know how to lead and inspire very different groups of people and would also know how to arrange the elements of his army in a way that took note of the different fighting styles of the different groups that composed it; one looked to place Celts, Greeks, Romans, Numidians, and others in positions where they would be more likely to manifest their virtues than to yield to their shortcomings.

The need to incorporate psychology into military strategy went beyond the battlefield. Pericles's order to the Athenians to avoid battle with the Spartan troops ravaging Attica, like Fabius's order to the Romans to avoid battle with Hannibal, ran counter to the culture of both cities, and the stress between a sound and necessary military strategy and the instincts of the people put the leadership of both men to a serious test.[6] The desperate hunger of the Spartans to recover the prisoners taken at Pylos compared to the frigid refusal of the Romans to seek the release of the prisoners taken by Hannibal after the disaster of Cannae illustrates the way that the different political cultures of the two cities affected the strategic options of their leaders. The kings of Sparta simply could not tell the Spartan assembly to forget their prisoners in Athens; the Romans had more choices after Cannae.

The final level of psychology is that of the individual, whether in a position of military or political leadership. The ancient historians believed that the character of a leader was one of the principal determinants of the outcome of military and civil contests. Courage, wiliness, eloquence, an appropriate mix of humility and pride, constancy, physical and emotional self-control: these qualities led some to success, while qualities like rashness, cowardice, vanity, avarice, and concupiscence led others to defeat. Ancient histories were written in part to illuminate the relationships between virtue and success, vice

5. Polybius, *Histories*, 1.39.

6. Thucydides, *The Peloponnesian War*, 2.13; Polybius, *Histories*, 3.89.

and failure. The historians thought that it was impossible to understand the course of events without understanding the characters of the principal leaders involved.

After nature and psychology, history was the third force that shaped the arena within which states competed, but history meant something different to the ancients than it does in our time. The concept of history in the modern world reflects the massive cultural impact of Abrahamic religion and the secular ideologies that grew up in its shadow. To the modern imagination, history almost always appears as a process of struggle from the abyss of ignorance and poverty toward a hoped-for utopia of abundance and peace. Judaism, Christianity, and Islam all present the human story as one of a fall from a primeval paradise into a realm of conflict and misery. However, all three religions also see divine providence working through the historical process in order to return humanity to a higher version of the prelapsarian bliss. This historical template is retained by secular ideologies like liberalism and Marxism, and the idea of progress toward a triumphant "end of history" is deeply engrained in the modern imagination.[7]

The ancients saw history in different terms. They were aware that the arts of civilization were developing, and that states were growing in power and wars growing in intensity. This awareness was not, however, yoked to a doctrine of progress. The historical imagination of the pre-Abrahamic Greco-Roman world was cyclical. Human societies rose from ignorance and savagery to civilization and sophistication, but as the strong and noble virtues of the savage were softened by the comforts of civilized life, society lost the virtues that enabled its rise. As societies became decadent and luxurious through their mastery of the arts of civilization, they became easy prey for new waves of strong, savage armies.

This approach led the ancient historians to a bifurcated view of the impact of history on international politics. The rise and fall of states on the one hand did not proceed on any kind of synchronized timetable. Rising states encountered states at their peak or states proceeding through decadence toward collapse in the mixed melees of world politics. On the other hand, a gradual enlargement of the playing field affected all states.

The Peloponnesian and Second Punic Wars are separated by almost exactly 200 years. Hostilities between Athens and Sparta erupted in 431 BCE and Athens capitulated in 401; Hannibal invaded Italy in 218 BCE and Carthage

---

7. Francis Fukuyama, "The End of History?" *The National Interest* (Summer 1989): 3–18.

accepted harsh Roman terms to end hostilities in 201. While there was some geographical overlap between the two wars as Syracuse played a significant role in both conflicts, and both wars saw battles in southern Italy and the Greek mainland, the Mediterranean world had changed dramatically between the two eras.

Over those two centuries, the center of gravity in the Mediterranean had shifted decisively to the west. In the time of Thucydides, Rome had been fighting for its life against Celtic invaders. Carthage had already established a significant Mediterranean empire but neither of these western powers mattered much in the Peloponnesian War. By 218 BCE, however, Rome and Carthage were clearly the two most powerful states in the Mediterranean world. As the master of Italy and most of Sicily, Rome controlled the largest and richest agricultural lands under cultivation. Carthaginian possessions in North Africa and Spain, together with its trading empire, made it much richer and more powerful than Athens at its peak.

While the west had grown in economic and military importance, the east had suffered an eclipse. The Greek city-states had fallen into irrelevance. Overshadowed by Macedonia and the other Hellenistic kingdoms, individual Greek cities retained cultural prestige and wealth, but, even when joined into multistate federations like the Achaean League, they were too small and weak to figure decisively in the power politics of the later era. The Hellenistic kingdoms that emerged from the wreckage of Alexander the Great's empire had neither the power of Persia nor the dynamism of Greece. The Greek world was largely a spectator in the Punic Wars that would determine its fate.

Polybius, whose career has some similarities with that of the later historian Josephus, was keenly aware of the changes between his era and what already in retrospect looked like a vanished golden age of Greek power.[8] As the son of a prominent official of the Achaean League of Peloponnesian city-states, Polybius was brought to Rome as a hostage. Thanks to his family's prominence and his own intelligence and culture, Polybius moved in aristocratic and powerful circles in Rome and even after the Achaean hostages were permitted to return home, he remained with the Scipio family. Following Rome's defeat of the Achaean League and the end of Greek independence, Polybius worked for reconciliation while assisting the establishment of Roman rule.

---

8. A. M. Eckstein, "Josephus and Polybius: A Reconsideration," *Classical Antiquity*, 9:2 (1990): 175–208.

But the changes were not just about political and military power shifting to the west. Polybius was an early chronicler of what we would now call globalization. Before the Second Punic War, he wrote:

> things happened in the world in a sporadic fashion, because every incident was specific, from start to finish, to the part of the world where it happened. But ever since then, history has resembled a body, in the sense that incidents in Italy and Libya and Asia and Greece are all interconnected, and everything tends towards a single outcome.[9]

The war between Rome and Carthage was clearly a competition to dominate the entire Mediterranean basin. As Polybius put it, "[O]nce the Romans had defeated the Carthaginians in the Hannibalic War, they came to think that they had completed the largest and most difficult part of their project of worldwide dominion," and turned immediately from Carthage to Greece for further expansion.[10]

Even in an earlier time, Thucydides discerned that the changing field of international politics was affecting Greek politics. The ancient rivalries of Greek city-states were increasingly being affected by the attitudes of "barbarian" states. Thucydides traced the origins of the Peloponnesian War to the impact of Persia on Greek politics, and throughout the war both Athens and Sparta found themselves constantly looking to the Great King and his satraps.[11] The expansion of the Greek world into southern Italy contributed both to the origin and the outcome of the Peloponnesian War. Corcyra, the city over whose destiny Athenian and pro-Spartan forces first came to blows, was important because of its location on a major trade route between the Greek mainland and the Greek colonies of Italy. The rising power of Syracuse and the growing strategic weight of Sicily in the Greek world drew Athens into the disastrous Sicilian Expedition. Athenian power depended on its lifeline to the granaries of the Black Sea, and its security depended on its ability to prevent the Persians, Macedonians, and other rival powers from controlling the islands and harbors through which Black Sea grain made its way to Athenian markets.

Nature, chance, human nature, culture (including both social and economic development), individual psychology, and the course of history constituted

9. Polybius, *The Histories: A New Translation*, trans. Robin Waterfield (Oxford: Oxford University Press, 2010), Book 1, Paragraph 3. Unless otherwise noted, citations of this source are given as Polybius, *Histories: A New Translation*, followed by book and paragraph number.

10. Polybius, *The Histories: A New Translation*, 1.3.

11. Thucydides, *The Peloponnesian War*, 1.18.

the givens with which both strategists and statecraft practitioners engaged. Our historians were careful to describe these elements and give them, so far as they could, their due weight, but the men's goal was not merely to analyze human affairs. They wanted to provide useful advice to future policymakers, and so sought to understand how different decision-makers struggled with the fates, and why some succeeded, and others failed.

The wars end badly for three of the four main protagonists. In the Peloponnesian War, the Athenians lost outright, and, while the Spartans won, their victory was hollow. Their war aims were achieved, but Sparta could not turn back the clock on the historical developments that were transforming the Mediterranean region and depriving the Greek city-states of control over their fate. Indeed, Sparta's victory over Athens ensured that no Greek city-state would be among the "rule makers" in the emerging Mediterranean world. In the Second Punic War, Carthage was defeated, while Rome lay the foundations for an enduring hegemony, uniting the formerly Carthaginian territories in Africa and Spain to Italy and the Hellenistic world in the state that, more than any other, shaped the political, legal, and cultural future of the Western world.

II

The Peloponnesian War played a role in Greek history comparable to what the First World War was to Europe. Both wars left the victors almost as exhausted as the vanquished and inaugurated a period of civilizational crisis and imperial decline. Thucydides could not see all the future consequences of the conflict, but he knew that the moral and political failures of Athens, that brilliant city then at the height of its cultural and intellectual glory, cast shadows over the whole Greek-speaking world, shadows that the victorious Spartans had no power to dispel.

Corcyra was the city that drew Corinth, Athens, and ultimately Sparta into conflict.[12] As outside actors supported internal factions, the social and political polarization in Corcyra spiraled into an uncontrollable cycle of atrocity. The oligarchical and democratic parties inside the city came to hate and fear one another more bitterly than either side feared foreigners and the civic life of a prosperous Greek outpost degenerated into a maelstrom of massacres and plots.

This sorry drama repeated itself in city after city across Greece. Meanwhile, the rival armies and navies of the major powers left destruction in their wake,

---

12. Thucydides, *The Peloponnesian War*, 1.24.

from Sicily to the Black Sea. Ancient cities were burned to the ground, their adult males massacred, and their women and children sold into slavery. The highest culture the Western world had ever seen turned on itself in a frenzy of hatred and rage. The hands that built the Parthenon would slaughter the citizens of Melos, and the cities whose courage had defeated Xerxes would turn as suppliants to his successors in order to seek Persian aid against their Greek rivals.

It is a complicated story. On the eve of the war, Athens was a revolutionary power pursuing a conservative policy, while Sparta was a status quo power prepared to wage a revisionist war. Athens sought security abroad by achieving hegemony in Greece; Sparta's quest for security against the consequences of a rising Athens would end by undermining the security of Greece as a whole.

Thucydides famously wrote that Spartan fear about the rising power of Athens was the root cause of the Peloponnesian War, and he was not wrong.[13] However, Athens also had its fears and the Athenian commitment to policies that increased its power, even at the cost of alienating Sparta, reflected those fears.

Athens was committed to an expansive view of security. The poor soil of Attica could not support a rising population, and the best sources of cheap grain were on the coast of the Black Sea. Its silver mines gave Athens the wealth to support a large fleet and a trading empire, but the needs of its trade forced Athens onto the path that aroused the jealously of Sparta. Maritime trade at the time was much cheaper and faster than trade overland, but given the primitive state of ship building, weather forecasting, and navigation equipment, ships preferred to travel in short hops and, when possible, to stay within sight of land. To ensure its grain supply, Athens needed to secure control over intermediary ports from Byzantium and beyond in the Black Sea down through the Sea of Marmara and the Hellespont down through the islands and continental ports of the Aegean.

This space could not be defended without a large and active fleet. At the same time, the security of its sea routes depended on either overawing or placating the powerful terrestrial states that bordered the waterways on which Athens depended. Barbarian and semi-barbarian rulers of states and quasi-states like Macedonia and Thrace preoccupied the Athenians on the European side of the waterways; on the Asian side, the menacing power of Persia confronted the Athenians at every turn. In addition to its naval strength, Athens

13. Thucydides, *The Peloponnesian War*, 1.23.

needed enough land-based military strength to deter these neighboring states from interfering with its commerce. A military establishment of this size was not cheap and indeed Athens could not maintain these forces on its own.

From this reality, and especially the need to keep any ambitious Persian satraps in check, came the need for the Delian League or, as it came to be known, the Athenian Empire. Including about 150 city-states at the outbreak of the Peloponnesian War, and stretching from the Bosporus to the Adriatic, the empire brought the most strategic waterways and coastal territories under Athenian control and the tribute paid by members provided Athens with the resources necessary to defend its far-flung interests.[14]

From the Athenian point of view, the development and defense of the empire was a noble, natural, and necessary aspect of any policy that sought to defend Greek independence. The connection between the well-being of Greece and the strength of the Athenian Empire was less clear to those members of the Delian League who resented the increasingly heavy hand of Athens. It was also less clear to Sparta.

If Athens was doomed to expansion by its history and geography, Sparta was made for conservatism. Located in the remote southern half of the Peloponnese, Sparta was, by Greek standards, well inland from the sea. The basic fact of Spartan life was the existence of a large class of so-called helots, a class of Greek-speaking, hereditary peasants and quasi-slaves who worked the fertile fields of the Spartan homeland for the benefit of their masters. Outnumbering the Spartans by as much as seven-to-one, and given to the occasional revolt, the helots were both the pillar and the nightmare of the Spartan state.[15] Their labor provided the wealth that enabled free Spartans to devote their lives to the military drills that made the Spartan army both the wonder and the terror of Greece. The need to keep the helots in subjugation forced the Spartans to organize their laws and institutions around the constant need for vigilance and military discipline.

Spartan life was organized under laws said to have come from the semi-legendary figure of Lycurgus, who lived between three and six hundred years before the Peloponnesian War and left Sparta organized for patriotism, military service, and rough economic equality among free Spartan citizens.[16] Taken from their mothers at age six, Spartan boys underwent years of military

14. Donald Kagan, *The Peloponnesian War* (New York, NY: Penguin, 2003), 8.
15. Thucydides, *The Peloponnesian War*, 4.80.
16. Polybius, *Histories*, 6.10.

training under conditions of constant hardship. The survivors of this process became the finest fighting force known to classical Greece and exploits like their defense of Thermopylae were legendary.

The possession of a quasi-invincible army did not, however, make Sparta an expansionist state. On the contrary, the long period of training meant that new Spartan soldiers could not be made quickly. The population base was a fraction of the more urban and commercially focused Greek states like Athens. Casualties in battle could not be quickly replaced. Moreover, the need to keep a large force at home to overawe the helots ensured that Sparta was reluctant to commit to hostilities far from its boundaries and thus limited the number of soldiers available for foreign campaigns.

These facts of Spartan life gave Spartan foreign policy a defensive orientation. It needed no long trading routes in the Aegean, and as long as the Persian Empire refrained from new conquests in Greece, Sparta had no necessary quarrel with the Great King. The Athenian-led transformation of the ancient Greek political order was more ominous. Sparta did not have the ability or the will to build an empire that could meet Athens on equal terms, but nor was it willing to sit passively by while Athens established an uncontestable hegemony over Greece.

The logic of Athenian security and of the independence of Greece as a whole ran counter to the logic of Spartan security. This was the hard fact that drove Athens down a path that increased the risk of war with Sparta, and that left Sparta with no option but war once Athenian power threatened the position of Sparta's key ally Corinth after Athens came to the defense of Corcyra, a renegade Corinthian colony in the far northwest.[17]

The two states were not wrong to see their clash as unavoidable, and while strong factions in both cities argued for compromise and peace from the first outbreak of hostilities on through the Athenian defeat, efforts at compromise repeatedly broke down.

There was another problem for Athens, one that Pericles might have surmounted but that his successors could not. The problem was that, from the beginning, the Peloponnesian War involved two very different conflicts. Athens was not only fighting Sparta; it was fighting for naval and commercial supremacy in and around the Adriatic Sea.

Corcyra, a city originally founded by Corinth, had become a powerful naval state on its own, thanks largely to its position as the closest city on the Greek

17. Thucydides, *The Peloponnesian War*, 1.38.

side of the Adriatic to the rich cities of southern Italy and Sicily. By the outbreak of the Peloponnesian War, Corcyra was said to possess the third largest navy in Greece. Athens, as the largest navy, in combination with Corcyra, could overawe Corinth, perhaps the most important city allied to Sparta.[18] An alliance between Corcyra and Athens dramatically weakened Corinth's position at sea; it also undercut Corinth's standing as a major trade emporium.

The war forced both Athens and Sparta into unfamiliar patterns of behavior and thought. Sparta's goal was to protect both its unique position of prestige and honor in Greece as well as the security of its way of life. To win the war it would have to engage in dramatic, even revolutionary changes. Before victory came, Sparta would send troops across much of Greece, welcome the unprincipled Athenian adventurer Alcibiades into its inner councils, take Persian gold to build a fleet that challenged Athens from Sicily to the Black Sea, and put that fleet under the command of Lysander, a rumored half-helot who wrenched Spartan policy out of its traditional channel to seek a short-lived hegemony over Greece.

The Athenian strategy that Pericles originally developed was as uncongenial to the Athenian spirit as Lysander's was to Sparta. Pericles understood that the status quo was favorable to Athens at the start of the war. Each year, the Athenian trading empire became larger and richer. Each year, the tribute from the cities in the Delian League flowed into the Athenian treasury. Fear of Persia and of larger neighbors would bring new cities into the Athenian orbit over time. As democratic movements came to power around the Greek world, those governments would seek Athenian protection and with Athenian support could likely sustain themselves against attempts by anti-democratic forces to regain power. To solidify its position, Athens needed to exhaust Sparta, not to conquer it. Secure behind the long walls that connected the city to its seaport at Piraeus, Athens could hit Sparta with pinprick attacks until, ultimately, the Lacedemonians decided to abandon the war. A relatively quiet war strategy had the additional advantage of not alarming Persia.

The difficulty was that a cautious war policy ran counter to the instincts of the war party in Athens. Right through the end of the war, Athens was divided into two parties: an oligarchical, or as they might put it, aristocratic party that favored peace with Sparta and a democratic party committed to the policy of expansion. Pericles had the political ability to keep the oligarchs out of power while imposing his strategic views on the populists, but after his death Athens

18. Thucydides, *The Peloponnesian War*, 1.36.

had no leader with his combination of political skill and strategic vision.[19] Over time, as the war became more difficult, the two parties each became more radical. The democrats threw off restraint in pursuit of the war, and the oligarchs were ultimately willing to accept defeat in the war if that could secure their power at home.

The factions in Athens aligned behind different foreign policies based on their economic and political interests at home. The popular party was largely composed of city-based merchants, workers, and sailors. These people depended on the commercial economy and the empire for their prosperity. The great merchants grew rich from international trade and supported a strong navy to protect their trade and to extend the range of their operations. To the extent that imports reduced food prices, most ordinary Athenians benefitted from the empire, and the revenues of the empire went either to the navy (and employment for the oarsmen manning the galleys) or to public works (providing jobs for ordinary Athenians).

The conservative oligarchs were not as enamored of the Athenian commercial boom. While some found their way into the new economy, for many of the older Athenian families, land was their wealth. Trade undercut the prices they received for their produce, reduced the dependency of the Athenian poor on powerful aristocratic patrons by offering more and better paying jobs, and stimulated the rise of powerful political rivals among the mercantile classes. The division between agricultural aristocrats and oligarchs and the participants in the mercantile trading economy was found throughout the Greek world and in Athens as elsewhere, the agricultural and aristocratic traditionalists tended to sympathize with the Spartan cause.

Pericles's war and political strategies meshed perfectly here. Sparta's war tactic, one they had every reason to believe would be effective, was to send their strongest forces against their strongest enemy: to invade Attica by land and lay waste to the fields and farms of Athens. Impelled by both honor and interest, the Athenians would come out to defend their property. The Spartans would, as usual, beat them in battle and make terms. Pericles saw no advantage in giving Sparta an easy victory and counseled the Athenians to keep their forces behind the walls as the Spartans ravaged the hinterland. This was extremely unpopular with old, landed Athenian aristoi. They were the ones who stood to lose the most as the Spartans burned their villas and farms; they were the ones whose old-fashioned sense of honor was most outraged by the

---

19. Thucydides, *The Peloponnesian War*, 2.65.

"cowardly" refusal to fight the Spartans head on. Pericles's core supporters among the commercial classes and the urban mass were probably not entirely displeased to see the wealthy oligarchs bear the brunt of the Spartan offensive, and, thanks to Athenian naval supremacy, trade carried on as usual. Wartime spending on naval construction and crewing naval vessels provided jobs for many voters, and not even the plague could force Pericles out of office—or force him to modify his policies.

It was the moderation his strategy required in the long term that proved too much for the Athenians, especially after Pericles died of the plague early in the war.[20] The urban democracy wanted a vigorous prosecution of the war and embraced maximum war aims, rather than the limited war for limited gains that Pericles wanted. The climax of this post-Periclean war policy was the Sicilian Expedition, when, with Spartan armies still in the field, Athens widened the scale of the war by attacking Syracuse, the greatest of the Greek colonies on that fertile island. Had the campaign succeeded (and, according to Thucydides, the Athenians came close to victory more than once), Athens would have been mistress of both the east and the west of the Greek world, and sooner or later Sparta would have had to come to terms.[21]

Thucydides reproached the democracy with inconstancy, but the democratic faction in Athens fought to the bitter end. The plague, the loss of Syracuse, revolts in the empire, the appearance of a Spartan fleet, Persian interference, and internal strife: none of this sufficed to break the fighting spirit of the Athenian democrats until, the navy defeated, the city besieged, Athens was literally starved into surrender.

What the democracy lacked was institutional coherence, not constancy. The Athenian state lacked the deep institutions that the Roman Republic brought to its contest with Carthage. Athens also lacked the depth and breadth of leadership that we will see in Rome. Athens was led, or misled, by individuals. Rome produced its share of great generals and political leaders, but the deeply institutionalized quality of Roman politics meant that Rome was less dependent on particular leaders. If one or even two consuls failed, others could always be found.

In any case, Sparta's victory in the Peloponnesian War led only to dead ends. For Sparta, a brief period of hegemony ended thirteen years after the Athenian surrender as a league of ambitious city-states led by Thebes reduced

---

20. Thucydides, *The Peloponnesian War*, 2.65.
21. Thucydides, *The Peloponnesian War*, 7.2.

Spartan power to its traditional limits. For Greece, the consequences were worse. Without a strong hegemonic city-state or an effective league of states, the Greek world could not maintain its independence in an age of rising superpowers. Most of Greece would fall to Philip of Macedon, and in the fullness of time, to Rome. Whether a victorious Athens could have built an empire strong enough to remain a factor in power politics against Macedonia, Carthage, and Rome cannot be known. But with the fall of Athens, the era of Greek power came to an end. Alexander the Great's Macedonian empire would spread Greek learning and ideas across western Asia and Egypt, but Greek culture traveled in the baggage trains of despotic kings, then and for many centuries to come.

III

If Thucydides's subject was the tragedy of the Greek world, Polybius's was the triumph of Rome. To be the chronicler of Rome's rise to supremacy was not, we can safely say, Polybius's original life goal. Like his father, Polybius had a distinguished career as an official in the Achaean League, an almost EU-like union of sovereign, equal city-states in the Peloponnese that, for a time, held off both Macedonia and Rome. After the Romans defeated the League, Polybius was taken to Rome as a prominent hostage, a status that allowed him to become intimately familiar with Roman life and institutions. Accompanying his friend Scipio the Younger, whose adoptive father Publius Cornelius Scipio was the eldest son of the Scipio Africanus who defeated Hannibal and ended the Second Punic War at the Battle of Zama, Polybius witnessed the final defeat of Carthage and the subsequent sack of the city. 146 BCE, the year Carthage fell, also marked the final defeat of the Achaean League, as the Romans won a crushing victory in the battle of Corinth and ended the era of Greek independence in the ancient world.[22]

The Mediterranean globalization so central to Polybius's historical vision was a real thing. The economic and institutional convergence launched by Alexander's conquests had struck deep roots in the east and was rapidly spreading across the west. The patterns of agriculture, trade, and city life originating in the Levant and Greece were being rapidly adopted by the Gauls of Italy and Southern France as well as the peoples of North Africa and Spain. Increasingly, the peoples of the Mediterranean basin were living in a single

22. Polybius, *The Histories: A New Translation*, i.

economic and political space, and that space was increasingly dominated by Rome.

If we compare the protagonists in the Peloponnesian and Punic Wars, certain parallels suggest themselves. Carthage was like Athens, both mercantile and mercurial. Rome, like Sparta, was originally a terrestrial power that built a fleet to counter the sea power of its great rival. Carthaginian leadership was personal and charismatic. As the Roman empire began to crack under Hannibal's attacks, the politics of empire were similar to what Thucydides described. In city after city, the landed and aristocratic upper classes supported the alignment with Rome, while the "mob" and the merchants felt the pull of a Carthaginian alliance.[23]

Carthaginian power struck like lightning. Expelled from Sicily and Sardinia after the First Punic War, Carthage rapidly built a formidable new power base in Spain. Knitting tribes together into a broad coalition, it established new cities that stimulated rapid growth and development. At the outbreak of the Second Punic War, Carthage was in a stronger position than it was at the start of the First. When Hannibal determined that the time had come to attack Rome, he chose an unconventional route—over the Alps—that brought him into the territory of the restive Cisalpine Gauls, peoples who resented Roman pressure and were ready to explore new alliances. A string of extraordinary victories culminating in the Battle of Cannae, a victory so complete that generations of generals have sought to emulate it, shattered the Roman armies, dented Roman prestige, and brought Hannibal into the heart of Italy as a conqueror. One of Rome's wealthiest and most important subject allies, the city of Capua, drove out its Roman garrison and welcomed Hannibal into its citadel.[24]

Yet Hannibal failed, and after almost two decades of fruitless campaigning, he was forced to return to North Africa to meet a Roman attack on the Carthaginian homeland. The result of the Second Punic War was much worse for Carthage than the First, and in the years before its final fall, the city of Dido never recovered its former power or wealth. While Polybius's text contains very little from Carthaginian sources, what we do know allows us to conclude that Hannibal's brilliance as a military commander was undercut by failures in national strategy and statecraft.

Carthage, like Athens, was a victim of the qualities that made it a success. The decentralized Carthaginian system conferred freedom on entrepreneurial

23. Polybius, *Histories*, 7.4.
24. Polybius, *Histories*, 7.1.

leaders like Hasdrubal and Hannibal. With little oversight—or support—from the central government, these war leaders were able to seize opportunities to expand Carthaginian power and relatively quickly they established their control over much of Spain south of the Ebro. The decentralized nature of this policymaking likely reflects the mercantile basis of Carthaginian culture and politics. Like Venice, Carthage was a city of traders and adventurers where generations of free-wheeling merchants made fortunes in unconventional ways and in places well beyond the reach of the authorities back home. The Carthaginian state gave its representatives more leeway than more highly institutionalized and law-bound states like Rome (or Sparta) did, but the price for this freedom was a potential lack of support at critical moments.

Rome, on the other hand, was organized for war. The interplay between the geography and politics of central Italy left it no choice. The soil of Italy was more fertile, the climate more favorable, and the landscape less mountainous than in any large area of Greece. That meant that Rome was surrounded by jealous neighbors, and from its earliest times, was engaged in conflicts with rival cities and towns. Worse, Italy was more exposed to invasion from the north. In 390 BCE, little more than a decade after the close of the Peloponnesian War, Celtic invaders occupied and burned Rome, extracting a large payment in gold before returning to the north. Rome emerged as the leading city, first of its immediate region and then of Italy as a whole, only after centuries of stiff competition with peer and near-peer competitors.

Schooled by war, Rome's culture and political institutions were shaped by the demands of conflict. Those demands led Rome down a different path than Sparta. To be ready for war, Rome needed two things: a class of highly trained leaders and officers, and a large enough population to raise the sizeable armies needed for victory against neighboring states. The need to maintain these two large groups, and to regulate their economic and political interactions with each other, led the Romans to develop a complex system of institutions, customs, and laws. That system in turn required skilled politicians and lawyers to operate, maintain, and, when necessary, alter the laws to meet changing conditions.

Out of these conditions and forces, the Romans developed three capacities that made them the most formidable power of the time. First, their citizen armies were better trained, better equipped, and better led (at the tactical if not always at the strategic level) than virtually any other force in the world. Second, their civic institutions were strong enough and flexible enough to withstand shocks that would have brought on revolution or collapse in most cities of the day. And third, the Romans developed a national culture around the conduct of war that informed the thinking both of elite policymakers and of ordinary citizens and soldiers in the ranks. Rome did not exactly yearn for war, but it was ready for war and it was built to succeed in war.

This Roman state and its traditions were the engine that enabled Quintus Fabius Maximus Verrucosus Cunctator (c. 280–203 BCE) and Publius Cornelius Scipio Africanus (236–183 BCE) to defeat Hannibal and make Rome the hegemon of the Mediterranean world. Both men came from patrician Roman families with long traditions of strategy and statecraft. Both understood Roman politics and the Roman art of war, and both were able to wield the full power of the Roman state in support of their objectives.

Fabius had the harder task. After Hannibal's army descended on Italy, destroying a major Roman army at the battle of Lake Trasimene, Fabius believed, correctly, that the way to resist Hannibal was to avoid direct battle while raiding Hannibal's supply trains and harassing his outlying forces.[25] This ran directly counter to Roman doctrine and Roman instincts, and it would ultimately take the disaster at Cannae to convince Roman opinion that "Fabian tactics" as they are still called were the best way to confront Hannibal's threat.[26] For the remainder of the war in Italy, Rome employed these tactics and successively wore down Hannibal's army, even as they neutralized the advantage of his superb generalship.

These tactics would not, however, have worked if Rome had been a less resilient state or had possessed a weaker empire. The disasters of the opening years of the war not only saw the killing or capturing of many of Rome's most able and experienced soldiers; those early years exhausted Rome's financial resources and signaled weakness to the many jealous states in Italy and beyond who hoped to exploit Rome's vulnerability in this rare moment of weakness. But Fabius steadied Roman opinion at the moments of gravest crisis. Under his leadership Rome was able to replace the lost armies, float loans among citizens for the growing costs of war, and project enough power to deter its enemies, even as it fought delaying actions against Hannibal.

Another major factor supporting Rome in these critical years was the loyalty of so many allied cities. This was not a universal phenomenon; a number of cities, most prominently Capua, cast their lots with Hannibal. However, Rome never faced the kind of mass defection that would have broken the

---

25. Polybius, *Histories*, 3.84.
26. Polybius, *Histories*, 3.118.

Republic. For this, Rome chiefly had the moderation of its rule and its reputation for ruthless vengeance to thank. The Roman yoke was, at this time, reasonably easy to bear. The aristocracy of allied cities mingled socially and intermarried with leading Romans. Taxes were not excessive and the security and prosperity that followed the Pax Romana were attractive for city-states long accustomed to war. The democratic elements in the Italian city-states were politically weaker and, on the whole, less organized than their counterparts in Greece, and with Roman support added to their own resources and political skills, the political establishments in the allied cities were (mostly) able to ride out the storm until Rome's survival seemed once more assured.

Fabius's generalship and his knowledge of Roman politics and culture enabled him to identify and pursue the path that saved Rome from the first shock of Hannibal's invasion, and the institutional strengths of the Roman state ensured that Fabius's strategy had time to work. It was, however, a strategy of resistance and denial. In the end, Rome would want a decisive victory, and this Fabius could not deliver. The coup de grace would be provided by Scipio, and he would do it by abandoning Fabian strategy and humiliating Fabius in the Senate.[27]

Here too the institutional strength of Rome was on display. Had Fabius been a purely personalistic ruler—a tyrant in the language of the time—either his views would have continued to guide Roman strategy even as they became obsolete or he could only be replaced by a destabilizing political revolution that would inevitably have divided and weakened the country.[28]

Elected consul at age thirty-one, Scipio naturally favored a more aggressive strategy, and assembled forces in Sicily for an expedition to North Africa in the belief that, faced with a threat to Carthage itself, Hannibal would have to leave Italy. In the ensuing debate, Fabius deployed all the prestige of his long career against the upstart's plan, and while Fabius succeeded in limiting funding for the expedition, Scipio did obtain senatorial permission for an African campaign. He reached Africa in 204, and, as predicted, Hannibal returned to defend his capital. Scipio defeated Hannibal at the Battle of Zama in 202, imposing a moderate peace on Carthage to bring the war to an end.

The controversy between Fabius and Scipio bore several resemblances to the struggle between Nicias and Alcibiades over the Sicilian Expedition in the earlier war. The Athenian solution, which left the cautious Nicias in command of an expedition that could only succeed by boldness, led to the single greatest

27. Polybius, *Histories*, 3.97.
28. Polybius, *Histories*, 3.94.

Athenian defeat in the war, and left Nicias dead and Alcibiades exiled as a traitor. Rome's ability to harness the talents of both Fabius and Scipio and to adjudicate the clash between them highlights the importance of strong institutions in war.

Polybius attributed Rome's victory to its constitution (by which he meant its political structure rather than a specific written document) and to the culture out of which it grew.[29] Polybius's constitutional analysis remains relevant today, and for two thousand years it has been consulted by state builders looking to organize their institutions in the most suitable way. Noting that monarchy, aristocracy, and democracy were the three most prevalent forms of government in the known world, and that each system had a mix of strengths and weaknesses, Polybius observed that the Roman constitution of his time effectively combined elements of all three systems. The consuls (and, in times of emergency, a dictator) represented the monarchical form of government. The Senate, composed of wealthy people of rank, brought an aristocratic element into governance, while the assembly of the people and the tribunate were more democratic. The three elements balanced one another and, at least to some degree, ensured against the decay and degeneracy that overtook so many states of the ancient world.

This is insightful and the mix of dynamism and stability that Rome drew from its constitution was a decisive factor in Rome's success, but the history of subsequent years suggests that too great a focus on the undoubted excellencies of the Roman constitution may blind us to other factors of equal or even greater importance to the rise and fall of great powers.

The problem for Polybius's approach is that the Roman constitution that he celebrated began to break down almost immediately following the Second Punic War. Scipio's daughter Cornelia is known to history as "the Mother of the Gracchi," two politicians who, until they met their violent ends, shook the Roman world with populist demands. In subsequent years the struggle between the "Optimates" and "Populares" would escalate into repeated outbreaks of civil war and massacre that ended only with the establishment of the Principate of Augustus Caesar. The institutions and laws that preserved stability while promoting strength for the Rome of 200 BCE were utterly useless at preventing the breakdown of the Republic in the era of civil wars.[30]

---

29. Polybius, *Histories*, 6.1.

30. For more on the breakdown in this era see Appian, *Roman History*, trans. Horace White (Cambridge, MA: Harvard University Press, 1912).

From the crisis of the Republic to the present, the discussion of Rome's constitutional breakdown has often followed a tradition of attributing the failure of Roman civil institutions to the moral decadence of the Roman people—in part due to the vast wealth that came to Rome following the destruction of Carthage.[31] But the correlation between moral decadence and the fall of great powers is not quite as simple as some suggest.

The Roman Republic did not fall simply because the morals of the Romans declined. It fell because the institutions of the state failed to adapt to changes in the condition of Rome. Some of those changes were external. As threats to Roman security receded, Roman society relaxed. A professional military recruited from the enormous territories under Roman control was better suited to the defense of the empire than a citizens' army recruited from the increasingly less warlike population of the capital city. The pressures to maintain the institutional balances between rich and poor through a complex web of legal and political norms also relaxed as external threats diminished. As many observers have noted, the shift from free peasants on small farms to large plantations worked by slaves undermined both the political and the military foundations of the old Roman system. The peasants had filled the armies of Rome with their sturdy sons; their votes helped balance the influence of the wealthy elites in Roman politics.

The old Roman system was also poorly suited to the task of administering a large empire. Institutions that worked for a city-state and its hinterland could, with difficulty, be stretched to cover an empire consisting of the lower two-thirds of Italy and a few patches of Spain. But for an empire that included all of Italy, the Levant, Greece, Spain, North Africa, and, ultimately, Gaul, the institutions of the old Republic could not be made to work. The interests of the provinces were largely ignored by both the Senate and the people of Rome. The principate, for all its faults, was better equipped to govern the empire than the republican system, and imperial Rome was as formidable an actor on the international stage as the Republic had been in its day. One can reasonably argue that the transformation from republic to principate was a manifestation of the health and resilience of the Roman state rather than evidence of its decline. Rome reinvented itself to adapt to the consequences of its republican success.

---

31. Even at the time, individuals such as Cato the Elder raised the alarm bells on the moral decline they perceived and the outside influences they blamed.

IV

Each generation ransacks the wisdom of the past in search of insight for the world it lives in, and today, the greatest contributions the ancients can offer Western policymakers flow from their insights into the relationship of strategy and statecraft. For the ancients, the two arts were intimately and inextricably connected, and success ultimately depended on forces like the cultural and institutional foundations of states, the genius (understood as a mix of intuitive perception and practical ability) of leaders, and the workings of fate and chance. The task of statecraft was to develop and, where possible, increase the strength of a given polity while ensuring the necessary political support to sustain a given national strategy; the task of strategy was to deploy the polity's resources in the ways and towards the ends most likely to secure the welfare of the political community.

Statecraft worked primarily in the medium of domestic politics, but domestic politics could never be separated from foreign affairs. During the Peloponnesian and Hannibalic wars, Greece and Italy were filled with domestic revolutions and discord linked to the wider conflicts. In city after city, political factions saw their fortunes at home as connected to the course of the international contest. Oligarchs and aristocrats supported Sparta and Rome; poorer citizens and, often, the mercantile interests, looked to Athens and Carthage. More critically still, the internal factions were willing to invite the interference of foreign powers, preferring security against their domestic enemies to the well-being of the state as a whole. Politics did not stop at the water's edge. Foreign policy was the continuation of domestic politics by other means.

In the end, the question of war strategy almost always came down to politics. Could Pericles impose his strategic vision on the restless Athenians? Could Sparta overcome the inertia of tradition to become a naval power? Would Rome support Fabius's unorthodox war strategy? Would Carthage sustain Hannibal's armies in the field? The most technically brilliant strategy in the world is worse than useless without the political support necessary to see it through.

In our age of stove-piped specialists whose formative years are spent almost entirely in academic settings, foreign policy is often made by people who have little knowledge of, and sometimes little sympathy for, the dizzyingly complex cultural and political instincts of the American people. And those dedicated to American domestic policy are often ignorant of the ways in which the prosperity and security of the American people at home depend on powers and developments far from home. From the perspective of the ancient historians, this division of labor is unlikely to serve the commonwealth well. This is not solely an American problem. Western democracies on the whole have not produced leaders of the caliber our times increasingly require.

The contemporary world increasingly resembles the Mediterranean world that the ancients knew. It is partly that globalization has made world politics the kind of unified arena that Polybius described in the Mediterranean of his day. Wherever they occur, events "are all interconnected, and everything tends towards a single outcome."[32] COVID lockdowns in China cause factory closures in Germany. Russian threats against Ukraine affect defense calculations in Japan. What happens in the Middle East affects the balance of power in East Asia.

As in the time of Thucydides, great-power competition has an ideological dimension. Democracy advanced following the fall of the Soviet Union and subsequently retreated globally as American foreign policy lost its way. Both democratic and anti-democratic powers see ideology as an important strategic tool, and democratic and anti-democratic factions in smaller states look for assistance from outside powers who share their political values.

The information revolution has thinned the always-permeable barriers between international and domestic space. The internet allows action at a distance. Hackers in Siberia can rob banks in Bermuda. Foreign governments can access the confidential information and disrupt the operations of individuals, firms, and governments around the world. Increasingly, strategic planning will have to take account of a new reality in which the homeland is a major theater of conflict.

The effective strategists and state-crafters of the twenty-first century will have more in common with leaders like Pericles, Lysander, Hannibal, Fabius, and Scipio than with the managerial politicians and technocratic planners of the more recent past. A knowledge of culture, history, and the realities of contemporary technology will matter more to them than even the most sophisticated attempts to theorize the international system. Twenty-first-century actors will need an intuitive understanding of the psychology of their fellow citizens and of their opponents; they will need to know how to gain and hold the trust of an always skeptical and often frightened populace. They will also need the kind of maturity and depth of character that young people rarely acquire in the halls of academe.

32. Polybius, *The Histories: A New Translation*, 1.3.

In the short term, strategists and state-crafters need to recalibrate their expectations and policies for a more Thucydidean and less post-historical world. For the longer term, reforming our process in order to prepare new generations of Western state-crafters and strategists must be one of our highest priorities. Encouraging the study of the ancient historians is an important first step along this necessary path.

CHAPTER 3

Sun Zi and the Search for a Timeless Logic of Strategy

Toshi Yoshihara

Sun Zi's *Art of War* is considered the oldest and the most widely read military treatise in the world. Its Chinese title, the *Sun Zi bingfa*, translates into "Master Sun's military methods." The work passed from oral tradition to written form over two millennia ago. The text likely cohered over decades, cobbled together by curators through a cumulative process. Comprising just over 6,600 classical Chinese characters, the *Sun Zi* is compact. It is filled with aphorisms and enigmatic phrases that have been held up as "the concentrated essence of wisdom on the conduct of war."[1]

The work's origins are obscure. Unlike Clausewitz's *On War* or Jomini's *Art of War* or even Mao's *On Protracted War*, the *Sun Zi bingfa* cannot be reliably attributed to a historical figure in a specific time and setting. It is not a book that was written by one author in a single act. The voice in the *Art of War* does not belong to the putative Master Sun. Rather, the anthology expresses the collective wisdom of faceless, nameless stewards of an emerging school of military thought in ancient China. Given the book's nebulous origins, the *Sun Zi* poses many analytical challenges to the modern reader.

The norms, culture, and language from which the work emerged were vastly different from those of the West and even from contemporary China. Readers can read the maxims out of context or project twenty-first-century meaning

---

1. B.H. Liddell Hart, "Foreword," in *Sun Tzu: The Art of War*, trans. Samuel B. Griffith (London: Oxford University Press, 1963), v.

onto the axioms. They can cherry pick phrases and employ them to suit their circumstances. Shorn of its historical context and the purpose for which it was originally written, the *Sun Zi bingfa* has been subjected to use and abuse. Western writers have promiscuously applied the *Sun Zi* to fields as diverse as business, medicine, and even interpersonal relationships.

To those in the strategic studies discipline, the *Sun Zi bingfa*'s proliferation is highly problematic—if everything is strategy, then nothing is strategy. This chapter's purpose is to locate the ancient text in the realm of strategy. Specifically, this chapter evaluates how the *Sun Zi* has helped advance the West's understanding of statecraft, strategy, and war. To do so, this chapter addresses two central questions: What does the *Sun Zi* say about strategy as a universal concept? What does the *Sun Zi bingfa* say about the peculiarities of Chinese strategy? To explore these two questions, this chapter first situates the military treatise in its historical context and summarizes a tantalizing theory about the true purpose behind the *Art of War*. It then examines select Sun Zian concepts that tap into the universal logic of strategy. Finally, the chapter assesses the extent to which the *Sun Zi* reveals a uniquely Chinese martial tradition.

I

Tradition attributes the *Sun Zi* to Sun Wu, a figure in Chinese antiquity. Sun Wu or Sun Zi, meaning Master Sun, purportedly lived during the later Spring and Autumn period in the late sixth century or early fifth century BCE, making him a contemporary of Confucius. Biographical details are sketchy. The thin records recount that Sun Wu, a great military strategist, was from the northeastern state of Qi, located in modern day Shandong Province. Sun fled his native land to seek refuge in the state of Wu, a fiefdom south of the Yangzi River led by King Helu. Upon learning of Sun Wu's military skills, Helu granted him an audience to gauge his abilities. In the famous but apocryphal tale, Sun Wu agreed to the king's request to train the court ladies in an experiment. Over the king's objections, Sun Wu ordered the beheading of Helu's two most beloved concubines, frightening the other women into following Master Sun's every drill order. Impressed by his ruthlessness, the king chose Sun Wu to lead the Wu armies.

Sun Wu and Wu Zixu, a high-ranking advisor to Helu and a fellow refugee from the state of Chu, joined forces to strengthen the kingdom of Wu. Together, the two men eventually led the Wu armies to victory against the powerful fiefdom of Chu to the west. As a result of Sun Wu's superior stewardship, along with that of Wu Zixu, the state of Wu grew so strong that it cowed the great powers of Qi and Jin in the north. This hazy biography is all that has been left to posterity. Doubts about the veracity of Sun Wu's story and of his very existence have swirled since the Song Dynasty in the tenth century. Scholars today continue to debate Sun Zi's identity and his life. In the absence of concrete evidence, Sun Wu, the man, will likely remain shrouded in mystery.

The *Art of War* was likely composed in the late Warring States period (475–221 BCE), at least a century after the Spring and Autumn period during which Sun Zi was supposed to have lived. The work's focus on large armies comprising hundreds of thousands of peasant conscripts was an exclusively Warring States phenomenon. The age of mass conscript armies required significant expansions in the administrative, logistical, and revenue-generating powers of the state in order to assemble, marshal, and direct these enormous forces. Mobilization, training, and supply of conscripts became central to war-making, and brought about far-reaching changes in the relations between state and society. A new social class—the military professional—emerged to lead an increasingly complex enterprise. The Warring States period saw the bulk production of standardized iron weaponry—superior in strength and sharpness to its bronze-age predecessors—to equip the immense armies. The introduction of calvary and the crossbow led to unparalleled carnage on the battlefield. Moreover, the relative ease with which individuals could learn to fire a crossbow enabled commanders to train and transform peasant boys into lethal infantry with speed and at scale.

During the preceding Spring and Autumn period, war and its conduct had belonged to the aristocrats. Generalship was based on royal lineage rather than professional merit and competence. The chariot-riding aristocratic commanders fought ritualistic battles, the casualties on the field akin to blood sacrifice. The Spring and Autumn armies were relatively small, averaging less than 10,000 troops, and they waged limited, short wars on a seasonal basis whereas Warring States forces fought year around. The chariot-infantry formations of the Spring and Autumn years were typically not tightly organized, and instead consisted primarily of lance-wielding foot soldiers supporting the noble charioteers. Crossbow-fired iron-tipped arrows did not exist in the earlier period. These sharp differences in the character of warfare furnish compelling evidence that the *Art of War* was compiled in a much later period than tradition maintains. As Victor Mair stated, "Everything that the *Sun Zi* has to say about the pattern of war, battle tactics, the conduct of armies, strategic planning, and

weaponry is irrelevant to the Spring and Autumn period but perfectly compatible with the Warring States period."[2]

This excursion is not meant to adjudicate the historical authenticity of Sun
Wu or the dating of the writings ascribed to Master Sun. Rather, it introduces
an intriguing hypothesis about the original purpose of the *Sun Zi bingfa*, that
is, to illuminate the military revolution that convulsed Warring States China.
Andrew Meyer and Andrew Wilson contend that the authors of the *Sun Zi
bingfa* projected Master Sun's military teachings backward from their own time
in the Warring States period to the Spring and Autumn period, akin to a
twenty-first-century author ghost writing a memoir ascribed to General
Ulysses S. Grant. This "purposive anachronism," Meyer and Wilson explain,
was a literary sleight of hand.[3] By claiming that Sun Wu was a contemporary
of Confucius and by conferring upon him the honorific title of Master, the
authors behind the *Art of War* sought to lend legitimacy to the arguments
they were advancing. They portrayed the enigmatic *Sun Zi* and the author's
credentials on military affairs as morally equivalent to that of Confucius and
other great philosophers, who had looked askance at martial matters. By doing
so, the later writers of the *Art of War* appropriated authority from the past as
a kind of analytic top cover to render judgments about their contemporaneous
concerns.

Meyer and Wilson further contend that the authors of *Sun Zi bingfa* used
this circuitous polemical device to advocate for a break from past military
practices. As noted previously, the Warring States period witnessed a radical
shift in the character of war, which required a professional military class to
oversee the complexities of mass warfare. The leading states of the era could
not count on aristocrats, whose hereditary credentials were inadequate to
manage war's growing scale. Yet, the strategic tradition that vested military
authority in the nobility proved resistant to change. The *Art of War*'s portrayal
of the sagacious general was, in part, an argument for the professional military
class to eclipse the lingering aristocratic influence on martial matters. To
Meyer and Wilson, the *Sun Zi* was meant to advance "a new paradigm that
placed a premium on the rational and cognitive faculties of the commander

2. "Introduction" to Sun Tzu, *The Art of War: Sun Zi's Military Methods*, trans. Victor H. Mair
(New York, NY: Columbia University Press, 2007), 28.

3. Andrew Meyer and Andrew Wilson, "Sunzi Bingfa as History and Theory," in *Strategic
Logic and Political Rationality: Essays in Honor of Michael I. Handel*, Bradford Lee and Kurt F.
Walling, eds. (London: Frank Cass, 2003), 100.

and one that invents a new social role for the 'general.'"[4] The *Sun Zi bingfa* can thus be seen as a subversive text that sought to displace the politically entrenched noblemen.

This interpretation of the military treatise is a powerful reminder that the *Sun Zi bingfa* was a product of—and a response to—the larger political, social, economic, and technological forces at work in the Warring States period. The milieu in which the *Art of War* coalesced reaffirms Michael Howard's insight that the operational, logistical, social, and technological dimensions of strategy and their interactions are essential to understanding warfare.[5] Just as the French *levee en masse* transformed the power of the state to wage war on an unprecedented scale in Europe, the advent of conscription, iron-forging technology, and expanded state powers ushered in internecine wars of extermination in ancient China.

II

While the *Sun Zi* emerged out of the unique intellectual, political, and historical contexts of ancient China, the text also illustrates the logic of strategy that transcends national and cultural boundaries. The text speaks to universal strategic principles that ought to resonate with policymakers and commanders, past and present alike. For this reason, the *Sun Zi bingfa* has attracted adherents in China, Asia, and across the world and over the course of generations. Its appeal lies less in its origins or in the presumed intent of its authors, but more in its potential applicability for practitioners of strategy. As Bradford Lee advises, the strategist should "make pragmatic forward-looking use of the texts, rather than let the texts make backward-looking philological use of" the strategist.[6]

The opening line of the *Sun Zi* makes clear that questions surrounding war are so vital to the well-being and survival of the state that war must be subjected to the closest scrutiny. Error in judgments about war can lead to ruin. The *Art of War* thus emphasizes the power of the intellect to study war in all its dimensions. The *Sun Zi*'s most important contribution is its insistence on

4. Andrew Meyer and Andrew Wilson, "Inventing the General: A Re-appraisal of the *Sun Zi bingfa*," in *War, Virtual War and Society*, Andrew Wilson and Mark Perry, eds. (New York, NY: Rodopi, 2008), 166.

5. Michael Howard, *The Causes of Wars and Other Essays* (Cambridge, MA: Harvard University Press, 1983), 101–15.

6. Bradford A. Lee, "Teaching Strategy: A Scenic View from Newport," in *Teaching Strategy: Challenge and Response*, Gabriel Marcella, ed. (Carlisle, PA: Strategic Studies Institute, 2010), 120.

rationality and the rational calculus when contemplating military affairs. References to the commander making estimates in the temple are not about divinations from supernatural sources. Rather, such sections concern the cool, dispassionate, and detailed evaluation of the security environment, balance of forces, moral factors, choices, courses of action, probabilities, costs, capabilities, and so forth. As Ralph Sawyer observed, "Sun-tzu stressed that warfare should be not undertaken unless the state is threatened. Haste, fear of being labeled a coward, and personal emotions such as anger and hatred should never be permitted to adversely influence state and command decision making."[7] In short, the *Sun Zi* advances a highly calculative approach to strategy focused exclusively on serving the state's interests.

The *Sun Zi bingfa* calls on statesmen and commanders alike to engage in "the careful, continuous correlation of means and ends" to ensure that the war aims do not outrun or undershoot the means available to achieve their objectives.[8] The text is particularly preoccupied with the costs of war and their enervating effects on the state. A war's enormous consumption of resources could expose a weakened state to grave danger. Internecine warfare in ancient China provided frequent opportunities for predatory states to exploit their enemies' exhaustion from prolonged conflict. In such contests for supremacy, defeat risked extinction. This unforgiving environment explains why the *Sun Zi* raises concerns about how wars drain blood and treasure, warns against protracted conflicts, and pays close attention to the morale of the people. States must be perpetually alert to the expenditure of scarce resources. A key corollary is to win with minimum cost to oneself. Put another way, a state must conserve its energy in a marathon contest for survival. Sensitivity to cost is vital to success in long-term rivalries.

The *Art of War* further urges strategists to carefully evaluate the "five fundamental factors"—the will of the people, weather, terrain, command, and doctrine—and to know oneself and to know the enemy, including each other's strengths and weaknesses. This close study of the strategic balance is an approach that should be instantly recognizable to those engaged in the modern process of net assessment. Such an appraisal of the correlation of forces can yield insights about comparative advantage. These findings, in turn, can inform competitive strategies that seek to pit one's enduring strengths against the adversary's structural weaknesses, allowing one to impose terms inherently

7. Sun-tzu, *The Art of War*, trans. Ralph Sawyer (New York, NY: Fall River Press, 1994), 131.

8. Michael I. Handel, *Masters of War: Classical Strategic Thought* (London: Frank Cass, 2001), 77.

favorable to one upon the other. An effective competitive strategy depends on deep knowledge of the enemy as well as a remarkable degree of self-awareness. Statesmen and command thus must possess the intellectual wherewithal to engage in the close study of all relevant factors that bear on victory. Practitioners of strategy must live the life of the mind.

The *Sun Zi* places a high premium on "foreknowledge" in war. Foreknowledge is neither magical nor mystical. As Roger Ames explained, foreknowledge is the kind of wisdom that "entails a cognitive understanding of those circumstances that bear on the local situation, an awareness of possible futures, and the capacity to manipulate the prevailing circumstances, and to dispose of them in such a way as to realize the desired future."[9] It is a cognitive process that leads to a choice among alternative courses of action. Contemporary strategists would recognize this as critical analysis, counterfactual reasoning that yields alternative strategies to achieve desired political outcomes. The search for foreknowledge drives the commander to acquire as much information and intelligence as possible in order to arrive at an optimal decision through a rational process.

The apparent dialectic between Clausewitz's *On War* and the *Sun Zi bingfa* reinforces the universal logic of strategy. The *Sun Zi's* preference for attacking the enemy's strategy and alliances over attacking their army or cities stands in evident contrast to Clausewitz's insistence that the destruction of the adversary's army is the ultimate key to victory. The *Art of War's* hierarchy of strategy appears to favor non-violent means of statecraft to achieve policy objectives. However, this is an overly narrow understanding of the *Sun Zi*. An attack on the enemy's strategy is as much about warfighting as it is about peacetime maneuvering. As Bradford Lee argued, the *Sun Zi bingfa* prods the strategist to conceive of operational concepts that would "induce the enemy to blunder into a self-defeating reaction."[10] In insurgencies, insurgents have employed tactics to provoke disproportionate reprisals by counterinsurgents that in turn alienated the local populace upon which the incumbent government's legitimacy rested.

The non-military ways of attacking the enemy's strategy should be seen as a supplement to the quest for decision on the battlefield. The *Sun Zi* makes clear that the commander should aim to deliver destructive and decisive blows against

9. See the "Introduction" to Sun-Tzu, *The Art of Warfare*, trans. Roger Ames (New York, NY: Ballantine Books, 1993), 92.

10. Bradford A. Lee, "Strategic Interaction: Theory and History for Practitioners," in *Competitive Strategies for the 21st Century: Theory, History, and Practice*, Thomas Mahnken, ed. (Stanford, CA: Stanford University Press, 2012), 30.

the enemy if deterrence were to fail. Similar to Clausewitz, the *Sun Zi bingfa* recognizes that diplomacy, including its coercive varieties, propaganda, political warfare, spy-craft, and economic measures are all operative before, during, and after any war. During the Chinese civil war, for example, Communist agents induced mass defections and surrenders that unraveled Nationalist operational plans, contributing to decisive battlefield victories by Mao Zedong's armies. The *Art of War* thus helps strategists to think beyond military means.

The *Sun Zi*'s treatment of civil-military relations would also seem to violate the Clausewitzian principle that policy and politics should reign supreme over strategy, as well as its formulation and execution. To Clausewitz, all military matters, down to the tactical details, are suffused with policy and political meaning. In apparent contrast, the *Sun Zi bingfa* states plainly that the commanders in the field, under certain circumstances, need not obey the sovereign's orders, if they are judged to be harmful to the conduct of operations. To be sure, the state of communications in antiquity precluded timely interaction and adaptation between the sovereign's wishes and the commander's plans, thereby explaining the *Sun Zi*'s ambivalence about interference from the capital. More importantly, the *Art of War* illustrates the inevitable tensions that arise between war aims and the operational design needed to achieve those aims in any conflict. The passages about the prerogatives of the general, if not read literally, also point to the predispositions of any military institution. The military's independent agency, its proclivity to jealously guard what it considers the exclusive realm of its professional expertise, and its natural inclination to resist or resent political interference are universally recognizable.

Clausewitz and the *Sun Zi* differ most sharply over the efficacy of intelligence, deception, and surprise in war. The former holds a dim view about the reliability of intelligence and the ability of the commander to deceive and surprise the opponent. The *Sun Zi*, in contrast, holds these instruments of warfare in high esteem. After all, the *Sun Zi bingfa* asserts that, "All warfare is based on deception." It further advises statesmen and commanders to obtain such intimate knowledge of the enemy and of themselves that they can virtually guarantee victory on the battlefield. Michael Handel attributed these divergences to the different planes of strategy that each text tends to occupy.[11] Clausewitz was largely concerned with war at the tactical and operational levels whereas the *Art of War* considered broader political, strategic, and prewar elements of armed conflict. At higher levels of strategy, for example, deception can be effective while intelligence can be

11. Handel, *Masters of War*, 225–28, 242–43.

quite valuable. In short, the two perspectives are not fundamentally incompatible but rather complement each other in the study of strategy.

Given the work's universal resonance, the *Art of War* has been employed as a powerful pedagogical device to teach strategy in the West. Considered a major strand of classical strategic thought, the *Sun Zi* is an essential part of the core curricula in many professional military education institutions in the United States. The US Naval War College's strategy course employs Clausewitz's *On War* and the *Sun Zi bingfa* as the foundational strategic theories upon which the rest of the curriculum depends. This pairing allows for a constructive dialogue between the two masters of war to discern the merits (or demerits) of different strategic approaches and to illustrate the enduring principles of strategy. The two texts provide useful analytic foils to reenact critical debates in contemporary US defense strategy. Clausewitz's pessimism and the *Sun Zi's* optimism about one's ability to control the battlefield parallels the discourse between the devotees of transformation in the first decade of the twenty-first century and those who expressed reservations about the power of information to fundamentally alter the conduct of war.[12]

The universalism of the *Sun Zi* was evident in the debates about US military strategy and doctrine in the 1990s. That decade saw the United States win a quick, limited war against Saddam Hussein and achieve a virtually bloodless victory over the air of Serbia and Kosovo. The fusion of precision strike and modern sensors, aided by the information revolution, enabled the US military to see, find, fix, target, and attack the enemy across the battlefield with unprecedented fidelity and lethality. The resulting operational successes in the Middle East and southeastern Europe produced a cottage industry of predictions about the prospective revolution in military affairs. Enthusiasts gushed about the power of technology to lift the fog of war, furnishing the US armed forces with virtual omniscience.[13]

In the early years of the twenty-first century, the United States embarked on a "defense transformation" that sought to maximize the potential of the information-based military revolution. *Joint Vision 2020*, published by the Office of the Joint Chiefs of Staff in June 2000, perhaps best exemplifies the Sun Zian optimism about war that pervaded the discourse.[14] The document's

12. Lee, "Teaching Strategy," 123.

13. William A. Owens, *Lifting the Fog of War* (Baltimore, MD: Johns Hopkins University Press, 2001).

14. Office of the Chairman of the Joint Chiefs of Staff, *Joint Vision 2020: America's Military—Preparing for Tomorrow* (Arlington, VA: Department of Defense, June 2000).

purpose was to "describe in broad terms" the operational capabilities and human capital necessary "for the joint force to succeed across the full range of military operations and accomplish its mission in 2020 and beyond." The overarching goal was to achieve "full spectrum dominance," a buzz phrase meant to convey a qualitative superiority that would outmatch any conceivable opponent in any warfighting scenario. *Joint Vision 2020* claimed that such dominance, underwritten by "superior information and knowledge," promised to produce "better decisions arrived at and implemented faster than an opponent can react" in war. Such "decision superiority" would, in turn, allow the armed forces to "shape the situation" and to "create frictional imbalance" whereby the friction inherent in any conflict would weigh more heavily on the opponent than on one's own forces. According to this reasoning, by acting and reacting faster than the adversary and by forcing upon the enemy a fast-moving series of events, the United States would be able to overwhelm the enemy.

The document saw maneuver as the central operational concept for winning future wars. It called on the armed forces to prepare for "dominant maneuver," jargon for the ability to act with "unmatched speed" to "gain positional advantage." *Joint Vision 2020* asserted that, "The capability to rapidly mass force or forces and the effects of dispersed forces allows the joint force commander to establish control of the battlespace at the proper time and place." The local commander would be able to assemble, dispatch, withdraw, move, attack, and scatter forces at will, conferring on them significant operational and tactical initiative. The enemy would have no choice but to react to events dictated to it. *Joint Vision 2020* further claimed that the mere potential of employing such a nimble and nearly irresistible force would alter the opponent's calculus. The framers of the vision averred, "Beyond the actual physical presence of the force, dominant maneuver creates an impact in the minds of opponents . . . In a conflict, for example, the presence or anticipated presence of a decisive force might well cause an enemy to surrender after minimal resistance." In short, the US military would become so powerful that it would intimidate the adversary into dropping its sword.

The ambitions and aspirations of *Joint Vision 2020* reflected the zeitgeist of the 1990s and early 2000s. Faith in the power of technology to be able to gather and process information was central to this vision of future warfare. Such confidence, bordering on hubris, shows how Sun Zian precepts had become very seductive as the character of warfare underwent a major change. The quest for information superiority paralleled the *Sun Zi bingfa*'s call to obtain foreknowledge. The twenty-first-century commander's expected ability to impose the terms of combat on the adversary dovetailed with the *Sun Zi's* observation that, "those skilled at making the enemy move do so by creating a situation to which he must conform."[15] Dominant maneuver conferred Sun Zian powers to perpetually keep the enemy guessing about where the battle might take place, thereby throwing the adversary off balance. The idea that overwhelming US military might would overawe the enemy into succumbing held out the promise of winning without fighting.

The extent to which the *Sun Zi* influenced the American defense establishment at the turn of the new century is unclear. But the US military's exuberant embrace of Sun Zian ideas—particularly the commander's ability to manage fog, friction, and uncertainty—reveals that the *Sun Zi's* optimism about warfare is not an exclusively Eastern or Chinese trait. A military steeped in Western thought can be just as susceptible to the *Sun Zu bingfa's* beguiling logic. Furthermore, this period in the US military's intellectual history demonstrates that the *Sun Zi's* teachings are a double-edged sword. On the one hand, the *Art of War* promises a way out of the Clausewitzian interaction between two living forces locked in hard fighting, each determined to impose its will on the other. In this view, speed, maneuver, stratagem, and intelligence, if employed creatively, can break the cycles of mutual escalation as well as of deadlock. On the other hand, the *Sun Zi bingfa's* reasoning, if taken too far, assumes a kind of one-sided game in which one combatant can act freely against a pliant, if not helpless, adversary. This view distorts the nature of war, introducing the kinds of fallacies that pervaded *Joint Vision 2020*. The *Sun Zi's* allure and its analytical traps are thus a cautionary tale that transcends nationality.

III

The flip side to the *Sun Zi's* universalism is the putative "Chineseness" of the ancient text. In recent decades, Western scholarship has sought to extract evidence of a "Chinese way of warfare" or, more ambitiously, a "system of Chinese strategic thought" from the *Sun Zi bingfa*.[16] The search for a Chinese martial tradition is premised on the idea that a nation's formative military experiences and their lessons leave a lasting influence on its elites' thinking about the use of force. This intellectual imprint—akin to DNA—persists over time and

---

15. *Sun Tzu: The Art of War*, trans. Griffith, 93.

16. Derek M.C. Yuen, *Deciphering Sun Tzu: How to Read "The Art of War"* (London: Oxford University Press, 2014), 13–39.

holds sway over decision-makers' thinking about force. A nation's leaders, owing to such deeply embedded beliefs about force, exhibit unique patterns in military thought.

The debate over whether China has displayed a distinctive approach to war has centered around the concept of strategic culture, defined here as a set of shared beliefs and values about the efficacy, role, and use of force that is shared among members of a state's national security community. These shared beliefs and values—drawn, in part, from narratives of a remembered past—establish a hierarchy of preferences about whether and how a state should employ force to deal with security threats. The theory of strategic culture posits that beliefs and values about force are relatively stable over time, and that they exert a discernable influence on how contemporary statesmen and commanders think about and employ force. Conversely, statesmen and commanders exhibit a pattern of preferences about force that can be linked to those enduring beliefs and values. According to this theory, an understanding of a nation's strategic culture could yield insights about how it might use force to deal with future security threats.

In applying strategic culture to identify Chinese predispositions about war, scholars have frequently turned to the classical Eastern military texts, including the *Sun Zi bingfa*. To them, the *Art of War* and other intellectual artefacts embody the enduring beliefs and values about force that have been passed down, disseminated, and accepted as received wisdom by generations of Chinese strategists. One school of thought, led first by John King Fairbank and followed by others, contends that Chinese strategic culture reveals a deeply rooted disinclination to use force as an instrument of statecraft. Writing in the early 1970s, Fairbank advanced the view that the Chinese way of warfare deprecated the role of violence in resolving interstate disputes. He argued that the *Sun Zi* reflected a "specific habit of mind and action" about the use of force that is unique to the Chinese experience. Specifically, he perceived a "pacifist bias of the Chinese tradition" that originated in Confucian thought, the basis of dynastic China's moral, normative, and political order. Fairbank contended that this "disesteem for physical coercion" can be found in the *Sun Zi bingfa*. He asserted:

As the Sun-tzu makes plain, violence is only one part of warfare and not even the preferred part. The aim of war is to subdue an opponent, in fine, to change his attitude and induce his compliance. The most economical means is the best: to get him—through deception, surprise, and his own ill-conceived pursuit of infeasible goals—to realize his inferiority, so that he surrenders or at least retreats without your having to fight him.[17]

The *Art of War*'s famous maxims would seem to affirm Fairbank's hypothesis. The *Sun Zi* proclaims that, "To subdue the enemy without fighting is the acme of skill." It further asserts that "those skilled in war subdue the enemy's army without battle. They capture his cities without assaulting them and overthrow his state without protracted operations."[18] As noted previously, in the hierarchy of strategies for defeating the opponent, the *Sun Zi bingfa* appears to favor non-military means, including attacks against the enemy's strategy and allies. Corollaries, such as the emphasis on deception, surprise, stratagem, and strikes against the enemy's weaknesses, dovetail with the notion that the *Sun Zi bingfa* frowns upon brute force.

Another school of thought, represented by Alastair Iain Johnston, argues that Chinese strategic culture accepts, if not embraces, the employment of military force to achieve policy goals. Johnston finds that the *Sun Zi* tells a very different story about the Chinese habit of mind from that told by Fairbank. Johnston dismisses the Confucian ethic in ancient Chinese writings as a rhetorical veneer beneath which lurks a "hard realpolitik" worldview. According to this interpretation, China's military classics, including the *Sun Zi bingfa*, see the use of force as highly efficacious. Rather than shying away from violence, these works encourage the overwhelming application of force as a normal implement of statecraft. Like the other Chinese military classics, the *Art of War* advances the idea that "the correct handling of security threats rests in large measure on the defeat of the enemy" and, in fact, welcomes "massive overproportionality in the use of violence."[19] The *Sun Zi*'s calls for deception, stratagem, surprise, and other non-military measures are meant to complement, rather than supplant, the use of devastating force. As Johnston explains:

It is, in the end, this act of attacking the enemy with massive force that directly creates the possibility of winning. It is only in the process of getting to the point where one is attacking from a position of superiority that stratagem plays a role. That is, political and military stratagem and deception are

17. John K. Fairbank, "Introduction: Varieties of the Chinese Military Experience," in *Chinese Ways in Warfare*, Frank Kierman, Jr., ed. (Cambridge, MA: Harvard University Press, 1974), 11.

18. *Sun Tzu: The Art of War*, trans. Griffith, 77, 79.

19. Alastair Iain Johnston, *Cultural Realism: Strategic Culture and Grand Strategy in Chinese History* (Princeton, NJ: Princeton University Press, 1995), 95–96.

elements in weakening, or attriting, the adversary short of its outright defeat and submission.[20]

Johnston further shatters the idea that China eschewed force in the past. Citing a Chinese study, he shows that internal conflicts and wars, including expeditionary wars of conquest, have been integral to Chinese history. From about 1100 BCE to 1911 CE, China was involved in nearly 3,800 wars. During the Ming dynasty alone, Chinese rulers fought about one external war per year over the course of some 270 years.[21] As Sawyer confirms, "From antiquity through the Ch'ing the frequency of warfare in China was overwhelming—at least one armed clash large enough to be recorded every eighteen months; a major battle every few years; and a large-scale campaign or prolonged war every decade."[22] He notes, "Ever since its inception China has continuously and systematically conducted aggressive, externally directed campaigns against contiguous peoples and foreign states."[23] Many led to the defeat, subjugation, or extermination of China's opponents. This is hardly a pacifist historical record.

That the same intellectual artefact can lead serious scholars to draw opposite conclusions testifies to the malleability of the *Sun Zi*. The *Sun Zi bingfa*'s plasticity has, in turn, invited reinterpretations and new hypotheses that have kept alive the debate. The view that China hews to a nonviolent outlook has proved resilient. Huiyun Feng carries Fairbank's perspective into the twenty-first century. She asserts, "The fundamental philosophical underpinning of *The Art of War* remains Confucian. In other words, Sun Tzu remains Chinese in nature and his articulation of the art of war maintains the preferences of war fighting strategies and tactics with Chinese characteristics."[24] To Feng, the *Sun Zi bingfa* expresses a quintessentially Confucian worldview that disfavors the use of force, sees the use of force as a last resort, and holds in high esteem a defensive strategy. Because the *Sun Zi* allows its readers to draw inferences that are virtually unfalsifiable, the text is unlikely to resolve the impasse over enduring Chinese beliefs about the efficacy of force.

20. Johnston, *Cultural Realism*, 97.

21. Johnston, *Cultural Realism*, 27.

22. Ralph Sawyer, "Chinese Warfare: The Paradox of the Unlearned Lesson," *American Diplomacy*, April 2001.

23. Ralph Sawyer, "Chinese Strategic Power: Myths, Intent, and Projections," *Journal of Military and Strategic Studies*, 9:2 (2006/07): 19.

24. Huiyun Feng, *Chinese Strategic Culture and Foreign-Policy Decision-Making: Confucianism, Leadership, and War* (London: Routledge, 2007), 22–23.

IV

Beyond debating Chinese views of force, Western scholars have examined the extent to which key ideas in the *Sun Zi* reflect a uniquely Chinese approach to operations and tactics. The concept of *shi* stands out as an object of fascination in the West.[25] Mair describes *shi* as "one of the most ineffable" concepts while Ames depicts *shi* as "a complex idea peculiar to the Chinese tradition, and [that] resists easy formulaic translation."[26] Sawyer concurs, describing *shi* as "a strategic concept whose complexities require a book-length study."[27] The concept connotes different meanings across different contexts. As such, translations of the term vary widely and include strategic configuration of power, strategic advantage, potential, configuration, energy, and combat power.[28] Tellingly, one study keeps the term untranslated, preferring to leave it merely Romanized.[29]

The *Sun Zi bingfa* employs four evocative metaphors to capture the meaning of *shi*. One likens *shi* to rushing water moving with such force that it sends boulders tumbling along, illustrating the power of momentum. Another compares *shi* to that of a diving hawk breaking the spine of its prey. The bird's agility and precision, combined with its speed of descent, can deliver a deadly blow. Still another metaphor equates *shi* to the latent power of a drawn crossbow about to fire the arrow. It demonstrates the accumulation of potential energy waiting to be released with devastating force against the target. Finally, *shi* is akin to a round boulder rolling down from a mountain summit. This final image combines the ideas of latent power and momentum: the boulder obtained its deadly force after it was set in motion. These metaphors convey the conversion of something soft like water or something

---

25. Henry Kissinger, *On China* (New York, NY: The Penguin Press, 2011), 30–32; Michael Pillsbury, *The Hundred-Year Marathon: China's Secret Plan to Replace America as the Global Superpower* (New York, NY: Henry Holt, 2015), 42–51.

26. Mair, *The Art of War*, xlv; and Ames, *The Art of Warfare*, 71.

27. Sawyer, *The Art of War*, 143.

28. Terms in order of appearance: Sawyer, *The Art of War*, 143; Ames, *The Art of Warfare*, 71; François Jullien, *A Treatise on Efficiency: Between Western and Chinese Thinking*, trans. Janet Lloyd (Honolulu, HI: University of Hawaii Press, 2004), 17; Mair, *The Art of War*, xlv; Griffith, *The Art of War*, 90; Lionel Giles, trans. *Sun Tzu on the Art of War: The Oldest Military Treatise in the World* (London: Luzac & Co., 1910) 33; and Sun-Tzu, *The Art of War*, trans. J.H. Huang, (New York, NY: Harper Perennial, 1993), 57.

29. Sun Tzu, *The Art of War*, trans. Denma Translation Group (Boulder, CO: Shambhala, 2009), 75.

light like a bird or an arrow or even something inert like a sitting rock into objects of explosive power.

Sawyer defines *shi* as the strategic configuration of power. *Shi*, in his view, is an advantage derived from positioning and mass. The boulder metaphor shows that the destructive power of a rock tumbling down from a mountain-top depends on the height from which the boulder began its descent, the speed of its descent as it gathers momentum over time, and its mass.[30] According to Arthur Waldron, *shi* "refers to the configuration and the tendency of all the factors (terrain, weather, forces, morale, and so forth) that bear on victory. The military commander must evaluate all these elements, and move only when they are in optimal alignment."[31] To Ames, *shi* is "the full concentrated release of that latent energy inherent in one's position, physical or otherwise" and encompasses "intangibles such as morale, opportunity, timing, psychology, and logistics."[32] The ability to harness and employ that latent energy allows the commander to "ride the force of circumstances to victory."[33] François Jullien describes *shi* as the "potential energy within the situation," including positioning, morale, and adaptation to circumstances.[34] The military commander shapes the potential energy of the troops' position and morale to allow the situation to bring about favorable outcomes. Another study observes that the commander can exploit *shi*—even small ones—inherent in any given situation to achieve success.[35]

One method for explaining *shi* in practice is to employ case studies on Chinese warfighting. This is a common analytical exercise in contemporary China. Chinese military writings frequently refer to China's many past battles, from the ancient to the recent, in order to illustrate the *Sun Zi's* key concepts, including *shi*. Indeed, Chinese strategists rely heavily, if not exclusively, on wars in premodern China to bring to life the *Sun Zi bingfa's* axioms. For example, a Chinese National Defense University study cites forty case studies of Chinese battles spanning nearly two thousand years to explain the *Art of War*.[36] A Chinese Academy of Military Science textbook similarly alludes to various

30. Sawyer, *The Art of War*, 145.

31. Waldron, "The Art of Shi," *The New Republic*, June 23, 1997, 39.

32. Ames, *The Art of Warfare*, 82.

33. Ames, *The Art of Warfare*, 78.

34. Jullien, *A Treatise on Efficiency: Between Western and Chinese Thinking*, 18.

35. *The Art of War*, trans. Denma Translation Group, 77.

36. 李殿仁 [Li Dianren, ed.], 孙子兵法通论 [*A General Theory of Sun Zi's Military Methods*] (Beijing: National Defense University, 2006), 7–251.

premodern clashes to explain key Sun Zian concepts.[37] The interplay between the *Sun Zi's* concepts and China's rich martial past continues to shape how China's national security community thinks about the use of force. Borrowing from this methodology, the following (taken from a Chinese analysis) briefly summarizes two famous battles in antiquity—celebrated in China to this day—that appear to exemplify *shi*.

Chinese strategists hold up the Battle of Maling (341 BCE) during the Warring States period between the armies of Qi and Wei as a classic military engagement.[38] It featured manipulations of morale, terrain, and psychology by Sun Bin, an advisor to the king of Qi, that resulted in decisive victory. The road to battle began when the state of Wei attacked the state of Han, forcing the latter to seek help from the state of Qi. To rescue Han from destruction, Qi dispatched its army to march on Daliang, the Wei capital. The threat to the capital forced the Wei army, led by General Pang Juan, to abandon its operations in Han and to hurry back to defend the homeland.

Sun Bin judged that Pang Juan's army, about 100,000 strong, was full of fighting spirit and assessed that Pang Juan deemed Qi an unworthy and craven opponent. To exploit the adversary's arrogance, Sun Bin devised a feigned retreat after crossing into Wei territory. He ordered the Qi army, as it withdrew, to light 100,000 cooking fires on the first day, 50,000 and 30,000 cooking fires on the second and third day, respectively. Pang Juan, on the heels of the enemy, saw the successive and drastic reductions in cooking fires as evidence that Qi's soldiers were deserting in droves. Buoyed by this apparent collapse in resistance, Pang Juan left his infantry behind and charged ahead with only light elite forces to chase down and destroy what he thought would be the remnant Qi army.

Sun Bin fell back and led Pang Juan to Maling, where the narrow road through the area was surrounded by crevasses from which Qi's forces could lay an ambush. Sun Bin then deployed 10,000 crossbowmen on both sides of the road. The troops were ordered to fire en masse when they saw a fire at dusk. To set the trap, Sun Bin chose a larger tree located along the road and wrote a message on its trunk that read, "Pang Juan will die beneath this tree." Pang Juan arrived at the tree just as night began to fall. To read the writing on the tree, Pang Juan lit a

37. 任力 [Ren Li], 孙子兵法教程 [*Course Materials on Sun Zi's Military Methods*] (Beijing: Academy of Military Science, 2013).

38. 陈宇 [Chen Yu], 孙子兵法: 精读 [*Sun Zi's Military Methods: A Close Reading*] (Beijing: Contemporary World Press, 2013), 294–300.

torch. Seeing the light, the Qi's crossbowmen unleashed their arrows. The mas-sive onslaught killed many and sowed chaos among the Wei troops. The Qi army descended upon an enemy in disarray and wiped it out. Seeing that defeat was inevitable, Pang Juan committed suicide. Sun Bin exploited this battlefield suc-cess to destroy the rest of the Wei army.

The Battle of Wei River (204 BCE) was part of a larger struggle for supremacy between Liu Bang's Han and Xiang Yu's Western Chu. The former's success paved the way for the Han dynasty to reign over China. The engagement, like the Battle of Maling, involved a scheme to ensnare the enemy in order to achieve operational success. Han Xin, a Han general of great sagacity, invaded the state of Qi and seized its capital with a meager and disorganized force of 30,000 men. When the king of Qi appealed to Xiang Yu for assistance, the king of Chu ap-pointed Long Ju, his best commander, to lead an army of 200,000 to rescue Qi. Since Han Xin was operating deep in enemy territory far from his home base, an advisor recommended that Long Ju go on the defensive and stoke uprisings among the people of Qi. Surrounded by a hostile population, in a distant foreign land, and cut off from local supplies, the advisor reasoned, Han Xin might be forced to surrender. Long Ju rejected the suggestion, believing that Han Xin was an inferior commander. Long Ju's superiority in numbers further convinced him that a great battlefield victory was within easy reach.

Han Xin, like Sun Bin before him, understood that his opponent was driven by hubris. He thus exploited Long Ju's overconfidence. As the two armies faced each other on opposite sides of the Wei River, Han Xin dispatched an element of his force upriver the night before the battle. He ordered those troops to build an improvised dam upstream—using more than 10,000 bags filled with sand and stone—to stop the river's flow. The next morning, Han Xin forded the shallow river to attack Long Ju. After a brief clash, the general contrived a retreat back across the river and fled before the enemy. Persuaded that Han Xin was indeed a coward, Long Ju gave chase and forded the Wei River. As Long Ju and a fraction of his army reached the other bank, Han Xin's men broke the makeshift dam, unleashing a column of rushing water. The tor-rent smashed into troops still attempting the river crossing, drowning many of them. The raging river severed Long Ju's small contingent from the rest of the army on the other bank. Han Xin then launched an assault that destroyed the trapped force and killed Long Ju. The victory opened the way for Han Xin to conquer the state of Qi.

While details of both clashes are likely apocryphal or at least embellish-ments, the core elements of operational success in each represent concrete manifestations of *shi* in combat. In both battles, the victorious commanders manipulated the potential of the circumstances facing them to their advantage. They redirected the existing momentum and trajectory of events in their favor. Employing a Chinese idiom to capture the essence of the Maling battle, a Chinese Academy of Military Science study on the *Sun Zi bingfa* depicts the engagement as a classic case of "exploiting a given situation for all possible favorable factors for one's benefit [因势利导]."[39]

Sun Bin and Han Xin knew their opponents' psychological profiles. They were thus able to manipulate their enemies' arrogance and confidence in superior numbers to set traps. They feigned retreats that confirmed the adversaries' misperceptions, thereby prodding the opponents to assume risks that they were already inclined to take. The winning generals maneuvered their enemies onto terrain that maximized their own positional advantages. In both instances, precise timing unleashed the arrows in Maling and the water at Wei River and thus delivered explosive and devastating power against the opponents. The blows, in turn, knocked the adversaries off balance, opening the way to annihilating enemy troops.

V

Western scholars have sought to trace the presence and employment of *shi* during the modern era to discern a Chinese way of warfare. They have long argued that the *Sun Zi* influenced Mao Zedong's thinking about war and strategy. After all, Mao cited the *Sun Zi bingfa* in some of his most important works, including *On Protracted War* and *Problems of Strategy in China's Revolutionary War*.[40] His emphasis on deception, surprise, and intelligence mirrored that of the *Sun Zi*. Mao's description of the interplay between regular and guerilla forces echoed the *Art of War*'s treatment of orthodox and unorthodox forces. Some analysts have thus turned to the decades-long Chinese civil war and Maoist China's violent clashes along its periphery from the 1950s to the 1960s to test the *Sun Zi*'s enduring impact. They claim that Communist strategy during and after the Chinese civil war is explicable in Sun Zian terms and, moreover, that Mao and his subordinates employed *shi* in key campaigns.

39. Ren Li, *Course Materials on Sun Zi's Military Methods*, 157.
40. Mao Zedong, "On Protracted War," in *Selected Military Writings of Mao Tse-Tung* (Beijing: Foreign Language Press, 1963), 238; Mao Zedong, "Problems of Strategy in China's Revolutionary War," in *Selected Military Writings of Mao Tse-Tung*, 86.

Gary Bjorge argues that the initial Communist strategy in the Huai-Hai Campaign (November 1948–January 1949) during the Chinese civil war epitomized the practice of *shi*. The climactic clash between Mao Zadong's armies and Chiang Kai-shek's forces led to a series of decisive battles in which the Communists wiped out five Nationalist armies, including over 550,000 troops, secured their position over the Central Plain, and opened a path to the Yangzi River, the gateway to South China. The Communist success in the Huai-Hai Campaign shattered Chiang's armies and sealed the fate of the Nationalists on the mainland.

Su Yu, the local Communist commander who conceived of the original plans for the Huai-Hai Campaign, made the case for the operation based on calculations of *shi*. Su believed that an earlier victory over the Nationalists defenders at the key city of Jinan had significantly buoyed the fighting morale of his own forces while it depressed that of his opponent. Su also saw that the Nationalists had been knocked off balance by the setback at Jinan, presenting an opportunity to press the advantage. A rapid transition from one operation to the next, in Su's view, would keep the Nationalists disoriented, prevent them from recovering and regrouping, and perhaps even open the door to crushing Communist victories. As Bjorge describes it, Su sought to "maintain the physical and psychological momentum the successful Jinan Campaign had generated and [to] use it to exploit existing opportunities and create new ones."[41] According to Bjorge, Su's calculus, informed as it was by estimates of morale on both sides and the momentum that the Communists had obtained, was a classic example of *shi*.

William Mott and Jae Chang Kim similarly contend that estimates of *shi* informed China's entry into the Korean War as well as the initial military campaigns that followed.[42] During the first Communist offensive, Mao and his theater commander, Peng Dehuai, employed deception to confuse the adversary. The initial contact with the enemy was also meant for Communist forces to gain experience and confidence on the battlefield. The Chinese People's Volunteers (CPV) moved across the border into North Korea in utmost secrecy. They traveled at night, took cover during the day to conceal their positions to evade detection from the air, and disguised themselves in

---

41. Gary J. Bjorge, *Moving the Enemy: Operational Art in the Chinese PLA's Huai Hai Campaign* (Fort Leavenworth, KS: Combat Studies Institute Press, 2003), 58.

42. William Mott and Jae Chang Kim, *The Philosophy of Chinese Military Culture: Shih vs. Li* (London: Palgrave Macmillan, 2006), esp. 103–30.

North Korean uniforms. The CPV were instructed to direct their assaults against the weaker South Korean units to achieve easy initial victories, thereby boosting their own morale while undercutting that of the adversary. The CPV launched a series of surprise attacks against the Korean forces, delivering heavy blows that cost the enemy 15,000 troops. Peng then broke contact and withdrew his forces, feigning a disorderly retreat; he even released prisoners of war who were made to believe that the Chinese side was suffering shortages.

Together, the initial collision of forces and the sudden withdrawal were intended to stoke the enemy's arrogance and to maneuver it into a trap during the second offensive. Mao and Peng hoped that such deception would convince General Douglas MacArthur that victory was within easy reach and lure him to press on. As Mott and Kim explain, "To exploit MacArthur's arrogance, Peng exploited UNC [United Nations Command] confusion by deceiving the enemy about Chinese weakness and his own intentions . . . To manipulate MacArthur, Peng's deception presented the possibility of final military victory."[43] Peng's apparent retreat and passivity in the face of US and South Korean advances were also designed to draw the US VIII Army and X Corps further north and thereby overextend them. As American forces drew near, Peng launched a massive assault involving eighteen divisions and nearly 390,000 troops. Employing large numbers of maneuver units, the Communists fought a series of outflanking and encirclement operations in a campaign of annihilation. This second offensive forced the VIII Army into the longest retreat in American military history and drove US-led forces back into South Korea.

As Mott and Kim see it, the first two offensives—and the thinking behind them—were in accord with *shi*. Mao and Peng sought to enhance the confidence and combat power of their forces, depress the morale of the enemy through initial battlefield victories, manipulate the over-confidence of the adversary's commander, and induce operational overreach by the opponent. These moves in turn brought about the opportunity to unleash overwhelming military power akin to the *Sun Zi*'s various metaphors about *shi*. Of course, Chinese intervention in the Korean War also demonstrated the limits of *shi*. Mao's hubris led to subsequent offensives that severely overextended the CPV. American successes in blunting the Communist advances and subsequent counter-moves forced Mao's armies to abandon battles of annihilation and to accept a bloody struggle of

43. Mott and Kim, *The Philosophy of Chinese Military Culture*, 118.

attrition and stalemate on the peninsula. The employment of *shi* ultimately failed to achieve Mao's objective of pushing American-led forces into the sea.

Other scholars are skeptical about *shi*'s uniqueness and its apparent role in Chinese strategy. Harold Tanner argues persuasively that the *Sun Zi*'s influence alone is insufficient to explain Mao's civil war victories. Tanner acknowledges that Communist operations "followed a number of precepts that can be found in Sunzi," including the concept of *shi*. Nevertheless, Tanner detects a quintessentially Clausewitzian ethos that guided Mao and his lieutenants.[44] Mao's theory of victory envisioned a three-stage war that would culminate in the complete obliteration of the enemy through decisive engagements conducted by regular forces. To Mao, annihilation campaigns were only possible through numerical superiority, the concentration of forces, maneuver, and conventional military power. Mao foresaw the physical destruction of adversary forces as the primary mechanism by which to achieve victory. He rejected the Sun Zian idea that one can win without fighting or that one can win by stratagem alone. Tanner's in-depth assessment of the Liao-Shen Campaign, which saw the Nationalists lose some 470,000 troops, vividly shows how Mao and his theater commander, Lin Biao, engaged in hard fighting through large-scale, conventional military operations in order to defeat the enemy.

Andrew Wilson similarly debunks *shi*'s presumed Chinese-ness. He points out that, far from being a peculiar or even mystical Chinese concept, *shi* is universally understandable. As Wilson observes, "*shi* sounds like something that either Caesar or Clausewitz might consider in assessing the surprising ways that discipline, morale, terrain, timing, change, and genius combine in battle."[45] Wilson concurs with Tanner that Western intellectual thought, including that of Marx, Lenin, and Clausewitz, exerted a more consequential influence on Mao's approach to war and politics. Marx introduced Mao to class struggle; Lenin offered Mao insights about party organization to win a revolutionary war; and Clausewitz advanced Mao's understanding of the relationship between policy and strategy. Arguably, the political lessons that Mao drew from Western thinkers contributed more to his strategic success than the *Sun Zi*'s contributions to his operations and tactics.

44. Harold M. Tanner, *Where Chiang Kai-shek Lost China: The Liao-Shen Campaign, 1948* (Bloomington, IN: Indiana University Press, 2015), 19.

45. Andrew R. Wilson, "The Chinese Way of War," in *Strategy in Asia*, Thomas Mahnken, ed. (Stanford, CA: Stanford University Press, 2014), 120.

VI

The *Sun Zi bingfa* remains a go-to text for military theorists and strategists for good reason. It elucidates enduring principles of strategy that apply universally. The treatise draws attention to the primacy of rationality in war and opens the door to a highly calculative strategy. Its discussion of non-military means in prewar and wartime circumstances encourages readers to consider strategy broadly and at higher planes. The work offers alternative and complementary warfighting approaches to Clausewitz that widen strategists' analytic aperture. The ancient text's relevance and resonance have grown following the information revolution. The US military's post-Cold War peacetime roles in maintaining forward presence and reassuring allies dovetail with the *Sun Zi*'s emphasis on shaping the situation. The book has helped generations of Western scholars to explore Chinese strategy and to speculate about a Chinese way of warfare. Its axioms have produced lively debates over enduring Chinese views about the efficacy of force and recurring patterns in China's use of force. To the extent that this discourse has forced academia and the policy community to wrestle with Chinese strategy and its potential implications for regional and global security, it has proved a net positive.

At the same time, the *Sun Zi bingfa* is a difficult and, in many ways, problematic work. Translations and interpretations run the gamut. The text is in perpetual flux, lacking the stability of other military classics. Its elasticity has allowed historians and analysts to draw diverse and often conflicting conclusions about the *Sun Zi*'s meaning and implications. Some see the *Art of War* as evidence that Chinese strategic culture deprecates the use of force while others detect a Chinese military tradition that embraces violence. Some see the Sun Zian concept of *shi* as a uniquely Chinese way of conceiving strategy that continues to exert an influence on Chinese statecraft and war-making. Others view *shi* as a universally explicable idea rather than an exotic species of strategy peculiar to China. Even those who concede *shi*'s role in Chinese decision-making doubt whether its impact on contemporary Chinese strategic thought is as significant as Western intellectual influences. In sum, the literature that relies on the *Sun Zi bingfa* to discern how China views force and its employment yields inconsistent, if not unsatisfactory, answers.

Moreover, it is easy to go too far with the *Sun Zi* and its presumed precepts. The Sun Zian optimism that confers on the sagacious general a near superhuman ability to control the battlefield is dangerous because it risks wishing away interaction, distorting the fundamental nature of war. The claim that Chinese military thought is profoundly different from that of its Western counterpart—owing in part to the influence of *Sun Zi bingfa* and other military classics—reduces Chinese or Eastern strategy to a caricature or, at worst, a stereotype. The philological insistence that the work must be tied to historical context crowds out worthy efforts to apply the *Sun Zi's* axioms to practical problems of strategy. Finally, there is a built-in tension between the work's universality and its peculiarities that appears unique to the Chinese tradition. Historians object to uncritical analysis that wrenches the maxims out of context while strategists chafe at textual readings that narrow room for creative thinking about strategy.

These analytic pitfalls are serious. Some may lead strategists astray while others might limit strategists' imagination. But they also mark the boundaries within which strategists can fruitfully evaluate the ancient text. Western scholarly debates suggest that strategists should avoid lazy generalizations of the *Sun Zi's* insights about strategy as a universal concept or about Chinese strategy. Strategists should also recognize that the *Sun Zi bingfa* will be perpetually subject to historical and textual reinterpretation. Therefore, they should accept the contingent nature of the work, stay clear of dogmatism, and keep an open mind. Strategists can make good use of the text so long as they approach it with caution and some humility.

CHAPTER 4

Machiavelli and the Naissance of Modern Strategy

Matthew Kroenig

Niccolò Machiavelli made modern political thought and in so doing, he made modern strategy.[1] He emphasized "the effectual truth," studying the world as it is, rather than how it should be.[2] By separating morality from political science, Machiavelli liberated subsequent strategists to examine political behavior for its effectiveness, rather than for its goodness. He also innovated in terms of method, looking to the empirical record to develop covering laws for effective political action that could travel across time and space.

1. This chapter considers Machiavelli's three major political works. *The Prince, The Discourses on Livy*, and *The Art of War* are all available in Niccolò Machiavelli, *The Essential Writings of Machiavelli*, trans. Peter Constantine (New York, NY: Modern Library, 2007). The commentary on Machiavelli over the centuries is voluminous. Machiavelli provoked responses from, among others, Frederick the Great and Voltaire, *Anti-Machiavel: Or, an Examination of Machiavel's Prince: With Notes Historical and Political* (Farmington Hills, MI: Gale ECCO, 2018); Isaiah Berlin, "The Originality of Machiavelli," in *Against the Current: Essays in the History of Ideas*, Isaiah Berlin, ed. (Princeton, NJ: Princeton University Press, 2013), 33–100; Leo Strauss, *Thoughts on Machiavelli* (Seattle, WA: University of Washington Press, 1969). The most prominent contemporary interpreters of Machiavelli include: Quentin Skinner, *Machiavelli: A Very Short Introduction* (New York, NY: Oxford University Press, 2019); and Harvey Mansfield, *Machiavelli's New Modes and Orders: A Study of the Discourses on Livy* (Chicago, IL: University of Chicago Press, 2001). For biographies, see Christopher S. Celenza, *Machiavelli: A Portrait* (Cambridge, MA: Harvard University Press, 2015); and Paul Strathern, *The Artist, the Philosopher, and the Warrior: The Intersecting Lives of Da Vinci, Machiavelli, and Borgia and the World They Shaped* (New York, NY: Bantam, 2009). This chapter was inspired by Felix Gilbert, "Machiavelli: The Renaissance of the Art of War," in *Makers of Modern Strategy from Machiavelli to the Nuclear Age*, Peter Paret, Gordon A. Craig, and Felix Gilbert, eds. (Princeton, NJ: Princeton University Press, 1986).

2. Machiavelli, *The Prince*, Chapter XV.

Machiavelli was a realist who understood the brutal realities of politics and the importance of military force in statecraft. He disdained traditional forms of morality due to what he saw as their undesirable political consequences. Machiavelli demolished the divine right basis for political authority and paved the way for successors, like Thomas Hobbes and John Locke, to conceptualize new theoretical foundations for the modern nation state. He was an early figure in the nationalist movement, who fantasized about creating a powerful and unified Italian state. Machiavelli also made foundational contributions to a wide range of other political debates, including on how domestic political regime type shapes national power and state behavior; military organization and civil-military relations; and the judicious application of military force. He even wrote histories, plays, and poems.

Machiavelli was the political genius of the Italian Renaissance. When we recall this remarkable period of human flourishing, we often think of the sculptors, scientists, painters, and architects: Michelangelo, Leonardo, Raphael, and Brunelleschi. But Machiavelli was the Michelangelo of politics and strategy. He brought his field into the modern world. Like the artists around him in his native Florence, Machiavelli looked to the ancient world, especially to the example of ancient Rome, to inform his views of politics.

In another sense, however, Machiavelli was revolutionary—and self-consciously so. He intended to break from what he saw as the naïve body of political thought that preceded him and to establish "new modes and orders" for understanding political life.[3]

Centuries before Henry Kissinger, Machiavelli was the ultimate scholar-practitioner. He served for over a decade as the leading national security official in the Florentine Republic during the Italian Wars. In that role, he conducted diplomatic missions, oversaw the creation of a Florentine militia, and served as a military commander in a successful operation to retake Florence's long-standing rival, Pisa. It was only through tragedy that he was forced from office, sent into exile, and thus became an accidental scholar. With his newly found free time, Machiavelli wrote books that were so profound that they are still widely read half a millennium later: *The Prince*, *The Discourses on Livy*, and *The Art of War*. His experience gives his writing a distinct authority. Machiavelli knew kings and popes. He was an insider. He wrote his pamphlet to the

---

3. Machiavelli, *The Discourses on Livy*, Preface.

new Medici prince with a tone of condescension. He seems to have been saying, "I've been doing this for years. You are new. Let me guide you."

And guide subsequent political thought he did. Machiavelli's *Art of War* was widely read as an authoritative manual on military matters in his lifetime. *The Prince* caused widespread controversy when it was published shortly after his death. Even today, many political theorists praise *The Discourses* as his greatest work. Shakespeare referred to the "murderous Machiavel" and the Catholic Church banned the Italian's writing for over two centuries.[4] That did not stop his ideas, however, from informing political thinkers and doers for over five centuries, including: Spinoza, Rousseau, Frederick the Great, the US Founding Fathers, Napoleon, Clausewitz, and senior government officials and political philosophers to this day.

Indeed, few political scientists become adjectives, but we all know what it means to be "Machiavellian." At least we think we know what it means. How Machiavellian was Machiavelli? What was the strategic context and personal biography that shaped Machiavelli's worldview and writing? Why was Machiavelli the founder of modern strategy? This chapter will address these questions.

I

The vast majority of scholarship on Machiavelli is produced by political theorists and they, understandably, situate Machiavelli in relation to other political theorists. To understand Machiavelli as a strategist, however, it is necessary to situate him within the geopolitical context in which he lived and wrote. It was a time of rapid change: European exploration, the Renaissance, cultural advancement, scientific discovery, and intense geopolitical competition among the major powers of Europe and the smaller powers on the Italian Peninsula.

Machiavelli's life coincided with the age of European exploration and the discovery of new worlds. In 1488, Portuguese navigator Bartolomeu Dias sailed around the Cape of Good Hope. In 1492, Christopher Columbus landed in the Americas. Spain and Portugal signed the Treaty of Tordesillas, and agreed to divide the new world outside of Europe between themselves in 1494. The African slave trade began in the early 1500s. In 1513, the Portuguese landed in Macao, China. From 1519 to 1522, a Spanish expedition commanded by Ferdinand Magellan was the first to circumnavigate the globe. In those same years,

4. William Shakespeare, *Henry VI* (New York, NY: Simon and Schuster, 2008), Act 3, Scene 2.

Hernán Cortés led the Spanish conquest of Mexico. This age of discovery and the opening of new worlds had a profound effect on many Europeans, including Machiavelli. Indeed, he explicitly compared himself to these explorers.[5] Just as Columbus had discovered new geographic worlds, Machiavelli hoped to discover and explore a new type of political thought.

Machiavelli also lived during a time of significant cultural and technological advancement. It was the Italian Renaissance. He was a contemporary of Michelangelo (1475–1564), Botticelli (1445–1510), Raphael (1483–1520), Titian (1488–1576), and Leonardo (1452–1519). Machiavelli knew his fellow intellectuals and artists personally and was influenced by them. They shared a basic method of disrupting their fields by turning to the ancient world for inspiration. They even collaborated. Machiavelli and da Vinci once conspired (unsuccessfully) to engineer a diversion of the Arno River around Pisa, so that Florence would be less dependent on its archrival's port for access to Mediterranean trade routes. These thinkers of the High Renaissance were, in turn, shaped by the cultural contributions that had preceded them. Machiavelli spoke Latin, but, following the path set out by Dante, Petrarch, and Bocaccio, he wrote in the vernacular, his native Italian.

Machiavelli challenged Christian thought, but he was not alone in this regard. In 1512, Copernicus wrote that the sun, and not the Earth, was at the center of the universe. Martin Luther confronted Catholic theology in 1517 when he posted his ninety-five theses on the church door in Saxony.

This was also a time of disruptive military technology. Machiavelli was living through the earliest days of one of the most significant military revolutions—the gunpowder revolution. France easily invaded Italy in 1494 thanks to the use of modern artillery. In 1503, at the Battle of Cerignola in southern Italy, firearms were employed effectively on the battlefield for the first time. Machiavelli was a careful student of these developments.

It was, however, the geopolitics of this era that had the greatest influence on Machiavelli's thought. It was the transition from the medieval to the modern world and smaller political entities were consolidating into larger state units. The Holy Roman Empire (HRE), reformed through the Diet of Worms (1495), lurked just over the Alps. In 1469, Aragon and Castille were united by the marriage of Ferdinand II and Isabella I, creating a unified Kingdom of Spain. In 1519, Charles V temporarily brought the HRE and the Kingdom of Spain together under a single crown. The War of Roses concluded in 1485,

---

5. Machiavelli, *The Discourses*, Preface.

leaving Henry VII as the undisputed King of England. In the southeast, the Ottoman Empire was a rising power, encroaching on European territory. In 1453, Constantinople fell to the Ottomans. Suleiman the Magnificent took Belgrade in 1521 and was narrowly beaten back at the gates of Vienna in 1529. In the east, Russia was also on the rise. After the Great Stand on the Ugra River in 1480, Muscovy gained independence from the Great Horde, and, by 1485, Ivan the Great had tripled the size of the Russian state.

This profound state consolidation beyond the Italian Peninsula led Machiavelli to fantasize about a new prince who could create a unified Italian state capable of holding its own among the major powers of Europe, just as the Roman Republic had been a major Italian geopolitical force in the ancient world.

Instead, at the time Machiavelli was writing, Italy was fragmented into its own multi-polar, balance-of-power system. The major Italian city-states in this period included: the Venetian Republic, the Papal States, Florence, the Kingdom of Naples, and the Duchy of Milan. Lesser powers were many and included Florence's long-standing rival, Pisa. (To this day, Florentines quip that it is better to have a death in one's family than a Pisan at your front door).

The Italian city-states were locked in geopolitical rivalries with each other, and, relatedly, they made for low-hanging fruit for the major European powers. The city-states were wealthy and indefensible. The dilemma facing the Italian city-states was always between inviting in the major European powers to help settle local disputes, but only at the risk of losing their autonomy to their stronger neighbors to the north. During Machiavelli's lifetime, France and the HRE conducted two major invasions each of the Italian Peninsula, and France and Spain used Italy as an arena to wage war against each other. Milan and Naples forever lost their independence in the process.

II

The Italian Wars may have been the most significant geopolitical development in Europe in the first half of the sixteenth century. The conflicts trace their origins to the Lombardy Wars (1423–54), a series of clashes between the Republic of Venice and the Duchy of Milan in a struggle for hegemony in northern Italy. The wars concluded with the 1454 Treaty of Lodi, which established the Italic League, a concert among the five major powers of Italy that locked in a balance of power and brought four decades of peace and stability to the Italian Peninsula.

This peace was shattered in 1494 when Ludovico Sforza of Milan, seeking an ally against Venice, encouraged Charles VIII of France to invade Italy. Charles VIII saw an opportunity to make a dynastic claim on the throne of Naples and launched the First Italian War. Italy's tall and thin medieval walls were no match for France's modern artillery, and the French easily ransacked the peninsula. Charles VIII made a triumphant entry into Pisa on November 8, 1494, freeing the city from Florence's rule. He took Florence on November 17, resulting in the Medici's subsequent collapse and Machiavelli's eventual rise to a position of authority. The French invasion continued to Rome on December 31, 1494, and on to a sack of Naples in February 1495.

Ludovico Sforza soon regretted his decision to invite the French into Italy and the balance of power kicked in. The League of Venice (consisting of Milan, Venice, Spain, and the HRE) formed in response to the threat of French hegemony on the peninsula. Florence, wracked by revolution, remained on the sidelines. The Battle of Fornovo was a victory for the League of Venice, but a pyrrhic one. Charles VIII retreated to France, but he had demonstrated to his successors and other major powers that Italy was vulnerable.

With the French gone and order restored at home, Florence was still stinging from its loss of Pisa. Florence attempted to retake the city, but Pisa received assistance from other Italian city-states, including Venice and Milan.

The next time, Florence (and Machiavelli) joined Venice in welcoming a French invasion. They understood that the new French king, Louis XII, was intent on returning to Italy. Venice wanted help combatting Milan, and Florence offered to align with France in exchange for assistance in re-conquering Pisa. The Second Italian War, or King Louis XII's War, began in July 1499, when the French army invaded Italy with 27,000 soldiers. On October 6, 1499, Louis conquered Milan. The city never regained its independence, save for a few brief years, as it was passed back and forth among various imperial powers. (Machiavelli took note of Sforza's leadership and cited him as an example of a weak prince who lost his state due to poor decision-making and military planning.)[6]

Consistent with its promise, a French army joined Florence to lay siege to Pisa in the summer of 1500. Within a day, French guns blasted a hole through Pisa's city walls, but the armies were unable to retake the city. Stiff resistance and lackluster initiative on the part of Florence's mercenary armies impeded the conquest. Paolo Vitelli, the captain of the mercenaries, delayed in following orders to enter the city. Florence suspected treason and had him executed.

6. See, for example, Machiavelli, *The Prince*, Chapter XIV.

In his later writings, Machiavelli cited the incident to support his deep mistrust of mercenary armies.

Aware of the anti-hegemonic alliance that had frustrated his predecessor's ambitions in Italy, Louis XII negotiated peace deals with potential major power rivals, including the HRE and Spain. In the 1500 Treaty of Granada, France agreed to split the Kingdom of Naples with Spain. By 1502, a combined French and Spanish force had seized control of southern Italy. Shortly thereafter, as might have been expected, the two powers disagreed about how Naples should be divided and turned on each other. The critical Battle of Cerignola (1503) was arguably the first battle in which firearms played a decisive role. Spain emerged victorious. Naples lost its independence and became part of the Spanish Empire for the next two centuries. France was once again forced to retreat from the peninsula. Machiavelli criticized Louis XII's decision to welcome the Spanish into Naples, calling it "foolish" to invite a competitor into territory that France could have possibly controlled by itself.[7]

The Second Italian War coincided with the pinnacle of Cesare Borgia's conquests in the Romagna. Borgia likely would have been forgotten (or at best been a brief historical footnote) had it not been for Machiavelli's lionization of him in The Prince. During the war, Pope Alexander VI had attempted to carve out a small territory from the Papal States to become a hereditary principality for his son. Cesare moved quickly to consolidate his rule, greatly impressing Machiavelli, but was unable ultimately to hold onto power after his father passed away in 1503; Cesare suffered an undignified death at the hands of enemies in Spain several years later.

Nevertheless, Machiavelli saw Borgia as the ideal prince who (had circumstances been different) could have (perhaps) succeeded in uniting all of Italy. As Machiavelli wrote:

> The Lord [Cesare] is very splendid and magnificent, and is so spirited at arms that it is no great matter that he seems small; and for the glory and to acquire states he never rests, nor does he know tiredness or danger. He reaches places first so that he can understand the game where it is played out; he endears himself to his soldiers, he has captains, he is the best man in Italy; all of which makes him victorious and formidable, to which is added perpetual luck.[8]

---

7. Machiavelli, The Prince, Chapter III.
8. Niccolò Machiavelli, Letter to the Florentine Signoria, 1502.

After a few years of relative tranquility, the Italian Wars resumed in 1508 with the War of the League of Cambrai. The new Pope Julius II (the Warrior Pope) wanted to re-establish control over the Romagna territories previously held by Cesare Borgia, but the local lords appealed to, and received offers of protection from, Venice. Angered by Venice's transgression, Julius II seized on the greed of the other major powers and proposed an alliance under which they would dismember Venice and divide its territories among themselves. The League of Cambrai united the papacy, France, Spain, and the HRE against Venice. By 1509, the League had succeeded in bringing Venice to its knees and the dodge signed a one-sided peace treaty with Julius II.

At this point, Julius II saw France as the bigger threat and turned the alliance, then including Venice, against Louis XII. In 1511, Julius II declared a new Holy League against France that included Spain, the HRE, Venice, and England—the last of which was eager to reclaim territory in Aquitaine. Since Florence was widely viewed as partial to France, Julius II sent in forces to overthrow the Republic and re-install the Medici. This was Machiavelli's greatest personal tragedy as he was removed from office and sent into exile, never again to return to public life.

The war continued for several years with France suffering a series of losses in Italy and northern Europe. In 1513, however, Julius II died, leaving the alliance without a leader. His successor, Leo X, was less interested in warfare. He famously said, "God gave us the papacy. We might as well enjoy it."[9] In 1515, Louis XII also passed away. His successor, Francis I, led a reinvigorated offensive and managed to reclaim most of France's lost territory. Separate peace agreements between France and the other major powers ended the war in 1515, with borders essentially returning to the pre-1508 status quo.

By this point, though Machiavelli had been removed from public life, he was a witness to the wars that continued to rage while he was in exile. With French hegemony of the Italian Peninsula checked, it was the HRE's turn to vie for dominance. In 1519, Charles V united Spain and the HRE, creating the largest European power since the time of Charlemagne. In 1521, Charles V ousted France from Milan and returned it to the Sforza family. In an effort to retake Milan, Francis I personally led the French army into Lombardy in 1525. His army was defeated at the Battle of Pavia, and Francis I was captured and imprisoned.

Out of desperation, Francis's family formed an alliance with Suleiman the Magnificent. The Ottoman army invaded Hungary to attack the HRE's eastern

---

9. William Samuel Lilly, *The Claims of Christianity* (New York, NY: Palala Press, 2016).

flank, but it was not enough to save France's position. In the 1526 Treaty of Madrid, France, in exchange for Francis I's release, surrendered all claims to Italy, Flanders, and Burgundy.

With France neutralized and the HRE ascendant, a new balance of power formed. In 1526, Pope Clement VII, alarmed at the growing power of the HRE, formed the League of Cognac. Members of the League included the Papal States, France under King Francis I, Henry VIII of England, Venice, Florence, and Milan. The League planned a war against the Empire to begin in early 1526, but, for a variety of reasons, it was unable to act decisively. Charles V struck first and, in May 1527, he sacked Rome. The sacking of Rome by imperial forces marks the unofficial end of the Italian Renaissance. Machiavelli died the next month. The Italian Wars continued in this manner for another thirty years, with no clear victors, but Machiavelli was not there to witness them.

III

Machiavelli was born in 1469 and raised in the Santo Spirito neighborhood of Florence, just south of the Arno River. His father, Bernardo, was a lawyer, and Machiavelli received a good education. He read and wrote in Latin and was deeply familiar with ancient texts, including Cicero and Seneca, as well as with more recent Italian works, such as Dante. Little else is known about Machiavelli's early life.

Machiavelli's childhood and early adulthood occurred during the rule of Lorenzo (the Magnificent) de Medici. At the age of twenty-five, Machiavelli was shocked by the French invasion of Florence, which led to the fall of Lorenzo's firstborn son and successor (Piero "the Unfortunate") and the creation of a new Florentine republic under the sway of Dominican Friar Savonarola. The friar advocated for a religious revival and staged large "bonfires of the vanities" in which Florentines were encouraged to burn their worldly possessions. Many Florentines bristled under Savonarola's theocratic rule, and this experience helped to instill in Machiavelli his lifelong disdain for Christianity. Savonarola's attacks on papal corruption went too far, however, and, in 1497, the Borgia Pope Alexander VI excommunicated the friar. The Florentines turned against Savonarola, and he was publicly hung and burned at the stake.

It was now Machiavelli's turn to rule. In 1498, Piero Soderini became the leader of a new Florentine Republic. Machiavelli was appointed secretary for both the Second Chancery and the Ten for Liberty and Peace. The former produced official Florentine government documents and the latter was a

council of ten men responsible for matters of war and diplomacy. To be selected for such important posts before his thirtieth birthday, one can presume
that Machiavelli had previous administrative experience, and that he was well-
connected and respected by influential Florentines, including Soderini.

Machiavelli had many accomplishments while in office. He played an important role as a diplomat. He traveled widely to represent his city-state in negotiations with foreign rulers. He conducted missions to meet with leaders such as
Caterina Sforza, King Louis XII, Cesare Borgia, Pandolfo Petrucci of Sienna,
Pope Julius II, and Emperor Maximilian I. Given the realities of travel in this period, these visits often resulted in lengthy stays in foreign courts where Machiavelli was able to observe and interact with foreign potentates. These meetings
helped to inform his views on leadership and these characters appear in Machiavelli's writings, not as distant figures, but as colleagues he knew personally.

Machiavelli also succeeded in creating a Florentine militia. Previously, Florence had relied heavily on hired mercenary armies, but they had failed to fight
effectively on Florence's behalf on numerous occasions, including in operations to retake Pisa. Machiavelli believed that citizen-soldiers would make for
a more effective fighting force, and he took great interest in establishing the
militia, involving himself down to such details as recruiting, training, and designing uniforms. He was also a successful military commander, leading the
Florentine militia in a campaign to recapture Pisa in 1509. These experiences
shaped Machiavelli's views on mercenaries, civil-military relations, and warfare, and infuse all of his major works, especially *The Art of War*.

In 1512, after fourteen years in office, Machiavelli's life as a high-ranking
public servant came to an abrupt end. With the military backing of Pope Julius
II and Spain, the Republic was overthrown and the Medici swept back into
power. The new princely rulers did not look kindly on the holdovers from the
previous government, and Machiavelli's name was included on a list of possible anti-Medici plotters. Machiavelli was imprisoned and tortured, including
with multiple rounds of the *strapaddo*. He felt viscerally, therefore, the effects
of "cruelty well used."

The Medici must have judged Machiavelli as not too great a threat because
they allowed him to live. He was exiled to his family's country farm in
Sant'Andrea in Percussina, roughly twenty kilometers southeast of downtown
Florence.

Machiavelli considered this exile his life's greatest tragedy. He longed to
return to a position of authority in the city that—on a clear day—he could see
from his country estate. It is a nice property and a tourist destination that one

can visit to this day, but Machiavelli was unhappy. He was out of power, and we know from his personal correspondence that he spent much of his time doing farm work, drinking wine, playing cards, and engaging in extramarital affairs. He lived with his wife, Marieta Corsini, and six children. It does not appear, however, that he was a devoted husband or father. Indeed, Machiavelli was Machiavellian in his personal life; he used a tunnel in the cellar of the house to sneak out undetected and visit the tavern across the street.

With little else to do, Machiavelli devoted himself to study and writing. As he wrote to his friend Francesco Vettori:

> When evening comes, I return home and enter my study; on the threshold I take off my workday clothes, covered with mud and dirt, and put on the garments of court and palace. Fitted out appropriately, I step inside the venerable courts of the ancients, where, solicitously received by them, I nourish myself on that food that alone is mine and for which I was born; where I am unashamed to converse with them and to question them about the motives for their actions, and they, out of their kindness, answer me. And for four hours at a time I feel no boredom, I forget all my troubles, I do not fear poverty, and I am not terrified by death. I absorb myself into them completely. And because Dante says that no one understands anything unless he retains what he has understood, I have jotted down what I have profited from in their conversation and composed a short study, *De Principatibus*, in which I delve as deeply as I can into the ideas concerning this topic, discussing the definition of the princedom, the categories of princedoms, how they are acquired, how they are retained, and why they are lost. And if ever any whimsy of mine has given you pleasure, this one should not displease you. It ought to be welcomed by a prince, especially a new prince; therefore I am dedicating it to His Magnificence Giuliano.[10]

Machiavelli used his evenings in exile to compose some of the greatest masterpieces in the Western cannon. *The Prince* was completed in 1513. It was a gift to the new Medici prince and something of a failed job application. Machiavelli had hoped that the new ruler would find his expertise useful and call him back into public service, but it was not to be. *The Prince* was not published in Machiavelli's lifetime, but its shocking arguments caused a worldwide sensation when it was released shortly after his death.

---

10. Niccolò Machiavelli, *Letter to Francesco Vettori*, December 10, 1513, in *The Essential Writings of Machiavelli*, trans. Peter Constantine (New York, NY: Modern Library, 2007).

The Discourses on Livy was completed in 1517 and also published posthumously. *The Art of War* was completed and published in 1520 and was immediately well-received and widely read given Machiavelli's obvious authority on the subject.

This was not the entirety of Machiavelli's opus. Many of his writings as a government official are still available. His *Discourse on Pisa* (1499), *On Pistoian Matters* (1502), and *On How to Treat the Populace of Valdichiana after their Rebellion* (1503), for example, are short, analytical pieces with clear recommendations on how Florence should handle various situations, not unlike a contemporary article in *Foreign Affairs*. His play *The Mandrake* (1524) is a comedy and a thinly veiled critique of the Church and Medici rule, and is still performed in Florence to this day.

While it was not quite what he had hoped for, the Medici did recall Machiavelli for official duties, albeit briefly. In 1520, Giulio de Medici sent him to Lucca to convince the government there to repay a loan. Inspired by the trip, Machiavelli wrote *The Life of Castruccio Castracani of Lucca*. Giulio was impressed by the work and appointed Machiavelli to a position at the University of Florence, as the city's official historian. Machiavelli completed the *Florentine Histories* in 1526. He died the next year at the age of fifty-eight, believing that his career since leaving government service had been mostly a failure.

IV

In his contribution on Machiavelli for the original *Makers of Modern Strategy*, Felix Gilbert focused almost exclusively on Machiavelli's *Art of War*. This was a reasonable choice. For some analysts, and in earlier time periods, strategy was conceived of in strictly military terms. The Merriam-Webster dictionary, for example offers as a definition of strategy—"the science and art of military command exercised to meet the enemy in combat under advantageous conditions."[11] There are, however, other, broader definitions for strategy. In fact, Merriam-Webster also defines strategy as "the science and art of employing the political, economic, psychological, and military forces of a nation or group of nations to afford the maximum support to adopted policies in peace or war."[12] As we will see shortly, Machiavelli's contributions to modern strategy

---

11. Merriam-Webster, "strategy," https://www.merriam-webster.com/dictionary/strategy, accessed November 26, 2021.

12. Merriam-Webster, "strategy."

are much broader and more fundamental than his writing on military affairs. Moreover, in a world of cyber threats, disinformation, economic sanctions, trade wars, large standing alliances, and competitive multilateralism, contemporary strategy must, by necessity, go beyond issues of military force. This chapter will, therefore, follow the broader definition of strategy and, accordingly, consider a broader range of Machiavelli's work.

Certainly, Machiavelli's most famous (and notorious) work is *The Prince*. The central question of the book is how can a new prince maintain their state? The answer is that a new prince can only maintain their state through virtue, but this is a different type of virtue than classical and biblical sources had extolled over the years. Rather, Machiavelli aimed to teach a prince "how not to be good."[13] An effective prince must be able to lie, deceive, murder, and apply "cruelty well used" (*crudeltà bene usata*) if they are to achieve their goals.[14] The book was ignored by the Medici, and seen as scandalous when it was published shortly after Machiavelli's death, but it was appreciated by subsequent political philosophers as the first modern work of political theory (and for our purposes, strategy) due to its focus on the way things are, rather than the way they should be.

The book begins with a dedication to the new Medici ruler. Machiavelli's hope was that the Medici prince would find the book (and Machiavelli's insights) useful and recall him to public service. It is not unlike an aspiring policy wonk in the United States writing a policy memo hoping to catch the eye of an incoming presidential administration.

Machiavelli stated at the outset of the work that there are only two major types of political systems: republics and principalities. In today's parlance, we would use the terms "democracies" and "autocracies." Machiavelli explained that he had written at length about republics elsewhere, by which he presumably means *The Discourses*, a book he had already started before he turned his attention to *The Prince*. This later book, therefore, will focus on principalities. He then explained that there are two major types of principalities: those led by established princes and those headed by new princes.

The Prince focuses on new princes and how they can maintain their state (*mantenere lo stato*). This focus was relevant to his intended audience of one: the new Medici ruler. But Machiavelli also saw this as an important and practical, real-world problem. In Machiavelli's decade in office, he had witnessed

13. Machiavelli, *The Prince*, Chapter XV.
14. Machiavelli, *The Prince*, Chapter VIII.

Cesare Borgia, the Sforzas, the Medici, the king of Naples, and several others lose their states. New princes can have a difficult time maintaining power in the face of constant threats of conspiracy, assassination, invasion, civil war, and *coup d'etat* (literally a strike against the state). How, therefore, can states be maintained in the face of these challenges?

The answer, according to Machiavelli, is that a new prince must be virtuous. Machiavelli set out a famous dichotomy between virtue and fortune, or what we might call today, skill and luck. He argued that some princes get lucky, and opportunity falls in their lap, but it is still difficult to maintain a state without skill. Moreover, even skill is insufficient if one is unfortunate, and never presented with the right opportunities. The key, therefore, is to be able to employ skill to harness circumstances to one's own ends. In essence, one must be able to create one's own luck. A good prince must be able to understand their times, spot opportunities, and be bold. As Machiavelli wrote in a passage that is jarring to modern sensibilities:

> Fortune is a woman. She will let herself be won by men who are impetuous rather than by those who step cautiously . . . She is partial to young men because they . . . command her with greater audacity.[15]

Machiavelli criticized Italian princes who lost their states, such as Ludovico Sforza, for lacking sufficient virtue. He claimed these princes blame luck for their fate, but the real cause for failure is poor leadership.

What then, other than boldness and spotting opportunities, are the key characteristics of virtue? Critics have argued that the term "virtue" is never clearly defined and even borders on the tautological. To maintain a state, a prince needs virtue, and virtue is the quality required to maintain a state. This criticism, however, is only partly fair.

Machiavelli's explanation for the requirements of a virtuous prince comes in the most critical chapters of the book (Chapters 15–19). This is his radical break with tradition, a direct revolt against the classical and Christian sources that preceded him. Aristotle, Cicero, Seneca, Augustine, Thomas Aquinas, and others, for centuries, had held up justice as the cardinal political virtue. Central to the concept of justice was honesty. Related virtues for a good ruler, according to previous scholars, were generosity and mercy. They argued these moral goods were categorical imperatives that should be followed without exception because the ruler is on a public stage. If rulers want a reputation for justice,

---

15. Machiavelli, *The Prince*, Chapter XXV.

then they must behave justly. Moreover, there is no hiding from God, and Christian rulers will eventually face an ultimate judgment day. Indeed, Machiavelli was not the first to write a book of advice to a prince. In fact, there was a large, preexisting genre of "mirrors of the prince" books in which authors instructed princes on why and how to behave justly. Machiavelli's *The Prince* followed this long-standing tradition, but with a radical twist. In Chapter 15, Machiavelli told us that he would:

> seek the truth of the matter rather than imaginary conceptions. Many have imagined republics and principalities that have never been seen or heard of, because how one lives and how one ought to live are so far apart that he who spurns what is actually done for what ought to be done will achieve ruin ... Hence it is necessary for a prince ... to learn how not to be good.[16]

Having set forth his approach, Machiavelli began Chapter 16 with an attack on the princely virtue of generosity. He argued that what is commonly praised as princely generosity (doling out benefits to one's subjects) is often wastefulness. Excessive spending can bankrupt the state. Moreover, for a prince to spend freely, they must acquire the resources from somewhere, often through predatory taxation. Excessive taxation, however, will cause one's subjects to hate the prince. Machiavelli instead saw stinginess as the greater princely virtue. He praised Louis XII of France for his parsimony, which allowed him to finance large armies without raising taxes.

Machiavelli set his sights on the princely virtue of mercy in Chapter 17. He argued that mercy is overrated and that an effective prince must develop the capacity to effectively employ cruelty. By striving for mercy, many princes unintentionally incentivize disorder, which ultimately results in greater pain and suffering. Machiavelli chastised Scipio, the Roman hero, for failing to punish a mutiny in his army, which only incentivized another mutiny. He blamed the Florentine government in which he served for not intervening in a civil war in Pistoia, a small city about thirty-six kilometers west of Florence. While in the government, Machiavelli had recommended that Florence use force to put down the uprising and kill the ringleaders. Instead, Florence stayed on the sidelines, the civil war raged, and many perished. Machiavelli wrote:

> Cesare Borgia was considered cruel; notwithstanding, his cruelty reconciled the Romagna, unified it, and restored it to peace and loyalty. And if

16. Machiavelli, *The Prince*, Chapter XV.

this be rightly considered, he will be seen to have been much more merciful than the Florentine people, who, to avoid a reputation for cruelty, permitted Pistoia to be destroyed.[17]

To be sure, he argued, a reputation for mercy can be advantageous, but its actual practice is often dangerous. Machiavelli was not, therefore, as is sometimes believed, a proponent of evil for its own sake. He thought princes must be judicious in their application of force so as not to become hated. Ultimately, however, if forced to choose, Machiavelli concluded, it is "better to be feared than loved."[18]

Finally, and perhaps most audaciously, Machiavelli took aim at justice in Chapter 18. He argued that, "if all men were good," a prince could afford to be just, but because "men are wicked and not prepared to keep their word to you, you have no need to keep your word to them."[19] To be an effective ruler, it was helpful to be *perceived* as "merciful, loyal, human, upright, and scrupulous," but that "if need be," a ruler must be able to "turn one's back on these qualities and become the opposite."[20] For Cicero and classical political theorists, a just ruler must apply human reason to overcome beastly emotions, but Machiavelli argued that a good ruler must sometimes be beastly and effectively "emulate both the [cunning of the] fox and the [strength of the] lion."[21]

In this and his other works, Machiavelli is a consequentialist. Nothing is good or bad in absolute terms. Rather, actions can only be judged with regard to their outcomes. Injustice, cruelty, and parsimony often produce desirable results. While Machiavelli never explicitly wrote "the ends justify the means," it is not a bad summation of his ethical worldview. If princes can maintain their states, through whatever means necessary, then they will be judged positively by their subjects and history.

Maintaining the state, however, was not the ultimate goal in Machiavelli's mind. The ultimate goal for a prince is to attain glory and everlasting fame, and to do that, a prince must do "great things" (*grande cose*).[22] As Machiavelli explained in the final chapter of *The Prince*, the great thing he desired is for a strong prince to unify all of Italy and to create the kind of powerful nation-state

17. Machiavelli, *The Prince*, Chapter XVII.
18. Machiavelli, *The Prince*, Chapter XVII.
19. Machiavelli, *The Prince*, Chapter XVIII.
20. Machiavelli, *The Prince*, Chapter XVIII.
21. Machiavelli, *The Prince*, Chapter XVIII.
22. Machiavelli, *The Prince*, Chapters XVI, XVIII.

that could stand up to the major powers of Europe and eventually dominate, just as the Roman Republic achieved mastery in ancient times. As Machiavelli once wrote about his cherished homeland, "I love my country more than my soul."[23]

V

For readers familiar with Machiavelli only through *The Prince*, *The Discourses on Livy* comes as something of a surprise. If *The Prince* is a handbook for dictators, *The Discourses* is a full-throated defense of democracy. How these two books can best be reconciled and Machiavelli's true beliefs understood is a puzzle that has occupied political philosophers for half a millennium.

The Discourses is so named because it is ostensibly Machiavelli's commentary on Titus Livius's (Livy in English) monumental *History of Rome*. Machiavelli focused on the first ten books (or chapters) of Livy, from Rome's mythical founding to its victory in the Third Samnite Wars in 293 BCE. In actuality, *The Discourses* is a highly original work of political theory. Machiavelli used *The Discourses* and Rome's ancient history to present lessons for the practice of contemporary international politics. *The Discourses* is a disjointed book. It is organized into 142 chapters, divided into three sections. Each chapter delivers its own lesson and often does not directly connect to adjacent chapters. There is no clear narrative or argument. When reading the work in its entirety, however, a larger set of ideas emerges.

The Discourses is consistent with the Renaissance method. Machiavelli looked to the ancient world to recover lost wisdom and inspire new truths. He explicitly made the case for this method, explaining how his contemporaries valued the possession of ancient art and wisdom, but had allowed the political lessons of the ancient world to go unheeded.

Machiavelli's motivation for writing the book and the central question it seeks to answer are quite clear. He wanted to understand how Rome rose from a small city-state on the Tiber River to become the dominant power over, first, the Italian Peninsula and, later, the entire Mediterranean basin. The Italy of his time was weak, divided, and constantly preyed upon by larger powers. Machiavelli lamented, "Whoever is born in Italy has reason to blame his own times and praise the past. The past could boast of much that was admirable, while

---

23. Machiavelli, *Letter to Francesco Vettori*, April 16, 1527, in *The Letters of Machiavelli*, trans. Allan Gilbert (Chicago, IL: University of Chicago Press, 1961).

the present has nothing that can raise it out of the greatest misery, infamy, and shame . . . every kind of filth."[24] There was a time, however, when Italy had been great. What was the secret of its success?

Machiavelli's answer is straightforward. Rome achieved everlasting glory due to its republican form of government, which was supported by Rome's pagan, civic religion. For Italy to recover from its current low state, it would need to unify under a new republican form of government, complete with a new civic religion. Machiavelli believed that a powerful prince was sometimes necessary to establish—and occasionally to renew the spirit of—a republic. Except for those situations, Machiavelli's review of history led him to conclude that republican systems of government are superior to principalities for achieving international power and influence. Following Aristotle, Polybius, Cicero, and other theorists in the republican tradition, Machiavelli believed that a mixed constitution—with elements of monarchy, aristocracy, and democracy—was the best form of government because the various elements balanced each other. He cited Rome's consuls, senate, and assemblies as a perfect example of such a mixed constitution.

Republican forms of government are better able to harness the energy and ambition of a broad cross section of society toward national greatness. Machiavelli explained:

> We have seen from experience that states have grown in land and wealth only if they are free: the greatness that Athens achieved within a century of liberating itself from the tyranny of Pisistratus is astonishing and even more astonishing the greatness that Rome achieved after it freed itself from its kings. The reason these cities flourished is easy to understand, because it is the pursuit of the public interest, not private interest, that will make a city great. . . . the opposite occurs when there is a prince because more often than not what he does in his own interest will harm the city and what he does for the city will harm his interests.[25]

Defenders of autocracy from Plato to the present argue that the whims of the people are too unstable and that a strong dictator would be better able to chart a clear strategic course. Moreover, they claim, the public does not have the education and judgment necessary for matters of state, which are best left to a wise central leader. Furthermore, democracy is messy. It results in clashes between factions, while a strong ruler can enforce societal stability.

---

24. Machiavelli, *The Discourses*, Book II, Preface.
25. Machiavelli, *The Discourses*, Book II, Chapter 2.

Machiavelli rebutted dictators' defenders. He argued that the competing interests in a republican system keep a country on a stable course, whereas unconstrained dictators can take countries in an extreme direction and, when they change their minds, back again. He wrote, "I therefore disagree with the common opinion that a populace in power is unstable, changeable, and ungrateful."[26] On the contrary, Machiavelli argued, "The prince . . . unchecked by laws will be more ungrateful, unstable, and imprudent than a populace."[27]

Machiavelli also believed that republican systems, not principalities, tend to produce better decisions. Dictators can take big, bold actions, true, but they also often make big, bold mistakes. A republican system balances competing points of view and prevents ill-considered policies. According to Machiavelli, "a populace . . . has better judgment than a prince." He continued, "One will see fewer mistakes in the populace than in the prince, and these will be less serious and easer to resolve."[28]

As it relates to the messiness of democracy, Machiavelli welcomed societal clashes as something that contributes both to greater liberty at home and enhanced influence abroad. In looking at the Conflict of the Orders (between the patricians and the plebeians in the Roman Republic), Machiavelli wrote, "If one examines the outcome of these clashes, one will find that they did not result in exile or violence . . . but in laws and institutions that benefited civil liberty."[29] Rome could have put in place a more tranquil domestic political system, like Sparta or Venice had, but "had the state of Rome become more peaceful it would have become weaker, as this would have blocked the path to the greatness it achieved." Machiavelli recommended that, if a prince creates a republic with the aim "to expand his dominion and power, like Rome," then "he has to follow the model of Rome and allow the tumult and popular discord to the extent he can."[30]

Indeed, in what might seem like a 180-degree reversal from *The Prince*, Machiavelli went so far as to advise a prince to use their fleeting power to establish a republic. He wrote, "Though to their everlasting honor they are able to found a republic . . . they turn to tyranny, not seeing how much fame, glory, honor, security, tranquility, and peace of mind they are rejecting, and how much

---

26. Machiavelli, *The Discourses*, Book I, Chapter 58.
27. Machiavelli, *The Discourses*, Book I, Chapter 58.
28. Machiavelli, *The Discourses*, Book I, Chapter 58.
29. Machiavelli, *The Discourses*, Book I, Chapter 4.
30. Machiavelli, *The Discourses*, Book I, Chapter 6.

infamy, vituperation, blame, danger, and insecurity they are bringing upon themselves."[31] Machiavelli blamed Julius Caesar for ruining Rome when he could have reordered and renewed the republic.

> In conclusion, he to whom the heavens give such an opportunity [to rule a state] should consider that there are two paths: one that will make him secure during his lifetime and glorious after his death, and the other that will make him lie in constant anguish and after his death leave behind a legacy of everlasting infamy.[32]

Instead, Machiavelli argued, "the security of a republic is not in having a prince who merely reins wisely during his lifetime, but in having one who can establish institutions in such a way that the state will be maintained after death."[33]

Machiavelli also believed that religion was necessary to hold a republic together. He wrote that, in the Roman Republic, religion served to "govern the armies, encourage the plebeians, keep good men good, and shame evil." He claimed that "Roman citizens were more afraid of breaking an oath than of breaking a law."[34]

According to Machiavelli, however, some types of religion were better than others. In his opinion, Roman pagan religions had prioritized worldly matters and thus had made people lovers of freedom, honor, and glory. Christianity, on the other hand, encouraged people to focus on the afterlife and to be humble and weak in this one. He concluded that this difference in religion was why there were more republics in the ancient world. People of his time were unwilling to fight for freedom. Machiavelli's conception of competing moral systems, with varying consequences for society, influenced Friedrich Nietzsche and other subsequent moral relativists.

The Discourses is certainly Machiavellian in its ethic. Republics and religion are not praised for their intrinsic merits. Machiavelli did not argue that democracy is beneficial because it protects human rights and dignity. He did not assess religious belief according to moral precepts or truth claims. Rather, he defended republicanism and civic religion because they were useful. And they were useful, specifically, to a particular end that Machiavelli held in the highest possible regard—helping a state (and his beloved Italy) achieve international power and glory.

---

31. Machiavelli, *The Discourses*, Book I, Chapter 10.
32. Machiavelli, *The Discourses*, Book I, Chapter 10.
33. Machiavelli, *The Discourses*, Book I, Chapter 11.
34. Machiavelli, *The Discourses*, Book I, Chapter 11.

Machiavelli's insights into whether democracy or autocracy better contributes to state expansion is as relevant today as when it was written. The United States and its democratic allies are entering a new period of great-power competition with autocratic rivals, Russia and China. In 2021, US President Joseph Biden declared an "inflection point" in which democracies must demonstrate that they can still deliver.[35] While Biden's White House may not be cognizant of these theoretical roots, Machiavelli has inspired a new generation of strategists who look to America's domestic political institutions as a fundamental source of its international power and influence.[36]

VI

Today, *The Art of War* is the least-known of Machiavelli's major political works, but it was the most widely read in his lifetime, and it influenced military thinkers for centuries thereafter. Frederick the Great, Napoleon, Clausewitz, and Thomas Jefferson all cited it approvingly. Voltaire even said, "Machiavelli taught Europe the art of war."[37]

The Art of War takes the form of a dialogue in which a famous mercenary, Fabrizio Collona, instructs several young gentlemen on military matters. Collona is a thinly veiled mouthpiece for the author, and the dialogue a rhetorical device Machiavelli used to espouse his views on warfare.

The method is similar to Machiavelli's other major works (and the Renaissance style) in that he looked to the ancient world for inspiration. The Roman Republic had mastered the art of war, and the answers for his contemporaries could be found by studying and imitating the military of ancient Rome. Like in the Roman Republic, Machiavelli believed that the best army would consist of citizen-soldiers, not mercenaries, foreign forces, or even a large professional standing army. He argued that the citizen-soldiers should be well trained and disciplined. A strong infantry, armed like Roman soldiers with armor, shields,

35. President Joseph R. Biden, Remarks at the 2021 Virtual Munich Security Conference, February 19, 2021.

36. Matthew Kroenig, "Why Democracies Dominate: America's Edge over Russia and China," *The National Interest* 138 (2015): 38–46; Hal Brands, "Democracy vs Authoritarianism: How Ideology Shapes Great-Power Conflict," *Survival*, 60:5 (2018): 61–114; Matthew Kroenig, *The Return of Great Power Rivalry: Democracy versus Autocracy from the Ancient World to the U.S. and China* (New York, NY: Oxford University Press, 2020).

37. Voltaire, "Battalion," in *The Works of Voltaire: A Contemporary Version: A Critique and Biography*, John Morley, ed. (New York, NY: E.R. DuMont, 1901), Volume III.

and swords and packed together in dense formations, was the key to battlefield success. Machiavelli was skeptical of cavalry and firearms. The book also highlights themes from previous books, including his arguments that good laws and good arms are mutually reinforcing and that republican governments and a strong civic religion help to make an effective and loyal army.

The Art of War is a difficult read. Most of the book deals with details of military organization, tactics, and training that might have been relevant to military officers at the time, but that lack enduring relevance. For example, there are pages and pages devoted to how to set up a military camp. Where should one place the captain's headquarters? How many roads should run through the camp? How much space should there be between them? Machiavelli had answers. Many of the passages remind one of contemporary debates about military procurement. Must the United States modernize its nuclear arsenal now or can it push the investments off a few years into the future? While there are real-world and important decisions that need to be made on this basis today, it is unlikely that readers five centuries from now will find reports on this subject interesting.

Perhaps Machiavelli's strongest belief on military matters was his disdain for mercenary armies and auxiliary forces (those lent by a foreign power). This theme runs through all three of his major works. His devotion to this issue is understandable given Florence's poor fortunes when employing soldiers of fortune, and the success achieved with the Florentine militia he himself established. Machiavelli argued that mercenary and auxiliary forces cannot be trusted and that they will not be motivated to fight. Ultimately, one must rely only "on one's own arms."[38]

Machiavelli also strongly emphasized the importance of good training and discipline. For example, he wrote, "he who in war is more vigilant in scrutinizing the enemy's designs and more tireless in training his army will face fewer dangers and have greater hope for victory." Similarly, "nature creates few brave men—diligence and training create many."[39]

There is the interesting question of whether Machiavelli best fits within Western or Eastern traditions of war. Some scholars point to a Western tradition best exemplified by Jomini and Clausewitz that emphasizes bringing to bear overwhelming force on the enemy's center of gravity in a decisive battle of annihilation. On the other hand, the Eastern tradition, epitomized in Sun

---

38. Machiavelli, *The Art of War*, Book I.
39. Machiavelli, *The Art of War*, Book VII.

Tzu, prioritizes deception and winning without fighting. One can find elements of both in Machiavelli, but he may lean East. In the Florentine's opinion, "good generals never engage in battle unless necessity compels or opportunity beckons." Moreover, "The best strategy is that which remains concealed from the enemy until it has been carried out."[40] He recommended deceiving the enemy by lighting many campfires to amplify the deterrent effect of a small force, while lighting few campfires in order to conceal a large force.

Some writers pan *The Art of War* and Machiavelli as a military strategist for his failure to understand that he was living through history's most important military revolution. At the risk of oversimplifying, from the dawn of recorded human history until Machiavelli's time, people fought by hitting each other with hand-held objects. This is precisely what Machiavelli recommended in *The Art of War*. But, beginning in the late 1400s and culminating in the military reforms of Maurice of Orange in the 1600s, the world experienced the gunpowder revolution. The signs were already visible in Machiavelli's time, from France's use of modern artillery to Spain's successful employment of arquebuses. Yet, as late as 1520, Machiavelli denigrated firearms. He admitted that they could be helpful in the opening stages of a battle and their loud noise could frighten an enemy, but once the battle was underway, they were of little use.

Machiavelli's defenders argue that he was writing a century before the revolution came to full fruition; his operational concepts did include a niche role for firearms; and he was reacting to a conventional wisdom that was unduly enthusiastic about new technology and unappreciative of warfare's fundamentals. Moreover, they rightly claim, *The Art of War* grapples with how to design fortifications to withstand modern artillery, and points in the direction of the successful *trace italienne*-style fortifications that arrived shortly thereafter.

VII

How can we make sense of Machiavelli? Did the same author really write a guidebook for dictators and a lengthy defense of republicanism? Before tackling this question, it is worth emphasizing that there are many common themes that transcend the three works: the consequentialist morality; the method of learning from the Roman Republic's example; the need for strong rulers to use violence to achieve their goals; the disdain for Christianity and mercenary armies; and the passionate ambition to unify Italy.

---

40. Machiavelli, *The Art of War*, Book VII.

But how do we make sense of the seeming contradictions between *The Prince* and *The Discourses*? The first possible interpretation is to discount *The Prince*, perhaps as satire or as a poison pill. In other words, Machiavelli did not really mean it. Spinoza and Rousseau believed that Machiavelli was truly a republican, and *The Prince* was a warning to the world of the depravations of which princes were capable. Or, perhaps Machiavelli was laying out a princely template so fundamentally flawed that it would surely fail miserably if any prince were foolish enough to try it.

A second interpretation holds that these were different books for different purposes. Machiavelli was cynical. He did not like dictatorships but he understood the prevailing political winds and thought this content would be helpful—and that it would allow him to ingratiate himself to the new Medici rulers. Relatedly, perhaps *The Prince* was devoted to the narrow question of what was required for a new dictator to maintain power, whereas *The Discourses* outlined Machiavelli's comprehensive political worldview.

Finally, and perhaps most persuasively, we can take Machiavelli at his word. He was, first and foremost, a man of action, and a scholar only second. He wanted to establish a new, unified Italian republic, modeled on ancient Rome, to stand up to, and eventually dominate, its neighbors. As he explained clearly in *The Discourses*, new republics are best founded by a single, bold leader. According to this interpretation, the books can be read as a step-by-step plan in the order in which they were written. *The Prince* is the guide to a new prince to help them maintain their state against myriad threats. Once the prince is firmly in control, *The Discourses* instructs them on how to establish republican institutions that can expand the state's power, unify Italy, and bring this heroic founder everlasting glory.

VIII

Machiavelli made modern strategy. This is not a statement about Machiavelli's insights into particular issues, though these are significant. Well-ordered and well-trained armies outperform their opponents. States governed by republican forms of government enjoy unique advantages in international power politics. Early and judicious applications of military force can forestall greater catastrophes later.

Machiavelli's contribution to modern strategy is more profound than that. Political philosophers recognize him as the founder of modern political thought, and strategy is but one small offshoot of this broader field. Strategy rests on the notion that there are general laws that can be learned from experience and that can be applied in new contexts. Strategy also requires one to make practical calculations about how best to pursue goals in a way that is not unduly constrained by unrealistic and idealistic ethical standards. Machiavelli separated politics from morality, paving the way for an amoral study of the political world. He also innovated with regard to method, looking to empirical evidence in order to develop general laws that would apply across time and space about how the world worked, and could be manipulated to one's own advantage.

These intellectual moves were necessary in order to make modern strategy. We cannot get to "war is a continuation of politics by other means," or "the threat that leaves something to chance" without "cruelty well used." Absent Machiavelli, there is no Clausewitz or Schelling.

CHAPTER 5

The Elusive Meaning and Enduring Relevance of Clausewitz

Hew Strachan

On January 29, 1943, General Friedrich Paulus, the commander of the German Sixth Army which was surrounded at Stalingrad, sent a signal to Adolf Hitler: "May our struggle serve as an example to this and future generations that one must never capitulate even in the most hopeless predicament. Then Germany will triumph." The next day, the tenth anniversary of the Nazi accession to power in Germany, Hitler replied: "Clausewitz's dictum shall be fulfilled. Only now is the German nation beginning to grasp the seriousness of this struggle; it will make the greatest sacrifices."[1]

Simultaneously, but on the other side of the Atlantic, at the Institute of Advanced Study at Princeton, Edward Mead Earle was overseeing the final stages of *Makers of Modern Strategy: Military Thought from Machiavelli to Hitler*. With the United States confronting modern war for the second time in thirty years, Earle was determined to explain its evolution the better to make strategy. The result was a book which became the founding text of contemporary strategic studies in the English-speaking world. Almost half of its chapters referenced Carl von Clausewitz (1780–1831) and it put him on America's mental map for the first time.[2]

---

1. As quoted and cited in Bernd Boll and Hans Sagrian, "On the Way to Stalingrad: The 6th Army in 1941–1942," in *Wars of Extermination: The German Military in World War II, 1941–1944*, Hannes Heer and Klaus Naumann, eds. (New York, NY: Berghahn, 2000), 238.

2. Christopher Bassford, *Clausewitz in English: The Reception of Clausewitz in Britain and America 1815–1945* (New York, NY: Oxford University Press, 1994), 174; see also Michael Finch's

How could the same strategic thinker inspire both a totalitarian state, which defined itself through the waging of an existential war, and its principal enemy, the world's leading democracy which liked to see war as irrational? Part of the answer lay in the fact that Hitler and Earle were inspired by different texts written at different stages of Clausewitz's life and for different purposes. The inspiration for the *Makers of Modern Strategy* was an instrumental view of war: Clausewitz's *Vom Kriege*, published posthumously in three volumes between 1832 and 1834. First translated into English as *On War* by J.J. Graham in 1873, *Vom Kriege* was not published in an American edition until it was again translated (in the most literal of the three English versions) by O.J. Matthijs Jolles, also in 1943. It is a work of theory, written by a Prussian in peacetime after the final defeat of Napoleonic France in 1815. Its best-known principle is that war is the continuation of policy by other means.

That, however, was not the "dictum" to which Hitler was referring when he signaled Paulus. The Clausewitz whom the Führer and his party venerated was less a theorist than a soldier, a radical nationalist who saw the purpose of the wars in which he fought not simply as an instrument of foreign policy but as an existential struggle. For Clausewitz, war was the means to reform Prussia and to create a German identity. Clausewitz first faced revolutionary France as an adolescent in the War of the First Coalition in 1792–95. He did not do so again for more than a decade, a period of peacetime soldiering which the young officer devoted to his professional education. He also began his courtship of Marie von Bruhl, whom he married in 1810. His intellectual equal, she stimulated his political awareness and, after his death, ensured the publication of *On War*. In 1805, Prussia held back from the alliance formed against France and by 1806 it was too late. Prussia faced Napoleon alone, and on October 14 its army was outmaneuvered and smashed in the twin battles of Jena and Auerstedt. So too was the Prussian state. Under the terms of the Treaty of Tilsit, signed on July 9, 1807, Prussia lost half its territory and accepted a French army of occupation, for which it was required to pay. A year later, the French capped Prussia's army at 42,000 men. Clausewitz, a prisoner of war for the first ten months of 1807, developed a visceral dislike of the French.

Serving a king, Friedrich Wilhelm III of Prussia, who preferred to appease Napoleon rather than to fight him, Clausewitz looked on in frustration at events elsewhere. In Spain, Switzerland, and Italy insurgents resisted French occupation.

---

forthcoming book, *Making Makers: The Past, the Present, and the Study of War* (Oxford: Oxford University Press, 2023), Chapter 2.

In 1809, Austria resumed its war with France and some Prussians, although not Clausewitz, rallied to its cause. In 1812, Napoleon demanded that Prussia provide troops for his invasion of Russia. The king's readiness to acquiesce in this ultimate humiliation pushed Clausewitz over the brink. He decided to switch sides and join the Russians. He penned a three-part memorandum which appealed to the German nation over the head of the Prussian king:

> I believe and confess that a people can value nothing more highly than the dignity and liberty of its existence; that it must defend these to the last drop of its blood; that there is no higher duty to fulfil, no higher law to obey; that the shameful blot of cowardly submission can never be erased; that this drop of poison in the blood of the nation is passed on to posterity, crippling and eroding the strength of future generations.[3]

In 1924, Hitler used these words in his defense at his trial after the beer cellar putsch; he referred to them again when he cited Clausewitz in *Mein Kampf*. Although Hitler was given *On War* when he was incarcerated in Landsberg prison, and although it remained on his shelves and was included in the first one hundred books for Nazi bookshops, Hitler continued to prefer Clausewitz the German nationalist over Clausewitz the theorist of war. On November 9, 1934, in his speech to mark the tenth anniversary of the putsch Hitler said, "Clausewitz writes that recovery is still always possible after a heroic collapse . . . It is always better to embrace an end with horror than to suffer horror without end."[4] As Germany—not just its Sixth Army—faced defeat in the Second World War, this message became more insistent. Clausewitz's declaration of 1812 was read on German radio before Hitler's midnight address on New Year's Eve 1944, and the plan for the defense of Berlin in 1945 was dubbed "Operation Clausewitz."

Paradoxically (an appreciation of paradox is essential to understanding Clausewitz's life and work), the juxtaposition between the heroic, self-sacrificial fighter deified by the Nazis and the strategic theorist who became such a powerful figure in Cold War thinking had a common origin. In January 1918, Hans Rothfels, who had been seriously wounded in the First World War, submitted his thesis, *Carl von Clausewitz. Politik und Krieg. Eine*

---

3. Carl von Clausewitz, *Historical and Political Writings*, Peter Paret and Daniel Moran, trans. and eds. (Princeton, NJ: Princeton University Press, 1992), 290; the full text of the three declarations is to be found in Carl von Clausewitz, *Schriften-Aufsätze-Studien-Briefe*, Werner Hahlweg, ed., Volume 1 (Göttingen: Vandenhoeck und Ruprecht, 1966–1990), 678–751.

4. Carl von Clausewitz, *Vom Kriege*, Friedrich von Cochenhausen, ed. (Leipzig: Insel, 1937), 5.

Ideengeschichtliche Studie. It put the development of Clausewitz's theories in the context of his experiences between 1792 and 1815, thus uniting the thinker with the soldier and thereby linking his military and political ideas. In November of 1918, faced with the shock of Germany's defeat, Rothfels was struck by the relevance of Clausewitz's predicament in 1812. Desperate and despondent, Clausewitz could not have anticipated that his decision to fight for the Russians would be vindicated by ultimate victory. Rothfels's thesis provided a historical example to inspire national recovery but, when that recovery came, it had no place for Rothfels. Although a German nationalist, he was also a Jew. Stripped of his academic posts from 1933 onwards, he made his way to the United States. When Herbert Rosinski, another German exile and the first choice to write the chapter on Clausewitz for *Makers of Modern Strategy,* failed to deliver, Earle selected Rothfels to plug the gap.

Clausewitz lived in an era when war was transformed not by technological change, but rather by political and social change. He recognized that he could not predict whether those changes would be lasting or not, although he suspected that they might be. Clausewitz therefore hesitated to anticipate war's future. Instead, his aim was to understand war as a phenomenon, one which he described at the book's outset in the simplest terms, not as the continuation of policy by other means, but as a clash of wills. He hoped to educate his readers, to develop their judgments, to help them recognize the irrational as well as the rational in war, and to think about strategy in order to better comprehend it and even to apply it. In these respects, *On War* remains pre-eminent, but how it is read and interpreted—like war itself—changes over time.

I

The Second World War both put American strategic studies on a new footing and Europeanized them, thanks to the influx of academic refugees from which *Makers of Modern Strategy* had profited. After 1945, the United States could not withdraw from international engagement, as it had done after 1919. Confronting the need to underpin its hegemony with grand strategy, the US had to address the problem of war despite its historic reluctance to do so. Clausewitz's *On War* became part of its strategic discourse, ultimately ousting the influence of his near-contemporary and hitherto more influential commentator on the Napoleonic Wars, Antoine-Henri Jomini.

By retaining armed forces at wartime levels in peace, the United States threatened the balance in civil-military relations which the Constitution had established. In 1957, Samuel P. Huntington addressed the challenge in *The Soldier and the State*. His argument depended on an understanding of military professionalism whose roots rested in early nineteenth-century Prussia and for which Clausewitz's *On War* had—in Huntington's words—"contributed the theoretical rationale." In Huntington's interpretation, Clausewitz saw war "as at one and the same time an autonomous science" (and so a defined area of professional competence) while also appreciating that it was "a subordinate science in that its ultimate purposes come from outside itself." These purposes were those set by politicians in accordance with state policy. As a result, Huntington claimed that "Clausewitz also contributed the first theoretical justification for civilian control."[5]

Although Clausewitz did see a duality in war (to which we shall turn in a moment), it was not that attributed to him by Huntington. Clausewitz regarded policy as an alien element in relation to war, able either to moderate its conduct or to march in step with its inbuilt capacity for escalation.[6] However, he rejected the notion that strategy (which he consistently defined as the use of fighting for the purposes of the war) could be separated from the policy which set war's ultimate aim. "The main lines of every major strategic plan are largely political," he wrote to Major Carl von Roeder of the Prussian General Staff on December 22, 1827, "and their political character increases the more the plan applies to the entire campaign and the whole state."[7] Not least because he rejected the idea that there could be "a purely military evaluation of a great strategic issue," Clausewitz also never developed a theory of civil-military relations that adhered to the rigid lines of demarcation suggested by Huntington. The American read Clausewitz as saying that "the soldier must always be subordinate to the statesman."[8] In fact, Clausewitz suggested the exact opposite.

---

5. Samuel P. Huntington, *The Soldier and the State: The Theory and Politics of Civil-Military Relations* (Cambridge, MA: Belknap Press, 1957), 31, 56, 58.

6. Carl von Clausewitz, "Strategische Kritik von Feldzugs von 1814 im Frankreich," in *Sämtliche hinterlassen Werke über Krieg und Kriegführung*, Volume 3, Wolfgang von Seidlitz, ed. (Stuttgart: Mundus, 1999), 235; Carl von Clausewitz, *On War*, Michael Howard and Peter Paret, trans. and eds. (Princeton, NJ: Princeton University Press, 1976), 608. For ease of reference, I have used this edition of *On War* but have corrected the text in line with the original German where Howard and Paret have omitted words or altered their meaning. I have used the Sixteenth German edition, the first to revert to the phrasing in the First German edition: Carl von Clausewitz, *Vom Krieg; hinterlassenes Werk*, Werner Hahlweg, ed. (Bonn: F. Dümmler: 1952).

7. Carl von Clausewitz, *Two Letters on Strategy*, Peter Paret and Daniel Moran, trans. and eds. (Carlisle Barracks, PA: US Army War College, 1984), 9.

8. Huntington, *The Soldier and the State*, 57.

We say that the general becomes a statesman, but he must not cease to be the general. On the one hand, he must comprehend in one glance all the political conditions; on the other, he knows exactly what he can do with the means at his disposal.[9]

The Korean War had given energy to Huntington's use of Clausewitz to support the arguments for military subordination to civil control. In 1951, General Douglas MacArthur challenged the primacy of the president by claiming the authority to escalate the conflict in the pursuit of victory, even beyond the nuclear threshold. In doing so, MacArthur exceeded the confines of professionalism as Huntington would later define them. So, when Harry S. Truman dismissed MacArthur, he did more than sanctify the use of Clausewitz to assert civilian control over the military. President Truman also ensured that the Korean War did not trigger the wider conflict between the democracies and communism which many feared. In an era which threatened total war, the Korean War provided the basis for the development of ideas about limited war.

Although both total war and limited war were twentieth-century concepts unfamiliar to Clausewitz, there was a second way in which *On War* could be made applicable to the United States' post-1945 security dilemmas. In this case, however, they were built on what Clausewitz had actually said about war's duality. In a prefatory note to *On War* dated July 10, 1827, Clausewitz claimed that war could be of two kinds. Either the objective was to "annihilate the enemy" so as to force him "to sign whatever peace we please" or it was "merely to occupy some of his frontier districts so that we can annex them or use them for bargaining at the peace negotiations."[10] This distinction allowed Clausewitz to recognize that not all the wars in history, and especially not those of the eighteenth century, had been fought with aims as extensive as those of Napoleon. It neatly balanced his experience of existential conflict with the aspiration that war might be simply instrumental by identifying a feature that was common to both—"that war is nothing but the continuation of state policy by other means."[11] This duality created a theoretical construction for wars with either expansive or limited aims without compromising the idea that the phenomenon of war had a unitary nature. It did not say anything specific about how the second type of aim might be pursued, thus allowing for the possibility

---

9. Carl von Clausewitz, *On War*, trans. O.S. Matthijs Jolles (Washington, DC: Infantry Journal Press, 1950), 45; see also Book 1, Chapter 3 and Book 2, Chapter 3, of Clausewitz, *Vom Kriege*.

10. Clausewitz, *On War*, 69.

11. Clausewitz, *On War*, 69.

that the military objective might still be "to annihilate the enemy," even if the ultimate aim was a compromise peace.

The duality of the prefatory note of 1827 had inspired two major thinkers about war prior to 1914. In Germany, Hans Delbrück developed Clausewitz's interpretation by identifying the sort of strategy adopted by commanders pursuing more limited objectives. His principal example—and the one which dominated Clausewitz's discussion of the defense in Book 6 of *On War*—was Frederick the Great in the Seven Years' War. Delbrück argued that Frederick, facing a stronger alliance and committed simply to holding what he had gained in previous wars, used maneuver to exhaust his militarily stronger opponents, engaging them in battle only when he could fight them in isolation. The title he gave this extension of Clausewitz's thinking, *Ermattungsstrategie*, could be translated as a strategy of attrition, although the application of attrition in the First World War—unlike Delbrück's version—elevated fighting, not maneuver, as its principal method. Moreover, the Seven Years' War left Prussia prostrate; in other words, the limited aim still called for maximum military effort.

The second thinker, Julian Corbett, aspired to achieve major effect in return for less effort. In *Some Principles of Maritime Strategy* (1911), he applied Clausewitz's duality to show how Britain could take a limited part in a major continental war, using its naval power to launch amphibious expeditions to points of its own choosing or to conduct economic war through blockade.[12] Again, the practice of the First World War contradicted the theory. Britain adopted both the maritime options, but it also raised a mass army to fight a major land war. The losses of the First World War prompted many of those who thought about war to seek to prevent it altogether, primarily through deterrence rather than to fight it in limited ways. To do that, they stressed that future war would be "total." However, for fascist states, this was how they proposed to fight war, not prevent it. Total war also became a synonym for "totalitarian war."[13] In 1939, Walther Malmsten Schering, a philosopher, Nazi, and the author of *Die Kriegsphilosophie von Clausewitz*, concluded that in future there would be only one kind of war—total war.[14]

12. Julian Corbett, *Some Principles of Maritime Strategy* (London: Longmans, 1911).

13. The English translation of Erich Ludendorff, *Der Totale* Krieg (Munich: Ludendorffs Verlag, 1935) is A.S. Rappoport, trans. *The Nation at War* (London: Hutchinson, 1935): Chapter 1, rendered "total war" as "totalitarian warfare."

14. Walther Malmsten Schering, *Wehrphilosophie* (Leipzig: Barth, 1939), 241, 246–76.

The revival of limited war thinking after the Korean War was driven not by the dualism in war's aims but rather by the incipient totality of its conduct, expressed not in the terms which German thought had espoused before 1939 but in response to the mass destruction enabled by nuclear weapons. In 1957, Robert Osgood's *Limited War* claimed that Clausewitz believed policy "was the essential basis for apprehending all war's complexities and contradictions from a single standpoint, without which one could not form consistent judgments."[15] Rather than the mastermind of "total" war—the interpretation imposed on Clausewitz by Basil Liddell Hart in 1933—Osgood saw Clausewitz as the theorist who wanted policy to be used to curb war's uncontrolled violence.[16] It was beholden on the United States to discard its distaste for war and to see its use as "a rational instrument of power" by putting Clausewitz's dictum into practice.

Osgood described limited wars as fought for "concrete, well-defined objectives that do not demand the utmost military effort"; major wars, by contrast, had no clear objectives beyond the destruction of the enemy.[17] For all his avowed enthusiasm for Clausewitz, Osgood was shifting the weight from a war limited by its ends to one limited by its means. Because wars would have to be fought in ways which remained below the nuclear threshold, their objectives would also have to be circumscribed. At one level, Osgood had no choice but to downplay the role of the political aim. The Cold War was a clash of competing ideologies that would brook no compromise. Clausewitz's discussion of the political aim had recognized its capacity to escalate war, but he had treated war's violence as inherent in war itself and applicable to both kinds of war. In his brief survey of the history of war in *On War* (Book 8, Chapter 3A), Clausewitz ascribed the expansion of war after the French Revolution in 1789 not to France's pursuit of ideologically open-ended aims like liberty, equality, and fraternity, but instead to the political and social transformation of the state itself. Nor had he seen Napoleon's lust for conquest in terms of totalitarianism. Instead Clausewitz argued that, because Napoleon's power rested on his achievements in war, his rule depended on his next victory, and so he was locked in a gamble of "double or quits" from which he could not escape.[18] The

---

15. Robert Endicott Osgood, *Limited War: The Challenge to American Strategy* (Chicago, IL: University of Chicago Press, 1957), 21, 22–23.

16. Basil Liddell Hart, *The Ghost of Napoleon* (London: Faber, 1933), 118–29.

17. Osgood, *Limited War*, 28.

18. Carl von Clausewitz, *The Campaign of 1812 in Russia*, foreword by Sir Michael Howard (New York, NY: De Capo, 1995 [1843]), 252–53.

extremes of war in his day, for all the rhetoric of the revolution in the 1790s, were not stoked by the fundamental incompatibility of regime types characteristic of the clashes between fascism and communism in the Second World War, or the competition between communism and liberal democracy in the Cold War.

In these circumstances the American application of limited war proved harder to direct than the theory suggested, not least in Vietnam. In *Nuclear Weapons and Foreign Policy*, also published in 1957, Henry Kissinger had praised Osgood's book and joined him in arguing that "a total war," conducted according to purely military considerations, "would have been to Clausewitz a contradiction in terms."[19] Here Kissinger drew on Clausewitz's discussion of absolute war in Book 1, Chapter 1, where it is treated as a philosophical concept which can never be achieved in reality. This is also where Clausewitz asserted the primacy of the political objective most strongly. Kissinger, therefore, criticized, "the separation of our strategic doctrine from diplomacy, its notion that victory is an end in itself achieved by rendering the enemy defenseless." Rather, limited war should both prevent extremes of violence and slow down "the tempo of modern war lest the rapidity with which operations succeed each other prevent the establishment of a relation between the political and military objectives."[20] That was roughly what Kissinger tried to do during the Vietnam War, first as national security advisor and then as secretary of state between 1969 and 1975. It did not work. Although Kissinger himself saw the conflict as peripheral to US interests, the effect of American failure was to make it central.

Apart from the prefatory note of 1827, Clausewitz's *On War* actually has little to say about limited war in any form, and particularly not that which shaped the United States' approach to Vietnam. In a second but undated prefatory note, Clausewitz described his manuscript as "a collection of materials from which a theory of *major* war was to have been distilled."[21] This might imply that Clausewitz had a plan to write a second book after *On War* and that it would have been on limited war, but most commentators reckon that the reference instead is to a possible book on "small wars." Clausewitz lectured on

---

19. Henry Kissinger, *Nuclear Weapons and Foreign Policy* (New York, NY: Council on Foreign Relations, 1957), 225.

20. Kissinger, *Nuclear Weapons*, 341, 440.

21. Clausewitz, *On War*, 70; I have italicized "major" as Howard and Paret omit the word "*großen*" from their translation of the original.

that subject at the war college in 1810 and 1811. He focused on the eighteenth-century patterns of what was then called "petty war," operations away from the main battlefield designed to harass lines of communications, to raid, and to reconnoiter, and included his own experience in 1792–95.[22] But at the same time, in collusion with August Neidhart von Gneisenau, who as a young officer had served in the American War of Independence in 1782–83, Clausewitz was secretly plotting a national insurgency against the French occupation. Such a struggle would have used terror and indiscriminate violence, blurring the division between civilian and soldier in its mobilization of the people. The tactics of "small war" would have been used in "major war" in ways that refute those critics of Clausewitz who see him solely as a student of major interstate wars with no appreciation of guerrilla warfare. Sibylle Scheipers has argued that through his engagement with partisan and people's war Clausewitz developed the themes of *On War* itself. A national insurrection would have been an "absolute war," which would have been more fully permeated by policy than any other form of war.[23]

If that is the case, then Book 6 of *On War*, on the defense, gives the best indication of the directions which Clausewitz was following. In Clausewitz's characterization, the aim of defense is negative but its means are stronger than those of the offensive. Guerrillas can harass the lines of communication of an advancing army and turn defense into popular insurrection. In the last resort, as Chapter 26 of Book 6 reveals, the mobilization of the people in arms and their commitment to fight to the bitter end, expressed in terms which evoke the 1812 declaration, would expand and deepen war, not limit it. If Vietnam was a war of Clausewitz's second kind, the response of the North Vietnamese was a better example of what he had in mind than the idea of the war constructed in Washington, in which the debate over the means created uncertainty over the ends.

Osgood and Kissinger both stressed how Clausewitz had impressed Marx, Engels, and—above all—Lenin. Marxists liked *On War*'s treatment of the relationship between war and policy and, in recognizing this, Osgood and Kissinger pressed its wisdom on skeptical Americans. Moreover, as the West collectively confronted what it called "revolutionary war," it took Mao Zedong's military writings as the basis for insurgent doctrine. Mao too had read

22. The lectures were published in Clausewitz, *Schriften*, Volume 1, 226–558.

23. Sibylle Scheipers, *On Small War: Carl von Clausewitz and People's War* (Oxford: Oxford University Press, 2018).

On War, and, like the Bolsheviks, he was inspired by its discussion of war and policy. In Osgood's words, "the whole purpose of revolutionary violence is political, and the whole tactic of revolutionary violence must be subordinated to political objectives and shaped in anticipation of political consequences."[24] But both he and others exaggerated the influence of Clausewitz on Mao, who drew on a wide range of other sources for his military thought. Moreover, the war which Mao envisaged was not limited in time or participation: it would be both protracted and popular (in the sense that it would mobilize the people).

The American presentation of the Communists' reading of *On War* also missed much of its relevance to the Soviet army. The responses to *On War* of Trotsky, the Red Army's principal founder, were more diverse and pragmatic than politically driven. They included a strong stress on war's inherent violence. Although *Vom Kriege* was first translated into Russian in 1902, the fullest edition wasn't published until 1931–32 and was overseen by Aleksandr Andreevich Svechin, a major Soviet strategic thinker of the early 1920s. A former tsarist officer, Svechin was stripped of his principal functions in 1931. Between then and his execution in 1938, he devoted himself to the study of Clausewitz. By 1941, 55,000 copies of *On War* were in circulation in the Soviet Union.[25] Svechin's own work on strategy supported *On War*'s stress on the greater strength of the defense and, influenced by Delbrück, he argued that the Soviet Union should adopt a strategy of attrition. Both suggestions were strongly criticized as inappropriate for a revolutionary army, particularly by Mikhail N. Tukhachevsky, who called for the offensive and a strategy of annihilation. Svechin embraced Clausewitz's two kinds of war, differentiated by their objectives, while at the same time not ducking war's true nature. In this respect, Svechin endorsed Clausewitz in ringing terms:

> We consider ourselves bound to Clausewitz's splendid definition of destruction, and it would be pitiful to replace his vivid, rich definition of destruction with some watered down concept of a half-destruction, which yields no corollaries or inferences, under the pretext that destruction in pure form is inapplicable today.[26]

24. Osgood, *Limited War*, 53–54.

25. Olaf Rose, "Swetschin und Clausewitz. Geistesverwandtschaft und Schicksalsparallelitätit," in *Clausewitz*, Alexander Swetschin, ed. (Bonn: F. Dümmler, 1997), 64–69.

26. Aleksandr A. Svechin, *Strategy*, Kent E. Lee, ed. (Minneapolis, MN: East View Publications, 1992), 65.

Svechin wrote before the Soviet Union suffered horrific losses fighting a defensive war in 1941–45. Clausewitz's reputation in Russia suffered in consequence. He was accused of "reactionary-idealist teaching" which had been adopted uncritically by German military ideology. Although the Soviet occupiers set about purging German libraries of books that promoted Nazi or militarist views, they only banned those works associated with Clausewitz which had come out between 1933 and 1945. *On War* began to regain readers in East Germany even before Stalin's death in 1956. Clausewitz's links to the Prussian reform movement between 1807 and 1811, and his radicalism in 1812, burnished his revolutionary credentials. In 1952, the Russians commemorated the 140th anniversary of their victory over the French. As Clausewitz had played a crucial role in the convention under whose terms the Prussian contingent serving Napoleon had changed sides, he could be cast as representative of Russian-German brotherhood. The officers of the East German National Volksarmee reported that, although they rarely encountered Clausewitz in their own academy, they were immersed in his thinking when they completed their military education in the Soviet Union. In 1971, 140 years after Clausewitz's death in Breslau, his body was exhumed and reburied with great ceremony in Burg, his hometown. On the bicentenary of his birth in 1980, he was feted as a "patriot, reformer, and theorist."[27]

Although Soviet military thinkers rejected any suggestion that the violence inherent in war's nature could be contained, they accepted the idea that war could be of two kinds, because—like Clausewitz—they saw the differentiation in terms of ends rather than means. The value of the objective would define how war would be fought. Both Lenin and Stalin had condoned retreat if the circumstances made that necessary—the former explicitly citing Clausewitz in support.[28] Even defeat was acceptable if the likely gains were incommensurate with the effort required. However, the point remained that, "where the motive underlying the war is not some material advantage" but is instead "a war of hatred—a war, that is to say, where the political objective is the extermination of the one side by the other," the war "would be literally a war to the death."[29]

The problem, as in the United States, was whether this sort of conflict could any longer be the continuation of policy by other means given the advent of

27. Andrée Türpe, *Der vernachlässigte General? Das Clausewitz-Bild in der DDR* (Berlin: C. Links, 2020), 25–31, 117–53, 278–82.

28. Raymond L. Garthoff, *Soviet Military Policy: A Historical Analysis* (London: Faber, 1966), 88.

29. Peter Vigor, *The Soviet View of War, Peace and Neutrality* (London: Routledge, 1975), 90.

nuclear weapons. In East Germany in 1986, Erich Hönecker, the first secretary of the Socialist Unity Party, asserted it could not. Wolfgang Scheler, professor of philosophy at the Volksarmee's military academy, responded that it could, at least in regional and local wars. He argued that a nuclear exchange was not really a war, as its outcome would not be peace but extermination.[30] In 1987, Mikhail Gorbachev, the Soviet leader and architect of *Perestroika*, endorsed Hönecker's view. Although some Soviet military thinkers disagreed, others exploited the opening in Gorbachev's statement which allowed for conventional wars in pursuit of limited aims. Andrei A. Kokoshin, who served as Russia's First Deputy Minister of Defense between 1992 and 1997, led the way in Svechin's rehabilitation and so in turn brought Clausewitz into the debate. Referring to Book 6 of *On War*, Kokoshin took the battle of Kursk in 1943 as an example of how tactical and strategic defense, using attrition, could lead to victory. He also argued that war was not just a conflict fought by armed forces but, in reality, the sum of all the intellectual, political, and economic means possessed by a state in the struggle for power. By asserting the role of domestic policy in a doctrine of defensive deterrence, Kokoshin redefined Clausewitz's dictum for a contemporary context not least because he and others were clear-headed about the violence inherent in war.[31] Russian thinkers were more open to the possibility of existential war, more adaptive in thinking of ways round the problem (the American argument for limited nuclear war, which once again prioritized means over ends, gained little traction), and more sympathetic to the conditioning effects of Clausewitz's own experience than was the postwar United States.[32]

In West Germany, the Nazi legacy remained an obstacle to the study of Clausewitz for longer than it did in the East but, in a paradox which mirrors that of Rothfels, it provided the foundation for the major leap in his adoption in the United States. In 1961, a group of retired officers set up the non-partisan Clausewitz-Gesellschaft, but it commented on current issues more than it used *Vom Kriege* to promote strategic thought. Only one university, Münster, had a chair in what it also called *Wehrwissenchaft* (so perpetuating the Nazi

---

30. Türpe, *Der vernachlässigte General?* 247–64.

31. Hans-Ulrich Seidt, "Swetschin als politischer und strategischer Denker," in *Clausewitz, Swetschin*, ed., 35–36.

32. Andrei A. Kokoshin, *Soviet Strategic Thought, 1917–1991* (Cambridge, MA: MIT Press, 1998), 71–73, 140–41, 147–57, 168–69, 173; Hans-Ulrich Seidt, "Swetschin als politischer und strategischer Denker," 38–48; see also the introductory essays by Andrei Kokoshin, Valentin V. Larionov, and Vladimir N. Lobov, in Svechin, *Strategy*.

name for defense studies)—and in 2012 its incumbent, Werner Hahlweg, who had retired three decades earlier, was posthumously "outed" as a former Nazi. However, Hahlweg was also the preeminent Clausewitz scholar of the postwar era. In 1952, when he edited the sixteenth edition of *Vom Kriege*, Hahlweg reverted to the original text of 1832–34, abandoning the second edition of 1853 which had become tarred with the brush of Prussian militarism. Hahlweg also edited Clausewitz's surviving unpublished papers, thus exposing the book's genesis and development. If Earle, Huntington, Osgood, and others had prepared the ground for a better appreciation of *On War* in the English-speaking world, Hahlweg provided its scholarly underpinnings.

III

In 1976, Michael Howard and Peter Paret produced the third translation of *On War* in English. They used Hahlweg's edition. It proved massively successful. Here was *On War* in a form that overturned the received wisdom that the text was difficult, contradictory, and prolix. English-language references to Clausewitz soared to new heights in the early 1980s. In Britain that peak was twice as great as the previous surges in references to *On War*, each of which had occurred in the two world wars; in the United States it had no previous precedent and was five times bigger than that in Britain.[33] Most contemporary Clausewitzian strategic commentary is based, at least in the English-speaking world, on Howard and Paret, not on Clausewitz.

Princeton University Press reduced its bulk, abandoning the three-volume structure of the original German edition—and of the Graham translation—for a single volume. It was also dramatically shorter in another sense. In her foreword to the 1832 edition, Marie von Bruhl had published an undated note in which her husband said that he regarded only Book 1, Chapter 1 of *On War* as finished. Hahlweg dated this note unhesitatingly to 1827, a year in which Clausewitz passed through a personal and intellectual crisis.[34] It was possibly prompted by the writing of Book 6 on defense, a theme which forced Clausewitz to address other forms of war than the Napoleonic and whose unresolved tensions made it—by some distance—the longest book of *On War*. Others have placed the key developmental phase in Clausewitz's thinking even earlier—to

33. I am grateful for these calculations to Connor Collins, who worked them out using a Google Books Ngram search and applied them in an essay for the M Litt in Strategic Studies at St Andrews in 2020.

34. Clausewitz, *Schriften*, Volume 2, Part 1, Hahlweg, ed., 625.

1825. Paret himself, in recognizing the formative effects on Clausewitz of his exposure to Gerhard von Scharnhorst, through the war school and a military discussion group to which the young officer was admitted, rightly traced the origins of some key ideas to the years 1802–5. Nonetheless, Paret and Howard dated the note to 1830, believing it was written as Clausewitz bundled his papers up before returning to active duty in Poland. He died the following year without reopening them. For Howard and Paret, Book 1, Chapter 1 became the final summative statement of Clausewitz's views on war, succinct, brief, aphoristic, and to the point. If they—and others, for they are not alone—are wrong, much more of *On War* is a final statement, and even finished, than the standard wisdom allows.[35]

Howard and Paret's *On War* was also more accessible in another way. Both had served in the Second World War, and Howard especially wanted to create a text, written by a soldier building on his own experience, that would be read by other soldiers. They brought it conceptually up to date by introducing words and phrases that were not in the original but which spoke to those concerned with war in the late twentieth century. Total war was but one of these. Clausewitz talked of "absolute war" and "whole war," meaning war in its purest forms, but he never addressed total war in the sense understood today. Another neologism was operations. By 1976, operational art was being accepted as a distinct level of war within military doctrine. By occasionally translating *Krieg* [war] and more frequently *Handeln* [dealings] as operations, Howard and Paret implied that operational art's origins lay in Prussia in the 1820s, not—as was actually the case—in Russia a century later.[36]

Howard and Paret had four interlocking themes which they used to fashion their interpretation. First, strategy should be understood in terms of ends, ways, and means. This tripartite division is one Clausewitz applied to war at every level—tactical and political, as well as strategic, but he was looser and less consistent in the German words he attached to the three terms than Howard and Paret implied, and he was less determinedly hierarchical in their treatment than were his translators. One of the reasons for that was their focus on

35. Herbert Roskinski and Raymond Aron agreed; see most recently Christian Müller, *Clausewitz Verstehen. Wirken, Werk und Wirkung* (Paderborn: Brill, 2021), 49–50.

36. Jan Willem Honig, "Clausewitz's *On War*: Problems of Text and Translation," in *Clausewitz in the Twenty-First Century*, Hew Strachan and Andreas Herberg-Rothe, eds. (Oxford: Oxford University Press, 2007); Hew Strachan, "Clausewitz en Anglaise: La Césure de 1976," in *De la Guerre? Clausewitz et la Pensée Stratégique Contemporaine*, Laure Bardiès and Martin Motte, eds. (Paris: Economica, 2008), 81–122.

the second theme: the idea that war is the continuation of policy by other means, a proposition which *On War* addresses directly only in Books 1 and 8, but which they suggested permeates the whole text, sometimes by inserting "political" when it is not present in the original. Policy was placed at the apex of *On War*, both methodologically and in setting war's objectives. Yet Clausewitz never clearly defined what policy was—in contrast to his sustained efforts to define war: some commentators sometimes seem to forget that the subject of the book is war, as its title makes abundantly clear, not war's causes.

Thirdly, and also consequently, Howard and Paret stressed that the state made war. Significantly, Paret called his own biography of Clausewitz, published in the same year as the translation, *Clausewitz and the State*. However, in Chapter 26 of Book 6, Clausewitz acknowledged that the people or the nation also made war and could so with greater determination than the state. Although he was reluctant to pontificate about the future shape of war, Clausewitz thought the nation in arms would probably cause war to expand, rather than revert to the more limited forms of the eighteenth century, because it would follow the precedent of the Revolutionary and Napoleonic Wars. Howard and Paret were determined to contain war and, by treating absolute war as an abstraction, as Kissinger had done, conscripted Clausewitz for their cause. This was their fourth theme: that Clausewitz's book, despite the fact that it originated in the experience of the most extensive and destructive war in Europe since the Thirty Years' War, could be read as supporting ideas of deterrence and limited, state-controlled wars. In 1977, the year after the publication of their translation, international law responded to insurgencies and civil wars by recognizing the belligerent status of those fighting in wars of national liberation. Howard saw the additional protocols to the Geneva Convention as a retrograde step in the progression to "a just, peaceable, and orderly society." War, he pronounced, "is instrumental, not elemental."[37]

The Howard and Paret translation had caught the bow-wave of the Cold War and the fear of a nuclear exchange. Raymond Aron's *Penser la Guerre, Clausewitz*, published in the same year, directly applied *On War* to contemporary problems and concluded that, if Clausewitz had still been alive, he would have developed a theory of conflict resolution.[38] Aron's preoccupations

---

37. Michael Howard, *"Temperamenta Belli:* Can War be Controlled?" in *Restraints on War: Studies in the Limitation of Armed Conflict*, Michael Howard, ed. (Oxford: Oxford University Press, 1979), 13–14.

38. Raymond Aron, *Penser la Guerre, Clausewitz* (Paris: Gallimard, 1976).

were those of Howard and Paret: how do you make what Aron called the "formula"—the idea that war is the continuation of policy by other means—relevant to a generation confronting what Aron dubbed "the planetary age?"

More parochially but even more pertinently, the Howard and Paret version spoke to Americans grappling with the legacy of the Vietnam War. In 1981, Colonel Harry Summers, a Vietnam veteran, wrote *On Strategy: A Critical Analysis of the Vietnam War*. It proved especially successful in military circles, perhaps unsurprisingly given that it portrayed an army that won the tactical war in Vietnam but was let down at the strategic level. "As military professionals," Summers wrote, "it was our job to judge the true nature of the Vietnam war, communicate those facts to our civilian decision-makers, and to recommend appropriate strategies." He used *On War* (in the Howard and Paret translation) as his template, quoting Clausewitz in support: "The first, the supreme, the most far-reaching act of judgement that the statesman and commander have to make is to establish . . . the kind of war on which they are embarking."[39]

The United States had failed to do that. Summers was not unsympathetic to the idea of limited war but he did not believe that a war could be contained by way of means rather than ends. For similar reasons, he abhorred the cult of counterinsurgency. It had been wrong to see the war as a "classic revolutionary war," because "the guerrillas did *not* achieve decisive results on their own."[40] Here Summers followed the Howard and Paret interpretation of *On War*, rather than what Clausewitz himself had suggested, not just in the heat of 1812 but also in the cooler analysis at the end of Book 6, Chapter 26.

Summers's handling of Clausewitz's trinity is particularly revealing. In Book 1, Chapter 1, after he set out the need to identify correctly the kind of war which is being undertaken, Clausewitz went on to show just how difficult that can be. In one of the most suggestive passages in *On War*, he likened war not only to a chameleon, because "it in some respects changes its *nature* in each concrete case," but also to a "strange trinity," composed: first, "of the original violence of its essence, the hate and enmity which are to be regarded as a blind, natural impulse"; second, "of the play of probabilities and chance, which make it a free activity of the emotions"; and third, "of the subordinate character of a

39. Harry G. Summers, *On Strategy: A Critical Analysis of the Vietnam War* (Novato: Presidio, 1982), 83.

40. Summers, *On Strategy*, 63–80. Emphasis in original.

political tool, through which it belongs to the province of pure intelligence."[41] This has come to be called the "primary" trinity. Clausewitz then proposed that each of these three attributes can be more often (but not exclusively) associated with the people, the commander and his army, and the government. These three groups constitute the "secondary" trinity. The so-called primary trinity has a numinous quality, just like the Christian trinity, an important consideration given that several of Clausewitz's forebears had been churchmen. What unites the three in one is war itself. Here war is not of two kinds but a single phenomenon—an adversarial business whose outcomes depend on the reciprocal and hostile actions of both sides and so can go in multiple directions with exponential effects. At the opening of Book 1, Chapter 1, Clausewitz defined war first and foremost as a clash of wills. The "secondary" trinity, with which he associated these elements, are actors within a nation and so make up the strategy which one country applies to a war, but they cannot encompass the whole war because that has to include the enemy's behavior and the interaction of the two opponents. The whole concept unites the instrumental with the existential. It has many moving parts and no theory can afford to leave any one of them out of account, nor can it fix the relations between them because they are in perpetual flux.

That was not how Howard and Paret presented the trinity in their translation. In order to bring it into line with the ideas that war is the continuation of policy by other means, and that war is a political instrument and so subordinate to policy, they stressed the link between policy and reason as well as the separation between the people and policy. Howard and Paret did not allow for a rational populace or a passionate government. Their preference when translating *Politik* was to call it policy, not politics. They prioritized what Clausewitz called *Staatspolitik*, despite the fact that he used the word only once, in his prefatory note of July 10, 1827, and not in the main body of *Vom Kriege*.[42] This approach both omits the adversarial aspects of political debates and overlooks Clausewitz's own definition of *Politik* in Book 8 as "the representative of all interests of the community."[43] As a result, Summers entirely excluded from his

---

41. Clausewitz, *On War*, Book 1, Chapter 1; most of the translation is that of Jolles, *On War*, 18, but the phrase on the chameleon is mine. Both Jolles and Howard and Paret translate the German, *Natur*, as "character." For the problems inherent in the Howard and Paret version, and Summers's use of it, see Christopher Bassford, "The Primacy of 'Policy' and the 'Trinity' in Clausewitz's Mature Thought," in *Clausewitz in the Twenty-First Century*, Strachan and Herberg–Rothe, eds.

42. Clausewitz, *Vom Kriege*, 77.

43. Clausewitz, *On War*, 607.

use of *On War* the primary trinity, thus also omitting one of Clausewitz's most profound characterizations of war. Instead, Summers focused on the secondary trinity, seeing it as the vehicle for making national strategy. His book stated at its outset that Clausewitz described the task of military theory as maintaining a balance between the people, the government, and the army, and then went on to apply the trinity in those terms.[44]

The effects on American strategy were profound, especially as the United States Army came to believe it had lost the Vietnam War at home because the government had failed to engage the people in an understanding of the war. Another Vietnam veteran, Colin Powell, also used his reading of *On War* to stress the importance of the secondary trinity. As military assistant to the defense secretary, Caspar Weinberger, in 1984, Powell ensured that Clausewitzian principles shaped the Weinberger doctrine and, when he himself became Chairman of the Joint Chiefs of Staff, the same principles informed his own doctrine. The United States should not start a war without a clear sense of its objectives or of how it might achieve them. It was the government's role to settle the former and that of the armed forces to deliver them. To do that, as Powell put it in 1992, they needed sufficient means to be decisive from the start.[45]

None of this was un-Clausewitzian in itself. Summers and Powell could quote chapter and verse in support. The problems were twofold. The first was how to manage the relationship between ends, ways, and means and what happened at the junctions between each, especially in a massive bureaucracy, obsessed as it was by the principle of civil-military subordination in theory but unsure of its practical application during war. The second was what selective quotation and free translation left out.

As the Cold War ended, the central challenge posed by nuclear war to the proposition that war was the continuation of policy by other means became less pressing. At the same time, however, civil wars and so-called new wars acquired increasing salience. The heavy identification of *On War* by Howard and Paret with what Clausewitz's critics now called "old" wars reduced his relevance when the principal protagonists were non-state actors. Clausewitz was caricatured as the product of a post-Westphalian order, established in 1648 at the end of the Thirty Years' War but now crumbling as states lost their

---

44. Summers, *On Strategy*, 5.

45. Colin Powell and Joseph Persico, *My American Journey* (New York, NY: Random House, 1995), 207–8.

monopoly of force. "New Wars" proponents argued that war was no longer a political instrument, not because nuclear weapons made that a nonsensical proposition, but because their aims were economic and social, waged by warlords who used armed conflict to make profits or to facilitate crime. To achieve their objectives, they shunned battle rather than sought it, thereby rendering the techniques of the guerrilla and insurgent central rather than peripheral to modern and future war. The aim of war was no longer victory and then peace, but rather its perpetuation for the purpose of profit.

The Clausewitz constructed and then deconstructed by his critics in the 1990s owed more to Howard and Paret than to a close reading of *Vom Kriege*. Their translation of *On War*, shaped by the apparent certainties of the Cold War, looked increasingly dated as the context for armed conflict changed. And it was not just those outside the military who reached that conclusion. So too did some of those in uniform. The American advocates of new technologies in the 1990s, who presented the "revolution in military affairs" as the recipe for the application of overwhelming military power for decisive effect in short wars, seemed vindicated after the 9/11 attacks in 2001 by the initial successes in Afghanistan and Iraq. As signals intelligence and satellite navigation enabled precision guidance and targeted effects, they saw Clausewitz's stress on the fog of war and the friction inherent in its conduct as redundant. They were elevating means over ends. When, by 2005–6, mounting insurgency fed civil war and reinvigorated the debates around guerrilla warfare, the ends for which the United States was fighting lost clarity. But Clausewitz was not necessarily vindicated as a result. Summers had rejected counterinsurgency for reasons that he presented as Clausewitzian. *On War*, according to much standard wisdom, said nothing about "small war," let alone terrorism. Thanks to Huntington, Clausewitz was also held responsible for the strict subordination of the military to the civil power, which resulted in the two pursuing parallel, rather than convergent, paths. Clausewitz was quoted back to himself: his injunction to the statesman and the commander first to identify the sort of war on which they were about to embark had been breached because each had failed to listen to the other. They read *On War* selectively, if at all.

Each of those who, from 1943 onwards, read Clausewitz in such different ways, whether Marxist or Fascist, liberal or democrat, was like the blind man trying to identify a camel by touch alone: they could not identify the whole. After 1815, when Clausewitz began to write *On War*, he addressed the war he had known, and which dominates Books 2 to 5. Faced—at the latest by 1827— by the realization that his own experience was insufficient to produce a general theory of war, and possibly driven by a pragmatic need to moderate his political radicalism, he shifted tack, most evidently in Books 1 and 8. As a result, Clausewitz did not see war as either existential or instrumental but instead as both. Moreover, the former had struck him with compelling force at a formative stage in his career, while the latter became dominant later, as he labored in peacetime to give context from above to what he had experienced and felt from below—and ultimately to use the idea of policy to give unity to the whole.[46]

IV

Strategic studies have struggled to define themselves, not least because they draw on so many other fields of enquiry. Anthropology, history, economics, political science, international relations, psychology, and sociology all offer perspectives on war but, as two political scientists have written, "military history is the only disciplinary perspective that is traditionally defined by the actual study of war and combat."[47]

Clausewitz shared that view. He too was eclectic in his use of disciplines. Mathematics and mechanics shaped much of his thinking and, from "friction" to the "center of gravity," gave wings to his metaphors. Because those metaphors are so powerful, we can be in danger of elevating the ideas over the realities in which they are grounded. His study of war grew in the first instance from his own experience. After writing his 1812 memorandum, he took part in the Russian campaign, the war of German liberation of 1813–14, and the Waterloo campaign. In all, Clausewitz fought for nine years between 1792 and 1815, but experience was not enough. Scharnhorst, whom Clausewitz saw as his second father, advised him that he had to put experience into context through military history.

Clausewitz did what he was told. He wrote accounts not only of all the wars in which he had participated (except that of 1792–95) but also of the French wars in Italy in 1796 and 1799. When shaping Book 6 of *On War*, he paid more attention to the wars of Frederick the Great, in whose army his father had served. In all, Clausewitz studied in excess of 130 wars reaching back to the late

---

46. Herfried Münkler, *Gewalt und Ordnung. Das Bild des Krieges im politischen Denken* (Frankfurt am Main: Fischer, 1992), 9, 92–110; see also Lennart Souchon, *Strategy in the 21st Century: The Continuing Relevance of Carl von Clausewitz* (Clam: Springer, 2020), 122–26.

47. Donald Alexander Downs and Ilia Murtazashivili, *Arms and the University: Military Presence and the Civic Education of Non-Military Students* (New York, NY: Cambridge University Press, 2012), 288–90.

sixteenth century.[48] Military history was the bedrock on which he built his ideas on war, testing them against reality and incorporating exceptions which both proved rules and undermined them.

As a result, in quantitative terms, Clausewitz wrote as much military history as strategic theory, but—as his drafts, redrafts, and failure to publish in his own lifetime show—he labored more self-critically on the latter than the former. His deep dives into military history were not ends in themselves but rather means to test and refine hypotheses. He therefore read more deeply in what today would be called strategic studies than he publicly revealed in *On War*. Strategy had only been identified as a distinct aspect of military thought in the late eighteenth century. The impassioned nationalist vocabulary of the 1812 memorandum quotes directly, but without acknowledgment, from the *Essai Général de Tactique* (first published in 1770) by Jacques-Antoine-Hippolyte de Guibert, a work often seen as anticipating the effects of both the French Revolution and Napoleon on war's conduct.[49] The impact of both and the need to explain them prompted the development of strategy as an analytical tool, even if it was conceived in more narrow terms than would be the case after 1945. Clausewitz's *On War* was not an isolated phenomenon but stood on the shoulders of others, although he rarely—if ever—acknowledged them.

Prussia's own post-Frederician study of war was shaped by Georg Heinrich von Berenhorst (1733–1814), who had emphasized, as Clausewitz would too, the roles of chance and of moral and psychological factors in war, and also by Adam Heinrich Dietrich von Bülow (1763–1807). Bülow, like Clausewitz, was influenced by Newtonian physics. In Book 7—that on the attack and the least developed of all the books of *On War*—Clausewitz followed Bülow in adopting the mechanical concept of equipoise to declare that an offensive, as it advances, drains its own momentum so that the advantage swings to the defensive. Without acknowledgment, he lifted from Bülow the idea of the culminating point of victory and concluded that defense is the stronger form of war. There is no allowance for the increasing power of an attack through its moral effects, through its control of territory and the exploitation of its resources, or for the disintegration of an army as it retreats.[50]

48. Müller, *Clausewitz Verstehen*, 233.
49. Clausewitz, *Schriften*, Volume 1, Hahlweg, ed., 710–11.
50. Clausewitz, *On War*, 143, 573.

Bülow, unlike Behrenhorst, was named by Clausewitz, but only so that the latter could bracket him with Antoine-Henri Jomini (1779–1869), both of whom Clausewitz criticized for their emphasis on geography and geometry. That did not stop him, when explaining the importance of bases and lines of communication, from leaning heavily on the systems which they had propounded. The pragmatist in Clausewitz recognized that armies needed positive doctrines to be able to act as cohesive bodies in consistent ways.[51] *On War* may be a book on how to think about war but, like Jomini, Clausewitz also sought to tell his readers how war should be conducted, and so sought to establish principles to guide a commander in his decisions.[52]

The differences between Clausewitz and Jomini were twofold. First, Clausewitz was readier to acknowledge the exceptions to what was generally true and to appreciate the need to embrace them as conferring their own insights, rather than reject them. Second, while Clausewitz was little known in his own lifetime, by the 1820s, Jomini was the dominant international figure in the field, recognized for his *Traité des Grandes Opérations Militaires,* a multivolume work which began to appear in 1805 and went through many accumulations and editions. An analytical account of the wars of Frederick the Great, the French Revolution, and Napoleon, it presented its theoretical points as conclusions, not as departure points. Not until 1830, the year in which Clausewitz stopped writing, did Jomini prioritize theory. His *Précis de l'Art de la Guerre* did not appear until seven years after Clausewitz's death and Jomini used its foreword to respond robustly to Clausewitz's attacks. Their contemporaries looked at Clausewitz through the prism of Jomini, but today the opposite happens.

These earlier texts reveal how commonplace Clausewitz's best-known dictum was. In 1806, Bülow had written that "war was only a means for reaching a diplomatic end."[53] Two of Clausewitz's contemporaries, Constantin von Lossau (1767–1848) and Rühle von Lilienstern (1780–1847), wrote books "on war," albeit at lesser length than Clausewitz, and both anticipated him in their attention to moral factors in war and by their conviction that war was a political

---

51. Clausewitz, *On War,* 153.

52. The distinction is nicely made by Jean-Jacques Langendorf, whose study of Jomini in two volumes is called *Faire la Guerre: Antoine-Henri Jomini* (Geneva: Georg, 2001–2004), in contradistinction to Aron's book on Clausewitz, *Penser la Guerre.*

53. Arthur Kuhle, *Die Preußische Kriegstheorie um 1800 und ihre Suche nach dynamischen Gleichgewichten* (Berlin: Duncker und Humblot, 2018), 27.

instrument.[54] Jomini's *Précis* explicitly included, as *On War* did not, a chapter on the different sorts of political objectives which might guide war.

The third discipline which shaped Clausewitz's approach was political philosophy. While Bülow and Jomini can be taken as the tail-end of the Enlightenment and its endeavor to impose rationality on war, Clausewitz lies on the cusp of Romanticism, venerating the hero and the genius in war, and embracing it as a medium in which both could thrive. With peace in 1795, he seized the opportunity to explore nearby libraries to extend his limited education. He wrote on Machiavelli in 1804 and referenced Montesquieu's *De l'Esprit des Lois* in 1818, saying he was inspired by its "concise, aphoristic chapters, which . . . would attract the intelligent reader by what they suggested as much as by what they expressed."[55] Book 1, Chapter 1 reflects that ambition, while Machiavelli's realism suffuses the whole of *On War*. In the absence of any evidence, it is tempting to wonder whether Clausewitz also read Thomas Hobbes's *Leviathan* (1651). Although less explicitly than Hobbes, Clausewitz suggested that the European state had created a monopoly in the use of war which contained conflict, not least by its use of strategy to define war's conduct. Whereas for Hobbes, the world before the state was characterized by perpetual war, for Clausewitz, this "other" was embodied in Asia, a continent in which war was "virtually permanent" and whose peoples were outstanding warriors but bereft of strategic thought.[56]

On his return from imprisonment in France in 1807, Clausewitz stayed in Switzerland with Madame de Staël. While there, he visited the school of the educationalist, Johann Heinrich Pestalozzi, who introduced Clausewitz to the Socratic method of question and answer as the basis for philosophical enquiry.[57] Lennart Souchon believes that the themes of the "primary trinity" were shaped by Plato's *Republic*.[58] Certainly *On War*'s method was Platonic in its bid to achieve understanding by a sustained dialogue, in which Clausewitz used military history to challenge theory, to point out that what was generally true was not always universally so, and to caution against the dangers of

54. Constantin von Lossau, *Der Krieg. Für wahre Krieger* (Leipzig, 1815; Reprint, Vienna: Carolinger, 2009); Johann Jakob Otto August Rühle von Lilienstern, *Vom Kriege* (1814) and *Apologie des Krieges* (1813; Reprint, Vienna: Carolinger, 1984).

55. Clausewitz, *On War*, 63.

56. Clausewitz, *On War*, 453, 586.

57. Peter Paret, *Clausewitz and the State* (Oxford: Clarendon Press, 1976) 123–36, 147–86; Müller, *Clausewitz Verstehen*, 20.

58. Souchon, *Strategy in the 21st Century*, 58.

allowing theory to accompany the general to the battlefield.[59] Some of Clausewitz's biographers have linked his philosophical approach to that of his contemporary, Georg Wilhelm Friedrich Hegel. Like Clausewitz, Hegel was deeply influenced by the events of 1806 and the impact of Napoleon. The two lived in Berlin and it is hard to believe their paths did not cross. Clausewitz's trinity, with its fusion of the rational and irrational and its conception of war as a whole, is Hegelian.[60] Each used history as a basis for his argument, but in different ways. Hegel's method was to answer a proposition with a counter and then to seek a resolution through a synthesis. To the frustration of many of his readers, that is not Clausewitz's approach—which is precisely why he can be so readily and selectively quoted to advance seemingly contradictory positions. A Hegelian synthesis was frequently only resolved through idealism, when Clausewitz—who after all was not a philosopher—sought to produce a result of practical, not philosophical, use. He juxtaposed discordant points to show real differences as a basis for better critical judgment, not as a route to a synthesis.

Immanuel Kant, not Hegel, was the greater influence on Clausewitz. At the war school, Clausewitz attended lectures given by Johann Gottfried Kiesewetter, who had written an outline of Kant's philosophy. *On War*'s view of the great commander—and specifically Napoleon—as a military genius owed not a little to Kant's essays on *Critical Judgement* and on art, which requires knowledge of the rules as well as an awareness of when to break them. Kant differentiated between logical truth and the actual truth, and sought to ensure that the former conformed with the latter, rather than spiraling off into self-referential argument. His use of the dialectic to seek an equipoise had underpinned Bülow's approach to war and, while at one level Scharnhorst's followers sought to break the Kantian consensus on war, Clausewitz's thinking on great-power relations reflected it. He saw the balance of power as a self-correcting mechanism, with the result that ultimately Napoleon's vaulting ambition and accretion of power had generated a coalition strong enough to defeat him.[61] *On War* does not demand a synthesis or a resolution; even the idea that war is the use of policy by other means is normative more than persistently true. Clausewitz's view that ultimately the end of war is peace, not more war, may be Kantian (Kant had written his

59. Clausewitz, *On War*, 141, 146–47, 168.
60. Souchon, *Strategy in the 21st Century*, 49, 63, 72.
61. Clausewitz, *On War*, 373–74.

essay on *Perpetual Peace* in 1795), but—unsurprisingly—Clausewitz recognized that was not the whole story: the animosities left by war could in fact lead to another war.[62]

V

Clausewitz provides an object lesson on the use and abuse of theory. It should be neither a prescription nor an interpretation into which evidence must be either forced or excluded, but its value is unequivocal. Theory "becomes a guide to anyone who wants to learn about war from books; it will light his way, ease his progress, train his judgment, and help to avoid pitfalls."[63] In other words, theory is a form of a shortcut, because it obviates the need "to start afresh each time" and clarifies "concepts and ideas that have become confused and entangled."[64]

At the same time, theory must not become dogmatic or doctrinaire. Rather than an end in itself, it is a tool. Theory helps the commander recognize "the point at which all lines converge," and provides "the thinking man with a frame of reference for the movements he has been trained to carry out."[65] Theory is therefore only useful when it is true, because, "while there may be no system, and no mechanical way of recognizing the truth, truth does exist."[66] Truth is when theories don't simply follow their own logic but also align with practice so that each provides confirmation of the other.[67]

The concept with which *On War* is principally engaged—apart from war itself—is strategy. Clausewitz consistently stressed that strategy in reality had to trump theory, that contingency in war demands decisions which are instinctive because those who take them have to respond to the situation in front of them. The function of theory is to alert them to the possible implications of those decisions, so that the past informs the present to shape the future. For Clausewitz's generation, strategy was the new way to look at war. For modern strategists, his understanding of strategy as the use of the engagement for the purposes of the war now seems too narrow, even too "operational," but it locates strategy firmly within war, not as superior or external to it.

62. Clausewitz, *On War*, 80, 91, 570, 603.
63. Clausewitz, *On War*, 141.
64. Clausewitz, *On War*, 152.
65. Clausewitz, *On War*, 132, 141.
66. Clausewitz, *On War*, 517.
67. Souchon, *Strategy in the 21st Century*, 61.

Clausewitz had reached this definition very early in his career and never wavered from it. In 1805, he rejected Bülow's idea that "strategy is the science of belligerent movements outside the enemy's field of vision." He believed that strategy achieved its results by fighting and so could not be separated from tactics.[68] "Strategy," Clausewitz wrote in Book 3 (which he devoted to the subject), "decides the time when, the place where, and the forces with which the engagement is to be fought, and through this threefold activity exercises considerable influence on its outcome."[69]

Some modern devotees of On War seem to want Clausewitz to have defined strategy—not war—as the continuation of policy by other means. To do so, they pass over the centrality of combat for Clausewitz, expressed most graphically in Book 4 (on the engagement). Because strategy in the Cold War sought to perpetuate peace by way of deterrence—in other words to avoid war, not to wage it, strategists after 1945 increasingly lost sight of war's most distinctive characteristic—its use of violence. The dialectic in Clausewitz is not that between war and policy, but that between war and peace. And policy presides over both. The problems of world order since 2001 have reinvigorated Clausewitz's relevance. The salience of actual war in a world where nuclear deterrence has diminishing purchase, as well as the West's wars of intervention and the prevalence of civil wars, demand that strategy recognizes its roots in war itself.

Doing so also requires a reexamination of Clausewitz's most famous, if also trite, dictum that war is the continuation by policy other means. If Politik can be translated narrowly as diplomacy or policy and so linked to the state, it can also be rendered more broadly to embrace the political community beyond the government.[70] Clausewitz's recognition of the need to mobilize the people in a war of national self-defense points to an inclusive, not an exclusive, view of what he meant by Politik. He was sufficiently committed to the reform of Prussia—a program which embraced the end of serfdom, the transforming power of education, and the creation of an effective scheme of mass military participation—to be seen by the Prussian court as a radical. The "trinity" shows his stress on the importance of public opinion in war. As Clausewitz put it in Book 1, Chapter 1, "When whole communities go to war—whole peoples, and especially *civilized* peoples—the reason always lies in some political situation." As a result, war "cannot be considered to have ended so long

68. Clausewitz, "Im Jahre 1804," in *Strategie*, 56, 62.
69. Clausewitz, *On War*, 194.
70. Clausewitz, *On War*, 606–7.

as the enemy's *will* has not been broken: in other words, so long as the enemy government and its allies have not been driven to ask for peace, or the population made to submit."[71]

Clausewitz lived in an autocracy, albeit one buffeted by the democratizing effects of the French Revolution. It is bizarre that modern democracies, when addressing what is today seen as Clausewitz's central theme—that is, the relationship between war and policy—have read him in ways which make the role of policy more restricted than he suggested. To be sure, they have done so for good reasons. The way to limit and contain war, Clausewitz consistently argued, was by limiting its aims. Being realistic about what war can achieve is one way of setting limited objectives and so containing the means allocated to its prosecution. Clausewitz accepted that the military aim might often set the complete defeat of the enemy as a precondition of peace, but he specifically rejected the idea that that should be raised "to the level of law," and suggested that, if such an outcome were likely, "the very faintest prospect of defeat might be enough to cause one side to yield."[72]

These calculations are both political and military, and—in so far as they are matters of strategy—they are proper subjects for the general as well as the politician or statesman to address. "If we keep in mind that war springs from some political purpose, it is natural that the prime cause of its existence will remain the supreme consideration in conducting it," Clausewitz wrote in Book 1, Chapter 1. "That, however, does not imply that the political aim is a tyrant. It must adapt to its chosen means, a process which can radically change it."[73]

The boundaries between policy and strategy are therefore as permeable as those between strategy and tactics. War—not least because of the roles of chance, friction, and probability—can change policy. Politicians may set out their purposes, albeit sometimes without the clarity or strategic awareness that the military would like, but they can then change them or themselves be changed by the operation of democratic politics. For Clausewitz, strategy is the business of the commander but that responsibility requires that he possesses political awareness. The commander alone can moderate or maximize the means in line with the political objectives or be in a position during war to exploit the opportunities presented by chance and probability. Clausewitz

---

71. Clausewitz, *On War*, 86, 90, 606–7. Emphasis in original.

72. Clausewitz, *On War*, 91.

73. Clausewitz, *On War*, 87; Antulio Echevarria, *Clausewitz and Contemporary War* (Oxford: Oxford University Press, 2007), 84–101.

expressed this thought both negatively and impersonally in his 1827 letter to Carl von Roeder:

> The right of war in relation to policy is thus above all to prevent policy from making demands *that are contrary to the nature of war*, to save it from misusing the military instrument from a failure to understand what it can and cannot do.[74]

Two centuries separate us from the creation of *On War*. Much has changed in the interim. Contemporary strategic studies have sought to make Clausewitz relevant by stressing that, while the character of war changes, the nature of war does not. The presumption of an underlying continuity within *On War* does little to convince those who see the effects of technological innovation on modern war as exponential and pervasive. Its advocates also elevate the importance of Books 1 and 8, because here the juxtaposition between war's nature and its character is most evident, and in doing so they derogate the insights of the intervening pages. The results can verge on the absurd. We are asked to believe, in Christopher Coker's words, that "unlike the character of war which is indefinable because it is always changing, the nature of war can be defined because it does not." Since "every war in changing its character transforms its past and appropriates it at the same time," Coker concludes, "the nature of war is made manifest in time."[75] Clausewitz would have agreed. He believed that only under one condition could we "see that all wars are things of the *same* nature." Both policy and war have to become "more ambitious and vigorous," to "the point where war reaches its absolute form."[76] And that is precisely the situation which contemporary strategy seeks to avoid.

---

74. Clausewitz, *Two Letters on Strategy*, 12. Emphasis in original.

75. Christopher Coker, *Barbarous Philosophers: Reflections on the Nature of War from Heraclitus to Heisenberg* (London: Hurst, 2010) 12–13.

76. Clausewitz, *On War*, 606. Emphasis in original.

CHAPTER 6

Jomini, Modern War, and Strategy

THE TRIUMPH OF THE ESSENTIAL

Antulio J. Echevarria II

In the 1986 edition of *Makers of Modern Strategy*, historian John Shy argued that the Swiss military writer, Antoine-Henri Jomini, rather than the Prussian military theorist, Carl von Clausewitz, deserved the "dubious title of founder of modern strategy."[1] Shy's claim has since disappointed many students of Clausewitz; they see him as the rightful founder of modern strategy. Clausewitz's masterwork, *Vom Kriege* (*On War*), though unfinished and frequently misinterpreted, is uncontestably superior in its treatment of armed conflict to Jomini's two major treatises—*Traité des grandes operations militaires* (*Treatise on Grand Military Operations*) and *Precis de l'art de la guerre* (*Summary of the Art of War*).[2] In fact, critics have gone so far as to liken Jomini's works, pejoratively, to "how-to" manuals. But Shy's essay also expresses a sense of disappointment with his own conclusions. He, too, seems to have preferred that the historical evidence had pointed to Clausewitz rather than Jomini.

1. John Shy, "Jomini," in *Makers of Modern Strategy from Machiavelli to the Nuclear Age*, Peter Paret, ed. (Princeton, NJ: Princeton University Press, 1986), 143–85.

2. Carl v. Clausewitz, *Hinterlasseneswerk Vom Kriege* (Berlin: Ferdinand Dümmler, 1832–34); Antoine-Henri Jomini, *Traité des grandes operations militaires, contenant l'histoire critique des campagnes de Frederic II, compares a celles de l'Empereur Napoleon, avec un recueil des principes generaux de l'art de la guerre* (Paris: Giguet et Michaud, Magimel, 1805–9); and Jomini, *Precis de l'art de la guerre, ou nouveau tableau analytique des principales combinaisons de la strategie, de la grande tactique et de la politique militaire*, 2 Volumes (Paris: Anselin, G. Laguionie, 1838–39). *Precis de l'art de la guerre, de la grande tactique et de la politique militaire* (Paris: Anselin, G. Laguionie, 1838–39).

Indeed, a mild animosity toward Jomini had been building since the mid-1970s with the "Clausewitz renaissance" brought about largely by the English translation of *On War* by Sir Michael Howard and Peter Paret.[3] This renaissance depicted Jomini as Clausewitz's rival and foil; the former was seen as prescriptive and doctrinaire, the latter as probing and open-minded. As an example, one of the period's more objective comparisons of the two writers likened Jomini to a "fox" and Clausewitz to a "hedgehog."[4] The fox, the author explained, "knows many things," but the "hedgehog knows one big thing." Clausewitz's big thing concerned the integral role of policy and politics in shaping war's nature; whereas Jomini's many things had to do with concepts that informed the operational conduct of war. In short, receiving credit for knowing many things was as good as it got for the Swiss military writer.

Shy's essay, though dated, remains relevant for twenty-first-century readers on at least two counts. First, the title of founder of modern strategy is a dubious one and so will not be used here; and second, Clausewitz's theories may enjoy more popularity due to their intellectual richness, but Jomini's core ideas have penetrated more deeply into modern military thinking and official doctrine and are still being used. Paradoxically, the complexity of the Prussian's military theories works against their full adoption. In contrast, the simplicity of Jomini's concepts makes them eminently more useful, though the degree to which the Swiss military writer was their sole author is questionable. The prevalence of Jomini's concepts persists in the present, moreover, even though military and policy practitioners have despised his name for decades and have upheld his treatises as exemplars of how *not* to think about war. The story of Jomini's success, therefore, is an all-too familiar, and all-too-often regrettable one in which the essential triumphs over the complex, and the simple vanquishes the sublime.

I

When Shy wrote his essay on Jomini in the 1980s, few critical biographies of the military writer existed.[5] Most accounts of Jomini's life had drawn heavily from the Swiss's personal recollections, which included, among other marvels,

---

3. Christopher Bassford, *Clausewitz in English: The Reception of Clausewitz in Britain and America 1815–1945* (Oxford: Oxford University Press, 1994), 197–211.

4. Col. Richard M. Swain, "The Hedgehog and the Fox: Jomini, Clausewitz, and History," *Naval War College Review* 43: 2 (1990): 98–109.

5. Compare: Bibliotheque historique Vaudois, *Le général. Antoine-Henri Jomini (1779–1869). Contributions a sa biographie* (Lausanne: Imprimeries reunites, 1969); Xavier de Courville,

a story of how he saved significant portions of the Grande Armée from destruction during the retreat from Moscow. One of his admiring biographers, Ferdinand Lecomte, managed to reprise words of praise from the French Emperor, Napoleon Bonaparte. After reading the first volumes of Jomini's *Treatise* (1805), for instance, Napoleon is purported to have said: "Here is a young *chef de bataillon*, and of all men a Swiss, who teaches us things which my professors never told me and which few Generals understand. How did Fouché allow the publication of such a book?! It betrays to the enemy the whole of my system of war!"[6] The fact that Jomini, albeit through Lecomte, expected readers to believe such statements is sure evidence of his narcissism. Jomini also held many conceits regarding his intelligence and abilities, which led him into numerous fracases with other staff officers, including Napoleon's incomparable chief of staff, Louis-Alexandre Berthier, whom Jomini later relentlessly sought to dishonor. He even turned on his erstwhile patron and benefactor, French Marshal Michel Ney, more than once, including in August 1813 when he left Ney's staff and defected to the Allied cause. After Jomini's defection, the tsar's chief quartermaster, Russian General Karl Fedorovich Toll, found the Swiss military writer unreliable and "not fit to serve during war."[7]

Clausewitz once said the thirst for glory and lust for renown are indispensable qualities in great commanders.[8] Perhaps so. But in Jomini's case they caused mostly resentment and mistrust among his contemporaries and prevented him from reaching the high-level command he desired and the glory he craved.[9] Much of the renown Jomini received as a military writer, in fact, he owed to having plagiarized the writings of others, albeit hardly an uncommon practice in his day. Little wonder, then, when the Duke of Wellington, victor of the Battle of Waterloo, referred to Jomini, quite perceptively, as a "pompous charlatan."[10]

Jomini ou le devin de Napoléon (Paris: Plon, 1935); Ferdinand Lecomte, *Le général Jomini: sa vie et ses écrits*. Esquisse biographique et strategique, 1st ed., (Paris: Chez Tanera, 1860). Newer, more objective accounts include: Jean-Jacques Langendorf, *Faire La Guerre: Antoine-Henri Jomini* (Paris: Georg, 2001); and Ami-Jacques Rapin, *Jomini et Stratègie: Une approche historique de l'oeuve* (Lausanne: Payot, 2002).

6. Lecomte, *Le général Jomini*, 10.

7. John R. Elting, "Jomini: Disciple of Napoleon?" *Military Affairs* (Spring 1964): 17–26.

8. Clausewitz, *On War*, Book I, Chap. 3.

9. Shy, "Jomini," 148.

10. J.H. Stocqueler, *The Life of Field Marshal the Duke of Wellington* (London: Ingram, Cooke, 1853), Volume II, 330.

Jomini was born in 1779, one year before Clausewitz and ten years after Napoleon, into a middle-class family living in the village of Payerne, in the French-speaking Canton of Vaud, Switzerland. Belonging to the Swiss middle class meant Jomini would have had reasonable financial opportunities and bright, if unspectacular, career prospects. His family expected him to become a banker or a commercial stockbroker, careers that would have benefitted from the local political connections his father and grandfather had developed; each, in turn, had served as mayors of Payerne. Already fluent in French, Jomini learned German at the age of fifteen while completing an apprenticeship in the city of Aarau, Switzerland. His facility in that language proved useful later when he began reading the military treatises of Wilhelm Dietrich von Bülow, Georg von Templehoff, Archduke Charles, and later Clausewitz. From 1795 to 1797, Jomini served as a banker's apprentice, first in Basel at *Hause Preiswerk* then in Paris at Bank Mosselmann.[11] After hearing news of Bonaparte's sweeping victories over the Austrians in Italy (1796–97), or so Jomini later claimed, he became obsessed with visions of glory and left banking altogether to pursue a military career.[12] In those days it was not unusual for news of Napoleon's triumphs to raise the aspirations of anyone who stood to gain from social and political reforms. The German philosopher Georg Wilhelm Friedrich Hegel and the literary genius Johann Wolfgang von Goethe, for instance, both admired the Corsican and hoped he would crush the Prussian monarchy in 1806, sweep away its rigid legal system, and replace it with a more egalitarian one.[13] Both were to be disappointed, however.

In 1798, Jomini managed to gain the favor of the Swiss Minister of War, who made him his adjutant and granted him a commission in Switzerland's "Army of the Helvetic Republic", with the rank of first lieutenant. Jomini received a promotion to captain in 1799 and to major and *chef de bataillon* (battalion commander) in 1800. He saw no combat in the campaigns of 1799 and 1800, which resulted in turning back a Russo-Austrian invasion, and by that point he had already acquired a reputation for causing friction among his compatriots. In addition, he accumulated serious gambling debts during this period, which led to a legal investigation and questions about his character. Jomini left

11. Kevin D. Stringer, "General Antoine-Henri Jomini," *Swiss-Made Heroes: Profiles in Military Leadership* (Ashland, OR: Hellgate Press, 2012), 57.

12. Shy, "Jomini," 148.

13. Clark Butler and Christine Seiler, trans., *Hegel: The Letters* (Bloomington, IN: Indiana University Press, 1984), esp. letters dated Oct. 13, 1806; Nov. 3, 1806; and Nov. 17, 1806; John R. Williams, *The Life of Goethe: A Critical Biography* (Oxford: Blackwell, 2001), 38–39, 42–34.

Switzerland for France in February 1801, before the investigation concluded, and found employment with Delpont, a military contracting firm. During this period, he read the *History of the Late War between the King of Prussia and the Empress of Germany and her Allies* (in French translation) by the Welsh military critic, Henry Humphrey Evans Lloyd, and *Geist des Neueren Kriegssystems* (*The Spirit of the New System of War*) by the Prussian military theorist, Wilhelm Dietrich von Bülow.[14] Both texts, which Jomini drew from heavily, provided the conceptual foundations for his later theories. He later claimed to have burned a previous manuscript he had penned on military principles after reading these texts; however, the story parallels too suspiciously that of Plato burning his scrolls after hearing the lectures of Socrates to be taken at face value.[15]

By 1804, Jomini had drafted another manuscript, *Traité de grande tactique* (*Treatise on Grand Tactics*) which borrowed from the aforementioned works, even as it critiqued them, as well as using Jacques-Francois de Chastenet de Puységur's *Art de la Guerre* (*Art of War*) and Jacques-Antoine-Hippolyte, Comte de Guibert's *Essai général de tactique* (*General Essay on Tactics*). Jomini managed to get volume one of the *Treatise* in front of French Marshal Michel Ney, to whom he had propitiously dedicated it. Ney, not known for his intellectual gifts, found the volume impressive, and agreed to subsidize its publication which occurred later in 1804 (though the publisher postdated parts of it to 1805 so it would appear newer). Ney also added its author, now just twenty-six years old, to his staff as an *aide-de-camp* in March 1805 (though in an unpaid status).[16] While Jomini's later recollections made much of this appointment, in reality it simply meant that he carried dispatches and ran errands for the French marshal.

Jomini served once again on Ney's staff, though still in a volunteer status, during the Ulm Campaign (October 1805) in which Napoleon's Grande Armée executed an extensive enveloping maneuver that annihilated the Austrian army of Karl Freiherr Mack von Leiberich. After the Battle of Austerlitz (December 1805), perhaps Napoleon's greatest victory, where the Grande Armée defeated a Russo-Austrian army, Jomini managed to get volumes one and two of his *Treatise* into the emperor's hands. Napoleon eventually read them and,

---

14. Azar Gat, *The Origins of Military Thought: From the Enlightenment to Clausewitz* (Oxford: Clarendon Press, 1989), 106.

15. Shy, "Jomini," 147.

16. John I. Alger, *Antoine-Henri Jomini: A Bibliographic Survey* (West Point, NY: US Military Academy, 1975), 10.

favorably impressed, ensured Jomini received a commission as "adjutant-commandant" (a staff-grade colonel, not a command grade) in the wave of promotions and awards that followed the French victories. Napoleon then added the Swiss to the imperial staff, but again as a courier; Jomini served in that position through the Grande Armée's successes over the Prussians at Jena-Auerstadt (October 1806) and Eylau (February 1807). In December 1806, be-tween these two campaigns, Jomini found time to publish a pamphlet on the fundamental principles of strategy, *L'art de la guerre*. The Swiss officer also caused a scandal during the Battle of Eylau, when he claimed he could turn the tide of the fighting if he assumed the place of the Russian commander; he was subsequently placed on sick leave for four months to calm the situation and so missed the Battle of Friedland (June 1807), which resulted in a French victory over the Russians. In the wave of awards that followed the French suc-cesses of 1806 and 1807, Jomini was awarded the *Légion d'honneur* (Legion of Honor) and received the title of *baron de l'empire français* (Baron of the French Empire), effective July 27, 1808.

In late summer of 1807, the emperor assigned Jomini to Ney's Sixth Corps as the marshal's chief of staff. From September 1808 to July 1809, Jomini served with Ney's Corps in Galicia, Spain, as the French army executed its ill-fated bid for control of the Iberian Peninsula. That experience exposed Jomini to what he later described as a "dangerous and deplorable" type of war, rife with atrocities; it was one that would challenge the Swiss military writer's funda-mental principle of strategy—concentration (about which more will be said later). The Spanish guerrillas, for instance, seemed to be everywhere and no-where at the same time, and possessed no decisive point against which to mass one's forces.[17] During this time, however, Jomini and Ney had a falling out, though the details are unclear. One reason for it was Jomini's instructions to Ney's staff to route all important decisions through himself, thereby usurping Ney's authority. In any event, the French marshal could no longer bear the presence of the Swiss officer, and hence appealed to Napoleon to have Jomini assigned elsewhere. The emperor did so, mildly reprimanding the Swiss officer in the process. Jomini thus found himself assigned to the French Ministry of War in Paris, with orders to write the histories of the French Revolutionary Wars and the Italian campaigns.[18] According to some scholars, these historical

17. Shy, "Jomini," 170–72.
18. Antoine de Jomini, *Histoire critique et militaire des campagnes de la révolution* (Paris: Mag-imel, 1811).

works rank among Jomini's best due in large part to the detailed information they contain. Still disgruntled, however, Jomini began actively seeking a position within the Russian army during the summer of 1810. Plans for his departure fell through, however, and a timely promotion to *général de brigade* (brigadier general) on December 7, 1810, kept the Swiss in French service.

Jomini participated in Napoleon's invasion of Russia in 1812. But he did so as an administrative governor of rear-area detachments and zones of occupation. He was first assigned to Vilna in August 1812, where he clashed with General Hogendorp, the Governor General of Lithuania. To avoid further frictions, he was quickly reassigned to Smolensk. Little glory was to be had in such assignments, though they were critical to the logistical sustainment of the Grande Armée, a fact Jomini should have appreciated. But the Swiss officer's letters to Napoleon during this period were full of complaints, excuses, and a sense of ingratitude, for which he was once again mildly rebuked by the emperor. Despite historical myths to the contrary, enough supplies had been amassed in the months preceding the invasion to feed and refit the Grand Armée for the Russian campaign. Unfortunately for Napoleon, the means of distribution, the echeloned-system of supply trains, broke down over the long distances.[19] Added to that, discipline in the rear areas, the responsibility of rear-echelon administrators such as Jomini, collapsed once the retreat from Moscow began and rumors of catastrophe spread. Looting became rampant and supplies meant for the front lines were raided and carried off by marauders. Jomini's negligence and self-absorption during this period make him complicit in the breakdown of the logistical system. Not all the blame for this debacle falls to Jomini, of course, as some French commanders made poor decisions that sent troops on fools' errands when they would have been better employed in and around Smolensk to guard the supply stores.[20] Jomini's own account of the retreat, by contrast, relates an epic tale in which he showed Napoleon a fordable location across the Berezina River and heroically guided a good portion of the French army safely from Smolensk to Orsha.[21] No other accounts of the crossing, however, mention Jomini's presence.

In the spring of 1813, Jomini returned to Ney's staff (their differences at least temporarily resolved) in time for the battles of Lützen (May 2) and Bautzen

19. David G. Chandler, *The Campaigns of Napoleon* (New York, NY: Macmillan Publishing, 1966), 755–59.

20. Martin Van Creveld, *Supplying War: Logistics from Wallenstein to Patton* (Cambridge: Cambridge University Press, 1980), 67–74.

21. John R. Elting, "Jomini: Disciple of Napoleon?" *Military Affairs* 28:1 (1964): 17–26.

(May 20–21). Both encounters resulted in French victories. Nevertheless, Napoleon's victory fell short of completely annihilating the Russian and Prussian armies, partly due to Ney's inability to execute a flank attack that would have blocked the Allies' route of retreat. According to Jomini, Ney failed to grasp the situation and to heed the Swiss officer's astute operational advice. Ney's abilities as a corps commander, such as they were, had surely declined since the Grande Armée's debilitating retreat from Russia. Shortly after the battle, Berthier placed Jomini under arrest because the Swiss officer had fallen egregiously behind in submitting his unit's situation reports. Jomini's devotees would later claim Berthier was merely harassing Jomini. But these situation reports contained valuable information Napoleon required for planning; failure to submit them was akin to insubordination.

Jomini defected to the Allied cause during the brief summer armistice of 1813, asserting he had suffered enough "humiliation." He was welcomed into the Russian army as a major general and eventually received a promotion to lieutenant general.[22] While accounts differ, as part of his defection Jomini appears to have conveyed intelligence about Napoleon's intention to advance against the army of the Crown Prince of Sweden Jean-Baptiste Bernadotte (who was also Bonaparte's brother-in-law) on or about August 22, 1813. This information was passed by letter to Prussian Marshal Gebhard von Blücher, who in turn passed it to Bernadotte. The Crown Prince not only believed it but also ensured it factored into the Allies' decision-making.[23] Readers will recall Clausewitz and several of his fellow officers had similarly resigned, and effectively defected, from the Prussian army in 1812 to assume commissions in the Russian army. Their defections carried with them the possibility of engaging in combat against their former compatriots. Nonetheless, Jomini's defection differed markedly from Clausewitz's in that the Prussian did not convey actionable intelligence to the enemy. A French tribunal tried Jomini in absentia for treason, found him guilty, and sentenced him to death. Naturally, the betrayal attracted the opprobrium of French officers. It also marred Jomini's legacy, despite the repeated attempts of his family and followers to exonerate him. Napoleon, who suffered through more than a few acts of treason in his day, including that of his brother-in-law Bernadotte, evidently held nothing against Jomini. As the emperor explained, Jomini was Swiss, not French, as if

22. Stringer, *Swiss-Made Heroes*, 63.

23. Michael V. Leggiere, *Napoleon and Berlin: The Franco-Prussian War in North Germany, 1813* (Norman, OK: Oklahoma University Press, 2001), 155.

to say the military writer owed him nothing. In any event, Napoleon might not have known the full extent of Jomini's betrayal.

Jomini participated in some of the Russian army's operational planning during the battles of Dresden (August 26–27), a French victory, and Leipzig (October 16–19), an Allied victory that forced Napoleon to begin withdrawing his forces from Germany. Jomini resigned his commission in the Russian army when it looked as if the Allies intended to march through Switzerland to attack France. He reentered Russian service in 1819, became military tutor to the Russian Crown Prince (Czar Nicholas I), was promoted to general in 1823, and was awarded the Grand Cordon of the Alexander Order in 1828 for his advice to the czar during the Russo-Turkish War (1828–29), which ended in a Russian victory. Jomini also assisted in establishing the Russian Imperial Military Academy (later General Staff Academy) in St. Petersburg. Jomini retired from Russian service once again in 1829 and relocated to Brussels, where he stayed until 1849. In 1838, he published his most influential military work, his *Summary of the Art of War*. He was later recalled to Russian service to advise the czar on the campaign plan for the Crimean War (1853–56), which failed and induced Russia to set aside its plans to expand into the Ottoman Empire. Jomini then returned to France and settled near Paris in the affluent town of Passy. In 1859, he was called upon to give advice to French Emperor Napoleon III on the Italian War (1859), in which France achieved its limited objectives. Jomini died in Passy in 1869 at the age of ninety.

Although Jomini had matured intellectually at a time when the passions behind the French Revolution were sweeping Europe, he joined the French army not to spread the ideals of liberty, equality, and fraternity, but rather to satisfy his personal ambitions and desire for military glory. As a writer and theorist, Jomini was influenced more by the Enlightenment emphasis on the foundational importance of scientific principles than the post-Enlightenment-Romanticist rediscovery of the power of human passions. The Enlightenment tradition believed positive doctrines were possible for most human affairs, including war. Military genius, therefore, was not an emergent quality for Jomini in the way it was for Clausewitz; rather, it came from mastering the immutable principles that governed the conduct of war. Jomini embraced the post-Enlightenment ideal of love of *la patrie*, but only so far as it did not hinder his opportunism. Indeed, he felt no patriotic conflict of interest when, as a Swiss citizen, he threw his lot in first with the French and later with the Russians, remaining in the service of the latter for what amounted to the bulk of his career.

As an opportunist, Jomini ensured volumes of his *Treatise*, evidence of his knowledge of war's scientific principles and thus his qualifications for high-level command, reached Ney and Napoleon, two individuals who obviously could advance his career. Ergo, the *Treatise* and indeed his other writings, had more than the didactic purpose historians have ascribed to them; in fact, Jomini's works represented specimens of genius. Ironically, however, much of that genius was borrowed from the works of others. While Jomini wished to believe that both Ney and Napoleon recognized his genius, and that it was only the abominable Berthier who blocked his advancement, in truth, the emperor, always quick to appropriate talent, could easily have overridden his chief of staff at any time. He never did. Napoleon must have sensed, in the Swiss's narcissistic personality and his presumptuous reduction of armed conflict to a few simple principles, a limited ability to command within the violent atmosphere of war. At the same time, he must have seen in Jomini an opportunity of his own; here was an ambitious historian and military critic who might contribute abundantly to Napoleon's own legacy as one of history's greatest commanders and strategists.

For his part, Jomini must have realized the great deeds he claimed to have accomplished and the fulsome praise he put into the mouths of others were nothing more than his own inventions. He was, therefore, an imposter in the grandest sense: neither the military genius, nor the brilliant commander, nor the talented staff officer he wanted others to believe he was. As experts have noted, Jomini's facial expressions in his later portraits seem to be those of a bitter, frustrated individual; one might also see them as the exasperated countenance of a charlatan, an impersonator unable to accept the failure of his deception.

II

Although Jomini's deceptions fell short in his lifetime, they succeeded in enlarging his legacy. Eminent scholars have affirmed Jomini's enduring reputation as the "principal interpreter of the Napoleonic era and the most influential strategic theorist of the entire nineteenth century."[24] One historian, whose cumulative work on Napoleon's campaigns remains unsurpassed, identified Jomini and Clausewitz as the only two of the period's critics who "came anywhere near to comprehending [Bonaparte's] military genius."[25] Other scholars have rightly classified Jomini as a synthesizer; he arranged popular operational concepts into a single system. Specifically, he borrowed the concept of lines of

---

24. Hew Strachan, "Operational Art and Britain, 1909–2009," in *The Evolution of Operational Art from Napoleon to the Present*, John Andreas Olsen and Martin van Creveld, eds. (Oxford: Oxford University Press, 2011), 98.

25. Chandler, *Campaigns of Napoleon*, 133.

operation from Henry Lloyd; combined it with the principle of concentration, which he saw as foundational to war; then added two complementary concepts he appropriated from von Bülow, namely, that of a base of operations ("those places which contain the means of an adversary's military power") and decisive points.[26] As readers will note, none of these concepts originated with Jomini.

Moreover, historians generally agree Napoleon had little in the way of a deliberate strategic or operational formula for Jomini to comprehend. Instead, Bonaparte used the tactics and organizational structures bequeathed to him by earlier military reformers—especially Guibert's emphasis on smaller, more maneuverable units and the use of citizen armies rather than mercenaries. Napoleon also repeatedly leveraged the military policy of *levée en masse* (mass conscription) to fill the ranks of his corps and certainly manipulated his troops' patriotic motivations, which the French Revolution had aroused. With such a fighting instrument at his disposal, Napoleon could wage a more aggressive style of war, one better suited to strategic improvisation, rapid operational movement, and battles of annihilation. In practice, Bonaparte typically followed the principle of concentration, bringing the most force possible to bear against an opponent's weakest point. But that was true of many of history's commanders and hardly unique to Napoleon.

Thus, while Jomini claimed to have divined Napoleon's formula for success, there was, in fact, none to divine. Each of Napoleon's campaigns conformed to, or took advantage of, the military, political, geographical, and logistical circumstances of the moment—except, of course, his invasion of Russia in 1812, which failed in part because he showed little inclination to adapt his political and military goals to the situation. Indeed, Napoleon's lack of a specific method amounted to an advantage since it made it more difficult for his adversaries to predict his moves. Rather, the Swiss military writer hammered the Corsican's approach into the existing eighteenth-century structure and labeled it modern. Upon closer inspection, the ingredient that made the system modern, particularly when compared to Frederick the Great's eighteenth-century model, was simply Napoleon's skill. Bonaparte possessed better *coup d'oeil*, moved his troops more quickly, and relentlessly sought decision by battle. These were hardly concepts foreign to Frederick the Great, the example of an eighteenth-century commander, whom Jomini repeatedly criticized. Jomini once stated "the art of war made but little progress under [Frederick]"; and

26. Dietrich von Bülow, *Spirit of the Modern System of War* (London: C. Mercier, 1806), 18.

the Prussian king had only succeeded because he made "fewer mistakes than his opponents."[27]

Although Jomini's synthesis of eighteenth-century operational concepts was not wholly original, it moved military thinking forward by rendering explicit what expert military commanders since Hannibal and Caesar had instinctively practiced. His operational-strategic synthesis also shows him to be a "system builder," though he denied such. Certainly, he was not a system builder to the extent of von Bülow, who constructed an inflexible system based on the inviolability of geometric principles. Clausewitz, as is well known, despised system builders for the rigidity and artificiality of their constructions, which seldom accorded with the realities of war. Nonetheless, Clausewitz, too, experimented with the possibility of organizing a few principles into a system of sorts, based on his concept of the center of gravity. Creating a system is almost an unavoidable outcome of military theorizing; systems undermine military strategy only if one allows them to become prescriptive.

The concept of lines of operation, though commonly attributed to Lloyd, had appeared in eighteenth-century military literature, especially after the Seven Years' War, and had many authors. In its standard sense, a line of operations consisted of a route of march—from one's base of communications and supply to one's objective. More than a physical line on a map, however, a line of operation also served as a justification, or planning rationale, for applying force effectively and efficiently. The side with shorter lines of operation, moreover, possessed superior advantages over the side with longer ones; shorter lines allowed for faster transmission of reports, orders, and supplies, and had the added benefit of requiring fewer troops to protect them, a phenomenon which later came to be known as strategic consumption. Lines of operation, accordingly, needed to be both as short and as secure as possible. The terms eventually became interchangeable in theory and in practice. Not surprisingly, the best rationale for applying force usually coincided with the best routes for communication and supply.

Jomini derived his understanding of war's principles from Lloyd and embraced the Welshman's definition with little modification. In 1781, Lloyd had stated that the military "art, like all others, is founded on certain and fixed principles, which are by their nature invariable; the application of them only

27. Jomini, *Treatise*, 445.

can be varied: but they are themselves constant."[28] Jomini repeatedly stressed the same qualities: "The fundamental principles upon which rest all good combinations of war have always existed . . . [and] are unchangeable; they are independent of the nature of the arms employed [and] of times and places."[29] As readers will see, immutability presents problems of its own that neither the Welshman nor the Swiss adequately addressed.

For Jomini, decisive points conveyed advantages by virtue of their position. They were physical sites or features "capable of exercising a marked influence either upon the result of the campaign or upon a single enterprise." Jomini referred to them in terms of three categories: strategic (or functional), operational (within a theater of war), and tactical (on the battlefield). Strategic points of maneuver were those whose "natural or artificial advantages favor the attack or defense," and which facilitated or hindered the movement and concentration of troops against a decisive point or strategic objective. Operational decisive points, that is, within a theater of war, can be either geographic, such as mountain passes whose "importance is permanent and a consequence of the configuration of the country"; or accidental, which resulted from the relative maneuvering and subsequent positioning of the troops on both sides. Battlefield, or tactical, decisive points were of three types: (a) terrain, as determined by "features of the ground"; (b) relative, determined by the "relation of the local features to the ultimate strategic aim"; and (c) accidental, determined by the "positions occupied by the respective forces."[30] For Jomini, then, decisive points clearly applied to what military practitioners currently recognize as the operational and tactical levels of war, though Jomini saw them more as functions or responsibilities than as levels.

Since Jomini's writings straddle twenty-first-century conceptions of operations and military strategy, it is useful to discuss briefly the Swiss military thinker's notions of strategy. He saw strategy chiefly in functional terms, that is, the "how" rather than the "why" one defeated an opponent. He defined it variously as the "art of properly directing masses upon the

---

28. Michael Howard, "Jomini and the Classical Tradition in Military Thought," in *The Theory and Practice of War*, Michael Howard, ed. (Bloomington, IN: Indiana University Press, 1965), 3–20; David G. Chandler, "Napoleon: Classical Military Theory and the Jominian Legacy," in Chandler, *On the Napoleonic Wars: Collected Essays* (London: Greenhill, 1999), 241–53.

29. Baron de Jomini, *Treatise on Grand Military Operations*, 2 Volumes, trans. Col. S.B. Holabird (New York, NY: D. Van Nostrand, 1865), 177, 278.

30. Baron de Jomini, *The Art of War*, trans. Capt. G.H. Mendell and Lieut. W.P. Craighill (Philadelphia, PA: J.P. Lippincott, 1862), 49–50.

theater of war either for defense or for invasion" and as the "art of making war on the map, and it comprehends the whole theater of operations."[31] But he also said, not unlike Clausewitz, "strategy decides where to act," that is, where the decisive point will be.[32] Logistics brought the troops to that point, grand tactics decided how the troops were to be arranged and employed at the point of decision. By comparison, Clausewitz saw strategy, much as his mentor Gerd von Scharnhorst did, as the use of "combats" to achieve the purpose of the war.

To be sure, both definitions of strategy concentrated on land warfare, but neither was limited to the use of ground forces. The American sea power theorist, Alfred Thayer Mahan, successfully adopted Jomini's definition of strategy to naval warfare, for instance. Clausewitz explicitly noted that strategy's role was to link military action to the purpose of the war; whereas Jomini, at best, included that role implicitly. For both, strategy actively involved the direction of forces as well as setting the conditions for success. Jomini, in fact, placed more emphasis on strategy's power to shape the outcome of battle by controlling decisive points and by maneuvering one's opponent into unfavorable positions. He was, thus, more terrain-oriented but obviously did not overlook the importance of battle, as that was the point of maneuver. Clausewitz was more force-oriented but did not eschew the advantages of decisive points or good lines of operation, as those put friendly forces in favorable positions for battle. The Prussian's definition, readers will recall, served as a direct counter to von Bülow's, which claimed battles had become unnecessary under the new system. Battles, even if they did not occur, represented a form of potential force resembling that described by Thomas Schelling, one that might provide important leverage in achieving one's aims.

III

From Jomini's perspective, the application of proven principles in strategy and operations could occur in three ways, or "combinations": (a) the "art of adjusting the lines of operations in the most advantageous manner"; (b) "strategy" or the "art of placing the masses of an army in the shortest space of time on the decisive point of the original line of operations"; and (c) "tactics" or the "art of combining the simultaneous employment of masses upon the important

31. Jomini, *Art of War*, 38.
32. Jomini, *Art of War*, 38.

point of the field of battle."[33] From a twenty-first-century perspective, the second combination can be thought of as strategic-operational in nature; the third can be seen as operational-tactical in nature.

Jomini's *Summary* offers a succinct articulation, a list, of his notion of the modern system of war, which he arranged in a series of logical steps. Following such a system, he urged, was more important than developing an entire plan of operations because it was impossible to anticipate friendly and enemy movements beyond the first stage of a conflict. Here his words echo those of Prussia's Chief of the Great General Staff, Helmuth von Moltke the Elder, who famously made a similar claim in the 1870s. A modern system of operations, Jomini explained, must account for the object of the war, the enemy's forces, the nature and resources of the country, the national characters of the belligerents, the personalities of their leaders, the psychological and material means available to each for attack and defense, as well as the likelihood of alliances or coalitions forming during the conflict and coming to the aid of one party or the other.[34] The steps for taking all these factors into account were the following:

1. Select the theater of war and discuss the various combinations it permits.
2. Determine decisive points within those combinations and the best direction for operations.
3. Select and establish the fixed base and zone of operations.
4. Select the offensive or defensive objective point.
5. Identify the strategic fronts, lines of defense, and fronts of operations.
6. Choose lines of operations leading to the objective point or strategic front.
7. Identify the best strategic line and maneuvers necessary to account for all possible cases.
8. Position eventual bases of operations and strategic reserves.
9. Decide upon the marches of armies, which are to be considered as maneuvers.
10. Consider the relation between the position of depots and the marches of the army.
11. Identify which fortresses will serve as strategic means, as refuges for an army, as obstacles, and the sieges that might be necessary.

33. Jomini, *Treatise*, 181, 277.
34. Jomini, *Art of War*, 25.

12. Identify points for entrenched camps.
13. Identify the diversions to be made and detachments necessary to make them.[35]

Lists of this sort abound in the *Summary*. Their simplicity and directness undoubtedly appealed to military practitioners of the nineteenth century, particularly as military organizations began to construct modern professional identities, and as systems of this sort became transferable across cultures by virtue of the replicability of the scientific method. In other words, if Jomini's system worked for officers in France's Grande Armée, military science meant it should also prove effective for officers in America's Army of the Potomac.

Other lists worth noting include Jomini's descriptions of types and branches of war. The former amounted to a brief typology, but it reveals the thrust and extent of Jomini's thinking. Unfortunately, Jomini missed an opportunity to make an original contribution to the art of war by discussing how one might modify his strategic-operational system to fit irregular or nontraditional types of conflict. For instance, in Articles VII through IX, he described "Wars of Opinion," "National Wars," and "Civil Wars and Wars of Religion," but dismissed their potential implications for military operations. Instead, Jomini concluded that searching for maxims in such wars "would be absurd."[36] An outspoken military critic who claimed to have discerned Napoleon's secret for success could not even suggest principles for some of the most prevalent types of wars in his day. Rather, he looked backward, to the "chivalrous" era of dynastic wars and preferred to use those as his models. Despite his experience in Spain, Jomini offered no principles comparable to what the nineteenth-century British military writer C. E. Callwell suggested in 1896 for so-called small wars, nor anything approaching the centers of gravity Clausewitz described some years earlier for defeating insurrections and rebellions. Jomini's strategic-operational system, thus, remained geared toward traditional or conventional wars, though he clearly recognized the qualitative differences between the two. He agreed with Clausewitz's claim that political aims should influence military objectives. Nevertheless, he refrained from discussing the nature or limits of that influence over war's so-called immutable principles, or what constituted appropriate modifications to them. Ultimately, he was as

35. Jomini, *Art of War*, 38.
36. Jomini, *Art of War*, 15.

vague as Clausewitz on this point; yet, the thrust of his argument suggests Jomini favored putting the grammar of war, its rules and principles, ahead of policy's logic.

Fortunately, Jomini's description of the branches of war is less disappointing. He discussed six such branches: (1) statesmanship in its relation to war; (2) strategy; (3) grand tactics; (4) logistics; (5) engineering; and (6) minor tactics. In contrast to the level of discussion one finds in Clausewitz, Jomini merely offered a list of political purposes and sketched, only broadly, the role of *politique*—usually translated into English as diplomacy or statesmanship, but perhaps better thought of as an equivalent to the German word *Politik*—in armed conflict. Contrary to popular opinion, Jomini's treatment of *politique* was published in 1829–30, a year or so before Clausewitz's *On War*, and thus it was not directly influenced by the Prussian's work.[37] *Politique*, Jomini said, amounted to an "essential branch" of war, and, as such, was of vital importance to army commanders and high-level staff officers, even though he thought it would be useless to subordinate commanders. Surely, though, subordinate commanders would need an understanding of *politique* to enable them to replace higher-level commanders who might suddenly be killed or wounded in action. Ultimately, Jomini saw *politique* as the responsibility of heads of state, and not military commanders, suggesting the demarcation between power and politics that Robert Osgood described in *Limited War* (1957) was more than an American outlook.

Jomini's strategic-operational system has at least two critical shortcomings important for modern readers to appreciate. His "Note upon the Means of Acquiring a Good Strategic *Coup-d'oeil*," practically a microcosm of his work, reveals the first of these.[38] The Note showed practitioners how they might partition a theater of operations and, by repeatedly performing its steps, develop greater instinctive insight, or *coup-d'oeil*. Unfortunately, the Note lacks both depth and explanatory power. It neglects to explain why, for instance, there could be only three zones of operations: left, center, and right. Moreover, Jomini's zones equaled each other in size, rather than being aligned with the major geographic features in the theater, a more pragmatic approach. Dividing the theater of war along rivers, roads, or mountain ranges would provide clear boundaries for each army's operations and thereby reduce confusion. Furthermore, Jomini's discussion of how armies might maneuver against one another

37. Gat, *Origins of Military Thought*, 126–27.
38. Jomini, *Art of War*, 222.

incorporated only one type of strategic decisive point, rivers. Other decisive points, such as cities or fortresses, might exert a counteracting influence important for military planners to consider, forcing them to decide which point is more important. In sum, the Note represents a critical problem for practitioners, namely, arbitrariness. An arbitrary system puts theory in opposition to practice, rather than making the two complementary. Jomini's approach, in other words, wedded itself too closely to science and yet was not properly anchored by it.

This arbitrariness uncovers the second shortcoming—balancing the presumed immutability of a principle against the assumption one could readily adapt it to the circumstances. Concentrating force at a decisive point clearly makes practical sense. But Jomini never discussed the considerations one might need to address when concentrating force strategically, operationally, or even tactically, in a given area, based, for instance, on the number of troops that area could support. France's Grande Armée of 1812 was one of the largest forces ever assembled in modern Europe. However, many of the areas the army would have to march through were not rich enough to enable living off the land. To be sure, Napoleon had enhanced his army's supply system, but it had not been tested against Russia's vast distances. Nor could the army receive sufficient supplies via the sea as Britain's Royal Navy patrolled the Baltic Sea. Ergo, a force smaller than the Grande Armée's 650,000 troops might have fit the strategic circumstances better, and it might have offered more mobility with lower logistical demands. In short, Jomini neglected to address second- and third-order issues that might have made his system work.

Despite its shortcomings, one ought not to dismiss Jomini's system outright. The manner in which he framed land warfare has merit (though he wrote a "Sketch of the Principal Maritime Expeditions," it did not address sea power directly and lacked analytical depth; Jomini's analyses were clearly land-centric). Moving armies, whether in ancient or modern times, has usually resulted in de facto lines of operation requiring foresight and coordination. It also has required a reliable flow of supplies, especially food and ammunition. Occasionally, such logistics have had to flow through or around decisive points, such as mountain passes or across rivers, the control of which either facilitated or hampered that flow. Even the French army, which could not wholly sustain itself by foraging or living off the land, required secure lines of communication and supply. One day, when military forces occupy positions in space, those troops, too, will need to be resupplied. This framework will, even with its shortcomings, likely endure for some time to come.

IV

Several concepts and principles Jomini synthesized and refined in the early Napoleonic era have survived into the twenty-first century. These include decisive points, lines of operation, interior and exterior lines, and the core principles of concentration, offensive action, and decision by battle. Many of these have been incorporated into modern Western military doctrine as "elements of operational art." The similarities between Jomini's version of these elements and their modern counterparts offer positive evidence for the triumph of the essential.

The definition of a decisive point has expanded since Jomini's day and now accommodates evolving military domains and capabilities. The basic concept, however, has remained unchanged. In 2020, for instance, Western military doctrine referred to a decisive point as "key terrain, key event, critical factor, or function that, when acted upon, enables a commander to gain a marked advantage over an enemy or contribute materially to achieving success (e.g., creating a desired effect, achieving an objective)."[39] By comparison, Jomini defined decisive points as "capable of exercising a marked influence either upon the result of the campaign or upon a single enterprise." Hence, the similarities are obvious.

In 2019, Western military doctrine described a line of operations as one that "defines the directional orientation of a force in time and space in relation to the enemy and links the force with its base of operations and objectives."[40] As Jomini instructed his readers, the "general will take a first objective point: he will select the line of operations leading to this point, either as a temporary or permanent line, giving it the most advantageous direction; namely, that which promises the greatest number of favorable opportunities with the least danger."[41] Again, the modern definition closely parallels Jomini's concept, particularly regarding the linkage between one's base of operations and one's objective.

Obvious, too, are the similarities between Jomini's concept of interior lines and the twenty-first-century definition, which states: "*Interior lines* are lines on which a force operates when its operations diverge from a central point. Interior

---

39. Joint Publication 5–0, *Joint Planning* (Washington, DC: Dec. 1, 2020), IV-32 (Hereafter JP 5–0); see also Dept. of Army, *Army Doctrine Publication 3–0* Operations (Washington, DC: July 31, 2019), 2–7 (Hereafter ADP 3–0).

40. ADP 3–0, 2–7.

41. Jomini, *Art of War*, 36.

lines usually represent a central position where a friendly force can reinforce or concentrate its elements faster than the enemy force can reposition."[42] Jomini defined interior lines as those "adopted by one or two armies to oppose several hostile bodies, and having such a direction that the general can concentrate the masses and maneuver with his [sic] whole force in a shorter period of time than it would require the enemy to oppose to them a greater force." He later rejected the idea that interior lines required a central position. "An army may occupy a central position in the presence of two masses of the enemy," Jomini wrote, "and not have interior lines of operations; these are two very different things." Conversely, exterior lines are those "formed by an army which operates at the same time on both flanks of the enemy, or against several of his [sic] masses."[43] These statements provide evidence of Jomini moving away, albeit not entirely, from using definitions based on the terminology of geometry, which he had come to see as too restrictive and a source of confusion. Physical relationships, one army's position in relation to another's, increasingly replaced abstract geometric descriptions.

Modern doctrine, however, sees the advantages of interior lines *viz-a-viz* exterior lines (when a friendly force's operations converge on an enemy) as relative to force ratio and factors such as space and time. The battles of encirclement and annihilation throughout the twentieth century, particularly the many such engagements that characterized the European theater of operations during the Second World War, raised the general awareness of the merits of exterior lines. Jomini, on the other hand, initially saw the advantages of interior lines as all but decisive because only from that position could one apply the "fundamental principle."[44] He was incorrect in this belief because, even with exterior lines, one can maneuver to apply superior quantities of combat power against the weakest point of an opponent's lines. Jomini eventually qualified his views, admitting central positions may be completely untenable if one's forces were seriously weaker than those of one's adversary.

Even in Jomini's day, lines of operation often coincided with lines of communication and supply. The reasons one might seize a city, port, or road network, for instance, were frequently the same as those that might drive one's opponent to defend them: such points facilitated the flow of communications and logistics and, hence, were integral to successful operations. Jomini, though,

---

42. JP 5–0, IV-29–30; see also ADP 3–0, 2–7; italics original.
43. Jomini, *Art of War*, 60.
44. Jomini, *Art of War*, 218.

at times indicated his concept of lines of operation—lines connecting decisive points to an objective—could amount to more than lines of communication and supply, which obviously only extend to an objective once it is seized, that is, after the fact. Nonetheless, his explanation also betrayed an inability to fully appreciate the value of logistics, which he viewed as the "art of moving armies." In Jomini's day, the field of logistics encompassed more than the art and science of keeping one's forces supplied with replacements, ammunition, rations, and so on. It also included such activities as the quartering of troops, finding camp sites, establishing and reconnoitering routes of march, and arranging orders of march. His discussion of logistics is, on the whole, tentative and uncertain; it is perhaps the weakest part of his *Treatise* and reflects a general bias toward—perhaps even a preoccupation with—combat operations, or his personal embarrassment over the fact that the majority of his successes came while serving in an administrative capacity.

In twenty-first-century military doctrine, the concept of lines of operation has undergone a crucial evolutionary development in the form of "lines of effort." Whereas lines of operations have remained associated with physical linkages, such as seizing and securing a town, lines of effort describe "logical linkages," such as the measures necessary to establish the rule of law in a province, or the steps needed to build regional and local governance. An example of such steps for establishing the rule of law, for instance, might consist of the following decisive points: (a) establish police forces training; (b) integrate trained police into operations; (c) counter organized crime; (d) establish judicial system; and (e) transition to host-nation police forces. Likewise, lines of effort for establishing local governance could consist of the following decisive steps: (a) identify and recruit leaders; (b) facilitate establishment of sector representation; (c) facilitate establishment of neighborhood councils; (d) facilitate establishment of district councils; and (e) support and secure elections.[45] Such lines of effort show a clear recognition that the tasks needed to accomplish policy objectives during armed interventions often extend beyond wartime military expertise. Military commands may need to coordinate and support such operations, even if they do not necessarily lead them.

Jomini's principle of concentration must also be listed among the essentials which have persisted through the ages. When Mahan developed his principles for naval strategy, for instance, he rightly identified concentration as Jomini's fundamental principle. But Mahan also correctly discerned two other

<hr>

45. JP 5–0, p. IV–31.

principles—offensive action and decision by battle—as core to Jomini's analysis of Napoleon and which supplemented concentration. Referred to by historians as a man of principles, and famous for naming his dog "Jomini," Mahan might seem extreme. However, Mahan's era was an age of principles—from the tenets of Taylorism and Fordism that enabled mass production, to the principles of good housekeeping that made homes into orderly "units of the state." The positivism that provided the foundation for Jomini's operational system also underpinned so many of the sciences of Mahan's day, especially economics, sociology, and psychology. They would do so, moreover, until middle of the twentieth century when Karl Popper's notion of the falsifiable hypothesis, the idea of arriving at knowledge through negation, began to replace positivist approaches in the social sciences.

But Jomini's core principles also informed air power theory, particularly as they were expressed by the American airpower evangelist, William (Billy) Mitchell. However, Mitchell had done little more than articulate what many military practitioners, regardless of their branch of service, had come to realize about fighting wars. One had to hit hard, hit fast, and keep hitting until one's opponent threw in the towel. That Jominian credo drove the thinking of such twentieth-century commanders as Ernest King, George S. Patton III, and Curtis LeMay.

With the advent of nuclear weapons in the mid-twentieth century, that credo had become dangerous. The concentration of land, sea, or air power provided lucrative targets for nuclear attacks. Offensive action, rather than knocking an opponent off balance, could lead to mutual destruction due to second-strike nuclear capabilities. Decision by battle was, therefore, meaningless. Accordingly, Bernard Brodie, Robert Osgood, and other limited-war theorists argued for rejecting Jomini's core principles—concentration, offensive action, and decision by battle—which had all but become instinctive among the West's military leaders.

Even in environments in which the risk of nuclear escalation was low, as in the Vietnam conflict, following the Jominian core principles yielded, at best, only tactical successes, not strategic ones. The US military could concentrate overwhelming combat power, pursue offensive "search and destroy" operations against Viet Cong and North Vietnamese Army formations, and defeat most of those forces in battle; yet strategic victory remained elusive. Instead, counterinsurgency doctrines, which in practice typically require considerable time, ran up against the realities of US domestic political struggles and economic challenges, which worked against long-term, open-ended commitments as in Korea. On this deficiency, the US military is not alone. Other armies have struggled to address war's apparent dual grammar as well. Meeting the requirements for each type of mission remains a challenge in the twenty-first century.

Indeed, counterinsurgency (and other) doctrines appear anathema to Jominian core principles. But are the actions required to defeat insurgencies truly anathema to concentration, offensive action, and decision by battle? Western militaries have yet to examine whether those core principles might apply if one could think of them differently. Concentration, for instance, should extend beyond directing military force against an enemy's weakness and could mean using assets appropriate to resolving particular problems. Similarly, one could think of offensive action as taking positive action to nip potential insurgencies in the bud, as it were, rather than attacking with conventional forces. Likewise, decision by battle could also mean gaining and maintaining decisive advantages in the diplomatic, informational, and economic dimensions of conflict. Such changes have less to do with preserving the core principles, than assisting modern militaries in modifying their instincts to confront nontraditional challenges more effectively.

V

This chapter may have indirectly given military and policy practitioners, as well as Clausewitz students, more reasons to despise Jomini. If so, they ought not to despise him or his works unreflectively. Even by modern accounts, Jomini was a competent military historian, even if his theoretical works were largely derivative and even if his narcissistic personality made him despicable to many of those with whom he associated. What he had to say about decisive points, lines of operation, interior and exterior lines, and war's principles bears reviewing; it suggests military science is as much a part of military practice as military art. As with any prominent writer, Jomini's works must be engaged and readers must draw their own conclusions. Practitioners may prefer to see war through a Clausewitzian lens and, indeed, they may well think of themselves as Clausewitzians. Nonetheless, they are also Jominian in ways they would do well to understand.

As Shy's essay noted, the title "founder of modern strategy" is ultimately a dubious one. Attempting to identify the military writer most responsible for the founding of modern strategy is an unrewarding enterprise. Strategic thought moved through the minds of multiple writers over the centuries. As this chapter has shown, Jomini's core ideas persist, but he was more their synthesizer and refiner than their author. The Swiss military writer owes much to his antecedents as well as his critics, but perhaps even more to his admirers, for they have created for him a legacy many times larger than the person. Jomini's antecedents, as discussed, provided him the raw framework for fitting out a strategic and operational system. At the same time, those antecedents, primarily Lloyd and Bülow, owed much to their predecessors as well.

Perhaps twenty-first-century readers will find a bit of poetic justice in the fact that Jomini's name has all but disappeared from the pages of modern military doctrine. To be sure, Jomini plagiarized many of the concepts he promoted. But plagiarism was not uncommon in his day, partly because procedures for giving credit to one's sources were underdeveloped. Jomini's plagiarism of Lloyd was extensive to the point of being word-for-word in some cases, not only of his ideas but also of his historical narrative of the Seven Years' War. On the other hand, Jomini wrote at a time when military writers sought legitimacy by grounding their work in scientific methodologies, which in turn invited imitation. Science at the time rested on the assumption one could arrive at incontrovertible truths through methods, such as induction, deduction, and various forms of the dialectic. Military science provided a factual foundation, albeit dubious in cases, aimed at freeing individuals to employ their creative skills to solve higher problems, that is, to realize the "art" in military art. With the rise of ever more destructive weaponry during the twentieth century, science turned increasingly toward reducing the opportunities for human error. One example of this development is the proliferation of systems or processes related to military decision-making.

One ought not to forget, therefore, that Jomini supplied the types of guidelines military and policy practitioners have historically demanded. To be sure, Clausewitz's *On War* offers readers a more sophisticated understanding of armed conflict than do Jomini's treatises. Unfortunately, what military and policy practitioners seem to want, as Shy warned, is simplicity—core essentials that lead to better decisions. In some ways, they are right to want such. But one hopes the triumph of the essential will not endure indefinitely. If the sublime cannot occasionally overcome the simple, tomorrow's practitioners will find it difficult to confront the complexities of future war.

CHAPTER 7

Alfred Thayer Mahan and the Strategy of Sea Power

John H. Maurer

"The history of Sea Power is largely, though by no means solely, a narrative of contests between nations, of mutual rivalries, of violence frequently culminating in war."[1] Thus Alfred Thayer Mahan began his most famous book, *The Influence of Sea Power Upon History*. Published in 1890, his history examined the contest among the great warring states of Europe—Spain, the Netherlands, France, and Britain—for naval mastery and leadership of the international system during the seventeenth and eighteenth centuries. He presented a dramatic vision of history, of intense rivalries among the great powers, of overseas expansion, of the rise and fall of empires, and of battles to achieve victory at sea. Mahan's history became an instant classic and garnered for him celebrity status as the world's leading authority on warfare at sea and naval strategy. The contests for empire and command of the seas recounted by Mahan did not appear confined to some distant past but were very much part of his times. Mahan's account of great-power clashes resonated with an age that viewed international politics as a Darwinian struggle in which only the fittest of peoples would find security and prosper. *The Influence of Sea Power Upon History* garnered such fame that it is widely considered the most influential work of nonfiction written by an American author during the nineteenth century.

---

1. A.T. Mahan, *The Influence of Sea Power Upon History, 1660–1783* (Boston, MA: Little, Brown, 1890), 1.

Mahan followed up this success with the two-volume *The Influence of Sea Power Upon the French Revolution and Empire, 1793–1812*, published in 1892.[2] These histories cemented his reputation as a serious historian. Mahan would serve as president of the American Historical Association, and he received honorary degrees from the universities of Oxford, Cambridge, Harvard, Yale, and Columbia. In his work, he aimed to relate the operations of navies to the larger sweep of history. He noted that "naval historians have troubled themselves little about the connection between general history and their own particular topic, limiting themselves generally to the duty of simple chroniclers of naval occurrences."[3] Mahan explored war and change in world politics, the search by great powers for security, well-being, and leadership in the international arena. He contended that the great commercial seafaring states had played a leading role in world politics because of the wealth they generated from international trade and access to resources from around the globe. Controlling major trade routes across the seas—what Mahan called a great highway and wide common—was the mission of navies in war.

In writing his histories, Mahan sought to apply the study of history to explain the strategic predicament and foreign policy choices before the United States as the nineteenth century ended. While his books started as lectures at the Naval War College, he was determined to reach a wider audience than that of his students in the classroom. Mahan believed that the study of strategy "has an interest and value for all citizens of a free country, but especially for those who are charged with its foreign and military relations."[4] Mahan proved a prolific author, publishing twenty books and 137 articles over his lifetime.[5] His stature

2. A.T. Mahan, *The Influence of Sea Power Upon the French Revolution and Empire, 1793–1812* (Boston, MA: Little Brown, 1892).

3. Mahan, *Sea Power, 1660–1783*, v.

4. Mahan, *Sea Power, 1660–1783*, 23.

5. For a list of Mahan's writings, see John B. Hattendorf and Lynn C. Hattendorf, *A Bibliography of the Works of Alfred Thayer Mahan* (Newport, RI: Naval War College Press, 1986). A useful selection of Mahan's writings is provided in John B. Hattendorf, ed., *Mahan on Naval Strategy* (Annapolis, MD: Naval Institute Press, 1991). Robert Seager and Doris Maguire, ed., *Letters and Papers of Alfred Thayer Mahan* (Annapolis, MD: Naval Institute Press, 1975), three volumes, provides insights into Mahan's life and work through his voluminous correspondence. Mahan has attracted several major biographies: Charles Carlisle Taylor, *The Life of Admiral Mahan* (New York, NY: George H. Doran, 1920); W.D. Puleston, *The Life and Work of Captain Alfred Thayer Mahan* (New Haven, CT: Yale University Press, 1939); Robert Seager, *Alfred Thayer Mahan: The Man and His Letters* (Annapolis, MD: Naval Institute Press, 1977); Suzanne Gessler, *God and Sea Power: The Influence of Religion on Alfred Thayer Mahan* (Annapolis, MD: Naval Institute Press, 2015). Earlier editions of *Makers of Modern Strategy* included valuable

as a strategic thinker was so great that, although retired from active duty, the secretary of the navy asked Mahan to serve on a special board to guide the navy's strategy during the Spanish-American War.

Mahan wanted to alert Americans of his generation to the coming dangers that the United States would face as a rising world power. He foresaw fierce geopolitical contests and the end of what the historian C. Vann Woodward would call "the age of free security" for the United States.[6] The United States could no longer depend for its security, as it largely did during the nineteenth century, on Britain's naval mastery, or on latent American military power, buttressed by the natural moat formed by the Atlantic and Pacific oceans and the icebound wastes of the Arctic. Instead, future international challenges would demand that the United States take on a more active role in world politics. Mahan declared, "I am frankly an imperialist, in the sense that I believe that no nation, certainly no great nation, should henceforth maintain the policy of isolation which fitted our early history."[7] To prepare for future trials of strength, he called for a buildup of naval power as America's first-line of defense. He maintained:

> Every danger of a military character to which the United States is exposed can be met best outside her own territory—at sea. Preparedness for naval war—preparedness against naval attack and for naval offence—is preparedness for anything that is likely to occur.[8]

---

assessments of Mahan's contribution to the history of strategic thought. In the original 1943 edition, Margaret Tuttle Sprout wrote "Mahan: Evangelist of Sea Power"; the 1986 edition featured Philip A. Crowl, "Alfred Thayer Mahan: The Naval Historian." Theodore Ropp's essay, "Continental Doctrines of Sea Power," also in the 1943 edition, describes the principal strategic tenets of the *Jeune École*. Walter LaFeber, "A Note on the 'Mercantilistic Imperialism' of Alfred Thayer Mahan," *The Mississippi Valley Historical Review* 48:4 (1982): 674–85, examined Mahan's understanding of the international economy and America's growing role in it. George W. Baer, *One Hundred Years of Sea Power: The U.S. Navy, 1890–1990* (Stanford, CA: Stanford University Press, 1994) appraised Mahan's strategic theories for explaining American naval history during the world wars and the Cold War. On the influence of Mahan's strategic thought in current-day China, see Toshi Yoshihara and James R. Holmes, *Red Star Over the Pacific: China's Rise and the Challenge to U.S. Maritime Strategy*. Second Edition (Annapolis, MD: Naval Institute Press, 2018). Paul Kennedy, *The Rise and Fall of British Naval Mastery* (London: Penguin, 2017), is itself a classic book on sea power that interprets Mahan's work.

6. C. Vann Woodward, "The Age of Reinterpretation," *American Historical Review* 66:1 (1960): 11–19.

7. A.T. Mahan, *From Sail to Steam: Recollections of Naval Life* (New York, NY: Harper, 1907), 324.

8. A.T. Mahan, *The Interest of America in Sea Power, Present and Future* (Boston, MA: Little, Brown, 1897), 214.

Mahan's message, while winning him admirers like Theodore Roosevelt, also attracted harsh critics, who railed against his stark depiction of the international environment and his call for overseas expansion, foreign entanglements, and a buildup of American arms. The famous author of the *Great Illusion*, Norman Angell, attacked Mahan's view of international politics, which "with whatever sophistry or eloquence it may be urged, is a doctrine of savagery."[9] Another fiery critic of a generation later, the famous historian Charles Beard, savaged Mahan, both as a shoddy historian and for preaching "the whole gospel" of imperialism. According to Beard, Mahan "used history, economics, and religion to defend and justify his new creed to America—the continental America of old times, now to be treated contemptuously by the new apostles of imperialism drunk with the wine of the lust for power." Beard lamented that Mahan's call for a naval buildup was taken up not only by the United States but by other countries. In Germany, Mahan's writings "went to the head of the Kaiser and [Admiral Alfred] von Tirpitz like heady wine" and moved them to build a powerful battle fleet. The spread of Mahan's ideas resulted in an escalating naval arms race among the great powers. "From year to year more and more billions were poured into armaments," Beard wrote. "The rivalries for power, territories, commerce, colonies, and sea bases grew ever more sharp, until they exploded in the world war in 1914." While Beard disdained Mahan and his ideas, he nonetheless considered him "the most successful propagandist ever produced in the United States."[10] To admirers and critics alike, Mahan was a voice to be reckoned with in the debates about American foreign policy and strategy during the turbulent era of the world wars.

I

Alfred Thayer Mahan was born at West Point on September 27, 1840. His father, Denis Hart Mahan, was a renowned and long-serving member of the Military Academy's faculty. While primarily an instructor of engineering, the elder Mahan also educated students on the art of warfare. In his teaching, he drew heavily upon the writings of Baron Antoine-Henri Jomini, the prominent military writer on strategy and operations of the early nineteenth century. The elder

---

9. Norman Angell, " 'The Great Illusion': A Reply to Rear-Admiral A.T. Mahan," *The North American Review* 195:679 (1912): 772.

10. Charles A. Beard, *A Foreign Policy for America* (New York, NY: Knopf, 1940), 39–40, 74–75; Beard, *The Navy: Defense or Portent?* (New York, NY: Harper, 1932), 19, 21.

Mahan saw to the education of his son, including two years of study as a teenager at Columbia College. In considering career options, the younger Mahan decided to follow the profession of arms and attended the United States Naval Academy. The elder Mahan questioned his son's decision to join the navy. In his autobiography, Mahan wrote that his father thought him "much less fit for a military than a civil profession." Despite the elder Mahan's misgivings, he used his network of contacts to obtain an appointment for his son to attend the Naval Academy. One of Denis Hart Mahan's former students who lobbied on behalf of the younger Mahan was none other than Jefferson Davis. Alfred Thayer Mahan would later recount "that I owed my entrance to the United States navy to the interposition of the first and only President of the Southern Confederacy."[11]

Commissioned as a naval officer on the eve of the Civil War's outbreak, Mahan served in the navy both afloat and ashore against the Confederacy. His assignments included serving as an instructor at the Naval Academy, temporarily relocated to Newport, Rhode Island, during the war. Mahan continued in the navy after the war and earned the rank of captain. Within the navy, however, he gained the reputation of being more a thinker and writer than a ship handler. When Mahan tried to avoid ship command toward the end of his career in uniform, preferring instead to devote his time to study and writing, the officer in charge of personnel assignments refused. Mahan was ordered to sea duty with the scathing remark: "It is not the business of a naval officer to write books."[12] In Mahan's last command at sea, as captain of the cruiser *Chicago*, flagship of an American squadron of warships visiting European waters, he drew harsh criticism from his superior officer, who sneered that "Capt. Mahan's interests lie wholly in the direction of literary work and in no other way connected with the service."[13]

Mahan's life took a radical turn "in the direction of literary work" when, in his mid-forties, Rear Admiral Stephen Bleecker Luce invited him to serve on the faculty of the newly established Naval War College in Newport, Rhode Island. Luce was a towering figure in the navy, with a career spanning some forty years of active duty. He was appalled by American naval weakness in the era following the Civil War, known as the "dark ages" of the navy. Not only was the fleet in poor material condition, but the service suffered from administrative shortcomings and poor leadership. Luce railed against the "crass ignorance" of naval officers,

11. Mahan, *Sail to Steam*, xiv, xvii.
12. Mahan, *Sail to Steam*, 311.
13. Seager and Maguire, eds., *Letters and Papers*, Volume 2, 210–12.

who had neither an appreciation for naval history nor a background in operational and strategic thought. For the service to progress out of darkness, Luce wanted the Naval War College to develop a science of naval warfare that would provide a guiding light for rebuilding the navy. "No less a task is proposed," Luce told the secretary of the navy, "than to apply modern scientific methods to the study and raise naval warfare from the empirical stage to the dignity of a science." Luce's high standing within the service and forceful personality induced a reluctant navy leadership to establish the Naval War College. As the College's first president, he declared its mission was a "place for the study of war and of all questions of statesmanship related to the prevention of war."[14]

Luce confidently looked to the College producing a "master mind who will lay the foundations of the [naval] science, and do for it what Jomini has done for the military science." In the cerebral Mahan, Luce found an officer suited to carrying out the College's mission. Mahan had already established a reputation for himself as an historian and an advocate of professional military education within the navy. He had written a detailed and well-regarded history of naval operations along the coast and rivers of the western theater of the Civil War, entitled *The Gulf and Inland Waters*.[15] A study he published on "Naval Education" had demonstrated his ability to develop programs of instruction for navy officers and enlisted personnel.[16] Luce tasked Mahan with formulating operational and strategic principles to govern the conduct of war at sea. Mahan would more than fulfill Luce's expectations. Luce would later recognize that the College did produce the master mind, who "appeared in the person of Captain A.T. Mahan, U.S.N." On taking over from Luce to serve as the College's president, Mahan's reputation saved the institution from being closed by a navy leadership that questioned its value. From that time to today, the College's reputation has been inextricably linked with Mahan's name.

II

On receiving orders to join the Naval War College's faculty, Mahan recalled that his father at the military academy had "introduced a course of strategy and grand tactics, which had commended itself to observers. I trusted, therefore, that

14. John H. Maurer, "The Giants of the Naval War College," *Naval War College Review* 37: 5 (1984).
15. A.T. Mahan, *The Gulf and Inland Waters* (New York, NY: Scribner, 1883).
16. A.T. Mahan, "Naval Education," *Proceedings of the United States Naval Institute* 5:9 (1879): 345–76.

heredity, too, might come to my aid."[17] Given a free rein by Luce, Mahan spent the next ten months in New York City doing research and writing. The lectures he prepared on naval history became the basis for *The Influence of Sea Power Upon History*. Mahan was pleased that the lectures, when delivered to the students, "met with a degree of success which surprised me and which still seems to me exaggerated." Buoyed up by the student response and encouraged by his wife Elly and by Luce, Mahan sought a publisher for his research. Finding a publisher, however, proved difficult, as publishing houses rejected the manuscript. In September 1889, after more than a year of trying, a despondent Mahan wrote to Luce:

> With these efforts I propose giving up. . . . I believe that the book to be, in the main, good and useful—and am therefore ready to work hard at its proper presentation, if a publisher turns up. . . . But I am not willing . . . to go on begging publishers. It both distracts, vexes and hinders me in my other work.[18]

Mahan's perseverance finally paid off when the Boston publishing house of Little, Brown accepted the manuscript.

The first American edition of *The Influence of Sea Power Upon History* appeared in May 1890 and met with an immediate success that confounded all expectations. The book's publication could not have been more auspicious. A generation had passed since the surrender of General Lee at Appomattox. In that time, the United States had made remarkable economic strides. The huge infrastructure projects of railway construction and laying a cable network were knitting together the country, facilitating the movement of goods and information. After the Civil War, the government's policy, Mahan observed, "has been effectively directed solely to what has been called the first link in the chain which makes sea power. Internal development, great production, with the accompanying aim and boast of self-sufficingness, such has been the object."[19] By 1890, the United States had surpassed Britain as the world's leading industrial power. Continued growth in industrial, energy, and agricultural production was transforming the United States into an economic superpower by the beginning of the twentieth century. The World's Columbian Exposition of 1893 in Chicago, occurring just after the publication of Mahan's histories, showcased the industrial and technological prowess of a rising great power.

17. Mahan, *Sail to Steam*, 273.
18. Seager, *Mahan*, 162–68, 191–218.
19. Mahan, *Sea Power, 1660–1783*, 84.

The publication of Mahan's volumes also foreshadowed the publication of Frederick Jackson Turner's famous essay on "The Significance of the Frontier in American History," presented at the World's Columbian Exposition in 1893. Turner contended that "four centuries from the discovery of America, at the end of a hundred years of life under the Constitution, the frontier has gone, and with its going has closed the first period of American history." The closing of the frontier, however, did not mean the end of history, or that "the expansive character of American life has now entirely ceased." Instead, Turner predicted, "American energy will continually demand a wider field for its exercise."[20] Mahan's work provided a window on the next period of American history, after the closing of the frontier, of increased involvement in the global economy, of an emerging great power operating on a wider field, caught up in the rough and tumble, and often violent, arena of world politics. "Whether they will or no," Mahan contended, "Americans must now begin to look outward. The growing production of the country demands it."[21]

The appearance of *The Influence of Sea Power* attracted an enthusiastic response from elite audiences in countries around the world. Theodore Roosevelt offered a glowing review. "Captain Mahan has written distinctively the best and most important, and also by far the most interesting, book on naval history which has been produced for many a long year." Roosevelt added, "Mahan shows very clearly the practical importance of the study of naval history to those who wish to estimate and use aright the navies of the present." Roosevelt captured the nature of Mahan's work: a study of history meant to guide policy on the navy's development and strategy for the application of naval force. Roosevelt and Mahan would form a close relationship, meeting and corresponding, if not always agreeing, with one another over the next quarter-century.

When Mahan visited Britain as captain of the cruiser *Chicago*, he was feted by the great and the good: Queen Victoria, her son the Prince of Wales (the future King Edward VII), Lord Rosebery, the prime minister, and other British leaders wanted to meet the celebrity American author. Britons saw in Mahan's histories a recognition of their own country's success in establishing the world's greatest empire and achieving naval mastery against rivals. In Britain, he also met Germany's Kaiser Wilhelm II, who was visiting his

---

20. Frederick J. Turner, "The Significance of the Frontier in American History," American Historical Association, 1893.

21. Mahan, *Interest of America in Sea Power*, 21–22.

grandmother Queen Victoria. The Kaiser admired Mahan's work. "I am just now not reading but devouring Captain Mahan's book, and am trying to learn it by heart," the Kaiser wrote an American friend. "It is a first-class work and classical in all points."[22] An American journalist in Berlin observed, "I have heard several times of the Emperor's references to Captain Mahan's doctrines. The Emperor is familiar with all that Mahan has written."[23] The Kaiser had Mahan's works translated and distributed widely within Germany. Japan's naval leaders, too, followed Mahan's writings. Japan was building up its naval power and would fight successful wars against China and Russia that established the Japanese empire. Admiral Tōgō Heihachirō, commander of the Japanese fleet that triumphed over the Russians at the Battle of Tsushima, expressed his "deep and cordial reverence" for Mahan's "far-reaching knowledge and keen judgment." Japan's naval hero declared, "Naval strategists of all nations are of one opinion that Admiral Mahan's works will forever occupy the highest position as a world-wide authority in the study of military science."[24]

Another enthusiastic admirer was Franklin D. Roosevelt, who became hooked after receiving a copy of Mahan's work as a young boy. As assistant secretary of the navy in the Woodrow Wilson administration, Roosevelt reached out to Mahan, asking him to write articles to sway public opinion on the topic of naval strategy and the necessity of keeping the battle fleet as a concentrated force in peace as well as in war. In enlisting Mahan to write articles, Roosevelt maintained, "People can be educated, but only if we all get together ahead of time and try to show the average 'man in the street' the military necessity of keeping the Fleet intact." To Mahan, Roosevelt wrote, "Your voice will carry more conviction than that of anybody else." The young Roosevelt considered Mahan an asset in the navy's ability to publicize the service's purpose and strategic employment to the American people. Mahan did write for Roosevelt; it was one of his last articles before his death.[25] When war broke out in Europe, with his life coming to an end, Mahan urged on Roosevelt that

22. John H. Maurer, "The Influence of Thinkers and Ideas on History: The Case of Alfred Thayer Mahan," *Foreign Policy Research Institute*, August 2016.

23. Albert Gleaves, *Life and Letters of Rear Admiral Stephen B. Luce* (New York: Putnam, 1925), 304.

24. Sadao Asada, *From Mahan to Pearl Harbor: The Imperial Japanese Navy and the United States* (Annapolis, MD: Naval Institute Press, 2006), 26.

25. A.T. Mahan, "The Panama Canal and the Distribution of the Fleet," *The North American Review* 200:706 (1914): 406–17.

"the fleet should be brought into immediate readiness, and so disposed as to permit of very rapid concentration."[26]

Another young political leader attracted to Mahan's work was Winston Churchill. Before the First World War, as first lord of the Admiralty, the civilian cabinet minister charged with responsibility for Britain's naval defense, Churchill drew upon Mahan's writings to guide British strategy to meet the pacing challenge posed by the German naval buildup. Churchill affirmed, "The standard work on Sea Power was written by an American Admiral [Mahan]."[27] When Mahan visited Britain in 1912, he met Churchill at the British Admiralty. The previous year, Mahan's book *Naval Strategy* had appeared in print.[28] Mahan crowed to his publishers, "It may interest you to know that when in England Mr. Winston Churchill, the head of the Admiralty, told me he was about to read the book upon the recommendation to him of one of the 'Sea Lords.' "[29] Churchill would later say "there is no more famous writer on naval affairs" than Mahan.[30]

III

Mahan emphasized the importance of strategy—"the queen of military sciences"—in determining the outcome of wars fought by the great powers. "Strategy underlies the fortunes of every campaign," he wrote. "If the strategy be wrong, the skill of the general on the battlefield, the valor of the soldier, the brilliancy of victory, however decisive, fail of their effect."[31] Strategy was not confined to directing wartime operations of armies and navies. For Mahan, strategic considerations should guide the actions of states in peace as well as in war. In examining the causes for Russia's defeat in the Russo-Japanese War of 1904–5, he criticized the Russian high command for strategic mistakes that it "made in time of peace, in the face of conditions threatening war. In fact, as

26. Mahan to Roosevelt, August 3, 1914, Assistant Secretary of the Navy Collection, Box 53, Franklin D. Roosevelt Library, Hyde Park, New York.

27. Winston S. Churchill, *The World Crisis, 1911–1914* (London: Thornton Butterworth, 1923), 93.

28. A.T. Mahan, *Naval Strategy: Compared and Contrasted with the Principles and Practice of Military Operations on Land* (Boston, MA: Little, Brown, 1911).

29. Seager and Maguire, *Mahan Letters*, Volume 3, 491.

30. Winston Churchill, "Military History," July 4, 1950, in *Winston S. Churchill: His Complete Speeches, 1987–1963*, Robert Rhodes James, ed. (New York, NY: Chelsea House Publishers, 1974), Volume 8, 8028–31.

31. A.T. Mahan, *Naval Administration and Warfare: Some General Principles* (Boston, MA: Little, Brown, 1908), 235.

is often the case, when war came it was already too late to remedy adequately the blunders or neglects of peace."[32] Strategy, to Mahan, encompassed the actions of civil and military leaders "to found, support, and increase, as well in peace as in war, the sea power of a country."[33]

Mahan wanted to show the importance of sea power for gaining competitive advantage over rivals. In one of his most famous passages, he observed:

> The first and most obvious light in which the sea presents itself from the political and social point of view is that of a great highway; or better, perhaps, of a wide common, over which men may pass in all directions, but on which some well-worn paths show that controlling reasons have led them to choose certain lines of travel rather than others. These lines of travel are called trade routes.[34]

Whereas Americans were long accustomed to looking upon the oceans as moats protecting the New World from the Old, Mahan instead saw the seas as highways for the United States to promote economic growth, to gain diplomatic influence, and to find greater security.

In Mahan's search for strategic principles, he turned to history. Like Luce, he believed that war has principles governing the conduct of operations, and that "their existence is detected by the study of the past, which reveals them in successes and in failures." Mahan's study of history reached as far back as the wars of Greece and Rome in the ancient world, along with the maritime contests of the sailing ship era involving the European great powers, down to the conflicts of his own day.[35]

In an age of rapid technological change, Mahan apprehended that "thoughtless prejudice" existed among some naval officers who did not see how the study of history would contribute to understanding modern warfare.[36] Since technology was changing the character of war at sea, he observed, "Hence the natural tendency on the part of many connected with maritime matters to think that no advantage is to be gained from the study of former experiences; that time so used is wasted." Mahan, however, rejected the view that studying history had no value. He asserted, "The battles of the past succeeded or failed

32. A.T. Mahan, *Naval Administration and Warfare*, 137, 167–68, 171–72.

33. Mahan, *Sea Power, 1660–1783*, 89.

34. Mahan, *Sea Power, 1660–1783*, 25.

35. Mahan, *Sea Power, 1660–1783*, 7.

36. Mahan, *Naval Administration*, 226.

according as they were fought in conformity with the principles of war." Strategic principles "belong to the unchangeable, or unchanging, order of things, remaining the same, in cause and effect, from age to age. They belong, as it were, to the Order of Nature; whereas tactics, using as its instruments the weapons made by man, shares in the change and progress of the race from generation to generation." Mahan concluded, "From time to time the superstructure of tactics has to be altered or wholly torn down; but the old foundations of strategy so far remain, as though laid upon a rock."[37] Despite the application of new technologies to naval warfare, history remained the best school for the study of strategy.

To Mahan, concentration of force and offensive action served as the cardinal strategic principles for the conduct of war at sea. Victory at sea would go to the side that possessed a superior naval force, capable of carrying out an offensive maritime strategy. Such a strategy would seek out the enemy's fleets, bring them to battle, and destroy them in decisive action. "Jomini's dictum that the organized forces of the enemy are the chief objective," Mahan asserted, "pierces like a two-edged sword to the joints and marrow of many specious propositions."[38] This strategy would typically require taking the offensive into the enemy's home waters. Concentration of force, followed by offensive action to seek out and annihilate the adversary's fleet, provided the road map for exerting "overbearing power on the sea which drives the enemy's flag from it, or allows it to appear only as a fugitive; and which, by controlling the great common, closes the highways by which commerce moves to and from the enemy's shores."[39]

Mahan used historical examples to illustrate his strategic principles. In *The Influence of Sea Power*, he criticized Britain's leaders for not undertaking a more aggressive, forward-deployed naval concentration against France and Spain during the American War for Independence. He contended, "Not without a risk, but with strong possibilities of success, the whole fortune of the war should at first have been staked on a concentration of the English fleet between Brest and Cadiz." British strategic missteps, failing to concentrate and act aggressively, enabled France, along with its ally Spain, to contest the maritime common and pave the way for American independence, thus weakening Britain as a sea power.[40] In contrast, Mahan praised British strategy during the crisis

---

37. Mahan, *Naval Administration*, 9.
38. Mahan, *Sail to Steam*, 283.
39. Mahan, *Sea Power, 1660–1783*, 138.
40. Mahan, *Sea Power, 1660–1783*, 415–17.

year of 1805, when Napoleon massed his army along the Channel coast with the intent of invading Britain. In one of Mahan's most famous passages, he praised how Britain's forward-deployed fleets on blockade duty off the French coast kept Napoleon at bay. "Dull, weary, eventless months, those months of watching and waiting of the big ships before the French arsenals saved England," he intoned. "The world has never seen a more impressive demonstration of the influence of sea power upon history. Those far distant, storm-beaten ships, upon which the Grand Army of Napoleon never looked, stood between it and the dominion of the world."[41] An aggressive maritime strategy provided the basis for the victory achieved by the famed naval hero Admiral Lord Nelson over the combined French and Spanish fleets at the Battle of Trafalgar.

Sir Julian Corbett, a naval historian and strategic theorist writing in this era, sought to temper Mahan's enthusiasm for offensive fleet operations. While Corbett agreed with Mahan that the destruction of the enemy's naval forces was generally the best strategy to pursue, he cautioned that strategic context matters and sometimes the risks of aggressive operations could outweigh the rewards. Corbett instructed his readers, "The maxim of 'seeking out' for all its moral exhilaration, for all its value as an expression of high and sound naval spirit, must not be permitted to displace well-reasoned judgment." Corbett held as a strategic axiom, "The object of naval warfare must always be directly or indirectly either to secure the command of the sea or to prevent the enemy from securing it."[42] A defensive, cautious strategy might sometimes best serve that purpose, rather than aggressive action. While Mahan understood the importance of strategic circumstances in choosing among alternative courses of action, he nonetheless believed that "war, once declared, must be waged offensively, aggressively. The enemy must not be fended off, but smitten down."[43]

Acquiring overbearing power on the sea would enable the dominant navy to protect trading links across the maritime commons. While the weaker navy could no longer fight for command of the sea, it might still try to disrupt maritime networks of trade, to cause as much damage as it could to shipping. The weaker navy's attacks, however, would only prove "irritating" and not seriously weaken the stronger sea power. At the same time, the stronger naval power could use its command at sea to interrupt the enemy's access to resources, to

41. Mahan, *Sea Power, 1793–1812*, Volume 2, 118.
42. Sir Julian S. Corbett, *Some Principles of Maritime Strategy* (London: Longmans, Green, 1911), 87, 171.
43. Mahan, *Interest of America in Sea Power*, 193.

impose a blockade, to damage its economy. By hurting the enemy's economy, the overall balance of power would shift in wartime to the country in command of the sea. Command of the maritime commons would translate into victory in war by providing the leading sea power with the ability to defeat its adversaries through economic exhaustion.[44] According to Mahan's sea-power model, naval strength is closely connected with a country's commercial activity. Trade creates wealth, which can be tapped to build naval power that, in turn, can be used to gain command of the seas.

Secure in the command of the maritime commons, a sea power could attract coalition partners to tie down on land an adversary continental state. Mahan argued that those countries with land frontiers, requiring them to devote substantial resources to fielding large armies, find themselves at a strategic disadvantage when competing on the maritime commons against a rival that "is neither forced to defend itself by land nor induced to seek extension of its territory by way of the land." He pointed out that Britain possessed a "great advantage" over "both France and Holland" because those countries needed to maintain large armies to secure their land frontiers. Mahan praised British leaders, like the father and son pair of the Earl of Chatham and Sir William Pitt, for pursuing a strategy of "subsidizing continental allies" to fight on land against Britain's "great enemy, France."[45] Corbett elaborated in his work how a maritime power could use the ground forces at its disposal to defeat a land power. The British writer highlighted that the "paramount concern" of maritime strategy is "to determine the mutual relations of your army and navy in a plan of war."[46] Corbett's emphasis on formulating an overarching strategy that joined together navy and army service strategies is a useful addition to Mahan's work that focused on naval operations.

During Mahan's lifetime, a group of naval strategists known as the *Jeune École* advocated a much different strategy for how to wage war at sea. The *Jeune École* aimed at the disruption of seaborne trading networks, upon which sea powers depended. This school of strategic thought gained prominence in France, where naval planners wanted to find a way to compete on the sea against Britain without going head-to-head in acquiring battleships to fight for command of the maritime commons. In the aftermath of France's humiliating defeat in the Franco-German War, French leaders faced the daunting task of funding a navy to fight Britain while at the same time trying to match Germany

44. Mahan, *Sea Power, 1793–1812*, Volume 2, 389–90.
45. Mahan, *Sea Power, 1793–1812*, 389–90.
46. Corbett, *Some Principles*, 14.

on land. To compete with Britain, leaders of the French navy thought that they could strike directly at the shipping and financial networks upon which the British economy depended. Fast cruisers could range out far on the world's oceans, avoiding Britain's superior battle fleet, to sink British merchant shipping. The disruption caused by these attacks on international supply chains crossing the seas would cause shock and panic, producing a meltdown of financial markets. By bringing about the collapse of British shipping and credit, France could defeat Britain without having to fight major fleet engagements. France could win without going to the expense of competing in battleships.

The *Jeune École* also put their faith in the lethality of mines, small surface craft and submarines armed with torpedoes, and coastal artillery to execute what is today called an anti-access, area-denial (A2/AD) strategy, as means to ward off Britain's surface fleet of capital ships. A relatively cheap torpedo boat or mine could sink a battleship. A swarm of torpedo boats would prevent the British battle fleet from undertaking forward-deployed operations in France's littoral waters and instituting a close blockade of French naval bases, such as Mahan praised in his histories. The increased lethality of naval weaponry was working to the competitive advantage of the weaker navy, according to the *Jeune École*. By increasing the danger to surface naval forces, inducing British admirals to more risk averse behavior in their operations, France would find opportunities to overturn Britain's lead on the high seas.

Mahan took seriously the challenge that the strategic views of the *Jeune École* offered to his own. He feared that the *Jeune École* doctrines for fighting at sea would take hold in the United States as it sought to rebuild the navy at the end of the nineteenth century. The American public and their leaders in government would forgo building a powerful battle fleet and, instead, acquire a coastal defense force and cruisers to carry out commerce-destruction raids. This alternative doctrine Mahan regarded as "a delusion, and a most dangerous delusion, when presented in the fascinating garb of cheapness to the representatives of a people." Mahan sought to counter what he considered the misleading strategic prescriptions and force structure recommendations of the *Jeune École*. "The harassment and distress caused to a country by serious interference with its commerce," he conceded, "is doubtless a most important secondary operation of naval war." Mahan denied, however, that the strategic nostrums proffered by the *Jeune École* would prove decisive against a country in possession of "the two requisites of a strong sea power—a wide-spread healthy commerce and a powerful navy."[47]

47. Mahan, *Sea Power, 1660–1783*, 539.

New technologies, however, did change how war was fought at sea, as the *Jeune École* predicted. In the First World War, a British and French battle fleet failed to force the rudimentary defenses of mines and coastal artillery erected by the Ottoman Empire at the Dardanelles. Six British and French battleships were sunk or heavily damaged in a single day when attacking the Ottoman defenses. In the North Sea, the main naval theater of the war, the sinking of battleships and cruisers by submarines and mines demonstrated the lethality of these weapons to large surface ships. Britain's admirals feared risking their Grand Fleet by attacking into German home waters in search of a new Trafalgar. Mahan's praise of aggressive, risk-taking admirals, like Nelson, did not resonate with Britain's naval leaders during the Great War. Better to preserve the Grand Fleet than to risk its loss by offensive action. Meanwhile, the risk-averse defensive mindset of the Kaiser and his admirals resulted in Germany's vaunted force of battleships steaming into captivity rather than going down in heroic fighting.

Germany's actual high-seas fleet acting on the offensive in the war was not the battleships but the submarines, which operated in the western seaborne approaches of the British Isles. This campaign of unrestricted submarine warfare inflicted staggering losses on the merchant shipping underpinning the war effort of the Allied and Associated Powers. While German submarines did not sever Britain's seaborne lifelines or produce a financial panic, the loss of 13-million tons of shipping was real enough in hobbling the war effort to defeat Germany. In the spring of 1917, with shipping losses to German submarines mounting, the first sea lord Admiral Sir John Jellicoe advised the British government that the war was lost. Winston Churchill characterized the fight to defeat the German submarines "a life-and-death struggle" on which the war's outcome turned.[48] Defeating "fugitive" German submarines in both world wars, and keeping the New World connected to the Old across the great highway of the North Atlantic required an extraordinary commitment of resources.

Mahan—who passed away just months after the war started—would undoubtedly have pointed to the contribution made by sea power in defeating Germany. Britain's geographic position and superior naval forces imposed a blockade that damaged the German economy and caused Germany's rulers to make strategic gambles—such as unrestricted submarine warfare—that

---

48. Winston S. Churchill, *Thoughts and Adventures*, James W. Muller, ed. (Wilmington, DE: ISI Books, 2009), 134.

eventually brought America into the fight. Furthermore, command of the seas allowed Britain to draw on resources and manpower from around the world, including the United States, to ensure Germany's defeat.

IV

Mahan enjoyed a reputation not only as a naval historian but also as a commentator on world politics and the international strategic environment. He was drawn to studying "the field of thought" concerned with "the external policy of nations, and of their mutual—international—relations." He wanted to highlight strategic factors in writing about international relations.[49] In his examination of world politics, Mahan also highlighted the field of international political economy. The growing output of American industry and agriculture would propel greater involvement in the world economy. The building of the Panama Canal would promote increased seaborne trade within the Western Hemisphere and across the Pacific, as well as facilitating the movements of naval forces. Along with increased trade, it would become a strategic requirement to acquire bases for the navy to protect commerce. Bases in the Caribbean, the isthmian canal, Hawaii, and the Philippines would support American naval forces. Mahan wrote that the "United States is to all intents an insular power, like Great Britain." Increased commerce, acquisition of bases, and a stronger navy would help underwrite American security in a world of competitive great powers.[50]

In examining the international arena, Mahan was greatly concerned by the decline of British power and how it would impact the security of the United States. Britain had been the leading great power, the workshop of the world, the world's foremost trading and financial state, possessing an empire on which the sun never set, and boasting a navy to rule the waves. As the nineteenth century ended, however, Britain's international position was threatened by the spread of industrialization, which enabled other great powers to build up their naval strength. The passing of the era when Britain was the world's leading industrial power pointed to a waning of its leadership as a naval power as well. To compensate for the decline of British power in the face of rising challengers, Mahan called for major increases in American naval strength. His study of history, and his efforts to apply what he learned from historical cases

49. Mahan, *Sail to Steam*, 324.
50. Mahan, *Interest of America in Sea Power*, 99–100, 210.

to understand the kaleidoscopic changes taking place in world politics, made him warn of impending conflicts. Like Mahan, Theodore Roosevelt believed that the United States needed to play a larger role on the international stage. He observed that "we ourselves are becoming, owing to our strength and geographical situation, more and more the balance of power of the whole world."[51]

Mahan saw Britain's international position being threatened from several directions. One clash was a showdown in Asia between Britain the sea power and Russia the land power. What might be called a Russian belt-and-road advance across the Eurasian landmass threatened to tilt the international balance of power in Russia's favor. Russian expansion was pushing against the weak states that existed on an arc stretching from the Ottoman Empire, Persia, and Afghanistan, to China and Northeast Asia. Before Halford Mackinder wrote his famous article on geopolitics, Mahan was bringing the contest to prevent one great power from dominating the Eurasian land mass to the attention of his readers.[52] Mahan argued for the United States to support Britain's efforts to contain Russian expansion and to prevent China from falling under the "preponderant political control" of outside great powers. The United States could assist Chinese economic and political development by promoting the open-door policy.[53] Mahan's geopolitical assessment matched that of Brooks Adams in his book *America's Economic Supremacy* published in 1900. "America must more or less completely assume the place once held by England," Adams argued, "for the United States could hardly contemplate with equanimity the successful organization of a hostile industrial system on the shore of the Pacific, based on Chinese labor."[54]

Later, after Russia's defeat in the Russo-Japanese War checked Russian geopolitical ambitions in Asia, Mahan identified imperial Germany as the most dangerous challenge to Britain and, hence, a looming security concern for the United States. "The rivalry between Germany and Great Britain today," he told his readers, "is the danger point, not only of European politics, but of world

51. As quoted in, Howard K. Beale, *Theodore Roosevelt and the Rise of America to World Power* (Baltimore, MD: Johns Hopkins University Press, 1956), 447.

52. H.J. Mackinder, "The Geographical Pivot of History," *The Geographical Journal* 23:4 (1904): 421–44.

53. A.T. Mahan, *The Problem of Asia and Its Effect upon International Policies* (Boston, MA: Little, Brown, 1900), 167.

54. Brooks Adams, *America's Economic Supremacy* (New York, NY: Macmillan, 1900), 197–98.

politics as well."[55] The famous "naval panic" of 1909 in Britain heightened Mahan's concern about Germany's foreign policy ambitions. Mahan alerted American readers to the growing German battle fleet in an article entitled, "Germany's Naval Ambition: Some Reasons Why the United States Should Wake Up to the Facts About the Kaiser's Battleship-Building Program—Great Britain's Danger Exaggerated, But Not Her Fright."[56] Mahan took note of Germany's rapidly rising population and industrial production, which would lead the German government and people to demand overseas territories to serve as markets for manufactured products, resources, and naval bases. He saw "an inevitable link in the chain of logical sequence: Industry, markets, control [of overseas territories], navy, bases."[57] What we might call the Mahan trap of great-power competition resulting in war was being sprung by Germany's growing economy, battle fleet, and the dreams of world power held by its rulers.

Mahan feared that Britain and the United States would fall behind Germany in the naval competition. He thought, "It seems as if the national life of Great Britain were waning at the same time that of Germany is waxing." Mahan doubted whether Britain and the United States, whose governments were in the hands of the people, would fund the armed forces required to deter Germany from going to war. While Britain and the United States possessed superior resources, their political systems appeared incapable of harnessing them. "The two English-speaking countries," he wrote, "have wealth vastly superior, each separately, to that of Germany; much more if acting together. But in neither is the efficiency of the Government for handling the resources comparable to that of Germany." Mahan argued that "the habits of individual liberty in England or America [do not] accept, unless under duress, the heavy yoke of organization, [or] of regulation of individual action, which constitutes the power of Germany among modern states."[58] The challenge from Germany was a test of societies, economies, and governments as much as navies, and Mahan harbored doubts about American and British democracy designing and executing a long-term strategic plan to thwart German ambitions.[59]

55. A.T. Mahan, *The Interest of America in International Conditions* (Boston, MA: Little, Brown, 1918 edition), 163–64.

56. A.T. Mahan, "Germany's Naval Ambitions: Some Reasons Why the United States Should Wake Up to the Facts About the Kaiser's Battleship-Building Program—Great Britain's Danger Exaggerated, But Not Her Fright," *Collier's Weekly*, April 24, 1909, 12–13.

57. Mahan, *Interest of America in International Conditions*, 87.

58. Mahan, *Naval Strategy*, 109; Mahan, *Interest of America in International Conditions*, 163.

59. *Britain and the German Navy: Admiral Mahan's Warning* (London: Associated Newspapers, 1910).

When war engulfed Europe in the summer of 1914, Mahan's nightmare scenario of a German triumph appeared imminent. In a newspaper interview, he warned, "If Germany succeeds in downing both France and Russia, she gains a respite by land, which may enable her to build up her sea power equal, or superior to that of Great Britain." The United States would then "be confronted by the naval power of a state, not, like Great Britain, sated with territory, but one eager and ambitious for expansion, eager also for influence."[60]

Mahan's public stance on the war contradicted President Woodrow Wilson's foreign policy of preserving American neutrality. Fearing that Mahan's pronouncements might influence public opinion against the government's policy, the president instructed Secretary of the Navy Josephus Daniels to "advise all officers of the Service, whether active or retired, to refrain from public comment of any kind upon the military or political situation on the other side of the water."[61] In failing health and close to death, Mahan resented the president's "muzzling order" and protested its application to him. He wanted "to show our people, as this wretched war goes on, the necessity for preparedness." Much to Mahan's chagrin, his protest proved of no avail, and the ban on public comment remained in force. In a sad ending to Mahan's life, he was silenced as a public commentator.[62]

V

Today, modern weaponry has changed strategic geography and assessments of national power in ways that Mahan could not imagine. To the maritime common that Mahan examined have been added contests in the air, space, and cyber domains. Countries once protected by their navies became vulnerable to air attack. In the Second World War, Hitler no more than Napoleon could transport an army across the Channel, but the German air force pounded British cities, inflicting heavy loss of life and immense damage. Air superiority became every bit a prerequisite for victory in wars involving the great powers as navies had been in the conflicts examined by Mahan. To exercise overbearing power on the seas required command of the air. Aircraft—operating either from ships or from land—were required to support navies and to project military power overseas. Since then, technology has only increased the lethality of naval combat by putting in danger

60. Seager and Maguire, *Mahan Letters*, Volume 3, 698–700.
61. Taylor, *Mahan*, 275.
62. Seager, *Mahan*, 689, note 31.

forward-deployed surface warships operating within range of land-based missiles. In Mahan's time, coastal artillery had limited range. In the twenty-first century, long-range, precision-guided ballistic and cruise missiles can strike surface ships far out to sea, as well as attack bases supporting forward-deployed naval forces.

The revolution in strategic affairs ushered in by the development of nuclear weapons atop long-range ballistic missiles has forced a fundamental rethinking of national strategy. Nothing perhaps better illustrates this than the work of Bernard Brodie. Published in 1941, his book *Sea Power in the Machine Age* stood very much in the tradition of Mahan. Brodie provided a thoughtful defense of the battleship as the weapon required to gain sea control through offensive operations by battle fleets. Soon after Hiroshima and Nagasaki, however, Brodie would orchestrate the seminal study *The Absolute Weapon* and later write *Strategy in the Missile Age*, books that reflect a much different, more frightening strategic reality and set of national security concerns.[63]

Nuclear weapons have forced naval war planners to rethink the teachings of Mahan and other classic works on maritime strategy about how navies fight and their strategic purpose. Great powers deploy nuclear weapons and long-range ballistic missiles in submarines (SSBNs), which serve as a stealthy undersea deterrent, the ultimate reserve force in the balance of terror. At a time when long-range precision strike weapons make land-based nuclear weapons more vulnerable to attack, SSBNs remain the most survivable of deterrents. The high strategic value placed on the survival of SSBNs dictates that naval planners add strategies for their defense and attack to Mahan's doctrines on the purpose of navies in wartime.

During the Cold War, the navies of the superpowers also carried nuclear weapons for use in naval combat. The United States Navy's maritime strategy of the 1980s, in the best traditions of Mahan, called for offensive operations "*to carry the fight to the enemy*," to bring Soviet naval forces to battle and, if ordered by national command authorities, to attack Soviet SSBNs. While American naval planners wanted to keep fighting at sea below the nuclear-use threshold, they did not discount the danger of escalation as an outcome of a superpower war.[64] On the other side, Soviet Admiral S.G. Gorshkov endorsed

63. Bernard Brodie, *Sea Power in the Machine Age* (Princeton, NJ: Princeton University Press, 1941); Bernard Brodie, ed., *The Absolute Weapon: Atomic Power and World Order* (New York, NY: Harcourt, Brace, 1946); Bernard Brodie, *Strategy in the Missile Age* (Princeton, NJ: Princeton University Press, 1959).

64. John B. Hattendorf and Peter M. Swartz, eds., *U.S. Naval Strategy in the 1980s: Selected Documents* (Newport, RI: Naval War College Press, 2008).

Mahan's tenet that sea battles—fleet-on-fleet engagements—have "nearly always been waged to destroy the enemy." In a grim understatement, he added, "The equipping of the forces of the fleets with nuclear weapons is further accentuating this feature."[65] In many ways American and Soviet war plans thus reflected Mahan's calls for offensive naval operations, but with nuclear weapons aboard ships rather than carronades to strike at the adversary.

Along with rapid technological change, the twenty-first century is witnessing a shift away from American dominance of the international system established after the Second World War and deepened after the end of the Cold War. The growth of China's power is transforming the international system. What Brooks Adams wrote in 1900 appears even more applicable in our time than in his—namely, that on "the fate of China may, perhaps, hinge the economic supremacy of the next century."[66] Mahan also imagined a future revival of Chinese power overcoming the foreign invasions and internal turmoil that kept China weak during the so-called century of humiliation. With technology and a strong government, he argued that China's rise as a great power "will go far to determine the future of the world."[67]

In 1892, Mahan addressed the students at the Naval War College, "All the world knows, gentlemen, that we are building a new navy." He asked them, "Well, when we get our navy, what are we going to do with it?"[68] Chinese military professionals now wrestle with the question that Mahan posed to American naval officers at a time when their country was a rising great power in world affairs. Mahan is currently widely read and studied in China. One Chinese naval officer maintains that the United States "benefited from the guidance of Mahan's theories of sea power, and unceasingly pressed forward in the maritime direction . . . [thus] establishing a firm foundation for its move into the world's first-rank powers." Another Chinese military officer contends that "America introduced the term 'sea power' and the United States was also the first country to realize the secret of sea power. Exactly because of holding such a secret, the United States has gradually approached being a superpower and accomplishing world hegemony."[69] Mahan's writings were

65. S.G. Gorshkov, *The Sea Power of the State* (Annapolis, MD: Naval Institute Press, 1979), 226.

66. Adams, *America's Economic Supremacy*, 196.

67. Mahan, *Problem of Asia*, 88.

68. Mahan, *Naval Administration*, 229.

69. Andrew S. Erickson and Lyle J. Goldstein, "China Studies the Rise of Great Powers," in *China Goes to Sea: Maritime Transformation in Comparative Historical Perspective*, Andrew S.

hardly a secret, and few would contend that America's rise to world power followed a coherent grand strategy. Nonetheless, some of Mahan's appeal in China comes from the notion that he provided a strategic blueprint for an ambitious, rising great power on the world stage. As Robert Kaplan has observed, "Tellingly . . . the Chinese avidly read [Mahan]; the Chinese are the Mahanians now."[70]

China's aspirations to assert itself as a superpower, to usher in an end to an American-led world order, are certainly manifest in Beijing's naval buildup. Projected increases in Chinese capabilities to fight on the maritime commons offer a telltale sign of the determination of China's rulers to compete in the world arena. China's reported ambitions to possess a high seas fleet of six or more aircraft carriers is a statement of foreign policy intent as well as one of enhanced naval capabilities. China's development of export industries, overseas trade, shipbuilding capacity, a commercial fleet, forward bases, and a navy illustrates Mahan's contention that an "absolute government" can marshal the resources to transform a country into a great sea power.

The Chinese regime's commitment to becoming a sea power and to building the navy of a superpower cannot be doubted. At a major fleet review in the South China Sea, ships and aircraft paraded before President Xi Jinping, seen wearing military fatigues, in a display that harkens back to the spectacles of naval nationalism exhibited by imperial Germany. Channeling his inner Kaiser for the fleet review, Xi proclaimed that China had "an urgent need" for "a strong and modern navy [which] is an important mark of a top-ranking global military."[71] It was Germany's naval buildup that had so alarmed Mahan and led him to warn about the danger of war posed by the Kaiser's world power aspirations. Xi's public pronouncements reflect faithfully his beliefs about the connection between sea power and national greatness. In an internal speech to China's Central Military Commission, he declared, "History and experience tell us that a country will rise if it commands the oceans well and will fall if it surrenders them. A powerful state possesses durable sea rights, and a weak state has vulnerable sea rights." In championing the accelerated "construction of a modernized navy," Xi sounds like a follower of Mahan.[72]

Erickson, Lyle J. Goldstein, and Carnes Lord, eds. (Annapolis, MD: Naval Institute Press, 2009), 409.

70. Robert D. Kaplan, "America's Elegant Decline," *The Atlantic*, November 2007.

71. John H. Maurer, "Kaiser Xi Jinping," *National Interest*, September–October 2018, 28–35.

72. John W. Lewis and Xue Litai, "China's Security Agenda Transcends the South China Sea," *Bulletin of the Atomic Scientists* 72:4 (2016): 218.

While read in China, Mahan is no longer a prophet honored by his own country's navy. In 2021, the Chief of Naval Operations Professional Reading Program dropped his writings. Pushing him aside surely makes no sense when America's principal competitor for sea power looks to him for strategic inspiration and guidance. Mahan belongs on the reading lists of national security professionals, strategic leaders, and naval planners. His writings are not for the faint of heart: his stark realism about world affairs warns that struggles for mastery of the global commons cannot be won on the cheap against determined great-power challengers. An American-led world order will depend on the United States keeping ahead of competitors in the global commons. Mahan remains the foremost thinker on sea power, the essential starting point for examining the conduct of naval warfare and for understanding the strategic importance of commanding the global commons in deciding the outcome of contests for world power.

CHAPTER 8

Kant, Paine, and Strategies of Liberal Transformation

Michael Cotey Morgan

According to a venerable tradition, the nature of statecraft has not changed throughout the centuries. The same dilemmas confronted leaders in the second century and in the twentieth century, and those dilemmas will endure. War is an eternal feature of international politics, whether because human beings are inherently sinful, as St. Augustine suggested, or because conflict is an integral component of relations between states, as Europe's Early Modern aristocrats believed. Wise leaders must therefore adapt themselves to the world, rather than trying to transform it.[1]

Rival schools of thought have long contested this view. Karl Marx argued that material forces constrain the choices available to individuals and governments alike, and that no human being can change the direction of history. In contrast, liberal thinkers have insisted that, by making the right choices, leaders and states can achieve lasting progress. As one historian put it, these figures "believe the world to be profoundly other than it should be, and . . . have faith in the power of human reason and human action so to change it that the inner potential of human beings can be more fully realized."[2]

These liberals looked for ways to escape the cycle of conflict and to establish lasting peace among states and just systems of government within them. They

---

1. Michael Howard, *The Invention of Peace: Reflections on War and International Order* (New Haven, CT: Yale University Press, 2000), 9–13.

2. Michael Howard, *War and the Liberal Conscience* (New Brunswick, NJ: Rutgers University Press, 1978), 11.

perceived a direct relationship between the proliferation of democratic self-government and the advent of international harmony. This argument gained momentum during the Enlightenment, when writers and philosophers began to question the inevitability of war. According to older ideas, such as the balance of power, the prospects for peace depended on how states conducted their foreign policies. If they formed or broke off alliances with the right countries or issued threats at the right time, states could deter aggression or, failing that, punish it. This system held out the possibility of stability, but not enduring peace.

By contrast, many Enlightenment thinkers—and the liberals whom they inspired—emphasized a state's internal character rather than its external behavior. They thought about transforming the international system, rather than seeking temporary relief from conflict. If citizens replaced their monarchies with republics and determined their own governments' policies rather than obeying a tyrant's commands, their countries would behave peacefully. The more countries that followed this model, the more peaceful the world would become, especially if the growing number of republics pledged to defend each other in the event of conflict with an undemocratic state. The expansion of international trade and the development of international law would reinforce these processes, and foster the emergence of an international society that protected common interests against selfish demands.

This line of reasoning defined the goals of a distinctly liberal grand strategy. But it also raised questions about the best way to achieve those goals. The two most salient problems concerned how democracy would take root in new countries, and the role that force should play in that process. Some, following the German philosopher Immanuel Kant, insisted that democracy would spread through the power of reason, without violence. Others, in the tradition of the Anglo-American writer Thomas Paine, embraced revolution and military intervention as essential tools in the democratic arsenal. The history of liberal statecraft from the French Revolution to the First World War illustrates the difficulties and contradictions of both approaches. Liberal strategists have repeatedly attempted to reconcile their commitment to peace with the reality of war. They have debated how to deal with non-democratic governments in the pursuit of democracy, and they have wrestled with the challenge of fashioning a cooperative international system out of the divergent interests of its members. Like all strategists, they have struggled to find a sustainable balance between ends and means.[3]

3. On the history of liberal and other approaches to international politics, see F.H. Hinsley, *Power and the Pursuit of Peace: Theory and Practice in the History of Relations between States*

I

In the eighteenth century, while European monarchs invested enormous energy in fighting wars, European thinkers pondered how to end them. In urging rulers to put down their weapons, the abbé de Saint-Pierre, a French cleric, proposed creating a "European Union." In this international organization, every state would enjoy equal representation, regardless of its military or economic power. Having agreed to preserve the continent's territorial status quo "for all time," the Union's members would resolve their disputes by mediation. If that failed, an international army would punish aggressors and enforce peace, though Saint-Pierre assumed that the mere threat of force would be enough to deter misbehavior. One of his contemporaries fused this commitment to peace with a belief in human progress. According to the Baron d'Holbach, a German-born philosopher, warfare was a relic of the "savage customs" of the past. The advance of reason would persuade rulers to stop chasing martial glory and focus on governing their countries well instead. These schemes, and others like them, emphasized the power of education: if rulers properly understood the wisdom of peace, then peace would prevail.[4]

That assumption did not satisfy every Enlightenment philosophe. Two of the era's most influential thinkers sought a more robust way to preserve peace. According to Thomas Paine and Immanuel Kant, trying to change the minds of individual monarchs would not solve the problem. More dramatic changes, which addressed the underlying causes of war, were needed. Rather than working within the existing system of monarchical states, they agreed, it was necessary to change the system.

(Cambridge: Cambridge University Press, 1963); and Michael W. Doyle, *Ways of War and Peace: Realism, Liberalism, and Socialism* (New York, NY: W. W. Norton, 1997). Readers interested in the history of the balance of power should consult Evan Luard, *The Balance of Power: The System of International Relations, 1648–1815* (New York, NY: St. Martin's Press, 1992). For an introduction to Kant's political thought, see the essays in Immanuel Kant, *Toward Perpetual Peace and Other Writings on Politics, Peace, and History*, Pauline Kleingeld, ed. (New Haven, CT: Yale University Press, 2006). T.C.W. Blanning, *The French Revolutionary Wars, 1787–1802* (New York, NY: Arnold, 1996) offers an excellent overview of its subject. On Italian unification, see Denis Mack Smith, *Cavour and Garibaldi 1860: A Study in Political Conflict* (Cambridge: Cambridge University Press, 1954). Roy Jenkins, *Gladstone: A Biography* (New York, NY: Random House, 1995) is the best one-volume treatment of the British prime minister. On the origins of Wilson's ideas, see Thomas J. Knock, *To End All Wars: Woodrow Wilson and the Quest for a New World Order* (New York, NY: Oxford University Press, 1992).

4. David A. Bell, *The First Total War: Napoleon's Europe and the Birth of Warfare as We Know It* (New York, NY: Houghton Mifflin Harcourt, 2007), 70.

Paine and Kant started from the assumption that peace constituted something more than the absence of conflict. Whenever monarchs grew "wearied with war, and tired with human butchery," Paine wrote, "they sat down to rest, and called it peace." For peace to mean something, however, it could not merely entail "the accidental respite of a few years' repose." It had to endure. Kant expressed a similar idea, albeit in less vivid language. The documents that governments called peace treaties did not deserve the name, he said. They were "actually only truces" because, sooner or later, another war would break out. Real peace required a permanent end to all wars. Peace in this sense would not come about automatically. It had to be built.[5]

The best way to build such a peace was to spread liberal democracy, or, to use Paine's and Kant's preferred term, republicanism. In a republican system, the government respects its citizens' freedom and equality, and its policies reflect their preferences. States that operate according to these principles behave peacefully because, as Paine put it, the decision whether to go to war "reside[s] . . . with those who are to pay the expense." Given the choice, they will choose peace.[6]

Kant pushed this idea further. Like Paine, he traced a state's external behavior to its domestic form of government. Because "the consent of the citizens is required to decide whether or not war is to be declared, it is very natural that they will have great hesitation in embarking on so dangerous an enterprise," Kant wrote. "For this would mean calling down on themselves all the miseries of war." The spread of republicanism, however, would not be sufficient to guarantee peace. Republics also had to establish a "pacific federation," which would preserve security by upholding its members' freedom "in accordance with the idea of international right." By settling disputes without resorting to violence, this federation would end not just one war, but all wars.[7]

International commerce would reinforce these patterns. The more that countries did business with each other, the better they would understand each other, and the lower their risk of stumbling into conflict by miscommunication. Trade would also encourage countries to resolve their disagreements amicably, since war would interrupt the flow of profits. "The spirit of commerce . . . cannot

---

5. Thomas Paine, *Political Writings*, revised edition, Bruce Kuklick, ed. (New York, NY: Cambridge University Press, 2000), 164; and Immanuel Kant, *Political Writings*, Hans Reiss, ed. (New York, NY: Cambridge University Press, 1991), 98 and 130.

6. Paine, *Political Writings*, 94 and 152.

7. Kant, *Political Writings*, 100, 104, and 123.

exist side by side with war," Kant observed. Besides, once states saw that they could obtain whatever resources they needed by trade, they would have no reason to conquer their neighbors. Commerce was "a pacific system" that made "nations, as well as individuals, useful to each other," Paine said. If governments allowed it to flourish without interference, it would eventually "extirpate the system of war."[8]

In making these arguments, Kant and Paine drew connections between freedom and peace, and between self-interest and moral obligation. When states were free from tyranny, and markets were free from governmental interference, peace could flourish. When citizens could pursue their own interests, they would act as reason commanded. However bloody the history of relations between states, they were not condemned to repeat it. States could get better at solving their problems, and their citizens could live freer, more peaceful, and more prosperous lives.

Behind these sunny promises lurked a number of difficult questions. To the extent that progress was possible, would it come about automatically, or did it depend on the course of events and the decisions that people made? Would some unstoppable mechanism convert every state to a republic sooner or later, or would the existing republics have to export their ideals? How should republics deal with their non-republican neighbors? Could they use force to spread their system of government and hasten the arrival of utopia? For all that they had in common, Paine and Kant answered these questions in different ways. Their disagreements represented a fork in the road for liberal strategy.

Down one path lay a strategy that expected only gradual progress and treated peace as both a means and an end. In Kant's view, nature and reason work together to steer human society away from war. By bringing people into conflict, nature pushes them to develop their powers of reason. In turn, reason helps people to recognize that they have an interest in living peacefully under laws that bind everyone. This mechanism operates both within states and among them, and produces "concord among men, even against their will and indeed by means of their very discord," Kant concluded. Because human beings are flawed, however, this process takes time. Peace would only be achieved "at a late stage and after many unsuccessful attempts." In the interim, even a single republic could serve as a "focal point" for building the pacific federation, Kant suggested, because the force of its example would inspire other states to join. Citizens had a "duty to work towards this goal," but under no circumstances

8. Kant, *Political Writings*, 114; and Paine, *Political Writings*, 208.

could they seek to topple undemocratic regimes by force or impose new institutions on them from abroad. Both domestic rebellions and military interference in the affairs of independent states contravened the principles of right. The goal of perpetual peace, however just it might be, could not justify starting a war.[9]

The other path pointed to a more self-confident and more violent strategy. Because democratic government benefited ordinary people, it would propagate everywhere. All attempts to stop the spread of democracy "will in the end prove fruitless," Paine assured his readers. "An army of principles will penetrate where an army of soldiers cannot. . . . [I]t will march on the horizon of the world, and it will conquer."[10] Education and the open discussion of public policy would contribute to the process, Paine suggested, because they "explode ignorance" and empower citizens to understand the business of government. But the export of democracy might need help from soldiers themselves.[11]

During the French Revolution, Paine welcomed the prospect of citizen armies marching abroad to spread freedom, and even called for an invasion of England to overthrow its monarchy. Military power would liberate those who had not yet achieved their freedom and improve the security of those who were already free. "When France shall be surrounded by revolutions," Paine wrote, "she will be in peace and safety." Spreading democracy by force was a matter of humanitarian duty as well as an imperative of self-defense.[12]

For Paine and Kant, liberalism constituted both a statement of faith and a program of action. It promised a world in which the triumph of reason would bring liberty and prosperity to all; in which states' self-interest and their ideals pointed in the same direction; and in which they could transcend their war-torn histories and achieve lasting peace and security. If the two thinkers agreed about the ultimate goal, however, they had different ideas about how to achieve it, and about how existing republics ought to behave while they waited for other states to catch up with them. During their lifetimes—and long after—the

9. Kant, *Political Writings*, 47, 108, 114, and 126–28.

10. Paine, *Political Writings*, 164 and 336; and David M. Fitzsimons, "Tom Paine's New World Order: Idealistic Internationalism in the Ideology of Early American Foreign Relations," *Diplomatic History* 19:4 (1995): 579.

11. Paine, *Political Writings*, 183; and Thomas C. Walker, "The Forgotten Prophet: Tom Paine's Cosmopolitanism and International Relations," *International Studies Quarterly* 44:1 (2000): 58–59.

12. Paine, *Political Writings*, 156; and Fitzsimons, "Tom Paine's New World Order," 580.

course of international politics highlighted the significance of their disagreement, with decisive consequences for the development of liberalism and attempts to establish lasting peace.

II

The French Revolution demonstrated, in an extreme form, the conflict between the two strategies of liberalism. In early 1790, as the National Assembly drafted a new constitution, its members grappled with a fundamental question of statecraft. Because King Louis XVI remained on the throne as a limited rather than an absolute monarch, the Assembly had to determine whether he retained the power to declare war, or if that prerogative should devolve to the French people's elected representatives. The ensuing debate pitted the new commitment to popular sovereignty, which the Declaration of the Rights of Man and the Citizen had affirmed the previous year, against the traditional concept of monarchical sovereignty. It also forced the Assembly to consider what its new approach to government implied for international politics and the utility of force.[13]

The representatives debated whether kings started more wars than republics, and which kind of government conducted foreign policy more effectively. Several suggested that, if the revolution lived up to its ideals, the debate about war powers would become moot. "May all nations be as free as we wish to be, and there will be no more war," said one representative. Another argued that France had to consider its responsibilities not only to its own people, but to the whole of humanity, which "form[ed] but a single and same society, whose object is the peace and happiness of each and all of its members." This cosmopolitan line of reasoning raised questions about the legitimacy of war itself. Maximilien Robespierre, who would soon emerge as one of the Revolution's leading radicals, proposed that the Assembly forswear war as an instrument of policy and commit France to live in peace "with all nations in the fraternity commanded by nature." After further back-and-forth, the representatives issued a proclamation, which became known as the "Declaration of Peace to the World"—"The French nation renounces the undertaking of any wars aimed at conquest, and will never employ its forces against the liberty of any people." The statement captured the spirit of what one historian has called "Enlightenment pacifism," which assumed—like Kant and Paine—that the spread of freedom and progress of reason would make war obsolete.[14]

13. Bell, *The First Total War*, 89.
14. Bell, *The First Total War*, 96, 98, 102, and 104–5.

The declaration did not claim, however, that France would never go to war. To the contrary, it implied that the country still required a military in order to defend itself. It also hinted at using force to liberate other peoples. Subsequent events put these ideas to the test. By the fall of 1791, tensions between France and its neighbors had been rising for months. Since the start of the Revolution, thousands of its opponents, mainly drawn from the ranks of the aristocracy, had fled the country. From their places of refuge in western Germany, they urged other European governments to act against the new regime in Paris. Meanwhile, the Revolution drew an entirely different group of migrants to Paris. These foreign radicals sought help to overthrow their own governments and establish new republics across Europe. Louis XVI's failed attempt to escape from Paris made matters worse. The episode convinced many in the capital that, far from accepting his new role as a constitutional monarch, the king was conspiring against the government. When the rulers of Austria and Prussia issued the Declaration of Pillnitz, calling on European sovereigns to help restore Louis's royal prerogatives, French radicals concluded that a "coalition of despots" threatened to destroy the Revolution.[15]

In the Assembly in Paris, the demands for war grew louder. The loudest of the hawks, the Girondins, made two arguments for attacking Austria. First, a war would propagate republican values and liberate the peoples that had not yet achieved their freedom. France had to undertake "a crusade for universal liberty," Girondin leader Jacques Pierre Brissot insisted. "Each soldier will say to his enemy: Brother, I am not going to cut your throat, I am going to free you from the yoke you labor under." Second, they promised that, by defeating the Revolution's foreign enemies, France could end war itself. "It is because I want peace that I am asking for war," Anacharsis Cloots said. Liberty would "triumph everywhere" and "seat itself on all thrones, after having crushed despotism," Charles-François Dumouriez promised. "This war will be the last war." Even Louis XVI supported the calls for war, but for different reasons. He expected that Austria would triumph over the revolutionaries and restore his own authority and prestige.[16]

Only a handful of voices dared to express a contrary view. Whereas Cloots had promised that every people in Europe eagerly awaited their liberation and

15. T.C.W. Blanning, *The Origins of the French Revolutionary Wars* (London: Longman, 1986), 73–74; and Marc Belissa, "War and Diplomacy (1792–95)," in *The Oxford Handbook of the French Revolution*, David Andress, ed. (New York, NY: Oxford University Press, 2015), 422–23.

16. Blanning, *Origins of the French Revolutionary Wars*, 111; Bell, *First Total War*, 112–15; speech by Dumouriez, October 10, 1792, *La Vie et les mémoires du général Dumouriez*, Volume 3 (Paris: Baudouin Frères, 1823), 405.

would rise up against their rulers as soon as the conflict began, Robespierre questioned whether the French could spread their political ideals by force. "No one loves armed missionaries," Robespierre said, "and the first counsel that nature and prudence give is to repulse them as enemies." Few heeded this warning. In April 1792, France declared war on Austria. The conflict soon expanded. Within twelve months, Prussia, Britain, the Netherlands, and Spain had entered the fight against France.[17]

Despite its lack of allies, the French army enjoyed remarkable success. As its troops advanced into neighboring countries and toppled governments in the name of liberty, however, they did not always receive a warm welcome. In Belgium, for example, deep disagreements over revolutionary principles had split the population even before the French arrived. Radicals wanted to establish a republic along Jacobin lines, but moderates rejected the redistribution of political and economic power that this program would have entailed. The French tried to appeal to both groups, but only managed to alienate them both instead. Besides, the Belgians refused to defray any of the costs of their liberation. The French government therefore pushed its revolutionary logic one step further. Wherever its forces went, they would overthrow the existing governments and laws in the name of popular sovereignty, and set up new administrations. Any objections from the local inhabitants would only confirm that they remained intellectually oppressed and required the enlightenment that only France could provide. During the 1790s, this story repeated itself in Belgium, the Netherlands, Switzerland, western Germany, and much of Italy, where liberation turned into occupation. The French either annexed these territories or turned them into satellite republics, where French control depended on the threat or use of force. These developments contrasted sharply with the revolutionaries' predictions about the universal appeal of liberty and the inherent connection between republicanism and peace.[18]

Despite mass conscription, battlefield success, the promise of liberation, and the hope of building a federation of independent republics, victory eluded the French revolutionaries. With only brief interruptions, the wars that they launched ravaged the continent for a generation. Even as the conflict continued,

17. Blanning, *Origins of the French Revolutionary Wars*, 110; and Robespierre's Speech to the Jacobin Club, January 2 and 11, 1792, in *The French Revolution: A Document Collection*, Laura Mason and Tracey Rizzo, eds. (Boston, MA: Houghton Mifflin, 1999), 161.

18. R.R. Palmer, *The Age of the Democratic Revolution: A Political History of Europe and America, 1760–1800* (Princeton, NJ: Princeton University Press, 2014), 425–37, 505–29, and 589–613.

however, their adversaries began thinking about a postwar settlement that would stop the bloodshed for good. Instead of trying to restore the prewar status quo, they devised a new concept for preserving peace. Because the leading allies remained committed monarchists, they had no interest in a peaceful federation of republics. Nonetheless, they embraced the liberal commitment to collective action and shared responsibility. British Prime Minister William Pitt described the outlines of this approach in an 1805 message to the Russian government. Once the war had ended, the great powers "should all bind themselves mutually to protect and support each other, against any attempt to infringe" the peace settlement, Pitt wrote, and "provide, as far as possible, for repressing future attempts to disturb the general Tranquility."[19]

The Congress of Vienna demonstrated how this concept could work in practice. When the exiled Napoleon Bonaparte fled Elba in 1815, the Congress was still in session. The victorious allies immediately grasped that his escape threatened to reignite the war, and resolved to work together, once again, to defeat him for good. They pledged to seek "calmness for Europe and general peace, and protected by it the rights, the freedom, and the independence of nations."[20] After the Battle of Waterloo, the powers agreed to extend their alliance into peacetime for a further twenty years, and to meet periodically to agree on new measures for protecting peace. The new German Confederation, which the Congress also established, operated on similar principles. This defensive league assembled a group of sovereign states with a mandate to band together in order to stop aggression. All told, the 1815 settlement represented something new in European statecraft. It set aside the eighteenth-century notion that a self-regulating balance of power could preserve peace. In its place, it created an integrated system, grounded in a more robust understanding of international law, in which states remained sovereign but also shared the responsibility to collaborate in solving international problems.[21]

The Concert system did not live up to all of its creators' hopes, but it still fulfilled its central purpose. To be sure, unexpected crises continued to erupt, challenging both the great powers' interests and their ability to work together.

19. "Official Communication made to the Russian Ambassador at London," January 19, 1805, *The Foreign Policy of Victorian England, 1830–1902*, Kenneth Bourne, ed. (Oxford: Oxford University Press, 1970), 198.

20. Wolfram Siemann, *Metternich: Strategist and Visionary*, trans. Daniel Steuer (Cambridge, MA: Harvard University Press, 2019), 547.

21. Paul Schroeder, *The Transformation of European Politics, 1763–1848* (New York, NY: Oxford University Press, 1994), 546–47, 557, and 575–82.

Over the four decades that followed the end of the Napoleonic Wars, nearly every corner of Europe—from Spain to Poland, and from Germany to Greece—experienced political turmoil and often violence. But while the great powers disagreed about how to respond, and sometimes stepped to the brink of conflict (as in 1840, when events in the Ottoman Empire almost brought France to blows with the other powers), the system nonetheless held together and prevented another cataclysmic war.

III

Despite this commitment to peace and international cooperation, many liberals sharply criticized the Concert system. They wanted to reform their countries' political systems by limiting the power of monarchs and aristocrats and, in some cases, by redrawing the map of the continent entirely. Some even wanted to replace the old monarchies with republics organized along ethnic, linguistic, or religious lines. If they realized these ambitions, the multinational Austrian and Russian empires would collapse into an assortment of nation-states, and smaller polities would merge to encompass those peoples that spilled across international frontiers, especially in Italy and Germany. This program promised to establish a freer, more just international order, but it raised difficult questions about how to reconcile the pursuit of liberty with the demands of peace.

Liberal nationalism's most incisive advocate was the Italian journalist Giuseppe Mazzini. He championed the unity of humankind, the equality of republican citizenship, and the existence of universal moral imperatives—all widespread liberal notions. Individuals had a duty to devote their lives to "the benefit of humanity," he argued. But Mazzini also insisted that God had divided humanity into separate peoples, each with its own character and mission. This division did not constitute an obstacle to overcome, Mazzini suggested, but was a "means to multiply your forces." As each nation pursued its own distinct calling, it would contribute to the good of humanity.[22]

From this perspective, the purpose of statecraft was to empower every people to fulfil its purpose. Every nation, therefore, required its own state, because the state provided the indispensable tools of political action. "Our

22. Giuseppe Mazzini, "On the Duties of Man," in *A Cosmopolitanism of Nations: Giuseppe Mazzini's Writings on Democracy, Nation Building, and International Relations*, Stefan Recchia and Nadia Urbinati, eds. (Princeton, NJ: Princeton University Press, 2009), 89, 93.

country is the pivot of the lever we have to wield for the common good," Mazzini wrote. "If we abandon that pivot, we run the risk of rendering ourselves useless not only to humanity but to our country itself."[23] The new states created on this basis also had to uphold the values of "equality and democracy," since without them, genuine self-government would be impossible.[24]

An international system organized along these lines would enjoy peace and prosperity. Conflict would not disappear, but states would be able manage it without violence. Democracies would deal openly with each other for both moral and pragmatic reasons. By eschewing secret diplomacy, they would educate their citizens, fortify their love of liberty, prevent officials from losing touch with the citizens they served, and rally the whole nation behind its foreign policy. "[P]ublicity is life. It is a source of energy, force, independence, and honor," Mazzini argued. "Every republican state should elevate the requirement of total publicity in foreign affairs into a defining characteristic of its existence." This approach to international affairs, strengthened by international trade and economic interdependence, would bring states into ever-closer cooperation. Eventually, the democracies would band together into a political federation and "create the United States of Europe."[25]

Building this peaceful system required war. For one thing, tyrants would not relinquish power without a fight. In many cases, Mazzini expected, revolutionaries would have to overthrow tyrants by force in order to establish republics. For another, Europe's borders would have to be redrawn, because "evil governments" had carved up the continent, ignoring the natural contours of its constituent peoples. Reuniting them meant breaking up some states and merging others. Nearly every people would have to take up arms to secure its unity and independence. "We disagree with those dreamers who preach peace at any cost, even that of dishonor," Mazzini wrote. "We believe war to be sacred under certain circumstances."[26]

Once these wars had been won, and democratic governments established along national lines, the new states would face a new set of dangers. Like the French revolutionaries, Mazzini reasoned that no democracy could be safe

23. Mazzini, "On the Duties of Man," 94.
24. Mazzini, "On the Duties of Man," 12.
25. Mazzini, "From a Revolutionary Alliance to the United States of Europe," in *A Cosmopolitanism of Nations*, Recchia and Urbinati, eds., 135; and Mazzini, "On Publicity in Foreign Affairs," in *A Cosmopolitanism of Nations*, Recchia and Urbinati, eds., 176.
26. Mazzini, "On the Duties of Man," 93; and Mazzini, "Neither Pacifism nor Terror," in *A Cosmopolitanism of Nations*, Recchia and Urbinati, eds., 157.

unless its neighbors were democratic too. Democratic leaders therefore ought to establish a "collective defensive pact" to protect themselves from undemocratic countries, which posed an inherent threat. Unlike the French, however, he denied that one nation could liberate another by force. Only in cases where a foreign great power had already intervened in a state to crush a nationalist uprising could other powers step in as a counterweight on the side of the revolutionaries, "so as to make good all prior infractions of the law of Noninterference." This exception, however, only proved the rule—that each people had to win its own freedom.[27]

In 1849, Mazzini seized the chance to put his ideas into practice. When he heard that a revolution had started in Rome, where a constituent assembly had proclaimed the advent of "pure democracy" under "the glorious name of The Roman Republic," he rushed to the city from his exile in Switzerland. Mazzini hoped that the new polity would inspire its neighbors to throw off their reactionary despots and establish a unified and democratic Italy. When the assembly chose Mazzini to lead the government, he implemented a sweeping program of reform—lifting censorship, ending religious discrimination, abolishing capital punishment, and slashing tariffs.[28]

Mazzini understood that the republic's survival depended on developments abroad. Pope Pius IX, who had fled to the Kingdom of the Two Sicilies, called for foreign military assistance to restore him to his rightful position as Rome's secular ruler. His host, Ferdinand II, rallied to the cause, as did the Spanish king and the Austrian emperor. The military balance weighed heavily against the Romans. Nevertheless, they hoped that the new French republic, which had overthrown the monarchy the previous year, would come to their aid. France's president, Louis-Napoleon Bonaparte, contemplated entering the fight against Austria in order to roll back Vienna's influence in northern Italy. Ultimately, however, he decided to take the pope's side in order to shore up his standing with French Catholics. Although France's 1848 Constitution incorporated, verbatim, the declaration of peace issued in 1790, which required the government to respect the liberty of other peoples, the National Assembly approved a military expedition to occupy Rome's port, under the pretense of protecting the city against the Austrians. Bonaparte, however, secretly ordered

27. Mazzini, "Principles of International Politics," and Mazzini, "On Nonintervention," in *A Cosmopolitanism of Nations*, Recchia and Urbinati, eds., 236, 216.

28. Mike Rapport, *1848: Year of Revolution* (New York, NY: Basic Books, 2008), 350–51; and Denis Mack Smith, *Mazzini* (New Haven, CT: Yale University Press, 1994), 67–69.

the commanding general to capture the city itself. At the end of April, the French attacked.[29]

Rome's defenders held their ground, but time was not on their side. In Paris, the news of the assault provoked outrage in the assembly, whose deputies were looking ahead to the elections scheduled for the end of May. Mazzini perceived that the best chance for his city's salvation lay in France's ballot boxes. If voters chose a government that opposed Bonaparte's operation, the Roman republic might survive. In the meantime, Mazzini negotiated a truce with the attackers and appealed for help from the revolutionary governments that had seized power in other Italian cities, but they too faced desperate military situations. When Bonaparte's supporters won the election, the French army renewed its offensive and the Roman assembly capitulated.[30]

The events of 1849, and the renewed campaign for unification a decade later, underscored the dilemmas of Mazzini's strategy. He had hoped that the example of the republic would inspire others to complete his unfinished project, and urged his followers to act "like men who are working for eternity."[31] Although he preached that republicanism and national self-determination demanded the use of force, Mazzini could not find a way to marshal the military power required to save Rome. Worse still, he had assumed that republics, once established, would defend each other from their shared monarchical adversaries. At the moment of truth, however, France's Second Republic violated Mazzini's theory. In 1859, when Piedmont-Sardinia launched a new effort to unite the peninsula—this time with French backing—its leaders claimed the mantle of Italian nationalism, but eschewed Mazzini's republicanism in favor of monarchy. Piedmont's early successes in northern Italy forced Giuseppe Garibaldi, who had worked with Mazzini to defend Rome, to choose between his republican ideals and his commitment to national unification. He opted for the latter. After liberating Sicily and Naples, Garibaldi handed the territory over to the Piedmontese, who incorporated it into the new Kingdom of Italy. According to Mazzini's theory, nationalism and republicanism constituted complementary aspects of the same political project. In the struggle to find the means to achieve these ends, however, the success of one entailed the sacrifice of the other.

29. Rapport, *1848*, 357; Smith, *Mazzini*, 69–70.
30. Rapport, *1848*, 358; Smith, *Mazzini*, 70–73.
31. Rapport, *1848*, 355.

IV

The British Radicals of the mid-nineteenth century posed some of the same questions as the French revolutionaries and Mazzini, but reached different conclusions. Their highest priority in foreign affairs was to establish lasting peace, but they denied that it could be achieved by exercising military power. Radical MP John Bright called the balance of power "a mischievous delusion," which provided a pretext for any conflict and ensured that peace could "never be secure."[32] International trade, not the threat of force, provided the best foundation for international stability. If governments embraced free trade and dedicated themselves to lowering the barriers to commerce, Richard Cobden argued, they would "secure the dependence of countries one upon another." As citizens gained a material stake in preventing conflict, they would compel their governments to avoid war. By treating other countries as partners rather than as competitors, and by democratizing control over foreign affairs, free trade would "snatch the power from the governments to plunge their people into wars." For these reasons, Cobden said, such a policy constituted "the means, and I believe the only human means, of effecting universal and permanent peace."[33]

The power of public opinion would reinforce the commercial incentives for peace. In this respect, the Radicals hoped to build on the success of the 1832 Reform Act, which dramatically expanded the franchise. Just as public sentiment could prevent a democratic government from acting undemocratically, they reasoned, international opinion could restrain a state from acting against the common interest and thus make war unnecessary. After Russian troops crushed the Polish uprising of 1830–31, Radical MP Richard Hume lamented the fate of the rebels, but insisted that the great powers could have defended them without having to use force. If only Britain and other likeminded states had expressed "a strong opinion" on the matter, they could have achieved their goals without "the necessity of going to war," he told the House of Commons.[34] Some reformers suggested that democratizing British politics would prompt similar changes abroad, as if popular sovereignty could spread through

---

32. Richard Cobden, *Russia* (Edinburgh: William Tait, 1836), 33; and 132 Parl. Deb. (Third Series) (1854) col. 257–58.

33. Letter from Richard Cobden to Henry Ashworth, April 12, 1842, *The Letters of Richard Cobden*, Volume I, Anthony Howe, ed. (New York, NY: Oxford University Press, 2007), 267; and Hinsley, *Power and the Pursuit of Peace*, 97.

34. 12 Parl. Deb. (Third Series) (1832) col. 661.

the force of example alone. Hume's colleague Maurice O'Connell argued that the Reform Act would compel France's "unpopular monarch . . . to sympathize with the feelings" of his citizens and subsequently show greater respect for democratic values.[35]

If liberty could spread without the use of force, the Radicals also insisted that force could do little to spread liberty. For this reason, the British government had no business meddling in the affairs of other countries, however worthy the cause or lofty the moral principle. For one thing, it lacked the wherewithal to reorder the world in its image. "Are we armed with the powers of Omnipotence?" Cobden asked. For another, the British government had no moral right to make the attempt. The injustices apparent everywhere in Britain itself demonstrated that the country lacked "the virtue and the wisdom essential to the possession of supreme power," he said. As his fellow Radical John Bright put it in the early days of the Crimean War, the country could not afford to behave like "the knight-errant of the human race."[36]

Nor should governments—even democratic ones—collaborate to preserve peace. Instead, they should let private citizens and businesses take the lead. "The progress of freedom depends more upon the maintenance of peace, the spread of commerce, and the diffusion of education, than upon the labours of cabinets and foreign offices," Cobden told the House of Commons. He distilled his views into a slogan: "As little intercourse as possible betwixt the governments, as much connection as possible between the nations of the world." This approach reduced foreign policy to a catalog of missteps that governments ought to avoid.[37]

Prime Minister William Gladstone, the dominant figure of nineteenth-century British liberalism, had a complex relationship with the Radical tradition. Like Cobden and Bright, he prioritized democratic rule and demanded that the government defer to public opinion in foreign policy. Furthermore, Gladstone echoed their criticism of excessive military spending, and denounced secret diplomacy. British foreign policy "should always be inspired by the love of freedom" and should endeavor to preserve "the blessings of peace" for all people and all states, he told an audience in 1879. It should respect the

---

35. 13 Parl. Deb. (Third Series) (1832) col. 1138.

36. 132 Parl. Deb. (Third Series) (1854) col. 262.

37. Speech to the House of Commons, June 28, 1850, *Speeches on Questions of Public Policy by Richard Cobden, MP*, Volume II, John Bright and James E. Thorold Rogers, eds. (London: Macmillan, 1870) 228.; and Cobden, *Russia*, 33.

equal rights of all countries. It should minimize the burdens imposed on British power, and avoid unnecessary commitments abroad. Unlike the Radicals, however, Gladstone believed that Britain should maintain the Concert of Europe so as to "fetter and bind up" each power's selfish goals, keep "common action" focused on "common objects," and prevent great-power conflict. He also accepted that wars were "among the necessities of our condition," and that states must not "shrink from the responsibility of undertaking them" when necessary. If states refused to use force, they stood no chance of upholding international law or the Concert's decisions.[38]

During his many years as prime minister, the course of events raised questions about how to implement these axioms. In 1870, Gladstone resolved to avoid military involvement in the Franco-Prussian War, but wanted to mediate a diplomatic settlement. Britain should pursue "a secured neutrality, a neutrality backed and sustained by an adequate condition of defensive establishments," he said. This approach would provide both the "moral authority" to uphold international law and also hasten a peace agreement. He demanded that both sides respect Belgian neutrality, a principle that the Concert of Europe had laid down in 1839, and backed this demand with the threat of force. In response, the French and Prussians signed a treaty promising to stay out of Belgium. The French army's collapse, however, frustrated Gladstone's hope of defending self-determination. When Prussia made clear that it intended to annex Alsace and Lorraine, the prime minister objected that territory should not change hands without consulting its inhabitants. Gladstone had hoped to rally a European coalition to press this claim, but his cabinet colleagues forced him to abandon it. In the absence of a serious threat to use force, they reasoned, diplomatic appeals would not change the Prussian position. Britain should not waste its prestige on a futile effort to vindicate a moral principle.[39]

After defeating Gladstone in the 1874 election, Conservative Prime Minister Benjamin Disraeli prioritized geopolitical calculation over self-determination. When nationalist uprisings erupted in the Ottoman Empire in 1875–76, Disraeli showed little sympathy for the rebels' efforts to liberate themselves. He

38. A.J.P. Taylor, *The Trouble Makers: Dissent over Foreign Policy, 1792–1939* (London: Pimlico, 1993), 69–70 and 84; and "Extract from Gladstone's Third Midlothian Campaign Speech, November 27, 1879," Bourne, ed., 420–22.

39. Richard Shannon, *Gladstone*, Volume II (Chapel Hill, NC: University of North Carolina Press, 1999), 87–89.

dismissed reports of Turkish atrocities in Bulgaria as "inventions" and "coffee-house babble," and resolved to stand by the Sultan. To complicate matters further, influential voices in Russia were pressing Tsar Alexander II to use force to help fellow Slavs. Disraeli feared two possible outcomes. If the Russians intervened to help the Bulgarians, the Ottoman Empire might collapse, creating a power vacuum in the eastern Mediterranean that officials in St. Petersburg would rush to fill. Alternatively, the intervention could draw in the other great powers and set off "another Thirty Years War," he warned. Either outcome would damage British interests. It was far preferable to stand aloof from the conflict and to deter the Russians from acting too. Great-power peace and Britain's strategic interests trumped humanitarian considerations.[40]

From the opposition benches, Gladstone bitterly denounced both the Ottoman Empire and Disraeli's support for it. Seeing the crisis as an opportunity to stand up for moral principle and revive his own political fortunes, Gladstone dashed off a pamphlet, which became a best-seller. The Ottomans were committing "crimes and outrages, so vast in scale as to exceed all modern example," he wrote. Meanwhile, the British government ignored "the broad and deep interests of humanity," preferring to "keep out of sight what was disagreeable and might be inconvenient." The country now had to rally the great powers to evict the Turks from Bulgaria. In contrast with Disraeli's concerns about tsarist expansion, Gladstone denied that Russian policy was "governed by aggressive or selfish views." Besides, if Britain failed to rescue the Bulgarians, they would have even more reason to look to St. Petersburg for help.[41]

This call to action brought several of Gladstone's core principles into conflict. The crisis forced him to choose between his commitment to international law, which demanded respect for Ottoman sovereignty, and his belief in self-determination and the Concert of Europe, which required (and would enable) military intervention. "There are states of affairs, in which human sympathy refuses to be confined by the rules, necessarily limited and conventional, of international law," he wrote. It also led him to support one autocracy in the hope of reining in another. Decades earlier, British Radicals had routinely backed the Ottomans against the Russians, on the grounds that tsarism posed a greater threat to liberty in Europe. Gladstone now reversed that logic, provoking

40. Gary Bass, *Freedom's Battle: The Origins of Humanitarian Intervention* (New York, NY: Knopf, 2008), 261–62 and 265.

41. William Gladstone, *Bulgarian Horrors and the Question of the East* (London: John Murray, 1876), 9, 11–12, and 31.

a rift with Parliament's leading Cobdenites, who would not countenance a war, even one waged on high principle and in the name of liberty. When Gladstone presented resolutions condemning Turkey and demanding joint action with Russia, they voted against him, as did a majority of MPs.[42]

Disraeli got his way, but at the expense of his own career. After pressing the Turks to halt their operations in Bulgaria, he urged the Russians to stop their preparations for war, but they ignored him. After the tsar declared war in April 1877, his forces advanced rapidly. Fearing that Constantinople itself might fall, Disraeli took a risk. He sent a Royal Navy fleet to the Dardanelles, and warned the tsar that Britain would enter the conflict if Russia seized the Turkish capital. The threat persuaded the tsar to stop. At the Congress of Berlin, the Russians abandoned their plan to establish a sprawling independent Bulgaria, which would project their power to the shores of the Aegean. They settled instead for a smaller state, autonomous but still within the Ottoman Empire. The result satisfied neither Gladstone nor the thousands of voters who had rallied to the Bulgarian cause. Gladstone prosecuted an unrelenting public campaign against Disraeli's foreign policy. Speaking before huge crowds, he denounced the prime minister's indifference to the fate of the Bulgarians and his failure to "fulfil those traditions of liberty which belong to the history of this country and the character of the people." In the 1880 election, Gladstone triumphed over his rival.[43]

This uncompromising approach to foreign policy yielded better results for Gladstone the campaigner than Gladstone the prime minister. Early in his new mandate, another revolt threatened the Ottoman Empire. After falling deeply into debt and defaulting on foreign loans, the Egyptian government accepted joint Franco-British control over its finances and slashed spending. In 1879, the khedive's austerity measures, combined with its deference to European demands, inspired a revolt by senior army officers. Within two years, their leader, Colonel Arabi, had sidelined the khedive and threatened to tear down the structures that gave France and Britain so much influence in Cairo. By endangering the route to India and threatening to wipe out foreign investments in Egypt, the crisis posed geopolitical and financial risks for Britain. It also forced Gladstone to grapple with the tensions inherent in his strategy.[44]

42. Shannon, *Gladstone*, 25; and Taylor, *Trouble Makers*, 45 and 82–83.

43. Bass, *Freedom's Battle*, 309.

44. Ronald Robinson and John Gallagher with Alice Denny, *Africa and the Victorians: The Climax of Imperialism in the Dark Continent* (New York, NY: St. Martin's Press, 1961), 76–89.

In keeping with his principles, the prime minister sought a peaceful solution, but the complexities of the situation frustrated his hopes. On the one hand, Gladstone had long sympathized with nationalist demands for self-determination and long opposed the expansion of the British empire. He had no desire to use force. On the other hand, he resolved to work with France and, if possible, the rest of the Concert of Europe. The goal of British policy, Gladstone said, was to defend "all established rights in Egypt, whether they be those of the Sultan, those of the Khedive, those of the people of Egypt, or those of the foreign bondholders."[45]

As the crisis escalated, Gladstone's priorities pulled him in opposite directions. When the French government insisted on threatening Arabi with military action, Gladstone reluctantly agreed to send a joint fleet to Alexandria. Rather than cowing the Egyptian nationalists, however, the ships' arrival provoked riots that killed dozens of European expatriates. The great powers met in Constantinople to discuss the situation, but failed to reach agreement, dashing Gladstone's hopes for a collective response. When the French lost their nerve and recalled their ships, the British government faced a choice between withdrawal and unilateral escalation. Under pressure from the more hawkish members of his government, Gladstone opted for the latter, prompting John Bright to resign from the cabinet in protest. In rapid succession, a naval bombardment led to a ground invasion, Arabi's capture, and the installation of a British agent-general in Cairo. The military success proved a strategic defeat for Gladstone's approach to foreign affairs. He vindicated the status quo and international order by sacrificing his commitments to freedom, self-determination, and the European Concert. He purchased stability at the cost of principle.[46]

V

In his youth, Woodrow Wilson hung a portrait of Gladstone above his desk and called him "the greatest statesman that ever lived," so it is unsurprising that, when he became president of the United States, his approach to foreign affairs resembled that of the Grand Old Man.[47] Wilson started from the conviction that peace depended on the spread of democracy. "If democracy fulfills the best and most characteristic of its promises," he wrote in 1885, "its coming will be

45. 270 Parl. Deb. (Third Series) (1882) col. 1146.
46. Robinson, Gallagher, and Denny, *Africa and the Victorians*, 94–121.
47. A. Scott Berg, *Wilson* (New York, NY: Berkley, 2003), 43.

the establishment of the most humane results of the world's peace and progress, [and] the substitution of agreement for command."[48] More than thirty years later, in asking Congress to declare war on Germany, Wilson placed this theme at the center of his appeal. Whereas autocracies pursue selfish goals instead of the common good, democracies "prefer the interests of mankind to any narrow interest of their own." For this reason, he said, a "steadfast concert for peace can never be maintained except by a partnership of democratic nations," who would "bring peace and safety to all nations and make the world itself at last free."[49]

Democracy, in turn, required national unity and self-determination. No system of self-government could function unless its citizens understood themselves to belong to a single people. Without that awareness, "they can form no common judgment; they can conceive no common end; they can contrive no common measure," Wilson argued.[50] By the same token, no government, whether democratic or otherwise, had the right to rule a foreign people. In 1919, he indicted the defeated imperial powers for doing just that. The solution, Wilson said, was to give the "suffering peoples" control over the territory they inhabited, and to tell them, "The land always should have been yours; it is now yours, and you can govern it as you please."[51] This tidy logic concealed a messy problem, however, as Wilson's secretary of state, Robert Lansing, pointed out. "When the President talks of 'self-determination' what unit has he in mind? Does he mean a race, a territorial area, or a community?" By his own admission, Wilson found it difficult to answer.[52]

Notwithstanding this conceptual difficulty, when Wilson arrived in the White House, he brought with him the conviction that democracy would take root slowly but inexorably worldwide. Like Kant, Wilson believed that human reason provided the engine of progress. "Ever since the rise of popular education in the last century has assured a thinking weight of the masses everywhere, the advance of democratic opinion and the spread of democratic institutions has been most marked and most significant," he wrote in 1889. "Democracy seems

---

48. Tony Smith, *Why Wilson Matters: The Origin of American Liberal Internationalism and Its Crisis Today* (Princeton, NJ: Princeton University Press, 2017), 68.

49. "Special Message Advising that Germany's Course Be Declared War," April 2, 1917, *The Messages and Papers of Woodrow Wilson*, Volume I, Albert Shaw, ed. (New York, NY: Review of Reviews, 1924), 379, 383.

50. Smith, *Why Wilson Matters*, 49.

51. Smith, *Why Wilson Matters*, 104.

52. Lansing as quoted in Margaret MacMillan, *Paris 1919: Six Months that Changed the World* (New York, NY: Random House, 2003), 11.

about universally to prevail." The United States could provide a model for the rest of the world to emulate, but it could not export self-government. "No result of value can ever be reached in politics except through slow and gradual development, the careful adaptations and nice modifications of growth. Nothing may be done by leaps." Each people had to develop the habits of democracy on its own, according to its own timetable.[53]

Just as citizens had to transform their societies in the name of democracy, governments had to transform the international system in the name of peace. Wilson rejected the idea that states could preserve order through calculations of power, with "one great force balanced against another great force." Instead, he proposed establishing a new order based on justice and the rule of law. States would build "a community of power," abandoning their "organized rivalries" in favor of "an organized common peace."[54]

In articulating this vision, Wilson drew on the efforts of previous administrations. During the late nineteenth century, the United States and Britain had settled several territorial and commercial disputes by legal arbitration. In 1897, they signed a permanent arbitration treaty, pledging to use this method to deal with any problems that they could not solve diplomatically. A decade later, Secretary of State Elihu Root tried to expand this mechanism to include American relations with Latin America, and invested considerable energy in trying to build a more robust system of international law. Inspired by these ideas, Wilson sought to incorporate them in the very foundations of the international system.[55]

Despite the force of his convictions, Wilson remained uncertain about how to translate them into policy. He believed that the United States had a preeminent role to play in international affairs, but he lacked a clear idea about how to bring its growing influence to bear. He authorized repeated military interventions in Latin America, sending troops into Mexico, Haiti, and the Dominican Republic. Wilson did not argue that the United States would export democracy to these countries, since no such thing was possible. Rather, he hoped to establish the conditions, especially public order, that were necessary for democracy to grow. Because the United States understood those conditions and had the means to act, it had a duty "to suffer neither our own people nor the citizens or governments of other countries . . . to violate them or render them impossible

53. Smith, *Why Wilson Matters*, 62 and 68.

54. Smith, *Why Wilson Matters*, 98.

55. G. John Ikenberry, *A World Safe for Democracy: Liberal Internationalism and the Crises of Global Order* (New Haven, CT: Yale University Press, 2020), 108–15.

of realization." Yet these interventions did little to improve the lives of the citizens they touched, or to improve the prospects for democracy and self-determination in any of the three countries.[56]

The First World War cast doubt on Wilson's faith in the inevitable progress of reason and the triumph of democracy. Nevertheless, he resolved to use the conflict to save a world that could no longer save itself.[57] His Fourteen Points, which Gladstone would have recognized, illustrated his ambitions. For almost three years, Wilson had insisted that the United States should stay out of the conflict in the hope of mediating a peace settlement, but in 1917, he decided to bring the full measure of American power to bear in an effort to remake the world in the image of American principles. Wilson's promises—including national self-determination, unfettered commerce, open diplomacy, and a "general association of nations" to guarantee "political independence and territorial integrity"—inspired people across Europe and far beyond. The United States had made a categorical commitment to these principles, Wilson said. "There can be no compromise. No halfway decision would be tolerable. No halfway decision is conceivable," he declared.[58]

At the Paris Peace Conference, however, the tensions inherent in Wilson's strategy became apparent. Despite the president's erstwhile certainty that each nation had to seize liberty for itself, and that democracy had to evolve slowly, the victorious allies now set about reconfiguring central Europe. They carved the Habsburgs' multiethnic empire up into a clutch of independent states, some brand new, others reborn after centuries of foreign rule. Setting aside the difficulty of drawing sharp lines between one ethnic group and another, this approach assumed that the massive application of military force by foreign powers could bestow freedom on previously subjugated peoples, and that, in the extraordinary circumstances that the war had created, new democracies could be born in a matter of months.[59]

The plans for the postwar settlement illustrated a similar ambivalence about the utility of force. During the negotiations, when French Prime Minister

---

56. George C. Herring, *From Colony to Superpower: U.S. Foreign Relations since 1776* (New York, NY: Oxford University Press, 2008), 388–96. Quotation from Smith, *Why Wilson Matters*, 79.

57. Ikenberry, *A World Safe for Democracy*, 123–24.

58. "Address of President Wilson Delivered at Mount Vernon," July 4, 1918, *Foreign Relations of the United States, 1918*, Supplement 1, Volume I (Washington, DC: US Government Printing Office, 1933), Document 206.

59. MacMillan, *Paris 1919*, 109–35 and 207–70.

Georges Clemenceau demanded harsh terms for Germany in order to handicap its future strength, Wilson warned him not to make "excessive demands," lest he "sow the seed of war." British Prime Minister David Lloyd George shared the president's view. After a bitter argument, the men struck a compromise deal. They agreed to cap the size of Germany's armed forces, extract an unprecedented sum in reparations payments, subject the Rhineland to foreign military occupation, and seize the country's overseas colonies. Writing these terms into the treaty was one thing, but making them stick was a different matter entirely.[60]

Wilson conceived the League of Nations as the vehicle for his ideas of collective security and the rule of international law, but he held conflicting views about how the organization would enforce these principles. The League Covenant bound its signatories to "respect and preserve as against external aggression the territorial integrity and existing political independence of all Members," but it did not compel them to take any specific action to this end. Wilson himself was reluctant to impose concrete obligations on League members, especially obligations involving a response to aggression with force, because he did not want to infringe any state's sovereign prerogatives. But he also believed that, over time, skeptical members would come to see the wisdom of collective security. They would slowly develop methods to keep the peace by "precedents" and "custom," much as the common law had emerged.[61]

Likewise, Wilson believed that the workings of the League would engender a new diplomatic culture, one in which states would show greater respect for the rule of law and self-government. In turn, the spread of these principles would put peace on a more secure footing, regardless of the military balance.[62] This faith in gradualism fit with Wilson's ideas about democratic development, but it sat uneasily with his reasons for entering the war in the first place, when he had concluded that only the application of immediate and overpowering force could save civilization.

VI

Woodrow Wilson inherited and enriched a long liberal tradition of seeking to transform international politics through the application of reason and human will. His track record and his legacy—especially the ultimate failure of the

60. Quotation from Smith, *Why Wilson Matters*, 119. See also MacMillan, *Paris 1919*, 157–203.
61. Ikenberry, *A World Safe for Democracy*, 131–32.
62. Smith, *Why Wilson Matters*, 124–25.

League of Nations, the structure in which he had invested so much energy—speak to the tradition's power, but they also underscore its inherent dilemmas. Like Kant, Paine, Brissot, Mazzini, Cobden, and Gladstone before him, Wilson believed in the possibility of abolishing war in favor of lasting peace. Like them, he believed that the spread of liberty and self-determination and the development of international society would make that ambition a reality.

The practice of liberal grand strategy between the late eighteenth and early twentieth centuries illustrates its internal tensions. Liberal thinkers and leaders wanted to abolish war, but they could not reach consensus about what role military force should play in the pursuit of that goal. Some eschewed the use of violence, either categorically or in all but the most extreme cases. Others regarded force as an essential tool, accepting short-term compromises for the sake of their long-term objective. The catalog of their successes and failures offers few clear lessons, and cannot resolve the enduring conflict between Kant's and Paine's approaches. It does emphasize, however, the danger of going too far in either direction. Neither pacifism nor militancy seems likely to bear much fruit. This history also offers an enduring reminder of the imperative of thinking clearly about the relationship between ends and means, which remains at the heart of the strategic enterprise.

CHAPTER 9

Alexander Hamilton and the Financial Sinews of Strategy

James Lacey

On September 2, 1781, under a scorching heat, 4,000 tattered, mostly unshod, and angry soldiers of the Continental Army marched into Philadelphia. The march from New York had been exhausting, and few soldiers were looking forward to continuing to march away from their homes to carry the war into the pestilence-ridden southern colonies. But what truly angered them was the knowledge that a large amount of silver had arrived from France and that all of it had gone to government creditors, and none of it to the army, which had had not been paid in months. Even the payment of paper money—the infamous "continentals"—was suspended after runaway inflation made them worthless. There had already been serious trouble over this issue when, in January 1781, regiments from Pennsylvania and New Jersey mutinied and threatened to march on Philadelphia to force the Continental Congress to meet their demands. Back pay was only one of their motives, but it was a crucial one. A combination of prudent concessions and the execution of a limited number of ringleaders sufficed to end the immediate problem. But even as new demands were placed on the army, pay was still not forthcoming and mutinous mutterings were again stalking the army.

Now, that threadbare army was in and near Philadelphia. It was not yet threatening Congress or the property of the city's rich inhabitants, but increasing numbers of soldiers were refusing to march further. Moreover, the soldiers were demanding their pay in specie—gold or silver—and not in worthless paper. Repeatedly, Washington begged Congress for help, writing to Robert Morris, the newly appointed Superintendent of Finance, in August:

> I must entreat you if possible to procure one months [*sic*] pay in specie for the detachment which I have under my command part of those troops have not been paid anything for a very long time past, and have upon several occasions shewn marks of great discontent.[1]

But Congress was bankrupt and Morris, who had been financing much of war's costs with his own money and personal credit, had nothing left to give. The great financial crisis of the war was at hand. Washington had seen it coming, writing to Joseph Reed, in May 1780, "In modern Wars the longest purse must chiefly determine the event—I fear that of the enemy will be found to be so."[2] Despite his foresight, the commanding general was powerless to reverse the slide into national insolvency.

Thankfully, Admiral Francois Joseph Paul, *comte* de Grasse had come north, with a French fleet and 3,000 reinforcing soldiers. Just as crucially, he had also brought barrels of silver raised by the citizens of Havana in less than six hours. Hat in hand, Robert Morris made a deal directly with the French commanding general in America, General Jean-Baptiste Rochambeau to secure a loan of 1.2 million livres of silver. Morris then ordered John Pierce, paymaster-general of the Continental Army, to pay the army and to make a spectacle of the event. As disgruntled soldiers approached, Pierce broke open one of the casks, dumped it over, and let the silver fall to the ground. As Joseph Plumb Martin remembered, "We each of us received a MONTH'S PAY in specie . . . This was the first that could be called money, which we had received as wages since the year '76, or that we ever did receive till the close of the war, or indeed, ever after, as wages."[3]

1. From George Washington to Robert Morris, August 27, 1781, *Founders Online,* National Archives, https://founders.archives.gov/documents/Washington/99-01-02-06802. [This is an Early Access document from The Papers of George Washington. It is not an authoritative final version.]

2. "From George Washington to Joseph Reed, 28 May 1780," *Founders Online*, National Archives, https://founders.archives.gov/documents/Washington/03-26-02-0150. [Original source: *The Papers of George Washington*, Revolutionary War Series, Volume 26, *13 May–4 July 1780*, Benjamin L. Huggins and Adrina Garbooshian–Huggins, eds. (Charlottesville, VA: University of Virginia Press, 2018), 220–25.]

3. Joseph Plumb Martin, *Yankee Doodle Boy* (New York, NY: Holiday House, 1995), 155.

Satisfied, the army continued on to Yorktown, to besiege and capture a British field army in a battle that decided the war's outcome. Conspicuous for his bravery at Yorktown was Lieutenant Colonel Alexander Hamilton, who led the assault on Redoubt No. 10, the loss of which finally cracked British resistance. Hamilton, a long-serving aide to Washington, was a witness to the constant penury of the Continental Army, as well as Congress's incapacity to force the respective thirteen colonies to properly fund the war. He knew as well as anyone how close the Patriot cause came to ruin simply because of Britain's ability to financially outlast its opponents. If General Cornwallis had managed to escape from Yorktown, the war would likely have ended in Britain's favor, as the fledgling nation's coffers were empty. Without pay, Washington's army would have melted away.

I

Since the start of organized warfare, the crucial sinew of war had been "endless streams of money."[4] The ability to mobilize huge amounts of capital has always been the single most important factor in waging successful wars. And for two and a half millennia—since the Battle of Marathon—rulers have been in constant search for new sources of capital, and better methods of getting their hands on it—almost always for employment in waging wars. But only in the modern era did governments begin to comprehend and employ the alchemy of debt financing to fund their military ambitions. In doing so, they proved the essential correctness of Charles Tilly's observation that "war made the state and the state made war." For the waging of modern wars required sums of money so vast that it required rulers to build effective central administrative apparatuses capable of collecting such funds and then efficiently managing their use. War, which has always been the dominate concern of every modern state, therefore, provided the catalyst for improving every state's administrative capacity, which was then employed to raise unprecedented amounts of revenue.

Over the centuries, the capacity of states to raise revenue for war grew so that it outstripped even the vast material bounty of the Industrial Revolution. As the world descended into the two cataclysmic conflicts of the twentieth

---

4. M. Tullius Cicero, *The Orations of Marcus Tullius Cicero*, trans. C. D. Yonge (London, 1903), 95. This quote may be an adaptation of the original, "First of all the sinews of war is money in abundance."

century, money was barely a concern of the major belligerents, as production capacity and manpower were exhausted long before the wherewithal to pay for them. Only when a state exhausted its production base and had to purchase munitions from other nations did finance become a crucial determinant of military strategy. The institutions required to implement this massive shift of money, so crucial to a state's grand and military strategies, first begun in the Dutch and British Financial Revolutions, were first implemented in the United States through the farsightedness and determination of Alexander Hamilton. What he bequeathed to the nation became the edifice upon which the United States built it financial, industrial, and military power.

Hamilton, an orphan and recent immigrant from the Caribbean, was recognized early on as possessing a first-rate mind, which caused a group of local businessmen to pay his expenses to New York so that he might continue his education, while also representing their trading interests. For a time, he was enrolled in King's College, but gave up his studies to form an artillery battery that was soon placed at the service of the Continental Army. Hamilton distinguished himself in the fighting around New York City, and particularly during Washington's Christmas offensive at Trenton and Princeton. He then spent the next four years as Washington's aide before receiving a battalion command at Yorktown. During the war Hamilton married the rich and socially connected Elizabeth Schuyler, a marriage that immediately promoted Hamilton into society's upper ranks. After the war, Hamilton practiced law and was instrumental—through his contributions to the Federalist Papers and the employment of his many political connections—in ensuring ratification of the American Constitution.

As his contributions to the Federalist Papers make clear, Hamilton was dismayed at the continuing anarchic state of Confederation government and was particularly appalled by the federal government's inability to get its financial house in order. In his writings, Hamilton put on display all of the psychic scars inflicted by the poverty that plagued the Revolution, as he made the case for a strong central power capable of putting America's fiscal house in order. How to accomplish this huge task was something Hamilton had already put much thought into, even as the war raged. In a series of three letters written in the months before Yorktown Hamilton set forth his ideas on how states could best finance themselves.

In his first undated letter, probably sent to Robert Morris in late 1779 or early 1780, Hamilton recognized the most practical method of funding the Revolution was through a foreign loan. He wrote, "The most opulent states of

Europe in a war of any duration are commonly obliged to have recourse to foreign loans or subsidies. How then could we expect to do without them[?]."[5] Hamilton then set forth his still forming ideas for a national bank—partially financed by a foreign loan—tasked to provide a stable currency to replace the rapidly depreciating continental dollars, as well as with providing loans to cover the cost of the war. In effect, Hamilton outlined the foundational structure of a modern state financial system.

In a second letter, this time to James Duane, one of New York's delegates to the Continental Congress, Hamilton identified the key to making any system of government finance and public credit possible—the power of the purse:

> The confederation too gives the power of the purse too intirely [sic] to the state legislatures. It should provide perpetual funds in the disposal of Congress—by a land tax, poll tax, or the like. All imposts upon commerce ought to be laid by Congress and appropriated to their use, for *without certain revenues, a government can have no power; that power, which holds the purse strings absolutely, must rule.* This seems to be a medium, which without making Congress altogether independent will tend to give reality to its authority.[6]

In the same letter, Hamilton further discussed the needs for a foreign loan, and the necessity for Congress to have the power to establish enforceable taxes that would underpin a national system of public credit.

Finally, in a letter to Robert Morris in April 1781, we see Hamilton's maturing ideas, starting with the crucial point that American independence rested upon "introducing order into our finances—by restoring public credit—not by gaining battles."[7] After a long discourse on how the continuing struggle could be funded, Hamilton turned to the future and laid out his recommendations for the creation of a national bank. Although Hamilton noted the danger

5. "From Alexander Hamilton to———, [December–March 1779–1780]," *Founders Online*, National Archives, https://founders.archives.gov/documents/Hamilton/01-02-02-0559-0002. [Original source: *The Papers of Alexander Hamilton*, Volume 2, *1779–1781*, Harold C. Syrett, ed. (New York, NY: Columbia University Press, 1961), 236–51.].

6. Emphasis added. Alexander Hamilton to James Duane, September 3, 1780, *Founders Online*, National Archives, https://founders.archives.gov/documents/Hamilton/01-02-02-0838, originally found in Syrett, ed., *Papers of Alexander Hamilton*, Volume 2, 400–18.

7. Hamilton to Robert Morris, April 30, 1781, *Founders Online*, National Archives, https://founders.archives.gov/documents/Hamilton/01-02-02-1167, originally found in Syrett, ed., *Papers of Alexander Hamilton*, Volume 2, 604–35.

of a national bank—that it could become the object of abuse—he believed the benefits of such an institution far outweighed the risks:

> The tendency of a national bank is to increase public and private credit. The former gives power to the state for the protection of its rights and interests, and the latter facilitates and extends the operations of commerce among individuals. Industry is increased, commodities are multiplied, agriculture and manufactures flourish, and herein consist the true wealth and prosperity of a state.
>
> Most commercial nations have found it necessary to institute banks and they have proved to be the happiest engines, that ever were invented for advancing trade.[8]

Hamilton concluded the letter with one of his most oft quoted comments:

> A national debt if it is not excessive will be to us a national blessing; it will be powerful cement of our union. It will also create a necessity for keeping up taxation to a degree which without being oppressive, will be a spur to industry.[9]

Hamilton was preaching to the converted, as Morris, with his business partner Thomas Willing, soon thereafter received the first Congressional banking charter, for the Bank of North America, which opened in Philadelphia in 1782. It was later chartered by Pennsylvania, removing it from consideration as a national bank under the Constitution. In the meantime, the bank provided loans of approximately $1.25 million which funded much of the war effort from Yorktown until the British departure from New York in November 1783.

Grasping the need to convince the general population of his ideas, Hamilton produced them in a more comprehendible form in a series of six essays, titled *The Continentalist*, published in the *New York Packet* between 1781 and 1782.[10] Many of these same arguments would emerge again later in the more widely circulated *Federalist Papers*. In these earlier essays, particularly the final three, Hamilton detailed his thoughts on how finance and economic growth underpinned state power, touching on almost every element of the financial system that remains the core of today's modern fiscal state.

---

8. Hamilton to Morris, April 30, 1781.

9. Hamilton to Morris, April 30, 1781.

10. For copies of each of these six essays see Syrett, ed., *Papers of Alexander Hamilton*, Volume 2, 649–74.

After the Constitution's ratification, Hamilton, Washington's choice as the nation's first secretary of the treasury, had the opportunity to put his ideas into action. After being approved in the position on September 11, 1789, Hamilton went right to work, securing two bank loans to cover government expenses until tax revenue started to come in. Later that same month, Congress asked for a full report on the state of the national debt and the means by which it could be repaid. Hamilton delivered his answer—*Report Relative to a Provision for the Support of Public Credit*—in early January 1790.[11] It was the first of two reports whose arguments underpinned a financial and commercial revolution in the United States.

Hamilton's report placed the total national debt, including arrears, at just north of $54 million dollars, which he listed in two broad categories—foreign and national. America owed $11.7 million to foreign lenders and a little over $42 million to domestic creditors. But those were just the debts incurred by Congress. The individual states had also incurred debts to the tune of $25 million, which Hamilton believed should be assumed by the federal government. The grand total was over $79 million, which represented over forty percent of the nation's Gross Domestic Product (GDP) in 1790.[12] That number may not seem frightening to modern readers, who are increasingly accustomed to state debts exceeding one hundred percent of GDP. It was, however, an appalling prospect for a government already in default on all its debts, without a national currency, and still devoid of an interstate banking system or regular securities markets.[13] Moreover, it would take time to install a federal revenue system capable of collecting sufficient funds to keep the government afloat and make even minimal payments on the debt. In fact, the US Treasury raised only slightly more than $162,000 in customs duties in 1789, meaning the total national debt was approximately five hundred times the nation's tax revenues.

According to Hamilton's report, the interest payments on this total debt load would be $549,599.66 on the foreign debt and $4,044,845.15 on the

11. Report Relative to a Provision for the Support of Public Credit, January 9,`1790, *Founders Online*, National Archives, https://founders.archives.gov/documents/Hamilton/01-06-02 -0076-0002-0001. [Original source: *The Papers of Alexander Hamilton*, Volume 6, *December 1789–August 1790*, Harold C. Syrett, ed. (New York, NY: Columbia University Press, 1962), 65–110.]

12. Louis Johnston and Samuel H. Williamson, *What Was the U.S. GDP Then?*, MeasuringWorth 2022, https://www.measuringworth.com/datasets/usgdp/.

13. Richard Sylla, "Financial Foundations: Public Credit, the National Bank, and Securities Markets," in *Founding Choices: American Economic Policy in the 1790s*, Douglas A. Irwin and Richard Sylla, eds. (Chicago, IL: University of Chicago Press, 2011), 59.

domestic debt. As Hamilton placed the operating costs of the US Government at approximately $600,000, interest payments alone would be more than seven times the cost of everything else in the government budget combined. To make this debt manageable, Hamilton proposed that the interest and principal due foreign creditors be paid in full, but advocated for refloating the domestic debt at four percent instead of its current six percent. Hamilton believed that most domestic creditors would accept this reduced interest rate—a "haircut" in financial parlance—in return for assured dividends paid on a regular schedule. By reducing the interest rates to four percent, Hamilton cut the annual expenditure for debt service to a more manageable $2.7 million, an immediate annual savings of $1.3 million. Hamilton also proposed the creation of a "sinking fund" that would apply excess government funds toward the purchase of the debt, until the entire debt had been extinguished.

While Hamilton was able to see the immediate and long-term impacts of his plan, they were invisible to many others. By paying foreigner creditors in full, Hamilton transformed a bankrupt United States into the world's best credit risk. Only a few years after the Revolution, America could borrow on Amsterdam's debt markets at less interest than what Great Britain was paying. By assuming all of the nation's debt and then reissuing new loans with assured regular payments, Hamilton also created the equivalent of a paper currency that added hugely to the nation's overall capital. At the time, many believed government loans destroyed a nation's capital, by removing cash from the economy. But Hamilton saw that the bonds could circulate as currency, helping to grow a specie-starved American economy. As his report stated:

> It is a well known fact, that in countries in which the national debt is properly funded, and an object of established confidence, it answers most of the purposes of money. Transfers of stock or public debt are there equivalent to payments in specie; or in other words, stock, in the principal transactions of business, passes current as specie.[14]

As long as the debt was securely funded, Hamilton recognized, it could act in the economy the same way as silver or gold. In the form of bonds, debt would be tradable and persons would accept government paper bonds in return for services and goods. Moreover, as the banking system developed, banks would feel safe holding bonds as part of their capital reserves, which in a fractional banking system allowed those banks to make commercial loans in

14. "Report Relative to a Provision for the Support of Public Credit."

multiples of their capital. These loans, in turn, would also be tradable, creating a virtuous cycle—some call financial alchemy—where the amount of capital available to fund investment grew in lockstep with the growth of the economy. For a specie-starved American economy, the securely funded US national debt was a godsend. The system was, of course, prone to both overheating and collapse, as it remains today, but by making the debt callable, Hamilton had established the rudiments of what we today call open-market operations, which allow the government to rapidly withdraw or add liquidity to the economy based on the situation. Yet Hamilton also issued a warning about the misuse of the public debts.

> But these good effects of a public debt are only to be looked for, when, by being well funded, it has acquired an *adequate* and *stable* value. Till then, it has rather a contrary tendency. The fluctuation and insecurity incident to it in an unfunded state, render it a mere commodity, and a precarious one. As such, being only an object of occasional and particular speculation, all the money applied to it is so much diverted from the more useful channels of circulation, for which the thing itself affords no substitute.[15]

In other words, an unfunded debt, or one the markets deemed beyond the government's ability to pay off would lead to a crisis of confidence that would make the debt impossible to sustain and wreak havoc, first in the financial markets and immediately thereafter in the wider economy.

The debate over the report—particularly the assumption of state debts and how to fund the debt—was prolonged and brutal. The southern states were mostly opposed to assumption, as their state debts were smaller than New England's and, in some cases, largely paid off. Congress was also concerned that speculators, who had bought up much of the debt when it was nearly worthless, would now enrich themselves at the expense of farmers and backwoodsmen if the debts were paid off at par. This, however, was part of Hamilton's plan, as by concentrating capital the hands of the rich, they would be more inclined to make commercial investments that would grow the overall economy. Surprisingly, James Madison, who, along with Hamilton, had been one of most prolific writers of the Federalist Papers advocating for a strong central government, was leading the opposition. But as an elected official, Madison deemed it prudent to argue for the position of his home state—Virginia—despite his personal beliefs. And Virginians were largely opposed to Hamilton's plans—until Hamilton agreed to use his influence to place the

---

15. "Report Relative to a Provision for the Support of Public Credit." Emphasis in original.

national capitol on the Potomac River, near Virginia, in return for their ceasing to oppose his financial program.

Most of Hamilton's program would likely have been adopted in any event, as almost everyone at the time understood the importance of creating and sustaining the public credit of the nation on good terms. President Washington, in a letter written during the Revolution acknowledged the importance of public credit to Britain's capacity to wage war:

> I fear that of the enemy will be found to be so—though the Government is deeply in debt & of course poor, the nation is rich and their riches afford a fund which will not be easily exhausted. Besides, their system of public credit is such that it is capable of greater exertions than that of any other nation—Specialists have been a long time foretelling its downfall, but we see no Symptoms of the catastrophe being very near. I am persuaded it will at least last out the War, and then in the opinion of many of the best politicians it will be a national advantage.[16]

Washington clearly grasped the importance of public credit to waging war. Hamilton demonstrated the same awareness in his surviving letters and essays which continually reference the earlier Dutch and British financial revolutions. After absorbing these lessons, Hamilton took on the task of adapting them to America's peculiar situation and politics, and then establishing the institutional foundations and intellectual paradigm that allowed the United States to harness this revolution. To understand what Hamilton had wrought, we, therefore, must turn our attention to the Dutch and, particularly, the British experiences in debt management.

II

When, in 1648, the Treaty of Westphalia ended the Thirty Years' War, the Dutch, despite eighty years of continuous conflict with Spain and the Hapsburg Empire, emerged in an enviable financial position. Despite the need to fund a per-capita national debt that was a multiple of the bankrupted Hapsburgs and Bourbons,

---

16. George Washington to Joseph Reed, May 28, 1780, *Founders Online*, National Archives, https://founders.archives.gov/documents/Washington/03-26-02-0150. [Original source: *The Papers of George Washington*, Revolutionary War Series, Volume 26, *13 May–4 July 1780*, Benjamin L. Huggins and Adrina Garbooshian-Huggins, eds. (Charlottesville, VA: University of Virginia Press, 2018), 220–25.]

it ended the conflict as the only state in Europe with its credit intact. In fact, it was still capable of borrowing huge sums if it became necessary fund a new major conflict, as well as pay for their unprecedented global commercial expansion. The Dutch had been able to wear down and eventually defeat powers possessing twenty times their population for one reason: they could more efficiently draw financial resources out of their economy than any other state in Europe.

This was a consequence of several factors. First and foremost, the Dutch gained from a global economic expansion that gave them a near monopoly on goods imported from the Mughal Empire and East Asia into Europe. The resultant growing wealth was available for ever greater levels of taxation, which the Dutch Estates General was rarely hesitant to impose upon its citizens. And this was the crux of the matter. Creditors were loaning money to a state, through its representative body—the Estates General—and there was no king involved. Kings were known to be capricious when it came to repaying their debts, as demonstrated by Spain's Phillip II, who defaulted on loans four times during his wars with the Dutch. Although Phillip was never completely cut off from European credit markets, creditors were forced to take many precautions to protect themselves from default, including setting exorbitant interest rates on any new funds Phillip requested. Throughout the Eighty Years' War, the Spanish paid an average long-term interest rate of 7.6 percent, while the Dutch, even as their debt burdens reached extraordinary levels (given the size of their population) were funding their long-term debt at 2.5 percent—a third the cost of Spain.[17]

Historians have offered many reasons why Spain, with monopoly access to the New World's silver, was never able to get its financial house in order. But recent research has narrowed the cause down to one overarching variable:

> Spain's difficulties do not reflect the evils of an unconstrained executive and were more about the failure to build a consensually strong state—one where those paying taxes gained some degree of control over expenditure in exchange for massively higher contributions.[18]

The Dutch, on the other hand, funded their debt through over 65,000 individual investors, who, through their representatives in the Estates General, had a say, or at least believed they had a say, in how their taxes were employed. Moreover, in

---

17. Paul Schmelzing, *Eight Centuries of Global Real Rates, R-G, and The "Suprasecular Decline,"* *1311–2018* (London: Bank of England, January 2020).

18. Mauricio Drelichman and Hans-Joachim Voth, *Lending to the Borrower from Hell: Debt, Taxes, and Default in the Age of Philip II* (Princeton, NJ: Princeton University Press, 2014), 280.

Antwerp and Amsterdam, creditors had access to the world's most liquid securities markets, making it possible to easily employ their debt holdings as security for funding globe-spanning commercial enterprises. In short, the debt acted as currency and was employed to grow the economy that, in turn, funded the war. Despite its financial advantages, the war with Spain pushed the small Dutch state to the wall. Moreover, even after the war ended, borrowing levels remained as high as during wartime. This time, however, the loans were paying for the Dutch Golden Age and the growth of Dutch industry and commerce.

France's Louis XIV's acquisitive designs did not allow the Dutch much time to recover their financial equilibrium before they were, once again, plunged into war. From 1672 to 1714, the Dutch were engaged in a long series of financially draining wars that, by 1688, brought them near the breaking point. Holland's financial system, despite being hugely more efficient than France's, still found it impossible to match the resources of Europe's mightiest state. Salvation came in 1688 through England's Glorious Revolution, which tied the British and Dutch together in the person of William of Orange, or William III.

By bringing England's financial wherewithal into the struggle against France, Holland saved itself and doomed Louis XIV's ambitions. But before that could happen, Britain's financial institutions needed to reform along the Dutch model. Once prompted, England's system of state finance, guided by an increasingly politically dominant Parliament, evolved rapidly. The pressing need to finance unprecedented war expenditures led to a series of financial innovations that far surpassed those instituted by the Dutch, or any other European power. Hence, 1688 is also marked as the advent of a "financial revolution" that ushered in the era of modern finance. At first, these innovations primarily underwrote the cost of war, but later they were employed to build and utilize the accumulations of the capital that propelled the Industrial Revolution.

In his remarkable work, *The Financial Revolution*, P.G.M. Dickson explained the impact of the creation of England's system of public debt:

> More important even then alliances, however, was the system of public borrowing . . . which enabled England to spend on war out of all proportion to its tax revenue, and thus throw into the struggle with France and its allies the decisive margin of ships and men without which the resources previously committed might have been committed in vain.[19]

19. P.G.M. Dickson, *The Financial Revolution in England: A Study in the Development of Public Credit, 1688–1756* (New York, NY: Macmillan, 1967), 9.

Dickson's great error was in claiming that the development of the English credit system was forced upon the government because of the limitations of the English tax system. This, however, is the opposite of reality. While 1688 remains a watershed year in terms of state financial policy, the policy's foundations rested upon the previous three decades of changes to the country's revenue system. Starting with John Pym's excise tax in 1664, England almost continuously added a series of new revenue measures that stabilized the nation's income at much higher levels than previously. By the end of the Nine Year's War (1697), Englishmen were already paying per capita taxes nearly double those of France, allowing the British central government to gather twice the revenue it collected before the Glorious Revolution. Four decades later, Britain was collecting twice that much again to pay for the War of Austrian Succession, and then doubled its tax revenues one more time by the end of the American Revolution, a sixfold increase in tax revenue in under a century.

England was able to collect such a large percentage of the nation's revenues without causing major social disruptions for several reasons. The first, and probably most crucial, was that the taxes were generally seen by the majority of the population as fair. For instance, a series of excise taxes enacted in the second half of the seventeenth century struck every segment of society, generally in line with an individual's respective wealth. Moreover, unlike England's leading rival, France, there were no legal exceptions to taxes based on rank. Second, the administration of the revenue system became increasingly professional, as centrally appointed government officials, held accountable for the fair and honest application of tax laws through regular audits, proved far more efficient than the tax-farming system that preceded it and was still employed in France.

Despite the tremendous surge in revenues, the totals were only enough to pay a fraction of the cost of the era's conflicts; a simultaneous military revolution had hugely increased the size and cost of military forces. As wars were now fought on a continental—even global—scale, the cost, when compared to previous centuries, was astronomical. For a time, the English tried to make up the delta between revenues and costs with a number of short-term borrowing expedients. But as the interest on these loans edged toward fifteen percent, and the state's capacity to raise sufficient short-term funds eroded, Parliament explored the implementation of long-term loans.

In the second half the eighteenth century, Britain introduced long-term bonds, called Consols—consolidated stock—with no redemption date. As such, they paid out a specified interest rate indefinitely. This allowed Britain to consolidate almost all its high interest rate debt into a stock of long-term bonds (Consols) that paid significantly less interest. As the principal on these loans never came due, there was no requirement for the government to continuously roll over old loans, even as new debt was issued in ever increasing amounts. This innovation allowed British governments, during the crisis of war, to ignore the size of the debt and focus on managing the cost of annual interest payments.

British Consols all paid three percent interest, but their price was allowed to fluctuate based on demand. For instance, in the midst of the Napoleonic Wars, creditors might require five rather than three percent interest to allow for the risk of a negative outcome of the war. In this case, they could purchase £1,000 in Consols for £600, giving them a real return of five percent. Moreover, at the war's end, when interest rates returned to par (three percent), creditors would be able to sell their Consols on established financial markets at the full £1,000, thus giving investors a capital gain of over twenty percent. The cost, of course was that to raise £1,000 to pay for an ongoing war, the Exchequer, by issuing Consols at sixty percent of par, would need to add £1,670 to its total debt. Still, there was an expectation that government postwar revenue surpluses would reduce and eventually eliminate the overall debt. Thus, British governments were willing to undertake prolonged periods of massive borrowing. But, even after Napoleon's defeat, there was never really much action taken on reducing war term debts, which at the end of the Napoleonic Wars were, in total, close to Britain's overall debt in 1914—a century later. Still, by 1914 the debt equaled only thirty percent of GDP compared to over 250 percent in the years after the Battle of Waterloo. With no similar borrowing capacity, France and its allies were unable to match the volume of British borrowing except at ruinous and politically destabilizing interest rates.

This, however, raises the question—why did British creditors demand so little interest when it was by no means certain Britain would win any of its eighteenth- and nineteenth-century conflicts? As with the Dutch, the British were not lending to a king, they were lending to a nation. In the wake of Charles II's infamous Stop of the Exchequer Order in 1672, which bankrupted many of the nation's creditors, it became almost impossible for the crown to raise new funds at anything approaching affordable rates. Thus, Parliament increasingly assumed responsibility for issuing debt and raising funds to pay the cost of that debt. By the War of Spanish Succession, Parliament was fully in control of state finances. Ministers, such as Sidney Godolphin and Robert

Harley, did such an outstanding job putting the nation's financial house in order that, when Queen Anne tried to remove Godolphin from his position as First Lord of the Treasury, the Duke of Marlborough threatened to resign his command of Britain's armies if the minister was not retained. In the end, the record speaks for itself; once Parliament took charge of Britain's public debt, the nation never again defaulted.

Another major factor was the government's concerted effort to massively increase the number of creditors, thereby giving a larger percentage of the population a greater vested interest in the stability of the government and its finances. In little more than a generation, starting in 1710, the number of creditors increased sixfold from 10,000 to 60,000 and continued to grow throughout the Napoleonic Wars. This increase could not have been accomplished without the simultaneous creation and growth of a secondary financial market with sufficient liquidity to assure creditors that they could add to or decrease their debt holdings at any time. Later, when government borrowing outpaced even the Bank of England's lending capacity, these markets were available to absorb the government Consols that were sold directly to investors. Peter Dickson laid out the importance of the developing securities markets:

> The development of a market in securities in London in the period 1688 to 1756 was one of the most important aspects of the financial revolution. For unless facilities had existed to enable lenders to sell to a third party their claim on the state to annual interest, the government's system of long-term borrowing would never have got off the ground. The State would have been obliged to promise repayment in a limited number of years—and to keep this promise. This would have effectually stopped it from borrowing on the scale needed.[20]

The Bank of England, mentioned previously, was chartered in 1694, and was the final major piece of the British Financial Revolution. Modeled on the Bank of Amsterdam (chartered in 1609), the Bank of England was created for the sole purpose of funding the government's wars. This was a job the bank took so seriously that Michael Godfrey, one of its first directors, joined the king in the trenches around the besieged city of Namur, intent on examining whether the bank's money was being properly employed. Godfrey was apparently unaware that the king's retinue attracted fire, and a careless Godfrey, in full view of the king, lost his head to a French canon ball. Since that incident,

---

20. Dickson, *The Financial Revolution in England*, 457.

no other bank director has ever again visited any of the battlefields the bank was financing.

The original subscription to the Bank of England—£1.2 million—was completed within a month. As the original shareholders were a who's who of the nobility and great financiers of the kingdom, the bank enjoyed instant credibility. It immediately loaned the government the full amount of its capitalization, minus a £4,000 management fee, in return for discounted Consols paying a "real" interest rate of eight percent, a rate that rapidly fell as the bank helped stabilize British financial markets. The bank was also given the power to sell notes, which traded like currency, up to the total it had leant to the government. These notes were given to depositors and were a promise to pay the bearer the full amount in specie, on demand. At first, the bank discounted these loans by six percent for British investors (four-and-a-half percent for foreign investors). These deposits were then loaned to the government at eight percent, giving the bank a guaranteed two percent profit. Because these notes traded as currency to supplement the specie already in circulation, they also added a wave of liquidity to burgeoning commercial markets. Inflation was kept mostly in check, despite vast war expenditures, by resisting the urge to print currency not backed by specie. Even when Britain went off the gold standard during the Napoleonic wars, it limited the use of fiat money to the greatest extent possible, and by adding the nation's first income tax, atop increased borrowing, the government managed to sterilize much of the newly issued notes. John Brewer masterfully summed up the impact of this financial revolution:

> Britain emerged in the later seventeenth and early eighteenth century as the military *wunderkind* of the age. Dutch admirals learnt to fear and then admire its navies, French generals reluctantly conferred respect on its officers and men, and Spanish governors trembled for the safety of their colonies and the sanctity of their trade. European armies, most notably those of Prussia, Austria and the minor German states marched if not to the beat of British drums, then to the colour of English money.[21]

In a remarkably short period of time, Britain, which had not been a true European power since the Middle Ages, was elevated into the first ranks of military powers. Cicero was right when he called "infinite money" the true and

---

21. John Brewer, *The Sinews of Power: War, Money, and the English State 1688–1783* (Boston, MA: Harvard University Press, 1990), xiv. Emphasis in original.

most crucial sinew of war, but the same was also true of commerce in the modern era. Even as the financial revolution was allowing tiny Britain to punch far above its weight in the contest for global military supremacy, it was also creating the capital pools paying for Britain's global commercial expansion, as well as covering the astronomical costs required for building the infrastructure—roads, canals, railroads, and factories—that underpinned the Industrial Revolution.

III

It was this system of state finance that Alexander Hamilton desired to replicate in the United States. After winning the battle to assume all of the state's Revolutionary War debt and to create a common national debt, he was ready to take the next crucial step. In December 1790, Hamilton issued his next major report to Congress, the *Second Report on the Further Provision Necessary for Establishing Public Credit*, better known as *The National Bank Report*.[22] In his report, Hamilton explained how a modern fractional banking system works to a Congress that was mostly ignorant of modern financial methods. He pointed out that without banks, merchants would horde their funds, waiting for an opportunity to present itself, thereby, effectively removing money from circulation and slowing the overall growth of the economy. But by placing those stored funds in a bank, the merchant would gain interest, and the bank would be able to lend the money out and keep it in circulation. In fact, as depositors in a bank would rarely want all of their funds back at the same time, banks would be able to lend multiples of the gold and silver they had on hand in the form of banknotes. These notes, by circulating alongside specie, would add liquidity to the economy and accelerate economic growth.

For Hamilton, such rapid economic growth was at the core of his thinking, as the weak post-Revolution economy could not handle the weight of taxes Britain imposed upon its more developed economy. Hamilton had sought and gained Congressional approval for a series of excise taxes, which secured at least the interest payments of the nation's refunded national debt. But to pay

---

22. "Final Version of the Second Report on the Further Provision Necessary for Establishing Public Credit (Report on a National Bank)," December 13, 1790, *Founders Online*, National Archives, https://founders.archives.gov/documents/Hamilton/01-07-02-0229-0003. [Original source: *The Papers of Alexander Hamilton*, Volume 7, September 1790–January 1791, Harold C. Syrett, ed. (New York, NY: Columbia University Press, 1963), 305–42.]

off the principal and to secure future debt issues required a rapidly growing economy.

Hamilton also recognized that a national bank would play a crucial role in "obtaining pecuniary aids, especially in sudden emergencies."[23] Here, Hamilton was clearly thinking about Britain's experiences in employing the Bank of England to fund its wars. In his view, only a powerful central national bank could provide loans of sufficient size to fight a war; no chartered state banks would ever possess the financial firepower to undertake a task of such magnitude. Finally, by holding a monopoly on the issue of federal banknotes, and as the manager of the nation's debt, the Bank of the United States would facilitate the formation of securities markets that would power a rapidly growing commercial sector.

Hamilton's proposal faced strong opposition in the southern United States, where many believed that the bank favored the commercial interests of the northern states over the south's predominately agricultural interests. In the end, only one southern delegate to Congress voted for the bill, which passed on a slim margin. But to stop the bill from becoming law, James Madison and Thomas Jefferson petitioned President Washington to veto it as unconstitutional. Both men argued that the Constitution only gave the federal government the power to pass laws that were "necessary and proper" for the execution of government responsibilities. And as the government was already functioning without a Bank, it was clearly not "necessary." Washington, who supported the creation of a national bank, took these arguments seriously and asked Hamilton to reply. Hamilton, after a week's thought, wrote out his lengthy reply in a single evening.[24] In it, he invented the idea of "implied powers," arguing that the United States Congress could not accomplish its enumerated duties if it was not permitted to decide how best to perform those duties.

Convinced, Washington signed the bank bill into law on February 25, 1791, and the Bank of the United States was duly chartered for twenty years—until 1811. Interestingly, Jefferson, the great proponent of a limited federal government,

23. "Final Version of the Second Report on the Further Provision Necessary for Establishing Public Credit (Report on a National Bank)."

24. "Final Version of an Opinion on the Constitutionality of an Act to Establish a Bank," February 23, 1791," *Founders Online*, National Archives, https://founders.archives.gov /documents/Hamilton/01-08-02-0060-0003. [Original source: *The Papers of Alexander Hamilton*, Volume 8, *February 1791–July 1791*, Harold C. Syrett, ed. (New York, NY: Columbia University Press, 1965), 97–134.]

did not hesitate to employ Hamilton's system of public debt to make the Louisiana Purchase. Jefferson even used many of Hamilton's arguments favoring implied powers to defend his own power to make the purchase, as he did again when he decided to wreck the American economy by forcing the Embargo Act through Congress in 1807. Madison, however, had the last word on the First Bank of the United States, when, as president, he allowed its charter to expire in 1811. Therefore, the bank no longer existed when the War of 1812 erupted. The war ushered in a period of unregulated currency expansion, made a shambles of the public debt, and did so much damage to the nation's economy that Madison was forced to reverse his position and approve legislation creating the Second Bank of the United States in 1816.

The Second Bank of the United States was effectively destroyed by the enmity of President Andrew Jackson, who undertook what became known as the "Bank War." The contest began in 1832, when Congress, led by Jackson's political rival Henry Clay, pushed through an extension to the bank's charter. Jackson vetoed the bill, and, after his reelection, he removed all US deposits from the Bank of the United States and spread the funds over ninety-one state-chartered banks. Congress censured him for this unilateral act but did not reverse it. For all practical purposes Jackson's removal of funds killed the bank, although its current charter still had four years to run.

The bank's demise led directly to the Panic of 1837, as state banks immediately began printing their own currency and overextending themselves with loans. The resulting depression lasted seven painful years, until the California Gold Rush vastly increased the amount of specie in circulation. But without a national bank, ready to act as a lender of last resort, the United States jumped from economic crisis to economic crisis for the next seventy-five years, including the Long Depression of 1873. It was not until the great Banking Crisis of 1907—ended when J. P. Morgan coordinated a financial rescue of the financial system—that there was, once again, substantial public support for a new central lender of last resort, capable of pumping liquidity into the banking system in any amount required. Thus, in 1913, the United States created the Federal Reserve System—the modern incarnation of Hamilton's bank. Unfortunately, the Federal Reserve was not ready in time to help finance World War I. Moreover, by mistakenly contracting the money supply in 1929, when it should have been expanding it, the Federal Reserve worsened the impact of the Great Depression. It did, however, come into its own at the start of World War II, when Federal Reserve President Marriner Eccles announced he would throw the entire power of the Federal Reserve behind the war effort and guaranteed that there would be enough money to pay for the total mobilization of the country for a war of any duration. As US Secretary of War Stimson said after the war:

> The one thing upon which the whole country was agreed was that the services must have enough money. At no time in the whole period of the emergency did I ever have to worry about funds; the appropriations from Congress were always prompt and generous. The pinch came in getting money turned into weapons.[25]

V

When Hamilton took office in 1789, the US Treasury was nearly empty. His great achievement was to give the United States a modern financial system that, within six years, ensured there were sufficient funds to pay government expenses, as well the interest on a debt of approximately $80 million. Hamilton also left the United States with an established mint issuing a new dollar currency in gold and silver, as well as a stable paper money system based on banknotes backed by specie and government debt obligations. This was all managed through the Bank of the United States, which stabilized the financial system sufficiently for states to charter twenty new banking corporations in less than half a decade. Finally, by combining all of these elements, Hamilton made it possible to create regularly functioning financial markets. Rudimentary financial markets had existed in the United States prior to Hamilton's modernization of the country's finances, but they were erratic. In the year after the formation of the Bank of the United States there were active markets in government securities and corporate stocks in Boston, New York, and Philadelphia in continuous operation.

Economist Frederic Mishkin explained the importance of Hamilton's creation:

> Why is finance so important to economic growth? *The answer is that the financial system is like the brain of the economy*: it is a coordinating mechanism that allocates capital to building factories, houses and roads. If capital goes to the wrong uses or does not flow at all, the economy will operate inefficiently, and economic growth will be very low. No work ethic can compensate for a misallocation of capital. Working hard will not make a country rich because hard-working workers will not be productive unless

---

25. Henry Stimson, *On Active Service in Peace and War* (New York, NY: Harper & Bros., 1971), 352.

they work with the right amount of capital. Brain is more important than brawn, and similarly an efficient financial system is more important than hard work to an economy's success.[26]

Robert Sylla further informed us that the United States grew at unprecedented rate because Alexander Hamilton provided it with a fully developed brain.[27] Despite many changes and adaptions over the past 200 years, the essentials of what Hamilton created remain with us, and its impact on strategy in peace and war remains immense.

Before the financial revolution, states were always bankrupted long before they ran out of productive capacity or manpower. The financial revolution reversed this historical truism in ways strategists and policymakers are still having trouble adjusting to. For example, before the onset of World War I, many Britons voiced considerable trepidation over German war reserves stored in gold within Spandau Fortress. By hording French reparations—£70 million in gold—after the Franco-Prussian War to defray the costs of a future war, Germany robbed itself of the opportunity to use this specie to underwrite a further expansion of its economy. Their thinking on specie was, in fact, no different than that of Persian rulers, who had stored vast hordes of silver and gold for Alexander the Great to pillage. As World War I approached, British Chancellor of the Exchequer Lloyd George was asked about this massive gold reserve. His response: "A mighty sum, but England will raise the last million."[28] Lloyd George had clearly absorbed the lessons of the financial revolution, even if few others had. It was a remarkable testament to his faith in Britain's capacity to finance a prolonged conflict, as well as proof that his government realized that its ability to increase its public debt was now the determining factor in war.[29]

---

26. Frederic S. Mishkin, *"Is Financial Globalization Beneficial?"* NBER Working Paper 11891 (December 2005). Emphasis added.

27. Richard Sylla, "Comparing the UK and US Financial Systems, 1790–1830," in *The Origins and Development of Financial Markets and Institutions: From Seventeenth Century to the Present* Jeremy Atack and Larry Neal, eds. (Cambridge: Cambridge University Press, 2009), 214.

28. B. M. Anderson, *Effects of the War on Money, Credit and Banking* (Washington, DC: Carnegie Endowment for International Peace, 1919), 6. The Germans began storing additional gold in the Reichsbank in 1912, but ceased collecting reserves at about $360 million when they apparently considered they had enough to finance a major war. In reality, it was enough to pay for (at best) a single month of heavy fighting in 1915. See also J. Laughlin, *Credit of Nations: A Study of the European War* (New York, NY: Charles Scribner's Sons, 1918), 202–5.

29. According to Niall Ferguson, "The British revenue side was exceptionally robust: as a consequence of the reforming budgets of 1907 and 1909/10—which had a far more decisive

In 1914, however, few could envision the colossal sums of cash that industrial warfare consumed. For instance, the much-feared Spandau gold reserves proved insufficient to cover even a single month's war expenses. Economists who did estimate the cost of modern warfare were convinced that no state could finance a war for more than six months. Even the great economist, Milton Keynes, believed Britain, despite being the financial center of the world, could not cover the cost of a single year of total war. Clearly, even the best economists could no longer comprehend how the coupling of the financial and industrial revolutions had impacted the overall wealth of modern societies as well as their governments' ability to draw upon that wealth. *Nations that could raise and sustain the largest amount of public debt now had a decisive advantage in war, as they were literally tapping into the wealth of future generations to fight a current conflict.*

While every major European state was pushed to the brink of financial disaster during the Great War, only Russia collapsed. Still, the other major participants—Germany, France, and Great Britain—all discovered that they ran out of industrial capacity long before they ran out of financial wherewithal. It was only when Britain could no longer finance the purchase of American war production that national bankruptcy threatened. That possibility disappeared when America entered the war and opened its financial spigots to full blast. A similar pattern was repeated in World War II, where states hit their industrial and manpower limits long before they were bankrupted. Famously, Britain went to the financial edge, but that was, once again, caused by the need to buy American production after their own industries were tapped out. In this case, America's Lend Lease program removed the financial stranglehold.

But it was America's entry into the war that changed the global fiscal picture. Through Lend Lease, America financed a huge percentage of the war materiel employed by its allies, while also financing its own massive mobilization and executing operations in multiple theaters. This was brought about by the remarkable cooperation between the US Treasury and the Federal Reserve. Treasury would issue the debt and the Federal Reserve would ensure that its member banks would purchase whatever the American public did not. The Federal Reserve, employing methods similar to what we now call "quantitative easing," sopped-up any debt the markets could not absorb. Any detailed

---

fiscal outcome than the comparable German finance bill of 1913." See Niall Ferguson, "Public Finance and National Security: The Domestic Origins of the First World War Revisited," *Past and Present* 142 (1994): 142.

discussion of the inner workings of this process is beyond the scope of this essay. But, for all practical purposes, America during World War II discovered how to tap into Cicero's "endless streams of money."

VI

Paul Kennedy, in his masterpiece *The Rise and Fall of Great Powers*, noted that victory in long-drawn out great-power wars has "repeatedly gone to the side with the most flourishing production base."[30] As this essay makes clear, it is not the size of the production base that counts; it is the efficiency with which a state can muster its financial resources that decides conflicts. Paul Kennedy also popularized the term "imperial overstretch," claiming that "that the sum total of the United States' [*sic*] global interests and obligations is nowadays far larger than the country's power to defend them all simultaneously."[31] Kennedy clearly identified the problem, but he misidentified the state. The US economy, thanks to Hamilton's gift to the nation, could have maintained its Cold War spending for generations. It was the Soviet Union that buckled under the economic and financial strain of the competition.

Yet at the start of the twenty-first century, strategists and policymakers must wonder if the United States and much of the world is not facing a problem of "entitlement overstretch." Hamilton, who called the national debt a "national blessing," in the same breath warned that this was only true "if it [was] not excessive." Hamilton envisioned the public debt as proof against a crisis. Today, we are conducting a great experiment to see if debt can be continuously expanded at wartime levels during peacetime. When the United States entered World War II, its debt was under forty percent of the GDP. The country finished the war with a debt-to-GDP ratio of 118 percent. We exceeded that level in 2020, and we, along with the rest of the world, continue to pile on more debt. The strategic question is, can a nation already pushing a debt-to-GDP ratio approximating 150 percent sustain the amount of new debt required to engage in a prolonged great state competition or conflict? In other words, at what point does the system Hamilton bequeathed to us break? The answer is unknowable as we are now in unchartered financial waters.

---

30. Paul Kennedy, *The Rise and Fall of the Great Powers: Economic Change and Military Conflict from 1500–2000* (New York, NY: Random House, 1987), xxiv.

31. Kennedy, *The Rise and Fall of Great Powers*, 515.

CHAPTER 10

Economic Foundations of Strategy

BEYOND SMITH, HAMILTON, AND LIST

Eric Helleiner and Jonathan Kirshner

In the twenty-first century, few students of international politics would fail to acknowledge the essential and inescapable economic aspects of strategy. At the most basic level, tectonic shifts in world politics are only intelligible in this context: economic distress contributed to the collapse of a military superpower (the Soviet Union), and the emergence of a new great power in the international system (China) was entirely facilitated by decades of fast-paced economic growth, which has fundamentally changed the contours of the international balance of power and the pattern of world politics. In addition, the oil shocks of the 1970s not only shook great-power geopolitical complacency, but also contributed to the fact that the Persian Gulf region would become the site of several large wars, and hold the continuing attention of numerous military establishments and defense strategists. Moreover, although many international relations scholars remain dismissive of the political consequences of economic interdependence, from the 1990s, the disruptive effects of globalization, often the catalysts or accelerators of conflict, are difficult to ignore. Indeed, attention to the "high security" implications of globalization has been steadily increasing, with one emergent school of thought exploring the prospects for and consequences of "weaponized interdependence."[1]

Nevertheless, for much of the past (and even more recently), attentiveness to economic aspects of national security strategy has been something of a

---

1. Daniel Drezner, Henry Farrell, and Abraham Newman, eds., *The Uses and Abuses of Weaponized Interdependence* (Washington, DC: Brookings Institution, 2021).

specialist's game. The classic first two editions of *Makers of Modern Strategy* focused largely on the pre-1945 era, and, not surprisingly, largely reflected the traditional separation between political economy and security studies. In addition, both editions were also almost entirely Euro-centric.

The original *Makers*, however, did feature a landmark statement on economics and strategy from Edward Meade Earle: "Adam Smith, Alexander Hamilton, Friedrich List: The Economic Foundations of Military Power." Earle's contribution called attention to the crucial and counterintuitive observation that, although these three celebrated thinkers are often positioned as being in opposition to one another, their differences can be overstated. Smith, certainly, was a cheerleader for liberalism and free trade whereas Hamilton and List are appropriately associated with protectionism and as champions of a powerful and autonomous state. But these stark differences obscure continuities across their thought and purpose. Importantly, and all-too-commonly overlooked, Hamilton and List did not reject Smith's scorching critique of mercantilist trade theory, rooted as it was in the leveling insight that a nation's wealth and power ultimately derived from its productive capacity, not its cache of precious metals. Rather, they embraced that innovation and located their objections to free trade elsewhere.

Indeed, repeatedly, both Hamilton and List paused to observe that they fully acknowledged the wisdom of much what Smith had to say. List stated plainly that "the power of producing wealth is . . . infinitely more important than wealth itself"; Hamilton characterized his dissent as "exceptions" to the general liberal rules Smith established. But they do offer sharp divergences from the free trade ideal. In particular, each articulated the "infant industry" argument. As Hamilton put it, "the United States cannot exchange with Europe on equal terms," because of the "difficulties incident" in initiating enterprise in the context of "superiority antecedently enjoyed by nations." More pointed still was the critique that Smith's policy prescriptions (conveniently, for the British thinker) failed to adequately account for the imperatives of national security. "The idea of a perpetual state of peace forms the foundation of all [Smith's] arguments," List parried. The abstract case for free trade was robust, but in practice the "influence of war" required deviations from that Platonic ideal. International trade had important consequences for national security that could not be disregarded—even at the cost of short-term economic sacrifice.[2]

---

2. Alexander Hamilton, "Report on the Subject of Manufactures" (1791), in *Industrial and Commercial Correspondence of Alexander Hamilton*, Arthur Cole, ed. (Chicago, IL: A.W. Shaw,

Conversely, regarding matters of national security, Smith's thinking was not so incongruous with that of his ostensible intellectual opponents. Rather, many of the differences between them derived (as List and other critics suggested) from distinct national circumstances. As Earle observed, Smith "clearly" believed that "the economic power of the nation should be used as an instrument of statecraft."[3] Moreover, in *The Wealth of Nations*, Smith went out of his way to explicitly endorse England's protectionist navigation acts and other interventionist measures, on the grounds that ensuring the defense of the realm "is of much more importance than opulence."[4]

Smith, Hamilton, and List, then, all understood the relationship between economics and strategy; all placed a high priority on national security; all shared the (Smithian) insight that both wealth and power ultimately derived from a nation's productive capacity; and all understood that, in the long run, the pursuit of wealth and the pursuit of power were each vital, intimately enmeshed, and not easily disentangled. Earle was not alone in observing this grand synthesis—the conclusion was also highlighted by Jacob Viner in his influential *World Politics* essay from 1948, "Power versus Plenty as Objectives of Statecraft in the Seventeenth and Eighteenth Centuries." Hamilton and List parted company with Smith in their insistence that for developing states or second tier powers with some aspiration to one day play a greater role on the world stage, deviations from the free trade ideal were necessary. They were not alone in these sentiments.

In this essay, we build on Earle's classic text in two ways. First, we seek to broaden the pre-1945 history of thought about economic aspects of national security strategy beyond the famous trio of Western thinkers Earle featured. Because of China's importance in the contemporary global political economy, we focus on a Chinese tradition of thought that reached its fullest and most influential expression in the ideas of Sun Yat-sen in the early twentieth century. Second, we extend Earle's analysis forward in time to highlight thinkers who explored this topic after World War II. We highlight the important contributions to postwar conceptions of economics and national security associated with Robert Gilpin, as well as Albert Hirschman and Susan Strange. Across

---

1928), 248, 265, 266; Friedrich List, *The National System of Political Economy* (London: Longmans, Green and Co., 1885), 120, 317, 347.

3. Edward Meade Earle, "Adam Smith, Alexander Hamilton, Friedrich List: The Economic Foundations of Military Power," in *Makers of Modern Strategy*, Peter Paret, ed. (Princeton, NJ: Princeton University Press, 1986), 225.

4. Adam Smith, *The Wealth of Nations* (New York, NY: Random House, 1776), 431.

the entire chapter, our goal is to introduce some additional "makers" of the economic foundations of strategy.

I

The ideas of Smith, Hamilton, and List about the economic aspects of strategy left important legacies in Western thought. But there were also many thinkers from outside the West in the pre-1945 era who developed important and innovative ideas on this topic. Among them were Chinese thinkers in the nineteenth and early twentieth centuries whose writings are rarely mentioned in Western textbooks of international relations or international political economy. Their ideas deserve more attention for a number of reasons. First, the links that some of them drew between economics and strategy were more ambitious than those of Smith, Hamilton, and List. Second, their thought left intellectual legacies in Chinese statecraft that continue to resonate in the contemporary era, when China has emerged as a dominant power in the global political economy.

Chinese thinkers in the pre-1945 era drew on a tradition of thought that was much deeper than the European mercantilist ideas with which Smith, Hamilton, and List engaged. Particularly important were the writings of Legalist thinkers from the period of the Warring States in China's history (453–221 BCE) who challenged the traditional Confucian focus on cultivating values such as frugality, benevolence, and moral leadership. In the context of the violent interstate rivalry of the time, the Legalists urged that attention be devoted to the goal of maximizing state power instead of cultivating Confucian values. For later Chinese thinkers interested in the economic aspects of national security strategy, a key reference point was *The Book of Lord Shang*, written in the third century BCE. Shang Yang had been an advisor to the ruler of the state of Qin that eventually emerged victorious from the wars of that age. Shang was well known for emphasizing that state power derived not just from a strong military but also from a state's wealth. As *The Book of Lord Shang* put it, "he who rules the state well consolidates force to attain a rich state and a strong army."[5]

In the wake of the Opium Wars (1839–42, 1856–60), many nineteenth-century Chinese thinkers echoed Shang's emphasis on the need for a "rich state

---

5. Shang Yang, *The Book of Lord Shang: Apologetics of State Power in Early China*, Yuri Pines, trans. and ed. (New York, NY: Columbia University Press, 2017), 174.

and a strong army" (*fuguo qiangbing*), a phrase that they often contracted to *fuqiang* (wealth and power). They even drew direct parallels between Shang's Warring States period and their own era, arguing that China as a whole faced military threats from Western powers that resembled the conflictual interstate environment within China during that earlier era. In their view, Western power rested not just on its military superiority but also on important economic foundations. If China was to fend off this new external threat, its leaders needed to recognize the tight interconnections between the wealth and power of Western states and launch appropriate domestic economic reforms.

The most important of these thinkers initially was the scholar Wei Yuan who published two key books after the First Opium War (and almost at the same time as List's most famous work, *The National System of Political Economy* published in 1841): *Military History of the Qing Dynasty* (1842) and *Illustrated Gazetteer on the Maritime Countries* (1843). Lamenting China's "humiliation" in the First Opium War, Wei urged Chinese leaders to respond to the new external threat by strengthening the empire's power through various reforms, including importing Western military technology and boosting China's study of Western knowledge and skills. Like Shang, Wei emphasized the interconnection between state wealth and power: "When the state is rich and powerful, it will be effective. . . . What then is there to fear about barbarians anywhere— what is there to worry about as to defense against aggression?"[6]

Wei's ideas about *how* to promote China's wealth, however, differed from those of Shang. Seeing agriculture as the basis of wealth, Shang was deeply skeptical of merchant activity, which he thought should be strongly discouraged. Shang's views on this topic did not reflect all Legalist thought in the BCE period. Some Legalists expressed pro-commerce views, including the authors of the well-known work *Guanzi* and thinkers in the Iron and Salt debates of 81 BCE. Closer to these latter views, Wei argued that Chinese authorities needed to recognize that foreign commerce formed a key basis of the power of Western states. In his *Illustrated Gazetteer*, Wei urged Chinese authorities to promote foreign commerce more actively, and with the support of an expanded Chinese naval presence in its region.

Wei's ideas built upon his earlier involvement in a "statecraft" school that had been concerned with growing problems confronting the Chinese empire before the First Opium War. Like others in this school, Wei combined Confucian ideas

---

6. William Theodore de Bary and Richard Lufrano, eds., *Sources of Chinese Tradition*, Volume 2: *1600–2000*, Second edition (New York, NY: Columbia University Press, 2000), 208.

about the importance of moral leadership with the practical study of economic and political reforms to address these problems. Wei argued forcefully that Confucian values were compatible with an emphasis on promoting *fuqiang*: "there is no kingly way without wealth and power."[7] This incorporation of *fuqiang* goals into Confucian thought echoed the ideas of some earlier Confucian thinkers, including the prominent eighteenth-century official Chen Hongmou who had also endorsed the promotion of foreign commerce and whose ideas were praised by statecraft thinkers and later Chinese reformers.

This line of argument became increasingly prominent in the Chinese intellectual circles after the Second Opium War, creating what Benjamin Schwartz called a "quasi-Legalist vein of Confucian thought."[8] It was particularly influential at that time within the "self-strengthening" movement that supported various reforms to the empire, including economic ones designed to bolster China's power. This movement drew inspiration from the ideas of Wei Yuan, the statecraft school, and earlier Chinese thinkers. Its most important intellectual advocate became the merchant-scholar Zheng Guanying, whose best-known work, *Words of Warning in a Flourishing Age* (1893), drew on ideas he had promoted since the 1870s.

Like Wei, Zheng insisted on the interconnected nature of state wealth and power: "strength can not be achieved without wealth, and wealth can not be secured without strength."[9] But Zheng had much more ambitious ideas about how the Chinese economy needed to be reformed to strengthen China's capacity to fend off Western power. In his view, new Chinese firms needed to be established and supported in sectors such as manufacturing, shipping, and mining to compete with foreign enterprises both within China and in global markets. Higher external tariffs were also needed to help local firms, even if that meant challenging the trade treaties imposed on China by Western powers. Zheng also urged the modernization of the country's agriculture, financial and monetary system, and infrastructure as well as the establishment of new diplomatic services abroad and educational institutions at home. In addition, he called for taxes on internal trade to be abolished and for merchants to be valued more highly within Chinese society.

7. Hao Chang, *Liang Ch'i-ch'ao and the Intellectual Tradition in China, 1890–1907* (Cambridge, MA: Harvard University Press, 1971), 30.

8. Benjamin Schwartz, *In Search of Wealth and Power* (Cambridge, MA: Harvard University Press, 1964), 17.

9. Wu Guo, *Zheng Guanying* (Amherst, NY: Cambria, 2010), 189.

This broad-based economic reform agenda to strengthen Chinese power bore some resemblance to List's ambitious ideas about the need to boost the overall productive power of a country. Zheng does not, however, appear to have had any awareness of List's writings or other Western political economy literature that expressed similar views. His rationale for the proposed reforms was that China needed to improve its ability to fight what he called "commercial warfare" (*shang-zhan*) against other states.[10] The phrase came not from Western thought, but had instead first been used in the early 1860s by another Chinese thinker associated with the self-strengthening movement, Zeng Guofan. That thinker, in turn, drew inspiration from a reference that Shang Yang had made to "agricultural warfare."[11] In Zheng Guanying's analysis, the phrase referred to a new kind of warfare in which states fought for profits and wealth on a worldwide scale. Those states which were less successful in this economic struggle saw their wealth drained in ways that left them severely weakened and open to being invaded militarily.

Zheng worried that China was increasingly in this position. He urged Chinese authorities to recognize this and compensate for the empire's military weakness by learning how to fight commercial warfare more successfully. As he put it, China needed to be "fighting with wealth rather than force."[12] Like other Chinese thinkers at the time, Zheng drew parallels between the conflictual nature of world politics in his age and during the period of the Warring States. In this dangerous context, he argued, the security of the empire depended on large-scale economic reforms.

Zheng also invoked Japan as a model of a country that had responded successfully to the Western challenge by cultivating wealth and power through economic reforms of the kind he recommended. He does not seem to have been familiar with the ideas of specific Japanese figures who promoted these reforms in Meiji Japan. It is worth noting, however, that many of these figures echoed Chinese reformers in invoking Shang's advocacy of a "rich state and a strong army." Indeed, the Japanese translation of the phrase—*fukoku kyōhei*—became very popular in the early Meiji era; it was even used by advocates of the importation of Western ideas, such as Fukuzawa Yukichi. Both Wei Yuan and Zheng's ideas were also read in Japan, highlighting once again the wider regional intellectual context in which Japanese ideas about economic aspects of national security strategy emerged.

10. Wu, *Zheng Guanying*, 188.
11. Eric Helleiner, *The Neomercantilists* (Ithaca, NY: Cornell University Press, 2021), 241.
12. Wu, *Zheng Guanying*, 190.

II

Zheng's ideas found support among some Chinese policymakers, such as Li Hongzhang who supported the creation of some state-sponsored firms in the 1870s and 1880s (one of which Zheng himself worked in briefly). In general, however, the conservativism of Chinese officialdom meant that Zheng's ideas did not find a wider audience in government circles until after Japan's military victory over China in 1895. The outcome of that war finally generated much stronger official interest in economic reform to strengthen the security of the Chinese empire, culminating in the short-lived 1898 reform movement in which Zheng's ideas were widely cited.

This new political context also generated new interest in Western literature about political economy. Most of the earlier Chinese thinkers, including Wei Yaun and Zheng Guanying, had very little knowledge of that Western literature. Even classic Western works on this topic such as *The Wealth of Nations* had not been translated into Chinese. Interestingly, when the first Chinese translation of Smith's work did finally appear in 1901, its content was interpreted in a way that highlighted Chinese preoccupations with the economic foundations of China's security.

The translator of *The Wealth of Nations* was Yan Fu, who had been become fascinated with British political economy while studying in England between 1877–79—very unusual for a Chinese scholar at the time. After returning to China, Yan became part of Li Hongzhang's brain trust and then became well known for publishing a set of essays in 1895 that argued that the basis of Western power was not its technology or political-economic arrangements but rather its ideas. His suggestion that Western ideas might be superior to Chinese ones, including Confucianism, was bold. To reinforce his message, Yan began to translate and comment on key Western scholarly works for a Chinese audience.

Yan's 1901 translation of *The Wealth of Nations* included considerable commentary for his Chinese audience. He argued that Smith deserved credit for laying the intellectual foundation for Britain's superior wealth and power in the world. In his reading, Smith's advocacy of individual economic liberty and the elimination of barriers to commerce had unleashed a dynamic energy among the British people. At the same time, Yan stressed how Smith's ideas were linked to a public spiritedness that successfully harnessed this new dynamic energy to serve collective national ends. From Yan's standpoint, this combination of individual energy and sense of national public spirit was at the core of Britain's successful cultivation of wealth and power. In Schwartz's words, Yan's message was that Smith's system of economic liberalism was "admirably designed to achieve the wealth and power of the state."[13]

This interpretation of Smith downplayed the Scottish thinker's liberal commitment to the idea of individual liberty as an end in and of itself. At the same time, Schwartz's analysis reminds us that Yan's interpretation was not entirely off the mark since, as Earle also emphasized, Smith was indeed very concerned with the wealth and power of the state. This concern of Smith's was often downplayed by nineteenth-century Western economic liberals who embraced a more cosmopolitan worldview. But it resonated with Yan Fu and other Chinese thinkers of his era who were deeply worried about the precarious security position of their own state. In Yan Fu's case, this worry was reinforced by his embrace of social Darwinist ideas and his belief that the Chinese people were engaged in an international struggle for their very survival. Yan saw economic liberal ideas instrumentally as a tool to boost China's wealth and power. This was similar to some of the sources of Fukuzawa's interest in Western economic liberalism several decades earlier in Japan.

While Yan Fu was attracted to Smith's ideas, other Chinese thinkers were drawn to Western political economists who were critical of Smith's liberal economic advice. The most important of these was Liang Qichao who became one of the most influential Chinese thinkers in the first decade of the twentieth century. Liang first began to read about Western political economy in detail after fleeing into exile in Japan because of his role in the 1898 reforms. Like Yan Fu, Liang was interested in the Western literature because he hoped it would help him to understand the ideas that underpinned Western wealth and power. In this period, Liang shared Yan Fu's interest in social Darwinism as well as his fears about the prospects for China's survival.

Liang was soon drawn to the nationalist ideas of the German historical school which carried on the criticism of free trade developed by List (whose work also first began to attract attention in China at this time). Like Zheng, Liang saw China as competing in an international "trade war" in which protectionist policies needed to play an important role.[14] In his words, "no private business firms in China can be strong enough to survive the competition with

13. Schwartz, *In Search of Wealth and Power*, 117.

14. Tang Xiaobing, *Global Space and the Nationalist Discourse of Modernity* (Stanford, CA: Stanford University Press, 1996), 167.

their western counterparts backed by their governments."[15] Liang depicted free trade as a tool of foreign domination: "Are not Shanghai, Hankou, and other [treaty ports] called concessions? What are concessions but colonies? If the whole country becomes a free-trade zone, then is that not equivalent to making the whole country a colony?"[16] In addition, Liang warned against the exploitation of China by large foreign companies, suggesting that foreign investment might serve as the first step to colonization.

Although Liang was interested in Western economic ideas, his thought was also rooted in some of the Chinese intellectual traditions already discussed. Well before arriving in Japan, Liang had embraced the ideas of the self-strengthening movement. In 1897, he had updated a famous collection of statecraft writings that Wei Yuan had edited in 1826. Once in Japan, his interest in Chinese economic thought endured, including in Legalist texts such as *Guanzi* and *The Book of Lord Shang* that had emphasized the importance of economics to national power. In 1903, Liang even declared, "I pray only that our country can have a Guanzi, a Shang Yang, a Lycurgus, a Cromwell alive today to carry out harsh rule, and with iron and fire to forge and temper our countrymen for twenty, thirty, even fifty years."[17]

III

After World War I, Liang became disillusioned with these ideas and, more generally, with nationalism, materialism, and social Darwinism in the context of the devastation caused by the war. Other Chinese thinkers, however, remained committed to the cultivation of China's wealth and power. Particularly important was Sun Yat-sen who, in the first decade of the century, had been Liang's political rival among Chinese in exile and who briefly became the first provisional president of the Chinese Republic after the 1911 Revolution. At the very moment that Liang lost interest in boosting China's wealth and power, Sun outlined some ideas about how to meet this goal that were more ambitious even than Zheng's (as well as Smith's, Hamilton's, and List's). Sun's ideas

---

15. Paul Trescott and Zhaoping Wang, "Liang Chi-chao and the Introduction of Western Economic Ideas into China," *Journal of the History of Economic Thought* 16:1 (1994): 135.

16. Rebecca Karl, *Staging the World* (Durham, NC: Duke University Press, 2002), 73.

17. Liang Qichao, "The Power and Threat of America," in *Land without Ghosts: Chinese Impressions of America from the Mid-Nineteenth Century to the Present*, R. David Arkush and Leo O. Lee, eds. (Berkeley, CA: University of California Press, 1993), 93.

subsequently had considerable influence in China and they continue to be invoked today, including by the top leaders of the country.

Sun was much more familiar with Western economic thought than were figures such as Wei Yuan and Zheng Guanying. But his ideas about the link between economics and national security strategy were also heavily influenced by the Chinese intellectual tradition. That influence was very evident in the first serious text that Sun wrote concerning economic issues. In this 1894 memo to Li Hongzhang, Sun emphasized the importance of cultivating China's power through economic reform. His arguments, and even some of his wording, bore strong similarities to ideas expressed on this topic by earlier Chinese thinkers associated with the self-strengthening movement, including Zheng Guanying. Like Zheng, Sun called attention to the economic foundations of Britain's power in its commercial prowess:

> The reason why Britain can conquer India, control Southeast Asia, seize Africa, and annex Australia is because of its commercial strength. National defense cannot function without money, and money for the military will not accumulate without commerce.[18]

The similarities to Zheng's ideas reflected the fact that the two men had become close since the late 1880s; Sun may even have made contributions to Zheng's 1893 book *Words of Warning*. When taking the memo to Li, Sun stopped to see Zheng, at which time his memo was edited by the latter's close colleague, Wang Tao.

In subsequent years, Sun's ideas continued to reflect core themes from Zheng and others from the self-strengthening movement. After the revolution of 1911, Sun also referred to older texts such as *Guanzi*, suggesting that the content of the latter showed that "economics initially originated in China."[19] The influence of earlier Chinese thought was also evident in his most ambitious ideas about economic reform that appeared in a number of publications after World War I. Particularly important at that time was a 1920 English-language book entitled *International Development of China* and a set of Sun's lectures from 1924, published later as *The Three Principles of the People*.

18. Sun Yat-sen, *Prescriptions for Saving China*, Julie Lee Wei, Ramon Myers, and Donald Gillin, eds., trans. Julie Lee Wei, E-su Zen, and Linda Chao (Stanford, CA: Hoover Institution Press, 1994), 11.

19. Zhao Jing, "*Fu Guo Xue* and the 'Economics' of Ancient China," in *A History of Ancient Chinese Economic Thought*, Cheng Lin, Terry Peach, and Wang Fang, eds. (London: Routledge, 2014), 66–81, esp. 80.

In this final stage of his life, Sun expressed much more serious worries about what he called China's "extremely perilous" position in world politics resulting from its weak economic state.[20] He highlighted how the latter was causing China to experience various forms of foreign "economic oppression."[21] Sun was particularly concerned about how the foreign-imposed trade treaties prevented China from protecting local firms against foreign imports with tariffs. As he put it, "Just as forts are built at the entrances of harbors for protection against foreign military invasion, so a tariff against foreign goods protects a nation's revenue and gives native industries to develop."[22] The trade treaties, Sun argued, contributed to China's "failure in the trade war" as foreigners came to dominate local markets and the country's trade deficits grew, causing the country to experience a "tremendous drain" of wealth.[23] Furthermore, Sun insisted that the trade treaties oppressed China economically in other ways, such as by granting foreigners special privileges in the treaty ports and elsewhere, allowing them to earn profits that would otherwise have gone to Chinese people.

Sun suggested China's economic oppression created huge economic losses for the country that could ultimately "spell the loss of our country as well as the annihilation of our race." It was, he argued, "more severe than imperialism or political oppression." But he also noted how the latter reinforced economic oppression. Referring to Europe and America, Sun argued, "If their economic arm is at times weak, they intervene with political force of navies and armies. The way their political power cooperates with their economic power is like the way in which the left arm helps the right arm."[24]

In Sun's view, the best way to combat China's oppression by foreign powers was to promote rapid economic development, just as Japan had done. Not only would this enable China to recapture lost markets and profits, it would also generate political and military power that could be used to reject the trade treaties and fend off political oppression. When invoking Japan as a model, Sun argued that China could become even more powerful: "China has ten times the population and thirty times the area of Japan, and her resources are much larger than Japan's. If China reaches the standard of Japan, she will be equal to ten Great Powers." Particularly important was the task of promoting

20. Sun Yat-sen, *San Min Chu I: The Three Principles of the People,* trans. Frank Price; L.T. Chen, ed. (Shanghai: Commercial, 1928), 12.

21. Sun, *San Min Chu I,* 37.

22. Sun, *San Min Chu I,* 41.

23. Helleiner, *The Neomercantilists,* 248.

24. Sun, *San Min Chu I,* 53, 37, 87–88.

China's industrialization because Sun thought it was key to generating both rising standards of living as well as political and military power. He also suggested that "in international trade an industrial nation has an advantage over an agricultural nation."[25]

Sun assigned the Chinese government a central role in promoting industrialization and economic development. In addition to raising tariffs to protect the development of local industries, it could create state-owned firms to foster new industrial sectors and enable profits from these sectors to be shared by the entire nation. The government also needed to support the building of new transportation and communications infrastructure, such as massive new railway networks, roads, ports, canals, and telegraph and telephone systems. In addition, Sun outlined plans for ambitious state-led initiatives to promote agricultural modernization, mining and energy, reforestation, and urban development. In his 1920 book, Sun went into enormous detail in outlining plans for these various initiatives, many of which were grandiose in scope. William Kirby described Sun's overall vision in the book as "the first attempt to design the integrated economic development of a unified China." In 2000, Kirby wrote, "Today, many Three-, Four-, Five-, and Ten-Year Plans later, it remains the most audacious and memorable of national development programs."[26]

Sun assigned one further important task to the Chinese government: the management of foreign capital. Sun was more positive about the potential role of foreign capital in supporting China's economic development than many Chinese thinkers at the time, including Liang. In his 1920 book Sun explained, "Europe and America are a hundred years ahead of us in industrial development; so in order to catch up in a very short time, we have to use their capital, mainly their machinery."[27] Sun had put the point more starkly in a work completed in late 1918 for a Chinese audience, tying the issue to China's national security: "to regenerate the State and to save the country from destruction at this critical moment, we must welcome the influx of large-scale foreign capital on the largest possible scale."[28]

But Sun was also very critical of how foreign financiers had "entirely disregarded the will of the Chinese people" and thus had contributed to the

25. Sun, *San Min Chu I*, 176, 41.

26. William Kirby, "Engineering China," in *Becoming Chinese: Passages to Modernity and Beyond*, Wen-hsin Yeh, ed. (Berkeley, CA: University of California Press, 2000), 138.

27. Sun Yat-sen, *The International Development of China* (New York, NY: G. P. Putnam's Sons 1920), 198.

28. Sun Yat-sen, *Memoirs of a Chinese Revolutionary* (New York, NY: AMS, 1970), 175.

country's economic oppression. For this reason, he insisted that the Chinese government manage all foreign borrowing and ensure that all Chinese projects that were financed with foreign capital would be "national undertakings." Although foreigners might help to manage and supervise these projects, they would do so only "under Chinese employment" and would be required "to undertake the training of Chinese assistants to take their places in the future." Sun also proposed that the Chinese state borrow, not from private financiers, but rather from a new kind of international public institution that would be managed by the "various Governments of the Capital-supplying Powers." Sun suggested that this "International Development Organization" would be part of the League of Nations and be required to secure "the confidence of the Chinese people" before any contract was signed between it and the Chinese government.[29]

One final aspect of Sun's ideas about China's wealth and power deserves mention. Looking to the future, Sun argued that China would have an important international role to play as its wealth and power grew. While Liang had hoped China might become an imperialist power in the future when writing before World War I, Sun opposed this idea, arguing that China should take on a quite different role:

> If we want China to rise to power, we must not only restore our national standing, but we must also assume a great responsibility towards the world.... We must aid the weaker and smaller peoples and oppose the great powers of the world.... Let us to-day, before China's development begins, pledge ourselves to lift up the fallen and to aid the weak; then when we become strong and look back upon our sufferings under the political and economic domination of the Powers and see weaker and smaller peoples undergoing similar treatment, we will rise and smite that imperialism.[30]

Sun died in 1925, but his economic ideas had enormous influence in China during the interwar years, and not just in the Nationalist government. Even the communists committed to them, including Mao who had also been inspired by Zheng Guanying's writings in his youth. After the conclusion of the Chinese civil war in 1949, Mao turned to a very different economic strategy, first following a Stalinist development model and then a more autarkic policy

---

29. Sun, *The International Development*, 9–12.
30. Sun, *San Min Chu I*, 147–48.

after his break with the Soviet Union. When Deng came to power in 1978, however, Sun's economic ideas gained renewed attention in China as the country's leadership turned to an outward-oriented, state-led industrialization strategy supported by foreign capital, including from multilateral development banks. Figures associated with the self-strengthening movement, including Zheng, also began to receive more positive assessments. More recently, Chinese President Xi Jinping has also celebrated Sun's economic ideas. In a 2016 speech honoring the 150th anniversary of Sun's birth, Xi boasted that Chinese Communist Party had surpassed the economic goals Sun set in his 1920 book.[31]

IV

After World War II, although economic diplomacy was commonly practiced—consider the Marshall Plan, one of the most expensive and ambitious peacetime allocations of resources to advance grand strategic goals—the study of economic statecraft was largely inhibited, especially in America. For the US in particular, the colossal size of its economy, relative insulation from international competition, and radically circumscribed commercial interaction with its Cold War adversary, all contributed to a reduced salience of and, in turn, vanishing academic emphasis regarding economic aspects of national security. A darker side of the Cold War also discouraged such studies—one chilling effect of McCarthyism in American universities was to dissuade scholars from trafficking in notions that were suggestive of a Marxist influence. And the idea that politics might shape the pattern of economic activity was (if obviously correct) nevertheless a notion at odds with the broadly held "neo-classical synthesis" in economics and associated with a minority dissent from the radical left.

One exception to this general rule was an important book by Albert Hirschman, *National Power and the Structure of Foreign Trade* (1945), which explored how, historically, countries could manipulate their commercial relations to enhance their national power. Hirschman explored lessons drawn from practices introduced by states before and during World War I, and, most notably, on the trade practices of Nazi Germany in the 1930s that were embedded in a larger strategy of economic preparation for World War II. In particular,

---

31. See "China Marks 150th Anniversary of Sun Yat-sen's Birth, Stressing National Integrity," *Xinhua*, November 12, 2016.

Germany was determined, in contrast to its experience of the Great War when the Allied blockade nearly starved the country into submission, to enter the next war assured of its economic sustainability, principally though the cultivation of a self-reliant sphere which it would dominate. Hirschman's insights, most easily visible when applied to interwar Germany and its relations with its small neighbors to the south and east in the context of a distressed international economy, were nevertheless generalizable, consequential, and of enduring importance.

Two of the conclusions of *National Power* are especially noteworthy. The first, with which the book would ultimately become most closely associated, was Hirschman's argument about the consequences of asymmetric economic relations, and the ways that politically motivated great powers could manipulate such relations. As Hirschman illustrated, Germany purposefully redirected the pattern of its international trade towards its smaller regional neighbors, often, counter-intuitively from an economistic perspective, by offering overly generous terms-of-trade—perhaps this was the price of cultivating considerable regional autarky. A potentially insidious effect of this was that trade between Germany and a much smaller economy (such as, for example, Bulgaria) could account for *most* of the international commerce of the latter but only a tiny percentage of the former's aggregate trade ledger. Thus, each smaller trading partner would, at least implicitly, become newly vulnerable to Germany's whims. A sudden termination of trade between the two would be ruinous for the smaller state yet barely register on the accounts of the latter—and the mutual awareness of this asymmetry meant that both knew this threat hovered like a sword of Damocles over the economy of the smaller state. This implied formidable coercive power.

A second conclusion, less emphasized during the book's initial reception but more fully developed decades later by scholars following in this tradition, had to do not with coercion but with political influence. This fascinating phenomenon, flagged by Hirschman, is of particular interest because it operates absent any of the relatively special factors of the interwar case: Nazis, depression, and the causal practice of overt intimidation, often in the shadow of looming military as well as economic asymmetry. Hirschman observed that, as trade is reoriented, the economy of the smaller state can be increasingly conditioned on that of the larger—something that will develop in the context of any asymmetric relationship (and can even, it should be noted, generate powerful incentives felt to some extent in important economic relationships that are not inherently asymmetric). Such conditioning can yield political benefits to the dominant state, not because of implicit coercive threats, but via a transformation of the smaller state's self-perception of its own interests. This is because certain sectors of the economy—often becoming more influential within the domestic political economy as their activities thrive and expand in this context—naturally see their interests converging with those of their vital trading partners. As Hirschman put it, this cultivates "a powerful influence in favor of a 'friendly' attitude towards the state to the imports of which they owe their interests," a phenomenon observed among Germany's trading partners not simply in Eastern Europe, but (to the dismay of strategic thinkers and policymakers in the US) in Latin America as well.[32]

The significance of the "Hirschman effects" articulated and elaborated in *National Power and the Structure of Foreign Trade* would not gain widespread currency for several decades after the book's initial publication, despite the fact that its logic arguably influenced the introduction of the Marshall Plan and would appear to be of obvious relevance for the postwar United States, most of whose bilateral economic relationships were inevitably asymmetric. This was not only due to the chilling Cold War effects on studies of economic strategy noted previously, but also because of the ideological context in which it was written. After the Second World War—especially in the United States, whose foreign policy elites increasingly came to rue the protectionist, isolationist, and "America First" policies that characterized the interwar years—it was the consensus view that closure, economic machinations, and the regimentation of the international economy had contributed to the war. The lesson was thus that all good things need go together: liberal free trade made sense from an economic perspective, and it would have an ameliorating effect on world politics. Greater attention to the practice of economic statecraft (and to the fact that even economic liberalization and "free trade" had profound and varied implications for "high politics" and the balance of power) would have to wait—for the invention of International Political Economy.

V

By the late 1960s and into the 1970s, even in the still hegemonic United States, the role of economic factors on international politics became too salient to ignore. Inflationary pressures associated with the financing of the Vietnam

---

32. Albert Hirschman, *National Power and the Structure of Foreign Trade* (Berkeley, CA: University of California Press, 1980 [1945]), 29; see also 18, 28, 34–37. For illustrations of this phenomenon more generally, see Rawi Abdelal and Jonathan Kirshner, "Strategy, Economic Relations, and the Definition of National Interests," *Security Studies* 9:1–2 (1999–2000): 119–56.

War threatened to (and ultimately would) undermine the American-orchestrated Bretton Woods international monetary system. International trade, which continued to thrive and expand, placed new competitive pressures on previously unrivaled industries. The first oil shock, a sudden, unexpected, and, for many societies, traumatic quadrupling of energy prices on import-dependent economies emerged directly from the 1973 Arab-Israeli War. With the end of a quarter-century of remarkable economic growth—the Golden Age of Capitalism—and from there to the distressed 1970s, economic pressures could not but be understood as having profound consequences for the pattern of world politics.

Unsurprisingly, the academic International Relations (IR) subfield of International Political Economy (IPE) emerged at this time in the Anglo-American world. At the forefront of this new specialization was the discovery—a novelty for the relatively insular United States—of the consequences of economic interdependence. Initial work in IPE emphasized this point of departure—notably in a special issue of the journal *International Organization* (1971) edited by Robert Keohane and Joseph Nye. That project, "Transnational Relations and World Politics," was initially conceived in 1968 (the same year that saw the publication of Richard N. Cooper's *The Economics of Interdependence*) and featured papers presented at a 1970 Harvard University conference. At the time many scholars were suggesting that interdependence was fundamentally transforming the nature of world politics; many contributions emphasized the purportedly novel consequences of the "multinational" corporation. In 1968, and in subsequent influential work, Raymond Vernon wrote about "Economic Sovereignty at Bay." In 1969, Charles Kindleberger (somewhat prematurely, it would seem) declared "the nation state is just about through as an economic unit."[33]

At least one participant at the Harvard conference saw things differently. In a series of seminal contributions over the following two decades, Robert Gilpin recreated the spirit (though not the particulars) of the implicit debate between Smithian liberalism and the neo-mercantilist dissents of Hamilton and List. In his contribution to the *International Organization* special issue, Gilpin parried the emerging conventional wisdom: "I think it is closer to the truth to argue that the role of the nation-state in economic as well as in political

---

33. Raymond Vernon, "Economic Sovereignty at Bay," *Foreign Affairs* 47:1 (1968): 110–22; Charles P. Kindleberger, *American Business Abroad* (New Haven, CT: Yale University Press, 1969), 207.

life is increasing and that the multinational corporation is actually a stimulant to the further extension of state power."[34] In contrast with what could be understood as liberal, or at least liberal-leaning theories of IPE, Gilpin articulated a more statist interpretation of the pattern and politics of international economic relations, in contributions ultimately summarized over the course of three important books. *U.S. Power and the Multinational Corporation* (1975) laid out three distinct paradigms of IPE: a liberal vision, a Marxist vision, and what Gilpin dubbed a "mercantilist" vision, though caution should be taken with the embrace of that term. "Mercantilist," for Gilpin, meant "the attempt of governments to manipulate economic arrangements in order to maximize their own interests, whether or not this is at the expense of others."[35]

Essentially, Gilpin was establishing a "statist" interpretation of IPE, which did have affinities with both classical and neo-mercantilism, approaches that, in contrast to liberalism, placed great emphasis on the importance of an autonomous state, with interests distinct from, and not reducible to, an aggregation of individual interests within society. Gilpin contrasted the liberal emphasis on individuals pursuing material interests in the context of unfettered market forces adjudicated by a neutral, passive government with a more statist conception that envisioned groups pursuing politically shaped goals guided by state authority in the context of international anarchy. Obviously, these were expressions of idealized types, or paradigms, but from the statist perspective, politics led and economics followed.

This primacy was reflected in Gilpin's magisterial *War and Change in World Politics* (1981), which argued that throughout modern history the pattern of global economic actively reflected the power, interest, and ideological disposition of the dominant state in the system. Likewise, his summary statement, *The Political Economy of International Relations* (1987) emphasized again, if more generally and comprehensively, the ways in which international politics formatively shaped the pattern of international economic activity. In all of these contributions, but most explicitly in the final two, Gilpin's perspective bears the influence of E. H. Carr, in particular his book *The Twenty Years' Crisis 1919–1939* (1939), whose critique of liberal economics plainly echoed that of

---

34. Robert Gilpin, "The Politics of Transnational Economic Relations," *International Organization* 25:3 (1971): 419.

35. Robert Gilpin, *U.S. Power and the Multinational Corporation* (New York, NY: Basic Books, 1975); Robert Gilpin, "Three Models of the Future," *International Organization* 29:1 (1975): 45.

List. Carr had argued that Smithian-inflected theories of mutually beneficial exchange assumed away the implications of power politics and the prospect for war; that some rather than others benefitted (or at least anticipated benefitting) disproportionately from free trade; and that implicit power structures, not the spontaneous operation of market forces, underpinned any system of economic organization and permitted it to function. As Carr insisted (and Gilpin repeatedly echoed throughout his own oeuvre), "the science of economics presupposes a given political order, and cannot be profitably studied in isolation from politics."[36]

Gilpin's approach to IPE was enormously influential, but it nevertheless remained a minority perspective within the subfield which remained predominantly liberal. Stephen Krasner was among those scholars who advanced the agenda suggested by Gilpin's contributions. In *Defending the National Interest: Raw Materials Investments and U.S. Foreign Policy* (1978)—note the purposeful double entendre of the title—and in *Structural Conflict: The Third World Against Global Liberalism* (1985), Krasner emphasized the distinct role of the state in shaping the pattern of economic activity—and called attention to how those preferences and outcomes diverged from the default settings implied by the pressures of pure and purposeless market forces.

Krasner's most notable and enduring contribution along these lines was his paper "State Power and the Structure of International Trade" (1976), which tied together several of the strands of this discussion. "State Power" (the title should sound familiar), was a statist conception of what would become known as "Hegemonic Stability Theory," first suggested by Charles Kindleberger in his one of his most influential books, *The World in Depression, 1929–1939* (1973). Kindleberger had argued that the Great Depression was so deep and so enduring due to the absence of a state willing and able to embrace a leadership role, and thus unable to take the measures necessary to stabilize and restore the world economy. Generalized, the theory of hegemonic stability associated a concentration of power (that is, a hegemon) with global economic openness, and thus greater efficiency and economic growth (one of the themes Gilpin emphasized in *War and Change*). Kindleberger, leaning Smithian, saw the problem as one of market failure—the world economy depended on the provision of public goods to thrive, and only a hegemon would be so large as to

---

36. Gilpin, *War and Change in International Politics* (Cambridge: Cambridge University Press, 1981); E. H. Carr, *The Twenty Years' Crisis 1919–1939* (London: Macmillan and Co., 2nd ed., 1946), 117.

see its particular interest in accord with the general interest, and thus take costly measures necessary to ensure systemic stability (such as maintaining an open market in times of distress, and orchestrating and supervising a system of global free trade more generally).

Krasner, profoundly influenced by Gilpin, reached instead for a Hirschman-esque explanation for the same pattern. Openness was associated with hegemony, Krasner argued, because the hegemon expected to thrive in a relative economic sense, but also, crucially, as a political calculation, from such an environment. The logic was the one set out by Hirschman in *National Power*:

> The relationship between political power and the international trading structure can be analyzed in terms of the relative opportunity costs of closure for trading partners. The higher the relative cost of closure, the weaker the political position of the state.[37]

Thus, after World War II, for example, the United States pushed for an open international trading system in part because it understood that it had the least to lose from closure, and would thus be politically empowered, relative to other states.

VI

Complementary to the notion of influence, à la Hirschman (and as deployed by Krasner), is the related but distinct concept of structural power, which can be associated with Susan Strange. In contributions that included "International Relations and International Economics: A Case of Mutual Neglect" (1970), and, especially, *Sterling and British Policy: A Political Study of an International Currency in Decline* (1971), the book that illustrated how issuing the currency widely used as the "world's money" first enhanced but later impinged upon British power, Strange was also present at the creation of IPE.

Strange defined structural power as "the power to decide how things shall be done, the power to shape frameworks within which states relate to each other."[38] Thus it is not about forcing others to bend to one's will, but, often implicitly, establishing the context within which actors make decisions about what measures

37. Stephen Krasner, "State Power and the Structure of International Trade," *World Politics* 28:3 (1976): 317, 320.

38. Susan Strange, "Finance, Information, and Power," *Review of International Studies* 16:3 (1990): 259–74.

will best serve their interests. As with Hirschman effects, structural power thus reflects how the pattern of economic relations between states influences calculations of political interest, narrowly defined, and, again, is distinct from coercive power—but is nevertheless commonly ubiquitous and generates incentive structures that are consequential for international politics.

Strange was a particularly astute observer of the politics of international monetary relations, and of the relationship between American power and the international role of the dollar. Most insightfully, in those difficult 1970s, while others saw the collapse of the Bretton Woods system as a harbinger of US weakness and decline, Strange, who would consistently challenge "the persistent myth of lost hegemony," saw the exercise of extraordinary strength.[39] With the ability to simply and unilaterally change the rules, the United States shed some of the costs and constraints of having the dollar serve as the world's money, while retaining the structural power garnered by its continued global role. The role of the US dollar as the "key currency," which was not a function of its convertibility into gold (accurately dismissed by Keynes as a "barbarous relic") but due to the breadth of its international use, as well as the extraordinary depth, security, and perceived stability of the American financial system—and, crucially, the paucity of plausible alternatives—meant that any consideration of the global macro-economy, for better or worse, took place in the context of dollar primacy. (The unique and central role of the dollar also has allowed the US to more easily impose financial sanctions on adversaries, and contributed to American "hard power" by loosening the disciplining macroeconomic constraints more promptly faced by other states, thus implicitly enabling its exercise of force abroad.)

A world that runs on the greenback is a world in which other countries can find their interests conditioned by their relationship with the dollar, even for states that did not purposefully sign on as "stakeholders" in an American system. It is thus not surprising to observe the US taking measures to bolster the international role of the dollar at moments when it appeared vulnerable, such as in the 1970s, when it reached secret agreements with Gulf states in apparent exchange for security guarantees, and in the late 1990s, when American officials moved aggressively to crush Japan's nascent agenda for an Asian Monetary Fund that might sidestep the influence of the International Monetary Fund (and enhance the regional role of the Yen).

39. Susan Strange, "The Persistent Myth of Lost Hegemony," *International Organization* 41:4 (1987): 551–74.

More generally, Strange would have no trouble recognizing, with Gilpin, that the emergence of economic globalization in the 1990s was not the affectless consequence of irresistible market forces, but rather was actively encouraged by a post-Cold War United States, which, as the superpower in a one-superpower world, assessed that it would be relatively advantaged in such an environment. The US push for globalization—with financial globalization leading the way—was in large part an expression of a geopolitical strategy, which went hand in hand with a complementary economic vision.[40]

The remarkable reach of American structural power was illustrated by the Global Financial Crisis of 2008. It is little short of breathtaking that a crisis with an American epicenter, rooted in its economic practices, and which exposed the rot of its entire financial edifice, was accompanied by a run *towards*, rather than a flight from, the US economy and the dollar. Similarly eye-opening was the fact that China, the most significant geopolitical rival of the United States, quickly understood that it was an essential stakeholder in the American order, and in the heat of that moment behaved in ways designed to stabilize rather than undermine the system. When a key political rival not only fails to take advantage of a self-inflicted catastrophe, and instead, if anything, takes measures to bolster the tottering status quo built and run by its adversary—that is structural power.

VII

But of course, even American power, as it must, has its limits. This can be seen in the changing balance of hard military power in the Western Pacific, and additionally and perhaps even more consequentially in practice, in the fact that regionally and globally, the currents of Hirschmanesque influence and Strange's structural power are increasingly running against US interests. We reject the enterprise of prediction in International Relations, an arena characterized by uncertainty and contingency, where crucial turning points are often formed by unanticipated shocks. Nevertheless, should current trends continue along plausible paths, likely consequences can be anticipated.

The emergence of China's economy as both a central pillar and an engine of the global economy, will, following the logics articulated previously,

---

40. It should be noted, however, that in his late writings Gilpin mistakenly—or prematurely?—anticipated an increasingly regionalized global economy as states sought to retain some degree of autonomy in an increasingly interconnected world.

fundamentally shape the emerging pattern of world politics. And should the key currency status of the dollar finally erode, for example, or if the US indeed renounces the pursuit of what Arnold Wolfers described as "milieu goals" in favor of a more short-sighted, transactionalist "America First" foreign policy, its structural power will atrophy.[41] The US may achieve greater success in extracting a larger share of concessions from others in bilateral negotiations, but those gains will come at the cost of America's broader international political influence.

At the same time, for many countries, the increasing importance of their economic relations with China will lead to a greater sensitivity to the foreign policy preferences of the People's Republic. Given that, short of war (always possible but relatively rare), the common currency of international political power—getting what one wants on the world stage—is influence rather than force, these shifts have the potential to be salient and consequential. But regardless of which direction the emerging pattern of world politics bends towards, scholars of international relations and international political economy have much to learn from the contributions of thinkers such as Hirschman, Gilpin, and Strange who advanced understandings of the economic dimensions of national security strategy beyond the insights of earlier Western thinkers such as Smith, Hamilton, and List.

Contemporary scholars also need a better understanding of Chinese perspectives on this topic. China's growing clout in the global economy itself has been fostered by strategic choices made by its policymakers since the late 1970s to prioritize the pursuit of economic development. Those choices, in turn, were consistent with a long-standing lineage of Chinese thinkers who emphasized the economic aspects of national security strategy. Those writing in the late nineteenth and early twentieth centuries developed even more ambitious ideas on this subject that those of Smith, Hamilton, and List. Witnessing the strategic consequences of China's economic weakness at the time, Chinese scholars prioritized a full-scale transformation of China's economy as the crucial first step on the road to fending off and eventually challenging Western power. Through the lenses of China's history in that period and these indigenous traditions of thought, we can better understand the enormous emphasis placed in the post-1978 period on economic foundations of strategy, including the pursuit of bold plans for state-led economic development.

---

41. Arnold Wolfers, "The Goals of Foreign Policy," in his *Discord and Collaboration* (Baltimore, MD: Johns Hopkins University Press, 1962), 73.

Whether China now uses its growing power to serve neo-imperialist or anti-imperialist goals also recalls the debate on this topic between Liang and Sun in the early twentieth century.

Earle's chapter in the original edition of *Makers* made a seminal contribution in highlighting some of the key Western classics that addressed the relationship between economics and national security. His intellectual history now needs to be complemented by analyses that explore traditions of thought on this topic from China and other parts of the world.

PART II

Strategy in an Age of Great-Power Rivalry

CHAPTER 11

Sully, Richelieu, and Mazarin

FRENCH STRATEGIES OF EQUILIBRIUM IN THE SEVENTEENTH CENTURY

Iskander Rehman

In early June 1660, Europe's two greatest powers finally came to terms after more than a century and a half of intense rivalry. The occasion was the formalization of the marriage of Maria Teresa of Spain to Louis XIV of France, a union which served to consummate, both symbolically and legally, the Peace of the Pyrenees—a laboriously crafted, seventy-nine-page treaty.

This had been a hard-earned settlement. For more than eleven years after the Peace of Westphalia had brought a fragile peace to much of Europe, Paris and Madrid had fought on. While both warring states were financially and morally exsanguinated, the protracted struggle had revealed Habsburg Spain as the weaker party, and the continental balance of power had decisively shifted in Bourbon France's favor. Not only had Madrid encountered a series of military reverses in the Spanish Netherlands—most notably at the Battle of the Dunes in 1658, when its army of Flanders had been trounced by an Anglo-French force—it was also staggering under the weight of an irretrievable debt burden while being mired in a vicious war against its former Portuguese subjects.

For the Spanish attendees, the peace gathering was therefore something of a bittersweet moment. Watching from the sidelines was a gnarled, crimson-clad figure—Cardinal Mazarin, the redoubtable chief-minister of France. Deploying his signature blend of cold *raison d'état* and Mediterranean avuncularity, the Italian-born polyglot had negotiated a treaty which marked an epochal shift in European geopolitics—all while eschewing the more maximalist approach to negotiations advocated by some hawkish French military figures, who had urged Mazarin to wrest the entirety of the Spanish Netherlands away from their enfeebled foe.

The Peace of the Pyrenees, which—among other things—obliged Madrid to formally recognize France's painfully negotiated gains at Westphalia and resulted in a sizable expansion of French territory, was an impressive achievement. It appears all the more remarkable when bookended against another landmark Franco-Spanish treaty, the treaty of Cateau-Cambrésis, negotiated exactly a hundred years prior, in 1559. With the signing of that earlier diplomatic compact, which had ended the bloody Italian Wars of the Renaissance, Henri II had reluctantly surrendered virtually all of France's territories in northern Italy, and agreed to evacuate most of its remaining transalpine garrisons.

The financially ruined Valois monarchy, already quietly seething with confessional tensions between its Catholic majority and Huguenot (Calvinist) minority, had then tumbled into a spiral of fratricidal violence, with no less than—depending on how one counts or delineates them—eight religious wars over thirty-six years. Foreign powers meddled in the nation's byzantine domestic politics and intervened in its civil wars. Philip II of Spain, in particular, had persistently sought to maintain France in a state of strife, with one of his advisors smugly observing that, "The wars in France bring peace for Spain, and peace in Spain brings war for France—thanks to the flow of our ducats."[1] Whereas Spain was initially content with providing covert military aid and subsidies to the rebel forces of the Catholic League, it eventually opted to engage in direct military intervention in an unsuccessful, last-ditch attempt to prevent Henri of Navarre, later crowned as Henri IV, from gaining the throne. It was only with this first Bourbon monarch's reign, from 1589 to 1610, that a tenuous peace was eventually reintroduced, and that France began the long and difficult process of salving its wounds and devising a coherent grand strategy.

The following chapter provides an in-depth examination of this recuperative process, and of what can best be described as France's pursuit of "primacy through equilibrium" from 1589 to the Peace of the Pyrenees in 1659. Over that critical seventy-year period, France gradually recovered its traditional primacy,

---

1. Geoffrey Parker, *The Grand Strategy of Philip II* (New Haven, CT: Yale University Press, 1998), 86.

and—through an adroit combination of internal and external balancing—permanently sapped the foundations of Spanish power. This is the intellectual history of one of Europe's greatest acts of national resurrection, and it is told through an analysis of three seminal figures in the history of French statecraft: Maximilien de Béthune, Duke of Sully, the Protestant lord who accumulated a variety of ministerial roles under Henri IV from 1589 to 1610; Armand Jean du Plessis, Cardinal-Duke of Richelieu, who served as chief minister under Louis XIII from 1624 to 1642; and Cardinal Jules Mazarin, who was France's chief minister, first during the tumultuous regency of Anne of Austria, from 1643 to 1651, and then during the first decade of Louis XIV's reign, from 1651 to 1661.[2]

These three individuals—all so different in their temperaments, skill sets, and personal backgrounds—were united in their desire to see a strengthened and unified French monarchy prevail over its Habsburg foe; and in their conviction that such a goal could only be achieved through the design of a new collective security architecture buttressed by international law and formalized via security guarantees. Yet, despite these overarching similarities, drastic improvements in circumstance—most notably in the Franco-Spanish balance of power from the 1640s onward—eventually prompted a degree of hubristic deviation from France's initial, more restrained conception of a pan-European equilibrium. Indeed, some of the very first warning signs of Louis XIV's voracious "earth-hunger" and hegemonic ambitions can already be discerned in aspects of Mazarin's statecraft. More broadly, France's subsequent overextension serves as a cautionary tale—whether on the tendency toward diplomatic intemperance following an earlier period of strategic success, or on the enduring challenge of marrying primacy with equanimity.[3]

2. Maximilien de Béthune was elevated to the rank of Duke of Sully in 1606. Armand-Jean du Plessis achieved the rank of cardinal in 1622 and was awarded the title of Duke of Richelieu in 1629. Jules Mazarin, for his part, was gifted the cardinal's hat in 1641. For purposes of clarity and readability, this chapter will primarily refer to each protagonist under their best-known title/appellation, i.e., as "Sully," "Richelieu," or "Mazarin."

3. For such a well-known figure of French history, there are surprisingly few full-length biographies of Sully. In English, the best source remains David Buisseret, *Sully and the Growth of Centralized Government in France: 1598–1610* (London: Eyre and Spottiswoode, 1968). For a more recent and extensive biography, see Bernard Barbiche and Ségolène de Dainville-Barbiche, *Sully: L'Homme et ses Fidèles* (Paris: Fayard, 1997). For a fascinating historiography of the potent mythology surrounding Sully, see Laurent Avezou, *Sully a Travers l'Histoire: Les Avatars d'un Mythe Politique* (Paris: Ecole des Chartes, 2001). For biographical treatments of Richelieu, this author would recommend beginning with Françoise Hildesheimer, *Richelieu* (Paris:

I

The period ranging from the late Renaissance to the early modern era was one of immense political, intellectual, and religious ferment. The increased complexity of the early modern state, its burgeoning centralization, the growing sophistication of its bureaucratic apparatus—all of these developments required chronically overworked monarchs to find safe and effective ways to delegate their authority. Institutionally, this found expression through the proliferation across Europe of small, ruling councils composed of tight cadres of ministers and secretaries, often each operating at the heart of their own intricate networks of patronage and clientele. The period also bore witness to the phenomenon of the rise of the favorite or chief minister—ruthless, larger-than-life figures such as the Count-Duke of Olivares in Spain, Axel Oxenstierna in Sweden, or Lord Buckingham in England. A favorite's influence and longevity, whether in France or any other European monarchy, revolved around the precise, oft-idiosyncratic nature of their relationship with their royal overseer. While Henri IV of France chose not to appoint a single chief minister over the course of his reign, relying instead on a small core of key advisors, the nature of his spirited friendship with the volcanic Sully, one of his most loyal youthhood companions and a fellow grizzled veteran of the wars of religion, was unique in its depth and intimacy, and undoubtedly contributed to Sully's unparalleled influence on matters of state. The rapport between Cardinal Richelieu and Louis XIII, while less casual and

Flammarion, 2004), Carl H. Burckhardt's classic three-volume series *Richelieu and His Age* (New York, NY: Helen and Kurt Wolff Book, 1967), Robert Jean Knecht's tersely elegant *Richelieu* (New York, NY: Routledge, 2007), Roland Mousnier, *L'Homme Rouge ou la Vie du Cardinal de Richelieu* (Paris: Robert Laffont, 1992), and Joseph Bergin, *The Rise of Richelieu* (New Haven, CT: Yale University Press, 1991). On Richelieu's grand strategy and its intellectual foundations, see Iskander Rehman, "Raison d'Etat: Richelieu's Grand Strategy During the Thirty Years' War," *Texas National Security Review* 2:3 (2019): 38–78; William Farr Church, *Richelieu and Reason of State* (Princeton, NJ: Princeton University Press, 1973); Etienne Thuau, *Raison d'Etat et Pensée Politique a l'Epoque de Richelieu* (Paris: Armand Colin, 1966); and Jörg Wollenberg, *Richelieu: Staatsräson und Kircheninteresse: zur Legitimation der Politik des Kardinalpremier* (Bielefeld: Pfeffersche Buchhandlung, 1977). For a granular assessment of French military reforms, strategy, and performance under Richelieu, see David Parrott, *Richelieu's Army: War, Government and Society in France, 1624–1642* (Cambridge: Cambridge University Press, 2006). On Mazarin's life and approach to foreign policy, see Pierre Goubert, *Mazarin* (Paris: Fayard, 1990); Derek Croxton, *Peacemaking in Early Modern Europe: Cardinal Mazarin and the Congress of Westphalia* (Selinsgrove: Susquehanna University Press, 1969); and Paul Sonnino, *Mazarin's Quest: The Congress of Westphalia and the Coming of the Fronde* (Cambridge, MA: Harvard University Press, 2008). On Mazarin's actions leading up to, and during the Fronde, see David Parrott, *1652: The Cardinal, The Prince, and the Crisis of the Fronde* (Oxford: Oxford University Press, 2020).

friendly than that between Sully and Henri IV, was also marked by a profound—if sometimes wary—level of mutual respect. And for the young Louis XIV, who had lost his father at the age of four, Mazarin was not only a trusted tutor and advisor, but also a beloved godfather and a reassuring paternal presence.

During the earlier phases of the Renaissance, the nature of statecraft had undergone a deep transformation, as the practice of establishing permanent embassies, which first came about in Italy in the mid-fifteenth century, spread across the European continent. The generalization of more sophisticated and permanent forms of diplomatic administration introduced a new climate of "mutual watchfulness," whereby resident ambassadors, finely attuned to every minute shift in the balance of power, continually funneled information to their capitals.[4] There was a widespread sense that European history was increasingly interconnected, and that an ill-considered military venture within the continent's cramped political space could have damaging ripple effects. Thus, when the French king Charles VIII had invaded Italy in 1494, careening through its fine-spun web of preexisting diplomatic ties and mutual security guarantees, Guicciardini famously noted that he had durably destroyed its preexisting balance of power.[5]

This revised conception of international relations was the reflection of broader intellectual trends. Galenic theories of medicine, which were extremely popular in the late medieval and early Renaissance eras, understood physical health to be the result of a continuous process of equalization of the humors within a dynamic and multivalent bodily system—a biological imperative which was then applied to describe the inner workings of "balanced" polities. Meanwhile, the discovery of Copernican heliocentrism appeared to further confirm the notion that international order was not necessarily expressed via a rigid and static hierarchy, but rather through a carefully synchronized ballet of perpetual movement. Last but not least, the advent of Cartesianism, along with its associated mechanical philosophy, was a pivotal moment in the intellectual history of the West, shaping the work of later political theorists such as Thomas Hobbes, who famously portrayed the state as a great, clanking machine—a gargantuan engine that, like the human body, moves itself "by springs and wheels as doth a watch."[6]

4. Garett Mattingly, *Renaissance Diplomacy* (Boston, MA: Houghton Mifflin Harcourt Books, 1971), 110.

5. Francesco Giucciardini, *The History of Italy, Book I* (Princeton, NJ: Princeton University Press, 1984), 98.

6. Thomas Hobbes, *Leviathan or the Matter, Forme and Power of a Common Wealth Ecclesiasticall* (London: Andrew Cooke, 1651), Introduction.

Equilibrist thinking was especially widespread in early seventeenth-century France. After the horror of France's religious wars, the urgency of establishing a lasting European peace, which would take the form of a self-adjusting equilibrium, was keenly felt by Sully, Richelieu, and Mazarin. Staunch believers in Gallic exceptionalism, all three statesmen were convinced that only a revived French monarchy possessed the historical mandate and latent capacity to engage in such an ambitious reordering of the international system—and that it was, therefore, the only actor worthy of attaining primacy.

The challenge was twofold. First, Paris needed to displace Madrid as Europe's leading power, and, if possible, isolate or sever Spain from its Austrian dynastic branch. Second, the new Bourbon monarchy needed to persuade lesser European powers to buy into its vision for regional security by proving that it could a play a stabilizing role as a benevolent arbiter. Paris thus would be simultaneously perceived both as one of the scales in the balance, and as the "holder of the [said] balance."[7]

II

Early in the morning on August 24, 1572, the young Maximilien de Béthune and future Duke of Sully was shaken out of his slumber by the clangor of alarm bells and bloodcurdling shrieks. Upon learning that raging mobs were roving street-to-street, pillaging Protestant homes and slaughtering their inhabitants, the young Huguenot sought shelter at a nearby Catholic school whose principal was a family friend. The terrified twelve-year-old wound his way through the torchlit alleyways and blood-spattered streets until he eventually reached the gates of the college sanctuary. In his memoirs, Sully recounted how he saw "houses broken open and plundered, and men, women, and children butchered, while a constant cry was kept up of 'Kill! Kill! O you Huguenots!' "[8]

Sully would be profoundly affected by his close escape from the Saint Bartholomew's massacre. It inculcated in the young survivor a passion for order, a disdain for fanaticism, and a strong desire to shield France from foreign interference, which he considered had played a leading role in exacerbating his

7. Per Mauserth, "Balance-of-Power Thinking from the Renaissance to the French Revolution," *Journal of Peace Research* 1:2 (1964): 120–36.

8. Maximilien de Béthune, *Memoirs of the Duke of Sully, Minister to Henry the Great—Originally Entitled Mémoires ou Oeconomies Royales D'Estat Domestiques, Politiques, et Militaires de Henry le Grand, Volume 1, Book I*, trans. Charlotte Lennox (London: William Miller, 1810), 39.

beloved *patrie*'s internal divisions. If he had his way, Sully later claimed, the continent's delicate preexisting confessional status would remain frozen in amber, for "it has always been my opinion that the true system of politics, that which may give and preserve tranquility in Europe, depended upon firmly fixing her in this equilibrium."[9]

In the years following the massacre, Sully continued his formal education, developing a particular fondness for mathematics. With a mind like a steel trap, the young noble's love of numbers, geometry, and statistics would serve him well in his future ministerial career. His second great lifelong passion was the study of ancient history. Devouring the morally uplifting works of classical historians, Sully was inspired less by the Neoplatonism of the earlier Renaissance, with its emphasis on mysticism and individual enlightenment, and more by the earthy, civically minded Neostoicism of writers such as Justus Lipsius and Guillaume du Vair.

In the spring of 1576, the sixteen-year-old Sully rode across the country to join the army of fellow Huguenot Henri de Navarre (later crowned as Henri IV) and began a distinguished career as a soldier, fighting under his lord's banner until his eventual victory in France's civil wars. As Sully rose through the ranks, he displayed a marked aptitude for military engineering, with a talent for trench warfare, sapping, and mining. Whereas Henri of Navarre was one of the era's finest cavalry officers, with an almost preternatural predilection for speed and shock tactics, Sully's punishingly methodical intellect was better suited to the grime and drudgery of siege warfare. He also took a nurturing interest in the development and implementation of new forms of artillery and fortification design. His increasingly technical expertise was to prove invaluable when subduing hostile strongholds or decimating larger enemy formations, such as at the battle of Coutras in 1587, when the mobile artillery train Sully co-commanded inflicted horrific casualties.

Due to his unique background, Sully would also come to play a vital role as an intermediary. In the early, troubled years of Henri IV's reign, when the new monarch sought to reunify the nobility by offering former League members generous bribes and terms of amnesty, Sully was often the go-between. The austere French Calvinist shrewdly leveraged his sprawling, trans-confessional network of contacts and clients, and personally ensured the rallying of a number of recalcitrant magnates to the Bourbon cause.

---

9. de Béthune, *Memoirs of the Duke of Sully, Volume 4, Book XXIII*, 101.

Sully was also a useful interlocutor with his fellow Protestants, many of whom had been deeply troubled by Henri IV's decision to convert to Catholicism in 1593. While some of the Huguenot grandees had desperately exhorted Henri not to abandon their shared faith, Sully, ever the pragmatist, had privately argued in favor of conversion. Indeed, the new ruler's belated embrace of Catholicism was in many ways what delivered the coup de grâce to the vacillatory opposition of the League, enabling France's divided Catholic elites to rally around the new Bourbon monarchy. This led to the progressive normalization of Henri IV's reign, with his formalized coronation taking place in 1594.

During those fraught years, Henri had been obliged, in the name of unity, to parcel out political and financial concessions to his former Catholic opponents. Understandably, these demonstrations of largesse generated mounting disquiet within France's heavily armed Huguenot minority, and eventually Henri IV found himself obliged to address his erstwhile co-religionaries' growing list of grievances. Peace was preserved through the issuance of the Edict of Nantes in 1598, a landmark document which accorded Huguenots freedom of worship in approximately two hundred designated towns. Separate articles discreetly provided for the maintenance of protective garrisons in certain key Protestant "security towns," at royal expense. In subsequent negotiations to secure acceptance of the Edict of Nantes, Sully frequently served as the Protestants' direct conduit to Henri IV—all while revealing himself to be an intransigent defender of royal authority, with little tolerance for any hint of religiously inspired separatism, whether Catholic or Protestant.

For all of Sully's diplomatic utility, it was his prodigious organizational talents that cemented his position, first as Henri IV's financial fixer, and then as his indispensable advisor. Indeed, to this day, Sully is still perceived as one of the Ancien Regime's most consequential drivers of state centralization and regulation.

During their years of incessant fighting across France, Henri IV had developed a strong respect for his younger subordinate's proficiency in military finance and resupply, gradually entrusting him with logistical oversight of his campaigns. With the winding down of France's wars of religion, Sully's administrative acumen was applied to the civilian domain. Gifted with almost boundless reserves of energy, Sully's roving intellect only truly found solace in the strict regimentation of every aspect of public and private existence. Upon assuming the reins of power, Henri IV entrusted Sully with the delicate task of salvaging the bankrupt kingdom's parlous finances. The young man set to the task with gusto, and— through a mixture of sly ingenuity and blunt intimidation—successfully renegotiated the bulk of the king's outstanding loans. By the mid- to late-1590s, Henri IV evidently felt that internal dynamics were sufficiently stabilized to allow a Huguenot lord access to the highest levels of officialdom. Sully thus began formally attending the meetings of the highest-level royal councils in 1596, before being nominated to the newly important position of superintendent of finance in 1598. Thereafter followed a flurry of new titles and ministerial roles, often in very rapid succession: superintendent of fortifications, *Grand Voyer de France* ("grand overseer," responsible for all major public works and infrastructure), grand master of artillery, all in 1599; superintendent of royal construction (*Surintendant des Bâtiments*) in 1602; and governor of the large, central region of Poitou in 1603.

As superintendent of finance, Sully prosecuted financial maladministration with a joyous zeal, dispatching commissioners across France to conduct detailed censuses of towns and parishes, and establishing an exhaustive inventory of every outstanding municipal debt. With an inordinate love for data and quantitative analysis, Sully drafted personal copies of the royal budget which he then meticulously coded and cross-referenced with the aid of a key comprising over two thousand symbols. He also encouraged a general shift from direct to indirect taxation, and, in 1604, instituted the *Paulette*, an annual tax on government and judicial office holders. Through the disbursement of this specially levied tax, officeholders acquired the right to transfer their positions to their progeny. This controversial initiative contributed more than any other measure to empower the new hereditary caste of government administrators—or *noblesse de robe*—that hoary traditionalists such as Sully affected to disdain. It was, however, highly profitable, ensuring a steady, reliable stream of revenue to the Crown. Sully also established a royal contingency fund for military operations, stabilized the notoriously volatile French currency, and left the kingdom with a rare budgetary surplus—all without massively increasing the burden of taxation on the less privileged categories of the population.

An avid aficionado of Xenophon's theories of household and property management, Sully has traditionally been viewed as one of France's most ardent champions of agriculture. The Huguenot lord viewed France's rarefied climate, bountiful resources, and fertile land as key comparative advantages over a more arid Spain, famously extolling the fact that "tillage and pasturage" were the "two breasts of France" and easily equaled in their worth all "the mines and treasures of [Spanish-controlled] Peru."[10] Yet Sully favored the development

10. de Béthune, *Memoirs of the Duke of Sully, Volume III, Book XVI*, 178.

of France's industry as well as its agriculture. He did not view the steady growth of European trade interdependence as a negative in and of itself, but rather as a reality to be carefully managed—and perhaps even exploited—by vigilant custodians of "sovereign" economic interests. When in 1603–4 France and Spain became embroiled in a tense trade war, Sully thus played a lead role in negotiating the agreement to arrest the cycle of duties and tariffs. By assuming the new position of *Grand Voyer de France*, Sully also oversaw a colossal nation-wide program of road, bridge, and canal construction; an effort unprecedented in its scope and scale which also had broader strategic ramifications. Indeed, strengthening the defense of the realm in preparation for a renewed, and more protracted conflict with the Habsburgs was always at the forefront of the veteran's mind.

As superintendent of fortifications, Sully engaged in a widespread effort to revamp France's border defenses—especially to the north and east—drawing inspiration from recent Dutch innovations in fortification design. Meanwhile, his headquarters at the Palais de l'Arsenal evolved into a massive armory and munitions depot, as well as a noisome hub of technological experimentation. As grand master of the artillery, Sully—dubbed *Le Cannonier* by foreign diplomats—labored to modernize and standardize the equipment of this veritable service arm of the French military. Last but not least, one English ambassador later recalled, Sully was "forever hammering for building a navy for the sea," advocating for France's transformation into a premier maritime power.[11] In Sully's mind, the primary purpose of an expanded navy was to challenge Spain in the Mediterranean—thereby threatening its communications with its Italian territories. In the event of a renewal of high-intensity warfare, France should also be able to strike Spain at its economic "heart and entrails," by mounting raids against its transatlantic colonial possessions.

The increasingly charged international environment lent Sully's initiatives a sense of urgency. In 1598, with the signing of the Treaty of Vervins, France and Spain agreed to a temporary reprieve in armed hostilities. For the next twelve years, and until Henri IV's assassination in 1610, the Franco-Spanish relationship morphed into a cold war, with long periods of simmering rivalry interspersed by episodes of white-knuckled tension. Philip III of Spain continued to covertly support and shelter rebellious French nobles, and in 1604,

---

11. Sir George Carew, "Relation of the State of France With the Characters of Henry IV and the Principal Persons of that Court," in *An Historical View of the Negotiations Between the Courts of England, France and Brussels, 1592–1617*, Thomas Birch, ed. (London: A. Millar, 1740), 487.

Paris was convulsed by a high-profile case of espionage when a clerk was found to have been funneling French cypher codes to the Spanish. Meanwhile, in 1602, Henri received an envoy from the restive Moriscos, the forcibly converted Moors of Granada, and signed a secret agreement of support for their rebellion. He also negotiated a treaty of revitalized cooperation with the Sublime Porte and continued to covertly provide subsidies to the Dutch, thus perpetuating two long-standing traditions in France's counter-containment strategy. Indeed, under the previous Valois dynasty, in their attempts to cripple or distract their Habsburg foes, French kings had not hesitated to support partners ranging from disgruntled Lutheran German princes to the Ottoman Empire. These alliances with heretics and infidels had been framed at the time as a necessary, albeit temporary, evil. In the volatile aftermath of France's religious wars, however, Henri IV was obliged to tread far more gingerly than his Valois predecessors, for fear of inciting renewed religious polarization over issues of foreign policy.

Although Sully was eager to preserve the post-Vervins peace, he was also resigned to its impermanence. And like so many political theorists of his era, he occasionally mused that a well-conducted foreign war, however tragic, would have the perverse side-effect of fostering greater internal cohesion, once confiding that, "the true means of setting the realm at rest is by keeping up a foreign war, toward which one can channel, like water in a drain, all the turbulent humors of the kingdom."[12] Spain, after all, still posed a serious threat along France's borders—with fifty thousand troops ominously poised in the Low Countries and five thousand more in Lombardy. From 1600–1, France, concerned over the security of its alpine perimeter, had waged a brief but successful punitive war against Spain's troublesome ally, the Duchy of Savoy. In so doing, French forces had wrested control of a large band of territory west of the Rhône overlooking the so-called Spanish road—the slender military corridor connecting Madrid's Italian possessions with the Spanish Netherlands. These developments, along with France's growing confidence and vigor following decades of relative infirmity, were a source of mounting anxiety for Philip III and his advisors. In his memoirs, Sully recounted the Spanish ruler's escalating disquiet over the fact that "the balance had begun to lean too much on the side of France."[13]

---

12. Quoted in Joseph Nouillac, *Villeroy: Secrétaire d'Etat et Ministre de Charles IX, Henri III et Henri IV* (1543-1610) (Paris: Honoré Champion, 1909), 390.

13. de Béthune, *Memoirs of the Duke of Sully, Volume 4, Book XXIV*, 311.

In 1610, these tensions came to a head over the right of succession to the United Duchies of Jülich-Cleves-Berg following the death of its Catholic ruler. Wedged between the Netherlands and the lower Rhineland, this congeries of strategically situated territories was claimed by two opposing coalitions: the Catholic League, led by the Holy Roman Emperor Rudolf II, and supported by Spain; and an Evangelical Union of German Protestant princes backed by France. Plunging into a sudden frenzy of activity, Henri IV declared himself determined to protect the "ancient liberties" of all smaller European states from the threat of Habsburg coercion. French diplomats were dispatched to mobilize financial and military support from overseas, while an army of over fifty thousand men was amassed under Sully's supervision. Yet just as he was preparing to leave Paris to lead his armies to the front, Henri IV was suddenly stabbed to death by a Catholic fanatic.

The most detailed ad hoc rationalization of Henri IV's hyperactive foreign policy was provided by his grief-stricken advisor close to thirty years later. Sully famously argued that France's first Bourbon monarch had been operating under the framework of an intricate "Grand Design" for countering Habsburg domination. Under the aegis of this "vast enterprise," France would forcibly reengineer the geopolitics of the continent for the collective good. It would stitch together new coalitions; arbitrate festering bilateral disputes; protect the age-old rights of the smaller, more vulnerable *stati liberi* ("free states"); and ensure that the "house of Austria (Habsburg)" was "divested of the empire and of all the possessions in Germany, Italy and the low countries." "In a word," Sully bluntly asserted, it would be reduced "to the sole kingdom of Spain, bounded by the ocean, the Mediterranean, and the Pyrenean mountains."[14] Contemporary historians have evinced a certain amount of skepticism regarding the retiree's grandiose post hoc characterizations of French strategy. Nevertheless, Sully's *Grand Design* remains a seminal text in the history of European statecraft.

The *Grand Design* called for a reorganization of Europe around fifteen political entities—six hereditary kingdoms, five elective states or monarchies, and four republics. While this continental remodeling would require the implementation of vast schemes of territorial readjustment, France, Sully pointedly noted, "would receive nothing for itself, apart from the glory of distributing them with equity."[15] Such a demonstration of selflessness would not only

---

14. de Béthune, *Memoirs of the Duke of Sully, Volume 5, Book XXVII*, x.
15. de Béthune, *Memoirs of the Duke of Sully, Volume 5, Book XXVII*, 405.

bolster France's reputation for magnanimity and equanimity as the "sole benefactor and arbitrator of Europe," it would also prevent it from engaging in ruinous overextension.[16]

A general council with delegates from across Europe would be charged with
mediating disputes between these newly balanced entities, and with levying
shared funds and troops in order to pursue that old pan-European dream—the
revival of a great crusade against the Turks. Sully's belief that a general European peace could, regrettably, only be achieved through system-shattering
force, differed greatly from the Renaissance's earlier, more Erasmian visions of
international concord. This somber conviction would be shared by the French
minister's two principal successors.

III

Henri IV's assassination was a traumatic moment in French history. After a
decade of relative tranquility, a deep sense of foreboding now rippled through
the body politic, with many fearing a return to civil war. Public concerns were
exacerbated by the young age of his son, Louis XIII, who was only eight, and
by the expectation of a renewal of the instability historically associated with
minority rule. These dire projections were not borne out entirely. Many Protestant and Catholic communities preemptively renewed their confessional
coexistence pacts, dampening the prospects of any immediate conflagration.
Queen Marie de Medici also moved fast to consolidate her authority as regent,
immediately confirming the Edict of Nantes and making a point of retaining
her late husband's core group of advisors.

Tensions soon flared, however, between Sully and his colleagues. While the
queen politely professed to take the proud Huguenot's recommendations into
consideration, she preferred the advice dispensed by his Catholic colleagues
or her Florentine favorites. Marie de Medici's administration was intent on
pursuing a more cautious policy of détente with Spain, and the pugnacious
Protestant was increasingly perceived as a diplomatic liability. In February 1611,
increasingly isolated and embittered, Sully left Paris. He would spend the final
three decades of his life in forced retirement, powerlessly observing the ebb
and flow of French grand strategy from his drafty castles along the Loire.

Marie de Medici was both an unpopular foreigner and deeply impression-
able—two traits which rendered her overly susceptible to the blandishments

16. de Béthune, *Memoirs of the Duke of Sully, Volume 5, Book XXVII*, 405–6.

of slithery courtiers. Sensing this vulnerability, aristocratic grandees jockeyed for influence, launched sporadic revolts, and blackmailed the Crown into granting them ever more political and monetary concessions. The Huguenots, already troubled by the advent of a new, more ardently pro-Catholic regime and by the resignation of Sully, became increasingly restive. Looking back on these years of collective confusion, backstabbing, and mediocrity, Richelieu would remark that:

> The times were so miserable that the ablest among the nobles were also those who were the most industrious in instigating quarrels; and the quarrels were such that . . . the ministers were more occupied in finding the necessary means to preserve themselves than the means that were necessary to govern the state.[17]

Indeed, it was only with the cardinal's ascent to chief minister, in 1624, that France's strategy of equilibrium began to recover its earlier vigor and purpose.

Richelieu first came to national attention in 1614, when, speaking as a representative for the clergy, he delivered a speech at the assembly of the Estates General. At that time, Richelieu had been serving for several years as bishop of Luçon, a small diocese in a war-ravaged corner of Poitou. These challenging early years of pastoral work shaped Richelieu's intellectual development. In his opening speeches and sermons, the twenty-three-year-old bishop had repeatedly emphasized the need for mutual concord and coexistence, stressing that his Huguenot and Catholic neighbors should "be united in affection and loyalty to their king."[18] Notwithstanding the heretical nature of their beliefs, Huguenots were first and foremost fellow French citizens. "In matters of state," Richelieu would later profess, "no French Catholic should be so blind as to prefer a Spaniard to a Huguenot."[19]

Richelieu's philosophy of moderation did not apply, however, to matters of state security. The counselor's conception of *raison d'état* was resolutely authoritarian and a reflection of his own absolutist tendencies, lifelong yearning

---

17. Armand Jean du Plessis de Richelieu, *Mémoires du Cardinal de Richelieu Sur Le Règne de Louis XIII Depuis 1610 Jusqu'à 1638* (Paris: Firmin Didot, 1837), 57.

18. Including in his theological treatises, such as Armand Jean du Plessis de Richelieu, *Instruction du Chrétien* (1618), and Armand Jean du Plessis de Richelieu, *Traité Qui Contient la Méthode la Plus Facile et la Plus Assurée Pour Convertir* (1657).

19. Richelieu to Schomberg, the French ambassador in Germany, in 1616, James Breck Perkins, *France Under Mazarin: With a Review of the Administration of Richelieu, Volume 1* (London: G.P. Putnam's Sons, 1887), 74.

for order, and contempt for factionalism. While a good Christian could show-case the virtues of charity and forgiveness in his private dealings, no such op-tions were available to a ruler confronted with the threat of sedition. Similarly, while a nation could display tactical flexibility in its diplomacy, its overarching objectives should remain undergirded by intellectual coherence and unity of purpose.[20] In a letter to one of his most trusted advisors, Richelieu claimed that upon taking office, "three things" had preoccupied him: "First to ruin the Huguenots and render the king absolute in his state; second, to abase the House of Austria (i.e., the House of Habsburg with both their dynastic branches); and third to discharge the French people of heavy subsidies and taxes."[21]

The repression of the Huguenot insurrection was one of Richelieu's first priorities. In December 1620, an assembly of Protestants had voted to enter into armed resistance against the government. Led by a group of talented gen-erals, this French Calvinist resistance, observed Richelieu, posed an existential threat to the French monarchy's legitimacy by appearing to form a "state within the state." In 1627, the Crown took decisive aim at the political epicenter of the uprising, and royal forces were dispatched to besiege La Rochelle. This was a massive military undertaking, overseen by Richelieu and involving the majority of the nation's military resources. The Bourbon monarchy's eventual victory over the rebels and their English sponsor accelerated the collapse of Protestant opposition to royal rule and considerably strengthened the young Louis XIII's military credentials in the eyes of his fellow European leaders. Victory was followed by the Peace of Alais, which did away with most of the Huguenots' past political privileges—and most notably their right to an au-tonomous military capability—while continuing to allow them relative free-dom of worship.

The chief minister's suppression of the revolt was part of a much wider ef-fort to reduce alternative power centers or codes of loyalty within France. The definition of treason (or of lèse-majesté) was expanded, and followed by a series of policies aimed at the French nobility's ability to resist royal authority. In 1626, the Crown ordered the destruction of all fortresses not positioned

20. See "Cardinal de Richelieu: His Letters and State Papers," in *Portraits of the Seventeenth Century: Historic and Literary*, C.A. Sainte-Beuve, ed., trans. Katharine P. Wormeley (London: Putnam & Sons, 1904), 234.

21. As quoted in, A. Lloyd Moote, *Louis XIII: The Just* (Berkeley, CA: University of California Press, 1989), 177.

along the nation's borders, regardless of the religion of their owners. In the same year, Richelieu issued a wildly unpopular edict against dueling in an effort do away with the vendetta culture that fueled internecine strife.

Over the course of the wars of religion, two broad constituencies had emerged within France's national security elite: the *politiques* or *bons français* who argued in favor of national unity, religious toleration, and vigorous containment of the Habsburgs; and the more dogmatically Catholic *dévots* who privileged the defeat of heresy, and promoted accommodation, or even alignment, with Madrid and Vienna. When Richelieu took office, the dévots, strengthened by the pro-Catholic interregnum of Marie de Medici, had come to wield a greater deal of influence. France was also in the throes of a major renaissance of reinvigorated Catholicism—a veritable golden age of spiritual revival which permeated society at all levels. The eruption of the Thirty Years' War, in 1618, only further polarized French opinion, stoking fears of an importation of confessional violence were France to get overly involved overseas. Meanwhile, Louis XIII—unlike his hyper-pragmatic father—was deeply devout, and occasionally wracked by pangs of conscience over the more morally controversial aspects of Richelieu's foreign policy. As Richelieu's earliest biographer memorably quipped, "The six square feet of the king's private study gave him more worries than all of Europe."[22] Surrounding himself with a "politico-literary strike force" of the nation's most talented polemicists and political theorists, the cardinal waged a relentless propaganda campaign in defense of France's grand strategy.[23] His goal was to demonstrate that, contrary to dévot critiques, "the good of the state coincided with that of religion," by contributing to the general *repos de la Chrétieneté* or "peace of Christendom," and to the strengthening of the French monarchy's divinely sanctioned ordering function.[24]

For Richelieu, time was the most precious commodity in the competition with Spain. As long as Paris could buy time and sap the strength of its Habsburg rivals through the subsidization of capable proxies, the cardinal was confident that France's more centralized system of government, along with its superior economic and demographic resources, would allow it to eventually prevail.[25]

22. Antoine Aubery, *L'Histoire du Cardinal Duc de Richelieu* (Cologne: Pierre Marteau, 1669), 589.

23. Marc Fumaroli, "Richelieu Patron of the Arts," in *Richelieu: Art and Power*, Hilliard Todd Goldfarb, ed. (Montreal: Montreal Museum of Fine Arts, 2002), 35.

24. William F. Church, *Richelieu and Reason of State* (Princeton, NJ: Princeton University Press, 1972), 44.

25. France's population at the time has been estimated at about sixteen million—about twice the size of Spain's.

Whereas Sully had highlighted the advantages proffered by France's food security and industrial self-sufficiency, Richelieu pointed to the additional military benefits to be derived from its unique geographic position. With its scattered territorial possessions, Spain was heavily dependent on the lines of communication which, whether by sea or by land, formed the connective tissue of its far-flung empire. France's seeming state of encirclement could, in fact, be leveraged to its advantage, as its centrality and superior interior lines of communication provided it with the means of selectively truncating the Spanish military system's clogged arteries.

Richelieu, like his predecessor Sully, emphasized the importance of sea power and of developing a strong navy. Not only would this pose a threat to Spain's trans-oceanic logistics system, it would also compel Spain to redirect its finite reserves of resources and manpower toward defending its coastal cities. Although the multitasking chief minister's naval expansion plan was not an unvarnished success, by 1635, Richelieu had succeeded in creating a navy which overshadowed England's and rivalled Spain's in the Mediterranean.

For the first decade of Richelieu's tenure, the chief minister privileged *la guerre couverte* (covert war) over *la guerre ouverte* (open war). He pursued a strategy of delay, limited military involvement, and measured assertiveness within France's near-abroad, all while seeking to sap Habsburg power from afar, via a policy of subsidized warfare. This was not only costly, necessitating increasingly large sums for France's proxies, but also diplomatically challenging. The most able French diplomats were dispatched to adjudicate disputes and cement agreements between Paris's allies and third parties, such as Poland and Sweden, so that the latter could transfer the bulk of its military assets back toward the German theater. With the aid of a sprawling network of spies and foreign envoys, Richelieu aimed to forestall any precipitate slide towards a full-spectrum and system-wide war against a unified Habsburg foe. With regard to the Holy Roman Empire, France's overarching objective was to maintain it in a state of managed disequilibrium—fomenting dissension among the prince-electors and weakening imperial authority.

The most serious crises during this period unfolded at the violent intersections of each great power's sphere of interest—whether for control of the Valtellina Valley connecting Lombardy to the Spanish Netherlands, or over the succession to the Duchy of Mantua abutting Spanish-controlled Milan. In each case, military action was undertaken in a tailored fashion, and within third-party territories, with the goal of preventing escalation to a formal declaration of war between France and Spain. Even though France's most militarily redoubtable partners, such as Sweden or the United Provinces, were Protestant, it was important that Paris's strategy be perceived as balanced, rather than overly weighted toward one confessional coalition. A great deal of energy was thus expended in the establishment of an opposing Catholic party in Germany under the leadership of Duke Maximilian of Bavaria, as well as in the building of an allied Italian League, with Venice and Savoy at its core. The management of such a heterogeneous set of partners, with competing territorial and religious ambitions, eventually became unworkable, with Richelieu forced to reluctantly prioritize the alliance with Sweden over that with Bavaria.

Surrounding himself with jurists, the cardinal emphasized a legalistic approach to the resolution of territorial disputes, refusing to entertain some of his compatriots' more outlandishly revisionist claims on foreign soil. Rather, he sought to weave a web of protectorates along France's frontiers, offering to ensure the defense of weaker entities in exchange for transit rights or the stationing of light garrisons in well-positioned strongholds—often overlooking key tracts of the Spanish road. Although French territory was enlarged under Richelieu, the cardinal's goal was primarily to secure gateways into enemy territory, rather than to pursue untrammeled expansionism.

In 1634, at the battle of Nördlingen, a combined Spanish-Imperial force won a crushing victory over the Swedes and their Protestant German allies. This constituted a drastic change in the European configuration of power, and forced Richelieu—under the combined pressure of increasingly desperate foreign allies and an ever-more vocal war party at home—to reluctantly transition from *guerre couverte* to *guerre ouverte*. In March 1635, Spain's occupation of the French protectorate of Trier—along with its massacre of the French garrison and abduction of its archbishop-elector—provided Richelieu with the perfect legal justification for French intervention. In May 1635, France formally declared war on Spain, proclaiming that the latter's naked act of aggression was both "against the law of nations" and "an offense against the interests of all princes of Christianity."[26] France was positioning itself once again as the valiant guarantor of smaller states' freedoms and as the great bulwark against Habsburg hegemony.

During Richelieu's tenure, France had engaged in a massive military build-up. Whereas Sully had painstakingly mustered fifty-five thousand troops for the war of the Jülich succession, France could now field over one hundred thousand men. The chief minister had also centralized control over France's forces to a greater

---

26. Randall Lesaffer, "Defensive Warfare, Prevention and Hegemony. The Justifications for the Franco-Spanish War of 1635 (Part I)," *Journal of the History of International Law* 8:1 (2006): 92.

degree, fashioning a corps of specialized civil servants who acted as agents of royal authority and operated alongside French generals in the field. Despite these reforms, France's performance at the outset of the war was middling, at best. In 1636, the nation flirted with disaster when a Habsburg army launched a deep thrust into French territory, capturing the town of Corbie, less than seventy miles from Paris. Under the gallant military leadership of Louis XIII, however, the beleaguered French forces eventually recovered, with the conflict evolving into a bruising war of attrition. Both Richelieu and his Spanish counterpart, the Count-Duke of Olivares, fully grasped the inadequacies of their respective state bureaucracies for the waging of such a protracted war. Each thus pinned their hopes on their adversary's regime being the first to buckle under centrifugal pressures.

While Richelieu had been markedly successful in expanding the scale and scope of taxation, his wide-ranging domestic reforms were deeply unpopular, not only within the fractious nobility, but also among the hard-pressed peasantry. As the war ground on, France was convulsed by large-scale rural uprisings, forcing the redeployment of thousands of French soldiers. Elite opposition to Richelieu's anti-Habsburg policies also steadily grew, and in 1642, the cardinal was nearly overthrown and murdered by a Spanish-abetted conspiracy.

In the end, however, Richelieu won his strategic wager. With the death of Emperor Ferdinand II and his replacement by his more pacifistic son, Ferdinand III, Spain could no longer rely on the same levels of imperial military support. The yield of its South American silver mines had begun to dwindle, and Spanish bullion shipments were now regularly intercepted by Dutch vessels. Meanwhile, secessionist movements, carefully cultivated and monitored by Richelieu's agents, had grown more virulent. In 1640, the Iberian Peninsula was engulfed by these fissiparous tensions, with both Portugal and Catalonia revolting against their Castilian rulers and allying with France. Three years later, in 1643, French forces annihilated a larger Spanish army at the battle of Rocroi, in northeastern France, a turning point in the Franco-Spanish competition.

Richelieu, however, was no longer there to witness it. In December 1642, exhausted and emaciated, he had succumbed to one of his many illnesses. When the king came to pay the fading counselor a final visit, the cardinal purportedly rasped that he could die comforted by the knowledge that he had left the "kingdom in the highest degree of glory and reputation it has ever been, and all the king's enemies cast down and humiliated."[27]

27. As quoted in Jean-Christian Petitfils, *Louis XIII: Tome II* (Paris: Perrin, 2008), Chapter XXIII.

IV

Originally from the Abruzzi, Mazzarini—later known as Mazarin—spent his formative years in Rome, working for influential noble families. During the Mantuan Succession Crisis, he had been tasked by Pope Urban VIII with mediating a truce between Spain and France. Over the course of their lengthy discussions, Cardinal Richelieu had been favorably impressed by his counterpart's supple mind and sparkling verve. Richelieu stealthily began luring Mazarin into France's orbit, commending him to the pope and pressing for him to be selected as papal nuncio to Paris. In 1639, the French chief minister's protégé was offered letters of naturalization—complete with the new, gallicized name Jules Mazarin—and formally embarked upon service to the French Crown. On his deathbed, Richelieu purportedly urged Louis XIII to make good use of his Italian creature's services, observing that "he had a mind sufficient to govern four empires."[28]

With Louis XIII following his advisor to the grave only six months later, France entered a new extended period of minority rule, with Queen Anne of Austria assuming the title of regent. To many contemporaries' surprise, Mazarin, who had been carefully, if quietly, cultivating the dowdy queen mother and her four-year-old boy, was soon named chief minister of the regency government.

Whereas Richelieu had relied on sheer force of personality to control France's government, Mazarin preferred to cajole, charm, and manipulate. A relative outsider to French politics, he was less familiar with the arcane traditions of some of its institutions. Perhaps in part because of this, he appears to have frequently resorted to improper inducements—whether financial or political—to purchase loyalty. Indeed, while no seventeenth-century administration was bereft of financial malpractice, there was far greater tolerance for corruption under Mazarin. Whereas both Sully and Richelieu had continuously paid attention to the complex interaction between internal and external balancing, Mazarin's focus was narrower and more self-interested, with the minister often delegating more mundane domestic policy issues to concentrate on diplomacy and higher level strategy. This more siloed and unethical approach to governance would end up costing the monarchy dearly, heightening factional division and stoking general unrest.

---

28. As quoted in Madeleine Laurain-Portemer, *Une Tête A Gouverner Quatre Empires, Etudes Mazarines Volume II* (Paris: Editions Laget, 1997), vii–viii.

Initially, however, Mazarin's policies appeared highly successful, and to demonstrate a strong continuity with those of his predecessor. Under a new generation of talented generals, French troops pushed deeper into Germany and the Low Countries, establishing an iron necklace of fortlets along the Rhine and capturing the vital port city of Dunkirk. France preserved its steady flow of military support to the guerrilla fighters in Portugal and Catalonia, tying up Spanish troops and thus preventing them from reinforcing their compatriots on the crumbling Flanders front. The cardinal-minister also perpetuated France's far-reaching policy of arbitration between rancorous neighbors, negotiating an important peace between Denmark and Sweden, and then drawing Copenhagen into its own alliance with Paris. Additional pressure was exerted on the Viennese Habsburgs' eastern flank by sponsoring the revolt of the Protestant Prince of Transylvania, George I Rákóczi, and through a marriage alliance between Wladislaus IV of Poland and a French princess.

Even as France continued its ruthless, continent-wide campaign against both branches of the Habsburg dynasty, the Thirty Years' War was winding to a close. As early as 1640, the war-weary Emperor Ferdinand III had called for a major international peace congress. Four years later, in 1644, national delegations began to trickle into the Westphalian cities of Münster and Osnabrück to commence negotiations.

In his final years, Richelieu had drafted a clear set of directives for the French negotiating team, providing a compelling blueprint for "the general peace of Christendom." The goal was to be a truly universal peace, enshrined in a common treaty, and in which all European powers would have a stake. A healthier equilibrium would be generated both through the humbling of the hegemonistic Habsburgs, and via the establishment of two separate leagues in the most politically fragmented and conflict-prone regions of Europe: Germany and Italy. Peace would be preserved not only through French military might, but also through some form of collective security guarantee. Crucially, the Bourbon monarchy's key allies were to be intimately involved in every aspect of its deliberations, and France's own territorial claims were to be limited and grounded in international law.

For the first few years of his tenure Mazarin seems to have largely followed his late predecessor's guidance. As time went by, however, his behavior displayed troubling signs of overconfidence. Whereas Henri IV and Louis XIII had studiously avoided projecting power beyond the Lombardy plains, Mazarin began to pour resources into Italy—an ultimately peripheral theater of operations. In 1646, over the course of a prohibitively expensive campaign,

France's newly expanded Mediterranean fleet was ordered to undertake a series of large-scale amphibious assaults along the Italian coastline. The first major naval engagement ended in disaster and subsequent positional gains were fleeting. The Neapolitan Revolt of 1647, which Mazarin had supported, was even more short-lived, with the Spanish taking a mere seven months to reconquer the city.

The clearest indication of Mazarin's growing hubris was in the diplomatic domain. In 1646, the cardinal concocted the idea of a grand territorial bargain with Spain. Overriding his envoys' objections, Mazarin secretly approached Madrid and offered to trade French-occupied Catalonia for the Spanish Netherlands. The "satisfaction with which he outlined his plan," grumbled de Lionne, the French secretary of state for foreign affairs, "led one to believe he had become intoxicated by its beauty."[29] Obsessed with the geographical vulnerabilities of France's northern heartland, France's chief minister hoped, in one masterstroke, to acquire greater strategic depth and absorb wealthy neighboring territories.

This sudden embrace of unabashed expansionism was a clear departure from both his predecessors' more limited conceptions of territorial security. It also went against Richelieu's repeated emphasis on the importance of allied consultation, and of striving for a universal peace. Madrid promptly and gleefully leaked the proposed arrangement to the Dutch. Incensed at having been left in the dark by their purported ally, the Dutch Republic reacted by signing a separate peace with Spain. This denouement was a diplomatic disaster for France. It emboldened Spain, which could now redirect its troops based in the Netherlands towards other operations, and durably alienated a key French ally. Most importantly, it precipitated the resumption of civil war in France.

Indeed, critics of Richelieu and Mazarin had long argued that the two cardinals had perpetuated the war with the Habsburgs for private gain, to bolster their influence with the king, and to preserve their own emergency powers. The costly Italian debacle and embarrassing imbroglio over the Spanish Netherlands lent credence to these views. Meanwhile, anger over wartime taxation and the predatory practices of Mazarin's financiers had been steadily escalating.

In August 1648, Paris erupted into revolt as enraged Parisians took to the streets in reaction to Mazarin's detention of three Parlement of Paris members who had opposed his policies. The resulting series of civil and "baronial" wars, known as *La Fronde*, constituted an existential threat to Mazarin's authority

29. Geoffrey Treasure, *Richelieu and Mazarin* (London: Routledge, 1998), 75.

(the cardinal was forced to flee twice into exile) and to the credibility and effectiveness of France's negotiating teams in Westphalia.[30] Spain unsurprisingly capitalized on its rival's descent into chaos, abruptly withdrawing from bilateral negotiations at Westphalia, pursuing combat operations with a renewed intensity, and supporting rebellious French magnates. France incurred severe military losses across every critical theater, with its increasingly ill-provisioned forts in Gravelines, Dunkirk, Barcelona, and Casale-Monferrato all falling like dominos.

When the wars of La Fronde finally ended in 1653, and Mazarin reassumed full control of the government, France was in a less favorable position than only five years prior. In October 1648, its delegates had signed the Treaty of Münster with the Holy Roman Empire which had, on balance, positively affirmed French interests by consolidating its presence in the Rhineland, and formally acknowledging its sovereignty over Metz, Toul, Verdun, as well as over the Alsatian fortress-cities of Breisach and Philippsbourg. Importantly, the Holy Roman Emperor had also yielded (albeit ambiguously) certain of his rights in Upper and Lower Alsace to the French Crown. Peace with Spain, however, now appeared more elusive than ever, as did Richelieu and Sully's dream of universal concord. France had lost some of its most strategically positioned fortresses and its most formidable general, the treacherous Prince de Condé, remained at the head of Spain's armies. Meanwhile, Philip IV had finally crushed the revolt in Catalonia and driven out French troops.

At the same time, however, France's monarchy had emerged politically fortified from its years of intestinal conflict—and with a charismatic young king who had now attained his majority. Spain, on the other hand, was governed by an ailing and increasingly erratic monarch, utterly consumed by his vengeful desire to reconquer Portugal. And for all of Spain's latest tactical triumphs, there was no eliding the structural causes behind its progressive decline: the steady diminution of its population; the underdevelopment of its local industry; the dwindling of its supplies of overseas wealth; and its lack of agricultural self-sufficiency. It was Spain's isolation on the international stage, however, that finally brought the country to its knees.

Eager to find some way to break out of their mutually debilitating stalemate, in the years following La Fronde, both France and Spain had begun to entertain the risqué notion of initiating a rapprochement with a hitherto pariah

---

30. On the "baronial" aspects of the Fronde, see David Parrott, *1652: The Cardinal, the Prince and the Crisis of the 'Fronde'* (Oxford: Oxford University Press, 2020), 28.

state—the new Cromwellian republic. With its highly professionalized New Model Army, and its ability to disrupt the flow of shipping off the coast of Flanders, England had emerged, after a decade of civil war, as the mid-seventeenth century's critical swing state. Mazarin, whose spies had been tracking Philip IV's own fumbling efforts to court Cromwell, was determined to preempt the Spanish, even at the cost of allying with a Protestant and a regicide. In 1655, Paris and London signed a treaty of "peace, friendship, and intercourse" at Westminster, and in 1657, this entente was further formalized under the aegis of the Treaty of Paris, with both parties agreeing to form a joint Franco-English army to wage war against Spain in Flanders. Interestingly, when privately justifying his decision to opt for an alliance with France over Spain, Oliver Cromwell had pointed to France's greater tradition of religious tolerance since the passage of the Edict of Nantes. Henri IV and Sully's quest for moderation and confessional coexistence had thus, over half a century later, emerged as a key source of competitive advantage.

For Spain, this new-fangled alliance was an unadulterated calamity. It was now, in the words of one despondent chronicler, "as surrounded by enemies as a honeypot is with flies."[31] Madrid had lost control of the seas between Spain and Flanders, and was pressed in the vise of a new triple entente between France, England, and Portugal. In June 1658, an Anglo-French army routed a Spanish army at the Battle of the Dunes, paving the way toward the Peace of the Pyrenees. As one English royalist writer wistfully noted several years later, Cromwell's decision to ally with Paris had, more than any other, helped propel France toward paramountcy, for it had "made the latter [France] too great for Christendom, and by that means broken the balance between the two Crowns of Spain and France."[32]

The same year as the Battle of the Dunes, Mazarin succeeded in another one of his key goals with the creation of the League of the Rhine, a defensive union of approximately fifty German princes and their cities across the Rhine, all bound to France. For all of the cardinal-minister's flaws, by the time of his passing, Paris found itself in a position of unparalleled strength. Sully, the great centralizer, had reknit the sinews of French power; Richelieu, the master planner, had perfected its strategy; and Mazarin, the expert—albeit imperfect—negotiator, had

31. Jerónimo de Barrionuevo, in *Avisos de Jerónimo de Barrionuevo 1654–1658*, A. Paz y Meliá, ed. (Madrid: Ediciones Atlas, 1968), 202.

32. Slingsby Bethel, "The World's Mistake in Oliver Cromwell," in *The Harleian Miscellany*, Volume 1, William Oldys, ed. (London: Robert Dutton 1808 [1668]), 289.

formalized its return to primacy. The question, both for France and Europe, was what use its swashbuckling young monarch would now choose to make of this laboriously acquired new dominance.

V

Louis XIV was initially disconsolate upon hearing the news of his godfather's death in 1661. Soon, however, his mood changed—he appeared reinvigorated, and almost relieved by his newfound independence. As he would later confess, Louis XIV now felt free to rule alone, and the "death of Cardinal Mazarin constrained [him] no longer from putting into execution the hopes and fears which [he] had entertained for so long."[33]

Summoning his cabinet, the king informed them that henceforth he intended to manage all major affairs of state by himself. Louis XIV's power would be both unfettered and deeply personalized, and in many ways the half-century of despotism that followed was the logical, albeit infelicitous, endpoint of Sully, Richelieu, and Mazarin's centralizing impulses. Where Louis XIV differed with his two royal predecessors and their advisors, however, was in his disregard for any notion of equilibrium in his single-minded pursuit of continental supremacy. The first manifestations of the king's approach to diplomacy occurred only a few months after Mazarin's death, when—in the wake of an ugly brawl between French and Spanish officials in London—Louis XIV threatened to annex the Spanish Netherlands unless Spain issued a groveling apology and ceded diplomatic precedence in all European courts. Philip IV was forced to concede, a humiliating demonstration of Europe's newly lopsided power dynamics.

For all its gilded grandiosity, the Sun King's long reign was also a period of great suffering and upheaval across Europe. Louis XIV waged war for fifty of the seventy-two years of his reign, triggering—through his acts of brazen assertiveness—France's gradual isolation by a series of counterbalancing coalitions. This tendency toward imbalance and immoderation was tragically reflected in French domestic policy. In 1685, Louis XIV formally revoked the Edict of Nantes, thus dismantling his grandfather's century-long tradition of religious tolerance. The savage repression of the Huguenots not only estranged the kingdom's long-standing Protestant allies, it also triggered a mass exodus

---

33. "A King's Lessons in Statecraft," in *Mémoires of Louis XIV*, Jean Longdon, ed. (London: Fisher Unwin, 1924), 41.

of many of the country's most talented artisans, financiers, and military officers—many of whom then went on to swell the ranks and buoy the economies of France's rivals.

In his final days, Louis XIV appears to have belatedly realized the errors of his ways, advising his successors to avoid succumbing to hubris, to maintain peace with France's neighbors, and to spare the common people the pain and expenses of perpetual war. By then, however, it was too late. The kingdom was bankrupt, and its wars of aggression had provoked the lasting enmity of neighboring countries, all while stimulating the long-term growth of a new, and deadly, form of anti-French German nationalism. Sully, Richelieu, and Mazarin's legacy of balance and caution in statecraft had been durably squandered, with disastrous consequences for the future of French national security.

CHAPTER 12

Generational Competition in a Multipolar World

WILLIAM III AND ANDRÉ-HERCULE DE FLEURY

Matt J. Schumann

European foreign relations experienced significant change in the early seventeenth century, with effects that would endure up to the present day. Often identified with the Peace of Westphalia (1648), the states system of this era has typically been viewed against papal and/or Habsburg endeavors to recapture hegemony in Europe, or "universal monarchy" as propagandists called it at the time.[1] As European power politics transcended earlier visions of Christian unity, social custom among states slowly acquired the force of law. In the process, new metrics emerged for assessing and affirming legitimate governments and dynasties, fair claims for territory, indemnity, and rituals of respect, and for regulating state actions ranging from commerce to warfare. International etiquette followed suit, so that successful states rested on robust institutions and diplomatic finesse as well as martial glory, and on generational strategies of domestic and foreign politics.

Britain and France were two of the more successful states under this regime. Their approaches to their own strategic rivalry, and to Europe's fluid alignments and multipolar power structure, often involved short-term expedients.

---

1. Andreas Osiander, "Sovereignty, International Relations, and the Westphalian Myth," *International Organization* 55:2 (2001): 251–87; Peter H. Wilson, *The Thirty Years' War: Europe's Tragedy* (Cambridge, MA: Belknap Press, 2009), 75, 106–67, 197–361, 716–78.

A few forward-thinking statesmen, however, understood the need to formulate, adopt, or advance more enduring strategic principles. King William III worked within the states system, first to bolster Dutch prestige, and later to confer international legitimacy on the future United Kingdom. Meanwhile, like his cardinal-statesman forebears, Cardinal André-Hercule de Fleury creatively reframed the rules and tools of the power-political game around France as a central player.

I

From the voyages of Dias and Columbus to the ravages of the Thirty Years' War, the long sixteenth century encompassed several challenges to European views of the world, and of foreign relations. The tumults of religious reformation and the vast scale of trans-oceanic exploration shattered earlier images of a universal church. The decline of "Christendom" as a unifying political construct under papal authority became more evident as scholars at Salamanca theorized a separation of clerical and political powers, and as Jean Bodin proposed a civil order founded upon state sovereignty.[2] While the fracturing of the Church informed violence across Europe, Alberico Gentili both observed and theorized the gradual accretion and codification of interstate social customs into a corpus of international law.[3]

Perhaps unknowingly, Bodin followed Salamanca scholars such as Francisco Suárez and Francisco de Vitoria in proposing that commonwealths held equal dignity and an equal right to exist, regardless of other considerations.[4] Émeric de Cructé theorized international society along similar lines, and Hugo Grotius likewise for international law. Together, these musings signal a trend in European thought by the early seventeenth century, envisioning a society of states transacting their relations and ambitions through broadly agreed ground rules.

Christianity retained a strong presence in European culture, but as a marker of common identity and aspiration, it entered a long period of decline. James

2. Mark L. Thompson, "Jean Bodin's *Six Books of the Commonwealth* and the Early Modern Nation," in *Statehood Before and Beyond Ethnicity*, Linas Eriksonas and Leos Müller, eds. (Brussels: PIE Peter Lang, 2005), 53–56.

3. Andreas Wagner, "Francisco de Vitoria and Alberico Gentili on the Legal Character of the Global Commonwealth." *Oxford Journal of Legal Studies* 31:3 (2011): 575–76.

4. Robert Knolles, *Six Bookes of a Commonweale* (London: G. Bishop, 1606), translation of Jean Bodin, *Les Six Livres de la République* (Paris, 1576), Book 1, 10.

VI of Scotland wrote on the divine right of kings in 1598, but differences of how to interpret the divine will prompted significant violence.[5] Zealous Catholics attempted to assassinate James (1605), Henri IV of France (1593–94, successfully in 1610), and Venetian statesman Paolo Sarpi (1607); Catholic-Lutheran-Utraquist fights drove the Imperial astronomer Johannes Kepler from Prague in 1612; and Calvinist-Arminian disputes killed the Dutch statesman Johan van Oldenbarnevelt in 1619, and sent Grotius to prison and then into exile.

Meanwhile, the image and prestige of the state—and of secular, quasi-social interstate relations—evidently arose in turn. Grotius articulated a rational morality of foreign relations in his *Law of War and Peace*, while Crucé advocated multilateralism and diplomatic congresses.[6] Conversely, Jean de Silhon mused on Richelieu's *raison d'étât* and conceived a cold-heartedly pragmatic approach to the distinctive moral logic of state-level security imperatives: "a [mathematical] mean between that which conscience permits and affairs require."[7]

Later theorists expanded on these basic ideas, but the axioms that grounded the emerging law of nations endured largely intact until the age of revolutions. Charles Irenée Castel de St. Pierre offered a bold project for perpetual peace to accompany the Utrecht Settlement in 1713, yet his scope and proposed institutions share much in common with Crucé, Gentili, and Vitoria.[8] Emmerich de Vattel published a celebrated work on the law of nations in 1758, yet he also drew repeatedly and deferentially from Grotius.[9]

In sum, theorists in the emerging discipline of international law glimpsed a system of interstate relations that harnessed fluid alignments and overlapping strategic ambitions within a power structure that was necessarily multipolar and socially constituted. Though it lost the substance, the system retained much of the form of earlier ideals of "Christian, universal, and perpetual peace."[10] Preservation of sovereign political units, if not exactly international

5. James VI and I, *The True Law of Free Monarchies* (Edinburgh: Robert Waldegrave, 1598).

6. Hugo Grotius, *The Law of War and Peace*, trans. Louise R. Loomis, (Roslyn, NY: Walter J. Black, 1949), 269; Émeric Crucé, *Le nouveau Cynée* (Paris: Chez Jacques Villery, 1623).

7. Jean de Silhon, *Letter à l'Evêsque de Nantes* (1626), in William Farr Church, *Richelieu and Reason of State* (Princeton, NJ: Princeton University Press, 1972), 167–71.

8. Charles Irenée Castel Abbé de St. Pierre, *Projet pour rendre la paix perpétuelle en Europe* (Utrecht: Chez Antoine Schouten, 1713).

9. Emmerich de Vattel, *Le Droit des Gens* (Leiden: Depens de la Compagnie, 1758).

10. The phrase and its cognates appear repeatedly in treaties of the era, including Ryswick (1697), Utrecht-Baden-Rastatt (1713), Nystadt (1721), Åbo (1743), and Aix-la-Chapelle (1748).

stability, seemed to have survived the paradigm shift in European power politics from Church unity and God's dominion to a more earthbound social reasoning.

European states also rarely disappeared, even before the seventeenth century. Grotius and Crucé may have observed international legitimism at work even as the Thirty Years' War raged across Germany and beyond. Institutions and traditions in the Holy Roman Empire remained largely intact, even as its political order collapsed into violence. Silhon also may have observed, as Thomas Hobbes did later, how utilitarian social ordering emerged from power-political anarchy: "the weakest having strength enough to kill the strongest . . . by secret machination, or by confederacy with others, that are in the same danger."[11] Beyond treaty and tradition, perhaps Europe's smaller states also survived because of the fluidity and potential for turnabout that inhered in having so many actors on the stage.

Consensus and legitimacy seem to have circumscribed even the worst excesses of the era. Battlefield defeat stripped Palatine Elector Frederick V of both his elected kingship of Bohemia and his own electorate; yet after decades of foreign intervention, the Peace of Westphalia restored his son, Charles I Louis, to the Palatine electorate—smaller, but still in existence. "The peacemakers also considered how Sweden acquired Pomerania upon the death of its last duke, Bogislaw XIV, in 1637: finding that Swedish military occupation may have influenced the Duke's will, they recognized Brandenburg's claims by splitting the duchy." Outside Germany, when it became clear in 1623 that Urbino's della Rovere line would end without heirs, Pope Urban VIII badgered Duke Francesco Maria II to surrender his titles. Ending nearly two centuries of autonomous vassalage, Urbino returned to Rome's direct control in 1631. Even the wild spiral of conflict over the Mantuan Succession after 1627 had origins in conflicting— yet legitimate—dynastic claims, and not international anarchy as such.

Further corollaries of the Thirty Years' War persisted until around 1660, with even major states experiencing acute political fragility and vulnerability to foreign intervention. The Wars of the Three Kingdoms left a very capable New Model Army and Commonwealth Navy, but neither could cement Oliver Cromwell's political legacy. Less than two years after his death in 1658, Britain welcomed a restored monarchy under Charles II. Cardinal Jules Mazarin meanwhile sought to centralize France and reduce its debts, provoking civil strife during a war with Spain. The wars of La Fronde that resulted saw two

---

11. Thomas Hobbes, *Leviathan* (London: Andrew Cooke, 1651), 60–61.

great captains—Turenne and Condé—turn briefly against their king. Like Charles II, however, Louis XIV emerged by 1660 with loyal generals, internal peace, and a stronger state. Poland-Lithuania was not so fortunate. A Cossack revolt known as Khmelnytsky's Uprising invited a *deluge* of foreign intervention by 1654. Forces from Russia, Sweden, Brandenburg, and several Romanian principalities overran, occupied, and sacked most of the country before Polish resistance, a wave of defections, and further foreign interference restored a much-weakened commonwealth.

Political education in the mid-seventeenth century drew as much from the political fragility and seeming lawlessness of the period as it did from early theorists. Both suggested that preservation of the state rested with man as much as with God, and that even divine-right monarchs needed wise counsel, capable spies, potent armed forces, and reliable allies. This chapter's two strategists, William of Orange, born in 1650, and Cardinal Fleury, born in 1653, carried personal experiences and insights from this period into their later careers.

II

As it emerged in early modern Europe, international law articulated both norms and optics of legitimate state action. Vitoria, Bodin, Grotius, and others attempted to codify and prescribe the law, but Gentili and Silhon may have observed correctly that it gained more force from accreted social practice over time. Thus, custom grounded the fluid, multipolar relations of early modern Europe—relations, and by extension, customs, that might appear all the more remarkable for their absence elsewhere.

By the mid-seventeenth century, European international custom seems increasingly to have protected property and human life. Despite the growth of the Atlantic slave trade, slavery in Europe itself was rare, and captive-taking virtually absent from European warfare. Likewise, monetary tribute appears in the Anglo-French treaties of Étaples (1492) and Boulogne (1550), but it was less common outside Northern and Eastern Europe by the mid-seventeenth century. Following Grotius's *Mare Liberum*, admiralty courts also became more rigorous in condemning prizes taken at sea; and while armies did sack cities like Magdeburg in 1630, the practice became far less common. Europe's international community also apparently disapproved of simply ending constituent states' laws and liberties by 1660, let alone their existence.

Much, however, remained permissible. Aggressors might still demand indemnity for specific damages, port access or trade concessions, or lands to which they held claims as affirmed by their neighbors. They could foment civil strife, repurpose territories for a new dynastic line, rearrange a succession, displace a dynasty altogether, or even overthrow a government—as in the Dutch revolutions of 1672 and 1747. Likewise, governments could renegotiate alliances more-or-less as it suited them, withhold ships or troops from a given campaign, or change sides in the middle of a war; treaty and kinship might mitigate such betrayals, but neither proved infallible for guaranteeing an ally's loyalty.

Explanations vary as to why European states behaved this way. Classical realists like A.J.P. Taylor illustrated shifting alignments by using the metaphor of the quadrille dance, in which participants changed partners.[12] Ironically, Europeans of the era had a quadrille metaphor of their own for the same phenomenon: a card game. By the deal of the cards, players never were, nor expected to be, equal beyond their mere presence at the table; their stakes and alignments shifted round by round. Editorialists even noted how the game mapped onto the era's power politics.[13] Duke Victor Amadeus II of Savoy offers a distinctive example of play, ending involvement in the War of the Grand Alliance through a separate peace with France in 1696, cementing the French tie in 1701 by marrying his daughter to Philip of Anjou—shortly to become Philip V of Spain—and switching sides against France in 1703, in the middle of the War of the Spanish Succession.

Closer to the geographic and ideological center of the European game lay the Holy Roman Empire and its traditional leaders, the Austrian Habsburgs. This house was proverbially masterful at marriage politics, not least through manipulating Imperial institutions to regulate that most divisive corollary of family politics: inheritance. Emperor Leopold allowed George William of Celle to claim the Saxe-Lauenburg inheritance by force in 1689, and Emperor Charles VI enfeoffed his successor, Britain's King George II, in 1728; yet the new rulers always had to reaffirm Lauenburg's local privileges, as George William did in 1702, and George III by writ in 1765. Meanwhile, when disputes over Saxe-Meiningen augured larger-scale violence in 1763, Emperor Francis affirmed an Imperial ruling from 1747 over and above the deceased duke's will. Francis threatened armed intervention, convened the Aulic Council, set the widowed duchess as regent, and shamed Saxe-Gotha and Saxe-Coburg for backing the wrong side.

---

12. A.J.P. Taylor, *The Struggle for Mastery in Europe, 1848–1918* (Oxford: Oxford University Press, 1954), xix.

13. Anonymous, "Political Quadrille: A Paper Handed about Paris," *South Carolina Gazette*, July 27 to August 3, 1734, 2.

As conquerors also, the Austrians balanced their monarchical prerogatives and the rights of conquest against Imperial and European jurisprudence on legitimate claims and local privileges. Joseph I briefly returned the Upper Palatinate to its earlier Palatine owners after defeating Bavaria in 1704; yet under French pressure he restored Bavarian lands by the 1714 Treaty of Rastatt. A second conquest in 1745 was quickly followed with the very lenient Treaty of Füssen: peace and the status quo ante bellum in exchange for Bavarian support in that year's Imperial election for Emperor Francis. Finally, at the height of their military fortunes against Prussia in 1759, Austrian leaders apparently pondered major reductions—stripping the royal title and reapportioning many lands—but neither possibility involved ending Hohenzollern rule in Brandenburg nor their status as Imperial electors.[14]

Two of Austria's major rivals, however, sought to test and stretch the affordances of both Imperial and international law: Louis XIV of France and Frederick II of Prussia. They were fortunate to combine diplomacy with war in ways that two Swedish contemporaries did not, much to the detriment of the latter state: Charles X Gustav trying to end Denmark's independence in 1658–59, and Charles XII refusing peace talks a half-century later. Louis and Frederick no more liked the dictates of international custom and consensus than did their Swedish counterparts, but they came a lot closer to playing by the rules.

Louis's many wars did expand French territory, but conquest may be too bold of a word. Instead, he won a limited exchange of enclaves with Savoy, concessions around his borders from the Austro-Imperial and Spanish Habsburgs, and an altered line of succession for the latter. He may have let slip his disdain for the law with the motto on a medal for the 1684 Treaty of Ratisbon—"rest follows victory"—but for the settlements of Nijmegen (1678), Ryswick (1697), and Utrecht (1713), he cast a public image of, respectively, "peace within their laws," "the security of Europe," and "hope for the joy of the world." Imperial law, meanwhile, hampered his anti-Protestant policies in Alsace and barred him from properly incorporating Lorraine, though both were legally French domains. International law and its enforcers, it seems, did indeed circumscribe the ambitions of one of early modern Europe's more powerful and belligerent monarchs.

So too with Frederick, who gained notoriety in 1740 for using flimsy legal pretexts to invade and annex the Austrian province of Silesia. Certifying his

---

14. "Peace project" was supposed to have been drawn up in Vienna following the Austro-Russian victory at Kunersdorf. See, Cressener to Holdernesse, February 6, 1760, SP 81/136, The National Archives (TNA), Kew, United Kingdom.

ill-gotten gain, however, required epic feats of arms in all three Silesian Wars, as well as shrewd, sustained diplomacy over nearly a quarter-century. Frederick privately opined that Saxony would make a great rampart for his state, but he doubted whether Prussia could annex the electorate in the face of international opposition.[15] In fact, though his troops occupied much of Saxony in 1745 and again after 1756, he yielded all claims to Saxon territory at the treaty tables of Dresden (1745) and Hubertusburg (1763). However potent Frederick's armies, however impressive his military feats, however crafty his jurists and diplomats, Imperial laws and the customs of Europe still constrained his actions and his strategy.

Such niceties seemed not to apply for Europeans far from home. In 1729, French colonial forces retaliated for an attack on Fort Rosalie, Louisiana, with a largely successful attempt to eradicate the Natchez people. In 1755, an edict in the Massachusetts Bay colony set bounties for Penobscot scalps, including those of children.[16] By the Treaty of Giyanti the same year, the Dutch East India Company concluded more than a decade of warfare in Java by disestablishing the moribund Sultanate of Mataram. A successor state based in Jogjakarta was notionally independent, but by 1760, the Dutch had erected a fort within cannon range of the sultan's palace. A similar arrangement had been in place with the Banten Sultanate since around 1680, with Benteng Speelwijk less than a mile from the Surosowan palace.

Like Louis and Frederick, leaders around the world sought expansion and hegemony when they thought they had means; yet international custom in these regions appears not to have shared Europe's emerging international jurisprudence. Although the practice of human sacrifice declined, Native American warfare continued to focus on seizing people. This was as true for the Iroqouis-Huron wars in the 1670s as it was for Cherokee and Shawnee raids on British settlements in Appalachia nearly a century later. In Africa, meanwhile, the Rozvi Empire apparently placed much of the Zimbabwean plateau under a tribute of goods by the late seventeenth century. Asantehene Osei Tutu did much the same in Ghana after 1701, when his emerging Ashanti Empire defeated the Denkyira Kingdom. In 1724, Alaafin Ojigi of Oyo imposed a tribute of men, women, and guns on Dahomey—forty-one of each being a symbolic insult to a favored number among the latter.

15. Frederick II, "Testament Politique [1752]," in *Die Politischen Testamente Friedrichs des Grossen*, Gustav Berthold Volz, ed. (Berlin: Verlag von Reimar Hobbing, 1920), 61–63.

16. Spencer Phips, "Proclamation Against the Tribe of the Penobscot Indians," Boston, November 3, 1755.

Different customs also reigned in eastern Asia. Facing Manchu invasion in 1644, Korea's Joseon Kingdom merely shifted its ritual tribute from the Ming dynasty to the Qing. The Kaanxi Emperor eradicated Ming influence with his invasion of Taiwan in 1683; his operatives meddled in Tibetan politics by the turn of the eighteenth century; and by the 1750s his great-grandson, the Qianlong Emperor, led a campaign to destroy the Dzunghar Khanate that left up to a million dead. Togugawa Japan opted out of the tributary system, but Dutch and Portuguese traders opted in from time to time, and European merchants generally deferred to the Chinese preference for trade and tribute in silver.

Regional Asian powers also held sway outside the sinosphere. From 1728 to 1747, Nader Shah subverted Safavid Persia, exacted immense tribute after sacking the Mughal capital at Delhi, and conquered Khiva, Bukhara, and Oman. A revived Oman in the 1750s took a large share of East Africa's slave trade, and during the same decade Alaungpaya Konbaung conquered Restored Hanthawaddy and several Shan states to reclaim Burmese hegemony in Southeast Asia. Prithvinarayan Shah of Gorkha worked over a longer period to unify Nepal, conquering Nuwakot in 1744, Kirtipur in 1765, and Kathmandu in 1768.

International systems outside Europe clearly observed their own customs, but what distinguished European foreign relations in this era was the relative restraint with which even the most bellicose leaders felt compelled to conduct themselves in the face of popular censure and armed resistance. Europe certainly saw wars, intrigues, concessions of land and trade rights, and humiliations during peace talks, but the kind of violence and conquest that Qianlong and Nader Shah visited upon their neighbors was simply unthinkable—or perhaps only barely thinkable—for the likes of Louis and Frederick. European leaders who sought to expand their states confronted a task involving many treaty talks, probably many wars and dynastic marriages, and certainly many years. Success required at least grudging adherence to the evolving house rules, and strategies for a longer game.

III

As described previously, the fates of Lorraine, Lauenburg, and Silesia evidenced the need for would-be conquerors within Europe to take their time, and to read social cues from the international community. The fate of these duchies fell subject to mediation under law, as did Spain's monarchy and empire in the 1690s, while King Charles II was still alive; even after his death, the final dispositions in Italy required forty-eight years and four wars![17] So what of the beneficiary of two short, largely conclusive, nearly bloodless revolutions—a Dutch one in 1672 and an English one sixteen years later—who spent most of his time and political capital forming and leading multinational coalitions?

Following the quadrille metaphor, William of Orange often played for high stakes with a few strong cards in a generally weak hand, yet he brought strong partners to bear both on the game itself, and on upholding the rules. For most of his thirty years in European politics, he formed the focal point of opposition against Louis XIV. William also overcame Dutch and British domestic opposition and built institutions that greatly increased the security of both domains. Though he did not live to see them, he laid the foundations for what became the United Kingdom, the British Empire, a close Anglo-Dutch relationship, British commercial and maritime hegemony, and an enduring British commitment to continental Europe.

William's story began with a strategic marriage in 1641. King Charles I of England, Scotland, and Ireland tied his daughter Mary Stuart to the Dutch stadtholder William II of Orange in a bid to bolster foreign support amid his own failing domestic policies. Ultimately defeated in the Wars of the Three Kingdoms, Charles was executed in 1649; William II died a year later, eight days before the birth of his son. Both states became full-fledged republics in 1649–50; three years later, they were at war.

Adriaan Pauw, Grand Pensionary of Holland, led the Dutch war effort until his death in February 1653. His deputy, Johan de Witt, took over the office and became the defining figure for the first stadtholderless period, perhaps for the entire Dutch Golden Age. He expanded Dutch trade, helped to professionalize its navy, navigated the Northern Seven Years' War with great success, and continued the colonial rivalry with Portugal. From the start, however, de Witt was also defined by his efforts—initially shared with Cromwell—to prevent the younger William from inheriting his father's offices.

De Witt walked a narrow line in opposing William's rise. Orangism remained popular across the country, and the young heir regained foreign support when Charles II ascended the English throne in 1660. De Witt took greater control over William's education, yet while the young man respected

---

17. Wouter Troost, "Leopold I, Louis XIV, William III and the Origins of the War of the Spanish Succession," *History* 103:357 (2018): 545–70.

his tutor's political instincts, they never overcame their mutual mistrust. De Witt also tried to separate William's intended offices of captain-general and stadtholder and abolish the latter, though by degrees he accepted the young man's political rise. Just in time for a foreign policy catastrophe, William became captain-general.

The disaster resulted directly from de Witt's balancing act on the international stage after 1660, between Charles and Louis XIV. His middle path offended both kings, informing tense talks for a French treaty in 1662, and war with England in 1664. A triumphal raid on the Medway in 1667 brought England to a quick peace and a tripartite pact with Sweden to rein in Louis's ambitions in the War of Devolution, but de Witt could not maintain these new ties, nor could he restore his earlier favor with France. Instead, in 1670, the two men whose ambitions he hoped to balance made their own agreement to destroy the Dutch Republic. Dutch isolation and vulnerability became clear as naval conflict with England resumed in March 1672, and as French troops invaded in May, backed by Cologne and Münster.

Thus began the *rampjaar*—a critical moment for the Dutch counselor-pensionary state, and a spur for an Orangist revolution. De Witt planned a spirited defense, at least for the province of Holland, but domestic pressure forced his resignation on August 4, passing his titles and powers to the capable Orangist Gaspar Fagel. William duly became stadtholder, seemingly verifying Louis's instinct that overwhelming force could overthrow the Republic and leave an Orangist rump. William's partisans even added icing to Louis's cake as Johan and Cornelis de Witt both suffered a grizzly death-by-mob on August 21. The panicked provinces eagerly sought terms, but the military situation soon stabilized as William gathered Dutch forces behind Holland's defensive Water Line and vowed to fight on.

As Spain, the Empire, and Brandenburg-Prussia came to recognize the need for an anti-French coalition, an Imperial-Brandenburg army duly formed on the right bank of the Rhine—just out of reach for joint operations. William thus struck out on his own across the Spanish Netherlands towards a French position at Charleroi. Though this raid also proved abortive, it demonstrated some of his strategic thought: patience did not mean passivity, and though he preferred to work with allies, he was not above going alone.

William successfully cemented his alliances in 1673, and he worked with another great captain of the age, Raimondo Montecuccoli, to besiege Bonn and cut French supply lines down the Rhine. William merged tactical and diplomatic prowess in 1674, leading a multinational army to fight Condé to a bloody standstill at Seneffe—not quite a victory, but enough that Louis ordered his generals to avoid further battles. Though William failed to carry the war into France, he had still emerged at the center of international opposition to Louis XIV—a role that would define his statecraft and strategic legacy.

Key to William's strategy was the effort to flip his other erstwhile enemy: England. Beyond his land operations, William sought sufficient victory at sea to transform Charles II from adversary to ally. William's senior admiral Michel de Ruyter scored repeated victories over English and French fleets in Dutch coastal waters; a trans-Atlantic venture briefly retook New York City, and a foray from the Dutch Cape Colony took St. Helena. By 1673, William's Stuart heritage, Protestant faith, and general support for Parliament also gave him a fair shot at the English throne, should anything happen to Charles and his brother James, Duke of York. With help from Dutch agents and perhaps Spain's treasury, parliamentary factions began forming around his interests— not least the incipient Whigs. For all of this, however, William chose merely to pursue peace for the moment: the 1674 Treaty of Westminster.

William still had to consolidate his Dutch base after all. As he would later in the British context, William substantially achieved his domestic goals by finding and placing the right people. The Prince of Orange was gifted with friends from youth whom he could not have chosen in anticipation of their roles. Among them were Hans Willem Bentinck, a close friend from the age of thirteen who proved to be a jack of many trades, and Gaspar Fagel, noted previously, who, together with his successor Anthonie Heinsius, proved exceptionally loyal and capable grand pensionaries.

Increasingly secure at home, William turned again to his English uncles. He hoped to turn England fully from enemy into ally, though this proved elusive for some time. The one breakthrough he achieved was visiting England after the campaign of 1677 and marrying his cousin Mary Stuart, the oldest daughter of James, Duke of York—for the moment, the most legitimate, and most likely, person of her generation to succeed the mainline Stuarts. Neither Charles nor Mary herself really cared for the match, but William pressed it in the short-term hope of drawing nearer to his uncles, and counterbalancing Louis's influence. The new English connection was enough, in the moment, to bring French diplomats to the table for what became the Peace of Nijmegen.

It is unclear whether, at this stage, William intended his marriage to strengthen his claim to the English Crown, any more than in 1673–74, yet the idea could not have been far from his mind. In England as in the Dutch lands, he built an impressive array of informers and apologists. His Protestantism, international clout, and opposition to Louis (and Louis's absolutism) certainly endeared him to the English public, yet he still chose to bide his time. Far above any popularity in Britain or aspirations to the throne, he remained focused on opposing France.

Several tests of William's resolve, and his relationship with his uncles, came from what might be called unintentional Orangists after 1678. As the Whigs gained popularity, for example, Parliament demanded James's exclusion from the throne. William stood to gain from the exclusion crisis, but the rift between Crown and Parliament troubled him deeply and he ultimately found it most politic to keep quiet. By 1681, Titus Oates's imaginary Papal Plot incited mass hysteria, but William again could not appear too eager. Still less could he be seen to take interest in the Rye House Plot of 1683, when radical Whigs sought to kill his English uncles outright. The incident may have sparked an Orangist revolution, but begging the counterfactual, how could William lead a legalist-legitimist coalition against France when his own rise to power in the British kingdoms rested on an act of banditry?

William also opposed Monmouth's Rebellion in 1685, after the Duke of York became King James II and VII. Though he could not actively intervene as a matter of Dutch policy, William did send English and Scots from Dutch service to help his father-in-law, and the latter shared details of the campaign.[18] Officially neutral and still burnishing his Protestant credentials, William could shelter some defeated and exiled rebels, as well as Huguenots expelled from France. However useful these exiles and partisans might be for his cause, he still needed the right circumstances to turn them to advantage. Exemplified by the Bloody Assizes, James's increasing misrule antagonized more of his subjects; but if William truly wanted to oust his father-in-law, he needed a more compelling reason.

William would have two. First, the military edge to Louis's diplomacy in the 1680s would turn to full-scale war as the Holy League continued from victory at Mohács in 1687 to the siege of Belgrade in 1688. Second and more immediate for William, James II and Mary of Modena welcomed a baby boy, reviving English fears of a Catholic, absolutist succession. With an invitation from the "immortal seven," William not only had more warrant for claiming the throne across the Channel, but also a greater need: the Holy League's progress against the Turks might be for naught, he believed, if Louis aggrandized France.

18. Wout Troost, *William III, the Stadholder-King: A Political Biography* (London: Routledge, 2017), 174–75.

The "Respectable Revolution of 1688" has been demythologized in recent decades, but its persistence in English memory bears witness to a piece of William's strategy for the long game of European politics. Well informed by his many agents, and prepared against most contingencies with a 14,000-man army, William exploited a combination of family connections, the English invitation, and the overall strategic situation to claim legitimacy for his invasion. James's flight without resistance helped William's cause in England, and he profited internationally from Louis's latest adventure into Germany.

Unquestionably, William sought to exploit British resources for his focus on France, and he did so with pragmatic measures that left Jacobitism in his rear. He responded in part by merging his Dutch and English intelligence networks, and both would remain among the best in Europe for generations. In Scotland, after Viscount Dundee died at Killiecrankie, William sought to allay most of his remaining opposition with a simple oath of loyalty; that failing in the region of Lochaber, his consolidation culminated in a massacre at Glencoe. Likewise in Ireland, William saw off his uncle again at the Boyne in July 1690, then left his friend Godert de Ginkel—later First Earl of Athlone—to mop up Irish Jacobite resistance in 1691. Ginkel duly won at Aughrim and offered generous terms at Galway and Limerick; yet while not as bad as Glencoe in the moment, longer-term exploitation, betrayal, and simple failure of good faith left Ireland only partly integrated into the post-Williamite British state.

Looking abroad, William had good reason to leave Ireland after his victory at the Boyne, and to bring his new kingdoms more deeply into the continental fray. On the same day as the Boyne, the French duc de Luxembourg won a victory at Fleurus in the Spanish Netherlands. William already had English troops there; he soon sent more, and some Scots. Despite defeats at Leuze in 1691, and under his personal command at Steenkirk (1692) and Landen (1693), there was no doubt of his troops' ability—Dutch and British alike—to stand their ground and both take and inflict galling casualties on the battlefield. William's Dutchmen already served as a core for allied armies in the Low Countries by 1673, but he set the stage in the 1690s for coalition building around Anglo-Dutch forces during the next decade, under John Churchill, First Duke of Marlborough. British troops also formed the core for multinational coalition armies in the 1740s and 1750s, in much the same way.

Meanwhile in the Channel, just nine days after William's triumph at the Boyne, the Comte de Tourville's naval victory at Beachy Head raised English fears of a French invasion. Though William had first hoped to govern with a mix of English parties, he soon saw the Whigs' value for promoting continental engagement, urban industry—not least exchanging the Stuarts' hearth tax for the Land Tax in 1692—and, by 1694, the Bank of England as a way to increase public revenue for government initiatives. This agreement of values and policies not only signaled the Whigs' long-term rise in British politics, but it also grounded the building and maintenance of a world-beating navy. A first victory at Barfleur-La Hogue in 1692 served as a harbinger of things to come.

Many of the naval and financial developments echoed de Witt's innovations during William's youth, and the financial markets and commercial networks of Amsterdam and London became deeply intertwined. Likewise, their diplomacy: England-Britain and the Dutch Republic were casually known in foreign relations circles as the "Maritime Powers" as late as the 1750s.[19] Some of William's Dutch friends also came over in the 1690s and left important legacies in the English aristocracy. Bentinck, the clear favorite for most of William's reign, became Earl of Portland; a later favorite, Arnold Joost van Keppel, became Earl of Albemarle; and Willem Nassau de Zuylestein became Earl of Rochford. Long after William's death, successive earls and later dukes of Portland, and generations of earls of Albemarle and Rochford kept both Dutch family names and English titles of nobility, and they continued to figure prominently in British political, diplomatic, and military circles.

Among his British subjects, meanwhile, William strove to promote a limited freedom of conscience and a smooth succession. Both were of interest to the political philosopher John Locke, who wrote to justify the Glorious Revolution of 1688–89, and soon served in the new government. As the 1688 Declaration of Right became the English Bill of Rights in 1689, William retained his Calvinist faith even while he led the Anglican Church; his Puritan and Presbyterian subjects also enjoyed relatively greater freedom of worship. He may also have had in mind that, if Parliament remained opposed to the Catholic Stuarts, the Lutheran Hanoverians might be next in line. This was certainly the case by 1700, when Princess Anne's son William, Duke of Gloucester died, and William of Orange and others managed to steer the Act of Settlement through a Tory-majority Parliament in 1701.

The Scots opposed the Act of Settlement and passed their own Act of Security in 1704, but William and the Whig junto had already assured one particular thread of Scottish insecurity that would bind the British kingdoms closer together. While William and the Whigs probably did not consciously strategize

19. E.g., Holdernesse to Keith, January 7, 1755, SP 80/195, TNA.

around William Paterson's financial and political odyssey in the 1690s, the latter's meandering from the Bank of England to seeking funding for a Scottish colony in Panama, to supporting an Anglo-Scottish union did ultimately coincide with their instincts. William and the Whigs opposed any English financial support for the Darien scheme; when it duly failed, it greatly indebted the Scottish government. William did not live to see the fruits of his malice toward Scotland's last colonial venture, but there is no question of its role in persuading the Scottish Parliament—grudgingly—to accept the Act of Union in 1707.

By the time of his death, staring down yet another coalition war against France, William had already set the strategic tone in his domains for a long time to come. He had subordinated his British kingdoms to Dutch ambitions informed by the experience of the *rampjaar*, yet he left these same British domains in 1702 at the political, financial, and military head of a broad legalist-legitimist coalition opposing French aggrandizement, ready to unify politically, fielding a first-class navy, and sufficiently committed to the continent that it supported Marlborough's campaigns for nearly a decade. The British kingdoms were so bound with the Dutch lands that a union of armed forces, finances, and strategic interests endured for a half-century, and the lingering, Jacobite-related insecurities that would persist for decades also informed some of the best intelligence services in Europe. As he had done for himself so many times, William III left at least his British domains positioned for the long game of European and global international relations under law that would characterize much of the eighteenth century.

IV

A quarter-century after the death of William III, the map of Europe had changed. Distant as it was from him, William may yet have understood the significance of Ottoman concessions in the 1699 Treaty of Karlowitz, but he may not yet have glimpsed a similar fate for Sweden in the Great Northern War, nor the corresponding rise of Austria and Russia. All of these were negative developments for a France exhausted and financially strained by Louis XIV's wars and fallout from the Mississippi Bubble. Adding insult to injury, the family ties with Spain that Louis had worked so hard to establish over almost his entire reign collapsed in 1725, leaving the two major Bourbon powers on the brink of war. Much like William, then, André Hercule de Fleury, Bishop of Fréjus and shortly a cardinal of the Roman Catholic Church, took over the making of French strategy at a pivotal moment.

In many respects, however, Fleury represents the opposite side of William's coin. France was still a wealthy and populous country in the first quarter of the eighteenth century, with a fearsome military reputation. It had, however, lost a dynamic head of state, critical strategic partners, and clear direction for its power-political ambitions. Fleury may have come to power with many good cards in hand, but he had an unusual set of partners, and no great reason to play for high stakes. Though his situation clearly differed from William's, Fleury played a patient, watchful game, and made a strong show of playing by the rules.

Almost immediately after he supplanted the Duc de Bourbon in June 1726, Fleury reaffirmed a peculiar alignment of major powers: the Alliance of Hanover with Britain and Prussia. Forged a decade earlier under the regent Philippe II Duc d'Orleans, the Anglo-French tie still appeared strange in the mid-1720s, and the two governments colluded to publish an anonymous pamphlet stressing its merits to other potential partners, including the Dutch.[20] British and French diplomats also collaborated to seek Danish, Swedish, and Sardinian accession. Despite fears that Fleury was not as pro-British as his regency-era predecessor, Cardinal Dubois, Fleury reaffirmed French pledges, not least against Spain.

Franco-Spanish antagonism in the mid-1720s claimed several origins, not least Spain's attempt to revise the Utrecht Settlement in what became the War of the Quadruple Alliance (1718–20). Many issues having been resolved by the Treaty of the Hague (1720), the regent sought to rebuild Franco-Spanish relations with a double marriage: first, Luis, Prince of Asturias with his daughter, Louise Élisabeth d'Orléans, and second, a young Louis XV with the Spanish Infanta, Maria Victoriana. The first marriage survived Orléans's death in 1723 and the rise of Louis XV with Bourbon as first minister; it seemed primed for success as Philip V abdicated his throne to Luis in 1724, but Louise Élisabeth was already falling into dementia and Luis was dead within nine months. Bourbon then jilted the second match, and he and Fleury—the young king's tutor at the time—settled on a marriage with Marie Leszczyńska, daughter of the exiled former king of Poland. Enraged at his French relatives, Philip V

20. Horatio Walpole to Delafaye, October 9, 1726, Fontainebleau, SP/184/114, TNA; H. Walpole to Newcastle, October 9, 1726, Fontainebleau, SP/184/115, TNA; Robinson to Delafaye, January 30, 1727 NS, Paris, SP 78/185/9, TNA; Anonymous, *Analyse du Traité d'Alliance, conclu á Hanover* (The Hague: chez Charles Levier), 1725. More generally, see G. C. Gibbs, "Britain and the Alliance of Hanover, Apr. 1725–Feb. 1726," *English Historical Review* 73:288 (1958): 404–30.

resumed his reign in Madrid and sought alliance with his former adversary, the Austrian Archduke and Holy Roman Emperor Charles VI.

Formalized in the First Treaty of Vienna, the Austro-Spanish alliance drove Britain and France to conclude the Alliance of Hanover. Though British diplomats aided efforts to bring the Dutch, Danes, and Swedes into their new coalition, the playing of their strongest card—the Royal Navy—in a show of gunboat diplomacy drove Russia into the opposite camp.[21] Anglo-Spanish commercial disputes also took on a military edge, auguring a large systemic war. With nothing to gain from such a conflict, and called to commit militarily on the Italian and Netherlands frontiers as well as against Spain, Fleury did something as bizarre for French geopolitics as it was brilliant: he withheld the French army.

Even before the British declared war on Spain in March 1727, Fleury struck the opposite chord. Despite strong words of support for France's allies, he never sent troops toward France's frontiers; instead, he drove the peace process by floating proposals for a general congress. No later than May, the Austrians and Spanish affirmed a lack of interest in large-scale fighting, and by the time Simon Slingelandt became Holland's grand pensionary in July—once again the highest Dutch office after William III's death inaugurated the second stadtholderless period—he differed with Fleury only in the priority and specifics of closing down a new commercial rival in the Austrian Netherlands: the Ostend Company.[22] While Spain's army continued to besiege Gibraltar and Britain kept a powerful fleet in the Caribbean, both belligerent powers felt themselves checked by their respective allies' reluctance to support them militarily.

Eventually, Fleury emerged as the major broker for the Anglo-Spanish Convention of the Pardo—an effective cease-fire—signed in March 1728. He also organized and dragged out larger-scale talks at Soissons from June 1728 to July 1729. Reconciling the belligerents was no easy task, and the Hanover allies lost Prussia to the Austro-Spanish-Russian camp in 1728; but Fleury continued to believe that winning over either Madrid or Vienna would be as good as a general peace. The two courts did this on their own as Charles VI refused a double marriage between his two daughters and the sons of Philip V and Elizabeth Farnese. In consequence, paralleling the proceedings at Soissons, Fleury's envoys led talks for the Treaty of Seville: an Anglo-French-Spanish alliance

21. Horatio Walpole to Delafaye, August 3, 1726 NS, Paris, SP 78/184/54 TNA; letter from "l'Ami," August 25, 1726, giving details of an Austro-Russian treaty, SP 78/184/78, TNA.

22. Adriaan Goslinga, *Slingelandt's Efforts Towards European Peace* (The Hague: Martinus Nijhoff, 1915), 118–23.

signed in November 1729 to which the Dutch soon acceded. Through diplomatic obstructionism and evident pacifism, Fleury cut the Madrid-Vienna axis, won a victory for his allies, and supported French merchants who valued peaceful trade, all without resorting to arms.[23]

Fleury also restored a place for Spain in the constellation of French diplomacy that aroused British envy. Spain had changed sides, but Anglo-Spanish commercial disputes remained unresolved. Despite some revisions in the 1716 Bubb Treaty, British merchants continued to abuse a Spanish trade concession at Utrecht known as the *Asiento*, and the violence with which Spanish authorities enforced their interpretation of the law continued to excite British anger. The new alliance could not last, even with Fleury's interposition, and the diplomats themselves soon changed: William Stanhope, First Baron Harrington had been a key player at Seville, and in 1730 he succeeded Charles, Second Viscount Townshend as the head of British foreign relations. Shortly thereafter, British policy took a new direction that Fleury might have anticipated: towards Vienna.[24]

The legacy of William III meant that the British betrayal was a Dutch one as well, but it was not all loss for Fleury. Discomfited as the French ministry may have been by shifting alignments in 1731, it was not 1725: Britain and Spain kept at peace; British and Dutch leaders remained cordial toward France; and a British pamphleteer even wrote of 1732 as the most peaceful year in recent memory.[25] Freed, in fact, from the demands of alliance with the British, Fleury and his protégé, Germain-Louis Chauvelin, found it easier to build better relations with Madrid. They needed to wait for events to concur in bringing the stronger bonds to full fruition, but they came in due course from an unusual quarter: Poland.

The death of King Augustus II in February 1733 catalyzed both French and Russian foreign policy. For hawks in the French ministry, it represented an opportunity for Poland's elective monarchy to restore Stanislaus Leszczynski, father-in-law of the now twenty-three-year-old Louis XV. On the far side of Europe, however, Czarina Anna had her own profoundly cynical ideas about elective monarchy; she ordered Russian troops to secure the election of her

23. Arthur McAndless Wilson, *French Foreign Policy During the Administration of Cardinal Fleury, 1726–43* (Cambridge, MA: Harvard University Press, 1936), 164–214.

24. Jeremy Black, *The Collapse of the Anglo-French Alliance, 1727–1731* (Gloucester: St. Martin's Press, 1987).

25. *The Natural Probability of a Lasting Peace in Europe* (London: J. Peele, 1732).

own candidate: Elector Augustus III of Saxony.[26] As both sides mobilized, Fleury concluded the First Family Compact with Spain and a separate alliance with the young King Charles Emmanuel III of Sardinia. Strangely for a struggle over elective kingship in Poland, Russian pressure on Austria to join the war opened the way for campaigns in Italy and on the Rhine.

Fleury looked on a still larger scale, however, and moved to limit French operations. He had a great bluff to play for limiting to Europe what might well have become a global war. Without question, his strongest cards were the French armies under Marshal Villars and the Duke of Berwick; but refusing to attack the Austrian Netherlands reaffirmed an early Dutch decision to declare neutrality. Fleury therefore challenged the other maritime power—Britain—to contemplate a war in the Low Countries and around the world without Dutch help, on the side that was trying to subvert a royal election. Would Britain expend its resources in such a venture, risking its trade, colonies, a friendly and demilitarized neutral territory, and even its own society and government to Jacobite revolt? Fleury gambled that they would not, and events proved him right.[27]

So much for limiting the war to Europe, but with armies taking the field, what would Fleury have French armies fight for? With French frontiers sheltered behind the iron belt of Vauban fortresses, what could he expect to gain? That too would have to wait for events. The French-Spanish-Sardinian bloc triumphed in southern Italy, much of northern Italy, and in a sliver of the Rhineland, while the Russians conquered and occupied much of Poland and Lithuania. A bloody but largely predictable stalemate ensued, broken in Fleury's distinctive way.

With Spanish forces away in Italy, Portugal's King Joao V may have seen a chance to profit from a double marriage in 1729 that had set his son José with Louis XV's jilted bride Mariana Victoria, and his daughter, Barbara of Portugal, with the younger son of Philip V and Maria Luisa of Savoy, the future King Ferdinand VI. Perhaps Joao pondered a palace coup in Madrid, favoring the latter couple, though the evidence is uncertain. Spanish authorities nevertheless believed that they had uncovered a plot early in 1735, roughly handled Portuguese embassy staff, and both sides withdrew their diplomats. The exchange stoked fears of a Spanish-Portuguese conflict in the middle of the War of the

26. John R. Sutton, *The King's Honor and the King's Cardinal: The War of the Polish Succession* (Lexington, KY: University of Kentucky Press, 1980), Chapter 1.

27. Richard Lodge, "English Neutrality in the War of the Polish Succession," *Transactions of the Royal Historical Society* 14 (1931): 141–13; Jeremy Black, "British Neutrality in the War of the Polish Succession, 1733–1735," *International History Review* 8:3 (1986): 345–66.

Polish Succession; Joao invoked the 1703 Treaty of Methuen, and the British ministry duly dispatched twenty-eight warships bearing 9,000 troops.[28]

A legal and logical British response to the Iberian emergency immediately undercut their bid to mediate the larger conflict, and gave Fleury the opening he sought. On a small scale, he rebuked the British for their gunboat diplomacy, and—withholding troops once again, this time from Spain—he immediately took the lead trying to repair the Iberian rift. On a larger scale, Fleury wrote a personal note to Britain's leading minister, Sir Robert Walpole, strongly selling a two-part agenda they shared in common: achieving European peace, to be sure, but also to a small degree humbling an Austrian regime that had largely progressed from triumph to triumph over the previous half-century.[29] Then he turned to Vienna.

The case was a persuasive one, and in time to avert ill effects from 30,000 Russians marching from Poland to the Rhine. Austria had already fared badly there, lost in northern Italy, lost Naples and Sicily altogether, and the Netherlands lay open to French conquest. However, Fleury could argue that French triumphs at Kehl, Trarbach, and Philippsburg were merely diversions; and despite Villars's activity during the first campaign in Italy, he could note just as easily that most of the activity there came from Spaniards and Sardinians whom he had also sought to restrain. Would the Austrians prefer to deal with him—and the reputation Fleury had already established at Soissons—or with a British "mediator" whose forces in Lisbon lay poised to expand the war?

Though some issues remained unsettled, Fleury brokered a cease-fire near the end of 1735. A restored Neapolitan kingdom passed to Don Carlos, the elder son of Philip V and Elizabeth Farnese. Sardinia made gains in the Milanese. French ambitions, including for Louis's father-in-law, required more time, finesse, and distinctive turns of circumstance. Perhaps Fleury could profit from the latest turn of European foreign affairs: the Russians returning east and dragging a reluctant Austrian ally into a fresh war against the Turks.[30]

28. The incident enters the British diplomatic record in Tyrawly to Newcastle, March 19, 1735 NS, SP 89/38/4, TNA. For the most complete history, see Visconde de Borges de Castro and Julio Firmino Judice Biker, *Collecçao dos Tratados, Convenções, Conttratos e Actos Publicos Celebrados entre Corôa de Portugal e as Mais Potencias desde 1640*, Volume X (Lisbon: Imprensa Nacional, 1873), 365–426.

29. Fleury to Robert Walpole, March 14, 1735 NS, SP 78/207/37, TNA. See also Jeremy Black, "French Foreign Policy in the Age of Fleury Reassessed," *English Historical Review* 103:407 (1988): 359–84.

30. Karl Roider, *The Reluctant Ally: Austria's Policy in the Austro-Turkish War, 1737–1739* (Baton Rouge, LA: Louisiana State University Press, 1972).

The Turkish war did not go well, and Gian Gastone de Medici, the last of his line among the Grand Dukes of Tuscany, died in July 1737. Fleury exploited these openings to work once again both with and against the Austrians. First, he turned his cease-fire into a firmer peace through a mutual transfer of claims in the Third Treaty of Vienna: Francis Stephen of Lorraine, husband of Charles VI's elder daughter Maria Theresa, would transfer sovereignty to the now-vacant Grand Duchy of Tuscany and allow a pro-French ruler to take Lorraine—Stanislaus Leszczynski, who in turn would recognize his defeat in Poland—and France could abandon a decade of efforts to undermine the lynchpin of Austrian diplomacy over the previous fifteen years: the Pragmatic Sanction of 1713. A year later, Fleury's envoys also arranged the Treaty of Belgrade, exchanging Austrian Serbia for peace in the Balkans.

In short, Fleury patiently exploited fluid multipolarity in European foreign relations, and repeatedly and effectively utilized diplomatic obstruction and non-commitment of forces to France's advantage. Beyond diplomatic achievements, he also promoted French logistics and commerce on local, European, and global scales.[31] He backed the Controller-General of Finances Philibert Orry mandating *corvée* labor to rebuild and expand France's road system. It was likely the best in Europe by the time Fleury died in 1743. Meanwhile, a sympathetic Marine minister, Jean-Frédéric Phélypeaux, Comte de Maurepas, enabled the expansion of French commerce in the Levant, and a shift from the French East India Company's abortive tobacco schemes in Louisiana to more profitable ventures in the Indian Ocean.

Fleury's interaction with the colonial realm also bears mention. He probably had no role in appointing Joseph François Dupleix to the superintendency of Chandannagar in 1730, but the latter's expansion of French profits and influence in India broadly accords with the cardinal's vision of French commerce and colonialism under conditions of European peace. Fleury and Maurepas also oversaw more fort construction in French North America, from a spate of exploratory outposts west of Lake Superior, to Fort de Tombecbé bolstering the Choctaw near Louisiana's eastern frontier, to Fort Vincennes along the Maumee-Wabash portage linking the Mississippi and St. Lawrence waterways. Intendant of commerce and physiocrat leader Jacques Claude Marie Vincent de Gournay may also have taken cues from Fleury, favoring commercial deregulation and—paralleling Dupleix—pondering how to maintain, manipulate, and exploit European peace to France's benefit overseas.

31. Wilson, *French Foreign Policy*, 64–68, 71–76.

Fleury's career has a tragic coda: the rise of the otherwise talented Duc de Belle-Isle. Notwithstanding his meddling in German politics and cunning diplomacy among allies and rivals, the cardinal built France's reputation for some fifteen years largely on peace-seeking and honest brokering. As Louis XV backed his hawks in 1741, Belle-Isle took the War of the Austrian Succession much deeper into Germany, and with far more ambitious aims than Fleury had dared eight years earlier. Moreover, by supporting Frederick's invasion of Silesia, Belle-Isle also affirmed a flagrant breach of international custom and broke France's good-faith assent to the Pragmatic Sanction.

In sum, the octogenarian Fleury bequeathed ideas of French strategy that were too subtle for younger generations to follow—much the same fate that befell Germany after Bismarck. Fleury sacked his own protégé in 1737; neither Orry nor Maurepas could step into his role, and Louis XV proved a poor leader on his own. Later first ministers—Choiseul, Vergennes, Talleyrand—were competent and creative men, but none quite observed, as Fleury had, the value of keeping an ace very visibly in reserve.

V

Roughly from the Peace of Westphalia to the Age of Revolutions, European foreign relations turned on peculiar interpretations of secular state sovereignty and quasi-social norms that gradually accreted into international law. Dynamic alignments among the system's many states often collapsed into violence, yet the selfsame traits of fluidity and multipolarity informed drives to codify a law of nations. Europe thus possessed a distinctive culture of war and diplomacy that guaranteed survival for almost all participants, even as conditions for specific states fell subject to contingency and whim.

Success in this regime depended on the careful building and constant maintenance not only of political and commercial bonds with other states, but also of a reputation that suited the system's social norms—playing by the rules, as it were. The wars of Louis XIV and Frederick the Great allowed great captains to emerge, such as Turenne and Henry of Prussia, but nobody quite like Osei Tutu, Alaungpaya, or Prithvinarayan Shah. Especially following Locke's logic, Europeans might resist poor government; yet the community of European states also needed time to accept change like the mainline Stuarts being ousted, the Pragmatic Sanction of 1713, or acquisitions of large territories like Pomerania, Silesia, and Lorraine.

Among the more successful strategists in this game of European politics, William III and Cardinal Fleury led what might fairly be called generational efforts to promote their states' interests. William emerged from the shadow of Johan de Witt to become, in many respects, the leading progenitor of the United Kingdom as such, and the strategy both of Britain-in-Europe and the British Empire. Conversely, Fleury inherited the advantages and limitations of decades of French growth, and arguably weaponized European peace as he pursued novel directions for the expansion of French prestige and commerce.

The examples set by these two strategists offer insights for our own times, when higher speeds and volumes of transport, communication, commerce, and force projection herald the possibility of a multipolar world. Beyond China-US dualism, a system that also recognizes the European Union, Russia, India, Brazil, and perhaps ASEAN and the African Union if and as they take more definite shape, may bear comparison with the world of William III and Cardinal Fleury. International alignments will likely be fluid, complex, contingent, and, without due care, attended by a high risk of conflict. Conversely, like the early modern Holy Roman Empire, contemporary Europe may yet house some institutions that inspire, model, and help to regulate the larger system. The example of William III highlights the role of smaller states for building international custom, consensus, and norm-enforcing coalitions, while that of Fleury hints at the rewards for carefully conceived strategic restraint. Above all, regardless of formal laws and endeavors for world peace, a multipolar global system will certainly develop its own social logic; today's strategists will do well to pay attention to its cues.

CHAPTER 13

Napoleon and the Strategy of the Single Point

Michael V. Leggiere

Napoleon ruled France as an enlightened despot from November 1799 to May 1804, and then as emperor until April 1814, followed by the inglorious Hundred Days of 1815. However, any discussion of his strategy must begin with an outline of the nearly quarter-century of conflict that commenced in 1792.

That year, Revolutionary France started the first of seven coalition wars that pitted the French against various combinations of great powers and secondary states. Including the Anglo-French War (1793–1802, 1803–14), the war in Iberia (1807–14), and Napoleon's 1812 invasion of Russia, these seven coalition wars constitute the "French Wars." Within this period are two separate epochs: the French Revolutionary Wars (1792–1802)—the wars started by France's revolutionary governments—and the Napoleonic Wars (1803–15), that is, the wars caused by Napoleon.

This chapter will discuss the Napoleonic Wars in the context of Napoleon's crucial innovation—his pursuit of the *Vernichtungsschlacht* (battle of annihilation) through the strategy of the single point. This strategy emphasized the advance along a single axis to engage the enemy decisively, at a single point and time. It worked wonders for a time. A combination of Napoleon's operational mastery, a qualitatively superior army, and his opponents' adherence to outmoded approaches produced overwhelming success against the Third (1805) and Fourth (1806–7) Coalitions. Yet the deteriorating capabilities of Napoleon's army, along with the tactical and strategic improvements of his enemies, led to failure against the Fifth (1809) and Sixth (1813–14) Coalitions.

These defeats, in turn, marked not simply Napoleon's downfall but also the end of the Napoleonic era in warfare. If the political and military changes wrought by the French Revolution had enabled Napoleon's conquests, the changes wrought by the Industrial Revolution would render the strategy of the single point defunct.

I

To better understand Napoleon's strategy, it is useful to take a glimpse at his foes. Until 1809, the Austrian, Prussian, and Russian armies that Napoleon faced dutifully respected the cult of Frederick the Great. After Frederick's death in 1786, military observers concluded that the Prussian king employed *Ermattungsstrategie* (strategy of exhaustion) in a *Stellungskrieg* (war of position). Lacking the resources to overwhelm and render a large state completely defenseless, Frederick limited his actions and objectives—hence the name: limited war. To obtain limited objectives that could be won just as easily at the peace table as on the battlefield, the *Ermattungsstrategie* employed battle, maneuver, position, and attrition—all of which he considered equally effective means of attaining the political ends of the war.[1] Frederick's strategy sought to exhaust the enemy by maneuvering his own army into an advantageous position. Examples of this include threatening the enemy's line of communications, besieging a critical fortress, occupying a rich province, destroying crops and commerce, and holding key road junctions or bridges. Like in chess, the Frederician general sought to force his opponent into checkmate while conserving as many pawns as possible, because he lacked the resources to replace them.[2]

Consequently, military theory experienced minimal change in Austria, Prussia, and Russia. In fact, many of the same officers who had served Frederick or fought against him held commands or senior advisory positions in their respective armies. Across Europe, a handful of them, as well as younger, enlightened officers such as Gerhard von Scharnhorst of Prussia, urged change. Moreover, their monarchs were not ignorant of the power unleashed by the French Revolution. Yet, in the absolutist framework of Old Regime Europe,

---

1. Dennis E. Showalter, "Hubertusberg to Auerstedt: The Prussian Army in Decline?" *German History*, 12:3 (1994): 308.

2. Hans Delbrück, *Die Strategie des Perikles erläutert durch die Strategie Friedrichs des Grossen. Mit einem Anhang über Thucydides und Kleon* (Berlin: Georg Reimer, 1890), 9–28.

army reform on par with the French remained out of the question; only drastic political and social change could affect the social composition of the army.[3]

A rigid system of discipline based on fear bound the armies of the eighteenth century. As obedience was based on fear, desertion plagued Frederician armies. Consequently, every aspect of a Frederician army—tactics, marching, logistics—was designed to prevent the individual from deserting.[4] Tactically, the armies employed a linear system that emphasized thin, rigid, close-order lines in order to maximize firepower through a closely supervised, cohesive infantry attack. The need to supervise the men, combined with the requirements of linear cohesion, limited the options and flexibility of Frederician generals. Night marches had to be avoided except when absolutely necessary.[5] Frederick had also advised against camping near forests and suggested that the men be led to bathe and supervised by an officer. Besides possibly enabling desertion, woods and hills undermined the effectiveness of the volleys, broke linear cohesion, and limited the tactical control of the commanding general.[6] Bound to Frederick's system of sophisticated maneuvers and tight formations, generals preferred to move their units slowly and methodically over open terrain. Unlike Napoleon, they held precision above speed and flexibility.

Linear tactics required the planning of the entire operation. Overwhelming the enemy through a single crushing blow served as the fundamental tactical concept. Orders of battle typically grouped the infantry in deep, massive waves with cavalry protecting the flanks and rear; artillery normally remained stationary throughout the course of the battle. As linear formations were highly susceptible to flanking attacks, Frederician generals often preferred flank security over a strong center. The entire army advanced as a unitary organism toward the enemy in a completely uniform manner. All rearward waves followed the movements of the first wave in a parallel direction. Firefights featured long thin lines of three-deep infantry exchanging mass, unaimed volleys with the enemy. Panic in the front lines easily spread rearward so that, if the frontline units broke and ran, they usually dragged the unbroken units with them.

3. Hans Delbrück, *Das Leben des Feldmarschalls Grafen Neidhardt von Gneisenau*, Volume 2 (Berlin: Hermann Walther, 1894), 211–12.

4. Delbrück, "Über den Unterschied der Strategie Friedrichs und Napoleons," in his *Historische und politische Aufsätz* (Berlin: Walter und Apolant, 1887), 20, 24.

5. Robert R. Palmer, "Frederick the Great, Guibert, Bülow: From Dynastic to National War," in *Makers of Modern Strategy: Military Thought from Machiavelli to Hitler*, Edward Mead Earle, ed. (Princeton, NJ: Princeton University Press, 1944), 55.

6. Delbrück, "Über den Unterschied der Strategie Friedrichs und Napoleons," 23, 28.

As for provisions, supplies came via a system of food and fodder magazines. This forced the army to advance with large quantities of victuals in huge supply trains. Soldiers could not be trusted to forage in small groups; many would simply never return. Desertion also occurred if the army did not provide the soldier "with a tolerable standard of living, since to make a living, not to fight or die for a cause, was the chief aim of the professional soldier."[7] Dependence on magazines and depots further added to the army's inflexibility. Because aristocratic officers traveled in style, and the morale of soldiers who lacked political passion would suffer without a steady supply of food, enormous baggage trains followed a slow moving, inflexible force.[8]

II

General Bonaparte toppled the French government in the Coup of 18–19 Brumaire (November 9–10, 1799). In so doing, he inherited an army that had been undergoing extensive evolutionary reform since the 1760s as well as revolutionary reform for the past decade. By producing new political and social systems, the French Revolution unlocked a new age of war.

Thanks to the *levée en masse* of 1793, France became the first "nation in arms," where the people, the army, and the government formed a triad to wage war, thus inaugurating the transition from limited war to total war. By sequestering the human and economic resources of the entire nation, France no longer had to wage limited war to attain limited objectives. The French nation in arms possessed the power to undertake an offensive with such force that victory could take the form of the complete destruction of the enemy army and the capture of its capital.[9]

As the Revolution changed France's social fabric, the social composition of the army likewise changed, resulting in nationalism underpinning its social cohesion rather than discipline enforcing it from above. From the chaos and bloodshed of the Revolution emerged a self-disciplined, independent citizen-soldier who served in a people's army that fought for the nation rather than the king.[10] Unlike the reluctant peasants and capricious mercenaries who filled the ranks

7. Palmer, "Frederick the Great," 50.

8. Delbrück, "Über den Unterschied der," 51.

9. Delbrück, *Gneisenau*, Volume 2, 211.

10. Aarden Bucholz, *Hans Delbrück and the German Military Establishment: War Images in Conflict* (Iowa City, IA: University of Iowa Press, 1985), 9.

of their enemies, French soldiers enjoyed the benefits of a constitution that provided them with civil rights and a society based on merit.[11] With a vested interest in defending this new society, the French soldier became the representative of national independence. In addition, troops no longer accepted officers whose only claim to leadership was a noble title.[12] Moreover, the mass exodus of nobility during the Revolution purged the army's officer corps, opening it to "natural-born" leaders such as General Bonaparte, who received command of the French Army of Italy in April 1796 at the age of twenty-seven.

The complimentary aspects of conscription and nationalism filled the ranks of Napoleon's armies. Between 1800 and 1811, 1.3 million men answered the summons to serve. In the wake of the disastrous Russian and German campaigns of 1812 and 1813, respectively, Napoleon drafted a further one million men. Although the army had transitioned back to a professional force by the end of the Revolution, Napoleon leveraged the intrinsic benefits of the French Revolution that had produced a highly motivated and ultra-patriotic citizenry. His comment that a marshal's baton could be found inside the knapsack of every soldier adequately describes the real possibility of promotion based on merit rather than a noble title. To further motivate his men, Napoleon awarded generous incentives such as medals, decorations, monetary grants, titles, and promotion to the Imperial Guard. Yet, despite his attempts to reinforce the nation-in-arms concept, war weariness and the revulsion over the butcher's bill led to high rates of draft dodging and desertion in 1813 and 1814.

Although conscription and troops from vassals and allies provided Napoleon with armies of unprecedented size, he needed to find solutions to the interrelated problems of distance, space, and time. For example, the distance from Paris to Berlin remained the same for an army of 50,000 men or 250,000.[13] Space on a single axis of advance from Paris to Berlin remained finite: only so many men, horses, cannon, and wagons could be found at any time at any single point on the march route. Napoleon solved both problems through speed and distributed maneuver. While the distance between Paris and Berlin did not change, the amount of time needed to cover this distance could. To increase speed, Napoleon's troops marched between twenty and

11. Gerhard Ritter, *Frederick the Great,* trans. Peter Paret (Berkeley, CA: University of California Press, 1974), 132.

12. Delbrück, *Gneisenau,* Volume 2, 211; Delbrück, "Über den Unterschied der Strategie Friedrichs und Napoleons," 24; Bucholz, *Hans Delbrück,* 25.

13. Delbrück, "Über den Unterschied der Strategie Friedrichs und Napoleons," 31–32.

thirty miles per day compared to the enemy, who typically covered seven to ten miles. French troops marched at night, traversed thick forests, navigated rugged terrain, and operated in small units. They also used a simple logistical system that dispensed with the traditional magazine and supply trains of the eighteenth century. In particular, French armies supplemented their meager supplies by foraging and requisitioning. This increased the flexibility, mobility, and speed of French armies. The soldiers knew that defeat brought misery, rags, and hunger but victory meant full bellies and the sating of their material and sexual needs. While this system worked well in the bountiful regions of Germany and Italy, French soldiers suffered horribly from privations in the barren regions of Eastern Europe and Iberia.

Napoleon overcame the problem of space by further developing the concept of dividing the army into smaller, combined-arms units that functioned as self-contained "mini-armies." The mini-army began as an ad hoc division that contained infantry and artillery, totaling between 5,000 and 7,000 men. As a combined-arms division, it could rapidly and independently deploy either to counter or to pose a threat. Napoleon distributed these mini-armies along a broad front but always within supporting distance of each other. By marching on parallel roads, the combined-arms divisions extended the range of the army's operations, facilitated envelopment maneuvers, and eased foraging by expanding the army's area of operations. While speed remained a primary objective, a combined-arms division could hold its ground against a typical eighteenth-century army. By attacking, the division could fix the enemy until other friendly divisions arrived along different routes to converge on the enemy. Equally if not more important, if one corps was destroyed, the army could survive and possibly even win the battle.

Napoleon first implemented ad hoc combined-arms divisions during his 1800 Italian campaign. During the period of continental peace between 1801 and 1805, he expanded the concept by adding cavalry to create the preeminent tool of Napoleonic warfare: the army corps. He based the army corps on the same idea as the combined-arms division: a mini-army consisting of infantry, cavalry, and artillery, but on a much larger scale. Truly a mini-army, a corps ranged in size from 15,000 to 40,000 men or even more—in 1813, Marshal Michel Ney's III Corps numbered 60,000 men. A French army corps contained all of the necessary elements to hold its ground against a conventional eighteenth-century army for twenty-four hours. A typical corps consisted of three infantry divisions with organic artillery, one cavalry brigade, one reserve battery of heavy artillery, and its own support personnel of staff, engineers, and liaison officers. Attaching the cavalry and reserve artillery to the corps allowed its commander to respond to the fluidity of the battlefield in real time. Thus, the corps system enabled the army to move with lightning speed, display extraordinary flexibility, and operate on a broad front. More so, it allowed Napoleon to strike with overwhelming force.

III

With the army divided, new needs of planning arose to enable the various corps to operate in unison. Napoleon referred to this level of war—the moving of combat assets to the battlefield and the battle order of those combat assets—as Grand Tactics; today we call it the operational art. Napoleon developed and perfected the principles of operational warfare that are still viewed as paramount today. Speed, flexibility, and the concentration of overwhelming force at the point of attack formed the most crucial elements of Napoleon's art of war. His operations consisted of deep flanking maneuvers to envelop the enemy's rear. His corps always advanced to the battlefield along different routes but within supporting distance: divide, converge, and unite on the battlefield. This approach enhanced flexibility, coordination, and combat power within the army and ensured unity of command under Napoleon. Moreover, the nature of battle changed from the all-destroying massive linear formation to the attrition of the enemy army by the constant arrival of fresh corps on the battlefield in preparation for the final blow to be delivered by a powerful reserve.

On the army level, Napoleon retained direct command of the infantry, cavalry, and artillery of his elite Imperial Guard, Reserve Cavalry Corps, and Reserve Artillery. This allowed him to direct overwhelming firepower and force against any point on the battlefield. His favorite march formation, the *bataillon carré* (battalion square), positioned the various corps in a diamond shape with one corps at each of the four points. Napoleon, with the Guard and Reserve, marched in the center, about a twenty-four-hour march from each point. With all four sides equally spaced, twenty-four hours separated each point while forty-eight hours separated the diagonals. Thus, forty-eight hours separated the van from the rear, and the left from the right. Theoretically, within twenty-four hours of the van engaging the enemy, the emperor and his Guard would arrive as well as the corps on the left and right wings. In another twenty-four hours, the entire army would be concentrated. Moreover, the diamond formation made the army equally effective in any direction by simply changing the responsibilities of each point. This formation provided Napoleon with the flexibility and speed necessary to achieve his strategic goal, the *Vernichtungsschlacht* (battle of annihilation).

For Napoleon, a successful campaign achieved the destruction of the main enemy army through the most economical expenditure of time and resources. Rather than focusing on the conquest and occupation of terrain, he placed overwhelming emphasis on force convergence in the shortest amount of time. "In war," he explained in 1806, "the loss of time is irreparable: the excuses that one gives are always bad because any delay is detrimental to operations." In 1809, Napoleon advised that, "as with mechanics, time is the great element between weight and force in the art of war."[14] Wanting rapid and decisive results, he almost always seized the initiative, launched the offensive, and attacked. His armies covered a far greater range than their adversaries because his troops traveled more lightly than those of the Frederician period. This provided Napoleon with far greater mobility than the armies he faced for most of his career. He used this mobility to impact all three levels of war but his greatest impact can be seen on the strategic and operational levels.

In his planning process, Napoleon positioned his army along a single front with a single line of communications. If he faced two armies, he would execute a *manœuvre sur position centrale* by placing himself between them. Next, he would identify which of the two armies posed the main threat to his line of communications and concentrate all available forces for a *Vernichtungsschlacht*. Minimum essential combat power would mask the other enemy army; at least in his early campaigns, Napoleon did not expend combat assets on nonessential targets such as cities. Screened by light cavalry, he would advance toward the enemy's most vulnerable flank, making sure that his own line of communications remained open and secure. If the conditions were right, Napoleon would execute his favorite operational maneuver, the *manœuvre sur les derrières*, to place his army on the enemy's flank and rear, thus enveloping him and cutting line of communications. On the operational level, Napoleon excelled at deploying and maneuvering large, independent forces simultaneously and then concentrating them on the battlefield to deliver maximum combat power.

---

14. Napoleon to Joseph, *Correspondance général* (Paris: Fayard, 2009), No. 11732, Volume 6, 247; Napoleon to Eugene, January 14, 1809, *Correspondance de Naploéon Ier* (Paris: Imprimerie Impériale, 1858–69), No. 14707, Volume 18, 256.

IV

Carl von Clausewitz referred to Napoleon as "the God of war himself." Clausewitz based this generous assessment on Napoleon's strategy. The French general instinctively recognized that the nation-in-arms provided the resources to replace the Frederician concept of maneuver, position, and attrition with a single principle: battle. To achieve political objectives, Napoleon sought to destroy the enemy's main army in a *Vernichtungsschlacht*; battle became the main component of his *Niederwerfungsstrategie* (strategy of annihilation). Napoleon's mastery of the operational level of war allowed him to perfect the concept of *Niederwerfungskrieg* (war of annihilation). He exploited the form of warfare waged by modern nation-states, where the power of universally conscripted mass armies was used "to break the enemy's will to resist through short, rapid, destructive strokes against the enemy's main force."[15] "Napoleon always subordinated secondary concerns to concentrate all of his forces for a single, devastating blow," concluded Hans Delbrück. "After destroying the enemy's forces, he invaded and conquered the enemy's country."[16] In his memoirs, General Pierre Berthezène provided the following quotation from a young General Bonaparte in 1797:

> There are many good generals in Europe, but they see too many things at once; I see only one thing; namely, the enemy's main body. I strive to destroy it, confident that secondary matters will work themselves out.[17]

Napoleon's campaigns exemplified the concept of the *Vernichtungsschlacht*, typically referred to as a "decisive" battle. To wage a decisive battle, he conducted a long approach march on one general axis with the objective of engaging the enemy at a single point at the decisive time.[18] Military theorists such as Antoine-Henri Jomini viewed the essence of Napoleon's operational and strategic genius as the "strategy of the single point."[19] The Soviet officer and theorist, Georgii Isserson (1898–1976), described a typical Napoleonic campaign as "a great, long approach, which engendered a long operational line, and a short

---

15. Ritter, *Frederick the Great*, 131.

16. Delbrück, *Gneisenau*, Volume 2, 212.

17. Pierre Berthezène, *Souvenirs militaires de la République et de l'Empire* (Paris, 1855), 2, 309.

18. John Shy, "Jomini" in *Makers of Modern Strategy: From Machiavelli to the Nuclear Age*, Peter Paret, ed. (Princeton, NJ: Princeton University Press, 1986), 154.

19. Bruce W. Menning, "Operational Art's Origins," in *Historical Perspectives of the Operational Art*, Michael D. Krause and R. Cody Phillips, eds. (Washington, DC: Center of Military History, United States Army, 2005), 4.

final engagement in a single area, which, with respect to the long operational line, is a single point in space and a single moment in time."[20] Thus, Napoleon's columns march-maneuvered within theater to force convergence with the enemy at a single point—finite in time and space—for a climactic battle that would determine the outcome of the campaign and, perhaps, even the war.[21]

V

On May 18, 1804, the French proclaimed Bonaparte "Napoleon I, Emperor of the French." His transformation of the Italian Republic into the Kingdom of Italy with himself as king one year later further alienated the Austrians and offended the Russians, in whose eyes Bonaparte had gone too far. His coronations as Emperor of the French and King of Italy were "affronts to the Austrian Holy Roman Emperor, by tradition successor to Charlemagne, and to legitimate monarchs generally."[22] Adroit British diplomacy led to Britain signing military conventions with Russia, followed by similar agreements with Austria and Naples. Although courted by both camps, Prussia remained an armed neutral.

After christening the Army of England "*La Grande Armée*," Bonaparte drove it from the Channel, where it had been training to invade Britain for several years, to the Rhine at an amazing speed. Departing their camps on August 27, 1805, the army's seven corps marched 450 miles along parallel roads to reach the Rhine on September 26. Meanwhile, a slow-moving Austrian army had opened the war by invading Bavaria. Not expecting to encounter the French until at least November, the Austrians lumbered west toward the city of Ulm. After giving each soldier fifty cartridges and rations for four days, Napoleon swiftly moved his army across the Rhine and marched east.[23] Through a *manœuvre sur les derrières*, Napoleon conducted one of the greatest envelopments in military history. By wheeling his army south, he emerged east of Ulm, completely cutting off the Austrian army from Vienna, trapping the majority of it in Ulm, and forcing it to surrender on October 20, 1805.

---

20. G. S. Isserson, "The Evolution of Operational Art," in *The Evolution of Soviet Operational Art: 1927–1991: The Documentary Basis*, H. S. Orenstein, ed. (London: Frank Cass, 1995), 55.

21. Menning, "Operational Art's Origins," 4.

22. Owen Connelly, *Napoleon's Satellite Kingdoms: Managing Conquered Peoples* (Malabar, FL: Krieger Publishing Company, 1990), 3.

23. Mark T. Gerges, "1805: Ulm and Austerlitz," in *Napoleon and the Operational Art of War: Essays in Honor of Donald T. Horward*, Michael Leggiere, eds. (Leiden and Boston, MA: Brill, 2021), 230.

At the same time, Napoleon executed a *manœuvre sur position centrale* by placing the Grande Armée between the Austrians at Ulm and an approaching Russian army. After receiving news of the events at Ulm, the Russians retreated. Napoleon pursued, taking Vienna along the way. He found the Austro-Russian army waiting for him near Brünn, in the modern Czech Republic. On December 2, 1805, Napoleon achieved his most brilliant tactical victory during the Battle of Austerlitz, a pitched battle in which both sides had time to prepare. With his III Corps en route, Napoleon baited the Allies by offering his right, which only a single regiment held. Tsar Alexander I fell for the ruse, shifting forces from his center to his left in order to crush the French right. Not only did III Corps arrive just in time to stop the Russian left, but Napoleon launched a massive assault on the weakened Allied center. To seal the victory, his Imperial Guard overwhelmed its Russian opposite. At that time, Austerlitz marked Napoleon's largest engagement and first *Vernichtungsschlacht*. The Russian army marched home without concluding a diplomatic settlement to officially end their participation in the war while the Austrians signed an armistice on December 6. The Third Coalition was over.

However, on the other side of the ledger, Admiral Horatio Nelson ended any chance of the French challenging British naval superiority by destroying a Franco-Spanish fleet off the coast of Spain at Trafalgar on October 21, 1805. Realizing that Trafalgar severely limited his ability to challenge the British in a fleet action and thus considerably eroded his chances of gaining control of the English Channel, Napoleon sought to exploit his victory on land. With French forces occupying the mainland portion of the Kingdom of Naples, he made his brother, Joseph, the new king while his younger brother, Louis, became the new king of Holland. In July 1806, Napoleon completed the reorganization of Germany by creating the *Rheinbund* (Confederation of the Rhine), consisting of fifteen autonomous German states joined in a military and political union under the protection of the French emperor. This provided the proverbial last straw for Prussia, which had pursued a policy of neutrality since 1795. King Frederick William III issued an ultimatum to Napoleon, summoned help from Russia, and secured assistance from Great Britain to form the Fourth Coalition. The next eleven months proved to be a nightmare for the Prussian ruler.

Marching north from Bavaria through the Thuringian Forest with the Grand Armée aligned in a *bataillon carré*, Napoleon assumed he would find the main Prussian army to the northwest, near Erfurt. He planned to march down the Saale River, using it to mask his movement and conduct a *manoeuvre sur les derrières* around the Prussian left to cut its line of communications that stretched 180 miles northeast to Berlin. His van, III Corps, made steady progress down the Saale as did his right-wing point: IV Corps. However, on October 10, Napoleon's left-wing point, V Corps, found and defeated the Prussians at Saalfeld, less than thirty miles east of Erfurt. Although still lacking a clear view of the situation, Napoleon continued the march north, believing that the Prussians remained to his left (west) at Erfurt. Three days later, V Corps again made contact with the Prussians, this time some twenty-five miles northeast of Saalfeld at Jena. After guessing Napoleon's plan, the main Prussian army of 65,000 men had started withdrawing along its line of communications, reaching the village of Auerstedt on August 13, while fifteen miles to the south a rearguard of 40,000 men held Jena as flank protection. Convinced that V Corps had found the main Prussian army at Jena, Napoleon swung the *bataillon carré* west so that V Corps became the van, III Corps the right, IV Corps the rear, and the former rear, VI Corps, the left. For the *manoeuvre sur les derrières*, he ordered III Corps followed by I Corps to envelope the Prussian left by marching west and swinging south. The rest of the army received instructions to converge on Jena.

By nightfall on October 13, some 30,000 men of V Corps and the Imperial Guard stood on the high ground at Jena overlooking the Prussian position. At 6:00 a.m. on October 14, the French attacked. Fresh troops continuously reached the battlefield in the form of IV Corps on Napoleon's right, VII on his left, and VI in the center. By one o'clock in the afternoon, Napoleon had 54,000 soldiers engaged in battle. Over the course of the next two hours another 42,000 men arrived. Suffering tremendously from combined-arms attacks, the Prussians began to yield. After their center broke around two o'clock, Napoleon unleashed his Reserve Cavalry to relentlessly pursue the retreating Prussians. By four o'clock, they were a mass of helpless fugitives; all resistance ended. Prussian losses had amounted to 10,000 killed and wounded, 15,000 prisoners, and 155 guns.[24]

Although the Battle of Jena marked Napoleon's second *Vernichtungsschlacht*, he had not defeated the main Prussian army, much to his disbelief. Instead, to

---

24. See, generally, Alain Pigeard, *Dictionnaire des batailles de Napoléon 1796–1815* (Paris: Tallandier, 2004), 399; Owen Connelly, *Blundering to Glory, Napoleon's Military Campaigns* (Wilmington, DE: Scholarly Resources, 1987), 101; Eduard von Höpfner, *Der Krieg von 1806 und 1807: Ein Beitrag zur Geschichte der Preußischen Armee nach den Quellen des Kriegs-Archivs*, Volume 1 (Berlin: Simon Schropp & Comp., 1850), 471–72.

the north, the 28,000 men and forty-four guns of Marshal Louis-Nicholas Davout's III Corps encountered it at Auerstedt as it retreated northeast. Although facing an enemy army that totaled 39,000 infantry, 9,200 cavalry, and 230 guns, the steady arrival of Davout's three divisions and combined-arms interplay held the Prussians at bay. Stymied, the Prussians commenced an orderly retreat at 12:30 p.m. after losing 13,000 killed or wounded, 3,000 prisoners, and 115 guns. French losses amounted to over 7,000 men for a twenty-five percent casualty rate but Davout's troops validated the role of the corps as a "mini-army."[25]

Late that night, the fugitives from Jena ran into the well-ordered Prussian troops retreating from Auerstedt. Panic quickly spread. Soon, both Prussian armies resembled a mob. At dawn, the French cavalry continued the pursuit, capturing thousands. Although Frederick William fled to Königsberg where a force of 10,000 Prussians had linked with the approaching Russian army, Prussia collapsed after a series of feeble and unparalleled surrenders. The Jena campaign ended with the fall of Magdeburg and its 22,000-man garrison on November 6. In a less than one month, the Prussian army lost 165,000 men, including over 30,000 killed and wounded. Unfortunately for the Prussians, they suffered the full effects of the emperor's *Niederwerfungskrieg*.[26]

From Berlin, the Grande Armée moved east to confront the Russians but the inhospitable weather of Prussian-Poland slowed operations and required the return to a conventional supply system for the winter. After the Russians launched a general offensive in late January, Napoleon responded with another *manœuvre sur les derrières* by advancing 115,000 men in a *bataillon carré* to turn the Russian left. However, his quarry started retreating in early February after learning the details of the French plan. Napoleon gave chase but fierce Russian rearguard actions on February 4, 5, and 6 prevented him from gaining an advantage. Yet, the Russians could go no further without abandoning their line of communications to Königsberg and its precious magazines that kept the army fed, albeit just barely. Consequently, they decided to make a stand at the village of Eylau with 67,000 men on the seventh. Napoleon reached Eylau that night with elements of the Guard, Reserve Cavalry, and IV and VII Corps, totaling 50,000 men. Anticipating the arrival of III and VI Corps on his right, Napoleon attacked on February 8.

25. Pigeard, *Dictionnaire des batailles de Napoléon*, 71; Connelly, *Blundering to Glory*, 101; Höpfner, *Der Krieg von 1806 und 1807*, Volume 1, 471.

26. Michael V. Leggiere, *Napoleon and Berlin: The Franco-Prussian War in North Germany* (Norman, OK: University of Oklahoma Press, 2002), 19.

The two sides waged a bloody slug-fest during an extended blizzard. Napoleon planned to pin the Russian army until Davout's III Corps arrived to envelop the Russian left. In whiteout conditions, Napoleon's VII Corps accidentally veered into the line of fire of massive French and Russian artillery batteries. In a matter of minutes, VII Corps ceased to exist. Again, validating the corps system, its loss did not lead to the collapse of the French army. Nevertheless, a Russian counterattack shattered the French center. With few infantry formations at hand, Napoleon ordered his Reserve Cavalry to break the Russian center. In one of the greatest cavalry charges in military history, the French shock and awe force of 10,000 cavalry smashed through the Russian army's center. Reaching its rear, the French reformed and charged back through the Russian lines to return to Eylau. In complete disarray, the Russians needed time to reorganize, in turn providing III Corps time to arrive and extend Napoleon's right. As Davout applied pressure, the Russian left bent back, practically forming a right angle with the center. Just before III Corps could move around the flank to cut the Russian line of retreat, 8,000 Prussians arrived to repulse Davout's assault. In a short time, the Russians and Prussians had turned the tables on Davout, threatening to envelop his exposed right. As night fell, the fighting ended; the arrival of VI Corps on Napoleon's left convinced the Russians to withdraw during the night. As the Russians relinquished their position, victory went to the French but both sides suffered horrendous casualties: over 25,000 for the Russians and somewhere between 20,000–30,000 for Napoleon. In its aftermath, both sides moved into winter quarters.[27]

After summoning reinforcements from his German vassals and resting his army, Napoleon prepared for a summer offensive. Before he could seize the initiative, the Russians attempted to destroy his VI Corps, which appeared isolated, in early June. The flexibility of the French corps system again proved its value. Instead of smashing the 16,000 men of III Corps, the Russians found themselves in the midst of a closing net. Per standard operating procedures, Napoleon had positioned the army so its various corps could concentrate within twenty-four to forty-eight hours. After the Russians withdrew, he launched a counteroffensive that aimed to deliver a *Vernichtungsschlacht* by executing a *manœuvre sur les derrières*. According to Napoleon's plan, the bulk of his army would pin the Russians while III and VIII Corps enveloped the

27. John H. Gill and Alexander Mikaberidze, "Napoleon's Operational Warfare During the First Polish Campaign, 1806–1807," in *Napoleon and the Operational Art of War*, Leggiere, ed., 292–94.

Russian right. On the morning of June 10, Napoleon engaged the Russians, whom he found strongly entrenched behind a ring of earthworks that included six redoubts on both banks of the Alle River. The bloody but inconclusive Battle of Heilsberg cost Napoleon 12,000 casualties while the Russians lost between 6,000 and 9,000 men. Although no fighting occurred on the eleventh, the Russians withdrew over the concern of being cut off from Königsberg. Napoleon pursued the Russians north toward Friedland, where a newly constituted formation, the "Reserve Corps" commanded by Marshal Jean Lannes, found the Russians on the west bank of the Alle.

Not knowing the rest of the Grande Armée would arrive so quickly, the Russians attacked. For three hours starting at six o'clock on the morning of June 14, Lannes's corps held its ground against the Russians, despite their three-to-one advantage in infantry. After 9:00 a.m., the lead elements of VIII Corps and the Reserve Cavalry started arriving on Lannes's left, I and VI Corps and the Guard to his right. Fresh troops continuously reached the "single point" so that, at the height of the battle, Napoleon commanded 80,000 French against 60,000 Russians. He launched a general attack at 5:30 p.m. His right drove the Russian left into Friedland; the interplay between French artillery and infantry caused havoc among the Russians' tightly packed masses. With their left shredded, the Russians withdrew across the Alle under severe duress caused by Napoleon's guns. With their morale broken and 20,000 dead or wounded, the Russians requested an armistice.[28] At 12,000 killed and wounded, French losses were not slight but Napoleon could designate the Battle of Friedland as another *Vernichtungsschlacht* because it knocked the Russians out of the war. In the aftermath, Tsar Alexander accepted the monumental Franco-Russian Treaty of Tilsit that ended the war and established an offensive-defensive alliance between the two empires. Moreover, the Russians joined the French emperor's Continental System: Napoleon's ambitious plan to defeat Britain through economic warfare. As for Frederick William III, the Franco-Prussian Treaty of Tilsit reduced his kingdom to a third-rate rump, stripped of half of its territory and population, and occupied indefinitely by the French.

Napoleon earned his signature victories over Frederician-style armies at Ulm and Austerlitz in 1805, Jena-Auerstedt in 1806, and Eylau and Friedland in 1807. In each battle, Napoleon maneuvered his army into position to

28. Gill and Mikaberidze, "Napoleon's Operational Warfare During the First Polish Campaign," 296–301.

confront the enemy's main army. In the head-to-head contests that followed, the emperor benefitted from the tremendous advantages offered by the corps system, his mastery of the operational art of war, his strategy of annihilation, and his adversary's adherence to the principles of linear warfare. Napoleon also had the luxury of having to face only one enemy army, in one theater of operations, in one theater of war. Thus, between 1805–7, Napoleon achieved decisive victories due in part to the continued adherence of his adversaries to linear warfare, which rendered their main army susceptible to his massive blows. With one main army operating in one main theater of operations, its ensuing defeat resulted in the end of the war.

VI

Following Tilsit, Napoleon assessed the overall situation in Iberia. Aside from the goal of ending Portuguese trade with the British, he viewed Spain as too corrupt and too inefficient to administer the Continental System. Thus, the emperor decided to deal with Portugal overtly and Spain covertly. On November 30, 1807, French forces entered Lisbon just as the Portuguese administration sailed for Brazil with most of the state's coin. The French established rule over Portugal, occupying its ports and fortresses, and dismantling its armed forces.

With the conquest of Portugal, Napoleon moved against Spain. Under the pretext of establishing a line of communication between France and Portugal, over 130,000 French troops crossed the Pyrenees. Instead of marching toward Lisbon, the army appeared at Madrid on March 24, 1808, while other French forces took control of Spain's major fortresses. On May 2, 1808, the people of Madrid violently protested against the French presence. Meanwhile, disagreement between King Charles IV and his son, Crown Prince Ferdinand, had resulted in an invitation from Napoleon for all concerned parties to meet with him at Bayonne in April 1808. There, Napoleon arrested father and son, compelling both to surrender their rights to the throne. He then summoned Joseph from Naples to be the new king of Spain.

In Madrid, the revolt of the common people against the unholy French invader escalated into a general insurgency. Revolutionary *Juntas* (assemblies) sprang up throughout the state and mobilized Spanish forces, both conventional and guerilla. In July 1808, French units deployed to Spain's larger cities, where they encountered fanatical resistance. Moreover, British troops that had landed in Portugal forced the French army to surrender. This rapidly deteriorating situation required Napoleon's presence. Assuming command of all

French forces in Spain on November 5, 1808, he conducted a short blitzkrieg that smashed the Spanish field armies and drove the British into the sea at Coruña. At this point, Napoleon should have turned south to drive the remaining redcoats out of Portugal but rumors over Austria's preparations for war had him back at Paris on January 19, 1809. He never returned to Iberia, leaving the war to his marshals and his brother—a grave error as that war considerably drained French resources. The British presence in Portugal and their support of the Spanish guerillas forced Napoleon to allocate over 500,000 men to Iberia over the course of the Peninsular War (1807–14). Two subsequent French invasions of Portugal were turned back by Arthur Wellesley's Anglo-Portuguese army in 1809 and 1810–11 respectively. The British exploited these victories with offensives into Spain that the French likewise parried. An adherent of *Ermattungsstrategie*, Wellesley, named Duke of Wellington in 1814, exploited the shortcomings of the marshals and never came close to being trapped in a *Vernichtungsschlacht*.

Although the British and the Spanish guerillas exhausted the French, Napoleon's resources seemed boundless; even after he withdrew forces for the buildup prior to the 1812 invasion of Russia, 200,000 imperial soldiers continued the war in Spain. The British managed to take Madrid in August 1812 as a result of the drawdown, but the French chased the redcoats back to Portugal before year's end. After receiving considerable reinforcements in the winter of 1812–13, the Anglo-Portuguese army invaded Spain in May 1813. Again, the British benefitted from the further drawdown of French forces as Napoleon summoned veteran units from Spain to replace the tens of thousands of soldiers lost in Russia. On July 21, 1813, the British defeated the French in the last great battle of the Peninsula War. In its aftermath, all the French armies retreated across the Pyrenees. The British invaded France in October 1813, reaching the French city of Toulouse by the time of Napoleon's abdication in April 1814. Estimates of French losses in both Spain and Portugal exceed 250,000 men, with some authorities placing the losses at over 400,000.[29]

Returning to central Europe, the tremendous advantages that Napoleon enjoyed in army organization, strategy, operations, and tactics started to fade in 1809. That year, the Austrians declared war. Proving that they had learned some lessons from the French, the Austrians implemented the corps system. Although the Austrian high command lacked sufficient training, and thus

29. Connelly, *Blundering to Glory*, 132; Jean Tulard, *Dictionnaire Napoléon*, Volume 1 (Paris: Fayard, 1987), 752.

comfort, in the new command structure, 200,000 men organized in eight corps invaded Bavaria in April. After Napoleon stopped their offensive there, the two armies moved into positions facing each other from across the Danube River in the vicinity of Vienna. At Aspern-Essling on May 21–22, 1809, the Austrians defeated Napoleon mainly because he underestimated his adversary and attempted to cross the Danube River without taking the proper precautions. However, Austrian failure to exploit the victory allowed Napoleon to recover and brutalize them at the July 5–6 Battle of Wagram. During two days of vicious fighting, some 188,000 imperial troops faced 155,000 Austrians. On the second day, Napoleon split the Austrian army in two, but to his surprise it did not break. Despite suffering a casualty rate of almost thirty percent, or 40,000 men, the Austrian army lived to fight another day, proving that the French no longer held a monopoly on tactical ability.[30]

Although technically a French victory, the Battle of Wagram was far from a *Vernichtungsschlacht*. The Austrians were the first major power to copy the French corps system, which allowed the Austrian army to survive such horrendous losses. Moreover, at Wagram we find no signs of Napoleon's usual tactical finesse or distributed maneuver. Instead, we see a growing preference for bloody, mass frontal attacks supported by massive batteries. This was indicative of the fact that the tactical skill of the French infantry was declining, in part because raw conscripts and non-French recruits had replaced the veterans of Austerlitz and Jena; those troops were fighting in Iberia along with some of his most experienced generals. Just as important, Napoleon held his enemies in contempt, unable to stretch the limits of linear warfare. Such overconfidence restricted his critical thinking.

After the end of the War of the Fifth Coalition in October 1809, Napoleon did not see battle again until he invaded Russia on June 16, 1812, with some 650,000 men in response to the tsar's withdrawal from the Continental System. In terms of strategy and operations, Napoleon attempted to conduct the war much like he had his earlier campaigns but on a much larger scale. Unable to use the superior speed and flexibility of his own forces to envelop and destroy the Russians, he fruitlessly pursued them 500 miles as they retreated in an impromptu Fabian strategy. On September 7, they finally engaged him

---

30. Ian Castle, "The Battle of Wagram" in *Zusammenfassung der Beiträge zum Napoleon Symposium "Feldzug 1809" im Heeresgeschichtlichen Museum,"* June 4–5, 2009, 198–99; Pigeard, *Dictionnaire des batailles de Napoléon,* 924; John H. Gill, "1809: The Most Brilliant and Skillful Maneuvers," in *Napoleon and the Operational Art of War,* Leggiere, ed., 365.

at Borodino in a pitched battle. The ensuing bloodbath saw the Russians group their infantry in deep, massive waves protected by earthworks, redoubts, and flèches, against which Napoleon, like at Wagram, hurled equally massive frontal assaults. Casualties amounted to 30,000–35,000 imperials and 40,000–45,000 Russians. On this occasion, Napoleon did not commit his Guard to deliver the knockout blow, which allowed the Russian army to limp away from Borodino and the French to reach Moscow one week later. To Napoleon's disbelief, the war did not end as the Russians refused to negotiate. He remained in Moscow with his 95,000 ill-equipped and under-supplied men until finally ordering the retreat to commence on October 9. Snow, starvation, disease, and the pursuing Russians ensured that only 23,000 men from Napoleon's main army of around 450,000 men emerged from Russia in late December.[31]

Driven by Tsar Alexander, the Russians carried the war westward in a great effort to drive the French from central Europe. In February 1813, Prussia joined Russia and Britain to form the Sixth Coalition. Undaunted by either the catastrophic losses his army had suffered in Russia or the new coalition, Napoleon ordered general mobilizations in France, Germany, and Italy. Although his unrivaled organizational skills produced a new field army of 200,000 men by the end of April, he could not replace the 180,000 horses that had been lost in Russia, meaning that the army lacked not only its main instrument for shock tactics, but its eyes and ears as well.

Strategically and operationally, the spring campaign of 1813 proved to be relatively routine for Napoleon, and he dominated his enemy. He again faced one main enemy army, which he made his primary target, and operations were limited to one theater. Victories over the Allies came at Lützen on May 2 and Bautzen on May 21. The Battle of Lützen again demonstrated Napoleon's operational supremacy. Advancing toward Leipzig in a *bataillon carré* enabled him to move his various corps to Lützen where and when they were needed. On May 2, the Allied army came within hours of being destroyed by a double envelopment that would have been so crushing it would have ended the war. Following Lützen, however, the shortage of cavalry prevented Napoleon from unleashing a deadly Jena-like pursuit to annihilate the Allies and achieve his *Vernichtungsschlacht*.

31. Alexander Mikaberidze, "The Limits of the Operational Art: Russia," in *Napoleon and the Operational Art of War*, Leggiere, ed., 406, 416–19; Pigeard, *Dictionnaire des batailles de Napoléon*, 586–97; Connelly, *Blundering to Glory*, 171–81.

On May 20, Napoleon assaulted the Allied army at Bautzen. As at Borodino the previous year, he found massive waves of Russians entrenched behind earth works and redoubts. To counter this, he planned for Marshal Ney to march east on May 21 and cross the Spree River north of the Allied position. While Napoleon fixed the Allied army with over 120,000 men, he wanted Ney to wheel southeast with more than 60,000 to envelop the Allied right. Despite the admonitions of his chief of staff, Jomini, the impetuous Ney turned south, after observing the Allied right "in the air." Running into the Prussian army entrenched atop a steep ridge line ended his advance. Had Ney wheeled southeast as instructed, the war would have ended with both Alexander and Frederick William being taken prisoner.

Organizationally, Napoleon's enemies had vastly improved. The development of combined-arms doctrine made them more flexible and fluid while the adoption of the corps system allowed them to absorb battlefield losses and still march away relatively intact. Napoleon's lack of cavalry assured his opponents' survival and limited the intelligence he received over their movements. Napoleon's oft-quoted statement that "the animals have learned something" reveals his reluctant admission that his adversaries had closed the gap in terms of tactical proficiency. For Napoleon, such parity meant that he had to retain his operational superiority. Lützen and Bautzen proved that the debacle in Russia did not affect his ability to conduct operations. The Allies could neither challenge him nor predict his movements; his shadow loomed large over their war planning. Thus, to defeat Napoleon, they needed a new and innovative plan.

VII

After both sides agreed to an Austrian-brokered armistice, Napoleon's intransigence at the negotiating table drove Vienna to join the Allies. The Sixth Coalition's war plan—the Trachenberg-Reichenbach Plan—called for a wide arc to be formed around French forces in Saxony and Silesia by three multinational armies: the main army, the Army of Bohemia—220,000 Austrians, Prussians, and Russians; the Army of Silesia—105,000 Russians and Prussians; and the Army of North Germany—140,000 Prussians, Russians, Swedes, and North Germans.[32] Accordingly, these armies would engage detached enemy corps only; pitched battles with Napoleon would be avoided. Should the

---

32. Barthold von Quistorp, *Geschichte der Nord-Armee im Jahre 1813*, Volume 3 (Berlin, 1894), 1–60.

emperor concentrate against any one army, it would retreat while the other two attacked his flanks and communications. The plan aimed to split and exhaust French forces. Although Napoleon had the advantage of interior lines, he would be forced to fight against armies advancing simultaneously against his center, flanks, and communications. Moreover, as Napoleon could personally challenge only one Allied army at a time, the other two would attack his flanks and lines of communication while the threatened army executed a Fabian strategy to induce the emperor to pursue, thus extending and exposing his line of communication.

Napoleon planned to assemble 300,000 men to oppose what he believed to be the Coalition's main army of 200,000 Russians and Prussians in Silesia. Timing would be crucial; he needed to deliver a *Vernichtungsschlacht* in Silesia before the Austrians advanced from Bohemia against his base at Dresden. Inconceivably, Napoleon violated the principle of allocating minimal essential combat to a secondary effort by forming the 70,000-man Army of Berlin (IV, VII, and XII Corps as well as III Cavalry Corps) under Marshal Nicolas Oudinot to conduct an offensive against the Prussian capital. As the end of the armistice approached, Napoleon received reports indicating that the Allied force in Bohemia represented the Coalition's main army. After the armistice expired on August 17, he wasted several days seeking confirmation rather than launching a blitzkrieg offensive. Although he received the necessary confirmation, Napoleon decided to attack a secondary army: the Army of Silesia. Yet, as soon as he established contact with it on August 20, it retreated eastward in compliance with the Trachenberg-Reichenbach Plan. After fruitlessly pursuing the Army of Silesia for three days, Napoleon learned that the Army of Bohemia had crossed the Saxon frontier en route to Dresden. He immediately issued orders for 200,000 men to converge on Dresden for a *Vernichtungsschlacht*. With the 75,000 troops that remained in Silesia (III, V, and XI Corps and II Cavalry Corps), he formed the Army of the Bober commanded by Marshal Jacques-Etienne Macdonald.[33]

While he herded his forces toward Dresden, the Army of North Germany stopped Oudinot's Army of Berlin at Großbeeren, eleven miles south of the city, on August 23. Although he lost only 3,000 men, Oudinot retreated all the way to Wittenberg on the Elbe River. Three days later, the Army of Silesia repulsed Macdonald's Army of the Bober along the banks of the Katzbach River; Macdonald lost over 30,000 men and 103 guns during his flight to

33. Michael V. Leggiere, "Prometheus Chained, 1813–1815," in *Napoleon and the Operational Art of War*, Leggiere, ed., 438–39.

Saxony. On that same day, August 26, the Army of Bohemia assailed Dresden. In the midst of the struggle, Napoleon and the Guard arrived to repel its assaults. During the night, II and VI Corps moved up, increasing Napoleon's combatants to 135,000 men against 215,000 Allied soldiers. Continuing the battle on the twenty-seventh, Napoleon enveloped the Allied left, crushing two Austrian corps. With the French also working around their right, the Allied army retreated after losing 38,000 men. Although the imperials sustained far fewer casualties in comparison (10,000), decisive victory had again evaded Napoleon. Despite having adequate cavalry, illness forced the emperor to leave the field rather than direct the ensuing pursuit. On August 30, the Allies trapped his overextended I Corps at Kulm, thirty-five miles south of Dresden. Imperial losses amounted to 25,000; Allied casualties numbered 11,000 men.[34]

Following the defeats at Großbeeren, the Katzbach, and Kulm, Napoleon decided on a second offensive against Berlin despite knowing that the main Allied army was in Bohemia. He planned to lead 30,000 men from Dresden, unite with the Army of Berlin on September 6, and resume the operation against the Prussian capital. Napoleon never executed the Berlin offensive; the impending collapse of Macdonald's beleaguered Army of the Bober required his personal intervention. After restoring discipline and moving up substantial reinforcements on September 3, Napoleon led the Army of the Bober against the Army of Silesia, which again retreated. As Napoleon pursued, the Army of Bohemia resumed its offensive against Dresden, forcing the emperor to rush back to the Saxon capital. Meanwhile, Ney, who had replaced Oudinot as commander of the Army of Berlin, collided with the Army of North Germany on the sixth. In the ensuing Battle of Dennewitz, Ney's losses amounted to 21,500 men, compared to 9,700 Prussians.[35]

Napoleon's situation had become critical after less than one month of campaigning. Since the expiration of the armistice, he had lost 150,000 men and 300 guns—an additional 50,000 names filled the sick list. While French commanders suffered defeats at Großbeeren, the Katzbach, Kulm, and Dennewitz, the emperor raced back and forth between the Elbe and the Bober Rivers in futile attempts to strike at one of the Allied armies. The constant marches and counter-marches exhausted his conscripts both mentally and physically.

34. Leggiere, "Prometheus Chained," 440–42; Pigeard, *Dictionnaire des batailles de Napoléon*, 253–54, 360–417, 434; Connelly, *Blundering to Glory*, 192.

35. Leggiere, "Prometheus Chained," 444; Pigeard, *Dictionnaire des batailles de Napoléon*, 241; Quistorp, *Geschichte der Nord-Armee im Jahre 1813*, Volume 1, 524–31.

Following the battle of Dennewitz, the Army of Silesia linked with the Army of North Germany after both crossed the Elbe. Napoleon made one final attempt to deliver a *Vernightungsschlacht* by surprising these armies south of Wittenberg. On October 9, he massed 150,000 soldiers in the region of Bad Düben and Dessau, but once again the Allies complied with their operation plan; both armies escaped by retreating west across the Saale River. At this juncture, Napoleon simply resolved to take a position at Leipzig, allow the Allies to encircle him, and wage an epic struggle. One week later, the Coalition's armies started converging concentrically on his position, resulting in a tremendous *Kesselschlacht* (encirclement battle). On the final day of the battle, the nineteenth, 365,000 Allied soldiers, supported by 1,500 guns, assaulted Napoleon's 195,000 men and 700 guns. The battle ended after staggering losses: 54,000 Allied casualties to 73,000 imperials, including 30,000 prisoners and 5,000 German deserters.[36] This disaster resulted in Napoleon's loss of Germany. In December 1813, the Allies invaded France, soon forcing him to abdicate. His brief return in 1815 led to his utter defeat at Waterloo.

VIII

The Grande Armée peaked in the years 1805–7 following the intense training it received in the years prior to the War of the Third Coalition. After sustaining irreplaceable losses in 1807, Napoleon committed many of the survivors to Iberia, from where they would never return. After exhausting this invaluable, highly trained force, he became increasingly dependent on German, Italian, and Polish manpower that had not received training on par with the original Grande Armée. The imperial forces that waged Napoleon's wars from 1809 onward simply could not match their predecessors' performance. Coinciding with this qualitative decline was a marked change in Napoleon's tactics. Instead of continuing the progression of his tactical innovations for battlefield problem-solving, he became increasingly dependent on the weight of massed batteries, huge infantry formations, and unimaginative frontal assaults, as illustrated by the battles of Aspern-Essling, Wagram, and Borodino.

Moreover, with the exception of Bautzen, Napoleon rarely sought to achieve victory through operational maneuver. Although he suffered no rival

---

36. Leggiere, "Prometheus Chained," 445, 447–50; Pigeard, *Dictionnaire des batailles de Napoléon*, 468–69; Connelly, *Blundering to Glory*, 193; Rudolph von Friederich, *Die Befreiungskriege, 1813–1815*, Volume 2 (Berlin: E. S. Mittler, 1903–9), 349–60.

in the operational art, the *Ermattungsstrategie* of the Trachenberg-Reichenbach Plan exhausted both him and his army, keeping him off-balance and wrecking his strategy of the single point. His defeat in 1813 reflects four important considerations concerning Napoleon's system of war during the last years of the empire. First, he understood that the qualitative decline of his army limited his options on all three levels of war. Second, Napoleon viewed his adversaries with utter contempt which, combined with his own sense of infallibility, stifled his novel approach to battlefield problem-solving. Third, he placed emphasis on securing secondary objectives rather than on achieving a *Vernichtungsschlacht*. Fourth, his aging marshalate and incompetent generals often rendered "out-of-the-box" thinking impractical. Lacking a proper general staff, the majority of his corps' commanders failed to formulate strategy and conduct operations on par with the emperor himself. Napoleon's system excelled at training great tacticians, but failed to prepare his officers for independent command.

In the evolution of warfare, the differences between *Ermattungsstrategie* and *Niederwerfungsstrategie* reflect the differences between two sociopolitical systems. The political and social changes caused by the French Revolution unlocked the forces that enabled Napoleon to develop the latter. His mastery of the operational art made it possible for him to engage the enemy at a single point and time—the strategy of the single point—and deliver a *Vernichtungsschlacht* using a combination of mass and firepower. The central theme of Napoleon's art of war—the blitzkrieg attack—aimed to destroy the enemy's center of gravity: his army.[37] For Napoleon, strategy always sought to force a decisive battle. Where *Ermattungsstrategie* sought to secure checkmate while conserving as many pawns as possible because it was too costly to replace them, *Niederwerfungsstrategie* recklessly sought to force checkmate regardless of the number of pawns lost because they could be replaced quickly and cheaply. For that very reason, the *Ermattungsstratege*— Prince Eugene of Savoy, Frederick the Great—had to be a genius on par or perhaps even greater than the *Niederwerfungsstratege*: Alexander the Great, Caesar, and Napoleon.[38]

As the French Revolution provided the tools that enabled Napoleon to perfect the strategy of the single point, another revolution—the Industrial Revolution—rendered those very same tools obsolete. The tremendous

---

37. David G. Chandler, "Napoleon, Operational Art, and the Jena Campaign," in *Historical Perspectives of the Operational Art*, Krause and Phillips, eds., 27.

38. Delbrück, *Die Strategie des Perikles*, 1, 22–23.

technological improvements in firearms and artillery during the nineteenth century increased the battlefield's killing zone exponentially. As the accuracy and range of rifled muskets made cover a necessity, battlefields became honeycombed with defensive lines and huge earth works that served as the blueprint for the trenches of the First World War. Thus entrenched, a single rifleman could kill or wound dozens of approaching soldiers with little-to-no danger to himself. Massing infantry in Napoleonic attack columns or Frederician lines and attacking frontally became tantamount to suicide. Instead of shock and awe, armies needed flexible, extended tactical formations, swift tactical maneuvers, rapidity of fire, and marksmanship.

As the increased lethality of the battlefield favored the defensive and challenged the feasibility of the Napoleonic *Vernichtungsschlacht*, a new conceptual framework for strategy emerged: the "extended line." To avoid deadly frontal confrontations, commanders employed "distributed operational strategy" to laterally stretch the Napoleonic "single point" of troop convergence to produce an "extended line." As flanks vanished, attacking armies sought to penetrate a continuous front. The speed and reliability of railways and steamships exploiting tight interior lines shortened distances creating a distributed battlefield.[39] In this sense, the Austro-Prussian War of 1866 provides the last salient nineteenth-century example of the strategy of the single point: all three Prussian armies advanced concentrically on Königgrätz to deliver a *Kesselschlacht*. Yet, just four years later during the Franco-Prussian War, the Prusso-German armies "required four discrete combat links to defeat France: Spichern-Werth, Metz, Sedan, and Paris, each of which represented a cluster of lesser battles of varying scale. This meant that battle, instead of occurring in a single place with the mass of the forces of both sides engaged, became distributed into a number of subordinate battles across an expanding front or 'line.' "[40] The culmination of this trend would come in World War I. In the human tragedy that was the Western Front, *Stellungskrieg* und *Ermattunskrieg* replaced *Niederwerfungsstrategie* and its prized *Vernichtungsschlacht* as decisive battle was no longer possible.[41]

39. Michael Evans, *The Continental School of Strategy: The Past, Present and Future of Land Power, Study Paper No. 305* (Duntroon, Australia: Land Warfare Studies Centre, 2004), 35, 61; Menning, "Operational Art's Origins," 5.

40. Justin Kelly and Mike Brennan, *Alien: How Operational Art Devoured Strategy* (Carlisle, PA: Strategic Studies Institute, US Army War College, 2009), 18.

41. Hans Delbrück, *Krieg und Politik*, Volume 2 (Berlin: Georg Stilke, 1919), 164.

CHAPTER 14

John Quincy Adams and the Challenges of a Democratic Strategy

Charles Edel

"The influence of our example has unsettled all the ancient governments of Europe," John Quincy Adams declared in a letter to his brother in 1823. He predicted that the power of that example would "overthrow them all without a single exception."[1] But, as Adams knew, it would take more than just influence to establish the United States as a force capable of influencing the world; it would also take power. Adams believed that quite apart from the power of its ideas, America's size and its capacity for growth meant that it had the potential to rival—perhaps even supersede—the European states that had dominated world politics for the previous several hundred years.

These ideas famously found expression in Adams's July Fourth Address of 1821, where he held that the American Revolution, embodied in the principles of the Declaration of Independence, was the first global ideology, bound "to cover the surface of the globe."[2] But claiming "destiny" was not the same thing as constructing a strategy that would guide his nation to power while also keeping it on a course towards justice.[3] In fact, Adams can plausibly lay claim to being the most important strategist of the early republic, as his career

1. John Quincy Adams to Charles Jared Ingersoll, June 19, 1823, in *Writings of John Quincy Adams*, Worthington C. Ford, ed., 7 vols. (New York, NY: The MacMillan Company, 1913–17), hereafter cited as John Quincy Adams, *Writings*.
2. John Quincy Adams, *Writings*, Volume 7, 12, 21.
3. Charles Edel, *Nation Builder: John Quincy Adams and the Grand Strategy of the Republic* (Cambridge, MA: Harvard University Press, 2014), 303.

was so wide-ranging, his ideas so influential, and his life spanned nearly the entirety of the antebellum period.

Adams's contemporaries recognized this. Speaking after Adams's abrupt death on the floor of the House of Representatives, one congressman declared that no other American had ever occupied "so large a space in his country's history, or . . . stamped so deeply his impress on her institutions." The congressman concluded that Adams had "stood out far beyond the rest of us, upon a broader and higher elevation."[4] Newspaper obituaries argued that "few men have filled a larger space or acted a more important part in the great civil affairs of their country."[5]

For Adams, the goal of American statecraft was preserving, protecting, and expanding the republic and the idea of republicanism. Goals, however, are not strategies. Adams, like most of the founding generation of American statesmen, sought answers to a series of basic challenges confronting the United States. How could it remain safe? How would it expand across the North American continent? How could it lay the foundations for long-term growth? And, how could it best influence the world with the power of its example?

Establishing a grand strategy for a republic, based on democratic principles, was, to a very large extent, unprecedented. Long before Dean Acheson laid claim to being present at the creation of American efforts to build a new world order, the founding generation of American statesmen believed that they were involved in a task of equal importance. Thomas Paine had urged Americans to understand that their task was to "begin the world anew," by establishing a republic, and thus lighting the way for others to follow. But, when they looked for historical examples that might instruct them on how to build a government that could preserve security, exercise power, increase prosperity, and expand its influence in a distinctly democratic manner, the Founders saw that the options were of limited utility. While the founding generation of policymakers were extraordinarily historically conscious, they were also clear-eyed about the limitations of what that history could tell them about building something new.

This challenge, therefore, was not unique to John Quincy Adams, nor was he the only American policymaker who sought answers to the multiple challenges

---

4. *Congressional Globe*, House of Reps, 30th Congress, 1st Session, February 24, 1848, 384 (Congressman Viton, OH).

5. *The National Intelligencer*, February 24, 1848.

facing the young republic. But the longevity of his career, the thoroughness of his thinking on America's strategic challenges, and the influence of his ideas during and after his lifetime marked him as distinctive. Examining John Quincy Adams's life offers ample opportunity to see how he grappled with the big questions confronting the founding generation of American policymakers as they struggled to fashion a distinctly democratic strategy.[6]

I

Adams may have been the most interesting American of the nineteenth century. He was a lawyer, a political essayist, a diplomat, a politician, a professor, a poet, an advocate of science and technology, an enthusiastic amateur astronomer, a wine expert, and a life-long gardener. In his youth, he knew Benjamin Franklin and Thomas Jefferson. As an adult, his contemporaries were Andrew Jackson, Henry Clay, and John Calhoun. In his later years, Adams served in Congress with a young Abraham Lincoln. Abroad, he rubbed shoulders with the greatest figures of his age, including Austria's Prince Metternich, Tzar Alexander of Russia, Viscount Castlereagh of England, and Napoleon Bonaparte. When they travelled to America, Charles Dickens, Alexis de Tocqueville, and the Marquis de Lafayette, all sought Adams's company. And with good reason—Adams authored the Monroe Doctrine and influenced the ideas in Washington's Farewell Address as well as Lincoln's Emancipation Proclamation.

The eldest son of John and Abigail Adams, John Quincy grew up during the American Revolution. After his father was appointed an American envoy

---

6. For more on John Quincy Adams and early American strategy, see Samuel Flagg Bemis, *John Quincy Adams and the Foundations of American Foreign Policy* (New York, NY: Knopf, 1949); Samuel Flagg Bemis, *John Quincy Adams and the Union* (New York, NY: Knopf, 1956); Charles Edel, *Nation Builder*; Edel, "Extending the Sphere: A Federalist Grand Strategy," in *Rethinking American Grand Strategy*, Elizabeth Borgwardt, Christopher McKnight Nicholas, and Andrew Preston, eds. (New York, NY: Oxford University Press, 2021); James Traub, *John Quincy Adams: Militant Spirit* (New York, NY: Basic Books, 2016); Fred Kaplan, *John Quincy Adams: American Visionary* (New York, NY: Harper Collins, 2014). For a comprehensive bibliography see David Waldstreicher, ed., *A Companion to John Adams and John Quincy Adams* (Oxford: Wiley-Blackwill, 2013). For broader works on the rise of United States in the nineteenth century, see John Lewis Gaddis, *Surprise, Security, and the American Experience* (Cambridge, MA: Harvard University Pres, 2004); Richard Immerman, *Empire for Liberty* (Princeton, NJ: Princeton University Press, 2010); Walter McDougall's *Promised Land, Crusader State* (Boston, MA: Houghton Mifflin, 1998); Walter Russell Mead's *Special Providence* (New York, NY: Knopf, 2001); and Robert Kagan's *Dangerous Nation: America's Place in the World from its Earliest Days to the Dawn of the Twentieth Century* (New York, NY: Knopf, 2006).

by the Continental Congress, he accompanied him to Europe as his personal secretary. At fourteen, John Quincy travelled to St. Petersburg, as part of the American effort to open diplomatic relations with Russia and, upon returning, was by his father and Thomas Jefferson's sides as they negotiated the 1783 Peace of Paris that concluded America's War for Independence. He returned to America for college as perhaps the most well-traveled American at that time, and was there to witness the debates surrounding the Constitutional Convention.

His early political essays defending President Washington's recall of French Minister Citizen Genêt in 1793, and advocating for American neutrality in European affairs earned him appointment as American Minister to the Hague— one of only five American diplomatic positions at the time. Posted abroad in the Netherlands and then in Prussia between 1794 and 1801, John Quincy returned to America following his father's loss of the presidency to Thomas Jefferson in 1800.

Upon his return, the younger Adams threw himself into politics, becoming a United States Senator in 1803. When his advocacy for a commercial embargo against the British in 1807 caused him to lose the support of his Massachusetts constituency, he resigned from the Senate, and was appointed American Minister to Russia by President James Madison, where he negotiated a commercial treaty between Tzar Alexander I's Russia and the United States. John Quincy was also there when the War of 1812 broke out between the United States and Great Britain and was appointed chairman of the American delegation responsible for negotiating an end to hostilities with London. Upon successfully concluding negotiations to preserve prewar boundaries, Adams was appointed American Minister to the Court of St. James in London.

Adams was then named US Secretary of State by James Monroe. In that role, he endeavored to push Spanish, Russian, and British interests out of, or nearly out of, North America and to project American power all the way to the Pacific. He managed relations with the new South American republics, secured American borders in Florida, and signed the Transcontinental Treaty with Spain that extended American territorial claims to the Pacific.

Adams was elected president in 1824, in a disputed contest. Despite an increasingly organized and vocal opposition, he pushed for a massive domestic investment into infrastructure, education, and industry with the hope of establishing a firmer footing for the long-term prosperity of the country and its citizens. His major initiatives failed, as did his reelection bid of 1828, due to deepening political divisions and his own political intransigence.

His post-presidential retirement was short-lived, as he was elected to the House of Representatives from Massachusetts in 1830. John Quincy remained in that post for the final seventeen years of his life, before dying of a cerebral hemorrhage on the floor of the House of Representatives. The final stage of his life and career saw Adams warring against what he decried as the slave power of the South and working to limit, constrain, and ultimately abolish slavery.

Adams's influence was so great that the evolution of America's democratic strategy in many ways can be traced by focusing on his career, his ideas, and his impact. But for all the successes he achieved, Adams encountered nearly equal amounts of failures and setbacks. Some were of his own doing, while others derived from the challenges inherent to the country's large, fractious, and often contradictory impulses. Attempting to translate the Founders' vision into actual polices that rendered the country not only powerful, but also prosperous and just, Adams showed what a democratic strategy could mean, and exposed what challenges it would encounter.

II

"Safety from external danger is the most powerful director of national conduct," Alexander Hamilton wrote in *Federalist 8*, echoing the common sentiment that the first challenge early American policymakers had to face was one of survival.[7] This was particularly acute in the country's first several decades as, from the outset, the country was vulnerable to European intervention, manipulation, and dismemberment. Even after America achieved independence and became a recognized sovereign state, it still had to deal with European powers' attempts to manipulate American policies to their advantage and to influence the trajectory of its development. And as the country grew stronger, larger, and richer, it had to deal with the prospect that European powers would encourage its breakup and attempt to limit its growth.

This challenge dominated American policymaking for at least the country's first half-century, although it arguably persisted through the American Civil War, and defined Lincoln's strategy for keeping the Union whole and foreign powers at bay. This challenge also dominated most of John Quincy Adams's career. Before sailing back from England to become secretary of state, an English

---

7. Alexander Hamilton, *Federalist 8*, November 20, 1787, https://avalon.law.yale.edu/18th _century/fed08.asp.

colleague underscored that looming danger, explaining to Adams that, from a European perspective:

> America . . . was the only country in the world enjoying happiness and with prospect of greatness. "Of too much greatness," said he, "if you should remain long united; but you will not. You will soon break up into several Governments: So extensive a country cannot long remain under one Government."[8]

Such sentiments assumed that the breakup of America was inevitable, and believed that it would be America's own internal tensions and centrifugal tendencies that would be the principal cause of that dissolution. Adams however, judged that external forces were just as likely to play such a role. Shortly after the Congress of Vienna had returned Europe to peace, Adams observed that, for a variety of reasons, "all the restored governments of Europe are deeply hostile to us."[9] Adams feared that increasing hostility would produce another violent conflict that threatened the security and integrity of the United States.

Without security from external threats, neither the country's republican principles nor its nascent democratic institutions were likely to survive. In response, the founding generation fashioned a threefold approach that they believed would secure the nation. This consisted of strengthening America's unity, remaining neutral in Europe's feuds, and pursuing a deterrent, appropriate in size, strength, and form to a democratic state.

The US Constitution sought to establish greater national unity to deal with the country's pressing security challenges. Prior to declaring its independence from Britain, America had been part of the world's most powerful empire. In order to unite in their struggle against Britain, the colonies had joined together in a loose confederation of states. But scarred by their experiences dealing with London, and fearful of trading a distant tyrant for a local one, the United States, arranged under the Articles of Confederation, found itself unable to fulfill many of the basic functions of a state, including defending its borders, reimbursing its creditors, and establishing a national trade policy. As these problems intensified, American leaders drafted the Constitution with the express purpose of establishing a unified government that could effectively meet the country's national security requirements. Even Thomas Jefferson, no fan of centralized government,

---

8. John Quincy Adams, Diary 30, May 27, 1817, 202 [electronic edition], in *The Diaries of John Quincy Adams: A Digital Collection* (Boston, MA: Massachusetts Historical Society, 2005), https://www.masshist.org/jqadiaries/php/.

9. John Quincy Adams to John Adams, August 1, 1816, *Writings*, Volume VI: 58 ff.

understood the importance of unity for foreign policy, expressing his opinion that, "I wish to see our states made one as to all foreign, and several as to all domestic matters."[10] The government the Constitution created would do so by regulating the military, setting the direction of US trade policy, and controlling the diplomatic orientation of the country through its treaty powers.

Security, in this conception, would come from domestic unity. Adams noted that he looked to "the *Union* of our country as to the sheet anchor of our hopes, and to its dissolution as to the most dreadful of our dangers."[11] To understand just how important this concept was to the founding generation of American policymakers requires looking not just at their historical experience under the Articles of Confederation; it also means understanding what fears lay underneath.

The ultimate fear of Adams and the Founders was that the political conditions of Europe would replicate themselves in America. If the United States divided, and multiple sovereign states took its place, North America would become a new Europe: a contested arena where multiple states competed for advantage in close proximity. Such rivalry would demand the creation of permanent military establishments, set off an arms race, and inevitably lead to the diminishment of civil liberties and respect for human rights. Moreover, the fracturing of the North American continent into several competing sovereign states increased the chances not only of foreign interference but also, perhaps, of military intervention.

Europe always loomed large in the American strategic imagination—both for the threat it presented, and because the prospect of European divisions taking root in North America was the harbinger of the future that Americans wanted to avoid at all costs. Adams spoke for an entire generation of American policymakers when he said that, if united, the country would "proceed with gigantic strides ... [towards] national greatness; but that if it is once broken, we shall soon divide into a parcel of petty tribes at perpetual war with one another, swayed by rival European powers."[12]

When Adams was criticized for supporting the Jefferson administration's response to the British attack on the USS *Chesapeake* in 1807 as undercutting

---

10. "From Thomas Jefferson to Joseph Jones, 14 August 1787," *Founders Online*, National Archives, https://founders.archives.gov/documents/Jefferson/01-12-02-0038. [Original source: *The Papers of Thomas Jefferson*, Volume 12, *7 August 1787–31 March 1788*, ed. Julian P. Boyd. (Princeton, NJ: Princeton University Press, 1955), 33–35.]

11. John Quincy Adams to Thomas Boylston Adams, February 14, 1801, *Writings*, Volume I, 499. Emphasis in original.

12. John Quincy Adams to Charles Adams, June 9, 1796, *Writings*, Volume I, 493.

New England's commercial interests, he responded that his—and the nation's—higher interest lay in avoiding political division in the face of foreign aggression. "My sense of duty shall never yield to pleasure of party," he wrote in one particularly high-handed letter explaining his actions.[13] Political unity demanded that commercial entities and political parties both needed to think of national interests, not just regional benefits. If they could not, Adams feared the fate of the United States was to become "an endless multitude of little insignificant clans and tribes at eternal war with one another for a rock, or a fish pond, the sport and fable of European masters and oppressors."[14]

To avoid this fate, to give the union time to mature and strengthen, Adams advocated a policy of neutrality in Europe's wars. Neutrality, early American statesmen of all political persuasions believed, would make America a smaller target for Europe and soothe, rather than exacerbate, internal divisions. It also played to America's commercial strengths and its geographical removal, and, furthermore, neutrality would allow the country to expand territorially. Moreover, if pursued with skill, neutrality could forestall further European encroachment in the Western Hemisphere.

Maintaining neutrality in the face of intensifying Anglo-French rivalry was easier said than done, given French and British actions in America and against American shipping. Additionally, as the country grew in size and strength, neutrality became more difficult as policymakers and the public found themselves eager—and increasingly able—to support democratic movements around the world. America's responses to the French Revolution, the Haitian Revolution, the Greek revolt against the Ottoman Empire, and the South American colonial rebellion against Spain all demonstrated the mounting pressure of maintaining the country's policy of neutrality.

Adams was an early advocate for neutrality. In his earliest public writings, John Quincy defended George Washington's Proclamation of Neutrality after Britain and France declared war on each other in 1792 and the subsequent recall of the French Minister Citizen Genêt in 1793 for the Frenchman's interference in American politics. A young Adams argued that:

> as the citizens of a nation at a vast distance from the continent of Europe; of a nation whose happiness consists in a real independence, disconnected

---

13. John Quincy Adams, Diary 27, July 11, 1807, 297 [electronic edition].
14. John Quincy Adams to Abigail Adams, June 30, 1811, in *Writings*, Volume IV, 128.

from all European interests and European politics, it is our duty to remain, the peaceable and silent.[15]

Neutrality, according to Adams, would reduce the nation's exposure to foreign influence. It also would act as a constraint on American enthusiasm for supporting revolutionary causes. These positions strengthened through Adams's career. Looking back at the debates surrounding the Anglo-French Wars of the 1790s a half-century later, Adams wrote that, "the duty of the United States in this war was *neutrality*—and their rights were those of neutrality. Their unquestionable policy and their vital interest was [*sic*] also neutrality."[16]

Maintaining neutrality in Europe's wars became so important that, when it was flagrantly violated—by the French in the 1790s and later by the British during the Napoleonic Wars—America took up arms in the Quasi War with France and in the War of 1812 to defend its neutral rights. Support for neutrality culminated in the Monroe Doctrine of 1823, which Adams authored, and which declared American neutrality in European affairs and non-interference in Europe's colonies. In the Monroe Doctrine, as elsewhere, the principles of neutrality and non-interference were based on the belief that any other policy would invite European intervention in the Western Hemisphere. They were also predicated on the hope—which came in the form of an assertion—of reciprocity. "Neutrality of the United States will be maintained," Adams declared to the Russians in an attempt to explain the Monroe Doctrine, "as long as that of Europe, apart from Spain, shall continue."[17]

Just as important, America's policy of neutrality between warring parties in Europe—or elsewhere—required more than just assertion; it needed to be respected to be useful, which necessitated building deterrent capabilities. This was an obvious point, but it was also a controversial one. How powerful of a military establishment was appropriate for a republic? What type of military was most suitable, and most likely to safeguard a free people and protect their civil liberties? Should it be local militias? A citizen's army? Or a large and powerful navy? How could the country's leaders ensure civilian control of a

15. John Quincy Adams, *Writings*, Volume I, 140.

16. John Quincy Adams, *Jubilee of the Constitution, A Discourse Delivered at the Request of The New York Historical Society, in the city of New York, on Tuesday, the 30th of April 1830* (New York, NY: Samuel Colman, 1839), 88. Emphasis in original.

17. John Quincy Adams, "Observations on the Communications recently received from the Minister from Russia," Department of State, November 27, 1823. Worthington Chauncey Ford's "John Quincy Adams and the Monroe Doctrine," *The American Historical Review* 8:1 (1902): 43.

professional military? Given the imbalance in the size and power projection capabilities of American and European militaries at the time, the question was whether American defense requirements should be weighed in absolute or relative terms. Additionally, given American antipathy towards taxing itself, how would the new nation be able to raise the necessary funds?

Although America was born in a violent struggle largely won by the army, early American strategy would be based more on a navy. A navy, after all, posed less of a threat to a republican government and citizens' rights, but would guard the Atlantic and help preserve American commerce. Arguing in *Federalist 11* for a powerful navy as both a safeguard of civil liberties and a deterrent against foreign invasion, Alexander Hamilton wrote that "a further resource for influencing the conduct of European nations toward us . . . would arise from the establishment of a federal navy." A sufficiently large naval force would protect the country's trade and underwrite a policy of neutrality. Hamilton underscored the point, arguing that "a nation, despicable by its weakness, forfeits even the privilege of being neutral."[18]

Hamilton's warning notwithstanding, the strengthening of the nation's defenses was highly uneven. Following the Revolutionary War, the army had been reduced to a single regiment. But as threats proliferated in the 1790s, Congress sanctioned expanding coastal fortifications and building six frigates. Then, with the advent of peace, Jefferson drastically cut the defense budget—with the navy's budget shrinking sixty-seven percent. After the British burning of Washington, DC, the hard experience of war caused American policymakers to once again rethink the requirements for putting the nation's defenses on a sounder footing.

John Quincy Adams, hypersensitive to shifts in the European balance of power and the necessity of the United States possessing a sufficiently powerful defense capability, decried such inconsistency in American thinking. On the eve of the War of 1812, he wrote, "we have not force to defend our rights upon the sea, or exercise our rights upon it at the pleasure of others."[19] As that war developed, this sentiment hardened into a belief that "no nation can enjoy freedom and independence without being always prepared to defend them by force of arms."[20] Once hostilities had ceased, Adams argued that, "the war may also be instructive . . . if it will teach us to cherish the defensive strength

18. Hamilton, *Federalist 11*, https://avalon.law.yale.edu/18th_century/fed11.asp.
19. John Quincy Adams to Abigail Adams, January 1, 1812, *Writings*, Volume IV, 286.
20. John Quincy Adams to Abigail Adams, January 17, 1814, *Writings*, Volume V, 7.

of a respectable navy."[21] And so, he continued to advocate for the growth of the American navy, although he cautioned that such a buildup should be undertaken in a manner that did not unduly provoke suspicion from stronger powers. An advocate of the navy throughout his career, Adams consistently pushed for the enlargement of a permanent naval peace establishment, the acquisition of new naval stores, the construction of new ports, and the advancement of the navy into the Pacific.

III

Unity, neutrality, and deterrence were meant to offset attempts to break up the United States as well as to put, and keep, the country on a path of democratic development. They were also meant to counteract efforts to limit American territorial expansion. Originally, arguments in favor of enlarging the nation's size were premised on the idea that consolidating the thirteen colonies into one nation would better protect its borders and provide for the common defense than could otherwise be achieved by thirteen sovereign states. The argument for expanding the country's size soon grew to include the motivation of securing American hegemony on the North American continent. As Hamilton would write in *Federalist 11*, the goal of the United States was "to become the arbiter of Europe in America, and to be able to incline the balance of European competitors in this part of the world as our interests may dictate."[22] The larger, and the more powerful America became, the less able Europe would be to constrain its ambitions.

Nearly all of America's early statesmen believed that America's republican principles and institutions were best served by establishing the United States as the dominant power in North America, preventing a rival from contesting its dominion, and, in effect, by establishing its own sphere of influence.[23] To resolve that challenge and to protect republicanism at home required that America "extend the sphere" by expanding the size of the republic.[24] As a result, much of early American strategy was predicated on simultaneously

---

21. John Quincy Adams to Peter Paul Francis De Grand, April 28, 1815, *Writings*, Volume V, 314.

22. Hamilton, *Federalist 11*.

23. Hal Brands and Charles Edel, "The Disharmony of the Spheres," *Commentary Magazine*, January 2018, 20–27.

24. James Madison, *Federalist 10*, November 23, 1787. https://avalon.law.yale.edu/18th _century/fed10.asp.

undercutting European assertions of sovereignty in North America and buttressing America's own claims. Squarely in line with this thinking was Adams's conviction that "the world shall [have] to be familiarized with the idea of considering our proper dominion to be the continent of North America."[25]

America's early history is a record of westward expansion. Even before the country gained its independence, leading colonial voices argued that the foremost objective of the British in North America should be "to secure Room enough, since the Room depends so much the Increase of her People." These were the words of Benjamin Franklin, who ceaselessly advocated that British security would be found by "Increasing her People, Territory, Strength, and Commerce" in North America."[26] Such impulses found expression in the basic structures of the US Constitution, with Article Four granting Congress the authority to admit new states into the Union.[27] Congress incorporated its first new territories with the creation of the Northwest Territories in 1789, and in 1790, with the Treaty of New York, which attempted to establish a stable border between the United States and the Creek tribe in the southwest. But the country's explosive demographic growth and the incessant pressure of Americans moving beyond the nation's demarcated borders proved too great for the federal government to restrain. "Scarcely anything short of a Chinese wall or a line of Troops," an exasperated George Washington opined, "will restrain . . . the encroachment of settlers, upon the Indian Country."[28] The removal of American Indians, however, was only one part of American expansion.

Geopolitics, and adroit manipulations of Europe's balance of power, were of equal consequence to the expansion of America's borders. Neutrality in Europe's quarrels did not mean that American policymakers were above threatening to tip the scales. Thomas Jefferson, perhaps the greatest advocate

25. John Quincy Adams, Diary 31, November 16, 1819, 205 [electronic edition].

26. "From Benjamin Franklin to George Whitefield, 2 July 1756," *Founders Online*, National Archives, https://founders.archives.gov/documents/Franklin/01-06-02-0210. [Original source: *The Papers of Benjamin Franklin*, Volume 6, *April 1, 1755, through September 30, 1756*, Leonard W. Labaree, ed. (New Haven, CT, and London: Yale University Press, 1963), 468–69.]

27. US Constitution, Article IV, Section III, https://www.archives.gov/founding-docs /constitution-transcript.

28. "From George Washington to Timothy Pickering, 1 July 1796," *Founders Online*, National Archives, https://founders.archives.gov/documents/Washington/05-20-02-0239. [Original source: *The Papers of George Washington*, Presidential Series, Volume 20, *1 April–21 September 1796*, David R. Hoth and William M. Ferraro, eds. (Charlottesville, VA: University of Virginia Press, 2019), 349–50.]

of sealing the country off from Europe, knew that doing so completely was "a theory which the servants of America are not at liberty to follow."[29] Not only did Jefferson know this, but as his actions during the Louisiana Purchase made clear, he acted upon it. His exquisite knowledge of the current state of the balance of power in Europe allowed him to turn it to America's advantage by threatening French negotiators "to marry ourselves to the British fleet and nation."[30]

This history informed John Quincy Adams's extensive record expanding American territory. He supported the Louisiana Purchase, arguing that "the acquisition of Louisiana adds an immense force" to the nation by moving the "centre of power" further west.[31] The further the country expanded across the continental landmass, the more it would find security by becoming the resident power in the Western Hemisphere and thus foreclosing Europe's ability to constrain its reach. In Europe, Adams supported balancing between the old world's powers. But in North America, he advocated a strategy intended to undermine their hold on power and, where feasible, replace them all together. In an early formulation, Adams imagined "a nation coextensive with the North American continent." [32] It was to this end that he lent himself during his eight-year tenure as secretary of state.

During Adams's time at the State Department, he worked to reduce Spanish, Russian, and British influence in North America, fill power vacuums, and project American power all the way to the Pacific Ocean. In this he achieved a fair amount of success by shrewdly combining diplomacy and force—dealing with the much-strengthened British Empire one way (diplomatically), and the much-diminished Spanish Empire another (the show of military force). The results had the desired effect; the Anglo-American Convention of 1818 established a US-Canadian border along the Rockies and declared that territory to the west of the Rockies would be opened for joint settlement for the following decade. Against the Spanish, Adams used the threat of war and annexation to push Madrid not only into ceding Florida, but also into signing the Transcontinental

29. "From Thomas Jefferson to G. K. van Hogendorp, 13 October 1785," *Founders Online*, National Archives, https://founders.archives.gov/documents/Jefferson/01-08-02-0497. [Original source: *The Papers of Thomas Jefferson*, Volume 8, *25 February–31 October 1785*, Julian P. Boyd, ed. (Princeton, NJ: Princeton University Press, 1953), 631–34.]

30. Walter Hixson, *American Diplomatic Relations: A New Diplomatic History* (New York, NY: Routledge, 2016), 36.

31. John Quincy Adams, published as Publius Valerius, *The Repertory*, October 30, 1804, in John Quincy Adams, *Writings*, Volume III, 57.

32. John Quincy Adams to Abigail Adams, June 30, 1811, John Quincy Adams, *Writings*, Volume IV, 128.

Treaty that extended the country's borders out to the Pacific Ocean. Security, Adams argued, required establishing the country's borders where it could and playing for time where it could not.

Expansion was the core component of Adams's strategy, as only a secure nation, he believed, could become a democratic one. Even with his mostly conciliatory policy towards the British, Adams made sure that London realized that "there would be neither policy nor profit in caviling with us about territory on this North American continent."[33] Under Adams's guidance, that final point become enshrined into formal declaratory policy with the language he inserted into President Monroe's 1823 message to Congress. Known forever after as the Monroe Doctrine, Adams held that henceforth the Western Hemisphere would remain off limits to European colonization and would serve as America's exclusive sphere of interest.

The following decades saw this vision largely fulfilled with the annexation of Texas in 1845, the acquisition of California and much of the southwest following the Mexican War of 1846, the 1846 Oregon Treaty establishing a border between the United States and the British in the Pacific Northwest, and the 1853 Gadsden Purchase of additional territory in modern-day Arizona and New Mexico.

But while territorial expansion was fervently pursued by American policymakers as necessary for the flourishing of their republic, it also increasingly conflicted with national unity. Contrary to the Founders' expectations, slavery did not fade away, but instead became more deeply entrenched as the country expanded and added more slave territory. Throughout his life, Adams detested slavery and often attempted to weaken its hold on the country's institutions. But prior to becoming president, he had not pushed the case too hard, fearing the breakup of the country—and wary of harming his own prospects. However, after the Missouri Crisis exposed the depth and intensity of the national divide over slavery, and after his lackluster presidency, Adams emerged as a full-throated opponent of slavery, calling it a stain on the country's republican character. He began to oppose territorial expansion, believing that it would further embed slavery in the fabric of American democracy. This was a contradiction that would not be resolved until Abraham Lincoln led the nation through the fiery trial of the Civil War, expunging slavery, ensuring the country's sovereignty was uncontested, and, in the process, establishing America as the preponderant force on the North American continent.

---

33. John Quincy Adams, Diary 31, January 27, 1821, 502 [electronic edition].

IV

If there was one lesson Adams learned early, it was that national prosperity was the foundation upon which American power and influence would rest. Taken to Europe with his father as a boy, he witnessed his father's frantic efforts to secure a solid line of credit from Dutch bankers and various European governments. But, if access to credit was a necessary lifeline, Adams understood that this was but one part of more comprehensive mechanism for building wealth and generating power.

Like many commercially minded American founding statesmen, Adams came to believe that good finances, a robust industrial base, access to distant markets, and strong trade—backed by a powerful navy—were the keys to the nation's economic health, and long-term prosperity. His reading of British history, his time spent traveling Europe and analyzing different markets, his experiences in commercial diplomacy, and his advocacy for market access all contributed to his understanding that economic power went hand-in-hand with, and in fact often set the terms for, American influence abroad.

In this, the Founders endeavored to adapt the British model to American circumstances. They identified commerce, manufacturing, infrastructure, and fiscal health as the key building blocks that would allow the country to unleash its full economic potential. And yet, even as they worked to advance those facets of economic power, they also had to grapple with how best to construct an economic system that was oriented not around the power of the state, but instead around individual welfare.

For a former colony that had rebelled, at least partially due to complaints with Britain's regulation and control of American trade, the importance of commerce was obvious. Hamilton believed that commerce was "the most powerful instrument in increasing the quantity of money in a state."[34] For some, the appeal of international trade—and, more specifically, what it had the potential to accomplish—went even further. Writing in *The American Crisis*, Thomas Paine asserted that because access to American ports was of such interest to Europe, the American colonies in their independence ought to pursue a foreign policy based on commerce. Doing so, Paine argued, would allow America to break free of the old mercantilist model and "shake hands with the world—live at peace

---

34. Hamilton, *Federalist 12*, November 27, 1787, https://avalon.law.yale.edu/18th_century/fed12.asp.

with the world—and trade to any market" interested in receiving it.[35] In Paine's rendering, commerce held the power to transform the international system, working as a "civilizing effect" on those who participated in it, and promoting peace by weaving the world into a web of mutual dependence.

Alexander Hamilton and others were less sure that commerce would lead to perpetual peace. Regardless of whether commerce halted or produced conflict between nations, there was broad consensus that increases in American commerce would make the country stronger and more able to affect world politics. Similarly, there was general agreement that for commerce to flourish in early America, the country would need a strong navy and access to markets. Both of those positions received broad support, even as visions for the future development of the country's economic and political development began diverging sharply.

Long-term prosperity also required good fiscal health, so that America could borrow money when it needed to do so, and so that it was seen as an attractive destination for capital. Servicing the national debt regularly was a means of accomplishing this goal. For a country born in debt, this was of the utmost importance. It had been borrowed money that had allowed the American colonies to wage war against Britain; those loans eventually amounted to $200 million to feed, equip, and pay the Continental army and state militias.[36] Of course, borrowed money had to be repaid. One solution was a national debt that, in Hamilton's formulation, "if it is not excessive, will be to us a national blessing."[37] Hamilton's idea was that regular interest payments to bondholders would service the debt, giving the wealthiest a stake in the solvency of the new government, and spurring taxation that, if not overly oppressive, would stimulate industrial growth.

That investment would be key for the other components of economic growth, which included supporting domestic manufacturing, protecting those industries, and building the necessary infrastructure to connect the country so that goods and services could move efficiently from farm to factory and then to ports and the global market. The creation of an industrial base was

35. Thomas Paine, *The American Crisis* (London: W.T. Sherwin, 1817), 40.

36. John Steele Gordon, *Hamilton's Blessing: The Extraordinary Life and Times of Our National Debt* (New York, NY: Walker Publishing Company, 1997), 12.

37. "From Alexander Hamilton to Robert Morris, [April 30, 1781]," *Founders Online*, National Archives, https://founders.archives.gov/documents/Hamilton/01-02-02-1167. [Original source: *The Papers of Alexander Hamilton*, Volume 2, 1779–1781, Harold C. Syrett, ed. (New York, NY: Columbia University Press, 1961), 604–35.]

intended simultaneously to power the country's growth and to buttress the country's security. And, while there was a consistent push for discovery of, and access to, new markets for American goods, there was also a recognition that certain key industries and technologies required investment, in the form of subsidies, and protection, in the form of tariffs. This, it was thought, would be good for American businesses trying to compete against established global competitors. A key component of this was protecting the integrity of Ameri can supply chains in critical goods "to render the United States independent of foreign nations for military and other essential supplies."[38]

Throughout his career, John Quincy Adams was very attuned to the priority of aiding the country's fiscal health and economic growth. His very first public address, given at his graduation from Harvard College, attests to the importance he placed on the interrelationship between a nation's robust commerce, strong navy, and the state of its finances. Adams argued that regularly servicing the national debt would enhance public credit and, as such, was "the foundation upon which the fabric of national grandeur has been erected."[39] In Adams's formulation, a weak country that regularly and reliably serviced its debts could become a strong nation that attracted investment. The early stages of his career saw him putting those instincts into practice. While abroad, he consistently pushed for a navy sufficiently powerful to protect American commerce and as Minister to the Netherlands, Prussia, Russia, and the United Kingdom, Adams administered American loans, obtained new lines of credit, ensured access to European markets, and negotiated new commercial treaties.

As Adams's career progressed, he became one of the leading proponents of using trade as a tool of American statecraft. The job of American diplomats, he came to believe, was not just engaging in what he initially disparaged as "pecuniary negotiation."[40] Their purpose was to wield commerce as a source of political leverage. The promise of access to American markets and the threat of exclusion from America's rich resources and growing population would make other nations "*feel* the necessity of our friendship." Virtually every European

---

38. Alexander Hamilton, *Report on Manufactures*, December 5, 1791. Edward Mead Earle, "Adam Smith, Alexander Hamilton, Friedrich List: The Economic Foundations of Military Power," in *Makers of Modern Strategy: From Machiavelli to the Nuclear Age*, Peter Paret, ed. (Princeton, NJ: Princeton University Press, 1986), 233.

39. John Quincy Adams, Diary 11, July 18, 1787, 296 [electronic edition].

40. John Quincy Adams to John Adams, July 27, 1794, *Adams Family Correspondence*, Volume X (Cambridge, MA: Belknap Press, 2011), 218.

power employed trade both as an inducement and as a weapon that could be wielded in service of political objectives. Adams advocated doing the same, and utilizing American trade to force other nations to "observe a more friendly line of conduct."[41]

The push to extend the reach of American commerce continued during his years at the State Department. In addition to drafting the Monroe Doctrine, Adams's tenure as secretary of state is most remembered for his obtaining Florida, extending US borders out to the Pacific with the Transcontinental Treaty, and negotiating a stable northern border with the British. However, arguably more important to the future growth of American trade were his actions in securing a Pacific foothold for the country's commercial interests and a launching pad for the forward projection of American commercial, diplomatic, and military across the Pacific and towards the Asian mainland.

Adams's support for domestic industry and infrastructure dated to his time as a senator, but it was during his presidency that he really threw his weight, and the country's resources, behind a program of internal improvements. Such work, in fact, stood at the heart of Adams's domestic agenda as president. He believed that such investments would knit together the country's distant regions, while enhancing the efficient movement of men, materials, and ideas around the country, and beyond its borders.[42] If enhancing national unity and accelerating the growth of American power were the ends, to Adams, "internal improvement, and domestic industry, [were] the means."[43]

The challenge for Adams, as it was for his predecessors, was in ensuring— or at least trying to ensure—that economic growth benefited the many, and not just the few, and that governmental policy was not primarily concerned with centralizing state power, but rather pushing it outward. As one historian wrote, Adams was "determined to use federal power . . . to plan and fund a rapid but orderly transition to a commercial and industrial society."[44] Adams's vision might have been more organized and coordinated than the alternative set of policies pushed by the Jacksonian Democrats. Yet it also encountered determined resistance as Americans had long objected to the idea that a

41. John Quincy Adams to John Adams, July 21, 1796, in John Quincy Adams, *Writings*, Volume II, 13. Emphasis in original.

42. Edel, *Nation Builder*, 191.

43. *Niles Weekly Register*, July 19, 1828.

44. Harry L. Watson, *Liberty and Power: The Politics of Jacksonian America* (New York, NY: Hill & Wang, 1990), 76.

government should organize their lives—or their economic activity. This tension was endemic to the early republic. It would only be resolved, and at that only temporarily, during the Civil War when virtually all proponents of small government seceded from the national government, paving the way for federal approval of a government-designed railroad route linking the entire country, and a massive infusion of governmental resources to power the country's industrialization.

V

From the very start, American aspirations have been enormously ambitious. Americans' ideas about the exceptional nature of their country and their political ideals predate the founding of the American nation. Best captured in John Winthrop's invocation of America as a "City on a Hill," the idea that America would influence the rest of the world as a beacon of liberty dates from the establishment of the North American colonies in the early seventeenth century. Such ideas pervaded early American thought and found expression in the universalizing impulses and language of the American Revolution, which was cast not merely as an anti-colonial struggle, but as a struggle for the future direction of history being waged on behalf of all mankind.

"The birthday of a new world is at hand," Paine proclaimed in 1775, equating the creation of a republic in the United States to a divine act that would revolutionize world politics. Such a providential view of America held that the ascendency of the United States was heaven-sent. In the words of John Quincy Adams, the United States was "destined by God and nature to be the most populous and most powerful people ever combined under one social compact."[45] Such beliefs equated American ideals with American influence.

Left open, however, was how the United States would best influence the world. Virtually all American statesmen believed that the country would be more secure in a world filled with democracies. The perennial question for American policymakers was how active of a role the country should play in shaping that world. Should America throw its weight behind democratic movements abroad? Should it intervene in anti-colonial struggles? Should it materially support those struggling for their own freedom, or just offer moral support and enthusiasm? Beyond these questions there was another debate, increasing in volume as the country grew more powerful, about how well America could

45. John Quincy Adams to AA, June 30, 1811, in John Quincy Adams, *Writings*, Volume IV, 128.

defend democratic values abroad given its own democratic shortcomings at home. Should democratic deficiencies at home disqualify the United States from democratic leadership abroad? At no time in American history was that question as glaring as in the antebellum period, when American ideals of liberty were constantly undercut by the country's reality of slavery.

To many of the Founders, not only had America set a modern precedent for colonial rebellion and opposition to authoritarian states, it also pointed the way for others to follow. Yet the question of whether America would lend a helping hand quickly came into focus. Even before the Constitution was written, Thomas Jefferson had written to John Jay, then secretary of foreign affairs, to advise him that the Brazilians had reached out to him in France to gauge American enthusiasm in supporting their plans for a revolution. They "consider," Jefferson wrote, "the North American Revolutions as a precedent for theirs [and] look to the United States as the most likely to give them honest support."[46] But, "without the aid of some powerful nation," the Brazilians had admitted, they were reluctant to launch a revolution, fearing a lack of popular enthusiasm. America denied that request, but the issue would return.

As the historian David Brion Davis has written, "news that republican principles were exportable ended Americans' sense of isolation and helped legitimate the lawless, and indeed treasonable, cause that the Declaration of Independence had sought to defend."[47] But this news was more than just legitimating; it also presented challenges for policymakers grappling with trying to define just what a democratic strategy would entail. Supporting foreign revolutions that purported to be carrying liberty's banner, and carrying on the work that America had started was certainly gratifying. It also played to American notions of exceptionalism. Yet experience would prove that, for a variety of reasons, not all revolutions were worthy of support; supporting revolutions abroad would dissipate American energies and divert its resources; and, if American support came in the form of armed intervention, it would change America's mission and its character.

The first real test occurred with the outbreak of the French Revolution. Many Americans viewed the unfolding events as a natural outgrowth of the

46. "From Thomas Jefferson to John Jay, 4 May 1787," *Founders Online*, National Archives, https://founders.archives.gov/documents/Jefferson/01-11-02-0322. [Original source: *The Papers of Thomas Jefferson*, Volume 11, *1 January–6 August 1787*, Julian P. Boyd, ed. (Princeton, NJ: Princeton University Press, 1955), 338–44.]

47. David Brion Davis, *Revolutions: Reflections on American Equality and Foreign Liberations* (Cambridge, MA: Harvard University Press, 1990), 37.

American Revolution. None were more enthusiastic than Thomas Jefferson, who declared that "all that old spirit of 1776 is rekindling."[48] As events unfolded in France, and as the revolution increased in violence, and then descended into a campaign of terror, others began expressing misgivings. John Quincy Adams, just launching his public career, was one of the first to do so.

Contrary to the enthusiasm the French Revolution was generating, Adams argued that overthrowing a government too easily was inherently dangerous, ridiculing the notion that "it [is] as easy for a nation to change its government, as for a man to change his coat."[49] Attacking the zeal with which both Thomas Paine and Thomas Jefferson cheered on the rapid spread of revolution throughout Europe, Adams urged caution, noting that different histories and cultures produced different societies. What had worked in America would not necessarily be replicable elsewhere, and while Adams thought that Europe's nations might one day evolve into republics, he later reflected that such a transformation would only be possible when social conditions supported local movements pressing for "the unalienable right of resistance against tyranny."[50]

Additionally, Adams charged that those who "advise us to engage voluntarily in the war," were willing "to aim a dagger at the heart of the country," as actions undertaken to support the French Republic would have the effect of "uniting all of Europe against us."[51] Adams was not yet in a position to affect American policy, but that would soon change as he headed to Europe and his subsequent counsel influenced thinking at both the State Department and the White House. His belief that America should morally support liberal movements, but ideally abstain from engaging in them, strengthened during his diplomatic postings abroad as he watched the French Republic morph into an empire that launched war after war in Europe, and later witnessed Europe's monarchies search for pretexts to snuff out the republican governments they claimed as ideological rivals and existential threats.

48. "From Thomas Jefferson to James Monroe, 5 May 1793," *Founders Online*, National Archives, https://founders.archives.gov/documents/Jefferson/01-25-02-0603. [Original source: *The Papers of Thomas Jefferson*, Volume 25, 1 January–10 May 1793, John Catanzariti, ed. (Princeton, NJ: Princeton University Press, 1992), 660–63.]

49. John Quincy Adams, *Columbian Centinel*, June 18, 1791, in John Quincy Adams, *Writings*, Volume I, 81.

50. John Quincy Adams, *Jubilee of the Constitution*, 77.

51. John Quincy Adams, Writing as Marcellus in the *Columbian Centinel*, May 11, 1793, in John Quincy Adams, *Writings*, Volume I, 146.

During Adams's tenure as secretary of state, America was offered opportunities to test its commitment to spreading liberty and republican governments abroad. The Greeks were rebelling from the oppressive rule of the Ottoman Turks, and various South American colonies were declaring independence from the Spanish Empire. Both groups of rebels claimed America as their model and demanded both recognition and assistance; and in both cases, support for the rebels was widespread and popular in the United States. Henry Clay, then serving as Speaker of the House, accused the administration of not doing enough for the revolutionaries, supported sending an American mission to Greece, and reminded his colleagues that those fighting for their freedom in South America had "adopted our principles, copied our institutions, and, in some instances, employed the very language and sentiments of our revolutionary papers."[52] Urging a more assertive and interventionist policy, Clay asked how could his fellow Americans "honorably turn away from their duty to share with the rest of mankind this most precious gift."[53]

Adams cautioned restraint to those advocating American armed intervention in support of Greek and South American independence. In his July 4, 1821, address, Adams argued that Americans were the well-wishers of all, but defenders only of their own, famously stating, "America goes not abroad in search of monsters to destroy." According to Adams, the central message of the Declaration of Independence, and indeed of American history, was "the successful resistance of a people against oppression, the downfall of the tyrant and tyranny itself." In a war between liberty and oppression, there would be no doubt which side America supported. But Adams recognized a choice between competing priorities. America could either continue to strengthen its own republican institutions, or it could aid those who claimed solidarity with America's principles. To those who would advocate a more activist foreign policy, Adams asserted that America "has seen that probably for centuries to come, all the contests of . . . the European world, will be contests of inveterate power, and emerging right."[54] If it were to avoid dissipating its strength, entangling itself in foreign wars of choice, supporting causes that lacked popular

52. *Annals of Congress*, 15th Cong., 1st sess., March 25, 1818, 1482.

53. *Annals of Congress*, 16th Cong., 1st sess., May 10, 1818, 2223.

54. John Quincy Adams, *An Address Delivered At the request of a Committee of the Citizens of Washington; On the Occasion of Reading The Declaration of Independence on the Fourth of July, 1821* (Washington, DC: Davis and Force, 1821).

support, and substituting force for influence, America could not afford to take on a more active foreign policy. America, Adams argued, would be on the side of emerging right, but not necessarily directly fighting for it.[55]

Adams's forceful words of restraint in the July Fourth Address mask that he was never shy about promoting American values or using military power aboard. Nor should they obscure his lifelong antipathy to authoritarian regimes and his willingness to combat their spread into new territories. In a letter accompanying the Monroe Doctrine—which Adams considered "the most important paper that ever went from my hands"—he underlined the point that "we could not see with indifference any attempt . . . to introduce monarchical principle into" the Western Hemisphere.[56] The Monroe Doctrine asserted that protection of American interests required the Western Hemisphere to remain America's exclusive sphere of influence. In the accompanying letter, Adams took that principle one step further, arguing that America should seek to shrink the international space for non-republican regimes by opposing efforts to create any new monarchies within the Western Hemisphere. For Adams, extending American influence abroad might necessitate restraining impulses to interfere in other nation's affairs. But in key locations, extending American influence would also be required to prevent authoritarian regimes from expanding onto democratic soil.

The question for America, Adams asked, was what should be done about the authoritarian challenge at home. Slavery was a glaring contradiction in America's attempt to hold itself up as a model for the rest of world. This had hardly gone unnoticed at the nation's founding. In fact, so glaring was the discrepancy between the promise of liberty and the reality of human bondage that mentions of slavery were excised from the Declaration of Independence and purposefully obscured in the Constitution. The omissions were notable. John Laurens, the son of one of America's wealthiest slave traders, an ardent opponent of slavery, and an aide to George Washington during the War for Independence, wanted to know how Americans could reconcile their "spirited Assertions of Rights of Mankind [with] the galling abject Slavery of our [slaves]."[57] When it came to fashioning a democratic strategy, this inconsistency was

55. Edel, *Nation Builder*, 162.

56. John Quincy Adams, Diary 34, November 26, 1823, 172. [electronic edition]; John Quincy Adams, Diary 34, November 25, 1823, 168. [electronic edition].

57. Robert Kagan, *Dangerous Nation: America's Place in the World from its Earliest Days to the Dawn of the Twentieth Century* (New York, NY: Knopf, 2006), 44.

explained away, or ignored. As slavery became woven ever more deeply into the fabric of America's institutions, friction between the country's aspirations and its reality became both more pronounced and more intractable. Just after the Missouri Compromise had been passed in 1820, Adams wrote, the "bargain between freedom and slavery contained in the Constitution of the United States is morally and politically vicious, [and] inconsistent with the principles upon which alone our Revolution can be justified."[58] As long as slavery remained embedded in American institutions, it would be a permanent deficit in the country's attempt to influence the world.

VI

The Founders attempted to secure, expand, and enrich the American republic while broadening its influence on the world stage. All these goals had to be pursued within the confines of a democratic system. This was an unprecedented act, and meant that the Founders had to diverge from the past practices of old world diplomacy by constraining the power of the state, and plot a course which allowed for divergent opinion.

Within this context, a series of questions presented themselves. How could they expand the country without losing its democratic nature? How could they build a sufficiently strong military without corrupting the nation's mission? How would they guide the economic development of the state without being too intrusive? And how could they influence the world with an imperfect democracy at home?

Adams's remarkable career as a politician, diplomat, and American statesman had a significant influence on the creation and direction of American grand strategy. At the beginning of his career, in the 1790s, he made the case for neutrality in foreign policy. With the turn of the century, he spent two decades pushing for continental and commercial expansion. While president, he led an energetic and activist government, with large-scale domestic investment into infrastructure and new trade policies. And in his final years in public life, Adams fought against slavery and its extension. His ideas weave through George Washington's Farewell Address, the Monroe Doctrine, and even Lincoln's Emancipation Proclamation, which drew from speeches Adams made on the Senate floor against slavery.

58. John Quincy Adams, Diary 31, March 3, 1820, 278 [electronic edition].

Adams stands as the bridge between the Founders and Abraham Lincoln. The country's founding generation of statesmen envisioned a mighty republic, but their circumstances rendered that a hope for the distant future. And Lincoln—in the midst of a Civil War that gave the government unprecedented power—accomplished much of that vision—forcefully uniting the country, establishing it as a two-ocean power, and ensuring that the republican government would endure. But it was Adams who can, and should, be credited with putting the country on a path towards becoming the preponderant power in the Western Hemisphere, laying the long-term foundations of economic growth, and offering the nation a vision for aligning its laws to its founding ideals.

Adams's influence extends well beyond the mid-nineteenth century. His forceful assertion of American values, his projection of American power and commerce further afield, his constant admonition that the source of American power is domestic, and his deep-seated antipathy towards authoritarian regimes, all continue to set the broad contours of America's approach to a distinctly democratic statecraft.

Adams did not solve the intractable problem of how the United States could reconcile liberty with power—either at home or abroad. This was a source of unending frustration to him and, more often than not, led him to believe that his life and career were a failure. And yet, his contemporaries viewed him as the most consequential American of the era. So too with historians, who consistently characterize John Quincy Adams as one of the greatest figures in American history, one who provided answers to the primary challenges confronting early American statecraft.

CHAPTER 15

Strategic Excellence

TECUMSEH AND THE SHAWNEE CONFEDERACY

Kori Schake

Strategists worry that America is incapable of the "whole of society" strategy that existential security challenges require. And it is rare for the fulgent diversity of the United States to be truly harnessed for a common purpose. Yet there is a powerful precedent, when Americans came together to design and execute a strategy with political, religious, economic, diplomatic, and military elements commensurate to the problem threatening them, and aligned the totality of their resources to achieve their desired outcome. That time was between 1807 and 1813, and the Americans who enacted the strategy were the Shawnee Confederacy, who coalesced in attempting to prevent domination by colonial settlers of the territory that would become the United States.[1]

Under the leadership of Tecumseh, the Shawnee Confederacy created an alliance of American Indians whose land stretched from Lake Erie to the Gulf of Mexico—a swath comprising the entire frontier north to south of what would become the United States. Tecumseh pulled together a larger fighting force than any other American Indian chief in history, creating a twelve-hundred-mile barricade to limit westward expansion of the United States.

---

1. For purposes of clarity and in order not to give either side precedence over the terminology American, since both were, Native Americans are here termed primarily American Indians, and occasionally also Native peoples and indigenous peoples, and colonial Americans with citizenship claims on the United States government are termed settlers.

Tecumseh combined military prowess with organizational skill and diplomatic finesse; he propagated centripetal religious beliefs that advanced political power within tribes and encouraged accession to the Confederacy; he used social suasion to reduce reliance on colonial-produced goods; he won foreign economic support that freed up fighters for military campaigns; he secured consequential European military involvement; and he produced an organized military force capable of defeating the US militarily. The Shawnee Confederacy threat precipitated the doubling of the size of the US military, and the Confederacy imposed the largest combat losses the US had known to that point.

The United States government defeated this elegant strategy not on the battlefield, but economically. By targeting Shawnee reliance on British sustenance to their families, the US government reduced the American Indian forces. Challenged to overcome the Shawnee Confederacy in combat, the US Navy cut the British supply lines to Shawnee villages, drawing fighters away from the battlefield. Without his charismatic leadership and strategic sensibilities, the Confederacy dissipated after Tecumseh's death at the Battle of the Thames in 1813.

Governments of what would become the United States were fighting Native peoples from the time Europeans set foot on the North American continent until the US wrested control of the entire landmass. Frontier wars were endemic to the establishment of the United States—the fight against the Shawnee Confederacy was only one of 943 military actions taken against American Indian tribes between 1768 and 1889.[2]

The Shawnee Confederacy wasn't the first American Indian political grouping to attempt a whole of society approach. Decades earlier, in 1763, the Lenape Neolin combined preaching spiritual purity, autarky from European goods and practices, and pan-tribal cooperation to resist American expansion. Ottawa Chief Pontiac contributed combat leadership so impressive that the British anointed him Chief of all Algonquin in 1776, a recognition unacknowledged by other native peoples and that fractured their cooperation.

The Confederacy was not even the start of Shawnee militant uprising. In 1791, Shawnee forces decimated a US military expedition intended to drive them out of the Ohio valley, killing 630 of the 1,700 US troops, an enormous casualty roster by the standards of frontier warfare.

---

2. R. Ernest Dupuy and Trevor N. Dupuy, *The Encyclopedia of Military History from 3500 B.C. to the Present* (New York, NY: Harper & Row, 1970), 905.

What made the Shawnee Confederacy that came together in 1807 different, and more dangerous from the US government's perspective, was that it used religious and social means to radicalize and unify tribes, popularized an economic model resistant to land cessation, developed a foreign policy that provided sustenance to communities while freeing up men for war, *and* was successful on the battlefield. The elements were mutually reinforcing. What the Shawnee under Tecumseh did was maximize their prospects of success through the shrewd orchestration of all available means—that is, they practiced with excellence the art of strategy.

Although enduring for only six years, Confederacy strategy came so near to establishing a fixed border preventing westward expansion that it cemented the idea for settlers that American Indians were incompatible with frontier settlements. This resulted in the forcible removal of American Indian tribes east of the Mississippi. The Shawnee Confederacy proved to be the last time American Indians had a genuine prospect of turning back dominance by settlers of the continent that would become the United States.

I

It was not inevitable that American colonization would become incompatible with coexistence with American Indians, in the same geographic space. The Narangasett had facilitated survival of early European arrivals; the Haudenosaunee (Iroquois) League fought alongside English settlers against other tribes as well as against the French. The Five Civilized Tribes (Cherokee, Chicksaw, Choctaw, Creek, and Seminole) were particularly well-disposed to coexistence, as they were centrally governed, multi-ethnic, farmed and hunted in ways similar to their settler counterparts, had market economies, and chose to be conversant in the English language. The United States' Founding Fathers even drew on American Indian models in developing their own ideas for democracy.

But one of the objections listed in the Declaration of Independence was that the British had "endeavored to bring on the inhabitants of our frontiers, the merciless Indian Savages." And although American Indians fought on both sides of the American Revolution, frictions were constant with various tribes whose lands and livelihoods were being displaced by settlers.[3]

---

3. Europeans were not, of course, the only displacers—American Indian tribes fought amongst themselves before Columbus arrived in the Americas. The Iroquois displaced the

The contest was particularly brutal in the Northwest Territory (which was then the Ohio River Valley). "Indian country" became synonymous with danger, but despite that danger, immigrants flowed first to the United States and then further west. In the northwest, American Indians fought predominantly alongside the British, pressuring the western frontier in attempts to regain their territories from settlers.

Ten months after Cornwallis's surrender to Washington in 1781, British and American Indian forces were still contesting the outcome in the northwest. As a teenager, Tecumseh and three hundred warriors provided the combat power for a British assault on Bryan's Station in 1782. Daniel Boone's account of the battle describes Shawnee fighting using conventional tactics of the time: "the enemy was so strong that they rushed up and broke the right wing at the first fire. Thus the enemy got in our rear and we were compelled to retreat."[4]

Boone's letter also gives a sense of foreboding at the strength of American Indian forces:

> I have encouraged the people in this country all that I could, but I can no longer justify them or myself to risk our lives here under such extraordinary hazards. The inhabitants of this county are very much alarmed at the thoughts of the Indians bringing another campaign into our country this fall. If this should be the case, it will break up these settlements.[5]

What followed the British and American Indian success in 1782 was British cessation of attacks against settlers. The Treaty of Paris, in which Britain ceded independence of the thirteen American colonies, also ceded sovereignty of the entire trans-Appalachian region south of the Great Lakes, north of Florida, and east of the Mississippi. The US government quickly offered land grants to veterans in an effort to populate the frontier with militias capable of defending it. And protection was necessary as the US government attempted to enforce its control of territory in which American Indian nations were living and had not been party to ceding. For example, settler militias conducted campaigns of destruction of Shawnee villages in 1782 and again in 1786.

Huron and other Algonquin tribes, Sioux forced Shoshone off plains hunting grounds, and Comanche murderously carved a swathe of territory equaling that of the United States in the mid-nineteenth century.

4. Letter from Daniel Boone to the Governor of Virginia, August 30, 1782, reproduced in John M. Trowbridge, " 'We Are All Slaughtered Men': the Battle of Blue Licks," *Kentucky Ancestors* 42:2 (2006): 60.

5. Letter from Boone to the Governor of Virginia, August 30, 1782.

George Washington's presidential administration attempted a more pacific policy, negotiating peace in the northeast with the Creek nation in 1790, but failing to get traction in the Ohio, where other tribes defeated repeated campaigns, including one in which the Shawnee imposed the largest battlefield losses the US military had sustained against any American Indian force. Nor were the casualties only soldiers. A 1790 report to President Washington assessed 1,500 settlers had been killed in Kentucky, hundreds more in what is now Ohio and Indiana. In response, Washington authorized the first war under the Constitution of the United States, against the Native American peoples of the Ohio River Valley.

In 1790, the US Army was comprised of only 700 men, mostly ill trained and ill equipped. After the Shawnee Confederacy and as a result of Shawnee success, Congress doubled the size of the army, creating a Legion of the United States to protect settlers on the frontier. General Anthony Wayne's training of the force to fight the tribes gathered under Shawnee leadership in 1793 was legendary. He organized the thousand troops into combined-arms combat teams, built forts as they advanced, and successfully engaged an enemy twice their own numbers at the Battle of Fallen Timbers in 1794, effectively ending near-term prospects for American Indian control of the Northwest Territory. Various tribes signed the Treaty of Greenville in 1795, ceding lands in what is now Ohio, Indiana, Illinois, and Michigan. In parallel, the British abandoned the forts they had maintained along the Great Lakes that had provided shelter and support to American Indian forces and inhabitants.

Haiti's successful revolution precipitated the US Government's 1803 Louisiana Purchase but also sounded alarms about the potential success of slave revolts and uprisings by indigenous populations. The Louisiana Purchase titularly doubled the territory of the United States, creating a bonanza of land in the Mississippi Valley for westward migration. But the land wasn't empty, it was populated by American Indians; and all the Louisiana Purchase did was secure for the US government the right to obtain the land without European claim.

II

The Shawnee Confederacy didn't begin with its great leader, Tecumseh; it began with Tenskwatawa, Tecumseh's brother.[6] Tenskwatawa claimed visions, preached that American Indians had been abandoned by the Great Spirit

---

6. Peter Cozzens considers Tenskwatawa and Tecumseh equal forces in the Shawnee strategy, but that's not how they were assessed at the time. For example, William Henry Harrison

because they had become too reliant on white people and that the only way to reclaim grace was repudiation: no alcohol, European clothing, firearms, and no further involvement with white people. The Governor of Indiana, William Henry Harrison, inadvertently legitimated Tenskwatawa's powers by setting him the challenge of making the sun stand still; having some knowledge of astronomy, Tenskwatawa accurately predicted an eclipse.

In 1805, Tenskwatawa and Tecumseh began recruiting people drawn to Tenskwatawa's preaching to migrate to his location along the Wabash River—land ceded to the US in the Treaty of Greenville—creating the largest community of American Indians on the continent, and including converts from the Shawnee, Iroquois, Chickamauga, Meskwaki, Miami, Mingo, Ojibwe, Ottawa, Kickapoo, Lenape Delaware, Mascouten, Potawatomi, Sauk, Tutelo, and Wyandot nations. They termed themselves Prophetstown, and were the genesis of the pan-tribal cooperation and essential to building a common fighting force. Lyman Draper acknowledged that, Tenskwatawa's "prophesying that the world would come to an end and the people must reform, abandon the habits and practices of the white—were to aid his brother and the British."[7]

Tecumseh was a minor figure among the Shawnee before the whole of society strategy came together. But he proved smart, courageous, and persuasive, capitalizing on his brother's spiritual magnetism to recruit an army. Tecumseh's first declaration at the Chillicothe council of military action against encroaching settlers makes reference to a confederation comprised of religious adherents to his brother's movement.

Religion was more than a unifying force and recruitment aide. Tecumseh's theory of victory over white encroachment was bound up with Tenskwatawa's

---

concluded that, "the Prophet is imprudent and audacious but is deficient in the judgment, talent, and firmness." Letter from William Henry Harrison to William Eustis, Secretary of War, Vincennes, August 7, 1811, Indiana Historical Society, William Henry Harrison Papers and Documents, 1791–1864, DC050, https://images.indianahistory.org/digital/collection/dc050/id/771. And as Sarah Nakasone has analyzed, "Tecumseh is unable to persuade many tribes to join his resistance using his brother's doctrine, adherents to the doctrine fall away from many of the central tenants, and Tenskwatawa (and his doctrine) are largely absent for the third of the book in which Tecumseh garners military successes." Sarah Nakasone, unpublished memorandum, September 12, 2021.

7. Draper's extensive correspondence and interviews constitute one of the most important contemporaneous primary sources on the Shawnee. Lyman C. Draper Manuscript Collection microfilm number 1 YY (microfilm edition, 1979), University of Chicago, Joseph Regenstein Library, Photoduplication Department, 168–69. Draper conducted interviews in 1868 with American Indians in Kansas (where the Shawnees settled after the Battle of the Thames).

religious zealotry. When Europeans made landfall in the territory of what would become the United States, American Indians numbered around five million people broken into over 500 tribes, many as distinct from each other as were European nations; unifying them to a common purpose was a herculean task. In attempting to win over the Osage, Tecumseh argued, "we must fight each others' [sic] battles; and more than all, we must love the Great Spirit; he is for us; he will destroy our enemies."[8]

III

Tecumseh's story is unexceptional at its start. Born in 1768, in the Northwest Territory (what is now Ohio), his father was killed in combat against Virginia militia at the Battle of Kanawa (Point Pleasant) in 1775, when Tecumseh was seven years old. Virginia militia had invaded the Ohio Valley to enforce a treaty they'd signed with the Iroquois ceding Shawnee and Mingo lands. The battle was significant because the Shawnee defeat resulted in their ceding all lands south of the Ohio River (what are today Kentucky and West Virginia).

Tecumseh began raiding boats provisioning settlements in the 1780s; his first combat came in 1792 when he was living among a branch of the Cherokee in Tennessee. Thirty American Indian tribes came together in 1793, uniting around the goal of reclaiming land from settlers; specifically, they wanted settlers to move north of the Ohio River (it was this alliance that General Wayne's force defeated decisively at the Battle of Fallen Timbers).

The Governor of the Ohio Country ascribed General Wayne's overall success as much to the fissiparousness of the American Indian alliance as to Wayne's army, writing after the Buchanan Station battle that:

> difference in opinion, as to the mode and place of attack, at the rendezvous after they passed at the Tennessee, probably was the cause of the delay; I have no other way to account for it; and it is a rock on which large parties of Indians have generally split, especially when consisting of more than one nation.[9]

8. Tecumseh, Speech to the Osages, in John D. Hunter, *Memoirs of a Captive Among the Indians of North America* (London: The Author, 1824), 43–48, reproduced in Bette-Jon Schrade, *Tecumseh: His Rhetoric and Oratory* (Charleston, IL: Eastern Illinois University, 1976), Appendix 8, 155.

9. Governor Blount to the Secretary of War, in *American State Papers: Documents, Legislative and Executive, of the Congress of the United States*, Walter Lowrie and Matthew St. Clair Clarke, eds., Volume IV (Washington, DC: Gales and Seaton, 1832), 294.

According to Blount, the American Indian military force—composed, as it was, of a number of different nations—lacked the political cohesiveness to act in unison.

As early as 1795 Tecumseh and his brother Tenskwatawa began traveling among the tribes. While biographers of Tecumseh debate when he was radicalized, the lived experiences of the Shawnee were so dire that it hardly matters; there doesn't appear to be a time before he resented settler encroachment into tribal lands and the brutality of US Government military campaigns against American Indian communities.

Although Tecumseh wasn't solely responsible for the convergence of various tribes, he was essential to it. Unlike others before him, Tecumseh was able to tirelessly stitch together the cooperation of a variety of American Indian peoples to a common political and military purpose. His main adversary, William Henry Harrison, afforded a window into the Shawnee leader's talents:

> The impatient obedience and respect which the followers of Tecumseh to pay to him is really astonishing, and more than any other circumstance bespeaks him one of those uncommon geniuses which spring up occasionally to produce revolutions and overthrow the established order of things. If it were not for the vicinity of the United States, he would perhaps be the founder of an Empire that would rival in glory that of a Mexico or Peru.
>
> No deficiencies deter him. His activity and industry supply the want of letters. For four years he has been in constant motion. You see him today on the wall, and then a short time you hear of him on the shores of Lake Erie or Michigan or on the banks of the Mississippi and wherever he goes he makes an impression favorable to his purposes.[10]

Within a year of founding Prophetstown, Tecumseh was utilizing his brother's religion to political advantage, eliminating chiefs who'd signed treaties ceding land by having Tenskwatawa declare them witches. Tecumseh canvassed from Lake Erie to the Gulf of Mexico, convincing tribes to join the Confederacy and take up arms against settler encroachment. He was so successful that by 1812, the tide had turned from him recruiting cooperation to the Huron beseeching him to admit them. Tecumseh's recruitment built a north-south Maginot line of American Indian militancy against further settler expansion along the whole landmass, something that had not been achieved before

10. Letter from Harrison to Eustis, Secretary of War, Vincennes, August 7, 1811.

and wouldn't be achieved again. Had the Shawnee Confederacy succeeded, it would have foreclosed European settlement west of Ohio, denied use of the Mississippi River as an economic engine of US development, prevented utilization of the west's natural resources, and constrained the United States to an eastern seaboard country rather than a continent-spanning behemoth.

IV

Tecumseh and Tenskwatawa drew on communal notions of land ownership traditional among the indigenous nations to negate the right of any tribe to cede its land to the US. Tecumseh's statement of economic philosophy was that:

> White people . . . are never contented, but always encroaching. The way, and the only way, to check and to stop this evil, is, for all the red men to unite in claiming a common and equal right in the land; as it was at first, and should be yet; for it never was divided, but belongs to all . . . the white people have no right to take the land from the Indians, because they had it first, it is theirs; they may sell, but all must join; any sale not made by all, is not valid.[11]

The approach served to delegitimize any leader, faction, or tribe that conceded territory. Because Tecumseh had a religious cause, an attractive and accepted economic model, and a coalition of scale, he could threaten into submission accommodationist chiefs. In negotiations with Harrison, Tecumseh was explicit about the economic model and its political purpose for both sides: "It has been the object of both myself and brother to prevent the lands being sold . . . You want by your distinctions of Indian tribes in allotting to each a particular tract of land to make them [go] to war with each other."[12] Because of course a tribe ceding territory would be displaced into the residence and hunting grounds of other tribes.

Tecumseh's denunciation of the ceding of land at the 1807 Chillicothe Conference with the Governor of Ohio catapulted the Shawnee to the forefront of American Indian leaders. The mayor of Chillicothe wrote:

11. Letter from Harrison to Eustis, Secretary of War, Vincennes, August 7, 1811. See also, J. Mark Hazlett, *American Indian Sovereignty: The Struggle for Religious, Cultural and Tribal Independence* (Jefferson, NC: MacFarland, 2020), 33.

12. As quoted in, Letter from Harrison to Eustis, Secretary of War, Vincennes, August 7, 1811.

While he [Tecumseh] fearlessly denied the validity of these pretended treaties, and openly avowed his intention to resist the further extension of the white settlements upon the Indian lands, he disclaimed all intention of making war upon the United States.[13]

Perceiving no threat, the governor disbanded the militia he'd called into service to march on Prophetstown, which by that time contained around fifteen hundred individuals.

V

Tecumseh used conferences with white leaders to great effect in coalition building, designing his speeches to appeal for allegiance from the other tribal leaders conveniently gathered for him by his adversaries, while also assuaging their concerns that his army gathered at Prophetstown posed an imminent threat.

Indiana Governor William Henry Harrison sought to isolate the Shawnee, negotiating with the Delaware, Potawatamie, Miami, Wea, and Kickapoo in 1809 to cede three million acres. At the Vincennes Conference organized by Harrison in 1810, to again assess whether to militarily move against Prophetstown, Tecumseh arrived with four hundred war-painted warriors, rejected the legitimacy of the treaty, and claimed to speak for a unified nation with this emotional appeal:

It is true I am a Shawanee. My forefathers were warriors; their son is a warrior. From them I only take my existence; from my tribe I take nothing. I am the maker of my own fortune; and oh! that I could make that of my red people and of my country, as great as the conceptions of my mind, when I think of the Spirit that rules the universe. I would not then come to Governor Harrison, to ask him to tear the treaty, and to obliterate the landmark: but I would say to him, Sir, you have permission to return to your own country.[14]

Tecumseh persuaded tribes that the settlement threat was existential. It was that "the annihilation of our race is at hand unless we unite in one common cause

13. Tecumseh, as quoted by John A. Fulton, formerly mayor of Chillicothe, communicated by General James T. Worthington, in Benjamin Drake, *The Life of Tecumseh and His Brother the Prophet* (Cincinnati, OH: E. Morgan and Company, 1841), Chapter IV, https://www.gutenberg.org/files/15581/15581-h/15581-h.htm#Page_082.

14. Tecumseh, as quoted in H. Marshall, *The History of Kentucky*, Volume II (Frankfort: The Author, 1824), 482–83, reproduced in Bette-Jon Schrade, *Tecumseh*, Appendix 4, 147. See also A.J. Langguth, *Union 1812: The Americans Who Fought the Second War of Independence* (New York, NY: Simon & Schuster, 2006), 165.

against the common foe." In his appeal to the Choctow, a reluctant tribe, Tecumseh argued:

> Where today is the Pequod? Where the Narragansetts, the Mohawks, Pocanokets, and many other once powerful tribes of our race? They have vanished before the avarice and oppression of the white men . . . The white usurpation in our common country must be stopped, or we, its rightful owners, [will] be forever destroyed and wiped out as a race of people. I am now at the head of many warriors backed by the strong arm of English soldiers . . . Let us form one body, one heart, and defend to the last warrior our country, our liberty, and the graves of our fathers. Choctaws and Chickasaws, you are among the few of our race who sit indolently at ease.[15]

It is a speech worthy of Thucydides's recounting, but it failed to cajole the Choctaw into joining the Confederacy, because what Tecumseh was asking for wasn't just tribes refusing treaties that allowed white settlement, or tribes defending their own settlements and hunting grounds. The Shawnee Confederacy was a mutual defense pact in which tribes would rush fighting forces to the defense of any tribe confronting a military expedition. The Confederacy had an Article 5 that magnified their power just as NATO does; none of the allies needed sufficient military forces to defend their territory because they could call on reinforcements from all the other tribes.

Part of refining Tecumseh's pitch was his framing of American Indian strategy as inherently defensive, and that of the settlers as insatiably aggressive. On his recruitment trips, Tecumseh described settlers as "a people fond of innovations, quick to contrive and quick to put their schemes into effectual execution, no matter how great the wrong and injury to us; while we are content to preserve what we already have."[16] He rallied those American Indians who'd converted to Christianity by invoking the tragedy of crucifixion: "How can we have confidence in the white people? When Jesus Christ came on earth, you killed him and nailed him on a cross."[17]

15. Tecumseh, Speech to the Choctaw Council, 1811, in H. B. Cushman, *History of the Choctaw, Chickasaw and Natchez Indians* (Greenville, TX: Headlight Printing House, 1899), 303–5, reproduced in Bette-Jon Schrade, *Tecumseh*, Appendix 7, 152.

16. Tecumseh, Speech to the Choctaw Council, in Schrade, *Tecumseh*, Appendix 7, 152.

17. Tecumseh, as quoted in Edward Egglestone and Lillie Egglestone Seelye, *The Shawnee Prophet; or The Story of Tecumseh* (London: The Authors, 1880), 182–86, reproduced in Schrade, *Tecumseh*, Appendix 4, 145–46.

Tecumseh even ominously raised the injustice of slavery and the American Indians' potential subjection to it:

> Are we not being stripped day by day of the little that remains of our ancient liberty? Do they not even now kick and strike us as they do their black-faces? How long will it be before they will tie us to a post and whip us, and make us work for them in their corn fields as they do them? Shall we wait for that moment, or shall we die fighting before submitting to such ignominy?[18]

Tecumseh was adroit enough to try to shift the burden of proof for land acquisition from tribes having to prove ownership to the US government having to prove the land was rightfully bought. He also shifted the moral burden, following his threat to kill chiefs that sold land with an appeal to Harrison, reminding the governor that, in 1810, "You said that if we could show that the land was sold by people that had no right to sell, you would restore it. If you do not restore the land, you will have a hand in killing them."[19]

At one point, Tecumseh even persuaded Governor Harrison to send food to supply Prophetstown. The Shawnee leader marshalled every argument that might persuade any allies into joining the Confederacy and plied every angle that might impose difficulty on his European American interlocutors. It wasn't enough—as late as 1811, Tecumseh was still encountering rejections in the south (Creek, Osage, Seminole, and Choctaw), and on the northeast and west. Expanding and solidifying the Confederacy required further expanding its appeal.

VI

Another important development in Tecumseh's strategy was the inversion of the relationship between warriors and leaders within the tribes. Traditionally, American Indian societies were ruled in peacetime by elected leaders, with war chiefs only chosen for campaigns and receding back into the tribe afterwards. But many tribes considered resistance to white encroachment futile or at least unsustainably costly, and land virtually unlimited; Tecumseh therefore needed multivariate ways to delegitimize accommodationist leaders.

One of Tecumseh's successful thrusts for consolidating his control over chiefs who urged cultural accommodation was encouraging the rise of a

---

18. Tecumseh, Speech to the Choctaw Council, in Schrade, *Tecumseh*, 152.
19. Tecumseh, as quoted in Egglestone and Seelye, in Schrade, *Tecumseh*, 182–86.

warrior class that rejected their subordination in peacetime. As a result, even when whole tribes wouldn't join the Confederacy, young warriors broke tribal discipline and did.[20] When negotiating with the British, Tecumseh could rightly claim "we the Warriors now manage the affairs of our Nation; and we sit at or near the Borders where the Contest will begin."[21]

And Tecumseh prided himself on its success, saying "since my residence at Tippecanoe we have endeavored to level all distinctions—to destroy village chiefs, by whom all mischief is done. It is they who sell out lands to the Americans. Our object is to let our affairs be transacted by warriors."[22]

VII

Matthew Elliott, a British Indian agent, described the American Indian anger at the continuing encroachment enforced by the Greenville treaty as creating a great opening for British foreign policy:

> From the present disposition of the Indians it appears evident that the least encouragement from our government would raise them all in arms and tribes who formerly with reluctance and others who never sent warriors against [settlers] would now with joy accept the invitation.[23]

William Henry Harrison would later recall British policy as actively taking that opportunity up: "the peace which concluded the following summer at Greenville was opposed by every exertion of British influence."[24]

The British plan in supporting American Indian forces had not been simply to force the US into a two-front war during the Revolution, but more ambitiously to foster an American Indian state as a buffer between Canada and the burgeoning expansionism of settlers.[25]

20. Peter Cozzens, *Tecumseh and the Prophet: The Shawnee Brothers Who Defied a Nation* (New York, NY: Knopf, 2020), 300.

21. Tecumseh, Speech to the British at Ft. Malden, November 15, 1810, from manuscripts in the Public Archives of Canada, "Q" series, 114-M.G.II., in Schrade, *Tecumseh*, 149.

22. Schrade, *Tecumseh*, 144.

23. Letter from Matthew Elliott to William Claus, June 10, 1810, National Archives of Canada RG 10, 27:16100, as quoted in Cozzens, *Tecumseh and the Prophet*, 233.

24. Draper Manuscript Collection microfilm number 1 YY, 18.

25. The Mexican government took the inverse approach, encouraging American settlers into what would become Texas, New Mexico, Arizona, Utah, Nevada, and California in an effort to create a buffer between Mexicans and southwest border tribes like the Comanche and Apache.

Tecumseh understood the value of British Canada as a potential sanctuary, armory, army, and economic lifeline for tribes while warriors were campaigning. In 1810, he secured an early British commitment by arriving in force at a meeting with a hundred tribal chiefs and a thousand warriors, not asking for troops, just supplies: "we think ourselves capable of defending our Country . . . We now are determined to defend it ourselves, and after raising you on your feet leave you behind, but expecting you will push forwards towards us what may be necessary to supply our Wants."[26]

VIII

Governor Harrison well understood the breadth of challenges Tecumseh posed, writing to the secretary of war in 1811:

> [Tecumseh] is now upon the last round to put a finishing stroke to his work. I hope, however, before his return that that part of the work which he considered complete will be demolished and even its foundation rooted up . . . his absence affords a most favorable opportunity for breaking up his Confederacy, and I have some expectations of being able to accomplish it without a recourse to actual hostility.[27]

Harrison endeavored to "organize an absolute disavowal of all connections with the Prophet, and as they are the owners of the land he occupies, I will endeavor to prevail upon them to express to him their disapprobation of his remaining there . . . But to ensure success a military force must be brought into view."[28] This attempt to break the political solidarity of the Confederacy did not succeed.

What did succeed was Harrison knowing in 1811 that the Confederacy's battlefield commander was away from Prophetstown recruiting, and so he attacked the settlement. Even without Tecumseh and against a numerically superior force, the Shawnee community held its own until running short of ammunition. And although US newspapers considered it a defeat for Harrison, and the residents of Prophetstown killed more US forces than they took casualties, the Battle of Tippecanoe did result in the Confederacy abandoning

---

26. Tecumseh, Speech to the British at Ft. Malden, in Schrade, *Tecumseh*, 151.
27. Letter from Harrison to Eustis, Secretary of War, Vincennes, August 7, 1811.
28. Letter from Harrison to Eustis, Secretary of War, Vincennes, August 7, 1811.

Prophetstown. The settlement was burned to the ground by Governor Harrison's troops, and its winter food supply subsequently destroyed.[29]

Tecumseh argued Tippecanoe proved that civilizational accommodation was impossible—"We, ourselves, are threatened with a great evil; nothing will pacify them but the destruction of all the red men."[30] Nor was he mistaken. Harrison's description of his subsequent policy was that "any Tribe [that] should dare take up the Tomahawk ... they need not expect that the same leniency would be shown them as they experienced at the close of the former war, but that they would be absolutely exterminated or driven beyond the Mississippi."[31]

But Harrison's destruction of Prophetstown achieved for Tecumseh what his own persuasive efforts had failed to do, which was bring in the hesitant tribes. And Harrison understood what Tecumseh was doing, explaining to the secretary of war that "there can be no doubt but his object is to excite the Southern Indians to war against us."[32]

Tecumseh undertook urgent recruiting trips to the Cherokee, Chicksaw, Choctaw, Creek, Potawawatamie, Wyandotte, Chippewa, Sauk, Osage, and Seminole. While he didn't get them all, he was so successful that William Henry Harrison acknowledged Tecumseh had successfully united the Confederacy and was the sole leader who could deliver their agreement to any treaty or their force in any battle. In the aftermath of Prophetstown's destruction, Tecumseh extended the line of resistance to the waters of the Gulf of Mexico. Settlers would have to either fight their way through the Confederacy or circumvent it via ocean-going vessels.

IX

Like any good strategist, Tecumseh adjusted his approach when circumstances changed. Sensing discouragement among tribes after Prophetstown was destroyed, he altered his recruiting pitch to emphasize that the war was winnable.

29. Tecumseh, Speech at Machekethie, in E. A. Cruikshank, *Documents Relating to the Invasion of Canada and the Surrender of Detroit, 1812, no. 7* (Ottawa: Publications of the Canadian Archives, 1912), 33–35, reproduced in Schrade, *Tecumseh*, 157. After defeat of the Shawnee Confederacy in 1813, US attitudes shifted, and Harrison was elected to the presidency as the hero of Tippecanoe.

30. Tecumseh, Speech to the Osages, in Schrade, *Tecumseh*, 153.

31. Letter from Harrison to Eustis, Secretary of War, Vincennes, August 7, 1811.

32. Letter from Harrison to Eustis, Secretary of War, Vincennes, August 7, 1811.

"Who are the white people that we should fear them? They cannot run fast, and are good marks to shoot at: they are only men; our fathers have killed many of them."[33]

And he was right. The US forces were not formidable. During the 1786 campaign against the Wabash, US troops had mutinied. William Henry Harrison complained in 1811 about his undisciplined forces, "The militia of the western country are only formidable when acting as mounted infantry."[34] Even with war against Britain looming in 1812, the United States was having difficulties gathering a force—enlistment was low, commanders were ill-prepared and untested in previous battles, and fellow officers were "swaggerers, dependents [and] decayed gentlemen . . . utterly unfit for any military purpose whatever."[35]

British support deepened as the Confederacy strengthened militarily and British frictions increased with the United States over the Napoleonic Wars; those frictions would burst into open conflict known as the War of 1812. The ranks of Tecumseh's forces expanded further after he began accruing military victories at the Canard River, Brownstown, Mongaugon, and Fort Detroit. Furthermore, those victories bolstered confidence that the British would back the Shawnee leader in the fight against settlers. While US forces were invading Canada in the east, the Shawnee alliance and British took Fort Detroit and attacked several others, forcing the United States into a two-front war of land engagements geographically disparate enough to require separate armies.

In 1813, at the Battle of River Raisin, the Confederacy achieved its most decisive victory. Tecumseh led an army of 800 Wyandot, Shawnee, Potawatomi, Odawa, Ojibwe, Delaware, Miami, Winnebago, Creek, Kickapoo, Sac, Fox, and other American Indian warriors into battle, destroying the US force in only twenty minutes; only thirty-three US soldiers escaped with their lives. Harrison, commanding a reinforcing force that hadn't arrived in time to salvage the engagement, called it "a national calamity."[36]

Together, the British and Shawnee Confederacy forces laid siege and attacked forts throughout the Northwest Territory. Their forces weren't integrated, but their operations were sophisticated—in combat for Fort Stephenson, the British attacked from the sea while two thousand Shawnee-led troops

33. Tecumseh, Speech to the Osages, in Schrade, *Tecumseh*, 155.
34. Letter from Harrison to Eustis, Secretary of War, Vincennes, August 7, 1811.
35. Cozzens, *Tecumseh and the Prophet*, 318.
36. National Park Service, "Battles of the River Raisin: Fall of the Michigan Territory, 1812," https://www.nps.gov/rira/index.htm.

attacked by land. The Shawnee constantly feared British defection, Tecumseh presciently worrying about the precedent from 1795 when "our father [the British] took them by the hand without our knowledge, and we are afraid our father will do so again at this time."[37]

In their alliance with the Shawnee Confederation, Britain controlled the timing and locations of combined attacks. They gained that leadership not by acknowledgment of any operational superiority, but instead by committing to supply Confederacy villages with food and clothing. And it was that reliance on British logistics that doomed the Shawnee Confederacy.

During the 1813 Battle of the Thames, a US naval squadron slipped through the British blockade of Lake Erie and severed the British sea lines of supply. The US commander triumphally signaled, "We have met the enemy and they are ours," while ferrying 2,500 of Harrison's troops to the front. Confederacy forces repaired to the highest navigable point of the Thames—but the British commander personally led the women and baggage retreating while the Shawnee fought.[38]

Seeing the British preparations to evacuate, Tecumseh attempted to shame the British commander:

> We are much astonished to see our father tying up everything and preparing to run away the other, without letting his red children know what his intentions are . . . You always told us you would never draw your foot off British ground; but now, father, we see you are drawing back, and we are sorry to see our father doing so without seeing the Enemy.[39]

That having no effect, Tecumseh pleaded for ammunition:

> The Americans have not yet defeated us by land; neither are we sure that they have done so by water; we therefore wish to remain here, and fight our enemy, should they make their appearance . . . You have got the arms and ammunition which our great father sent for his red children. If you have any idea of going away, give them to us.[40]

37. Tecumseh, Speech to General Procter Before Leaving Ft. Malden, in John Richardson, *War of 1812* (London: Brockville, Ltd., Inc., 1842), 119–20, reproduced in Schrade, *Tecumseh*, 158.

38. Katherine B. Coutts, "Thamesville and the Battle of the Thames," in Morris Zaslow, ed., *The Defended Border* (Toronto: Macmillan of Canada, 1964), 116.

39. Tecumseh, Speech to General Procter Before Leaving Ft. Malden, in Schrade, *Tecumseh*, 158.

40. Tecumseh, Speech to General Procter Before Leaving Ft. Malden, in Schrade, *Tecumseh*, 158.

That, too, was an unsuccessful appeal.

Even before Perry severed British supply lines, Britain had been reducing their promised support to Confederacy villages. Families sent word they were hungry and frightened, begging the British for food and clothing.[41] Wellington's army was fighting the Peninsular Campaign and needed both the ammunition and food; the balance of power on the European continent mattered more to British interests than the balance of power on the North American continent.

A first-hand Shawnee account of the climactic Thames battle recounted that, "In the fight Tecumseh was among the foremost—and did as he counseled others, that when the Americans fired, they would fire too high and then for the Indians to rush up, and use the tomahawk."[42] Harrison's after-action report to the secretary of war concluded that the British inflicted only three American casualties in the battle, all others were by American Indian troops.[43]

Shawnee scout Charr-he-nee recounted that, when the Confederacy forces saw Tecumseh fall, the cry went forth, "our chief is fallen, let's retreat."[44] The Battle of the Thames ended the war in the west. Tecumseh's death removed the glue of the Confederacy; troops scattered, and tribes returned to their villages.

The near success of the Shawnee Confederacy embittered settlers. As Darren R. Reid concluded, "twenty years of psychological warfare, sieges, and wilderness domination failed to drive European Americans out of that country, but it did succeed in fundamentally souring Western perspectives of the Indians and, as a result, drew a conceptual line down the spine of the Appalachians."[45]

The magnitude and pace of settlement moving westward continued to generate demands from settlers for both protection and the legitimation of claims to land possession.[46] Michigan Governor Lewis Cass spent fifteen years after

---

41. Cozzens, *Tecumseh and the Prophet*, 379.

42. Interview with Shawnee scout Charr-he-nee, Draper Manuscript Collection, 186.

43. John Sugden, *Tecumseh's Last Stand* (Norman, OK: University of Oklahoma Press, 1985), 127.

44. Interview with Shawnee scout Charr-he-nee, Draper Manuscript Collection, 188.

45. Darren R. Reid, "Anti-Indian Radicalization in the Early American West, 1774–1795," *Journal of the American Revolution*, Annual Volume, 2018.

46. Around six hundred treaties were negotiated between the US government and American Indian tribes, resulting in the transfer of two square miles per hour from 1784 to 1911. Arthur Spirling, "US Treaty-Making with American Indians: Institutional Change and Relative Power, 1784–1911," *American Journal of Political Science* 56:1 (2012): 84–97.

the Shawnee Confederacy's collapse agitating for the removal of the local tribes, eventually becoming President Andrew Jackson's secretary of war. In 1830, he carried out the Indian Removal Act. This saw the forcible removal of forty-six thousand natives of the Five Civilized Tribes that had been the most reluctant to join the Confederacy. These American Indians were forcibly depopulated from their twenty-five million acres of homes and hunting grounds to reservations west of the Mississippi.

X

The Confederacy's proximity to success, despite the significant political, technological, economic, and demographic advantages of their adversaries demonstrates the value of good strategy. The Shawnee and their Confederacy allies needed to utilize their resources creatively, efficiently, and with extraordinary virtuosity in order not to be quickly overwhelmed. And they did.

As the magnitude of settler challenge became manifest, particularly the sheer numbers of settlers willing to risk the hardships and dangers of the frontier, Tecumseh had to surmount the resignation of American Indians that there was no better alternative than submission. His principal strategic challenge was domestic: creating and sustaining a willingness to unify and resist settler expansion. Tecumseh oriented his political, religious, economic, and diplomatic efforts to foster and enforce cohesion among Confederacy tribes. That unity proved decisive while he lived.

Although the great man theory of history is unfashionable, it is nonetheless true that the individual Tecumseh was essential to the coming together of the Shawnee Confederacy. Central elements of the strategy had been attempted previously, and unsuccessfully. It was Tecumseh who saw the potential of drawing on religion as a political tool and then ruthlessly utilized it to delegitimize domestic opponents. He was the one willing to destroy the traditional power relationships between elected leaders and warriors to achieve his ends. It was his rhetoric in conferences with settlers that catalyzed (and solidified) American Indian opposition to accommodation. Tecumseh frenetically traveled to personally cement the alliances and he was the one who could discern variegated arguments and persuade tribes to take up arms. It was his courage and fighting ability that won battlefield victories, and it was he who capitalized on those victories with diplomacy in securing British alliance to provide the needed support so villages could do without their male populace. There would have been no Shawnee Confederacy without Tecumseh.

Strategy failures tend to be failures of imagination. The Shawnee strategy failed because Tecumseh could imagine neither the volume of immigrants that would come to the United States and disperse out into the Northwest Territory and beyond, nor the breadth of global interests tugging for British interest and resources. While the accommodationist chiefs could not assess the magnitude of settler immigration either, their strategy might have produced better outcomes for the tribes of the Confederacy. Ceding some of their lands and sustaining the prospect of coexistence rather than wholesale deportation might have been possible. Perhaps not, though, given General Andrew Jackson's betrayal of the American Indians that had fought with his forces in that same war, the insatiable land requirements for a cotton economy, and the desperation of settlers for land of their own that drove the incessancy of westward expansion.

War on the scale being fought in Europe during the Napoleonic Wars would be difficult to imagine for populations the size and geographic dispersal of American Indians. Tribes fought land wars with very limited maritime operations because they largely lived away from bodies of water; the great sea battles of the Napoleonic Wars had little relevance to the battles for control of the North American interior. And while the similarities of the close-in infantry fight might not differ too much between the continents, the scale of firepower being developed and amassed by European and European American societies was so far from American Indian's experience as to be unimaginable. Still, indigenous tribes seldom massed troops in ways that would have made those weapons efficient. Moreover, they were often brilliant insurgents and so could continually drive up the incremental costs of success while populations remained interspersed which, again, suggests the unlikelihood of an accommodationist strategy succeeding.

The experience of the Shawnee Confederacy validates the time-honored military maxim that logistics win wars. The Confederacy dominated the battlefield, effectively put forts and settlements under siege, and was societally resilient to losses. What decimated their prospects was losing access to food supplies for non-combatants. The warriors of the Shawnee Confederacy could claim to have never lost a battle, but their strategy's reliance on external supplies lost them the war.

One discouraging conclusion from the collapse of the Shawnee Confederacy is that even excellent strategies fail. Short of developing indigenous gunsmithing and more nutrition-intensive indigenous food production, there is little Tecumseh could have done to improve Confederacy prospects. Even

British battlefield abandonments in the later stages of the campaign weren't decisive. Reliance on British commissary for American Indian villages was the Confederacy's vulnerability; the US government found and exploited it to strategic success. The sad truth is that there is not likely to have been any strategy that could have succeeded against the onslaught of westward expansion. Sir Lawrence Freedman argued in *Strategy: A History* that Adam and Eve had no successful strategy other than obedience to God.[47] American Indians were caught in an even less forgiving vice, because even accommodating settler demands was unlikely to preserve their lands, their societies, or their freedoms. Different tribes attempted different strategies, and none of them succeeded.

Another discouraging conclusion is that failed attempts prejudice future prospects. The Trail of Tears that deracinated American Indian communities east of the Mississippi was a direct result of the near success of the Shawnee Confederacy. As such, it cast a long shadow over the fates of tribes beyond those of the Confederacy, setting the policies that would be sustained by settlers and the US government until American Indian independence was effectively extinguished.

That the Shawnee-led coalition was capable of practicing strategy ought not to require proof. Yet the persistence of racist derogation and of competing serendipitous explanations for their achievements justifies providing evidence not only of apparent strategic design but also acknowledgment by the Shawnee that they were thinking in strategic terms. So, for example, when negotiating with William Henry Harrison in 1812, Tecumseh clearly linked elements of the Shawnee approach, refusing high-level political engagement without legitimation of their economic system:

> You wish to prevent the Indians doing as we wish them—to unite, and let them consider their lands as the common property of the whole; you take tribes aside and advise them not to come into this measure; and until our design is accomplished we do not wish to accept of your invitation to go and see the President.[48]

Indeed, Tecumseh and the American Indian nations that he led had what in contemporary parlance is termed a "whole of society strategy." There was a religious line of operations to foster commonality among tribes and create a

---

47. Lawrence Freedman, *Strategy: A History* (New York, NY: Oxford University Press, 2013).
48. Schrade, *Tecumseh*, 144.

sense of inevitable success; a domestic political line of operations to unite various tribes; an economic line of operations to end reliance on European goods and cut off trade lucrative to settlers; a diplomatic line of operations to secure British support and supplies; and a military line of operations to defeat armies in the field and starve forts into closure—all organized by a leader of magnetism and battlefield courage.

Had the Shawnee Confederacy succeeded in stringing an enduring barricade from Canada to the Gulf of Mexico, the United States may not have come to dominate North America. Settlers could have emigrated by sea around the Confederacy's lands, and pushed in with settlements from both east and west of the American Indian states, forcing the Shawnee to defend on both borders, but success in 1813, at a minimum, would have bought the Confederacy crucial time to figure out how to manage that challenge. Perhaps it would have even allowed Tecumseh to become the founder of an empire that would rival the glory of a Mexico or Peru, as William Henry Harrison envisioned.

CHAPTER 16

Francis Lieber, the Laws of War, and the Origins of the Liberal International Order

Wayne Wei-siang Hsieh

In the introduction of the first edition of *Makers of Modern Strategy*, Edward Meade Earle defined strategy as "the art of controlling and utilizing the re-sources of a nation—or a coalition of nations—including its armed forces, to the end that its vital interests shall be effectively promoted and secured against enemies, actual, potential, or merely presumed."[1] Eighty years have elapsed since the first printing of the first iteration *Makers of Modern Strategy*, but most scholars and policy professionals would still consider his definition a reason-able one. Both the first and second editions of *Makers of Modern Strategy* sought to help educate the American public in the vital task of rationally di-recting instruments of power on behalf of democratic statecraft; the second volume also had to contend with the prospect of nuclear Armageddon. The specter of global communism has departed the world stage, but the so-called liberal international order led by the United States finds itself beset by chal-lenges such as global pandemics, climate change, migration, and alternative visions of political order ranging from the Chinese Communist Party's au-thoritarian developmental state to the religious millenarianism of the self-styled Islamic State.

---

1. Edward Mead Earle, ed., *Makers of Modern Strategy: Military Thought from Machiavelli to Hitler* (Princeton, NJ: Princeton University Press, 1961), viii.

The liberal international order can no longer claim the almost automatic ideological assent described by Francis Fukuyama, but amidst this era of ideological fracture, historians can better understand the intellectual foundations of the postwar liberal order. The modern law of war remains one of the originating strands of that liberal order, with mid-nineteenth-century origins amidst the American Civil War and other related conflicts. That legal regime both enabled and limited violence, while rooting dreams of a just peace in the fire and blood of righteous war. Its complex roots in Christian Just War doctrine, Enlightenment philosophy, post-French Revolution nationalism, and nineteenth-century power politics all contributed to this dualist character, and no complete understanding of our own era's debates over the legal basis of concepts such as the Responsibility to Protect is possible without understanding these historical origins. The German-American political theorist Francis Lieber stands at the center of this story, because the code of conduct—the Lieber Code—he produced for the Union armies during the Civil War established crucial precedents for the Hague Peace Conferences and the Geneva Conventions. Lieber thus holds a position in the story of the liberal international order akin to Carl von Clausewitz's looming presence in the first two editions of the *Makers of Modern Strategy*.

I

Peter Paret highlighted Clausewitz's importance during the Cold War as a theorist who seemed to mark a path by which war could still be a rational instrument of policy in the nuclear age. Lieber, in contrast, spoke to an era where the crucial question was not whether war could be a rational instrument of policy, but whether it could be moral and ethical in the first place. Like Clausewitz, Lieber wrote in the wake of the tumult of Napoleon and had himself fought in the wars surrounding the French emperor's bid for mastery of Europe, and both believed in the power of nationalism while accepting the inevitable presence of war. Lieber's older brothers had belonged to the reformist military circle led by Gerhard von Scharnhorst, Clausewitz's mentor, and the famed military theorist had also opposed the dissolution of the Landwehr, which had drawn its officer corps from the Lieber family's middle-class strata. Nevertheless, while Clausewitz was, by Prussian standards at least, relatively sympathetic to liberalism, he abhorred the circle of student radicals that became implicated in the assassination of the reactionary dramatist August von Kotzebue, and it was Lieber's membership in these circles that led to the younger man's eventual political exile. The older man also proved mostly indifferent to the question of ethics or codes of conduct in war, dismissing them as "imperceptible limitations hardly worth mentioning, known as international law and custom." Unlike most Americans, Lieber knew of Clausewitz's work when he became a full-blown academic, and he directly criticized Clausewitz's definition of war in *Vom Kriege*, but Lieber also acknowledged that the Prussian general possessed a "powerful mind."[2]

Both men thus represented related but different facets of a common Napoleonic legacy, and because we remain heirs to the nation-state international system created in that period, both have remained relevant. However, many of their modern heirs have arguably misused the men's ideas to some degree, as they sought to apply their ideas to new circumstances. In the case of Clausewitz, Cold War readers in the United States emphasized his oft-cited dictum of war as an instrument of political policy in order to defuse the danger of escalation—but arguably at the cost of understating the escalatory dynamic that Clausewitz himself embedded in his analysis of war. Clausewitz may not have anticipated the rise of nuclear weapons, but he certainly anticipated several centuries worth of escalating violence paired with the technological advances and globalizing forces of modernity. Lieber sought to tame and domesticate those processes for the sake of liberal nationalism with his code of conduct and his access to state power, and epigones such as Samantha Power saw an opportunity in post-Cold War American hegemony to master war for liberal ends such as the Responsibility to Protect. In short, Lieber dismissed Clausewitz, which many of his Cold War American readers in turn misread, and that misreading set the stage for liberal disappointment with the challenge of making war into a rationalist and legalistic instrument of policy.

Ironically enough, self-styled American strategists might have avoided a good deal of grief if they had paid more attention to French readings of Clausewitz—in particular the interpretations of both René Girard and Michel Foucault. Writing in the aftermath of post-Cold War atrocities—the collapse of

---

2. Peter Paret, "Clausewitz," in *Makers of Modern Strategy: From Machiavelli to the Nuclear Age*, Peter Paret, ed. (Princeton, NJ: Princeton University Press, 1986), 186–213; Frank Freidel, *Francis Lieber: Nineteenth-Century Liberal* (Baton Rouge, LA: Louisiana State University Press, 1947), 3–8, 24–26; Peter Paret, "Clausewitz's Politics," in his *Understanding War: Essays on Clausewitz and the History of Military Power* (Princeton, NJ: Princeton University Press, 1992), 172–73; Carl von Clausewitz, *On War*, Michael Howard and Peter Paret, eds. (Princeton, NJ: Princeton University Press, 1989), 75; Francis Lieber, *Manual of Political Ethics* (London: Smith, 1839), 631.

Yugoslavia, genocide in Rwanda, and sectarian warfare in Iraq—Girard believed that the modern condition had in fact accelerated the escalatory dynamic of violence Clausewitz had first identified—"Do we not now destroy simply to destroy? Violence now seems deliberate, and the escalation to extremes is served by science and politics." Globalization created uncontrollable networks over which terrorists and pandemics traveled, exacerbated by climate change—"violence has been unleashed across the whole world, creating what the apocalyptic texts predicted: confusion between disasters caused by nature and those caused by humans."[3] In 2007 self-styled strategists within the Beltway might have dismissed this all as quasi-mystical rhetoric from a peculiar French intellectual. However, it reads differently after the Fall of Mosul in 2014 to an extremist movement that combined seemingly atavistic conceptions of religion with social media fluency, the Taliban seizure of Afghanistan in 2021, and the worldwide struggle to control COVID.

Thirty-some odd years before Girard surveyed the post-Cold War order, Michel Foucault provided his own reinterpretation of Clausewitz that highlighted the problem of politics and violence within a polity—the same problem Lieber had hoped to ameliorate with his code of conduct. Foucault inverted the orthodox interpretation of Clausewitz and argued that "politics is the continuation of war by other means." In Foucault's view:

> The law is born of real battles, victories, massacres and conquests which can be dated and which have their horrific heroes ... Law is not pacification, for beneath the law, war continues to rage in all the mechanisms of power, even in the most the regular. War is the motor behind institutions and order. ... We are therefore at war with one another; a battlefront runs through the whole of society, continuously and permanently, and it is this battlefront that puts us all on one side or the other.

Foucault's reading echoes Carl Schmitt's interpretation of Clausewitz, anticipating his friend/enemy distinction in politics, which seems all the more germane in an era of seemingly increased polarization in the Western world.[4]

3. René Girard and Benoît Chantre, *Battling to the End: Conversations with Benoît Chantre*, trans. Mary Baker (East Lansing, MI: Michigan State University Press, 2010 [2007]), 20, 23–24, x.

4. Michel Foucault, *"Society Must Be Defended": Lectures at the College de France, 1975–76*, Mauro Bertani, Alessandro Fontana, and François Ewald, eds., trans. David Macey (New York, NY: Picador, 2003), 15, 50–51; Wolfgang Palaver and Gabriel Borrud, "War and Politics: Clausewitz and Schmitt in the Light of Girard's Mimetic Theory," *Contagion: Journal of Violence, Mimesis, and Culture* 24:1 (2017): 104.

One can certainly acknowledge that Foucault might have overdrawn his point, but the "civil" aspect of the Civil War makes his analysis especially germane to the circumstances in which Lieber found himself. The American state, after all, had emerged from a voluntary constitutional compact rooted in early modern notions of sovereignty and popular consent. But embedded in that constitutional order were aggressive and expansionist wars against various groups of American Indians. Furthermore, the sectional controversy over slavery and the federal nature of the American constitutional order both loomed over the federal compact. In the case of Civil War America, part of the promise of war was that it would finally end the long-running sectional conflict over slavery—to end the vexatious process to which we can apply Foucault's analysis of Henri de Boulainvilliers's *ancien regime* historical writing that considered "war to be a sort of permanent state that exists between groups, fronts, and tactical units as they in some sense civilize one another, come into conflict with one another, or on the contrary, form alliances. There are no more multiple and stable great masses, but there is a multiple war."[5] American historians still call the period before the Civil War the antebellum era, but, within that peace, violence remained persistent. There were outright wars against indigenous peoples that concluded with dubious peace treaties; an early naval conflict with republican France (the "Quasi-War"); chronic low-level political violence that did not involve slavery but ranged from riots against Federalists during the War of 1812 to ethnic clashes in Baltimore; and political violence that did involve slavery such as Bleeding Kansas and John Brown's Harpers Ferry raid. The decentralized nature of the American political order helped make possible this "multiple war," culminating in the Confederate bid for independence. The desperate nature of that struggle, together with Lieber's desire to subjugate the Confederacy and restore the Union, helps explain how his code could both enable and restrain the war's violence at the same time.

Both Girard and Foucault did not see Clausewitz as a curio of his era who wrote a theoretical work of interest only to what we would now call "national security professionals." Nor did they see their own projects as a means of educating the American demos in order to prepare it for the burden of world hegemony, which was the original impetus for the first edition of the *Makers of Modern Strategy*. They instead saw Clausewitz as a prophet of modernity and its associated violence. Lieber, in contrast, represented a dissenting tradition that saw more reasons for optimism regarding the modern human condition.

5. Foucault, *Society Must Be Defended*, 162.

While Foucault found fame in Western academia by connecting armies, prisons, schools, and insane asylums into an interlinked theory of modern political power wielded by disciplinary institutions themselves marked by a degree of deception and hypocrisy, Lieber (himself a former political prisoner in Prussia) had counted prison reform as one of his causes, along with antislavery and military law. One sees in Lieber's own thinking the connections between nation, state, army, school, and prisons within the liberal political order, and his code of conduct for armies was a piece with his larger vision.[6] While Lieber's code helped build a liberal scaffolding that aided in limiting violence, it also endorsed war as a means of creating peace and enforcing order on enemies within a polity, especially if that peace involved liberal causes such as antislavery.

II

In 2009, Barack Obama cited a nineteenth-century historical narrative in his Nobel Peace Prize address, presenting the liberal international order at its peak moment of power and prestige:

> Let me make one final point about the use of force. Even as we make difficult decisions about going to war, we must also think clearly about how we fight it. The Nobel Committee recognized this truth in awarding its first prize for peace to Henry Dunant—the founder of the Red Cross, and a driving force behind the Geneva Conventions. Where force is necessary, we have a moral and strategic interest in binding ourselves to certain rules of conduct. And even as we confront a vicious adversary that abides by no rules, I believe the United States of America must remain a standard bearer in the conduct of war.[7]

Obama's narrative drew from a memo written by Samantha Power on just war doctrine, which cited David Hume, Immanuel Kant, Martin Luther

6. M. Russell Thayer, "The Life, Character, and Writings of Francis Lieber," in *The Miscellaneous Writings of Francis Lieber*, Volume 1, Daniel Coit Gilman, ed. (Philadelphia, PA: Lippincott, 1880), 31; Francis Lieber, "The Necessity of Continued Self-Education," in *Miscellaneous Writings*, Volume 1, 291; Michael O'Brien, *Conjectures of Order: Intellectual Life and the American South, 1810–1860* (Chapel Hill, NC: University of North Carolina Press, 2004), 1–83; Francis Lieber, "History and Political Science Necessary Studies in Free Countries," in *Miscellaneous Writings*, Volume 1, 331–32.

7. Barack Obama, "Remarks by the President at the Acceptance of the Nobel Peace Prize," December 10, 2009, https://obamawhitehouse.archives.gov/the-press-office/remarks-president-acceptance-nobel-peace-prize.

King, Jr., Reinhold Niebuhr, and Henry Dunant as authorities and influences. Perhaps due to her Irish-American background, Power's historical gloss did not include Lieber and the American Civil War, although two years before the American war broke out, Henry Dunant surveyed the carnage at the Battle of Solferino and was inspired to establish what became the International Committee of the Red Cross. Four years later, the Lieber Code was issued by Union military authorities as General Orders No. 100, which in turn served as the basis of the Brussels *projet* of 1874 and the binding treaty that came out of the First Hague Peace Conference of 1899.[8] The Hague Rules then heavily influenced the Geneva Conventions that Obama commemorated in his Nobel address.

The Hague Rules and the Geneva Conventions focused on the conduct of nation-state armies fighting each other, while the Lieber Code had served an army fighting what it defined to be a large, organized, but illegitimate domestic insurrection. The Lieber Code thus authorized violence as a righteous means to suppress villainy and comprised part of the legal tradition that Obama drew from when he declared that war was legitimate "to prevent the slaughter of civilians by their own government, or to stop a civil war whose violence and suffering can engulf an entire region."[9] Furthermore, the code had arisen out of an internal civil conflict—Obama's wars were also civil wars to some degree in Iraq, Afghanistan, and Libya—where reformation had been an important wartime objective and justification.

The Lieber Code spoke to the Janus-faced nature of the Western law of war, and its origins in a chaotic civil war echo Girard's and Foucault's skepticism about the subordination of war's violence to rational policy. In the orthodox liberal narrative, the Lieber Code's appeals to humanitarianism and its attempt to distinguish between combatants and non-combatants dovetail nicely with Clausewitz's argument that war should be subordinate to policy. The Lieber Code thus seemed to provide a means of ensuring that Clausewitz's warnings about escalation in war could be restrained by both political rationality and liberal ethics. In the wake of the world wars and with the rise of atomic weapons, this seemed all the more important.

From at least the vantage of point of 2021, Obama's presidency represents both the recent peak of this liberal model of war and the beginning of the

---

8. Samantha Power, *The Education of an Idealist: A Memoir* (New York, NY: Dey Street Books, 2019), 262–63; Stephen C. Neff, *War and the Law of Nations: A General History* (New York, NY: Cambridge University Press, 2005), 186–87.

9. Obama, "Remarks by the President."

doctrine's decline in influence. One can find it in Obama himself when he rebuffed Power's request that he include in his Nobel address an explicit endorsement of the "responsibility to protect" (R2P)—defined by Power as the doctrine that "genocide and mass atrocity are monstrous crimes that require governments to act to stop them." Such arguments swayed Obama in 2011, when the US intervened militarily in Libya, but this was an operation he later soured on. When faced with the Syrian civil war in his second term, Obama would refuse to be swayed by Power's arguments and citations of R2P. Obama's successors, Donald Trump and Joseph Biden, have proved even less amenable to such arguments. Others formerly sympathetic to Obama have even grown disenchanted with the Nobel Prize-winning president. In Samuel Moyn's 2021 philippic against the recent melding of American air power with humanitarian legalism, he savagely contrasted a well-heeled Connecticut wedding attended by Obama voters with the dark legacy of Afghan weddings being bombed by US drone strikes.[10] The recent US withdrawal from Afghanistan, punctuated by a final botched American drone strike in Kabul, represents a denouement of sorts for Obama's Nobel Prize-winning synthesis of liberalism and precision-guided munitions.

The modern law of war, and the larger liberal international order, partly ground their legitimacy in a larger narrative of historical progress. A full understanding of their historical origins thus has stakes that go beyond purely disinterested scholarly curiosity, in the same way so many of our current culture wars involve conflicts over the moral standing of historical narratives. Indeed, the historical narrative Obama drew on for his Nobel address reflected prior historical scholarship that tended to see the development of the law of war as a fundamentally progressive phenomenon, with an advancing humanitarian sensibility attempting to keep pace with advancing weapons technology. That era then gave way to the carnage of the twentieth century's ideologically driven world wars and the nuclear-armed standoff of the Cold War. However, the fall of the Soviet Union seemed to usher in a new era where the Cold War liberalism of Reinhold Niebuhr (cited by Obama as an influence) could be

---

10. Barack Obama, *A Promised Land* (New York, NY: Crown, 2020), 445, 655; Samantha Power, "Foreword," in *Responsibility to Protect*, Richard H. Cooper and Juliette Voïnov Kohler, eds. (New York, NY: Palgrave Macmillan US, 2009), vii; Power, *The Education of an Idealist*, 511–12; Samuel Moyn, *Humane: How the United States Abandoned Peace and Reinvented War* (New York, NY: Farrar, Straus and Giroux, 2021), 4–6. For a more balanced recent treatment of Lieber and his legacy, see John Fabian Witt, *Lincoln's Code: The Laws of War in American History* (New York, NY: Free Press, 2012).

married with precision-guided munitions to produce a humanized form of war akin to policing and that culminated in the targeted raid to kill Osama bin Laden.[11] These attempts to blur the line between war and policing—or at least to see the two as existing along a continuum as opposed to conflicting forces separated by a chasm—drew from nineteenth-century precedents solidified in many ways by Lieber's codification of the laws of war amidst what was legally, in the Union's eyes, an illegitimate insurrection.

Nevertheless, despite the violence and chaos in Libya, Syria, Iraq, and Afghanistan during Obama's second term, followed by Trump's election in 2016, the law of war regime did not crumble. When a group of notable German writers and political figures—including the philosopher Jürgen Habermas and the politician Friedrich Merz (a prominent contender to lead the CDU in the opposition after its 2021 electoral defeat)—called for a European Army in 2018 to help defend the EU against external adversaries such as Trump, Russia, and China, they cited the same essay of Kant on perpetual peace that Power must have referenced in her pre-Nobel memo to Obama. The German writers claimed that this new military force would not be "directed against anyone" and would be "combined with arms control and disarmament initiatives."[12] Lieber's legacy remains alive and influential.

III

Lieber inhabited a longer tradition of Western thought on just and unjust war that stretched back to classical antiquity. The Greeks and Romans had seen war as a routine occurrence, with the latter's conception of war and peace as a distinction "between a state of passive or notional hostility as opposed to a state of *active* conflict." Early classical theorists of natural law, however, conceived of a general law of nature applicable to all of humanity and saw war as an aberrant disruption to a larger global community bound together by reason. The rise of Western Christianity merged with these earlier, Stoic-influenced

11. Michael Howard, "Constraints on Warfare," in *The Laws of War: Constraints on Warfare in the Western World*, Michael Howard, George J. Andreopoulos, and Mark R. Shulman, eds. (New Haven, CT: Yale University Press, 1994), 5–7; Geoffrey Best, *Humanity in Warfare* (New York, NY: Columbia University Press, 1980), 171; Moyn, *Humane*, 294, 298.

12. Hans Eichel et al., "Time to Wake up: We Are Deeply Concerned about the Future of Europe and Germany," *Handelsblatt Today*, October 25, 2018, https://www.handelsblatt.com /english/opinion/time-to-wake-up-we-are-deeply-concerned-about-the-future-of-europe-and -germany/23583722.html.

views and produced a viable and durable just war doctrine in the medieval period that viewed war as a means for crushing evil and denied any sort of legal and moral equality between belligerents based on their status as states.[13] Either one combatant had God and justice on its side, or it did not, and the moral absolutism of the doctrine contributed to the violence of early modern Europe's religious wars.

A new conception of the law of war emerged after the Westphalian settlement of 1648, which sought to govern a conflict between sovereign states whose legitimacy flowed not from the justness of their cause, but, to use the words of the political and legal theorist Carl Schmitt, from their "adherence to a specific procedure (effected by bracketing the struggle), and, especially, in the inclusion of witnesses on an equal footing."[14] These witnesses were sovereign states whose special legal status both authorized and limited violence, because "the equality of sovereigns made them equally legal partners in war and prevented military methods of annihilation."[15] The legal status of states and their role in recognizing other states' legitimacy would prove to be a major point of legal controversy during the Civil War. Schmitt, moreover, argued that such a conception made interstate war akin to dueling, where "men of honor have found a satisfactory means of dealing with a matter of honor in a prescribed form and before impartial witnesses."[16]

Dueling represented a different model for regulating violence than the Christian just war tradition. Instead of citing abstract moral principles grounded in universal reason and God's will, dueling assumed the moral equality of aristocratic equals whose shared commitment to a code of rituals allowed them to resolve their disagreements by a form of controlled violence. Those disagreements frequently centered on arguments over prestige, status, and honor in the eyes of their peers, and the *code duello* helped regulate aristocratic desires to assert and defend their reputations through displays of courage and violent dominance. In Europe after the Peace of Westphalia, where the dream of reuniting Christendom had perished amidst bloody religious wars that plagued relations between and within states, those states took on the role of aristocratic nobles who vied for status and honor, and who channeled that

13. Neff, *War and the Law of Nations*, 30–33, 49, 62. Emphasis in original.

14. Carl Schmitt, *The Nomos of the Earth in the International Law of the Jus Publicum Europaeum*, trans. G. L. Ulmen (New York, NY: Telos Press, 2006), 143.

15. Schmitt, *The Nomos of the Earth*, 142.

16. Schmitt, *The Nomos of the Earth*, 143.

competition through the ritualized violence of a developing law of war that helped lead to Lieber's code of conduct for the Union Army. This system proved durable within Europe as a means of war and violence, although it also enabled imperial state violence outside of the European periphery, where these quasi-aristocratic rituals did not apply. In North America, for example, where European states fought each other directly with their military forces while engaged in conflicts involving colonial settlers and indigenous peoples outside of the European cultural remit, this system did little to restrain the racialized violence that demarcated imperial peripheries. The American republic inherited this decidedly mixed legacy. Even in Europe itself, the wars of the French Revolution and Napoleon overturned many of the political premises of state war being anthropomorphized as duelists on a public field of honor. Aristocratic restrictions on wartime violence did not fully evaporate in the hothouse of revolutionary and Napoleonic Europe, but the ideas certainly suffered body blows. However, some of the French Revolution's violence found its roots in the reformist visions of the Enlightenment, which, while dreaming of perpetual peace, opened the road to total war.[17]

IV

Francis Lieber came of age amidst the tumult of the Napoleonic Wars. While Hegel believed that history culminated in Napoleon's defeat of the Prussian armies at Jena-Auerstedt, the eight-year-old Lieber bitterly wept at the sight of France's victorious troops parading through Berlin. His older brothers served in the campaigns of 1813 and 1814, and the sixteen-year-old Lieber enlisted in a regiment in 1815 after Napoleon's return from exile. Lieber saw combat at the Battle of Ligny in what is now Belgium; he described his company of younger troops as overeager for action. Their veteran colonel had cautioned his unit, "Riflemen, you are young, I am afraid too ardent; calmness makes the soldier, hold yourselves in order." After fierce fighting, Lieber recounted that his unit began to lose their cohesion, but the colonel calmed his men: "As if he were on the drilling place, he said, 'Your beat is bad; have we drilled so long for nothing? down your guns; now, Ready;' and every man was calm again." Lieber's later code of conduct would emphasize the importance of good order and discipline in an army, values he learned as a teenager during the Waterloo

---

17. David A. Bell, *The First Total War: Napoleon's Europe and the Birth of Warfare as We Know It* (Boston, MA: Houghton Mifflin Harcourt, 2007), 35–36, 48–51, 77.

campaign. Lieber would be grievously wounded by a musket ball passing through his neck at the Battle of Namur during the pursuit of the retreating French forces after Napoleon's defeat at Waterloo. He suffered so badly that he begged a comrade to put him out of his misery but survived the ordeal.[18]

Lieber was a rifleman, and with his first shot in battle he felled a French grenadier with a ball aimed at his adversary's face, only fifteen paces away. The open order formations and more individualistic aimed fire of the rifleman acquired political connotations associated with the tumult of the revolutionary period, as opposed to the precise machine-like drill of Frederick the Great's absolutist regime. Lieber himself criticized the Prussian military model of Frederick II, which used a regime of "degrading discipline" that led to armies comprised of "mere machines, without any moral incentive." Such rotten material was swept aside by the Napoleonic wars, with all the European armies now raised from native citizenry, as opposed to "the refuse of foreign nations." However, the light infantry formations Lieber served in proved incapable of producing the political change a committed liberal such as Lieber desired. As a young veteran, Lieber joined the Turner Movement of Frederick Lewis Jahn, which espoused the value of physical and moral conditioning via gymnastics and the nationalistic Protestantism of Schleiermacher. Lieber became impatient with Jahn's political conservatism and Prussian authorities arrested Lieber in 1819 because of his association with radical student politics. While they released him due to a lack of evidence, the powers-that-be frustrated Lieber's attempts to become an academic in his native country. The outbreak of the Greek Revolution inspired Lieber to join their cause and he left on this new adventure in 1822.[19]

Lieber did not see himself bound by his sovereign's will, and he hoped to help the Greeks overthrow their Ottoman rulers. However, he remained committed to the military discipline learned during his prior military service. He proudly claimed to his parents, "You can judge from our first rule what good discipline is maintained, namely: all, irrespective of rank, must submit to the

18. Freidel, *Francis Lieber*, 1–11; Francis Lieber, "Of the Battle of Waterloo," in *Miscellaneous Writings*, Volume 1, 155, 158, 162. Lieber did not think much of Hegel, as argued for in Merle Curti, "Francis Lieber and Nationalism," *Huntington Library Quarterly* 4:3 (1941): 270.

19. Lieber, "Of the Battle of Waterloo," 151, 156; Peter Paret, *Yorck and the Era of Prussian Reform, 1807–1815* (Princeton, NJ: Princeton University Press, 1966), 215–18, 244; T. G. Bradford, E. Wigglesworth, and Francis Lieber, *Encyclopædia Americana; a Popular Dictionary of Arts, Sciences, Literature, History, Politics, and Biography, Brought down to the Present Time* (Philadelphia, PA: Desilver, Thomas, 1836), 1–381; Freidel, *Francis Lieber*, 19–31.

regulations." Lieber fully accepted the legitimacy of revolutionary movements and wars, but he also believed that only organized armies and warfare could possess moral sanction. The Greek expedition went poorly, and the small band of self-styled European freedom fighters eventually found themselves robbed by armed peasants and forced into selling their arms. In Lieber's view, "the cowardice and incapacity of the Greeks made them unfit to defend or free their country." Scholars have sometimes expressed confusion at Lieber's later belligerency and hostility to the peace movement, which in their view seemed discordant with his bloody experience of war as a teenager, but it was clear that Lieber had experienced in battle the sort of transcendent experience that has marked modern military culture. Having gone to Greece to engage in martial exploits with the aim of freeing the Greeks, he now simply hoped to find some edifying tourism. In the end, Lieber would not be able to manage even that and he left Greece for Rome.[20]

There Lieber came under the tutelage of Barthold George Niebuhr, the noted Prussian historian of Rome who also moderated Lieber's youthful radicalism. Despite his considerable influence, however, Niebuhr could not protect Lieber from the Prussian regime's reactionary tendencies and its suspicion of the latter's youthful activism. After further harassment, including periods of time in solitary confinement, Lieber finally emigrated to England. From there, he acquired a teaching position at a gymnasium and swimming school in Boston, where some enterprising Americans hoped to import the new German ideas about physical education that Lieber had learned from Jahn as a young veteran. Lieber arrived in America in 1827, but the Boston school failed. Lieber managed to make a name for himself as a noted writer and academic and even came under serious consideration for a history professorship at Harvard, but he was only able to find his first stable faculty appointment when the controversy-plagued South Carolina College in Columbia offered him its chair of history and political economy.[21]

Lieber spent twenty-one fraught years in South Carolina. Despite his antislavery beliefs, he became a slaveowner and broke off relations with some of his northern friends with abolitionist inclinations. He exhibited some of the same callous racism that marked the slaveholding society that surrounded

20. Thomas Sergeant Perry, ed., *The Life and Letters of Francis Lieber* (Boston, MA: J. R. Osgood and Company, 1882), 32, 38–39, 41; Witt, *Lincoln's Code*, 174–79; Freidel, *Francis Lieber*, 33–34, 305.

21. Freidel, *Francis Lieber*, 36–45, 52–61, 111–22.

him. Nevertheless, Lieber never completely assimilated to the views of his employers. He never used his considerable intellectual abilities to defend slavery in print, even if he did not publicly denounce it, and his employers rightly interpreted his silence as a sign of his true convictions. Lieber wrote his major academic works, which laid out a theoretical basis for the liberal nationalism that went back to his youth. While committed to individual rights and development like a good liberal, Lieber also emphasized the importance of the state and of citizen participation in self-governance. The Liebers raised their children in South Carolina—Matilda Lieber in particular made closer personal associations than her bookish husband—but Francis Lieber could never shake off well-justified suspicions from pro-slavery South Carolinians that the German émigré was not fully loyal to their regime. In 1855 South Carolina College passed over Lieber for its vacant presidency position, despite his academic credentials, and Lieber left for a new chair at Columbia University in New York City. Due to his long southern sojourn, Lieber became a staunch defender of individual conscience and immigration.[22] Just as he had once departed his native Prussia due to its hostile political climate, Lieber now departed the hotbed of proslavery secessionism.

Lieber's long exile in South Carolina—the epicenter of proslavery thought and secession—certainly adds irony to his later role as Union theorist and adviser to the military occupiers of recaptured secessionist territory. It also split his family apart—one of his three sons joined the Confederate Army and fell in action at Williamsburg in 1862, cursing his estranged father as he expired. Two other sons fought in the Union Army, and one lost his arm at Fort Donelson in 1862. While a calamity for his nation and personal life, the Civil War thrust Lieber into the position of political and intellectual influence that he had long craved. No longer forced to teach and write at what was, for a well-educated German scholar, a provincial finishing school for the sons of planters, he was now free to express his convictions. After South Carolina seceded, Lieber republished an address he had given in 1851 arguing against secession; he also gave two new lectures arguing the Union's case at Columbia—all three garnered considerable attention from notable Unionist politicians and writers.[23]

Whatever Lieber thought of secession's legality within the American constitutional order, the Confederacy obviously presented ambiguous difficulties to scholars of international law. Citing various legal authorities and historical

22. O'Brien, *Conjectures of Order*, 1–86.
23. Freidel, *Francis Lieber*, 301–5, 324–26.

precedents including the Greek Revolution of 1821, the British and French governments recognized the Confederacy as a belligerent state. Lieber condemned the British decision in a private letter to Sumner, and cited Great Britain's own internal political troubles: "How bitterly the cup she is brewing now may one day be pressed to her mouth by the Irish, that her lips will bleed and her teeth will ache."[24] The Union government obviously took great umbrage at this recognition and Secretary of State William Seward wrote Charles Francis Adams, US Ambassador to England, the following explanation of the Union government's position:

> There is, of course, the employment of force by the government to suppress the insurrection, as every other government necessarily employs force in such cases. But these incidents by no means constitute a state of war impairing the sovereignty of the government, creating belligerent sections, and entitling foreign States to intervene or to act as neutrals between them, or in any other way to cast off their lawful obligations to the nation thus for the moment disturbed.[25]

In his antebellum ethics manual, Lieber himself listed "insurrection" and "wars of independence" as two possible forms of just war. However, he also listed "wars to unite distracted states of the same nation, or in a country destined by nature to form one political society"—criteria he obviously later applied to the Union.[26]

Lieber and Union authorities might have inveighed against British and French recognition, but neither could do much more than complain about the affront. As one might expect of a former soldier, Lieber proved to be a pragmatist, and when the question of the disposition of Union and Confederate prisoners presented itself, he considered the issue from the empiricist school of positivist international law that dominated nineteenth-century international law. This school of jurisprudence cited the practical conduct of states and the agreements between them, as opposed to the abstract moral principles of medieval Just War theorists. Lieber cited various historical examples when he argued that the federal government's willingness to exchange prisoners did not represent any sort of tacit recognition of the Confederate cause's legitimacy,

24. Francis Lieber, *Letter to Charles Sumner*, June 2, 1861, Box 42, Francis Lieber Papers, Henry E. Huntington Library, San Marino, CA.

25. William H. Seward, "Message of the President of the United States to the Two Houses of Congress, at the Commencement of the Second Session of the Thirty-Seventh Congress," history.state.gov/historicaldocuments/frus1861/d55.

26. Lieber, *Manual of Political Ethics*, 654.

but rather "a simple recognition of fact and reality; and nothing remains to be decided except the expediency of advantage, which we leave to the proper authorities." The violence of the French Revolution's civil war in the Vendée was not some dark premonition of what nationalist feeling might enable, but a case where the combatants "were simply infuriated against one another." In Lieber's view, there was no reason to make the question of recognition overly abstract— "the two parties, whatever their differences are, will, at all events, acknowledge one another as men in arms, accustomed to go straightforward to the point in question. Soldiers settle matters of this sort readily enough."[27]

Despite various controversies, in the summer of 1862, the Union and Confederate governments would formally organize a cartel to govern the exchange and paroling of prisoners of war. The escalating violence of the war would show the limits of soldierly pragmatism, however. The legal cartel and regime would collapse by the summer of 1863, partly due to an error Lieber himself made in the wording of General Orders No. 100 that Confederate authorities would exploit for pragmatic military advantage, but more importantly, by the unwillingness of Confederate military authorities to recognize African-American Union troops as legitimate combatants protected by the law of war. That unwillingness led to a multitude of infamous massacres of black Union troops by enraged Confederate soldiers after the former had duly surrendered.[28]

Even as the war's violence inexorably escalated, Lieber sought to codify and guide the legal basis of the Union's war efforts. It helped that Major General Henry Wager Halleck, a notable legal authority himself, had become general-in-chief of the Union Army in the summer of 1862. Lieber had corresponded with Halleck beforehand, and the two had met when Lieber sought out his wounded son in Union hospitals in the aftermath of Fort Donelson. In December 1862, Halleck agreed to convene a board chaired by Major General Ethan Allen Hitchcock that included Lieber in order to draft the proposed code. Lieber led the process, but the entire board contributed to its production, including comments by Halleck. For the sake of brevity, the board also cut some explanatory sections Lieber had included. In April 1863, the secretary of war issued the now famous Lieber Code to the Union armies as General Orders No. 100.[29]

27. Francis Lieber, "The Disposal of Prisoners," *New York Times*, August 19, 1861.

28. Witt, *Lincoln's Code*, 254–58.

29. Freidel, *Francis Lieber*, 324–27; James F Childress, "Francis Lieber's Interpretation of the Laws of War: General Orders No. 100 in the Context of His Life and Thought," *American Journal of Jurisprudence* 21:1 (1976): 37–39.

Indeed, the nineteenth-century naturalization of war as a legitimate—even ordinary—activity naturally lent itself to regulation via codes of conduct, of which Lieber's was the initial model, because it synthesized and regularized legal thinking in an easily digestible manner. The Lieber Code drew on earlier analogies of war as a form of dueling, where the moral obligations of both combatants centered on their willingness to abide by mutually agreed upon rules and rituals of violence. Lieber took the *ancien regime* analogy of war as a duel and combined it with nationalist mass politics. Moreover, while Lieber's conduct of conduct sought to limit and control violence, it also included a concept—"military necessity"—that gave tremendous discretion to soldiers:

> Military necessity admits of all direct destruction of life or limb of *armed* enemies, and of other persons whose destruction is incidentally *unavoidable* in the armed contests of the war; it allows of the capturing of every armed enemy, and every enemy of importance to the hostile government, or of peculiar danger to the captor; it allows of all destruction of property, and obstruction of the ways and channels of traffic, travel, or communication, and of all withholding of sustenance or means of life from the enemy; of the appropriation of whatever an enemy's country affords necessary for the subsistence and safety of the army, and of such deception as does not involve the breaking of good faith either positively pledged, regarding agreements entered into during the war, or supposed by the modern law of war to exist.

At the end of this long clause—one of the lengthier articles in Lieber's Code—Lieber added a cautionary, but almost perfunctorily, "Men who take up arms against one another in public war do not cease on this account to be moral beings, responsible to one another and to God." Lieber gave further definition in the following article to what bound the principle of necessity by excluding "cruelty—that is, the infliction of suffering for the sake of suffering or for revenge, nor of maiming or wounding except in fight, nor of torture to extort confessions. . . . in general, military necessity does not include any act of hostility which makes the return to peace unnecessarily difficult."[30]

Lieber and General Orders No. 100 still looked forward to the end of hostilities, and drawing on conventional Just War rhetoric from the medieval period argued, "Peace is their normal condition; war is the exception. The

30. Neff, *War and the Law of Nations*, 186; Leon Friedman, ed., *The Law of War, a Documentary History*, Volume 1 (New York, NY: Random House, 1972), 161, emphasis in original.

ultimate object of all modern war is a renewed state of peace."[31] Lieber explicitly laid claim to the progressive historical narrative his successors would also cite:

> as civilization has advanced during the last centuries, so has likewise steadily advanced, especially in war on land, the distinction between the private individual belonging to a hostile country and the hostile country itself, with its men in arms. The principle has been more and acknowledged that the unarmed citizen is to be spared in person, property, and honor as much as the exigencies of war will admit.

Lieber thus laid down one of the core distinctions of the current law of war—the distinction between combatants and non-combatants, with special protection for the latter. As the St. Petersburg Resolution of 1868 put it, "the only legitimate object which states should endeavor to accomplish during war is to weaken the military forces of the enemy."[32]

However, a sharp edge closely shadowed that borderline bromide—"exigencies" and "military necessity" limited civilian protections. Lieber bluntly stated, "The more vigorously wars are pursued, the better it is for humanity. Sharp wars are brief." Helmuth von Moltke would later echo Lieber's sentiment: "The greatest benefit in war is that it be ended promptly." However, the Prussian general would use that very idea to repudiate specifically the St. Petersburg declaration, asserting that "it was necessary to attack all the resources of the enemy *government*, its finances, its railroads, its provisions and even its prestige." Moltke wrote those lines to Johann K. Bluntschi, one of Lieber's early imitators in the codification of the law of war. On this point, though Lieber and Moltke diverged, their differences were not hard and fast. Indeed, Halleck himself had earlier subscribed to an English-language tradition of military lawyers seeing war as a contest between whole populations, "that every member of the one nation is authorized to commit hostilities against every member of the other . . . permitted by the general laws of war, and subject only to the limitations and exceptions permitted by such laws."[33] Moreover, both Lieber and Moltke repudiated pacificism; the latter dismissed

---

31. Friedman, *The Law of War*, 192

32. Friedman, *The Law of War*, 164, 162, 192.

33. Friedman, *The Law of War*, 164; Neff, *War and the Law of Nations*, 205, emphasis in original; H. W. Halleck, *International Law; or, Rules Regulating the Intercourse of States in Peace and War* (New York, NY: D. Van Nostrand, 1861), 345; Francis Lieber to Charles Sumner and George Hillard, March 16, 1844, Francis Lieber Papers.

perpetual peace as "not even a beautiful dream" and declared war "an element of the order of the world established by God" in which "the noblest virtues of man are developed."[34] Even before the Civil War, Lieber had declared war a civilizing force:

> Imagine mankind without coercion into states. Millions upon millions in solitary and selfish contentment on insulated patches of banana fields. Is that civilization. Blood is occasionally the rich dew of History.[35]

In the Lieber Code itself, Lieber declared that "it is a law and requisite of civilized existence that men live in political, continuous societies, forming organized units, called states or nations, whose constituents bear, enjoy, and suffer, advance and retrograde together, in peace and in war."[36] Lieber disagreed with the atomized individuals of social contract theory, and it is hardly surprising that he unabashedly spoke of "coercion into states" and conceived of military discipline in stringent terms. In Lieber's view, "the very meaning of an army is founded upon obedience. He therefore destroys his own character if he does not obey, and does not do it entirely as a duty."[37] Lieber did argue that soldiers in exceptional revolutionary circumstances could resist "unlawful and ruinous decrees of government."[38] For that reason, Lieber could still admire his boyhood hero, Ferdinand von Schill, as a German patriot, despite his willingness to fight against Napoleon in 1809 without orders from his sovereign. Obedience had its limits, in the same way Lieber believed individuals could leave their native states and emigrate abroad, as he had done. Schill fell in battle in his failed bid to defy Napoleon's regime, but a French court martial sentenced twelve of his captured officers to death, deeming them "common robbers."[39]

The question of obedience to state authority intersected with the issue of lawful combatants. While uniformed Confederate armies fought pitched

---

34. "Les Lois de La Guerre Sur Terre: Lettres de M. Le Comte de Moltke et de M. Bluntschli," *Revue de Droit International et de Législation Comparée* 13:1 (1881): 79–84. For the earlier quotation of Moltke, I used Neff's translation. This quotation is my own translation.

35. Francis Lieber, *Letters to Charles Sumner and George Hillard*, March 16, 1844, Box 41, Francis Lieber Papers.

36. Friedman, *The Law of War*, 162.

37. Lieber, *Manual of Political Ethics*, 667.

38. Lieber, *Manual of Political Ethics*, 667.

39. Francis Lieber, "A Reminiscence," *Southern Literary Messenger* 2:9 (August 1836): 537; Alexander Mikaberidze, *The Napoleonic Wars: A Global History* (New York, NY: Oxford University Press, 2020), 317.

battles with Union armies, large numbers of secessionist guerrillas harassed federal authorities in territory that was recaptured from the Confederacy. In the wide geographic expanses of the western theater, this proved to be an especially vexatious problem, where Union armies found it difficult to distinguish between inoffensive civilians and guerillas, because the latter did not wear uniforms and concealed their weapons when federal authorities approached. Guerrillas frequently verged into banditry, theft, and violence disconnected from any political cause. Indeed, on balance, guerrillas hurt the Confederate war effort more than they assisted it due to the long-term dislocations they inflicted on the Confederate civilian population. But this was no comfort to Union authorities who sought to pacify formerly Confederate territory. Lieber sought to better define the distinction between legitimate soldiers fighting under discipline and guerrillas, and what special measures federal military authorities could utilize toward the latter. He defined illegitimate guerrillas as:

> Men, or squads of men, who commit hostilities, whether by fighting, or inroads for destruction or plunder, or by raids of any kind, without commission, without being part and portion of the organized hostile army, and without sharing continuously in the war, but who do so with intermitting returns to their homes and avocations, or with the occasional assumption of the semblance of peaceful pursuits, divesting themselves of the character or appearance of soldiers—such men, or squads of men, are not public enemies, and, therefore, if captured, are not entitled to the privileges of prisoners of war, but shall be treated summarily as highway robbers or pirates.

In contrast, partisans fighting in small groups, separate from the main body of the army retained their protected status as potential prisoners of war as long as they wore their uniforms. Scouts and spies, however—defined as individuals who did not wear their own country's uniforms—"are treated as spies, and suffer death."[40]

Prisoners of war, in contrast, were to be "subject to no punishment for being a public enemy, nor is any revenge wreaked upon him by the intentional infliction of any suffering, or disgrace, by cruel imprisonment, want

---

40. Daniel E. Sutherland, *A Savage Conflict: The Decisive Role of Guerrillas in the American Civil War* (Chapel Hill, NC: University of North Carolina Press, 2009), x; Friedman, *The Law of War*, 173–74.

of food, by mutilation, death, or any barbarity." Lieber also stipulated that prisoners of war "shall be fed upon [sic] plain and wholesome food, whenever practicable, and treated with humanity." Furthermore, "every captured wounded enemy shall be medically treated, according to the ability of the medical staff." Lieber's attempt to codify protections for the wounded harkened back to his own experiences fighting in a pitched battle where having "to assist in getting a cannon over the mangled bodies of comrades or enemies, leaping in agony when the heavy wheel crossed over them, has impressed itself with indelible horror upon on my mind." He himself had nearly been buried with the dead after being robbed by peasants scavenging amidst the wounded and the dead, but Lieber had also experienced the sympathy and kindness of strangers.[41]

Lieber's code of conduct included specific measures to protect civilians. It declared that "the United States acknowledge and protect, in hostile countries occupied by them, religion and morality; strictly private property, the persons of the inhabitants, especially those of women: and the sacredness of domestic relations. Offenses to the contrary shall be rigorously punished." It also gave special protections to churches, hospitals, educational institutions, and other charitable organizations, along with protections for works of art and cultural collections. Nevertheless, the imperious nature of military necessity still hovered over these provisions. Lieber made that explicitly clear: "When a commander of a besieged place expels the noncombatants, in order to lessen the number of those who consume his stock of provisions, it is lawful, though an extreme measure, to drive them back, so as to hasten on the surrender."[42]

Lieber's own description of a child caught in the crossfire at Ligny haunts his code's attempts to protect noncombatants—"I observed a hog and a child both equally bewildered; they must have soon been killed, and as I never can omit observing contrasts, I noticed a bird anxiously flying about its young ones and striving to protect them in this tremendous uproar and carnage." Lieber also experienced the consequences of hungry soldiers searching for food. After eating some raw pork, he went out with a foraging party and "in one house, stripped of everything, we found a young woman with an infant, by the side of her father, who had been beaten and wounded by some marauding enemies. She asked us for a piece of bread; we had none. We gave her some

---

41. Friedman, *The Law of War*, 169, 172–73; Lieber, "Of the Battle of Waterloo," 157, 164–67.
42. Friedman, *The Law of War*, 162, 165.

potatoes which we had just found, but she said she had nothing to cook them with." In a darker episode, Lieber admitted to threatening a peasant who at first claimed to have no food for some bread—"I told my comrade to hold him, while I would seem to prepare to shoot him; he brought us a small loaf." While matter-of-fact in his description, Lieber also remarked that "no one knows what the enjoyments of the palate are who has not really suffered from hunger or thirst." Once again, in the code he developed in his old age, Lieber made provisions for an army's pragmatic need for supplies, and while private property was protected in principle, his code also declared that military necessity authorized the seizure of private property.[43]

Like his American contemporaries, Lieber's conception of warfare and armies involved the nation-state, organization, discipline, and scientific organization. Union soldiers should wear uniforms and obey their lawful superiors, who in turn were guided by the rationally derived code of conduct Lieber had helped devise. That code in turn came out of a positivist legal tradition that saw itself as allied with the sciences. Indeed, Lieber later recounted that, during his planning for his misadventure in Greece, "an engineer officer had procured in Paris the best and most useful instruments, and, besides these, we possessed several maps, box-compasses, spy-glasses, and other things required in war." Shortly before that ill-fated venture, Sylvanus Thayer had also traveled to Europe to collect scientific instruments and books for the United States Military Academy at West Point, whose scientific curriculum then educated Halleck.[44]

While historians looking back at this period have seen a tension between the law of war and technological advance, nineteenth-century actors would not necessarily have recognized such an opposition. For example, during the Mexican War then-Lt. Col. Hitchcock (future chair of the board that produced the Lieber Code) boasted of the invading US Army's technical skills at the siege of Veracruz even as he denigrated the war's larger morality:

> Our approach and our entire proceedings have been conducted under the direction of scientific Engineers & everything has proceeded according to known rules of the art of war. Hence the loss has been very slight—of course

43. Lieber, "Of the Battle of Waterloo," 156, 159–60; Friedman, *The Law of War*, 165.

44. Perry, *The Life and Letters of Francis Lieber*, 34–35; Wayne Wei-siang Hsieh, *West Pointers and the Civil War: The Old Army in War and Peace* (Chapel Hill, NC: University of North Carolina Press, 2009), 17–20.

I mean comparatively. No loss in this infamous war is slight. We have not acted neighborly towards our weak brother, but you know all I think of this.

As Lieber himself put it when describing his own faculty appointment at Columbia, "to me have been assigned the sciences which treat of man in his social relations, of humanity in all its phases in society."[45]

In Lieber's view, Union victory vindicated his progressive and liberal visions of history. It certainly assuaged the grief and loss suffered by his own family during the war. Nevertheless, despite its later influence in the legal sphere, we should not overstate the Lieber Code's actual direct effect on the conduct of the Union armies. In many respects, the code ratified prior federal military practice regarding problems such as guerrillas, and customary practices related to flags of truce and the like. Local Union military commanders possessed a great deal of practical autonomy in how they dealt with civilians— an autonomy that Lieber himself had recognized with his provisions on military necessity. Indeed, part of the reason the code became so influential later on was that it simply codified in a more systematic way the common practice of most Western military professionals. It could thus never satisfy the desires of pacifists who hoped to ban war outright, but it might serve as a more plausible brake on Clausewitz's dynamic of escalating violence than utopian pacifism.

Those wartime practices helped protect the college campus where Lieber once taught when the war came directly to Columbia, South Carolina. In February 1865, the city surrendered to William T. Sherman's forces, and in the ensuing chaos, approximately a third of the town burned down due to fires set by retreating Confederate forces seeking to destroy state property, drunken rioting by both civilians and Union troops, and the general chaos that advocates of order such as Lieber feared. In the end, a fresh and sober brigade of Union troops led by Major General O. O. Howard, who later became known for various postwar humanitarian efforts, restored order by force. Because it had been converted into a hospital, Union forces physically protected the South Carolina College campus, which thus escaped the fire and devastation. The war had saved the Union and destroyed slavery, but it had not brought about an end to political strife nor had it created a regime of perfect justice. Its violence had maimed and killed countless Americans, including two of

45. Ethan Allen Hitchcock to Elizabeth Nicholls, March 27, 1847, Ethan Allen Hitchcock Papers, Manuscript Division, Library of Congress, Washington DC; Lieber, "History and Political Science Necessary Studies in Free Countries," 336.

Lieber's own sons, but amidst all the chaos, the Union Army had obeyed the precepts of Lieber's code and protected a college-campus-turned-hospital from the torch.[46]

Critics then and now of the liberal international order that Lieber helped midwife focus on its shortcoming and failings. Yet the ghosts of violent escalation discerned by Clausewitz haunt any Kantian dream of perpetual peace. While Clausewitz sought to understand the fundamental essence of war, Lieber sought to bind it with rules and rituals rooted in the disciplinary institutions Foucault cited as the crucible sources of modernity—just as his commander had steadied Lieber's nerves at Ligny with drill and discipline. However, in a world where climate change, pandemics, resurgent great power conflict, and various brands of political extremism have compounded the Cold War's risk of nuclear annihilation, it remains to be seen as to whether any form of order—liberal or not—can contain "the violence that we ourselves are in the process of amassing and that is looming over our own heads."[47]

46. Marion Brunson Lucas, *Sherman and the Burning of Columbia* (College Station, TX: Texas A & M University Press, 1988) 12–13, 117, 100–1.

47. Girard and Chantre, *Battling to the End*, xvi.

CHAPTER 17

Japan Caught between Maritime and Continental Imperialism

S.C.M. Paine[1]

Imperial Japan's leaders agreed on the policy objective of transforming Japan into a great power, but disagreed over whether to emphasize force or persuasion, to act unilaterally or in concert with allies, to follow a maritime or a continental security paradigm. In other words, theirs was a difference over the strategy, not the strategic objective. They fought two pairs of wars as means to the ends. When they followed a maritime security paradigm, as they did in the First Sino-Japanese War (1894–95) and the Russo-Japanese War (1904–5), they furthered their strategic objective. When they followed a continental security paradigm, as they did in the Second Sino-Japanese War (1931–45) that escalated into World War II Pacific (1941–45), they destroyed their country.

Three features distinguish sea powers from land powers: (1) the ability versus inability to defend primarily at sea, (2) the reliance on exterior versus interior lines of communication in wartime, and (3) the resulting focus on access to versus insulation from neighbors.[2] As an island power, an oceanic moat

---

1. The views expressed are those of the author, not necessarily of the US Government, the US Department of Defense, the US Navy Department, or the US Naval War College. This chapter draws on S.C.M. Paine, *The Japanese Empire: Grand Strategy from the Meiji Restoration to the Pacific War* (New York, NY: Cambridge University Press, 2017), as well as other sources cited in the notes that follow.

2. S.C.M. Paine, "Maritime Solutions to Continental Conundrums," *Proceedings of the U.S. Naval Institute* 147:1422 (2021), https://www.usni.org/magazines/proceedings/2021/august/maritime-solutions-continental-conundrums.

protected Japan from invasion, so, unlike a continental power, Japan could defend itself primarily at sea, but access to neighbors required crossing the sea on exterior lines. Import dependence meant exterior lines loomed large for trade as well. In contrast, China and Russia were great continental powers. Both had repeatedly leveraged interior lines and resource self-sufficiency to survive devastating overland invasions by multiple neighbors. Huge distances and topographical barriers insulated virtually all of Russia and most of China from temperate seas. A continental power must prioritize defense against landward threats. So, a continental security paradigm relies on territorial control, large armies, exclusive zones, and overmatching neighbors in order to wall off threats. In contrast, the comparative security bestowed by a moat allows maritime powers to follow a security paradigm leveraging trade, alliances, international laws to minimize transaction costs, and connections with others to create wealth and derive national security from wealth and friends. Unlike armies, navies are rarely decisive in wartime. Therefore, maritime powers must integrate multiple instruments of power.

In the first two wars, Japanese leaders crafted a grand strategy—grand in its integration of multiple instruments of national power. In the second pair, Japanese leaders reduced strategy to the operational level of war where they incorrectly assumed strategic victory would be found. Instead, they ruined themselves and their neighbors, who have neither forgotten nor forgiven the consequences—a multigenerational, negative strategic effect. In the interwar period separating these two pairs of wars, the Japanese army scored a big bureaucratic win by gradually taking over the government. This skewed civil-military relations toward military solutions for political problems, ultimately ruining the army, the country, and the citizenry. Winning is always defined at the strategic level by the attainment of national objectives, never at the operational level by the attainment of military objectives. Wars and bureaucratic fights are a means, not an end. Those who lose sight of this put their nation at risk.

I

In the nineteenth century, in the face of an unprecedented national security threat, the Japanese made a careful assessment of the world as it was, not as they wished it were. Based on that assessment, they set a feasible policy objective and tailored a strategy integrating all instruments of national power to achieve it. For Japan as a maritime power and in distinction to continental powers, the navy was central to these plans.

The Industrial Revolution posed an unprecedented national security threat to the unindustrialized world. The compounding effects of economic growth, institutional changes, and technological innovations in industrializing societies overturned the international balance of power, rendering traditional security paradigms ineffective. Japan watched in horror as the West projected force on exterior lines from the far side of the globe in the two opium wars to defeat China, the theretofore eternally dominant power of Asia. Unlike China, which focused on modernizing the military instrument of national power, only to lose a succession of wars, the Japanese conducted a detailed assessment of the national security threat.

Even before the Boshin War (1868–69) that brought the Meiji Restoration generation to power, both the fading Tokugawa Shogunate and the large feudal domains sent students abroad, initially to study technical subjects, but soon encompassing Western civil and military institutions. The new Meiji government sent top leaders on fact-finding missions. The most famous was the two-year Iwakura mission, which visited eleven European countries plus the United States to examine their military, political, economic, legal, social, and educational institutions. Prussia impressed the mission's members most.[3]

The Iwakura mission arrived in Europe just as Otto von Bismarck completed the unification of the numerous Germanic principalities under Prussian hegemony to create the modern state of Germany. At the time Japan was also divided into numerous competing semi-independent domains. So, the Prussian model of asserting central control through dual lines of authority from its emperor and legislature in order to win incremental limited wars for territorial unification seemed highly relevant to the quest to transform Japan into a unified state and regional power.

During these missions, the extensive railway and telegraph systems, the gas-lit cities, and steam-powered factories produced the realization that a strategy of resistance would result in military defeat as had occurred in China, and the conclusion that the sources of Western power were not merely technological or military, but also institutional and civilian. Japan's problem was not simply modernization, meaning the acquisition of the most up-to-date technology (let alone just armaments), but also westernization, meaning the introduction

3. Marius B. Jansen, "The Meiji Restoration," in *The Cambridge History of Japan*, Marius B. Jansen, ed. (Cambridge: Cambridge University Press, 1989), 336; Sukehiro Hirakawa, "Japan's Turn to the West," in *Cambridge History of Japan*, Jansen, ed., 459; W. G. Beasley, *The Meiji Restoration* (Stanford, CA: Stanford University Press, 1972), 370.

of westernized civil and military institutions. Without westernization Japan could not become an innovator of state-of-the-art technologies, but instead would remain a mere consumer. So, it must westernize in order to modernize.

Based on this assessment of Japanese weaknesses and Western strengths, the Meiji leadership set aside the Chinese leadership's prized but unfeasible objective of retaining a civilization unaltered. Instead, it set the contentious but feasible objective of transforming Japan into a great power capable of defending its national security. It formulated a two-stage strategy, beginning with a domestic phase entailing the selective westernization of Japan's civil and military institutions in order to modernize its military and economy. This would achieve the intermediary diplomatic objective of treaty revision to regain sovereignty over its economic policy. A foreign phase followed, entailing the creation of an empire of sufficient size to parry the Western threat.

Within two decades, the Meiji generation had westernized an impressive array of institutions. In 1869, a year after assuming power, the new government upended the domestic power structure by eliminating the feudal domains long fragmenting Japan. It then turned from the top to the bottom of the social pyramid—from feudal lords to children. In 1872, elementary education became compulsory in recognition that productivity required literacy. Higher education came in 1886 with the founding of the first imperial university. Major military reforms included universal conscription (1873), the bifurcation of the War Ministry to establish a separate Navy Ministry (1873), the creation of the army General Staff (1878), the founding of the Staff College (1883), and the reorganization of the army into mobile divisions (1888). Japan modeled its army on Prussia and its fleet on Britain. The political system emulated Europe with the creation of a cabinet subordinate to a prime minister (1885), introduction of a civil service examination system (1887), promulgation of a constitution (1889), and the convening of the Diet (1890). The government also westernized the financial system with the creation of the Bank of Japan (1882) and its legal system with a new criminal code (1882), code of civil procedure (1890), and a reorganized judiciary (1890). These collectively became known as the Meiji Reforms in deference to the reigning (and therefore legitimating) Meiji emperor.[4]

Once the domestic reforms were in place, the government turned to renegotiating its treaties on the basis of juridical equality. As in China, the Western-imposed treaty port system entailed trade in designated treaty ports,

---

4. S.C.M. Paine, *The Sino-Japanese War of 1894–1895* (Cambridge: Cambridge University Press, 2003), 87.

most-favored-nation treaty clauses guaranteeing that any benefits negotiated by one foreign power accrued to all, and extraterritoriality granting home-country (not host-country) legal protections to Westerners, who also set, collected, and delivered customs duties to the host government, China. There were no reciprocal rights for Asians in Europe, hence the name "unequal treaties." The westernization of Japanese political and legal institutions removed the rationale for unequal treaties and on July 16, 1894, Britain concluded a new treaty with Japan on the basis of juridical equality. The other great powers soon followed suit.[5] Treaty revision marked the culmination of the domestic phase of Japan's grand strategy. During this phase, the government carefully eschewed foreign wars to avoid derailing the reforms, whereas China lurched from one military or diplomatic loss to the next and did not eliminate the treaty port system until the 1940s with the West and the 1950s with Russia.

II

Immediately after finishing the domestic phase of its grand strategy, the Meiji generation embarked on the foreign policy phase, which vacillated between a continental empire on the Asian mainland and a maritime empire along island chains to Taiwan. Japan emulated the strategy of Prussia's Otto von Bismarck, whose succession of short, regional wars for limited objectives—the Danish War (1864), the Austro-Prussian War (1866), and the Franco-Prussian War (1870–71)—together elevated Prussia from the weakest of the five European great powers (Britain, Russia, France, Austria, and Prussia) to the number two spot behind Britain without these competitors realizing what was happening until it was done. Bismarck's objectives were limited to land outside core Danish or Austrian territory, and only a small part of French territory, not the unlimited objective of regime change in any of these countries.

On July 25, 1894, nine days after treaty revision with Britain, Japan went to war with China to control Korea. Instability in Korea, China's most important tributary and nearest invasion route to Japan, had already invited foreign intervention with British management of customs collection and Russian ambitions for empire. Russian plans, announced in 1891, to build a trans-Siberian railway stretching to Vladivostok would enable efficient troop deployments where no one else could. This threatened to close Japan's window of opportunity for empire, a window that had only just opened with treaty revision. The

5. Paine, *The Sino-Japanese War of 1894–1895*, 101.

First Sino-Japanese War would be Japan's first in the series of three aimed at the containment of Russia in order to create and then preserve an empire meant to defend Japan.

In the first war, Japan's stated objective was to expel China from the Korean Peninsula on the pretext that Chinese intrusions violated Korean sovereignty (so did Japan's) in order to impose a Meiji reform package that would fix Korea's endemic instability. Unstated goals included the negative objective of preventing Russian expansion and the positive objective of overturning the regional balance of power by supplanting China as the dominant power.[6] No one but the Japanese saw this coming. To achieve these strategic objectives, Japanese leaders set three operational objectives: expel China from Korea, permanently secure Japanese sea lines of communications to Korea, and maximize imperial winnings, which the navy and diplomats thought should be Taiwan but the army thought should be Manchuria's Liaodong Peninsula.

A tall order requires an accurate assessment of available opportunities and unavoidable constraints—the strategic cards dealt. The choices on how to play the hand constitute the strategy. Treaty revision opened an opportunity for Japan to settle its foreign policy. In addition, a century of internal rebellions, killing tens of millions and wrecking entire provinces, had gravely weakened China's Qing dynasty and undermined the legitimacy of continued Manchu minority rule over the subjugated Han majority. Simultaneously, Korea suffered even greater governmental dysfunction and unrest. The long-suffering peasantry erupted in the largest uprising in its history. When the ruling house invited China, its suzerain, to intervene, Japan stepped in to protect its nationals.

A strategy of military intervention entailed huge risks. The sheer size of the Korean theater would stretch Japan's limited manpower, in contrast to China's bottomless manpower and resource potential. China's problem was its difficulty mobilizing its forces. Japan could lose either on land or at sea, whereas China could lose only on land because interior lines meant it did not require the sea to reach the theater. So, it could afford to risk its fleet in ways that Japan could not. Japan also faced time constraints; it must conclude hostilities before its window of opportunity slammed shut with completion of the Trans-Siberian Railway, anticipated soon after 1900. By definition, a window of opportunity means that time is on someone else's side.

---

6. A positive objective makes something happen, while a negative objective prevents something from happening. The former is visible, while the latter is invisible and therefore disputable.

The war was comprised of two pairs of key battles plus a naval coda. The first pair occurred in a three-day period in mid-September 1894, when the Japanese army defeated the Chinese at Pyongyang. This resulted in the expulsion of Chinese forces from the Korean Peninsula, the original stated war aim. Meanwhile, the Japanese navy defeated the state-of-the-art Chinese Beiyang Fleet in the Battle of the Yalu. This resulted in Japanese command of the sea because China avoided engaging the opposing navy again.

After the Korean Campaign, Japan launched a succession of three others. The first two, the Manchurian and Shandong Campaigns (over the winter of 1894–95), focused on the land and sea approaches to Beijing, threatening a pincer movement on the capital. The Japanese army took the state-of-the-art naval base at Lüshun (Port Arthur) by land and the Japanese navy blockaded the remaining Chinese naval base at Weihaiwei. Both services jointly destroyed the trapped fleet, ending Chinese naval power for the next century because China could not afford a replacement. The naval coda, the Battle for the Pescadores, which secured a maritime empire, coincided with the peace negotiations.

China followed Japan's script by fighting incompetently in predictable places, blunders Japan leveraged. China ceded the initiative by defending such cities as Pyongyang behind its walls, which crumbled before modern artillery, instead of defending at river crossings and mountain passes that Japanese troops had to traverse—locations that geography made both predictable and dangerous and that China had ample time to leverage. The Chinese Beiyang Fleet sat out the war instead of destroying troop transports and supply ships at sea. Rather than fleeing from Pyongyang to the Yalu River, Chinese forces could have combined with Koreans to deliver an insurgency to threaten Japanese supply lines. Had China exacerbated Japan's logistical problems by always fighting inland, cold and starvation would have weakened Japan. China also botched war termination. Its failure to send duly accredited negotiators gave Japan the opportunity to send them home and use the extra time to capture the Pescadores and successfully demand sovereignty over Taiwan. In other words, China was a "cooperative adversary" in the sense that it played its available cards poorly, unwittingly following the Japanese script, thus producing an optimal outcome for Japan, not China.

The Japanese army overreached with demands for the Liaodong Peninsula—an area Russia proclaimed off limits to others. When Russia, France, and Germany intervened to demand Japan withdraw in return for a higher indemnity from China, Japan had to back down. It could not take on three great European powers. Despite the humiliation, the indemnity made the war profitable. Domestically, the outcome validated the very controversial westernization program that had appalled traditionalists. Military prestige emerged greatly enhanced. Regionally, Japan supplanted China as the dominant power—unprecedented in Asian history. Internationally, Japan became a recognized great power as demonstrated by the Anglo-Japanese Alliance of 1902, Britain's only long-term alliance between the Napoleonic Wars and World War I. But Japan's victory on Russia's vulnerable Siberian frontier precipitated an arms race with Russia, which made an unprecedented (and misguided) shift in foreign policy priorities from Europe to Asia, setting the stage for another war.

III

Russia's occupation of Manchuria, a region exceeding the combined area of France and Germany, in response to the Boxer Uprising (1899–1900) threatened Japan's plans for empire. Japan exhausted diplomacy when Russia pocket vetoed its final proposal to exchange recognition of Russia's primacy in Manchuria for Japan's in Korea. So, Japan prepared to take militarily what Russia would not cede diplomatically. This required victory within another tight window of opportunity that opened with the Anglo-Japanese Alliance but would close upon completion of the Trans-Siberian Railway, when Russian could bring its material superiority to bear—its three times Japan's population, seven times the soldiers, and eight times the gross national product.[7] But like the Qing dynasty, the Romanov dynasty was past its prime. Russia, Turkey, and Montenegro remained the only European states without a parliament. Assassinations of public figures resumed when Tsar Nicholas II stonewalled demands for political representation from his increasingly well-educated urban population.

As in the previous war, Japan marshalled and integrated multiple instruments of national power into a coherent strategy. Diplomacy had isolated Russian through the Anglo-Japanese alliance. The treaty terms promised British intervention should Russia combine with another power against Japan. The terms went into effect for five years, until 1907. By 1904, Japan had used the previous war's indemnity to rearm before Russia did. But Russian naval

---

7. B.R. Mitchell, ed., *European Historical Statistics 1750–1970* (New York, NY: Columbia University Press, 1978), 7; Ian Nish, *The Russo-Japanese War, 1904–5*, Volume 1 (Kent, UK: Global Oriental, 2003), 19; Ono Keishi, "Japan's Monetary Mobilization for War," in *The Russo-Japanese War in Global Perspective*, John W. Steinberg, et al., eds. Volume 2 (Leiden: Brill, 2007), 253.

capabilities in Asia would surpass Japan's soon after 1904.[8] Japan also secured a succession of foreign loans that ultimately financed thirty-eight percent of the war.[9] At war's start, Russia had yet to repair two thirds of the Manchurian section of the Trans-Siberian Railway that the Boxers had damaged.[10] The railway was not double-tracked and lacked a link around Lake Baikal, which approximated Switzerland in size. At the onset of hostilities, it could transport 20,000 to 40,000 men per month to the front; that capacity reached 100,000 men per month by the end. If this carrying capacity had been available from the start, Russia would have had numerical superiority throughout.[11]

Japanese reconnaissance included Chinese scouting units behind Russian lines, Chinese spies within Russian camps, and the deployment of Colonel (later General) Akashi Motojirō to coordinate spies from the Japanese legation in Stockholm, funding Russian, Polish, and Finnish revolutionaries to stir up trouble throughout the Russian empire.[12] The Japanese cultivated Chinese loyalties by paying for local goods, creating a wartime economic boom in Manchuria.[13] Japan located Russian ships by intercepting fleet communications.[14] Japan also pre-positioned representatives in the United States to request mediation at the appropriate moment.

The army's 1903 war plan emphasized speed and initiative so that Japan could leverage its initial, but temporary, numerical superiority in order to swarm northward up the Korean Peninsula by foot and up the Liaodong Peninsula by rail to converge in a war-winning battle, perhaps in the vicinity of Liaoyang, before Russian could adequately mobilize. It would be a replay of the Franco-Prussian War's double envelopment at the Battle of Sedan.[15] On

8. Donald Keene, *Emperor of Japan* (New York, NY: Columbia University Press, 2002), 581, 589.

9. Janet Hunter, "The Limits of Financial Power: Japanese Foreign Borrowing and the Russo-Japanese War," in *Great Powers and Little Wars*, Hamish Ion and E.J. Errington, eds. (Westport, CT: Praeger, 1993), 152.

10. S.C.M. Paine, *Imperial Rivals: China, Russia, and Their Disputed Frontier* (Armonk, NY: M. E. Sharpe, 1996), 215.

11. E.L.V. Cordonnier, *The Japanese in Manchuria 1904*, Volume 1, trans. Capt. C. F. Atkinson (London: Hugh Rees, 1912), 1, 38.

12. Denis and Peggy Warner, *The Tide at Sunrise: A History of the Russo-Japanese War, 1904–1905* (New York, NY: Charterhouse, 1974), 451–52; Donald Keene, *Emperor of Japan*, 845.

13. James Reardon-Anderson, *Reluctant Pioneers* (Stanford, CA: Stanford University Press, 2005), 190)

14. Eduard J. Drea, *MacArthur's ULTRA* (Lawrence, KS: University of Kansas Press, 1992), 13.

15. Y. Tak Matsusaka, "Human Bullets, General Nogi, and the Myth of Port Arthur," in *The Russo-Japanese War in Global Perspective*, David Wolff et al., eds. Volume 1 (London: Brill, 2007), 181–82.

February 8, 1904, Japan opened hostilities with a surprise attack to destroy Russia's Port Arthur Squadron in its homeport of Lüshun (Port Arthur) at the tip of the Liaodong Peninsula. Neither country anticipated that the battle for Lüshun would become so difficult, nor so essential, to the war's outcome. Complicating Japan's plans was the small Vladivostok Squadron. Complicating Russia's plans were the 625 miles separating Lüshun and Vladivostok, which ran by Japan.

Admiral Tōgō Heihachirō and General Nogi Maresuke's joint solution—the former to cork the Port Arthur Squadron in port until the latter destroyed it by land—was the high-water mark of Japanese army-navy coordination. Though the surprise attack failed to destroy the squadron, which remained a fleet in being, posing a potential threat to Japan's sea lines of communication, the attack did insure safe simultaneous troop landings on the Korean Peninsula for the long hike northward to Shenyang (Mukden), the Qing dynasty's ancestral home. The inability to block the port entrance forced a continuous blockade.

Given the tsar's insistence on relieving Lüshun, from late May to mid-June, Russia fought (and lost) the battles of Nanshan (forty-five miles north of Lüshun) and Delisi (Te-li-ssu, eighty miles north of Lüshun) on the railway line to Harbin, located at the T-intersection between the east-west line connecting European Russia with the port of Vladivostok, and the southwestward line to Lüshun. Japan cut land access to Lüshun and soon took the nearby commercial port of Dalian to serve as its logistical hub. The tsar's forward strategy undermined field commander General Aleksei N. Kuropatkin's plans to fight only after building his forces and doing so much closer to Harbin (over 600 miles north of Lüshun) in order to force Japan to fight both outnumbered and on extended lines.[16] On June 20, the tsar doubled down by ordering the Baltic Fleet to prepare to relieve Lüshun, a quixotic mission given the distance and lack of intermediary basing for coaling or refitting.[17] The Baltic Fleet would not arrive in theater until the following May.

Meanwhile, the Port Arthur Squadron unsuccessfully tried to escape to Vladivostok on June 23 and August 10, the latter known as the Battle of the Yellow Sea, which cost numerous ships and the commanding admiral.[18] It took

16. John W. Steinberg, *All the Tsar's Men* (Baltimore, MD: John's Hopkins University Press, 2010), 123–25, 127.

17. Warner and Warner, *Tide at Sunrise*, 304–5.

18. Vladimir A. Zolotarev and Iurii F. Sokolov, Трагедия на Дальнем Востоке [*Tragedy in the Far East*, Volume 2], (Moscow: «Аними Фортудо», 2004), 2, 415; Ian Nish, *The Russo-Japanese War*, Volume 5, 617.

two successive incoming tides for the whole squadron to exit Lüshun's narrow entrance, leaving little mystery to its movements.[19] Meanwhile, in the seven sorties of the much smaller Vladivostok Squadron before its destruction at the Battle of Ulsan on August 14, it sank troop transports and Krupp siege guns reluctantly removed from Japan's own coastal defenses. Replacement guns essential to sink the Port Arthur Squadron would not be emplaced for six months.[20]

Nine days after the Battle of the Yellow Sea that had threatened a more active Russian fleet, General Nogi doubled down with the first of four manpower-murdering assaults on Lüshun. Japan could not concentrate its forces deep in Manchuria for the anticipated a battle of annihilation as long as one army out of four remained pinned at Lüshun. Similarly, the blockade pinned the navy, which could not refit in preparation for the approaching Baltic Fleet. The first two assaults immediately preceded major land battles, the battles of Liaoyang (August 26–September 4) and Shahe (October 5–17). Liaoyang, located over 200 miles north of Lüshun and fifty-five miles south of Shenyang, was the second largest battle in history after the Battle of Sedan that the Japanese so wanted to emulate, but it left victorious Japan unable to pursue given its desperate lack of munitions, irreplaceable losses of officers, and shortage of horses.[21] The Russians counter attacked about fifteen miles south of Shenyang in the Battle of Shahe, where unbeknownst to the Russians, Japanese supplies and forces verged on collapse. But Russian morale suffered from peculating officers, inadequate clothing, incompetent command, and rampant alcoholism.

Japan followed with two more costly assaults on Lüshun, having belatedly realized the importance of a highpoint necessary to place spotters in order to adjust Japan's line of fire on the squadron trapped in port. The necessary Krupp siege guns were not in place until the fourth assault finally captured the highpoint, allowing Japan to sink the squadron within the week. Lüshun surrendered on January 2, 1905. Nogi's army was soon off to Shenyang for the long-anticipated annihilating battle. Sadly for Japan, the assaults on Lüshun had cost

19. Zolotarev and Sokolov, *Tragedy in the Far East*, Volume 1, 221–22, 240–41.

20. 田中健一 [Tanaka Kenichi] and 氷室千春 [Himuro Chiharu], eds., 東郷平八郎目で みる明治の海軍 [*The Meiji Navy in the Eyes of Tōgō Heihachirō*], (Tokyo: 東郷会社・東郷, 1995), 92–93; Warner and Warner, *The Tide as Sunrise*, 284–85, 376, 381, 427, 436.

21. Zolotarev and Sokolov, *Tragedy in the Far East*, Volume 2, 417–18; Warner and Warner, *Tide at Sunrise*, 354, 365, 373; Shumpei Okamoto, *The Japanese Oligarchy and the Russo-Japanese War* (New York, NY: Columbia University Press, 1970), 105–6.

the equivalent of an entire army.[22] Sadly for Russia, it no longer had a base capable of refitting the Baltic Fleet. With the fall of Lüshun, the fleet had only one possible destination, Vladivostok, sending it right past Japan.

General Ōyama Iwao, commander of the Manchurian forces, was desperate for an annihilating battle. In the Battle of Shenyang (February 19–March 10, 1905), the largest battle in history to that date, he committed everything Japan had left. Even so, Japan deployed only 250,000 against Russia's 375,000. At battle's end, Japan verged on both military and financial exhaustion, while Russia's troop buildup continued apace. Japan requested US mediation to end the war.[23] One more land battle would have shattered the Japanese army for lack of men, arms, and horses.

Yet the tsar placed his hopes on the navy. In the Battle of Tsushima (May 27–28, 1905), Tōgō's Combined Fleet made short work of the Baltic Fleet in one of history's most lopsided naval battles. As in the first war, Japan destroyed the enemy navy virtually in toto. Tsushima was the rare decisive battle that led directly to war termination and the achievement of the war's objective. The tsar folded in the face of a gathering revolution throughout his empire over his incompetent military and political leadership. He feared that riotous reserves would join rather than suppress the unrest.[24] The United States played its scripted role to host the negotiations. As in the first war, Japan's navy took islands during the peace negotiations to gain leverage—the Pescadores in the first, and Sakhalin Island in the second.

The Portsmouth Peace Treaty confirmed the outcome of the First Sino-Japanese War yielding Japan, not China or Russia, as the dominant regional power of Asia. Whereas at war's outset, Japan had been willing to trade Manchuria for Korea, in the end it got the southern halves of Manchuria and Sakhalin, too.[25] Russia lost influence in Korea, which soon became a Japanese

22. Shumpei Okamoto, *The Japanese Oligarchy*, 106; Warner and Warner, *Tide at Sunrise*, 388–90, 427; Bruce W. Menning, *Bayonets Before Bullets* (Bloomington, IN: Indiana University Press, 1992), 164–71, 304; Y. Tak Matsusaka, "Human Bullets, General Nogi, and the Myth of Port Arthur," 180, 182–83, 188, 190; Ian H. Nish, *The Russo-Japanese War*, Volume 6, 274, 328, 336, 4.

23. Warner and Warner, *Tide at Sunrise*, 466–67; Shumpei Okamoto, *The Japanese Oligarchy*, 108–9, 111, 153; E.L.V. Cordonnier, *The Japanese in Manchuria 1904*, Volume 1, 68.

24. John Bushnell, "The Specter of Mutinous Reserves: How the War Produced the October Manifesto," in *The Russo-Japanese War in Global Perspective*, Steinberg et al., eds., Volume 1 (London: Brill, 2005), 333–49.

25. Imperial Japanese Ministry of Foreign Affairs, *Correspondence Regarding the Negotiations between Japan and Russia (1903-1904)*, presented to the Imperial Diet, March 1904, 3–4, 28–33; S.C.M. Paine, *Imperial Rivals*, 243–44.

protectorate. Russia's very expensive south Manchurian railway concessions became an indemnity in kind for Japan, which had secured its strategic objective of a continental empire.

In reality, first Chinese and then Russian incompetence had saved Japan. Like the failing Qing dynasty, the failing Romanov dynasty was a cooperative adversary that could have played its cards quite differently. Had Russia spent its defense budgets on the railway systems to deploy its armies, as a continental power should, instead of on capital ships that it could not reliably deploy in wartime, this would have yielded numerical superiority of ground troops from start to finish. As it was, Russia increased its troop levels in theater from 98,000 in February 1904 to 149,000 in August 1904 at the Battle of Liaoyang, when its numbers creeped past Japan's, and reached 788,000 in August 1905, just one month before the conclusion of the peace treaty. At that time, Russia had deployed just forty percent of its army to the theater, while Japan had deployed 670,000, virtually its entire army.[26] Moreover, in both wars, the population in theater was at worst neutral and often supportive of the Japanese versus the Manchus or Russians. Nevertheless, the Japanese chalked up their victories to what they had done right, not to what their enemies had done wrong. This self-deception was one of multiple unpromising trendlines that would bear cumulative long-term effects. Japan became comfortable with risk-accepting strategies. Had it not defeated the world's two largest continental powers? Clearly, will power trumped material inferiority, or so the Japanese believed. The army and navy failed to recognize that victory depended on their coordination at Lüshun. Postwar, they developed separate war plans against different adversaries, fought bitter budget battles, and refused to consult—let alone cooperate—with each other.

War had become an increasingly expensive instrument of policy. In the first one, the indemnity had yielded a fifty percent profit.[27] In the second, Japan suffered more casualties and expended more ammunition at the relatively small Battle of Nanshan than during the entire previous war.[28] Estimates differ on the relative costs of the two conflicts—multiples range from five to over eight times more expensive.[29]

---

26. Ono Keishi, "Japan's Monetary Mobilization for War," 253, 256.

27. Peter Duus, *The Rise of Modern Japan*, 2nd ed. (Boston, MA: Houghton Mifflin, 1998), 142.

28. Warner and Warner, *Tide at Sunrise*, 297.

29. 大江志乃夫 [Ōei Shinobu], 東アジやとしての日露戦争 [*East Asia's Russo-Japanese War*], (Tokyo: 立風書房, 1998), 170, 456–5; Shumpei Okamoto, *The Japanese Oligarchy*, 127.

IV

Japan, surrounded entirely by seas, could never become a continental power capable of ingesting expansive continental neighbors over great-power objections. Great continental powers generally are self-sufficient in food, energy, and war materiel, and surrounded by protective geographic barriers because they have already expanded into the most accessible contiguous areas. Often, they whittle away at neighbors. Although continental powers can suffer catastrophic defeats, their geography and resources allow the great ones to rise again.

In the interwar period, Japan's ability to profit from its mainland holdings declined as nationalism energized Korean and Chinese hostility. In East Asia, the interwar period began in 1905 with the Portsmouth Peace Treaty, not in 1919 with the Treaty of Versailles, and ended in 1931 with Japan's invasion of Manchuria, not in 1939 with Germany's invasion of Poland. Chinese and Russian decline had made the international environment of the Meiji era hospitable to Japanese ambitions for great powerhood. Rising hostile neighbors and cascading economic depressions of the interwar period threatened these ambitions.

The Bolshevik Revolution of 1917 added an ideological dimension to Russian expansion, with communism increasingly popular among laborers across Asia. Russia's Communist International (Comintern) soon established communist parties worldwide: in India, Iran, and Turkey (1921); China and Outer Mongolia (1921); Japan (1922); Korea (1925); and Laos, Malaya, the Philippines, Siam, and Vietnam (1930). As in the Boxer Uprising, Russia again invaded Manchuria with the Railway War of 1929 in an effort to regain its railway concessions renounced in its Karakhan Manifesto of 1919, promising but not delivering liberation from imperialism.[30]

Anti-Japanese nationalism increasingly unified China. Japan's Twenty-One Demands of 1915, arrogating extensive concession areas and commercial privileges throughout central and northern China, became recognized as National Humiliation Day. The convoluted post–World War I return to China by Japan of Germany's Shandong concession areas also enraged the Chinese.[31] Japan's funding of multiple warlords—who ultimately lost—along with its assassination of

---

30. S.C.M. Paine, *Imperial Rivals*, 320; Bruce A. Elleman, *Modern Chinese Warfare, 1795–1989* (London: Routledge, 2001), 182–89.

31. Bruce A. Elleman, *Wilson and China* (Armonk, NY: M.E. Sharpe, 2002).

the one in Manchuria (Zhang Zuolin) and a dustup with Nationalist troops in Jinan, both in 1928, did not raise its stock in Chinese estimations.[32]

On a platform of nationalism to unify the faction-riven country, the Nationalist Party in China oversaw the Northern Expedition (1926–28), a nationwide military campaign eliminating or coopting competing warlords. Tariff autonomy and railway nationalization became the new Nationalist government's priorities. Tariff increases swelled Nationalist customs revenues from 46 million yuan in 1927 to 385 million in 1931. Much of this trade was with Japan. The railway nationalization campaign focused on Manchuria—the location of Japan's railways.[33] Another Nationalist priority was reunification. With a succession of five encirclement campaigns (1930–34), it forced the Communists to evacuate to the far north in the Long March to desolate Yan'an. Japan feared Chinese reunification.

Simultaneously, Japan faced three economic depressions: one in 1920–21 savaging its exports as Europeans reclaimed Asia markets forfeited in World War I; another in 1927 from a run on banks over bonds issued after the Great Kantō earthquake (1923); and, the capstone event, the 1929 Great Depression, ruining trade and prospects for prosperity globally. Japan's primary trade partner, the United States, responded with the 1930 Hawley-Smoot Tariff, raising tariffs to historic highs. Between 1929 and 1931, Japanese exports halved.[34]

The brilliant Meiji generation had passed away. Nine of its members, known as the oligarchs, had set policy and strategy, but the Meiji Constitution made no mention of them, so their deaths left an institutional void. Their preeminent civil leader, Itō Hirobumi—a member of the Iwakura mission, the author of the Meiji Constitution, and the first prime minister—died in 1909. The preeminent military leader, Marshal Yamagata Aritomo—an author of the First Sino-Japanese and Russo-Japanese war plans, and founding father of the Imperial Japanese Army and police force—lived until 1922, over a decade longer, allowing him to appoint proteges throughout the government, skewing power from civil to military authority. Itō and his followers had favored civilian control over the military, party prime ministers, foreign policy in cooperation with Britain and the United States, and a constitutional monarchy ruling

32. Bruce A. Elleman and S.C.M. Paine, *Modern China: Continuity and Change, 1644 to the Present*, 2nd ed. (Lanham, MD: Rowman & Littlefield, 2019), 323.

33. S.C.M. Paine, *The Wars for Asia, 1911–1949* (New York, NY: Cambridge University Press, 2012), 20.

34. S.C.M. Paine, *The Wars for Asia*, 20–21.

through the House of Representatives. In keeping with a maritime security paradigm, Itō had focused on the economic underpinnings of power: Japan required stable, productive neighbors both to promote trade and to preclude a hostile power from invading.

The military favored military rule on the basis of imperial prerogatives, non-party cabinets, (eventually) cooperation with the Axis, national economic mobilization, and day-to-day administration through the War Ministry.[35] Yamagata's institutional legacy left the military accountable only to one man, a figurehead emperor isolated in his palace and under the thumb of the Imperial Household Ministry. The army fixated on the operational means of military occupation and operational ends of killing those who resisted, with ever less understanding that these operational means and ends, by fueling Chinese and Korean hatred, precluded the strategic end of protecting national security, let alone of promoting national prosperity.

Although the next generation had better formal educations than their parents, their very professionalism narrowed their career paths. The Meiji generation was composed of civil and military, army and navy leaders who knew each other personally. These personal connections bridged institutional divides that, upon their deaths, entrenched to become insurmountable. A wave of assassinations cemented army control over strategic objectives and operational strategy. In addition to Prime Ministers Hamaguchi Osachi (1931) and Inukai Tsuyoshi (1932), and Admiral Saitō Makoto (1936), the assassinations included Finance Ministers Inoue Junnosuke (1932) and Takahashi Korekiyo (1936), who dared suggest the financial unfeasibility of the army's preferred plans. Grand strategy was a casualty of the elimination of the civilian elements of national power.

Japan's army reverted to its samurai tradition of ground warfare, applicable when the warfare was within Japan and in order to dominate Japan, but inapplicable to expeditionary warfare crossing the sea to dominate China. Naval support is inescapable for expeditionary warfare. Crossing seas brings a host of vulnerabilities requiring instruments of national power beyond the army, most particularly finance, production, logistics, trade, and diplomacy. Mobility of all kinds—air, land, and sea—depended on oil, which Japan lacked. Armaments depended on industry that required natural resources that Japan also mostly lacked. Exterior lines of communication opened vulnerabilities that a continental security paradigm did not address.

---

35. David Anson Titus, *Palace and Politics in Prewar Japan* (New York, NY: Columbia University Press, 1974), 32–36, 138–39.

V

The primary policy objective of maintaining Japan as a great power capable of defending its national interests remained unchanged. The opportunities of the Meiji period—an opening window of opportunity with treaty revision; Korean, Chinese, and Russian domestic weakness; Japan's comparative military preparedness; and unfinished opposing railways—vanished during the interwar period. No new opportunities appeared while the old constraints remained: the huge size of Japan's theater of ambitions; its relative resource and population inferiority; and its requirement for command of the sea. Moreover, new constraints emerged—Soviet Communism, Chinese nationalism, and economic depression—requiring the addition of intervening objectives to reach the original goal.

With prosperity through trade a non-starter, Japan's army charted a course of autarky, which required having an empire of sufficient size. Manchuria, already the focus of Japanese investments, fit the bill. Within a year of the Hawley-Smoot tariff, Japan's army invaded and occupied Manchuria in a matter of months on a trumped-up charge of railway sabotage actually perpetrated by its own officers.[36] Soon afterward, the military assassinated the prime minister, eliminating party governments with the appointment of an admiral. In 1932, the Japanese navy opened a second theater in Shanghai in an attempt to pressure the Nationalists to cede Manchuria.

To legitimize the invasion, Japan installed the last Qing emperor as titular head of Manchuland (Manchukuo), but the local branch of the Imperial Japanese Army (the Kwantung or Kantō Army) actually ran the economy through the South Manchuria Railway Company. Massive investments in infrastructure, mining, and heavy industry, as well as significant investments in education followed.[37] In 1935, Russia sold Japan its Manchurian railway concessions, rolling back Russian imperialism—an important intermediary goal. Manchuria soon became the most industrialized part of Asia outside of Japan's home islands. In 1938, Japan applied the Manchukuo development formula to North China.[38] Japan could not have prosecuted its long war against China, let alone World War II Pacific, without these resources.

The Chinese were not idle. An anti-Japanese insurgency broke out in Manchuria. Once suppressed, it migrated to North China. The Nationalist government,

---

36. S.C.M. Paine, *The Wars for Asia*, 13.

37. S.C.M. Paine, "Japanese Puppet-State Building in Manchukuo" in *Nation Building, State Building, and Economic Development*, Paine, ed. (Armonk, NY: M.E. Sharpe, 2010), 66–82.

38. Paine, *Wars for Asia*, 29, 40–41.

fully preoccupied militarily in anti-Communist encirclement campaigns, resisted Japan diplomatically at the League of Nations, which denounced the invasion, whereupon Japan withdrew from the League, leaving itself diplomatically isolated. China's citizenry retaliated by boycotting Japanese goods, tanking Japan's trade with its second most important market. Most boycotts centered in south and central China, safely outside the range of the Kantō Army. Japan responded with escalatory military pressure, occupying the adjoining Rehe province in 1933, followed by a creeping North China Campaign through 1936. While China could not defeat Japan, denying it victory through guerrilla warfare was sufficient to prevent the peace that prosperity required.

Russia had other concerns. In 1936, Japan and Germany allied, signing the Anti-Comintern Pact to combat communism. To avoid a two-front war with them, Russia set up China to fight Japan. Russia promised both the Chinese Communists and Nationalists, dire enemies in the Chinese Civil War, conventional military aid if they joined a United Front against Japan. When they did, on July 7, 1937, Japan doubled down with a full-scale invasion via China's railway grid and waterways, and unleashed a bombing campaign. The Japanese army expected a Nationalist capitulation within a few months. Instead, by the end of 1937, Japan had suffered 100,000 casualties, doubled the number of divisions deployed to twenty-one, and committed 600,000 men. By the end of 1938, it had deployed thirty-four divisions totaling 1.1 million men, and by 1941, fifty-one divisions. Yet the Chinese fought on.[39]

With the escalation, Japan converted to a command economy. In 1937, the military commandeered factories and the government took over capital and commodity allocation. In 1939, the government froze prices and wages, and in 1940, imposed rationing. The military portion of the budget rose from 30.8 percent in 1931, to 69.2 percent in 1937, 75.6 percent in 1941, and finally to an economy-busting 85.3 percent in 1944. The balance between heavy and light industry changed from 38.2 percent for heavy industry in 1930, to 57.8 percent in 1937, and to a standard-of-living killing 72.7 percent in 1942. No light industry meant no consumer goods. Wages, indexed to purchasing power and set at 100 for the 1934–36 period, fell to 79.1 in 1941, and to 41.2 in 1945. The military got the planned economy it coveted as well as the hyperinflation and resource bottlenecks that the assassinated finance minister, Takahashi Korekiyo, had predicted.[40] These were the economic costs China imposed on Japan.

39. Paine, *Wars for Asia*, 21, 101–3, 128–29.
40. Paine, *Wars for Asia*, 168–69.

During the campaigns from 1937 to 1941, Japan targeted a succession of supposed Chinese centers of gravity, meaning targets that if destroyed should have caused capitulation. It beset China's receding capitals at Nanjing (1937), Wuhan (1938), and Chongqing (1938), but the last, located beyond the railway net, behind mountains, and protected by the Yangzi River rapids, survived. Japan attacked the will to resist through escalatory brutality put on horrifying display during the Rape of Nanjing (1937). It tried to eliminate the economic capacity to continue fighting. By the fall of 1938 Japan occupied China's main industrial centers (Manchuria, the Beijing-Tianjin area, Shanghai, Wuhan, and Guangzhou).[41] It destroyed Nationalist conventional forces in a succession of bitterly fought, huge battles, including Shanghai (1937), Nanjing (1937), Xuzhou (1937–38), and Wuhan (1938). Finally, Japan targeted trade and aid from the outside, starting with a full coastal blockade (1937), the occupation of Guangzhou, China's last unoccupied port (1938), and the invasion of French Indochina, the last remaining external railway link (1940).[42]

The Chinese, rather than capitulate—as the Japanese had assumed they would—traded space for time in keeping with plans developed after the first Battle for Shanghai in 1932. These plans anticipated a protracted war of attrition fought deep inland to force Japanese overextension and impose unsustainable costs.[43] The Chinese delivered a costly combination of conventional and insurgent operations. The former required Japanese forces to concentrate, the latter to disperse, and the deployment dilemma imposed spiraling costs precluding prosperity. The conventional battles included: Nanchang (1939), Suixian-Zaoyang (1939), Nanning (1939), the Nationalist Winter Offensive (1939–40), Zaoyang-Yichang (1940), the Communist Hundred Regiments Campaign(1940), Southern Henan (1941), and the Gogō Offensive (1941–43). In the second half of 1937, Japanese forces had advanced 17.4 kilometers per day. This declined to 7.6 kilometers per day in 1938, 1.1 kilometers in 1939, and finally to 0.6 kilometers in 1940.[44] The war had stalemated.

Japan's peace demands became a function of these increasing costs. Soon after the 1937 escalation, it upgraded the limited objective of the cession of

41. George E. Taylor, *The Struggle for North China* (New York, NY: Institution of Pacific Relations, 1940), 178.

42. Arakawa Ken-ichi, "Japanese Naval Blockade of China in the Second Sino-Japanese War, 1937–41," in *Naval Blockades and Seapower*, Bruce A. Elleman and S.C.M. Paine, eds. (London: Routledge, 2006), 107–9.

43. Paine, *Wars for Asia*, 133.

44. Diana Lary, *The Chinese People at War* (Cambridge: Cambridge University Press, 2010), 78.

Manchukuo to the unlimited objective of regime change for China. Unlike during the wars of the Meiji period, Japan no longer fought for remote parts of opposing empires or against Han conscripts indifferent to Manchu rule or even against Russian conscripts indifferent to Manchurian conquests, but it demanded a punitive peace inimical to Chinese interests. Japan's strategy of compounding military coercion, indiscriminate reprisals, living off the land, and deploying chemical and biological weapons enflamed hatreds, swelled enemy recruitments, and united even the most hostile Chinese factions.[45] Merciless means and unlimited objectives left the Chinese nothing to negotiate, but only to fight on, producing a protracted war across a huge theater that Japan lacked the resources to win.

Prior to Pearl Harbor, Japan had suffered 600,000 casualties, a sunk cost of stupendous proportions that its leaders tried to justify by promising citizens expanded conquests. The outbreak of war in Europe in 1939 opened a perceived window of opportunity, akin to those of the Meiji period. Perhaps Japan could compensate itself with the Asian colonies of France, Britain, and the Netherlands, then immobilized by Nazi aggression. In 1940, Japan joined the Axis powers. Yet neither Germany nor Japan could support each other over extended exterior lines. Instead, the alliance transformed Japan from a regional nuisance into a threat to the global order.

The United States threatened Japan's plans with its widening trade embargo and its appropriations aimed at building a two-ocean navy by 1943. Japan's relative naval strength would peak in 1941 before rapidly declining. In 1940, when Japan invaded French Indochina to sever China's last major supply route to the outside, the United States, the supplier of 75.2 percent of Japan's oil, imposed a total oil embargo. At the time, Japan had a one-and-a-half-year's supply at stable consumption rates, after which its window of opportunity would slam shut.[46] Within the week, the Japanese army favored war in the Pacific to take the Dutch East Indies' oil fields. Japan's leaders concluded that peace on American terms, entailing a withdrawal from China, would gradually impoverish Japan, undoing the work of the Meiji generation. War with the United States, on the other hand, offered a fifty-fifty chance of success. Finance

45. 单冠初 [Shan Guanchu], "日本侵华的'以战养战'政策" ["The Japanese Policy of 'Providing for the War with War' during the Invasion of China"], 历史研究 [*Historical Research*] 4 (1991): 77–91.

46. Paine, *Wars for Asia*, 175–76, 182, 185.

Minister Kaya Okinori alone repeatedly raised economic concerns indicating the unfeasibility of the war plans.[47] The army and navy doubled down.

VI

On December 7–8, 1941, to halt Western aid to China and expropriate the entirety of Dutch East Indies oil production, Japan conducted roughly simultaneous attacks against Hawaii, Thailand, Malaya, the Philippines, Wake Island, Guam, Hong Kong, and the international settlement at Shanghai. These actions elicited declarations of war from Germany (pro) and the United States, Britain, Australia, New Zealand, and the Netherlands (anti), and delivered China great-power allies. Japan and the United States would fight their war in a series of peripheral theaters, not in the main theater that remained China.

The author of the operational war plan, Admiral Yamamoto Isoroku, the commander of the Combined Fleet, scripted the destruction of the US fleet based at Pearl Harbor, Hawaii, then an American territory, not yet a state. The fleet's elimination would allow Japan rapidly to occupy the minimally defended Western colonies in Asia and to build an impregnable defensive perimeter of airbases to defend the far edges of this expanded empire. The United States would recognize the insignificance of its Asian interests, the costs and futility of a counterattack, and would finally abandon China. The Japanese did not see their actions as a frontal attack on the maritime order organizing international relations, an object of enormous value to US policymakers. Nor did the Japanese perceive that the defensive-perimeter strategy was a continental strategy applied to the sea. The strategy worked on land by leveraging interior lines through occupied areas surrounded by defensible terrain with limited and known access points, but would have real trouble across a vast ocean that no one could occupy and where the perimeter could be punctured from any number of directions. Seas grant both access to the world and insulation from it, but the seas themselves, unlike land, are unconquerable.

After Japan wrecked the US Navy at Pearl Harbor, Japanese forces advanced on two prongs, one through the Southeast Asian mainland to take Thailand, Malaya, Singapore, and Burma, and the other through the Pacific to take the Philippines, Guam, Borneo, Java, and Sumatra. In the first five months of 1942,

---

47. David J. Lu, *Japan a Documentary History*, Volume 2 (Armonk, NY: M.E. Sharpe, 1997), 427; Meirion Harries and Susie Harries, *Soldiers of the Sun*, 295; Nobutaka Ike, ed., *Japan's Decision for War* (Stanford, CA: Stanford University Press, 1967), 223.

Japan took more territory over a greater area than had any country in history. Japan captured 250,000 Allied prisoners of war, sunk 105 Allied ships, and seriously damaged 91 others, while it lost only 7,000 dead, 14,000 wounded, 562 planes, and 27 ships, but not a single cruiser, battleship, or carrier.[48] General Terauchi Hisaichi was credited with the success and promoted to field marshal.

On the strategic level, Pearl Harbor was a disaster because it transformed an isolationist, great naval power into one bent on regime change in Japan. The United States responded with a series of resource-consuming peripheral operations including: the Battle of the Coral Sea (May 4–8, 1942) to impede Japanese progress toward Australia; the Battle of Midway (June 3–7, 1942) to degrade the Japanese fleet; the Guadalcanal Campaign (August 7, 1942–February 9, 1943) to wall off Japan from Australia; the Battles of Makin and Tarawa in the Gilbert Islands (November 20–23, 1943) to acquire stepping stones on the way to Japan's home islands; the Battles of Kwajalein and Majura Atolls of the Marshall Islands (January 31–February 7, 1944) to extend the stepping stones toward Japan; the Mariana and Palau Islands Campaign (June–November 1944) to acquire airfields on the stepping stones of Saipan and Tinian to bomb Japan's home islands; Leyte Gulf (October 23–26, 1944) to neutralize Japan's fleet; and the Battles of Iwo Jima (February 19–March 26, 1945) and Okinawa (April 1–June 22, 1945) to acquire airfields even closer to Japan's home islands necessary for their invasion. Other large campaigns in New Guinea and the Philippines served to protect Australia and to attrite Japanese forces, but the main event was the tightening of the noose around Japan's home islands, where most amazingly of all, the United States never fought.

Simultaneous with the infamous day in Hawaii, the Japanese army launched the first in a sequence of battles from December 1941 through December 1942 intended to take over the Central China railway system and to culminate in the war-winning Gogō Campaign to flush the Nationalists from their capital in Chongqing. But the Pacific theater sucked so many Japanese troops and planes out of the China theater that, in December 1942, Japan called off the Gogō Campaign. Instead, throughout 1943, Japan conducted offensives along broad fronts, taking territory, but only temporarily for a lack of manpower to garrison the vastness of China.[49] In 1943, the United States began its

---

48. Takafusa Nakamura, *History of Shōwa Japan, 1926–1989*, trans. Edwin Whenmouth (Tokyo: University of Tokyo Press, 1998), 204.

49. Diana Lary, *The Chinese People at War*, 89, 112; Edward J. Drea and Hans van de Ven, "An Overview of Major Military Campaigns during the Sino-Japanese War, 1937–1945," in *The Battle*

two-pronged offensive, one led by General Douglas MacArthur to reclaim the Philippines and another led by Admiral Chester Nimitz to follow the island chains and establish bomber bases within range of Japan.

The Japanese planned to fight to the death for each position on the way to Tokyo in order to impose unsustainable costs. Instead, the United States bypassed most of those positions, only taking those necessary for naval logistics and bomber bases. Simultaneously, the United States deployed submarines to eliminate merchant traffic. By war's end, Japan's merchant marine had been reduced to one-ninth of its pre-Pearl Harbor capacity. Only half the men and supplies sent from Japan and Manchuria reached the Pacific theater, leaving scattered armies insufficient supplies to sustain the fight.[50] Had Japan surrendered in 1944, it would have avoided most fatalities. It had suffered 28,000 military deaths in 1941, 66,000 in 1942, 100,000 in 1943, 146,000 in 1944, but a stunning 1,127,000 in 1945.[51]

Instead, Japan doubled down again with the Ichigō Campaign in 1944, its largest campaign ever. The operational goals were: establish a submarine-proof inland supply route from Indochina to Korea; remove US airfields in China within range of Japan; and destroy Nationalist forces. But a win in China no longer contributed to homeland defense given the rapid approach of the US Navy to Japan—through the Marshall Islands in January 1944, the Caroline Islands in February, and the Marianas, from which US bombing raids against the home islands began in November 1944. Firebombing targeting civilians proved brutally successful, burning to the ground sixteen square miles of downtown Tokyo in a single night and killing more people than the atomic bombing of Nagasaki. By war's end, sixty-six Japanese cities lay in ruins, leaving 9.2 million homeless.[52]

When Japan did not accept the Potsdam Declaration demanding unconditional surrender, the atomic bombings of Hiroshima (August 6) and Nagasaki (August 9) followed. Simultaneously, Russia declared war, sending 1.5 million soldiers into Manchuria in anticipation of a postwar Japan divided between Russia and the United States.[53] Prime Minister Suzuki Kantarō concluded, "If

for China: Essays on the Military History of the Sino-Japanese War of 1937–1945, Mark Peattie et al., eds. (Stanford, CA: Stanford University Press, 2010), 44; Dagfinn Gatu, *Village China at War* (Vancouver: University of British Columbia Press, 2008), 31.

50. Paine, *Wars for Asia*, 195.

51. 江口圭一 [Eguchi Kei-ichi], 十五年戦争小史 [*A Short History of the Fifteen Year War*] (Tokyo: 青木書店, 1996), 172, 226; Takafusa Nakamura, *History of Shōwa Japan*, 253–54.

52. Paine, *Wars for Asia*, 201–2, 204–5.

53. David M. Glantz, *The Soviet Strategic Offensive in Manchuria, 1945: "August Storm"* (London: Frank Cass, 2003), xviii, xxv, 49, 143.

we don't act now, the Russians will penetrate not only Manchuria and Korea but northern Japan as well. . . . We must act now, while our chief adversary is still only the United States."[54] Emperor Hirohito agreed and called for acceptance of the Potsdam Declaration. With Japan's capitulation, China succeeded in outlasting Japan.

In the Second Sino-Japanese War, Japan descended into terminal overextension, step-by-step. Had army and navy officers coordinated on national defense, they would have realized the inadequacy of their resources instead of double counting them in war plans they refused to share and failing to account for sister-service expenditures. Had officers not assassinated Prime Minister Inukai in 1932, he could have negotiated a settlement for the invasion of Manchuria. Had the Japanese coordinated with the virulently anti-Communist Chiang Kai-shek, together they could have destroyed the Chinese Communists, who had retreated to Yan'an, within striking range of the Kantō Army. Alternatively, had Japan coordinated with its ally, Germany, they could have leveraged interior lines to defeat Russia in a two-front war. These were the feasible choices. Instead, the Japanese army conducted diplomacy through successive ultimatums on the false equation that operational victory equated to strategic victory. The outcome of the war proved that this was not so. Japan won most battles of the regional war but lost the fatal commerce war at sea that cut supplies to the army, navy, industry, and the people. Japan's attempt to follow a continental security paradigm of conquest from an island position, reliant on a single instrument of power—its military—proved ruinous to all concerned. It even predisposed a Communist victory in the Chinese Civil War—an outcome still endangering Japan's security.[55]

VII

Throughout the imperial period, Japan followed a series of high-risk, high-reward strategies that succeeded when the adversaries were incompetent, the wars were short, the objectives were limited, the locals were not hostile, the value of the contested spoils was higher for Japan than for its enemies, and when the peace terms were generous to the defeated. In the wars of the Meiji period, Japanese civil and military leaders made careful prewar assessments of the capabilities of all parties concerned in order to calibrate objectives to

54. Yukiko Koshiro, *Imperial Eclipse* (Ithaca, NY: Cornell University Press, 2013), 243.
55. Yukiko Koshiro, *Imperial Eclipse*, Chapter 24.

capabilities and to avoid third-party interventions. They coordinated all instruments of national power—military and civilian—prepared exit strategies, and stuck within a maritime security paradigm sensitive to the trade of others.

In the 1930s, Japan applied a continental solution to the Great Depression and resurgent neighbors. It took territory dwarfing its own and separated by oceans in order to guarantee resource self-sufficiency. It did so without allied support against an opposing alliance that eventually including the United States, the dominant naval power, as well as China, its great continental neighbor. Japan's conquests were operationally impressive, but economically unsustainable, morally repellant, and strategically unworkable. China never could threaten the home islands; the United States wrecked them.

Japan applied a continental strategy of conquest, oblivious to the differences between land and sea. Land powers radiate power outward to absorb contiguous, generally smaller neighbors. Armies garrison the conquered. Seas cannot be occupied like land. Presence is a problem at sea. Presence was a problem for Japan even on land. Given its resource and population inferiority, there were too many places to be present and too many people present in China. What was the point? The fighting impoverished everyone.

Overextension in the Pacific was no solution to overextension in China. As a maritime power, the seas insulated Japan from attack, that is, until it attacked the dominant naval power. Japan's notional outer defensive perimeter was a continental game played at sea, where it could not work. Geography on land usually constrains feasible directions of attack, whereas the sea is open in most directions. The perimeter Japan chose to defend by sea was immense—Japan had to be strong everywhere but could be attacked anywhere without interior land lines to reinforce quickly and safely. It was much easier to puncture a maritime perimeter than a continental one because the puncture opened onto ungoverned seas, not garrisoned enemy home territory. In the age of nationalism, land conquests were expensive. Unlike land, seas cannot be conquered. The only economical solution is to share them. The maritime order is based on win-win, wealth-producing trade, not the negative-sum, wealth-destroying battle for land preoccupying continental powers.

CHAPTER 18

Strategies of Anti-Imperial Resistance

GANDHI, BHAGAT SINGH, AND FANON

Priya Satia

Resistance to modern imperialism has shaped the world since the era of indigenous resistance to settler colonialism in the Americas. Enslaved Africans drew on military practices derived from West Africa, and transatlantic political ideals infused eighteenth-century revolts in the Americas. Their memory drove later West Indian risings. In South Asia, the British struggled for control in the face of frequent and vehement pushback. After brutally crushing the massive uprising, or ghadar, of 1857, the British invested even more in divide-and-rule strategies aimed at preventing unified resistance. Around the empire, illicit writing and illicit action, smuggled pamphlets and smuggled rifles, shaped resistance.

Peaceful protests turned violent, as in Jamaica in 1865. Irish anti-colonialists waged psychological warfare with terror tactics, invaded British Canada, *and* used peaceful methods such as giant processions, rent strikes, boycotts, and land repossession. Collective withdrawal of labor, consumption, or services was a long-standing means of colonial protest, acquiring the name "boycott" when the Irish Land League targeted the English land agent Charles Boycott's violent tactics of tenant eviction in 1880. Strikes—in industrial and agricultural settings—and street protests were part of the repertoire of resistance. So were everyday acts like pilfering, crop concealment, gestures of contempt, and tax resistance.[1]

---

1. On such resistance, see Vincent Brown, *Tacky's Revolt: The Story of an Atlantic Slave War* (Cambridge, MA: Harvard University Press, 2020); Ranajit Guha, *Elementary Aspects of Peasant*

In the Middle East, South Asia, the Caucasus, and Africa, pushback against empire drew on Islamic thought and peasant and military discontent. Prophetic figures led resistance movements in Africa and North America. East Asian polities strove to shut out European intervention and faced it with religiously informed rebellion. There, and elsewhere, communism infused anticolonial struggle in tandem with rival outlooks. Guerrilla tactics mattered everywhere, driving the British to coin the term "small war" to encompass the stubborn military resistance to their self-proclaimed Pax Britannica. Resistance often incorporated multiple elements: boycotts accompanied by marches; violence against planters alongside desertions; military challenges stiffened with moral righteousness. Even when resistance did not overthrow or loosen the imperial grip, it informed the evolution of the tactics of both rule and later resistance.

Transnational networks, including Pan-Africanism, Pan-Islamism, and the League Against Imperialism, were central to resistance, generating counterpublics that challenged the networks and spatial imaginaries of both empire and nation. Such spaces of solidarity enabled debates about ends and means when resistance met with coercion, disarmament, and concessions from colonial powers.

Here I focus on the ideas and actions of key theorists of anti-colonial resistance particularly preoccupied with what form such resistance should take. Though the question was strategic, it was always also moral, given its investment in opposing the immorality of empire. Debates about strategies (means) were simultaneously debates about goals (ends), about what ought

---

Insurgency in Colonial India (Durham, NC: Duke University Press, 1983); Antoinette Burton, *The Trouble with Empire: Challenges to Modern British Imperialism* (Oxford: Oxford University Press, 2015); Richard Gott, *Britain's Empire: Resistance, Repression and Revolt* (Brooklyn, NY: Verso Books, 2012). Other key works informing this chapter include: Priyamvada Gopal, *Insurgent Empire: Anticolonial Resistance and British Dissent* (Brooklyn, NY: Verso Books, 2019); Shruti Kapila, *Violent Fraternity: Indian Political Thought in the Global Age* (Princeton, NJ: Princeton University Press, 2021); Faisal Devji, *The Impossible Indian: Gandhi and the Temptation of Violence* (Cambridge, MA: Harvard University Press, 2012); Tim Harper, *Underground Asia: Global Revolutionaries and the Assault on Empire* (Cambridge, MA: Belknap Press, 2020); Joel Cabrita, *Text and Authority in the South African Nazaretha Church* (Cambridge: Cambridge University Press, 2014); Satia, *Time's Monster: How History Makes History* (Cambridge, MA: Belknap Press, 2020); James Vernon, *Hunger: A Modern History* (Cambridge, MA: Harvard University Press, 2007), 60; Kevin Grant, *Last Weapons: Hunger Strikes and Fasts in the British Empire, 1890–1948* (Berkley, CA: University of California Press, 2019); Yasmin Saikia, "*Hijrat* and *Azadi* in Indian Muslim Imagination and Practice: Connecting Nationalism, Internationalism, and Cosmopolitanism," *Comparative Studies of South Asia, Africa and the Middle East* 37:2 (2017): 201–12; Kama Maclean, *A Revolutionary History of Interwar India: Violence, Image, Voice*

to replace empire. My purpose here is not to assess strategies' relative justness or effectiveness. Instead, taking contestation of and dissent from modern racial empire as constitutive of its violent and insecure reality, this essay validates the view of many prominent thinkers—that empire's shapeshifting capacity meant permanent anti-colonial struggle, rather than a moment of decisive victory against it. Liberation would be experienced in rather than as a result of that unresolved struggle. In short, debates about anti colonial "strategy" included attacks on strategic thinking itself, as the instrumental logic that justified empire in the first place; key thinkers urged ethical over "strategic" action based on the calculus of future effect.

This is clear in the contest between two approaches to resistance in British India: the revolutionary Bhagat Singh's challenge to Gandhian nonviolence (which itself responded to the constitutional and violent tactics of earlier resistance efforts). After laying out this seeming clash nurtured by global currents of pacifist and socialist thought, the essay examines the Martiniquan thinker Frantz Fanon's diagnosis of the way this very debate enabled colonial renewal and his prescription for a "new humanism" that might release us from this shattering cycle. Although forms of anti-colonial resistance were framed in opposition to one another, *as* a dispute about strategy and aims, they dialectically shaped one other—and the incomplete unfolding of decolonization Fanon perceived. The dissonant form of postcolonial life today can be traced to their unresolved contradictions.

---

and Text (Oxford: Oxford University Press, 2015); Rudrangshu Mukherjee, *Tagore & Gandhi: Walking Alone, Walking Together* (New Dehli: Aleph Book Company, 2021); J. Daniel Elam, Kama Maclean, and Christopher Moffat, eds., *Writing Revolution in South Asia: History, Practice, Politics* (Milton Park: Routledge, 2018); Kama Maclean and J. Daniel Elam, eds., *Revolutionary Lives in South Asia: Acts and Afterlives of Anticolonial Political Action* (Milton Park: Routledge, 2016); Simona Sawhney, "Bhagat Singh: A Politics of Death and Hope," in *Punjab Reconsidered: History, Culture, and Practice*, Anshu Malhotra and Farina Mir, eds. (Oxford: Oxford University Press, 2012); Barbara Metcalf, *Husain Ahmad Madani: The Jihad for Islam and India's Freedom* (London: Oneworld Publications, 2008); Faisal Devjji, "From Minority to Nation," in *Partitions: A Transnational History of Twentieth-Century Territorial Separatism*, Arie Dubnov and Laura Robson, eds. (Palo Alto, CA: Stanford University Press, 2019); Noor-Aiman I. Khan, *Egyptian-Indian Nationalist Collaboration and the British Empire* (London: Palgrave Macmillan, 2011); Peter Hudis, "The Revolutionary Humanism of Frantz Fanon," *Jacobin*, December 26, 2020, https://jacobinmag.com /2020/12/humanism-frantz-fanon-philosophy-revolutionary-algeria; Neeti Nair, *Changing Homelands: Hindu Politics and the Partition of India* (Cambridge, MA: Harvard University Press, 2011).

I

Indian and British elites established the Indian National Congress in 1885, the latter hoping it would provide an outlet for grievances and prevent more unruly rebellion. One of its founders, Dadabhai Naoroji, also became the first Asian member of Britain's parliament in hopes of appealing to British conscience. But as famine stalked India, many Congress members urged more radical goals and means. The partitioning of Bengal on religious lines in 1905 provoked widespread rebellion, goaded in 1907 by the commemoration of the fiftieth anniversary of 1857. The resulting Swadeshi movement entailed the boycott and destruction of British goods and the promotion of home-grown enterprise—coinciding with Chinese boycott of American goods in protest of the 1882 Chinese Exclusion Act and Mohandas Gandhi's boycott tactics in South Africa. Religious practices such as fasts and bathing in the Ganges were also part of the resistance. As British violence mounted, revolutionary groups retaliated with assassinations and armed revolt.

Colonial officials had faced assassination before, but the Irish example and the burgeoning global anarchist movement made it a sensational recourse. In 1908, two Bengali men bombed a carriage at Muzaffarpur, killing two women instead of the targeted British magistrate. Bal Gangadhar Tilak, a Congress radical, defended them. He read the *Gita*, the work of Hindu scripture derived from the *Mahabharata*, as licensing violence against an oppressor when undertaken without thought of reward. Jailed for sedition, he wrote an important commentary amplifying this reading.

Anti-colonial violence extended to London through India House, a student residence founded in 1905 that doubled as a hub for political activism, most famously when Madan Lal Dhingra assassinated Sir William Curzon Wyllie of the India Office in 1909. Dhingra was a member of V. D. Savarkar's Revolutionary Society of Hindustan, which stressed the importance of self-sacrifice for the nation, and the role of secret societies in this work. Savarkar's revisionist account of the 1857 rebellion, prompted by British celebration of the fiftieth anniversary, circulated from 1909 as a banned-but-much-read book.

In this context, in 1909, Gandhi spelled out a rival, nonviolent approach to anti-colonial resistance, recognizing, as he later wrote, that "violence is the keystone of the Government edifice."[2] From the 1890s, Gandhi had developed civil disobedience practices against racial discrimination in South Africa,

---

2. Nirmal Kumar Bose, ed., *Selections from Gandhi* (Ahmedabad: Navajivan, 1948), 203.

where he worked as a lawyer, terming them "satyagraha," or "insistence on truth." On news of Wyllie's assassination, Gandhi described Dhingra in the South African journal *Indian Opinion* as a piteous "coward" who had acted in a "state of intoxication" induced by "ill-digested reading of worthless writing" by the truly guilty who had "egged" him on.[3] Landing in England a week before Dhingra's trial, which ended in his execution, Gandhi had a provoking meeting with Savarkar. Traveling back to South Africa, having encountered "every known Indian anarchist in London," Gandhi elaborated his philosophy of nonviolent anti-colonialism in *Hind Swaraj* (also banned in 1910).[4] This opening of a public dialogue itself took the form of a dialogue between a reader and editor—perhaps inspired by the dialogue structure of the *Gita*, which fascinated Gandhi as a work of "pure ethics" and a way out of the instrumental ethics that anchored British imperialism: the idea that destructive means might be a necessary evil in pursuit of constructive ends, which drove its adherents to forgo ethical accountability in the present.[5]

In this text, Gandhi wrote that, "Dhingra was a patriot, but . . . [h]e gave his body in a wrong way." Assassination was "cowardly." "What we need to do is to sacrifice ourselves." Unlike underground activity, there was "nothing reserved and nothing secret" in satyagraha.[6] Its purpose was to make the normalized power relations between Indians and those who exploited them visible.

Nonviolent resistance was not an idea plucked from the wind; it had its own currency as a morally fitting and strategic means of countering empire. In late-nineteenth-century Punjab, Namdhari Sikhs had used non-cooperation as an anti-colonial weapon. In Russia, while violent anarchism flourished, Leo Tolstoy cleaved to pacifism, partly through study of East and South Asian religious thought. He too questioned liberal justifications of empire as a lesser evil that would shepherd the progress of benighted parts of the world. This "law of necessity in history" destroyed "the concept of the soul, of good and evil."[7] Gandhi was deeply impressed when reading Tolstoy in 1894—again as part of a dialogue: Indian revolutionary networks extended to North America, where the journal *Free Hindustan* engaged Tolstoy in open correspondence. Gandhi translated this

3. Kapila, *Violent Fraternity*, 92.

4. Mohandas Gandhi, *Hind Swaraj or Indian Home Rule* (Ahmedabad: Navajivan, 1938), 11. This quotation is from the 1921 preface to this work.

5. Devji, *Impossible Indian*, 105.

6. Gandhi, *Hind Swaraj*, 50, 12. This quotation is from the 1921 preface to this work.

7. Leo Tolstoy, *War and Peace*, trans. Ann Dunnigan (London: Signet Classics, 1968), 1454–55.

"Letter to a Hindu" (1908) by Tolstoy into Gujarati on his voyage back to South Africa and corresponded with the author until the latter's death in 1910. Gandhi even named his ashram for communal living "Tolstoy Farm."

Gandhi's dream of an India of village republics owed something to Tolstoy's idealization of small, self-governing communities. He read Henry David Thoreau's 1849 essay on civil disobedience (after coining "satyagraha"), John Ruskin, and Edward Carpenter; Jain influences in Gujarat were formative. Gandhi's ideas were also influenced by his South African context where the mineral revolution and the Boer War were causing upheaval. Gandhi's base, the Phoenix Settlement, was in Natal, home to a dynamic religious culture, including an Order of Trappist monks and, from 1910, the Nazareth Baptist Church. John Dube established the Ohlange Institute, modeled on the Tuskegee Institute, in the same valley as Gandhi's settlement, becoming founding president of the African National Congress in 1912.

Gandhi saw violence as morally unsound and tactically unwise, liable to extend rather than end colonial rule. His version of nonviolent resistance entailed non-cooperation with British economic dominance and unjust laws, repurposing boycott towards promoting Indian goods over colonial ones *and* rejecting the dehumanizing machine civilization the British had brought. Satyagraha included hartal: stoppage combining strike and boycott to disrupt imperial economic life. Marches and traffic-stopping were part of satyagraha's toolkit, as were spinning khadi, walking, and fasting, practices that "took the everyday as the only temporal framework."[8] The movement was not about sacrificing now towards some future goal but rather sacrificing now for the sake of now. The objective was repossession of the self, recovering the self from Western notions of civilization, including the idea that violence is necessary for progress, which elided love's actual centrality in civilization. Nonviolence sought to create new future possibilities by demanding moral accountability in the present.

Such politics were "impossible to institutionalise," relying on inner transformation automatically clearing the way for transformation of the world.[9] Gandhi assured that people had only to recognize the evil of machinery, and "it would ultimately go."[10] Effective as he had already proven as an activist, he was adamant that satyagraha did not require organization:

8. Kapila, *Violent Fraternity*, 149.
9. Kapila, *Violent Fraternity*, 162.
10. Gandhi, *Hind Swaraj*, 70.

What the leaders do, the populace will gladly do in turn . . . You and I need not wait until we can carry others with us. Those will be the losers who will not do it.[11]

Gandhi's favorite song, Rabindranath Tagore's "Ekla Cholo Re" ("Walk Alone"), expressed this core belief.

Noncooperation may require imprisonment or death, Gandhi warned; suffering was necessary for freedom. All this was for each to consider for themselves: "Let each do his duty. If I . . . serve myself, I shall be able to serve others."[12] "Real home-rule is self-rule or self-control" and was achievable through soul-force, for which swadeshi in every sense was required. The objective was an "enlightened anarchy in which each person will become his own ruler," he explained in 1939. Government would be redundant, as each individual would "conduct himself in such a way that his behaviour will not hamper the well-being of his neighbours." His approach was anti-institutional because fundamentally anti-statist: "In an ideal State there will be no political institution and therefore no political power."[13] Such utopianism was necessary to decolonization: "To believe that what has not occurred in history will not occur at all is to argue disbelief in the dignity of man."[14] Straining after the ideal mattered more than arriving at it. "Let India live for the true picture, though never realizable in its completeness," Gandhi affirmed in 1946.[15]

In this view, freedom was something that might be attained instantly, entailing only refusal to be ruled by another and rejection of the colonial idea of gradual progress towards freedom based on material measures of civilizational maturity. "Civilization" was rather about ethical being, something achievable now, not the end of some developmental process. "It is Swaraj [self-rule] when we learn to rule ourselves. It is, therefore, in the palm of our hands."[16] Recognizing the role of colonial, liberal education in propagating belief in necessary evils, Gandhi called for its rejection in favor of religious, or ethical, education.

This idea that independence comes from the bottom-up resembled Tolstoy's insistence that, "There can be only one permanent revolution—a moral

11. Gandhi, *Hind Swaraj*, 70.

12. Gandhi, *Hind Swaraj*, 76.

13. Mukherjee, *Tagore & Gandhi*, 171.

14. Gandhi, *Hind Swaraj*, 47.

15. Gandhi, "Gandhi's Political Vision: The Pyramid vs. the Oceanic Circle (1946)," in *"Hind Swaraj," and Other Writings*, Anthony Parel, ed. (Cambridge: Cambridge University Press, 1997), 189.

16. Gandhi, *Hind Swaraj*, 47.

one: the regeneration of the inner man," and that anarchism will be fulfilled "only by there being more and more people who do not require the protection of governmental power."[17] Nonviolence was refracted through a religious idiom—hence Gandhi's sobriquet as "Mahatma" ("great soul")—but its moral appeal transcended religion itself. The Christian minister Martin Luther King, Jr., could also embrace it, as could the piously Muslim Abdul Ghaffar Khan. Religious ideas were important to anti-colonialism's challenge to colonialism's irreligious logic of suspending everyday ethics in the service of history.

For Gandhi, nonviolence, insofar as it was about being ethical now, was itself the end, not a means to achieving some other political end. This was a dispute not only about the means of decolonization but also about the relationship between means and ends. Against the assassins of his time, Gandhi insisted on the "inviolable connection between the means and the end." Violent means extracted concessions only as long as fear held, and such concessions themselves bred violence. If those who would extort freedom through violence prevailed, Gandhi warned, "they will want you and me to obey their laws," which, if they went against the conscience, they would also have to disobey. It would be freedom got by "others" and thus still "not Home Rule but foreign rule."[18]

Thus, in 1909, Gandhi recognized the risk of the colonial *national* rule that would dismay Fanon in 1961. Gandhi was explicit that Indians' enmity was not with the English but rather with English civilization's centering of material desire as the key to progress. Freedom was thus not about expelling the British but about attaining self-reliance and recovering a life based on the "recognized reciprocity of interests," rather than on the commodity-based industrialism driven by individual self-interest.[19]

Gandhi also criticized the moderate mode of patient petition. Petitioning was a helpful means of education but, he argued, could achieve change only if backed by passive resistance: refusal to be governed by authorities that did not heed the petition. It depended on understanding that British rule could not operate if Indians refused to "play the part of the ruled."[20] Gandhi asked

17. Leo Tolstoy, "On Anarchy," 1900. https://theanarchistlibrary.org/library/leo-tolstoy-on-anarchy.

18. Gandhi, *Hind Swaraj*, 51, 59, 71.

19. Mukherjee, *Tagore & Gandhi*, 33.

20. Gandhi, *Hind Swaraj*, 73.

Indians to withhold the self from the Raj in a dialogic way, drawing it into conversation while also compelling it. Moderates who persistently petitioned the British despite the latter's evident immovability implied that the British were indispensable, like God.

His reputation established from South Africa, Gandhi arrived in India in the midst of World War I and helped connect the Congress movement to a mass base. Indians endured many wartime deprivations, and the 1919 Montagu Chelmsford reforms fell far short of expectations for just reward. Moreover, the accompanying Rowlatt Act extended wartime emergency procedures for trying anti-colonial revolutionaries in closed, expedited, jury-less trials. As much as Gandhi disapproved revolutionaries' violent tactics, he capitalized on anger against the repressive law by launching a massive satyagraha campaign. Participation in Punjab was widespread, given intense wartime suffering there, setting the stage for Reginald Dyer's massacre of a peaceful gathering at Jallianwala Bagh, which Gandhi called the state's "resort to terror."[21] The British also bombed protests in Punjab from the air. The Air Ministry embraced "terror" as the new technology's tactical principle, building on established colonial practice: in 1872, the British Lieutenant-Governor of Punjab defended blowing rebels from cannons as "an impressive and merciful" act "calculated to strike terror into the bystanders."[22] Such defenses of terror were precisely the instrumentalizing of the present from which Gandhi wanted Indians to recover their minds and souls.

Gandhi launched another movement in 1920. Despite his call for nonviolence, colonial officials were attacked; to the extent that satyagraha was about noncooperation with authority, it implicitly licensed all manner of anti-governmental activity. He contended with skepticism, too. In a 1920 Congress speech, Mohammed Ali Jinnah, the future leader of the movement to create Pakistan, insisted that independence could not be won without bloodshed.

In November 1921, during another movement including boycott of the royal tour, Gandhian volunteers enforcing hartal turned violent, prompting riots. An ashamed Gandhi launched a fast to restore order. It was perhaps these events that prompted him to write in the 1921 preface to *Hind Swaraj* that he was no longer aiming for the swaraj the book had envisioned, as India was "not

21. Durba Ghosh, "Gandhi and the Terrorists," *Journal of South Asian Studies* 39:3 (2016): 567.
22. Kim Wagner, " 'Calculated to Strike Terror:' The Amritsar Massacre and the Spectacle of Colonial Violence," *Past & Present* 233:1 (2016), 194. https://academic.oup.com/past/article/233/1/185/2915150.

ripe for it."[23] Though Gandhi continued to work for swaraj at an individual level, his "corporate activity" was instead "devoted to the attainment of Parliamentary Swaraj, in accordance with the wishes of the people." Letting go of parliament, railways, and mills required "a higher simplicity and renunciation than the people are today prepared for." Thus, Gandhi compromised on the very sort of "stagist" understanding of history that his philosophy questioned. His doubts were renewed during the 1922 campaign when satyagrahis at Chauri Chaura in the United Provinces fought police violence with violence. Gandhi called off the campaign and fasted in atonement: protestors at Chauri Chaura had called out his name.

Gandhi's recourse to fasting was another arrow in satyagraha's quiver. Fasting was related to the hunger strike, a strategy first used in the empire by suffragettes, also in 1909—borrowing from the example of Russian prisoners, whose struggles against tzarist tyranny Russian exiles popularized in Britain. Groups who could not wage their struggles in the streets or battlefield took them to "spaces . . . within the state itself."[24] Gandhi referenced the "growing suffragette movement" in *Hind Swaraj*, having attended a reception for suffragettes released from prison on hunger strike and noted the tactic's effectiveness.[25] The hunger strike became an anti-colonial tactic in Ireland and India in 1912. Gandhi turned to it in South Africa in 1913, as did the jailed Indian revolutionaries Bhai Parmanand and Randhir Singh during World War I. The government effort to undermine such protests by transferring prisoners between provinces only helped spread the tactic. Indian and Irish activists often expressed solidarity with one another's strikes. A British subject who chose death over life under British rule depleted the government's moral capital and claim to liberal rule.

Hunger strikers exposed the state's tyranny and violence by drawing on locally specific political and cultural resources. As an exemplary tactic of self-sacrifice, the hunger strike possessed religious dimensions (Catholic notions of purity and sacrifice, for instance) and found local roots in older practices of protest, such as dharna in India. In Russia, India, Ireland, and Britain, hunger strikes emerged in communities in which fasting was a recognized religious practice; British depictions of Gandhi's fasts played on long-standing stereotypes about Indian mystical asceticism.

23. For quotations in this paragraph, see Gandhi, 1921 preface, *Hind Swaraj*, 10–11.
24. Grant, *Last Weapons*, 3–4, 105.
25. Gandhi, *Hind Swaraj*, 27.

For all these resemblances, Gandhi assiduously distinguished his fasts from those aimed at extorting personal political or material advantage. He saw the suffragettes' hunger strikes as a form of political violence and disputed revolutionary hunger strikers' claims as satyagrahis. Though at times his own fasts blurred the distinction, they took the practice in a new direction and generated more media attention. For him, fasting was central to self-rule: freedom "achieved through the ethical government of the self in the pursuit of truth."[26] It was about self-purification, not militancy. Fasting asserted an individual's sovereignty over themselves, abetting the self-transformation that was Gandhism's goal. The audiences for Gandhi's fasts were fellow Indians. Fasting expiated Indian moral failure, tested his own self-discipline, *and* posed a moral challenge to British rule. Gandhi insisted that his 1932 fast against separate electoral representation for untouchables was directed not against the government but rather the Hindu community that had failed to end untouchability: an "act of conscience, not a political gesture." But his challenger B. R. Ambedkar branded it a kind of "terrorism."[27] In his 1947 fast to stop Partition violence in Bengal, Gandhi made religious leaders swear to prevent violence, else he would fast unto death—another consummately coercive use of self-starvation, whatever else it also was.

II

Gandhism unfolded in a roiling society in which colonialism was being resisted in manifold ways. Theory aside, it was a hybrid approach in practice. When Gandhi rejected this hybridity, others worried that his obsession with means might stifle the ends. The exile Lala Har Dayal landed in California in 1911. In a 1912 biography, he portrayed Karl Marx as a campaigner against poverty and inequality; it was often in this general way, because of Communism's resonance with traditions of communal living, that Marxism informed socialist anticolonial thought. In 1913, Har Dayal helped found the Ghadar Party, named for the rebels of 1857. Though largely Punjabi, its center in San Francisco, "Yugantar Ashram," was named in homage to the Bengali revolutionaries. Its journal, including much revolutionary poetry, acquired a global readership. The group was marked by a "revolutionary eclecticism" informed by its global concerns and reach. It was part of the international "underground" that offered mass

26. Vernon, *Hunger*, 69.
27. Kapila, *Violent Fraternity*, 158.

political education from 1905 to the twenties through intense exchange and nurtured an ethos of patience.[28] Like Pan-Africanism, the group's networks worked beyond not only the spatial but also the temporal limits of empire and nation "for a world in which racialized imperial state power was no more."[29] Rather than Congress's goal of "home rule" within the empire, Ghadarites sought total independence and were willing to use violent tactics.

In an anonymous pamphlet, Har Dayal celebrated the "philosophy of the bomb" as a means by which slaves might obtain freedom: "The bomb and the pistol are so full of magic that they . . . can awaken the sleeping and can destroy tyrants."[30] The party's call for personal sacrifice resonated with South Asian traditions of sacred violence and martial memory. It, too, was about remaking selves, forging new kinds of agency. Ghadarites plotted to free India during World War I through an Indian Army-wide revolt. With the help of American intelligence, British agencies imprisoned and hanged many who landed in India. Still, the network struck a major blow with the 1915 mutiny in Singapore, threatening Britain's Asian empire.

Ghadar martyrologues and shrines to the men of 1915 across Punjab helped fuel the mass anti-colonial awakening in India, inspiring a new generation, while exposure of army disloyalty convinced the British that they could not hold India by force. Many of Dyer's victims were Ghadarites' relatives protesting the rebels' harsh sentences. In the United Provinces, the young student Ram Prasad Bismil read of their executions, with long-lasting effects.

Like earlier revolutionaries, Ghadarites relied on a combination of secret networks and highly visible spectacular violence. They too called for sacrifice oriented "to the 'event,' " as partisans waging war from behind enemy lines.[31] Ghadar was about dying for a historical cause greater than the subject, while Gandhism saw no historical cause greater than the subject. If Gandhism collapsed ends and means, Ghadarism saw chaos as a means that at once undid the sovereign and territorial claims of the colonial state. Gandhi arrived in India on the heels of the Ghadarite failure, offering an alternative vision of sacrifice for freedom. But Ghadarites did not disappear.

Har Dayal helped found the wartime Provisional Government of India in Kabul, with the support (including arms) of the German and Ottoman

28. Harper, *Underground Asia*, 187.
29. Burton, *Trouble with Empire*, 199.
30. Harper, *Underground Asia*, 185–86.
31. Kapila, *Violent Fraternity*, 149.

empires, and Pan-Islamic networks. The Ghadarite Muhamed Barkatullah Bhopali was prime minister; the president, the Pan-Asianist Raja Mahendra Pratap, was a Hindu who understood his freedom struggle as jihad, also embracing "prem dharma" (an ethic of love), internationalism, and Communism. Thousands of Indian Muslims arrived in Afghanistan, many later deported and punished. Discovering their plans to create an Army of God to liberate Islamic countries under infidel rule—the "Silk Letter Conspiracy"—British policing agencies worked to stop what they saw as a malicious plot.

Many involved reappeared in later anti-colonial efforts (including the future Congress leader Abul Kalam Azad). Indeed, many of them, too, saw means and ends as inseparable, conceiving their international partnerships mixing Muslims and non-Muslims in a manner recalling the Prophet Muhammad's Medina as the very experience of azadi (freedom)—something encompassing a recovery of full humanity rather than mere political freedom. The experience of common effort towards freedom was, for these activists, freedom itself. This capacity for common cause made the war a harrowing time for the British, who confronted anti-colonial forces on multiple fronts. Their repressive responses in turn instigated new alliances and reconsideration of strategy.

Later Communists, Pan-Islamists, anarchists, and nationalists all claimed to be Ghadar's heirs. The Khilafat movement extended such revolutionary modes of thought into partnership with the Gandhian movement. Threats to Ottoman power had long stirred anti-colonial feeling among Indian Muslims. Prewar revolutionary Bengal was home to Pan-Islamic secret societies concerned about the Balkan Wars. After World War I, a movement emerged to save the Turkish Caliphate from destruction at the hands of European division of the Ottoman empire and the Turkish nationalist movement. Gandhi's movement joined this Khilafat movement. Bhopali enthusiastically supported the joint effort, also hoping for a Ghadar revival with Russian support under his and the Congress leader Jawaharlal Nehru's leadership. In short, Gandhism at times drew strength from and found philosophical intersection with seemingly distinct kinds of anti-colonial activism.

Partnerships induced shifts in thinking. Har Dayal came to see imperialism's cyclical production of violence as Gandhi did. On his release from jail, the Ghadarite Bhai Parmanand looked to Gandhi, whom he had known in South Africa, as "a new Avatar."[32] The war's nationalistic violence also prompted

---

32. Harper, *Underground Asia*, 437–38.

reflection on goals, as the new Soviet Union offered a vision of alternative, federal futures. Har Dayal repudiated nationalism entirely, worrying, like Gandhi (and later Fanon), that purely nationalist leaders sought a mere "change in masters." He even praised the empire as a healthier, because more international, framework, before committing to the dream of a "World State."[33] The Khilafat movement called for an Asiatic federation in 1922. Gandhi conceived of the "Indian" itself as an international category, dreaming of interdependent village republics.

In some ways, Gandhism, with its own international roots, channeled Ghadar's self-sacrificing vision in a nonviolent, "aboveground" direction, while Ghadar's violent ethos found further expression in socialist anti-colonialism. In general, postwar anti-colonialism bore the imprint of the Russian Revolution. That revolution and the Leninist theory behind it challenged the stagist historical assumptions undergirding empire, that every society must undergo certain phases of development—industrialism, capitalism, nationalism—before achieving proletarian rule. They also strengthened the idea that the Indian struggle was part of a global cause. Praise for Lenin as an anti-imperialist and a model of sacrifice was widespread; Gandhi called him a "master-spirit."[34] Moscow also provided practical support to Indian revolutionary networks.

And so, alongside, and entangled with, the Gandhian movement were movements indebted to global socialism and Ghadarism. Prewar networks in California had included the Communist M. N. Roy, who started out as a Bengali revolutionary in 1905 but turned during the war toward the pacifist internationalism he discovered in New York. Before arms, Roy concluded, revolution required "intelligent understanding of the idea of revolution."[35] Hoping to bring revolution to India via the Northwest Frontier, Roy moved from Mexico, where he had established a Communist party, to Moscow where he debated Lenin on the colonial question.

In 1920, Roy headed to Tashkent where an Indian Revolutionary Association nurtured dreams of recovering democratic institutions like the panchayat (village council) and the egalitarianism of frontier peoples. This was not far from the Gandhian utopia of village republics—perhaps one reason why Roy partnered with the Congress Party, despite his doubts about its revolutionary

33. Harper, *Underground Asia*, 383; Kapila, *Violent Fraternity*, 87.

34. Harper, *Underground Asia*, 412.

35. Harper, *Underground Asia*, 379.

potential. Counting on the muhajirin already training in Afghanistan, he asked the Congress politician Lala Lajpat Rai (who had met Ghadarites in California) to come there, reached out to leaders of the 1915 rising, *and* invited Gandhi to an All-India Revolutionary Congress in Tashkent or Kabul in 1921. In September 1921, Roy's manifesto reached the Congress meeting in Ahmedabad through a messenger.

While serious Communists made overtures to Gandhi, others saw the news from Russia as a rebuke to Gandhian passivity. In 1921, S. A. Dange's pamphlet *Gandhi vs. Lenin* faulted the Congress strategy. Rival approaches did not merely trundle along in parallel; they influenced one another. The challenge posed by the Communist approach radicalized the Gandhian movement. This continual dialogue and debate, pitting Gandhi against other thinkers and leaders, was integral to actual decolonization, as Fanon would explain.

Bismil was among those at the 1921 Congress meeting who urged a resolution in favor of purna swaraj (complete self-rule) rather than home rule. Gandhi demurred and called off the noncooperation movement after the events of Chauri Chaura in 1922. There was a feeling that Gandhi was holding India's masses back, making them choose, as Roy's wife Evelyn put it, between "their crying earthly needs and real love for this saintly man."[36] Even Tagore, a fellow critic of violence, was dismayed by Gandhi's obsession with spinning and his insistence on blind obedience to that call—another public dialogue in which Gandhi engaged.

As Gandhi had articulated his vision against the revolutionary outlook of 1909, frustrated youths of the 1920s framed an updated revolutionary approach in opposition to his. Veterans of old revolutionary circles were emerging from jail and becoming involved in arms procurement. Bengal saw armed robberies in 1923–24 as well as attempts to assassinate the commissioner of police, Charles Tegart (fresh from suppressing Sinn Fein). Gandhi engaged in a long public dialogue with the revolutionary Sachindranath Sanyal. In 1923, with Har Dayal's encouragement, Sanyal, Bismil, and others founded the Hindustan Republican Association (HRA), aiming to create a federated United States of India through armed revolution, inspired by Irish (IRA) and Russian examples. Their "actions" strove to wrest independence in sharp contrast to "passive" resistance. In 1925, Bismil was hanged for participating in a plot to rob a train carrying government money. That year, HRA figures helped found the

---

36. Harper, *Underground Asia*, 471–72.

Communist Party of India (CPI), dedicated to the overthrow of colonialism and social revolution in India.[37]

Savarkar, too, reemerged, launching the Hindutva movement, which drew on the revolutionary past and the interwar fascist turn. It embraced violence as a productive historical and natural law, and institutionalized the "form and logic of secret societies."[38] The structure of its cultlike paramilitary organization, the Rashtriya Swayamsevak Sangh (RSS), was inspired partly by the HRA and was designed to foster bonding in opposition to the mainstream Congress movement.

Bhagat Singh was part of both the HRA and the CPI. Inspired by the Ghadarites, with whom his uncle had worked while organizing Punjabi laborers on the American west coast, he hero-worshiped Kartar Singh Sarabha, who had been executed in 1915.[39] Singh's Marxism was, however, grounded in study of canonical texts. He was educated at National College in Lahore, which Rai had helped establish as part of the boycott of colonial education (inspired partly after visiting Tuskegee). Through his Marxist commitments, Singh nevertheless absorbed the Western view, common to liberalism and socialism, that fulfilling history's mission at times demanded an instrumental attitude towards the present. In 1924, the teenaged Singh argued that, to achieve universal brotherhood, "we will have to sacrifice the real present. For that imagined peace we will have to create chaos."[40] Singh, like Gandhi, understood anti-colonial struggle as permanent, per the slogan "Inquilab Zindabad" ("Long Live Revolution"), but believed that the future demanded continual sacrifice of the present. Singh defended HRA violence as impersonal, aimed at the "capitalist and imperialist system," citing Dhingra's last words that a "nation held down by foreign bayonets is in a perpetual state of war."[41] HRA terrorism was counter-terrorism. In 1928, at Singh's urging, the group was renamed the Hindustan Socialist Republican Association (HSRA).

37. Women were also part of this activity.

38. Kapila, *Violent Fraternity*, 97.

39. Singh was also particularly inspired by Mazzini, hero to earlier Indian revolutionaries too, which Gandhi addressed in *Hind Swaraj*.

40. J. Daniel Elam, "The 'Arch Priestess of Anarchy' Visits Lahore: Violence, Love, and the Worldliness of Revolutionary Texts," in *Revolutionary Lives*, Maclean and Elam, eds., 36.

41. Maclean, *A Revolutionary History*, 15; Sawhney, "Bhagat Singh: A Politics of Death and Hope."

The HSRA was grateful for the awakening Gandhism had caused, but its 1929 manifesto painted Gandhi as an "impossible visionary" given that "the world is armed to the very teeth. And the world is too much with us."[42] With this (Romantic) Wordsworthian line, the HSRA positioned themselves as realists about the violent forces ranged against a plan of redemption at the level of individuals. The present was a "time of confrontation," to shock the victims of capitalist militarism out of inertia.[43]

Still, this aim echoed the satyagrahi determination to render empire visible. Indeed, the manifesto called on satyagrahis to admit that HSRA members also knew "how to suffer for and to act up to our convictions."[44] Singh wore khadi and embraced anarchism in terms close to the Gandhian understanding of true freedom, albeit as an atheist. HSRA texts show the influence of Marxism, nationalism, internationalism, but also Gandhism. After all, its members included many disenchanted workers from that movement. Singh openly admired Nehru's revolutionary internationalism.[45] The group's ideology was not systematic but continuously evolving in response to events. Congress, for its part, exploited the group's outlook and actions, thanks partly to clandestine ties. Nehru wielded the threat of revolutionary violence in 1928 and 1929 to get the British to negotiate. Congress made political capital from HSRA sacrifices, gaining popular support and appeasing party radicals.

In 1928, the all-white Simon Commission on constitutional reform triggered massive protest. The authorities lathi-charged the protestors, and Rai died of his wounds. HSRA members Bhagat Singh, Sukhdev, Rajguru, and Chandrashekhar Azad were not in particular accord with Rai's politics but determined to avenge his death—mistakenly assassinating the police officer J. P. Saunders, rather than the intended police superintendent. Influenced by the French anarchist Auguste Vaillant's 1893 bombing of the Paris Chamber of Deputies, Singh and Batukeshwar Dutt bombed the Central Legislative Assembly in Delhi, taking care to avoid casualties and courting arrest to create an opportunity to defend their outlook. The assembly was discussing trade disputes bills during a time of strikes and persecution of labor leaders, including

---

42. Chris Moffat, "Experiments in Political Truth," in *Revolutionary Lives*, Maclean and Elam, eds., 78.

43. Moffat, "Experiments in Political Truth," 78.

44. Moffat, "Experiments in Political Truth," 79.

45. Bhagat Singh, "Naye Netaon ke Alag-Alag Vichaar," *Kirti*, July 1928, https://www.marxists.org/hindi/bhagat-singh/1928/naye-netaon.htm.

British Communists. Singh knew the West was divided and imagined himself fulfilling a destined role in an unfolding global history. His atheism apart, he was influenced by Sikh and Arya Samaji (broadly Punjabi religious) notions of sacrifice and militancy. During the bombing trial, Singh and Dutt asserted the justness of violence that furthered a legitimate cause, reaching behind the nonviolent movement to the memory of "Guru Gobind Singh and Shivaji, Kamal Pasha and Riza Khan, Washington and Garibaldi, Lafayette and Lenin."[46] Against Gandhi's claims of nonviolence's particular Indianness, they asserted historical legitimacy for their means.

Still, HSRA violence was different from that of prewar revolutionaries, indebted as it was to Gandhian lessons in the power of visibility and persuasion. In 1929, Singh affirmed his willingness to "renounce all," praising, like Gandhi, love's power to elevate man and the importance of a love not confined to an individual but that was "universal."[47] Though the HSRA attacked British officials, the purpose of this violence was new: propagandistic, and, increasingly, focused on violence without harm (though the assembly bombing caused injuries). Ignored by the British and Indian leaders, the revolutionaries turned to the bomb to "sound a warning"—"an attack directed against no individual but against an institution in itself." The bomb strove to awaken England and end "an era of Utopian non-violence, of whose futility the rising generation has been convinced."[48]

Their methods careened closer to Gandhi's as they launched a hunger strike for the rights of political prisoners. Singh grew as popular as Gandhi, not as a contrastingly violent persona but an "unequivocally anticolonial" one.[49] Gandhi denounced such militants in "The Bomb and the Knife" (1929) and criticized revolutionaries' hunger strikes as coercive acts unlike fasts motivated by satyagraha, ahimsa, love, and self-purification.[50] But many imprisoned satyagrahis were also undertaking hunger strikes for similar reasons.

The HSRA's actions helped radicalize and thus strengthen the mainstream movement. Against this backdrop, in 1929, as the global stock market crashed,

46. *Joint Statement* of Bhagat Singh and B.K. Dutt in the Assembly Bomb Case, read in court June 6, 1929, June 8, 1929, https://www.marxists.org/archive/bhagat-singh/1929/06/06.htm.

47. Bhagat Singh, Letter to Shaheed Sukhdev, April 5, 1929, https://www.marxists.org/archive/bhagat-singh/1929/04/05.htm.

48. Bhagat Singh and B.K. Dutt, *Joint Statement*, June 1929.

49. Nair, *Changing Homelands*, 130.

50. Grant, *Last Weapons*, 115.

the Congress movement finally adopted purna swaraj as its aim. Masses turned out the next year when Gandhi launched another bout of civil disobedience, a reassertion of leadership prompted partly by Congress's growing intimacies with the HSRA. Again, the movement was accompanied by violence in Bengal and Punjab.

When Gandhi again condemned the HSRA's cult of the bomb in a 1930 essay, the group defended it as a complement to Gandhian methods in a pamphlet on "The Philosophy of the Bomb," replete with homages to Ghadar. The text, too, criticized Gandhi's insistence on his own authority rather than an egalitarian relationship with the masses, arguing that HSRA violence was precisely a means of mass communication, of shocking the masses into action.[51]

HSRA's defense of its violence as merely propaganda was slippery, however, given the distinction between the two ongoing trials. In the 1930 statement Singh authored for five accused in the murder, he called imperialism "a vast conspiracy . . . with predatory motives." Justifying conspiracy with conspiracy, Singh asserted the moral justness of any means used to destroy such a government, defending bombs and pistols "as a measure of terrible necessity, as a last recourse."[52]

Arguing that the government's laws protected its interests rather than the people's, Singh, like Gandhi, urged Indians to "defy and disobey" them. Later that year, he described his evolution from early religious belief, through his days as a "romantic revolutionary" and his education through the works of Marx, Bakunin, Lenin, Trotsky, and others. Such independent thinking was essential to revolution, Singh explained, for, "As Mahatmaji [Gandhi] is great, he is above criticism," an obstacle to "constructive thinking." Moreover, belief in God kept men from recognizing their own ability to confront distress. Nevertheless, this emphasis on independent thought landed Singh near Gandhi's conclusion that the British had subjugated Indians "above all because of our apathy."[53]

Late in 1930, Singh, Sukhdev, and Rajguru were sentenced to death. Committees for their appeal appeared all over Punjab; thousands signed petitions. Acknowledging his evolution, Singh affirmed, "I am not a terrorist and I never

51. Kama Maclean, "Returning Insurgency to the Archive: The Dissemination of the 'Philosophy of the Bomb,'" *History Workshop Journal* 89 (2020): 154.

52. Bhagat Singh, "Statement of the Undefended Accused," May 5, 1930, available at, https://www.marxists.org/archive/bhagat-singh/1930/05/05.htm.

53. Bhagat Singh, "Why I Am an Atheist," October 5–6, 1930, published 1931, available at, https://www.marxists.org/archive/bhagat-singh/1930/10/05.htm.

was, excepted perhaps in the beginning of my revolutionary career."[54] They had learned that bomb-throwing was useless and sometimes harmful but that so were utopic Gandhian promises of swaraj in a year and embrace of compromise, which kept Congress from organizing the peasantry and laborers. Ghadar had failed in 1915 because of mass apathy, Singh deduced, urging mass education to spread the theory behind the revolutionary effort. Revolution was "an organized and systematic work" requiring the direction of "professional revolutionaries" (not underground) committed to constant struggle and sacrifice. In a widely disseminated manifesto written just before his death, Singh called on youth not to turn to violent acts meant only for the chosen few to publicize the movement. Such outrages could not fulfill the larger goal of getting power "by the masses for the masses."[55] This doubt was tactical, not just principled. Singh worried that terrorism would drive the empire to compromise with moderates and simply replace white rule with brown rule. To him, this was Gandhism's goal, but, we know, that was a compromise of which Gandhi himself was wary.

Indeed, Gandhism was also about constant struggle and federal aims. Its distance from Singh's socialist goals mirrored Tolstoy's from Russian Communists' goals. Tolstoy opposed private land ownership but also a soulless planned socialist economy, favoring autonomous local communities. For Gandhi, too, socialism remained rooted in industrialism and a historical vision that countenanced ethical compromise in the present in the name of material progress. The philosopher-poet Muhammad Iqbal agreed with Gandhi, discerning that this vision paradoxically foregrounded the "interests" produced historically by the establishment of property as the driving force of history itself. Perceiving modern nation-states' separation of the material and spiritual realms, Iqbal hoped that Muslim political autonomy might instead foster a society on the basis of an Islamic moral system that would serve Muslims and non-Muslims. Iqbal, too, believed man's purpose was to remake himself ethically rather than to remake the world, and that pursuit of truth depended on love. Thus, at the end of that momentous year of 1930, Iqbal landed at the idea of a "Muslim India within India"—later co-opted into a movement for Pakistan. The idea of partition emerged from a brainstorm about anti-colonial goals among skeptics of socialism and the nation-state.

---

54. Bhagat Singh, "To Young Political Workers," February 2, 1931, available at, https://www.marxists.org/archive/bhagat-singh/1931/02/02.htm.

55. Maclean, *Revolutionary History*, 216–17.

In March 1931, Singh (aged twenty-three) and his companions were hanged. For some, this moment pivotally exposed Gandhism's uselessness. In Punjab, many were alienated by Congress's failure to address the pain of Singh's hanging. "Gandhi did not see the truth of his opponents' satyagraha," writes Neeti Nair; but Singh offered "a window into a different and inclusionary anticolonial nationalism," of the sort "needed to weld together truly disparate segments of Indian political society" in a manner that might have fortified it against the divisive leanings that led to Partition.[56]

Singh's possible trajectory has long been an object of speculation. The thought of Gandhi, Barkatullah, Har Dayal, Roy, and others evolved over lifetimes. But more than imagining a convergence between Singh and Gandhi or freezing them in an opposing binary (as the British did), it is important to understand their mutual shaping. Gandhism always relied on dialogue—with imperialists and other anti-colonialists—to clarify its means and ends. Singh thought nonviolence needed to be supplemented with efforts to awaken the masses. But it was not nonviolence but truth that Gandhi offered as violence's opposite, something more active and confrontational than signified by satyagraha's English cognate, "passive resistance." If the HSRA was about heroes committing actions that drew the masses in, Gandhian actions were designed for collective participation by ordinary people. The HSRA did more than violence, and Congress did more than nonviolence. The HSRA did not seek to negate Gandhi, but to push him to take the radical possibility of his approach further. The HSRA thought of themselves as operating alongside the Congress movement and felt that their interventions contributed strategically to that broader struggle. That a key demand of Singh's hunger strike was reading material, even after his death sentence, testifies to his value for non-instrumental action, too: the desire to read purely for self-cultivation.

All this explains why many Indians revered both Singh and Gandhi at once. Popular art depicted Gandhi and the revolutionaries united, imagining Gandhi's tacit support for revolutionary violence as sustaining Singh's legitimacy. Singh was famous because he used violence *and* despite his violence. The underground culture of defiance intersected with the ethos of civil disobedience. The reinvigoration of the Gandhian movement in the 1930s was the product of the dialectical tension between it and its challengers. Insofar as Gandhism opposed violence with truth, contradiction was immanent to it. Many felt no

56. Nair, *Changing Homelands*, 130–31.

cognitive dissonance in supporting both strategies. The organizations shared overlapping memberships. HSRA members attended Congress meetings, designing their work around Congress activities. Friendships between individual members were strong, thanks also to common ties to institutions like National College. In 1926, Singh modeled the Naujawan Bharat Sabha on the Congress format; its leaders also led the Congress in Punjab. Many Congress members were themselves ambivalent about means. For example, Nehru committed unequivocally to nonviolence only in 1931, partly from fear of communal violence, and later downplayed the overlap between the groups. After 1931, Congress no longer publicly endorsed violence. Individuals inspired by the HSRA undertook assassinations in the early 1930s, but the HSRA itself began to rethink the role of violence, disappearing altogether in 1934 (excepting Udham Singh's 1940 assassination of Michael O'Dwyer). Congress's legal, moral, and financial support had always been essential to HSRA work; intensified repression shrank the scope for violent acts, while the renewed Congress struggle offered an outlet for revolutionary sentiment.

Rather than rival approaches, then, these movements were parts of a single anti-colonial formation, linked "by complex discursive and organisational connections."[57] The productive tension, the "promiscuous alliances," between approaches persisted.[58] Roy was popular throughout the 1930s (though Gandhi abhorred his anti-religion stance) and continued to push socialist aims, urging Congress leaders at the 1936 convention to adopt a social and economic program. After the British ceded provincial government control in 1935, Indians were in charge of jails full of hunger-strikers. Gandhi secured release for political prisoners who renounced violence—becoming useful to the British this way.

During World War II, Indians navigated the choices of noncooperation; neutrality; cooperation with the British, whether to confront fascism, gain postwar rewards, or support the Soviet cause; and cooperation with Britain's enemies. In 1942, Congress opted for noncooperation, launching the Quit India movement. As its members were then jailed and killed, more violent and sectarian movements gained traction. Subhas Chandra Bose organized an army among Indian prisoners of war and civilians in Southeast Asia to liberate India with Japanese help, nurturing the old ethos of martial sacrifice.

57. Partha Chatterjee, as quoted in Maclean, *Revolutionary History*, 221.
58. Leela Gandhi, as quoted in Maclean and Elam, "Reading Revolutionaries," in *Revolutionary Lives*, 8.

The ascendance of violent ideals was evident upon independence in 1947 but directed against Indians rather than Britons. Some grasped the historic entanglement of violent and nonviolent anti-colonialism. In 1949, when Prime Minister Nehru refused to lay the foundation stone for a memorial to the 1908 bombers of Muzaffarpur, Roy, who had himself repudiated violence in favor of Radical Humanism, countered that, as a beneficiary, Nehru was "not morally entitled to be censorious about acts of violence prompted by selfless idealism."[59] But the price of the double helix of violent and nonviolent anti-colonialism had been too high, to Nehru: Gandhi had been assassinated the year before by the RSS, an echo of the assassination that had prompted his formal theorization of nonviolence. (Savarkar was implicated but acquitted.)

III

As it began beyond the subcontinent, so Gandhism spilled beyond it, becoming an instrument of popular instruction in Asia, Africa, and beyond. Khadi and the Gandhi cap were mass circulated symbols of anti-colonialism. Interest in the Indian movement was based on a sense of shared obstacles and colonial brotherhood. Some questioned the viability of nonviolence in the face of British violence. African-American leaders applied Gandhi's methods to the anti-racist struggle in the United States, where they also remained in tension with violent approaches.

Indeed, though satyagraha was an anti-colonial strategy, it was essentially about reclaiming the self from oppressive rule. As soon as Congress began to wield institutional power after 1935, Gandhi distanced himself from it, maintaining his anti-statist stance. As we have seen, the concern for many anti-colonial thinkers was state oppression, not national emancipation.

Given the destruction of the self at the heart of colonialism, it is no surprise that it was a psychiatrist who ultimately analyzed the dangerous dance of nonviolent and violent anti-colonialism. Fanon was in Algeria after World War II. In that brutal settler colonial society, he joined the side of those fighting for freedom, becoming deeply involved in FLN (National Liberation Front) discussions of strategy. From there he became an advocate for other African anti-colonial struggles.

The Ghanaian struggle—the first to succeed in Sub-Saharan Africa—drew on Gandhian ideas, but Fanon doubted their viability, backing the development of a militia corps to support African revolutionary movements. Fanon's

---

59. Harper, *Underground Asia*, 656–57.

tolerance for violent means echoed Singh's logic: colonized people, like mental patients, needed a shock to enable their reconstruction. This conclusion emerged, however, from his observation of nonviolence's reliance on and provocation of violent anti-colonialism—as in India—and of the way in which this contest then limited the scope of decolonization.

Accepting the inevitability of violence, Fanon's writing on violent decolonization was descriptive more than prescriptive, explaining the mental processes that made violence inescapable. *The Wretched of the Earth* (1961) opened with an empirical observation: "whatever may be . . . the new formulas introduced, decolonization is always a violent phenomenon." The objective of replacing one set of men with another could "only triumph if we use all means . . . including . . . violence" because colonial agents brought violence "into the home and . . . mind of the native." Colonialism was "violence in its natural state."[60]

This truth had driven Gandhi to nonviolence as an antidote. But Fanon was skeptical after what he had seen: for, empirically, colonialism yielded only "when confronted with greater violence." His focus was, importantly, settler colonialism, in which the settler makes even dreams of liberty impossible for the native, who then imagines "all possible methods for destroying the settler." He first turns his aggression towards his own people and, eventually, identifying his enemy and recognizing all his misfortunes, the native throws "all the exacerbated might of his hate and anger into this new channel." Those who colonizers long claimed understood only the language of force then "give utterance by force," finding "freedom in and through violence." Their violence responds to colonial violence with "an extraordinary reciprocal homogeneity," unifying those that colonialism works to separate. It functions as "a cleansing force," freeing each from his inferiority complex, despair, and inaction.[61]

Though *Wretched of the Earth* opens by explaining anti-colonial violence, its central concern was the dehumanizing violence of colonialism. Its prescriptive arguments, about the need for reparations and new consciousness, derived from Fanon's observations of the way anti-colonialism fared absent those changes, given the "pitfalls" of bourgeoisies bent on preserving the power structures spawned by colonialism. Fanon showed how anti-colonial action driven spontaneously by dynamics of survival and realism succeeds somewhat because colonial powers simply cannot undertake "prolonged establishment of large forces of occupation." But the independence thus produced could not bring

60. Frantz Fanon, *The Wretched of the Earth* (New York, NY: Grove, 1963), 35, 37–38, 61.
61. Fanon, *Wretched of the Earth*, 71, 84, 86, 88, 93, 94.

change for most people because the will to break colonialism remained linked with the will to come to "friendly agreement with it." While jailed revolutionaries launched hunger strikes, colonialism compromised with moderates, who, in turn, became absorbed in the details of government conceded to them. Echoing Singh, Fanon wrote that moderates' pacifist commitments exploited the violence automatically erupting in the colonized society to extort compromises. He, too, complained of moderates' disregard for the inherently "revolutionary" peasantry and the way they later disowned anti-colonial violence as that of "adventurers and anarchists." Moreover, whatever their intentions, moderates were forced to spend much time merely warding off neocolonial threats. As a result, despite independence, colonialism, "the rule of violence," persists. The struggle against it morphs into struggle against poverty, illiteracy, underdevelopment, neocolonialism; life remains an "unending contest."[62]

If anti-colonialism was not enough, neither was economic transformation, given the racism underpinning colonialism. The world needed "a new humanism," involving transformation of our most intimate relations, whose potential emerged from the very dynamics of anti-colonialism. When people find that some settlers are sympathetic and some colonized people unsympathetic to the struggle, "barriers of blood and race-prejudice" start to break down. Echoing Khilafat leaders, Fanon saw the struggle as not only the means but the end of internal rehabilitation: the Algerian movement had drawn Arabs, Black Africans, Kabyles, and white Algerians into a single struggle. The forms of collective organization that enable the struggle themselves allow the colonized to recover the vocabulary of kinship and coexistence: "community triumphs, and . . . spreads its own light."[63]

Like many anti-colonial thinkers, Fanon believed human nature was essentially intersubjective, that solidarities (which racism broke down) were integral to lived experience. His earlier book, *Black Skin, White Masks* (1951), declared that freedom was a "world of reciprocal recognitions" and that a desire "to touch the other, feel the other, discover each other" was essential to humanity.[64] Hence peasants' whole way of life was anti-colonial by nature. Colonialism hammered into the native mind "the idea of a society of individuals where each person shuts himself up in his own subjectivity," and decolonization shows it the "falseness of this theory."[65]

62. Fanon, *Wretched of the Earth*, 61, 74, 78, 94, 124.
63. Fanon, *Wretched of the Earth*, 48, 146, 246.
64. Fanon, *Black Skin, White Masks* (New York, NY: Grove, 2008 [1951]), 193, 206.
65. Fanon, *Wretched of the Earth*, 47.

The Wretched of the Earth spelled out the dangers of a middle class "glad to accept the dividends that the former colonial power hands out to it," so that the masses might bar their way. "If you really wish your country to avoid regression," Fanon urged, "a rapid step must be taken from national consciousness to political and social consciousness." They must move from rediscovering national culture—an important part of challenging colonialism—to *creating* it by working with "the people" to construct a new future. This was national culture based not on folklore but rather on the "whole body of efforts made by a people in the sphere of thought to describe, justify, and praise the action through which that people has created itself and keeps itself in existence." It was a national consciousness that bred international consciousness.[66]

Like Gandhi, Fanon called for transformation of selves to enable new human relationships. "Decolonization is the veritable creation of new men": it turned what colonialism had made a "thing" into "man." The colonized mock the "Western values" that had legitimized their subjugation "and vomit them up." The "Third World" must thus refuse to define itself "in the terms of values which have preceded it," Fanon concluded, dreaming (like Gandhi) of a postcolonial way of life based on anti-statist decentralization—an independent Africa without capital cities.[67]

Fanon, too, recognized the risk of formal freedom without substantive change, especially given the propensity for continued economic dominance by former colonial rulers—neocolonialism. Thus, he called for "redistribution of wealth." Just as European nations had received reparations and restitution from the Nazis, they must do likewise for colonialism. "The wealth of the imperial countries is our wealth too," he affirmed. Rather than "nuclearizing the world," Europe must aid newly decolonized countries—which depended on that shift in consciousness: Europeans no longer "playing the stupid game of the Sleeping Beauty."[68] Fanon's intended audience included Europeans, hence the preface by Jean-Paul Sartre.

The demand for reparations persists. As does the call for a new humanism— made also by Gandhi, Roy, Har Dayal, and Tagore, whose "last testament," composed as he witnessed the destruction of World War II, looked toward

66. Fanon, *Wretched of the Earth*, 175, 203, 233.
67. Fanon, *Wretched of the Earth*, 36–37, 43, 99.
68. Fanon, *Wretched of the Earth*, 98, 102, 105–6.

"unvanquished Man arising from the ashes of destruction."[69] Ghadar poetry belongs to such a humanistic effort, as does the work of the Indian Progressive Writers' Movement. Literary and poetic language had a primary role in forming anti-colonial subjectivity and shaped responses to traumas of decolonization like Partition. Those who recognized the new border as colonialism's enduring imprint drew strength from continued connection across it, an ethics of love, of interpersonal subjectivity, serving as both means and end of their activism.

The works of anti-colonial thinkers like Gandhi, Singh, and Fanon were themselves part of this new humanism, which triggered change even in old humanistic endeavors like history. In 1932, the Indonesian anti-colonial revolutionary Tan Malaka warned the British that his voice would be even "louder from the grave," and, indeed, such thinkers' work sustains anti-colonialism today.[70] It has also nurtured the rise of postcolonial, indigenous, gender, and other studies making up "the new humanities."[71] Yet, new humanities do not on their own offer the new humanism required to confront inequality and climate crisis. The work of repair and self-examination that Fanon demanded of those who profited from empire—Europeans, Americans, and colonial bourgeoisies—remains to be done.

Anti-colonialism thrived on utopianism: Muslim utopia, village utopia, socialist utopia, cross-border friendship utopia. This is a way of living in a state of constant aspiration, aware that fulfilment of the struggle lies in the struggle itself, akin to experiences of the divine in many mystical traditions.

The global horizons of Ghadar continue to inform anti-colonialism, in transnational solidarities with Palestinians and Indian farmers as well as in the global reach of Black Lives Matter and movements for climate justice. In India, the farmers' protest of 2020–21 challenged the colonialism that Gandhi, Singh, and Fanon warned would persist in a postcolonial order still tethered to the mindset of colonialism. Prime Minister Narendra Modi crafts an image of the sacrificial, abstinent leader idealized by the RSS (which he joined as a youth). His henchmen exemplify Hindutva's conversion of the principle of sacrifice "into a collective, anonymous . . . force suffused by a heightened awareness of organisation and institutional perpetuation."[72] The "intoxication" induced by "worthless reading" that led Dhingra on his violent path continues to radicalize

69. Mukherjee, *Tagore & Gandhi*, 159.

70. Harper, *Underground Asia*, 658.

71. K. Ruthven, quoted in Dipesh Chakrabarty, *The Climate of History in a Planetary Age* (Chicago, IL: University of Chicago Press, 2021), 2.

72. Kapila, *Violent Fraternity*, 121.

youth into acts of spectacular violence. And consumer boycotts extend anti-colonial traditions, often without any awareness of doing so.

It was in evolving anti-colonial practices that thinkers like Gandhi and Fanon decolonized themselves. Debate about how to be anti-colonial *is* the process of decolonization. State power confronts plural forms of dissent and resistance wherever and whenever it acts coercively, imperiously. But anti-colonial thinkers remind us that the key to decolonization is recovering the capacity for ethical as *opposed* to "strategic"—consequentialist—thought.

PART III

Strategy in an Age of Global War

CHAPTER 19

Strategy, War Plans, and the First World War

Margaret MacMillan

"War is Right, Peace is Wrong, says German General." In the spring of 1912, just two years before the Great War, the *New York Times* was shocked at the views expressed by the leading German military theorist, General Friedrich von Bernhardi, in his latest book *Germany and the Next War*. For Bernhardi, war was "not only a necessary factor in civilization, but the highest expression, among civilized people, of power and life."[1] While they might not have engaged in the same sort of philosophizing, many, perhaps a majority, of Europe's political and military leaders before 1914, thought of war as an effective tool of state which could be used to achieve national goals with acceptable costs. The century since the end of the Napoleonic wars appeared to bear this out. The wars of Italian and German unification had been fought between only two powers at a time, had seen decisive battles, and had ended with definitive outcomes. The many colonial wars from those between the United States and American Indians to Germany's wars in southwest Africa were further evidence of the possibility of limited wars with beneficial results for the victors.

As they formulated the strategies that they would adopt before the First World War, European policymakers started with the fundamental assumption that war remained an option to achieve national goals, whether these were

---

1. "War Is Right, Peace Wrong, Says German General," *New York Times*, April 21, 1912.

expansionist or defensive.[2] Strategy still was understood largely as war-making, and defeating the enemy to the point of surrender remained the goal. The enemy in question of course shifted in response to domestic and international changes so, for example, where Britain saw France and Russia as future potential enemies in the 1890s, it swung around in the following decade to identify Germany as the primary enemy in the face of German naval and economic rivalry and so moved closer to both France and Russia, even if it continued to avoid military alliances. The sorts of economic issues now so familiar in war planning—ensuring that the nation's resources would be effectively used or undermining the enemy's economy—were not yet seen as part of strategy. Army general staffs and those political leaders involved in planning saw no need to consult with their bankers or industrialists.

The military also attempted to argue, with more success in Germany than in other countries, that strategy was largely their business and that once war had started, entirely theirs. Too often civilian leaders accepted this and failed to inform themselves of what their militaries were planning. In 1900, when Friedrich von Holstein, the eminence grise of German foreign policy, discovered that General Alfred von Schlieffen contemplated violating Belgium's neutrality in war, he simply said, "If the Chief of the General Staff, particularly such a preeminent strategical authority as Schlieffen, considers such a measure imperative, then it is the duty of diplomacy to concur in it and to facilitate it

2. There is a vast and ever-growing literature on strategic thinking and war planning before the First World War. For strategic thinking in the period see Azar Gat, *The Development of Military Thought: The Nineteenth Century* (Oxford: Oxford University Press, 1992); Beatrice Heuser, *The Evolution of Strategy: Thinking War from Antiquity to the Present* (Cambridge: Cambridge University Press, 2010); Peter Paret, Gordon A. Craig, and Felix Gilbert, eds., *Makers of Modern Strategy from Machiavelli to the Nuclear Age* (Princeton, NJ: Princeton University Press, 2010); Martin Van Creveld, *Command in War* (Cambridge, MA: Harvard University Press, 1985). On the cult of the offensive the following are useful: Robert Citino, *Quest for Decisive Victory: From Stalemate to Blitzkrieg in Europe, 1899–1940* (Lawrence, KS: University Press of Kansas, 2002) and Steven Miller, Sean M. Lynn-Jones, and Stephen Van Evera, eds., *Military Strategy and the Origins of The First World War* (Princeton, NJ: Princeton University Press, 1991). The impact of the Russo-Japanese war on contemporary thinking is covered in Frank Jacob, *The Russo-Japanese War and Its Shaping of the Twentieth Century* (New York, NY: Routledge, 2017) and Rotem Kowner, *The Impact of the Russo-Japanese War* (New York, NY: Routledge, 2006). Christopher Clark, *Sleepwalkers: How Europe Went to War in 1914* (New York, NY: HarperCollins Publishers LLC, 2012) and Margaret MacMillan, *The War That Ended Peace: The Road to 1914* (New York, NY: Random House, 2013) cover the diplomacy of the period. Hew Strachan's *The First World War*, Volume 1: *To Arms* (Oxford: Oxford University Press, 2001) is indispensable for the war plans. Richard F. Hamilton and Holger Herwig, eds. *War Planning 1914* (Cambridge: Cambridge University Press, 2009) and

in every possible manner."[3] Communication among armies and navies was often little better. At a 1911 meeting of the Committee of Imperial Defence to review Britain's strategy (the last such meeting before 1914), the politicians were dismayed to find that, while the army had plans to send an expeditionary force to the Continent in the event of an attack on France, the navy intended to blockade German ports and carry out occasional amphibious raids but did not think its role included getting the military safely to the Continent.

The strategies and choices each power adopted were, as they have always been, influenced by a range of considerations, from the nature of each nation's society to geography. Where the British had an aversion to standing armies for historical reasons, in Germany the army was seen, at least by its officers and supporters, as the noblest part of the nation. Additionally, while the British and the Japanese thought of sea power as crucial for defense and the projection of power and influence, the Germans, French, Russians, and Austrians, with their vulnerable land borders, had to rely largely on their armies for security.

History was yet another factor. In particular, the putative lessons of the Napoleonic wars were studied and disseminated widely in the course of the nineteenth century. They appeared to show that wars were won by strategic brilliance and boldness, exercised by inspiring leaders. The offensive was therefore generally preferable to the defensive in both strategic and tactical terms. War itself, even if its aims were limited, should be waged, on the Napoleonic model of *guerre à outrance*, with utmost ruthlessness, to destroy the enemy. Battles such as Austerlitz, Trafalgar, and Waterloo exerted a powerful hold on nineteenth-century

---

Richard Fr. Hamilton and Holger Herwig, *Decisions for War, 1914–1917* (Cambridge: Cambridge University Press, 2004) have excellent essays on specific powers. For more on the Triple Entente, see Samuel Williamson, *The Politics of Grand Strategy: Britain and France Prepare for War, 1904–1914* (London: Ashfield Press, 1990); Douglas Porch, *The March to the Marne: The French Army 1871–1914* (Cambridge: Cambridge University Press, 2010); and John Gooch, *The Plans of War: The General Staff and British Military Strategy c.1900–1916* (London: Routledge, 1974). For the Triple Alliance see, Gordon Craig, *The Politics of the Prussian Army 1640–1945* (Oxford: Oxford University Press, 1964); Holger Herwig, "Disjointed Allies: Coalition Warfare in Berlin and Vienna, 1914," in *War Studies Reader: From the Seventeenth Century to the Present Day and Beyond*, Gary Sheffield, ed. (London: Continuum, 2010); Marcus Jones, "The Alliance That Wasn't: Austria-Hungary and Germany in World War I," in *Grand Strategy and Military Alliances*, Peter Mansoor and Williamson Murray, eds. (Cambridge: Cambridge University Press, 2016); Norman Stone, "Moltke-Conrad: Relations between the Austro-Hungarian and German General Staffs, 1909–14," *The Historical Journal* 9:2 (1966): 201–28; and Graydon Tunstall, *Planning for War against Russia and Serbia: Austro-Hungarian and German Military Strategies, 1871–1914* (New York, NY: Columbia University Press, 1993).

3. MacMillan, *The War That Ended Peace*, 346.

imaginations and too few military planners stopped to reflect that Napoleon was finally defeated by superior forces in a war of attrition. On land and sea, the ability of forces to maneuver, dividing the enemy forces or outflanking and bringing about decisive battles, remained the key to ultimate victory over the enemy. Yet what if the enemy refused to surrender even after defeat on the battlefield? The French nation, as opposed to its armies, had fought on against the German Confederation after the battle of Sedan in 1870. As his colleagues planned for new decisive battles at the start of the twentieth century, a German general warned, "You cannot carry away the armed strength of a great Power like a cat in a bag."[4]

Naval strategy, thanks in part to the highly influential American theorist Alfred Thayer Mahan, mirrored that on land. While Mahan argued that Britain's global dominance in the eighteenth century rested on its command of the seas and its power to seize France's colonies, blockade its key ports, and to interdict its trade, he also believed that the primary purpose of a navy was to seek out the enemy battle fleet and either render it useless through blockade or destroy it in battle. He and his many followers dismissed the ideas put forward by the French Jeune Ecole which advocated mines and swarms of fast torpedo boats to attack enemy navies and raid enemy commerce in a *guerre de course*.

For all their admiration of Napoleon and his great interpreters, Clausewitz and Antoine-Henri Jomini, those responsible for making strategy were uneasily aware that they were doing so in a rapidly changing world, with new technologies, new ideas, and a new mass politics. This was a world where the Napoleonic battle with fast-moving columns attacking the enemy might not be easily achievable. Advances in infantry weapons and artillery as a result of improvements in explosives and metallurgy, rifling, and breechloading meant that the field of fire through which attacking troops moved gave an increasing edge to defenders, who were largely invisible thanks to smokeless gunpowder and trenches. Europe's military planners tried to accommodate to this by changes at the tactical rather than the strategic level. According to the French Infantry Field Regulations of 1904, troops should spread out more as they moved forward, utilizing natural cover. The corresponding German regulations stressed enveloping the enemy lines rather than frontal attacks. (Few imagined a situation such as the Western Front, in which it was impossible to envelop a line stretching from the Swiss border to the sea.) If losses were greater as a result of increased and more deadly firepower, then the attackers must also expect to assemble and employ overwhelming strengths of artillery and infantry. Crucially, leaders must so motivate their troops that they could endure great losses but still push forward in the face of the fire being rained down on them.

---

4. Craig, *The Politics of the Prussian Army 1640–1945*, 280.

The scaling up in the size of armies, which the Industrial Revolution made possible, brought its own problems of moving and controlling vast numbers on a greatly expanded battlefield. Bernhardi and Schlieffen both painted a rosy future where balloons, telegraphs, couriers with fast motor vehicles, telephones, or special optical signaling devices would allow commanders of great armies to sit far in the rear in a comfortable set of offices directing the movements on the ground. There, said Schlieffen, "the Modern Alexander will have the entire battlefield under his eyes on a map."[5] By 1914, the technology was not yet up to that task. Telegraph and telephone wires were easily cut and difficult to roll out as armies advanced. As the experience of the German advance in the summer of 1914 showed, headquarters many miles in the rear struggled to find out what was happening on the ground. Radios, which were going to play such an important part in the Second World War, were still too cumbersome and the coding and decoding too slow, to be a substitute means of communication.

The prolonged period of peace in Europe before 1914, when the military could carry out maneuvers or war games under controlled conditions, also allowed them to minimize the growing difficulties faced by the attack. Observers at Austria-Hungary's annual war games were struck by the absence of war conditions. Cavalry charged about as if there was no need to worry about gunfire and infantry advanced upright and en masse against defenders who were also standing. The very professionalism of general staffs, with their reliance on statistics, maps, and railway timetables to make elaborate plans, served to blind them to what Clausewitz called "friction" in actual war: the uncertainty, confusion, accidents, or mistakes, "the force that makes the apparently easy so difficult."[6] Schlieffen, whose influence and thought continued to shape the work of the German High Command even after his retirement in 1905, saw a seamless progression through from mobilization to victory. As a German general later complained of his education at the war academy, no order that would have been given in real combat was ever discussed.

I

For all that they often saw themselves as somehow apart from society, Europe's militaries were affected by the intellectual currents and assumptions of their times. The great advances in science in the nineteenth century fostered

5. Van Creveld, *Command in War*, 153.
6. Paret, ed., *Makers of Modern Strategy*, 202–3.

positivism, the hope that all human activity could be studied and measured. Commodore Stephen Luce, the founder of the US Naval War College and a mentor to Mahan, held that "it seems only natural and reasonable that we should call science to our aid to lead us to a truer comprehension of naval warfare."[7] Across Europe, military thinkers tried to discover the laws governing war and victory. Clausewitz and Jomini were poured over in search of clear guidance. In France, the experts argued over whether there were twenty-four or perhaps forty-one laws. Increasingly, strategy was seen as a formula rather than a set of guidelines adaptable in changing circumstances.

On the Continent, planning the mobilization of the vast armies which were being created through conscription and the use of reserves became an important element of strategy. The examples of French failures in mobilization in 1870 and, more recently, the Russians in 1904 were studied as examples of the dangers in not concentrating forces effectively and in time. As the French Chief Staff Joseph Joffre claimed to the French president in 1914, every day's delay in mobilization meant the loss of between fifteen and twenty kilometers of French territory to the advancing Germans. The mechanics of mobilization were properly "scientific" and general staffs threw themselves into making detailed mobilization timetables, utilizing the growing railway networks and indeed pressuring governments to build lines to fit their plans. By 1914, the Railway Section of the German General Staff had a staff of sixty, among them some of the brightest and most ambitious officers, whose detailed plans to mobilize and move 2.1 million men and their supplies, including 600,000 horses, would be disseminated when the time came by hundreds of thousands of railway, telegraph, and telephone employees.

While romanticism with its cult of the emotions and of the individual seemed to be the opposite of positivism, the military took from it the faith that, with the right training and inspiration, humans could develop the will and the capacity to counter the growing preponderance of weapons on the battlefield. The right spirit could enable soldiers to face the storm of fire. Colonel F. N. Maude, an enthusiast for Clausewitz, wrote that "success in the assault is all a case of how you train your soldiers beforehand to know how to die or to avoid dying."[8] The new discipline of psychology and, in particular, the work of Henri Bergson, who argued for the animating life force—*élan vital*—in human beings, influenced major military thinkers such as Colonel

---

7. Gat, *The Development of Military Thought*, 175–78.
8. Paret, ed., *Makers of Modern Strategy*, 511.

Louis de Grandmaison, France's Director of Military Operations before the war. "We are rightly told," he wrote in his classic 1906 work on infantry training, "that psychological factors are paramount in combat. But this is not all: properly speaking, there are no other factors, for all others—weaponry, maneuverability—influence only indirectly by provoking moral reactions . . . the human heart is the starting point in all questions of war."[9]

Positivism and romanticism nourished those other great trends of the prewar years: Social Darwinism, nationalism, and militarism. The first of the three misapplied Darwin's theories of evolution to posit a "scientific" taxonomy of races arranged in a hierarchy from the least evolved to the most. Nationalism mobilized emotions through myth, often disguised as history, symbols, and culture to weld individuals into a mystical thing called the nation. Since the time was one of intense imperialist competition among the powers, the seizing of colonies and the subduing of their inhabitants by force was often read as another marker of national vitality and power. The nation that was not prepared to fight for its existence did not deserve to survive. Indeed, in the act of war the nation would become stronger still. What worried Europe's leaders was the question of whether their young would fight as their forefathers had done. Had modern life made the youth soft and passive? Perhaps, as some leading thinkers argued, war was a necessary tonic, to toughen them up and instill patriotism. Militarism was partly a response to such concerns, to encourage military values among civilians—think of all those school children in miniature uniforms—but it also served to elevate the mystique and the position of the military and war itself within society.

The decades before 1914 were marked by growing academic and public interest in military matters. Oxford got its first professor of military history in 1909 and the war correspondent became an admired contributor to the new mass newspapers and magazines. Across Europe, army and navy leagues, sometimes with covert support from the military, mobilized civilians to demand more, whether bigger armies or new battleships. Governments, sometimes reluctantly, responded to public pressures. The period also saw an arms race which heightened tensions among the powers and helped to set off sudden waves of panic in their citizens about surprise attacks or invasions.

Russia's turmoil and near revolution in 1905–6, after its defeat in the Russo-Japanese War, sent shivers through Europe for it demonstrated that nations that lost wars or failed to prosecute them with sufficient vigor risked internal

9. Porch, *The March to the Marne*, 120.

collapse. The longer the war, the greater the strain and so it was widely assumed that future wars had to be short. Most policymakers also assumed that
Europe's economies were so closely intertwined that the economic dislocation
caused by war would bring economies to a standstill in a matter of months.
Nations had to plan for and fight short, decisive wars. This suited the traditions
and ethos of the officer classes which customarily came from the landed and
aristocratic classes and were acculturated to war from childhood. In the rapidly
changing Europe of the nineteenth century, they feared for their social status
in the face of a rising middle class and growing socialist movements. Defensive
wars, in their view, led to weakness and division while offensive wars were not
only glorious and noble but also brought and kept the nation together. As
guardians of the nation, the social position of the officer class was thus
ensured.

In the highly globalized world before 1914, ideas and assumptions as much
as goods and capital flowed across borders and the militaries shared similar
education, views, and institutions. The Prussian—later the German—General
Staff was a model for the others that were set up in Europe and as far away as
Japan in the second half of the nineteenth century. The manual on the duties
of the General Staff by General Bronsart von Schellendorff, Prussia's war minister in the 1880s, went through several editions in various languages and was
issued even to British officers for their edification. Officers read the same
works, from Clausewitz to Mahan, and studied the same battles. (Cannae, with
its classic envelopment of Roman forces by Hannibal was a favorite, while
Quintus Fabius Maximus, who harassed the Carthaginian armies in a long
campaign of attrition, was largely ignored.) Military journals kept officers up-
to-date on developments in each other's countries. In London, the Royal
United Services Institute Journal frequently carried translations of articles
originally in German, French, or Russian and by 1900 had a regular feature on
the contents of foreign military journals. The posting of military attachés to
foreign capitals and the growth in observers at each other's maneuvers or at
the wars before 1914 further helped to create a community linked by shared
knowledge and outlook. The Russo-Japanese War, which was to have a significant impact on the planning before 1914, attracted over eighty officers from
sixteen countries who spent considerable time in each other's company and
often drew similar conclusions about Japanese strengths and Russian
weaknesses.

There were plenty of wars to observe before 1914 and indications enough
that attacks in modern war were costlier and decisive victories in battle more

difficult to achieve. The European military largely explained inconvenient examples away and picked the "lessons" to suit their own preference for offensive war. As Jack Snyder and Barry Posen, among others, have suggested, their training and very cohesiveness inclined them to "group-think" and a reluctance to challenge prevailing orthodoxies. Ivan Bloch, the Polish-Russian financier who wrote a major study in the 1890s of war, described the military as a priestly caste. Of the American Civil War, where time and again attacking forces had suffered disproportionate casualties against well-armed and well-dug-in defenders, a European general told Bloch that it had not been a proper war and that he discouraged his officers from reading about it. The British military persuaded themselves that their initial losses in South Africa to the Afrikaans farmers who lay concealed in the ground were an aberration from which no useful lessons could be drawn. As a British major-general proudly said, his compatriots did not find being on the defensive acceptable and therefore made little study of it.[10] While the observers could not fail to notice how in the more recent Russo-Japanese war the Japanese forces besieging Port Arthur had nearly twice the number of casualties as the Russian defenders, the lesson largely drawn then and in the voluminous official histories that followed was that the Japanese triumphed because they had the right spirit. As Grandmaison maintained, the Japanese victory was due to "the absolute and unreserved offensive spirit, animating officers and men alike."[11] In 1913, France adopted a new regulation which said "the French army, returning to its traditions, accepts no law in the conduct of operations other than the offensive."[12] The Balkan Wars of 1912 and 1913 apparently provided confirmation of the superiority of French offensive élan: Bulgarian and Serbian armies, trained by French, triumphed over the Ottomans, who had been trained by the Germans.

Bloch presciently warned that the growing advantage of the defense and the capacity of modern nations to mobilize their resources would lead to stalemates on the battlefields and wars that lasted for years. "Namby-pamby so-called humanitarianism," was the reaction of a British general who heard him talk and the great German historian Hans Delbrück called Bloch's work "amateurish" without much to recommend it. Jean Jaurès, the leading French socialist, made arguments similar to Bloch's in his 1910 L'armée nouvelle. The French

10. Gat, *The Development of Military Thought*, 219.
11. Kowner, *The Impact of the Russo-Japanese War*, 265.
12. Hamilton and Herwig, eds., *War Planning 1914*, 160.

military, Jaurès warned, had been beguiled by Napoleon into thinking that the offensive was the only way to fight a war and that the defensive was dishonorable and unworthy of the French nation. In calling on Clausewitz, they ignored his teaching on the value of the defense. The British historian Julian Corbett also saw a place for the defensive in naval war and criticized the overemphasis of naval strategists on decisive battles and command of the seas. Furthermore, Corbett took on those experts, Mahan foremost among them, who argued that sea power could determine the outcome of wars. "Since men live upon the land and not upon the sea," Corbett wrote, "great issues between nations at war have always been decided—except in the rarest cases—either by what your army can do against your enemy's territory and national life or else by the fear of what the fleet makes it possible for your army to do."[13] Because of the British navy's long experience with economic, amphibious and defensive warfare, Corbett's arguments received a hearing within naval circles but came in for strenuous criticism as well.

Businessmen, socialists, or science fiction writers such as H.G. Wells, all could be dismissed because they were civilians. If any among the senior military had doubts about the future of war, they largely kept quiet but one can sense in their repeated assurances that the offensive was the key to success that they were gambling that their plans would succeed and quickly. They were not planning for long wars of attrition and by 1914, they had mostly scrapped alternate, defensive, strategies and plans. Only small European nations such as Switzerland, Belgium, or Serbia, which faced much larger enemies, continued to think and plan defensively.

II

The remaining offensive plans of the Great Powers were not, as historians such as Barbara Tuchman and A.J.P. Taylor later held, so rigid that they took Europe to war in 1914. That view has long since been challenged by those who argue that longer term forces such as nationalism or militarism played a key part, as well as the decisions made by those in power in the particular circumstances of 1914. Another persistent myth about the outbreak of the Great War is that what is misleadingly described as "the alliance system," with its balance of power, ensured that what began as a conflict in the Balkans between Austria-Hungary and Serbia would almost inevitably lead to a general war. In both the

---

13. Gat, *The Development of Military Thought*, 487.

Triple Alliance of Germany, Austria-Hungary, and Italy and the Triple Entente of Britain, France, and Russia, the treaties were defensive and only came into effect if there were an unprovoked attack on a member. Italy stayed out of the war in 1914 because Austria-Hungary initiated the war with Serbia. In the Triple Entente, the treaty was bilateral, between France and Russia. Britain had understandings with each but no formal agreement with either, although in the event the foreign secretary, Sir Edward Grey, was to talk of "obligations of honor." Nor were all the plans as thoroughly worked out as Germany's, commonly known as the Schlieffen Plan. While that plan was an elaborate and detailed mobilization and deployment scheme, France merely had overall general directions which left much to the initiative of theatre commanders. Britain had scarcely any plans at all for engagement in a major continental war.

The strategies and plans that the powers had by 1914 were the product of many years of discussion within the military and sometimes with their civilian leaders and of changes and modifications in response to a variety of factors from domestic politics, new technologies and tactics, and shifts in the international scene. By 1914, France had made seventeen mobilization plans against Germany while Austria-Hungary, with its multiplicity of possible enemies, had made plans against Italy, Russia, Serbia, Montenegro, and Albania, sometimes singly but more often in combinations. Significantly, all the powers were moving towards offensive war and abandoning the option of a defensive war or, in the case of Russia, Germany, and Austria-Hungary, a war against just one enemy at a time. While the evolution of the different strategies is a fascinating story, to make sense of what happened in 1914 we need to understand what Europe's leaders were thinking and planning then. By 1915, if the Great War had not intervened, the strategies and plans might well have changed again. Britain, for example, was growing ever more concerned about imperial competition from Russia while a number of Russian statesmen were arguing for a rapprochement with the other conservative monarchies of Germany and Austria-Hungary.

III

Prior to the First World War, the Triple Alliance was a marriage of convenience which seemed to be heading for the rocks with its members' strategic interests increasingly at odds. Italy, the most lukewarm member, was also the weakest. A new arrival on the international scene, it was a great power more by courtesy than reality, with its deeply divided society and a weak economy. If civil-military relations were imperfect all over Europe, those in Italy were abysmal. Politicians discouraged military leaders from talking directly to government ministers and rarely consulted with them on policy. The attitude of Giovanni Giolitti, prime minister on three occasions before 1914, was typical of many civilian leaders: "The generals are worth little; they came out of the ranks at a time when families sent their most stupid sons into the army because they did not know what to do with them."[14] The military had little of idea of the government's foreign policy or what agreements it had made with other powers. When the Triple Alliance was renewed in 1912, the Chief of the Italian General Staff complained that no one had told him what its clauses were. The Italian military resigned itself to planning for war, probably an offensive war, and waiting for the government to let it know who the enemy was.

Geography and history gave Italy two potential rivals, France and Austria-Hungary, and, although Italy was allied to the latter, its leaders contemplated war with it and worked to improve relations with the former. The existence of Italian-speaking territories still under Austrian rule was a particular sore point and Italian ambitions to acquire Italy's "natural" borders along the high points of the Alps and the Dolomites were unlikely to be achieved short of war with its neighbor. Austria-Hungary had no intention of losing any more territory and its general staff continued to update its plans for a war with Italy. The Chief of Staff, Franz Conrad von Hötzendorf, had a particular hatred for the Italians and strengthened Austria-Hungary's fortifications and military presence along the common border. The Italian military responded by creating mobilization plans for its northeastern frontier.

Nevertheless, Italy continued to discuss its possible military contributions to the Triple Alliance in the event of a general war. These included disrupting movements of troops from France's North African colonies across the Mediterranean to France, either via an amphibious landing on France's southern coast or an offensive through the French Alps. The option that received the most attention was for Italy to send infantry and cavalry divisions to the Upper Rhine in support of the German left wing. The problem was how to get them there. Switzerland had a good railway system but was neutral and unlikely to agree. The German High Command, which had no compunctions about breaching Belgium's neutrality, hesitated largely because Switzerland, with its mountainous terrain and strong defenses, was a harder target. The alternative route was through Austria-Hungary which, understandably, was reluctant to

14. Hamilton and Herwig, *War Planning 1914*, 190.

see a large force from a potential enemy entering its territory. The Italians themselves were divided and indecisive and support for Germany on the Rhine became even more problematic after the Italian invasion of Ottoman Libya in 1911 proved very costly for the Italian military. At the start of the 1914 crisis, however, the Italian military at least was still planning to attack France and send a force into Germany. The civilians, however, were having second thoughts and, on August 3, Italy declared its neutrality, surprising both its allies and its own military. Moltke wrote in anger to Conrad about Italy's "crime" which had serious implications for Germany's own war plans.[15]

For decades, Germany had been obsessed by the notion that it was encircled, between a vengeful France on the west and Russia, with its vast resources, to the east. While Britain was a potential enemy, most German strategists felt that Germany's fate would be settled on land. Despite attempts to mend fences with Russia, the growing closeness between Russia and France—marked by a treaty of mutual defense, joint military planning, and massive French investment in Russian railways—persuaded the Germans that they almost certainly faced a two-front war. The question for the General Staff, therefore, was how to win it.

Schlieffen, Chief of the General Staff from 1891 to 1906, has given his name to the plan with which Germany entered the war in 1914. Although Terence Zuber has called into question the very existence of a "Schlieffen Plan" and instead argued that Germany's strategy was essentially defensive, his critics have made a convincing case that Germany intended to protect itself if war came by taking the offensive, and taking it first.[16] Schlieffen had initially envisaged a major campaign in the east against Russia, with a holding action against France, but growing French military strength and the development of its railway network persuaded him that the first and decisive blow should be struck in the west, against France. Germany's armies in East Prussia would stay on the defensive against Russian forces whose mobilization would necessarily be slow because of Russia's vast distances and rudimentary railways. Then, using Germany's efficient railway system, troops fresh from victory over France would be sent eastwards to defeat Russia, which might in any case be inclined to make peace after the loss of its ally.

Since the French had been strengthening their common frontier, an attack through the traditional route of Lorraine was yearly less appealing. With the

15. On these issues, see MacMillan, *The War That Ended Peace*.
16. Terrence Zuber, *Inventing the Schlieffen Plan: German War Planning, 1871–1914* (New York, NY: Oxford University Press, 2002).

alluring precedent of Cannae in mind, Schlieffen envisaged instead a great sweeping movement by a massive right wing which would advance through the flat lands of the Netherlands, Luxembourg, and Belgium to fall on the French from behind. Both Schlieffen and his successor, Moltke, knew that violating the neutrality of the Low Countries, especially that of Belgium which Germany, along with the other European powers, was committed to upholding, would constitute a cause of war for Britain but both men assumed the British deployment would be too slow and too small to make a significant difference.

Schlieffen's concept and his influence continued to shape the thinking and plans of the General Staff long after his retirement and his death in 1913. Throughout his long tenure the mobilization plans were constantly being worked on and his successor as Chief of the General Staff, General Helmut von Moltke the Younger (Moltke), likewise introduced modifications, so that what Germany had by 1914 was effectively a Schlieffen-Moltke plan. After the war, the German military found it convenient to argue that Schlieffen had created a masterpiece that ensured victory, and that Moltke had fatally changed it to create failure. In reality, Moltke was responding to changes in Germany's circumstances. Indications that the French were planning their own offensive into Germany from Lorraine had persuaded Moltke to strengthen his left wing. He also decided that the great right hook would bypass the Netherlands and move only through Belgium and Luxembourg. His reasoning reflects his fundamental pessimism about Germany's chances of swift success. If, as he feared, the war turned into a long one, it would be essential for Germany to be able to get much needed supplies through the "windpipe" of the Netherland's ports. That decision in turn meant that Germany's advancing forces were going to be jammed into a much narrower space and could not avoid, as had earlier been possible, the strong Belgian fortress at Liège. In the crisis of 1914, the need to take Liège first added pressure on the government to initiate hostilities.

As Hew Strachan has pointed out, the changes also reflected Moltke's doubts about the chances of Germany successfully defeating both France and Russia. Strachan also argued that, while Moltke's failure to impose a single strategic vision on the German commanders compromised Germany's war fighting capacity in the first months of the war, he was not responsible for Germany's fundamental dilemma: that it and its partner Austria-Hungary would have 136 divisions against 182 for France and Russia.[17] Less defensibly, the High Command effectively abandoned its Eastern Deployment Plan in

17. Strachan, *First World War*.

1913, which would have enabled it to fight a one-front war against Russia alone as the kaiser was to discover to his dismay the following year. After 1913, the mobilization schedule stated, *"Only one deployment is prepared in which the German main forces deploy on the western front against France."*[18]

German plans for the east had come to take second place, even though Russia's recovery and growing military strength after 1905 raised doubts about whether the small part of the German army designated for East Prussia could hold off the Russian "steamroller." The prospect of a German strategic retreat, with the resultant loss of considerable territory, was politically unpalatable. It was also becoming clear to the Germans, if not to their Austrian allies, that Schlieffen's timetable of defeating France rapidly and switching reinforcements to the east twenty-seven days after war started was slipping and that those reinforcements were unlikely to arrive for several more weeks. The German military had a low opinion of Austria-Hungary's forces and little confidence that their ally could withstand a Russian offensive, yet Germany continued to urge them to plan their own offensives. Moltke allowed Conrad to indulge in rosy pictures of a German thrust from the north into Russian Poland with an Austrian one from the south to surround and destroy Russian forces there. Significantly, no detailed plans were ever made for this modern Cannae and Moltke dodged the question of when German forces would start their offensive into Poland. Moltke's often-quoted remark of 1913 to Conrad echoed what Schlieffen had once said to his predecessor: that the fate of Austria-Hungary would be settled on the Seine River near Paris not the Bug in Poland. German strategy was a great gamble and Moltke knew it, even if many of his officers and the Austrians did not.

From the moment they signed a treaty in 1879, the relationship between Austria-Hungary and Germany had been under strain. After all, Prussia had defeated Austria-Hungary on its way to creating Germany. It was only the continuing enmity of France and the growing distance from Russia by the 1890s that made Germany depend on what one German statesman called "that corpse on the Danube."[19] The alliance partners did not trust each other and often went for long periods without consulting on a common strategy or sharing information about their military plans. Geography and interests meant that their goals tended to diverge. Germany saw France as its major enemy, while Austria-Hungary looked east at its rival Russia and south to Serbia, especially

18. Italics in original. Hamilton and Herwig, *War Planning 1914*, 63.
19. MacMillan, *The War That Ended Peace*, 229.

after the 1903 Serbian coup which put an anti-Austrian, pro-Russian dynasty in power in Belgrade. Where Germany saw Italy as a useful ally, capable of putting pressure on France in the event of a war, Austria-Hungary saw a rival with designs on Austrian territories.

By 1914, Austria-Hungary's strategic position had weakened significantly. Not only did it face a stronger Russia, it now had to deal with Serbia, which had nearly doubled in size as a result of the Balkan Wars of 1912 and 1913. Montenegro was likely to support Serbia. Romania, which had once been an ally, had switched sides and so its sixteen-and-a-half divisions might well be added to the Entente forces. Austria-Hungary's domestic situation had developed equally unfavorably. As a multi-national empire, its very existence was under threat by the growth of different nationalisms, including Polish, Romanian, and Czech. The Austrian authorities were particularly concerned about their own South Slavs for whom Serbia acted as a magnet and a siren with visions of a large, independent, new state to bring all South Slavs together. Austria-Hungary's leadership feared, with reason, that if war came and the empire lost territory, it might well fall to pieces altogether. Moreover, the compromise of 1867 had weakened the ties between Hungary and the Austrian territories to the point that the two were virtually separate entities with the military as one of the few remaining imperial institutions. Even the empire's railway network, a critical factor in the wars of the period, consisted of two different systems with few linking lines. The Hungarian parliament repeatedly blocked increases in the common military budget. As a result, Austria-Hungary had been able to train fewer conscripts proportionate to its population, and its forces were under-equipped and their weapons out-of-date. Reforms started in 1912 had only started to make an impact by 1914, and the empire was still spending significantly less than Russia on its armed forces. In addition, while two of its possible enemies, Russia and Serbia, had recently fought major wars and so benefitted from the lessons and experience gained there, Austria-Hungary's last major war had been against Prussia in 1866.

These handicaps did not deter Conrad who, apart from a brief spell out of office, was Chief of General Staff from 1906 to 1917 and thus dominated Austria-Hungary's military planning. Although he was aware of the military's deficiencies and the empire's weakness, he felt that the only way for Austria-Hungary to remain a great power and, indeed, to survive at all, was for it to be prepared to fight its enemies. Like many of his contemporaries, Conrad had absorbed the ideas of Social Darwinism and was an enthusiast for the offensive, making one plan after another for sweeping victories. He had enormous energy and self-confidence, and inspired generations of younger officers; yet his superiors, notably the Archduke Franz Ferdinand, heir to the throne, were wary of his repeated calls for preventive war on Austria-Hungary's enemies. Initially, Italy was the main target, but from 1909 onwards, Conrad fixated increasingly on Serbia as the chief threat, and, if Russia fulfilled its role as the little Balkan state's protector, war became more likely with it as well. The General Staff continued to update plans for separate wars on Italy and Russia and also had a plan for a two-front war against both until 1913 when an apparent improvement in relations between Italy and its alliance partners made that seem unnecessary.

If it attacked Serbia and Montenegro and Russia remained neutral, Austria-Hungary had a fair chance of winning. Even if Russia entered the war, Conrad thought, with unwarranted optimism, that he would have time to handle both enemies. Ideally, the war would happen in sequence with Serbia defeated first in a few weeks and then Russia, expected to be slower to mobilize, would face Austrian forces strengthened by the rapid movement of troops from the Balkans as well as a German attack into the Polish territories. Conrad divided his armies into three in order to give Austria-Hungary as much flexibility as possible. A-Group, with about half the available infantry divisions, would be stationed in Galicia by the Russian border in anticipation of what was assumed to be the major Russian attack. (If Italy became a likely enemy, A-Group could be sent south.) Minimal Group Balkan, consisting of about eight infantry divisions, was based largely near Serbia and a dozen remaining infantry divisions formed B-Group, which could be deployed to either theatre as needed. This assumed, optimistically, that the railways and staff could manage the logistics. By 1914, Russia's mobilization, thanks in part to new railway lines, was much faster, while Austria-Hungary's remained inadequate and key lines were vulnerable to attack. What is more, the Russians knew the Austrian deployment plans as well as details about its forts as a result of the treachery of Colonel Alfred Redl which was only discovered in 1913. Perhaps for this reason and to shorten Austria-Hungary's line in Galicia, Conrad decided to deploy his forces further back from the frontier. That meant that if an offensive was launched eastwards, the Austrian armies would have further to march.

As they entered the fateful year of 1914, there was no better coordination between Germany and Austria-Hungary about their overall strategy. Neither side was open with the other about the size of the forces to be deployed or about timetables for getting their armies into position. If Moltke was less than frank about German plans for an offensive against Russia, so too was Conrad, who never made it clear to the Germans that his intention was to defeat Serbia quickly before turning to take on Russia further north. The two chiefs of staff "beat about the bush concerning the heart of the matter" according to the official Austrian history after the war; the official German one said "Neither Moltke nor Conrad always spoke their innermost thoughts."[20] Even the sensible idea of a single commander for the eastern front, floated from time to time, foundered on Austria-Hungary's and Conrad's unwillingness to be subordinate to Germany. Each country assumed the other was going to do more than it was capable of doing given its available forces. The German High Command needed Austria-Hungary to bear the brunt of the expected Russian attack in the east in the opening weeks of the war while Austria-Hungary needed German forces to even the odds, somewhat, against Russia.

IV

The core relationship in the Triple Entente, that between France and Russia, was much stronger. Based on an agreement first made in 1892, it was confirmed and elaborated in subsequent years. French capital helped to fund the development of Russia's economic growth and infrastructure including the all-important railway networks. The two parties pledged to come to the other's aid if attacked by Germany, whether on its own or supporting a third power, in the case of France, Italy, and in Russia's, Austria-Hungary. Given Germany's power, the French and Russians came to agree that defeating Berlin should be their primary goal and, by 1914, that offensives against Germany would be key to defeating it. French and Russian staffs met regularly and exchanged information on their plans.

By 1914, the French and Russians also had a good idea of what their enemies were planning. Apart from Redl's invaluable intelligence about Austria-Hungary's plans, the Russians had concluded from German preparations and army maneuvers in East Prussia that its main attack would go against France. The French were drawing the same conclusions. They had kept track of the German railway lines being run up to the frontiers of Belgium and Luxembourg and the strengthening the bridges over the Rhine. Furthermore, French intelligence had managed to obtain details of German war games and mobilization plans, including that for the spring of 1914. In 1913, France and Russia agreed that, if Germany started hostilities against the former, the latter would

---

20. Herwig, *Disjointed Allies*, 99.

start an offensive two weeks later which would involve a very rapid Russian mobilization and deployment.

As was the case in the Triple Alliance with Italy, France and Russia could not be sure what their other partner, Britain, would do. The British themselves did not know and, as much as was possible, they preferred to keep their options open. Alone among the powers who went into the war in 1914, as Keith Neilson has pointed out, the British had no firm plans and no binding commitments. British strategy was determined by two main considerations: its imperial obligations and concerns, and what was happening closer to home. Although Britain had both the world's biggest navy and empire, its difficulties in the South African war had made it realize its lack of friends and the dangers of "Splendid Isolation." Moreover, growing German naval power challenged Britain's command of the seas, both globally and in its home waters, while German military and economic power raised the prospect of a German-dominated Continent which would be closed to British commerce and investment. To safeguard its empire in the East, Britain made a naval treaty with the rising power of Japan in 1902, and, to enhance its security at home and protect its routes to the East, it mended fences with two potential enemies. In the Entente Cordiale it settled outstanding colonial issues with France and then, in 1907, with France's ally, Russia.

While the British civilian and military leadership remained wary of Russia, only agreeing to naval talks in the summer of 1914, they were more open to discussions with the French. In what later became a matter of contention, from 1906 onwards the British army held a series of confidential talks with their French counterparts in which they discussed matters such as where a British expeditionary force might arrive and be deployed should a major war break out. The British never made a firm promise to send a force but the very nature of the talks and the evident and warm enthusiasm for France of General Henry Wilson, director of Military Operations at the War Office from 1911, encouraged the French to count on them. In 1913, naval talks between the two countries resulted in an agreement that the French navy would concentrate the majority of its fleet in the Mediterranean and the British would take care of the French Atlantic coast. All of these fell short of a full-blown military alliance but the French and key figures in the British government including Grey felt that, collectively, they added up to a commitment as war approached in 1914. Even after it entered the war, Britain did not decide to send an expeditionary force to France until two days later and did not settle on where to send it—to Maubeuge on the French left wing or further south to Amiens where it could maintain its freedom of action—until August 12.

France did not have Britain's freedom to choose its allies or to enter the war. While it had considered the possibilities of war with Italy or with Britain over a number of colonial disputes, Germany remained France's main preoccupation after the humiliating defeat and loss of Alsace and Lorraine in 1870–71. Growing German economic and military power, its higher birth rate, and the divisions within France meant that the French initially had no alternative but to think defensively. In the last quarter of the nineteenth century France put considerable resources into constructing fortifications and a railway network in the east along their border with Germany. The border with Luxembourg and Belgium seemed less of a threat, partly because of the latter's neutrality and also because French planners did not see how Germany could have sufficient forces to sweep down on its right into France unless it used its reserves. Since the French had a low opinion of their own reserves, they presumed, wrongly, that the Germans felt the same. As a result, French planners, including, crucially General Joseph Joffre, Chief of Staff from 1911, assumed that the German right wing would not move to the west of the Meuse River on the eastern side of Belgium.

A series of scandals, notably the Dreyfus affair, and crises between the military and the government lowered the prestige and morale of the military and hindered strategic planning, as did the rapid turnover of war ministers in the Third Republic. Additionally, control of the armed forces and consultation between those and the government were incoherent. By 1911, however, as France faced a renewed challenge from Germany over Morocco, there were grounds for optimism, even a national revival. France's long isolation had ended and it now had two powerful friends in Britain and Russia. A new generation of reformers were overhauling the armed forces and introducing new offensive tactical doctrines. In 1913, a new law which raised the length of service of conscripts promised to solve France's manpower deficiency against Germany. The relationship between the civilian and military leadership had improved and a new Superior Council of National Defense, with a membership that included the senior members of the government and the top military leadership, helped to consider and better coordinate national defense.

Although France did not intend to initiate hostilities with Germany, like the other continental powers it too had abandoned the strategy of fighting a defensive war, in its case by 1913. Under the direction of Joffre, France's last prewar plan—Plan XVII—was issued in April 1914, and concentrated the main French forces in the northeast, ready to swing, as the German attack unfolded, either along the eastern border north or south of French fortifications there, or towards the north along a front which included Belgium and Luxembourg. In either case, as Plan XVII said, "the intention of the commander-in-chief is to deliver with the forces assembled, an attack against the German armies."[21] In order not to alienate the British, the government refused Joffre's request to be allowed to send troops into Belgium before the Germans did. Unlike the German plan, the final French one did not try to prescribe in detail the direction of the battles to come. Rather, it outlined possible courses of action depending on what the enemy did and left considerable discretion to the army commanders.

France's ally, Russia, had been through a similar catastrophic defeat and regeneration, although the latter had taken place in a much shorter time frame. The Russian regime had survived an insurrection and started to make much needed reforms including to the military; the lessons of the recent war with Japan were absorbed to improve training, tactics, and equipment. Although an influential school of "Easterners" continued to focus on Japan while others were for moving into the Black Sea and on land against the Ottoman empire, Russian strategists increasingly concentrated on the threat from Germany and Austria-Hungary, in combination or separately. With its vast territory, Russia had the option of fighting a defensive war until the enemy attacks ran out of momentum and it could counterattack, as had happened in the Napoleonic Wars. Vladimir Sukhomlinov, Russia's energetic and capable minister of war from 1909, proposed effectively abandoning Russia's vulnerable salient in the west, the Polish lands which jutted out some 230 miles between East Prussia in the north and Galicia in the south. His mobilization plan for 1910 proposed withdrawing Russian forces there back to the interior of Russia as well as abandoning a costly line of fortresses. This led to a revolt by senior generals which reached as high as the tsar and his uncle, the Grand Duke Nicholas, chair of the State Defense Council. By 1912, moreover, Russian military planners had fallen victim to the general enthusiasm for offensive war from the start and, if necessary, against both Germany and Austria-Hungary at once. And like other observers of the Russo-Japanese war, Russian reform-minded officers concluded that the Japanese had won because they attacked no matter how much it cost. Increasingly, Russian orders, regulations, and military education stressed the power of the offensive.

The strategic choice that now preoccupied the Russians was whether to strike first and in force against Germany or Austria-Hungary. France was pushing for the former course while in favor of the latter was an assumption, wrong

---

21. Herwig and Hamilton, *War Planning 1914*, 157.

as it turned out, that Russia would have a significant preponderance of troops. In addition, defeat at the hand of the Russians might lead some of Austria-Hungary's many nationalities to rebel. Conversely if Austria-Hungary was initially successful, Russia's Polish subjects might rise up. While General Mikhail Alekseev, the head of the Kiev Military District which was responsible for the front with Austria-Hungary, argued for directing the bulk of Russia's forces "without hesitation" there when a general war started, Russia's Quartermaster General, Yuri Danilov, was for reversing the deployment and mounting a full-on attack in East Prussia. In 1912, at a meeting presided over by Sukhomlinov, an unsatisfactory compromise was reached "to direct the main forces against Austria, while not generally rejecting an offensive into East Prussia." As a Russian general later said, it was the worst possible decision.[22]

The new mobilization plan, Plan XIX, that emerged in the course of 1912 had two variants: "A" for a major attack on Austria-Hungary with simultaneous action against Germany and "G" for using the greater part of the Russian armies against Germany in the event of its being able to attack Russia early and in force. Of course, much depended on what the French could do if Germany, as Russia expected, tried for victory in the west first. Plan XIX expected, but did not spell out, how to achieve coordination and communication among the different Russian armies but its greatest weakness was that Russian forces were divided and would not have an overwhelming advantage in either theatre. In East Prussia, attacking Russian armies would be jammed into corridors on either side of the Masurian lakes where the Germans had been strengthening their fortifications. Yet a further problem was that Russia's spate of railway building had not created lines running north and south near the frontier to make it possible for more troops from one of the two main theatres to get to the other. Finally, although there was meant to be a third option, where Russia mobilized against just one enemy, that was never worked out and the tsar discovered, as his cousin Wilhelm II did in Berlin in 1914, that the war could only be a two-front one.

V

In 1914, the strategies each power had as well as their plans, some detailed like the German and some mere sketches like those of the British, narrowed the options for those making the decisions by focusing on the offensive and the

---

22. Bruce Menning, "War Planning and Initial Operations in the Russian Context," in *War Planning 1914*, Hamilton and Herwig, eds., 121.

winning of decisive battles and by not preparing for defensive war, or even for war on only one front. But the plans did not exist in a vacuum. National rivalries, fears, pride, Social Darwinian theories about the rise and fall of nations, a belief that the war would be short and decisive, all helped to create the context and assumptions that produced the strategies and plans. The plans, apparently so scientific, helped to make war seem more likely, even inevitable.

We must also consider the decisions, taken or not taken, by those who in 1914 had the power to authorize the steps towards war or to refuse to do so. Honor and obligation played a part in a world where aristocratic values still permeated the ruling classes. Breaking promises, whether for Russia and France to mobilize as soon as the other was attacked or for Russia to defend Serbia, was dishonorable. It is telling that on August 1, 1914, the French ambassador to London even said that the word "honor" should be struck from the English language if Britain failed to come to France's support.[23]

The plans and preparations added to the pressure to go to war, because for the continental powers, the timetables for mobilizing huge armies had to be set in motion in order not to be left unready if the enemy attacked. In fixing on likely enemies, Europe's planners allowed themselves to draw conclusions about the actions and thinking of the other side which fit the scenarios they were developing. As the French chose to believe that the Germans would not use reserves in their right wing, so the Germans hoped that the invasion of Belgium would not bring Britain in against them. It might be better to fight, too, while you still had a chance of winning. In 1914, the German high command feared that by 1917 Germany would no longer be a match for Russia. In Vienna the same year, Conrad wondered whether it would not be best to fight now before France and Russia were strong enough to invade Austria-Hungary or Germany. Just before war broke out in 1914, Conrad met Moltke at a spa and asked what would happen if he lost against France. "Well," said Moltke, "I'll do what I can. We're not superior to the French."[24]

What is also important to remember about the decisions of 1914 is that the repeated international crises that had shaken Europe since 1900—and which were getting closer together—had accustomed Europeans to two contradictory ideas. The first was that, when war came, as it might well, it would be a general one involving most or all of the major powers. The second, conversely, was that, since the diplomats, aided by the threat of military force, had

23. MacMillan, *The War That Ended Peace*, 616.
24. Stone, *Moltke-Conrad*, 214–16.

managed to come up with solutions to maintain the peace up until 1914, they would be able to do so again. Even if some powers were to initiate preparations for war, as Austria-Hungary and Russia had done in the Balkan Wars, the threat of escalation would again bring Europe's powers together to maintain the peace. If not, well, war might be like a thunderstorm clearing the air or, as the Prussian minister of war said on August 4, 1914, "Even if we will perish, it was nice."[25] In the end, a mix of fatalism and unwonted optimism, as well as assumptions about the nature of the war to come, helped lead Europe over the edge.

25. MacMillan, *The War That Ended Peace*, 252.

CHAPTER 20

The Strategy of Decisive War versus the Strategy of Attrition

Williamson Murray

One of the ironies of history has been the fact that almost invariably those who initiate wars believe that they are embarking on a course that will result in a short, decisive victory. In one of his most ironic comments, Clausewitz underlined the almost infinite capacity for politicians and military leaders to place hope for the best over the harsh realities in which they lived. "No one starts a war—or rather, no one in their senses ought to do so—without being clear in his mind what he intends to achieve by that war and how he intends to conduct it."[1] The problem has been that, since the Industrial and French Revolutions, the capacity of great states to mobilize their populations and resources has made decisive victory a chimera, one that all too many have sought to achieve.

In fact, wars rarely turn out to be either short or decisive. The military truism that the enemy always gets a vote intrudes to influence the outcome. Initial calculations invariably prove to be faulty; the enemy has unexpected options open to them; chance, or what the Greeks referred to as *tyché*, intervenes to skew the results; or, finally, friction interferes with the best laid plans. What almost always determines the result is the influence of attrition. Superior manpower and resources do not always make the results inevitable, but their weight certainly affects the outcome. In the end, attrition affects both sides

---

1. Carl von Clausewitz, *On War*, Michael Howard and Peter Paret, trans. and eds. (Princeton, NJ: Princeton University Press, 1975), 579.

and in cases where superiority does not determine the outcome, the result comes from the political impact that attrition imposes on the stronger side.

Some historians have suggested that strategy is a new concept, because it rarely appears before the nineteenth century and has really come into general usage only in the twentieth century. What such quibbling misses is the fact one does not to have to possess the word "strategy" in order to have an understanding of the concept. Nothing makes that clearer than the debate that took place in Sparta in 431 BC between the Spartan king Archidamnus and the ephor Sthenelaidas. In that contest the basic realities of the strategic conundrum, which has haunted Western war ever since, emerge in full clarity. On one hand stands the latter's belief that the war will be short, swift, and decisive. On the other side stands the king's clear warning that there will be no decisive initial battle, but rather Sparta will confront a long, drawn-out conflict that will demand that it adapt to conditions that it has never confronted in war before.

It is worth examining the arguments which Archidamnus set forth, because they underline the difficulties inherent in waging a war of attrition as well as the reality that there may be *no other choice*. Archidamnus began his address to the Spartan assembly with a grim warning as to the fundamental nature of war:

> Spartans, in the course of my life I have taken part in many wars and I see among you people of the same age as I am. They and I have had experience, and so are not likely to share in what may be a general enthusiasm for war, nor to think that war is a good or safe thing.[2]

Archidamnus warned the assembly that a war against Athens would be like none other they had fought. It would not involve simply lining up their hoplite phalanx and crushing the Athenians as they had done to those cities on the Peloponnesus who had dared to challenge the Spartan hegemony over the previous 300 years. Instead, the Spartans would confront an Athenian state, the power of which rested on its control on the seas, and which possessed great wealth with the largest population in Greece, as well as Athenian allies who paid substantial amounts of tribute.

Archidamnus then asked the crucial strategic questions: "How, then, can we irresponsibly start a war with such a people? What have we to reply upon if we rush in unprepared? Our navy? . . . Or are we relying on our wealth? . . .

---

2. Thucydides, *History of the Peloponnesian War*, trans. Rex Warner (London: Penguin, 1954), 82.

What sort of war are we going to fight?" The Spartan king then provided his fellow warriors with the clearest of warnings:

> For we must not bolster ourselves up with the false hope that if we devastate their land, the war will soon be over. I fear that it is more likely that we shall be leaving it to our children after us.[3]

What Archidamnus then laid before the assembly was a strategy aimed at building up Spartan power, economically and financially, and particularly by addressing its weakness in sea power. It was a strategy aimed at the long haul, one that recognized what a modern historian has called "a war like no other."[4] In judging the crucial issue as to whether to go to war, there always appear reasonable arguments for the possibility of a quick, decisive victory. The problem is that in almost every case they are wrong. And that is precisely the point, because few statesmen and powers have begun conflicts believing that the war on which they were embarking was going to be anything other than swift and decisive. In fact, virtually all the wars since 1500 among the Western powers have been long, drawn-out wars of attrition, wars about which, as Napoleon is reputed to have commented, "God was on the side of the big battalions." Since 1813, we might note, God has also been on the side with the greatest resources.

I

The contrast between the search for decisive victory and the terrible burden of a war of attrition comes to the forefront in the French Revolutionary and Napoleonic Wars. The wars initially began when a portion of the more radical revolutionaries in France declared war on Prussia and Austria in the belief that a quick victory would solidify their own position. It did nothing of the sort, but, instead, encouraged the Prussians and Austrians—to that point largely focused on helping the Russians devour the remnants of the Polish state—to involve themselves in the threat the French Revolution represented.

In fact, the wars of Revolutionary France only served to knock the other major powers back on their heels. Calling up their manpower and resources, the French were able to drive the Austrians, Prussians, and Russians back. Starting with what was largely a rabble, French armies learned by filling body

---

3. Thucydides, *History of the Peloponnesian War*, 83.
4. Victor David Hanson, *A War Like No Other: How the Athenians and Spartans Fought the Peloponnesian War* (New York, NY: Penguin, 2006).

bags. Through their ability to suffer a higher rate of attrition, they created an increasing dominance over Western Europe. But the arrival of Napoleon, undoubtedly the greatest general in history, altered the battlefield in an extraordinary fashion. By 1800, the Corsican had seized power in France. For a period, he accepted peace, while he dealt with France's political, economic, and military problems. But peace with Britain lasted barely a year.

Napoleon brought to the table an operational genius that no other general in history, except perhaps Alexander, had equaled. Moreover, he possessed a political and administrative genius that was extraordinary. What he lacked was a sense of limits. Initially, Napoleon focused on launching an invasion of the British Isles. But by summer 1805, it was clear the invasion was a nonstarter while the Austrians and Russians were gathering to strike at France.[5] Thus, Napoleon launched the Grand Army in a sweeping drive into Germany, where he swept up "the unfortunate" General Mack and his Austrian army at Ulm in October 1805. In December 1805, Napoleon utterly destroyed the combined armies of Austria and Russia at the Battle of Austerlitz. That victory eliminated the Austrians. In 1806, in a single day, at the Battle of Jena-Auerstädt he destroyed the entire Prussian army and state. In 1807, it would be the turn of the Russians, and at the Battle of Friedland the emperor destroyed a Russian army and forced Tsar Alexander to make peace. No general in history has equaled the performance of the emperor on the battlefield in those three years.

By 1813 Napoleon's world had changed. As he attempted to recover from disaster in Russia, he discovered that battlefield victories were no longer sufficient to achieve even temporary success. During the first half of the campaign, before the Austrians brokered a truce in spring 1813, Napoleon won two major victories, Bautzen and Lützen. Still the Prussians and Russians remained in the field. With the collapse of the armistice, the Austrians joined in late summer 1813. Allied strategy aimed to avoid Napoleon, but to batter his other armies. Again, the emperor won an impressive victory at Dresden. Seven weeks later, the combined allied armies brought the French to bay at Leipzig. By the time the French abandoned the fight, the two sides had fired off 200,000 rounds of artillery ammunition. Allied losses were 54,000; the French nearly 70,000.[6]

How did the allies not collapse before Napoleon's victories in 1813? The allied powers were able to fight a war of attrition against the French army

5. The foremost history of Napoleon's military campaigns remains David Chandler, *The Campaigns of Napoleon* (London: Weidenfeld and Nicolson Ltd., 1966).

6. Chandler, *The Campaigns of Napoleon*, 935–36.

because of the massive financial and economic help supplied by the British. Over the course of 1813, in addition to their financial aid, the British supplied 100,000 muskets to the Prussians and Russians, while the Swedes received 40,000 muskets.[7] At the same time, the British were equipping the Spanish and Portuguese as well as Wellington's army on the peninsula. The British were able to provide this massive aid as a result of their own revolution—the Industrial Revolution. The upsurge in the British economy had begun in the 1770s. By 1800, British coal production exceeded that of the French by a factor of twenty.[8] Nothing indicates the growth in British economic power more than that of its mercantile strength. In 1761, the tonnage of Britain's merchant fleet had been 460,000 tons; by 1800, it had grown to 1,656,000 tons.[9] The irony of the Napoleonic Wars lay in the fact that, by their end, decisive victory was no longer possible in a world where the enemy possessed the manpower, resources, and will to continue the fight.

II

Clausewitz asked the hard question toward the end of his seminal work: "Will this always be the case in [the] future? From now on will every war in Europe be waged with the full resources of the state, and therefore have to be fought only over major issues that affect the people?"[10] The answer would prove to be ambiguous. After the catastrophe of the terrible wars of 1792–1815, the great powers attempted, with some success, to put the genie of nationalism back in the box. But events across the Atlantic provided a warning that long wars of attrition were a distinct possibility.

In 1861, the American Civil War burst like a nightmare over the polity of the new nation, splitting it into two ferocious contestants. The war that occurred would see the two great military-social revolutions of the late eighteenth century—the French and Industrial Revolutions—fuse together.[11] At the war's

---

7. John M. Sherwig, *Guineas and Gunpowder, British Foreign Aid and the Wars with France, 1793–1815* (Cambridge, MA: Harvard University Press, 1969), 287–88.

8. C.W. Crawley, ed., *The New Cambridge Modern History: War and Peace in an Age of Upheaval, 1793–1830* (Cambridge: Cambridge University Press, 1965), Volume 9, 40.

9. Stephen B. Broadberry and Kevin H. O'Rourke, eds., *The Cambridge Economic History of Modern Europe* (Cambridge: Cambridge University Press, 2010), Volume 1, 199.

10. Clausewitz, *On War*, 593.

11. For the most outstanding history of the war, see James McPherson, *Battle Cry of Freedom, The Civil War Era* (Oxford: Oxford University Press, 1988). For a military history of the war, see

outset the opposing sides had little understanding of war, and even less understanding of their opponents. To Southern whites, their opponents in the North were a bunch of mudsills (factory workers) and greedy capitalists, while the general opinion in the North was that most Southern whites were loyal to the Union, but had been misled by the plantation owners. Both sides expected a quick, decisive victory that would end the war.

Ulysses Grant appears to have been among the first to understand what the war might actually entail. After winning a stunning set of victories in February 1862, in which his army captured a whole Confederate army and Forts Henry and Donelson, thereby opening the Tennessee and Cumberland Rivers as well as the heartland of the Confederacy, Grant's Army of the Tennessee ran into a fierce Confederate counterattack at the Battle of Shiloh in April 1862. It was the first killing battle of the Civil War that saw over 1,700 killed and over 8,000 wounded in the two-day struggle.

Grant noted in his memoirs that:

> Up to the Battle of Shiloh, I, as well as thousands of other citizens, believed that the rebellion against the government would collapse suddenly and soon, if a decisive victory could be gained against any of its armies. Donelson and Henry were such victories. . . . But when Confederate armies were collected which not only attempted to hold a line farther south . . . but assumed the offensive and made such a gallant effort to regain what had been lost, then, indeed, I gave up all idea of saving the Union except by complete conquest.[12]

What one sees in Grant is a general who recognized reality, who increasingly understood the larger strategic and political framework of the war, and who possessed a dogged willingness to pursue the conflict on its terms, even if those involved a strategy of attrition.

If Grant saw the dark reality, the greatest general on the Confederate side— Robert E. Lee—did not. Lee took over what would become the Army of Northern Virginia after Joe Johnston, commander of Confederate forces in the east had been wounded at the Battle of Seven Pines in late May 1862. Lee would seek a decisive victory over the Army of the Potomac from that moment to the end of the war. His first campaign drove General George McClellan's

Williamson Murray and Wayne Wei-siang Hsieh, *A Savage War: A Military History of the Civil War* (Princeton, NJ: Princeton University Press, 2017).

12. Ulysses S. Grant, *The Personal Memoirs of U.S. Grant* (New York, NY: Charles L. Webster and Company, 1885), 368–69.

army back from the gates of Richmond in a humiliating fashion. Yet, however impressive Lee's victories, the casualty bill suggests that he had beaten Mc-Clellan and the Union generals opposing him, but not the Union soldiers. By the time the fighting on the peninsula was over, the Confederates had suffered 29,298 casualties, while the Union casualties were 23,119.

In retrospect, there were battles that Lee had to fight, especially when the Army of the Potomac crossed into central Virginia in attempts to break the Army of Northern Virginia and capture Richmond. Fredericksburg, Chancellorsville, and the 1864 Union offensive in Northern Virginia were such battles and campaigns. But there was an aggressiveness in Lee's approach to war that clearly aimed at achieving a decisive victory that in Napoleonic terms would end the war. After the Peninsula Campaign, he set off to strike Union armies in Northern Virginia. The Second Battle of Manassas inflicted a humiliating defeat on General John Pope's ill-fated Army of Virginia. From there, Lee's search for a decisive victory led him to invade Maryland in September 1862 in a campaign that ended with the disastrous Battle of Antietam. The casualty figures were the worst for any single day in American military history: Union, 12,410 (2,108 dead); Confederate 10,316 (1,546 dead).[13] In nearly all of these battles, while Union losses were heavier in strictly numerical terms, the Army of Northern Virginia losses were heavier in percentage terms.

Nothing indicates more clearly the cost that Lee's search for decisive victory imposed on the Confederacy than the Gettysburg Campaign. On May 18, 1863, shortly after his impressive victory at Chancellorsville, Lee journeyed to Richmond to meet with the Confederate president, Jefferson Davis, and the Secretary of War, James Seddon. The two civilians urged Lee to release Longstreet's corps to bolster Confederate armies in the west, which were clearly in difficulty with Grant's Army of the Tennessee on the east bank of the Mississippi threatening Jackson, the state capital, and Vicksburg. Lee demurred and urged his political masters to allow him to take his army and invade Maryland and Pennsylvania so that he might seek a decisive victory over the Army of the Potomac that would end the war.[14]

Ironically, on that same day, Grant was defeating Pemberton's Army of Mississippi at the Battle of Champion's Hill and turning the strategic situation in the west from serious to disastrous. Lee's adventure into Pennsylvania turned

13. For Antietam, see Stephen W. Sears, *The Landscape Turned Red: The Battle of Antietam* (New York, NY: Houghton Mifflin, 1983).

14. For a discussion of this meeting, see Murray and Hsieh, *A Savage War*, 268.

out badly at the Battle of Gettysburg. From July 1–3, the Army of Northern Virginia launched a series of savage attacks on the Army of the Potomac. By the time it was over, the Confederates had lost 4,436 dead and 22,625 casualties, while Union losses were 22,813 casualties with 3,179 dead.[15]

While Lee was seeking decisive victory in the east, Union armies were slowly but surely strangling the Confederate position in the west, in effect breaking the heartland of the Confederacy. Though the rivers in the west provided access to some of the most productive agricultural areas in the South, the larger strategic difficulties revolved around the distances, which were an order of magnitude greater than those in Europe.[16] The problem for Union armies, then, largely revolved around the projection of military power over considerable distances.

In his memoirs, Grant mentioned that there were generals who, early in the conflict, propagated complex theories of war (obviously referring to Henry Halleck, who was a disciple of Jomini), but that from Grant's perspective such theorizing was irrelevant. What mattered to Grant and his hard-nosed lieutenant, William Sherman, was the solving of a series of difficult, interrelated problems: the projection of military power over great distances; the logistical support required; and the response of the enemy to Union moves. In other words, rather than theorists of war, Grant and Sherman were problem solvers involved in adapting to the conditions they confronted. The point where Grant emerged from being a tactical and then operational commander came after his victory over the Army of Tennessee at the Battle of Chattanooga in November 1863. The defeat of the Army of the Cumberland at the Battle of Chickamauga had forced the Lincoln administration to appoint Grant as the overall commander of Union forces in the western theater of operations, and he had more than lived up to their hopes. Nevertheless, Lincoln would not promote Grant to overall command of Union armies until the end of February 1864.

For the three months that Grant remained in command in the west, he and Sherman hammered out the strategy that the latter would execute in 1864. The advance on Atlanta required major logistical preparations, which depended on the industrial resources in the North being able to provide the supply dumps of ties, rails, telegraph wiring, rations, as well as major orders in

15. For the best account of the Battle of Gettysburg, see Stephen Sears, *Gettysburg* (Boston, MA: Harper Collins, 2003).

16. For a comparison of the size of Europe to that of the United States, see Murray and Hsieh, *A Savage War*, 42.

locomotives and freight cars. During the winter Grant and Sherman had the major rail line between Nashville and Chattanooga totally rebuilt, while they stationed engineer repair units at critical locations and built forts to protect the bridges over every major water crossing. In Chattanooga they also built up supply dumps, so that, as Sherman's army advanced southward on Atlanta, his engineers could extend that logistical line along with his advance. The result was that Confederate raiders were never able to break Sherman's rail lines of communications for more than a single day.[17]

The logistical support that Sherman received for his drive on Atlanta underlines the extent to which the Civil War had turned into a battle of material and attrition. The Ohioan calculated that his armies, in the advance on Atlanta, required receiving no less than sixteen trains per day, each pulling approximately fourteen freight cars, for a total of 1,600 tons per day arriving at the front. In total these supply lines supported an army of 100,000 soldiers and 35,000 horses and mules from the beginning of May through November 12, when Sherman broke his supply lines and began his advance into the heart of Georgia. He noted in his memoirs that the Atlanta campaign was an impossibility without these railroads, and that even then, victory was attainable only because "we had the means to maintain and defend them, in addition to what was necessary to overcome the enemy."[18]

Once in command of Union armies, Grant devised a twofold strategy that aimed at breaking the Southern will to continue the war through the ruthless attrition of Confederate armies and the destruction of their war-making capabilities—manufacturing as well as agriculture. He made his overall strategy clear to Sherman: "It is my design, if the enemy keep quiet and allow me to take the initiative to work all parts of the army together and somewhat toward a common center." Sherman's task was to "move against Johnston's Army, to break it up and to get into the enemy's country as far as you can, inflicting all the damage you can against their war resources." Grant's direction to the commander of the Army of the Potomac was that "Lee's army will be your objective point. Wherever Lee goes, there you will go also."[19]

The advance in Northern Virginia turned into one long, terrible, killing match. From its opening moments, Lee could not resist attacking. The fighting

17. Murray and Hsieh, *A Savage War*, 415.

18. William T. Sherman, *The Memoirs of William T. Sherman* (New York, NY: D. Appleton, 1875), Volume 2, 399.

19. Murray and Hsieh, *A Savage War*, 361–62.

in Virginia ended in a draw, while the casualties steadily sucked the lifeblood out of the Confederacy. In the west, Joe Johnston fought a far less aggressive campaign, but one which saw Sherman's armies draw close to Atlanta. But Johnston's Fabian strategy annoyed Jefferson Davis enormously, and in July 1864, the president of the Confederacy disastrously replaced Johnston with John Bell Hood. The new commander of the Army of Tennessee possessed an aggressive approach that mirrored that of Lee, without the latter's competence. Hood soon lost Atlanta and then exposed Georgia to Sherman's March to the Sea. In looking for a decisive victory, Hood destroyed what was left of his army in the Battles of Franklin and Nashville in November and December 1864.

With no opposition in front of him, Sherman and the elite of his armies destroyed Georgia and arrived in Savannah none the worse for wear at the end of December 1864. There he received 600,000 rations from the Union navy's supply ships that were waiting for him. Sherman estimated that, in the March to the Sea, his troops had inflicted $100,000,000 damage on Georgia (an extraordinary sum for the time); $20,000,000 had supported his troops—the remainder was the result of sheer, wanton destruction.[20] In February 1865, Sherman would follow up his March to the Sea with a devastating campaign through South Carolina in which few buildings were left standing.

In the end, it had been the superiority in manpower and material resources that determined the outcome of the Civil War by wearing the white Southerners down to the point where surrender was their only choice. But we should not think that by following a strategy of attrition Grant was somehow following a mindless approach that aimed only at crushing his opponents by utilizing the North's superior manpower and resources. The strategy of 1864 aimed to place maximum pressure on the Confederacy and its military forces in the belief that such an approach would lead to a breakdown in the Confederacy's defenses and eventually in its very will to resist.

That strategy took longer than it should have because three key pieces—the advance down the Shenandoah Valley, an offensive against Mobile, and a strike at Richmond from Bermuda Hundred—were all commanded by political generals who, whatever their level of military incompetence, were necessary for Lincoln's reelection. Moreover, the generals leading the Army of the Potomac possessed a military culture that proved incapable of initiative, lacked drive, and consistently failed to follow instructions. In spite of these weaknesses, Grant's strategy eventually broke the dam of resistance by placing an intolerable

20. Murray and Hsieh, *A Savage War*, 466–67.

pressure on the Confederacy and its armies. In the end, his strategy aimed to force the Confederacy to fight a sustained war of attrition that it possessed neither the manpower nor the resources to survive. In effect, Grant created a successful strategy that utilized the North's strengths to full advantage, while recognizing the political realities of reelecting Lincoln as president.

III

While the American Civil War was burning itself out on the North American continent, a series of wars broke out in Central Europe that would leave a profoundly different impression on the Europeans. Beginning in 1864 with a war between Prussia and Austria on one side and Denmark on the other, the Prussian Chancellor, Otto von Bismarck, would fundamentally alter the European balance of power. What makes Bismarck so interesting is that he possessed an extraordinary mind—he spoke and wrote in English, Latin, French, Russian, and Italian—and also understood his limitations. As one historian has described him, "surprising for a man who struck all who knew him as supremely prideful and arrogant, he [Bismarck] exhibited a modest view of his own capacities, a recognition of just how limited was the understanding and agency of statesmen."[21] While the Prussian army would win a series of stunning victories, its wars took place under the covering shield of the Iron Chancellor's deep perception of the European diplomatic and strategic environment within which Prussia existed. Above all, one must understand that Bismarck possessed no grand strategic plan. As he once noted, "[m]an cannot create the current of events. He can only float with it and steer."[22]

Bismarck was able to take advantage of the peculiarities of his time and the weaknesses of those who opposed him. Above all, he aimed to enhance the power and prestige of the monarchy he served. In terms of his most important war—the war of 1866 against Austria—Bismarck was able to maneuver Austria into declaring war, which made it appear the aggressor. Moreover, he ensured that the other major European powers remained on the sideline, while the Prussians fought it out with the Austrians for control of Central Europe.

21. Marcus Jones, "Strategy as Character," in *The Shaping of Grand Strategy, Policy, Diplomacy, and War,* Williamson Murray, Richard Hart Sinnreich, and James Lacey, eds. (Cambridge: Cambridge University Press, 2011), 86.

22. A.J.P. Taylor, *Bismarck, The Man and the Statesman* (New York, NY: Hamish Hamilton, 1967), 70.

The military analysts assumed that the Austrians possessed the stronger military. They were wrong. The crushing Austrian defeat at the battle of Königgratz was not only the result of the Prussian army's battlefield performance, but also because Bismarck's policies, as well as Austrian incompetency, had isolated Vienna. Bismarck then stepped in to prevent the elder Moltke and his generals from marching on the Austrian capital. They were furious to find themselves denied the opportunity to hold a victory parade down Vienna's Ringstrasse. But what Bismarck was able to do in molding the peace was to ensure Prussia's control of the Germanies, either directly or indirectly, while Austria lost none of her territory and did not have to pay an indemnity.

Bismarck's aim in settling the war was that the Austrians would not suffer too heavily for their defeat and therefore would accept defeat without a desire for revenge. Moreover, he had every reason to suspect that Napoleon III, emperor of the French, would not be able to restrain himself from intervening in the affairs of the south German states, which had retained their independence. In the Franco-Prussian war that broke out in summer 1870, Bismarck's strategic cloak covered the Prussian and German armies in their war against France. Austria and Russia remained on the sidelines, while Bismarck ordered Moltke to keep the army from the Belgian frontier and the English Channel in order to ensure that the British stayed out of the war.

Moltke and his generals took full advantage of the one-front war they were waging to surround and then destroy Napoleon III's armies at Metz and Sedan. But the war was not over. While the pseudo-Empire collapsed, those who assumed power in Paris declared a Republic and unleashed revolutionary nationalism in order to meet the invader. In fact, Bismarck had already unleashed German nationalism as a means to bring the south German states into a German Reich. Thus, there was every possibility of the kind of war that the Americans had just ended five years earlier. But with their armies entombed in the fortress cities of Metz and Sedan, there were few junior officers and NCOs available to train the recruits the French Republic was calling up. As a result, though the war technically ended the following spring, in reality, it had been over by the late summer of the previous year. If one is to speak of decisive victories, the German wars of reunification represent one of the few times in the last 500 years where the results—the creation of the German Reich— proved lasting in spite of the appalling strategic leadership of the kaiser and Hitlerian Reichs that followed Bismarck. The unfortunate aspect of the wars of German unification was that they gave the impression that future wars among the major European powers would be short and decisive.

IV

Before the catastrophe of 1914, the Europeans received another warning, but one that was largely ambiguous. In 1904, the Russo-Japanese War broke out over which power was going to have the larger say in Manchuria. On the tactical level, the conflict underlined that firepower was going to have a far more deadly effect on the battlefield than had ever been the case. On the strategic level, the war only helped to reinforce the belief among many military leaders and their political masters that the next war absolutely had to be short and decisive.

The two powers stumbled into the conflict. On the part of the Russians, Tsar Nicholas II proved particularly obtuse, among other things describing the Japanese as "yellow monkeys."[23] The Japanese for their part were also optimistic. From its opening battles at Port Arthur and in Manchuria, the fighting turned into a war of attrition. By blockading Port Arthur and by fierce, almost suicidal attacks, the Japanese eventually forced the Russians to surrender the port. Meanwhile, the fight in Manchuria turned into a vicious slugfest in which the Japanese slowly but steadily drove the Russians back. But there was nothing that resembled a decisive victory.

With nothing like a significant battlefield success in view, both sides agreed to have American President Theodore Roosevelt stand in as an arbitrator to end the conflict. Two factors forced the contestants to the peace table. On the Russian side, massive demonstrations verging on civil war had broken out across the major cities, threatening the regime's stability. Quite simply, the war was unpopular to begin with, a factor which a series of Russian defeats on land and at sea only served to exacerbate. On the Japanese side, despite considerable loans from the British and Americans, the Imperial regime was confronting major financial difficulties.

The lesson that many European military analysts drew was that the Russo-Japanese War had underlined that the failure of either side to achieve a decisive victory indicated the next war had better be short and decisive. If their military failed to achieve that success, there was a real danger of either bankruptcy or revolution or both. Thus, while virtually all the powers recognized the tactical and operational realities of modern firepower that the war had underlined, that factor was subsumed by the larger strategic belief that it would be necessary to sacrifice massive numbers of soldiers to achieve the political necessity of

23. Geoffrey Jukes, *The Russo-Japanese War, 1904–1905* (Wellingborough: Osprey, 2002), 16–20.

decisive victory. The result of such beliefs was that by December 1914, the European armies had sacrificed approximately *three million* of their soldiers in pursuit of an illusion, decisive victory.

The tragedy for Germany was that no statesman followed Bismarck. Rather, Kaiser Wilhelm II displayed no ability to understand the strategic problems confronting Germany. Even more dangerous was the fact that in examining the wars of reunification, the German "general staff's writers attributed victory solely to the regular army . . . and particularly to its staff officers."[24] German military culture simply dismissed strategy and Clausewitz's dictum that "war is a continuation of policy by other means." In effect, they no longer bothered to read, much less study, strategic historians. General Geyer von Schweppenburg, who graduated from the Kriegsakademie immediately before the First World War, wrote Liddell Hart after the Second World War that "you will be horrified to hear that I have never read Clausewitz or Delbrück or Haushofer. The opinion on Clausewitz in our General Staff was that [he was] a theoretician to be read by professors."[25]

The period from 1871 to 1914 was one of relative peace among the great powers. For most of the military pundits and theorists of the time, the German wars of reunification suggested that the next war would be short. Nevertheless, there were those who saw the future in a Cassandra-like fashion. The elder Moltke, who had led the German armies to victory in the wars of unification, warned in his last years as Chief of the General Staff:

> If war breaks out, one cannot foresee how long it will last or how it will end . . . There is not one of these [great powers] that can be so completely overcome in one or even two campaigns that it will be forced to declare itself vanquished or to conclude an onerous peace . . . Gentlemen, it may be the Seven Years War, it may be the Thirty Years War; and woe to him who sets Europe in flames, who first casts the match into the powder barrel.[26]

After the catastrophe of World War I, historians and other commentators argued that the general staffs and their plans had aimed to achieve short, decisive

---

24. Holger H. Herwig, "The Immorality of Expediency, the German Military from Ludendorff to Hitler," in *Civilians in the Path of War*, Mark Grimsley and Clifford J. Rogers, eds. (Lincoln, NE: University of Nebraska Press, 2002).

25. Letter from Geyer von Schweppenburg to Basil Liddell Hart, 1948, B.H. Liddell Hart Archives, King's College, London, September 24, 1961, 32.

26. Azar Gat, *A History of Military Thought, from the Enlightenment to the Cold War* (Oxford: Oxford University Press, 2001), 331.

victories and had missed the killing power of modern rifles, machine guns, and artillery. In fact, the military had been well aware of the killing power of modern technology. The problem lay in the fact that the economists and financiers of the time argued strenuously that the modern world was extraordinarily fragile and incapable of sustaining a lengthy conflict.[27] Thus, the failure to achieve a decisive victory would result in either revolution or financial collapse.

Perhaps the most important general in forming the war's initial movements was Alfred von Schlieffen, Chief of the Prussian General Staff until 1905. Given Germany's geographic position—with two hostile great powers on its frontiers—he saw "an exhausting trench warfare possible and even probable," one in which a blockade would present considerable difficulties to the Reich's position. Moreover, he recognized that such a conflict might well lead to a revolutionary outcome, which would threaten the Reich's political stability.[28] From Schlieffen's point of view, however, a war of attrition was "impossible at a time when a nation's existence is founded on the uninterrupted continuation of trade and industry: indeed a rapid decision is essential if the machinery that has been brought to a standstill is to be set in motion again."[29] Schlieffen's solution was to concentrate the Reich's military power on crushing France in a decisive campaign that would eliminate the French at the beginning of the war.

But the Germans were not the only ones basing their planning—and their hopes—on a short, decisive war. The French cobbled together an even more unrealistic set of plans that would see their forces go on the offensive across the Franco-German frontier and suffer catastrophic casualties as a result of a tactical doctrine that insured massive losses.[30] What is clear is that virtually no one prepared for a long war of attrition. So inept was their planning that the French lost much of their most important industrial areas in the first months of the war. On the German side, an examination of the 900 largest industrial firms in the Reich in August 1914 discovered that, on average, they

27. For a thoughtful unravelling of prewar thinking and strategy, see particularly Michael Howard, "Men against Fire: The Doctrine of the Offensive in 1914," in *The Makers of Modern Strategy from Machiavelli to the Nuclear Age*, Peter Paret, ed. (Princeton, NJ: Princeton University Press, 1984).

28. Gerhard P. Gross, *The Myth and Reality of German Warfare: Operational Thinking from Moltke the Elder to Heusinger* (Lexington, KY: University Press of Kentucky, 2016), 68.

29. Gerd Hardack, *The First World War, 1914–1918* (Berkley, CA: University of California Press, 1977), 55.

30. For the most recent study of the campaign in the west and the defeat of the Schlieffen Plan, see Holger H. Herwig, *The Marne 1914: The Opening of World War I and the Battle that Changed the World* (New York, NY: Random House, 2009).

possessed stockpiles barely sufficient to support continued production for six months.[31] Only the Royal Navy had done substantial work in preparing to wage an economic war of attrition against the Germans, but it had neglected to prepare the political framework in Britain to execute such an approach successfully.[32]

In the smoldering ruins of flawed assumptions at the end of 1914, the European powers found themselves stuck in a massive war of attrition from which there were neither military nor political possibilities that offered pathways of escape. There was no alternative to continuing the terrible attrition of men and resources. What had happened was that two great military-social revolutions of the eighteenth century—the Industrial and French Revolutions—had combined to provide European states with the unheard-of ability to mobilize and utilize its population and resources; and both had grown by an order of magnitude since the end of the Napoleonic Wars. Moreover, the First Industrial Revolution had mutated into a Second Industrial Revolution that had altered entirely the nature of manufacturing. In fact, the modern state of 1914 was by no means a fragile human edifice. It possessed enormous economic and political strength, which the participants of the war now focused on killing or starving their opponents. Moreover, both the British and French were able to draw on the agricultural revolution that had taken place not just across the Atlantic, but as far away as Australia and New Zealand.[33]

Beside the economic and political strengths of the opposing states lay the fact that a vast number of changes had occurred in the technologies that supported both the civilian societies and their military organizations. Smokeless powder, nitroglycerine, and artillery that fired over a distance of miles rather than yards, simple civilian inventions like barbed wire, machine guns, motorized vehicles, and aircraft had made their appearance. But how those pieces would actually fit together on the battlefield no one, including the military, fully understood. The admirals, who would command great battleships with speeds over twenty knots, had gone to sea as midshipmen in vessels partially powered by sail. Moreover, to make the problem even more difficult, over the course of the war, the opposing forces would introduce, as one historian has

31. Gerald D. Feldman, *Army, Industry, and Labor, 1914–1918* (Oxford: Oxford University Press, 1996), 46.

32. Nicholas A. Lambert, *Planning Armageddon: British Economic Warfare and the First World War* (Cambridge, MA: Harvard University Press, 2012).

33. See Avner Offer, *The First World War: An Agricultural Interpretation* (Oxford: Oxford University Press, 1989).

calculated, no less than forty-four technological changes on the battlefields, each of which would have a significant impact on the conduct of tactics and operations.[34]

The result, as underlined by the great graveyards and memorials in Flanders and France, was a terrible war of attrition. It was not that the generals were stupid; in fact, in some ways, they were superior to their counterparts in the next great war, because they had to adapt to a world in which both sides were changing on the fly as they attempted to develop entirely new ways of war at the same time that vast technological changes were taking place.

Until recently, much of the British historical depiction of the Somme has been one of a disastrous defeat. What that picture misses is the steady adaptation of the British army to the conditions it confronted on the Western Front. In August 1916 one British officer noted:

> Observation balloons, ammunition dumps, light railways, camps of prefabricated "Adrian" barracks; nothing improvised, every possibility anticipated, the front seems to work like a huge factory, following a plan no one can derail.[35]

Outside of the catastrophic losses suffered by the British on the first day of the Somme, Anglo-French casualties were approximately 560,000, while the Germans lost 465,000 soldiers. But in the harsh balance of attrition warfare, the Germans were in effect the losers, because they were far less able to accept the casualty bill.

Nevertheless, in spite of the reality of the attrition war that the contestants were fighting, a number of the leading generals persisted in seeking a decisive victory to end the conflict. For both his Somme and Flanders offensives, Douglas Haig, commander of the British Expeditionary Force, persisted in believing that a great breakthrough was possible and would lead to decisive victory over the Germans. Ludendorff was just as optimistic in his 1918 spring offensives. Yet, while he believed a complete breakthrough was possible, he refused to assign operational, much less strategic, goals to the attacking troops.

In spring 1918, the Germans achieved what appeared to be a stunning series of tactical victories. For the first time on the Western Front, they succeeded in

---

34. David Zabecki, *The Generals' War: Operational Level Command on the Western Front in 1918* (Bloomington, IN: Indiana University Press, 2018), 13–14.

35. William Philpott, *Three Armies on the Somme: The First Battle of the Twentieth Century* (New York, NY: Penguin, 2010), 261.

not only breaking through the enemies' front lines, but also in driving deep into the enemies' rear areas.[36] However, the casualties were so high—nearly one million—that Ludendorff's offensives bled the army white, and those losses would play a major role in the German army's collapse in the fall. A recent history of the British Third Army sums up the attritional framework of this terrible conflict:

> The Hundred Days of 1918 was punctuated by no Waterloo. The First World War ended, as it had mostly been fought, in a succession of dour attritional struggles rather than a thrilling climatic battle. The intensity of the campaign, hard fought almost to the end, shows that the battered and bruised German army, while down was definitely not yet out. When it finally collapsed in November, it did so more quickly and completely than anyone had expected even a month previously.[37]

V

The wreckage from the massive attrition of manpower and resources left both military experts and civilian commentators deeply puzzled as to what had happened. Perhaps not surprisingly, for the most part the Germans paid little attention to the strategic factors that had contributed so much to their defeat. Their general explanation was that the army had stood unbroken and undefeated in the field, only to be stabbed in the back by the Jews and the Communists. The army under the first chief of the disguised general staff did undertake a thorough examination of the tactical lessons of the war, which played a major role in the initial victories that the Wehrmacht achieved in the next war.[38] He concluded that the Germans were so dangerous in the early years of the war because they combined their decentralized, aggressive tactical system, with armored, mechanized forces.

There were those within the German military who recognized the larger strategic problem, namely that the Reich was poorly placed geographically to access the raw material requirements that a modern war of attrition required,

---

36. For the German spring offensives of 1918, see David Zabecki, *The German 1918 Offensives: A Case Study in the Operational History of War* (London: Routledge, 2006).

37. Jonathan Boff, *Winning and Losing on the Western Front: The British Third Army and the Defeat of Germany in 1918* (Cambridge: Cambridge University Press, 2012), 243.

38. See Robert Corum, *The Roots of Blitzkrieg: Hans von Seeckt and German Military Reform* (Lawrence, KS: University Press of Kansas, 1992).

particularly petroleum products.[39] But such views played no role in German thinking or in preparation for the possibility of a long-term war of attrition. In fact, there was no strategic or economic framework for the massive rearmament program that Hitler initiated upon coming to power in late January 1933. Rather the Führer simply gave the services vast resources and, rather than provide them overall guidance to coordinate, allowed them to go their independent way. After the war, General Georg Thomas, chief of the *Oberkommando der Wehrmacht*'s economic section, described the prewar economic system in the following terms: "I can only repeat that in Hitler's so-called Leadership State there subsisted a complete absence of leadership, and an indescribable duplication of effort and working at cross purposes."[40]

Having abandoned any effort to think seriously about their strategic position, in the 1930s the Germans engaged in a desperate effort to prevent a financial collapse, while scrounging for the raw materials they needed for rearmament. Hitler, confronting Germany's lack of access to the raw materials, embarked on a "Four-Year Plan" in 1936, which only served to waste resources and further exacerbate the economic difficulties the Reich was facing. Meanwhile, the services continued on their massive, and wholly independent, rearmament programs.

In Britain, thinking about the next war remained largely the purview of external commentators. The government, supported by the great majority of the population until March 1939, remained firmly committed to a policy of nonintervention by the army on the Continent. J.F.C. Fuller and B.H. Liddell Hart argued vociferously in favor of a mechanization of the army and the creation of a tank force. The British army did execute a number of interesting maneuvers on the Salisbury Plain, but ironically the Germans seem to have gained more from these experiments than did the British themselves. In the end, Liddell Hart undermined his own case for a mechanized army by arguing that Britain should return to its supposed strategy of the eighteenth century, where it had committed minimum forces to the Continent and emphasized a blue-water school of attacking its enemies on the periphery. In fact, he was wrong about Britain's strategy in the eighteenth century. In the end Liddell Hart provided the Chamberlain government with ammunition to undermine the arguments of those arguing for a strategy of a Continental commitment.

---

39. For Germany's economic problems see Williamson Murray, *The Change in the European Balance of Power, 1938–1939: The Path to Ruin* (Princeton, NJ: Princeton University Press, 1984), Chapter 1.

40. Berenice Carroll, *Design for Total War* (The Hague: Mouton, 1968), 73.

Only the Soviets and the Americans devoted serious thinking to the problems involved in a future war of attrition. Deeply affected by the paranoia of Bolshevism, Stalin would embark on the great Five-Year Plan in 1929, a time when the Soviet Union confronted no real military threats. The cost of those plans was inexcusably high, particularly in terms of lives lost. But in the end, they did provide the economic base on which the Soviet Union would hold out and then drive back the Wehrmacht's ferocious offensive of summer and fall 1941. The Soviet attitude toward a future war also reflected the nature of Marxist ideology with its emphasis on industrial strength. The serious study that took place in the Red Army before Stalin's disastrous purges of the late 1930s emphasized the conduct of military operations over the vast distances of the Soviet Union, seen in the thinking of generals like Vladimir Triandafillov and Mikhail Tukhachevsky. It was not an approach that emphasized decisive victory.

While a substantial portion of the American people remained with their heads firmly stuck in the ground, the army studied the problems involved in a long war of attrition, beginning with the creation of the Army Industrial College (today the Dwight D. Eisenhower School for National Security and Resource Strategy) to study the problems involved in mobilization. The army's effort in this regard reflected the wretched performance of American mobilization in 1917, as well as the fact that any participation of the United States in a major war was going to involve the projection of military power over oceanic distances.

The one area where there was sustained interest and advocacy for the possibility of a decisive battle came in the advocates of air power. Generally, with the exception of the Germans, those arguing for air power argued that the aircraft would prevent a repetition of the terrible attrition of manpower and resources that had characterized the First World War.[41] Those who advocated air power in the interwar period paid virtually no attention to the experiences of the last war. The first significant theorist of air power, the Italian Giulio Douhet, argued both during and after the war that fleets of bombers would both shorten war and make it less costly. In his works, there was no place for defending against air attacks. The only defense was attacking the enemy; a nation need not devote anything to its army or navy.

Douhet was to exercise little influence outside of Italy until 1943, but similar ideas about the possibility of air power as a decisive weapon emerged in both

---

41. There was considerable irony in such arguments; the air war from 1914 to 1918 had been immensely costly in pilots and aircraft.

Britain and the United States. In Britain, the first head of the Royal Air Force (RAF) would argue that the bomber was the crucial element of air power and that Britain should use it as its primary, even only, weapon of attack. Air defense made little sense except to reassure the general public. The target of the bomber should be enemy population centers, since, as the last war had proven, civilian morale would break quickly under the pressure of bombing. Inherent in his conception of war was a belief that the bomber would always get through. Luckily for the British, the Chamberlain government would stress air defense in the late 1930s and invest in Fighter Command, not necessarily because they believed in the efficacy of air defense, but rather because it was cheaper.

American airmen also placed their emphasis on strategic bombing, although in their case they focused on the potential impact of attacks on what they termed the enemy's industrial web.[42] In their view, attacks on industries such as ball bearings, petroleum, transportation, and the electrical grid would create widespread dislocations that would extend throughout the enemy economic system. Long-range bombers, epitomized by aircraft like the B-17, would be able to fly deep into enemy territory, unprotected by escort fighters, and destroy their targets without suffering "unacceptable losses." Inherent in both British and American thinking was the belief that strategic bombing would prove to be the decisive weapon of the next war and that it would achieve its effects without significant losses in either aircraft or crews. There would be no repetition of the terrible attrition of the trenches that had marked the last war, if air power received the support it deserved.

The navies represent an interesting contrast. The Japanese recognized the enormous economic superiority that the Americans possessed and calculated their own strategic approach on the belief that a few hard blows at the onset of a conflict would persuade the otherwise-weak Americans to quit. The Americans began the 1920s with the Mahanian belief that the US Navy's battle fleet would cross the Pacific and deal the Japanese a decisive defeat. By the late 1930s, that belief had disappeared into a far more sophisticated conception of a war in the Pacific in which the Americans would have to cross the Pacific in a series of amphibious operations to seize bases to enable a continued advance. The considerable worry that naval planners confronted was that the cost of

42. For a brief summation of air power thinking within those two countries, see Williamson Murray, *Luftwaffe* (Baltimore, MD: Nautical & Aviation Publishing Company of America, 1983), appendix 1.

such a campaign would involve manpower and resources that might not prove supportable among the American population. Pearl Harbor removed that problem.

In Europe, the Royal Navy prepared intelligently for the next war with an understanding that a blockade of Germany represented the crucial strategic piece. The one area where its leaders missed the mark lay in their underestimation of the submarine threat. Luckily for the British, they confronted a Kriegsmarine that seemed to have learned nothing from the last war. The conception of building a fleet of battleships and battle cruisers to attack British commerce was even more unimaginative than the High Seas Fleet of World War I. The conduct of the U-boat war by Admiral Karl Dönitz exhibited an extraordinary lack of imagination, while it is well to remember that the Germans, having had their codes broken in the last war, managed to repeat the failure with even greater consequences in the Second World War.

VI

The Third Reich embarked on World War II with neither a grand strategy nor a joint military strategy. There was no such thing as a Blitzkrieg strategy; instead, the three services developed their own tactical and operational concepts of war, and there were virtually no discussions about how the services might cooperate.[43] Moreover, the military left the issue of national strategy entirely in the hands of the Führer. As the future Field Marshal Erich von Manstein suggested in August 1938, the Führer had proven right thus far in his political and strategic judgments, and the military should not interfere. Hitler certainly had a grand strategic vision of what he wanted the Reich to achieve in creating a Greater Germany, *Judenfrei*, but there was no sense of strategy as a method to judge means and ends realistically, much less to recognize the strengths that others might possess.[44]

Hitler did have a far better sense of Germany's economic weaknesses than did his generals. To a considerable extent his policy was ad hoc, aimed to take advantage of circumstances, and he certainly grasped the unwillingness of the democracies to take a serious stand. He believed that Britain and France would not go to war over Poland, especially after the signing of the Nazi-Soviet

---

43. For a thorough destruction of the Blitzkrieg Theory, see Murray, *The Change in the European Balance of Power*, Chapter 1.

44. Hitler held to his strategic vision right to the bitter end in April 1945.

Nonaggression Pact. But he was willing to take the risk of a war against powers he believed were led by weaklings. As Hitler commented in 1939, given the major rearmament programs on which the Western powers had embarked, Germany needed to strike quickly to take advantage of her current military strength.

Britain and France went to war in September 1939 with a strategic approach that would eventually win the war, but the failure of their strategy in the short term would have disastrous consequences. Entirely defensive, their strategy aimed to use their economic strength and the blockade to starve the Germans into submission. To all intents and purposes, it was a strategy of attrition. In their strategic approach Britain and France possessed distinct possibilities that would have placed major economic and military pressure on the Germans.[45] They could have mined the Norwegian Leeds, which would have blocked the transportation of crucial Swedish ore to Germany over the winter of 1939–40. They might have placed sufficient economic and psychological pressure on Italy to force Mussolini to enter the war. They even might have launched a limited offensive on the Saar, an important economic region on the Franco-German border.

They did none of these options. The British and French approach was an attrition war without any serious attempt to undertake military operations. In April 1940, an Anglo-French strategic memorandum warned the alliances leaders:

> Hence the Reich appears to have suffered little wear and tear during the first six months of the war . . . Meanwhile, it has profited from the interval to perfect the degree of equipment of its land and air forces, to increase the officer strength and complete the training of its troops, and to add further divisions to those in the field.[46]

The analysis was spot on. Allied inaction led the Germans to maximize their resources for one great throw of the dice that resulted in one of the greatest catastrophes in history.

The German victory had as much to do with chance and gross French incompetence, as with the excellence of the Wehrmacht's battlefield performance.[47] Churchill described the years between 1934 and 1938 as the "locust

---

45. For those possibilities, see particularly Murray, *The Change in the European Balance of Power*, Chapter 11.

46. Murray, *The Change in the European Balance of Power*, 352.

47. For an examination of how close-run a thing the 1940 campaign in the west was, see Williamson Murray, "May 1940: Contingency and Fragility of the German RMA," in *The*

years," in which the Western powers abandoned their strategic and military advantages. Thus, they allowed the Germans, with their extraordinary financial and economic weaknesses, to escape a war of attrition until they decided to invade the Soviet Union in June 1941 and declare war on the United States in December of that year.

Slightly more than a year later Hitler launched the invasion of the Soviet Union, confident in his belief that Stalin's evil empire would collapse in a matter of weeks. The army's estimate for how long it would take to defeat the Soviet Union was seventeen weeks. The assumption was that the Wehrmacht's initial blow would destroy the Red Army in the first weeks of the offensive and then the rest of the campaign would turn into a problem of occupying the vast distances. Certainly, the initial operations appeared to justify such estimates. Massive victories followed on massive victories in a deadening sequence: 300,000 prisoners captured at Minsk in June; 300,000 captured at Smolensk in July; 600,000 captured in the Kiev pocket in early September; and a further 600,000 captured at the double victory of Bryansk-Vyazma. Yet none of these battles proved decisive.[48]

The strategic problem was that victories of this extent were irrelevant when weighed against the reality of the economic power arrayed against the Germans, not just by the Soviets but also by the Anglo-American powers. In spite of the immense dislocation caused by the German invasion, in 1942, the Soviets managed to outproduce the Germans by a four-to-one margin in tanks and a three-to-one margin in artillery.[49] Over the winter and spring of 1942, the Soviets produced 4,000 tanks and 14,000 artillery tubes, an order of magnitude greater than what the Germans were producing.[50]

The crucial strategists in defeating the Germans and the Japanese would prove to be Churchill and the American president, Franklin Delano Roosevelt. Both recognized that their countries had no choice but to fight a war of attrition.

Dynamics of Military Revolution, 1350–2050, MacGregor Knox and Williamson Murray, eds. (Cambridge: Cambridge University Press, 2001).

48. For a brilliant examination of the German Campaign in the Soviet Union in 1941, see the David Stahel, *Operation Barbarossa and Hitler's Defeat in the East* (Cambridge: Cambridge University Press, 2011); David Stahel, *Kiev, 1941, Hitler's Battle for Supremacy in the East* (Cambridge: Cambridge University Press, 2013); David Stahel, *Operation Typhoon, Hitler's March on Moscow, October 1941* (Cambridge: Cambridge University Press, 2015); and David Stahel, *The Battle for Moscow* (Cambridge: Cambridge University Press, 2015).

49. Tooze, *The Wages of Destruction*, 588.

50. David Glantz and Jonathan House, *When Titans Clashed: How the Red Army Stopped Hitler* (Lawrence, KS: University Press of Kansas, 1995), 101.

In the largest sense, the geographic position of their nations as island powers and the circumstances of their entrance into the conflict made a war of attrition inevitable. But the choices they made in how they mobilized their nations and how they brought that power to bear on the Axis underlined an ability to mold strategy to the military and political realities they confronted. In particular, the two men placed an emphasis on launching a great air war against their opponents. Initially their hope was that an aerial war would prove quick and decisive—or at least that was what the airmen were promised. But when confronted with a terrible war of attrition in the air, Churchill and Roosevelt stayed the course.

And it was in aircraft production that the Axis powers confronted impossible odds. As early as the Battle of Britain, the Luftwaffe was already substantially behind the power curve. In the last six months of 1940, British factories averaged 491 Spitfires and Hurricanes produced every month, while the Germans averaged only 146 Bf 109s every month.[51] The addition of the American economy to the production curve would place the Germans in an even more desperate situation. By the first half of 1942, the Anglo-Americans were outproducing the Germans by approximately three-to-one (1,092 to 373) in fighters. In four-engine bombers the totals were even more starkly set against the Germans, 268 to 15.[52]

Military historians have attempted to minimize the contribution the air war made to the defeat of Nazi Germany. In actuality, it played one of the most important roles in the eventual defeat of the Germans and Japanese. The air war quickly turned into a massive battle of attrition, one quite unlike the prophesies of air power prophets before the war. It began to have a major impact on the German economy only in spring 1943, when RAF Bomber Command savaged the Ruhr by dropping 34,000 tons of bombs on its major cities. The Wehrmacht's Armaments Inspectorate reported that because of the bombing, coal production dropped by 813,278 tons from April 1 to June 30, 1943.[53] Steel production fell 400,000 tons below the target for the same period. The damage cascaded into a number of other areas, affecting the availability of castings, forgings, and parts.[54] The Combined Bomber Offensive

---

51. The numbers are based on Sir Charles Webster and Noble Frankland, *The Strategic Air Offensive against Germany*, Volume 4, *Appendices* (London: Her Majesties Stationary Office, 1961), appendix XXXIV, 497.

52. Murray, *Luftwaffe*, tables XXII and XXIV.

53. Bundesarchiv, Militärarchiv, RW 20, 6/9, Kriegstagebuch der Rüstungsinsektion VI, 1 April bis 30 Juni 1943.

54. Tooze, *The Wages of Destruction*, 598.

(CBO), particularly targeted American raids on industries that were essential to German aircraft production, would begin to have a significant impact in the last six months of 1943. In July, the number of new and reconditioned Fw 190s and Bf 109s was 1,263; in December, the production had slipped almost in half, to 687.[55]

The overall impact of the bombing of Germany forced the Germans to address the CBO directly not only by building fighter aircraft, but also in a massive distortion of the overall German war effort. From 1943 on, approximately sixty percent of the German war economy was devoted to the production of aircraft, anti-aircraft weapons, the ammunition to support that effort, and the V-1 and V-2 revenge weapons.[56] Yet, though the CBO played a crucial part in the winning of the Second World War, the cost was extraordinarily high. Eighth Air Force lost thirty percent of its aircrew nearly every month from April 1943 through May 1944.[57] Of the approximately 125,000 air crew who served in Bomber Command during the war, 55,573 (over forty-four percent) were killed on operations; 8,403 were wounded; and 9,838 became POWs.[58] The CBO represented massive attrition of the most talented and eager on a scale that was every bit as horrific as had occurred in the last war. The cost in material in terms of air frames was an order of magnitude above the costs involved in the First World War.

VII

The seeming irony in our story is that in August 1945 two atomic bombs brought the war against Japan to a halt within a matter of days. The "Tall Boy" and "Fat Man" weapons appeared to be decisive weapons of war. Yet, within five years, the Soviet Union had emerged as a rival of the United States in a terrifying arms race. By 1960, both sides possessed sufficient numbers of nuclear weapons so that they might claim to be able to defeat their opponents decisively, leaving nothing but a nuclear wasteland in the wreckage. The only problem was that, if they managed to survive, they would be living in a nuclear wasteland.

55. Murray, *Luftwaffe*, table XLV.

56. Phillips Payson O'Brien, *How the War Was Won: Air-Sea Power and Allied Victory in World War II* (Cambridge: Cambridge University Press, 2015), 484.

57. For crew and bomber losses in the Eighth Air Force in 1943 and 1944, see Murray, *Luftwaffe*, tables XXXIII, XXXIV, and XL.

58. Andrew Roberts, "High Courage on the Axe of War," *The Times*, March 31, 2007.

Not even possession of the absolute weapon offered an escape from the dilemma that frequently there existed no rapid, decisive path to victory in the industrial age. Churchill, who had seen an earlier war of attrition through to a successful conclusion, put it best:

> Never, never, never believe war will be smooth or easy, or that anyone who embarks on that strange voyage can measure the tides and hurricanes he will encounter. The Statesman who yields to war fever must realize that once the signal is given, he is no longer the master of policy, but the slave of unforeseeable and uncontrollable events. . . . Always remember, however sure you are that you can easily win, that there would be no war if the other man did not think he also had a chance.[59]

59. Paul A. Rahe, *Sparta's Second Attic War, The Grand Strategy of Classical Sparta, 446–418 B.C.* (New Haven, CT: Yale University Press, 2019), 127.

CHAPTER 21

Strategy and Total War

Williamson Murray

One might best define "total war," which Clausewitz termed "absolute war," as a state's ability to mobilize to the greatest extent possible its manpower, resources, and industrial potential in order to wage a conflict against a single or multiple opponents. In its purest form, total war was a child of the first half of the twentieth century. But one can discern its appearance during the French Revolution and the American Civil War. Total war invariably involves a war against an enemy that is unconstrained by limits, either moral or political. In its course, the nations that have pursued total war have dismissed or discarded standards that appeared in peacetime as essential to their cultures. Thus, total war is more than military operations. It also involves various means to attack the enemy's economy and civilians.

Total war has been a phenomenon only of the past two centuries. History records innumerable cases where states have waged unconstrained warfare against opponents. Yet, such wars were not total war because they did not require the wholesale commitment of a society to wage war. The Roman response to the destruction of Varus's three legions early in the first century CE was to launch a series of campaigns under Tiberius and Germanicus that destroyed everything in the tribal areas lying across the Rhine. However, so constrained was Rome, which existed barely above the subsistence level, that Emperor Augustus failed to rebuild a single one of the legions the Germans had destroyed. Unconstrained warfare against an opponent may well form a part of total war, but it is a quite different phenomenon.

Total war requires something much more complex. Only a state with the bureaucratic and administrative ability to reach into the depths of its society is capable of waging total war. Required also is a level of popular commitment that supports the state's demands for the conscription of the society's young men and the imposition of taxes and demands far above normal. Only extraordinary circumstances—namely existential threats posed by foreign enemies—can call forth the willingness to support total war. Its appearance involves a recognition that the only alternative to a nation's destruction lies in the mobilization of the entirety of its resources. In some cases this involves a recognition of strategic possibilities. In summer 1940, Churchill understood that Britain's hope for survival rested on whether the United States and, to a lesser extent, the Soviet Union would recognize that it was not in their interest to allow Britain's defeat. Thus, his mobilization of British resources involved a strategic belief that other powers would find themselves involved in war against Nazi Germany.

I

We might date the appearance of "total war" to the French Revolutionaries, confronted by the Austrian and Prussian invasions of 1793. In August of that year, the Republic's Committee of Public Safety, confronted by a desperate military situation, declared a *leveé en masse*. Its initial pronouncement has echoed through the following years:

> From this moment until the enemy has been chased from the territory of the Republic, all the French are in permanent requisition for service in the armies. Young men will go into battle, married men will forge arms and transport supplies; women will make uniforms, tents, and serve in the hospitals; children will pick rags; old men will have themselves carried to the public squares to inspire the courage of warriors, and to preach the hatred of kings and the unity of the Republic.[1]

The opening comments of the decree are well known. Not so well known is the fact that the decree specifically spelled out the right of the French state to restrict the rights of its citizens. "Coalitions or meeting of any kind are forbidden ... In no case are workers allowed to meet in order to express their complaints; meetings are to be dispersed; instigators and ringleaders will be

---

1. John Lynn, *Bayonets of the Republic, Motivation and Tactics in the Army of Revolutionary France, 1791–1794* (Champagne, IL: University of Illinois Press, 1984), 56.

arrested and punished according to the law."[2] The impact of these restrictions on French armament production would prove as important as the increased size of French armies.

In effect, the French Revolution was in the process of creating the modern bureaucratic and authoritarian state, one in which the individual and his or her property were at its disposal. Republican leaders called for the extermination of internal as well as external enemies. As one deputy declaimed:

> This is a war of Frenchmen against Frenchmen, brother against brother, combined with a war of prince against nation; it is a civil war combined with a foreign war. This is a war of nobility against equality; a war of privileges against the common good; a war of the vices against public and private morality; of all tyrannies against liberties and personal security.[3]

The result of the *leveé en masse* was an unheard-of mobilization of the French nation. In his classic study, *On War*, Clausewitz summed up the results:

> There seemed no end to resources mobilized; all limits disappeared in the vigor and enthusiasm shown by the governments and their subjects. . . . Suddenly war again became the business of the people—a people of thirty million, all of whom considered themselves to be citizens. . . . The people had become a participant in war; instead of governments and armies as heretofore, the full weight of the nation was thrown into the balance. The resources and efforts now available for use surpassed all conventional limits; nothing now impeded the vigor with which war could be waged, and consequently the opponents of France faced the utmost peril.[4]

By the fall of 1793 the French had put over 750,000 soldiers in the field.[5]

The soldiers available to French armies had an immense impact on the battlefield. The untrained levees, whatever their initial weaknesses, rapidly learned the business of war. But their successes soon removed the need for the

2. Wolfgang Kruse, "Revolutionary France and the Meaning of the Leveé en Masse," in *War in the Age of Revolution, 1775–1815*, Roger Chickering and Stig Förster, eds. (Cambridge: Cambridge University Press, 2010), 311.

3. Kruse, "Revolutionary France and the Meaning of the Leveé en Masse," 302.

4. Carl von Clausewitz, *On War*, Michael Howard and Peter Paret, trans. and eds. (Princeton, NJ: Princeton University Press, 1975), 467, 591–92.

5. John Lynn, "A Nation at Arms," in *The Cambridge History of War*, Geoffrey Parker, ed. (Cambridge: Cambridge University Press, 2020), 199.

stringent enforcement of the decrees that the Republic had set forth in the dire moments of 1793. While the language of the French Revolutionaries had called for a "total war" against the internal and external enemies of France, the administrative and legal controls required to implement such a concept did not yet exist. They were beginning to emerge during the Revolution and under Napoleon, but not until the twentieth century can one talk of total war as completely realizable. For the century after the Napoleonic Wars had ended, Clausewitz was the only commentator who recognized what had happened:

> [T]hese changes did not come about because the French government freed itself, so to speak, from the harness of policy; they were caused by the new political conditions which the French Revolution had created both in France and in Europe as a whole, conditions that set in motion new means and new forces, and have thus made possible a degree of energy in war that otherwise would have been considered inconceivable.[6]

After the Thermidorian coup, one can no longer speak of total war. There simply was not the political basis on which to impose such ferocious demands on the population. Napoleon succeeded in seizing power at the end of the century. In many ways he was the Revolution's child. He brought extraordinary skill to innumerable endeavors, but the fairies at his christening neglected to give him the skills of a grand strategist. Whatever the strategic or political problem, the emperor's answer was always war. Until the end of 1812, Napoleon had no need to resort to total war. The conscription laws of the Directory supplied the manpower and the countries he occupied provided the finances.

That changed in December 1812 as the remnants of the Grand Army straggled back from Russia. In effect, Napoleon lost his army and its equipment. His opponents were gathering to overthrow the empire he had created. Confronted with an existential threat, Napoleon resorted to a mass mobilization of the nation, drawing on the administrative and legal framework the French Revolutionaries and he had established. His aide de camp, Colonel Armand-Augustin-Louis Caulaincourt, reported on the effort to remobilize the nation for the struggle:

> The entire French nation overlooked his reverses and vied with one another in displaying zeal and devotion. It was a[s] glorious [an] example of the French character as it was a personal triumph for the Emperor, who with

6. Clausewitz, *On War*, 610.

amazing energy directed all the resources of which his genius was capable into organizing and guiding the great national endeavor. Things seemed to come into existence as if by magic.[7]

If that effort was not yet total war, it was certainly on the road.

In 1813, Napoleon won a series of impressive victories, but victories no longer sufficed. As he commented after one of his battles, "These animals have learned something."[8] In fact, they had. They had learned how to deal with the French on the strategic and political levels. As Clausewitz wrote, "Not until statesmen had at least perceived the nature of the forces that had emerged in France and had grasped the new political conditions now obtained in Europe, could they foresee the broad effect all this would have on war; and only in that way could they appreciate the scale of the means that would have to be employed, and how best to employ them."[9]

Backed by British resources, the European powers possessed the staying power to suffer defeats, yet remain in the field and wear down the Imperial army. If the Austrians and Russians did not approach total war in 1813, the Prussians, drawing on the wellspring of nascent German nationalism, certainly did. In their reaction to Napoleon's invasion of 1812, the Russians had waged an unconstrained war in reverse, laying waste to their own food stuffs and dumps as they retreated. But given the primitive nature of their administrative capabilities, the Russians were hardly in a position to wage total war. Austria, for its part, was a multinational state, where many of its components were as hostile to Hapsburg rule as to the French. The Prussians, on the other hand, consisted of a single nationality, possessed an effective bureaucracy, and had felt the hard hand of French occupation for six years. Thus, while the smallest of the three Eastern European powers, Prussia and its subjects were the most amenable to waging what its leading military intellectual would term "absolute war."

II

The ending of the French Revolutionary and Napoleonic Wars in 1815 brought a period of unparalleled peace to Europe. However, across the Atlantic, the descendants of the English settlers waged a ferocious war, foreshadowing what would emerge during the course of the First World War half a century later.

7. David Chandler, *The Campaigns of Napoleon* (London: Scribner, 1966), 867.

8. Chandler, *The Campaigns of Napoleon*, 867.

9. Clausewitz, *On War*, 609.

The American war began with the decision of the Southern slave states to secede from the United States. By firing on Fort Sumter, the newly established Confederacy ensured that the North would reply in kind. Both sides entered the fight with the belief that it would be short and decisive, with their side the victor.

In retrospect, a quick, decisive victory for the North should have been the case, given the disparity in populations and resources. The North was a rapidly industrializing powerhouse, while the Confederacy possessed little industry. A growing network of railroads knit the Northern states from the Midwest to the Atlantic seaboard; on the other hand, there were fewer railroads in the South, even fewer interconnected and most poorly constructed and maintained. The North had well over twice the population (and forty percent of the Confederacy's population consisted of slaves). But numbers are deceiving. The Southern states encompassed a vast amount of territory, in total 780,000 square miles, much of that with few roads.[10]

The war's first years involved a series of battles along the border states. In the east, military operations from 1861 to 1863 largely resulted in stalemate. In the west, Union armies broke open Confederate control of the Tennessee, Cumberland, and Mississippi Rivers, exposing most of Tennessee to Union control. Nevertheless, the Confederates held most of the territory they claimed. By 1862, the Southern states had declared a draft and mobilized the majority of their manpower, except for those required to work in their few factories and to control the slaves. Merely to hold out, the Confederacy was as far along to creating total war as one could expect from an agrarian society, especially one based politically on states' rights.

By the end of 1863, the Northern states had enlisted or drafted an army of 1,000,000 men, with 600,000 in the field. However, in the words of the noted Civil War historian Shelby Foote, the North was fighting the war with one arm tied behind its back. While its armies were fighting the war against the Confederacy, the Northern industrial economy increased its GDP by a significant amount. By 1864, iron production was twenty-five percent greater than any year for the whole nation before the war; furthermore, manufacturing had increased by thirteen percent. Union expenses in support of the army jumped from twenty-three million to over 1.03 billion dollars for the war's last year.[11]

10. Williamson Murray and Wayne Wei-siang Hsieh, *A Savage War: A Military History of the Civil War* (Princeton, NJ: Princeton University Press, 2016), 61.

11. Murray and Hsieh, *A Savage War*, 516.

Yet, the effort that the Confederacy had mounted seemingly stalemated the struggle. The Union general, William Tecumseh Sherman, put the North's frustration in a letter to his wife in late 1863:

> No amount of poverty or adversity seems to have shaken their faith— [slaves] gone—wealth & luxury gone, money worthless, starvation in view within a period of two or three years, are causes enough to make the bravest tremble, yet I see no signs of let up—some few deserters—plenty tired of war, but the masses determined to fight it out.[12]

At the end of February 1864, Lincoln appointed Ulysses S. Grant to command Union armies. Within two months the general had articulated a military and political strategy aimed at breaking Confederate will. The main Union armies were to strike into the heart of the Confederacy. At the same time, Grant addressed the strength of Confederate will by making clear these drives were to destroy the South's agricultural and industrial infrastructure. His instructions to Sherman were explicit. After laying out the western armies' military objective "to move against Johnston's Army [of the Tennessee], to break it up," Grant instructed Sherman that he was to inflict *"all the damage you can against their war resources."*[13]

While the campaign did not turn out exactly as Grant had hoped, largely because the political generals floundered in their tasks, the two main armies essentially succeeded. Despite its insipid leadership, the Army of the Potomac pinned Lee into the environs of Petersburg and Richmond. But it would be Sherman's army that would rip the heart out of the Confederacy. In early May 1864, the western armies began their drive against Atlanta. The fighting eventually drove the Army of the Tennessee back on Atlanta, but skilled defensive moves by its commander, Joe Johnston, prevented Sherman from achieving a decisive success. Nevertheless, in mid-July, Jefferson Davis replaced Johnston with John Bell Hood, a fateful decision.

Hood's catastrophic generalship opened Georgia to Sherman. In effect, Hood allowed Sherman to divide his army. The Union general kept 60,000 of the toughest soldiers for his advance through central and southern Georgia to

12. Brooks Simpson and Jean V. Berlin, eds., *Sherman's Civil War: Selected Correspondence of William T. Sherman, 1860–1865* (Chapel Hill, NC: University of North Carolina Press, 1999), 609.

13. Emphasis added. Simpson and Berlin, *Sherman's Civil War: Selected Correspondence of William T. Sherman, 1860–1865*, 252.

Savannah. The remainder he sent north to cover Hood and reinforce Union forces in Nashville. In a telegram to Grant, the Ohioan made clear his intentions: "It is overwhelming to my mind that there are thousands of people abroad and in the South who will reason thus: If the North can march an army right through the South, it is proof positive that the North can prevail."[14] Sherman was a man of his word. With virtually no defenders in front of him, his army seized most of the foodstuffs in Georgia, wrecked what manufacturing existed, and burned virtually every plantation. By the time they arrived in Savannah on December 9, 1864, Sherman's troops had decimated Georgia. In his memoirs, Sherman estimated that the March to the Sea had inflicted as much as one hundred million dollars of damage; only twenty million of which had gone to the support of the soldiers, the rest was sheer wanton destruction.[15]

If Georgia suffered, it was nothing compared to South Carolina, which the soldiers regarded as the fountainhead of the Confederacy. Sherman spelled out for Grant his intentions for the Palmetto State: "I look upon Columbia as quite as bad as Charleston, and I doubt if I shall spare the public buildings."[16] Shortly before he left Georgia to invade South Carolina, Sherman noted that:

> I attach more importance to these deep incursions into the enemy's country, because this war differs from European wars in this particular: we are not only fight[ing] hostile armies, but a hostile people, and must make old and young, rich and poor, feel the hard hand of war, as well as these organized armies.[17]

The North had not felt it necessary to wage a total war by mobilizing all its manpower and resources to the fullest. Nevertheless, it had found itself in the position where it had to wage a fierce war requiring mobilization of huge numbers of soldiers, as well as a massive logistical structure in order to support military operations over continental distances. As Clausewitz noted, "war is

---

14. *The War of the Rebellion: A Compilation of the Official Records of the Union and Confederate Armies*, Part III, Volume 39, 660, available through the HathiTrust Database, https://www.hathitrust.org/.

15. Sherman's troops particularly targeted the plantation owners who possessed hounds to pursue escaped slaves. When the war came, those owners used the dogs to hunt down escaped Union soldiers. Simply owning a collection of hounds was a sufficient cause for Union soldiers to destroy the entire plantation complex.

16. William T. Sherman, *Memoirs of General William T. Sherman, By Himself* (New York, NY: D. Appleton and Company, 1887), Volume 2, 228.

17. Sherman, *Memoirs of General William T. Sherman, By Himself*, Volume 2, 227.

an act of force, and there is no logical limit to the application of that force."[18] By 1865, Northern armies had waged a war that completely destroyed the South, from Virginia to the Mississippi. Though the Union did not wage war against civilians per se—as was the case in the two world wars of the next century—its soldiers did destroy the Confederacy's infrastructure and wreck its cities. It was war unconstrained, and it left a sense of bitterness among the South's whites that lasted into the next century, and beyond.

On the other side and given the disparity in manpower and resources, the Confederates conducted a conflict that approached total war. They sacrificed nearly everything of worth, including much of their population. By war's end they had lost fifty percent of their men, dead, wounded, or missing. A Confederate woman summed up the result:

> We never yielded in the struggle until we were bound hand & foot & the heel of the despot was on our throats. Bankrupt in men, in money, & in provisions, the wail of the bereaved & the cry of hunger rising all over the land, our cities burned with fire and our pleasant things laid waste, the best & bravest of our sons in captivity, and the entire resources of our county exhausted—what else could we do but give up.[19]

III

Between 1861 and 1865, the Europeans gave hardly a thought to what had happened in the American Civil War. For a brief period after the collapse of Napoleon III's empire, the French had launched a *leveé en masse*, but the disastrous defeats at Sedan and Metz had stripped the country of the officer and NCO infrastructure required to rebuild a new army. Continuing defeats of the ill-trained conscripts as well as internal rebellion by the left in Paris forced the French to make peace in spring 1871. In the period before the First World War there were several small wars—the Boer War and the Russo-Japanese War—but none led to total war. In the case of the former, the Boers simply lacked the resources, if not the will. In the Russo-Japanese War, the opposing sides lacked either the will or the financial strength to mobilize manpower or resources fully.

When the First World War broke out, there were few who recognized that a war among the great powers would result in a long and costly conflict. Even

---

18. Clausewitz, *On War*, 77.
19. Murray and Hsieh, *A Savage War*, 468.

those leaders who feared the political and financial consequences of a long war, placed their bets on a short, decisive war, and hoped for the best. There were increases in defense spending immediately before the war as international tensions mounted, but these were miniscule compared to what was to come. No one was preparing for a long war, much less a total war.

In fact, none of the powers had even developed a strategy of total war before 1914. Nor did they do so once the war began. Instead, as they floundered their way through a conflict that failed to meet their prewar expectations, the various leaders found that circumstances forced them to up the ante in reply to their opponents' actions. In other words, instead of attempting to develop strategies that allowed for some form of long-range planning, the powers focused on the immediate threat, with little thought for the future. Thus, the Germans focused entirely on the next major campaign. The British and French at least paid attention to the difficulties involved in gaining America's financial and economic support. In other words, the great powers moved towards total war in stages which circumstances and their short-range choices forced upon them. Strategy played little-to-no role in the German conduct of the war. Their opponents made some effort to focus on the strategic, but even French mobilization was more circumstantial than strategic.

Before the war, the Royal Navy had prepared a plan to launch a ruthless blockade of the Central Powers as an assault on Germany's financial stability and economy. However, navy planners failed to consider the possibility that there would be substantial portions of their government—for example, the Foreign Office and Board of Trade—which would oppose stringent measures against the Germans. Thus, the naval leaders found their efforts sabotaged in a matter of days.[20] In fact, by February 1915, when the Germans declared unrestricted submarine warfare, the blockade leaked like a sieve.

On the strategic level, there were numerous indicators of how unprepared the powers were to fight a war of indeterminant length, perhaps stretching into years, much less a total war. In their military plans, the French made no effort to defend their industrial regions in the northwest. The British were so unprepared that they failed to field an army of Continental size until July 1916, and even then, suffered heavy casualties because their troops were so ill trained. On the German side, their industrial stocks in August 1914 consisted of barely sufficient raw materials for half a year.

20. Nicholas A. Lambert, *Planning for Armageddon: British Economic Warfare and the First World War* (Cambridge, MA: Harvard University Press, 2013).

The Germans, however great their reputation for all things military, proved particularly obtuse in refusing to recognize the importance of political and strategic concerns. Having dismissed the British as a nonfactor, the Germans blithely invaded Belgium and Luxembourg, thereby ensuring that Britain entered the war. Underlying the German approach to strategic issues was the principle of military necessity, which they believed should overrule all concerns about politics, strategy, and morality.[21] This resulted in a series of decisions that exacerbated the negative consequences the Germans had already accrued by invading the Low Countries. The most egregious case came in April 1915 when Germany unleashed gas warfare on the Western Front to test its efficacy. It worked, but added to anti-German feeling among the neutrals. As for the military necessity of gas warfare, winds on the Western Front blow from west to east, putting the Germans at a disadvantage. Even worse was the fact gas masks depend on rubber, and rubber was already in short supply in the Central Powers because of Britain's blockade.

The recognition that the war was not going to end in a sudden, decisive victory led the major powers into a scramble to mobilize manpower and industrial resources to handle the steadily growing demands for weapons and ammunition. What followed as a steady approach to total war. In their mobilization, the French came closest to total war. In a strategic sense, they had no choice, considering the ruthlessness with which the Germans had invaded France. Given the occupation of their industry in the north, the French confronted an especially difficult task. On their effort rested the Allied cause, at least until the British arrived in numbers in 1916 and the Americans in 1918.

Besides the 1914 mobilization, the French found themselves squeezed not only by an army engaged in constant operations but also by a steady increase in demand for armaments production. In retrospect, they made extraordinary strides. New production capabilities increased steel output by two million tons and cast iron by 600,000 tons.[22] By early 1916, French artillery factories hit full stride, producing one thousand 75mm artillery pieces per month, as many as in all of 1915.[23] But it was in aircraft production the French reached truly impressive numbers. From 4,489 aircraft in 1915, French industry rose to 24,632

---

21. For an outstanding examination of the German concept of "military necessity," see Isabel V. Hull, *Absolute Destruction: Military Culture and the Practices of War in Imperial Germany* (Ithaca, NY: Cornell University Press, 2005).

22. Hull, *Absolute Destruction*, 1,051.

23. Hull, *Absolute Destruction*, 1,055–58.

aircraft and 44,563 engines in 1918.[24] In 1918, the French provided much of the artillery (heavy and light), machine guns, and aircraft that the Americans required. If any power could claim that it came close to total war, it was France, but the French had only done so by degree, making the "pips squeak," without a strategic vision of absolute war.

Because production of ground armaments was low with the prewar all-professional army, the British had to scramble to reach the production totals demanded by the much larger British Expeditionary Force (BEF). By 1916, British production was finally hitting reasonable levels. From ninety-one artillery tubes in 1914, they reached 3,390 in 1915, and 8,039 by war's end. Shell production rose from 500 thousand to 67.3 million; machine guns from 300 to 120,900. In 1914 the British had produced no tanks; in 1918 the number produced had risen to 1,359.[25] By 1918, the British had reached an impressive level of mobilization that began to approach that of total war. Perhaps in 1919 they would have reached that level, but by then Germany had collapsed. At the strategic level, the problem for the British was that the war against Germany demanded that they concentrate on the Western Front, a focus which required their mobilization to the fullest extent.

The associated power, the United States, came nowhere close to reaching a state of total war. This was the result of the appallingly bad strategic leadership of Woodrow Wilson, who until April of 1917 had done everything he could do to prevent America from being prepared to enter the conflict.[26] That effort included strictures against serious military planning for potentially joining the war by either the army or the navy. Thus, American mobilization was a shambles. Only the provision of British and French military equipment to the American Expeditionary Force (AEF) allowed the Americans to participate significantly in the war's final months. Franklin Roosevelt, then serving as Assistant Secretary of the Navy, would not forget the confusion and chaos of 1917 and would ensure that the US military was better prepared for war when it came again twenty years later.

And then we have the Germans. In terms of manpower, the Germans were the quickest to mobilize. With an array of barracks and training facilities for

---

24. William H. Morrow, Jr., *The Great War in the Air: Military Aviation from 1909 to 1921* (Washington, DC: Smithsonian Institution Press, 1993), 102, 122, 329.

25. Gerd Hardach, *The First World War, 1914–1918* (Berkeley, CA: University of California Press, 1977), 77.

26. This included Wilson's order to the American military that they do nothing, including planning, to prepare their forces for the possibility that they might enter the European War.

their conscript army, Germany quickly conscripted those who had escaped the prewar draft. By 1916, they had largely mobilized their manpower and were confronting major shortages in filling the needs of the army, agriculture, and an exploding war economy. As with their opponents, the Germans made extensive use of women in factories; women were also an essential component on farms. Nevertheless, shortages of farm workers combined with a lack of fertilizer to cause increasing food scarcities. For the last three war years, it was a case of robbing Peter to pay Paul. In one sense, the blockade, which German actions during the war exacerbated, constrained their ability to realize what might have been possible with greater access to raw materials.

Nevertheless, the initial German industrialization was impressive. Between August and December of 1914 shell production increased by a factor of seven; by the next year it had doubled again in number.[27] However, the Battle of the Somme in summer 1916 represented a wakeup call. For the first time, Germany became aware of Allied material strength. Hindenburg and Ludendorff assumed command of the war effort in August of that year and immediately visited the Somme. Ludendorff's impressions are revealing:

> [On] the Somme the enemy's powerful artillery . . . fed by enormous supplies of ammunition, had kept down our own fire and destroyed our artillery. The defense of our infantry had become so flabby that the massed attacks of our enemy always succeeded.[28]

The Germans were to term what was occurring as a *Materialschlacht* (battle of material).

Their response was a major effort to increase German output of weapons and ammunition to meet Allied material superiority.[29] Ironically, at the same time Ludendorff was attempting to close the gap in ammunition production, he was supporting the navy's efforts to resume unrestricted submarine warfare, a decision that in April 1917 led to America's declaration of war. The armament program aimed to double production of ammunition and trench mortars, and

27. Hew Strachan, *The First World War*, Volume 1: *To Arms* (Oxford: Oxford University Press, 2003), 1,036.

28. Erich Ludendorff, *Ludendorff's Own Story, August 1914–November 1918* (New York, NY: Harper, 1919), 313.

29. For the tactical adaptations that would take place on the Western Front during the First World War, see Williamson Murray, "Complex Adaptation, The Western Front, 1914–1918," in his, *Military Adaptation in War: For Fear of Change* (Cambridge: Cambridge University Press, 2017), chapter 3.

to triple that of machine guns and artillery. Such goals, given economic constraints—manpower, resources, factory capacity, and raw materials—were impossible. Ludendorff and his staff simply decreed goals without paying attention as to whether they were possible. In so doing they caused confusion, duplication of effort, and a working at cross purposes.

As one senior bureaucrat described the impact of the military in interfering in areas where they had no expertise:

> The program was decreed by the military without examining whether or not it could be carried out. Today there are everywhere half finished and finished factories that cannot produce because there is no coal and because there are no workers available. Coal and iron were expended for these constructions and the result was that munitions production would be greater today if no master program had been set up, but rather production had been demanded according to the capacity of those factories already existing.[30]

Whatever the Allied superiority in economic and financial strength (and they had both), the real explanation for their victory lay in the conduct of a more effective war at the political and strategic levels. One can quarrel with the tactical and operational effort of French armies and the BEF, but the emphasis that the Allies—with the British kicking and screaming—placed on the war on the Western Front eventually broke the German army and resulted in victory. Their strategic focus was crucial.

IV

From our twenty-first-century perspective, the largest lesson from the First World War was that a major conflict between great powers would almost inevitably approach what Clausewitz termed "absolute war" and what we term "total war." However, the idealists of the time seemed to believe that nostrums—such as the League of Nations, various pacificist movements, world disarmament, and neutrality legislation—would prevent another occurrence of a conflict that involved total war. For others, like the British pundit Basil Liddell Hart, analysts focused on tactical answers such as the tank or the airplane that would provide quick and decisive victories to prevent the long, costly stalemate of World War I.

30. Gerald D. Feldman, *Army, Industry, and Labor* (London: Bloomsbury, 1992), 259.

In fact, once the major powers embarked on the Second World War, total war became an absolute necessity for the British, the Soviets, and eventually the Germans, faced as the powers were by the existential threat of total defeat. The Americans, however, even with the extraordinary performance of their war economy, never confronted the necessity of mobilizing their powers to the same extent as the others. As in the Great War, total war emerged as a necessary response to desperate circumstances rather than as a thought-out strategy. In some respects, one might term total war more as desperate expediency than strategy.

Ludendorff spent much of his postwar time arguing that Germany must prepare for total war; in effect, he turned Clausewitz on his head by claiming that "politics should be a continuation of war by other means," and that Germany should mobilize its entire society in peacetime for war. Not surprisingly, the majority of the Germans and their military focused almost exclusively on the *tactical* lessons of the last war. They displayed little interest in studying the *strategic* reasons for their defeat.[31] After all, the widespread belief throughout the middle and upper classes was that the army had stood unbroken in the field until it had been stabbed in the back by Jews and Communists.

The early success of the Germans and the Japanese in the next war was largely due to the fact that they began their rearmament programs earlier than the democracies. Thus, for a short period, they enjoyed an advantage. German rearmament began five days after Hitler's accession to power on January 30, 1933. On that day the Führer met with the senior serving officers, simply giving them a blank check, and making clear his intentions not just to overthrow the Versailles Treaty, but also to acquire all the *Lebensraum* (living spaces) the German people required.[32] From that point on, Germany under Hitler focused on fighting two wars: the first ideological, to make Europe *Judenfrei* and enslave the subhuman races in the east; the second being the military contest against the Reich's enemies.

Tragically, for the millions of civilians the Nazi regime slaughtered, the Germans did a better job in the ideological war than in the war against a disparate

---

31. One should mention that General Ludwig Beck, Chief of the General Staff until summer of 1938, did compose a series of strategic criticisms of Hitler's preparations to launch an offensive to conquer Czechoslovakia. Those efforts are sophisticated analyses of Germany's strategic situation, but they received virtually no response from the remainder of the army's strategic leadership. See Williamson Murray, *The Change in the European Balance of Power, 1938–1939: The Path to Ruin* (Princeton, NJ: Princeton University Press, 1984), Chapters 6, 7, and 8.

32. "Aufzeichnung Liebmann," *Vierteljahrshefte für Zeitgeschichte*, 2:4 (October 1954).

Allied coalition with little in common except hatred for the Nazi regime.[33] In the war against the Jews, the Nazi regime exterminated the great majority of those who fell within the nations their military forces occupied between 1939 and 1942.[34] As for those whom the Nazis characterized as subhuman, their fate was less terminal, but the occupation drove increasing numbers of the occupied into the resistance.

In preparing for the next war—namely destroying the military might of the powers arrayed against the Reich—the Germans mounted a massive effort of rearmament, but there was no coherent strategy, as Hitler maneuvered through the shoals of international relations. By skillfully playing on the appeasers in the Western powers, Hitler destroyed the Versailles Treaty and, by March 1939, had brought Austria and Czechoslovakia under Germany's control. Yet Hitler never laid out what his strategic vision for the war, if he had one. On the other hand, the generals and admirals displayed little or no interest in strategy. The so-called Blitzkrieg strategy did not exist, because Hitler ruled with no greater guide than his intuition, while his generals focused on creating more effective tactics and operations than their opponents.[35]

Compared to the efforts of the Western powers before the war, the Germans mounted a massive effort to rearm and escape the strictures of the Versailles Treaty. They started in 1933 with armament industries producing a minimum number of weapons. By 1938 the economy was devoting nearly fifty-five percent (54.7%) of state expenditures to the military, nearly sixteen-and-a-half percent of the national income.[36] The fact that from September 1937 through February 1939, industry could fulfill only about fifty-eight percent (58.6%) of the Wehrmacht's orders reveals the impact of raw material shortages caused by the financial difficulties as well as the lack of industrial capacity.[37]

Once the war began, the Germans achieved striking success over the first two years, but on a shoestring. There was nothing like a mobilization for total war. The economy continued to confront shortages, particularly in petroleum,

33. For the intersection of these two wars, See Adam Tooze, *The Wages of Destruction: The Making and Breaking of the Nazi Economy* (London: Penguin Books, 2007), Chapter 14.

34. The extermination of substantial numbers of Jews was entirely counterproductive from the viewpoint of Germany's desperate need for workers. Adam Tooze estimates that the Holocaust robbed the German economy of 2.4 million potential workers. Tooze, *The Wages of Destruction*, 522.

35. Even at the operational level, the Germans paid no attention to either intelligence or logistics, crucial factors to success on the operational level.

36. Murray, *The Change in the European Balance of Power*, table I–5, 20–21.

37. Gerhard Förster, *Totaler Krieg und Blitzkrieg* (Berlin: Deutscher Militärverlag, 1967), 101.

rubber, and specialized metals. Coal was a significant problem because of worker shortages. Armament factories remained on a one shift basis, and there was no effort made to rationalize and increase output by means of mass production. Operation Barbarossa, the invasion of the Soviet Union, achieved striking successes, but by December 1941, the army in the east was a shadow of its former force. It had lost over a third of its manpower, while its panzer divisions, which had begun the invasion with 3,486 armored fighting vehicles, counted only 140 tanks.[38] Confronted by the situation on the Eastern Front, as well as Hitler's decision to declare war on the United States, the Germans had to scramble not only to make up the gigantic losses suffered in the east, but also to match the swelling totals of weapons the Americans, British, and Russians were grinding out. Even then the Germans failed to move toward total war. To meet desperate worker shortages due to insatiable demands for troops to replace mounting combat losses, the Germans began the wholesale dragooning of slave laborers from the occupied territories. By 1944, some eight million guest workers were employed throughout Wehrmacht armament factories. Yet even that massive number hardly met the need. Miserably housed, badly fed, and refused access to shelters during air raids, the guest workers were less-than-enthusiastic laborers. Even Stalingrad failed to change Hitler's attitudes towards total war. Joseph Goebbels may have proclaimed "total war" before a handpicked audience at the *Sportspalast* in February 1943, but a German approach to it only came at the very end, when invading armies threatened the homeland, while massive bomber formations were quite literally ripping the roof off the Reich. Even then, the Führer's state could only patch together a haphazard approach.

In almost every respect British efforts to mobilize manpower and resources were more impressive and thorough. Winston Churchill's appointment as prime minister marked the tipping point in Britain's war. The brilliance of his oratory in those dark days of May 1940 through the Blitz of 1941 played a major role in the mobilization of the British people. Yet the existential threat to Britain from the fall of France in June 1940 and the bombardment of the Luftwaffe helped Churchill focus the British on supporting an extraordinary effort. Moreover, after its lackadaisical approach to rearmament through March 1939, the Chamberlain government had finally gotten serious, and Churchill inherited a country already embarked on major rearmament programs.[39]

---

38. Klaus Reinhardt, *Die Wende vor Moskau: Das Scheitern der Strategie Hitlers im Winter 1941/1942* (Stuttgart: Deutsche Verlags-Anstalt, 1972), 258.

39. Murray, *The Change in the European Balance of Power, 1938–1939*, Chapters 8 and 9.

Britain's effort approached as close to total war in this conflict as any democratic country is likely to be able. First of all, its military was responsible for the defense of the British Isles, and through May 1941 the Luftwaffe represented a major threat. Throughout the war the Royal Navy carried much of the burden of the Battle of the Atlantic. Until November 1942, the British were wholly responsible for the war in the Mediterranean. Additionally, beginning in December 1941, they were responsible for defending India against the Japanese, and through summer 1943, the Royal Air Force's Bomber Command was carrying the major effort in the Combined Bomber offensive against Nazi Germany; it continued to carry a major portion until the war's end.[40] Finally, the British made major contributions to the land campaigns in Italy, beginning in 1943, and northern France, beginning in June 1944. Again, we are dealing with a response to what Britain's leaders and the majority of its people believed represented a clear and present danger. That they were then able to mold a set of sensible strategic approaches—with American help—that saw them through to victory speaks to the importance of leadership in a world of chaotic imponderables.

The two most important British military efforts were the Battle of the Atlantic and the efforts of RAF Bomber Command. The former made possible the Anglo-American air effort against the German economy and air defenses as well as the eventual invasion of northern France in 1944. The latter broke the rapid German expansion of its war economy. Simply put, while the Germans would be able to keep their armament production going, its upward curve had screeched to a halt in spring 1943.[41] Given their economic and political position as a declining imperial power—which would become apparent in the postwar period—the British punched above their weight in contributing to Allied victory.

In 1944, a senior civil servant described civilian life in wartime Britain, revealing how close the country came to total war:

> The British civilian had had five years of blackout and four years of intermittent blitz. The privacy of his home has been periodically invaded by soldiers or evacuees or workers requiring billets. In five years of drastic labor mobilization nearly every man and every woman under fifty without young

---

40. For the effort of Britain and its armed forces in the war, see Williamson Murray, "British Military Effectiveness in the Second World War," in *Military Effectiveness*, Volume 3: *The Second World War*, Allan R. Millett and Williamson Murray, eds. (Boston, MA: Allen and Unwin, 1988).

41. See Tooze, *The Wages of Destruction*.

children has been subject to direction to work, often far from home. The hours of work average fifty-three for men and fifty overall; when work is done, every citizen who is not excused for reasons of family circumstances, work, etc. has had to do forty-eight hours a month duty in the Home Guard or Civil Defense. Supplies of all kind have been limited by shipping and manpower shortage; the queue is part of normal life. . . . The scarce supplies, both of goods and services, must be shared with hundreds of thousands of United States, Dominion, and Allied troops; in preparation of Britain first as the base and then the bridgehead, the civilian has invariably suffered hardships spread over almost every aspect of his daily life.[42]

In no way did the American effort approach that of total war. Admittedly, the American mobilization of manpower for the military and the workforce was crucial to the winning of the war. The Americans outproduced the other powers in virtually every category. Its Lend-Lease Program supported the British and Soviet militaries. The foodstuffs it sent to the Soviet Union prevented the starvation of a substantial portion of its population. After the war, Stalin was to admit to his henchmen that, without American help, the Soviets could not have beaten the Germans.[43] American turned out Liberty ships in such quantities that they overwhelmed the U-boats. Beginning in July 1943 an Essex-class carrier with a full complement of aircraft and trained aircrew arrived every month at Pearl Harbor until the war's end.

Yet it is hard to talk about the United States as waging total war compared to the war efforts conducted by Britain and the Soviet Union. This is especially true when one considers the fact that coal strikes in the United States resulted in a loss in production of twenty million tons of coal and delayed the production of 100,000 tons of steel.[44] Moreover, it is hard to speak of an American total war when ninety-five percent of Americans ate substantially better than the rest of the world; when, with the exception of the cities on the eastern seaboard, there were no blackouts; and when substantial numbers of Americans had access to gasoline for their automobiles throughout the war. In the

42. W. K. Hancock and M. M. Gowing, *British War Economy* (London: His Majesty's Stationary Office, 1949), 519.

43. "[I]f the United States had not helped us, we would not have won the war. If we had had to fight Nazi Germany one on one, we could not have stood up against Germany's pressure, and we would have lost the war." Nikita Khrushchev, *Memoirs of Nikita Khrushchev*, Volume 1, *Commissar, 1914–1945* (College Park, PA: Penn State University Press, 2005), 675–76.

44. James Lacey, *The Washington Wars: FDR's Inner Circle and the Politics of Power that Won World War II* (New York, NY: Bantam, 2019), 367.

case of the Americans, total war was not in the cards because there was no existential threat, except for a few months after the surprise Japanese attack on Pearl Harbor.

Even though the American effort did not approach total war, Roosevelt's handling of strategy was, for the most part, masterful. As early as the Munich crisis, he recognized that if matters in Europe were to continue on the same path, there was going to be a major war. Thus, he focused first on preparing the army air forces and the navy for war. If his cautious handling of the crisis of 1940, with the fall of most of Western Europe into Nazi hands was somewhat cold-blooded, it was also realistic given the strength of American isolationism. His decision to limit the size of the army in October 1942 reflected a recognition that there were limits on the capability of the American economy. Perhaps most importantly, Roosevelt recognized that to extract the maximum out of the economic system, the war had to be popular with Americans and that reality meant that butter was an essential component to the making of guns. Above all, strategy is a matter of recognizing limits to what is possible.

In the case of the Russians, we see a different picture. There was an existential threat from June 22, 1941, when the Wehrmacht invaded the Soviet Union right through to the end of the war. To a considerable extent, the Soviets were already on a war footing when the invasion began, but the extensive incursion of Wehrmacht spearheads deep into European Russia forced the Soviets to make major adjustments to their entire industrial infrastructure. Despite the rapidity of the German advance, the governmental bureaucracy managed to relocate no fewer than 1,360 factories to the east of Moscow along the Volga, to the Urals, and even farther to Siberia.[45] Some of these factories began operating in tents and subzero temperatures almost immediately on their arrival at the new locations.

But as the German army's geographic section had warned in July 1940, Stalin's Five-Year Plans already had moved substantial portions of Soviet heavy industry to the east of Moscow, particularly to the Urals. The factories transported to the east after the German invasion then fell into an industrial infrastructure capable of absorbing them. By the end of 1942, the Soviets had outproduced the Germans by a four-to-one margin in tanks and by a three-to-one margin in artillery over the year.[46] From 1942 to 1944, the Soviets increased the

45. David M. Glantz and Jonathan M. House, *When Titans Clashed: How the Red Army Stopped Hitler* (Lawrence, KS: University Press of Kansas, 2015), 71–72.

46. Tooze, *Wages of Destruction*, 588.

number of tanks their factories turned out yearly from 24,000 to 29,000.[47] To achieve production numbers sufficient to overwhelm the Wehrmacht, the Soviets placed enormous burdens on their population, which Stalin's cruel and malicious rule only served to exacerbate. But that rule was able to impose a draconian regime on the Soviet peoples that allowed them to absorb over seven million soldier deaths and to see the war through to victory in Berlin in May 1945.

V

One definition of strategy is that it must attempt to connect the military aims with the means available, and in the modern era that means economic as well as military. It is hard to speak of total war as a theoretical construct. Its appearance in the past has come in almost every case as a reaction to existential threats that have appeared to menace states and their populations with catastrophic defeat. The French Revolutionaries of 1793 did not frame their *leveé en masse* in theoretical terms, because they confronted palpable dangers that threatened the continued existence of the Republic and its ideology.

Ironically, in its efforts to free the French people from the shackles of the monarchy, the French Revolutionaries tightened control by the state to a degree unimagined before 1789. It would take a considerable period for these changes in the relationship between the citizen and the state to set, but by the twentieth century, they had set in concrete. As one modern commentator has noted:

> The new politics abolished, along with the society of orders, all theoretical limits on the state's actions. Individual lives and property were now unconditionally at the nation's service. Pervasive police surveillance, persecution, and extermination of real and unimagined enemies on a scale and with a brutality unseen again in Europe until 1917–45, and quasi-universal military service became the order of the day.[48]

The American Civil War provides a useful stop on the road to total war. Given the disparity between the resources and population available to the

---

47. Glantz and House, *When Titans Clashed: How the Red Army Stopped Hitler*, Table D, 306.
48. MacGregor Knox, "Mass Politics and Nationalism as Military Revolution: The French Revolution and After," in *The Dynamics of Military Revolution, 1350–2050*, MacGregor Knox and Williamson Murray, eds. (Cambridge: Cambridge University Press, 2001), 65.

North in comparison to those of the South, it took an extraordinary effort by the Confederacy to hold off the pressure of Northern armies. Even with the advantages that terrain and geographic expanse provided the Confederacy, the fact that the war lasted four terrible years underlines the extraordinary effort white Southerners were able to mount in attempting to gain their independence. But there was no strategic framework underlying the Confederate effort. If anything, the emphasis on seeking a decisive victory to end the war ensured that the North would win the long, drawn-out war of attrition. But what allowed the South to remain in the struggle for as long as it did largely rested on the commitment of the society to something that approached total war.

The reality of total war would come into its own in the catastrophic conflicts that would mark the history of the first half of the twentieth century. In the first of these conflicts, total war emerged as necessity rather than strategy. The French, again by necessity, found themselves mobilizing their population and industrial resources to the extent that, by 1918, they were able to support the AEF as well as their own forces. One suspects that the catastrophe of 1940 reflected the long-term impact of the psychological price the French nation had paid to participate in the winning of the Great War. The British found themselves forced to mobilize their nation in a fashion that flew in the face of Victorian and Edwardian culture, but in the end they were able to field a BEF that broke the back of the German army in fall 1918. The Germans, of course, were responsible for starting the war. In some respects, their approach to total war was impressive. Both their initial mobilization and their approach to the battlefield ensured that the Allies would find no easy solution to the conflict. Nevertheless, Germany's obtuse emphasis on military necessity ensured that they would lose a war they had little chance of winning. In the end total war in the 1914–18 conflict was more the result of desperate expedients than of conscious design.

The Second World War saw the Germans repeat every major strategic mistake they had made in the prior conflict. And it was not simply Hitler who made the mistakes. The military were fully culpable in the disasters, especially the invasion of the Soviet Union. But while the Germans waged a war of ideology, total war emerged only towards the end of the murderous course of the Third Reich. The Soviets and the British were remarkable in the degree to which they forced their societies toward total war. What made them so different from the Germans was the strategic frameworks within which they were fighting the conflict. Admittedly, the threat that the Third Reich represented helped in framing an approach to strategy that connected military and economic reality to the actual conditions of the battlefield.

Finally, we have the Americans, who, though they never had to fight a total war, at least possessed a willingness to adapt their strategy to a world in chaos. In spite of the weight of American isolationism, Roosevelt maneuvered the United States into a war, which it had no choice but to fight. Moreover, the president's recognition of the fact that the United States had entered a world dominated by mechanization, and particularly by air power, allowed the American military to begin playing a significant role in 1942. Even though the victorious Allied powers possessed overwhelming economic and military power by 1943, they still played the strategic hand they were dealt with considerable skill. And it was the superiority of Allied strategy that was as important to victory as the hard factors involved in superiority on the battlefield.

CHAPTER 22

Woodrow Wilson and the Rise of Modern American Grand Strategy

Robert Kagan

Not many historians or international relations theorists would list Woodrow Wilson as the first grand strategist of the new America era. That honor is generally reserved for his predecessor, Theodore Roosevelt. Roosevelt was the "warrior-statesman," Henry Kissinger writes in *Diplomacy*, the practitioner of "geopolitical realism," who "approached the global balance of power with a sophistication matched by no other American president." Wilson was the "prophet-priest," the purveyor of "high-minded altruism," the rejecter of "power politics." Or as another historian has put it, "Wilson imagined the way to serve God was by sacrificing US national interest on the altar of humanity."[1] This caricature remains popular today.

In fact, Wilson was no more or less idealistic than most Americans in his time, including Roosevelt. The chief difference between the two presidents was more a matter of timing and circumstance than of philosophy. The world order that had so benefited the United States and allowed Americans to remain generally aloof from international affairs suffered its final collapse on Wilson's watch and it was left to Wilson to devise a response to the new geopolitical circumstances.

The old order had rested on three pillars: a rough balance of power on the European continent; the absence of great powers outside Europe; and a satisfied

---

1. Henry Kissinger, *Diplomacy* (New York, NY: Simon and Schuster, 1995), 41–47; Walter McDougall, *The Tragedy of U.S. Foreign Policy* (New Haven, CT: Yale University Press, 2016), 137.

and relatively friendly naval superpower, Britain, which presided almost un-challenged over the oceans and the world's trade routes. This order did not provide the United States "free security," as is often alleged—geography, geol-ogy, and a feisty American belligerence over the course of the nineteenth century convinced other great powers to steer clear of challenging America's regional hegemony. But it had provided the United States with all the benefits of a generally liberal order without requiring America doing anything to up-hold it.

Yet the rise of Germany in Europe and of Japan in East Asia put an end to the Europe-dominated world and thrust the United States into a new position in the international system. With power shifting away from Britain and the European democracies, the capacity to maintain any kind of world order was shifting. If the Americans wanted to continue enjoying the benefits of a liberal world—with friendly democracies on the other shores of the Atlantic, with a generally open trading and financial system, and with the rising powers de-terred from aggression, they would have to step in themselves. Early on, Roo-sevelt saw this shift coming, but it was Wilson who had to lead Americans through this revolution in their thinking about their role in the world.

I

Kissinger praised Roosevelt for his "European" approach to diplomacy and geopolitics, a fitting description as Roosevelt was the last American president of the European era. When Roosevelt imagined the United States taking on the role of a world power, it was as an adjunct to the existing European order. He had a distant vision of American global leadership, but he did not actually imagine that the United States would have to step in and take over the role that had been so conveniently played by Britain. He preferred the British-led world, but he also assumed, as most Americans did, that the European great powers were "civilized." He saw the threat to world peace as coming chiefly from the backward, "barbaric" races, which for Roosevelt sometimes included Russia but not, he hoped, Japan. But even in these visions, the responsibility of the United States was to be limited to "policing" its own hemisphere.

The common view that America became a "world power" because of the war with Spain and the acquisition of the Philippines mistakes capability for state of mind. While the United States had acquired sufficient economic and demographic strength to be a world power in the late nineteenth century, Americans, including American diplomats, did not act like a world power, and did not wish to be a world power. James Bryce, the historian and British ambassador to Washington, once remarked of the United States: "She sails upon a summer sea . . . safe from attack, safe even from menace, she hears from afar the warring cries of European races and faiths, as the gods of Epicurus listened to the murmurs of the unhappy earth spread out beneath their golden dwellings."[2] To continue sailing on that summer sea remained the chief goal of Americans after 1900, and it seemed possible.

Even after the turn of the century the United States remained all but self-sufficient economically, at least compared with the other great powers, and enjoyed a far higher degree of security, as well. The European great powers all lived on top of each other and in a perpetual state of insecurity. The Asian powers, either the formerly great, like China, or the aspiring to be great, like Japan, competed for control of land and resources with each other and also with the British, French, Russian, and, more recently, German empires. From the end of the nineteenth century, the strategic contest among empires and great powers only intensified until the whole European great power system erupted into mutually destructive conflict. Only the United States remained outside this intensifying international struggle.

Americans did little to prepare themselves for a greater role in the world, even after defeating Spain and taking the Philippines in 1898. At the dawn of the new century, Russia's peacetime army numbered almost two million; Germany had 600,000 men under arms; France had 575,000; Austria-Hungary, a second-rank power, had 360,000. The United States, though it inhabited a territory almost as large as Russia's and had the world's third largest population, kept a regular army numbering in the tens of thousands. Yet this seemed adequate at a time when British intelligence officers assessed that "a land war on the American Continent would be perhaps the most hazardous military enterprise that we could possibly be driven to engage in."[3]

The "New Navy" built in the late 1880s and 1890s did not equip the United States for world power status. The handful of armored cruisers and, eventually, seven modern battleships put the United States in the upper tier, but in 1901 the British Royal Navy had 50 battleships cruising the oceans; France had 28, Germany had 21, and even Italy had 15. This despite the fact that the US Navy,

2. James Bryce, *The American Commonwealth* (London: MacMillan and Co., 1891), Volume 1, 303.

3. Robert Kagan, *Dangerous Nation: America's Place in the World From its Earliest Days to the Dawn of the Twentieth Century* (New York, NY: Knopf, 2006), 302.

unlike the army, theoretically had a big job. It had to operate in two oceans and the Caribbean as well as protect thousands of miles of coastline. Alfred Thayer Mahan wanted a battle fleet able to take on any other navy on the high seas. Yet Roosevelt could not get Congress to approve more than a handful of new battleships during his seven years in office. Indeed, by 1914, congressional authorizers had even revived the nineteenth-century notion of building ships for "coast and harbor defense." On the eve of the great European conflict, American naval strategy focused not on global expansion but on snuggling safely behind the two oceans.

British officials liked to tease their American colleagues that the United States was most fortunate "in being untroubled by any foreign policy," but the evidence suggests that was the way most Americans liked it.[4] Americans' failure to build on the acquisition of the Philippines reflected both a lack of ambition and a paucity of perceived interests in Asia. Unlike Britain, the United States did not have an "export economy" dependent on foreign markets. In 1910, exports made up just over five percent of the nation's gross domestic product, compared to twenty-five percent of Britain's.[5] Americans exported less than seven percent of their manufactured goods.

The public's indifference to foreign affairs disappointed and worried Roosevelt, but he did not challenge it. He took few actions that might run afoul of popular attitudes. He eschewed any thought of war, and even worked to cool the dangerous tensions arising from California voters' hostility to Japanese immigration. Even in the Western Hemisphere he deployed US forces reluctantly and only after other methods failed. His most controversial action, the acquisition of land in Panama for the canal, did not require US troops and was widely popular.

Roosevelt's relative inaction did not imply a lack of concern. Although he and the Republican Senator Henry Cabot Lodge feared that the other great powers were pushing out "in all directions," grabbing the remaining "waste spaces of the earth," scrambling for Africa, divvying up the prostrate Chinese Empire, and that it was only a matter time before this global competition brought them "into contact with American interest" in the Western Hemisphere, the two men did not want the United States to join in that competition.

---

4. William C. Widenor, *Henry Cabot Lodge and the Search for an American Foreign Policy* (Berkeley, CA: University of California Press, 1980), 106.

5. "U.S. International Trade in Goods and Services, monthly, 1992–Present," accessed May 28, 2015, http://www.econdataus.com/tradeall.html.

Rather, they hoped to shield the United States from it by consolidating and strengthening America's position within the hemisphere. The "Large Policy" that Lodge and Roosevelt had pursued in 1898 was not a new departure in American imperialism but rather the fulfillment of nineteenth-century ambitions. Building the Panama Canal, securing its approaches with naval bases in both the Pacific and the Caribbean, obtaining Hawaii and other islands in what Lodge called "the outworks" of America's defenses—these all had long pedigrees.[6] The McKinley and Roosevelt administrations repeatedly passed up chances to gain a foothold in China, as all the other great powers were doing. Roosevelt knew that the "open door" was unenforceable unless the American people were willing to "go to extremes," which they weren't. He therefore hoped other powers would keep the door open for them. Roosevelt supported Japan in the 1904 war with Russia, which he originally considered the real threat to China, only to find the Japanese to be an even bigger problem. In the end Roosevelt hoped the two powers would check each other, but when that failed and Japan emerged as the dominant power in East Asia, Roosevelt and his successors simply accommodated to this new reality and acceded to Tokyo's territorial claims on the Asian continent. As Taft's secretary of state put it, Americans were content to "stand consistently by our principles even though we fail in getting them generally adopted."[7]

For all his reputation as a "war lover," Roosevelt did not order a shot fired anywhere in the world throughout his seven years as president. He did nothing to expand American involvement in Asia, Africa, the Middle East, or Europe. He also rejected any discussion of alliances, although these had become a common feature of great power diplomacy since the late nineteenth century. In this respect, at least, Roosevelt did not pursue "European-style" diplomacy. While even Britain abandoned "splendid isolation" to forge an alliance with Japan in 1902, Roosevelt rejected entreaties from both the Japanese and the British to join their pact. British diplomats concluded that the United States was not "a major factor in world politics beyond the western hemisphere."[8]

American thinking about internationalism in this period reflected these constraints. While those who called themselves "internationalists" agreed that the United States could no longer remain apart from the world beyond the Western

6. Widenor, *Henry Cabot Lodge*, 105.

7. Akira Iriye, *Across the Pacific* (New York, NY: Harcourt, Brace, and World, 1967), 123.

8. Zara Steiner and Keith Neilson, *Britain and the Origins of the First World War* (New York, NY: St. Martin's Press, 1977), 175–76.

Hemisphere, even the most committed did not seek full and active participation in world affairs prior to World War I. Most sought the creation of international tribunals to arbitrate among states. The Republican Party's leading statesman, Elihu Root, hoped the gradual accretion of laws and institutions would eventually bring peace among the "civilized nations," and thus realize Tennyson's vision of a "Parliament of man, and Federation of the world."[9] American internationalists put much faith in international public opinion, which they believed only had to be mobilized to keep the great powers at peace. Josiah Strong, one of the leaders of the Social Gospel movement, preached the motto, "the whole world a neighborhood and every man a neighbor."[10] Nicholas Murray Butler, President of Columbia University, wrote of the emergence of an "international mind" that would increasingly govern the behavior of nations.[11]

The United States had to be more than a "successful national shop," Lodge argued, and most internationalists believed that with growing power came growing responsibility. But that responsibility did not entail use of that power, except in the Western Hemisphere. In Lodge's view, the United States should become a world power, but a "world power in the finer sense"—one whose "active participation and beneficent influence were recognized and desired by other nations in those great questions which concerned the welfare and happiness of all mankind."[12] The United States enjoyed a superior moral standing, Americans believed, precisely because it was not engaged in the scramble for territory in Africa, Central Asia, the Near East, or China, and because it was not part of the European system of alliances and arms races. (Few Americans at the time regarded the acquisition of the Philippines as a significant aberration from America's general abstention from world affairs.) This very disinterest made it possible for the United States to act as "the supreme moral factor in the world's progress."[13]

This self-image of the United States as a neutral arbiter of global disputes did not imply anything like the role played by the United States after 1945.

9. Walter F. Kuehl, *Seeking World Order: United States and the International Order to 1920* (Nashville, TN: Vanderbilt University Press, 1969), 48, 211.

10. Andrew Preston, *Sword of the Spirit, Shield of Faith: Religion in American War and Democracy* (New York, NY: Anchor, 2012), 185.

11. Dubin, "Elihu Root and the Advocacy of a League of Nations, 1914–1917," *The Western Political Quarterly* 19:3 (1966): 440.

12. Widenor, *Henry Cabot Lodge*, 134.

13. Robert E, Osgood, *Ideals and Self-Interest in American Foreign Policy* (Chicago, IL: University of Chicago Press, 1953), 87.

Before the war, Elihu Root argued that what was needed was not an "international policeman," but a permanent court to decide "upon rights in accordance with the facts and law."[14] No one suggested that justice depended on the exercise of American power, not even as part of a league. Most internationalists opposed the idea of a consortium of the great powers to enforce peace.

Americans were slow to recognize that the order which afforded them the luxury of musing about institutions of world peace from behind the safety of two oceans was already in an advanced state of collapse. This included Roosevelt. Although he believed American interests were best served by Britain "keeping up the balance of power in Europe," he was slow to see that Britain's ability to do so was rapidly diminishing. He tended to dismiss British fears of rising German power, to the point where British officials sometimes regarded him as pro-German. Americans persisted in believing that the trend of the world was toward "international unity"—as late as December 1913 President Wilson declared that a "sense of community of interests among nations" was producing "an age of settled peace."[15] Even as tensions in Europe rose, with two Balkan wars and a rampant arms race, the Taft administration made it clear to all concerned that Europe's problems were Europe's, not America's.

II

Such was the national mood when Woodrow Wilson took office. The Princeton scholar came to the presidency with few well-formed thoughts about foreign policy. Like most political leaders, he borrowed from a common reservoir of thinking about international questions. Despite the usual partisan campaign critiques, Wilson approached international issues much as his predecessors had. Like them, he focused most of his energies on the Western Hemisphere, dispatching troops to Haiti and the Dominican Republic and becoming deeply embroiled in an inept attempt to steer Mexico in a democratic direction after its revolution had produced political chaos and threatened Americans with property and investments south of the border. As a son of the South who remembered the Civil War from his childhood, Wilson inherited some of that region's aversion to war. As the leader of the Southern-dominated Democratic Party, he also had to grapple with the party's traditional aversion to an

---

14. Dubin, "Elihu Root," 441–42.

15. Kuehl, *Seeking World Order*, 144; Harley Notter, *The Origins of the Foreign Policy of Woodrow Wilson* (Baltimore, MD: The Johns Hopkins Press, 1937), 276.

expansive foreign policy. He was therefore cautious about proposing any grandiose ideas for international peace that might entail a deep involvement by the United States. Before August 1914, Wilson "gave scant attention to European affairs."[16]

The outbreak of the European war changed everything, including what many internationalists thought about both the possibilities of international law and institutions and about the role the United States must play. Some internationalists, like Root, who had opposed the idea of sanctions to compel obedience to international courts and councils, came to believe, in light of Germany's behavior, that some enforcement mechanisms would be necessary.

In the meantime, however, there was little for the United States to do. Once war broke out, Wilson at first pursued the only policy possible for an American president: neutrality. German and Irish Americans complained about the objectively pro-British quality of Wilson's neutrality, and Jewish Americans complained about aiding an alliance that included the anti-Semitic tsarist regime, but that was also the only possible course. Anglo-American commercial and financial relations were too important to both countries to allow them to be severed by the war. With the exception of those ethnic groups, most Americans preferred Britain and France and what they stood for to Germany and what it stood for. Especially in the influential eastern corridor of the United States, many regarded the European war as a struggle between liberal democratic "civilization" on the one side, and "Prussian" militarism and autocracy on the other. Ironically, given the consensus view of later historians that Lodge, Roosevelt, and their group were the "realists," during the war it was they who tended to make the most idealistic arguments for helping the Allies—short of entering the war, of course—while Wilson tended to downplay the differences between the two sides, at least publicly, to the point where the French leader, George Clemenceau, complained that the "moral side of the war has escaped President Wilson."[17]

In the first months of the war, neither Wilson nor anyone else in a position of influence believed the United States could get pulled into the conflict. The Germans certainly had no plans for fighting the United States. For Wilson, the

16. Arthur S. Link, *Wilson*, Volume III: *The Struggle for Neutrality, 1914–1915* (Princeton, NJ: Princeton University Press, 1960), 1.

17. *Americanism: Woodrow Wilson's Speeches on the War*, Oliver Marble Gale, ed. (New York, NY: The Baldwin Syndicate, 1918), 20.

only conceivable role for the United States would be to help the two sides achieve peace when they became exhausted by the conflict. It was only a matter of time, he told an audience in January 1915, before the warring nations turned to the United States and said, "You were right and we were wrong. You kept your heads when we lost ours. . . . Now, in your self-possession, in your coolness, in your strength, may we not turn to you for counsel and assistance?"[18]

This, again, was a common view among internationalists. Lodge also looked forward to "the right moment" when the United States could wield its influence on behalf of "a peace that will be lasting." So did Root.[19] In a series of essays published beginning in the fall of 1914, Roosevelt broached the idea of an international "League" to support and sustain the peace after the present war had ended. The international system, he argued, needed an enforcement mechanism for upholding treaties and deterring aggression. The great civilized powers had to work together, all of them "solemnly covenanted" to use "their entire military force" against any aggressor or would-be aggressor. Of course, the United States had a critical role to play in such a League. It had to become "one of the joint guarantors of world peace," to play its part as "a member of the international *posse comitatus* to enforce the peace of righteousness."[20]

Wilson did not have such elaborate plans. Although he wanted the United States to play a mediating role once the two sides were ready to talk, as president he was not about to commit the United States to the enforcement of a postwar peace. In January 1915, Wilson sent his most trusted adviser, Edward M. House, to Europe to sound out the belligerents but with no instructions other than the assurance that House would "know what to do."

Everything changed in 1915. When the Schlieffen Plan, designed to win the war in weeks, stalled and the war settled into a stalemate by the end of 1914, the United States suddenly and unexpectedly became a critical factor in the conflict. The United States "loomed so gigantic on the horizon of industrial and diplomatic competition," one contemporary observed."[21] In the long war of attrition that the struggle had now become, Britain and France would

18. Woodrow Wilson, "Jackson Day," Speech in Indianapolis, January 8, 1915, American Presidency Project.

19. Philip C. Jessup, *Elihu Root* (New York, NY: Dodd Mead, 1938), Volume 2, 313–14.

20. Theodore Roosevelt, "The International Posse Comitatus," *New York Times*, November 8, 1914. Emphasis in original.

21. Carl Russell Fish, *American Diplomacy* (New York, NY: Henry Holt and Co., 1938), 427.

rely on the United States for food, munitions, and the other sinews of war, including financing. Germany would at some point need access to American resources, as well. But the real problem for Germany was that so long as Britain could rely on an unlimited American supply of goods and money, it could stay in the war indefinitely. Cutting Britain off from the United States became Germany's only hope of victory.

None of this would have mattered very much had not the Germans, at that very moment, and almost accidentally, found a new, potent weapon suited for precisely that purpose: the submarine. Never having seen submarine warfare before, Wilson and other Americans were at first incredulous that Germans would actually use their "U-boats" to sink ships without warning. But that was the only way the submarine could operate, and the Germans soon proved themselves impervious to American notions of morality. The sinking of the Lusitania in May 1915, with almost 2,000 men, women, and children aboard, the great majority of whom drowned or froze in the waters of the Celtic Sea, heralded a new phase of the war for the United States. Whether Americans liked it or not, the United States was directly affected by the European conflict. It was clear to Wilson that, even after the sinking, Americans were not ready to go to war, but he also believed there were limits to what Americans would tolerate. Another such sinking, he feared, would force his hand.

For the next twenty-one months, Wilson worked to keep the United States out of the war. This first entailed convincing the Germans to cease submarine warfare altogether, or at least to abide by humane rules and refrain from sinking American vessels and civilian ocean liners. This he finally accomplished in May 1916, when the German government agreed to the Sussex Pledge against the indiscriminate sinking of non-military vessels. Wilson knew this was only a temporary reprieve, however. If the war continued and Britain continued to deny Germany access to American goods while receiving the full benefits of trade with the United States, then Germany would eventually return to unrestricted submarine warfare and Wilson would then have no choice but to take the United States to war.

Wilson's next task, therefore, was to convince the British to seek peace. But how? The answer, he hoped, was the League. In House's discussions with the British Foreign Secretary Edward Grey in early 1915, Grey had hinted that the British might be amenable to negotiations to end the war if the United States would commit to join an international league to secure the peace. Grey believed that had such an institution been in place in 1914, war might have been avoided. He and other British officials also believed that the balance of forces in the world had shifted such that only the United States could restore it. Germany's rise after its unification in 1871 had proved to be more than the other European powers and Britain combined could manage. The only answer was to bring the United States into the equation.

When Grey had first broached the idea, House had waved it off. No president could make such a commitment. But that was before the unleashing of unrestricted submarine warfare, before the Lusitania, and before the Sussex Pledge. By the spring of 1916, Wilson believed that the only way to keep the United States out of the war was to bring the British to the table, and the only way to do that was to agree to the idea of a League.

Wilson was a latecomer to the idea. The first stirrings of support for the idea were in Britain. In the United States, Roosevelt had laid out his thoughts on a League in 1914, and in June of 1915, a group of mostly Republican leaders, including former President William Howard Taft, had put more flesh on the bones. Their proposal of a League to Enforce Peace included the controversial provision that the signatory powers would use economic and military force against any member that went to war without first taking its case to the international court or to the League Council. That was further than Wilson was prepared to go. But he was willing to make a more general commitment to the idea of a League, if that was what was necessary to move the British. Soon after winning the Sussex Pledge from Germany, therefore, Wilson spoke to the second annual meeting of the League to Enforce Peace. The president announced that the United States was "willing to become a partner" in a "universal association of nations" that would act "in concert" to protect the rights of nations, to "maintain the inviolate security of the highway of the seas" and to "prevent any war" begun without warning, in violation of treaties, or without "full submission . . . to the opinion of the world." Wilson offered no specifics and avoided the question of how and when the United States might be called upon to use force. The truth was, he had no plan in mind at this point. For the time being Wilson wished only to "avow a creed."[22]

When the British nevertheless resisted, a furious Wilson turned his guns on London, firing rhetorical volleys about the absurdity of the war and eventually bringing financial pressure to bear on the vulnerable British war effort. His campaign to force the British to accept mediation culminated with a note to the belligerents in December 1916 and then what would become famous as his

---

22. Arthur S. Link, *Wilson*, Volume V: *Campaigns for Progressivism and Peace, 1916–1917* (Princeton, NJ: Princeton University Press, 1965), 23–24.

"Peace Without Victory" speech at the end of January 1917. Believing, with good reason, that the war was locked in a stalemate, and declaring the United States "indifferent" to the terms of a final settlement, Wilson called on both warring sides to accept a "peace without victory."[23] In return, he announced that the United States was prepared to join a "concert of power" and serve as "guarantor" of the peace. Echoing Roosevelt and others, Wilson declared that no "covenant of cooperative peace" would be powerful enough "to keep the future safe against war" without the participation of the United States. The American people, he said, were prepared to "add their authority and their power" to that of other nations in order to "guarantee peace and justice throughout the world."[24]

The *New York Times* called it "one of the most startling declarations of policy ever enunciated in the history of the United States." [25] Republicans and Democrats alike lashed Wilson for abandoning Washington's "great rule" and leading Americans into "the storm center of European politics." William Borah, the Republican senator from Idaho, accused the president of "moral treason."[26]

Wilson, uncharacteristically, had gotten himself out in front of public opinion. Why? It was not because he was so committed to the idea of a League, which at this point he clearly wasn't. It was because he hoped the offer would entice the British to accept his mediation and end the war. Wilson was in fact quite conscious of the moral issues at play in the war, but he regarded it as in America's paramount interest, not to mention the American people's clearly expressed desire, to stay out. As he put it to Walter Lippmann, "We've got to stop it before we're pulled in."[27]

Unfortunately, the Berlin government had already made its decision. On February 1, 1917, Germany announced a return to "ruthless" unrestricted submarine warfare. This thunderbolt, which left Wilson reeling, was almost immediately followed by the revelation of the so-called Zimmerman telegram, in which the German foreign minister proposed an alliance with Mexico against the United States and dangled the return of Texas and other southwestern territories taken from Mexico in 1848 as a reward. Wilson was aghast at

23. Link, *Wilson*, Volume V, 217.

24. "Scene in the Senate as the President Speaks," *New York Times*, January 23, 1917.

25. "Scene in the Senate as the President Speaks."

26. John Milton Cooper, *The Vanity of Power: American Isolationism and the First World War, 1914–1917* (Westport, CT: Greenwood Publishing, 1969), 136.

27. Ronald Steel, *Walter Lippmann and the American Century* (London: Routledge, 1980), 108.

German duplicity more than at any tangible threat posed by such a far-fetched scheme. He still held out hope that the Germans would avoid sinking American ships, but in March that hope was dashed too. As Spring Rice put it, Wilson had "done everything possible to put a stop to the war, in order to prevent the war reaching this country," and now he faced the choice he had worked so desperately to avoid, between "an ignominious surrender or a rupture of relations with Germany."[28] At this point, that was no choice at all as far as Wilson was concerned. As he told Congress in his war statement of April 2, the United States could "not choose the path of submission and suffer the most sacred rights of our nation and our people to be ignored or violated."[29] Republican leaders agreed, as did large bipartisan majorities in both the House and Senate, and as did the great majority of Americans.

Wilson's rationale for war was neither utopian nor even especially idealistic. In laying out his case for war, he pointed to Germany's aggressive actions, the need to protect Americans and their rights on the high seas, and also the need to safeguard "civilization" against "the domination of Prussian militarism."[30] That was what he meant when he spoke of making the world "safe for democracy." He did not mean transforming every nation in the world, or even every nation in Europe, into a democracy. For Wilson, the war was about defending the existing democracies against "autocratic governments backed by organized force." So long as an autocratic Germany remained powerful, "always lying in wait to accomplish we know not what purpose," there could be "no assured security for the democratic governments of the world."[31]

The larger point in Wilson's war speech concerned the role of the United States in the new era. With the British-led world order in shambles, the great powers at each other's throats, and the United States holding the balance among them, Wilson insisted, the old dream of disinterested neutrality was no "longer feasible or desirable." The United States had a stake in the outcome of the European struggle, if only to prevent the next war, into which the United States would invariably be drawn, just as it had been drawn into this one. This had been an increasingly common theme of his speeches over the previous two years. The world was "on fire," with "tinder everywhere," and Americans

28. Stephen Gwynn, ed., *The Letters and Friendships of Sir Cecil Spring Rice, a Record* (Boston, MA: Houghton Mifflin Company, 1929), Volume 2, 376.

29. See "War Message," April 2, 1917, available at https://www.mtholyoke.edu/acad/intrel/ww18.htm.

30. Link, *Wilson*, Volume V, 402–5.

31. See "War Message," April 2, 1917.

deluded themselves if they imagined they could remain "untouched by the sparks and embers." It was, he suggested, no longer a matter of choice. There were forces "lying outside our own life as a nation and over which we had no control" that were pulling the United States "more and more irresistibly into their own current and influence." Americans could be "provincials no longer," the president insisted. Their "fortunes as a nation" had become caught up in the European war, and there was "no turning back."[32]

Finally fleshing out his views of a future League, Wilson argued that a "steadfast concert of peace" could be maintained only by a "partnership of democratic nations." No autocratic government "could be trusted to keep faith within it or observe its covenants." He also made clear that he was on Roosevelt's side of the argument over the role of force in preserving peace. At various occasions over the previous months, Wilson had scolded "peace progressives" for imagining that peace could be preserved by international goodwill, international public opinion, or even by law and tribunals. "In the last analysis," he told the peace activist Lillian Wald, "the peace of society is obtained by force." [33] In his war address Wilson declared it a "fearful thing to lead this great peaceful people into war, into the most terrible and disastrous of all wars, civilization itself seeming to be in the balance. But the right is more precious than peace."[34]

It ought to have been clear enough that his earlier call for a "peace without victory" was no longer operative. Without acknowledging any inconsistency, Wilson, now that the United States was in the war, was determined on military victory. He knew the American public would not accept less, and that his Republican critics would have a field day with any outcome short of a German surrender. But it was also clear that he did not believe there was any satisfactory peace to be made with the present German government. Once Germany forced him into the war, Wilson sought only victory, and not a partial victory but a "complete" and "decisive" victory.[35]

32. Speech excepts, January 27–February 3, 1916, in *Americanism: Woodrow Wilson's Speeches on the War*, Oliver Marble Gale, ed. (Chicago, IL: Baldwin, 1918), 14; Arthur S. Link, *Wilson, Volume IV: Confusion and Crises* (Princeton, NJ: Princeton University Press, 1964), 46–48; Thomas Knock, *To End All Wars: Woodrow Wilson and the Quest for New World Order* (Princeton, NJ: Princeton University Press, 1995), 66; John M. Cooper, *Woodrow Wilson: A Biography* (New York, NY: Knopf, 2009), 326.

33. Knock, *To End All Wars*, 66; Cooper, *Woodrow Wilson*, 326.

34. "War Message," April 2, 1917.

35. Klaus Schwabe, *Woodrow Wilson, Revolutionary Germany, and Peacemaking, 1918–1919: Missionary Diplomacy and the Realities of Power* (Chapel Hill, NC: University of North Carolina Press, 2011), 20.

While focused on victory, Wilson remained careful to safeguard what he regarded as America's distinct interests. Those interests, he recognized, were different from those of the Allies, despite their common objective of defeating Germany. By the time the United States entered the war, for instance, Britain, France, and Russia had already made secret agreements with each other and with others enlisted against Germany (Japan and Italy, in particular), parceling out portions of the German and Ottoman empires after the war. When Lenin and Trotsky revealed these agreements from the tsarist government's diplomatic archives, the Allies were not only embarrassed but feared losing support for the war among their own populations, especially among liberals and progressives and the workers on whom the war effort depended. David Lloyd George tried to limit the damage with a speech in which he championed the cause of "self-determination," by which he meant chiefly giving people a say in their own governance rather than being traded about by the great powers. But both British officials and Wilson's advisers agreed that only the American president had sufficient credibility with the transatlantic Left to rally them behind the war effort. Wilson obliged in a speech of his own in January 1918, which became famous for the Fourteen Points he laid out as principles to guide a future peace settlement.

III

Although the Fourteen Points were widely misunderstood at the time, as well as by later historians, as a reaffirmation of Wilson's earlier call for a "peace without victory," they were in fact a renewed summons to war. The United States, he argued, had a profound interest in a "stable and enduring peace" in Europe, but that could only be achieved when the German menace had been removed. Belgium had to be liberated. The "wrong done to France by Prussia in 1871 in the matter of Alsace-Lorraine" had to be "righted." The already independent states of Romania, Serbia, and Montenegro, currently occupied by German and Austrian forces, were to be emptied of foreign forces, as was all the occupied Russian territory. An independent Polish state was to be created—in keeping with the French desire to create a check against Germany in the east. Wilson knew that only a defeated Germany would ever accept such terms, and, indeed, the kaiser called the Fourteen Points a "death knell" for Germany.[36]

36. Schwabe, *Woodrow Wilson, Revolutionary Germany, and Peacemaking*, 33, 24.

Wilson did not even want to negotiate with the present German government, which had proven itself "without conscience or honor or capacity for covenanted peace." The Prussian autocracy had to be "crushed." Only then, when Germany was led by the people's "properly accredited representatives," and was ready to accept a just settlement and pay reparation for the "wrongs" the previous rulers had done—only then could the war be considered "won."[37]

This was so contrary to the spirit of a "peace without victory" that some on the Left in both Britain and the United States were dismayed at what Ramsay MacDonald called the "complete reversal" of Wilson's "old views regarding the war and its settlement."[38] They were right. Wilson had reversed his views in response to changing circumstances. His "peace without victory" speech had aimed at avoiding war. After April 2, 1917, his speeches were about winning the war. Speaking to the American Federation of Labor in November 1917, Wilson affirmed that although he wanted peace, he believed the only route to a genuine, durable peace was to defeat Germany and remove its "military masters."[39] On this fundamental point, Wilson and the Allies were in accord. Wilson insisted they would all stand together until Germany was defeated.

On other matters, however, Wilson recognized that American and Allied interests diverged. The biggest of these concerned the disposition of German, Austro-Hungarian, and Ottoman territories after the war and, related to that but even more significant, the question of what to do with Germany proper once it was defeated. The French, not surprisingly, took a maximalist view. Having been attacked by Germany twice over the previous four decades, the French, led by "The Tiger," Clemenceau, wanted a guarantee that Germany would never rise up to threaten France again. The only guarantee possible, the French believed, was to dismantle Germany, hive off the Rhineland as either an autonomous or independent region under French control, take away German territories in the east in order to create new nations that could serve as France's allies against Germany, transfer to French control several regions with critical resources and industrial capacity, and parcel out Germany's few colonies among the victors.

Clemenceau liked to say that he put his faith in that "old system" called "the Balance of Power," but what the French really wanted was a permanent

37. Woodrow Wilson, "Fifth Annual Message," December 4, 1917, *The American Presidency Project*, available at https://www.presidency.ucsb.edu/documents/fifth-annual-message-6.

38. Allan Nevins, *Henry White: Thirty Years of American Diplomacy* (New York, NY: Harper and Bros., 1930), 344–45.

39. John A. Thompson, *Woodrow Wilson* (London: Routledge, 2002), 160.

imbalance of power that would leave Germany crippled forever.[40] To Anglo-American eyes, the French goal was not only unwise but reflected a return to old French ambitions. The British and Americans preferred to keep Germany intact and get it back on its feet economically. Germany had become an engine of the European economy and a significant purchaser of British and American exports. Only an economically healthy Germany would be able to pay reparations to Britain, which in turn would allow the British to pay off their huge debt to the United States. As Lloyd George put it, "We cannot both cripple her and expect her to pay."[41]

Unlike the French, moreover, the British really did want a balance of power on the Continent. They saw Germany as a necessary bulwark against Soviet Russia, *and* against an ambitious France. American goals were similar. When Wilson declared that the United States had "no jealousy of German greatness," it was not as an idealist but because the United States had an interest in a stable Europe requiring the minimum amount of American intervention. American soldiers were not fighting for *la gloire de la France* or to satisfy French (utopian?) desires for absolute and permanent security against Germany. Nor were they fighting to support Italian claims on the Dalmatian Coast or to expand British imperial influence in Mesopotamia. When Wilson insisted that any peace settlement not serve the "selfish claims" of the victors, it was not out of piety but because the United States was not making any claims at all. Wilson did not want the Allies aggrandizing themselves too much at America's expense.

Other points later derided as utopian and idealistic also reflected American interests that clashed with those of the Allies. Consider Wilson's call for "freedom of the seas." The British opposed "freedom of the seas" because they depended on wartime blockades to compensate for their weakness on land, but Americans in 1918 had neither the ability nor did they perceive the need to impose blockades. "Open covenants openly arrived it" was also a natural American preference because it was the only option available to an American president. European governments could make secret treaties, but an American president often had to submit not only the treaties but also the negotiating record to Congress for public debate and approval. Wilson's insistence on an

40. Margaret MacMillan, *Paris 1919: Six Months that Changed the World* (New York, NY: Random House, 2003), 23.

41. Peter J. Yearwood, *Guarantee of Peace: The League of Nations in British Policy 1914–1925* (Oxford: Oxford University Press, 2009), 127.

"impartial adjustment of all colonial claims" in accord with the wishes of subject peoples cost Americans nothing but potentially deprived Britain and France of the new territories they sought. As for "self-determination," Wilson's enthusiasm for that principle waxed and waned depending on the circumstances and on his view of American interests. He initially opposed breaking up the Austro-Hungarian Empire, for instance, hoping to entice the Vienna government away from Berlin, while the strongest support for "self-determination" came, ironically, from the French in their quest for new states to check Germany in the east. If the Allies, and especially the French, took a skeptical view of the Fourteen Points, it was not because they found Wilson's principles unrealistic but because they understood all too well the considerations of American interest that lay behind them.

IV

It wasn't until the war ended and Wilson got to Paris, however, that he and the members of the delegation fully comprehended the magnitude of the practical dilemma that Wilson would have to solve. Theoretical debates about world government did not have much relevance on a continent where vast numbers of people were homeless and destitute, where fighting continued over contested borders, and where empires were collapsing and revolutions were brewing. The internationalists' pet projects provided no security or reassurance to France or Belgium, to a newly independent Poland or the new state of Czechoslovakia, or even to Germany. What Europeans wanted were not theories of international relations but tangible and immediate responses to their predicament: armies, money, food, and, yes, commitments. Contact with the "terrible realities of Europe" compelled Wilson and his advisers to search for real-world answers to real-world crises.[42]

These inescapable realities forced Wilson to modify his views of the American role in the peace settlement and of the meaning, purpose, and structure of the League. It was in the effort to resolve the dilemma of the European peace that Wilson arrived at a model of American strategy in the new era.

Even on the voyage over, Wilson was still musing about a League of Nations that would demand little of the United States. Offering his thoughts to members of the delegation as they sailed to Paris on board the *George Washington*, Wilson spoke of an organization of powers that *might* impose an economic

42. Nevins, *Henry White*, 357.

embargo on a nation threatening to go to war, if the members agreed, but would have "no authority" for further action. Each member state "would be free to decide for itself" what additional steps "if any" should be taken.[43]

At Paris, Wilson remained dogged in protecting American interests. When the French sought forgiveness of the war debt and the continuation of wartime economic cooperation, Wilson refused. The war debts would have to be repaid in full, and he would "not agree to any program that even looks like inter-Allied control of our economic resources after peace."[44] When it came to the terms of the peace settlement, Americans shared Britain's interest in a moderate peace, a Germany that was punished but also restored and capable of paying reparations and buying American goods. Above all, Americans shared Britain's desire for a settlement that would require as little American involvement in Europe as possible.

But the problem of French insecurity hung over everything. To the French, Wilson's League was no answer. Clemenceau and other French military and civilian leaders had been suspicious from the beginning about any American promise to come to their defense. "America is distant," Clemenceau repeatedly remarked during the first days of the conference. American forces had taken "a long time to get here," even after the decision to enter the war, and during that time the French people had suffered terribly. Clemenceau insisted he could rely only on a "system of alliances."[45] If Wilson was insisting on a league, then the league itself would have to operate like an alliance. There had to be an international force of sufficient strength with contingents provided by the various members. There had to be a permanent "general staff" headed by a chief chosen for three-year terms. In case of war, this international army would be led by a "commander-in-chief" designated by the member states. The force would have to be "ready to act" with little or no advance warning.[46] Otherwise, the French complained, any league would be nothing "but a dangerous façade."[47]

43. Knock, *To End All Wars*, 149–50, 153; Nevins, *Henry White*, 359; Kuehl, *Seeking World Order*, 227, 256.

44. Yearwood, *Guarantee of Peace*, 92.

45. George Bernard Noble, *Policies and Opinions at Paris, 1919: Wilsonian Diplomacy, the Versailles Peace and the French Public Opinion* (New York, NY: The MacMillan Company, 1935), 88, 200.

46. David Hunter Miller, *The Drafting of the Covenant* (New York, NY: G.P. Putnam Son's, 1928), Volume 2, 242–43.

47. Miller, *The Drafting of the Covenant*, Volume 2, 210; David Hunter Miller, *The Drafting of the Covenant* (New York, NY: G.P. Putnam Son's, 1928), Volume 1, 256.

The American and British delegations naturally balked at such proposals—one American delegate at Paris called it a plan for "international control of our Army and Navy *in war and in peace.*" Wilson politely explained that what Clemenceau was asking was "impossible."[48] After several weeks of bargaining, the final language of what would become Article 10 of the League Covenant remained a carefully hedged commitment. It guaranteed the independence and territorial integrity of all member states, but stipulated only that, "in case of any aggression," an Executive Council of great powers would "advise the plan and the means by which this obligation shall be fulfilled." Wilson went out of his way to note that the commitment could be fulfilled in many cases "without the necessity of war."[49] Among the virtues of a league, for both Britons and Americans, was precisely that it was not an alliance. As the delegation's international legal expert, David Hunter Miller, put it, Article 10 entailed a "very limited obligation," which was why it was "certain to be regarded by the French as not enough."[50] Even the most committed American internationalists balked at anything suggesting "a defensive alliance with European nations."[51] Lodge opposed "permanent alliances of any kind."[52] Peace would have to be established on "a new basis," Root argued, one that would be "free from the old virus," by which he meant the European alliance system.[53]

Indeed, some American internationalists rejected Wilson's league precisely because it seemed too much like an old-fashioned great power alliance. Wilson's league was a concert of the great powers, a *posse comitatus*, as Roosevelt had put it. There was no international court or tribunal, no new body of international law. From Wilson's point of view, it was a practical response to the fact that the great powers, in going to war, had ignored laws and treaties, rejected arbitration, and been unmoved by any "international mind." After 1914, even a legalist like Root had come to believe that laws had to have "sanctions behind them."[54] Wilson wanted his League to have "teeth," even as he insisted that it was the opposite of an "entangling alliance."[55] Wilson's League was a halfway house between making a commitment and keeping options open.

48. Miller, *The Drafting of the Covenant*, Volume 1, 209. Emphasis in original.

49. Miller, *The Drafting of the Covenant*, Volume1, 169–70.

50. John M. Cooper, *Breaking the Heart of the World: Woodrow Wilson and the Fight for the League of Nations* (Cambridge: Cambridge University Press, 2001), 155.

51. Kuehl, *Seeking World Order*, 189.

52. John A. Garraty, *Henry Cabot Lodge: A Biography* (New York, NY: Knopf, 1953), 349.

53. Jessup, *Elihu Root*, Volume 2, 313–14.

54. Jessup, *Elihu Root*, Volume 2, 373.

55. Woodrow Wilson address, September 27, 1918; Woodrow Wilson Address, March 4, 1919; Woodrow Wilson Address, January 22, 1917, American Presidency Project.

This was too much for many Americans, but it was not nearly enough for the French. Wilson pleaded with Clemenceau to have "confidence in the good faith of the nations who belong to the League." Although he could not offer more than he had proposed in the way of guarantees, Wilson assured the French leader that "when danger comes, we too will come, and we will help you, but you must trust us."[56] But French trust at this point was in short supply.

The struggle between Wilson and the French has often been characterized as one between the hard-headed European's "realism" and the American president's "idealism." That was how Clemenceau and his allies portrayed it— Wilson, the "prophet," putting his faith in the "new diplomacy," while the French prime minister relied on the "old diplomacy" of alliances and the "balance of power." Even Wilson and his most ardent defenders drew this contrast—the virtuous Americans seeking a new and better world while Europe remained mired in power politics. But behind the façade of clashing philosophies lay a more fundamental clash of national interests and perspectives. What the French called "idealism" was really just America's reluctance, shared by the British, to be tied down by a binding security pact. The French wanted the Americans and the British to treat France's security as a vital interest—as one French senator put it, "The problem of the defense of civilization is the problem of the defense of France."[57] But while the Americans and British believed they had an interest in providing reassurance to France and deterring future German aggression, they also had an interest in protecting the right to make their own choices.

Wilson compromised some in the peace talks in order to keep the French and British on board with the League idea, but he never agreed with his liberal and progressive critics that the peace was simply a reaffirmation of the old power politics, imperialism, and greed. Nor was John Maynard Keynes right in accusing Wilson of being a naïve idealist "bamboozled" by his more ruthless and savvy European colleagues. In the Paris talks, Wilson prevailed in most of the arguments that mattered to him. He did not agree with critics that Germany was treated too harshly by the peace, partly because he knew how much worse it would have been treated by France had he not resisted. Those issues where he failed to have his way—in allowing Japan to take Shantung, for instance—he regarded as an unavoidable consequence of compromise among friendly powers. Some of the flaws in the agreement could be fixed by the

56. Noble, *Policies and Opinions at Paris*, 116; and Knock, *To End All Wars*, 222.
57. Noble, *Policies and Opinions at Paris*, 220.

League itself over time. Meanwhile, Wilson was willing to tolerate a flawed settlement of the last war if he could put in place the means of preventing the next one.

And the key to that, he believed, was American participation in a concert of powers committed to deterring and resisting aggression. The League was vital because America's commitment to a share of global responsibility was vital, and the League was the only possible vehicle for bringing American power consistently to bear on the international system. If the United States simply returned home after making the peace and reserved its power for "narrow, selfish, provincial purposes," Wilson warned, the nations of Europe would once again divide into "hostile camps" and the result would be a war far more destructive than even the last.[58] "If you want to quiet the world," he told American audiences on his ill-fated tour to sell the League in September 1919, "you have got to reassure the world, and the only way in which you can reassure it is to let it know that all the great fighting powers of the world are going to maintain that quiet."[59]

V

Wilson's strategy was a response to the seismic shift in the geopolitical terrain since the late nineteenth century. The British and European orders were gone, undermined by the rising power of Germany on the Continent, by the rising power of Japan in East Asia, and of course by the new and almost unimaginable power of the United States. Roosevelt and others had seen this change coming, but they had not had to reorient American strategy. "As long as England succeeds in keeping up the balance of power in Europe, not only in principle but in reality, well and good," Roosevelt remarked in 1912. But within four years it was clear that Britain no longer had that capacity, and it was Wilson, not Roosevelt, who had to make the adjustment to a new role. The world was increasingly going to "turn on the Great Republic as on a pivot," the British foreign secretary Arthur Balfour observed.[60]

It was left to Wilson to try to fulfill these great responsibilities. The League was his most important contribution but it was not his only answer. In 1916,

---

58. Woodrow Wilson, "Address at Boston," February 24, 1919, Cary T. Grayson Papers, Woodrow Wilson Presidential Library, http://presidentwilson.org/items/show/22126.

59. Woodrow Wilson, "War and Peace," in *The Public Papers of Woodrow Wilson*, Arthur S. Link et al., eds. (Princeton, NJ: Princeton University Press, 1967), Volume 2, 304–10.

60. Jason Tomes, *Balfour and Foreign Policy: The International Thought of a Conservative Statesman* (Cambridge: Cambridge University Press, 1997), 189; Yearwood, *Guarantee of Peace*, 60.

Wilson proposed and Congress agreed to an unprecedented naval buildup that aimed not only at winning the present war but at establishing the United States as by far the greatest naval power in the postwar world. If carried through and fully funded, by the mid-1920s the United States would have a "monster battle force" of over fifty first-line battleships, outstripping the Royal Navy and even the Imperial (Japanese) Navy's most ambitious plans.[61] The buildup, moreover, was aimed as much at Japan, and to a lesser extent at Britain, as at Germany. Both powers were in a panic, with neither able to afford to keep up with the massive buildup that the Americans seemed to undertake effortlessly. Both would plead for arms control measures soon after the end of the war. But both also seemed prepared to accept a de facto American naval hegemony. As the Japanese Navy Minister put it, Wilson's naval program, if carried to completion, would "create such a great disparity in the balance of naval power as to reduce the Pacific Ocean to an American lake." The buildup was enough to convince the Japanese to forego any attempt to catch up.[62]

But of course the American people quickly rejected Wilson's attempt to adjust to new realities. The League was defeated in Congress in 1920 and the naval buildup halted, even reversed, two years later by the Harding administration. Wilson's Republican opponents, led by Lodge and Borah, convinced many Americans that the United States was better off trying to stay where it was. In a very nineteenth-century manner, they returned to fanning suspicions of greedy European empires trying to pull the United States into battles that did not concern it. Indeed, while historians and international relations theorists persist in regarding Lodge and Roosevelt as conservative "realists," it was Lodge and his colleagues who employed the rhetoric of utopianism and American exceptionalism, contrasting the "New World's" moral superiority with the debased and corrupt "old world" of Europe. The League, they warned, would suck America into "the rapacious power of the imperial system of Europe." Instead of "Americanizing Europe," it would "Europeanize America."[63]

This was largely a partisan exercise, and while it would be easy enough to argue that Wilson's international strategy was simply too ambitious for Americans, Lodge knew that public opinion was at first overwhelmingly favorable

---

61. David C. Evans and Mark R. Peattie, *Kaigun: Strategy, Tactics, and Technology in Imperial Japanese Navy, 1887–1941* (Annapolis, MD: Naval Institute Press, 2012), 192.

62. Sadao Asada, "From Washington to London: The Imperial Japanese Navy and the Politics of Arms Limitation, 1921–1930," *Diplomacy & Statecraft*, 4:3 (1993): 146, 151.

63. Cooper, *Breaking the Heart of the World*, 227.

both to the treaty and to the League. Even the Republican party was deeply divided, at first. Republican internationalists like William Howard Taft saw things as Wilson did. The United States had been "driven" into the war, because, "with the dependence of all the world upon our resources of food, raw material and manufacture, with our closeness, under modern conditions of transportation and communication, to Europe," the possibility of isolation no longer existed. It would be "equally impossible for us to keep out of another general European war," therefore, and so the United States had just as much interest in preventing another war as if it were part of Europe.[64] With such views prevalent even among Republican "internationalists," it took all of Lodge's powers and legislative skill to defeat the treaty.

His efforts were significantly aided by liberals and progressives disillusioned by the Paris settlement. But it is interesting to consider what *their* complaint was: that Wilson had not lived up to his own lofty principles (as they understood them), that the peace was not, in fact, a "peace without victory," and largely because the peace had been shaped by great powers pursuing traditional power politics. "We had such high hopes of this adventure," one commented. "We believed God called us, and now at the end we are put to doing hell's dirtiest work."[65] Wilson himself had had more modest expectations.

In the end, Wilson's League wasn't defeated because it was too otherworldly, but because it was all too worldly. On reflection, and under the sway of Lodge's determined influence, Americans ultimately rejected the responsibilities and commitments of preserving the peace anywhere beyond their own hemisphere, and increasingly not even there. They preferred to return to the "summer sea," even though that sea no longer existed. It would take two decades, and the near conquest of Europe by a revived Germany and of Asia by an emboldened Japan, for Americans to return to Wilson's strategy under far more demanding and less favorable circumstances.

---

64. William Howard Taft, Address to the National Congress for a League of Nations, February 25, 1919, St. Louis.

65. Gordon Martel, "A Comment," in *The Treaty of Versailles: A Reassessment after 75 Years*, Manfred F. Boemecke, Gerald D. Feldman, and Elisabeth Glaser, eds. (Cambridge: Cambridge University Press, 2006), 627.

CHAPTER 23

Democratic Leaders and Strategies of Coalition Warfare

CHURCHILL AND ROOSEVELT IN WORLD WAR II

Tami Davis Biddle

When democratic states go to war against nondemocratic states, they may perceive themselves to be at a disadvantage. The latter are not slowed down or burdened by legislatures wishing to have a say in wartime decision-making; nor are they constrained by domestic opinion, courts, and international norms of behavior. Democracies, however, have advantages of their own. Indeed, they have an array of strengths that can be leveraged to powerful effect in wartime—and these can create resiliency, innovation, adaptability, and efficiency.

Sound civil-military norms within democratic states facilitate communication between key decision-makers, allowing them to craft plans and shape strategies driven by political aims, and adaptable to the changing fortunes of war. This interaction can drive out questionable or unsound ideas. Democracies can build trust with their democratic allies, and then rely on them to offer cooperative advantages often unavailable to nondemocratic actors.[1] And the collective wisdom of their deliberations can elevate reasoned over rash decisions. Because democracies often develop workable bureaucracies and business models, and because they promote education and analytical thinking

---

1. On the failed efforts of the Axis powers to cooperate, see Gerhard Weinberg, *A World at Arms* (Cambridge: Cambridge University Press, 1994), 744–49.

in citizens, they can rely upon these for success in wartime tasks in science and technology, intelligence, communication, and administration.

None of this is simple or automatic. Leveraging the inherent advantages of a democratic society at war requires astute, adroit leadership at the highest levels, and the establishment of mechanisms and institutions to implement choices made by those leaders. And even when good choices are made and sound institutions are set up, the vicissitudes of war will cause disruptions and failures. Democratic leaders must be prepared to invest tireless energy in the pursuit of military victory, the consolidation of gains, and the achievement of a sustainable peace. They must be clear-eyed, determined, and courageous in the face of setbacks. Similarly, democratic societies at war must recognize that their leaders will face daunting challenges, painful tradeoffs, and breathtaking risks. And they must understand that those same leaders often will be over-worked, anxious, and, on occasion, full of doubt.

Coalition warfare poses serious challenges because political actors fighting for a common cause nonetheless will have divergent interests that introduce friction into their strategic preferences and long-term aims. States in a coalition, even if democracies, will differ in their governance, decision-making styles, civil-military relations, and foreign policy goals. This ensures that when actors attempt to pool their resources and abilities to defeat a common foe, the work will be fraught with opportunities for miscommunication and mis-alignment. When democracies fight in coalition with nondemocratic actors, they must know when to extend trust and when to refrain from doing so. And they must seek agreements designed to hold the alliance together through the war.

War is a force unto itself, creating its own contingency-based narrative and unpredictable results. Like powerful flood waters, wars can create entirely new landscapes. Actors can rise or fall in strength and standing; they can emerge with positions far different than those they held at the opening of a conflict. Indeed, power shifts are likely—and these will affect the way states within a coalition interact with one another. Consequently, leaders must be foresighted and agile as they envision strategic ends, adjust them in real time, and struggle for the kind of "better peace" that will serve their people. But no mortal men and women will anticipate *everything*. In the wake of every war there will be questions—and disappointments—about choices not taken and events not foreseen.

In size, scope, and intensity, the Second World War was the largest and most demanding war ever fought by allied democratic states. But the politics of the war against Germany and Japan meant that the democratic partners at the forefront of the battle—Great Britain led by Winston Churchill and the United States led by Franklin Delano Roosevelt—were joined in coalition with a totalitarian state led by Joseph Stalin. Each had its own strengths, weaknesses, and priorities. Every wartime coalition is a coalition of short-term convenience, and this was true for the Allies of the Second World War. "Allies are the most aggravating of people, and never more so than in war," Alex Danchev once argued.[2] But they are also exceptionally useful. Actors in a competitive political system have many ways to provide security for themselves, to include military and economic power, scientific and technical ability, and industrial might. Alliances and coalitions are essential too.

If the war against Japan was fought primarily by the United States, the war in Europe required the sustained interaction of all three partners. The linkages between the three, and the cooperation among them, however, was uneven. While Britain and the US had an overlapping political heritage and a common tongue, the nondemocratic Soviet Union was a mysterious and enigmatic partner with a turbulent history and a culture shaped by invasion and upheaval. Thus, the Anglo-Americans kept an "arm's length war partnership" with Stalin, extending to him only a fraction of the trust they extended to one another.[3] If each of the three leaders had powerful incentives to cooperate, they also had reasons to be watchful of one another, particularly as victory drew near.

This essay examines strategies of coalition warfare in the Second World War, as waged by Churchill and Roosevelt.[4] It will highlight how democracies

2. Alex Danchev, "Being Friends: The Combined Chiefs of Staff and the Making of Allied Strategy in the Second World War," in *War, Strategy, and International Politics: Essays in Honour of Sir Michael Howard*, Lawrence Freedman, Paul Hayes, and Robert O'Neill, eds. (Oxford: Clarendon Press, 1992), 204.

3. Maurice Matloff, "Allied Strategy in Europe," in *Makers of Modern Strategy from Machiavelli to the Nuclear Age*, Peter Paret, ed. (Princeton, NJ: Princeton University Press, 1986), 682.

4. The literature on this topic is immense. See Richard Overy, *Why the Allies Won* (London: Jonathan Cape, 1995); Warren Kimball, *Forged in War: Roosevelt, Churchill, and the Second World War* (New York, NY: William Morrow, 1997); Warren Kimball, *Churchill and Roosevelt: The Complete Correspondence* (Princeton, NJ: Princeton University Press, 1984). Still essential are Robert Sherwood, *Roosevelt and Hopkins* (New York, NY: Grosset and Dunlap, 1950) and Herbert Feis, *Churchill, Roosevelt, Stalin: The War They Waged and the Peace they Sought* (Princeton, NJ: Princeton University Press, 1967). Max Hastings, *Finest Years: Churchill as Warlord, 1940–1945* (London: Harper Collins 2009) is illuminating. On Roosevelt, see Doris Kearns Goodwin, *No Ordinary Time* (New York, NY: Simon & Schuster, 1994); Robert Dallek, *Franklin D. Roosevelt and American Foreign Policy, 1932–1945* (New York, NY: Oxford University Press, 1979). Essential too is Mark Stoler, *Allies and Adversaries: The Joint Chiefs of Staff, the Grand Alliance, a US*

can successfully extract resources and skills from their populations, work with one another, and wrestle with the challenge of nondemocratic partners. It will focus on the leadership attributes and abilities needed by those who oversee coalition efforts in war, and the means and mechanisms needed to build cooperation and mutual support. If the narrative speaks to a specific period in time, many of the insights can be generalized to different circumstances and prove useful to contemporary students of war and strategy.

I

When Winston Churchill became prime minister in May 1940, Britain was in peril: national self-determination and survival were at stake. Churchill's belligerence toward Hitler had not been popular in the 1930s, when the combined effects of the First World War and the Great Depression produced financial strain, fear, and an unwillingness to fully countenance threats. But by the spring of 1940 it was abundantly clear that previous efforts to appease Germany had been a fool's errand. Churchill was able to play a strong moral hand because Adolf Hitler had proven himself unreliable and insatiable in his dealings with those who had sought to accommodate his desires without war. The prime minister argued that fighting was the only acceptable—and noble— choice left to Britain. His urgent task was to rally the confidence of a people who were uncertain of their fate, and he proved exceptionally capable in this realm. Churchill's rousing speeches, fierce political arguments, and well-crafted image of stubborn defiance combined to stiffen the resolve of his compatriots at a moment when such resolve was vital.

Of course, Churchill was never quite so certain about his choices as he appeared to be, and behind the scenes he carried an immense private burden. With his ministers and military leaders, he was obliged to craft and organize a strategy for national survival, and then muster the ways and means to give it life. He believed Britain's best chance relied on sea power and air power (particularly long-range bombing) to pressure Germany; the utilization of special forces to hearten resistance movements and sow discontent; and cooperation with potential allies, in particular the United States. Max Hastings has written

---

Strategy in World War II (Chapel Hill, NC: University of North Carolina Press, 2000). Useful official histories include Maurice Matloff and John Snell, *Strategic Planning for Coalition Warfare, 1941–1942* (Washington, DC: Office of the Chief of Military History, 1953); Matloff, *Strategic Planning for Coalition Warfare, 1943–1944* (1958).

that Churchill served as "suitor of the United States on behalf of the British nation," adding, "[t]o fulfill this, he was obliged to overcome intense prejudices on both sides of the Atlantic."[5] A master of imagination, influence, and the written word, Churchill would conjure the "Special Relationship" to reframe the Anglo-American narrative, downplaying the suspicions and rivalries that had shaped it for generations.

In support of this, the prime minister engaged in an energetic—and ultimately voluminous—correspondence with Franklin Roosevelt. Initially it dealt with the defense of Britain; later it focused on warfighting, and shaping the postwar world. Many of Churchill's early letters sought to make clear to Roosevelt that the survival of Britain was in the vital interest of the United States, and that the survival of Britain rested in no small part upon choices the president would make.[6]

When Churchill came to power, Roosevelt's nation was experiencing its own period of fear, paralysis, and unwillingness to countenance external threats. As in Britain earlier, the reasons included the financial toll of the Great Depression and the bitter memory of the First World War, which had provoked in many Americans a powerful resistance to future involvement in European affairs. By the late 1930s, Roosevelt had become keenly aware of the risk Hitler posed. He had to tread carefully however, since too brazen an action might cost him his position and influence—and perhaps far more. Reflecting on that moment, Roosevelt's speechwriter Robert Sherwood explained, "It is not easy for the average citizen to appreciate the extent to which every word . . . uttered by the President of the United States . . . may bolster the courage or deepen the despair of hundreds of millions of people in lands overseas." Contesting the idea that FDR might have demanded a declaration of war against Hitler earlier, Sherwood observed, "Had he done so in the summer of 1940 . . . when Britain was fighting alone, he would undoubtedly have been repudiated by the Congress and that might well have been the signal to the British people that their cause was hopeless and that they had no choice but surrender."[7]

Within the tight constraints that bound him, FDR nonetheless began to clear a path that would enable US aid to Britain. Churchill's letters made clear

5. Max Hastings, *Finest Years: Churchill as Warlord, 1940–1945* (London: HarperCollins, 2009), xviii.

6. See, for instance, Churchill to Roosevelt, May 20, 1940, in *Churchill and Roosevelt: The Complete Correspondence*, Kimball ed., Volume I, 40

7. Robert Sherwood, *Roosevelt and Hopkins: An Intimate History*, revised edition (New York, NY: Grosset and Dunlap, 1950), 133.

that his nation was determined to fight on, allowing the president to resist pressure from his own advisors, many of them in the military, who were pessimistic about Britain's chances.[8] In June, Roosevelt named Henry Stimson and Frank Knox, both Republicans and both committed to aiding Britain, to serve respectively as the new Secretaries of War and the Navy. With Gen. George C. Marshall, whom Roosevelt had appointed Chief of Staff of the Army in 1939, they worked energetically to put US national defense on a sound footing.

The president sought ways to dramatically expand American defense production—a project begun after the 1938 Munich crisis—by calling for a vast increase in aircraft construction, and then seeking to get much of it into British hands. In the short term, he scraped together an eclectic array of war material and transferred it to Britain by means of "legal manipulation."[9] The president was pushing against Congress and his own military, but in taking these risks he was placing what he believed was the best long-term bet for US defense—the survival of Britain as a combatant. British Chief of Air Staff Sir Cyril Newall put the case bluntly when he told his American counterparts that economic and industrial support from the United States was "fundamental to our whole strategy."[10] Later in 1940, FDR managed to edge around Congress again, delivering old but still seaworthy destroyers to Britain in exchange for leases (for US bases) on eight of their possessions in the Western Atlantic. The deal was less important for its military impact than for "its catalytic effect on cementing the Anglo-American alliance."[11]

For Britain, the situation was increasingly dire: not for much longer would the Treasury be able to cover the cost of badly needed war material. The full extent of Britain's economic plight was not made known to Americans until after FDR had been reelected in November. Seeking an alternative means of business transaction, the president envisioned a plan to lease to Britain and her allies whatever portion of US production "that events demanded."[12] The president, insisting on broad authority unbound by specific dollar figures,

8. Sherwood, *Roosevelt and Hopkins*, 150; Maurice Matloff and Edwin Snell, *Strategic Planning for Coalition Warfare, 1941–1942* (Washington, DC: Office of the Chief of Military History, Department of the Army, 1953), 13–21.

9. Sherwood, *Roosevelt and Hopkins*, 149; David Kennedy, *Freedom from Fear: The American People in Depression and War, 1929–1945* (New York, NY: Oxford University Press, 1999), 449–52.

10. Newall as quoted in Matloff and Snell, *Strategic Planning for Coalition Warfare*, 22.

11. Kennedy, *Freedom from Fear*, 451.

12. John Morton Blum, *Roosevelt and Morgenthau* (Boston, MA: Houghton Mifflin, 1972), 348.

asked US Treasury Secretary Henry Morgenthau to draft the "Lend-Lease" bill, knowing a herculean effort would be needed to usher it through Congress. The domestic debate was raucous and strident, but in early March 1941, the bill passed both houses. Oversight of the new program was entrusted to FDR's closest advisor, Harry Hopkins. No legislative action the Roosevelt administration took during the war would prove so important to Allied victory as Lend-Lease. A wise strategic initiative, it would provide vital munitions, and a vast array of other goods needed urgently by US allies throughout the war, including food, trucks, clothing, gasoline, and spare parts.

II

On June 22, 1941, Hitler stunned Stalin with a sweeping invasion of the USSR. Since the Bolshevik Revolution of 1917, Russia's Communist government had been feared and despised by most democratic states. After consolidating power following Lenin's death, Stalin did nothing to dispel those feelings; indeed, his forced collectivization, and routine killing and imprisoning of perceived enemies in the 1930s had made him a pariah in the West. In a stroke, though, Hitler's invasion changed this. Churchill argued immediately that the USSR should be considered an ally in the fight against the Third Reich.[13] Roosevelt, though he agreed, was careful in his language; he realized the American people needed time to adapt their view. Indeed, not until November 1941 would the US announce its extension of Lend-Lease aid to the USSR. In the meantime, however, the president dispatched Hopkins to Moscow to ascertain the USSR's most immediate needs.

An early draft of Anglo-American principles was publicly articulated in August 1941, following a meeting of the president and the prime minister, at sea, off the coast of Newfoundland. Both leaders had desired an in-person meeting, albeit for different reasons. Churchill, wishing to build stronger ties to the US, sought to stimulate conversations between Anglo-American military leaders. Moreover, he wanted to persuade FDR to make a firm statement to deter the Japanese from further aggression in the Far East. Roosevelt's primary aim was to create a joint statement of the principles at stake in the global contest. Keen to rule out postwar territorial and/or economic deals between Britain, Russia, and their allies, FDR also wanted to set down a clear statement of Anglo-American goals for the postwar world. He sought to shape American opinion

---

13. See Kimball, *Churchill and Roosevelt: The Complete Correspondence*, Volume I, 211.

by highlighting the distinctions between the Anglo-American cause and Hitler's objectives, hoping to stress the danger posed by the Third Reich and thereby stiffen American resolve.

The "Atlantic Charter" contained eight principles, including rejection of Anglo-American territorial aggrandizement; self-government for all peoples; international collaboration for economic advancement and social security; freedom of the seas; and a "wider system of general security" that would seek the disarmament of aggressors and a reduction of "the crushing burden of armaments."[14] The text of the Charter would become the basis of the alliance formed, on January 1, 1942, among the twenty-six nations then at war with the Axis powers. They pledged to use their full resources against the enemy, and to refrain from a separate peace.

At the August meeting Churchill did not get the detailed strategic discussion he had hoped for since US military leaders were not authorized to make any commitments. But the risk of sailing across the U-boat-infested Atlantic had not been without reward. Harry Hopkins had crossed the ocean with him, briefing Churchill on his July meeting with Stalin, and absorbing his views so they could be conveyed in detail to the president. Moreover, though FDR knew it involved risk, he promised to escort British convoys between Iceland and the US, freeing up British destroyers for other routes. On Labor Day 1941, Roosevelt told Americans that enemies of freedom would be emboldened "unless we step up the total of our production and more greatly safeguard it on its journeys to the battlefields."[15]

Ultimately, action in the Pacific, not the North Atlantic, brought the US into war. The day after the Japanese assault on Pearl Harbor, Hitler ordered his navy to sink US ships at any opportunity.[16] On December 9, Roosevelt merged the Far Eastern and European theaters in the American mind, arguing, "The course that Japan has followed for the past ten years in Asia has paralleled the course of Hitler and Mussolini in Europe and Africa. . . . all the continents of the world, and all the oceans, are now considered by the Axis strategists as one gigantic battlefield." He reinforced US coalition ties, explaining, "Precious months were gained by sending vast quantities of our war material to the

14. See "Message to Congress on the 'Atlantic Charter' " (August 21, 1941) in *Nothing to Fear: The Selected Addresses of Franklin Delano Roosevelt, 1932–1945*, B.D. Zevin, ed. (Boston, MA: Houghton Mifflin, 1946), 284–86.

15. Dallek, *Franklin D. Roosevelt*, 287.

16. Gerhard Weinberg, *Germany, Hitler, and World War II* (Cambridge: Cambridge University Press, 1995), 195.

nations of the world still able to resist Axis aggression. Our policy rested on the fundamental truth that the defense of any country resisting Hitler or Japan was in the long run the defense of our own country."[17]

III

The Pearl Harbor attack dealt a severe blow to the isolationist movement and shocked the US into a full war posture. A galvanized nation accelerated production and mobilization efforts beyond anything that had been possible earlier. On the day of the attack, Henry Stimson wrote in his diary that, while the news had been discouraging and worrying, it also brought a sense of relief. Gone was the limbo and uncertainty of 1940–41 as well as the poisonous political atmosphere it had provoked.[18]

By attacking nations that had made efforts to avoid war, Hitler, Mussolini, Hirohito, Yamamoto, and others placed their own strategy on a perilous foundation. Their actions infused energy into that ethereal but vital component of warfare that was Allied "will to fight," solidifying the linkages of the Clausewitzian wartime trinity between the people, the government, and the military—and helping the Anglo-Americans overcome years of hostility towards Stalin and the USSR. Like Churchill in 1940, FDR now had to channel and sustain popular anger and energy to make possible the sacrifice required for victory. Because political action in the US depends heavily on domestic opinion, Roosevelt needed all the communication and leadership skills he had honed during the Depression years.

After Pearl Harbor, Churchill wasted little time. On December 14, he and his key advisors boarded the HMS *Duke of York*, bound for the US. He wanted to shape Anglo-American grand strategy before the Americans could crystalize their own ideas. In addition, Churchill wanted to reinforce the politics of alliance by speaking before Congress, meeting with Congressional leaders, and generally exploiting his own celebrity status to solidify popular ties with the US. Churchill also wanted to reinforce the US commitment to the European war, and to take a hand in establishing the joint institutions for administering and implementing an Anglo-American grand strategy.

17. Franklin Roosevelt, "Fireside Chat on the Entrance of the United States into the War," December 9, 1941, in *Nothing to Fear*, Zevin, ed., 305, 308.

18. Henry Stimson and McGeorge Bundy, *On Active Service in Peace and War* (New York, NY: Harper & Brothers, 1947), 393.

During the weeks in which Churchill and his party were in North America, the fundamentals of early strategy were discussed, and the architecture of Anglo-American communication and cooperation was established. The prime minister hoped to see enhanced US support to the Atlantic naval battle, and he wanted US bomber forces to join ongoing strikes against Germany's sources of power. He hoped a near-term objective would be to "gain possession of, or conquer, the whole of the North African shore" and to provide for "free passage through the Mediterranean to the Levant and the Suez Canal." Churchill did not envision a ground offensive on a vast scale. Determined to avoid a repeat of the massive casualties of the First World War, he was opposed to an army-oriented strategy. Above all, he understood that Hitler had been shocked by his own failure to achieve an "easily and cheaply won" success on the Eastern Front, and that the smart play for the Anglo-Americans was to "make sure that we send, without fail and punctually, the supplies we have promised."[19]

Much of what Churchill envisioned would be made manifest, but not all of it. And at times his preferences would set up sharp divisions between the British and the Americans—and occasionally between FDR and the American military. A foreshadowing of Anglo-American conflict could be found in the early studies done by Maj. Gen. Stanley Embick, a senior advisor to Marshall, who opposed an emphasis on North Africa and the Mediterranean, and who felt that British priority of this theater was "motivated more largely by political than by sound strategic purposes."[20] Embick exemplified a type of instinctive (and often shortsighted) Anglophobia that pervaded much of the US military at the time. And while the Americans recognized and respected the "Germany first" principle—Hitler was clearly the more dangerous enemy—they were not prepared to wholly subordinate the war in the Far East—or, in certain respects, to subordinate it at all.

The main executive and administrative mechanisms for guiding Anglo-American strategic priorities also followed lines influenced heavily by the British. On January 10, 1942, they proposed a "Combined Chiefs of Staff" (CCS) to link the work of British and American military leaders. This body would decide on the requirements of strategy, issue directives governing the distribution of available weapons, and establish the priority of overseas movements. "It was essentially a proposal to institutionalize in committees the 'combined'

19. Churchill to Roosevelt, December 16–17, 1941, in *Churchill and Roosevelt*, Kimball, ed., Volume I, 294, 297–98.
20. Matloff and Snell, *Strategic Planning for Coalition Warfare, 1941–1942*, 104.

approach to prosecuting the war."[21] If some senior American military officers worried this would give the British too much influence over American decisions, they were overruled by Marshall and Hopkins who supported the proposal. Some on the British side were skeptical too, above all General Sir Alan Brooke, Chief of the Imperial General Staff and Chairman of the British Chiefs of Staff, who had low regard for American strategic ability, and was nervous of the growing power of the United States.

In order to facilitate sustained Anglo-American coordination, Churchill asked the outgoing Chief of the Imperial General Staff, Sir John Dill, to remain behind in Washington. Dill became head of the British Joint Staff Mission (JSM), ready to receive guidance from the British chiefs in London, and represent to high-level Americans the views of the prime minister. This decision would prove fortuitous and wise. Marshall and Dill had met in August 1941 and had established a friendship based on mutual respect. Hopkins too had met Dill and formed a high opinion of him. In the end, Dill would do remarkable work in Washington. Indeed, "Dill showed Marshall virtually all the telegrams he received from London, and many of the replies. . . . In return Marshall showed Dill much of his correspondence with the other members of the Joint Chiefs of Staff, with the White House, and with theater commanders like Eisenhower in Europe and Stilwell in China."[22] Dill's openness helped solve puzzles created by FDR's highly personalized and often opaque leadership style. Alex Danchev did not exaggerate when he argued that Dill was not only "influential in the central direction of the war" but also "the fulcrum of its combined machinery."[23] The secretariat of the CCS, too, was initially headed by two immensely talented individuals who established a powerful friendship. British Brigadier Vivian Dykes and US Brigadier Geneneral Walter Bedell Smith shared integrity and professionalism in equal measure.[24] On the American side, Marshall protégé Dwight Eisenhower, the future Supreme Allied Commander, would work to facilitate Anglo-American cooperation. Comprehending the value of allies—and the need for sound relations to produce salutary battlefield outcomes—Eisenhower was quick to turn a fire extinguisher on any persistent embers of Anglo-American antagonism.

21. Danchev, "Being Friends," 196–97; Stoler, *Allies and Adversaries*, 64–65.

22. Danchev, "Being Friends," 202.

23. Alex Danchev, *Very Special Relationship: Field Marshal Sir John Dill and the Anglo-American Alliance* (London: Brassey's, 1986), 11.

24. Danchev, "Being Friends," 200.

A crucial task of British and American staff officers was to prepare for the ongoing series of wartime conferences in which senior civilian and military leaders would meet to hammer out coalition grand strategy. After their initial August 1941 meeting, Churchill, Roosevelt, and their staffs met in Washington on three occasions, and in Quebec twice. They also met at Casablanca and Cairo in 1943, and at Malta in 1945. Though the Russians were not invited into the CCS system, Churchill met with Stalin on two occasions in Moscow (1942 and 1944), and all three titans met together at Teheran in 1943 and at Yalta in 1945.

If democratic committee and staff structures sometimes feel bulky and slow to those working inside them, they nonetheless facilitate a useful, and indeed essential, scrutiny of ideas—identifying weak and/or rash choices. And these committee structures also possess the infinite advantage of preventing a single individual from imposing impetuous, gut-based decisions, as Hitler and Mussolini both did. Such whims can lose wars and cost countless lives.

IV

Britain had entered the war "reliant for her very survival on the ability of her navy to defend the arteries of trade, and to shepherd troops and supplies worldwide."[25] In early 1942, the most urgent issue was Germany's campaign to cut Britain off from the resources needed to survive and continue the fight. Britain's naval position had been greatly compromised by German and Japanese advances, in particular by the real estate the Germans had gained on the Scandinavian and French coasts. By the end of 1941, the British merchant fleet was in trouble: no less than 1,299 ships had gone down, with fully half the crews lost.[26] Canada, with her small navy, was doing what she could to assist, but by the time of Pearl Harbor the situation was dire. A full-on effort was needed to combine the Anglo-American navies in a pitched, running battle against German U-boats, surface raiders, and auxiliary cruisers. In the end, it would be a fierce fight, testing the nerves, determination, and courage of those engaged in it. A battle of technology and a battle of attrition, it reached a breathtaking climax in the winter of 1942–43 before culminating in an Allied victory that summer.

If the Allies were to win the war, they *had* to win the war at sea. At the end of the day, the roots of this victory were found in the development and

25. Overy, *Why the Allies Won*, 28.
26. Overy, *Why the Allies Won*, 32.

production of useful weapons and methods of employment; in scientific discoveries; in evolving naval doctrine, techniques, and practices; in the new realm of operations analysis; and in bureaucratic administration. The discoveries, breakthroughs, and methods were put towards the collective benefit of Britain, the US, and Russia (which was dependent on sea supply from her allies). Brilliant, bold commanders like British submariner Admiral Sir Max Horton played a role, but equally important were the scientists and inventors who developed such instruments as high intensity lights for use by anti-submarine aircraft (Leigh lights), a mortar for slinging depth charges in an arc from the front of ships (Hedgehog), and High Frequency Direction Finding (HF/DF) which could locate enemy submarines daring to use their radios.[27]

Behind the scientists and inventors stood serried ranks of cryptanalysts who worked tirelessly to break German codes. Many of these, including the immensely talented mathematicians Gordon Welchman and Alan Turing, were recruited from Britain's leading universities. Before becoming a chief intelligence planner for the Royal Navy, Ian Fleming had been a maverick stockbroker. Similarly talented individuals in the US—most located in an American higher education system which was increasingly involved in war work—made their own vast contributions.

While conceding that there were inevitable moments of tension between the Anglo-American intelligence establishments, Christopher Andrew has argued that cooperation between the British and the Americans on this front was both remarkable and unprecedented. "American cryptanalysts actually worked with British cryptanalysts at Bletchley Park on ULTRA, the most valuable raw intelligence in British history." And US counterintelligence officers "followed in all its operational detail the entire Double Cross system, the most important system of deception in British history." ULTRA was critical to the long and complex sea campaign in the North Atlantic, but its decisive contribution was possible only because of transatlantic collaboration. Close cooperation in intelligence, Andrew has argued, was the "most special part of the 'special relationship.'"[28]

27. See Craig Symonds, *World War II at Sea* (New York, NY: Oxford University Press, 2018), 103–29; Overy, *Why the Allies Won*, 25–62.

28. Christopher Andrew, "Intelligence Collaboration between Britain and the United States during the Second World War," in *The Intelligence Revolution: A Historical Perspective*, Lt. Col. Walter T. Hitchcock, ed. (Washington, DC: Office of Air Force History, 1991), 111, 115; David Reynolds, *From World War to Cold War: Churchill, Roosevelt, and the International History of the*

As First Lord of the Admiralty in 1914 Churchill had overseen the resurrection of British SIGINT (signals intelligence) in Room 40 of the Old Admiralty Building. Roosevelt had an equal enthusiasm for intelligence, if less experience. When Colonel William "Wild Bill" Donovan arrived in London in June 1940 as FDR's special representative, Churchill gave him access to most of Britain's intelligence chiefs; Donovan returned to Washington ready to urge full cooperation with Britain. In the spring of 1943, a framework was negotiated for Anglo-American collaboration in land and air warfare, facilitating the exchange of information concerning the detection and interception of Axis signals. ULTRA would play a crucial role too in the Normandy landing in 1944, and in the deception operations that protected it. But it could not have done so without comprehensive Anglo-American collaboration.[29]

Women, who increasingly found opportunities in war work, proved particularly adept in intelligence and signals realms. Indeed, members of the Women's Royal Navy Service could sometimes recognize, through diligent listening, the characteristic patterns of particular German key operators.[30] Adding crucial support to the success of the Atlantic campaign were the economists, lawyers, and statisticians who used the tools available to them to carefully chart sea traffic, and to track and graph patterns of loss and success in naval interaction. In early 1942, the British sent a member of the Admiralty's Operational Intelligence Center to Washington to help establish a U-boat tracking room built on the British model. A similar center was built in Ottawa, and the result was integration so smooth and tight that they "operated virtually as a single operation."[31]

Another vital puzzle piece for success in the Battle of the Atlantic was the long-range airplane that could seek out U-boats, prohibit their action, and attack them outright. Converted B-24 bombers, designed by Consolidated Aircraft in the US, would have an outsized role in this effort. It proved challenging, however, to persuade long-range-bomber advocates on both sides of the Atlantic to release aircraft for naval and anti-submarine duty. They believed so passionately that their bombers could erode Germany's ability and will to fight, that they found it difficult to appreciate the fuller pattern of the war and the unforgiving priorities dictating resource allocation.

1940s (New York, NY: Oxford University Press, 2006), 66. ULTRA referred to the successful effort to break high-level German codes.

29. Andrew, "Intelligence Collaboration," 114–17.

30. Symonds, *World War II at Sea*, 245.

31. Sir Harry Hinsley as quoted in Andrew, "Intelligence Collaboration," 115.

When the Americans joined the bomber war staged from Britain in 1942, the Royal Air Force (RAF) already had a serious campaign underway, shaped by hard lessons. Effective German defenses had made it difficult for RAF bombers to sustain daylight campaigns against the oil and transport targets they initially preferred, forcing them into night attacks on urban areas—the only targets they could find and hit reliably in darkness. In the autumn of 1942, Churchill pushed hard for American airmen to join the nighttime offensive, but they—wedded to a doctrine of high-altitude, daylight "precision" bombing of specific factories—insisted on going their own way.[32]

The Americans would learn their own hard lessons in 1942–43, and would themselves be forced to switch tactics. Later, relying on long-range fighters equipped with self-sealing, droppable auxiliary tanks, they engaged the Luftwaffe in aerial battles of attrition over targets they knew the Germans felt compelled to defend. By late 1943, the US, with its prodigious industrial production at full speed, was able to turn out staggeringly large numbers of aircraft, and also large numbers of qualified pilots. Their dramatic aerial offensive, begun in early 1944, placed serious pressure on Germany's supply of both day and night fighter pilots, thus benefitting both the American and British bomber campaigns.

The Anglo-American bomber campaign proved far more difficult to execute than its proponents had anticipated, however, and this meant less accurate bombing than air commanders had hoped for.[33] The strategic bomber offensive was inefficient, and ultimately controversial. Two points deserve emphasis however. The grim experience of the First World War all but guaranteed that Anglo-American leaders would place a heavy bet on strategic bombing, in preference to ground warfare. And, in the end, it had some powerful effects, not least by keeping a ceiling on German munitions production, by pummeling the Luftwaffe ahead of the Normandy landing, by attacking secret German weapons sites, and by starving Germany of fuel (for mechanized weapons and for industrial production) in the late stages of the war.[34]

32. Sir Charles Webster and Noble Frankland, *The Strategic Air Offensive Against Germany, 1939–1945*, Volume I (London: HMSO, 1961), 353–63; Tami Davis Biddle, *Rhetoric and Reality in Air Warfare* (Princeton, NJ: Princeton University Press, 2004), 211–13.

33. In 1943, the Americans also began bombing through cloud cover when weather permitted little else. In the mid-1940s, no air force was capable of anything approaching "precision" bombing as we understand the term today.

34. Adam Tooze, *The Wages of Destruction: The Making and Breaking of the Nazi Economy* (London: Allen Lane, 2006), 598–603; Phillips Payson O'Brien, *How the War Was Won: Air Sea*

Through the Anglo-American "Combined Bomber Offensive" (CBO), senior air leaders created synergistic effects. Their efforts were enhanced by shared engineering and production efforts—which led to important advances like placing the British Rolls Royce engine in the North American P-51 fighter—and by the merger of British and American strategic photo-reconnaissance flown from bases in the UK. The expanding might and fury of the night and day campaigns against Germany forced that nation, increasingly, to draw men and weapons away from the Eastern Front and back to the home front to wage a defensive campaign. And this lifted some of the pressure on Russian troops.[35]

Many other uses of airplanes contributed to Allied victory. Aircraft in every part of the world provided vital support to ground troops and naval forces. For this to happen, however, the Allies had to stay ahead of enemy aircraft in terms of numbers and capabilities. Here, too, cooperation between the British and the Americans paid major dividends. An extraordinary leap forward took place early when a special mission—the "British Technical Mission to the United States" or "Tizard Mission"—arrived in the US in the late summer of 1940 for the explicit purpose of sharing sensitive technology with the Americans. A handful of British civilians and military officers, headed by noted scientist Sir Henry Tizard, made an unprecedented bet on cooperation among Anglo-American scientists, government officials, military officers, and industrial leaders. Those backing the mission, including Lord Lothian, British Ambassador to the US, had to overcome hesitancy on both sides of the Atlantic—but persistence paid off. Among the closely guarded secrets that crossed the Atlantic that summer, perhaps the greatest was the cavity magnetron, which would greatly enhance the roles of radar and was in many respects "the future of electronic warfare."[36] Once the arriving British convinced the Americans that they had a great deal to offer, the scope of their discussions ranged across a wealth of topics, including radar operational methods and technical details, anti-aircraft gunnery, aircraft armament, proximity fuses, and methods of distinguishing friends from foes.

Secretary of War Stimson's cousin, Alfred Loomis, who had created a cutting-edge laboratory in the 1930s, facilitated prompt agreements between

Power and Allied Victory in World War II (Cambridge: Cambridge University Press, 2015), 349–57.

35. Richard G. Davis, *Carl A. Spaatz and the Air War in Europe* (Washington, DC: Center for Air Force History, 1993), 590.

36. Stephen Phelps, *The Tizard Mission: The Top-Secret Operation that Changed the Course of World War II* (Yardley, PA: Westholme Publishing, 2012), 143.

the British representatives and leading US manufacturers like Bell Labs, RCA, and Sperry; he then catalyzed the highly productive Radiation Laboratory at MIT. The Tizard Mission was remarkable for the amazing array of weapons and instruments it spawned. But perhaps its greatest legacy is to show us how interallied cooperation can be an exceptionally powerful force multiplier.[37]

V

Even allies that have extensive common ground will find, invariably, realms of disagreement and dispute—in operations, strategy, and war aims. A sustained argument between the US and Britain transpired over land power strategy for the war in Europe. It caused, as well, serious tension with Stalin who pushed hard for a "second front" to relieve pressure on Russian troops fighting the Wehrmacht. In the US, General Marshall wished to prepare for a cross-Channel assault in 1942 and launch it against the French coast in 1943. This rested upon his every instinct as a soldier: he believed, simply, that victories are won when one takes the fight directly to the enemy. President Roosevelt had not precluded any strategic possibilities in early 1942 but, as was often the case, he was hard to read and harder to predict. Churchill—seared by memories of trench stalemate, and more recently by the fighting ahead of Dunkirk in 1940—was determined to shepherd the Anglo-Americans in a different direction. In this he was supported by General Sir Alan Brooke; both men opposed hurling their thinly stretched army against a heavily fortified French coast with complicated tides and currents, and both were intrigued by the possibilities of campaigns in the Mediterranean.[38]

Churchill's close relationship with FDR—and the president's own desire to get American troops into the European theater in 1942—enabled him to persuade FDR to back an Anglo-American landing in North Africa in November. This decision, Marshall knew, would upend preparations for a cross-Channel assault in 1943, and would instead entangle the US Army in the Mediterranean theater, as Churchill preferred. A bitter blow to Marshall, it was one of the few times the president overrode the wishes of his senior military advisor. But FDR's choice was providential. By that point in the war, the US Army

---

37. Jennet Conant, *Tuxedo Park* (New York, NY: Simon and Schuster, 2003), 208.

38. Michael Howard, *The Mediterranean Strategy in the Second World War* (New York, NY: Praeger, 1968); Andrew Roberts, *Masters and Commanders: How Four Titans Won the War in the West* (New York, NY: Harper Perennial, 2008).

had not gained enough experience in battle to know just how optimistic its own assumptions were. Commenting in April 1942 on the American desire for an early cross-Channel attack, Brooke had noted that the Americans "have not begun to realize all the implications of this plan and all the difficulties that lie ahead of us."[39] Looking back, it is not clear that the Anglo-Americans could have established the conditions or marshaled the resources for a successful cross-Channel attack in 1943. Above all, the Americans were overly optimistic about gaining air superiority—a requirement for amphibious operations—by 1943. In the event, such superiority was just barely achieved in the late spring of 1944. American optimism unchecked by British pessimism would have been dangerous indeed.

The prospects for a cross-Channel attack began to rise, however, as the balance of power within the coalition shifted. Ever-increasing industrial output, growing experience, and improvements in the "tactics of strategic planning" enabled the Americans to gain enhanced authority.[40] For Churchill, the downside of reliance on the US was the increasing difficulty he faced in bending plans and preferences to his will. And the Soviet position in the coalition was shifting as well. Caught flat-footed in 1941, Stalin had no choice but to fight a defensive war that relied on Russian geography and climate—and the fierce determination of a population facing an existential threat. For him, neither the Anglo-American bomber offensive nor the Mediterranean campaign were adequate substitutes for a landing in France. By 1943, Russian armies, relying on experience, steady Lend-Lease support, and domestic industrial production, had won hard-fought victories at Stalingrad and Kursk—and began to slowly push the Wehrmacht westward.

General Marshall was determined not to allow FDR to privilege Churchill's preferences again, and by this time in the war, the military Chief of Staff to the President, Admiral William Leahy, was gaining his own increasing influence over FDR and grand strategy. Leahy "became convinced that the Churchill government was not fighting to defeat the Germans and Japanese as quickly as possible—but instead that they were primarily concerned with protecting British strength, maintaining the empire, and protecting Britain's global position after the war."[41] This attitude, which tapped into long-held American suspicions of the British, was shared by many senior US officers, particularly Chief of Naval Operations Admiral Ernest King.

---

39. Brooke as quoted by Brian Bond in "Alanbrooke and Britain's Mediterranean Strategy, 1942–1944" in *War, Strategy, and International Politics*, Freedman, ed., 180.

40. Matloff, "Allied Strategy in Europe," in *Makers of Modern Strategy*, Paret, ed., 688.

41. Phillips O'Brien, *How the War was Won*, 208.

Through 1943, the British and the Americans waged a running battle over the Second Front. Finally, at the Teheran summit in November—where Churchill, Roosevelt, and Stalin all met together for the first time—the latter two joined forces and pinned Churchill into a commitment he had worked hard to avoid. This was, again, the right decision, even if it left one party unhappy. As Gerhard Weinberg has argued, "any substantial further operations in the Mediterranean would not only have made any invasion in the West impossible in 1944 but would have done far less to defeat the Germans militarily and would also and most dramatically have prejudiced the future of Europe and the world in the postwar era."[42]

Another issue plaguing the Anglo-American relationship centered on Chiang Kai-Shek's China. An ally in the war against Japan, China had received only limited support because Anglo-American attention had been elsewhere. After the fall of Singapore in early 1942, the British had pulled most of their resources out of the Pacific and pursued a defensive strategy in that theater, focused on the protection of India. FDR, however, was adamant that China should be helped; specifically, he and his military leaders wanted to see the British open a land route in Burma through which supplies could be moved to China. At the same time, though, Americans including Admiral King and General Douglas MacArthur (the latter then leading US efforts in the southwest Pacific), were wary of British interests in Asia, and anxious "to keep future British activities under close surveillance."[43] None of these conflicts were trivial. On more than one occasion the CCS resorted to closed, off-the-record sessions to resolve their differences.[44] Future strategists must realize that all alliances will face conflicts—some of them serious. What matters is whether—and how—they are resolved.

VI

As victory drew closer, tensions over the prospective peace began to intrude into the space once occupied fully by a robust consensus on the need to defeat Hitler. In late 1944, for instance, problems arising from the internal politics of Greece and Italy produced sharp words between the prime minister and the

---

42. Gerhard Weinberg, "Who Won World War II and How?," *Journal of Mississippi History* LVII:4 (1995): 279; Weinberg, *A World at Arms*, 611–12, 682–83.

43. Matloff, *Strategic Planning for Coalition Warfare, 1943–1944*, 495.

44. See Bond, "Alanbrooke," 183, 185; and Danchev, "Being Friends," 208.

president. Fear of public disagreement prompted Churchill to tell FDR, "In the very dangerous situation in which the war is now it will be most unfortunate if we have to reveal in public controversy the natural tensions which arise inevitably in the movement of so great an alliance."[45] The dominating issue in this phase of the war, however, was managing Stalin and his aspirations for the postwar world.

Michael Howard observed, presciently, that "one might have considered it difficult to present the peoples of the Soviet Union with an alternative more disagreeable than the regime which they had endured for the past twenty years, but it was a difficulty which the Nazi leadership very successfully overcame."[46] His comment captures the nub of the dilemma faced by the Anglo-Americans: the Soviet Union was, for a time, the lesser of two evils. If Churchill and Roosevelt felt it essential to aid Russia in its titanic struggle—so as to greatly reduce the burden on their own fighting forces—they did not want their ally to dominate European postwar politics. But they had different approaches to the problem. FDR's preference was to win the war first and settle the political issues later; Churchill wanted agreements settled sooner. Roosevelt believed he might constrain Stalin within the boundaries of an international framework—one that also would ease the American people into a sustained role in global politics. The absence of clear political aims was problematic for the US military, and inclined them to prioritize operational needs, or the "Unconditional Surrender" policy announced by FDR in January 1943.

The president had announced the policy because he believed it would eliminate a repeat of the unsuccessful postwar settlement of World War I, when self-interested German leaders were able to argue (falsely) that their nation had not actually been defeated, but instead "stabbed in the back" by domestic enemies including socialists and Jews. An unconditional surrender would create a clean slate, allowing Axis powers to be weaned away from the militarism, nationalism, and violent politics that had come to shape and define their behavior. Finally, FDR felt it would serve as an important form of reassurance to Stalin. "I am responsible for keeping the grand alliance together," he once told Marshall.[47]

45. See Churchill to Roosevelt, December 6, 1944, in *Churchill and Roosevelt*, Kimball, ed., Volume III, 438.

46. Michael Howard, "Total War in the Twentieth Century: Participation and Consensus in the Second World War," in *War and Society: A Yearbook of Military History*, Brian Bond and Ian Roy, eds. (New York, NY: Holmes and Meier, 1975), 221.

47. Overy, *Why the Allies Won*, 261.

In 1944, the Red Army commenced an offensive that drove forward 500 miles, destroying thirty German divisions, and bringing Soviet armies to the gates of Warsaw. Throughout the war the Soviet Union had borne the great bulk of the casualties in the fight against the Wehrmacht; indeed, more than ninety percent of the combat losses inflicted on Germany between June 1941 and June 1944 were inflicted by the Red Army.[48] Stalin believed this sacrifice justified a major voice in the peace. His quest for security was driven by the long Russian experience of incursions and invasions that had included Napoleon in the nineteenth century and Germany in the twentieth century. Even Britain and the United States had sent troops into the fledgling USSR in the aftermath of the Russian Revolution, seeking to aid anti-Bolshevik forces.

Churchill, acutely aware of Britain's waning power, became so anxious about Soviet intentions that he flew to Moscow to meet with Stalin in October 1944. Churchill felt concern not only for the European balance of power, but also for perceived moral obligations that weighed on him. Britain had, after all, gone to war over Poland in 1939. London was the home of the Polish government-in-exile; Polish mathematicians had given British intelligence officers information that greatly expedited key British codebreaking efforts during the war; and Polish pilots helped the RAF hold a narrow margin over the Luftwaffe during the Battle of Britain in 1940. FDR's reluctance to engage with difficult political questions at this moment in the European war exasperated Churchill—and would be criticized by an array of voices during the early Cold War. The president wanted to hold the alliance together—in part to bring the Russians into the war against Japan, and in part to preserve the prospect of postwar cooperation. In the near term, climactic battles against the Japanese home islands weighed on his mind. But both Churchill and Roosevelt were unsettled by the Soviet refusal to support the uprising of Warsaw Poles against Hitler's forces in the late summer of 1944.[49]

Postwar critics would point to the Yalta summit of February 1945 as a particular moment of lost opportunity. FDR and Churchill had conceded to Stalin on the location of the meeting, but in doing so imposed on themselves great physical challenges, particularly for Roosevelt, who was then suffering

---

48. David Reynolds, *Summits: Six Meetings that Shaped the Twentieth Century* (New York, NY: Basic Books, 2007), 106. Forrest Pogue observed that the Germans had suffered some 900,000 casualties on the Eastern Front in June–August 1944. He also explained that the Russian offensives were assisted in no small measure by Lend-Lease aid. See, *The Supreme Command* (Washington, DC: Center of Military History, 1954), 247.

49. Weinberg, *A World at Arms*, 709–11, 731–34.

anemia, high blood pressure, and heart failure, and was but two months from death. To reach Yalta, the president sailed for ten days to Malta, undertook a seven-hour flight to Saki, and then endured a five-hour drive over the mountains to Yalta on the southeast coast of the Crimea.

At the conference, the Anglo-Americans actually got much of what its leaders wanted, including a renewed commitment to enter the war against Japan, a basic agreement on terms for entry into the future "United Nations" organization, a role for France in the future occupation of Germany, and acceptance in principle of the US State Department's "Declaration on Liberated Europe." And they postponed agreements on the future dismemberment of Germany, and reparations (two high priority items for Stalin). On the question of Poland's fate, however, the result was much less satisfactory. When the Yalta conference took place, Stalin's forces held half of Poland, and this gave him the lion's share of leverage.[50]

Some greater influence might have been obtained if the Americans had been willing to bargain with cash, specifically regarding the extension of credit enabling the Russians to buy US industrial equipment after the war—an outcome that Stalin badly wanted. Perhaps sensing difficulties with Congress, FDR was not willing to play that card, at least not then. He assumed there would be further opportunities to settle the issue. If FDR's belief that he could manage Stalin was naïve, it was also genuine. But the president's unwillingness to fully countenance the state of his own health was a serious strategic error. As Pericles discovered early in the Peloponnesian War, no strategy ought to rest on the survival of a single decision-maker.

We know from Stalin's behavior that establishing a security zone between Russia and Germany (and between Russia and capitalist influence) was his highest priority as the war drew to a close. Supporting the Soviet Union unquestionably was the right choice for the Anglo-Americans in 1941, but it meant accepting risk regarding the war's settlement—risk that could not be fully estimated then. The Anglo-Americans had placed principal reliance on sea power and air power, but neither power can control terrain. In 1945, the physical disposition of troops in Europe would have a powerful influence over the peace then being contested.

Later, in the wake of the atomic bomb, the need for Russian entry into the war in Japan would seem less urgent than it had in February 1945. And this

50. S.M. Plokhy, *Yalta: The Price of Peace* (New York, NY: Penguin, 2011), xix, xx, 152–65; 196–206; 392–404.

would influence the way the war's final "Big Three" conference would be interpreted. Always, there are questions at the ends of wars about assumptions, choices, and agreements (made or not made). These are raised by observers who often forget that they possess the omniscience of hindsight, seeing choices or patterns after the fact that may not have been discernable, or politically feasible, at the time.

VII

Casualties matter in democratic states, and their leaders always will feel a compulsion to fight for political aims with ways and means they believe will limit the cost in blood. This was true for Britain and the United States in World War II, and it shaped strategy. For the first two years of the war in Europe, FDR was constrained as well by the bitterly divided domestic politics of his nation. He had little choice but to proceed with deliberation—educating his population, and bringing them along by degrees to understand the realities of their own national security.

FDR's offer of an exchange of information with Churchill—and Churchill's decision, in turn, to trust the power of his formidable pen—set a foundation upon which a sound fortress of war was built. Richard Overy observed that, "The decision of both men to build a common cause between their two states ranks as the most important political explanation of ultimate Allied success."[51] Their mutual decision to support Stalin in 1941 was equally determining for the defeat of Hitler. All three Allied leaders grew into able wartime commanders, building sound, honest relationships with their respective military leaders. In the crucible of war, even Stalin managed to shed his paranoia enough to trust his most talented generals, including Georgi Zhukov and Aleksei Antonov, temporarily eschewing the obsequiousness that dictators expect—and that is always their undoing. During the war all three Allied leaders stood apart from Hitler, who neither valued professional expertise nor welcomed news that vexed him.

For the Anglo-Americans, the Combined Chiefs of Staff system facilitated important debates and reasoned compromises. If hot tempers were sometimes inevitable, "a mutually acceptable master bargain was always produced."[52] The CCS was built around the personalities that formed it, and much of its

51. Overy, *Why the Allies Won*, 249–51.
52. Danchev, "Being Friends," 209.

success rested on the mutual respect of Dill and Marshall. Still, it is difficult to pull from the annals of warfare a better example of an institution supporting and sustaining allied strategy, and producing—through free exchange and expert staff work—the ways and means required for victory. The trust built by Churchill and Roosevelt made it possible, too, for them to share the abilities and energies of their talented, creative populations. Education is a powerful weapon of war, particularly the kind of analytical education fostered and protected by the universities of liberal societies.

Finally, the ties between Churchill and Roosevelt helped alter American thinking. Together, the two men battled isolationism and Anglophobia, and sowed the seeds of Atlanticism and internationalism in the American mind. Always afraid that the "betrayal of 1919–1920" would be repeated and the Americans would run from postwar international obligations, the British were glad to see the United States commit itself increasingly to forms of internationalism. Surely there were serious Anglo-American tensions over such things as commercial aviation, colonial territories, and merchant shipping, but, as David Reynolds has pointed out, the increased trust built by the "Special Relationship" laid the groundwork for Marshall Aid, relief loans, overseas military spending, the Berlin airlift, NATO—and many other agreements and interactions that helped bring postwar security. It is indeed fair to argue that "the wartime Anglo-American relationship was probably the most remarkable alliance of modern history" and an object lesson for democratic strategists in any era.[53]

53. Reynolds, *From World War to Cold War* (New York, NY: Oxford University Press), 70.

CHAPTER 24

The Hidden Hand of History

TOYNBEE AND THE SEARCH FOR WORLD ORDER

Andrew Ehrhardt and John Bew

In explaining what he saw as an intellectual rot at the heart of American foreign policy, the activist and conspiracy theorist Lyndon LaRouche, writing in the early years of the Reagan presidency, fastened on an unlikely source. The late Arnold J. Toynbee (1889–1975), the esteemed British scholar and best-selling historian was, according to LaRouche, a largely hidden but highly significant factor in the pollution of the American strategic mind over the course of the twentieth century. "No analyst nor government could possibly have a competent strategic assessment today unless it understood the significance of historian Arnold Toynbee's rather long tenure at the head of the British foreign-intelligence service," LaRouche claimed in a book published in 1982, entitled *The Toynbee Factor in British Grand Strategy*. According to this account, the British Empire had set out to change American culture and infect it with its own prejudices, with figures like Toynbee crafting a strategic script, based around the idea of civilizational history and the unification of the world through technology. It was a theory that, LeRouche believed, America's foreign policy elite had unwittingly imbibed.[1]

Toynbee never held such a position at the head of British intelligence. And yet, like many conspiracy theorists, LaRouche unwittingly stumbled upon an important theme—the role that historical and civilizational assumptions play

---

1. Lyndon Hermyle LaRouche, Jr., *The Toynbee Factor is British Grand Strategy: An Executive Intelligence Review Strategic Study* (New York, NY: EIR News Service, 1982).

in the formulation of strategy—and an ideal subject through which to explore this connection, in Toynbee himself. Indeed, there was another habit of the Western strategic mind that LaRouche identified which is also worthy of further consideration. This was the way in which certain ingrained and unexamined assumptions—about the nature of historical development and the way that different civilizations interact—could become an unconscious bias in the minds of strategists themselves.

Toynbee's primary contributions to the intellectual life of the twentieth century were as a scholar rather than a policymaker. He was known, above all, for his twelve-volume work, *A Study of History* (1934–61), first treated as a masterpiece although criticized by later historians as too influenced by Toynbee's Christian faith, too dependent on generalizations, and insufficiently empirical. Notably, it was Toynbee's work as a philosopher of history rather than as a strategist that captured the attention of Henry Kissinger in his 1951 undergraduate thesis at Harvard, on "The Meaning of History: Reflections on Spengler, Toynbee, and Kant." And yet Toynbee, while never attaining the heights ascribed to him by LaRouche, was also a significant figure in policymaking circles in his own right. This ranged from his close involvement in the Royal Institute of International Affairs (Chatham House) in the interwar years to his service for the British Foreign Office during the Second World War, as part of a team of scholars generating theories about the structural causes of international anarchy and the potential architecture on which to build an enduring peace. In 1940, at the apogee of his policymaking involvement, Toynbee participated in the influential British Cabinet War Aims Committee. In this position he was well known to those at the sharper end of British military and diplomatic strategy. Some, like Churchill and gnarly-handed diplomats at the Foreign Office like Gladwyn Jebb, regarded Toynbee as too much of a dreamer to serve their immediate political needs. Nonetheless, his policy contributions from this period sketched the outlines of a vision for a postwar world that have aged well in the course of time.[2]

2. One scholar has even gone so far as to say that Toynbee's wartime memoranda "laid down the foundations" for Britain's approach to the creation of the United Nations. This favorable view of Toynbee's output is made in Raymond Douglas, *The Labour Party, Nationalism and Internationalism, 1939–1951* (London: Routledge, 2004), 106–7, 112, 118–19. In reality, Toynbee's influence was much more limited and indirect. Credit for the UN policy, in particular, is owed chiefly to Gladwyn Jebb, head of the Foreign Office's Economic and Reconstruction Department, as well as one of Toynbee's colleagues in the Foreign Research and Press Service, the historian Charles Webster. See Andrew Ehrhardt, "The British Foreign Office and the Creation of the United Nations Organization, 1941–1945," doctoral thesis submitted to King's College London, November 2020.

It was as a thinker about world order—from the collapse of the post-1918 international system into anarchy to an attempt to articulate how the future world order might take shape after the defeat of Nazism—that Toynbee's place in an anthology to strategy-making is best understood. The conundrum to which he set his mind was how to manage civilizational relations—both within and between civilizational blocs—in a world which was evermore connected by technology and economic interdependence. More than that, Toynbee's influence on policymaking demonstrated how the pursuit of world order, from conceptualization to the building of a new international architecture, gave purpose and shape to foreign policy and medium-term strategic aims.[3] Indeed, one of the major themes of his writing was that the very act of being able to impose the human spirit on the historical environment, and to shape it to one's will, was the driving force of civilizational development. Toynbee's work also shines light on an overlooked but essential aspect of statecraft— namely, the way that notions of historical process, as well as an understanding of the pattern of historical events, influence one's approach to high policy. This chapter seeks to assert Toynbee's role as a serious and consequential strategist of the mid-twentieth century. Ultimately, it describes Toynbee as the archetype of a grand strategic thinker—that is, someone whose unique contribution was to think on a broader vista, to place international events on a continuum of long-term historical development, to place interstate relations in civilizational context, and to relate immediate foreign policy goals to a higher vision of a peaceful and stable world order.

I

A graduate of Balliol College, Oxford, Toynbee excelled in the classics and graduated near the top of his class in 1911, upon which time he was offered a full-time academic position to stay at the university. The sense in which the ancient world could provide lessons for the empire was something that had appeal in Edwardian Britain. Toynbee was particularly influenced by the prodigious Gilbert Murray, another classicist and best-selling author, who would coincidentally later become his father-in-law. As Toynbee's biographer William McNeill notes of Murray's influence, "To treat the ancients as though they were contemporaries with things to say to twentieth century audiences

---

3. John Bew, "World Order: Many-Headed Monster or Noble Pursuit?," *Texas National Security Review* 1:1 (2017): 14–35.

was both novel and intriguing at the time."[4] Like Murray and many English liberals before him, Toynbee's classical education gave him a strong belief in the powers of constitutional government and he entered adulthood as someone with what might be called classic liberal internationalist views.[5] Personally, he was a critic of colonialism, though he came to see the potential for the multi-ethnic British Empire to adapt and recreate itself as a voluntary association of nations, or Commonwealth.

The First World War marked an important staging post in Toynbee's intellectual and professional career. In 1914, he came to national prominence with his second book, a liberal internationalist text entitled *Nationality & the War*. "This normal life of ours," he wrote in the opening pages, "has suddenly been bewitched by the war, and in the 'revaluing of all our values' the right reading of the riddle of Nationality has become an affair of life and death."[6] In this 500-page work there were a number of practical recommendations for the building of a new European order out of the war, among them: the creation of new independent political units based around nationalities; the protection of minority populations within territories; and the creation of a new international architecture to facilitate relations between states. Underlying these suggestions were deeper reflections which provide some insight into Toynbee's developing view of international relations, his conception of European civilization, as well as the nature and purpose of international institutions. The strongest theme in the work, a familiar one among liberal internationalists at the time, was a bitter critique of nationalism as a scourge of stability in Europe and beyond. In an assessment that he would return to in the following decades, Toynbee wrote that the world had become far more economically interdependent than ever before, a reality which diplomats and militaries guided by nationalist impulses did not seem to grasp.[7] It led him to conclude that the idea of the sovereign nation state was "bankrupt" and that populations needed to move towards basic structures of international authority to reflect this new reality.[8]

A second argument put forward by Toynbee reflected his evolving conception of European politics, culture, and society. Drawing on the work of Leopold

4. William H. McNeill, *Arnold J. Toynbee: A Life* (New York, NY: Oxford University Press, 1989), 26.

5. Arnold Toynbee and Philip Toynbee, *Comparing Notes: A Dialogue Across a Generation* (London: Weidenfeld and Nicolson, 1963), 114, 118.

6. Arnold Toynbee, *Nationality & The War* (London: J.M. Dent, 1915), v.

7. Toynbee, *Nationality & The War*, 6.

8. Toynbee, *Nationality & The War*, 7, 10–11.

von Ranke, Toynbee spoke of the European Continent, despite its collection of diverse nationalities, as composing a "wider organism" or "system," bound by a common civilization. Therefore, he saw the war not as a battle between sovereign entities (nation-states) but rather as an internecine struggle (between nationalities) within one loose civilizational body. This European organism, Toynbee wrote, was "as full of life, as perpetually in transformation, as the individual national molecules of which it is woven." But a central problem for European statesmen since at least the 1814–15 Congress of Vienna was that outdated remedies had been instituted for new problems. "We are always mistaking the dead clothes for the living creature," he argued. For Toynbee, the essence of the problem in European society was psychological: there was insufficient toleration of different national ambitions, even if Toynbee was not particularly sympathetic to them himself. It was a challenge which he thought could be addressed not by developing rigid guarantees or institutions to last in perpetuity, but instead by erecting temporary structures of international authority—in this case guarantees for minorities within national units—which might allow for a "spiritual convalescence" across European society. "As soon as [Europe] has trained herself to national toleration, she will discard the guarantees and walk unaided."[9]

These passages reveal what would become a fundamental precept within Toynbee's wider thinking on international affairs. There was, he held, a purpose to societies and civilizations that went beyond material necessity and interest. And importantly, it was the role of institutions to provide the "transitory scaffolding" which would allow space for societies to "liberate their energy for higher ends." It was a position, Toynbee gladly acknowledged, which ran in stark contrast to his understanding of how Germans had conceived of the national unit. Here the allegiance to state interest (*raison d'état*) as the highest calling would logically lead to endless conflict between national groupings and, in the case of Europe, the "failure" of a shared civilization.[10]

In 1916, Toynbee had his initial experience of government service, first in the propaganda arm of the Foreign Office and then as a researcher and advisor on questions concerning the Armenian question, another fundamental issue for liberal internationalists. By the time of the armistice in 1918, he was one of the historians asked to accompany the British delegation to the forthcoming

9. Toynbee, *Nationality & The War*, 488.
10. Toynbee, *Nationality & The War*, 499–500.

peace conference in Paris.[11] Though he played a marginal role at the meetings, Toynbee was in close proximity to the leaders who met to structure the post-war continent. Taken together, his experiences during the war served as the initial adhesive bringing together his historical and contemporary interests.

Toynbee's conception of the present would come to be molded by his exploration of the past. The basic idea for what would become his magnum opus, *A Study of History*, had been gestating in his mind since his undergraduate days at Balliol. Though the Greek and Roman civilizations had long been central to his academic study, their contemporary relevance had come more into focus. In a lecture at Oxford in May 1920, he described the First World War, which he saw as a self-inflicted disaster that had befallen Western Civilization, as "like a conflagration lighting up the dim past and throwing it into perspective." The direct analogy he drew in this case was the Peloponnesian War between Athens and Sparta which, after beginning in 431 BC, led to roughly 400 years of instability before the Roman Empire was founded. The study of civilizations heralded some common themes that were present in every era—such as the cross-fertilization and cross-contamination of ideas and the role of human endeavor—as civilizations merged and divided over time, shaped above all by interaction with each other. "Each civilization—for instance, the civilization of Mediaeval and Modern Europe and again that of Ancient Greece—is probably a variant of a single theme."[12]

Lurking in the depths of this argument were themes that would become central to Toynbee's conception of history and order. The first was his emphasis on the "spirit of man" which, as his earlier work on nationalism had indicated, he saw as the pulsating force giving rise to larger civilization. The latter structure, in turn, became his second great focus of scholarly study. The civilizational unit of analysis was, for Toynbee, the proper way to comprehend both world history and the operative forces of contemporary international affairs. Nevertheless, within these structures, there was still ample room for human agency to shape the world, albeit as a collective endeavor. The extent to which man was able to impose this "spirit" on historical circumstances was the ultimate test of the vitality of a civilization:

11. See Erik Goldstein, "Historians Outside the Academy: G. W. Prothero and the Experience of the Foreign Office Historical Section, 1917–20," *IHR Historical Research* 63:151 (1990): 195–211.

12. Arnold Toynbee, *The Tragedy of Greece: A Lecture delivered for the Professor of Greek to Candidates for Honours in Literae Humaniores at Oxford in May 1920* (Oxford: Clarendon Press, 1921), 6, 9.

There are two constant factors in social life—the spirit of man and its environment. Social life is the relation between them, and life only rises to the height of civilization when the spirit of man is the dominant partner in the relationship—when instead of being moulded by the environment . . . it moulds the environment to its own purpose, or "expresses" itself by "impressing" itself upon the world.

Civilization, therefore, like literature or theatre, "is a social work of art, expressed in social action, like a ritual or play. I cannot describe it better than by calling it a tragedy."[13]

II

Alongside this growing scholarly body of work, Toynbee became more involved in the debates around the future of British foreign policy in the postwar era. From 1924, he served as editor of the Royal Institute of International Affairs' annual *Survey of International Affairs*, the premium foreign policy journal of the era.[14] This was the setting for some of the major strategic debates on British foreign policy in the next decade and a half. The British Empire's strength, as Toynbee was acutely aware, had declined in relative economic terms compared to other powers in the decades preceding 1914, before taking a further dent by the impact of the war. Other nations had matched, and indeed surpassed, the industrial advantage which Britain had long enjoyed. As such, Britain had "lost her strategic isolation," he wrote, particularly as a result of the technologies of modern warfare that had shrunk the distance of the English Channel.[15]

Despite these changing dynamics, Toynbee still considered his country to be asset rich, based largely on its geographical position, historical fortune, and "informal" model of commercial empire which held out, at least in principle, the prospect of self-governance for its dominions. In the decades ahead, Britain was destined to play an active global role, by necessity as much as by design.

---

13. Toynbee, *Tragedy of Greece*, 5–6.

14. Mark Mazower, *Governing the World: The History of an Idea* (New York, NY: Penguin, 2012), 194.

15. Arnold Toynbee, "America, England, and World Affairs," *Harper's Monthly Magazine*, December 1, 1925, 488. He wrote elsewhere that "Great Britain was . . . gradually being welded, by the irresistible progress of Western scientific invention, on to the most dangerous of the continents." Arnold Toynbee, *The Conduct of British Empire Foreign Relations Since the Peace Settlement* (London: Oxford University Press, 1928), 8.

Its proximity to Europe—which he considered to be the home of a Western Civilization with increasing global reach—combined with its connections to overseas areas, namely the Dominions and United States, meant that "England's role as a link will be magnified."[16] The linkages between Britain and the Dominions within the Commonwealth—entities that shared political and cultural similarities across vast expanses of ocean—Toynbee considered to be a profound creation in the "political life of mankind," one that could serve as a model to future conceptions of world order.[17] Among other achievements, it had shown the benefits of "the overseas principle of partnership," in contrast to the "continental principle of centralization." Toynbee suggested that this oceanic approach "might come to be regarded as the secret of strength in international affairs."[18] He credited British statesmen, who, while not perfect, he believed displayed an "empirical habit of mind" and were thus able to discern and respond to changing realities.[19]

Another potential asset—one which was likely to become more important—resided in the fact that the British Empire already bridged elements of Western and Eastern civilizations. The "contact between civilizations" more generally, Toynbee posited, "was perhaps the greatest of all movements in the contemporary world."[20] And he saw in the British Empire and Commonwealth, albeit with a considerable degree of bias, the only political body in which different civilizations were currently developing in peaceful cooperation. "A Commonwealth in which Westerners and Orientals live in free and equal partnership . . . might be of supreme value to a world in which conflicts on cultural and racial lines are one of the principal dangers of the coming era," he wrote.[21] Much would depend, however, on the intentions of the United States, and specifically on its policy in the Pacific and Indian Oceans. These regions of the world, Toynbee noted, contained a large of number of English-speaking populations who were interacting with other nations—among them Japan, China, and India. Although it might be able to play a mediating role, Britain's power in these regions remained limited. For

16. Toynbee, "America, England, and World Affairs," 488.

17. Toynbee, *The Conduct of British Empire Foreign Relations*, 15–24.

18. Arnold Toynbee, *The World After the Peace Conference* (London: Oxford University Press, 1925), 56.

19. Toynbee, *The Conduct of British Empire Foreign Relations*, 29–30.

20. Toynbee, *The World After the Peace Conference*, 91.

21. Toynbee noted that this was based on the assumption that the British Empire would be able to "establish . . . a commonwealth on an enduring basis." Toynbee, "America, England, and World Affairs," 489.

Toynbee, the United States was the essential representative of the "English-speaking peoples" in these parts of the world, and as such, its actions and behavior would profoundly affect the status of the United Kingdom.[22]

Toynbee had first visited America in 1925 on a lecture tour.[23] Following the First World War, he thought it had risen to "the highest degree of potency among the surviving Great Powers."[24] What was unclear to him was the nature of the role that the United States was prepared to play, in both psychological and material terms, in the future world order. In this respect, he drew a parallel between England after the Napoleonic Wars and the United States after the most recent conflict. Where England, economically and industrially more powerful, had sought to distance itself from the European Continent following the Napoleonic Wars, so too the United States would aim to maintain its distance from the European continent in the current postwar period. In this way, the Atlantic would play the role of the English Channel in the nineteenth century, in that the former body of water would both insulate and isolate the United States from the immediate effects of European politics. Meanwhile, just as the United Kingdom had done a century earlier, the United States would expand its connections and influences across the non-European world. "The psychological inhibition, half rational and half instinctive, which restrained [England] from meddling in Europe, abandoned her completely when she had to deal with other regions; and this is just the psychology which an English visitor observes in Americans today."[25]

Between America's uncertainty about assuming an international leadership role and the growing strain on the post-1918 settlement in Europe, Toynbee became increasingly concerned about the future of the international order as a whole. In December 1930, he took to the airwaves of the BBC for a series of lectures under the label "World Order or Downfall." He opened with a stark message:

> The ship on which we are sailing—to destruction or to the next port—has a Western rig, but it has become the ship of humanity. And the fate of humanity depends on whether we are going to let our Noah's Ark sink or keep it still afloat.[26]

22. Toynbee, "America, England, and World Affairs," 490.

23. William H. McNeill, *Arnold J. Toynbee: A Life* (New York, NY: Oxford University Press, 1989), 128.

24. Toynbee, *The Conduct of British Empire Foreign Relations*, 10.

25. Toynbee, "America, England, and World Affairs," 488.

26. Arnold Toynbee, "World Order or Downfall?" *BBC*, November 10–December 15, 1930, MS. 13967/80, Toynbee Papers, Bodleian Library, University of Oxford.

Within this warning were two themes Toynbee had trialed in his writings throughout the 1920s and which would become central ideas in the first six volumes of his magnum opus, *A Study of History*. Though *A Study of History* sought to trace the birth, growth, breakdown, and disintegration of twenty-plus civilizations across more than two millennia, Toynbee's study, even in its first iterations, also had much to say about the contemporary period.[27] He saw the extension of Western Civilization as one of the defining characteristics of the modern world. There were a number of other "living" civilizations including the Islamic, Hindu, Far Eastern, and Orthodox Christian, but because of the adoption of Western technical and, later, political techniques, the "westernization" of the world was occurring at a rapid clip:[28]

> It is as though this Western spirit were a kind of psychic electricity which had now electrified the whole of Mankind with such effect that there could no longer be any exertion of human psychic force which was not either a positive or a negative charge of this all-pervasive Western current.[29]

Despite its expansion, however, Western Civilization had entered a precarious state: it was undergoing a profound crisis. Toynbee came to see the West as experiencing a "Time of Troubles" and treading the same path as the "dead" civilizations that had come before it. The precedents he held foremost in his mind continued to be from ancient history, and specifically how the start of the Peloponnesian War in 431 BCE. had led to a time of troubles only ended by the founding of the Roman Empire in the first century BC. Just as ancient Greece had "brought itself to ruin by an inveterate idolization of City-State sovereignty," Toynbee warned, so too would modern Western Civilization see its end as a result of an "infatuation with the sovereignty of national states."[30] Indeed, since the breakdown of the "politico-religious unity" maintained by medieval Christendom, Western Civilization had been passing through a period of stagnation caused by the idolization of the nation-state. This period would end, he believed, when political unification was achieved, most likely in the form of a universal state. But importantly, the nature of this universal

27. McNeill notes that the first three volumes, in particular, "served as a grandiose background argument for the advocacy of collective security." McNeill, *Arnold J. Toynbee*, 160.

28. Arnold Toynbee, *A Study of History*, Volume III (London: Oxford University Press, 1934), 133.

29. Toynbee, *A Study of History*, Volume III, 204.

30. Arnold Toynbee, *A Study of History*, Volume IV (London: Oxford University Press, 1939), 319.

state—either in the form of a tyrannical body or a constitutional world order—would determine the continuance of Western Civilization.[31]

Here one gets closer to some of the underlying assumptions of Toynbee's views on British strategy which were to shape his contribution to the British foreign policy debates of the 1930s. As a starting point, he believed that as a civilization expanded outwards, its central bonds began to disintegrate. In the case of Western Civilization, as European powers came into contact with distant populations—either through conquest or the exchange of goods and ideas—expansion had begun to upset the delicate arrangement of political forces at the center. "We Europeans," he noted, "have called a new world into being not to *redress* but to *upset* the balance of the old."[32] Here the balance of power, a concept which he thought inherently destabilizing, served to both intensify competition on the European Continent and also to stifle creative diplomatic efforts aimed at transcending it.[33] The result was a decline in influence of states at the center and a dramatic increase in influence of states on the periphery. Being central to a civilization—as its originator or heartbeat—required an activist role in policing the bounds of that civilization. This notion took on particular significance with the failure of the guarantors of the post-1918 settlement to make their voices heard in defense of the League of Nations. Toynbee wrote:

> If the pygmy states at the centre take no preventive action . . . the creators and sustainers of the common civilization will lose their power of initiative and perhaps their independence, and that the sceptre will pass to the outer "barbarians" who are not yet fit to wield it.[34]

The potential salvation Toynbee saw in existing interstate structures—federations—which could help to overcome the problem of national sovereignty by giving precedent to some shared "higher law." Building on conceptions he had spoken of in the decade prior, Toynbee held up the British Commonwealth and, strikingly, the Soviet Union, as political experiments which might lead to new ideas concerning the association of states. "Will these

---

31. Toynbee, *A Study of History*, Volume IV, 3–4.

32. His emphasis. Toynbee, *A Study of History*, Volume III, 304.

33. Thus, where Ranke had viewed the balance of power as the mechanism which would keep the distinct and unique societies of European civilization together in an ordered whole, Toynbee saw the balance of power as fatally flawed, an arrangement which, despite the efforts of skillful and well-intentioned statesmen, would lead eventually to war.

34. Toynbee, *A Study of History*, Volume III, 305.

and such-like bodies politic, on the outskirts of our modern Western cosmos of sovereign nations, eventually produce some form of political structure that will enable us to give more substance, before it is too late, to our inchoate League of Nations?"[35]

At one level, then, Toynbee had begun to develop a vision of a future world order, based on federation, as an antidote to the growing prospect of international anarchy and the weakness of the League of Nations. More immediately, he had growing concerns about the inadequacy of British foreign policy in the short term and its ability to navigate the current crisis with any success. Strikingly, and in concert with a number of other prominent British historians such as A.J.P. Taylor and Harold Nicolson, Toynbee argued that one of the problems that Britain faced was its lack of strategic culture. In 1938, he gave a lecture on "The Issues in British Foreign Policy" in which he argued that Britons sometimes failed to see the "extraordinary good fortune" that the nation had enjoyed in its historical development. Since the Glorious Revolution of 1688, the country had acquired the largest empire ever seen in human history at "an astonishingly low cost to ourselves." It was also blessed with relative security and had spent much less time than other nations worrying about attack and invasion. In contrast to nearly every European power, only at one point in its history—the First World War—had it been forced to impose universal conscription on its people. A combination of "sea-power and money-power" had allowed Britain to establish "a world-wide *Pax Britannica*"—an international order that was suited to its own interests.[36]

Second, in a plea for historical and strategic self-awareness, Toynbee noted how the British often failed to see how others saw them. The British spoke of their sense of responsibility to higher ideals of common humanity, but many other nations saw them as uniquely self-interested. Both friends and foes tended to label this as "British hypocrisy," by which the British dressed up their motives in humanitarian affectation. Rather than being disingenuous, Toynbee believed that it was more accurate to say that the British deluded themselves. Indeed, this self-regarding delusion was sometimes more of an asset than was often recognized, "because it may help us to do what we want with great moral assurance." The League of Nations was an example of "British hypocrisy" at its most effective. This was by virtue of the fact that it suited British

35. Toynbee, *A Study of History*, Volume IV, 320.

36. Toynbee, "The Issues in British Foreign Policy," *Royal Institute of International Affairs* 17:3 (1938): 307–407, esp. 309–10.

national interests but could also be presented as something that could benefit mankind as a whole. "One feature of this 'British hypocrisy' is the knack of making British interests and ideals harmonise with each other and also with the interests and ideals of a majority of the rest of the world," Toynbee explained.[37]

There came moments, however, in which such delusions could become deeply dangerous to the future of the nation. Toynbee warned that the lack of self-knowledge could be damaging if it prevented Britons from realizing that the modern world around them was increasingly hostile to Britain's vital interests. There were rivals who were determined to challenge the existing order, leading to the prospect of anarchy. More than that, because the international system was structured in British interests, it was "impossible" for the British to somehow abdicate the international stage. Even as the country became comparatively weaker, the British were "prisoners . . . of our own past greatness." Thus, Toynbee captured the essence of the challenge facing a status quo power. It was, in the face of revanchism and with the prospect of anarchy, the need to engage in efforts to maintain some "collective kind of world order."[38]

By 1938, Toynbee described British foreign policy approaching a fork in the road. To engage in the game of preserving or building international order required the summoning of a national collective will to attempt to shape the future. As he put it, this was to "try to look ahead right down the whole length of it and consider whether this is a road that one is able and willing to follow to the end." Without that sense of direction and overarching strategy, the country would be courting disaster. "I think we are going to fall into mortal danger in our present situation if we indulge once more in our British bad habit," Toynbee warned, "of refusing to look more than one step ahead."[39]

III

It was the responsibility to look more than one step ahead—in fact, to think in five-to-ten-year leaps ahead from the cut and thrust of foreign policy—that defined Toynbee's output on the future of British strategy from that point. As early as February 1939, the scholars associated with Chatham House began a program of work to determine the nature and structure of future regional and

37. Toynbee, "The Issues in British Foreign Policy," 308, 318.
38. Toynbee, "The Issues in British Foreign Policy," 331–32.
39. Toynbee, "The Issues in British Foreign Policy," 332.

international order. Toynbee wrote to Gilbert Murray suggesting that "if we get through the present crisis and are given a further chance to put the world in order, we shall feel a need to take a broader and deeper view of our problem than we were inclined to take after the war of 1914–18."[40] Spurred on by Toynbee and others including Lionel Curtis, historians, economists, and political scientists associated with Chatham House moved to set up a body called the World Order Study Group in 1940.[41] Originally intended to deliver publications which would help to inform public opinion, this amalgamation of scholars and the papers they produced became one of the earliest formal groupings dedicated to planning for the postwar world.[42] It also led to more formal association with government departments, under the heading the Foreign Research and Press Service (FRPS).[43] Initially a kind of intelligence body responsible for tracking and distilling foreign newspapers and publications, the FRPS also came to serve as a kind of incubator for larger policy ideas.

In his earlier writings, Toynbee had painted a sharp distinction between leaders responsible for military strategy and those charged with diplomatic planning. His experience at the Paris Peace Conference had led him, in part, to the view that those responsible for winning wars were rarely the best choices for designing peace settlements. "The war-maker's virtues are the peacemaker's vices, and vice versa," Toynbee wrote. Where the statesmen at the Congress of Vienna had erred in elevating the principle of dynastic legitimacy

40. Christopher Brewin, "Arnold Toynbee, Chatham House, and Research in a Global Context," in *Thinkers of the Twenty Years' Crisis*, David Long and Peter Wilson, eds. (Oxford: Clarendon Press, 1995), 277–301, here 277.

41. Memorandum by Lionel Curtis, January 25, 1940, in Papers of Lionel Curtis, Bodleian Archives, University of Oxford; Michael Cox, "Review Essay: E. H. Carr, Chatham House and Nationalism," *International Affairs* 97:1 (2021): 219–28; Lionel Curtis, "World Order," *International Affairs* 18:3 (1939): 301–20. The World Order Preparatory Group was created in July 1939 and soon renamed the World Order Study Group. Lionel Curtis to John Fischer Williams, November 8, 1939, MS, Curtis 111, Papers of Lionel Curtis, Bodleian Archives, University of Oxford.

42. The first round of papers was published in April 1940. They included: Sir John Fischer Williams on "World Order: An Attempt at an Outline"; Gilbert Murray on "Federation and the League"; Sir William Beveridge on "Peace By Federation"; J.A. Spender commenting on the papers of Murray and Beveridge; and P. Horsfall on "Some Doubts as to the Imminence of the Millennium."

43. For background on the establishment of the Foreign Research and Press Service, see Andrea Bosco, *Federal Union and the Origins of the "Churchill Proposal"* (London: Lothian Foundation Press, 1992), 144, 154–58; Robert Keyserlingk, "Arnold Toynbee's Foreign Research and Press Service, 1939–43 and Its Post-War Plans for South-East Europe," *Journal of Contemporary History* 21:4 (1986): 542–46.

over national self-determination, the leaders at Paris had over relied on the latter principle, which by 1919 was antiquated. These historical precedents had shown, in Toynbee's view, that those responsible for political and diplomatic strategy in the aftermath of a war needed to have "the intellectual gift of seeing all round a problem, leaving no element out of account, and estimating all the elements in their relative proportions, and the moral gift of an aptitude for cautious conservatism, ripe deliberation, taking long views, and working for distant ends."[44]

This preference for thinking about the long-term future of both British foreign policy and world order came at a time when there was a distinct lack of such thinking within the government. Adolf Hitler's announcement in July 1940 of a "new order" for Europe and the subsequent propaganda campaign led senior British and Commonwealth leaders to call for a more concerted effort to develop postwar objectives. Jan Smuts, then in his second stint as the Prime Minister of South Africa, wrote to officials in London recommending the creation of "brain trusts" which might aid in this planning endeavor.[45] The government minister put in charge of carrying out this recommendation was Duff Cooper, who had recently been handed a copy of a paper published by the World Order Study Group. Echoing a theme which was to become more common throughout the Second World War, Cooper found that the opinions of academics were helpful, but they must be managed efficiently. Writing to the Foreign Secretary Lord Halifax, Cooper suggested that they find an appropriate medium between vision and practicality. "We do not want to have a lot of professors, out of touch with realities, thinking brilliantly in an academic void, nor do we want purely opportunist propagandists, changing their views from day to day with the course of events." Instead, the goal was to have individuals "capable of taking long views and planning for the future."[46]

Towards the end of August 1940, the British War Cabinet moved to create a committee dedicated to exploring postwar aims.[47] Duff Cooper remained

---

44. Toynbee, *A Study of History*, Volume IV, 298.

45. Copy of telegram from the Minister of External Affairs, Pretoria, to the High Commissioner, London, July 17, 1940, Number 547, FO 371/25207/W8805, Foreign Office Records, The National Archives, Kew, United Kingdom.

46. Duff Cooper to Foreign Secretary Lord Halifax, July 29, 1940, FO 800/325.

47. The Committee was chaired by Clement Attlee and included the Lord President of the Council, the Lord Privy Seal (Attlee), the Secretary of State for Air, the Secretary of State for Foreign Affairs, the Minister of Labour and National Service, and the Minister of Information. War Cabinet conclusions, August 23, 1940, W.M. (40) 233 Conclusions, CAB 65/8, The National Archives.

one of the key organizers, and in his efforts to facilitate an exchange of ideas, he approached Toynbee whose group had built a reputation as "learned men" with ambitious, if sometimes abstract, ideas on a future world order. The result of their meeting was a memorandum outlining the terms of reference for the new committee. Though most of the document contained specific questions of policy—for example, "Should the British Empire take the responsibility for order in Europe?"—it also weighed the benefits and drawbacks of international structures, including federal unions, associations of states like the League of Nations, and an international police force. Perhaps the most important point of reference, however, came at the very beginning. The committee, Toynbee and Duff Cooper acknowledged, would need "to make suggestions in regard to a post-war European and World system with particular regard to the economic needs of the various nations, and to the problem of adjusting the free life of small countries in a durable international order."[48]

As a result of this early consultation, Toynbee was invited into the new War Aims Committee, as one of the only non-ministerial members.[49] Similar to the terms of reference which he had outlined with Duff Cooper, one of Toynbee's earliest productions for the group became a basis for the committee's later work. In a paper entitled "Suggestions for a Statement on War Aims," he wrote, "Our own experience in the British Commonwealth of Nations has taught us that it is possible for nations differing greatly in numbers and wealth, in race and in social structure, to be freely associated as equals in status though differing in function." Added to this was Britain's position as a "bridge" between the European Continent and other parts of the world. Toynbee warned against the construction of continental blocs which he thought ran counter to the principle of freedom of the seas and exchange of commodities between global populations. The paper went on to suggest more specific proposals related to the preservation of peace and the promotion of prosperity. Highlighting the recent agreements between the United States and Canada regarding defense of the Western Hemisphere, Toynbee suggested that these kinds of "common defence boards" might be developed between European countries as well.[50] The paper even recommended that Britain encourage "economic co-operation on a world-wide scale," including bodies

48. Duff Cooper, "Committee on War Aims: Proposed Terms of Reference," Note by the Minister of Information, W.A. (40) 2, October 7, 1940, copy in CAB 21/1581.

49. Clement Attlee to Arnold Toynbee, October 9, 1940, CAB 21/1581.

50. Toynbee was referring to the Ogdensburg Agreement signed between Franklin Roosevelt and Mackenzie King on August 17, 1940.

which might oversee currency fluctuations, development, the administration of colonies, labor standards, and the exchange of raw materials.[51]

A second paper which Toynbee produced for the committee—which grew out of the central theme of his historical work—attempted to outline the "Spiritual Basis of Our War Aims." As broad and abstract a construction as any, Toynbee's memorandum brought forward certain religious principles in a way that his previous memoranda had largely avoided. He made clear that the United Kingdom was "fighting for our way of life" which he said was "derived from the belief that all men are brothers because they are all children of one God who loves them and wants them to love one another." This was directly challenged by what he saw as the principles of Hitlerism which held that individuals were not "the child of God, but the slave of a human body politic."[52] Though seemingly too abstract to be useful, Lord Halifax agreed with the fundamental proposition and reorganized the paper to be shorter and more explicit. Writing to Clement Attlee, then the chair of the committee, Lord Halifax suggested that if they were to "assert our value in the spiritual basis of life," then something like Toynbee's comments would need to be brought in as an introduction to any statement of war aims.[53]

Despite such high-level discussion between senior ministers, the War Aims Committee did not get very far in achieving its original objective. A lack of interest, especially from Churchill, meant that an articulation of postwar plans would have to wait. By the New Year 1941, the brief of the committee was transferred to another, more technical body of ministers and officials. Yet, though Toynbee would not return to such an influential position for the remainder of the war, he and his colleagues in the FRPS continued to be consulted on postwar questions. The ministerial Committee on Reconstruction Problems, which had taken on the original brief of the War Aims Committee, developed a close working relationship with Toynbee and other scholars in the FRPS.[54] A series of papers which Toynbee produced in the spring and

51. Arnold Toynbee, "Suggestions for a Statement on War Aims." This was circulated to the War Aims Committee by the Lord Privy Seal Clement Attlee on December 6, 1940. See CAB 87/90.

52. Arnold Toynbee, "The Spiritual Basis of Our War Aims," undated, CAB 21/1581.

53. Lord Halifax to Clement Attlee, October 23, 1940, CAB 21/1581; see also Lord Halifax, "The Spiritual Basis of Our War Aims." Months later, Halifax would submit a longer memorandum filled with religious references. See Draft Statement on War Aims, circulated by the Secretary of State for Foreign Affairs, W.A. (40) 14, November 13, 1940, CAB 87/90.

54. George Crystal to Arnold Toynbee, February 12, 1941, CAB 117/78.

summer of 1941 marked what would become his most ambitious and detailed work to date. More so than even his work for the initial Cabinet committee, Toynbee's writings in these months are the best representation of the way in which his historical expertise and his view of international affairs translated to specific strategic recommendations.

In the covering note which introduced these papers, Toynbee outlined what he felt to be current British agency within a larger movement of history. Many of these points borrowed from his writings in the decades leading up to the war but this iteration, targeting as it did officials within government, carried both a dose of realism and a clarion call. "Statesmen are only partially free agents," he wrote. "They find their freedom of choice, in working out and carrying out policies, severely restricted by intractable facts which have to be accepted as they stand." These intractable facts, in Toynbee's telling, were the larger forces which operated over a longer period of time and which were usually unobserved by the majority of practitioners. "Forces of this intractable kind are those 'long-term' tendencies towards unification and integration in one direction and, in the reverse direction, towards division and differentiation, which run through the history of a civilisation." For Western Civilization, it was clear to Toynbee that the movement, at least since the end of the Middle Ages, was towards division and differentiation. Importantly, however, he also suggested that a countermovement in the direction of "unification and integration" had grown up in recent decades. And here is where human endeavor and the spirit of man could play a constructive of role. "Time is of the essence," he exulted. For the English-speaking populations, in particular, it was necessary to lay the foundations of a new world order "at high speed, by rather rough-handed methods and with a certain amount of imperfect workmanship."[55]

Across the three memoranda which followed, Toynbee made a case for a future constitutional world order centered on Anglo-American cooperation. Echoing arguments he had made throughout the 1930s, Toynbee wrote that the world's "economic unification" had become a modern reality, and it was soon to be followed by "political unification."[56] But the latter development, he warned, would either be brought about by a "world order through constitution or world order through world tyranny." The English-speaking peoples, as he referred to the United Kingdom, United States, and the Dominion powers,

---

55. Arnold Toynbee, "Prolegomena to Peace Aims," April 5, 1941, CAB 117/79.

56. See for example Arnold Toynbee, "World Sovereignty and World Culture: The Trend of International Affairs Since the War," *Pacific Affairs*, 4:9 (1931): 753–78.

should take the opportunity to establish a constitutional order which, in the years immediately after the war would be supported by Anglo-American moral leadership, industrial power, and air and sea power.[57]

A crucial dimension of Toynbee's conception of a future international order rested on the significance of an oceanic, as opposed to continental, system. Where Germany was attempting to create continental blocs under the control of a dominant power, Toynbee suggested that "an oceanic commonwealth with its main concentration of power in North America and a secondary one in Great Britain" might serve the dual purpose of balancing against Germany while "providing the geographical basis of an ultimately world-wide association of states on a footing of equality." Thus, a world organization, underpinned by a "Pax Americano-Britannica" combining political, economic, and military dimensions, would serve as the new model of international order. Crucially, this system would depend on the extent to which the United States and United Kingdom were able to draw states of continental Europe, Asia, Africa, and Latin America into this new association of nations. In opposition to an oceanic system, a Eurasian continental system would only lead to instability, Toynbee argued.[58] Here the United Kingdom would play an indispensable role as a bridge to the European Continent:

> The way to get a stable peaceful order is, not to try to insulate the overseas world from the mainland of Europe either economically, politically or strategically, but to try to bring the two regions into partnership under the auspices of Powers strong enough to guarantee peace and at the same time wise enough to use force underlying the guarantee with tact, justice and moderation. This is a partnership which Great Britain, as the bridge between Europe and the overseas countries, would be capable of bringing into being.[59]

Toynbee's memoranda in these months represented both the value of grand strategic thinking—the leap from the confines of immediate challenges to paint on a larger canvas—and its limitations, slipping into the theoretical or abstract version of a potential future. Sometimes, as he developed his propositions for a future world order, Toynbee failed to keep pace with the movement

57. Memorandum by Arnold J Toynbee, "British-American World Order," July 25, 1941, FO 371/28902/W9336.

58. Memorandum by Arnold Toynbee, "The Oceanic versus the Continental Road to World Organisation: The Two Roads and their History," June 30, 1941, FO 371/28902/W9336.

59. Memorandum by Arnold Toynbee, "Why Great Britain Cannot Cut Herself off from the Continent," June 30, 1941, FO 371/28902/W9336.

on the physical battlefield. The paper covering the oceanic versus continental road to world order, for example, based its assessments on a German-dominated Europe, even as many of the officials concerned with the postwar world were planning for a victory on the Continent. Thus, although the oceanic versus continental dimension might have been a valuable strategic framework, it was difficult to see how Toynbee's writings could translate into more practical policy. And these points did not go unnoticed.

Foreign Office officials were the most critical of Toynbee's thinking. Gladwyn Jebb, who would go on to lead Britain's postwar planning machine as head of the Economic and Reconstruction Department, grew increasingly frustrated with Toynbee's recommendations, describing them as the work of "sentimentalists and idealists."[60] Other officials within the Foreign Office traded barbed and dismissive comments, writing in the margins of one memoranda: "a typical Toynbee production."[61] Notably, Jebb chose the historian Charles Webster, one of Toynbee's colleagues in the FRPS but a more "realist" diplomatic historian of European Congress diplomacy (a biographer of Lord Castlereagh), as his historical advisor in the months when planning for a postwar international organization become more advanced.[62]

Nevertheless, Toynbee influenced British postwar planning in this critical era, partly by virtue of his ability to maintain some academic distance from the immediate demands of the war. The breadth of his focus—thinking in terms of centuries and continents, for example—combined with concerns for both material and nonmaterial factors shaped the scope of later thinking. In truth, though he did not fully acknowledge it, much of Jebb's later work in drawing the outline for the United Nations Organization drew heavily on Toynbee's earlier productions. The oceanic versus continental framing and the incorporation of civilizational considerations, as well as the idea of an Anglo-American nucleus at the heart of a constitutional world order, were all themes which appeared in Jebb and Webster's memoranda addressing future regional and international order.[63] Indeed, one could go further and say that they were

60. Gladwyn Jebb minute, November 4, 1942, FCO 73/264/Pwp/42/48, as quoted in Sean Greenwood, *Titan at the Foreign Office: Gladwyn Jebb and the Shaping of the Modern World* (Leiden: Martinus Nijhoff Publishers, 2008), 164.

61. Minute by Laurence Collier, September 28, 1940, FO 371/25208/W10484.

62. P.A. Reynolds and E.J. Hughes, *The Historian as Diplomat: Charles Kingsley Webster and the United Nations, 1939–1946* (London: Martin Robertson, 1976).

63. In one of the most important memoranda concerning postwar planning, Jebb wrote that Western Europe was the "cradle and matrix of the civilization which has now spread to almost

fundamental pillars of Western strategy-making for decades after the end of the Second World War.

IV

Arnold Toynbee is an unlikely hero of modern strategy. As we have seen, to some contemporary military strategists and unsentimental diplomats, Toynbee could appear as an idealist or as someone who dealt primarily in such sweeping theoretical brushstrokes that they seemed remote from the challenges of the day. Yet the very act of thinking in this way meant that Toynbee illuminated the strategic horizon in a way that others were not capable of. His historical approach brought into consideration larger economic, political, technical, moral, and even spiritual phenomena. This ability to synthesize, to think in the big picture and long-term, was something that he consciously championed. This contribution to strategic thinking was born from his academic training and career as a public intellectual. During the interwar period, Toynbee had argued against what he considered the atomization of historical thinking. There was, he believed, a degenerative tendency among scholars of history to focus on ever more narrow topics and—worst still—to treat these subjects with the same methods as those used in natural science. Instead, he valued the "deep impulse to envisage and comprehend the whole of life."[64]

While Toynbee was later criticized for his lack of empiricism and granularity, and his brand of civilizational history became unfashionable among scholars, these are words that have a strong resonance today. He was not alone in thinking that the world had become more unified, complex, and in need of structured relations. But more so than other thinkers of his time, Toynbee's wartime work reflects how aspirational visions of world order could give purpose and form to practical strategy. Indeed, without such considerations, he believed, strategic thinking would become static and reactive, a reality at odds with his own appreciation for dynamic and inspired societies. It was a view which subtly but markedly influenced the wider community of academics and

---

every corner of the globe." He also placed great importance on the United Kingdom serving in a leadership role. If they refused to do so, he warned that there was a risk that "our particular type of civilization must inevitably crumble, or merge into something very new and strange." Memorandum by Gladwyn Jebb, "The 'Four-Power' Plan," October 20, 1942, 10–11, copy in FO 371/31525/U783.

64. Toynbee, *A Study of History*, Volume I (London: Oxford University Press, 1934), 8.

officials concentrating their minds on planning for the postwar world—impelled as they were by a sense of civilizational and spiritual purpose.

At the peak of Toynbee's influence, he provided ballast to the idea—which became received wisdom in British and American strategy from the time of the Atlantic Charter—that what was at play in the war was a struggle between a continental, authoritarian vision of a future world order, versus one that was maritime, commercial, and based on fundamental liberal values. This idea crystallized into the idea of an Anglo-American bedrock for the international architecture that would be needed to manage interstate relations after the end of the war. Yet an equally important characteristic of Toynbee's thinking involved his conception of human agency and historical process; or, in other words, how he understood history to be unfolding in real time and how collective or individual endeavor could be used to shape it. This intellectual framework, built on his own historical research and analysis of more than twenty civilizations over thousands of years, fundamentally shaped his anticipation of the future.

Importantly, Toynbee was not deterministic; he believed that societies, and especially "creative" individuals within them, could work to avoid or stave off disintegration and collapse. Yet his view of human and societal agency was shaped by what he saw as discernible, living patterns across vast expanses of space and time. The result was a consideration with which strategists of all responsibilities must grapple—namely the nature of their own influence and their afforded window of opportunity. Toynbee's own approach raises a fundamental if sometimes avoided question facing all strategic thinkers: How, if at all, do theories of history shape strategic planning?

Toynbee would have understood that his own contribution to modern strategy was itself a product of time and place—the challenges facing British strategy makers in the first half of the twentieth century, the pursuit of a new world order out of the Second World War, and the civilizational angst that began with the decline of the British Empire and manifested itself in different forms during the Cold War, under the shadow of the bomb. His way of thinking about the world—on the broadest imaginable geographic and historical scale—fell out of fashion in the last two decades of his life, before his death in 1975. By the time of his 1953 book, *The World and the West*—in which he argued that the aggression of the West was the single most destabilizing factor in the postwar world—seemed out of step with the mainstream of strategic thinking in the Cold War. In the sharpest criticism of his qualities as a historian, the famous scholar of the Middle East, Elie Kedourie, bemoaned the "Chatham

House version" propagated by Toynbee which Kedourie saw as the handmaid to decades of disastrous British foreign policy decisions in the Middle East.[65] The criticisms of Toynbee's work—that it was insufficiently grounded in empiricism and had little immediate relevance to those asked to align ends, ways, and means—were similar to the criticisms made by scholars and practitioners of the idea of "grand strategy." Yet, as the notion of world order is reimagined and contested once more today, there is value in returning to Toynbee. To think as big and as long-term as Toynbee did is to open oneself to the risk of generalization or abstraction. Ultimately, however, Toynbee's approach remains a necessary antidote to the atomization or over rationalization of strategic thought. Toynbee's theory of civilizational development—and the pursuit of a new world order to which he himself devoted considerable energy in the middle of the twentieth century—remind us of the vital importance of nonmaterial factors, such as societal spirit and civilizational purpose, in the shaping of world affairs.

65. Elie Kedourie, *The Chatham House Version and Other Middle Eastern Studies* (New York, NY: Praeger, 1970).

CHAPTER 25

Strategies of Geopolitical Revolution

HITLER AND STALIN

Brendan Simms

Hitler and Stalin's grand strategies were largely, but not exclusively, driven by their respective world views.[1] Though these were in some respects very different, they enjoyed enough similarities to warrant considering them together. Both visions were profoundly affected by the two men's experiences of the First World War and its shattering aftermath, especially, in Stalin's case, intervention and civil war. Both dictators faced related problems and shared the same enemy—objectively and in their own subjective perceptions—for much of their careers. Their resulting strategies, though differing in some very

---

1. Hitler's strategy and world view have been widely discussed by historians. The most recent overview is Brendan Simms, *Hitler: Only the World Was Enough* (London: Penguin 2019). The best overall account of Stalin is the continuing three-volume biography by Stephen Kotkin. See Stephen Kotkin, *Stalin:* Volume I: *Paradoxes of Power, 1878–1928* (New York, NY: Penguin, 2014); and Stephen Kotkin, *Stalin:* Volume II: *Waiting for Hitler, 1928–1941* (New York, NY: Penguin, 2017); as well as Oleg Khlevniuk, *Stalin. New Biography of a Dictator* (New Haven, CT: Yale University Press, 2007). A great deal has been written on Hitler's strategy. The best place to orient oneself in the debates is the chapter in "Nazi Foreign Policy. Hitler's Programme or 'Expansion without Object,'" in Ian Kershaw's *The Nazi Dictatorship: Problems and Perspectives of Interpretation* (London: Bloomsbury, 1985). The idea that Hitler had a worked out a "Blitzkrieg" concept before the invasion of France is laid to rest in Karl-Heinz Frieser, *The Blitzkrieg Legend: The 1940 Campaign in the West* (Annapolis, MD: Naval Institute Press, 2005). The German

important ways, were strikingly similar in others. Of the two, Hitler was the more original and, of course, the less successful.

Despite their aggressive policies, which ultimately led to the deaths of tens of millions, the principal emotion motivating Hitler and Stalin was not confidence but fear. Both men regarded their countries as victims of history. Hitler believed that Germany had taken a wrong turn in the early modern period, failing to build her own empire and thus falling easy prey to other empires. Likewise, Stalin saw Russia as the eternal plaything of outside powers. But if Germany and Russia had suffered from the attentions of various powers in the past, there was no doubt in the mind of either man where the biggest threat now lay. It was the British Empire and, increasingly, the United States which dominated the world, both territorially and, more importantly, through the structures of international capitalism.

I

Neither Hitler nor Stalin developed their strategic visions entirely from first principles. Hitler rarely cited influences, but close readings of his writings reveal borrowings from a variety of sources, including the American racist

war economy and Hitler's role in it is discussed by Adam Tooze in his classic *The Wages of Destruction: The Making and Breaking of the Nazi Economy* (London: Penguin, 2006). See also David Stahel, *Operation Barbarossa and Germany's Defeat in the East* (Cambridge: Cambridge University Press, 2009); Klaus Schmider, *Hitler's Greatest Miscalculation* (Cambridge: Cambridge University Press, 2011); Brendan Simms and Charlie Laderman, *Hitler's American Gamble: Pearl Harbor and the German March to Global War* (London: Basic Books, 2021). Less is available on Stalin, at least in English, but see Alexander Hill, "Stalin and the West," in *Companion to International History*, Gordon Martel, ed. (Hoboken, NJ: Wiley-Blackwell, 2007), 257–68; Sean McMeakin, *Stalin's War* (London: Basic Books, 2021); Milan Hauner, "Stalin's Big-Fleet Program," *Naval War College Review* 57 (2004): 87–120; Jonathan Haslam, *The Soviet Union and the Threat from the East, 1933–1941: Moscow, Tokyo and the Prelude to the Pacific War* (Pittsburgh, PA: Palgrave MacMillan, 1992). For the early Cold War see R.C. Raack, *Stalin's Drive to the West, 1938–1945: The Origins of the Cold War* (Stanford, CA: Stanford University Press, 1995); David Holloway, *Stalin and the Bomb: The Soviet Union and Atomic Energy, 1939–1956* (New Haven, CT: Yale University Press) and Silvio Pons, "Stalin, Togliatti, and the Origins of the Cold War in Europe," *Journal of Cold War Studies* 3:2 (2001): 3–27. Alfred J Rieber's *Stalin as Warlord* (New Haven, CT; London: Yale University Press, 2022) appeared too late to be used in this piece. Finally, there is a lively comparative literature on the two men. See Richard Overy, *The Dictators. Hitler's Germany. Stalin's Russia* (London: W.W. Norton, 2004); Alan Bullock's *Hitler and Stalin: Parallel Lives* (London: Vintage Books, 1991); Ian Kershaw and Moshe Lewin, eds., *Stalinism and Nazism: Dictatorships in Comparison* (Cambridge: Cambridge University Press, 1997); Roger Moorhouse, *The Devil's Alliance: Hitler's Pact with Stalin: 1939–1941* (New York, NY: Basic Books, 2014).

Madison Grant, and perhaps also the geopolitician Karl Haushofer. Stalin, for his part, was explicit about standing in the tradition of Lenin, with whose thought he grappled throughout his career. Above all, though, both Hitler and Stalin drew on their own experiences and on their understandings of their national history. Here the central experience for the two men was the First World War and its immediate aftermath, the crucible within which their strategic vision was shaped.

Hitler, who served in the German imperial army throughout the First World War, took away key lessons from that conflict and the years of turbulence which followed. So did Stalin, who spent that period first as a revolutionary agitator and then as a senior figure in the new Bolshevik government after the October Revolution. In his lengthy inquest, Hitler blamed the defeat on a combination of internal and external factors. Since the Reformation, he argued, German unity had been shattered by a variety of elements, including socialists, Catholics, and Bavarian separatists.

This German weakness, Hitler believed, had rendered the Reich helpless to resist the overwhelming power of Anglo-America, international capitalism, and "world Jewry," forces which were sometimes distinct and sometimes symbiotic in his mind. Germany had been so fissured by religious tension, regional differences, and class conflict that it had failed to match Anglo-American empire-building over the past three hundred years or so. This meant that Germany could not feed its growing population, which was exported as emigrants to the new world, "fertilizing" as Hitler put it, the British Empire and the United States—and even returning to fight the fatherland as American soldiers in the First World War. This crushing sense of demographic weakness was to drive much of Hitler's subsequent strategy.

Stalin, for his part, saw the Soviet Union in the tradition of a historical Russia which had taken regular "beatings" due to her "backwardness." "Those who fall behind," Stalin warned, "get beat up." Russia, Stalin continued, had been "beaten up" and "enslaved" by the "Mongol Khans," the "Turkish beys," the "Polish-Lithuanian pans," the "Anglo-French capitalists," and the "Japanese Lords."[2] He also believed the Soviet Union to be threatened by a combination of domestic and foreign enemies; the two fronts were closely related in his view.

At home, Stalin saw the cohesion of the young state as imperiled by tsarist sympathizers, nationalist separatists, uncooperative farmers, and party dissidents, both real and imagined. The external threats facing the Soviet Union came from many quarters. As a Communist true believer, Stalin lumped them

2. Kotkin, *Stalin*, Volume II, 73–74.

all together as the "capitalist world," with which no lasting coexistence was possible. At different moments in his career, the danger from Germany, Japan, and Poland waxed and waned. But Stalin's most consistent threat enemy, over time, was the same as that faced by Hitler: the British Empire, the United States, and world capitalism. Just as Hitler saw Bolshevism as the instrument of international capitalism, Stalin saw Nazism as its catspaw.

Fear and deprivation, especially hunger, were central to both worldviews. Cut off from food imports by the British blockade, Germany had starved during the First World War and its position remained precarious thereafter. This want was contrasted with the abundance of the Anglo-Saxon world. Hitler portrayed himself as the leader of the global "have-nots" against the satiated "haves." Similarly, Russia had starved during the civil war. Both men, therefore, sought a global redistribution of power and resources on what they regarded as a more "equitable" basis.

Neither man thought that they could simply stand still in a changing and dangerous world. Weimar Germany, Hitler believed, was too small to survive in a world where "space"—for settlement and food production—was at a premium. In fact, he bitterly criticized traditional German nationalists for merely wanting to return to the borders of 1914. These had been far too constraining, Hitler argued, to sustain the Wilhelmine empire, which collapsed four years later under the strain of the First World War. "Only a sufficiently large space on this earth secures a people's freedom of existence and for this reason [Hitler] called for the elimination of the 'discrepancy between our population and the size of our territory.' "[3]

Likewise, Stalin did not believe that the Russian Revolution could survive unless it was followed by revolutions in the heart of the capitalist world. Contrary to widespread belief, he did not hold that "Socialism in One Country" was a viable long-term strategy. In his keynote speech on the subject in December 1925, Stalin specifically stated "the impossibility of the complete, final victory of socialism in one country without the victory of the revolution in other countries." That said, he believed that the Soviet Union would be capable of "building socialism" within Russia on its own, indeed he had no choice but to do so.

If both Hitler and Stalin were primarily driven by fear of hunger, there was already at this stage an important difference in their answers. Unlike some contemporaries, the Fuehrer explicitly rejected "internal colonization" as the answer to the German predicament. From the beginning Hitler found the answer

3. Simms, *Hitler*, 96.

to the lack of "bread" for his people in external expansion and expropriation on the Anglo-American settler model (as he saw it). Because the predominance of the Royal Navy ruled out overseas colonies, Hitler saw the future in the seizure of living space—*Lebensraum*—in the east, which he defined in his manifesto *Mein Kampf* as "Russia and its vassal states." This would provide Germany with critical raw materials and, above all, with the "space" to accommodate its surplus population. This impulse underlay Hitler's entire grand strategy.

The Soviet leader, by contrast, tried to address his (self-inflicted) food security vulnerability through radical action within his own borders. His rural program, which deprived peasants of their land and created vast "collective farms"—the Kolkhoz—was designed to ensure that the population at large, especially the cities, would be fed, thus avoiding the famines of the civil war period. In this respect, Stalin did not hanker after more "space" but rather was determined to make better use, as he saw it, of the territory he already had.

That said, there was a curious symmetry between the spatial strategies of both dictators. If the German leader was obsessed with Russia, the Soviet dictator was fixated on Germany. "The victory of the revolution in Germany," Stalin said, "would have more substantive significance for the proletariat of Europe and America than the victory of the Russian Revolution six years ago."[4] In both cases, the purpose of the strategy was not enmity or friendship with the space per se, but rather in securing it in order to hedge against the might of Anglo-America and international capitalism.

Despite their common enmity against the forces of Anglo-American-led international capitalism, both Hitler and Stalin were hopeful that they could maneuver to exploit divisions within the enemy bloc. Hitler's strategy was partly based on the hope that he could use British fears of American hegemony to secure an arrangement with London. Likewise, Stalin believed that he could play off one imperialist side against the other, or at least wait until the bloc shattered due to its own "internal contradictions."

Conceptually, Hitler and Stalin shared some key strategic rhetoric and frameworks. Both feared the threat of encirclement. Hitler saw Germany as historically vulnerable on all sides. In the 1930s, he spoke repeatedly of the need to escape "British encirclement," by which he meant the ring of powers—such as France, Poland, and Czechoslovakia—which London had supposedly assembled to hem in the Reich at the heart of the Continent. Stalin, for his part, also referred regularly to "capitalist," and especially "British," encirclement. Stalin argued:

4. Kotkin, *Stalin*, Volume 1, 515.

Capitalist encirclement is not simply a geographical conception. It means that around the USSR there are hostile class forces, ready to support our class enemies within the USSR morally, materially, by means of financial blockade, and when the opportunity arises by means of military intervention.[5]

It was London, Stalin believed, which lay behind the ring of hostile powers which menaced the Soviet Union on every side: Poland, Japan, and of course the British Empire itself in Central Asia. To this extent both men saw breaking out of encirclement as a strategic priority.

Hitler and Stalin, the former much more so than the latter, were prepared to engage in maneuver and opportunistic *coups de main*; of this, more presently. That said, both men fundamentally regarded international struggle and military contests as processes of attrition: human, industrial, and moral. The Blitzkrieg strategy often attributed to Hitler is in many ways a subsequent construct; likewise, Stalin. In a famous phrase, spoken during the dark days of the German invasion, when Russia seemed on the verge of being overrun by Hitler, Stalin dubbed the conflict a "war of engines" in which the joint productive power of the Soviet Union, Britain, and, especially, the United States, would eventually overwhelm that of Germany.

So, while both men pursued essentially ideological grand strategies, they were also deeply conscious of their national histories and current economic and military realities, as they understood them. This tension between ideology and realpolitik resulted in a symbiotic policy. With Hitler, we might speak of a "racial-imperial" paradigm which sought territorial expansion for the racial "betterment" of the German people; in Stalin's case some historians see a "Revolutionary-imperial paradigm," which drew on the tsars as much as Lenin.[6] Their grand strategies were ideologically based, to be sure, but historically and geopolitically inflected.

II

The implementation of grand strategy was, or at least was intended to be, by stages. Some have attributed a clear master plan to Hitler, dubbed the *Stufenplan*. In fact, no specific document of that name or content exists either for him or for Stalin. That said, both men did have a broad idea of what they were

5. Kotkin, *Stalin*, Volume 2, 44.

6. Vladislav Zubok and Constantine Pleshakov, *Inside the Kremlin's Cold War: From Stalin to Khrushchev* (Cambridge, MA: Harvard University Press, 1996), 4.

doing, why they were doing it, and the order in which, ideally, they wanted to do it.

First came the strengthening of the home front in order to prepare state and society for the international struggles that lay ahead. This was partly a matter of eliminating potential (or alleged) domestic threats, partly of mobilizing the population for war, and partly of increasing economic development to meet the demands of modern warfare. Hitler, for example, pursued policies of "negative" eugenics designed to weed out supposedly harmful elements such as the Jews, gypsies, and the disabled. This began with discriminatory measures and ultimately ended in mass murder. He also promoted "positive eugenics" intended to bring out the "Nordic" strain in the German people which would be needed to prevail among a world of enemies. Finally, the Fuehrer ramped up investment in German heavy industry in order to support the rearmament programs necessary to implement his expansionist plans.

Stalin adopted a broadly similar approach. Domestic threats, real and imagined, were dealt with ruthlessly. National minorities deemed susceptible to foreign subversion were repressed, deported, and often murdered. "Bourgeois wreckers" were tried on trumped-up charges and often executed. Supposed enemies in the army and party were purged. At the same time, Stalin sought to create a Soviet "new man," who would be sufficiently robust both to resist the blandishments of capitalism and to wage the class war with vigor. All this was accompanied by a program of forced industrialization under the two "Five Year Plans" designed to strengthen the Soviet Union against its capitalist enemies.

Interestingly, Stalin did not react violently to Hitler's rise to power, at least not at first. That rise had taken place at a time when Stalin was distracted by other matters. Domestically, Stalin was preoccupied by the famine caused by his collectivization policies, which cost millions of lives. Internationally, the Soviet dictator was more worried by Japan in the Far East and the Anglo-French threat globally. He showed no interest, at this point, in an anti-Nazi regional pact.

The Soviet dictator was much more concerned, in fact, about the activities of his old party rival, Leon Trotsky, whom he had driven into exile. It was the latter's potential to act as an ideological counterpoint which concerned Stalin. Likewise, Hitler was more exercised during this period about the threat of a Habsburg restoration in his native Austria than is often realized. Neither Trotsky nor Otto von Habsburg had any divisions but they had a brand which was to be reckoned with.

It was only in Spain that Nazi Germany and the Soviet Union clashed militarily in the 1930s, and only via proxies. Hitler sent the "Condor Legion" to support the nationalist forces under General Franco in his civil war against the legitimate Republican government. Stalin sent military aid and advisors to the other side. Both men were motivated by the desire to secure an ideological ally in Spain, or at least to prevent the triumph of a hostile force. This intervention was flanked by support for "Popular Front" movements designed to rally non-Communists behind the struggle against "fascism."

The next stage was to emerge from isolation and break up the enemy "encirclement." Hitler did this by unexpectedly concluding a nonaggression pact with Poland in 1934. Then in 1936, he established what became known as the "Axis" with Mussolini's Italy; in due course this was expanded to include Japan. Stalin concluded agreements with France and Czechoslovakia in 1935, which were likewise intended to subvert the *cordon sanitaire* which had been erected to keep his country hemmed in after the Russian Revolution. Both men, in other words, were conscious of the need for allies, and, if necessary, were amenable to coming to terms with ideologically inimical powers.

Hitler and Stalin had differing views on the strategic value of the non-European world. Both had, or developed, a healthy respect for Imperial Japan, and were aware of the potential of China. When it came to the colonized peoples, though, Hitler was skeptical, even contemptuous. Unlike some Nazis, he saw no serious revolutionary potential among Indian, Arab, or other nationalist groups. He feared that any engagement with them would merely irritate the British to no effect. Stalin, by contrast, followed Lenin. He had seen the oppressed colonial and semi-colonial populations as a "strategic reserve" of the revolution against the capitalist world. Here the alliances Stalin sought were with bourgeois movements and he spent much of his efforts trying to dissuade local Communist forces from launching "premature" insurrections. In China, for example, Stalin initially vested most of his hopes with the Nationalist leader Chiang Kai-shek rather than with the Marxist Mao Zedong.

Hitler's next stage was the ingathering of German territories on the margin of the Reich. First, he harvested low-hanging fruit. In 1935, the Saar was returned to Germany after a plebiscite planned before Hitler's takeover of power. A year later, he forced the pace with the remilitarization of the Rhineland. This greatly increased his room for maneuver because it substantially reduced the amount of pressure France could exert on his western flank. In 1938, he annexed Austria and the largely German-settled areas of Czechoslovakia. Then, in March 1939, Hitler marched into what was left of the Czech lands.

Stalin's strategy was in some ways more modest. The Soviet leader initially sought to secure his borders through influence and, if possible, territorial expansion. In the 1920s and for most of the 1930s, this meant a campaign of subversion, but little overt military action. The exception was the proxy war against fascism which Stalin fought in Spain, but unlike Hitler and Mussolini, who supplied their men and equipment free of charge, Stalin insisted on payment in gold. Still, for neighboring countries such as the Baltic States, Finland, and Poland, Stalin's policies were an existential threat. It was the classic security dilemma. His demand for absolute security meant the absolute insecurity of all others in the vicinity.

The only major military confrontation Stalin engaged in before the outbreak of the Second World War was the standoff with Japan in the Far East in 1938–39. In two sharp encounters—at Lake Khasan near the Korean border and at Nomonhan in Inner Mongolia—the Red Army inflicted stinging defeats on the Japanese. The threat was still not entirely banished, but Stalin had given Tokyo something to think about and strengthened his own hand in the looming conflict in Europe.

Ultimately, though, both Hitler and Stalin aimed at nothing less than the complete transformation of the international system. The Fuehrer imagined a world of four or five superpowers—though he did not use that word himself— of which Germany would be one alongside the British Empire, the French Empire, and perhaps Russia and China (later replaced by Japan). If that was ambitious enough given the restrictions which Germany still labored under in 1933, Stalin's vision was even more grandiose. He wanted to bring about the collapse of the entire capitalist world and its replacement by socialism. This he expected to be achieved partly by exploiting the tensions between the capitalist powers and partly though Soviet strength.

III

The timelines for the implementation of these strategies varied. Hitler's shortened and lengthened depending on the circumstances. At first, he thought of himself as a "drummer," a John the Baptist, heralding the way for some future messiah. Moreover, his entire program was very much a multi-generational one which envisaged a slow process of racial renewal over centuries, similar to the one which had produced the hardy "Anglo-Saxons" who ran the British Empire. In 1923, Hitler had briefly thought he could seize the moment. When his coup failed, Hitler reverted to a longer timeline. Then, in 1933, he grasped the opportunity to take power. Towards the end of the decade, he became increasingly convinced that the window to achieve his aims was closing and that he had to take the initiative before it was too late.

Ideally, domestic transformation and geopolitical engagement would have been sequential, but in reality, they were simultaneous. Britain resisted Hitler's plans more strongly than he had hoped; the United States loomed as an enemy earlier than he expected. By the end of 1936, Hitler had clearly identified the British as a major roadblock; "Britain," he would say three years later, "is the motor of all opposition to us." In the autumn of 1937, Roosevelt came out as an enemy in a speech in which the American president called for the "quarantine" of Germany, along with Japan and Italy. Conflict with the "Anglo-Saxons," it appeared, was not far off, and the Fuehrer attributed it to the machinations of the Jews. In a series of public statements, he warned Roosevelt that he would hold "the Jews" responsible for the outbreak of any new "world war."

By his own logic, Hitler was now compelled not only to move swiftly on the international scene, and to secure living space, but also to speed up his program for domestic transformation. This had profound implications for the Fuehrer's "negative eugenics." What had previously been envisaged as a process of gradual elimination soon became one of mass murder.

In 1938–39, as the clash with Anglo-America loomed, Hitler moved to secure the living space and resources he would need for the contest ahead. Whether he intended to strike east first and then west or to move on directly against Russia is disputed. What is clear is that Hitler hoped to secure Polish participation in the despoliation of the Soviet Union. This proved to be a miscalculation. The Poles resisted his blandishments and were soon strengthened by an Anglo-French guarantee. Hitler believed, or at least hoped, that the Western allies would stand aside, not least because in the infamous Hitler-Stalin Pact of August 1939 he had secured Stalin's agreement to the carve-up of Eastern Europe. This proved to be another miscalculation and European conflict followed. When Hitler invaded Poland at the start of September 1939, the British and French declared war on him two days later.

Initially, Hitler proved a much better military strategist than diplomat. His plan was to crush the Poles and then turn to face the Western powers. Hitler's intention was to capture air bases along the Channel from which he could deliver a shock and awe bombing campaign which would bring Britain to its senses quickly. Poland was overrun in short order, a campaign largely planned by the German generals. In the following spring, Hitler authorized a risky but successful occupation of Denmark and Norway. Shortly after, the

Wehrmacht—using an innovative plan backed by Hitler—crushed France and drove the British off of the Continent. Though he failed to subdue Britain from the air, the Fuehrer subsequently overran most of the Balkans and sent German forces to support his embattled Italian ally in North Africa.

Stalin did not initiate the resulting great territorial realignment in Europe but he did take advantage of it. The Soviet leader refused to "take the chestnuts out of the fire" for the West, as he put it, by opposing Germany and instead cut the deal with Hitler. In September 1939, Stalin took his share of Poland and not long after forced the Baltic states to accept garrisons which rendered them defenseless. In the winter of 1939–40, he attacked Finland. The campaign was an abject failure, at first, but through sheer force of numbers Stalin managed to secure his principal objective, which was to increase the buffer around Leningrad. In the summer of 1940, partly exploiting the opportunity provided by the fall of France and partly trying to balance Hitler's gains, Stalin occupied Bessarabia and the Baltic states.

In order to implement their plans, both dictators required particular kinds of military instruments. The two were devotees of mechanized warfare and quick to recognize the importance of air power. If defeating the near enemy required huge land armies, the ultimate adversary for both men lay overseas. This is why they pursued grandiose projects of naval construction. Stalin's "big fleet" program of the 1930s was designed to overtake the British and US fleets within ten years. In January 1939, Hitler secretly authorized the "Z-Plan," a massive program of construction designed to culminate in the mid-1940s, the moment by which Hitler expected the confrontation with the United States to be unavoidable.

IV

The grand strategies of Hitler and Stalin were ultimately incompatible with each other, of course, but they converged for two important years at the start of the Second World War. In 1939–41, Hitler and Stalin divided Eastern Europe into Nazi and Soviet spheres of influence and, by eliminating Poland, temporarily relieved both dictators of their fear of "encirclement." The arrangement provided Hitler with vital raw materials no longer available on the world market because of the British blockade, and Stalin with at least the prospect of critical military technology.

It was certainly an alliance of convenience, but for some time it was much more than that. Two of the main "have-not" powers were now in a common front against the "Anglo-Saxons." The Nazi Foreign Minister, Joachim von Rib-bentrop, tried to extend this in a pact which stretched from Yokohama to Brest. In 1940, the three Axis powers formed the Tripartite Pact of Germany, Italy, and Japan which was directed against the British Empire and, especially, the United States. Stalin was invited to join them, but the price he demanded—in effect Finland, Bulgaria, and the Turkish Straits—was too high.

Stalin covered his eastern flank by concluding a Japanese-Russian nonag-gression pact in April 1941. This was negotiated by Matsuoka on his return journey to Japan via the Soviet Union. Stalin's explicit hope was to deflect Japanese aggression away from his eastern border and against what he pejora-tively called the "Anglo-Saxons." It is likely that the Soviet dictator also agreed with the Japanese Foreign Minister's contention that the Chinese Nationalist Chiang was the "agent of Anglo-Saxon capital." For the time, though, Stalin kept strong forces in the Far East, just in case.[7]

When Britain refused to yield, Hitler decided to break the deadlock through an attack on Russia. He did so not because he considered Stalin his main enemy, quite the contrary. Hitler still had the "Anglo-Saxon" and "pluto-cratic" powers firmly in his sights. Rather, the elimination of the Soviet Union, in his view, would kill several birds with one stone. First, it would force the British to give up any hopes of Stalin entering the war on their side, and thus make them amenable to a negotiated peace. Secondly, it would deter the United States from intervening by creating an overwhelming German prepon-derance in Europe and denying Roosevelt a potential major ally on the main-land. Thirdly, control of the cornfields of Ukraine and the minerals of the Donbas and Caucasus would allow the Reich to outlast the British blockade. Finally, the seizure of "living space" in the east would put the future of the German people on the sounder footing he had been calling for since the 1920s.

Strangely, the blow would catch Stalin unawares. This was not because, as myth has it, he "trusted" the German dictator. On the contrary, Stalin had been expecting a showdown for some time. His miscalculation was a matter of tim-ing and judgment. He thought that a German attack was some way off, and that in any case, Hitler's usual modus operandi, as per the Austrian, Czech, and Polish playbooks, would give him a chance to prepare. In one of the great intel-ligence failures of the regime, Stalin dismissed all warnings of imminent attack as British provocations designed to embroil him in a conflict with Hitler.

---

7. Simms and Laderman, *Hitler's American Gamble*, 35.

V

In June 1941, Hitler launched Operation Barbarossa, the invasion of the Soviet Union. The great grain robbery had begun; the Soviet population, regarded as useless mouths, would be left to starve in order to feed the German people from the granaries of Ukraine. Behind the lines, SS Einsatzgruppen murdered a million Jews—men, women, and children. In Hitler's eyes, these individuals were pillars of the Soviet regime and thus effectively enemy combatants. The millions of Jews already under Hitler's control in Central and Western Europe were spared for now, because they served as hostages for the good behavior of Roosevelt's United States.

From the start of the invasion until the end of the war, Stalin's main enemy was Hitler. At first, things went disastrously for Stalin as the Wehrmacht penetrated deeper and deeper into the Soviet Union, killing and capturing millions of Red Army soldiers. But in November 1941, due to the weather, supply difficulties, and stiffening Soviet resistance, the German advance slowed. Thanks to intelligence from his master spy Richard Sorge in Tokyo, which suggested that Japan would strike south and east against the Anglo-Americans and not west against him, Stalin was able to withdraw substantial forces from Siberia and send them to fight Hitler. Then, in early December 1941, the Soviet leader authorized a large-scale counterattack which soon forced the Wehrmacht to retreat from Moscow's approaches.

Despite his travails in Russia, the contest with Stalin was not, or at least not usually, Hitler's principal concern. Throughout the summer and autumn of 1941, his strategy remained steadily focused on the war with Britain and the imminent conflict with the United States. When victory in Russia seemed close, in the late summer of 1941, Hitler began to refocus the German war economy away from land warfare and towards naval and aerial war against the Anglo-Americans. Then, in August 1941, Churchill and Roosevelt announced their Atlantic Charter which specifically looked forward to a world after the defeat of Nazism. Though the United States was still formally at peace, it seemed clear to Hitler that its entrance into the war was imminent.

In these circumstances, Hitler adopted a three-pronged strategy. First, he encouraged the Japanese to attack in the Pacific in order to tie the US—and the British Empire—down there. Secondly, he stepped up his campaign against the Jews in order to intensify his "warning" to Roosevelt. Thirdly, Hitler decided to preempt the United States by declaring war at a time of his own choosing. When the Japanese bombed Pearl Harbor on December 7, 1941,

Hitler's declaration followed four days later. The day after that he told a secret meeting of his gauleiters that now that the "world war" was "here," the extermination of the Jews must surely follow.[8]

Hitler's declaration of war on the United States was both the culmination of his strategy and its nadir. He drew up no serious common military plan with his Axis allies. Hitler's intention was to capture enough resources in the next few months to enable him to outlast the Western blockade and to wear them down in a war of attrition. The best he could hope for was survival; victory was beyond his grasp. Hitler admitted as much to the Japanese ambassador in early 1942 when he confessed that he "did not yet know" how to defeat the United States.[9]

VI

If the first half of the war had already been extremely brutal, its second half was waged by both Hitler and Stalin as one of annihilation, though in this instance the ferocity of the former far outstripped that of the latter. The bulk of the Fuehrer's destructive force was felt by the Jews, who were subjected to genocide, and the Slavs, who suffered occupation, exploitation, and mass murder. But Hitler also believed himself to be engaged in a total war with the Western allies. German cities were the target of British area bombing which sometimes killed tens of thousands of civilians in a single night; the rocket program designed to deliver "retribution" was directed against Britain not the Soviet Union. Likewise, Stalin saw himself locked in a life-and-death struggle with Hitler. He warned that if the Germans, who he said had sunk to the level of "wild beasts," wanted a "war of extermination," they would "get it."[10]

Over the next three years, Hitler's military leadership steadily deteriorated while Stalin's gradually improved. During the traumatic winter of 1941–42, Hitler probably saved the Wehrmacht from rout by insisting that the men stand fast. In the summer of 1942, he launched a fresh offensive against Stalin, this time heading for Stalingrad on the Volga and for the oil fields of the Caucasus without which he could not hope to continue the struggle. Both attacks bogged down in the autumn and, in November 1942, a massive Soviet counterattack cut off the German Sixth Army in Stalingrad. Disastrously, Hitler

8. Simms and Laderman, *Hitler's American Gamble*, 361.
9. Simms, *Hitler*, 450.
10. Simms and Laderman, *Hitler's American Gamble*, 60.

once again demanded that the men stay put rather than break out. This time, though, there was no relief. The entire army, or what was left of it, was forced to surrender in February 1943.

Despite the intensity of the fighting on the Eastern Front, Hitler always kept the wider strategic and geopolitical picture, as he saw it, in view. For example, he reacted violently to the Allied landing in North Africa in November 1942, because he knew that Sicily would soon follow and this would provide bases for the Anglo-Americans to attack southern Germany from the air. Hitler therefore mounted a larger airlift there than to Stalingrad, and while many more Germans were killed in the city, a greater number went into captivity when "Tunisgrad" finally fell in May 1943.

If the Eastern Front absorbed most of German manpower, the main effort of Hitler's war economy was increasingly directed against the Anglo-Americans. Production of aircraft, submarines and anti-aircraft artillery, most of which was deployed in the west, far outweighed that of tanks. Moreover, much of the effort in the east was conducted with western priorities in mind.

As the enemy coalition closed in on the Reich, Hitler hoped to fragment it through political maneuver. He planned to make the Anglo-Americans sicken of the fight and to split the enemy coalition. It was for this reason that Hitler ordered the German evacuation of the Balkans in the autumn of 1944; he sought to widen the fissures on the enemy side as they squabbled over the resulting vacuum.

To the end, in fact, Hitler's military dispositions were not driven by classic strategic considerations, but rather by politico-economic ones. "Modern war," he told the head of the Germany Navy, Admiral Dönitz, in February 1945, "was principally an economic war whose needs must be given priority."[11] Hitler laid down as the priorities on the Eastern Front, not the Vistula or East Prussia, where the Soviet military threat was greatest, but rather first the industrial Vienna basin and the Hungarian oil fields (which by then provided the bulk of Germany's requirements), and then the Upper Silesian industrial area and the Bay of Danzig, which was vital for the submarine war.

Despite Hitler's hopes and stratagems, three-power unity between Roosevelt, Churchill, and Stalin was reaffirmed at the Yalta conference in February 1945. The Fuehrer then reluctantly blessed Ribbentrop's overtures to the Western powers. The main addressee of the initiative was Britain. It was in her "own deepest interest" to establish a front in Germany against the Soviet Union on the first

11. Simms, Hitler, 533.

day after the "possible" defeat of the Third Reich, especially as the United States would probably lapse back into "isolationism." London, therefore, would need to abandon "the old British idea of a balance inside Europe," and accept that "every further weakening of Germany through the Anglo-American air force and through the advance of the British and Americans would in the long term be a policy of self-destruction from the British point of view." The Allies showed no interest, and Hitler's plan came to nothing.[12]

Stalin, too, had an eye on the broader political picture throughout the war. He secured Allied commitments on his western border early on. Then, despite two decades of mutual suspicion, Stalin and Churchill agreed to divide southeastern Europe into spheres of influence. In the "percentages agreement" of October 1944, Romania and Bulgaria fell to the Soviet Union. By contrast, Greece was assigned to the Anglo-Americans, while both sides would share influence in Yugoslavia and Hungary equally. As Hitler had expected, the withdrawal of German troops led to mayhem in Yugoslavia—where Tito's partisans battled it out with various rightwing and centrist forces—and Greece, where British troops promptly found themselves embroiled in fighting with the Communist Party of Greece (KKE) in December 1944. Stalin, however, honored his commitments and told the Greek left to make its peace with the new regime.

In April 1945, the unequal struggle began to draw to a close. The Red Army fought its way into Berlin and was approaching Hitler's bunker when the dictator committed suicide. On May 8, Germany surrendered. Stalin had triumphed.

VII

With Hitler out of the way, Stalin was determined to prevent the recreation of the interwar *cordon sanitaire* on his western border. In particular, he refused pointblank to countenance any potentially hostile government in Warsaw. At the Yalta Conference of 1945, the three powers agreed that the Polish eastern border should be moved closer to Warsaw according to the old "Curzon line," which more or less reflected the linguistic boundary between Polish and Ukrainian or White Russia; in return Russia would gain a substantial accession of territory in the north and west at Germany's expense.

Stalin's grand strategy, of course, did not end with Hitler's defeat. He was plunged, or plunged himself, into a new Cold War with the West, which began well before the guns fell silent in Europe. The old struggle was resumed, with

12. Simms, *Hitler*, 534.

Stalin's playbook pretty much unchanged. Once again, he expected to profit from the internal rivalries of the imperialist powers as they fell out over the spoils. Once again, his principal focus was Germany, where he occupied the eastern half and tried to detach the western half from the democratic-capitalist embrace.

Stalin kept his options open. He argued that while the Hitlers came and went, the German people would remain. "Give them twelve to fifteen years," he remarked in April 1945, "and they'll be on their feet again."[13] On the one hand, this made him fearful about the reemergence of Weimar-style revanchism. For this reason, Stalin hoped for a longer-term American presence in, or at least engagement with, Europe. To be on the safe side, however, Stalin concluded a series of alliances designed to contain the threat: a Czecho-Soviet treaty in late 1943; a Franco-Soviet treaty with de Gaulle in December 1944; and treaties with Poland and Yugoslavia in April of the following year.

On the other hand, Stalin was quick to spot the potential accretion of power which control of Germany would bring him. He set up the *National Komitee Freies Deutschland*, made up of captured senior officers, including the commander at Stalingrad, Friedrich Paulus. This initiative was designed to revive traditional Prusso-Russian friendship and harness the power of German nationalism for Soviet ends. Stalin also kept the cadres of the powerful Communist Party of Germany (KPD), or at least those who had survived Hitler and the Moscow purges, in reserve in order to effect the Communist transformation of as much of Germany as required. Finally, Stalin deliberately left open the question of whether the Polish gains in the west would be confirmed or be returned to Germany on terms acceptable to him.

In the summer of 1945, Stalin turned to secure his Asian flank. He attacked Japanese forces in Manchuria, consolidated his hold on Mongolia, and pushed into Korea. He halted at the Thirty-Eighth Parallel, as previously agreed upon with the Americans. Stalin's main interest, though, remained Europe: all he wanted to secure in the Korean Peninsula, he said, was an independence "effective enough to prevent Korea from being turned into a staging ground for future aggression against the USSR, not only from Japan, but from any other power which would attempt to put pressure on the USSR from the east."[14]

13. Hannes Adomeit, "The German factor in Soviet Westpolitik," *Annals of the American Academy* 481 (1985): 17.

14. Kathryn Weathersby, *The Soviet Aims in Korea and the Origins of the Korean War, 1945–1950: New Evidence from Russian Archives*, Cold War International History Project, Woodrow Wilson International Center for Scholars, Working Paper Number 8, November 1993, 7.

Stalin was the great victor in Europe in 1945, securing most of the borders he had long sought. He held on to his gains of 1939–40: the formerly Finnish Karelia, the formerly Romanian Bessarabia, the Baltic states, and of course eastern Poland. As Stalin explained at Yalta, the annexation of Polish territory was driven by his sense of geopolitical insecurity. "Throughout history," he explained, "Poland was always a corridor through which the enemy has come to attack Russia. . . . the Germans have twice come through Poland in order to attack our country."[15]

Between them, Hitler and Stalin left a brutal legacy in Europe. With the exception of the Bulgarian, Danish, and Albanian communities, virtually the entire Jewish population between the Don and the Bay of Biscay had been murdered. The Germans of Pomerania, Silesia, and East Prussia were expelled en masse westwards into the occupation zones, as were the Sudeten Germans. The Polish populations of Pinsk, Lemberg. and Brest-Litovsk were deported westwards, and settled in the regions vacated by Germans. With a few substantial exceptions, the ethnic diversity that had characterized Central and Eastern Europe for hundreds of years was no more.

Indeed, in July 1945, Stalin made clear at the Potsdam Conference between the victorious powers that he had no intention of allowing Central and Eastern Europeans to decide their own destiny. "A freely elected government in every one of these countries," he announced, "would be anti-Soviet and we cannot permit that."[16] For the moment, however, Stalin only interfered directly in the strategically vital areas of Poland and Germany. He allowed elections in Czechoslovakia, Hungary, and Romania to go ahead. One way or the other, the new Europe—and certainly its eastern half—bore Stalin's imprint.

VIII

So did the post-World War II international system. Stalin sought to underpin his enhanced geopolitical position by putting his stamp on the new structure of international governance agreed at the San Francisco Conference in May–June 1945. The new United Nations would consist of a General Assembly and a Security Council made up of representatives from the victorious wartime coalition: Great Britain, France, the United States, the Soviet Union, and China.

15. Jonathan Haslam, "Soviet War Aims," in *The Rise and Fall of the Grand Alliance, 1941–45*, Ann Lane and Howard Temperley, eds. (London: Palgrave MacMillan, 1995), 27.

16. Andreas Hillgruber, *Die Zerstoerung Europas: Beitraege zur Weltkriegsepoche, 1914 bis 1945* (Frankfurt: Propyläen, 1988), 363.

At Stalin's insistence, the permanent members of the Security Council were granted a veto. As the British civil servant and historian Charles Webster, who was intimately involved in drafting the Charter, remarked, this made the UN "an alliance of the Great Powers embedded in a universal organization."[17] Thanks to the Soviet leader, the USSR would be one of them.

By the fall of 1945, however, Stalin faced a new and deadly challenge. The United States had ended the war in the Far East by dropping two atomic bombs on Japanese cities. Despite having been forewarned by both his spy network and President Truman, their destructive force shocked him. "Hiroshima has shaken the whole world," Stalin remarked shortly afterwards. "The balance has been broken."[18] "They are killing the Japanese," Stalin warned, "but they are intimidating us."[19] The key thing, as he repeatedly said, was to keep one's nerve. "Washington and London are hoping we won't be able to develop the bomb ourselves for some time," he remarked. "And meanwhile, using America's monopoly . . . they want to force us to accept their plans on questions affecting Europe and the world. Well, that is not going to happen."[20] Stalin instructed his scientists to build a Soviet bomb without delay.

Relations between Stalin and the West soon deteriorated sharply. His paranoia was stoked by the fact that the British kept hundreds of thousands of German prisoners of war under arms in Schleswig-Holstein and even allowed Doenitz's government to remain in place for more than a month; Stalin was fearful that this force would be deployed against him. Stalin's mood was not improved by being denied a share in the administration of Italy and Belgium, or an occupation zone in Japan. Worse still, his grip on large tracts of Eastern Europe was not yet secure: guerrilla formations such as the Baltic "forest brethren" and Ukrainian nationalists holding out in eastern Poland and the western Soviet Union were a constant headache. Stalin strongly suspected that such groups were receiving support from the capitalist powers.

The Soviet dictator responded to these threats by redoubling his efforts to create buffers along his western and southern periphery. He ruthlessly crushed all independent political expression in Poland—thus violating the letter of the Yalta Agreement—as well as in his zone of occupation in Germany. In Hungary,

17. Mark Mazower, *No Enchanted Palace: The End of Empire and the Ideological Origins of the United Nations* (Princeton, NJ: Princeton University Press, 2009), 7.

18. Caroline Kennedy-Pipe, *Russia and the World, 1917–1991* (London: Bloomsbury, 1998), 84.

19. Jonathan Haslam, "The Cold War as History," *Annual Review of Political Science* 6 (2003): 77–98, 92.

20. Melvyn P. Leffler, "Inside Enemy Archives," *Foreign Affairs* (July–August 1996), 132.

Romania, and Czechoslovakia, on the other hand, the Soviet dictator was inclined, for the moment, to allow some room for democratic politics, so long as those states remained strategically firmly within his orbit. Finland, whose capacity for resistance Stalin knew to his cost, was allowed to choose its own domestic orientation so long as it maintained a strict neutrality in foreign policy, thus serving as a buffer in the northwest.

As the Cold War got underway, Stalin's focus remained on Germany. Right at the end of the war he had signaled his willingness to cut a deal with German nationalism by delaying the handover of Stettin to the Poles as long as possible. He stalled on Western demands for the formal abolition of Prussia. Stalin also authorized the German Communists to take a strong stand against French ambitions. In late April 1946, he merged the old German Communist and Social Democratic Parties in his zone with the intent of using the new "Socialist Unity Party" to extend Soviet influence throughout the Western-occupied areas as well.

Stalin made less headway than he had hoped, however, partly because the behavior of Soviet forces—which was initially characterized by killings, mass rape, and the systematic dismantling of German industry—antagonized the local population, and partly because Communism was itself inherently antipathetic to most of the population, even the working class. The possibility of ending partition appealed to nationalists, but fewer and fewer Germans were attracted to the idea of living in a unified country under Communist hegemony. It was not just that Stalin's right hand in Germany did not know what his left hand was doing; the Soviet dictator himself does not seem to have made up his mind whether he was aiming for a single Soviet-dominated country, a militarily defanged neutral state, or some combination of the two possibilities.

Stalin's moves also provoked a balancing coalition in Europe. The United States embarked on a policy of "containment" designed to keep the Soviets out of areas Stalin did not already control. A program of economic assistance—"Marshall Aid"—was mounted to strengthen European countries domestically against the Communist virus. It also threatened to undermine Soviet control in Eastern Europe, if those countries accepted Western aid. In Germany, the British and Americans merged their occupation zones and introduced a currency reform in a clear sign that they were planning the establishment of a West German state. In the Mediterranean, an embattled Britain passed the baton to the Americans. Far from splintering, the capitalist world was rallying against the revolution.

Faced with a concerted Western attempt to contain him in Europe, Stalin reacted by consolidating his hold on Central and Eastern Europe. His control of eastern Germany and Poland was already complete, and in 1947–48, Stalin strengthened his control over Hungary, Bulgaria, Romania, and Czechoslovakia through the imposition of one-party Communist rule. Stalin also founded the Cominform—a successor organization to the old Comintern—to keep the Eastern European parties in line and to ensure that the activities of international Communism conformed with the interest of Moscow. Stalin did not, however, attempt to promote Communist revolution in France or Italy, on the grounds that this would be premature and give the capitalists a pretext to crush the parties there.

The really crucial arena, as always, was Germany. Stalin regarded the merging of the Western zones of occupation, the currency reform, and the Marshall Plan, rightly, as steps preparatory to the creation of a West German state and ultimately to the reunification of Germany under Allied aegis. Determined to forestall such a mortal threat to his European position, Stalin imposed a blockade—cutting off water, electricity, and all land routes into the city—on the Allied sectors of Berlin in June 1948. This was designed not so much to drive the Allies out of the former German capital, as to force them to desist from moves to draw Germany into their camp.

In the last four years of his life, Stalin stepped up the pressure on the West. In August 1949, the Soviet Union exploded its first atomic bomb, and although its arsenal was to remain markedly inferior of the United States for many years, the specter of being blackmailed by the American nuclear monopoly was banished. At the same time, Stalin—who had until recently had regarded the rest of the world largely as an unwelcome distraction from European matters—sought to harass the United States globally in order to force them to relax their grip in Europe, and especially in Germany. In March 1949, with defeat in the Berlin crisis looming, the Soviet dictator agreed to supply the North Korean leader Kim Il Sung with large quantities of modern armaments. The resulting invasion was part of Stalin's strategy of fighting for European objectives in Asia.

In 1952, the Soviet leader embarked on his last major geopolitical gambit. Tellingly, this was in Germany. In a series of what came to be known as "Stalin Notes," he sought to explore the possibility of German reunification in return for the neutralization of the country. The West German Chancellor, Konrad Adenauer—who was a firm advocate of a Western orientation—did not bite. Germany remained divided and the Soviet western flank remained exposed. Stalin died in 1953 with that fundamental geopolitical question unresolved.

By then, the Soviet dictator had provoked balancing acts not merely in Europe but across the world. In 1949, the Western powers set created the Federal Republic of Germany out of their occupation zones. That same year, they set up the North Atlantic Treaty Organization (NATO), whose function was to deliver collective security against the Soviet threat. This was followed by German rearmament. The project of European unification, though partly driven by fear of a resurgent Germany, was primarily intended to strengthen the Continent against the Soviet Union. Like Hitler, Stalin brought on the unbeatable coalition he so feared.

IX

There were, of course, many differences between Hitler and Stalin's grand strategies. Hitler's was both more restrained and more radical. He never—except perhaps for a brief moment in 1941–42—planned or hoped for world domination. The Fuehrer could not imagine completely obliterating or supplanting Anglo-America, which he admired as much as he feared. The best Hitler hoped for a was a position of equality as one of four or five global powers. Here Stalin was more ambitious, because as a good Communist his ultimate aim was the subversion and absorption of the entire "capitalist" (that is, the rest of the) world.

Yet Hitler's methods were far more radical, both in terms of external aggression and in his murderousness. Unlike Stalin, he was also gambler who self-confessedly stated that it was better to try when there was only a five-percent chance of success, if inaction meant certain death.[21] In fact, the German dictator precipitated the very danger he sought to anticipate. Hitler's strategic legacy is thus clear: it is a warning against hubris and overreach.

By comparison, Stalin's strategy was more successful, but it was far from being a success. To be sure, his more cautious approach paid dividends. If Hitler brought down a global coalition on his own head, Stalin managed to deal with the Germans and Japanese sequentially. But the Soviet dictator did not achieve his ultimate aim of world revolution, or even his narrower one of taking over or neutralizing the whole of Germany. He also provoked the Western balancing coalition which eventually wore down the USSR. In that sense, both men created the threat they hoped to preempt. The difference between them was that while Hitler lived to witness his own failure, Stalin's was deferred until many years after his death.

---

21. Simms, *Hitler*, 269.

CHAPTER 26

Mao Zedong and Strategies of Nested War

S.C.M. Paine[1]

The Chinese Communist Party's rise to power resulted from understanding China's strategic predicament better than its political and military rivals did. Mao Zedong differentiated among all three layers of the nested warfare, which were (1) a multi-generational civil war from 1911 to 1949 that coalesced into a bilateral Nationalist-Communist fight soon after the Northern Expedition nominally unified warlord-torn China in 1928; (2) a regional Sino-Japanese war from 1931 to 1945 that escalated to the third level; (3) a global war from 1941 to 1945 when Japan attacked Western interests across the Pacific in an attempt to eliminate outside aid to the Nationalists. Mao used warfare to assert his leadership and reunify China under Communist Party rule by minimizing cross-cutting strategies between the layers that ruined his adversaries.

Mao focused on founding and transforming the Chinese Communist Party into a shadow government to replace the Nationalist Party government under General Chiang Kai-shek. Mao leveraged the Second Sino-Japanese War to emerge victorious in the overlapping Nationalist-Communist civil war (1927–49) by building base areas or soviets in the ungoverned hinterland behind and beyond Japanese lines while the Japanese annihilated Nationalist armies, and then by awaiting the US annihilation of Japanese armies in the intervening world war, before resuming the civil war under more favorable conditions.

1. The views expressed are those of the author, not necessarily of the US Government, the US Department of Defense, the US Navy Department, or the US Naval War College.

Those who discounted any of the nested wars (civil, regional, or global), conflated operational victory with strategic victory, or who failed to track the primary adversaries of others, sacrificed their strategic objectives.

I

The warfare occurred against the backdrop of collapsing central governmental institutions—a circumstance essential to the success of Mao's strategy to take power within a failed state beset by an intervening power. It was not a strategy to take power within a democracy or a strong authoritarian state. The Chinese state failed slowly and comprehensively.[2] Manchu minority rule under the Qing dynasty (1644–1911) weakened over time. When the Qing belatedly unified the armed forces under Han commanders, the army promptly turned on the dynasty. Three revolutions ensued: the First Revolution (1911–12) overthrew the dynasty with twenty-one provinces declaring independence, but the centralized armed forces based in Beijing maintained nominal control. A Second Revolution (1913) followed with seven southeastern provinces unsuccessfully attempting to secede. Eight southwestern provinces tried again in the Third Revolution (1916), after the ruling general, Yuan Shikai, attempted to crown himself emperor. His sudden death that same year left a country shattered into pieces, each under an officer with a personal army. These were the warlords. Some aspired only to regional control, others to dominate the country through seizure of the capital. The fighting escalated into regional wars concentrated in North China, initially involving tens of thousands and eventually hundreds of thousands of combatants. The wars, named by province or warlord, included the Anhui-Zhili War (1920), the First Zhili-Fengtian War (1922), the Second Zhili-Fengtian War (1925), the Fengtian-Zhejiang War (1925), and the Fengtian-Feng Yuxiang War (1925–26). Both Russia and Japan tried to influence the outcomes by funding different generals.

The fighting weakened the North China warlords to such an extent that it allowed an unusual reunification from the south. Sun Yat-sen, the founding father of the Nationalist Party and of modern China (in both its Nationalist and Communist variants) unsuccessfully tried to establish a South China government in 1917–18, 1921–22, and 1923–25. He failed for a lack of proficient

2. For a more detailed discussion of state collapse in China, see Bruce A. Elleman and S.C.M. Paine, *Modern China: Continuity and Change, 1644 to the Present*, 2nd ed. (Lanham, MD: Rowman & Littlefield, 2019), 259–97, 323–29.

military forces. Russia intervened to change this balance of power by establishing the Whampoa Military Academy in Guangdong to train and arm officers able to command armies capable of reunifying China. The agreed upon price for the Russian aid was inclusion of Chinese Communist Party members in a united front within the Nationalist government and armies. Chiang Kai-shek served as the Whampoa Military Academy's first commandant, while his paired political commissar was Zhou Enlai, who would become the Communists' quasi-foreign minister until his death in 1976. During the First United Front, Mao joined the Nationalist Party in 1923, became the acting head of the Propaganda Department of the Nationalist Party Central Executive Committee in 1925, and the secretary of the Nationalist Party's Central Commission on the Peasant Movement in 1926. He conducted detailed field work that would be published in his seminal *Report on the Peasant Movement in Hunan* (1927).[3]

In the 1920s, the Nationalists and Communists shared a common adversary: the warlords commanding the regional armies and thus preventing national reunification under a central government. The Northern Expedition (1926–28) under Chiang Kai-shek defeated or coopted the warlords of South and Central China. The combat involved over one million belligerents. As his armies swept north, Chiang correctly perceived a Communist attempt to take over the Nationalist government from within by establishing an alternate government in Wuhan. So, his armies paused upon reaching Shanghai in 1927, turning on the Communists and massacring them, and thus ending the First United Front. This transformed the Nationalists into the primary adversary of the Communists. Mao's military career began inauspiciously at this time with his failed Autumn Harvest Uprising to create a base area in his native Hunan in defiance of the Nationalist purge of the Communists. In 1928, Chiang resumed the Northern Expedition to take Beijing, the internationally recognized capital. As the defeated Manchurian warlord, Zhang Zuolin, abandoned the capital and fled, the Japanese murdered him, making Japan and not the Nationalists the primary adversary of the Zhang family. The son and political heir of the dead warlord, Zhang Xueliang, allied with the Nationalists, producing the nominal reunification of China.

The Nationalists followed a strategy of defeating enemies sequentially, first the South China warlords, then the North China warlords, and then the

---

3. Stuart R. Schram, ed., *Mao's Road to Power: Revolutionary Writings 1912–1949*, Volume 2 (Armonk, NY: M.E. Sharpe, 1994), xxx, xxxix, xlvi, xlix, 411, 425, 429.

Communists, leaving the Japanese for last. From 1929 to 1936, Chiang fought off a succession of warlord attempts to reverse the outcome of the Northern Expedition. The most dangerous was the Central Plains War (1930) involving over a million combatants. Increasingly, the Nationalists focused on the Communists, who were building base areas in rural China. From 1930 to 1934, Chiang launched a succession of five encirclement campaigns to eliminate these South and Central China base areas, and especially the main one, known as the Jiangxi Soviet, where Mao Zedong served as the political commissar and Zhu De as the military commissar.[4]

The Communists' expulsion from urban areas in 1927 had forced them to develop bases in the inaccessible hinterland, often in the difficult geography along provincial boundaries. According to Mao, a viable base area required: 1) a party organization; 2) numerous organized workers and peasants; 3) strong Red Army and Red Guard units; and 4) "a strategic terrain which enables a smaller force to defeat a larger one."[5] Small guerrilla detachments played a critical role building the civil and military institutions that ran the base areas. They served both as a disposal force—a force whose loss would not jeopardize Communist survival and so could be risked in dangerous but promising missions—and also as the nucleus of the future army and government in new base areas. In 1940 Mao wrote, "[I]n small guerrilla groups, Party members are toughened, cadres trained, and the Party, government, and mass organizations consolidated."[6] After small guerrilla detachments began building new bases in ungoverned areas, the Red Army began engaging in the higher-level tasks of institution building and base area expansion. These tasks included "organizing the masses, arming the masses, establishing political regimes, destroying the reactionary forces, and promoting the revolutionary upsurge."[7]

The base areas were an adaptation of the Soviet export version of its strategy to win the civil wars characterizing failed states by shifting popular loyalties through a social revolution. The strategy paired military commissars (officers) with political commissars (party loyalists) connected to the secret police, the ultimate enforcers of command and control through the execution of noncompliant officers. Shifting popular loyalties entailed a bait-and-switch land reform strategy, promising land to the peasantry in return for loyalty

4. Schram, *Mao's Road to Power*, Volume 3, lv.
5. Schram, *Mao's Road to Power*, Volume 3, 124.
6. Schram, *Mao's Road to Power*, Volume 7, 375.
7. Schram, *Mao's Road to Power*, Volume 3, 214.

during the civil war. Peasants manned and supplied Communist armies, only to lose the land they fought to own to collectivization upon victory, when these newly independent farmers were treated as a reactionary class.

Along the way to revolution, instant gratification came via widespread land redistribution and the public executions of wealthy entrepreneurs and landowners. The incremental dividend from the propaganda of such deadly deeds then built the Communist base. Mao adapted the strategy to emphasize, not the proletariat that China lacked, but rather the peasantry that it had in abundance. His strategy began with building the Communist Party and training its members to create and control a guerrilla force, and then to field the conventional armies necessary to win the civil war. The Soviets had avoided the guerrilla phase by repurposing tsarist officers and conscripts, the veterans of the First World War.

Mao needed allies and made unprecedented selections in choosing them. In addition to peasants, he recommended cultivating the allegiance of women, minorities, youth, intellectuals, and enemy prisoners. The Communists gained peasant support not only through land reform and education, but also through army discipline aimed at preventing the looting and ill treatment that were tolerated by Nationalist armies.[8] Mao calculated that "women account for half the population" and suffered "special exploitation," proving "not only that women have an urgent need for revolution but also that they are a force that will decide the success or failure of the revolution."[9] He offered women previously unthinkable gains:

> Men and women are absolutely equal under the Soviet Government. Not only do working women have . . . the right to vote and be elected, but they should be recruited to participate in all the work of the government.[10]

To minorities Mao offered the previously un-offerable—self-determination:

> In all areas of Muslim people, independent and autonomous regimes are to be established by the Muslim people themselves to manage all matters of politics, economics, religion, customs, morality, education, and all other affairs. . . . Our policy is unequivocally national self-determination. . . . [F]orce will never be used against them. . . . This is true whether we are dealing with

8. Schram, *Mao's Road to Power*, Volume 3, 216, 283.
9. Schram, *Mao's Road to Power*, Volume 3, 217.
10. Schram, *Mao's Road to Power*, Volume 3, 227.

Muslims, Turks, Tibetans, Lolos, Miaos, Mongols, Lisus, or other tribal minorities of China.[11]

The minorities did not grasp that an offer made during a desperate war did not equate to an enforceable promise after victory when the Communists would be free to turn their guns on minorities tempted to secede.

Mao also cultivated the allegiance of youth and intellectuals, and, most imaginatively of all, the allegiance of enemy officers and soldiers. This was his strategy of disintegrating the enemy army that began by infiltrating Communists into the Nationalist armed forces. "Every *xian* [county] should select a large number of worker and peasant comrades, in a planned and organized way, and send them to the reactionary army to become soldiers, porters, cooks, and so on, and thus play a role within the enemy's forces."[12] Communist propaganda should target enemy soldiers. Cadres should secretly organize within enemy forces; "inconspicuous" cadres and women should agitate and propagandize in rural areas. This would have cumulative effects on enemy morale, leading the enemy army "to wavering and ultimately to collapse."[13] Shifting the allegiance of peasants, women, minorities, youth, intellectuals, and enemy forces together would tip the balance in the civil war to yield a Communist victory.

To swing loyalties, Mao leveraged the powers of persuasion and coercion, words and force. As he proclaimed in 1928, "the Communist Party can overthrow the enemy only by holding propaganda pamphlets in its left hand and rifles and bullets in its right hand."[14] The Communists tailored their message to the audience via acceptable messengers through accessible media—message, messenger, medium.[15] They cultivated allegiance by matching the message to local grievances, using propaganda personnel (political commissars) to identify "local bullies and all reactionary elements" and then to dispatch military personnel—those with the guns—to take care of the problem.[16] Political commissars also organized mass rallies, doubled as medics during

11. Schram, *Mao's Road to Power*, Volume 3, 202, 254.

12. Schram, *Mao's Road to Power*, Volume 3, 76.

13. Schram, *Mao's Road to Power*, Volume 3, 76.

14. Schram, *Mao's Road to Power*, Volume 3, 77.

15. The framework comes from Andrea J. Dew and Marc Genest in our tri-edited book, *From Quills to Tweets: How America Communicates about War and Revolution* (Washington, DC: Georgetown University Press, 2019), 1, 8.

16. Srikanth Kondapalli, "China's Political Commissars and Commanders: Trends & Dynamics," No. 88, Institute of Defence and Strategic Studies, Singapore, October 2005, 45, 29.

battle, propagandized enemy prisoners of war, and assumed responsibility for their own troop morale.[17] They were the eyes of the Communist Party. According to Mao, "The propaganda work of the Red Army is therefore first-priority work for the Red Army."[18] He used numerous media to spread his message: "[b]y word of mouth; by leaflets and bulletins; by newspapers, books, and pamphlets; through plays and films; through schools; through the mass organizations; and through our cadres."[19] Mao also leveraged his experience as a former primary school teacher to get the messages out via educating the illiterate—schools for children and cadres, and winter schools for peasants.[20]

Mao crafted his message based on a deep understanding of the countryside. In 1926, he presciently observed, "The peasant problem is the central problem of the national revolution. If the peasants do not rise up and join and support the national revolution, the national revolution cannot succeed."[21] He understood that "peasants are the foundation of agriculture and the foundation of China."[22]

From 1926 through 1933, Mao became an expert on the rural economy by conducting numerous data-driven surveys revealing who owned what, who tilled where, and who worked for whom.[23] In 1941, he summed up his findings:

> I learned that . . . 6 percent of the population owned 80 percent of the land, and . . . 80 percent of the population owned only 20 percent of the land. Therefore there is only one word for the conclusion I drew: revolution.[24]

From these surveys and the military experience of fighting off the first three Encirclement Campaigns against the Jiangxi Soviets, Mao learned how to calibrate land reform to meet the needs of the Communist Party to produce recruits, revenue, intelligence, and food to fund and defend a base area.

---

https://www.rsis.edu.sg/wpcontent/uploads/rsispubs/WP88.pdf. For the second quotation see, Schram, *Mao's Road to Power*, Volume 3, 294.

17. Schram, *Mao's Road to Power*, Volume 3, 294–95.

18. Schram, *Mao's Road to Power*, Volume 3, 214.

19. Schram, *Mao's Road to Power*, Volume 6, 358.

20. Schram, *Mao's Road to Power*, Volume 3, 221.

21. Schram, *Mao's Road to Power*, Volume 2, 387.

22. Schram, *Mao's Road to Power*, Volume 2, 386.

23. Schram, *Mao's Road to Power*, Volume 1, xviii; Schram, *Mao's Road to Power*, Volume 2, 425, 429–64; Schram, *Mao's Road to Power*, Volume 3, 296–418, 594–655, 658–67; Schram, *Mao's Road to Power*, Volume 4, 413–30, 504–18, 550–67, 584–622, 623–40.

24. Schram, *Mao's Road to Power*, Volume 7, 816.

Mao identified landlords as the lynchpin of the old order:

These four authorities—political, clan, religious, and masculine—are the embodiment of the whole feudal-patriarchal ideological system, and are the four thick ropes binding the Chinese people, particularly the peasants. . . . The political authority of the landlords is the backbone of all the other systems of authority.[25]

Take away land from landlords and the system would collapse, but land reform required extreme coercion, "terror," in his words.[26] "To put it bluntly, it is necessary to bring about a brief reign of terror in every rural area; otherwise we could never suppress the activities of the counterrevolutionaries in the countryside or overthrow the authority of the gentry."[27] Mao intended to shatter landlord authority and power.

Based on his assessment, Mao developed an operational plan: "The significance of bringing about a land revolution is not only to rid the peasant masses . . . of feudal exploitation, but also to incite this 80 percent of the people into actively taking part in national liberation."[28] Mao used class to cultivate loyalties by inverting the social pyramid to rally those at the bottom to crush those at the top: "The tactics for the Land Investigation Movement are to place the workers in the leading position, rely on the poor peasants, unite with the middle peasants, weaken the rich peasants, and wipe out the landlords."[29] He explained: "We must make the land reform penetrate deeply, for only thus will it be possible . . . to draw the hundreds of millions of bitterly poor peasant masses into a solid alliance, and win victory for the Chinese revolution. The Red Army was born from the struggles of the land revolution."[30]

He planned his operations sequentially: "Before the class investigation gets under way, there must be a phase of propaganda, namely, the phase of discussing the notion of class. To launch the investigation without open and widespread discussion of class will arouse panic among the masses."[31] Mao cultivated allegiance by encouraging broad local participation to determine class

25. Schram, *Mao's Road to Power*, Volume 2, 453.
26. Schram, *Mao's Road to Power*, Volume 3, 74.
27. Schram, *Mao's Road to Power*, Volume 4, 435.
28. Schram, *Mao's Road to Power*, Volume 5, 281.
29. Schram, *Mao's Road to Power*, Volume 4, 434.
30. Schram, *Mao's Road to Power*, Volume 3, 559.
31. Schram, *Mao's Road to Power*, Volume 4, 436.

status, "a life-and-death decision for the person in question."[32] To maximize buy-in and, thus, party legitimacy, he chose a highly bureaucratic process, starting with a majority vote at the local level and requiring layers of party approval before the final cathartic announcement of class status at a mass meeting. He made sure to leverage the incremental dividend from land re-distribution by seizing the moment to recruit for the party and the army.[33]

Although Mao intended to collectivize all land eventually, he recognized that the time was not yet ripe because of the intense desire of all peasants to own land. "Collectivization must be a thing of the future. . . . In order to win the support of the peasants for the national cause it is necessary to satisfy their demand for land."[34] Likewise, Mao did not immediately eliminate rich peasants *"because rich peasant production is indispensable for a certain period of time."*[35]

Mao carefully calibrated the violence to maximize both loyalties and pro-duction, and thereby to survive and win the civil war. He also kept careful track of his shifting primary adversary—initially the warlords, then the Nationalists, then the Japanese, then back to the Nationalists. In 1928, when the Nationalists were the primary adversary, Mao exhorted cadres:

> Unite the poor peasants; pay attention to the middle peasants; plunge into the land revolution; strictly impose Red terror; massacre the landlords and the despotic gentry as well as their running dogs without the slightest com-punction; threaten the rich peasants by means of the Red terror so that they will not dare assist the landlord class.[36]

However, when the Nationalists and Communists formed the Second United Front to fight Japan, he suspended land reform until Japan's defeat, lest land reform deflect the Nationalists from fighting Japan, enabling Japan to turn its attention to the Communists.[37]

Both the Communists and Nationalists intended to win the civil war and to restore China to its historic position as the dominant power of Asia—the former by asserting power from the bottom up and the latter from the top down.

32. Schram, *Mao's Road to Power*, Volume 4, 437.

33. Schram, *Mao's Road to Power*, Volume 4, 437, 440.

34. Schram, *Mao's Road to Power*, Volume 5, 272–73.

35. Schram, *Mao's Road to Power*, Volume 7, 298–99. The italics show text cut in later editions of the document.

36. Schram, *Mao's Road to Power*, Volume 3, 74.

37. Schram, *Mao's Road to Power*, Volume 1, xix; Schram, *Mao's Road to Power*, Volume 3, xix.

II

Japan was not agnostic about these developments. It feared the restoration of China as a neighboring great power. Russia was also on the march with a Communist government intent on world revolution. Friends abandoned Japan during the Great Depression. Cascading effects ensued. After the United States raised its tariffs to historic highs with the Hawley-Smoot Tariff of 1930 (an America-first solution to the Great Depression), trade-dependent Japan responded by invading Manchuria and pressuring the Nationalists to recognize the loss by launching a campaign in Shanghai. Japan intended to create a buffer against Soviet expansion while simultaneously cutting China down to size in an effort to preclude full reunification, while also puffing the Japanese Empire up to size to practice self-sufficiency in an age of tariff walls. Japan rapidly stabilized Manchuria, which its investments soon made the most industrialized part of Asia outside the home islands, a stark contrast to the war-riven rest of China.

Japan's policy objective was to protect its national security and prosperity in a hostile international environment; if others would not trade, it needed an empire of sufficient size to practice autarky. Its leaders correctly anticipated that the war to occupy Manchuria would be quick, with the rapid defeat of Chinese conventional forces, but they incorrectly conflated this operational victory with a formal Chinese cession of Manchuria. They failed to envision a militarily defeated adversary exploiting a prevent-defeat, deny-victory strategy through an interminable insurgency that would preclude the economic stability necessary for Japan's prosperity. As long as the insurgency continued, the war was not over. Japan soon discovered that a weak enemy did not necessarily equate to an affordable war. It turned out that there was more to strategic victory than military victory, that strategic objectives such as prosperity and security were not the same as operational battlefield objectives.

Chinese outside Manchuria responded by boycotting Japanese goods, undermining the Japanese economy from an unexpected direction. The Nationalists protested the invasion to a sympathetic League of Nations, Japan soon walked out, and Chinese under Japanese occupation launched an insurgency. Japan then doubled down militarily, as it would do time and again, to expand ever more deeply into China in search of the illusive operational victory that would somehow yield strategic victory. Although the Nationalists had intended to eliminate the Communists before taking on Japan, the vivisection of China conjured such viscerally anti-Japanese nationalism that the prudent military strategy became an untenable political strategy.

For the Nationalists to defeat a great power like Japan entailed domestic reforms to develop the necessary industrial and financial capacity in their overwhelmingly rural country. Conventional warfare required conventional arms and conventional arms required industry. The Nationalists understood the importance of the peasant question earlier than did the Communists, who for many years fixated on the virtually nonexistent urban proletariat. Sun Yat-sen had emphasized the slogan "land to the tiller" and the Nationalists had established organizations to study peasant land tenure and to reform the land tax—the organizations where Mao got his start during the First Nationalist-Communist United Front.[38] Like the Communists, the Nationalists also made a concerted effort to educate.

In the decade from 1927 to 1937, like Japan of the Meiji period and the Qing dynasty in the last decade of its rule, the Nationalist government attempted to westernize its political, financial, legal, and civil service institutions; to invest in heavy industry, infrastructure, technology, and education; to conduct land reform; and to regularize tax collection.[39] The government secured tariff autonomy allowing it to set the tariffs on its trade (promptly raising them on Japan's), but Russia rejected attempts to negotiate the return of Manchurian railways to Chinese sovereignty by fighting and winning the Railway War of 1929.[40] Thereafter regional war with Japan would derail both the reform program and Chiang Kai-shek's sequential military strategy. The invasion of Manchuria cut short the Nationalists' Third Encirclement Campaign to eject the Communists from South China—a goal that Japan might have shared had it not feared a united China under the Nationalists.

The Communist leadership disagreed over the best military strategy to survive the successive Nationalist encirclement campaigns that unleashed hundreds of thousands of troops against them. The leadership followed Soviet

38. Schram, *Mao's Road to Power*, Volume 2, xlvii; 陈梅芳 [Chen Meifang], "试论十年内战时期国民党政府的农村经济政策" ["On the Rural Economic Policy of the Nationalist Government, 1927–1937"], 中国经济史研究 [*Research in Chinese Economic History Quarterly*], 4 (1991): 63–76; 邱松庆 [Qiu Songqing], "简评南京国民 政府初建时期的农业政策" ["Comment on the Agricultural Policy of the Early Nanjing Government"], 中国社会经济史研究 [*Research on Chinese Social and Economic History*], 4 (1999): 72–76.

39. S.C.M. Paine, *The Wars for Asia, 1911–1949* (New York, NY: Cambridge University Press, 2012), 57–69.

40. 张生 [Zhang Sheng], "南京民国政府初期关税改革述评" ["A Discussion of Customs Reform in the Early Nanjing Nationalist Government"], 近代史研究 [*Modern Chinese History Studies*], 74:2 (1993): 208–12.

teachings to prioritize cities and territorial control.[41] Mao prioritized soldiers: the preservation of his and the annihilation of his enemy's. He explained how, "when facing the enemy's large-scale 'encirclement and suppression' campaigns, the general principle is to lure him in deep and retreat to fight in the soviet area because this provides us with the greatest certainty of smashing the enemy's offensive."[42] He emphasized the concept of the "terminal point of retreat."[43] When defending or losing a base area, the Communists needed to identify an optimal terminal point of retreat—for instance, Yan'an, within reach of Russia aid, in the case of the Long March.

Mao matched types of military units to types of territory. Territory was divided into: 1) base areas; 2) enemy-occupied areas; and 3) guerrilla areas, meaning the ungoverned interface in-between. Mao believed that the Red Army should deploy mainly in the comparatively safe base areas and that guerrilla detachments should operate mainly in the surrounding guerrilla areas. Only small guerrilla detachments should attempt to penetrate enemy-held territory.[44]

According to Mao, the Communists should fight only under favorable conditions in order to preserve their forces while eliminating entire enemy units.[45] In his mathematical world, the weak became strong from the cumulative effects of destroying entire enemy units one at a time. "It is better to destroy one enemy regiment completely than to rout many enemy regiments."[46] Only the strong had the resources to endure an attrition strategy.

The Communists had two military services: guerrilla forces and conventional forces. The former served to disrupt occupied areas, denying the enemy stable rear areas, and forcing enemy troops to disperse, which then made them vulnerable to annihilation.[47] This would impose unsustainable costs.[48] Mao wrote:

[Guerrillas'] primary field of activity is in the enemy's rear areas. They themselves have no rear. . . . As to the matter of military responsibilities, those of

41. Schram, *Mao's Road to Power*, Volume 3, 656; Schram, *Mao's Road to Power*, Volume 5, 476: Bruce A. Elleman and S.C.M. Paine, *Modern China*, 356–57.

42. Schram, *Mao's Road to Power*, Volume 5, 505.

43. Schram, *Mao's Road to Power*, Volume 5, 503.

44. Schram, *Mao's Road to Power*, Volume 7, 374, 376.

45. Schram, *Mao's Road to Power*, Volume 5, 489, 495, 501.

46. Schram, *Mao's Road to Power*, Volume 5, 456–57; 536–37.

47. Schram, *Mao's Road to Power*, Volume 6, 178–80, 324–25, 342–43; Schram, *Mao's Road to Power*, Volume 7, 375, 505.

48. Schram, *Mao's Road to Power*, Volume 5, 265–66.

the guerrillas are to exterminate small forces of the enemy; to harass and weaken large forces; to attack enemy lines of communication; to establish bases capable of supporting independent operations in the enemy's rear; to force the enemy to disperse his strength; and to coordinate all these activities with those of the regular armies on distant battle fronts. . . . [Nevertheless] there can be no doubt that our regular forces are of primary importance, because it is they who are alone capable of producing the decision. Guerrilla warfare assists them in producing this favorable decision.[49]

Unlike conventional warfare, "[t]here is in guerrilla warfare no such thing as a decisive battle."[50]

In the first three encirclement campaigns, Mao followed these convictions over the objections of the Communist leadership which finally sent an emissary, Xiang Ying, to fire him personally.[51] Xiang Ying's strategy to defend territory culminated in the Long March upon defeat in the Fifth Encirclement Campaign that ejected the Communists from South and Central China.[52] In reality, it was the Long Rout; the Communists lost over ninety percent of their forces.[53]

Russia, like Japan, was not agnostic about these events. Bordering countries rarely are. The Soviets had made no progress in fomenting communist revolutions in Western Europe, though they had helped establish Communist parties all along their borders. Fascists were on the march: Italy, Germany, Japan, and indeed Nationalist China all potentially fit the bill if fascism is defined as "an authoritarian nationalistic right-wing system of government and social organization."[54] Such governments were antithetical to the authoritarian, nationalistic left-wing system of government and social organization favored by the Communists. Disagreements between fascists and communists centered on ideology, property rights, and the favored social class, not on plans for dictatorship or the brutal means to get there.

49. Mao Tsetung, *On Guerrilla Warfare,* trans. Samuel B. Griffith II (Urbana, IL: University of Illinois Press, 1961), 52, 53, 56. Although Mao took credit for the book, it was probably written by his subordinates.

50. Mao Tse-tung, *On Guerrilla Warfare,* 52–53, 56.

51. Schram, *Mao's Road to Power,* Volume 3, lx; Schram, *Mao's Road to Power,* Volume 4, xxviii, xxxii–xxxiv, xciv; Schram, *Mao's Road to Power,* Volume 5, xxxviii, 488–89.

52. Schram, *Mao's Road to Power,* Volume 5, 505.

53. S.C.M. Paine, *The Wars for Asia,* 116.

54. "Facism," *Oxford Reference* (Oxford: Oxford University Press, 2002), https://www.oxford reference.com/view/10.1093/oi/authority.20110803095811414.

When Germany and Japan initialed the Anti-Comintern Pact in 1936 (the Comintern or Communist International being the Soviet outreach program to spread Communism globally), Joseph Stalin feared a fascist two-front war, with Germans in the west and Japanese in the east. Adolf Hitler's *Mein Kampf* and the Imperial Japanese Army's long-standing Northern Advance war plan bore him out. Territorial expansion at Russian expense was central to both neighbors. Soviet leaders had carefully cultivated both the Communist and Nationalist Parties from the Whampoa Military Academy days onward. Leaders from both parties had been educated in Moscow. Stalin had also funded key warlords along his borders.

Within weeks of the Anti-Comintern Pact, Stalin played all of his China cards to broker a truce in the Chinese civil war by creating a Second Nationalist-Communist United Front, this time to fight Japan, not warlords, on the correct assumption that Japan could not simultaneously take on both China and Russia. With China's urban population demanding action against Japan's creeping encroachments, Chiang Kai-shek abandoned his sequential strategy to finish off the Communists before taking on the Japanese because, however wise militarily, the sequential strategy was no longer feasible politically. The Communists and Nationalists agreed to combine against Japan in return for the Russian conventional military aid necessary to fight Japan and on the false assumption that Russian troops would join the war. Had they considered the war from a Russian perspective, the Chinese might have foreseen that once they were in, Russia was out.[55] They might have realized that Japan was the primary adversary of China, not Russia, whose greatest threats lay in Europe.

At the next dustup between Nationalist and Japanese forces, rather than back down as had been past Nationalist practice, they resisted, and Japan again doubled down, this time massively. Appalled by the Nationalist-Communist collusion that its own strategy of unending expansion had unwittingly precipitated, in 1937, Japanese forces swept down the Chinese coast, along the trainlines, and up the Yangzi River to take all of China accessible by rail or river. But however the Japanese escalated, neither the Communists nor the Nationalists would capitulate.

Japan's error was one of assessment. It fought a regional war with no consideration of the underlying civil war. Its assassination of the Manchurian warlord, Zhang Zuolin, glued his anti-Nationalist son to the Nationalists. Its creeping invasion unified the Chinese, a chronically divided people, by transforming Japan into the primary adversary of each faction, which then combined

55. Paine, *Wars for Asia*, 90–105.

against their common enemy. When the Chinese would not back down and the Japanese doubled down, their brutality supercharged Chinese nationalism. The Japanese also failed to consider likely countermoves of their adversaries: the Nationalists and the Communists, who combined against them; the Russians, who brokered the Second United Front; let alone the Western powers, which soon embargoed Japan. The Japanese assumed the war would be short as they poured armies into coastal and riverine China. Although the fighting ended quickly in Manchuria, it protracted in North China. The Japanese failed to consider nationalism, the theater size, the stakes for the Chinese, the Han will to fight, or even Japan's own increasing overextension. Their way of war depended on rivers and railways, but only Manchuria had a dense railway grid. Before long, the tab for the war was not worth the meal.

The Nationalists executed their long-standing war plan for a slow, orderly retreat intended to inflict unsustainable costs on the Japanese, while holding out in the impregnable Sichuan Basin beyond the railways, upstream from the Yangzi River rapids, and behind the mountains.[56] These conventional battles engaged hundreds of thousands of combatants. An incomplete list includes: Shanghai (1937), Nanjing (1937), Taierzhuang (1938), Wuhan (1938), Suixian-Zaoyang (1939), Changsha (1939), Nanchang (1939), the Nationalist Winter Offensive (1939–40), Zaoyang-Yichang (1940), Hundred Regiments (1940), Southern Henan (1941), Changsha (1941), and Gogō (1941–43).

Of the campaigns, the Communists fought only one—the One Hundred Regiments Campaign—that decimated Mao's conventional forces and triggered Japanese reprisals against civilians that wrecked base areas across North China.[57] Mao never scheduled a rematch, preferring to leave the fighting and dying to others. In January 1940, Zhou Enlai estimated that, of China's one million plus military casualties from 1937 to August 1938, only 31,000 were Communists. By December 1944, the total number of Communists killed in action remained shy of 110,000.[58]

56. Paine, *The Wars for Asia*, 133.

57. 石島紀之 [Ishijima Noriyuki], 中国抗日戦争史 [*A History of China's Anti-Japanese War*] (Tokyo: 青木書店, 1984), 171; 江口圭一 [Eguchi Kei-ichi], "中国戦線の日本軍" ["The Japanese Army on the China Front"] in 十五年戦争史 [*A History of the Fifteen Year War*, Volume 2], 藤原 彰 [Fujiwara Akira] and 今井清一 [Imai Seiichi], eds. (Tokyo: 青木書店, 1989), 60–62; Edward L. Dreyer, *China at War, 1901–1949* (London: Longman, 1995), 253–54; Dagfinn Gatu, *Village China at War: The Impact of Resistance to Japan 1937–1945* (Vancouver, Canada: UBC Press, 2008), 357–60.

58. Jay Taylor, *The Generalissimo: Chiang Kai-shek and the Struggle for Modern China* (Cambridge, MA: Harvard University Press, 2009), 169, 298.

The Nationalists' prevent-defeat-to-deny-victory strategy proved economically ruinous for Japan. It negated Japan's strategy of autarky by making Japan ever more import dependent. It negated Japanese prosperity by imposing huge costs. And it negated Japanese security by creating both massive overextension and adversaries across the globe as the atrocities mounted. Since China was too large to occupy, the Communists availed themselves of the regional war to cultivated peasant loyalties in the huge ungoverned spaces behind and beyond Japanese lines, where they were comparatively free from both Nationalist and Japanese persecution.

Chiang Kai-shek, like Japan's military leaders, focused on the military and not the political, economic, let alone human, aspects of the war. In 1938, as Japanese armies converged on Wuhan, the main inland economic center, Chiang ordered the breach of the Yellow River dikes in multiple places, inundating 70,000 square kilometers of mainly prime farmland, killing nearly 900,000 people and transforming 3.9 million into refugees. The river ran outside the dikes for the next decade, but the mayhem only slightly delayed the fall of Wuhan. Yet this one act killed more Chinese than Japan had killed since 1931.[59] Not only did the Nationalists lack the carefully integrated civil-military strategy of the Communists, but the Nationalists brutalized the very people they needed to man their armies.

III

In 1939, when the regional war (but not its costs) stalemated, Japan turned to an economic strategy to cut off the Nationalists' last supplies from the outside. The 1937 escalation had triggered intensifying Western trade embargoes on strategic goods, weakening Japan from another unexpected direction. Japan's invasion of French Indochina to cut the last Nationalist land route to the outside precipitated the total US oil embargo. This loss suddenly prioritized the immediate capture of the Dutch East Indies oil fields before Japan's year-and-a-half oil stockpile ran out. This led to cascading conquests to capture the oil, secure the sea lines of communication to deliver the oil, and build an impregnable outer perimeter to wall off the new maritime empire from all foes—all in order to cut supplies to China while retaining its own.

The attack on Pearl Harbor was but one out of many roughly simultaneous attacks across the Pacific and Southeast Asia. Japan rapidly achieved its

59. Paine, *Wars for Asia*, 140.

operational objectives in the Pacific Theater of the Second World War. From December 7–8, 1941, through May 1942, it occupied Hong Kong, Guam, Wake Island, Thailand, Malaya, Singapore, the Dutch East Indies, the Philippines, and Burma. No country ever had taken so much territory over such a vast theater in such a short time, inflicting such disproportionate losses. These were the territorial winnings the Japanese government hoped would justify to its people the decade of carnage produced by its strategy of warfare in the pursuit of national welfare. The winnings included the Dutch East Indies oil fields necessary to compensate for the Allied oil embargo and to keep Japan's modern forces mobile, and Burma to shut down the Nationalists' latest last land route, known as the Burma Road, which connected the railhead in Lashio, Burma, to Kunming, China. The Allies soon substituted an air route from Assam, India, to Kunming, by flying over the Himalayas ("the Hump"), but sustained bulk transport goes by land or sea, not by air, so little Lend-Lease aid ever made it into China.

As in the regional war, Japan's problem in the global war remained: the governments of the defeated forces refused to capitulate, so the war protracted and the theater of hostilities expanded. Japan already suffered overextension in the stalemated regional war where it struggled to hold territory. The new strategy delivered great power allies to the Nationalists: the United States, Britain, Australia, and New Zealand, which developed a combined attrition strategy that Japan's resource limitations could not overcome. With World War II, Japan soon had to redeploy troops and planes from China to the Pacific Theater, where it faced even greater impediments to hold territory over extended sea lines of communication, and to defend its far-flung perimeter, let alone to extract enough resources to make this feasible.

The strategy of escalation had made Japan more, not less, reliant on imports—67 percent of its oil in 1935, 74 percent in 1937, and 90 percent in 1939. At the same time, oil consumption in the Southern Theater of the Pacific war exploded in tandem with military operations from 15.4 million barrels in 1942 to 35.1 million barrels 1943. Most of the oil came from the Dutch East Indies, which provided 8.1 million barrels in 1942, 9.8 million barrels in 1943, but only 1.6 million barrels in 1944 due to losses from US submarine attacks. After May 1944, these oil shipping routes were cut. By 1945, even transportation to Korea had become dangerous.[60]

China played a crucial role in keeping nearly 1.8 million Japanese soldiers fully preoccupied with the regional war and far away from US forces homing

60. Paine, *The Wars for Asia*, 169, 219.

in on Japan. Another two million men defended Japan, Korea, and Taiwan, the nucleus of the prewar Japanese Empire. This left about one million men facing the United States in the Pacific Theater. Thus, the theaters where US fighting concentrated had comparatively small numbers of Japanese troops: 100,000 in the Philippines and 186,100 in the Central Pacific.[61] This is why the United States provided Lend-Lease aid to China, stationed bombers there, and treated China as a great power with an invitation to the Cairo Conference. China played an essential role for victory in the global war by pinning the bulk of the Japanese army to the mainland.

The United States, in turn, played an essential role in Japan's defeat in the regional war. It cut Japan off from its empire, starving its armies and people. The Japanese government capitulated from the cumulative effects of the naval blockade cutting it off from the world, the submarine campaign gutting its commerce, the fire- and atomic bombing wrecking its urban areas and modern economy, the impending invasion of the home islands by the Soviet Union (which took Manchuria in a matter of weeks), and the exhaustion from fifteen years of high-tempo warfare ruinous to living standards throughout Asia. Japan had been much better off in 1931 or 1937, or even 1941, than it was in 1945.

Japan and the United States fought the World War II without consideration of the civil war in China. In Japan's last attempt to wrap up the regional war so that it could survive the global war, it blazed a trail through Central China in the Ichigō Campaign (April 1944–February 1945), wiping out Nationalist armies. It was Japan's largest land campaign ever, intended to create landward supply routes impervious to maritime interdiction and to preclude any bombing of Japan from China. But the campaign was irrelevant to the world war, which ultimately was won via the Pacific, not via China. Nevertheless, Japan so weakened the Nationalist armies and so wrecked their morale and morality with fifteen years of merciless fighting that it facilitated a Communist victory in the long civil war.[62] In the 1970s, Mao congratulated the visiting Japanese prime minister, Tanaka Kakuei, for Japan's great contribution to the Chinese Communist victory.[63]

61. 防衛庁防衛研修所戦史部 [Japan Defense Agency, National Defense College and Military History Department], eds., 関東軍 [The Kantō Army, Volume 2] (Tokyo: 朝雲新聞社, 1974), 296.

62. Paine, The Wars for Asia, 200–3.

63. Li Zhisui, The Private Life of Chairman Mao, trans. Tai Hung-chao (New York, NY: Random House, 1994), 567–68.

The United States made a similar oversight that compounded Japan's error. US officers deployed in China wanted theirs to be the decisive theater in the world war. So, they demanded: (1) an unfeasible bombing campaign of Japanese cities from China that depended on fuel, planes, and parts being flown in over the Himalayas; and (2) an irrelevant land campaign in Burma, ostensibly to protect India, that even Britain rejected.[64] The United States forced the Nationalists to deploy their most modern armies and equipment to Burma. As Chiang Kai-shek predicted, Japan took advantage of their absence to target China, which soon occurred in the Ichigō Campaign.[65] Had the United States used its planes in China for close air support of Nationalist troops and left the Nationalists' modern armies in China, Chiang would have been much better positioned to win the ensuing civil war. In the final year of the global war, he might have even scored major military victories against the increasingly beleaguered Japanese forces that would have made him a victor in the eyes of his own people and greatly improved morale. When his equipment held out, his forces stood strong and sometimes defeated Japanese main forces—something the Communists never accomplished. Chiang had defeated Japanese main forces in the first three battles of Changsha—all major battles involving hundreds of thousands of combatants—only to lose the city in the fourth Battle of Changsha during the Ichigō Campaign.

Russia, however, understood all three layers of the warfare. It brokered a truce in the civil war that produced a regional war that fully preoccupied Japan, sending it south deep into China, not north into Siberia to cooperate with its German and Italian allies against Russia. The Russian-brokered Second United Front prevented Russia's defeat in World War II and even delayed the postwar rise of China as a potential competitor by ruining it in warfare.

IV

Mao also understood all three layers of warfare. He deliberately sat out most of the regional and global wars to continue organizing behind and beyond Japanese lines in preparation for the post-regional/global-war, showdown phase of the civil war. Although he developed his theory of a people's war to fight Japan, in reality, it applied much more closely to the long civil war.

---

64. Jonathan Templin Ritter, *Stilwell and Mountbatten in Burma: Allies at War, 1943–1944* (Denton, TX: University of North Texas Press, 2017), 33–34, 42, 56.

65. Paine, *The Wars for Asia*, 196–200.

Mao understood that his revolutionary war occurred in the context of an overarching regional war, which in turn occurred within an overarching struggle between the exploiting imperialist powers and their victims. To defeat Japan, Mao highlighted three prerequisites: "The first is progress by China [i.e., the civil war], which is the basic and primary thing. The second is difficulties for Japan [i.e., the regional war]. The third is international support [i.e., the Big Friend]."[66] He identified four key characteristics of the revolutionary war: (1) China was a large, unevenly developed, semi-colonial country emerging from a great revolution; (2) facing a powerful enemy; (3) with a small Red Army; (4) in the midst of an agrarian revolution.[67] The first and fourth characteristics (the vastness of China and the agrarian revolution) made a Communist victory possible, but the second and third (Japan's strength and China's weakness) would make the war protracted and the outcome unpredictable. Japan's weaknesses opened opportunities. Its inadequate manpower meant guerrillas could roam far and wide. Its intruder status and cruelty to the local population fed Communist recruitments. Its leaders' underestimation of the Chinese created difficulties that resulted in blunder-inducing infighting, which the Communist guerrillas could then exploit.[68] These weaknesses and opportunities also applied to the Nationalists.

On the basis of this assessment, Mao developed a strategy for protracted war. He wrote:

> The first stage is the period of the enemy's strategic offensive and our strategic defense. The second stage will be the period of the enemy's strategic consolidation and our preparation for the counteroffensive. The third stage will be the period of our strategic counteroffensive and the enemy's strategic retreat.[69]

Mao tried to apply this three-phased model of a people's war to the war against Japan, but US, not Communist, conventional forces won that war. The phases actually applied to the long civil war with phase one aligning with the First United Front (1923–27), phase two with the Second Sino-Japanese War, and phase three with the post-World War II resumption of the civil war (1945–49).

According to Mao, a people's war began with the strategic defensive (the prevent-defeat stage) and ended with the strategic offensive (the deliver-victory

66. Schram, *Mao's Road to Power*, Volume 6, 465.
67. Schram, *Mao's Road to Power*, Volume 5, 481–83.
68. Mao Tse-tung, *On Guerrilla Warfare*, 100; Schram, *Mao's Road to Power*, Volume 6, 468.
69. Schram, *Mao's Road to Power*, Volume 6, 341.

stage). The middle period was the stalemate when, after a long struggle, the balance of forces would finally favor the insurgent. The first phase emphasized civil and military institution building through popular mobilization, base area building, and guerrilla warfare. These activities continued through all three phases, with new activities added as capacity developed.

A critical mass of these activities yielded the transition to the second phase with the addition of mobile warfare, conventional warfare, and diplomacy. Communist efforts in the first two phases concentrated on shifting the allegiance of the peasantry to support them. In this phase, "the enemy's objective is to have us concentrate our main forces for a decisive engagement. Our objective is exactly the opposite. We want to choose conditions favorable to us, concentrate superior forces, and fight . . . only when we are sure of victory."[70]

In phase three, the focus of Communist activities shifted from mobilizing peasant friends to eliminating enemy armies, so military strategy shifted from the avoidance of enemy main forces through guerrilla and mobile warfare, to positional warfare to take and hold territory, and to defeat the Nationalist armies in huge battles:

> The third stage will . . . depend mainly upon the strength which China has built up in the preceding stage. . . . But China's strength alone will not be sufficient, and we shall also have to rely on the support of international forces and on the changes that will take place inside the country of the enemy, or otherwise we shall not be able to win; this adds to China's tasks in international propaganda and diplomacy.[71]

Thus, in phase two, diplomacy became essential to line up an industrialized ally that could provide the conventional weapons that China lacked in order to transition to phase three and win the conventional battles characterizing the final stage. Russia played the role of Big Friend the world over. It was for this reason that Mao made Yan'an his terminal point of retreat on the Long March—he was "fighting a way through to the Soviet Union."[72]

In the final phase, the Communists' strategy of "disintegrating" the enemy army reached a new level with soldiers defecting in droves. This outcome depended on a strategy of leniency. Rather than executing enemy prisoners or spies, the Communists propagandized to all a little, recruited the willing, and

70. Schram, *Mao's Road to Power*, Volume 6, 381.

71. Schram, *Mao's Road to Power*, Volume 6, 344.

72. Schram, *Mao's Road to Power*, Volume 5, 78.

returned the unwilling to create an image of Communist human decency in an otherwise pitiless war. The contrast between Communist leniency and Nationalist brutality would become stark, argued Mao.

> [I]n principle it is not permitted to execute any [captured] officers, soldiers, spies, special agents, and traitor elements of the domestic anti-Communist factions ... no matter how ... heinous the crimes they commit. This policy is the best way to isolate and disintegrate the anti-Communist factions, and the entire Party and army from top to bottom should be made to have a widespread and thorough understanding of it. . . . [A]ll reactionary elements and those who are of no use should be treated well and set free, and any soldiers who can join our army and those who can be useful to us should be kept, and it is forbidden to humiliate them (by beating, verbal abuse, writing of confessions, and so on) or to take revenge on them.[73]

Phase three worked as planned. It began immediately upon Japanese capitulation but Russia did not immediately provide much conventional military aid. Russia first focused on securing the territorial settlement in Europe and indemnifying itself for the war by shipping to Siberia hundreds of thousands of Japanese prisoners of war along with the industrial base of Manchuria. While this occurred, Nationalist armies swept through China and deep into Manchuria, crossing the Songhua (Sungari) River in June 1947. They were on the verge of taking Manchuria's central railway junction at Harbin when the United States insisted on a cease-fire under the illusion that a coalition government could be brokered. The United States failed to inquire into primary adversaries. If it had, it would have realized that the Nationalists and Communists were the primary adversaries of each other, so a coalition government was a nonstarter.

Mao lured Chiang deep into Manchuria, a Communist cul-de-sac with a single railway line providing access to the rest of China, making Nationalist troop movements predictable. The Communists denied the Nationalists port access to the theater and flooded the Nationalist-held cities with refugees, blockading them in to starve all and blame the Nationalists for the ensuing humanitarian catastrophe. The Communist destroyed Chiang's best remaining armies in Manchuria in four years of bitter fighting. In 1948, the Communists won the six-month Shandong Campaign that had precluded a Nationalist reinforcement of their beleaguered armies in Manchuria. The Communists soon

---

73. Schram, *Mao's Road to Power*, Volume 5, 525.

won the seven-week-long Liaoning-Shenyang Campaign, involving hundreds of thousands of combatants on both sides, that marked the Nationalist loss of Manchuria.

Two other huge campaigns rapidly ensued in North China, Beiping-Tianjin and Huai-Hai in early 1949, which involved millions of combatants. With these defeats, Nationalist armies defected en masse—disintegrating as Mao anticipated. The Communists mopped up the rest of the country within the year. The Nationalists made no preparations for fallback positions on the Yellow or Yangzi rivers. Instead, Chiang fled to Taiwan in December.

V

Japan and the United States focused on only one layer of the warfare. Japan lost everything in the regional war that metastasized into a global war. The United States won the world war only to lose the peace in Asia for a lack of attention to the civil war. US demands to syphon off scarce conventional assets from China to bomb Japan or to fight in Burma were irrelevant to the global war but consequential for the ensuing civil war. In the regional war, Japan ruined the armies of Nationalist China, the most likely bulwark against communist expansion in Asia. These US and Japanese choices set favorable conditions for a Communist victory in the civil war—the worst possible outcome for Japan and bad news for the United States, whose primary hot wars of the Cold War occurred in Asia, specifically in Korea and Vietnam. A Nationalist victory in the civil war in all likelihood would have precluded the hot wars in Korea and Vietnam.

In contrast, Russia and the Chinese Communists tracked all three layers of warfare and won. The Russians won in Asia at minimal cost by outsourcing the fight against Japan to the Chinese. Although the Chinese Communists skipped most of the regional and global wars, the Chinese people could not skip the regional or civil wars. Their homes became the battleground. They manned China's conventional armies and paid the price for the Communist victory.

The overly operational focus of the Japanese and the Nationalists did not further their causes. Japan's killing spree fed the Chinese determination to resist. Chiang Kai-shek, like the leadership of Japan, the country where he received his formal military education, also took an operational view of victory, equating battlefield victory with strategic victory. He too planned to kill his way to power—the body-count strategy that would get General William

Westmoreland into trouble in the Vietnam War. Chiang incorrectly believed that once his operational victories orchestrated from the top won the war, state-building of civilian institutions could resume. But the peasantry was unwilling to man his armies for endless promissory notes.

Mao Zedong, the political commissar, understood that Communist victory required a much broader set of instruments of national power than the military instrument alone. Mao rejected the Nationalists' sequential, top-down approach and instead engaged in simultaneous reforms and warfare, orchestrated from the bottom up. As he proved, there is more to allegiance than victory in battle. His grand strategy integrated such diverse elements of national power as the peasantry (both men and women), propaganda, land reform, base areas, institution building, warfare, and diplomacy. As Mao described it:

> All our experiences in the past have proved: only after the land question is correctly resolved, and the flame of class struggle in the countryside rises to its highest point under resolute class slogans, can we mobilize the broad masses of the peasants under the leadership of the proletariat to participate in the revolutionary war and in all aspects of building the soviets; build a solid revolutionary base; increase the power of the soviet movement; and achieve greater development and greater victories.[74]

While the Nationalists were dragooning peasants into their armies to fight the Japanese, the Communists were educating and redistributing land to the peasants beyond Japanese lines. Over the course of the Second Sino-Japanese War, for peasants the choice of whether to align with Nationalists or Communists became a no-brainer. Although Mao required peasant allegiance to win the wars, victory allowed him to turn his armies on the peasantry in order to collectivize agriculture. Peasants lost the land they had fought to gain. Landowning peasants had not understood that they were actually class enemies of the Communists.

It is important to correctly identify the sequence of primary adversaries as one is defeated and another emerges or as priorities shift. As the Japanese discovered postwar, neighboring Communism, not nationalism, posed their greatest security threat. Had they combined with the Nationalists to minimize Communism, Japan would be much more secure today, let alone back in the day when Japan's descent into military and economic overextension cost so many lives and destroyed Imperial Japan. Likewise, the United States incorrectly rank

---

74. Schram, *Mao's Road to Power*, Volume 4, 413.

ordered Communist and Nationalist enemies, just as the Communists and Nationalists incorrectly rank ordered Russian enemies, and as the Nationalists incorrectly rank ordered US enemies. The mistakes were costly. The United States, rather than trying to broker an unfeasible Chinese coalition government between two primary adversaries, needed to think of ways to position the Nationalists to win at least part of China. Both the Communists and the Nationalists, rather than expecting direct Russian military intervention in the war against Japan, should have understood that Russia's deployments would focus on its primary adversaries, which as always were in the west not the east. Likewise, the Nationalists, rather than expecting direct US military intervention in the post-World War II resumption of the civil war, should have understood that US reconstruction efforts and troop deployments would focus on Europe in order to contain Russia, not risk overextension in the morass of China. Mao correctly identified his primary adversary: the Nationalists not the Japanese. So, he leveraged the Japanese to inflict maximum damage on the Nationalists.

Mao did not simply win the civil war; he also positioned himself to become the leader of the international Communist movement after Joseph Stalin's death in 1953. Mao entered the Pantheon of great Marxist thinkers with his Sinification of Marxism that made it more relevant to the predominantly rural, newly independent countries after World War II. As he made clear, "So-called wholesale Westernization is wrong. China has suffered a great deal in the past from the formalist absorption of foreign things. . . . [T]he universal truth of Marxism must have a national form if it is to be useful, and in no circumstances can it be applied subjectively as a mere formula."[75] He also made clear, "We are certainly not fighting for an emancipated China in order to turn the country over to Moscow!"[76] Mao's strategy yielded military victory, and the Communist monopoly of power, but not prosperity.

75. Schram, *Mao's Road to Power*, Volume 7, 368.
76. Schram, *Mao's Road to Power*, Volume 5, 285.

PART IV

Strategy in a Bipolar Era

CHAPTER 27

Nuclear Strategy in Theory and Practice

THE GREAT DIVERGENCE

Eric S. Edelman

Thus, the first and most vital step in any American security program for the age of atomic bombs is to take measures to guarantee to ourselves in case of attack the possibility of retaliation in kind. . . . Thus far the chief purpose of our military establishment has been to win wars. From now on its chief purpose must be to avert them. It can have almost no other useful purpose.

—BERNARD BRODIE[1]

Deterrence seeks to prevent a given course by making it seem less attractive than all possible alternatives. It therefore ultimately depends on an intangible quality: the state of mind of the potential aggressor. From the point of view of deterrence a seeming weakness will have the same consequences as an actual one. A gesture intended as a bluff but taken seriously is more useful as a deterrent than a bona fide threat interpreted as a bluff.

—HENRY A. KISSINGER[2]

1. Bernard Brodie, ed. *The Absolute Weapon: Atomic Power and World Order* (New York, NY: Harcourt, Brace and Company, 1946), 76.
2. Henry A. Kissinger, *The Necessity of Choice* (New York, NY: Harper Brothers, 1961), 12.

The first edition of *Makers of Modern Strategy* was published when there were no nuclear weapons. The second edition appeared at the very height of the strategic antagonism between the nuclear-armed superpowers. A few years later, the Soviet Union collapsed, the Cold War ended, and scholars were heralding the "essential irrelevance" of nuclear weapons.[3]

Writing about, studying, and teaching nuclear strategy rapidly went out of fashion. In the US, thinking about nuclear weapons largely fell into desuetude (save for those specifically charged with that task at US Strategic Command). By 2008, a study by the Defense Science Board concluded that, due to a lack of focus and attention, the US was losing its nuclear deterrence skills. Although quite a bit of good historical scholarship has emerged about Cold War nuclear history (and the theorizing that emerged as a result), the slender attention devoted to questions of nuclear strategy during the post-Cold War era seemed to freeze in amber the concerns for "strategic stability" and arms control that marked the very end of the Cold War.[4]

It is true, as Frank Gavin argues, that there is great uncertainty about the degree to which "nuclear strategists" actually were responsible for much of what emerged as nuclear strategy. Moreover, as time went by, the actual practice of nuclear strategy by senior government officials stubbornly and persistently diverged from what strategists saw as the "illogic" of US nuclear posture—both the declaratory policies and the force structure that underpinned them. There does not appear to be a through line connecting the emergence of the nuclear forces of any of the nuclear-weapons states and the writings of nuclear strategists. Rather, much of what emerged was driven by the standard operating procedures of the uniformed military services, by bureaucratic and budgetary politics, and by the efforts of policymakers to anticipate and assuage public opinion. Moreover, because nuclear weapons were only used twice—both in

3. Lawrence Freedman, "The First Two Generations of Nuclear Strategists," in *Makers of Modern Strategy: From Machiavelli to the Nuclear Age*, Peter Paret, ed. (Princeton, NJ: Princeton University Press, 1986), 735–79; Lawrence Freedman and Jeffrey Michaels, *The Evolution of Nuclear Strategy*, Fourth Edition (New York, NY: Palgrave MacMillan, 2019); John Mueller, "The Essential Irrelevance of Nuclear Weapons: Stability in the Post War World," *International Security* 13:2 (1988): 55–79.

4. See James Schesinger's letter of transmittal covering Report of the Secretary of Defense Task Force on DoD Nuclear Weapons Management, Phase II, *Review of the DoD Nuclear Mission*, December 2008, located at https://apps.dtic.mil/sti/pdfs/ADA492647.pdf; and *Report of the Defense Science Board Task Force on Nuclear Deterrence Skills*, September 2008, located at https://dod.defense.gov/Portals/1/features/defenseReviews/NPR/DSB_Nuclear_Deterrence_Skills_Chiles.pdf.

1945—writing about nuclear strategy took place in the absence of direct evidence and hence was inherently speculative.[5]

Nevertheless, the first generation of nuclear strategists created a vocabulary and a grammar for thinking about and justifying nuclear weapons programs to a broader public. Even if the direct influence of nuclear strategists is hard to trace—with the exception of a few years in the early 1960s—their indirect influence was enduring, and it is worth excavating the now-lost language of nuclear deterrence that they created in order to grapple with the reemerging challenges of nuclear competition in a new era of great-power rivalry. Today, emerging disruptive technologies including but not limited to artificial intelligence, quantum computing, hypersonic missiles, as well as more multipolar, long-term strategic competition among the US, a rising China, and a revanchist Russia undoubtedly will complicate rigorous strategic thinking, but it would be foolish not to consider the "massive intellectual achievement" of the Cold War era strategists.[6]

I

At the height of the Cold War, the late Robert Jervis wrote, "Very little new has been said since 1946. In that year Bernard Brodie published his essays as *The Absolute Weapon* and William Borden published *There Will Be No Time* . . . Forty years of thought have not taken us very far." Brodie's important insight, written in late 1945, and cited as the epigraph to this chapter, is oft and appropriately cited as the starting point for discussions about nuclear strategy. Ken Booth has suggested that, "It is hardly an exaggeration to say that other nuclear strategists, in the years following, have simply written footnotes—long and short, spare and rococo—to these five sentences written in the shadow of the first mushroom cloud."[7]

5. See Francis Gavin, "The Elusive Nature of Nuclear Strategy," Chapter 28 in this volume; Robert Jervis, *The Illogic of American Nuclear Strategy* (Ithaca, NY: Cornell University Press, 1984).

6. Michael Quinlan, *Thinking About Nuclear Weapons: Principles, Problems, Prospects* (New York, NY: Oxford University Press, 2009) 15. The current essay deals with the Anglo-American discussion and debate about nuclear strategy. Important contributions by French strategic thinkers were largely focused on the specific requirements of France's contribution to Western nuclear deterrence. For readers interested in their contribution, see, for example, Raymond Aron, *The Great Debate: Theories of Nuclear Strategy*, (New York, NY: Anchor Press, 1965), 100–44.

7. Robert Jervis, "Strategic Theory: What New and What's True," *Journal of Strategic Studies* 9:4 (1986): 135–62; Ken Booth, "Bernard Brodie," in *Makers of Nuclear Strategy*, John Baylis and John Garnett, eds. (London: Pinter, 1991), 24.

Booth's statement notwithstanding, there was early dissent from Brodie's judgment that the atomic bomb was the "absolute weapon." Serious challenges were mounted from both the right and the left by William L. Borden and British Nobel Prize-winning physicist P.M.S. Blackett.

Borden's book appeared almost simultaneously with Brodie's. Borden argued that nuclear weapons would soon be plentiful and spread to other countries. He correctly anticipated that the wartime grand alliance would give way to two blocs dominated respectively by the United States and the Soviet Union. He rightly suggested that atomic weapons would become more powerful by an order of magnitude in a few short years. He accurately predicted that even jet-powered aviation would ultimately give way to rockets and ballistic missiles. He recognized that, at least initially, there would be no defense against missile attacks but he did hold out hope that eventually sensor technology, powerful computers, and telemetry would enable at least some defensive capability. He anticipated hardened missile silos, nuclear missiles on submarines, and even drones and precision guided munitions. As Colin Gray noted, today, Borden's work is "almost totally unknown to the current generation of strategists" and "no doubt suffered in terms of public and official acceptability because it was, in detail, too far ahead of its time."[8]

Borden's main contention and most important contribution to nuclear strategy in the long run was his notion that strategists needed to contemplate what kind of salvo competition would occur if nuclear war did happen and what kind of targeting would be most effective. "The central thesis of this book . . . is that strategic bombing will not decide atomic war, that military installations and not cities will form the key targets." Herein lay the seeds of the deep divide that underpinned so much of the debate about nuclear strategy in the Cold War between those who believed that the prospect of nuclear war was so horrific that antagonists would be deterred by the sheer prospect and those who believed that one needed to consider how nuclear war would be waged if deterrence failed and policymakers were forced to limit the damage. The best course, Borden believed, was targeting the adversary's nuclear forces rather than their cities and population—a distinction that would come to be called counterforce as opposed to counter-value targeting.[9]

---

8. William Liscum Borden, *There Will Be No Time: The Revolution in Strategy* (New York, NY: The Macmillan Company, 1946); Colin Gray, *Strategic Studies and Public Policy* (Lexington, KY: University of Kentucky Press, 1982), 29–30; Gregg Herken, *Counsels of War* (New York, NY: Alfred A. Knopf, 1985), 6–79.

9. Borden, *There Will Be No Time*, 61.

For his part, Blackett dissented from Brodie's position that the bomb was "the Absolute weapon." Blackett was one of the first to charge, based on the findings of the postwar US Strategic Bombing Survey, that the US atomic bombing of Hiroshima and Nagasaki had been unnecessary from a military point of view but had been done, instead, to intimidate the Soviets. Blackett concluded that, "the dropping of the atomic bomb was not so much the last military act of the Second World War [as] the first act of the cold diplomatic war with Russia now in progress." These views would become a staple of liberal and left-wing criticism of US nuclear policy.[10]

Blackett's critique of Brodie, however, reflected more than anti-Americanism and a life-long tendency to make arguments that were sympathetic to Soviet positions on nuclear issues. He initially rejected Brodie's notion that the atomic bomb marked a total revolution in warfare. Reflecting his distrust of strategic bombing theories that had been current during the war, Blackett downplayed the idea that there was no defense against atomic weapons and that their use would break the will and morale of the adversary's population. He suggested a war with Russia would be long and drawn out, and that the US arsenal was too small to defeat a determined Russian conventional assault on Europe. He believed the atomic monopoly was a wasting asset and, once both sides had atomic weapons at their disposal, it would be difficult for either side to derive a decisive military advantage. Over time, with the advent of thermonuclear weapons in the early 1950s, Blackett ultimately arrived at Brodie's original position that nuclear weapons could only be used for deterrence. Moreover, Blackett argued that maintaining deterrence required only a nuclear force capable of retaliating against a nuclear aggressor, and that this would only require extremely small nuclear forces on both sides. In essence, Blackett was the first apostle of "minimum deterrence" which became a standard position for critics of US (and UK) nuclear strategy.

Borden's view was that technological change made the potential nuclear balance between adversaries unstable and difficult to maintain and that an adversary needed to be convinced that its opponent had usable operational capabilities for deterrence to survive. Blackett eventually arrived at a radically different view—that the inherent difficulties in organizing a first-strike by adversaries made the balance relatively easy to maintain. In the long run, both Borden and Blackett's initial dissents suggesting that deterrence was hard or

10. PMS Blackett, *Fear, War, and the Bomb* (New York, NY: Whittlesey House, 1949), 127.

easy to maintain, made during the period of US atomic monopoly, would be echoed in debates about nuclear strategy for the entire Cold War.[11]

II

In retrospect it seems shocking how little attention was paid to the size of America's nuclear arsenal during the country's atomic monopoly. The conventional wisdom seemed to be that the US monopoly would last at least a decade, and that there was no urgency in thinking through the consequences of a possible nuclear war with the Soviet Union or even to provide the military with an arsenal large enough to prevail in a potential war. It was almost a decade after Brodie and Borden wrote before another major work on nuclear strategy would appear. In the meantime, nuclear strategy was shaped by the exigencies of rapidly cascading events and the work of government practitioners rather than outside strategic thinkers.

John Baylis and John Garnett have offered a useful distinction between the work and thought of "makers of nuclear strategy" and those of "applied strategists." From 1949–54, the work of nuclear strategy was the handiwork of the latter—those practitioners who had to turn the preliminary concepts discussed previously into programs, budgets, doctrine, and force posture—which is to say the actual weapons, delivery systems, their geographic disposition, and the declaratory policy about how the nation will use them if necessary.[12]

As the French philosopher and strategist Raymond Aron observed, before 1949, "confident that the stock pile [sic] of bombs would suffice to prevent the Soviet Union from employing regular armies in any part of the world, the United States reduced to minimum" its own armed forces. "Paradoxically the American stock pile [sic] became really useful when it was no longer a monopoly." No one engaged more directly with this puzzle than Paul Nitze, the director of the State Department Policy Planning Staff, who was charged with

---

11. Michael Howard, "P.M.S. Blackett," in *Makers of Nuclear Strategy*, Baylis and Garnett, eds., 153–56. Blackett's conclusions that the US arsenal was insufficient to win a decisive war with the Soviets was not far off from similar judgments reached by senior US officers who reviewed early US planning for an "atomic air offensive" against the USSR. See the text of the Harmon Committee Report—Ad Hoc Committee, consisting of Lieut. General H.R. Harmon, USAF et al. to the Joint Chiefs of Staff, J.C.S. 1953–1 (May 12, 1949), located at https://nsarchive.gwu.edu/sites/default/files/documents/6895250/National-Security-Archive-Doc-02-Report-by-the.pdf.

12. Baylis and Garnett, *Makers of Nuclear Strategy*, 2.

assessing the global balance of power and producing a strategy for responding to the enormous double shocks of autumn 1949, when the Soviet Union tested its own atomic bomb and when the collapse of the Nationalist regime in China created a Sino-Soviet alliance astride the heartland of Eurasia.[13]

Winston Churchill's remark in 1955 that, "but for American nuclear superiority, Europe would already have been reduced to satellite status and the Iron Curtain would have reached the Atlantic and the Channel" captured well the prevailing sentiments in the US before the Soviet nuclear test. Afterwards, however, the durability of American nuclear superiority, as well as the wisdom of the reductions in defense spending and military readiness that had followed in the wake of World War II, seemed increasingly in question. Nitze and his small team concluded in their famous strategy document—NSC 68—that the de facto reliance on America's nuclear force to offset the Soviet Union's manpower advantage and proximity to Europe was a policy with rapidly diminishing returns.[14]

Nitze and his colleagues were preparing NSC 68 against a backdrop of broader questions about nuclear strategy. By this point, the Joint Chiefs of Staff were pressing for increased production of nuclear weapons in order to bring America's military means into better balance with the commitments it had taken on in Europe as part of the North Atlantic Treaty Organization (NATO). Simultaneously, the president was being pressed to determine whether, in the wake of the Soviet test, the US should proceed with the development of thermonuclear weapons (the so-called Super) that would increase the explosive power of nuclear weapons by an order of magnitude. At issue with these decisions was whether a large arsenal of atomic weapons should be the cornerstone of American defense policy or if a smaller arsenal would suffice to deter the USSR.[15]

The scientists who had worked on the atomic bomb project were divided on the question of the "Super" but the General Advisory Committee (including Robert Oppenheimer) charged with reviewing the question voted unanimously against proceeding. The majority argued that proceeding would set off an arms race with the Soviet Union. George Kennan believed this as well. In a long memo, he suggested that placing atomic weapons at the heart of US

13. Raymond Aron, *The Century of Total War* (Boston, MA: The Beacon Press, 1954), 154.

14. Churchill Remarks to Parliament, March 1, 1955, Hansard, 5th Series, Volume 537, cc1893–2012.

15. Samuel F. Wells, *Fearing the Worst: How Korea Transformed the Cold War* (New York, NY: Columbia University Press, 2019), 81–107.

military strategy would be a mistake. "Are we," he wrote, "to rely upon weapons of mass destruction as an integral and vitally important component of our military strength, which we would expect to employ deliberately, immediately, and unhesitatingly in the event that we become involved in a military conflict with the Soviet Union?" Or, would it not be better to simply hold atomic weapons for deterrence and, if deterrence failed, for retaliation. In that case, "we may regard them as something superfluous to our basic military posture—as something which we are compelled to hold against the possibility that they might be used by our opponents. In this case, of course, we take care not to build up a reliance upon them in our military planning. Since they then represent only a burdensome expenditure of funds and effort, we hold only the minimum required for the deterrent-retaliatory purpose." Kennan's memo made the case for what would come to be called "no first use" and "minimum deterrence," paralleling the arguments of Brodie and Blackett. Kennan also argued for the primacy of arms control. Shortly after receiving Kennan's memo, Truman approved proceeding with the hydrogen bomb. In essence, debates about a scarce or plentiful nuclear arsenal were resolved in favor of quantitative and qualitative increases in the stockpile.[16]

In April, Nitze's report was presented to the National Security Council (NSC). It drew attention to the prospect that the USSR, even with the US nuclear build up already underway, would be able to field an arsenal of some 200 nuclear weapons by 1954, categorized by some as the "year of maximum danger." Allowing the Soviets some degree of parity in atomic weapons (including potentially thermonuclear weapons) would not only negate the US strategic offset to overwhelming Soviet conventional military power but would not yield a stable balance of deterrence either. With the experience of Pearl Harbor less than a decade removed, NSC 68 noted that "in the initial phases of an atomic war, the advantages of initiative and surprise would be very great. A police state living behind an iron curtain has an enormous advantage in maintaining the necessary security and centralization of decision required to capitalize on this advantage." Moreover, although the US nuclear arsenal was currently sufficient to deter Moscow, it might not be indefinitely into the future. Because policymakers feared first-mover advantages in

16. David Rosenberg, "American Atomic Strategy and Hydrogen Bomb Decision," *Journal of American History* 66:1 (1979): 62–87; Kennan, "Memorandum by the Counselor," January 20, 1950, in *Foreign Relations of the United States, 1950, National Security Affairs; Foreign Economic Policy*, Volume I, Document 7, located at https://history.state.gov/historicaldocuments /frus1950v01/d7.

nuclear warfare (what would later be called "the reciprocal fear of surprise attack") they concluded that once the USSR believed it had sufficient forces to execute a surprise attack it might no longer be deterred. In fact, NSC 68 argued, "[t]he existence of two large atomic capabilities in such a relationship might well act, therefore, not as a deterrent, but as an incitement to war."[17]

Nitze recommended a dramatic buildup of US nuclear and conventional capabilities to reduce US dependence on atomic weapons while sustaining its existing defense commitments. NSC 68 was punctuated, as it were, with a third big shock of 1949–50—the North Korean invasion of the South. The decision to defend the South in the Korean War blew away the bureaucratic and domestic political obstacles to acceptance of NSC 68's recommendations, which led in short order to tripling the defense budget and setting the US on the path of pursuing a symmetric strategy to counter the advent of Soviet nuclear weapons. It also began to embed in the nuclear strategies adopted by "applied strategists" the notion that deterrence was not easily achieved but required the right mix of capabilities and policies to make it work.[18]

III

The Korean War profoundly influenced British and American thinking about the role of nuclear weapons. The decision to defend South Korea was driven in no small part by concerns about how US allies in Europe would assess the value of American defense guarantees recently provided in the North Atlantic Treaty. It also raised questions about prospective Communist gains in Asia and the Middle East.

As it happened, senior officials in the UK, soon to have its own nuclear forces, were also thinking about these issues. The original project to develop the atomic bomb had begun as a joint Anglo-American effort, and British senior officials, in the aftermath of Hiroshima, had reached the same conclusion as Brodie. In October 1945, the British chiefs of staff reported to Prime Minister Clement Atlee that "the best method of defence against the new weapon is likely to be the deterrent effect that the possession of the means of retaliation would have on a potential aggressor." When Winston Churchill returned to

---

17. "A Report to the National Security Council by the Executive Secretary (Lay), NSC-68," April 14, 1950, *Foreign Relations of the United States, 1950m National Security Affairs; Foreign Economic Policy*, Volume 1, available at https://history.state.gov/historicaldocuments/frus1950v01/d85. Hereafter, this is referred to as NSC 68.

18. Wells, *Fearing the Worst*, 81–107.

office in 1951, the review of UK defense policy he set in motion concluded that Britain's deteriorating financial situation precluded the rearmament program launched by the Atlee government as well as the conventional force goals set for NATO by the February 1952 Lisbon Conference. Churchill's discussions with Truman in January 1952 included a very general brief on planning for the "atomic air offensive," and the prime minister came away convinced that British defense plans took insufficient account of atomic weapons. His subsequent instructions to the British military produced a Global Strategy Paper in spring 1952 that put nuclear deterrence at the heart of UK defense strategy.[19]

Anglo-American consultations with military and political leaders after the British paper was issued revealed differences of emphasis over whether the struggle with the Soviet Union would be a long cold war or if a hot war was more imminent. The Americans were inclined to the latter view, although they recognized that "the cold war would probably be the condition of man for a long period of time." No doubt reflecting skepticism about the dispositive role of nuclear weapons in a war with the Soviet Union, General Omar Bradley told the British that even with the accelerated production of nuclear weapons authorized by President Truman, "really sizable increases . . . were not due to come in for some time." The Americans, reflecting the view expressed in Nitze's NSC 68, "considered the degree of risk of a hot war through 1954 to be higher than was the case with the United Kingdom."[20]

The British annoyed their US military colleagues by proselytizing for a declaratory policy of nuclear deterrence, and that view found echoes in some precincts of the American press. After the 1952 US election brought to office policymakers who shared the acute British concern about a defense posture that was economically sustainable over the long term, an American view more parallel to that of the British emerged concerning the central role nuclear weapons played in national strategy.[21]

19. John Baylis and Kristn Stoddart, *The British Nuclear Experience: The Roles of Belief, Culture and Identity* (Oxford: Oxford University Press, 2014), 42–59; John Baylis and Alan Macmillan, "The British Global Strategy Paper of 1952, *Journal of Strategic Studies* 16:2 (1993): 200–26.

20. Ian Clark and Nicholas Wheeler, *The British Origins of Nuclear Strategy 1945–1955* (Oxford: Oxford University Press, 1989), 160–83; Richard Rosecrance, *Defense of the Realm: British Strategy in the Nuclear Epoch* (New York, NY: Columbia University Press, 1968), 134–81. General Bradley remarks in "United States-United Kingdom Politico-Military Meeting on Report by United Kingdom Chiefs of Staff re 'Defence Policy and Global Strategy,' dated July 9, 1952," located at https://nsarchive2.gwu.edu/nukevault/special/doco4.pdf.

21. Andrew M. Johnston, "Mr. Slessor Goes to Washington: The Influence of the British Global Strategy Paper on The Eisenhower New Look," *Diplomatic History* 30:2 (1998): 361–98.

The Korean conflict had kicked off controversy over the idea of "limited war" in two different senses. First, could conflicts, including between proxies of the two sides in the Cold War, be limited to conventional means? Although there were several moments when it appeared that the US was considering the use of nuclear weapons, allied concerns about the potential defense of Europe, lack of appropriate targets in North Korea or the PRC (the People's Republic of China), and concerns about a general war managed to keep the conflict confined to conventional means. A second sense of "limited war" as "limited nuclear war" would become a preoccupation of nuclear strategists and policymakers by the end of the decade.

The unsatisfactory nature of the limited war in Korea, the attendant inflation that accompanied the arms buildup, and the heavy government spending the buildup entailed, undermined popular support for Truman. To head off a return to isolationism in the Republican Party, Dwight Eisenhower decided to quit his post as Supreme Allied Commander in NATO and make himself available for a draft as the Republican presidential candidate. He was able to wrest the Republican nomination from Senator Robert Taft, who had expressed reservations about the US taking on alliance commitments, and then handily won the election.

No president has entered office with more knowledge about nuclear matters than Eisenhower. He began his tenure by ordering a large-scale strategy review that would ultimately shape the development of nuclear strategy for the rest of the Cold War. Eisenhower and his colleagues wrestled with the question of how to get some political benefit out of the new era of "nuclear plenty" that he had inherited from his predecessor. Simultaneously, the new president sought to put the US on a path where defense expenditures would be sustainable for the "long haul"—the protracted strategic competition with the Soviet Union. His initial instinct (along with Secretary of State John Foster Dulles) was that it would be necessary to get over the emerging sense that atomic weapons were unusable. In private deliberations (and some public comments) Eisenhower argued that nuclear weapons should be available for military operations like any other ordnance. Yet, as he absorbed reports analyzing the results of thermonuclear weapons tests (the first of which took place shortly before he assumed office), Eisenhower significantly revised his views.

As president, Eisenhower had to solve several vexing policy problems at once. What would be the basis for defending NATO since it had become abundantly clear that the European allies would not soon be able to dramatically increase their conventional military capabilities? Moreover, the accession of the Federal

Republic of Germany to NATO meant that NATO and the Soviet bloc would now be cheek by jowl. Altogether, these developments raised the problem of what would come to be called "extended deterrence." Simply put, how could the US deter not only an attack on itself but also one on its allies?

Eisenhower's strategy review brought together senior officials of his own administration with those, like Kennan and Nitze, who had been protagonists in the crucial debates of the 1940s. At the heart of the review was Eisenhower's fear that the enormous US military build-up, which now consumed over fourteen percent (14.2%) of the Gross National Product, would turn America into a garrison-state. The result was a revised defense strategy that would, as had the British a year earlier, prioritize the nuclear deterrent as the centerpiece of a US strategy that sought to reduce spending on conventional forces while at the same time holding off the advances of Soviet bloc.

The so-called Solarium review led to the adoption of NSC 162/2 in October 1953. It concluded that, "within the free world, only the United States can provide and maintain, for a period of years to come, the atomic capability to counterbalance Soviet atomic power." But the document stressed that the US required allies to be able to execute this strategy:

> The effective use of U.S. strategic air power against the USSR will require overseas bases on foreign territory for some years to come . . . The availability of such bases and their use by the United States in case of need will depend, in most cases, on the consent and cooperation of the nations where they are located. Such nations will assume the risks entailed only if convinced that their own security will thereby be best served.[22]

These concerns put a high premium on Secretary of State John Foster Dulles's efforts to convince America's European allies. In April 1954, Dulles told a closed session of the allied foreign ministers that the "primary purpose of the United States. . . . was to deter aggression and prevent the outbreak of war." He went on to argue that offsetting "the great concentration of military power within the Soviet bloc" could only be accomplished with "the integration of effective atomic means within our overall capability." Dulles stressed that the US would consult closely with allies and "cooperate with them fully . . . that is

22. The text of NSC 162/2 can be found at "Report to the National Security Council by the Executive Secretary (Lay)," October 30, 1954, *Foreign Relations of the United States, 1952–1954*, Volume II, Part 1, Document 101, located at https://history.state.gov/historicaldocuments/frus1952-54v02p1/d101.

the essence of collective security." In December, the North Atlantic Council approved MC48 which, as Dulles reported to President Eisenhower, codified that, "if an all-out Soviet attack occurred, whether atomic or otherwise, the NATO response would be a defense employing atomic weapons." The fundamental NATO strategy of using nuclear weapons to repel massive conventional aggression in Europe has remained in place until this day.[23]

Secretary Dulles spelled out this "New Look" policy in detail in two speeches and a subsequent article in *Foreign Affairs*. Dulles noted that, although the Truman administration had met the "emergency" created by aggressive Soviet behavior, emergency measures did not necessarily make for good permanent policies. Since the Soviets were thinking in terms of historical epochs it was essential for US policy to "serve our long-time interests" and to do so in a way that avoided "exhausting ourselves" or "practical bankruptcy."

To that end, Dulles endorsed an internationalist approach. "We need allies and collective security. Our purpose is to make these relations more effective, less costly. This can be done by placing more reliance on deterrent power and less dependence on local defensive power." The US and its allies should seek, Dulles argued, "a maximum deterrent at a bearable cost." As a result, and in consultation with his military commanders and senior advisors, the president decided that henceforth the nation's defense would "depend primarily upon a great capacity to retaliate, instantly, by means and at places of our choosing." Dulles's speech was met with an outpouring of criticism both at home and abroad. Critics feared that the administration was suggesting that the US would be forced to choose between nuclear war and accepting the kind of limited Communist aggression that was going on in Southeast Asia. Some allies initially even feared the US would be dragging them into a nuclear war.[24]

In response to these concerns, Dulles used a more measured tone in his *Foreign Affairs* article. He noted that without allies, the US would "not be in a position to depend primarily upon a great capacity to retaliate, instantly, by means and at places of our choosing." To quiet the concerns of both foreign

23. See Dulles's Statement to the North Atlantic Council, April 24, 1954, in *Foreign Relations of the United States, 1952–1954*, Volume V, Part 1, Document 264; Memorandum of Discussion at the National Security Council, December 21, 1954, in *Foreign Relations of the United States, 1952–1954*, Volume V, Part 1, Document 294. The text of MC-48 can be found at "M.C. 48 (FINAL)," November 22, 1954, *NATO Strategy Documents, 1949–69*, available at https://www.nato.int/docu/stratdoc/eng/a541122a.pdf.

24. John Foster Dulles, "The Evolution of Foreign Policy," *Department of State Bulletin* (January 25, 1954): 107–10.

and domestic critics Dulles also noted that, "furthermore, massive atomic and thermonuclear retaliation is not the kind of power which could most usefully be evoked under all circumstances."

Collective defense, however, required organization and coordination and Dulles suggested that, in order to operationalize the system of collective security and provide "maximum protection at minimum cost," it was imperative that "a potential aggressor be left in no doubt that he would be certain to suffer damage outweighing any possible gains from aggression." Dulles stressed that this concept "for the long haul" had been presented to and accepted by the NATO allies. He pushed back against the critics who argued that the US and its allies were relying solely on "large-scale strategic bombing" as the sole means of deterring aggression. Aid to allies, developing countries, and the example of freedom and liberty were also essential he argued. Massive retaliation made the possible use of US nuclear power the centerpiece of American strategy.[25]

"Massive retaliation" would be codified in US defense planning when Eisenhower asked the military services to create a plan to integrate and coordinate land- and sea-based ballistic missiles with US bombers for possible use, in extremis, at the order of the president. The result was the Single Integrated Operational Plan (SIOP) which called for a massive retaliatory strike on the USSR. Yet, when Eisenhower was briefed on the SIOP near the end of this presidency, he confided to one aide that it "frightened the devil out of me." It is not too much to say that the subsequent development of nuclear strategic thinking was guided by the need to make the nuclear arsenal politically useful as well as in response to the critiques of "massive retaliation" that now emerged.[26]

IV

Even before the emergence of massive retaliation as the US and NATO nuclear strategy, work was underway that would reshape how experts in and out of government thought about nuclear deterrence. From that ferment emerged ideas about second-strike retaliatory capability as the underpinning of strategic stability, the stability-instability paradox, debates about limited nuclear war and limited nuclear options, the idea of "graduated deterrence" or "flexible response," deterrence by denial and deterrence by punishment, debates about counterforce or

25. John Foster Dulles, "Policy for Security and Peace," *Foreign Affairs* 32:3 (1954): 353–64.

26. David Alan Rosenberg, "U.S. Nuclear War Planning, 1945–1960," in *Strategic Nuclear Targeting*, Desmond Ball and Jeffrey Richelson, eds. (Ithaca, NY: Cornell University Press, 1986) 35–56.

counter-value targeting how to manage escalation dynamics (the "escalation ladder" and "escalation dominance"), damage limitation if deterrence failed, the role of passive and active defenses, the notion that deterrence was a competition in risk-taking, and finally, the ideas of "assured destruction," "mutual assured destruction," and the importance of arms control as a means of limiting and bounding the strategic competition. These theories and concepts continue to provide the basic language with which we discuss nuclear weapons issues.

Much, but not all, of the thinking about nuclear strategy emerged not from the military but rather from a handful of universities and from the RAND Corporation. Project RAND (short for, Research and Development) was initially established at the command of Army Air Forces Chief General Hap Arnold and subsequently spun off as the non-profit RAND Corporation in 1948. In those early years, RAND brought together a team of intellects from different disciplines (economics, sociology, mathematics, and political science) including Bernard Brodie, William W. Kaufman, Andrew Marshall, Thomas Schelling, Albert Wohlstetter, and Herman Kahn, to think about the strategic problems facing the defense establishment.

The pioneering work at the "think tank" included Albert Wohlstetter's studies on the location of bomber bases. Overseas bases featured prominently in the "air atomic offensive" that Air Force planners considered a crucial element of the next war. As US nuclear weapons began to flow into Europe as part of the "massive retaliation" strategy, overseas bases assumed even greater importance. The Wohlstetter studies suggested that US bomber bases were vulnerable to preemptive Soviet attack and would be at even greater risk as ballistic missiles entered the future Soviet inventory. Meeting with Air Force resistance to his findings, a frustrated Wohlstetter ultimately published his views in a *Foreign Affairs* article entitled, "The Delicate Balance of Terror." It was the most thorough and influential statement concerning the proposition that deterrence might be harder than it looked. The problem facing policymakers, Wohlstetter argued, was not just to have enough nuclear forces to deter an adversary but also to have enough forces to retaliate after a first strike had degraded the US force. This notion of assured second-strike retaliatory capability would become a dominant concept in government and would come to underpin later notions of what constituted "strategic stability" in the arms race.[27]

27. Fred Kaplan, *The Wizards of Armageddon* (New York, NY: Simon and Schuster, 1983), 90–124; Albert Wohlstetter, "The Delicate Balance of Terror," *Foreign Affairs* 37:2 (1958): 211–34; Richard Rosecrance, "Albert Wohlstetter," in *Makers of Nuclear Strategy*, Baylis and Garnett, eds., 57–69.

One of the first explicit critiques of massive retaliation came from another RAND intellectual, William W. Kaufman. He would later note that "in principle ... the requirements of deterrence are relatively simple. In practice, however, they turn out to be exceptionally complex, expensive, and difficult to obtain." In a 1956 essay, Kaufman argued that deterrence required communicating to an adversary what actions the US would take if it pursued a course of action inimical to American interests. Moreover, it would be necessary to "surround the proposal with an air of credibility." Credibility, in turn, required that "the enemy must be persuaded that we have the capability to act; that, in acting, we could inflict costs greater than the advantage to be won from attaining the objective; and that we really would act as specified in the stated contingency." Since the Soviets were developing active and passive air defenses as well as their own strategic striking power, "if we are challenged to fulfill the threat of massive retaliation, we will be likely to suffer costs as great as those we inflict." Moreover, the US track record in Korea and Indochina suggested that "we are not prepared in cases of this sort to do more than limit and contain Communist thrusts by means of local applications of counterforce."[28]

If the point of US policy was to prevent further expansion of Communism in so-called gray areas, it would be better to build up American ground and tactical air forces, as well as passive and active defenses and to work with partners and allies. Kaufman concluded that "we must not delude ourselves that deterrents can be constructed on the cheap or that we will be taken at our word when we threaten massive retaliation indiscriminately."[29]

The critique of massive retaliation as unlikely to deter the Sino-Soviet bloc in Third World conflicts where US objectives were not inherently existential was one part of the problem. Yet plans to use theater nuclear weapons to blunt a Soviet invasion of Europe and the idea of "limited nuclear war" also came in for scrutiny.

Strategists who were critical of massive retaliation, such as Robert Osgood, Brodie, and Kaufman, all recognized that NATO was committed to the early use of nuclear weapons and struggled with the implications of that commitment. Many Europeans hoped that the Soviets could be persuaded that NATO's pledge to the early use of the weapons would almost immediately precipitate

---

28. Austin Long, *Deterrence: From Cold War to Long War* (Santa Monica, CA: RAND, 2008), 2; William W. Kaufman, "The Requirements of Deterrence." Memorandum Number 7, Center of International Studies, Princeton University, November 15, 1954.

29. Kaufman, "The Requirements of Deterrence."

a strategic nuclear exchange between the US and the Soviet Union—and hence deter Moscow from starting down that path in the first place. Many American and British critics of massive retaliation, on the other hand, tried to articulate a strategy in which limited use of nuclear weapons might make sense.[30]

A young American academic at Harvard, Henry Kissinger, was asked to summarize the thinking that emerged from a Council on Foreign Relations study group on nuclear weapons. The result was Kissinger's massive study *Nuclear Weapons and American Foreign Policy*, which articulated a strategy for limited nuclear war. In particular, Kissinger focused on how a limited use of nuclear weapons might force a pause in conflict and allow diplomacy to resume. He stated, "[i]n a limited war the problem is to apply graduated amounts of destruction for limited objectives and also to permit the necessary breathing spaces for political contacts." Kissinger suggested thinking about the tactics of limited nuclear warfighting more along the lines of naval rather than land warfare and advocated the use of small, self-contained mobile units to execute this approach.[31]

Proposals, notably Kissinger's, concerning the use of so-called tactical nuclear weapons for limited nuclear war were controversial from the outset. Brodie, who had initially supported the idea of using nuclear weapons in Europe to blunt an advance, began to have second thoughts. "The use of any kind of nuclear weapon probably increases markedly the difficulties in the way of maintaining limitations on war," he wrote. "For one thing, it is much easier to distinguish between [the] use and non-use of nuclear weapons than between the use of a nuclear weapon below some arbitrary limit of size and one well above the limit." Brodie noted that the use of nuclear weapons would carry political downsides and thus would require a degree of restraint, once the nuclear threshold was crossed, in exercising an efficient means of warfare that was virtually unprecedented historically.[32]

In the face of criticism, Kissinger soon reversed himself. Although he continued to insist that "no war in the nuclear age can ever be completely free of the specter of nuclear weapons," he conceded that the inherent difficulty of

30. Morton Halperin, "Nuclear Weapons and Limited War," *Journal of Conflict Resolution* 5:2 (1961): 146–66.

31. Henry A. Kissinger, *Nuclear Weapons and American Foreign Policy* (New York, NY: Harper, 1957), 156–57.

32. Bernard Brodie, *Strategy in the Missile Age* (Princeton, NJ: Princeton University Press, 1959), 323.

limiting nuclear use once such weapons had been employed, the growing Soviet arsenal, and disagreement among American military leaders and the allies
about strategies for limited nuclear war, undercut his earlier arguments for
limited war. Reflecting an emerging consensus that would soon be reflected in
the doctrine of "flexible response," Kissinger noted that, "at a minimum, the
conventional capability of the free world should be of such a size that a nuclear
defense becomes the *last* and not the *only* recourse. The best situation is one
in which the conventional forces of the free world can be overcome *only* by
nuclear weapons."[33]

The debate about limited war seemed more urgent after the USSR launched
the Sputnik satellite into earth orbit in fall 1957. The successful space launch
suggested that the Soviets had solved the problems of missile staging, and that
would enable them, in short order, to develop missiles of intercontinental
range, raising concerns in several quarters of a potential "missile gap." Fears
about US bomber bases being vulnerable were now augmented by concerns
that the US homeland might be subject to a devastating nuclear strike, with
only a thirty-minute warning. The possibility of a conflict in Europe moving
from a limited nuclear exchange to one that devastated the continental United
States appeared less of a theoretical and more of a practical concern. Eisenhower, privy to intelligence from US secret surveillance of the USSR, remained sanguine, but a classified report—the Gaither Report—he received
one month after Sputnik called for a dramatic acceleration of US efforts to
develop ICBMs (intercontinental ballistic missiles) and submarine-launched
ballistic missiles (SLBMs). The report also argued for ramping up efforts to
protect the civilian population from a nuclear attack. Despite its Top Secret
classification, many of the report's recommendations would become campaign
talking points for John F. Kennedy in 1960. They would also spark additional
speculation and intellectual innovation by nuclear strategists.[34]

Perhaps the most well-known discussion of escalation dynamics came from
another RAND figure, Herman Kahn. He sought to use arresting metaphors and
scenarios to illustrate the kinds of situations, forces, and behaviors that might
lead one side or another to increase the level of force, including potentially to

33. Henry Kissinger, "Limited War: Conventional or Nuclear? A Reappraisal," *Daedalus* 89:4
(1960): 800–17. Emphasis in original.

34. "Deterrence and Survival in the Nuclear Age" (also known as the Gaither Committee
Report) remained classified until 1973. "Deterrence and Survival in the Nuclear Age," November 7, 1957, Security Resources Panel of the Science Advisory Committee, available at https://
nsarchive2.gwu.edu/NSAEBB/NSAEBB139/nitze02.pdf.

the point of using nuclear weapons. Kahn's use of analogies like the labor strike and the teenage drag-racing game of chicken were colorful introductions to some of the psychological aspects of escalation. Yet his most lasting contribution was the elaborate metaphor of the "escalation ladder" (which in Kahn's construct contained forty-four "rungs" culminating in "war by spasm," or as he sometimes more colorfully and provocatively described it in public lectures—a "wargasm") and the notion of "escalation dominance." Escalation dominance was a function of one side or another having an asymmetric advantage in capabilities that, as Kahn wrote, "enable[s] the side possessing it to enjoy marked advantages in a given region of the escalation ladder." Whichever side had the greater fear of the other's ability to impose its will through these capabilities was more likely to yield.[35] Kahn, in essence, was describing what economists would call the risk tolerance of different national leaderships under different conditions.

One RAND economist, Thomas Schelling, would make risk management the centerpiece of a more sophisticated, formal deterrence theory. Schelling used game theory to make explicit assumptions about rationality combined with cost-benefit calculations borrowed from economics in order to enrich our understanding of deterrence. Schelling's point of departure was that what differentiated nuclear from conventional weapons was not so much the massive numbers of potential victims but rather the speed with which those victims could be killed, the centralization of the decision-making necessary to make that happen, and the prospect that war would be disconnected from political processes. Both sides, he pointed out, distrusted one another. Moreover, because most people assumed that in nuclear war a distinct advantage resided with the side that struck first, there was a "reciprocal fear of surprise attack." Since, borrowing from Brodie, the point was to deter war, the battlefield had now given way to "the diplomacy of violence." As Schelling argued, this state of affairs "enhances the importance of war and threats of war as techniques of influence, not of destruction; of coercion and deterrence, not of conquest defense; of bargaining and intimidation." Bargaining between nuclear-armed nations became a competition in risk-taking and the ability to manipulate the adversary's perception of risk as the key to winning the game. For Schelling, at the end of the day, the key to deterrence was "the threat that leaves something to chance"—the notion that it was imperative to convey to

35. Herman Kahn, *On Escalation: Metaphors and Scenarios* (New York, NY: Frederick A. Praeger, 1965), 39, 290.

opponents that government decision-making might not be totally in one's control, and that an inadvertent slide into war was a possible consequence of steps taken by their side to escalate in a crisis. Schelling's views exerted enormous influence, not least because his musings on shared risks and concern for stability led him to pioneer the arguments for arms control as a solution to the paradoxes that he explored so powerfully in his writing.[36]

Glenn Snyder made two important contributions to deterrence theory. He pointed out that deterrence by punishment—or retaliation—which had received the most attention from nuclear theorists, was only one part of the equation. It was also possible to deter by denying the adversary the ability to achieve its objectives. Snyder made clear that deterrence by punishment would remain the prime recourse for defending the American homeland. Yet for the vexing problem of extended deterrence, deterrence by denial provided not so much an alternative to deterrence by punishment as a complement and enhancement. Providing sufficient conventional forces in Europe or Asia would complicate Soviet planning for a fait accompli and could also enhance the prospect that their defeat would call forth a substantial retaliatory strike— thus strengthening the credibility of the massive retaliation threat. Some years later Snyder would add an additional wrinkle by pointing out that while a nuclear standoff between the superpowers might promote stability at the strategic level, it would incentivize adversaries to seek advantage at the conventional level. This stability-instability paradox is a concept that has had the most vigorous post-Cold War afterlife, particularly because the paradox seems to explain quite neatly the ongoing nuclear standoff that has allowed conventional and even sub-conventional conflicts between India and Pakistan in the years since they both tested nuclear weapons in 1998.[37]

As nuclear strategy became more sophisticated and complex, one author above all began to insist that thinking about deterrence had to consider the possibility that deterrence might fail. The potential of a nuclear war seemed so horrendous to most observers that it spawned an entire genre of post-apocalyptic

36. Thomas Schelling, "The Reciprocal Fear of Surprise Attack," RAND Corporation, 1958, located at https://www.rand.org/content/dam/rand/pubs/papers/2007/P1342.pdf; Thomas Schelling, *Arms and Influence* (New Haven, CT: Yale University Press, 1966), 1, 33; and Thomas Schelling, *Strategy of Conflict* (New York, NY: Oxford University Press, 1960), 187–203.

37. Glenn H. Snyder, "Deterrence by Denial and Punishment," Research Monograph No. 1, Princeton University Center for International Studies, 1959; Snyder, "The Balance of Power and the Balance of Terror," in *The Balance of Power*, Paul Seabury, ed. (San Francisco, CA: Chandler Publishing Co., 1965), 184–201.

fiction, much of it suggesting that the survivors of a nuclear conflict would envy the dead. Herman Kahn used this notion as a leitmotif for his books *On Thermonuclear War* and *Thinking about the Unthinkable*. Kahn argued that imagining a post-nuclear world would depend on what steps had been taken to prepare for it beforehand. It mattered whether one assumed that 10 million or 50 million people were killed in a nuclear exchange. Contrary to the emerging conventional wisdom, he insisted that prewar efforts at damage limitation, whether through targeting of the adversary's offensive forces or through vigorous efforts at civil defense, could make a significant difference in the number of deaths in a nuclear war. The latter, Kahn argued, could not contribute much to deterrence but might make a significant difference to the recuperative ability of the nation after a nuclear war. Kahn sought to provide assurance, almost always with greater certainty than the speculative nature of the subject warranted, that although nuclear war would be horrifically damaging, it would not spell the end of life on earth as we know it. This conclusion outraged a legion of critics, but Kahn touched on something fundamental. Although it was easy to stop thinking about nuclear war at the point at which deterrence fails, government officials charged with defending the nation had to contend with the questions: What would they do, and how would they use US nuclear forces, if deterrence failed?[38]

Kahn's colleagues at RAND had been worrying about this problem for some time. Massive retaliation, as Brodie and other critics had pointed out, raised both moral and practical concerns. Was it moral to hold civilian populations at risk? How credible were such threats? Andrew Marshall and Herbert Goldhammer produced a tour-de-force study that suggested attacking Soviet forces rather than population centers would produce better results. In a series of projects and studies building on Wohlstetter's earlier work, RAND analysts—foremost among them William Kaufman—argued for invulnerable strategic forces, a targeting policy that focused on military objects rather than urban areas, and that sought to maintain intact the command apparatus of both sides so that nuclear war, if deterrence failed, could be carried out in the least destructive way possible and terminated as quickly as possible.[39]

---

38. Herman Kahn, *On Thermonuclear War* (Princeton, NJ: Princeton University Press, 1960) 21; Herman Kahn, *Thinking about the Unthinkable* (New York, NY: Avon, 1962).

39. Kaplan, *Wizards of Armageddon*; Herbert Goldhamer, Andrew Marshall, and Nathan Leites, "The Deterrence and Strategy of Total War, 1959–1961: A Method of Analysis," RAND Research Memorandum RM-2301, April 30, 1959; Andrew May, "The RAND Corporation and

Although there were significant differences among the RAND strategists, there was a consensus that the US needed a counterforce strategy—even as some believed it would exist in tension with the idea of stable deterrence. Counterforce was often described as a war fighting strategy and critics of US counterforce nuclear strategy have, since the 1960s, argued that its advocates sought to fight a nuclear war. More sophisticated critics of "the illogic of American nuclear strategy" have not imputed ill motives to its proponents but instead have argued that, since nuclear war is suicidal, any attempt to escape from the fundamental paradox of deterrence—that nuclear weapons are only useful to deter the use of the adversary's nuclear weapons—was simply wrong-headed. Henry Rowen, one of those at RAND involved in the counterforce studies, preferred to call it a posture of "deterrence plus insurance." He noted in a paper prepared for the Joint Economic Committee of Congress that "the deterrence-plus-insurance view focuses on the possibility that war may occur in spite of our best attempts to avoid it and aims at alleviating the catastrophe." The appeal of this view to policymakers would soon be apparent as many of the RAND crew joined the Kennedy administration and staffed Secretary Robert McNamara's Department of Defense.[40]

V

Even before running for president, Kennedy had criticized massive retaliation as inflexible and lacking credibility. In 1958, he called for new strategic policies, arguing, "we must now be prepared to demonstrate that we have other courses besides military action and no action at all." In the same speech he decried the alleged missile gap and argued for accelerating production of ICBMs and SLBMs. Upon taking office, Kennedy directed Secretary McNamara to develop a new approach that was dubbed "flexible response."[41]

McNamara, an automotive CEO with a passion for quantitative methods, gravitated to the systems and operations analysts from RAND. Early in his

the Dynamics of American Strategic Thought, 1946–1962," Emory University, Unpublished PhD dissertation, 1998.

40. Andrew May, "The RAND Corporation," 317; Kaplan, *The Wizards of Armageddon*; Jervis, *The Illogic of American Nuclear Strategy*.

41. "Remarks of Senator John F. Kennedy, in the Senate, August 14, 1958" as found in "U.S. Military Power, Senate floor, 14 August 1958," Papers of John F. Kennedy. Pre-Presidential Papers. Senate Files, Box 901, John F. Kennedy Presidential Library, available at https://www.jfklibrary.org/archives/other-resources/john-f-kennedy-speeches/united-states-senate-military-power-19580814.

tenure William Kaufman briefed McNamara on the counterforce ideas that had been circulating at RAND. Kaufman argued that counterforce would complement deterrence by making US nuclear threats more credible and dismissed any tension between pursuing a damage limitation approach and a stable nuclear balance. McNamara was intrigued by the concepts which promised greater flexibility than he found in the existing SIOP which offered only a single massive attack on the Communist bloc and promised casualties in the range of 365–425 million people. McNamara began to reshape both US strategic doctrine and forces to incorporate the counterforce concepts, including targeting enemy forces, avoiding cities, and preserving Soviet command and control for purposes of intrawar deterrence into a package of options under the SIOP. Those elements largely would remain part of the SIOP throughout the remainder of the Cold War.[42]

McNamara used a NATO defense ministerial meeting in Athens and a subsequent speech in Ann Arbor to lay out the elements of the counterforce nuclear strategy. He told the allies that:

> Our principal military objectives, in the event of a nuclear war stemming from a major attack on the Alliance, should be the destruction of the enemy's military forces while attempting to preserve the fabric as well as the integrity of allied society. Specifically, our studies indicate that a strategy which targets nuclear force only against cities or a mixture of civil and military targets has serious limitations for the purpose of deterrence and for the conduct of general nuclear war.

McNamara's public exposition in Ann Arbor was less nuanced than the classified report to allies and opened him up to the criticism that he was trying to "conventionalize" nuclear war or was seeking a first strike capability. As the Kennedy administration buildup continued and the margin of US strategic advantage seemed to increase, McNamara was forced to address the question of "how much is enough" to deter. He ultimately concluded that an effort to develop an exquisite "first strike capability" was doomed to face the law of diminishing returns and generate a spiraling or an "action-reaction" arms race.

---

42. Lawrence S. Kaplan, Ronald D. Landa, and Edward J. Drea, *The McNamara Ascendancy, 1961–65* (Washington, DC: Historical Office, Office of the Secretary of Defense, 2006); Desmond Ball, "The Development of the SIOP: 1960–1983," in *Strategic Nuclear Targeting*, Ball and Richelson, eds., 57–83; May, "The RAND Corporation," 356–57; Fred Kaplan, *The Bomb: Presidents, Generals and the Secret History of Nuclear War* (New York, NY: Simon and Schuster, 2020).

After all, the Soviets could easily add additional forces that would make it hard for US planners to be certain that they could disarm the USSR in a first strike.[43]

McNamara found the limiting principle he was seeking for US strategic forces in the notion of "assured destruction." In the first instance, assured destruction was defined as the ability of US strategic forces to destroy thirty percent of the Soviet population and fifty percent of Soviet industrial production (later modified to 25% and 66% respectively) in a retaliatory strike. A stable nuclear balance would be assured when both sides had a similar assured-destruction capability, hence a situation that gave birth to the famous acronym of MAD—mutual assured destruction. Although McNamara's first effort to sell this concept to the Soviets at the Glassboro Summit in 1967 was a conspicuous failure, over time, the Soviets too would argue that defenses were dangerously destabilizing and undermined the fundamental nuclear balance.[44]

The logic of MAD, however, was in fundamental tension with counterforce, especially the question of active and passive defenses which could undermine "strategic stability" by calling into question one side or another's ability to inflict assured destruction on the other. It was also, writes Hal Brands, "lethal to a military strategy that required nuclear escalation to compensate for America's inability to defend far-flung allies conventionally." As Robert Jervis would describe it, MAD was less a strategy of deterrence than a reality from which there was no escape. It was a lasting source of perplexity to Jervis that policymakers persisted in the fruitless effort to pursue counterforce despite its apparent "illogic" according to MAD.[45]

As the Cold War played out, the divergence between theory and practice widened. The logic of MAD and the search for "strategic stability" became the mantra of most writing about nuclear strategy, even as counterforce remained embedded in the actual practice of nuclear strategy. Although one explanation for this gap was bureaucratic inertia, another was the ethic of responsibility that guided those charged with maintaining the nation's security. Perhaps no

43. Keith Payne, *The Great American Gamble: Deterrence Theory and Practice from the Cold War to the Twenty-First Century* (Fairfax, VA: National Institute Press, 2008), 83–148.

44. Payne, *The Great American Gamble*; "Memorandum of Conversation, June 23, 1967," in *Foreign Relations of the United States, 1964–1986*, Volume XIV: *Soviet Union*, Document 231, available at https://history.state.gov/historicaldocuments/frus1964-68v14/d231.

45. Hal Brands, *The Twilight Struggle: What the Cold War Teaches Us About Great Power Rivalry Today* (New Haven, CT: Yale University Press, 2022), 61; Robert Jervis, *The Meaning of the Nuclear Revolution: Statecraft and the Prospect of Armageddon* (Ithaca, NY: Cornell University Press, 1989), 74–106.

one expressed this better than the late Michael Quinlan, a senior British civil servant who spent his life immersed in the world of nuclear targeting and strategy. Quinlan noted that "a structure of deterrence cannot be built upon a state policy of absolute non-use, or without genuine concepts of possible use." As technology evolved this required that:

> plans and capabilities had to provide options for use that could be credible. This meant, for example, developing weapons of greater accuracy and lower explosive yield, and plans for a more limited scale of use and more constrained selection of targets, than might feature in an unconstrained apocalyptic holocaust. The development of such weapons and plans was intermittently assailed by anti-nuclear campaigners in the West as implying that nuclear warfare was thought probable, or as betokening a dangerously increased inclination to regard it as a tolerable enterprise. The assault sometimes seemed to be seeking to imprison defenders of nuclear deterrence in a manufactured dilemma: if nuclear weapons were too powerful, they were indiscriminate, and that was wicked; if measures were taken to make them less indiscriminate, this would make them more usable, and that too was wicked. But such criticisms failed to recognize the inevitability of the paradox. Ultimately, accepting them would lead towards less credible deterrence and thus more risk of war, not less. The evident possession of practical options was directed entirely to making war as remote an eventuality as possible.[46]

VI

There was, of course, one other way out of the dilemmas created by deterrence and increasing arsenals—the pursuit of arms control. For the bulk of the strategic community, promoting strategic stability required not counterforce strategies but rather steps towards disarmament, perhaps leading to the outright abolition of nuclear weapons.[47]

46. Quinlan, *Thinking About Nuclear Weapons*, 25–27. The Carter administration's review of nuclear strategy led to a "countervailing strategy" that focused on holding Soviet leadership targets at risk. See Walter Slocombe, "The Countervailing Strategy," *International Security* 5:4 (1981): 18–27.

47. The first of a series of op eds by Henry Kissinger, George Shultz, William Perry, and Sam Nunn calling for nuclear abolition appeared in the *Wall Street Journal* on January 4, 2007. The collection of editorials can be found at https://media.nti.org/pdfs/NSP_op-eds_final_.pdf.

Schelling and Morton Halperin argued in *Strategy and Arms Control* that there was a mutual interest in avoiding war, minimizing the costs of the arms race, and "curtailing the scope of violence of war in the event that it occurs." Since potential adversaries shared an interest in military cooperation as well as in competition, "the essential feature of arms control is the recognition of the common interest, of the possibility of reciprocation and cooperation." The two men remained agnostic as to "whether the most promising areas of arms control involve reductions in certain kinds of military force, increases in certain kinds of military force, qualitative changes in weaponry, different modes of deployment, or arrangements superimposed on existing military systems."[48]

Schelling and Halperin also anticipated one of the most serious objections to arms control, "that armaments are only a reflection of existing conflicts and not a cause of them." The question of which comes first—arms races or international rivalries that prompt them—is the gravamen of the critique of arms control that was most capably mounted by the late Colin Gray. He argued that the states most in need of arms control are unlikely to reach agreement because of the underlying political differences that cause them to arm in the first place. Moreover, since it is not the weapons per se that cause war, the control of weapons is not likely to cause peace. Moreover, although Gray acknowledged the vaunted concept of "strategic stability"—the proposition that a stable nuclear balance required both sides to maintain a secure, second-strike nuclear retaliatory force—he also knew that it is meaningless unless considered in the broadest political perspective with a granular understanding of the causes of national rivalries. "Countries arm," Gray wrote, "in order to deter, to defend if they must, and sometimes to secure the assets of others, but they do not fight because they are armed." The record of arms control was a mixed bag. As the Cold War came to an end with the Soviet-American rivalry receding, the two sides reached significant agreements to limit and reduce nuclear arms. As relations soured later, however, the "golden age" of arms control came to an end and many if not most of the agreements were undone.[49]

48. Thomas Schelling and Morton Halperin, *Strategy and Arms Control* (New York, NY: The Twentieth-Century Fund, 1961), 4.

49. Colin S. Gray, *House of Cards: Why Arms Control Must Fail* (Ithaca, NY: Cornell University Press, 1992), 37. For strategic stability see, John Steinbruner "National Security and the Concept of Strategic Stability," *Journal of Conflict Resolution* 22:3 (1978): 411–28. Also, Eric S. Edelman, "Arms Control: Can Its Future be Found in its Past?," Center for Strategic and

Even during the Cold War, the idea of nuclear "strategic stability" raised questions. The notion rested on an assumption that adversaries thought about the problems of deterrence and stability in much the same way, even though different historical experiences would inevitably incline different states to think differently about how, when, and why to use nuclear weapons. Today, the search for strategic stability is challenged by a plethora of complicating geopolitical and technological factors. The emergence of new and aspiring nuclear powers like North Korea and, potentially, Iran will create new proliferation pressures and regional security dynamics. A trilateral regional nuclear competition in South Asia among India, Pakistan, and China may create additional instability and the emergence of China as a nuclear peer could present a totally novel strategic challenge for the United States. Managing deterrence and arms control with three near-peers will be an enormously complicated question. Moreover, new technologies in the areas of cyberwarfare, artificial intelligence, and additive manufacturing will raise even more questions about the prospects for nuclear deterrence to survive the decade without the potential use of these weapons in anger for the first time since 1945.[50]

Under these circumstances the study of nuclear strategy is likely to make a comeback from the neglect into which it fell after the Cold War ended. Undoubtedly, new concepts, new ideas, and new strategies will be called for. But those who will be called upon to face up to these novel challenges could do worse than to study the work of those who had to contend with the consequences of nuclear weapons when the tasks ahead seemed fresh and new.

Budgetary Assessments, September 17, 2021 located at https://csbaonline.org/research/publications/arms-control-can-its-future-be-found-in-its-past-1/publication/1.

50. Colin Gray, "Strategic Stability Reconsidered," *Daedalus* 109:4 (1980): 135–54; Hal Brands, "U.S. Isn't Ready for Nuclear Rivalry with China and Russia," *Bloomberg Opinion*, January 30, 2022.

CHAPTER 28

The Elusive Nature of Nuclear Strategy

Francis J. Gavin

Assessing the makers of nuclear strategy presents at least three challenges. First, applying a strategic lens to nuclear weapons generates difficulties and dilemmas. Strategy, in a narrow sense, involves employing force or the threat of force to achieve military goals on the battlefield. Since the start of the nuclear age, and certainly since thermonuclear weapons were developed, any rational, *strategic*, use of the bomb has remained largely elusive. Short of a threat to a state's survival, launching nuclear weapons against an adversary has seemed incredible. History has borne this out; nuclear weapons have not been employed in battle since their only use over eight decades ago, soon after they were first developed, when the United States dropped two atomic weapons against Japan. In fact, the likelihood of nuclear use appears to have waned considerably in the years since 1945.

The second puzzle involves the makers of nuclear strategy. Identifying the true makers is difficult. On the one hand, the nuclear revolution generated an extraordinary community of intellectuals, many in the United States, working in major universities and think tanks like RAND. They produced the foundations of a new academic field—security studies—which flourished after World War II and retains remarkable prestige and following to this day. Strangly, however, much of this academic work—while impressive in its own right—was often disconnected from how policymakers thought about and deployed nuclear weapons to advance America's interest in the world. This is especially surprising given that, since its founding, the mission of security studies has been predicated on helping decision-makers understand the consequences of nuclear weapons on world politics.

This leads to a third dilemma. While nuclear weapons are difficult to employ for narrow strategic purposes, they have profound consequences for a state's *grand strategy*—its approach to generating security and advancing its political interests. In other words, regardless of whether their use on the battlefield is credible, nuclear weapons have played a central role in shaping world politics. The line between strategy and grand strategy is not always clear; the distinction, however, is important. Viewing nuclear weapons primarily through a narrow strategic frame, or simply as a military tool, has led some in the nuclear strategy community to misunderstand the origins and consequences of important US nuclear policies, from its force posture to a grand strategy of inhibition.

This chapter will examine the dilemmas of nuclear strategy in three sections. First, I will explore why locating the makers of nuclear strategy is challenging. Second, I will identify the core questions surrounding nuclear weapons, statecraft, and world politics with which any making of nuclear strategy must wrestle. Finally, I will analyze how understanding nuclear weapons through the lens of strategy—as opposed to grand strategy—generates different and at times contrasting insights. In particular, I will focus on the American case by evaluating how emphasizing a bedrock concern of many US nuclear strategists— achieving strategic stability—often led to misunderstandings of the role the bomb plays in American grand strategy.

I

The first question surrounding the making of nuclear strategy is an imposing one: How can we identify and then analyze a nuclear strategy? Atomic weapons were only deployed twice, and their use by the United States against Japan in August 1945 generated a difficult debate. Many questioned whether the atomic bombings of Hiroshima and Nagasaki provided any strategic benefit, or rather, a strategic benefit worth the enormous ethical cost of using weapons of mass slaughter. President Harry S. Truman appeared shocked by the damage caused by the first two bombs and moved to prevent their further use. Historians later questioned the rationale behind the decision to use atomic weapons against Japan. Would other strategies, from continued blockade and conventional bombing to invasion, have been preferable? Should the United States have relaxed its demands for unconditional surrender from Japan? Was the bomb used more to threaten a future adversary, such as the Soviet Union, than to defeat a current one, Japan? Scholars still debate these questions.

More consequentially for understanding strategy, nuclear weapons have never again been detonated in war since August 1945. Since that time, there have been many competing ideas and policies for what makes for the best nuclear strategy. It is not entirely clear, however, how to evaluate a military strategy if it has never been used in a conflict. Imagine if the German idea of blitzkrieg or Corbett's naval principles had never been implemented during a war; how would we assess their utility or value versus other strategies? It is unlikely we would we have ever discussed these insights and innovations if they had remained strategies only on paper and were never tested in combat. Strategy is an applied field, or as Bernard Brodie, one of the fathers of nuclear strategy, argued, "strategic thinking," or "theory" if one prefers, is nothing if not pragmatic. Strategy is a "how to do it" study, a guide for accomplishing something and doing it efficiently. The question that matters in strategy—as in many other branches of politics—is, will the idea work? More specifically, will it be likely to work under the precise and inevitably special circumstances under which it will next be tested?[1] It is not obvious that we've ever been able to answer Brodie's questions when it comes to nuclear strategy.

Furthermore, the best strategies allow for those implementing them to innovate and adapt after a conflict begins; few strategies remain untouched by the complex and unexpected realities of battle. Many nuclear strategies—especially those that focus on so-called limited options or signaling to an adversary—were based on speculation about how an atomic war would unfold, but the truth is, we have no idea what would happen after a nuclear detonation. All these factors make identifying, to say nothing of evaluating, nuclear strategy difficult. As Sir Lawrence Freedman wrote in his 1986 piece on nuclear strategy:

> The study of nuclear strategy is therefore the study of the nonuse of these weapons. Suppositions about their actual employment in combat may influence their peacetime role, but historical experience provides minimal guidance.[2]

---

1. Bernard Brodie, "Why Were We So (Strategically) Wrong?," *Foreign Policy* 5 (1971): 151–61.

2. Lawrence Freedman, "The First Two Generations of Nuclear Strategists," *Makers of Modern Strategy from Machiavelli to the Nuclear Age*, in Peter Paret, ed. (Princeton, NJ: Princeton University Press, 1986), 735.

Of course, the overwhelming consensus holds that the primary goal of most nuclear strategies is deterrence, that is, preventing something from happening. The actual use of nuclear weapons in such a scenario would mean that the strategy had failed, meaning we can only evaluate the strategy of deterrence ex post. If nothing happens, if a nuclear exchange or larger conflict is avoided, it *might* mean the strategy of deterrence succeeded. Or nuclear deterrence might be only partly or not at all responsible for the absence of war. Nuclear deterrence may have prevented a Soviet invasion of Western Europe during the Cold War, for example, but we can never prove it. In a counterfactual world where nuclear weapons never existed, the Soviets may not have wanted to invade or may have been prevented by factors unrelated to the bomb.

This does not mean nuclear strategy does not exist or is not consequential. People obviously thought in sophisticated ways about how nuclear weapons could best be used to achieve strategic goals. But the unique characteristics of nuclear weapons make both identifying the makers and assessing the content of nuclear strategy far different, and more difficult, than other elements of strategy. For example, which person, institution, or activity determines what the nuclear strategy of a particular state is, and in the absence of nuclear use, how can we assess whether it is working as intended? The case of American nuclear strategy during the Cold War is both instructive and important. Not only did the United States develop atomic weapons first and become the only country to detonate them against an enemy, it also, perhaps more than any other state, appeared to emphasize the role of nuclear weapons as a tool to protect its interests and accomplish its goals in the world.

Who was responsible for crafting, implementing, and communicating American nuclear strategy during the Cold War? There are at least four different sources. The first and most studied source is intellectual/scholarly, or what important thinkers and strategists said about the bomb and its uses. The second set of sources might be thought of as rhetorical/declaratory, or what major US government officials said, publicly and privately, about the role of nuclear weapons in American strategy. The third source to explore is operational: what nuclear weapons systems are developed and acquired, placed where and in which configurations, and under what plans for use. The fourth source of nuclear strategy consists of the views on nuclear weapons held by the individual who mattered most, the President of the United States. Depending how you define what nuclear strategy is, there is a case for each of these sources being the key driver. And while there are overlaps and connections, the meaning and consequences of these four often cut in different directions.

If you were to answer the question—"Who is the maker of nuclear strategy?"—by looking at university syllabi or academic journals, your answer might focus on the group of intellectuals from leading American research universities and think tanks like the RAND corporation. This extraordinary collection of intellectual firepower was multidisciplinary, including economists, historians, political scientists, lawyers, engineers, and natural scientists, and involved such renowned figures as Bernard Brodie, Roger Fisher, Richard Garwin, Herman Khan, Henry Kissinger, Thomas Schelling, Albert Wohlstetter, and Herbert York. Their intense debates and discussions were often sophisticated and meant to influence policy. Many served in or had close connections with the United States government. This first generation trained and influenced others and successfully created the sub-field of security studies, as well as the founding of important university research centers at top institutions like Harvard, MIT, and Stanford. These intellectuals certainly helped shape elite opinion and public debate.

There are robust studies of this group, labelled by Fred Kaplan as the "wizards of Armageddon," as well as scores of books and articles containing their arguments.[3] It should not be surprising that scholars and strategists put themselves and others like them at the center of the story when trying to identify the makers of modern strategy. There is reason to question, however, the actual influence this group had. Many of their theories and predictions were often at odds with more consequential, if less apparent, makers of nuclear strategy.[4]

The second source of nuclear strategy might be called rhetorical and declaratory. High-level national security officials have, from time to time, produced documents and given speeches laying out their views on how nuclear weapons advance American interests. Often, these statements have been meant to signal important changes in nuclear strategy. Key examples include US Secretary of State John Foster Dulles's so called "massive retaliation" remarks to the Council on Foreign Relations in 1954, Secretary of Defense Robert McNamara's "no cities" doctrine laid out in a speech in 1962, and Secretary of Defense Harold Brown's August 1980 address spelling out the "countervailing"

3. Fred M. Kaplan, *The Wizards of Armageddon* (New York, NY: Simon and Schuster, 1983).

4. Bruce Kuklick, *Blind Oracles: Intellectuals and War from Kennan to Kissinger* (Princeton, NJ: Princeton University Press, 2006).

strategy.[5] In more recent years, the congressionally mandated Nuclear Posture Review has been meant to establish US nuclear policy, strategy, capabilities, and force posture.

These speeches and documents, however, present certain challenges. First, government officials often used them to signal and satisfy multiple audiences— potential adversaries, allies, the US Congress, the national security bureaucracy, as well as the larger public. Different audiences took different meanings from these declarations, as was often intended. More importantly, it was not always clear that these rhetorical shifts reflected equivalent changes in the third source of nuclear strategy—operational strategy or nuclear posture. In other words, what key decision-makers said or wrote about their nuclear policies was not always reflected in the realities of what types of weapons the United States possessed, how they were deployed and managed, and what the plans for their use were if a war broke out. While the historical record on nuclear posture is often highly classified, it seems that major rhetorical shifts in strategy were not always matched by concurrent changes in weapons procurement and placement or targeting. There were few if any significant changes in US nuclear targeting or plans for use as a result of McNamara's various speeches and documents laying out the so-called strategy of "flexible response," for example.[6]

It can be argued that the most important "maker" of nuclear strategy was, in many ways, the most elusive—the various American presidents during the nuclear era. Under the command-and-control arrangements established in the United States, sole authority for the decision to use nuclear weapons lies in the hands of the Chief Executive. How have presidents thought about nuclear weapons since 1945? The evidence is mixed. Some presidents, like Eisenhower, Kennedy, Carter, and Nixon, engaged in the details surrounding nuclear strategy; Truman, Johnson, and Reagan seemed less hands on. How they thought about nuclear use, however, is harder to discern. Reading declassified documents, one could make a case that presidents such as Eisenhower, Kennedy,

5. John Foster Dulles, "Massive Retaliation," Speech before the Council on Foreign Relations, January 12, 1954, locaged at https://www.airforcemag.com/PDF/MagazineArchive/Documents/2013/September%202013/0913keeperfull.pdf; Robert McNamara, "No Cities," Speech before the University of Michigan, July 9, 1962, located at https://pages.ucsd.edu/~bslantchev/courses/nss/documents/mcnamara-no-cities.html. Harold Brown, "Countervailing Strategy," Speech before the US Naval War College, August 20, 1980.

6. Francis J. Gavin, "The Myth of Flexible Response: United States Strategy in Europe during the 1960s," *The International History Review* 23:4 (2001): 847–75.

and Nixon seriously considered the circumstances under which they might be forced to use nuclear weapons and how that process might unfold. Yet you can look at other documents involving these same presidents and their advisors and conclude that they would never have made the decision to employ the bomb. Scholars disagree on how close any president came to nuclear use.

Further complicating matters is that there were strong incentives for the nation's leader to keep various audiences, even their closest advisors, guessing as to their true intentions regarding nuclear weapons. Generating uncertainty about what the President of the United States might do in certain circumstances was thought to enhance deterrence. What is not in doubt is that no president relished the thought of using the bomb, and short of a threat to the survival of the American homeland (and perhaps not even then), it is reasonable to wonder how likely and in what circumstances the presidents who served in the thermonuclear age would have authorized the use of nuclear weapons.

Which of these four sources, alone or in combination, should we focus on to identify and assess by whom and how American nuclear strategy was made during the Cold War? Given that nuclear weapons were never used on the battlefield after August 1945, it is hard to say. Nuclear strategists developed elaborate, sophisticated theories, but how influential they were in determining what kinds of weapons were acquired and how they were deployed and targeted remains uncertain. Top officials often offered public and written explanations on nuclear strategy, though these documents were sometimes in tension with what we now know about the nation's operational posture. After Truman dropped atom bombs on Japan in August 1945, the thoughts and beliefs and the primary decision-maker, the president, remained largely in his private thoughts, never tested. Nuclear strategy exists and matters, but identifying its source and parameters is elusive.

II

Regardless of which person, group, or institution, alone or in combination, "made" American nuclear strategy, they all had to contend with several fundamental and recurring questions that were, in many ways, unique to nuclear weapons. The scholarly literature on nuclear strategy—which understandably, if unfortunately, focuses primarily on the American experience—is impressive, often contentious, and enormous. Despite its complexity and breadth, most of it can be boiled down into arguments and debates over four simple and persistent questions.

The first question is technological. How does the technology behind nuclear weapons work, how has it changed over time, and how do these technological issues shape nuclear strategy? There has been far more technological change, with greater political consequences, surrounding the science and engineering of nuclear weapons than is often recognized. Second, what is the strategic utility of nuclear weapons? In other words, as a tool of a state's strategy and statecraft, what can nuclear weapons accomplish and what are they unable to do? Third, who has the bomb and why (and why not)? Both the number of nuclear weapons states—and the efforts the United States has made to keep that number low—would have surprised early nuclear strategists. Fourth, are nuclear weapons "good or bad," at least in terms of strategy, grand strategy, and international security? In other words, have the world and the United States been better off for their creation, or would certain states or even the world be better off without them? Relatedly, can a nuclear strategy capture the benefits of atomic weapons while minimizing, if not eliminating, their risks and downsides?

On the first question, there are excellent primers describing the fundamental technology surrounding nuclear weapons, involving nuclear science and engineering.[7] Four points are worth highlighting for thinking about how evolving technology affects the making of nuclear strategy.

First, the history of early efforts to develop atomic weapons, and in particular, the US-led Manhattan project, is extraordinary. The creation of atomic bombs was the result of a massive top-secret effort, shaped in large measure by scientists who had fled Fascist Europe, and whose outcome was not inevitable and required grand strategic tradeoffs.[8] To an extent rarely recognized, the American effort to develop, build, improve, and secure nuclear weapons has had a profound effect on how science and technology operates in the United States to this day. The effort transformed institutions ranging from research universities to the intelligence community. It has also reshaped our norms and practices surrounding secrecy and national security.

Second, it is important to highlight the difference between the early atomic weapons developed by the United States for use against Japan and the

7. See Jeremy Bernstein, *One Physicist's Guide to Nuclear Weapons: A Global Perspective* (Bristol: IOP Publishing, 2016); Wisconsin Project on Nuclear Arms Control, "Nuclear Weapons Primer," located at https://www.wisconsinproject.org/nuclear-weapons/.

8. Richard Rhodes, *The Making of the Atomic Bomb* (New York, NY: Simon & Schuster, 1988).

thermonuclear weapons created by the United States and the Soviet Union in the 1950s, and developed by other nuclear powers in the following years. The two bombs dropped on Hiroshima and Nagasaki in August 1945 generated catastrophic damage, immediately killing 110–220,000 people. The so-called Mike Shot detonated by the United States in November 1952 was estimated to be 1,000 times more powerful than the bombs used against Japan. As horrific as fission bombs were, there were still those who believed they might have some military utility in battle. The explosive power of hydrogen bombs, however, is in a completely different category, with the ability to generate unthinkable damage. A full-scale thermonuclear war, in addition to potentially killing tens of millions through blast, radiation, and fire, could cripple societies' ability to function. The effects of a large-scale thermonuclear exchange would have unknown but potentially civilization-crippling effects on the earth's environment and atmosphere. The issue that Robert Jervis, building on Bernard Brodie, termed "conventionalization," or thinking about atomic weapons as simply bigger bombs, began to lessen with the thermonuclear revolution.[9] Hydrogen bombs are unlike any other weapon ever created.

Third, nuclear bombs are a relatively old technology, and how to build one is fairly well known, accessible, and within the abilities of even modestly competent states. That said, there has been enormous expenditure and innovation surrounding what might be thought of as the nuclear weapons complex— the institutions and infrastructure needed to build, control, and deliver nuclear weapons or anticipate and potentially defend against a nuclear attack. There have been profound technological changes in the ability to delivery nuclear weapons at increased distances, speed, and accuracy. There have been similar advances in the ability to defend against missiles and aircraft, track and identify an adversary's weapons and delivery systems, and evade detection. Similar investments have also been made in the safety and control of nuclear weapons, as well as command, communications, and intelligence. While there remains an argument over how much political and military advantage these technological changes provide, they all require enormous financial and engineering/ scientific investment and are available only to the most advanced, innovative states.

This leads to a fourth point—profound shifts in technology and changes in the different states' nuclear weapons complexes suggest that it makes sense to

9. Robert Jervis, *The Meaning of the Nuclear Revolution: Statecraft and the Prospect of Armageddon* (Ithaca, NY: Cornell University Press 1989).

divide the nuclear age into different periods. The late-1950s and early-1960s was a key pivot point, when the development of two technologies—intercontinental ballistic missiles (ICBMs) and satellites—fundamentally altered the politics of nuclear weapons. These technologies had cross-cutting consequences. ICBMs allowed the catastrophic devastation of thermonuclear weapons to be delivered to anywhere on the globe in less than an hour, compressing time and eliminating geographic constraints. Satellites allowed a state to better see an adversary's capabilities and potentially recognize a mobilization or preparation for an attack, reducing the danger of surprise attack. A second pivot point came in the late-1970s and early-1980s, as massive investments in qualitative and counterforce capabilities—increased accuracy, speed, miniaturization, stealth, and mobility—dramatically altered the nuclear balance. The United States invested large efforts into building sophisticated command, control, communications, and intelligence capabilities while also constructing elaborate safety and security procedures. We could be entering a third pivot during the 2020s, as new technologies in cyber, artificial intelligence and machine-learning, nano-technology, hypersonics, and additive manufacturing, among other changes, could once again shake up the nuclear weapons complex and the strategies surrounding it.

The key point is that there is an interactive, feedback loop between the development of new technologies and state strategies and grand strategies. Different strategies—and indeed, different grand strategies—demand different technologies, and different technologies allow for different strategies. A state whose goal is simply to deter an invasion or nuclear attack upon itself from a contiguous neighbor might have minimal technical requirements. If some element of its nuclear forces and its ability to survive and respond to an attack is secure, fairly basic nuclear forces and technology might suffice. On the other hand, a more ambitious nuclear strategy might require more sophisticated, advanced forces. The United States had grand strategic ambitions—namely, defending far-flung allies while also keeping them non-nuclear—that arguably required the possession of forces that went well beyond what was needed for simple mutual nuclear deterrence. These grand strategic requirements drove the development of preemptive capabilities—in other words, nuclear forces that could target and destroy the nuclear forces of other states before they were launched. That preemptive mission demanded more accuracy and better intelligence, as well as measures to protect American forces and even defend against a nuclear attack. Controversially, such a strategy also reserved the right to launch nuclear weapons first.

At times, novel technologies emerged that allowed for more expansive grand strategic aims, and at other times, grand strategic needs drove the technological process. The key is to understand that when we speak of nuclear technology, we need to analyze capabilities that go well beyond the bombs themselves, and include a wide range of complex, interconnected systems. These technologies did not remain the same for long, and the nuclear complex evolved and continues to evolve in dynamic and often unexpected ways, with important consequences for both strategy and grand strategy.

III

How might nuclear weapons be used to advance a nation's strategy? The United States originally developed atomic weapons in order to defeat Germany during the Second World War. The war in Europe ended before the bomb was complete, but with the war in the Pacific still ongoing, focus shifted to use against Japan. The decision to drop atomic weapons on the cities of Hiroshima and Nagasaki in August 1945 generated controversial questions that persist to this day.

In the aftermath of World War II, debates emerged in the United States over the strategic purposes of nuclear weapons moving forward. The debates fell into four broad categories.

First, there were those that believed the bomb could be used like any other weapon, such as a tank or a battleship, to defeat the enemy on the battlefield. In other words, nuclear weapons were seen as simply bigger bombs, integrated into war plans with other weapons and military forces. The utility of nuclear weapons was seen as especially important given the primary military challenge the United States faced in Europe during the Cold War. After the end of the Second World War, the United States had demobilized most of its military and redeployed the overwhelming part of its forces back home (and the few that remained in Europe were focused on policing the occupation of the American zone in Germany). The countries of Western Europe, ravaged by the war, were unable to quickly rebuild their forces and thus lay vulnerable to a Soviet conventional onslaught. The country with the greatest potential military power was a defeated, disgraced, and divided Germany, with no one eager to see it rebuild an independent military. To defend Europe under these trying strategic circumstances, early US military plans focused on aerial atomic bombardment of Russian forces, cities, and industrial capabilities to win a war against the Soviet Union.

The use of nuclear weapons as "bigger bombs" was problematic from the start. Ironically, given their devastating power, it was not clear that an atomic bombardment could actually defeat what was seen as a Soviet colossus whose territory covered eleven time zones. Furthermore, before the advent of longer-range bombers and intercontinental missiles, the United States would need bases in or near Europe—in the United Kingdom or North Africa—to deliver atomic bombs; yet it was not always certain these countries would allow such attacks from their territories if a war broke out. It was also impractical to use atomic bombs if the Soviet Union invaded Western Europe, as the bombs might devastate the very territories the United States and its allies sought to defend or liberate. And there was the growing sense that using atomic weapons generated deep moral challenges.

These moral considerations informed the second view—that the destructive power of nuclear forces and the misery they would bring on civilian populations and societies made them militarily unusable. For some, this meant that nuclear disarmament was the answer.[10] Sometimes this manifested itself through civil society efforts, such as the worldwide, grassroots effort to ban the testing of nuclear weapons in the atmosphere. Even at the highest levels of American government, the idea of international oversight of atomic weapons was explored, first in the Acheson-Lilienthal and Baruch plans of 1946. Nuclear disarmament enjoyed support from important segments of both American and global public opinion, even if many top-level American policymakers remained skeptical.

Was there a way to extract strategic benefits from nuclear weapons while lessening the practical and moral concerns that burdened nuclear use? The third strategic purpose of nuclear weapons—deterrence—over time became the centerpiece of American nuclear strategy and was emulated by other nuclear weapons states. Nuclear weapons could be used to discourage an adversary from taking an action, such as invading Western Europe, out of fear of the consequences generated by a nuclear response. At the start of the nuclear age, the idea of deterring large-scale war was a powerful and important consideration. After all, the first part of the twentieth century had been dominated by deadly world wars started and largely fought in Europe. Most of modern history had been shaped by invasion and conquest. Nuclear deterrence promised

10. Lawrence S. Wittner, *The Struggle against the Bomb: One World or None: A History of the World Nuclear Disarmament Movement through 1953* (Stanford, CA: Stanford University Press, 1993).

to reduce, if not eliminate, this scourge. What adversary would risk the unimaginable damage to their invading forces or home country by attempting to conquer or destroy another state?

Deterrence, over time, came to be seen as the most important strategic function of nuclear weapons.[11] Questions and debates about specific elements of the strategy, however, soon followed. Which actors, scenarios, and situations might nuclear weapons deter, and where, when, and against whom would nuclear deterrence be less relevant? Was the power to deter with atomic weapons narrow—for example, persuading an adversary not to launch a nuclear strike against you—or could nuclear strategy be used to deter broader phenomena, like a purely conventional attack against far away allies you had promised to protect? Relatedly, how credible were the promises to use nuclear weapons that were the foundation of nuclear deterrence? While responding to a nuclear attack upon your soil with your own nuclear weapons might be plausible, would using nuclear weapons (and exposing your homeland to a nuclear attack) against a conventional attack on your allies be credible? Analysts wondered which steps, weapons, or deployments would strengthen a strategy of nuclear deterrence. Many of the strategic debates within the United States about nuclear strategy surrounded the question of "how much was enough" to credibly deter, especially when it involved if and how deterrence could be "extended" to non-nuclear allies.

A fourth debate emerged over whether nuclear weapons could be used for purposes beyond deterrence. Could nuclear strategies be developed that not only prevented an adversary from taking an unwanted action, but also compelled a change in their behavior or policies?[12] This was a controversial subject for a few reasons. First, many believed that nuclear coercion or compellence was not possible, and even if it was, it required strategies and forces that were dangerous and destabilizing. Second, distinguishing between which actions deterred and which compelled was often difficult and in the eye of the beholder. During the four-year crisis over the status of West Berlin between 1958 and 1962, the United States believed it was using nuclear weapons to deter the Soviet Union, whom it saw as trying to compel a change in

11. Bernard Brodie et al., *The Absolute Weapon: Atomic Power and World Order* (New York, NY: Harcourt, Brace and Company, 1954).

12. See Francis J. Gavin, *Nuclear Weapons and American Grand Strategy* (Washington, DC: Brookings Institution Press, 2020).

the situation with atomic threats.[13] The Soviets, on the other hand, may have believed that by employing nuclear threats over Berlin they were deterring Washington from changing the non-nuclear status of the Federal Republic of Germany; for the Russians, any effort to provide West Germany with access to the bomb was a coercive act. In other words, both sides believed that they were pursuing nuclear deterrence while the other side was attempting nuclear compellence.

Relatedly, a debate emerged over how nuclear weapons affected crises and whether certain types of nuclear strategies and postures would help one side or another prevail in a standoff between nuclear-armed adversaries. Which factor most shaped the outcome of a nuclear crisis: superiority in the balance of nuclear forces, resolve, or interest?

The scholarly literature has struggled with these issues. It is unclear what counts for nuclear superiority, how it should be measured, and whether it matters in a world of mutual vulnerability. Most security studies scholars have been skeptical, short of a so-called splendid first strike capability that would be difficult if not impossible to obtain, that numerical superiority would be decisive in a crisis. There is evidence, however, that some American presidents believed that the number, kind, and types of deployments of nuclear weapons could drive outcomes in the world beyond simply deterring an adversary from attacking. Moreover, it is unclear how to comparatively measure state resolve or interest ex ante. Finally—and perhaps most essentially—how should we define a nuclear crisis? Is any dispute where one or more sides possess the bomb, even if no nuclear threats are made, a nuclear crisis?[14] Or must the use of nuclear weapons, explicit or implied, be in play?

These four different views of the strategic purposes of nuclear weapons are, of course, interconnected. The credibility of a strategy of nuclear deterrence, and to a greater extent, nuclear compellence, depends upon a willingness to actually use the bomb under certain scenarios. This logic also drives those who seek disarmament. If the weapons are unusable and deterrence based on a fiction, they are an enormous waste of resources. If certain kinds of nuclear strategies make the use of nuclear weapons not only possible but also plausible, it is a dangerous situation many want to eliminate.

---

13. Marc Trachtenberg, *History and Strategy* (Princeton, NJ: Princeton University Press, 1991), 169–234.

14. Mark S. Bell and Julia Macdonald, "How to Think About Nuclear Crises," *Texas National Security Review* 2:2 (2019).

IV

What about the question of who has—and can have—the bomb? Perhaps nowhere have the predictions from past policymakers and strategists been more off the mark than on the question of who would come to possess nuclear weapons. This issue had two components. First, which states (or non-state actors) have the interest and means to develop and incorporate atomic weapons into their military strategy? Second, could any strategy, pursued by a state, international organization, or regime, inhibit actors from acquiring those weapons?

Most analysts expected that, over time, many independent nuclear weapons programs would emerge and that there was little that could be done to stop or even slow what came to be called nuclear proliferation.[15] Consider the perspective of a strategist looking at the world in 1945. Both recent and longer global political and military history had been dominated by bloody and costly imperialism, total war, invasion, and conquest. Given that the first strategic goal of any state was to avoid being destroyed or conquered, nuclear weapons—and the existential deterrence they supplied—should have been desired by almost every state in the international system. Relatedly, history has demonstrated that states compete ruthlessly for any strategic advantage to guarantee their security, especially if it involves acquiring technology that provides protection or power. The American-led effort to develop the bomb was technologically and scientifically complex, but history offered few examples of such an appealing and powerful technology remaining secret and out of the hands of competitors. Nor were efforts by the creator of a new technology to prevent others from copying it successful over the long run. Efforts to limit the spread of military technology to other states was fruitless at best and counterproductive at worst.

Given such circumstances, the analyst in 1945 might have predicted that the number of nuclear weapons states would increase dramatically over time and that there was little the United States could or would do to prevent it. The early years of the nuclear age bore this out. The Soviet Union developed the bomb in 1949, the United Kingdom in 1952, and France in 1960. By the beginning of the 1960s, a wide range of countries, from Australia to Sweden, had active nuclear programs or were exploring nuclear weapons capabilities. The United

---

15. Kenneth Waltz, *The Spread of Nuclear Weapons: More May Be Better* (London: International Institute for Strategic Studies, 1981).

States had expressed an interest in limiting the spread of nuclear weapons, though its policies were often inconsistent. Any reasonable forecast of nuclear proliferation in 1961, focusing both on a state's strategic desire for the bomb and its ability to acquire one, would have predicted twenty, forty, or even sixty nuclear weapons states by the start of the twenty-first century. Few would have suggested there was much the United States, or even the international community, could do to inhibit proliferation.

Contrary to most predictions, the pace of nuclear proliferation slowed considerably in the ensuing decades. The United States made inhibiting the spread of independent nuclear weapons programs a core element of its grand strategy, employing a number of tools, including nuclear strategy, to achieve this goal.[16] This was not the only reason the number of nuclear weapons states in the world stayed, to everyone's surprise, in the single digits. Nuclear weapons were expensive and difficult to build. They had less strategic utility for many of the challenges states have faced over the last half-century, and in fact, may have generated unwanted vulnerabilities in a world where the threat of invasion and conquest appeared to shrink. American's grand strategy of inhibition, however, was a crucial and decisive factor.

The United States had hoped to keep the number of nuclear weapons states low from the beginning of the nuclear age. But American strategists did not think the goal of inhibition was worth sacrificing its other grand strategic goals, such as containing the Soviets and winning over allies. As America's experience with France in the 1950s demonstrated, half-hearted efforts to inhibit proliferation were not only unlikely to succeed; they also alienated friends and allies. If nuclear proliferation was inevitable, perhaps the right strategy was to get ahead of the curve and provide nuclear assistance and even weapons to allies in the struggle against the Soviet Union. High level officials even suggested providing nuclear aid to India and Japan. Most controversial were those who recommended bringing West Germany closer to nuclear decision-making. How could the United States accept a nuclear Great Britain and France, they asked, while not allowing loyal ally West Germany access to the bomb? The uncertainty around the German nuclear question, however, was a driving force behind Khrushchev's aggressiveness in the late-1950s and early-1960s.

Instead of remaining passive or even supporting proliferation, American grand strategy redoubled its focus on inhibition in the early and mid-1960s

---

16. Francis Gavin, "Strategies of Inhibition: US Grand Strategy, the Nuclear Revolution, and Nonproliferation," *International Security* 40:1 (2015), 9–46.

and has maintained it ever since. After the Cuban Missile Crisis in 1962 and China's detonation of a nuclear device in 1964, the shared sense of responsibility and national interest caused the superpowers to put aside their geopolitical and ideological competition to collude on nuclear nonproliferation. The international system appeared to be at a nuclear "tipping point": in the absence of action, dozens of states might acquire the bomb in the years following. The United States recognized that the Soviet Union's (and America's own allies') concerns about West Germany getting nuclear weapons were legitimate, while also understanding that West Germany could not (as Germany had been in the interwar period) be singled out. The United States incorporated a number of strategic tools to satisfy its grand strategy goal of inhibition, including cooperating with its bitter adversary, the Soviet Union, to limit the spread of nuclear weapons. Coercion and threats of abandonment were explored. International norms surrounding nonproliferation were supported, and arms control arrangements such as the Partial Test Ban Treaty and the Nuclear Nonproliferation Treaty were prioritized. Security guarantees to non-nuclear states were strengthened.

Nuclear strategy was also an important tool in the larger grand strategy of inhibition. Despite what appeared to be the inevitable emergence of mutual vulnerability between the Soviet Union and the United States—a condition where no first strike of nuclear weapons would be successful enough to avoid being annihilated by a devastating response—the United States still refused to close off potential paths to primacy.[17] The United States eschewed a no-first use policy, since its security guarantees were promises to use its nuclear weapons on behalf of allies who were attacked. In order to make those strategies credible, US nuclear force posture consisted of weapons, deployments, and plans of use that sought what was euphemistically called "damage limitation," that is, an ability to come out of a nuclear war better off than an adversary. There were other reasons for the United States to embrace forward-leaning nuclear strategies, including a belief that certain postures might allow it to prevail in a nuclear crisis with the Soviets (even as it, ironically, cooperated with the Soviets on inhibition). At heart, however, the drive to acquire nuclear weapons of a certain sort—more accurate, speedy, and stealthy—and place them in strategies that did not eliminate the possibility of using nuclear weapons first and targeting an adversary's nuclear

---

17. Austin Long and Brendan Rittenhouse Green, "Stalking the Secure Second Strike: Intelligence, Counterforce, and Nuclear Strategy," *Journal of Strategic Studies* 38:1–2 (2015): 38–73.

forces was shaped by a desire to make the security guarantees that helped inhibit nuclear spread more credible.

V

Finally, are nuclear weapons good or bad? Typically, a weapon either demonstrates battlefield utility that helps an actor achieve military victory or it does not. As we have seen, nuclear weapons have limited battlefield utility, and in many if not most cases, using them in war would indicate a profound failure of strategy. A better question might be—how do nuclear weapons affect the strategic environment and grand strategic circumstances of major states? There are two ways of getting at this. First, how have nuclear weapons influenced international security and world politics? Have they made the world more stable and safer than in the past? Second, how have nuclear weapons affected the strategic and grand strategic calculations of individual states, and in particular, the United States? Have nuclear weapons helped advance America's interests and goals?

Globally, it is hard to deny that nuclear weapons have played an important, perhaps even a decisive role in the near disappearance of world wars and the marked decrease in wars of conquest. Correlation is obviously not causation. There could be many reasons for the fading of fully mobilized total war, ranging from changes in norms to economic interdependence to shifting demographics. Furthermore, wars have continued in the nuclear age, and civil wars have been especially deadly. But while it cannot be proven, nuclear weapons and nuclear deterrence likely played a role in decreasing massive invasions and wars of conquest. Given that there had been two world wars that had killed tens of millions in the three decades before the first atomic bomb, as well as unbridled imperial conquest in the years before the world wars, this was not an outcome many expected.

The role of nuclear weapons in reducing if not eliminating total world war is obviously a desirable outcome. That said, this so-called long peace has been accomplished under the shadow of a terrifying fear and thinking about the unthinkable—using nuclear weapons should deterrence fail. It is difficult to calculate the hidden and not-so-hidden damage of a world order premised upon the possible use of catastrophic, murderous weapons. There is the lesser but not insignificant cost of making a strategic commitment to use nuclear weapons that may not be credible. Furthermore, the global nuclear order that emerged in the later part of the twentieth century is inherently unfair, a system that allows certain states to possess nuclear weapons while preventing most other states from obtaining the same privilege. It is fair to ask whether this system, based upon nuclear deterrence and nonproliferation, in the long run can withstand the inherent moral dilemmas and political inequities.

Have nuclear weapons improved the strategic and grand strategic circumstances of individual states? Another way to think about this question is to ask whether the country in question would have achieved its grand strategic interests more easily in a world without nuclear weapons. Ironically, this improved security environment has, arguably, diminished the whole practice of making strategy (or at least military strategy) in many medium and small powers. With many types of war on the decline, strategy rarely occupies the thinking of the most influential thinkers or policymakers in countries like it once did, particularly in countries like Germany or Japan, to say nothing of the Netherlands, Brazil, or Indonesia. For the major powers, however, nuclear weapons have had a profound and not always welcome effect on making strategy and especially grand strategy.

It is especially interesting to apply this question to the United States. Nuclear weapons helped solve a difficult strategic problem that confronted the United States during the Cold War—how to deter and, if necessary, defend against attacks on Western Europe and East Asia, facing an adversary with superior conventional military capabilities, without making conventional military commitments whose costs may have been prohibitive as well as unpopular with the American public. Extending America's nuclear umbrella to allies in Europe and East Asia also provided a compelling organizing principle for what became effective, long-lasting alliances.

On the other hand, a world with nuclear weapons often put the United States at a grand strategic disadvantage. After the Second World War, the United States possessed historically unparalleled economic, conventional military, and soft power. In a non-nuclear world, there would have been few constraints on America's freedom of action (including, ironically, the freedom to return to its traditionally isolationist posture). The extraordinary deterrent power of nuclear weapons meant that countries with far less conventional, economic, or soft power—but possessing nuclear weapons—could affect how the United States behaved. In some ways, the atomic bomb is a weapon of the weak, allowing a state with few other forms of projectile power but with nuclear weapons to punch above its weight in the international system. Few Americans would give much thought about the strategic goals North Korea, for example, nor worry about Pakistan as much, in a non-nuclear world.

Nuclear weapons and the ability to deliver them from far distances always exposed the United States to a level of existential vulnerability that it had rarely experienced since the early nineteenth century.

In the American case, a nuclearized world both expanded and constrained strategic options, allowing it to defend exposed allies while opening itself up to vulnerabilities and having its other forms of power minimized or cancelled out by others possessing the bomb. Much of American grand strategy has been driven by efforts to capture the strategic benefits of nuclear weapons while escaping their constraints.

VI

Nuclear weapons thus present a dilemma for strategy. According to Joshua Rovner, strategy is a state's *theory of victory*.[18] Nuclear weapons are terrible instruments to achieve that goal. In a nuclearized world, there is unlikely to be a strategic objective worth risking a nuclear response on your own territory nor the moral outrage if used against a non-nuclear state. Even absent mutual vulnerability, the catastrophic destruction wrought by nuclear weapons rend them ethically and strategically useless in most military circumstances. The major strategic use of nuclear weapons, ironically, is to prevent their use. To achieve that goal—nuclear deterrence—a state does not need expansive forces or sophisticated strategies. Moreover, given that nuclear weapons reduced if not eliminated the fear of invasion and conquest, other nuclear weapons states could be sanguine about the prospect of other state's acquiring nuclear weapons.

The blunting of strategy, however, did not eliminate a state's goals or interests in the world. States still need and must pursue a grand strategy, which, according to Rovner, is a state's *theory of security*. Even in normal circumstances, a state's military strategy can be at odds with its grand strategy; history contains numerous episodes where military victory does not necessarily increase a state's security.[19] Nuclear weapons, by precluding the possibility of military victory, present a particular challenge to a state's grand strategy.

This tension can be found within the nuclear strategy community in the United States. Led initially by such intellectual giants as Bernard Brodie—who

18. Joshua Rovner, "Was There a Nuclear Revolution? Strategy, Grand Strategy, and the Ultimate Weapon," *War on the Rocks*, March 6, 2018.

19. French support of the American Revolution resulted in a military victory against Britain but also helped bankrupt the French state and usher in the French Revolution.

argued that nuclear weapons meant that the whole point of military strategy was no longer to "win wars" but to "avert them"—and Thomas Schelling, and followed by leading international relations theorists such as Kenneth Waltz and Robert Jervis, strategists argued that nuclear strategy could and should be built around the core idea that atomic weapons served no other purpose than to deter war.[20] While a precise definition remains elusive, this was roughly what people meant when they used the term "strategic stability."

How could strategic stability be established? In a nuclear competition between two adversaries, once both sides achieved mutual vulnerability or second-strike survivability, attacking the other became pointless, as there were no political objectives worth risking a catastrophic nuclear response against your territory. War would be avoided. While the strategic logic behind this reasoning was powerful, several important questions remained unanswered.

First, what level and types of forces, deployed in what strategies, were required to achieve mutual deterrence? Did you need a significant number of forces to survive a first-strike, or would only a handful of weapons be enough? Second, some advocates believed that mutual vulnerability would emerge naturally, since as states developed their ability to deliver the bomb, defending against a nuclear attack would become close to impossible. Others thought that achieving second strike vulnerability was harder, that the nuclear balance was sensitive to change, and that without political intervention like arms control, countries would engage in expensive and potentially dangerous arms races. Based on certain readings of past crises that led to war, such as the July 1914 crisis in Europe and both Japan and Germany's surprise attacks against the United States and the Soviet Union in 1941, many analysts believed forces had to be mutually constrained to avoid temptations to launch a first strike or to inadvertently escalate a conflict to a full-scale nuclear exchange.

Third, which actions by an adversary could various nuclear strategies deter? Was nuclear deterrence limited to preventing a nuclear attack from an adversary on your homeland, or would it also deter large-scale conventional attacks? If nuclear deterrence only applied to preventing atomic attacks, might the so-called stability-instability paradox make conventional war more likely? Could nuclear strategies be developed that deter attacks by proxies? Were there

---

20. See Brodie et al., *The Absolute Weapon*, 76; Thomas Schelling, "Nuclear Strategy in the Berlin Crisis," July 5, 1961, *Foreign Relations of the United States, 1961–1963*, Volume XIV, available at https://history.state.gov/historicaldocuments/frus1961-63v14/d56; Waltz, *The Spread of Nuclear Weapons*; Jervis, *The Meaning of the Nuclear Revolution*.

nuclear strategies that could deter nuclear, or even conventional attacks against a state's allies? Efforts to "extend" deterrence or expand the range of activities and actors that could be protected by nuclear deterrence became the focus of the strategic community.

There was an even larger, unresolved issue, however—the goal of achieving strategic stability through nuclear strategy appeared to work at cross purposes with America's grand strategic goals. America's grand strategy required the United States to do much more than simply deter a nuclear attack against its homeland. US grand strategy sought to defend far away, vulnerable allies against an adversary with tremendous conventional superiority. American grand strategy also sought to accomplish this mission without allowing those allies to acquire their own nuclear weapons. Additionally, it sought to do this without bankrupting the American economy by deploying a massive army abroad. Settling for a nuclear strategy that simply accepted strategic stability would not accomplish these grand strategic goals. A nuclear strategy that focused on primacy and preemption, however, might blunt the Soviet conventional advantage and negate the need for independent nuclear forces amongst allies, all at a cost that would not overly tax the American economy. The preferred nuclear strategy of the top strategists was at odds with what the United States needed from nuclear weapons in order to achieve its grand strategic goals.

This tension emerged as the United States sought nuclear forces, arrayed in strategies, that went well beyond what was required for strategic stability. Even after it appeared to embrace mutual vulnerability and strategic stability through the Antiballistic Missile and Strategic Arms Limitation Treaties, the United States government continued to build forces and design operational plans that emphasized accuracy, speed, and stealth, qualities more appropriate for a strategy that targeted an adversary's nuclear forces and that went first, or preemptively. Nuclear weapons and operational plans that strategists often saw as "illogical" because they threatened strategic stability were, in retrospect, likely shaped to some degree by America's ambitious grand strategic goals.

VII

Nuclear weapons challenge the very notion of strategy. It is difficult to find a strategic use for nuclear weapons, since it is hard to imagine how using them can achieve victory on the battlefield. It is even harder to definitively identify who is responsible for making nuclear strategy, such as it is.

Imagine you were a visitor from outer space, tasked with determining what the Kennedy administration's nuclear strategy was in 1961 and 1962. This would be a good test. In its short time, the Kennedy administration was confronted with a number of issues surrounding the role of nuclear weapons and faced arguably the most dangerous period in nuclear history, as the ongoing crisis with the Soviets over Berlin reached a climax in the October 1962 Cuban Missile Crisis. Where would you find US nuclear strategy and how would you evaluate it?

You might first look at the work of Thomas Schelling, the brilliant and influential strategist with close connections to the administration. In 1960 and 1961, he published two classics: *The Strategy of Conflict* and, with Mort Halperin, *Strategy and Arms Control*. The latter focused on the "mutual interest in the avoidance of a war" and avoiding "false alarms and misunderstandings" through political arrangements like arms control.[21] *The Strategy of Conflict*, on the other hand, highlighted the "threat that leaves something to chance" as a way to enhance deterrence, as part of a limited war strategy that holds out the risk of inadvertent escalation and general nuclear war.[22] To add to the confusion, you would find a memo from Schelling, read by President John F. Kennedy at the height of the 1961 Berlin crisis, recommending launching a nuclear weapon against the Soviets, not to gain any military advantage on the battlefield, but to signal resolve to the adversary.[23] For Schelling, was US nuclear strategy about achieving strategic stability based on mutual understanding, arms control, and vulnerability, or by exploiting the uncertainty and danger of nuclear weapons for geopolitical gain? This contradiction—on the one hand, encouraging states to seek stability through arms control and mutual vulnerability, and on the other, recommending strategies that might engender and exploit instability to achieve political goals—ran right through the work of one of America's most incisive strategists.

After this confusion, you might look to speeches and documents. Deputy Secretary of Defense Roswell Gilpatric gave a speech in the fall of 1961 which warned that the United States possessed nuclear forces which could "bring to bear even after a Soviet surprise attack upon our forces [a force that] would be as great as—perhaps greater than—the total undamaged force which the enemy

---

21. Thomas C. Schelling and Morton H. Halperin. *Strategy and Arms Control* (New York, NY: Twentieth Century Fund, 1961).

22. See Thomas Schelling, *The Strategy of Conflict* (Cambridge, MA: Harvard University Press, 1960); Thomas Schelling, *Arms and Influence* (New Haven, CT: Yale University Press, 1966).

23. Schelling, "Nuclear Strategy in the Berlin Crisis."

can threaten to launch against the United States in a first strike."[24] Was this a second strike threat, as the text indicates, or was Gilpatric making a not-too-veiled threat that the United States possessed meaningful nuclear superiority and was willing to use these forces preemptively in a crisis? This is how many, including some in the Soviet Union, understood the message. A few months later, Robert McNamara's "no cities" speech laid out the strategy of flexible response, which called for increased reliance on conventional forces and high-lighted that smaller, independent nuclear forces operated by allies were "dangerous, expensive, [and] prone to obsolescence."[25] You would be surprised to find that contemporaneous to this speech, the secretary of defense was recommending reducing US conventional forces, was willing to help the French nuclear program, and appeared to order no significant change to America's war plan. That plan—the Single Intergrated Operational Plan (SIOP)—was briefed by the Chairman of the Joint Chiefs of Staff, Lyman Lemnitzer to President Kennedy in September 1961. According to Scott Sagan, it was "a highly inflexible plan" for "massive preemption."[26] While the SIOP was modified in future years, it remained inflexible and preemptive. Nor is it clear that it was the actual war plan of the Kennedy administration, as documents reveal the administration explored a more flexible, smaller strategy, not to fight a limited war as flexible response suggested, but rather to neutralize Soviet military forces with a first strike attack.[27]

The final and most important place you might look is President Kennedy's views. Kennedy spent as much time and effort as any president trying to wrestle with the realities of nuclear use. What conclusions did he come to? When Kennedy asked former Secretary of State Dean Acheson when he should use nuclear weapons, Acheson replied that the president should give it the "most careful and private consideration, well before the time when the choice might present itself," and that "he should tell no one at all what that conclusion was."[28] Looking over the documents, President Kennedy appears to have

24. Roswell L. Gilpatric, Speech before the Business Council at the Homestead, Hot Springs, Virginia, October 21, 1961, available at https://archive.org/stream/RoswellGilpatricSpeechBeforeTheBusinessCouncil/ELS000-010_djvu.txt.

25. McNamara, "No Cities."

26. Scott Sagan, "SIOP-62: The Nuclear War Plan Briefing to President Kennedy," *International Security* 12:1 (1987): 22–51.

27. Fred Kaplan, "JFK's First Strike Plan," *The Atlantic*, October 2001, https://www.theatlantic.com/magazine/archive/2001/10/jfks-first-strike-plan/376432/.

28. Kai Bird, *The Color of Truth: McGeorge Bundy and William Bundy: Brothers in Arms* (New York, NY: Simon and Schuster, 2000).

followed that advice; it is unclear whether he would have authorized the use of nuclear weapons, even if the Cuban Missile Crisis had spun out of control.

Nuclear strategy is elusive. Both the sources and purposes of strategies around the bomb are hard to identify and evaluate, not the least because the actual use of nuclear weapons would, in most cases, be a strategic disaster. Nuclear strategy is also consequential, and not only because it involves the one weapon that could destroy whole cities and societies. Nuclear weapons provide both opportunities and challenges to grand strategy. To identify, understand, and assess any nuclear strategy, we must first understand what the state hopes to accomplish in the world with these fearsome weapons.

CHAPTER 29

Limited War in the Nuclear Age

AMERICAN STRATEGY IN KOREA

Daniel Marston

The Korean War (1950–53) was the first major conventional war fought in the nuclear shadow.[1] It was also the first military test of America's Cold War containment policy. This chapter will assess the performance of three US commanders—Generals Douglas MacArthur, Matthew Ridgway, and Mark Clark—as they attempted to create and implement strategies that were consistent with shifting US policy aims. The generals had to be cognizant at

1. I wish to thank Prof Raymond Callahan, Sir Lawrence Freedman, Prof Robert O'Neill, and Sir Hew Strachan for reviewing and offering important feedback on earlier versions of this chapter. For further reading on the Korean War, see Rosemary Foot, *The Wrong War: American Policy and the Dimensions of the Korean Conflict, 1950–1953* (Ithaca, NY: Cornell University Press), 1985; Chen Jian, *China's Road to the Korean War* (New York, NY: Columbia University Press, 1994); Allan Millett, *The War for Korea, 1945–1950: A House Burning* (Lawrence, KS: University Press of Kansas, 2005); and Allan Millett, *The War for Korea, 1950–1951: They Came from the North* (Lawrence, KS: University Press of Kansas, 2010); James F. Schnabel and Robert J. Watson, *History of the Joint Chiefs of Staff: The Joint Chiefs of Staff and National Policy 1950–1951: The Korean War Part One* (Washington, DC: Office of Joint History, 1998); and James F. Schnabel, *History of the Joint Chiefs of Staff The Joint Chiefs of Staff and National Policy, 1951–1953: The Korean War, Part Two* (Washington, DC: Office of Joint History, 1998); William Stueck, *The Korean War: An International History* (Princeton, NJ: Princeton University Press, 1995); William Stueck, *Rethinking the Korean War: A New Diplomatic and Strategic History* (Princeton, NJ: Princeton University Press, 2002); Vladislav Zubok and Constantine Pleshakov, *Inside the Kremlin's Cold War: From Stalin to Khrushchev* (Cambridge, MA: Harvard University Press, 1996); Samuel F. Wells Jr., *Fearing the Worst: How Korea Transformed the Cold War* (New York, NY: Columbia University Press, 2019).

all times of the wider implications of their strategies, and whether their decisions might lead to dramatic escalation outside of the Korean Peninsula.

"Strategy," writes Hew Strachan, "has two principal tasks":

> The first is to identify the character of the war in hand. A misidentification is pregnant with consequences: it would be just as mistaken to fight a major war on the assumption that it is a smaller, more limited war, as the other way round. Moreover, what begins as one sort of war can, obviously enough, transmogrify into another. So recognising the character of the war and understanding it is a constant interrogative process. . . . not just something to be undertaken at its outset. But the second task of strategy, once the character of the war has been plumbed, is to manage the war and direct it. The first process is more reactive, the second more proactive. It is perfectly possible for the policy-makers of one belligerent to decide to escalate a war, to make a local conflict into a global one.[2]

The reciprocal nature of war and strategy becomes clear from an examination of the American experience in Korea. In early 1950, the United States was in the process of crafting a containment strategy to counter the threat of Soviet expansion; at that point, Korea was deemed to be a peripheral interest. The shock of the North Korean invasion, however, shifted American estimations of Korea's strategic importance, and by the summer of 1950, the United States was heavily involved in a conventional war on the peninsula.

Partially as a result of the success of US military operations, the United States escalated the war to a point that triggered Chinese intervention and widespread fears of global war. The challenge for American commanders was to design a strategy that would secure US policy objectives in Korea without unleashing an even broader conflict. If World War II had been a nearly total war fought to achieve a nearly total victory, the Korean War became a limited conflict, fought for limited aims, with politically imposed—and often-shifting—limits on the intensity of the violence American military leaders could apply. This experience in the Korean War, and the lessons it holds regarding the reciprocal nature of war and strategy, is worth revisiting as the great powers again confront the prospect of local wars that could escalate in unpredictable ways.

---

2. Hew Strachan, *The Direction of War: Contemporary Strategy in Historical Perspective* (Cambridge: Cambridge University Press, 2011).

I

During the Korean War, two different US presidents—Harry Truman and Dwight Eisenhower, were the Commanders in Chief and exercised control of all US military forces. The top advisory organizations for the president consisted of the Joint Chiefs, the National Security Council, and the Secretaries of Defense and State. The Joint Chiefs, also known as the JCS, included the Chairman of the JCS; the Chief of Staff, US Army; the Chief of Staff, US Air Force; and the Chief of Naval Operations. The National Security Council (NSC) had been created in 1947 to advise the president on the integration of domestic, foreign, and military policies dealing with national security. The Secretary of Defense and Secretary of State both sat on the NSC and in the Cabinet.

The generals' strategic implementation and attempts to deal with the theme of reciprocity in the Korean War occurred at different levels of command. Generals MacArthur, Ridgway, and Clark commanded both Far East Command (FECOM) and United Nations Command (UNC) as CINCUNC (Commander in Chief of the UNC) and reported directly to the JCS; they also interacted with the Secretary of Defense. All the South Korean, US, and UN forces fighting in Korea fell under the command of the UNC.

The background to the war itself, as with many conflicts, highlights shifting aims, national interests, and attempts by national security agencies to develop coherent policies. The Soviet Union and the US had divided occupation of the Korean Peninsula following the fall of Japan in 1945. The Soviet Union occupied the northern half and the US the southern half, with the thirty-eighth parallel as the line of demarcation. South Korea was established as an independent republic in 1948; North Korea then organized an insurgency to undermine its neighbor's stability. In response to this unsettled state of affairs, on April 4, 1948, President Harry Truman approved a JCS position stating:

> The United States should not become so irrevocably involved in the Korean situation that an action taken by any faction in Korea or by any other power in Korea could be considered a "casus belli" for the United States.[3]

---

3. Report by the National Security Council on the Position of the United States with Respect to Korea, April 2, 1948, *Foreign Relations of the United States (FRUS), 1948, The Far East and Australasia*, Volume VI, Document 776, hereafter cited as *FRUS* followed by year, volume, and document number.

US Secretary of State Dean Acheson reinforced this position in his early 1950 "Perimeter Speech" where he discussed US vital national interests in the Western Pacific, and excluded South Korea. At a time when US defense resources were still severely limited by the post-World War II drawdown, Truman's emphasis was on carefully bounding American military commitments and focusing US resources on Western Europe and, to a lesser extent, Japan.

This position was duly noted by Chairman Mao Zedong in a statement to a senior North Korean diplomat in the spring of 1950. Mao stated that "unification of Korea by peaceful means is not possible, solely military means are required to unify Korea. As regards the Americans, there is no need to be afraid of them. The Americans will not enter a third world war for such a small territory."[4] In the end, Mao was partially correct. The United States would not fight a third world war over South Korea, although the conflict did drag both China and the US into a major confrontation.

II

The North Koreans attacked South Korea at 4AM on June 25, 1950, local time, with the approval of the Soviet Union.[5] General MacArthur as CINCFEC (Commander in Chief of the Far East Command) informed Washington leadership that the North Korean invasion was an act of war. Secretary Acheson and President Truman agreed that the UN Security Council (UNSC) needed to be convened to deal with the act of war, and the Security Council met on the twenty-fifth without the Soviet Ambassador, who had absented himself from the proceedings in protest of the UN's refusal to admit the People's Republic of China to the UN. The UNSC Resolution stated that the North Korean attack "constitutes a breach of the peace," but did not yet authorize a military response.[6] The JCS held a teletype conference on the twenty-fifth, authorizing Gen MacArthur to extend his authority over any US operations in South Korea, and to be ready to send air and sea forces to protect US nationals as well as sea routes to South Korea in the event of deployment of US ground forces from Japan to stabilize the situation.

4. Document 13, Cold War International History Project (CWIHP) *Bulletin*, 6–7 (1995–96).

5. Document 14, CWIHP *Bulletin*, 6–7.

6. Resolution Adopted by the United Nations Security Council, June 25, 1950, *FRUS, 1950, Korea*, Volume VII, Document 84.

A subsequent meeting involving the president, JCS, Secretary of Defense Louis Johnson, Secretary of State Acheson, and the secretaries of the military departments was primarily a vigorous debate about what could be done and the potential US contribution. The outcome of the discussion was unanimous agreement that the US needed to take on the challenge, including the use of force, to stop North Korean aggression.

One reason why the US decided to intervene relates to the core theme of this chapter—the interaction between war and policy. As noted previously, US leaders had not planned to defend South Korea from aggression, but the North Korean attack led Truman to conclude that even peripheral interests had to be defended, lest their abandonment in the face of subversion or aggression lead to the weakening of more important allies in Europe and Japan. The invasion also dovetailed with mounting fears of Soviet militancy following Moscow's acquisition of nuclear weapons in 1949. As John Lewis Gaddis writes, the attack seemed to confirm "that the Soviet Union might resort to a war by proxy, even in the face of American nuclear superiority."[7] North Korea's assault thus contributed to a major reshaping of US global strategy. Washington made new commitments to non-Communist governments in South and Southeast Asia, as well as to a dramatic buildup of military power elsewhere, especially in Europe, with the aim of providing greater security against the threat of additional aggression—all while preparing to fight a localized war in Korea.

Initially, General MacArthur received authorization to use both air and sea assets in order to keep open various land routes in South Korea with the intent that ground forces might be used. This was all done without any consultation with the UN Security Council. On June 27, President Truman issued a formal statement: "The Security Council called upon all members of the United Nations to render every assistance to the United Nations in the execution of this resolution. In these circumstances I have ordered United States air and sea forces to give the Korean Government troops cover and support."[8] The British government announced on June 28 that British ships in the Far Eastern Station would support the USN and the ROK (Republic of Korea) as well. From the start, the British stayed close to the US position, and played a major role as a junior partner in strategic decision-making.

7. John Lewis Gaddis, *Strategies of Containment* (Oxford: Oxford University Press, 2005), 107.

8. Statement Issued by the President, June 27, 1950, *FRUS*, VII, *Korea, 1950*, Document 119.

By June 28, Seoul had fallen to the rapidly advancing North Koreans, and President Truman held another meeting on the twenty-ninth with many of the principal civilian and military leaders. Secretary Johnson presented a draft directive that hinted at the possibility of war with the USSR, a prospect the president rejected, making it clear that he wanted future directives to focus solely on regional concerns. Truman did approve air attacks on North Korean military targets north of the thirty-eight parallel, clear from the USSR and Chinese borders. This was followed, on the thirtieth, by a wider directive that all restrictions on the use of US ground forces being sent to Korea had been lifted. Stalin reacted to this development on July 5 with a telegram to the Chinese foreign minister hinting at major escalation:

> We consider it correct to concentrate immediately 9 Chinese divisions on the Chinese-Korean border for volunteer actions in North Korea in case the enemy crosses the 38th parallel. We will try to provide air cover for these units.[9]

On July 7, President Truman was made the "executive agent" by a UN Security Council resolution in waging a war against aggression in Korea. President Truman designated the JCS "his agents for Korea"; the JCS, in turn, requested that General MacArthur be appointed commander of all UN forces (later established as the United Nations Command or UNC).[10] MacArthur was given command on the July 10, and President Rhee immediately placed all ROK military forces under his and the UN's command.[11]

Yet even as the United States committed forces to combat in Korea, the need to keep that commitment in global perspective remained. On the tenth—the same day MacArthur was given command of the UNC—the JCS, in a note to Secretary Johnson, highlighted the need to avoid outright confrontation with the Soviets, stating, "it would be unsound for the United States to commit large forces against the USSR, in an area of slight strategic importance, as well as one of Soviet choice."[12] North Koreans were pushing the ROK military and US forces towards Pusan; the situation was ominous. By the end of July, the US military was shifting many assets to the Korean Peninsula, putting military

---

9. See Document 18, CWIHP *Bulletin*, 6–7.

10. James Schnabel, *United States Army in the Korean War: Policy and Direction—the First Year* (Washington, DC: Center of Military History, 1973), 102.

11. Schnabel, *United States Army in the Korean War*, 85–103.

12. Gaddis, *Strategies of Containment*, 108.

commands and interests in other parts of the world at risk. Some Truman administration officials feared that this could be a proxy war by the Soviets to distract the US from a larger campaign elsewhere. A part of the world which only a few months previously had been deemed non-essential to US national interests was already becoming a major drain on global planning and strategy—highlighting the difficulty of planning and forecasting future threats and contingencies accurately, particularly unexpected developments that can reposition situations previously considered peripheral.

III

The period between September and December 1950 highlights the dilemmas of strategy implementation. In June and July, the aims for the US had been to limit the ground war to south of the thirty-eighth parallel. In July, General MacArthur and his staff began planning an amphibious landing at Inchon (Operation CHROMITE); its aim was to dislocate North Korean forces in and around the Pusan perimeter.[13] On the eve of launching the Inchon operation, CHROMITE introduced the possibility that a successful operation could open the way for US troops to move into North Korea—a potential policy shift that was not universally supported.

A draft NSC document written on September 1 attempted to lay out the potential pitfalls of a UNC crossing of the thirty-eighth parallel, should the UNC be successful at Inchon and drive back the North Koreans from the Pusan region. The key issue requiring attention related to the USSR or Communist China entering the arena in support of the North Koreans. General MacArthur had already received intelligence on August 31 that the Chinese had moved more than 200,000 troops into Manchuria, readily able to proceed into North Korea. On September 7, General Omar Bradley, Chairman of the Joint Chiefs, stated:

> The JCS, after consultation by two of its members with General MacArthur, agree [sic] with his concept that the initial objective to be attained is the destruction of North Korean forces. We believe, after the strength of the North Korean forces has been broken, which is anticipated will occur south of the 38th parallel, that subsequently operations must take place

13. See Memorandum of Conversation by Lieutenant General Matthew B. Ridgway, Deputy Chief of Staff for Administration, United States Army, August 8, 1950, FRUS, 1950 Korea, VII, Document 402 for an interesting assessment of the plan for Operation CHROMITE.

both north and south of the 38th parallel. Such operations on the ground should be conducted by South Korean forces since it is assumed that the actions will probably be of a guerrilla character.[14]

At this stage, the JCS's stated policy was still that US forces would remain south of the thirty-eighth parallel, and that only ROK forces would enter North Korea. General MacArthur and his staff in FEC planned accordingly, yet they also hinted at the possibility of US forces crossing into the North. MacArthur was already on the record as saying at a meeting in July that, "I may need to occupy all of North Korea."[15] The US X Corps landed at Inchon on September 15, and the US 8th Army in the Pusan perimeter launched its counter-offensive on the sixteenth. Following intense fighting, the 8th Army pushed out of the perimeter on the twenty-third and marched north towards X Corps, with elements linking up on the twenty-sixth. The North Koreans were routed and streaming north.

With the success of the Inchon landing and the subsequent rolling back of the North Korean forces in and around the Pusan perimeter, policy aims—influenced by success on the battlefield—shifted to encompass the potential unification of the peninsula under UN auspices. UN resolutions hinted at the need to cross the thirty-eighth parallel, but the UK and others voiced concerns regarding a potential Soviet and Chinese Communist military response. Many advisors to President Truman feared that crossing the thirty-eighth parallel could trigger a wider general war, while the JCS and General MacArthur saw an opportunity to unify Korea politically and end the tensions on the peninsula once and for all.

On September 27, the JCS gave MacArthur the directive to cross the thirty-eighth parallel and to destroy the North Korean military. This directive was to be executed as long as the Soviets and/or Chinese had not entered North Korea or threatened to do so, and also on condition that only ROK troops would be used near the Soviet or Manchurian borders. On the same day as this directive arrived, MacArthur's planning team presented the strategy for the crossing of the thirty-eighth. It called for X Corps to re-embark and land on the east coast at Wonsan in North Korea, while the 8th Army would cross, drive north, and seize the North Korean capital, P'yongyang. The ROK forces would be in the vanguard of the US and Western forces.

14. Memorandum by the Joint Chiefs of Staff to the Secretary of Defense, September 7, 1950, *FRUS, 1950 Korea*, VII, Document 500.

15. Schnabel, *United States Army in the Korean War*, 179.

On the twenty-eighth MacArthur briefed his plan to the JCS, and advised that there was no intelligence that Soviet or Chinese Communist forces had entered North Korea. His plan of splitting his forces was approved by the secretary of defense and President Truman on the twenty-ninth. The same day, the new Secretary of Defense, George Marshall, sent a personal note to General MacArthur reinforcing the orders from the JCS and hinting at a wider role for US/UK forces:

> Report of supposed announcement by Eighth Army that ROK Divisions would halt on 38th parallel for regrouping: We want you to feel unhampered tactically and strategically to proceed north of 38th parallel. Announcement above referred to may precipitate embarrassment in UN where evident desire is not to be confronted with necessity of a vote on passage of 38th parallel, rather to find you have found it militarily necessary to do so.[16]

The US formally sought UN approval for the occupation of North Korea in October. On October 1, South Korean forces crossed the thirty-eighth parallel, and the G-2 intel officer of the 8th Army reported that hundreds of thousands of Chinese troops were massing on the Manchuria/North Korean border. The UNC intelligence branch reported that Chinese troops had already entered North Korea. These reports were dismissed by General MacArthur and others in FECOM, and on the seventh of October, the UN General Assembly passed a resolution that gave "implicit assent" to the conquest and occupation of North Korea.[17]

The war was clearly escalating from its original form. On October 9, the same day that the first US troops crossed into North Korea, the JCS sent a note to Gen MacArthur:

> Hereafter in the event of the open or covert employment anywhere in Korea of major Chinese Communist units, without prior announcement, you should continue the action as long as, in your judgment, action by forces now under your control offers a reasonable chance of success. In any case, you will obtain authorization from Washington prior to taking any military action against objectives in Chinese territory.[18]

16. The Secretary of Defense (Marshall) to the Commander in Chief, Far East (MacArthur), September 29, 1950, *FRUS, 1950, Korea*, VII, Document 573.

17. Schnabel, *United States Army in the Korean War*, 194.

18. The Joint Chiefs of Staff to the Commander in Chief, Far East (MacArthur), October 9, 1950, *FRUS, 1950, Korea*, VII, Document 648.

Intelligence reports and information from other countries, such as India, indicated "noise" from the Chinese and their intent to enter North Korea in order to oppose the presence of the UNC so close to their own borders. The ROK I Corps advance up the east coast of North Korea went faster than expected; they took Wonsan on October 11, before X Corps made their planned landing and struck out in support of the ROK, which was already moving quickly towards the Soviet border. The Chinese Foreign Office described the UNC actions "as a serious menace to the security of China."[19] The Chinese started to move their troops into North Korea on October 14.

As the 8th Army and ROK formations crossed and advanced into North Korea, President Truman called for a one-day meeting on Wake Island for October 15, summoning both General MacArthur and General Bradley, Chief of the JCS. General MacArthur briefed that North Korean resistance would end by Thanksgiving, and that many of the American forces would be able to withdraw from North Korea by Christmas. General Bradley was pleased to hear this, as he was hoping to move some forces from Korea to other "hot spots," such as Europe.[20]

One of the final issues raised during the Wake Island meeting was the Chinese. On October 15, General MacArthur stated that, although they may have hundreds of thousands of troops in Manchuria, they had not crossed into North Korea; he was unaware that they had crossed into the North the day prior. Moreover, MacArthur argued, even if they did, the Chinese had no air force and would be destroyed by UN air forces and UNC ground forces. This stark assessment proved to be incorrect in myriad ways, and also illustrates a critical mistake that military leaders make regularly: underestimating the opposition. MacArthur and his staff had underestimated the ability of the Chinese to organize, and questioned their fighting capability so soon after the conclusion of the Chinese civil war. As a result of this underestimation, MacArthur failed to develop and implement a revised strategy to prepare for the possibility that the Chinese might in fact intervene and even be able to inflict major damage upon the UNC.[21]

On October 24, General MacArthur made a critical overreach, one that some historians and military practitioners have characterized as disobeying

19. Schnabel, *United States Army in the Korean War*, 233.

20. See, Substance of Statements Made at Wake Island Conference on October 15, 1950, *FRUS, 1950, Korea*, VII, Document 680.

21. Substance of Statements Made at Wake Island Conference on October 15, 1950, *FRUS, 1950, Korea*, VII, Document 680.

orders. As noted previously, the ROK troops were the only forces which had been authorized to move beyond a specific line, much less anywhere near the Soviet and Manchurian borders. MacArthur lifted this restriction and ordered the commanders of the 8th Army, Lieutenant General Walton Walker, and the X Corps, Lieutenant General Edward Almond, to drive forward in support of the ROK formations. The JCS were surprised by this order; they sought clarification from General MacArthur, but their communication was not robust. They stated "that [MacArthur] undoubtedly had sound reasons for issuing these instructions [and they] would like to be informed of them, as [this] action is a matter of some concern here."[22]

General Walker pushed his two corps north towards the Yalu River. On October 25, the first Chinese troops engaged and defeated elements of the 6th ROK Division, fifty miles south of the Yalu River. The Chinese met elements of the US 1st Cavalry Division on the evening of November 1–2, and General Walker ordered the 8th Army to pull back to the south to defend along better terrain. Contrary to earlier reports, it was already clear that this was a significant Chinese incursion into the conflict, regardless of dismissals from Washington and Tokyo of these first Chinese units as a small vanguard. The G-2 intel officer in FECOM made it clear that the Chinese had close to twenty-nine divisions along the Yalu River and could easily bring them into the fight.

On November 5, General MacArthur ordered the Far East Air Force's Lt. General George Stratemeyer to "destroy every means of communication and every installation, city and village" along the Yalu River.[23] On the sixth, this order was expanded to include destroying the bridges across the Yalu River. The commander of the Far East Air Force informed USAF officials in Washington, DC, about these orders, and this information was conveyed to the Under-Secretary of Defense, Robert Lovett, who took it to Acheson. Both State and Defense officials understood that if bombs accidently fell in China, the stakes would get much higher, potentially drawing in the Soviets to support Beijing. Secretary of Defense Marshall was duly informed, and all agreed that the planned air attacks needed to be halted before they started, unless MacArthur's forces were in jeopardy of being destroyed.

General MacArthur responded that the air attacks had to go ahead, and that "every hour that this is postponed will be paid for dearly in American and

---

22. Schnabel, *United States Army in the Korean War*, 218.

23. Robert Frank Futrell, *The United States Air Force in Korea, 1950–1953* (Washington, DC: US Government Printing Office, 1983), 221.

other United Nations blood."[24] The president, his advisors, and the JCS were concerned about panicked messaging suddenly coming from General MacArthur; they gave approval for the air attacks, but imposed very tight restrictions for fear of spreading the war beyond Korea.[25] The first air attacks went out on November 8, but were soon suspended as the Yalu River froze and the use of the bridges became less important.[26]

As the war entered a dangerous new phase, discussions of escalation were debated heavily within the DoD (Department of Defense) and State Department. The JCS stated in a memo to Secretary Marshall on November 9 that America must avoid a protracted, let alone expanded, war in Korea.

> The continued involvement of the United States forces in Korea would be in the interests of the USSR and of world communism by imposing a heavy drain on United States military and economic strengths; it would also be in the interests of the USSR for the meager military forces in being of the United States to be committed in a strategically unimportant area. From the viewpoint of a global war, the United States would thus be off balance while the USSR perfects and completes its plans for global conquest and prepares to deliver a surprise blow.... The United States should develop its plans and make its preparations on the basis that the risk of global war is increased.[27]

Meanwhile, President Truman and his national security team attempted to de-escalate tensions with the UK and France that had been exacerbated by shifting policy aims and reactive decision-making. General MacArthur had been dismissive of British diplomatic efforts to de-escalate the situation, often describing the British as appeasing the Chinese as Chamberlain had done in 1938 with Germany.[28] The entry of the Chinese into the conflict demonstrated that the US had failed to "win" the war in Korea with limited assets. The US was now clear that it did not intend to expand the war beyond Korea; it merely

---

24. The Joint Chiefs of Staff to the Commander in Chief, Far East (MacArthur), November 6, 1950, *FRUS, 1950, Korea*, VII, Document 758.

25. See, The Joint Chiefs of Staff to the Commander in Chief, Far East (MacArthur), November 6, 1950, *FRUS, 1950, Korea*, VII, Document 773 for "restrictive tone" from the JCS.

26. See, The Commander in Chief, Far East (MacArthur) to the Joint Chiefs of Staff, November 9, 1950, *FRUS, 1950, Korea*, VII, Document 792, for a blistering attack by General MacArthur on the UK position of trying to de-escalate the situation with the Chinese.

27. Memorandum by the Joint Chiefs of Staff to the Secretary of Defense (Marshall), November 9, 1950, *FRUS, 1950, Korea*, VII, Document 797.

28. See, Commander in Chief, Far East (MacArthur) to the Joint Chiefs of Staff, November 9, 1950.

wished to gain support in the UN to resist the Chinese intervention, but only so far as to contain the threat. It would still be a difficult tightrope to walk. There had been some debate concerning the use of nuclear weapons at this period; many military and policy leaders in Washington responded to this with unease and skepticism, highlighting not only a lack of key targets, but also, and more importantly, fear of escalation to global war with the Soviets.[29] The US and its European allies were not prepared for a general war, and feared a defeat in Europe due to the imbalance of conventional forces. The Korean War needed to remain a limited war; the risk for an expanded war in Europe or anywhere in the world was simply too great. MacArthur's failing was his inability to recognize, or adapt to, this fundamental limitation.

That issue began to surface as the scope of Chinese intervention, and the scale of the resulting American defeat, became apparent. After the Battle of the Ch'Ongch'on, November 25–28, 1950, the 8th Army was in retreat towards the thirty-eighth parallel, as was X Corps in the east. General MacArthur tried to claim that the war had shifted once again on November 28. In a memo to the JCS, he stated, "All hope of localization of the Korean conflict to enemy forces composed of North Korean troops with alien token elements can now be completely abandoned. The Chinese military forces are committed in North Korea in great and ever increasing strength . . . We face an entirely new war."[30] On November 29, General MacArthur asked for reinforcements from Nationalist China to be sent to Korea to support the UNC; the JCS immediately refused the request, recognizing its potential to trigger a larger general war with China, and possibly the Soviets.[31]

President Truman and the British Prime Minister, Clement Attlee, met on December 4 to discuss the need for limitation of the conflict.[32] They reached two definite decisions: to fight a limited war confined to the Korean Peninsula only; and to seek a negotiated settlement to the crisis and reestablish a status quo ante June 25, 1950.[33] By December 25, the UNC forces had withdrawn

---

29. Lawrence Freedman, *Evolution of Nuclear Strategy* (London: Palgrave, 2019).

30. The Commander in Chief, Far East (MacArthur) to the Joint Chiefs of Staff, November 28, 1950, *FRUS, 1950, Korea,* VII, Document 888.

31. See, The Ambassador in Korea (Muccio) to the Secretary of State, November 28, 1950, *FRUS, 1950, Korea,* VII, Document 898 for more detail.

32. Robert O'Neill, *Australia in the Korean War 1950–53* (Canberra: Australian War Memorial and Australian Government Publishing Service, 1981).

33. See, United States Delegation Minutes of the First Meeting of President Truman and Prime Minister Attlee, December 4, 1950, *FRUS, 1950, Korea,* VII, Document 967.

beyond the thirty-eighth parallel. Seoul was overrun in January 1951, and then reoccupied by the UNC in March. General Walker was killed in a road accident, and Lieutenant General Matthew Ridgway was sent to replace him. The Chinese had succeeded in pushing the UNC back from their own border, while the 8th Army was digging in south of the thirty-eighth parallel, and needed time to rest and recuperate.

General MacArthur's strategy implementation in September and October had succeeded in pushing the North Koreans out of South Korea. However, the expansive nature of his strategy, supported by some policymakers in Washington, DC, had resulted in over-extension. The strategy also failed to take into account the strategic interests of the Chinese, supported by the Soviets, across the Yalu River and, most importantly, their capabilities to disrupt America's strategic aims. General MacArthur would maintain this "expansive" approach from late 1950 into 1951; he specifically made clear to various officials in the JCS the need "to carry the war to China, through bombing, blockade and other measures."[34] MacArthur also formally questioned the focus upon the security of Western Europe and the newly established North Atlantic Treaty Organization (NATO). He stated the following to the Army Staff on December 30:

> I understand thoroughly the demand for European security and fully concur in doing everything possible in that sector, but not to the point of accepting defeat anywhere else—an acceptance which I am sure could not fail to insure later defeat in Europe itself. The preparations for the defense of Europe, however, by the most optimistic estimate are aimed at a condition of readiness two years hence. The use of forces in the present emergency in the Far East would not in any way prejudice this basic concept.[35]

While he initially expressed these points of view through official channels, in February and March, MacArthur started to state these positions even more publicly, which eventually led to his firing.

It was evident by the spring of 1951 that General MacArthur clearly misunderstood both the nature of the conflict and how to manage it. When policymakers made it clear that he would need to reevaluate his strategy if there were signs of PRC (People's Republic of China) or Soviet intervention, MacArthur disregarded their advice and pushed his UNC/US forces further into North

34. Schnabel, *United States Army in the Korean War*, 373.
35. See, *FRUS, 1950, Korea*, VII, Document 1101 for more details.

Korea, hoping for a North Korean surrender. When intelligence reports came in that the Chinese might already be in North Korea, he actually pushed his UNC forces even harder. He did not recognize that while battlefield or tactical success may be occurring, those very successes could change the strategic context of the war in dangerous ways. MacArthur was not able, or willing, to adapt his preferred strategy as the geopolitical context of the war dramatically changed.

IV

After General Matthew Ridgway took over the 8th Army, he set out to refit and reorganize it. During this period Ridgway developed his concept of "attrition" against the Chinese and North Koreans. Along with General MacArthur, Ridgway understood that the enemy had a major numerical advantage; however, the UNC could cause attrition through their superior firepower from the air, sea, and ground, which might force the Chinese and North Koreans to seek the negotiated settlement outlined by Truman and Atlee in December 1950. This approach constituted a notable departure from strategies of the Second World War and its focus on total war and victory. The focus on attrition underlined the need to respect limitations, seek a negotiated settlement, and, not incidentally, reintroduce the concept of limited war into the US military and policy lexicon.

General Ridgway received support for his approach to attrition from Washington, DC, in early January. The National Intelligence Special Estimate noted:

> In the event that large scale operations against China become necessary, Korea would be favorable for joint UN-US ground operations because: (a) the superior air and sea power of the UN forces could be brought to bear effectively against the numerically superior ground forces; (b) Chinese Communist attrition would be relatively high in the confined battle area in Korea.[36]

General MacArthur was in agreement with General Ridgway; he stated to the press in February that, "our strategic plan involving constant movement to keep the enemy off balance with [a] corresponding limit on upon his initiative

---

36. National Intelligence Special Estimate, January 11, 1951, *FRUS, 1951, Korea*, VII, Part I, Document 48. See, Carter Malkasian, *A Modern History of Wars of Attrition* (Westport, CT: Praeger, 2002), Chapters 7–9 for a deep analysis of the use of an attritional strategy.

remains unaltered . . . There has been a resultant continuing and exhausting attrition upon his manpower and supply."[37]

While General MacArthur had stated the purpose of attrition, the question that remained for many inside the JCS and the Defense and State Departments was, "not only how long will the Chinese be willing to take punishment but also how long will the US public be willing to take American losses, even at the ratio of 20 Chinese to one American."[38] After a series of UNC withdrawals and counterattacks—Operations THUNDERBOLT, KILLER, RIPPER, COURAGEOUS, and DAUNTLESS—the front started to stabilize along the thirty-eighth parallel in early April 1951. The apparent success of attrition used by the 8th Army appeared to convince the American public and its leadership that this approach could work, at least for the time being.[39]

April 1951 would be an eventful month in the war. On April 5, the JCS debated a potential general war with the Soviets. The Chairman of the JCS, General Omar Bradley, argued:

> The Korean problem cannot be resolved in a manner satisfactory to the United States by military action alone. Further, because the Korean problem is a symptom of world tension, a satisfactory resolution of that problem probably cannot be achieved by politico-military action which is confined to Korea; rather, a resolution of that problem in a manner satisfactory to the United States is not to be expected unless and until there is a general relaxation of world tensions.[40]

In effect, a military solution either had to be limited, or else had to have the potential to escalate to a level to which the US was not prepared to commit. While the JCS was debating fundamental questions regarding containment worldwide and the role of the Korean War, General MacArthur—following a long series of statements and actions that bordered on insubordination—was fired and replaced by General Ridgeway as CINCUNC.[41]

37. Malkasian, *A Modern History of Wars of Attrition*, 126–27.

38. Memorandum for the Record of a Department of State—Joint Chiefs of Staff Meeting, February 13, 1951, *FRUS, 1951, Korea*, VII, Part I, Document 133.

39. See, Secretary of State to the Secretary of Defense (Marshall), February 23, 1951, *FRUS, 1951, Korea*, VII, Part I, Document 142 for an in-depth discussion of the situation in late February 1951, including future plans.

40. Memorandum by the Joint Chiefs of Staff to the Secretary of Defense (Marshall), April 5, 1951, *FRUS, 1951, Korea*, VII, Part I, Document 204.

41. There are many sources on the "firing" of MacArthur that can be consulted for a more in-depth analysis. A good starting point is James Schnabel and Robert Watson, *The Joint Chiefs*

His successor, General Ridgway, clearly understood the policy aim to de-escalate and limit the war; as he declared to his commanders, "the grave and present danger that the conduct of our current operations may result in an extension of hostilities, and so lead to a world-wide conflagration, places a heavy responsibility upon all elements of this command, but particularly upon those capable of offensive action."[42] General Bradley confirmed that Ridgway, as the 8th Army commander, was operating under a simple directive: "to kill all the Chinese he can while taking prudent measures to protect the safety of his troops."[43]

The second major event was the Chinese launch of their fifth and final major offensive of the war on the evening of April 21–22. The UNC was pushed back from KANSAS Line—which generally ran east/west along the thirty-eighth—to south of the thirty-eighth parallel once again; Seoul was at risk, but would hold. After a series of back-and-forth communiques and meetings between FECOM and JCS, General Ridgway received a revised set of directives on May 1, in keeping with the limiting aims of the war and attrition of the enemy:

> You are authorized to conduct air and naval operations within [the] geographic boundaries of Korea and waters . . . [this] does not include authority to conduct air or naval action against Manchuria, against USSR territory, or against North Korean electrical power complex including the Yalu River power installations, and as a matter of policy no operations will be conducted within 15 miles of USSR territory.[44]

The president, NSC, and JCS were supportive of General Ridgway's efforts in Korea, and NSC-48/5 was written to reiterate US policy in the region in May 1951. It specifically stated:

> [For] the protection of the security of US and UN forces [in Korea], [you are to] seek to avoid the extension of hostilities in Korea into a general war with the Soviet Union, and seek to avoid the extension beyond Korea of

---

of Staff and National Policy, 1950–1951: The Korean War, Volume III (Washington, DC: Office of Joint History, 1998).

42. Schnabel, United States Army in the Korean War, 381.

43. Memorandum on the Substance of Discussions at a Department of State—Joint Chiefs of Staff Meeting, April 18, 1951, FRUS, 1951, Korea, VII, Part I, Document 242.

44. The Joint Chiefs of Staff to the Commander in Chief, Far East (Ridgway), May 1, 1951, FRUS, 1951, Korea, VII, Part I, Document 268.

hostilities with Communist China, particularly without the support of our major allies. . . . Seek an acceptable political settlement in Korea that does not jeopardize the United States position with respect to the USSR, to Formosa, or to seating Communist China in the UN. . . . In the absence of such a settlement, and recognizing that currently there is no other acceptable alternative, continue the current military course of action in Korea, without commitment to unify Korea by military force, but designed to: (*a*) inflict maximum losses on the enemy. (*b*) prevent the overrunning of South Korea by military aggression. (*c*) limit communist capabilities for aggression elsewhere in Asia.[45]

General Ridgway had reiterated these points to his commanders in the UNC, stating, "you will direct the efforts of your forces toward inflicting maximum personnel casualties and material losses on hostile forces in Korea, consistent with the maintenance . . . and safety of your troops."[46]

The final major Chinese offensive petered out, and the UNC went back on the offensive in mid-May. The new 8th Army commander, Lieutenant General James Van Fleet, proposed an amphibious landing well beyond the old KANSAS Line. General Ridgway opposed the plan on the grounds that the risks would be too great. With his strategy of attrition, he felt that he could achieve his aim with limited objective attacks, chiefly an advance to the KANSAS/WYOMING Line, north of the KANSAS Line. By early June the KANSAS Line had been reached and was being fortified, and small advances towards the WYOMING Line were given approval. While the Chinese and North Koreans were expected to counter attack, the UNC fortified the lines and inflicted piecemeal damage on the enemy.

General Ridgway's strategy of attrition had won the support of US policymakers, and by late summer the consensus was that he had crafted a strategy that supported the limited policy aims set by Washington. The attrition strategy also produced a key diplomatic breakthrough. On June 23, the Soviet Ambassador to the UN requested cease-fire talks, and on July 2, the Chinese and North Koreans agreed.

While Ridgway had defined the strategy for the coming months and years, the complexity of maintaining pressure and achieving successes at the negotiation table would prove an ongoing series of headaches. The Chinese and North

45. Memorandum containing the sections dealing with Korea from NSC 48/5, May 17, 1951, *FRUS, 1951, Korea*, VII, Part I, Document 291.

46. Matthew Ridgway, *The Korean War* (New York, NY: Da Capo Press, 1967), 167.

Koreans broke off the initial negotiations in August, and limited objective attacks on both sides resumed. Some of these operations, such as the battles at the Punchbowl and Heartbreak Ridge, created tensions within the UNC. Other operations, such as COMMANDO, achieved some important gains, including the resumption of armistice talks in October 1951.

The war entered into its final phase in late 1951: stalemate and limited objective attacks for both sides. Air and sea operations increased over this time period, as ground operations were minimized to address issues and force concessions at the negotiation table. The questions for both sides were how much attrition was feasible, and how many concessions to allow at the negotiating table. While the strategy of attrition was limiting and supported the effort to de-escalate the war, the fact that there appeared to be no specific "light at the end of the tunnel" started to take a domestic toll within the United States. War-weariness was setting in among the population and the continuing feasibility of the war was a topic of significant debate in the run-up to the 1952 presidential election.

V

Both sides had dug in heavily along the KANSAS/WYOMING Line as negotiations continued into 1952. Major logistic nodes were created to support both sides' appetite for "firepower" attrition and limited ground attacks, or "outpost battles," such as Old Baldy and Triangle Hill. In May 1952, General Mark Clark took over command from General Ridgway as both CINCUNC and CICFECOM, while General Van Fleet remained as 8th Army commander. General Clark initially implemented the same strategy as General Ridgway, but soon picked up on tensions in DC regarding the use of attrition. The first signs that General Clark was thinking of expanding and escalating the war, in hopes of precipitating a decision, came when he sent a memo to the Army Staff on September 29, 1952, outlining the dilemma the UNC was facing:

> I am of the firm conviction that the basic, underlying reason for failure thus far to achieve an armistice is that we have not exerted sufficient military pressure to impose the requirement for an armistice on the enemy . . . It appears evident that positive aggressive action, designed to obtain military victory and achieve an armistice on our terms, is not feasible by this command with current forces operating under current restrictions [limitations on air strikes and naval engagements] . . . In any event, but subsequent to

arrival in the theater of force augmentations, I would wish to implement this extension of the war before launching a major ground offensive.[47]

In October 1952, General Clark and his staff formally created a plan for expansion of the war, which envisioned an advance to the Yalu River and the blockade of China. After reaching the Yalu, the advance would then continue into China, if the Chinese and North Koreans had not agreed to an armistice. This concept became known as OPLAN 8–52. General Van Fleet and other commanders were in support of such an operation, as they were becoming more and more critical of the perceived lack of offensive spirit in the UNC. While OPLAN 8–52 was escalatory in nature, it still did not introduce the use of nuclear weapons; that would come later. Dwight Eisenhower stated on October 25 that, if elected president, he would travel to Korea, and that "the first task for the new administration will be to reviews and re-examine every course of action open to us with one goal in view: to bring the Korean War to early and honorable end."[48]

President Eisenhower was elected in November 1952; the Soviets, Chinese, and North Koreans wondered if this would lead to a major escalation, given his campaign's previous rhetoric and incoming Secretary of State John Foster Dulles's emphasis on using asymmetric nuclear responses to deter Communist aggression. Clark's OPLAN 8–52 was briefed to the newly elected president in November. Eisenhower and the JCS did not support the plan, as it was clearly too escalatory in nature and the resources required would put pressure on other commitments. However, a deadlock within the armistice negotiations prompted the Eisenhower administration to raise the stakes dramatically in February 1953, noting that "in the absence of satisfactory progress [in the armistice talks] we intended to move decisively without inhibition in our use of weapons, and would no longer be responsible for confining hostilities to the Peninsula."[49]

The death of Joseph Stalin on March 5, 1953, provided the possibility of a breakthrough, but as the negotiations dragged on, the United States continued to debate escalatory options in hopes of forcing the Chinese and North

---

47. The Commander in Chief, United Nations Command (Clark) to the Joint Chiefs of Staff, September 29, 1952, *FRUS, 1952–1954, Korea*, XV, Part I, Document 283.

48. Speech, October 24, 1952, Papers of Dwight D. Eisenhower, Speech Series, Box 2, Oct 23, 1952 to Nov 3, 1952 and Dec 1952 (1), NAID #12012607, Dwight Eisenhower Presidential Library.

49. Freedman, *Evolution of Nuclear Strategy*, 112.

Koreans to accept an armistice. The first major discussion between the secretary of state's team and the JCS was held on March 27, 1953. At that point, General Collins stated that:

> In the new paper on alternative courses of action in Korea that we have just sent forward, we had a section which indicated that consideration should be given to use of atomic weapons. Personally, I am very skeptical about the value of using atomic weapons tactically in Korea. . . . Right now we present ideal targets for atomic weapons in Pusan and Inchon. An atomic weapon in Pusan harbor could do serious damage to our military position in Korea. We would again present an ideal target if we should undertake a major amphibious operation. An amphibious landing fleet would be a perfect target for an atomic weapon at the time when it was putting the troops ashore. On the other hand, the Commies, scattered over one hundred fifty miles of front, and well dug in, don't present nearly as profitable a target to us as we do to them.[50]

The Director of Policy Planning in the State Dept, Paul Nitze, also the chief architect of NSC-68, questioned the use of nuclear weapons on the battlefield and raised the fear that Soviets would respond in kind.

The debate continued at an NSC meeting on March 31. The president focused on discussions about the possibility of an advance towards the North Korean capital and across the "waist" of North Korea, as well as the use of nuclear weapons. Eisenhower noted that "it would be worth the cost if, through use of atomic weapons, we could (1) achieve a substantial victory over the Communist forces and (2) get to a line at the waist of Korea."[51] The conclusions from this meeting became known as NSC 147. The JSC did not initially okay the plan, but did so in May 1953, endorsing many of the key elements of NSC 147, including the use of nuclear weapons. The JCS asked General Clark to revise his original OPLAN 8–52 and, most importantly, to plan formally for the additional use of nuclear weapons, if need be.

The revised OPLAN 8–52 was never acted upon because the armistice negotiations finally gained momentum in May–July (partially as a result of significant US pressure on its own ally, South Korean President Rhee, to accept

---

50. Memorandum of the Substance of Discussion at a Department of State Joint Chiefs of Staff Meeting, March 27, 1953, *FRUS, 1952–1954, Korea*, XV, Part I, Document 419.

51. Memorandum of Discussion at a Special Meeting of the National Security Council on Tuesday, March 31, 1953, *FRUS, 1952–1954, Korea*, XV, Part I, Document 427.

the emerging terms), and because the resources needed for the revised OPLAN 8–52 would not be ready in Korea for a number of months. While the final months of the war saw an escalation in terms of ground combat as the Chinese and North Koreans mounted multiple attacks against the UNC, a cease-fire was signed and enacted on July 27, 1953, ending hostilities for the time being.

VI

The Korean War was a limited conflict, but its outcome cast a long shadow over the remainder of the twentieth century, and beyond. Limited war was a somewhat unfamiliar discipline for the US after World War II, which was one reason why the strategy-war relationship in Korea proved so complex. In the nuclear age, strategy and operations had to be consistently subordinated to political and global concerns in a fraught great-power context. Local wars were no longer localized; all strategic and operational decisions had to be taken in the context of wider political considerations.

The three commanding generals produced widely varying records in resolving the resulting dilemmas. General MacArthur was able to use his apparent battlefield success, post-Inchon, to escalate the war. When policymakers made it clear that he would need to reevaluate his strategy if confronted with the prospect of Soviet or Chinese intervention, he disregarded their thinking and pushed further into North Korea, hoping for a surrender. When he was faced with the reality of Chinese intervention, he overreached, attempting to expand the war rather than follow advice and withdraw an already overextended force. On the eve of his firing, MacArthur had still not grasped the need to limit the war due to the wider global and political implications.

General Ridgway, by contrast, demonstrated a better grasp of Strachan's two principal tasks of strategy. Ridgway came in as an operational/tactical commander; he recognized the limitations of his force and the fact that US policymakers, after the intervention of the Chinese, clearly hoped for a limited war. He successfully applied an operational approach of attrition as the commanding general of the 8th Army. When he took over as CINCUNC, Ridgway raised his experiences and knowledge to a strategic level. He sought guidance from his military and political masters; he asked tough questions regarding escalation. There was a robust and honest dialogue between the civilian and military leadership. Ridgway was clear that the UNC was fighting a limited war; he made this clear to the commanders below him, and to the senior leadership above him. At the strategic level, he applied attrition that was clearly tied to the policy aims of a limited war in order to achieve an armistice agreement. Ridgway's approach helped reshape some of the policy debates in DC, as he was clear about the limitations of his forces in achieving more than limited objectives. While this was an important development in strategy implementation, by 1952, attrition had become a negative word in the US political and public vocabulary, implying a costly, long campaign with no clear end-state. Attrition can be an effective strategy in a limited war, albeit one that can be exhausting for both sides—particularly if the enemy has a higher tolerance for taking casualties.

General Clark understood the experiences of MacArthur and Ridgway before he took command. He saw the war in the summer of 1952 as limited, but was also cognizant of the tensions with the US public, notably the mantra of "dying for a tie." The idea of "total victory" which had dominated strategic thinking during the Second World War had been replaced with acceptance of the need for a more ambiguous outcome. By October 1952, it appeared that even that result might require significant military escalation in and around Korea—General Clark and his civilian superiors began to move towards abandoning prior limits, although that move was never consummated thanks to the success of negotiations.

This case study highlights fundamental debates regarding the reciprocal relationship between war and strategy. In early 1950, America's containment strategy was still taking shape; the Korean Peninsula was not seen as a vital US interest. Despite this, by the summer of 1950 the United States was heavily involved in a conventional war on the Korean Peninsula, a conflict which threatened to spiral into a wider global conflict. It was not the first time, and may not be the last, that a regional conventional conflict escalates and draws in larger states. The key difference between this conflict and those that had come before was that it was the first regional war in which escalation was inextricably linked with the possibility of nuclear confrontation. The fact that the war remained limited, and resulted in the restoration of the status quo ante, appears in hindsight to have been a greater achievement than it may have seemed at the time.

In the same vein, the experience in Korea highlighted how quickly the character of war could change in response to shifting policy aims—and how quickly policy aims could shift in response to events on the battlefield. The agenda and decisions of the "enemy"—in this case North Korea and Communist China—played a role in escalating and shifting the war into areas previously unanticipated. War and strategy influence one another, and both sides have a say in the relationship and interactions. Policy and strategy implementation were and remain complex and frustrating; the need for adaptability is paramount.

Generations after it ended, the Korean War retains relevant lessons. We have now returned to an era in which great-power war is all too conceivable, and in which local conflicts could escalate rapidly and ensnare other powers. All future wars between major powers, moreover, will be waged in the shadow of nuclear weapons. This being the case, policymakers and military commanders must constantly weigh strategic and operational decisions not just on the basis of their immediate effectiveness, but also on whether they are likely to escalate or de-escalate already dangerous situations.

War and strategy are not linear processes, and history presents us with two enduring takeaways. First, a war may begin as one thing and quickly become another; and second, policy aims may shift due to the inescapable reciprocity between strategy and war. Nothing is simple regarding war and strategy; it can be messy, frustrating, and, most importantly, bloody for all sides.

CHAPTER 30

Ben-Gurion, Nasser, and Strategy in the Arab-Israeli Conflict

Guy Laron

One could scarcely imagine two people so different. One was born in Eastern Europe, the other in the Middle East. One was entering the last decade of his political career, the other just starting. One rose slowly through the ranks in a workers' party, the other reached the apex of power when he was only thirty-four, after a decisive coup. History destined them to become enemies.

Although coming from different backgrounds, David Ben-Gurion, Israel's Prime Minister, and Gamal Abd al-Nasser, the Egyptian President, shared, as strategists, one trait: they both understood that they would have to think globally to win locally. Both realized that whatever the capabilities of their own countries, the size and strength of the regional and international coalition that would support them would matter a great deal.

In addition, Nasser and Ben-Gurion had to come up with a military strategy which would play to each country's advantage and prey on the other country's weaknesses. Neither Ban-Gurion nor Nasser came to power with these blueprints in mind. The concepts the Israeli premier and the Egyptian military dictator developed were the result of a learning process each went through as they grappled with economic, diplomatic, technological, and military aspects of the conflict between the nations they led.

Their confrontation took place during a formative decade in the history of the modern Middle East. Hence, the decisions they made have shaped the region for many decades to come. Every Israeli leader adopted in some form or another Ben-Gurion's methods. And any Arab leader who sought to rise to regional prominence had Nasser in the back of his mind.[1]

I

Initially, neither Ben-Gurion nor Nasser sought confrontation. When the Free Officers Movement, headed by Nasser, came to power in 1952, Ben-Gurion welcomed the new Egyptian regime. In a speech to the Israeli Parliament, Ben-Gurion wished the Egyptian junta success. Ben-Gurion was probably genuine. While he had inner musings about expanding Israel's borders, Egypt was a low priority. His eyes were turned toward Israel's long and serpentine border with the Kingdom of Jordan. At some points the eastern border was only a dozen miles from Israel's coastline. Israelis always feared a scenario in which the Jordanian Legion, at a moment's notice, would make a run for the beaches, and cut communications between Israel's southern and northern parts.

Likewise, Nasser had other priorities. First, he had to survive the postcoup repercussions and take control over the levers of power. Second, he was focused on the problem that had destabilized Egyptian politics since 1945: the presence of 80,000 British troops on the western bank of the Suez Canal. They were the legacy of World War II, when Britain turned Egypt into its main logistical center in the Middle East. In 1942, British units had marched on Cairo and forced King Farouk to fire the government and appoint a cabinet to London's liking. It was this humiliating experience that made clear to the Egyptians that their country would never be free as long as the British garrison was there. Nasser involved himself in hectic negotiations with the British and the Americans to resolve this issue.

Yet the reality of the Arab-Israeli conflict forced itself upon Ben-Gurion and Nasser. Tensions between the two neighboring countries started to increase from the early-1950s. Israel suspected that Egypt was not doing enough to stop the movement of Palestinian refugees across the border. The refugees resided in camps in the Gaza Strip, then controlled by Egypt. Up to the War of 1948, the refugees had lived in Palestine. When the war erupted, hundreds of thousands of Palestinians left the country, sometimes willingly and sometimes under duress, and fled to neighboring Arab countries. When the war ended,

---

1. For overviews of the Arab-Israeli conflict, see Benny Morris, *Righteous Victims* (New York, NY: Vintage, 2001); and Avi Shlaim, *The Iron Wall* (New York, NY: Penguin, 2014).

the newly established state of Israel, controlling the territory that had once been known as Palestine, refused to let the refugees come back.

For those Palestinians, the new border separating them from the land they called home was an artificial line. They crossed the border by night, seeking to steal goods (often they would harvest their former fields). When they encountered Israeli settlers, violent clashes occurred, ending with dead Israelis and Palestinians. Israelis perceived this as an existential struggle regarding their right to establish sovereignty over a country they had fought long and hard to possess.

Infiltration from Gaza to Israel grew apace, especially from 1954. The Egyptian police were doing as much as they could to stop it, but were not able to hermetically seal the border. When Ben-Gurion assumed his role as the Israeli Minister of Defense in February 1955, he wanted to take a bold move. He authorized the 101 Commando Unit to penetrate deep into Gaza and blow up a water pump. The operation—code named Black Arrow—spun out of control. By the time it was over, thirty-four Egyptian officers and enlisted men lay dead. It was the worst border skirmish since 1948.

II

It was at that moment that Nasser had to form a strategy that would address the threat he was facing. He decided to spread his wings over the Palestinian refugees who wanted to cross the border. The Egyptian military intelligence began training and organizing the infiltrators who were dubbed *fidayeen* (loosely translated as "those who are willing to sacrifice themselves"). The *fidayeen* were sent out to penetrate deep inside Israel and to serve as Egypt's eyes and ears. More skilled in the art of warfare, the *fidayeen* were also more lethal when they encountered Israeli settlers and soldiers along the sandy landscape of the Negev. Nasser believed that he could use the *fidayeen* to deter Israel from launching operations such as Black Arrow.

Nasser's response to Israeli commando raids was to commence low-intensity warfare. Israel's response harked back to its experience in the 1948 War which had started off as a civil war in which Palestinian irregular units attacked Jewish convoys. Many Jewish settlements, including Jerusalem, found themselves under siege. Initially waiting until the last British soldier left the country, the Jewish armed forces, known then as the Hagana, planned ahead. Once the British withdrawal was complete, the Hagana implemented Plan D, the aim of which was to take advantage of their logistical edge. Plan D outlined how the Jewish forces would be mobilized in order to concentrate them in specific fronts. That way the Jewish army could have a numerical advantage on the battlefield, although overall there were more Palestinian irregulars then Jewish soldiers. The plan was decisive in ensuring Israel's victory in the first phase of the war.

The Israeli Defense Forces (IDF)—the successors to the Hagana—responded in the same manner to the challenge of Palestinian infiltration. Rather than adopt defensive measures that would stop the refugees from entering Israel, IDF generals preferred to take advantage of Israel's organizational edge. Following the doctrine developed in 1948, the IDF strategy that emerged in the early-1950s emphasized the concentrated use of force. Instead of dispersing its units along the border, the IDF planned to hit targets inside Arab countries, taking advantage of the Israelis' superior ability to plan, execute, and fight at night. Rather than respond in kind, Israel preferred massive retaliation, inflicting a painful price for any act of infiltration.

Following this logic, the IDF responded to *fidayeen* raids with three large operations in October and November 1955, all meant to humiliate Nasser. And they were quite successful. The Egyptian outposts were easily taken, and eighty-four Egyptian officers and enlisted men were taken prisoner, while ninety-three others were killed. Militarily, Nasser was powerless to stop Israel's escalation. As a result, he responded by suspending *fidayeen* operations inside Israel. His army was too weak, and Nasser knew it. However, he decided to take a step in the international arena that would send Israel reeling.

III

In September 1955, Nasser made an announcement broadcast around the world. He proclaimed that Egypt and Communist Czechoslovakia had signed a contract for a large arms deal. It was clear to all that Egypt was actually making the deal with the Soviet Union, thus tying itself to the Communist bloc. By doing so, Nasser turned his back on the informal alliance he had maintained with the US since he came to power. Indeed, Washington had been hoping to make Egypt the cornerstone of a regional defense alliance modeled on NATO; the planned acronym was MEDO—Middle East Defense Organization. But there was another reason why the Czech-Egyptian arms deal was such a game changer. It included eighty jets and a hundred and fifty tanks. These were items that Egypt had sought to purchase since the end of World War II; they were the bare minimum for creating a modern army. The jets would allow Egypt to have an air force worthy of its name and the tanks would enable the creation of Egypt's first armored division. The main conclusion that the Israelis drew from this was that the military balance was tipping in Egypt's favor.

Moscow had not been Nasser's first choice, but after months of haggling with Washington, he had realized that the Americans were making demands— such as signing a formal military alliance—that he could not accept. Any commitment to a Western power would have enraged Egyptian public opinion. Furthermore, the Americans were trying to weaken Nasser's negotiating position by devising an alternative: a regional defense alliance which would be led by Iraq. It came into life in February 1955 and became known as the Baghdad Pact.

Despite his disappointments, Nasser would have been willing to haggle some more with the West had Israel not intervened. The humiliations suffered by the Egyptian armed forces at the hands of Israeli troops made Egyptian officers accuse Nasser of not delivering on his promise to conclude a large arms deal. The officers alleged that better weapons would have produced a better response to the Israeli menace. Fear that the army would turn against him pushed Nasser into the Russian bear hug.

What started as a stopgap would develop in later years into a strategic alliance. One could say that Nasser came for the weapons but stayed for the overall package the Soviet Union could offer to developing countries: economic aid, turn-key installations, barter trade, and advisors who came to Egypt to offer advice on how to operate Soviet weapons, run a command economy, build the secret services, and create a one-party state. The Russian package was a perfect fit for Nasser's needs. He believed from an early stage in his career that the solution to Egypt's woes was a strong interventionist state. Nasser claimed he was practicing an ideology he called Arab Socialism. In reality, what Nasser espoused was Communism with Arab characteristics. For instance, by the early-1960s most of the Egyptian economy was nationalized.

In any case, the ball was in Israel's court. The first public response came in the form of a speech by Prime Minister Moshe Sharett, who served between late 1953 and November 1955, in which he announced that Israel would save no effort to make a counter-arms deal. At the time Sharett made his speech, it was unclear whether this would even be possible. Israel had friendly relations with the US and received generous economic aid from Washington, but the Eisenhower administration refused to sell weapons to Israel. It was clear to the officials in Washington that any signal that suggested stronger bonds with Israel would weaken American influence in the Arab world. For the same reason, London's approach towards Israel remained polite yet reserved.

Nevertheless, there was one European power that felt compelled to strengthen the Jewish state at that particular time. Paris shared Jerusalem's fear of Nasser. At that time, Egypt was supporting the underground movement in Algeria that aimed to expel France from North Africa. In truth, that support amounted to no more than some cash and a small amount of light weapons, but the cabinet of Guy Mollet had convinced itself that toppling Nasser would end the rebellion in Algeria, and so, Israel and France established their own strategic alliance.

Paris agreed to sell Israel jets (Dassult-made Mysteres and Ouragans) and tanks (AMX-type) that would make the advantage Egypt had gained when it signed a deal with Czechoslovakia null and void. It was clear to Ben-Gurion that by buying these weapons from France, Israel was committing to a future confrontation with Egypt and he saw no problem in that. Ben-Gurion believed that Israel's fate would be secure only if it was allied with a major Western power. He had tried to talk the US into accepting this role and failed; teaming up with France was second-best. Egypt and Israel were now armed and loaded. They shared a border and held a grudge toward each other. It was a recipe for war and war indeed erupted in late October 1956.

IV

When Nasser decided to nationalize the Suez Canal Company in July 1956, he made several overoptimistic assumptions. He believed that London and Paris would be slow to respond to the expropriation of their property and that Washington would oppose a Western European military intervention. Likewise, Nasser thought that Israel would not take part in the conflict and, even if it did, Israel would only try to bite off a small slice of the Sinai. If worse came to worst, Nasser assumed that Egyptian fortifications in the northeastern Sinai would delay any Israeli ground invasion.

On the other side of the border, Ben-Gurion was slow to understand the ramifications of the Suez Crisis. In July 1956, he thought Israel had no dog in the fight. But as summer turned to winter, Ben-Gurion realized that the crisis over the nationalization of the Suez Canal company was a window of opportunity. It presented Israel with a chance to punish Egypt for supporting Palestinian guerilla groups, to destroy the weapons Egypt bought from Czechoslovakia, and even to annex the Sinai Peninsula. Furthermore, Israel would be able do all that backed by two major European powers.

By invading Egypt, Israel would provide a valuable service to France and, as a result, cement the alliance between them. And that was just the beginning. During his discussions with British and French officials, Ben-Gurion argued that the war could be an opportunity to redraw the map of the Middle East. Thus, the Israeli prime minister suggested dividing Jordan between Iraq and Israel, which would allow Israel to occupy the West Bank. He also proposed attaching southern Lebanon to Israel and creating a Maronite-Christian state north of the Litani River. London and Paris, however, politely ignored these proposals.

At the end of October 1956, the Egyptian and Israeli armies went into the battle with two different strategies. The Egyptian army relied on static and mutually supporting lines of defense. The Israeli army, true to its offensive predisposition, was planning to use its armored troops to break through Egyptian fortifications. While each made careful preparations for the war, neither army fought particularly well. Ultimately, what decided the fate of the campaign was the fact that the Egyptian army was no match for the tripartite military coalition between Israel, Britain, and France.

Egyptian generals understood that they could not defend both the Sinai and the Suez Canal. For that reason, weeks before hostilities began, the Egyptians had thinned down the number of troops in the Sinai and pulled their units toward the Suez Canal, as they anticipated an Anglo-French landing there. As a result, when IDF troops entered the Sinai on October 29, the Israelis enjoyed numerical superiority. Yet even under these auspicious circumstances, the IDF had trouble conquering the Egyptian compound at Umm-Qatef, overlooking the road to the Suez Canal.

The IDF were able to accomplish that mission only when Nasser, alarmed by the onset of an Anglo-French air offensive against Egyptian airfields on the evening of October 31, gave the order to withdraw all Egyptian troops in the Sinai. Once Egyptian forces began their retreat, Israeli cavalry was quick to exploit success. By November 2, Israeli tanks, meeting little resistance, were within a few miles of the Suez Canal. On November 5, when Israeli troops reached the southern tip of the Sinai, at Sharm al-Sheikh, Ben-Gurion ordered his Chief of Staff, Moshe Dayan, to begin preparations for a permanent Israeli presence in the peninsula. However, no sooner had Ben-Gurion uttered these words than sharp American pressure to withdraw from Egyptian territory began. By March 1957, Israel had reluctantly pulled out all Israeli units from the Sinai—a withdrawal that showed how limited international support for Israeli expansion remained.

Even so, the 1956 War foreshadowed the emerging Cold War in the Middle East. Israel attacked Egypt as part of a Western coalition that included Britain and France. Egypt received Soviet support in the form of nuclear threats against its adversaries. The war revolved around control of the Suez Canal, the main waterway through which oil flowed to Western Europe.[2] The West wanted the jugular vein of the Western European economy to not be held by a nationalist dictator allied with Moscow. However, that goal was not achieved during the war in 1956. This end result made Western Europe and the US even more suspicious about Nasser and his rising stature in the region. Thus, this short war unsettled the Middle East and made both Ben-Gurion and Nasser reassess and reshape their strategies.

V

Nasser had espoused the ideology of Pan-Arabism before the Suez Crisis, but he would actually put the ideology into practice after 1956. Pan-Arabism was a vision not of one man, but of an entire social group. The urban, educated, white-collar workers in the Arab world believed that the ills that plagued their societies would be cured with the creation of a super-state encompassing most of the Middle East and North Africa. Such a state could use oil revenue to spur industrialization and create a union powerful enough to face Western or Eastern pressure. Nasser, who defied the West when he nationalized the Anglo-French Suez Company in July 1956 and withstood international pressure throughout that summer, became the personification of that vision.

In 1957, the Eisenhower administration tried to curtail Nasser's growing regional influence by creating an alliance of conservative Arab regimes which included Jordan, Saudi Arabia, and Iraq. It then made efforts to convince that coalition to threaten Syria with invasion, a punishment for Syria's friendly relations with Moscow. This crisis reached a crescendo toward the end of the year. Eventually the threat of invasion receded but a significant part of the Syrian command was shaken by the experience.

Nationalist officers in the Syrian armed forces feared both Washington's interference and the growing power of the Syrian Communist Party. In January 1958, a group of Syrian officers, without consulting elected officials,

---

2. On the war and is aftermath see, BennyMorris, *Israel's Border Wars* (Oxford: Clarendon, 1997); Mordechai Bar-On, *The Gates of Gaza* (New York, NY: Palgrave, 1994); Laura James, *Nasser at War* (New York, NY: Palgrave, 2006).

traveled to Cairo and handed Syria to Nasser on a silver platter. The Syrian president and the prime minister did not like any of it. Yet enthusiasm on the streets of Damascus was so strong that the two leaders had no choice but to proclaim their support for the Egyptian-Syrian union. The new political entity was formally established in February 1958.

Pan-Arabist zeal proved contagious. In May, a constitutional crisis in Lebanon brought ethnic tensions to the surface. The President of Lebanon, a Christian, Camille Chamoun, was trying to cling to power despite term limits. From his newly won base in Syria, Nasser supplied the Sunni opposition movements in Lebanon with cash and light weapons. Unrest and bloody battles continued to simmer in the Land of Cedars until the end of the year. Outside observers believed the country was drifting toward the Nasserite orbit.

At the end of June, a coup plot by pro-Nasserite officers was uncovered in Amman, the capital of Jordan. In response, King Hussein of Jordan asked his Iraqi ally to send troops to support his regime, setting the stage for a new and more dramatic development. In early July, Iraqi troops that were set to enter Jordan, passed first through Baghdad. This gave cover for a coup plan that was already under way. It turned out that parts of the Iraqi army were led by a Free Officers' Movement modeled on the one that Nasser had established in Egypt. Following the coup, the royal family of Iraq was slaughtered at its palace and Iraq was turned from a constitutional democracy into a military dictatorship.

The events of July 1958 were the high point of Pan-Arabism. The Egyptian dictator seemed to have a finger in every pie: Lebanon, Syria, Jordan, and Iraq. For a brief moment it seemed that Egypt would control not just one significant route through which oil flowed to Europe—the Suez Canal—but all of them. Had all of these countries fallen under Nasser's sway, as Syria had, Nasser would have controlled a vast area stretching from the Levant to the Persian Gulf. This moment of grandeur was not accidental. Many resources had gone into the powerful radio station *The Voice of the Arabs* which, broadcasting from Cairo, spread Pan-Arab propaganda to the entire region. Moreover, Egyptian spies were active in several Arab capitals.

Yet Nasser's ambition was more modest than it seemed. The Egyptian dictator wanted to be seen by the two superpowers as a regional boss. In that way he could extract aid from both the Soviet Union and the United States. However, he understood that governing the Arab world was beyond the capability of Egypt, a country facing many social challenges of its own. Indeed, though the events in Lebanon, Jordan, and Iraq were inspired by Nasser and his vision, they were not controlled by him. And when the dust settled in those countries, they remained independent and showed no real desire to join the Syrian-Egyptian union.[3]

It was against this background that Ben-Gurion came up with his regional vision. Known as the alliance of the periphery or Belt B, its aim was to envelop and encircle Nasser's Pan-Arab Bloc. The scheme moved through various permutations over time but the essential principle was to create an alliance with non-Arab countries such as Turkey and Iran. Another component of Ben-Gurion's strategy was to deepen Israel's involvement in Africa and strengthen its relationships with countries that shared a border with Arab states. Israel referred to its relations with Turkey and Iran as "the northern triangle." It also tried to form a "southern triangle" in Africa with states such Ethiopia and Sudan.

Formal steps towards the creation of the northern triangle were taken during the highly volatile summer of 1958. In June of that year Israeli and Turkish representatives met to discuss growing Soviet and Egyptian influence in the region. As a result of these meetings, Ben Gurion signed a pact with Turkey to coordinate their political strategies. In parallel, there were also joint Israeli-Iranian meetings. At the end of July, Ben-Gurion could report in a letter to Eisenhower, "We have begun to strengthen our links with four neighboring countries on the outer ring of the Middle East . . . with the object of establishing a strong dam against the Nasserist-Soviet torrent."[4]

In August, Israel signed bilateral agreements with the Turkish and the Iranian secret services. Turkey and Iran committed to share intelligence about Egyptian activities, while Israel promised to supply information about Soviet policies in the region. Another component was Israeli willingness to train Turkish and Iranian spies. By the end of the year, Israel, Turkey, and Iran had agreed to hold tripartite meetings of their intelligence services. These joint meetings, which received the code name "Trident," were convened once a month in Tel-Aviv, Tehran, or Ankara in the years 1958–68.

---

3. Salim Yaqub wrote an excellent study of the 1958 crisis: Salim Yaqub, *Containing Arab Nationalism: The Eisenhower Doctrine and the Middle East* (Chapel Hill, NC: North Carolina University Press, 2004). For a smart treatment of the politics of Pan-Arabism see, Malik Mufti, *Sovereign Creations: Pan-Arabism and Political Order in Syria and Iraq* (Ithaca, NY: Cornell University Press, 1996).

4. Jacob Abadi, *Israel's Quest for Recognition and Acceptance in Asia* (New York, NY: Routledge, 2004), 13.

However, things had been set in motion even before the summer of 1958. In fact, measures to create a strategic alliance with Iran preceded the establishment of the peripheral alliance. They emanated directly from the geopolitical consequences of the Suez Crisis. In early 1957, Israel withdrew from the Sinai in exchange for a tacit Egyptian promise to stop obstructing the movement of vessels headed for Israel. This agreement, reached thanks to American mediation, opened the naval route for trade between Israel and the Persian Gulf. As a result, Israel and Iran had forged their trade ties and military alliance already in that year. The first oil tanker from Iran arrived to the Israeli port of Eilat in mid-1957.[5]

VI

As Egypt and Israel sought regional and international solutions to their local conflict, they also placed their faith in the acquisition of advanced military technology—but with very different results. Before the onset of World War II, Ben-Gurion had thought about harnessing science mainly for agricultural and industrial purposes. It was only during the war that he grasped the crucial role of technology on the battlefield. The change happened when he stayed for a year in the United States where he witnessed first-hand how the Roosevelt administration pulled together the country's industrial and scientific capabilities to produce cutting-edge military technology. With the war coming to an end, Ben-Gurion began calling on scientists at Jewish Palestine's higher education institutions—Hebrew University, the Technion, and the Weizmann Institute—to serve the needs of the Israeli military industry.

It was around this time that Ben-Gurion realized that scientific prowess could be another way to overcome Arab numerical superiority. If the Israelis had more sophisticated weapons, they could offset the Arabs' manpower advantage. In the end of 1947, Ben-Gurion decided to create a large scientific department within the Hagana. During the 1948 War, the scientific institutions in Palestine became fully committed to harness technology in the service of Israeli victory. Out of this activity grew the science corps within the Israeli Armed Forces (IDF). In 1951, the science corps was one of the largest research institutions in Israel, having five institutes, 560 employees, and a budget of 900,000 Israeli pounds.

5. Abadi, *Israel's Quest for Recognition and Acceptance in Asia*; Trita Parsi, *Treacherous Alliance: The Secret Dealings of Israel, Iran, and the United States* (New Haven, CT: Yale University Press, 2007).

In 1952, Ben-Gurion initiated the creation of an Atomic Energy Committee (AEC), a civilian entity, but in practical terms nuclear research was done within the R & D department at the Ministry of Defense. Ben-Gurion closely monitored the day-to-day management of this department and supported its rapid expansion. However, due to domestic disputes and lack of access to crucial components, by the mid-1950s, Israel's nuclear project had hit a snag.

Again, the Suez Crisis proved pivotal. Israel's strategic alliance with France provided a way to overcome the nuclear impasse. During a summit meeting that preceded the war with Egypt in 1956, Israeli officials received a verbal commitment from French ministers for a major nuclear deal. What the Israelis wanted was a turn-key installation. They would pay full price and in return the French would come to Israel and build a reactor and a plutonium separation installation. The French assented. France also enabled Israel to advance the development of a delivery system. As a result, Israel was allowed to buy missile technology from the same manufacturer that supplied its air force: Dassault.[6]

All this was to cost a lot of money. The exact numbers are a still kept under lock-and-key in Israeli archives but estimates of contemporaries ranged between $180 and $340 million.[7] In the late-1950s, Israel was still a developing country with many other urgent needs. What, then, made Ben-Gurion pursue, with typical single-mindedness, the nuclear project? A close advisor claimed that the Suez Crisis led to a sea change in Ben-Gurion's thinking. It made him realize that Israel needed to jettison the "strategy of dominance," which sought to protect Israel by expanding its borders and instead to adopt a "strategy of deterrence," with the nuclear bomb being a chief tool. It was a strategy, claimed the advisor, suitable for "a castle under siege."[8]

At the other side of the border, Nasser's thinking about missiles was no less formed by the Suez Crisis. At the end of October 1956, French and British planes surprised the Egyptian air force and destroyed its aircraft on the ground. This debacle highlighted for Nasser how limited the value of his air force would be when confronting a technologically advanced adversary. Improving the

6. On Israel's nuclear policy see, Avner Cohen, *Israel and the Bomb* (New York, NY: Columbia University Press, 1998) and Michael Karpin, *The Bomb in the Basement: How Israel Went Nuclear and What that Means for the World* (New York, NY: Simon and Schuster, 2007).

7. Adam Raz, "The Meetings that Created Israel Nuclear Opacity," *Haaretz*, January 16, 2019, https://www.haaretz.co.il/magazine/the-edge/.premium-MAGAZINE-1.6847647, accessed October 12, 2021.

8. Adam Raz, *The Struggle for the Bomb* (Jerusalem: Carmel, 2015), 206–7 [Hebrew].

capabilities of the Egyptian air force would necessitate time and effort. Missiles offered a quicker way to solve the problem.

In May 1958, Nasser asked Nikita Khrushchev, the Soviet Chairman, for "medium-range missiles and bombers." Nasser clearly wanted weapons that would allow him to threaten Israel's rear. He received a categorical "Nyet" in response.[9] Unable to get help from Moscow, Nasser tried to pursue a missile program on his own. From 1960 on, Egyptian officials recruited German scientists who had been involved in the Nazi missiles project. They were offered generous salaries should they move to Egypt and help it create its missile program.

This proved to be a futile endeavor. Egypt had trouble putting enough resources behind the project. Moreover, Egyptian access to the relevant equipment on the world market was limited and prices were exorbitantly high. Furthermore, the missile factory which the Egyptians built had trouble manufacturing a functioning engine. In addition, the German scientists who arrived at Egypt brought with them outmoded knowledge of missile design and did not take advantage of recent breakthroughs. In particular, their understanding of guidance systems was limited and, therefore, the missiles could fly but could not be aimed, rendering the missiles useless as weapons. The missiles were, however, valuable as propaganda showpieces. In July 1962, the made-in-Egypt missiles were launched in the desert to much publicity in the Egyptian media. In July 1963, they were also exhibited during a military parade. This was the high point of the program. By 1965, the missile project had ground to a halt.[10]

Nasser did not find more success when it came to nuclear weapons. In the mid-1950s, he created the Atomic Energy Agency (AEA) and established the Center for Nuclear Research. But it seems that up to the end of 1960, Nasser was mainly interested in the peaceful research of the atom and its potential to solve Egypt's growing energy needs. In January 1958, Nasser agreed with the Soviet ambassador when the latter suggested creating a nuclear-free zone in the Middle East.[11] However, following revelations in the American media at the end of 1960 about the existence of an atomic reactor in Dimona, Israel,

9. V.V. Naumkin et al., *Blizhnevostochny Konflikt: 1957–1967* (Metrik: Moscow, 2003) Documents Number 77 and 108.

10. Owen L. Sirrs, *Nasser and the Missile Age in the Middle East* (New York, NY: Routledge, 2006).

11. Maria Rost Rublee, "Egypt's Nuclear Weapons Program," *Nonproliferation Review* 13:3 (2006); Naumkin et al., *Blizhnivostochny Konflikt, 1957–1967*, Document Number 66.

Nasser changed his tune. He instructed the AEA to start exploring the possibility of producing nuclear weapons. Nasser made it clear that the main factor behind the policy shift was his fear that Israel would get the bomb first.

In January 1961, two low-level officials at the Egyptian Embassy in Washington approached a Soviet diplomat and inquired whether the Soviet Union would be willing to sell a bomb to Egypt. Again, the response was negative.[12] In the same year, Egypt's two-megawatt reactor at Inshas went critical. It was, though, a small research reactor which could not produce significant amounts of weapon-grade material. Moreover, the Soviets, who built the reactor had demanded that all spent fuel would be sent back to the Soviet Union.

One year later, in 1962, Egypt signed a cooperation agreement with the Indian Atomic Energy Commission. Egypt hoped to benefit from scientific cooperation with a friendly country that had a more developed academic and technological infrastructure. In October 1964, enthused by China's first successful atomic test, Nasser sent a delegation there. Its members were to congratulate the Chinese government on being the first developing country to produce nuclear weapons and to ask for help in moving forward the Egyptian efforts in that field. The Chinese allowed the delegation to visit several atomic installations but refused the request to pass a nuclear device to Egyptian hands. The Chinese advice was crystal clear: "You have to build you own infrastructure."[13] By 1965, the Egyptian nuclear program was at the same place as the missile project—in a cul-de-sac.

Nasser failed where Ben-Gurion succeeded for a number of reasons. Chief among them was that, while Ben-Gurion found an ally willing to sell crucial equipment, Nasser did not. Beyond that was the fact that Israel had the scientific infrastructure to support indigenous production. These capabilities relied on efforts to establish top-notch higher education institutions which had preceded the establishment of Israel. Prior to the creation of Israel, Jewish universities in Palestine had become the refuge of leading Jewish chemistry and physics professors who fled Hitler's Europe. In time, those institutions trained and educated the Israeli technicians and scientists that would operate the Dimona reactor and further develop the missile technology bought from France. Egypt lacked the same intellectual and technological infrastructure. For that

12. Naumkin et al., *Blizhnivostochny Konflikt, 1957–1967*, Document Number 147.

13. Yair Evron, "The Arab Position in the Nuclear Field: A Study of Policies up to 1967," *Cooperation and Conflict* VIII (1973): 19–32; Gawdat Bahgat, "The Proliferation of Weapons of Mass Destruction: Egypt," *Arab Studies Quarterly* 29:2 (Spring 2007).

reason, Egyptian scientists could not complete the missile project that the ex-Nazi experts had begun.

VII

Ben-Gurion resigned as prime minister in 1963, though he remained an active backbencher until 1970 and died shortly after the 1973 October War. Three years earlier, in September 1970, Nasser had died of a massive heart attack while still serving as the President of Egypt. Thus ended their era in Middle East politics. However, the strategies the two men crafted remained templates that their successors could use. They also left large legacies in a more ironic way—the decisions Ben-Gurion and Nasser made limited the options of the Arab and Israeli leaders who followed their footsteps.

The conclusion that the IDF drew from its experiences in the years 1948–56 was that its offensive doctrine worked. Twice, the offensive-centered strategy had enabled Israel to vanquish its foes. Israeli generals also determined that the IDF was the strongest army in the region. Therefore, there was a unique window of opportunity to realize the objectives Ben-Gurion had laid out prior to the 1956 War. The planning department at the IDF maintained that by conquering the West Bank, the Sinai, and the Golan Heights, the IDF would create "defensible borders." In the years leading to the 1967 War, a blueprint had emerged detailing how it could be done.

In the meantime, the land forces should become fully mechanized. Tanks would become the main tool to break the formidable fortifications that the Syrians had built on the Golan Heights and the Egyptians had constructed in the Sinai. Strengthening the air force would enable the Israelis to repeat what French and British jets did during the Suez Crisis: launch a surprise air attack and bomb Arab aircraft while they were still on the ground. Air superiority would allow Israeli land forces to advance as quickly as possible.

The rise of the radical Baath regime in Syria in 1963 created the circumstances in which this scenario could unfold. The Syrians gave aid and refuge to the Palestinian Fatah. They hosted Fatah units in Syrian territory, trained them, and instructed them as to how to sneak into Israel through the Lebanese and Jordanian borders. Once they were inside Israel, Fatah units committed acts of sabotage. Israel responded as it did in the 1950s—by conducting across-the-border retaliation raids.

The Syrians also constructed works to divert the tributaries of the Jordan River away from Galilee and thus deprive Israel of water. Israel reciprocated by bombing Syrian water-diversion sites. Toward May 1967, Israeli leaders publicly threatened Syria with a major operation against it. The signal was received in Cairo and Nasser decided he would respond by moving his army into the Sinai in order to deter Israel from attacking his military ally, Syria. As in the 1950s, massive retaliation escalated tensions in the Middle East.

However, in the 1960s, Israel had an alternative to massive retaliation. The Syrian water-diversion plan was technically complicated and dependent on cooperation from other Arab countries, which was not forthcoming. Israel could have refrained from taking action. As for the Fatah guerilla campaign, Israel could have erected a fence in parts of its eastern and northern borders to prevent Palestinian units from entering. However, Israeli generals looked askance on anything that required a major expenditure to defend the current borders, opting to enlarge them instead.

During the war that ensued in June 1967, Israeli contingency plans worked even better than expected. The Israeli air force effectively destroyed the Egyptian, Jordanian, Syrian, and Iraqi forces within the first four hours of the war. In tandem, Israeli land forces went into action.

In the preceding years, Israeli tank operators had trained in driving through exceedingly difficult terrain so that they would be able to take enemy forces by surprise. In June 1967, this worked astoundingly well in the Sinai. Israeli tanks were able to drive over the crest of sand dunes in order to appear at the rear of the fortified Egyptian compound in Umm-Qatef. As a result, Israel won a decisive victory and gained control over the strategic road to Ismailia. That was the point when the Egyptian Chief of Staff, Abd al-Hakim Amer, panicked and ordered a hasty retreat. In response, the Egyptian army in the Sinai disintegrated, just as it had in 1956.

At that point the Israeli general staff realized it could pull troops out of the Sinai and shift them towards other fronts. Unfortunately for Jordan and Syria, they had already committed themselves to the war and exchanged artillery fire with Israel. No one in Amman and Damascus expected to face Israel alone. Yet this was just what happened, once the Egyptian army collapsed. The Jordanian army was too small and the Syrian too torn by ethnic tensions to confront the Israeli war machine. Each folded within forty-eight hours of the first engagement with Israeli armored divisions.

This quick turn of affairs allowed Israel to conquer the Sinai, the West Bank, and the Golan Heights within six days. However, it turned out that it was far easier to acquire new territory than to defend it. Artillery exchanges and commando raids by both Israeli and Egyptian troops started in the summer of 1967 and went into a more intensive phase between 1969 and 1970. Both sides depicted the campaign as a war of attrition. A protracted affair, it played to the strength of the Egyptian army.

Egyptian troops were able to absorb the daring raids and the deep bombing inflicted on them by the Israelis and keep on fighting. When a cease-fire was signed in August 1970 it was the Egyptians who achieved their main goal. They pushed their surface-to-air missile (SAM) batteries up to the Suez Canal. These batteries could prevent Israeli aircraft from harassing Egyptian troops should they decide to cross the canal.

During the three years of lull, between 1970 and 1973, the IDF's devotion to its offensive doctrine became a cult. Although the post-1967 lines were amenable to a defensive strategy, Israeli generals invested in fortifications only half-heartedly. The infamous "Bar-Lev Line" which the Israelis built on the eastern bank of the Suez Canal was series of outposts with large gaps between them. There was not enough manpower in them to stop the Egyptian army, half-a-million-strong, that was camping on the opposite bank.

There were other defensive options. An IDF-technology unit created a device that could throw diesel fuel into the canal and ignite it, turning any crossing into a death trap. However, the general staff deemed the system too costly. Instead, Israeli generals preferred to beef up on tanks and jets. In seeing every defensive weapon as wasteful and ineffectual, Israeli officers also failed to understand the revolutionary effect which Soviet-made anti-tank and anti-aircraft missiles would have on the battlefield.

Although Mossad had been able to gather intelligence on the crucial role that these weapons played in Egyptian preparations for the coming clash, that information was not widely understood. Subsequently, Israeli tank drivers and pilots were taken by surprise as they encountered the Egyptians' devastating efficiency on October 6, 1973, the day on which the Egyptian rubber boats crossed the canal and Syrian cavalry stormed the Golan Heights. This time around, Arab armies took a page from the IDF playbook and attacked without any advance warning. Initially, the plan worked well. The Syrian army was able to bite off large chunks of the Golan Heights and Egyptian units took over a strip of the Sinai, ten kilometers in depth, adjacent to the canal.

Israeli troops suffered heavy casualties in the first forty-eight hours of the war, but after that period, the IDF launched a counteroffensive in the north. By October 10, the Israeli forces were able to push Syrian tanks out of the Golan Heights. The next day, Israeli troops shifted the battle to Syrian territory and came within forty kilometers of Damascus. In the Sinai, the Israelis had to wait longer for a breakthrough. As long as the Egyptians defended the stretch of the Sinai they had conquered in those first two days, the Egyptians had the upper hand. An IDF counteroffensive on October 8 failed miserably and during the following days the Israelis focused on defending their positions.

However, when the Egyptian command made a serious error by launching a major offensive on October 14, the Israelis, having foreknowledge through a Mossad spy, were ready. The great tank battles on October 14—the biggest the world had seen since the end of World War II—involved the elements in which Israeli cavalry excelled: swift maneuver, improvisation, and superb gunnery. The failure of the Egyptian offensive allowed the IDF to exploit a breach in Egyptian defenses and to cross the canal on October 16. In the days that followed, the IDF was able to expand its beachhead on the western bank of the canal. Moving south from Ismailia, Israeli troops were able to reach the outskirts of the city of Suez and encircle the Egyptian Third Army. At that point, Egyptian President Anwar al-Sadat was compelled to seek an immediate cease-fire.

Before the war, IDF generals had insisted that the army's main goal would be to prevent the enemy from gaining any territorial advancement whatsoever. While they achieved that goal in the fighting against the Syrians, the situation in the southern front was closer to a draw. The Israelis may have ensconced themselves on the western bank of the canal, yet the Egyptians maintained a strong presence on the eastern bank. The price of (partial) victory was heavy, in casualties and lost equipment, and the war brought about some soul-searching within the IDF.[14]

Nevertheless, the Israeli general staff held on to its tried-and-true methods when facing Palestinian Liberation Organization (PLO) units in southern Lebanon. Those units had been harassing Israeli civilian population since the early-1970s. Massive retaliation operations did not deter the PLO from shooting Katyusha rockets at the Galilee. Eventually, Israeli tank columns entered Lebanon in June 1982 to settle the matter; their goal harked back to Ben-Gurion's designs from the 1950s. The Israeli Minister of Defense Ariel Sharon, a protégé of Ben-Gurion back in the day, hoped to push the PLO out of Lebanon entirely and to install a Maronite-Christian family, the Jumayyils, in power. Sharon succeeded in achieving the first goal but failed to accomplish

14. Ephraim Enbar, "Israeli Strategic Thinking After 1973," *Journal of Strategic Studies* 6:1 (1983).

the second. As a result, Israel found itself sinking into the Lebanese quagmire for the next two decades.

VIII

All the while, the linkage between the Cold War and the Arab-Israeli conflict had grown stronger during the 1960s—an outgrowth of Israeli and Egyptian strategies for securing foreign support. Lyndon Johnson, who came to office at the end of 1963, did what no American president had done before: he allowed Israel to purchase not only defensive but also offensive weapons. If, up to that point, the majority of Israel's arsenal was made in Western Europe, from the mid-1960s the United States became the main supplier. It was also under Johnson that Israel and Washington formalized their alliance by signing a strategic memorandum of understanding which enabled the first American-Israeli tank deal.

On the other side of the border, Egypt was becoming more attached to the Soviet Union. After the Suez Crisis, the Soviet Union committed to fund and construct the most important development project in Egypt's modern history: the Aswan Dam. Up until Khrushchev's ouster in 1964, Moscow showed nothing but steadfast devotion to its most important trade partner in the Middle East and Africa. It gave logistical and military support to Egypt's war in Yemen and lavishly funded Egyptian industrial growth. After 1964, the new leaders in the Kremlin showed some tough love toward Egypt's ever-growing needs, and they strengthened their relations with Syria. Among other support, the Russians agreed to fund and build a dam over the Euphrates.

The blooming affair between Moscow and Damascus, as well as the Baath regime's penchant for extorting high taxes from British and American oil corporations, led officials in the Lyndon Johnson administration to call on their Israeli counterparts to act against Syria. The resulting border skirmishes between Israel and Syria made a war in the Middle East much more likely. Each superpower stood behind its proxy, a tendency especially pronounced during the last day of the war (June 10, 1967). The Soviets became alarmed by Israel's swift movement across the Golan Heights and threatened to intervene militarily. President Johnson responded by sending the Sixth Fleet into the eastern Mediterranean. A crisis was averted only because on the same afternoon, Israel accepted the UN's cease-fire resolution.

The guns never really fell silent, even after the war ended. As no peace settlement emerged out of the wreckage, both the local players and the superpowers prepared for the next war. The Soviet Union and the United States increased their military sales in the area and understood the Arab-Israeli conflict as an opportunity to test their newest weapons, especially electronic warfare equipment. Indeed, the years that followed the Six-Day War were the hot years of the Cold War in the Middle East.

The arms race between Israel on the one hand, and Egypt, Syria, and Iraq on the other, fueled tensions. Furthermore, in response to entreaties by its Egyptian ally, and because it served its own needs, the Soviet Union sent expeditionary forces, 10,000-strong, to Egypt in March 1970. As a result, Israeli and Soviet troops found themselves fighting each other. At times, Israeli and Soviet pilots engaged in dogfights above the Suez Canal. In the summer of 1970, Soviet teams manning surface-to-air batteries fulfilled a key role in doing away with Israeli air superiority, something that forced Jerusalem to accept a cease-fire in August. Soviet forces would remain in Egypt until the summer of 1972, when Nasser's successor, Anwar Sadat, asked them to leave. However, even after their forced departure, there was a Soviet advisor embedded in every battalion in the Egyptian army.

Throughout the years 1967–73 both superpowers made half-hearted attempts to move the warring parties towards the negotiations table. But the price of applying pressure on their clients seemed too high to Washington and Moscow, the disagreements between Israel and Egypt too deep. Besides, the two superpowers had more pressing concerns to attend to (for example, Vietnam). It turned out, though, that not doing enough to force a settlement was also risky. Indeed, Egypt's and Syria's decision to go to war against Israel in October 1973 brought the superpowers to a crisis point, when Moscow's threats of intervention resulted in an American strategic nuclear alert.

The 1973 War highlighted that the strategy which Ben-Gurion and Nasser had pioneered—of relying on outside powers—came with a price. The more Israel and Egypt leaned on their superpower-patrons, the less autonomy they had. Israel, for instance, avoided launching a preemptive air strike on the first day of the war because it had a prior understanding with Washington that under no circumstances would Israel be the aggressor. Likewise, Sadat agreed to authorize a disastrous armored offensive in the Sinai on October 14 only because the Soviets were pressing him to do so.

The last Arab-Israeli war to be fought along Cold War lines was the 1982 Lebanon War. The Israeli invasion was tacitly approved by American Secretary of State Alexander Haig, on account of the fact that both Syria and the PLO were Soviet clients. Soviet advisors were present in Syrian army headquarters and in several units during the fighting, and an unknown number were killed and injured. As in the Yom-Kippur War, the Soviets did their best to supply the Syrian army. Nevertheless, the Russians frustrated their Palestinian and Syrian allies by not doing more to stop the fighting, largely out of concern about a potential confrontation with the United States.[15]

IX

Pan-Arabism as a plan of action was dying already during Nasser's last years in power. In 1961, Syria seceded from the union because Egypt treated it like a colony. Nasser ignored the Syrian officers that had helped to annex their country. He sought to turn Syria into Egypt's breadbasket, while ensuring that Syria would buy finished goods only from Egypt. What happened to Syria served as a cautionary tale for other Arab countries. Arab rulers learned that Pan-Arabism was actually Egyptian imperialism in disguise. In the following decades, Arab kings and presidents spoke the language of Pan-Arabism, but only paid lip service to the cause.

After the union with Syria collapsed, Nasser still looked for ways to secure himself as a regional leader. Each time he came up short. In fact, Nasser's bid for hegemony in the Arab world brought to the fore countervailing forces, chief among them were conservative Saudi Arabia and radical Syria.

In 1962, Cairo intervened in Yemen's civil war by supporting the republican forces. Beyond the ideological affinity between the Yemeni Free Officers and Nasserism stood Nasser's grudge against the house of Saud. Nasser believed that the Saudis had bribed Syrian officers in 1961 to dismantle the Egyptian-Syrian union. Through its intervention in Yemen, Cairo was able to leapfrog over the Red Sea and establish a large military presence—at their peak, Egyptian expeditionary forces were 70,000-strong—in Saudi Arabia's back yard. This decision, which initially looked like a brilliant move on the regional chessboard, turned out to be too clever by half. Egypt quickly found itself involved in a bloody and protracted low-intensity conflict with no end in sight. When Nasser made another fateful mistake in May 1967—remilitarizing the Sinai in

15. On superpowers' policies toward the region see, Galia Golan, *Soviet Policies in the Middle East: From World War II to Gorbachev* (Cambridge: Cambridge University Press, 1990) and Douglas Little, *American Orientalism: The United States and the Middle East since 1945* (Chapel Hill, NC: North Carolina University Press, 2008).

hopes of resuscitating his faltering regional ambitions—the result was a devasting defeat for both Egypt and the Pan-Arab vision.

The last Arab leader that tried to utilize Pan-Arabism was Saddam Hussein, who believed that the end of the Cold War and the demise of the Soviet Union opened a new window of opportunity. However, his hopes that his act of defiance towards the US—the occupation of Kuwait in August 1990— would unite the Arab world behind his leadership were dashed, and he, too, went down to a crushing military defeat. Moreover, by that time, a new aspiration for regional unity had swept the Middle East. Pan-Islam was a cause that was adopted and adapted by the Muslim Brotherhood and revolutionary Iran. In the decades that followed Nasser's death, it was this religious vision, rather than the nationalist one, that proved more enduring and more consequential.

The concept of the peripheral alliance proved far more enduring. After Ban-Gurion left office, his successor, Levi Eshkol, was able to further develop secret ties with Iran. Up to 1979, Iran, with its oil wealth, was second only to the US in Israel's list of allies. Iran, for instance, enabled Israel to establish a Mossad station in Iraqi Kurdistan in 1965. Thus, Israel established an alliance with another "peripheral" ally—the Kurdish nationalist movement. Up to 1975, Israel's involvement with the Kurds enabled it to weaken Iraq considerably. Iran also funded Israel's missile program and allowed it to conduct trials on its territory. The alliance worked so well that it continued to exist well into the mid-1980s, Khomeini's fundamentalist Islamism notwithstanding. Here and in other cases, notably Yemen and Lebanon, the search for peripheral allies never ceased.

Neither did the reliance on ballistic missiles and non-conventional weapons diminish. Although the use of nuclear weapons was discussed by the Israeli leadership both in 1967 and 1973, it was decided in both cases that Israel's conventional might was effective enough and that the use of a doomsday weapon would be counter-productive. Nasser used chemical weapons against the royalist forces in Yemen and Saddam did the same during the Iran-Iraq War. Yet neither country used non-conventional weapons against Israel, which had, in the meantime, become committed to ensuring that it remained the only nuclear power in the Middle East.

In 1981, Israel adopted the so-called Begin Doctrine which stipulated that Israel would function as a regional enforcer of the Non-Proliferation Treaty and would put a stop to any attempt by regional players to manufacture a nuclear weapon. The same year, Israel bombed an Iraqi reactor, named

"Osirak," at the Tuwaitha complex. Israel's attack supplied Saddam with a pretext to order his team of nuclear scientists to embark on a clandestine program which could have produced a bomb circa-1995. However, Saddam felt compelled to confront the US even sooner and invaded Kuwait in August 1990. Much of Iraq's nuclear infrastructure was destroyed during the war that ensued. Since Saddam was more successful than Nasser in developing ballistic missiles, he was able to use them during the Gulf War against Israel—as he had used them against Iran in the 1980s. His SCUD missiles hit some targets in Israel, thereby allowing Saddam to claim a moral victory. But the damage was too limited to provoke a major Israeli response.

X

Dean Acheson, the American Secretary of State between 1949 and 1953, titled his memoir *Present at the Creation*. His meaning was that his time in power had been the crucial moment when the modern international order emerged. Like Acheson, Ben-Gurion and Nasser were present at the creation of a new regional order in the Middle East.

Ben-Gurion and Nasser held office while the region was undergoing dramatic historical processes. A world war had ended, the British and French empires were disintegrating, and the Cold War was taking shape. In these circumstances, Ben-Gurion and Nasser took decisions that reverberated long after they left office.

Ben-Gurion refined and tested the IDF's military doctrine amid the confrontation between Israel and Egypt in the 1950s. Nasser's cry for help from the Soviet Union pushed Ben-Gurion from his perch on the proverbial fence and convinced the Israeli leader to seek an alliance with the West. Additionally, the challenge that Nasser's Pan-Arab ideology posed to the regional order led Ben-Gurion to seek allies in the Middle Eastern periphery. Ben-Gurion's pursuit of non-conventional weapons sent Nasser on a wild goose chase.

In the process, the main features of the Arab-Israeli confrontation were set. While Israel relied on its superior abilities in the fields of logistics, technology, and execution to win wars, the Arab side adopted defensive measures to break the teeth of Israeli offensives as well as guerilla warfare in order to embroil Israel in long wars of attrition. As Israel succeeded in expanding its borders, Arab military and political coordination increased. Israel attached itself firmly to the capitalist camp in the Cold War, while Arab countries created an alliance with Moscow and borrowed some elements from the Soviet economic system.

While most Arab countries viewed Israel's existence with a mix of frustration and anger, Israel always found regional allies who were willing to break ranks. Moreover, while Israel was able to survive and thrive in a hostile environment, Arab countries proved capable of setting a limit to Israeli overreach. Ben-Gurion and Nasser established these contours of regional politics. Even after they departed the scene, the same patterns would continue to shape conflict and rivalry in the Middle East.

CHAPTER 31

Nehru and the Strategy of Non-Alignment

Tanvi Madan

In June 1956, US Secretary of State John Foster Dulles infamously said neutralism was "immoral and shortsighted."[1] This was seen as a broadside against the countries pursuing non-alignment, which many conflated with neutrality. Shortly after, however, Dulles clarified that he was referring to "very few neutrals, if any." This left a bemused Walter Lippmann commenting that, for the secretary of state, "neutrality is immoral but . . . there are no neutrals who are immoral."[2]

Dulles's clarification may have reflected the Eisenhower administration's changing perception of non-alignment, as well as of India, its most prominent proponent. But it also reflected the fact that, to many observers, non-alignment was quite amorphous. At the time and since then, non-alignment has represented different things to different people—to some a prism, to others a critique of the Cold War, and to yet others an approach to international affairs.[3]

1. John Foster Dulles, "The Cost of Peace: Address by the Secretary of State at the Commencement Exercises," Speech at Iowa State College, Ames, Iowa, June 9, 1956.

2. Dennis Merrill, *Bread and the Ballot: The United States and India's Economic Development, 1947–1963* (Chapel Hill, NC: University of North Carolina Press, 1990), 132.

3. Relevant works on this subject include Tanvi Madan, *Fateful Triangle: How China Shaped U.S.-India Relations During the Cold War* (Washington, DC: Brookings Institution Press, 2020); Srinath Raghavan, *War and Peace in Modern India: A Strategic History of the Nehru Years* (Ranikhet: Permanent Black, 2010); Rudra Chaudhuri, *Forged in Crisis: India And The United States Since 1947* (London: Hurst, 2013); Zorawar Daulet Singh, *Power and Diplomacy: India's Foreign Policies During the Cold War* (New Delhi: Oxford University Press, 2019); and Swapna

For India's first Prime Minister Jawaharlal Nehru, considered the architect of non-alignment, it was not a passive, neutral, immoral, or indifferent concept. A year before India became free from British imperial rule, Nehru had already previewed the approach that would lie at the heart of Indian foreign policy:

> For too long we of Asia have been petitioners in Western courts and chancelleries. That story must now belong to the past. We propose to stand on our own feet and cooperate with all others who are prepared to cooperate with us.[4]

Years later, the prime minister explained that non-alignment was "essentially . . . freedom of action which is a part of independence . . . a policy of friendship toward all nations, uncompromised by adherence to any military pacts." He stressed that, for India, non-alignment was not an "arbitrary choice," but rather rooted "in our past history and way of thinking as well as in fundamental national exigencies."[5] And for independent India's first generation of leaders in the 1940s and 1950s, those imperatives involved nation-building at home, at the very time the Cold War was unfurling abroad.

Among other things, non-alignment was Nehru's approach to the world as he found it. Nehru believed that the new nation he was leading did not have the luxury of isolation. The world—and its wars—would inevitably come to India. But the world did not just present challenges; it also offered opportunities to a country that needed to develop economically. Thus, for India, international engagement was not a choice, but a necessity. Nehru, however, rejected the idea that the only way to approach the world was the alliance way. He did not accept that the only two options were joining either the American or the Soviet bloc—even as he recognized that the superpower competition was a key, if not the dominant, feature of the international order at the time.

Nehru's response was not a third bloc, but a third way—what came to be called non-alignment. As it evolved as an approach, non-alignment came to involve two elements: a strategy of deterrence, and a strategy of diversification.

Nayudu Kona, *The Nehru Years: Indian Non-Alignment as the Critique, Discourse and Practice of Security (1947–1964)*, thesis submitted for the degree of Doctor of Philosophy to King's College London, University of London, 2015.

4. Jawaharlal Nehru, "Speech at the Plenary Session of the Asian Relations Conference," New Delhi, March 23, 1947 in *Selected Works of Jawaharlal Nehru, Second Series*, Volume 2, Sarvepalli Gopal et al., eds. (Oxford: Oxford University Press, 1985), 503–9.

5. Jawaharlal Nehru, "Changing India," *Foreign Affairs* 41:3 (April 1963), 453–65.

They were designed to meet India's objectives of security, development, *and* autonomy in a Cold War context.

Non-alignment was not just an Indian choice. By 1960, *Time* covered its spread and influence, commenting, "The neutrals have made their weight felt [and] no longer consider themselves mere spear carriers but movers and shakers."[6] The magazine even noted that the group had its own "Big Five"— besides Nehru, Egypt's Gamal Abdel Nasser, Ghana's Kwame Nkrumah, Indonesia's Sukarno, and Yugoslavia's Josip Broz Tito. A few years later, Nehru observed in *Foreign Affairs* that non-alignment had become "an integral part of the international pattern and is widely conceded to be a comprehensible and legitimate policy, particularly for the emergent Afro-Asian states."[7]

That pointed to the confluence of at least two trends in which non-alignment was rooted: the Cold War and decolonization. The non-aligned countries, many of them recently emerging from colonial rule, shared a "similar outlook," as Nehru put it.[8] However, each also interpreted non-alignment in their own way. This chapter focuses on non-alignment as conceived of and practiced by Nehru, particularly his understanding of its underlying strategies of deterrence and diversification. Both were a response to and a recognition of India's exposure to the Cold War, and were designed to avoid war and dependence. But the strategies were not merely defensive or reactive. Rather, Nehru proactively sought to deter an escalation of tensions between the two blocs that could hurt India, and to take advantage of superpower competition when it could help India.

I

What non-alignment was—and was not—was much debated during the Cold War. It continues to be a subject of discussion. This was evident when an influential group of scholars and former practitioners in India released a report in 2012 outlining a foreign policy for the country labeled, "Non-Alignment 2.0." The title and the term "non-alignment," in particular, provoked several responses in both India and abroad. Some commentators conflated non-alignment with the Non-Aligned Movement that had been formed in 1961. Others interpreted

6. "A New Look at Neutralism," *Time*, October 24, 1960, http://content.time.com/time /subscriber/article/0,33009,871750,00.html.
7. Nehru, "Changing India."
8. Nehru, "Changing India."

non-alignment as neutrality, or equidistance, or even a "go-it-alone attitude." Yet others derided it as a concept that was about weak nations "hid[ing] behind principles," or an "archaic concept," or even an "abstract doctrine" that was developed with little relation to Indian national interest.[9]

While the interpretations varied, almost all the commentators acknowledged that non-alignment emerged in significant part as a response to the Cold War. Some argued that that context in which it emerged made non-alignment irrelevant for India in the twenty-first century. Others asserted that it should remain a valid touchstone for New Delhi and be the path India should continue to follow.

Within the Cold War context, non-alignment has been interpreted either as a defensive reaction to or a rejection of the bipolar security framework, or as an offensive approach to gain leverage. Some have argued it was a strategy of isolation, noting, "Nonalignment as a foreign policy was designed to keep India out of the way of the storms and stresses of the Cold War, allowing India to concentrate on its economic development."[10] Others have asserted it was a declaration of independence—"the ultimate expression of a newly independent nation's reluctance to be bound by any other actor's strategic needs and preferences."[11]

As conceptualized and practiced during the Cold War, Nehru's non-alignment approach had elements of both defense and offense. Non-alignment was as much about shunning dependence—and avoiding its entanglements and vulnerabilities—as it was about asserting independence. Early in independent India's history, the ruling Indian National Congress party had, as Rudra Chaudhuri put it, "agreed that India was to enjoy complete and uncompromising autonomy

---

9. Sunil Khilnani et al, *Nonalignment 2.0: A Foreign and Strategic Policy for India in the 21st Century* (Delhi: Centre for Policy Research, 2012); T. P. Sreenivasan, "Nonalignment Misconceived," *New Indian Express*, April 1, 2012; Ram Jethmalani, "Non-Alignment Is Over: This Is No Time to Be Neutral," *The Sunday Guardian*, March 4, 2012, http://www.sunday-guardian .com/analysis/non-alignment-is-over-this-is-no-time-to-be-neutral; Sadanand Dhume, "Failure 2.0," *Foreign Policy*, March 16, 2012; Ashley Tellis, *Nonalignment Redux: The Perils of Old Wine in New Skins* (Washington, DC: Carnegie Endowment for International Peace, July 2012); W.P.S. Sidhu, "Non-Alignment: Back to the Future?" *Mint*, March 4, 2012, https://www.livemint.com /Opinion/3Got8cVnKnpmtnGNqKMarM/Nonalignment-back-to-the-future.html.

10. Pramit Pal Chaudhuri, "The Day India and the U.S. Didn't Ally," *Hindustan Times's Foreign Hand*, November 25, 2010, https://rhg.com/research/the-day-india-and-the-us-didnt -ally/.

11. Rudra Chaudhuri, "Why Culture Matters: Revisiting the Sino-Indian Border Conflict of 1962," *Journal of Strategic Studies* 32:6 (2009): 847.

in its strategic decision-making process."[12] But Indian policymakers soon acknowledged reality—even if India wanted to, it could not isolate itself, and, moreover, it was likely to be dependent on others for a while. Moreover, as much as India wanted to be self-sufficient and unaffected by others' decisions, the reality was different: to achieve its goals, India had to engage with the world. And what emerged and evolved over time was a strategy that Indian leaders—acting from weakness and operating under political and economic constraints—employed to shape the international environment and expand their options.

Two decades after the Cold War ended, influential scholar-practitioner K. Subrahmanyam asserted that non-alignment had been a "strategy to safeguard India's security."[13] Indeed, security was a key objective, but for many in the Indian leadership, that involved more than protecting national security in the traditional sense of the term. The dominant Indian concept of security—as shaped and reflected by Nehru—did not just envision protection of the country's territorial integrity as an objective, but also achieving economic security and protecting India's autonomy, that is, its freedom of action. A desire for autonomy was not incomprehensible for a country just emerging from colonial rule. Yet, it meant that the Indian leadership needed a pragmatic plan that could reconcile these multiple goals to the greatest extent possible in the context of the Cold War.

There was no consensus on the best approach to achieve India's objectives in a divided world. Within and outside of the Indian government, views differed based on which partners or goals individuals thought should be prioritized or preferred. Some, particularly among the left, argued for a much closer relationship with the Soviet Union. For some on the right, aligning with the US or the West was the better path. Leaders such as India's first Deputy Prime Minister and Home Minister Vallabhbhai Patel saw the situation through the prism of a new India's objectives. He, too, wanted not to "compromis[e] our stand against imperialism" or Indian autonomy. But, Patel asserted, "we shall have to depend on outside sympathy and support" if "we have to safeguard our frontiers against Communist infiltration and encroachments."[14]

Patel and others concurred with India's broader foreign policy approach of not joining a bloc, but recommended tilting towards one or the other

---

12. Chaudhuri, "Why Culture Matters: Revisiting the Sino-Indian Border Conflict of 1962," 847.

13. K. Subrahmanyam, "That Night of November 19," *Indian Express*, November 18, 2010.

14. Vallabhbhai Patel to Nehru, June 4, 1949, in *Sardar Patel's Correspondence, 1945–50*, Volume VIII, Durga Das, ed. (Ahmedabad: Navajivan Publishing House, 1971), 135–36.

superpower. Patel felt American "support in men, money and machinery" would be crucial to industrial policy and thus India's "progress." He, therefore, wanted to pursue a closer relationship with the US.[15] India's first High Commissioner in London, V.K. Krishna Menon, credited with being among the first to use the term "non-alignment," preferred the Soviet Union. The different emphases are also seen in the exchanges between the first generation of India's foreign policy officials, including Girija Shankar Bajpai and K.P.S Menon, as well as Nehru's sister Vijaya Lakshmi Pandit (these three served in key positions at home and abroad, including in Washington, Moscow, Beijing, and London).

While its practice was debated and, over time, evolved, and New Delhi did tilt at times, India remained on the non-aligned path that Nehru preferred. And his dominant role in and influence on foreign policymaking—as both prime minister and foreign minister—from 1947–64 ensured that it took hold. The approach featured two intertwined tracks, one a strategy of deterrence and the other a strategy of diversification.

II

In the Nehru years, a key line of effort involved deterring war and entanglement. This resulted simultaneously in active Indian diplomatic engagement and in an avoidance of alliances.

In 1947, when India became independent, Nehru's focus was nation-building. His government's priorities, particularly in the aftermath of partition, were political, social, and economic development, as well as national consolidation. For this, the Indian leadership needed a peaceful environment, particularly in Asia. What India wanted "above all," according to Nehru, was "some time and some peace to build."[16]

Yet the international landscape was becoming more contested. Only a few months before Nehru declared in August 1947 that India was "awake[ning] to life and freedom," the American president had delivered the "Truman doctrine" remarks, which reflected and hardened Cold War lines. Moreover, Indian policymakers had to grapple with security concerns related to the newly

---

15. Patel to Nehru, May 6, 1948, in *Sardar Patel's Correspondence*, Volume VI, Durga Das, ed.(Ahmedabad: Navajivan Publishing House, 1971), 371.

16. Nehru to Vijay Lakshmi Pandit, January 23, 1948, Nehru Memorial Museum and Library, Vijaya Lakshmi Pandit Papers (1st Installment), Subject File Number 54.

formed Pakistan; additional conflict near or far had the potential to disrupt their development plans even more.

Indian leaders had seen the impact of a world conflagration on India. For many American policymakers, one of the key lessons of the Second World War had been that aggressors should be confronted, not appeased. Nehru learned different lessons: the way an India yoked to Britain had become entangled in a war not of Indians' choosing; the drain on Indian resources and the consequences for its development; and the adverse impact on many countries' economies. From the prime minister's perspective, "India has not yet recovered from the effects of the last war. India, therefore, does not want to get itself entangled in another war if it comes."[17]

And Indian policymakers believed another war could come. Nehru has often been labeled an idealist, but his view of the world in which independent India found itself was quite bleak. He was not the only one. In 1948, Patel called the situation between the West and East one of "unrelieved gloom."[18] And Bajpai, Secretary General in the Indian Ministry of External Affairs, outlined his "fear that some stray spark may ignite the gunpowder that is lying about any time."[19]

This concern led to a two-pronged approach. First, in order to decrease the likelihood of entanglement, India needed to stay out of the Western and Eastern blocs. Second, to contribute to conflict prevention, India needed to follow a policy of de-escalation and resolution, which required engagement with all parties. Both these elements were reflected in Nehru's speech at the Asian Relations Conference in Delhi in March–April 1947, the lesser-known precursor to the 1955 Bandung conference:

> In this crisis in world history, Asia will necessarily play a vital role. The countries of Asia can no longer be used as pawns by others; they are bound to have their own policies in world affairs. Europe and America have contributed very greatly to human progress . . . But the West has also driven us into wars and conflicts without number and even now, the

17. Nehru, Speech, Sambalpur, April 12, 1948, in *Selected Works of Jawaharlal Nehru, Second Series*, Volume 6, Sarvepalli Gopal et al., eds. (Oxford: Oxford University Press, 1987), 3; Nehru, Speech on October 27, 1949, in *Selected Works of Jawaharlal Nehru, Second Series*, Volume 13, Sarvepalli Gopal et al., eds. (Oxford: Oxford University Press, 1993), 364.

18. Patel to Premiers of Provinces, October 31, 1948, in *Sardar Patel's Correspondence*, Volume VI, Durga Das, ed. (Ahmedabad: Navajivan Publishing House, 1971), 446.

19. GS Bajpai to Pandit, June 4, 1948, Nehru Memorial Museum and Library, Vijaya Lakshmi Pandit Papers (1st Installment), Subject File Number 56.

day after a terrible war, there is talk of further wars in the atomic age that is upon us. In this atomic age, Asia will have to function effectively in the maintenance of peace. Indeed, there can be no peace unless Asia plays her part.[20]

The first element of the strategy of deterrence entailed avoiding alliances. Even before Indian independence, as a member of the interim government, Nehru had noted, "We propose, as far as possible, to keep away from the power politics of groups, aligned against one another, which have led in the past to world wars and which may again lead to disasters on an even vaster scale." Alliances, in his view, increased the likelihood of war. And alliance membership would increase the likelihood of India getting drawn into any global war that broke out. That would not just impinge on Indian security and development, but also its autonomy, that is, its "independence in action both in our domestic affairs and our foreign relations." Members of the Indian National Congress recalled that decisions about Indian participation in the world wars had not been made in Delhi but in London. They did not want to be in that position again—to be the "playthings of others," as Nehru put it.[21] He was clear—"It would not be in the interest of India to engage herself in any pact which would automatically involve her in war."[22]

Nehru—and others since—have compared this stance with George Washington's advice in his 1796 farewell address to "steer clear of permanent alliances." The Indian prime minister's writings and remarks are replete with questions akin to Washington's: "Why, by interweaving our destiny with that of any part of Europe, entangle our peace and prosperity in the toils of European ambition, rivalship, interest, humor or caprice?"[23]

This concern about getting entangled and losing freedom of action also meant that, while Nehru did see non-alignment as a third way, he did not want to form a third bloc. He was instrumental in bringing together African and Asian nations at Bandung in 1955, but he rejected calls for a commonwealth of

20. Nehru, "Speech at the Plenary Session of the Asian Relations Conference," 503–9.

21. Nehru, "First Broadcast Over All India Radio as Vice-President of the Interim Government," September 7, 1946, in *Selected Works of Jawaharlal Nehru, Second Series,* Volume 1, Sarvepalli Gopal et al., eds. (Oxford: Oxford University Press, 1984), 404–8.

22. Nehru's Interview with G. Ward Price (Correspondent of the *Daily Mail,* London), April 10, 1949, in *Selected Works of Jawaharlal Nehru, Second Series,* Volume 10, Sarvepalli Gopal et al., eds. (Oxford: Oxford University Press, 1990), 161.

23. George Washington, "Farewell Address," September 17, 1796, The American Presidency Project, https://www.presidency.ucsb.edu/documents/farewell-address.

African and Asian states. He felt it was "impracticable."[24] Moreover, the idea of a "third force" had "no relation to reality."[25] This sentiment was also evident in Nehru's later lack of enthusiasm to convene a non-aligned conference in the early-1960s—in contrast to Egypt, Indonesia, and Yugoslavia's advocacy for such an initiative.

Yet, staying out of blocs was insufficient. Nehru realized that due in part to geography, unlike eighteenth-century America, India did not have the luxury of being "detached and distant." If war broke out, particularly in Asia, "all our schemes of progress would have to be pushed aside for many, many years." Nehru did not think India would be able to stay aloof. It would likely get "entangled" by virtue of its independence, its integration with the world, and its "potential power in world affairs." Even if the country managed not to get "directly involved, it will still be powerfully affected."[26]

By the early-to-mid-1950s, it was clear that superpower competition was affecting the subcontinent, with the Soviet Union supporting a China that had taken over Tibet, and the US backing Pakistan. For Nehru, American military assistance to its neighbor and rival made Pakistan more assertive and required India to invest more in defense and in relationships with foreign military suppliers. To the east, the Korean War had heightened Indian concerns about superpower tensions spilling over. In Nehru's mind, if competition intensified further, it could lead to more military assistance to India's rivals or even to regional conflict, which would require even greater Indian expenditure on defense that would distract from development. And global war would reduce the resources that might be available for India from the world.

That is where the second element of the strategy of deterrence came in— making the world safe for Indian nation-building. This involved New Delhi working to prevent the Cold War turning hot through efforts to avert conflict or its escalation, and to de-escalate or resolve conflict when it did break out. This also fit with Nehru's desire for Indians to go beyond being "passive

24. Nehru to MEA Joint Secretary (West), March 9, 1957, in *Selected Works of Jawaharlal Nehru, Second Series*, Volume 37, Sarvepalli Gopal et al, eds. (Oxford: Oxford University Press, 2006), 555.

25. Nehru, Statement in Lok Sabha, New Delhi, December 17, 1957, in *Selected Works of Jawaharlal Nehru, Second Series*, Volume 40, Sarvepalli Gopal et al., eds. (Oxford: Oxford University Press, 2009), 580.

26. Nehru to the Premiers of Provinces, November 2, 1947, in *Selected Works of Jawaharlal Nehru, Second Series*, Volume 4, Sarvepalli Gopal et al., eds. (Oxford: Oxford University Press, 1986), 446; Nehru to Pandit, January 23, 1948, Nehru Memorial Museum and Library, Vijaya Lakshmi Pandit Papers (1st Installment), Subject File Number 54.

spectators of events," as he felt had been the case under colonialism.[27] Thus, India got involved in peacemaking efforts in Korea and in Southeast Asia, serving as a channel between the US and China (including presciently warning Washington in 1950 that crossing the thirty-eighth parallel would lead to an escalation of the Korean War). India also became active diplomatically during the Suez, Hungary, and Berlin crises and on disarmament, as well as by chairing the Neutral Nations Repatriation Commission in Korea and contributing to peacekeeping efforts in the Congo. More parochially, Nehru engaged Mao's China and advocated its inclusion in the international community and the United Nations (UN). And this led to New Delhi propounding, along with Beijing, the five principles of peaceful co-existence.

The Indian government believed its peacemaking efforts would be aided by—and indeed required—an active Indian role at the UN, engagement with countries across the two blocs and in the Third World, as well as coordination with like-minded countries. The latter not only helped lead to Bandung, but also to the inaugural Belgrade Conference of the Non-Aligned Movement— despite Nehru's reluctance about such formalization.

This diplomacy-first and negotiations-heavy aspect has led to some conflation of non-alignment with non-violence. As Srinath Raghavan has argued, however, Nehru did not reject the use of force as an idea or in practice. Indeed, when it came to India's security and its own neighborhood, as C. Raja Mohan has pointed out, Nehru's government had security alliances with Bhutan and Nepal. Furthermore, as Swapna Nayudu Kona has outlined, Nehru's non-alignment evolved to include using instruments of force to enforce the peace in Korea and the Congo.[28]

From Nehru's perspective, India's peacemaking efforts and its staying out of alliances also enhanced the country's stature. As a foreign minister would put it years later, it gave the country "a role in international affairs which was perhaps disproportionate to our military and economic strength."[29] This

27. Nehru, "First Broadcast Over All India Radio as Vice-President of the Interim Government."

28. Raghavan, *War and Peace in Modern India*; C. Raja Mohan, "India and the Balance of Power," *Foreign Affairs* 85:4 (2006): 17–32; and Kona, *The Nehru Years*.

29. Indian External Affairs Minister Yashwant Sinha, "Speech on India's Foreign Policy: Successes, Failures and Vision in the Changing World Order," National Defence College, New Delhi, November 18, 2002, available at http://www.mea.gov.in/Speeches-Statements.htm?dtl /9285/Indias+Foreign+Policy+Successes+Failures+and+Vision+in+the+Changing+World+ Order+Talk+by+External+Affairs+Minister+Shri+Yashwant+Sinha++on+18112002+at+Natio nal+Defence+College+New+Delhi.

role also gave multiple major powers incentive to engage with—and even assist—India.

III

The efforts to deter war and Indian entanglement stemmed from Nehru's concerns about what the world could do *to* India. That, as well as a recognition of what the world could do *for* India, led to another element of Nehru's nonaligned approach: a strategy of diversification. This, too, involved maintaining ties with countries in both blocs, and beyond.

Emerging from years of subjugation and dependence, many of independent India's first generation of policymakers preferred self-reliance as they sought to protect India's security and ensure its economic development. However, they soon realized that, at that early stage, it was not feasible to avoid dependence on external actors entirely if they wanted to achieve their goals—or even to build the country's own capabilities. The challenge was how to take advantage of what other countries offered without letting them take advantage of India.

So, Nehru and his colleagues came up with a strategy to diversify India's dependence. They hoped that this (a) would allow India to maximize benefits from various partners, (b) would minimize overdependence on any one source, (c) would reduce the demands of dependence in terms of the strings attached to external assistance or the necessity to go along with a particular donor or supplier's interests and actions because India had no choice, and (d) could protect them against the questionable reliability of external benefactors.

India's need for external partners was clear to Nehru's government. India had external and internal security challenges and Britain continued to be the main source for military equipment and training. The government also needed food as well as economic and technical assistance—preferably from multiple benefactors. Thus, visiting New York and Washington in 1949, Nehru welcomed aid from the US, which he believed had the capacity to aid India's development plans. Ideally, he would have liked assistance from the Soviet Union as well. Nehru reached out to Moscow, seeking to diversify India's relationships—and thus any potential dependence—and maximize the country's options in terms of sources of aid. But he found that Joseph Stalin's Soviet Union had little interest in India, which it considered a Western stooge. The India-Soviet relationship was quite strained at the time (due in part to Soviet encouragement of Indian Communists, who Nehru and Patel considered a threat). Furthermore, some of Nehru's aides believed that "the condition of Soviet friendship is political subservience."[30]

This made aid from the US crucial—important enough that it had Nehru contemplating a "tilt," reportedly saying to close confidante Krishna Menon, "Why not align with the United States somewhat and build up our economic and military strength?"[31] Nehru had also noted to others that he was not above making "some inclination towards this group or that" when necessary.[32]

In the late-1940s and early-1950s, it became clear to Indian policymakers that their country's importance to the US—and thus American willingness to aid India—was linked to a desire to see democratic India play a role as a contrast, and potentially a counterweight, to Communist China. They also realized that if they did not get on board the countering-Communist China bandwagon, there was limited appetite for aiding India in the Truman administration or on Capitol Hill.

Indian officials discussed using, and indeed did use, the "fall" of China to highlight the importance of India to American policymakers. The Indian chargé in Moscow, for instance, suggested, "The China situation will alter the balance in Asia, and it seems to me that this is a good time to take up seriously the question of opening trade talks with the USSR. One result will be to stir up the Ang[l]o-Americans who have been treating our requests for capital goods rather cavalierly."[33]

Despite their desire to use the China challenge instrumentally, Indian policymakers made clear to their American interlocutors that India had little interest in aligning with them and playing the role vis-à-vis China that the US envisioned for it. This reluctance frustrated American officials. And Indian actions such as the recognition of the Communist regime in Beijing in 1950 had commentators lamenting that, though India "h[eld] the key" to any defense of Asia, its attitude was "dangerous."[34]

30. KPS Menon, as quoted in Paul M. McGarr, *The Cold War in South Asia: Britain, the United States and the Indian Subcontinent 1945–1965* (Cambridge: Cambridge University Press, 2013), 32.

31. Krishna Menon's account of a conversation with Nehru. As quoted in *Selected Works of Jawaharlal Nehru, Second Series*, Volume 2, Sarvepalli Gopal et al., eds. (Oxford: Oxford University Press, 1985), 59.

32. Nehru to Pandit, January 23, 1948.

33. Rajeshwar Dayal to Pandit, December 21, 1948 in Nehru Memorial Museum and Library, Vijaya Lakshmi Pandit Papers (2nd Installment), Subject File Number 3.

34. C.L. Sulzberger, "Kremlin Opens Cold War Second Front in Asia," *New York Times*, February 5, 1950.

When India first requested American aid, India-US differences related to the Korean War, especially India's attitude toward China, negatively affected the response from Capitol Hill. An aid bill stalled in Congress for months as representatives debated whether to give India aid and—since Delhi was not going to support or aid US foreign policy—what to demand in return. The debate gave members a forum to criticize repeatedly and vociferously India's China policy. The India-bashing in Congress and the columns of newspapers, in turn, had repercussions in India. Congressional criticism and linkage between India's foreign policy and US food assistance, in particular, adversely affected Indian views of the US. Congress eventually passed the aid bill, but Indian policymakers realized not just the downside and demands of dependence, but also the disadvantage of not having multiple partnership options.[35]

India's options subsequently expanded in the mid-1950s thanks to changes in Moscow. In 1953, Nehru noted that in the aftermath of Stalin's death there had been "a definite change" in Soviet policy, which was "likely to endure for the next few years."[36] And the change lasted, as the new Soviet leadership reached out to India and other non-aligned countries in order to counter Western power and influence. They offered New Delhi assistance and acceptance. Indian policymakers found that Moscow offered more economic assistance at better terms; certain kinds of aid (especially scientific and technical aid) that the West had been more reluctant to provide; large infrastructure projects that would build internal capacity, including in the state-owned sector; trade; offers of military equipment; and support for India's position on Kashmir and its claim to Goa.

The Soviet option allowed Indian leadership to diversify the country's dependence and thus expand New Delhi's space. Furthermore, as the Indian ambassador to Moscow stressed, India could try to generate "a little competition" between the two blocs to elicit more aid from both. Nehru understood

---

35. Indian policymakers commented that they felt "isolated." See, Henderson to Acheson, January 27, 1951, in *Foreign Policy of the United States 1951*, Volume VII-1, Frederick Aandahl, ed. (Washington, DC: United States Government Printing Office, 1983), 141–42. Pandit, by then ambassador to the US, noted the effort "to play down India and Nehru"; Bajpai noted "the venom and the universality of the change in tone." See, Pandit to Bajpai, October 16 and December 11, 1950 and Bajpai to Pandit, October 29, 1950, Nehru Memorial Museum and Library, Vijaya Lakshmi Pandit Papers (1st Installment), Subject File Number 56.

36. Nehru Conversation with Norman Cousins, September 3, 1953, in *Selected Works of Jawaharlal Nehru, Second Series*, Volume 23, Sarvepalli Gopal et al., eds. (Oxford: Oxford University Press, 1998), 11.

that there would be an "angry reaction" in the US if India accepted Soviet assistance, but he believed it also might create in Washington "a feeling that India being even more important than they thought, far greater efforts should be made to win her on their side."[37]

Simultaneously and paradoxically, the improved India-Soviet relationship—as well as a budding Sino-Indian one—made it more important to maintain India's relationship with the US. Nehru was both wary of becoming too dependent on the Communist bloc and aware of the scale of assistance that India needed. Maintaining the American option would allow India to balance out the Soviet one, to play one bloc off against the other and thus to cope with the questionable reliability of benefactors, and preserve some freedom of action by diversifying its dependence.

These last two elements were especially important because of continuing Indian concerns about Soviet support for Indian Communists and what Nehru and others saw as the domineering Soviet attitude toward newly independent nations. Thus, in the second half of the 1950s, the Indian government reached out to the US (including with an invitation for President Eisenhower to visit India), tried to stop or limit visiting Soviet leaders' public criticism of the US, and even rejected a Soviet offer of aircraft, partly because American officials asserted this would negatively affect India's prospects of getting economic assistance from the US.

A change in the American attitude toward India and its non-aligned position from 1956 onwards made India's diversification more feasible. In the second Eisenhower administration and through the Kennedy administration, the US was much more tolerant of India's non-aligned approach. The Cold War battleground had expanded beyond Europe—especially to the uncommitted world—and involved a struggle not just for territory, but for hearts, minds, and stomachs. In this context, Washington did not want to see Soviet-backed Communist China succeed while "free" India failed or fell to Communism. Thus, it offered to assist Nehru's government with its nation-building project.

By the mid-to-late-1950s, Nehru's government had its own geopolitical and ideological concerns about China. American assistance—food and financial—was critical, even indispensable, not only for its own sake, but also because it would help demonstrate that democracy could deliver. Nehru worried that the Indian public would contrast democratic India's performance with that of

37. McGarr, *The Cold War in South Asia*, 35.

Communist China, and his government needed to show that democracy and development were not mutually exclusive. Thus, Indian policymakers played along with the role the US envisioned for it as a contrast or counterbalance vis-à-vis China. This convergence brought with it greater importance in and aid from the US.

With both Moscow and Washington interested in and assisting the country, Indian policymakers enjoyed the benefits of diversification and avoided many of the costs of dependence. Furthermore, the aid India received included the kind that would help internal capacity building, which policymakers hoped would reduce India's dependence over time.

The period of the late-1950s and early-1960s seemed to reinforce the Indian belief that the benefits of staying outside an alliance outweighed the risks of not being in one. Simultaneously, by this point, Nehru had become more tolerant of other countries choosing the alliance route. He acknowledged that for some countries, it might be less risky to be in an alliance than out of it; for others, who did not have the capacity to defend themselves, he understood that they might even want foreign troops in their country.[38] However, Nehru did not believe this was the case for India. New Delhi was successfully deriving military and economic benefits from both Washington and Moscow. Its non-aligned approach seemed to be paying dividends.

IV

When the Sino-Indian War broke out in October 1962, Nehru's non-alignment—and his cost-benefit analysis—came under attack. There were questions about the effectiveness and wisdom of India's approach at home and abroad. The strategy of deterrence, with its friends-with-all approach, had failed to restrain China or to prevent war. Moreover, few of the non-aligned vocally supported India, preferring to remain non-aligned, even between New Delhi and Beijing.[39] Contemporary and present-day critics asserted that Nehru's global and

---

38. Nehru, "Intervention during the Debate on the Address by the President," May 16, 1957, in *Selected Works of Jawaharlal Nehru, Second Series*, Volume 38, Sarvepalli Gopal et al., eds. (Oxford: Oxford University Press, 2006), 21–22; Nehru's Interview with Finnish Radio, June 19, 1957, in ibid., 537–38; Nehru's TV Interview, Tokyo, October 6, 1957, in *Selected Works of Jawaharlal Nehru, Second Series*, Volume 39, Sarvepalli Gopal et al., eds. (Oxford: Oxford University Press, 2007), 565–66.

39. Chinmaya R. Gharekhan, "Rediscovery of Non-Alignment," *The Hindu*, March 24, 2012, https://www.thehindu.com/opinion/op-ed/rediscovery-of-nonalignment/article3206917.ece.

regional efforts might have enhanced India's status briefly, but they had come at the expense of efforts and approaches that could have been better for India's security.

As for the strategy of diversification, for Nehru's critics, at best, the war had exposed the approach's key flaw. At worst, India's pleas for military assistance from the Western bloc showed that the strategy had collapsed. Diversification required more than one available option and the Soviet option had disappeared during the war. Moscow at first stayed neutral and then chose to tilt towards its ally China rather than its friend India, particularly because the USSR needed Beijing's support as it dealt with the Cuban missile crisis. India had little choice but to tilt towards the US and depend on Western bloc aid, which began to flow that October.

As the military situation became more dire in November, India's needs increased. Nehru asked President John F. Kennedy for "more comprehensive assistance."[40] The US ambassador in India thought Nehru's specific requests "amount ... to joint air defense."[41] Secretary of State Dean Rusk went even further, noting that Nehru "in effect proposes not only a military alliance between India and the United States but complete commitment by us to a fighting war ... it is a proposal which cannot be reconciled with any further pretense of non-alignment."[42]

China declared a cease-fire even as Washington was discussing the Indian request, but at the time and since, some wondered whether non-alignment died in November 1962. Nehru himself had believed that a rejection of military assistance was part and parcel of non-alignment, and his request to Washington violated that principle. After the war, India asked for and received additional military assistance from the US, subsequently signing an Air Defense Agreement in 1963 that included a provision that the Kennedy administration interpreted as a commitment—"The United States Government will consult with the Government of India, in the event of a Chinese Communist attack on India, regarding possible United States assistance in strengthening India's

---

40. Nehru to John F. Kennedy, November 19, 1962 in Papers of John F. Kennedy, Presidential Papers, NSC Box 111, India: Nehru Correspondence November 11, 1962–November 19, 1962.

41. John Kenneth Galbraith to Kennedy, Dean Rusk and Robert McNamara, November 19, 1962, in Papers of John F. Kennedy, Presidential Papers, President's Office Files, India: Security, 1962.

42. Rusk to Galbraith, November 20, 1962, in *Foreign Policy of the United States 1961–63*, Volume XIX (Washington, DC: United States Government Printing Office, 1996), 401. Hereafter, *FRUS*.

air defenses."[43] Nehru even admitted at the time, "There is no nonalignment vis-à-vis China."[44] The Indian ambassador in the US later recalled that "we had become in fact the allies of the United States in their confrontation *at least against China*."[45]

Nonetheless, India had managed to avoid a formal alliance. And American policymakers, on their part, did not expect India to jettison non-alignment. National Security Council (NSC) official Carl Kaysen believed, "We can expect the Indians to redefine their nonalignment policy, but we do not expect India to abandon this policy."[46]

Kaysen's assessment was accurate. Had the Soviet option remained unavailable, there might have been an Indian strategic rethink away from non-alignment, given that Nehru's India was not in a position where internal balancing would suffice against China. But Moscow's outreach to India after the war made that a moot point.

The resurrection of the Soviet option—and thus non-alignment—also precluded other questions about the wisdom of the path Nehru had taken and those of paths not taken, such as: What if the US had not been willing to assist non-ally India? (NSC official Robert Komer also highlighted a related risk of the lack of a formal commitment or at least "prior preparations" that allies regularly undertook: the danger that the US would have been unable to help in time.[47]) What would Nehru have done had the US made its assistance contingent on an alliance? And, while Nehru believed that alliances dragged countries into war, would an alliance have deterred a Chinese attack?

V

While India did not abandon non-alignment, as Kaysen had predicted, Nehru and his successors did adapt non-alignment. The *Washington Post*'s South Asia bureau chief's description of the shift was, "Non-alignment has been succeeded by bi-alignment."[48] More broadly, the redefined non-alignment involved

---

43. Galbraith to the Department of State, July 10, 1963, in *FRUS 1961–63*, Volume XIX, 615–17.

44. Nehru in December 1962, as quoted in A.G. Noorani, "India's Quest for a Nuclear Guarantee," *Asian Survey* 7:7 (July 1967): 490.

45. B.K. Nehru, *Nice Guys Finish Second* (Delhi: Penguin, 1997), 407. Emphasis in original.

46. Kaysen to Kennedy enclosing Sino-Indian war situation report, November 3, 1962, in *FRUS 1961–63*, Volume XIX, 366.

47. Komer to Kennedy, December 16, 1962, in *FRUS 1961–63*, Volume XIX, 437.

48. As quoted in Michael Brecher, "Non-Alignment Under Stress: The West and the India-China Border War," *Pacific Affairs* 52:4 (1979): 612–30.

doubling down on the strategy of diversification, while de-emphasizing the strategy of deterrence.

The war had made clear that India needed more from both external benefactors, and not only in economic aid but in military assistance (equipment, spare parts, training, intelligence, and the like) as well. But Indian policymakers' experience with the US and the Soviet Union during and after the war had also reinforced their desire to diversify India's dependence, and to reduce it over time. Soviet behavior during the war had made it evident that partners were not always reliable. And the American and British approach demonstrated that dependence—and particularly overreliance on one bloc—came with conditions that constrained India's choices. Washington and London had come to India's assistance during the war. But Nehru resented their postwar pressure on him to reach a settlement with Pakistan on Kashmir while discussions about further military assistance were underway. American officials also seemed to indicate that the extent and nature of Western military assistance would be contingent on the Indian government limiting the postwar increase in defense expenditure that it was planning. This American and British pressure reinforced the idea in India that dependence brought with it unwelcome demands—demands that India only ended up being able to resist somewhat due to the Soviet Union's competing offers.

Thus, this strategy of diversification continued under Lal Bahadur Shastri, who took office after Nehru's death in May 1964. Beyond policy considerations, it was also the politically popular choice. In a survey of Indian legislators taken after the Sino-Indian War, while US favorability rose, pollsters found that neutrality continued to be "a very real concept"—eighty-three percent did not want India to side with either the US or Soviet bloc.[49] Thus, there might have been costs for Shastri and his successors to depart from this approach. Scholar-practitioner Shashi Tharoor has observed that, over the years, Nehru had successfully conveyed his government's international approach not as his foreign policy or that of the Congress party, but rather as the country's foreign policy. By doing so, he had "transform[ed] opposition to its fundamentals into opposition to India's very independence."[50]

Shastri sought military and economic assistance from both blocs. After China's nuclear test in October 1964, he also sought a nuclear umbrella from

49. Indian Institute for Public Opinion (IIPO), "The Impact of the Sino-Indian Border Clash," *Monthly Public Opinion Surveys* IX:1 (1963): 16.

50. Shashi Tharoor, *Reasons of State: Political Development and India's Foreign Policy under Indira Gandhi, 1966–1977* (New Delhi: Vikas Publishing House, 1982), 44.

the other nuclear powers—noting this was the only alternative to Indian nuclearization. Eventually, this evolved into a request for an assurance to all non-nuclear states.[51] This, and seeking a joint rather than a unilateral guarantee, was more desirable to the Shastri government. It would not require India to join an alliance and would also avoid the appearance of India joining an alliance.

New Delhi also did not want a unilateral guarantee, which it discussed with Washington, because of its uncertainty about the US. This downside of dependence—as well as its continued necessity—became evident during the 1965 India-Pakistan War. On the one hand, Indian policymakers had the ability to turn to the US when China threatened to intervene in the war on behalf of Pakistan. On the other hand, developments during the war fueled questions about American reliability including mixed messages about whether Washington would indeed act if Beijing did; the inability of the US to follow through on its assurance that Pakistan would not be allowed to use American-supplied weapons against India; and the suspension of economic aid and military assistance and sales to India and Pakistan. New Delhi continued to have access to military supplies from the Soviet Union—which policymakers believed highlighted the benefits of having kept a diversified portfolio of partners rather than depending solely on the US.

Shastri's successor, Indira Gandhi, also maintained this preference for diversification. In the mid-to-late-1960s, the country was more dependent on the Eastern bloc for military assistance and the Western bloc for economic assistance, but, overall, her government tried to balance the relationships. She also looked beyond the superpowers—one of which (the US) was losing interest in India due to its economic performance and the other (the Soviet Union) which was flirting with rival Pakistan. So, she sought to deepen ties with several Asian and European partners.

Even when it became clear toward the end of the 1960s that India was losing its significance for Washington, Gandhi resisted Moscow's 1969 offer of a treaty that could have brought additional benefits. The prime minister hesitated because of the potential domestic and Chinese reaction, questions about Soviet reliability and fear of overdependence on them, and her concern that the treaty would be seen as a move away from non-alignment or as directed against a third party.

---

51. Andrew B. Kennedy, "India's Nuclear Odyssey: Implicit Umbrellas, Diplomatic Disappointments, and the Bomb," *International Security* 36:2 (2011): 120–53.

Gandhi's government did, however, sign that treaty with the Soviet Union in summer 1971 when circumstances changed. India found that it had lost its implicit US security assurance against China, thanks to Sino-US rapprochement, just as it was facing a crisis with China's partner, Pakistan. Just as India had tilted toward the US when the Soviet option had disappeared during the 1962 War, India tilted toward the Soviet Union for insurance against China when the American option went missing in 1971.

However, a few months after the India-Pakistan War of 1971, Indian policymakers moved to restore some balance and reached out to the US. As senior American officials predicted, Gandhi did so because she did not want to become overly dependent on the Soviet Union, and India was still in no position to manage without external assistance. Yet by then, with India's economic performance suffering and no American need for it to serve as a contrast or counterbalance to China, the country had little value for the US. So, Gandhi found herself having to look to partnerships with other countries to balance Delhi's relations with Moscow to some degree. To hedge against Soviet unreliability, her government also took key steps on the path to exercising its nuclear weapons program option—an option that Indian leaders had kept open, given the potential it had to provide an independent deterrent to protect the country's security.

When the first non-Congress party government came to power in the late-1970s, it also reiterated its support for a strategy of diversification. The leaders of the Janata party government indeed criticized Gandhi for having moved away from it, saying that she had made India too dependent on the Soviet Union. Prime Minister Morarji Desai labeled his approach to the world "genuine non-alignment," stating that "foreign policy should not be based on the fear that its pursuit might annoy others."[52] Foreign Minister Atal Bihari Vajpayee emphasized that India should neither get caught up in others' commitments, nor be pressured into accepting another country's ideology or policies, nor leave its defense to another country.[53] Years later when he was prime minister, Vajpayee would note, "we were ready to follow the policy of non-alignment because non-alignment was not the policy of just one party. During an argument once I told Pandit Jawaharlal Nehru

52. Anjali Ghosh et al., eds. *India's Foreign Policy* (Delhi: Dorling Kindersley, 2009), 271.

53. Priya Chacko, *Indian Foreign Policy: The Politics of Postcolonial Identity from 1947 to 2004* (Oxford: Routledge, 2012), 148.

that even if you had not followed non-alignment, the country would have tread it."[54]

VI

Intentions aside, the Desai government had a problem that the next two Congress governments led by Indira and then Rajiv Gandhi would also face—even as they tried to balance out their dependence on the Soviet Union, there were few other takers to substantially assist India. Thus, India's overdependence on the Eastern bloc remained through the 1980s, bringing with it limits on India's freedom of action. For instance, despite Delhi's dismay about the Soviet invasion of Afghanistan that brought the Cold War to South Asia and led to deeper American engagement with India's rivals, Pakistan and China, New Delhi had to hold back its criticism of Moscow. Beyond the reduced autonomy, the downside of alignment with one bloc, and particularly the lack of a diversified portfolio of partners, became shockingly apparent when the Soviet Union collapsed. India was left with no backup plan and facing a financial crisis.

The last decade of the Cold War only highlighted the drawback of non-alignment that had become evident to India earlier: for a strategy designed to increase India's flexibility, it depended a great deal on the willingness of other countries to be effective. Those countries' choices depended on their priorities and their perceptions of India's importance relative to others in their own strategies. Thus, for example, India could use a diversified Soviet-US balance against China only as along as both the Soviet Union and the US sought to balance China with India. When Moscow had chosen ally China over friend India in 1962 or when Washington's China policy changed and it sought to engage Beijing, diversification became difficult for India. In crises, India then had little choice but to align with one partner or bloc.

Non-alignment also did not always succeed in keeping India insulated from others' rivalries or interests. Indeed, the need to maintain multiple relationships and balance often opened India up to getting entangled with, affected by, or even influenced by several countries. Nehru had also found that his efforts to diversify and to deter war sometimes left India in situations where it had

---

54. Indian Ministry of External Affairs, "Interview of Prime Minister Atal Bihari Vajpayee to ITAR TASS," December 2, 2002, https://www.mea.gov.in/interviews.htm?dtl/4854/Interview+of+Prime+Minister+Shri+Atal+Bihari+Vajpayee+to+ITAR+TASS+Russian+news+channel.

pleased none of its partners and annoyed all of them. So did Indira Gandhi. She held back on criticizing the US approach in Vietnam because of India's need for American economic assistance, but then, facing criticism at home and in Moscow about shifting away from non-alignment, she reversed course when visiting the Soviet Union—which did not help the Indian case for aid in Washington.

Indian governments have also seen that non-alignment, when treated as an objective in its own right rather than an approach, can lead to suboptimal results vis-à-vis other goals such as security and prosperity. It can do this either by minimizing rewards or by tying policymakers' hands. For instance, in 1963, Nehru had agreed to the US setting up a Voice of America transmitter in eastern India that would transmit anti-China propaganda into China, but reversed that decision when he received blowback at home that this would be a violation of non-alignment.

VII

Nonetheless, elements of non-alignment persisted. In 2003, long after the Cold War had ended, the foreign minister of a Bharatiya Janata Party-led coalition government asserted that India's non-alignment "was not an act of passivity. It was a desire for balance, for non-interference, and for independence of action."[55] The national security advisor in the subsequent Congress-led coalition government reiterated the "continuing relevance of nonalignment as a strategy; not as an ideology . . . [It] remains a guide to what we should be doing with the rest of the world and for the foreseeable future."[56] In 2021, the Indian foreign secretary, while not using the term "non-alignment," noted that a key pillar of Indian foreign policy has been to maintain "comprehensive strategic relations with major powers while maintaining strategic autonomy."[57] Prime Minister Narendra Modi had earlier elaborated on this, noting, "We will

---

55. External Affairs Minister Yashwant Sinha, "Address at the Tajik National State University," January 29, 2003, https://www.mea.gov.in/Speeches-Statements.htm?dtl/4157/External+Affairs+Minister+Shri+Yashwant+Sinhas+Address+at+the+Tajik+National+State+University.

56. National Security Advisor Shivshankar Menon at Launch of *Non-Alignment 2.0*, New Delhi, February 28, 2012, http://youtu.be/TS9rZi6zers, uploaded March 6, 2012.

57. Indian Ministry of External Affairs, "Foreign Secretary's Remarks on 'India's Foreign Policy and Its Strategic Imperative: The Way Forward,'" 6th JP Morgan India Investor Summit, September 20, 2021, available at https://www.mea.gov.in/Speeches-Statements.htm?dtl/34287/foreign+secretarys+remarks+on+indias+foreign+policy+and+its+strategic+imperative+the+way+forward+at+the+6th+jp+morgan+india+investor+summit+september+20+2021.

work with [India's many partners], individually or in formats of three or more, for a stable and peaceful region. But, our friendships are not alliances of containment. We choose the side of principles and values, of peace and progress, not one side of a divide or the other."[58] And when pressed on whether New Delhi would take a stand on or pick a side in US-China competition, the Indian foreign minister had asserted, "India should take a stand and should take a side—our side."[59]

As New Delhi's China challenge has intensified, that "side" has led to India tilting or aligning to balance its rival—as it did in the 1960s with the US and in the 1970s with the Soviet Union. Just like the Vajpayee and Manmohan Singh governments before it, the Modi government has found a close partnership with the US to be crucial in managing India's China challenge. Washington helps enhance India's capabilities and influence and serves as a regional balancer and global partner. This is particularly important for India since Russia is not the strategic option it used to be, given Moscow's close ties with Beijing. Nonetheless, even as New Delhi has tilted toward Washington as US-China competition intensifies, it continues to pursue diversification—not to hedge between Washington and Beijing, but to hedge against uncertainty about the US relationship with China and its commitment to the Indo-Pacific, as well as to maintain Indian autonomy. This has meant deepening ties with like-minded partners such as Australia, France, Japan, Singapore, South Korea, Vietnam, and the United Kingdom, as well as maintaining a relationship with Russia.

Thus, despite the drawbacks of non-alignment and the fact that it was very much a product of its time, its underlying strategy of diversification at least outlasted the Cold War. Even as India moved from a context of dependence to interdependence, for Indian policymakers the rationale for diversification remained strong. It remained policymakers' preferred path given the persistent desire for strategic autonomy. Simultaneously, the strategy was flexible enough to be adapted to evolving situations, allowing India to tilt or align when necessary. For Indian policymakers, this approach allowed them to maintain a certain degree of freedom of action, keep options open, insulate India to the extent possible, and maximize benefits. Non-alignment could also help them not

58. Narendra Modi, "Prime Minister's Keynote Address at Shangri La Dialogue," Singapore, June 1, 2018, Ministry of External Affairs, Government of India, https://bit.ly/2zlllXA.

59. Indian External Affairs Minister S. Jaishankar's comments at Observer Research Foundation, "The World in a Moment: Looking Back, Looking Ahead, Looking Hard," Raisina Dialogue, New Delhi, India, January 9, 2019, https://youtu.be/FH2el8qEM4A, uploaded January 9, 2019.

to get dragged into other's crises or commitments—and to hedge against the questionable reliability of partners who have their own interests and priorities. Thus, particularly given the fluidity of the global situation in recent years, maintaining a diversified portfolio of partners remained desirable. And with several major and middle powers on the scene, and India's rise and position in Asia, this approach also remained feasible as other countries sought partnerships with New Delhi. But, as policymakers discovered in the past, crisis can put a strategy of non-alignment under strain, and they might once again have to adapt it to more trying circumstances.

CHAPTER 32

Lyndon Johnson and Robert McNamara

THEORY OVER HISTORY AND EXPERTISE

Mark Moyar

By virtue of its Constitution, the United States has always recognized the subordination of military leadership to civilian leadership, in war as well as in peace. American presidents make the highest-level decisions—whether, for instance, the administration should seek congressional authorization for the use of force. They delegate low-level decision-making authority to the military, knowing that directing the movement of platoons from the White House would be a fool's errand. Between the top and bottom levels of decision-making, however, lies a multitude of decisions that both the president and the generals may believe themselves best qualified to make. Some choices are strategic, such as whether a new military offensive should be launched, or which elements of the nation's armed forces should be committed to a theater. Others are tactical, like the restrictions the nation's aircraft should observe near the air space of a hostile power, or the rules of engagement the navy should follow during a blockade. The president may believe that a particular decision is too politically sensitive to leave in the hands of the military, while the generals may think that only they possess the military expertise necessary to make a decision in a timely and well-informed fashion.

Controversies over the division of labor between civilian and military authorities have bedeviled civil-military relations since the American Revolution, but they have become much more prominent as modern communications technologies have enabled civilian authorities to transmit and receive information more rapidly. Prior to the advent of the telegraph, messages could take weeks or months to travel from the nation's capital to the commander of a distant military expedition, making it all but impossible for the chief of state to give more than very general guidance to a commander. By the Vietnam War, encrypted radio and telephone communications allowed the president and secretary of defense to issue detailed orders to the other side of the planet instantaneously, and to require military commanders to send them vast quantities of reports with similar speed. These conditions made it even more important for presidents to differentiate properly between decisions that they should make themselves without regard for military judgments, decisions they should make in consultation with the military, decisions they should allow the military to make after receiving civilian approval, and decisions they should let the military make without civilian approval.

Presidents like George Washington, Abraham Lincoln, and Dwight Eisenhower excelled at the triage of national security decisions because they possessed a deep knowledge of military affairs and military history. Many of the problems encountered by the United States during the Vietnam War can be attributed to the failure of President Lyndon Johnson and his chief strategist, Secretary of Defense Robert McNamara, to manage the triage process effectively. Lacking both military expertise and an awareness of the value of such expertise, Johnson and McNamara made too many decisions without considering the views of the military, and too often ignored the military's insights when they did consult the generals. Their lack of military knowledge also made the two civilians less effective than other knowledgeable leaders at finding the optimal decisions, and, in the case of McNamara, led him to seek answers in the ahistorical theories of academics.

The net result of Johnson and McNamara's disregard for military history and military expertise was disastrous strategic decision-making. By imposing unilateral limits on the use of force, they ended up triggering the very escalation they were seeking to avoid. Their relentless rejections of strategic recommendations from the military leadership squandered numerous opportunities to obtain military and diplomatic advantages, setting America on the path to defeat in one of the longest, and most divisive, conflicts in its history.

I

Lyndon Johnson never served in the military, and he had always been more interested in domestic affairs than foreign policy. When the assassination of John F. Kennedy on November 22, 1963, thrust Johnson into the presidency, he resolved to inscribe his name in history through sweeping civil rights and anti-poverty legislation. His focus on domestic issues put diplomatic and military concerns on the back burner, and thus ensured that his modest military knowledge would be slow to increase, even as the Vietnam War came to overshadow everything else. Moreover, Johnson's domestic focus inclined him to defer to the judgment of McNamara on most military matters.[1]

McNamara was a man who inspired confidence. A graduate of the Harvard Business School, he had become the first person outside the Ford family to serve as the Chief Executive Officer of the Ford Motor Company. He combined a sharp mind and extraordinary memory with a voice that conveyed authority, even when he was less than completely certain of the truth of what he was saying. These qualities had endeared him to the president who had appointed him, John F. Kennedy, and would do the same with Johnson. Alexander Haig, one of McNamara's assistants at the outset of the Johnson administration, recalled, "Men who had been listening to testimony all their lives listened to McNamara's briefings with the rapt faces of religious converts. Standing behind McNamara as I placed the charts on the easel, I saw that Lyndon Johnson was one of them."[2]

1. Noteworthy histories of the Vietnam decision-making of Johnson and McNamara include David M. Barrett, *Uncertain Warriors: Lyndon Johnson and His Vietnam Advisers* (Lawrence, KS: University Press of Kansas, 1993); Larry Berman, *Lyndon Johnson's War* (New York, NY: W. W. Norton, 1989); Edward J. Drea, *McNamara, Clifford, and the Burdens of Vietnam, 1965–1969* (Washington, DC: Office of the Secretary of Defense Historical Office, 2011); Lloyd C. Gardner, *Pay Any Price: Lyndon Johnson and the Wars for Vietnam* (Chicago, IL: Ivan R. Dee, 1995); William C. Gibbons, *The U.S. Government and the Vietnam War: Executive and Legislative Roles and Relationships*, Volumes 1–4 (Princeton, NJ: Princeton University Press, 1986–95); George C. Herring, *LBJ and Vietnam: A Different Kind of War* (Austin, TX: University of Texas Press, 1994); David E. Kaiser, *American Tragedy: Kennedy, Johnson, and the Origins of the Vietnam War* (Cambridge, MA: Harvard University Press, 2000); Fredrik Logevall, *Choosing War: The Lost Chance for Peace and the Escalation of War in Vietnam* (Berkeley, CA: University of California Press, 1999); H. R. McMaster, *Dereliction of Duty: Lyndon Johnson, Robert McNamara, the Joint Chiefs of Staff and the Lies that Led to Vietnam* (New York, NY: HarperCollins, 1997); Brian VanDeMark, *Road to Disaster: A New History of America's Descent into Vietnam* (New York, NY: Custom House, 2018).

2. Alexander Haig, *Inner Circles: How America Changed the World* (New York, NY: Warner Books, 1992), 146.

The National Security Act of 1947 had transferred executive authority over combat forces from the Joint Chiefs of Staff to the secretary of defense, turning the former from commanders of extraordinary influence into advisers whose influence depended on their ability to sway the secretary of defense. If the secretary of defense wished to disempower the Joint Chiefs of Staff, he could ignore what they had to say and restrict their access to the president. That is precisely what McNamara had been doing since 1961.

McNamara had chosen to marginalize the Joint Chiefs because he saw them as hidebound and unsophisticated in their thinking, prevented by convention and tradition from capitalizing on the latest techniques of quantitative analysis and the latest academic theories. During the Second World War, McNamara had served in the US Army Air Forces as a statistician, before taking his statistical skills to Ford, where his use of statistics to manage operations and measure profitability had helped propel him to the top. When McNamara arrived at the Defense Department in January 1961, he was convinced that the same quantitative rigor that had made Ford a world-renowned corporation should be used to reform a stodgy Pentagon bureaucracy.

To implement his vision, McNamara brought brainy statisticians from Ford and other civilian institutions to the Department of Defense. Known as the "Whiz Kids," they required the Pentagon's bureaucrats to become more systematic in their collection and analysis of quantitative data. In some areas of the Pentagon's business, the drive for quantification made good sense; in others, however, it created more problems than it solved. A large private sector corporation could quantify nearly everything it did, including its return on investment, the ultimate indicator of success. National security, however, did not lend itself as well to numbers. There is no equivalent to return on investment, no unassailable gauge of effectiveness. The statistics most relevant to progress in a war—casualty counts, territorial control, etc.—were often subject to deliberate distortions or inadvertent inaccuracies. Others, like the impact of bombing on a hostile country, were short on hard data, and statisticians who made assumptions to generate data could veer wildly from the mark.

McNamara's time in the military had not imbued him with a deep understanding of military strategy. His education in economics at the University of California-Berkley and in business at Harvard had taught him little about the history of military strategy, or about history more generally, and instead had instilled in him a preference for the a priori theories and inductive reasoning of economics. When his appointment as secretary of defense required him to grapple with the complexities of military strategy, McNamara looked to economic theory and not to historical facts and analysis.

By the 1950s, leading academic economists had concluded that their sophisticated theories could solve problems far beyond the economic realm. International relations and conflict management became particularly popular topics for American economists, because the Korean War and the nuclear arms race had generated hunger among the military, the government, and the public for ideas on limiting and avoiding war. To meet this demand, economists and political scientists wrote a profusion of theoretical books and articles on what became known as "limited war" theory.

The most influential treatise on limited war was the book *Strategy of Conflict*, published in 1960 by Harvard economist Thomas Schelling.[3] He relied on an economist's assumptions and game scenarios to predict how nations would react in a conflict setting. Schelling's assumptions were derived from abstract reasoning, and not from any historical experience. Nations, Schelling assumed, acted rationally in response to their surroundings. Rational aversion to harm would cause modern nations to exercise restraint, for they would know that escalation of military conflict against a determined adversary could lead to nuclear war. To make sure the other side understood the nature of their commitment and would thus avoid pushing too far, Schelling posited, nations should undertake limited demonstrations of force when the opponent showed signs of escalating. Restraint by one nation would beget restraint by its adversary.

Schelling's theory of conflict limitation appeared to have been vindicated by the seminal international event of the Kennedy presidency—the Cuban Missile Crisis. After Kennedy's generals had recommended the use of overwhelming force against Cuba, Kennedy had opted instead for a naval blockade, and the Soviets had backed off without a fight. McNamara interpreted the Soviet reaction as a rational response to the limited American show of force. The Soviets had not, in reality, formulated their response based on an accurate perception of American intentions, but instead on ill-informed fears that Kennedy was about to use overwhelming force.[4] That truth, however, would remain hidden from the outside world until the collapse of the Soviet Union three decades later.

The recommendations of the Joint Chiefs for military strikes on Cuba convinced McNamara that the military leaders were too eager to employ overwhelming force, in any situation. Other events of the Kennedy presidency

3. Thomas C. Schelling, *Strategy of Conflict* (Cambridge, MA: Harvard University Press, 1960).

4. Vladislav Zubok and Constantine Pleshakov, *Inside the Kremlin's Cold War* (Cambridge, MA: Harvard University Press, 1996); Aleksandr Fursenko and Timothy Naftali, *"One Hell of a Gamble": Khrushchev, Castro, and Kennedy, 1958–1964* (New York, NY: W. W. Norton, 1997).

seemed to lend additional credence to this conclusion. The Joint Chiefs favored military intervention in Laos as a means of halting the advances of North Vietnamese forces and their Laotian allies, but under pointed questioning from Kennedy the generals failed to explain cogently how potential pitfalls could be avoided. Kennedy then reached a diplomatic agreement to neutralize Laos, whereby American and North Vietnamese personnel withdrew from the country. Only later, and inconspicuously, did it become clear that the North Vietnamese had no intention of living up to the agreement. The logistical routes built by the North Vietnamese in Laos in order to infiltrate men and materiel into South Vietnam would become known as the Ho Chi Minh Trail.

The generals of the 1960s had been the lieutenants and captains of World War II, and then the colonels of the Korean War. Through those experiences, the military leaders had absorbed practical, historical knowledge about how human adversaries employed force on the ground, and how they reacted to perceptions of strength, indecision, and weakness. The historical actions and events they had witnessed confounded the theories of twentieth-century economics. Humans had routinely defied predictions of what someone else considered rational behavior. Demonstrations of restraint had often invited aggression rather than mutual restraint. To the generals, limited war theories and simulations that were divorced from actual experiences were, in the words of one general, "academic and useless exercises played by a bunch of eggheads."[5]

II

Politics also led Johnson and McNamara to diverge strategically from the generals. This truth was particularly evident during Johnson's first year in office, when concerns about the November presidential election routinely took precedence over geopolitics. As the frontrunner in the race, Johnson worried that voters would blame him if they noticed worsening conditions in Vietnam, and that public attention to Vietnam would come at the expense of attention to his ambitious domestic agenda. He therefore decided to do everything possible to keep Vietnam out of the newspapers. To this end, Johnson tried to slow the deterioration of the South Vietnamese war effort by quietly sending additional resources and authorizing covert actions against North Vietnam while avoiding conspicuous initiatives.

5. Philip B. Davidson, *Vietnam at War: The History, 1946–1975* (Novato, CA: Presidio Press, 1988), 338.

Infighting among the leaders of South Vietnam, stemming from the assassination of President Ngo Dinh Diem in November 1963, was diminishing the effectiveness of the South Vietnamese armed forces and government. The Joint Chiefs urged bold measures to shore up the South Vietnamese and thereby discourage the North Vietnamese from pressing their advantage. They recommended attacking North Vietnam with US forces and moving South Vietnamese ground troops into Laos to disrupt North Vietnamese supply routes. "The United States," the chiefs asserted, "must be prepared to put aside many of the self-imposed restrictions which now limit our efforts, and to undertake bolder actions which may embody greater risks." In addition to forfeiting opportunities to harm the enemy, they noted, these restrictions "may well now be conveying signals of irresolution to our enemies—encouraging them to higher levels of vigor and greater risks."[6]

Political considerations aside, the most serious risk inherent in the actions proposed by the Joint Chiefs was the triggering of Chinese intervention in Vietnam. When American forces had pushed into North Korea in 1950, Mao Zedong had sent hundreds of thousands of Chinese combat forces to stop them, leading to several years of bloody military stalemate on the Korean Peninsula. The Joint Chiefs argued that the chances of Chinese troops entering North Vietnam were very low because the Chinese had been debilitated by severe economic problems at home.[7]

Johnson and McNamara repeatedly turned down the military proposals as 1964 moved along. The president admitted to subordinates that he wished to avoid such highly visible measures before November because it could adversely affect him and other Democrats in the election. He would consider them once he had been reelected, as it would then be easier to obtain public support.[8] Even after the election, though, Johnson would remain wary, for both he and McNamara worried that Chinese intervention was much more likely than the generals were saying.

6. *Pentagon Papers: The Defense Department History of United States Decision Making on Vietnam*, Senator Gravel, ed., Volume 3 (Boston, MA: Beacon Press, 1971), 496–99.

7. See, for instance, Taylor to McNamara, March 14, 1964, *Foreign Relations of the United States (FRUS), 1964–1968*, Volume 1: *Vietnam, 1961*, Ronald D. Landa and Charles S. Sampson, eds. (Washington, DC: United States Government Printing Office, 1988), 82; *Pentagon Papers*, Volume 3, 165–66.

8. Clifton, Memo for the Record, March 4, 1964, Declassified Document Reference System (DDRS), 1999, 91; Greene, meeting notes, March 4, 1964, MCHD, Greene Papers; memcon, March 4, 1964, *FRUS, 1964–1968*, Volume 1, 70.

McNamara and his Whiz Kids also objected to the military's recommendations on purely military grounds. According to the civilians' analysis, the Joint Chiefs greatly overestimated the benefits of the proposed military actions against North Vietnam. Influenced by counterinsurgency theorists who emphasized the ability of insurgents to sustain themselves locally, McNamara and his team concluded that the Communists in South Vietnam did not rely heavily on the support coming from North Vietnam into South Vietnam through Laotian infiltration routes; cutting off their supply lines from the north, therefore, would do little practical good.

Postwar disclosures would confirm that the generals, and not the civilians, had been correct about the importance of North Vietnamese infiltration of supplies via Laos. The quantity of supplies moved via the Ho Chi Minh Trail quadrupled over the course of 1964, and it would multiply again in the years to come as North Vietnamese military activity surged and the US Navy shut down North Vietnam's maritime infiltration operations.[9] North Vietnamese and Soviet sources both stated that cutting the Laotian routes would have suffocated the insurgency in South Vietnam. Moreover, both sets of sources asserted that such a shutdown could have been accomplished with only a few divisions of troops—a much smaller force than what the United States ultimately deployed to South Vietnam.[10]

Two incidents in early August 1964 disrupted President Johnson's plans for keeping the war on the back burner before the election. On August 2 and 4, US warships operating in the Tonkin Gulf reported coming under attack by North Vietnamese vessels. The circumstances surrounding the events remain shrouded in uncertainty, but at the time, nearly everyone in the American government was convinced that both attacks had occurred and that some type of retaliation was necessary.

The Joint Chiefs and the two principal combatant commanders—Admiral Ulysses G. Sharp and General William Westmoreland—called for the president

9. Nguyen Viet Phuong, *Van Tai Quan Su Chien Luoc Tren Duong Ho Chi Minh Trong Khang Chien Chong My*, Second Edition (Hanoi: General Department of Rear Services, 1988), 55; Military History Institute of Vietnam, *Victory in Vietnam: The Official History of the People's Army of Vietnam, 1954–1975*, trans. Merle L. Pribbenow (Lawrence, KS: University Press of Kansas, 2002), 126–27.

10. Bui Tin, *From Enemy to Friend: A North Vietnamese Perspective on the War*, trans. Nguyen Ngoc Bich (Annapolis, MD: Naval Institute Press, 2002), 82, 86–87, 157; London to State, June 22, 1965, Lyndon Baines Johnson Library (LBJL), NSF, Country File, United Kingdom, box 207.

to initiate a sustained bombing campaign against North Vietnam and the Ho Chi Minh Trail. McNamara and other civilian leaders recommended a much more limited response, and invoked limited war theory explicitly in making the case. Johnson chose the advice of the civilians. He ordered a single bombing raid on North Vietnamese naval facilities and stressed the limited nature of the military action in a public statement.[11]

Johnson's response did not produce the results foreseen by the theoreticians of limited war. The Chinese took the air strike as a sign that Johnson was prepared to invade North Vietnam, and possibly even China. Unbeknownst to the outside world, Mao had no appetite for another war with the United States; he dreaded a repetition of the lopsided bloodletting that had befallen Chinese forces in Korea. The Chinese promptly notified Hanoi that, if American forces invaded North Vietnam, China would not send its troops to fight the Americans. The Chinese further advised that, if the Americans invaded, the North Vietnamese should avoid the terrifying might of American firepower by withdrawing from installations and population centers and retreating to the mountains.[12] The North Vietnamese were distressed, to say the least, that their foremost ally was unwilling to stand up to their foremost enemy, but they heeded the advice of the Chinese and planned for a retreat into the mountains.

American intelligence agencies obtained no inkling of China's true reaction to the Tonkin Gulf incidents. Had the Americans been privy to it, Johnson and McNamara would have been hard pressed to avoid the conclusion of the Joint Chiefs that China would not intervene in North Vietnam in response to an American invasion. The fact that the North Vietnamese intended to respond by taking to the hills as they had done against the French also bolstered the case for invasion, for it would have put the United States in a much better military situation than the one it ultimately faced. Flight into the mountains would have stripped the North Vietnamese of most of their logistical infrastructure and much of the population base from which they obtained manpower. The French had nearly defeated the Vietnamese Communists under similar conditions and with just 150,000 troops, less than a third of what the United States eventually committed.

11. *Department of State Bulletin,* August 24, 1964, 259.

12. Memcon, Mao Zedong and Pham Van Dong, Hoang Van Hoan, October 5, 1964, Cold War International History Project.

The North Vietnamese interpreted Johnson's limited measure in exactly the opposite of the way predicted by the limited war theorists. Rather than viewing the American limitation as an indicator of resolve that demanded reciprocal limitation, the North Vietnamese saw it as an indicator of weakness that they could exploit through aggressive action. In September 1964, North Vietnamese leaders concluded that the absence of further American military action after the Tonkin Gulf incidents proved that the United States lacked the will to respond forcefully to North Vietnamese escalation. For the past decade, the North Vietnamese had avoided committing large North Vietnamese combat units into South Vietnam for fear that it would provoke a massive American military response. With that fear now dissipated, Hanoi began preparing entire North Vietnamese divisions for an invasion of South Vietnam, aimed at winning a decisive military victory.[13]

In the late summer and fall, Johnson's campaign rhetoric gave Hanoi additional reason to believe he would not intervene to save South Vietnam. While denouncing Republican nominee Barry Goldwater as a reckless warmonger, Johnson portrayed himself as the candidate of peace. At campaign events, Johnson vowed that he had no intention of sending American boys to fight in Asia.[14]

On November 1, two days before the US presidential election, a Viet Cong mortar company fired 100 rounds at the Bien Hoa Air Base, where large numbers of US aircraft were based. The bombardment killed four Americans and wounded thirty more, in addition to destroying twenty-seven aircraft. General Westmoreland and Admiral Sharp called for immediate retaliation against the North Vietnamese. The Joint Chiefs warned Johnson, via McNamara, that if the United States did not retaliate in the face of such a provocation, then it ought to leave Vietnam.

Before making up his mind, Johnson consulted political pollster Louis Harris. The president feared that retaliation would upset some voters, but was also concerned that a lack of retaliation would turn other voters against him. Harris responded that few voters would shift their vote away from him if Johnson did not retaliate right away.[15] Reassured, Johnson avoided any military response.

13. Luu van Loi and Nguyen Anh Vu, *Tiep Xuc Bi Mat Viet Nam-Hoa Ky Truoc Hoi Nghi Pa-Ri* (Hanoi: International Relations Institute, 1990), 26–28; Military History Institute of Vietnam, *Victory in Vietnam*, 137.

14. *Public Papers of the Presidents, Lyndon B. Johnson, 1963–1964*, Volume 2, 1387–93.

15. Louis Harris, *Anguish of Change* (New York, NY: W. W. Norton, 1973), 23; Gibbons, *U.S. Government and the Vietnam War*, Volume 2, 364.

The North Vietnamese took it as yet another sign that the Americans would not intervene to save South Vietnam.

News of Johnson's victory in the presidential election on November 3 confirmed for the North Vietnamese that Johnson, and not the bellicose Goldwater, would occupy the White House for the next four years. With the potential obstacle of a Goldwater presidency now out of the way, the North Vietnamese were ready to move forward with escalation. Within a few days, they ordered the first elements of the invasion forces to head immediately for the Ho Chi Minh Trail. These troops would wear the garb of Southern guerrillas and minimize communications to conceal their Northern origins; Hanoi knew that Johnson would face greater domestic and international pressure to intervene if the world noticed a foreign invasion rather than what looked like a home-grown insurgency.[16]

III

After the election, Johnson became more open to escalation, though he still believed that limited escalation would be sufficient to discourage the North Vietnamese from escalating too far. He charged McNamara with developing a plan to bomb North Vietnam. The secretary formulated a plan based on the concept of "gradual escalation," a principle derived from the abstract reasoning of limited war theory. The bombing would start with modest numbers of strikes on targets of modest significance and slowly, over time, would increase in intensity and target importance. For McNamara and other civilian proponents, this strategy was better than beginning with high intensity attacks on the most lucrative targets because it would be less likely to provoke the Chinese. Additionally, a strategy of gradual escalation would leave open the option of threatening the enemy with heavier strikes in the future. According to McNamara, the military damage caused by an intensive air campaign against North Vietnam would be inconsequential, for he and the other civilian advisors did not believe that the insurgents in South Vietnam depended heavily on assistance from the North.

The Joint Chiefs protested strenuously against gradual escalation. Taking a more pessimistic and historically-based view of human nature, they argued that the slow start of gradual escalation would convince the enemy that the

---

16. Military History Institute of Vietnam, *Victory in Vietnam*, 126–42; Pham Gia Duc, *Su Doan 325*, Volume 2 (Hanoi: People's Army Publishing House, 1986), 41–49.

United States lacked resolve, and hence, instead of leading the enemy to show restraint, it would cause them to escalate. If the United States commenced high-intensity bombing of critical targets at once, the generals argued, it would discourage the North Vietnamese from escalating.[17] The chiefs pointed to growing signs that the Chinese would not intervene in response to heavy attacks on North Vietnam, including Chinese public statements to that effect. The bluntest pronouncement came on January 9, 1965, when Mao told the American journalist Edgar Snow:

> China's armies will not go beyond her borders to fight. That is clear enough. Only if the United States attacked China would we fight.[18]

These arguments failed to sway Johnson. He began bombing North Vietnam in February 1965 in conformance with McNamara's strategy of gradual escalation. The bombing program—codenamed Operation Rolling Thunder—was to continue on and off for the next three and half years.

The limited nature of the initial strikes did nothing to curb the ambitions of Hanoi. As the Joint Chiefs had predicted, the North Vietnamese pressed ahead with the invasion, believing that Johnson would not step in to stop them. When the American president tendered an offer to negotiate, the North Vietnamese interpreted it as yet another sign that he lacked the will to fight. With a hint of impudence, Hanoi replied that it would negotiate only after the United States had agreed to leave South Vietnam and let the Communists take over.[19]

As it became apparent that the low-intensity bombing was not causing Hanoi to yield, Johnson showed symptoms of despair. His unfamiliarity with military affairs left him ill-prepared to question the merits of gradual escalation and to weigh the current strategy against alternatives. While pushing McNamara for a strategic silver bullet, Johnson laid bare how little he understood the military environment that dictated the viability of the strategic options. "I don't guess there's any way," Johnson said, "that through your small planes or helicopters . . . you could spot these people and then radio back and let the planes come in and bomb the hell out of them." The Americans and South

17. JCS to McNamara, "Courses of Action in Southeast Asia," November 23, 1964, DDRS, 1999, 9.

18. Edward Snow, "An Interview with Mao Tse-Tung," n.d., DDRS, 1977, 318B.

19. CIA, "North Vietnamese References to Negotiations on Vietnam," April 23, 1965, DDRS, 1983, 92.

Vietnamese had been doing just that for years, but McNamara was diplomatic enough to avoid mentioning that fact. Instead, he merely replied, "This is what we are trying to do, but it's very difficult when they're under the trees."[20]

With McNamara unable to produce a surefire solution, President Johnson turned to the Joint Chiefs for ideas. Army Chief of Staff Harold K. Johnson recommended the deployment of four US divisions across the seventeenth parallel into Laos in order to block the Ho Chi Minh Trail. The chiefs also called for closing North Vietnamese and Cambodian harbors by mining or blockades, a matter given new urgency in February 1965 by the discovery of a North Vietnamese transport ship on the South Vietnamese coast. McNamara persuaded Johnson to turn these recommendations down, repeating his claim that the Communist armed forces in South Vietnam did not need extensive external support, and arguing that obstructing Haiphong could provoke a crisis with the Soviets.[21]

Following additional North Vietnamese attacks, McNamara did convince Johnson to authorize the deployment of US Marines to defend American installations in the northern section of South Vietnam. The first of these Marines arrived at Da Nang on March 8. Neither McNamara nor Johnson anticipated that the deployment would be the first step toward direct American participation in the ground war; neither was aware that the North Vietnamese invasion forces were already on the Ho Chi Minh Trail. Johnson was so convinced that the American forces would avoid combat that he considered portraying them to the American people as "security battalions," rather than Marine combat battalions. McNamara was hardly opposed to such misrepresentation in principle, but he believed that in this instance the press would easily see through the deception and the administration would look the worse for attempting to mislead. As a less risky alternative, McNamara persuaded Johnson to minimize the attention given to the Marines by announcing the deployment on a Saturday night, which kept the news out of the morning papers on Sunday, the only day when no papers published afternoon editions.[22] This obfuscation would work for a time, and it might have succeeded in the end had it not been for the fact that the enemy's invasion would eventually draw the

20. Telcon, February 26, 1965, in *Reaching for Glory: Lyndon Johnson's Secret White House Tapes, 1964–1965*, Michael Beschloss, ed. (New York, NY: Simon & Schuster, 2001), 194.

21. Bundy to McNamara, June 30, 1965, *FRUS, 1964–1968*, Volume 3, 35; Greene, "Escalation of effort in South Vietnam," July 10, 1965, MCHC, Greene Papers; McNamara to Johnson, July 30, 1965, *FRUS, 1964–1968*, Volume 3, 100.

22. Telcon, March 6, 1965, Beschloss, ed., *Reaching for Glory*, 213–16.

American forces into mortal combat. Over time, the administration's efforts to conceal the truth would invite scathing criticism from Americans across the political spectrum.

The confinement of US forces to base security in the South, the inoffensive nature of Rolling Thunder, and the public statements by Johnson forswearing attacks on North Vietnam and China eased Chinese fears of a direct clash with the United States over North Vietnam. At the same time, the Soviets were boosting their military aid to North Vietnam, raising concerns in Beijing that North Vietnam would become too close to the Soviets. Because of these developments, the Chinese decided to send seven divisions of troops to North Vietnam, mainly to serve in construction and other support functions that would be far removed from current or probable future combat. Their presence did nothing to diminish Mao's determination to avoid war with the United States, or his willingness to say as much to numerous audiences.[23]

Not until April 1965 did the Johnson administration realize that the North Vietnamese had shifted to a strategy of decisive conventional warfare. The American intelligence community came to that conclusion after obtaining compelling evidence that the first North Vietnamese army division had entered the South. The news convinced McNamara and Johnson to accede to requests from the military to send more combat troops to South Vietnam, increasing the US military personnel strength from 33,000 to 82,000. Had Johnson authorized such a deployment in the summer or fall of 1964, when the generals had started recommending it, he would have shown the North Vietnamese that they could not win a rapid military victory in the South. Now, however, it was too late to stop the North Vietnamese invasion.

Hanoi's spring offensive began in May with a string of large-scale attacks on South Vietnamese cities and bases. Holding the tactical and strategic initiatives, the North Vietnamese attacked at the times and places of their choosing, in weather conditions and terrain that impaired American air support. The South Vietnamese armed forces, still reeling from coups and purges, sustained crippling losses. The attacks accelerated in the first week of June, inflicting 1,876 casualties on the South Vietnamese, the highest one-week tally of the war to this point.[24]

23. Chen Jian, *Mao's China and the Cold War* (Chapel Hill, NC: University of North Carolina Press, 2001), 219; Qiang Zhai, *China and the Vietnam Wars, 1950–1975* (Chapel Hill, NC: University of North Carolina Press, 2000), 134–35.

24. CIA, "The Situation in South Vietnam," June 9, 1965, LBJL, NSF, VNCF, box 18.

IV

On June 7, Westmoreland urged Washington to insert US ground forces into the war as the only way to stop the North Vietnamese army from obliterating its South Vietnamese opponents. American intervention would avert defeat, Westmoreland argued, but it would not bring about rapid victory. Rather, intervention would buy time to restore the strength of the South Vietnamese government and regain control of the South Vietnamese countryside.

President Johnson knew that a war would cost him dearly in material resources as well as in political capital, but he believed that abandoning South Vietnam would also come at enormous cost. Allowing South Vietnam to fall, he feared, would cause other Asian "dominoes" to fall to Communism, which would severely damage America's interests in Asia as well as undermine its credibility around the globe. The domino theory was well supported by the evidence available at the time and since. In late July, Johnson decided that the strategic ends of preserving South Vietnam were worth employing a massive US military commitment. The United States would enter the ground war.

While Johnson and McNamara had constrained and managed the use of American force in North Vietnam, Laos, and Cambodia, they deferred to the judgment of General Westmoreland on military operations within South Vietnam. Westmoreland's strategy for South Vietnam combined mobile military operations against North Vietnamese units with the securing of the South Vietnamese rural population and the rehabilitation of the South Vietnamese armed forces and government. Had McNamara and Johnson been more familiar with military affairs, they might have been more inclined to second-guess Westmoreland's strategy, although it was a sound strategy given the conditions and constraints that the general faced. Seeking out and destroying North Vietnamese forces—the strategic component of Westmoreland's plan that came under the most criticism—was essential in preventing the North Vietnamese from mounting massive attacks on South Vietnamese forces, bases, and cities.

During the late summer and fall of 1965, American combat troops found and engaged several large concentrations of North Vietnamese forces. Exploiting their superior mobility and firepower, the Americans inflicted heavy losses on the North Vietnamese each time, at relatively low cost to themselves. These defeats damaged many of the North Vietnamese units that Hanoi had earmarked for the decisive battles, and made clear the punishment awaiting other North Vietnamese units that had massed for the attack. The North Vietnamese leadership decided to abort its plans for a decisive military victory. They shifted to a strategy of protracted attrition, intended to wear down America's will.[25]

Once the immediate danger to South Vietnam had passed, the Joint Chiefs and McNamara resumed their struggles over strategy beyond South Vietnam's borders. The Joint Chiefs urged President Johnson to double the pace of Rolling Thunder, noting that the longer the bombing campaign took, the easier the enemy could relocate targets and strengthen air defenses. Additionally, the generals advocated mining North Vietnam's harbors. Former President Dwight D. Eisenhower weighed in with Johnson in favor of these measures. "We should not base our action on minimum needs," said the mastermind behind the defeat of the Axis powers in World War II. Instead, the United States "should swamp the enemy with overwhelming force."[26]

McNamara convinced Johnson to reject these recommendations by raising the same objections as before. McNamara clung to the hope that American restraint would be matched by North Vietnamese restraint. The United States did not yet know that Hanoi already had decided to set its 1965 invasion in motion back in November 1964, and therefore, Americans could still believe—as McNamara did—that the American bombing of North Vietnam in February 1965, rather than American weakness in late 1964, had triggered North Vietnam's springtime offensive.

At the same time that McNamara was arguing for limited war, the US intelligence community was predicting North Vietnamese and Chinese reactions that were diametrically opposed to McNamara's. In a unified estimate, the CIA, the Defense Intelligence Agency, the National Security Agency, and the US Intelligence Board augured that intensification of American bombing in North Vietnam or Laos would cause Hanoi to de-escalate, and would not cause the Chinese to intervene in the war.[27] In one of the most striking examples of his strategic closemindedness, McNamara refused to reconsider his views, and instead orchestrated the creation of a new estimate that was certain to demonstrate the soundness of his strategy. McNamara entrusted the estimate not to other intelligence professionals, but rather to his own policy experts,

25. Vo Cong Luan and Tran Hanh, eds., *May Van De ve Tong Ket Chien Tranh va Viet Su Quan Su* (Hanoi: Military History Institute of Vietnam and Ministry of Defense, 1987), 285; Pham Thi Vinh, ed., *Van Kien Dang*, Tap 24, 1965 (Hanoi: Nha Xuat Ban Chinh Tri Quoc Gia, 2003), 637.

26. Goodpaster, "Meeting with General Eisenhower," August 3, 1965, *FRUS, 1964–1968*, Volume 3, 104.

27. Special National Intelligence Estimate 10-11-65, "Probable Communist Reactions to a US Course of Action," September 22, 1965, *FRUS, 1964–1968*, Volume 3, 148.

breaching the segregation of intelligence from policy that normally impedes the slanting of intelligence for policy purposes. In their estimate, McNamara's policy staff concluded that American escalation would not achieve favorable changes in North Vietnamese behavior and, in fact, would dangerously antagonize the Chinese and Soviets.[28]

Debate over North Vietnam's openness to mutual self-limitation came to an end in November 1965 with the intelligence community's discovery of surging North Vietnamese troop infiltration. New information showed that young North Vietnamese men were coming down the Ho Chi Minh Trail at rates much higher than previously believed, and that enemy strength was increasing twice as fast. The North Vietnamese were estimated to have 90,000 regulars in the South at the end of 1965, up from 50,000 six months earlier.[29]

V

American restraint, it was now clear, was being answered by North Vietnamese escalation. McNamara's confidence in limited war theory was badly shaken, and it would never fully recover. Johnson, who had never been as fond of academic ideas as McNamara, lost whatever confidence he had possessed in the notion that one combatant's restraint caused the other to exercise restraint. Both McNamara and Johnson decided that the time had come to escalate. They would match the influx of North Vietnamese troops by increasing the American troop strength in South Vietnam to 400,000.

The generals favored this troop increase, believing it would be militarily and psychologically advantageous, but they told President Johnson that he needed to call up the reserve units of the US armed forces if he wished to raise the troop ceiling to 400,000. With a deep reservoir of experienced manpower, the reserves were intended for use in the type of wartime military expansion being contemplated. Johnson, however, opposed summoning the reserves for fear that it would rile up the American population, to the detriment of his domestic agenda and his personal popularity. He asked McNamara to come up with an

28. Gibbons, *The U.S. Government and the Vietnam War*, Volume 4, 77–80; Drea, *McNamara, Clifford, and the Burdens of Vietnam*, 63–64.

29. COMUSMACV to CINCPAC, November 21, 1965, LBJL, NSF, VNCF, box 24; Westmoreland to Sharp, December 9, 1965, National Archives II, RG 59, Lot Files, Entry 5408, box 2; USMACV, "1965 Command History," April 20, 1966, 44.

alternative plan for fielding the 400,000 troops without using the reserves. McNamara's solution was to send large numbers of draftees and junior officers to Vietnam. The Joint Chiefs protested that combat leadership and technical competence would suffer, but their words failed to dissuade Johnson from approving McNamara's plan.[30]

In November, the Joint Chiefs met with the president to advocate harder blows against North Vietnam, which they deemed necessary to compel North Vietnam to end—or at least curtail—its involvement in South Vietnam. Without a powerful hammering of the North, the chiefs told the president, the war would drag on without hope of decisive victory. In response, Johnson exploded with a ferocity greater than any he had ever evidenced toward the North Vietnamese. As retold by a junior officer who was present, the president "screamed obscenities, he cursed them personally, he ridiculed them for coming to his office with their 'military advice.'" Johnson "called them filthy names—sh__heads, dumbsh__s, pompous assh__s—and used 'the F-word' as an adjective more freely than a Marine at boot camp." The president castigated the chiefs for discounting the possibility of Chinese intervention and for "trying to pass the buck for World War III to him."[31]

Johnson's reaction was the antithesis of sound strategic contemplation. The president was supposed to question the advice of the military on an issue of this strategic magnitude, and to disregard that advice if he deemed it unsound, but he hurt himself and the country by demeaning the generals. Such venom could only discourage the presentation of dissenting opinions in the future, and, as events would show, the strategic counsel of the generals was often wiser than the preconceived notions of Johnson and McNamara.

Johnson's seething rage on the question of Chinese intervention was particularly striking in light of mounting evidence that China did not, in fact, intend to go to war over American actions in North Vietnam. In October 1965, the Chinese again had said publicly they would not fight the United States unless it attacked Chinese territory.[32] Near year's end, the Chinese government communicated privately to the North Vietnamese that they should not

30. JCS to McNamara, JCSM 811–65, November 10, 1965, DDRS, Document Number CK3100292141; *Pentagon Papers*, Volume 4, 347.

31. Charles G. Cooper, "The Day It Became the Longest War," *Proceedings* 122:5 (May 1996): 77–80.

32. CIA, "Chen Yi's Press Conference," October 1, 1965, LBJL, NSF, Country File, China, box 238.

expect much military help from China because they were fighting "paper ti-gers" that could be defeated through "self-reliance."[33]

During 1966 and 1967, the war in South Vietnam was one of protracted at-trition, with American forces dealing heavy losses to the North Vietnamese but unable to prevent Hanoi from replenishing its forces with fresh troops from North Vietnam. As the intractability of the conflict appeared to mount, the Joint Chiefs occasionally returned to recommendations to intensify Roll-ing Thunder and undertake ground operations in Laos and Cambodia. Each time, McNamara and his civilian analysts at the Pentagon batted them away with their usual arguments.

As time went on, disputes between civilian and military authorities over the effectiveness of Rolling Thunder became increasingly bitter. A scarcity of information on North Vietnamese logistics forced American analysts to rely on past experience, common sense, and a priori assumptions in estimating North Vietnamese logistical capabilities and requirements. The Whiz Kids relied little on the first two, and heavily on the third. Their assumptions con-sistently led to estimates of great excess capacity in the North Vietnamese logistical system, which the Whiz Kids then cited as evidence that no amount of bombing could diminish the North Vietnamese capacity enough to reduce the infiltration of supplies below Hanoi's desired levels. The generals and their analysts questioned the assumptions and logic of the Whiz Kids. Based on history and personal experience, they argued that the bombing of North Viet-namese logistics had to exert a larger impact than the Whiz Kids thought.

After the war, Hanoi would publish histories that settled the matter. During 1966 and 1967, the histories stated, Rolling Thunder had frequently damaged North Vietnam's logistical system to the point that no unused capacity re-mained. North Vietnamese forces regularly ran short of supplies, preventing them from undertaking some military operations and limiting the intensity of the operations they were able to undertake.[34]

---

33. Lin Piao, "Long Live the Victory of the People's War," *New China News Agency Interna-tional Service,* September 2, 1965, Texas Tech University Vietnam Archive, Pike Collection, Unit 3, box 13; Robert Garson, "Lyndon B. Johnson and the China Enigma," *Journal of Contemporary History,* 32:1 (January 1997): 73; Thomas Kennedy Latimer, "Hanoi's Leaders and Their South Vietnam Policies, 1954–1968" (Ph.D. diss., Georgetown University, 1972), 227.

34. For instance, Nguyen, *Van Tai Quan Su Chien Luoc Tren Duong Ho Chi Minh Trong Khang Chien Chong My,* 64; Nguyen Huu An with Nguyen Tu Duong, *Chien Truong Moi* (Hanoi: People's Army Publishing House, 2002), 52; Dang Van Nhung et al., *Su Doan 7: Ky Su* (Hanoi: People's Army Publishing House, 1986), 14, 22–30.

The United States was also accumulating evidence that North Vietnam was increasing the shipment of supplies through Cambodia. Ships from North Vietnam, China, and the Soviet Union brought the supplies to the port of Sihanoukville, and from there Cambodian soldiers helped the North Vietnamese sneak them into South Vietnam. In an attempt to cut off this supply line, Westmoreland and the Joint Chiefs called for ground operations into Cambodia as well as a blockade of Sihanoukville. CIA analysts, however, expressed doubts that the amount of support coming through Cambodia was as significant as the military claimed. In the CIA's view, the North Vietnamese forces in the South still depended mainly on supplies acquired locally and from Laos. McNamara and other civilian officials used the CIA's interpretation to reject the military's proposals for Cambodia. Westmoreland was so disturbed that he accused the CIA of "reflecting what Washington wanted to hear."[35]

Lyndon Johnson fell out with McNamara in the fall of 1967, in part because of his growing doubts about the wisdom of McNamara's advice on Vietnam. Earlier in the year, the president had begun questioning McNamara's argument that bombing North Vietnam had no military value and little other strategic value. Johnson's concern increased in the fall when McNamara argued that, because the bombing offered nothing of military value, Rolling Thunder should be curtailed, or even ended. Fueling Johnson's skepticism of McNamara's arguments were the strenuous efforts of the North Vietnamese to get the United States to end the bombing, the pleas of American allies to intensify the bombing, and the insistence of an increasing number of US civilian officials that the bombing had both military and political benefits. The US military and most of the intelligence community were in agreement—ending the bombing would convey American irresolution and hence discourage North Vietnam from negotiating an end to the war.

The controversy over bombing came to a head with the Stennis hearings of August 1967. Senator John Stennis of Mississippi, a conservative Democrat, had called the hearings out of dissatisfaction with the strategy of gradual escalation. With American involvement in the ground war now more than two years old, he, many others in the Congress, and much of the general public had reached the same conclusion as the generals—the administration needed to scrap gradual escalation in order to hasten the enemy's defeat.

35. William C. Westmoreland, *A Soldier Reports* (Garden City, NY: Doubleday, 1976), 181–82.

Johnson, the elected politician, was more concerned about the public and congressional discontent than McNamara, the unelected cabinet official. On the morning the Stennis hearings began, Johnson authorized strikes on several lucrative North Vietnamese targets that he had avoided hitting previously. Though the maneuver was to have significant military benefit in the long term, in the short term it merely stoked the anger of the hawks, who denounced it as a cheap political stunt.[36]

During the hearings, the Joint Chiefs and five other general officers testified that they had opposed gradual escalation from the start. The strategy, they said, had afforded the North Vietnamese time to build up their air defenses and to relocate supplies to less vulnerable locations. They noted that the bombing had achieved some valuable results, such as diverting half a million North Vietnamese from other activities to repairing bomb damage and rerouting logistics, and these effects could be amplified if the administration stepped up the bombing. The generals also advocated mining North Vietnam's harbors.[37]

McNamara appeared before the committee after the generals, on August 25. Stepping up the bombing or mining the harbors, he argued, would have little impact on the war. In an unapologetic defense of Operation Rolling Thunder, McNamara asserted that the bombing would not have saved American lives had it been pursued more intensively at the outset. Senator Stuart Symington, Democrat of Missouri, interjected that a senior Marine commander had testified that bombing was crucial to disrupting the enemy's movement of heavy equipment, and that when bombing had been suspended, the United States had incurred higher US casualties.

To bolster his claim that the bombing was not hindering the North Vietnamese war effort, McNamara asserted that the North Vietnamese supply system was operating far below its maximum capacity. The North Vietnamese, he said, were moving seventy-five tons of supplies to the South per day, enough for the average North Vietnamese battalion in the South to fight one day out of thirty, whereas their infiltration system had the capacity to move more than 200 tons per day. Even if bombing seriously reduced the 200-ton ceiling,

---

36. US Grant Sharp, *Strategy for Defeat: Vietnam in Retrospect* (San Rafael, CA: Presidio Press, 1978), 194; Drea, *McNamara, Clifford, and the Burdens of Vietnam,* 215–16.

37. US Senate, Preparedness Investigating Subcommittee of the Committee on Armed Services, *Air War Against North Vietnam,* 90th Cong., 1st sess. (Washington, DC: Government Printing Office, 1967), 236, 416.

therefore, the North Vietnamese would still be able to move their seventy-five tons per day.[38]

The generals, however, had exposed the flaws in this reasoning during their testimony. If the North Vietnamese had been able to move more than seventy-five tons per day, they surely would have done so, for they would have preferred to fight more often than one day in thirty. If indeed the North Vietnamese infiltration system did not have excess capacity, then bombing it would reduce further the North Vietnamese capabilities for waging war in the South.[39] After the war, North Vietnamese accounts would confirm that their units remained short on supplies during this period and, for that reason, were unable to operate as often as they wanted.[40]

As the senators kept pressing McNamara to explain why he had consistently ignored the advice of the generals, he asserted, "I don't believe that there is this gulf between the military leaders and the civilian leaders in the executive branch."[41] He told the press during a break, "My policies don't differ with those of the Joint Chiefs and I think they would be the first to say it."[42]

McNamara's dubious assertions about military strategy and his false denial of differences of opinion infuriated the Joint Chiefs as well as the senators. According to one account, the chiefs resolved to resign together in protest, but then backed off after tempers cooled.[43] The Stennis committee blasted McNamara and the administration in a report issued at the end of the hearings. In a unanimous verdict, the committee's Democrats and Republicans assailed the gradualism of Rolling Thunder and denounced the Johnson administration for disregarding the advice of the uniformed military. The military witnesses, the committee observed, had all believed that a combination of intensive bombing and mining "was the single most important thing which could have been done." Moreover,

38. US Senate, Preparedness Investigating Subcommittee of the Committee on Armed Services, *Air War Against North Vietnam*, 277, 299, 309.

39. US Senate, Preparedness Investigating Subcommittee of the Committee on Armed Services, *Air War Against North Vietnam*, 68.

40. See the sources in note 34.

41. US Senate, Preparedness Investigating Subcommittee of the Committee on Armed Services, *Air War Against North Vietnam*, 435.

42. Deborah Shapley, *Promise and Power: The Life and Times of Robert McNamara* (Boston, MA: Little, Brown and Company, 1993), 432.

43. Mark Perry, *Four Stars* (Boston, MA: Houghton Mifflin, 1989), 162–66. Several knowledgeable sources reportedly confirmed this account, but two of the Joint Chiefs denied it. Herring, *LBJ and Vietnam*, 56–57; Sorley, *Honorable Warrior*, 285–87.

the generals had argued, it could still "have a substantial impact on the course of the war and the American and allied casualties in the South."[44]

The Rolling Thunder strikes Johnson had authorized in early August turned out to be the most effective to date. By knocking out critical transportation targets in North Vietnam, they disrupted the importation and distribution of military goods and food. The population of Hanoi, which had become dependent on food imported from China because of agricultural labor shortages, verged on starvation. John Colvin, the British Consul-General in Hanoi, observed that "the country and its people were close to a collapse which, for the first time, no amount of excited exhortation could correct." Colvin believed that if the Americans continued their program of intensified bombing much longer, the North Vietnamese would have to end their war in South Vietnam.[45]

Had Johnson and McNamara been more familiar with military history, they might have known that the United States owed much of its success in several previous wars to strategies that deprived the enemy of food. Union forces had starved the Confederacy during the final year of the Civil War by systematically destroying its crops. During the closing stages of World War I, the effectiveness of the Allies in blocking food shipments had produced the famines that compelled the Central Powers to capitulate. The United States had launched Operation Starvation in April 1945 for the express purpose of starving Japan into submission, though the strategy was cut short by the atomic bombs. With such knowledge, Johnson and McNamara might have seized on the fragmentary reports of food deprivation in North Vietnam to accelerate the attacks on North Vietnam's logistics.

Instead, both men were fixated on diplomacy. Liberal Democrats were badgering Johnson and McNamara to negotiate an end to the war, and although Johnson had pointedly told the members of his party that the North Vietnamese had demonstrated no willingness to negotiate in earnest, he was still eager to pursue any possible indication that Hanoi was changing its mind. McNamara, having previously convinced Johnson to halt Rolling Thunder several times in order to encourage Hanoi to negotiate, made the same case again, with his customary claim that the United States would not give up much since the bombing campaign was militarily unimportant. In late August, when the

44. E. W. Kenworthy, "Senate Unit Asks Johnson to Widen Bombing in North," *New York Times*, September 1, 1967.

45. John Colvin, *Twice Around the World: Some Memoirs of Diplomatic Life in North Vietnam and Outer Mongolia* (London: Leo Cooper, 1991), 113–16.

North Vietnamese sent word through an intermediary that they would negotiate if Johnson stopped the bombing of North Vietnam, Johnson agreed to suspend bombing in the Hanoi area as a gesture of serious intent.[46]

This time, as on previous occasions, the North Vietnamese neither deescalated nor made a sincere effort to negotiate. By late September, Johnson threw up his hands in frustration. "I think they are playing us for suckers," the president exclaimed. "They have no more intention of talking than we have of surrendering."[47] Johnson kept the bombing campaign going, but did not resume the intensive strikes of the summer nor did he heed other recommendations from the Joint Chiefs for escalation. These decisions allowed the North Vietnamese to recover from their supply crisis.

VI

In mid-October, McNamara called for the complete suspension of Operation Rolling Thunder. By this point, the failure of previous bombing halts had convinced nearly every other senior official that another halt would be counterproductive. The CIA, which in the past had often been skeptical of the value of Rolling Thunder, predicted that the North Vietnamese would view another pause as "a sign the US will was weakening," and therefore would adopt an even more intransigent diplomatic stance.[48]

Among those who had given up hope in bombing pauses was Johnson himself. At the end of October, he authorized the extension of Rolling Thunder to sites he had rejected in the past. Johnson's loss of faith in the pause coincided with the completion of his loss of faith in McNamara. Near the end of the year, by mutual consent, McNamara agreed to step down as secretary of defense. Clark Clifford took his place in early 1968.

Clifford turned out to be closer to McNamara in his views than Johnson had anticipated. Influenced by Whiz Kids who remained at the Pentagon, Clifford adopted the view that stepping up the bombing would not cause serious harm to North Vietnamese infiltration, and hence could easily be reduced or discontinued to encourage the North Vietnamese to negotiate. He also seemed

---

46. *The Joint Chiefs of Staff and the War in Vietnam* (Christiansburg, VA: Dalley Book Service, 2001), 3; Helms to Johnson, "The Kissinger Project," September 7, 1967, CREST document number CIA-RDP79B01737A001800170001-7.

47. Johnson, meeting notes, September 26, 1967, *FRUS, 1964–1968*, Volume 5, 336.

48. CIA Intelligence Memorandum 1391/67, "The Consequences of a Halt in the Bombardment of North Vietnam," October 9, 1967, DDRS, document number CK2349074218.

to have doubts that the strategic objective of containing Communism in Asia warranted a huge US military commitment in South Vietnam. Soon Clifford was urging Johnson to stop the bombing campaign altogether and to draw down American forces in Vietnam. Johnson, with new confidence in his own ideas, flatly rejected Clifford's proposals.

At the end of March, Johnson suspended bombing in northern North Vietnam in another attempt to produce negotiations, though only because bad weather would preclude bombing in that area for the next few months anyway. To general surprise, Hanoi promptly agreed to enter into negotiations. The talks began in Paris the following month. The North Vietnamese, however, demonstrated no interest in finding a diplomatic resolution for the conflict, using the Paris venue solely for polemical propaganda.

The Joint Chiefs, seeing only deceit in the North Vietnamese, were soon recommending the full resumption of Operation Rolling Thunder. Clifford countered with the argument that resumption would damage prospects for the negotiations and, besides, it would have little military benefit. Johnson dismissed Clifford's claims as absurd.[49] The North Vietnamese themselves had escalated a few weeks earlier with a major urban offensive. General Abrams was sending Johnson information showing that the bombing was indeed saving American lives by damaging the North Vietnamese transportation network and forcing the North Vietnamese to divert military manpower to air defense. In reference to Clifford and like-minded officials, Johnson told Governor Richard Hughes of New Jersey:

> What they're asking me to do is be the biggest boob of our time. Just as the Communists get ready to hit us, they want me to do what I did at Tet—take a vacation, let our men accept a Tet holiday, and as I do it, and call off our bombing, let them hit me full length, and I just—I just—I just don't see it.[50]

Postwar Communist histories would reveal that Rolling Thunder, despite its confinement to southern North Vietnam, severely damaged North Vietnamese logistics in the middle of 1968. North Vietnamese trucks still had to pass through a few key intersections in southern North Vietnam, and concentration of the bombing at these points was destroying large numbers of trucks, and causing most others to turn back. During the late summer of 1968, only

49. Tom Johnson, "Notes of the Tuesday Lunch Meeting with Foreign Policy Advisers," May 21, 1968, LBJL, Tom Johnson Notes of Meetings, box 3.

50. Telcon, Johnson and Hughes, July 30, 1968, *FRUS, 1964–1968*, Volume 6, 315n.

twenty percent of the supplies intended for delivery to the Ho Chi Minh Trail reached their destination.[51]

Within South Vietnam, American and South Vietnamese forces dealt crushing losses to the North Vietnamese Army during 1968. The Tet Offensive of January and two subsequent large North Vietnamese offensives ended in total military defeat. The improvements in the military situation and the murders of several thousand South Vietnamese civilians at Hue in February and March spurred the South Vietnamese people to rally behind the Saigon government and send more of their sons into its armed forces. In November 1968, the South Vietnamese government embarked on an intensive pacification campaign, which proved spectacularly effective in reclaiming the South Vietnamese countryside.

During Lyndon Johnson's presidency, the American expeditionary forces in South Vietnam achieved the principal objectives that General Westmoreland had laid out in 1965—wearing down North Vietnamese forces, reestablishing rural population security, and reviving the South Vietnamese government and armed forces. These achievements laid the groundwork for the shifting of burdens from American to South Vietnamese forces, which was to take place successfully during the Nixon administration. It was no coincidence that the war within South Vietnam—the one part of the war that the Johnson administration had prosecuted effectively— was the part where Johnson and McNamara had left the strategy to the generals. Where Johnson and McNamara had ignored the generals, the United States had fared much worse. The politicians' refusals to intensify the bombing of North Vietnam and to conduct ground operations in Laos and Cambodia were strategic errors of the first order, allowing the North Vietnamese freedom to move men and materiel and to choose the times and places of battle.

VII

McNamara's failures in the central activity of strategy—identifying the optimal ways and means for achieving the strategic ends—were primarily the result of close-mindedness and overconfidence in abstract theories. When new information and events emerged that contradicted his initial opinions, McNamara

---

51. Nguyen, *Van Tai Quan Su Chien Luoc Tren Duong Ho Chi Minh Trong Khang Chien Chong My*, 77–79.

refused to change his mind, and instead found people who would reassure him that his initial thinking had been correct. By clinging to limited war theory in the face of mounting evidence that American restraint was leading only to North Vietnamese escalation, he precipitated the massive influx of North Vietnamese troops into South Vietnam during 1965. McNamara held on even longer to the erroneous belief that intensive bombing of North Vietnam would not impose high costs on the enemy's war effort and carried a high risk of provoking the enemy.

Lyndon Johnson heeded Robert McNamara's advice on Vietnam until late 1967, when the president came to realize the flaws in McNamara's bombing strategy. He was neither the first nor the last president to have too much faith in an adviser whose confidence and demeanor outpaced the quality of their judgment. Although Johnson had been as disinterested in dissenting views as McNamara for nearly four years, the president eventually proved more willing to change his mind as new information surfaced. His ability to obtain and process that information was always inhibited by his lack of military knowledge, his distrust of the generals, and his dependency on civilian advisers to interpret military affairs. Had Johnson recognized the weaknesses of McNamara's abstract and ahistorical thinking in 1964 or 1965, he probably would have intensified the bombing earlier, which might have compelled Hanoi to end or scale back its war in the South, and definitely would have reduced the strength of the invading North Vietnamese forces.

Johnson never came to appreciate the wisdom of the military's requests to conduct ground operations in Laos, Cambodia, or North Vietnam. By confining American ground operations to South Vietnam, he left General Westmoreland no choice but to fight a defensive war that depended upon continuous attrition of an enemy army that could always be replenished with new youth from North Vietnam. The protracted war of attrition, and the accompanying American casualties, intensified opposition to the war within the United States, among both those who wanted to get out and those who favored a more aggressive military strategy.

Though the American people had not turned decidedly against the war by the time Johnson left office, their loss of patience would loom large in the decisions of his successor. Richard Nixon's strategy would prove capable of preserving South Vietnam without American ground forces, and likely would have sustained South Vietnam indefinitely had the United States not cut its support to South Vietnam, which was in part the product of American impatience, fatigue, and distrust of government. The Johnson administration's strategy thus deserves some of the blame for the fall of South Vietnam in 1975, and the resultant damage to the global reputation of the United States.

At the same time, Johnson's strategy deserves much of the credit for America's broader strategic success in containing Communism in Asia. Most of the Asian dominos did not fall in 1975, whereas some of them almost certainly would have fallen had Johnson abandoned South Vietnam in 1965. By making a prolonged stand in South Vietnam, Johnson emboldened the anti-Communists in neighboring countries, most importantly in Indonesia, and derailed collaboration between China and North Vietnam in spreading the international Communist revolution. The preservation of anti-Communist and anti-Chinese nations in Asia has been enormously beneficial to the United States in its ongoing competition with China, something that today ranks at the top of nearly every American's list of national security priorities.

Johnson's Vietnam strategy also had lasting, and largely negative, consequences for American culture and politics. The protracted war of attrition necessitated by his strategic errors, and the prolonged military conscription that went with it, broke apart the national consensus on the Cold War. For much of the American Left, Vietnam became a symbol of American hubris and overreach. That interpretation would influence the foreign policy of the Democratic Party for decades to come. It would result, in addition, in the downgrading of foreign policy and military strategy at American colleges and universities, the places that had previously served as the leading incubators of national security strategists. As scholars in these fields retired, they were replaced by scholars in unrelated fields, and the courses they had taught disappeared. One cannot help but conclude that strategic decision-making in Washington has suffered in the twenty-first century because few of the nation's senior leaders have received any serious education in the history or principles of national security strategy.

CHAPTER 33

Strategies of Détente and Competition

BREZHNEV AND MOSCOW'S COLD WAR

Sergey Radchenko

Did the Soviet Union have a grand strategy? To early US Cold War policymakers, the answer would have seemed patently obvious. "The fundamental design of those who control the Soviet Union and the international Communist movement is to retain and solidify their absolute power," NSC-68 famously said.[1] The basic premise was never in doubt: the Soviet ideology was fundamentally hostile to the West. The Soviet leaders did not believe in the possibility of permanent accommodation, and all agreements they were party to were just temporary expedients to be discarded at the earliest opportunity. The Cold War thus became a long-term game until the Soviet ideology burned itself out, and the Russians rejoined the society of civilized states. Until then, the United States had to stay ahead in the competition while pushing back against Soviet encroachment. If the long game for the Soviets was expansion, for the Americans it was containment of Soviet expansion.

The problem with this narrative is that it fails to account for the fact that, for much of the Cold War, the Soviet leaders sought to reach accommodation with the West. Of course, expansionism and accommodation could be

---

1. "A Report to the National Security Council by the Executive Secretary (Lay)," April 14, 1950, *Foreign Relations of the United States (hereafter FRUS), 1950, National Security Affairs; Foreign Economic Policy*, Volume I, Document 85.

compatible aims. One could argue, for example, that by accommodation Moscow merely sought America's recognition of the legitimacy of Soviet geopolitical gains. In this reading, a Soviet-American détente, which briefly blossomed in the early-1970s, was that moment in history when America, reeling from its foreign defeats and its domestic upheaval, had reluctantly yielded to Soviet demands. This was how détente was often viewed by Nixon's American critics. But this was not the narrative to which Moscow could relate. The Soviet leaders, desperate for self-legitimation, pursued détente because it afforded them the glory of recognition by those greater still.[2]

The meaning of détente for the USSR was in attaining American recognition of Soviet superpower equality. This in turn required lavish spending on nuclear weapons, military interventions to defend one's ostensible sphere of influence, support of a far-flung clientele of make-believe socialist regimes, and—most importantly—summitry, for sharing the stage with American leaders imbued the Soviets with the much-needed sense of self-confidence and legitimacy. The less convincingly the Soviets performed domestically (and already by the late-1960s it had become patently clear to policymakers that they faced daunting economic prospects), the more weight was given to symbols of power: the might of the nuclear shield, the number of overseas clients, and the bombast of sweeping peace-loving initiatives meant to win the Kremlin the admiration of the humankind. A highly unfavorable international environment (especially the trauma of the Sino-Soviet split and the ensuing

2. For earlier treatments of Soviet approach to détente, see especially Vladislav Zubok, *A Failed Empire: The Soviet Union in the Cold War from Stalin to Gorbachev* (Chapel Hill, NC: North Carolina University Press, 2009). See also Svetlana Savranskaya and William Taubman, "Soviet Foreign Policy, 1962–1975," in *Cambridge History of the Cold War*, Volume 2, Melvyn P. Leffler and Odd Arne Westad, eds. (Cambridge: Cambridge University Press, 2010), 134–57. Raymond Garthoff's mammoth study of the subject has not lost its relevance, and is especially good for arms control negotiations. Raymond Garthoff, *Détente and Confrontation: American-Soviet relations from Nixon to Reagan* (Washington, DC: Brookings, 1994). Specific aspects of détente are explored in the following books: Odd Arne Westad, *The Global Cold War* (Cambridge: Cambridge University Press, 2009); Michael Cotey Morgan, *The Final Act: The Helsinki Accords and the Transformation of the Cold War* (Princeton, NJ: Princeton University Press, 2020); Viktor Israelyan, *Inside the Kremlin during the Yom Kippur War* (University Park, PA: The Pennsylvania State University Press, 1995). Henry Kissinger's memoirs contain marvellous detail on the Soviet-US summitry during the 1970s; there is nothing comparable on the Russian side, though the National Security Archive's translation of Anatolii Chernyaev's diary (https://nsarchive.gwu.edu/anatoly-chernyaev-diary) provides important insights. The best primary source collection is Douglas Selvage et al., eds., *Soviet-American Relations: The Detente Years, 1969–1972* (Washington, DC: Government Printing Office, 2007).

fragmentation of the international Communist movement) gave Moscow a further important reason to mend fences with the West. In this sense, détente signified not so much growing Soviet confidence as the increasingly obvious Soviet weakness. Détente was an effort to pocket the gains before share prices dwindled.

Unfortunately for the Soviets, détente would not—and could not—work. Détente was an inherently unstable condition; the Soviet-American relationship remained fundamentally competitive. One could argue that this was because the United States and the Soviet Union represented very different ideological poles—capitalism and socialism—and these simply could not be reconciled within the framework of détente. While useful, such a framing misses out on a problem of a more basic kind: rivalry between two centers of power in an essentially hierarchical global order. Could this rivalry have reached an equilibrium, where one side's recognition and accommodation were matched by the other side's self-restraint?

This isn't simply a matter of historical interest. It has broader relevance for our understanding of strategy and rivalry. We often think of competition and cooperation as polar opposites. But Brezhnev's strategy aimed to blend the two—to pursue Soviet interests while still limiting superpower hostility, and perhaps even developing shared management of the global system. The fact that he ultimately failed to strike this balance does not simply reveal the limitations of détente. It also testifies to many of the issues that can make it difficult for rivals to achieve mutually acceptable terms of coexistence.

Conflicting perceptions of status were one problem. The Kremlin's perception of what it meant to be seen as an "equal" of the United States did not accord with the views held by successive American presidents. Second, comanagement of the world required an implicit agreement as to what constituted each side's sphere of legitimate interests. Such an agreement was attainable in some areas but much of the world remained in the grey zone, which led to competition that put détente under stress. Third, the desires of allies and partners got in the way. Neither side's Third World clients, with their incessant demands, showed much appreciation for maintaining the superpower equilibrium. This was particularly the case in the Middle East and in Africa, where the Soviet leaders found themselves under pressure to live up to their clients' expectations even at the risk of undermining détente.

Fourth, entrenched bureaucratic interests often worked in accordance with their own logic and out of sync with the requirements of détente. In the Soviet case, the military, the intelligence services, and the Party apparatus sometimes worked at cross purposes, and collectively pursued policies that undercut détente. This was even more true for the United States, where presidents had to contend with the domestic public opinion (a problem the Soviets did not have to worry about), and the often-obstructionist Congress. Finally, individuals mattered. It took strong personalities to cut through decades of hostility, but it was also hard to maintain amity at the top for long. Key proponents of détente—President Richard Nixon and General Secretary Leonid Brezhnev—faced, in Nixon's case, debilitating political troubles (Watergate) or, in Brezhnev's case, progressively serious health problems. Nixon's resignation in August 1974 took the most prominent US advocate of détente out of the picture. Meanwhile, as the general secretary faded into senility, Soviet foreign policy went adrift, and superpower competition returned in all its fury.

I

When the chief Soviet proponent of détente, Leonid Il'yich Brezhnev, climbed to the pinnacle of political power in the USSR, he was not quite fifty-eight. A son of the Russian-Ukrainian borderlands, he had rapidly risen through the Party ranks decimated by Stalin's purges. Brezhnev had served in the Soviet army during the Second World War, which took him all the way to Prague—the first time he saw Europe. "I really miss the Motherland, mama," he recalled writing to his mother at the end of war. "When I get to Paris, I will climb the Eiffel Tower, and spit from it at all of Europe!"[3] (He did not go to Paris until much later in his life.) A protégé of Nikita Khrushchev, Brezhnev headed Party hierarchies in Moldova and Kazakhstan, distinguishing himself as a suave apparatchik, skilled in the art of back-stabbing and intrigue. This skill he put to good use in October 1964, when he ungratefully toppled Khrushchev and installed himself in his place as the First Secretary (later to become General Secretary) of the Soviet Communist Party.

Not known for intellectual prowess, Brezhnev was nevertheless a capable administrator. He could work long hours, wearing himself out (this would eventually have disastrous consequences for his health). He was a consensual policymaker who generally shunned confrontation and tried to smooth corners and arrive at compromise solutions. This was especially the case early in Brezhnev's tenure, since he had a power-sharing arrangement with two other

---

3. Vadim Pechenev, *Vzlet i Padenie Gorbacheva: Glazami Ochevidtsa* (Moscow: Respublika, 1996), 61.

players, Prime Minister Aleksei Kosygin and Chairman of the Presidium Nikolai Podgorny. The latter was never much of a threat, but the former was a real rival for a time, and even tried to play the central role in the making of Soviet foreign policy. It was not until the late-1960s that Brezhnev consolidated his authority, in large part by pursuing détente with the West as his personal political project.

Détente was not a new idea. Its key elements (as understood in Moscow) were already discernible at the outset of the Cold War, and, indeed, preceded its outbreak. Central to the idea was a more or less explicit division of the postwar world into spheres of influence, with the United States (or the West) recognizing Moscow's legitimate interests in Eastern Europe, parts of the Middle East, and in East Asia, with the Soviet Union returning the favor for parts of the world where it had no interests or ambitions. That vision (articulated in memoranda for Stalin by Soviet postwar planners like Maksim Litvinov and Ivan Maisky, and generally embraced by Stalin himself) had a fatal flaw that also plagued Brezhnev's détente: an assumption that what the Soviet Union perceived to be its "legitimate interests" would be seen as legitimate in Washington. In the meantime, US atomic monopoly undercut Moscow's claims to superpower equality and convinced the deeply neurotic, insecure Stalin that no accommodation with the American foe was possible or desirable.

The Soviet Union tested its first atomic weapon in August 1949, and within a few years built up a substantial nuclear capability, which emboldened Stalin's successor Nikita Khrushchev and supported the latter's conviction that, as much as the American leaders were unwilling to see the Soviets as "equals," they'd have no choice but to acknowledge such equality in view of the "realities" of the nuclear age. Such acknowledgment would then pave way to the end of the Cold War since (in the Kremlin's interpretation) the Cold War was itself merely a consequence of a consistent US effort to deny the Soviets their rightful place in the sun. "Love us as we are," Khrushchev once proposed to his Western interlocutors, and what he meant was that now that the Soviet Union had become a nuclear superpower, it would have to be given a seat at the high table on par with the United States.[4]

Some of the most audacious Soviet foreign policy moves in the late-1950s and early-1960s—from Khrushchev's successive Berlin ultimatums to the

4. For context, see Sergey Radchenko, "Love Us as We Are: Khrushchev's 1956 Charm Offensive in the UK," *CWIHP Dossier* No. 71 (April 2016).

deployment of Soviet nuclear weapons to Cuba—stemmed from the Soviet leader's nuclear-inspired confidence combined with an acute perception of being the underdog of international politics. How could the Americans have an outpost in the heart of *our* Germany? Why was it that the Americans had missiles in Turkey but *we* could not have them in Cuba? Such perceived injustices could no longer be tolerated now that the Soviet Union had the potential to destroy every and all adversaries. But was the game worth playing? Khrushchev thought the risks of war were minimal—no more than five percent, he estimated, in the case of the Berlin crisis.[5] Yet when push came to shove, Khrushchev backed off in Berlin. Nor did he test his luck in Cuba, withdrawing quickly when his reckless ploy to install nuclear missiles on the island brought the Soviet Union to the precipice of a war with the United States. It was a complete humiliation for the Soviet leader but the Cuban experience did have a silver lining in that it encouraged both Khrushchev and US President John F. Kennedy to redouble their quest for détente, which was nearly within grasp before it was derailed by Kennedy's assasination, Khrushchev's dethronement, and, above all, Vietnam.

Vietnam posed an enormous challenge for détente, and it highlights why détente proved so elusive within the broader context of Soviet-American competition. The escalation of the US military effort in this Cold War theatre (in late 1964–early 1965) coincided with Brezhnev's rise to power. In addition to taking the helm in the Soviet Union, Brezhnev rose to leadership of the entire Socialist camp, from which he needed and expected deferral and approval, and to which he promised a more principled application of ideological solidarity than Khrushchev, with his inconsistencies, was ever able to deliver. Such commitment was necessary in view of the toxic quarrel with China, which had challenged Moscow's authority and undermined Soviet positions in the socialist camp. Since the Chinese claimed that the Soviet Union had abandoned their struggle against American imperialism, Brezhnev had to show that this was not the case, that, in contrast, he was true to Marxist principles and so deserving of the mantle of leadership in the Communist world. This commitment showed in particular in the Soviet support for North Vietnam in its deepening confrontation with the United States, even if such support also undermined promises of détente with Washington.

---

5. Nikita Khrushchev's comments at the Presidium meeting, May 26, 1961, in *Prezidium TsK KPSS 1954–1964: Stenogrammy*, Volume 1, A.A. Fursenko, ed. (Moscow: Rosspen, 2003), 503.

Moscow's military aid to North Vietnam thus increased dramatically from 1965 for reasons that had much more to do with the ups and downs of the Sino-Soviet struggle for leadership than with Vietnam's strategic position. For a year or two, Brezhnev and his comrades tried to use Vietnam as the ground for repairing relations with China. If this were to happen (and it could only happen if Beijing agreed to defer to Soviet leadership), it would have given a marvellous boost to the Soviet sense of self-confidence. To this end, Premier Kosygin even ventured out to China in February 1965 and met with Chairman Mao Zedong (the last time a Soviet leader would meet with Mao). But in response to Kosygin's plea to bridge the gap over Vietnam, Mao promised that the Sino-Soviet struggle would continue for "10,000 years."[6] Having failed in the attempted rapprochement with the Chinese, the Soviet leaders then tried to outbid them in supplying aid to Vietnam while loudly condemning the US war effort. There were of course strict limits on the Kremlin's quest for revolutionary legitimacy. "What are we supposed to do," Brezhnev complained in July 1965, "resort to atomic weapons? Is this what peoples of the world would want? . . . This would not be aid to Vietnam but an assured war. We cannot allow this."[7]

While Moscow's growing commitment to North Vietnam was a consequence of the need to defend Soviet credibility against Chinese attacks, this commitment undoubtedly frustrated other aims of Soviet foreign policy—especially the need for a dialogue with the United States.

Overall, it was the idea of détente as the high table of international politics that underpinned Brezhnev's broader foreign policy agenda much as it had done for Khrushchev. By the late-1960s, détente seemed more attainable than it ever was for Khrushchev. There were three reasons for this. First, the Soviet Union had become weaker internally and stronger externally. Internal weakness refers here to Moscow's growing inability to deliver on growth targets in the context of the economic competition between the East and the West. During his infamous "kitchen debate" with Richard Nixon (in July 1959), Khrushchev had boasted of outstripping the US in economic production; a decade later, his successor Brezhnev could not have had any illusions on this score. In

6. "Minutes from a Conversation between A.N. Kosygin and Mao Zedong," February 11, 1965, History and Public Policy Program Digital Archive, AAN, KC PZPR, XI A/10, 517, 524, obtained by Douglas Selvage and translated by Malgorzata Gnoinska.

7. Conversation between Leonid Brezhnev and Nicolae Ceausescu and Ion Maurer, July 20, 1965, Russian State Archive of Contemporary History (RGANI): fond 80, opis 1, delo 758, list 34.

July 1968, Brezhnev received a memorandum from KGB Chairman Yurii Andropov discussing Soviet economic problems in brutally frank terms: wastefulness, low labour efficiency, and an inability to keep up with the US in R&D, education, and the use of computers.[8] Brezhnev locked away the offending document in his drawer, where it was discovered on his death in 1982. But the problems were there for everyone to see. Kosygin had attempted to address them through his ill-fated reform of 1965, but he barely scratched the surface. Creeping stagnation made it all the more important to lock in gains by winding down the Cold War on acceptable terms, that is, through détente.

At the same time, Brezhnev was in a much better position than Khrushchev had been to leverage Soviet military power. The Soviet Union had relentlessly continued its nuclear buildup. By 1970, it had accumulated almost half as many warheads as the United States (and continued stockpiling, overtaking the US later in the decade). The quality of its nuclear triad had also significantly improved and in some areas—for example, heavy ICBMs—begun to rival that of the United States. This awesome power to destroy translated for Brezhnev into a renewed sense of confidence that he could speak to the US president on equal terms.

Second, the successful Soviet invasion of Czechoslovakia in August 1968 (accompanied by a very tame US response) reassured Brezhnev that Washington would respect his sphere of influence. US woes in Vietnam convinced Moscow that Washington would be more amenable to an accommodation than at any prior point in the Cold War. And third, a rapidly worsening relationship with China underscored the need for mending relations with the West. In March 1969, the Chinese provoked a skirmish at the tiny islet of Zhenbaodao, along the eastern section of the heavily militarized Sino-Soviet border, and for a while it seemed that spiralling tensions would lead to an all-out war between the erstwhile allies. Not since the Second World War had "US imperialism" appeared in a friendlier light to the edgy policymakers in the Kremlin.

By then, Brezhnev had developed a distinctly civilizational approach to international politics—one that did not at all square with the principles of Marxism-Leninism but which was aligned with the Soviet leader's gut feelings. The central idea was that the Soviet Union was "European" and the Soviet leaders "Europeans." As such, the Soviets and the Americans (who were also

8. Memorandum from Yurii Andropov to Leonid Brezhnev, July 6, 1968, RGANI: fond 80, opis 1, delo 314 , listy 10–40.

"Europeans" as far as Brezhnev was concerned) had an affinity of interests, of which the most important one was to keep peace among themselves for fear that if a war broke out, "the whites will be gone, only the blacks and the yellows will remain."[9] The Chinese were especially suspect. Like Khrushchev before him, Brezhnev deeply distrusted Mao Zedong and his comrades. "These are people who can craftily conceal their real aims," the Soviet leader would say. "I am not proposing anything, but any student of China feels the same way."[10]

Brezhnev's fear of China, then, provided a kind of a civilizational reference point in his efforts to achieve détente with the United States. He was concerned that the Americans did not seem to share his apprehension of Beijing's far-reaching designs. Instead, President Nixon and his National Security Adviser Henry Kissinger seemed to be opportunistically exploiting the Soviet difficulties with China, even while tirelessly and somewhat mockingly reassuring Moscow that the Sino-American rapprochement was in no way directed against Moscow. No one in Moscow was reassured, of course, but the pace of Nixon's engagement with China in the early-1970s undoubtedly contributed to Brezhnev's eagerness to build up détente without waiting for the United States to leave Vietnam.

This was all the more interesting given that Nixon's visit to Beijing caused major frictions in Sino-Vietnamese relations, and made it next to impossible for the Chinese to defend their ostensibly "revolutionary" image in the Third World. Brezhnev could have scored points in Hanoi and among various "revolutionary" audiences around the world by exploiting the Chinese "betrayal" and confronting the US over its escalation in Vietnam. Some of his comrades—Kosygin included—argued in favor of precisely this course of action. Instead, Brezhnev rolled out the red carpet for Nixon in May 1972. Why? Because "revolutionary" prestige was of far less importance to Brezhnev than the prestige to be had from Soviet-US summitry. Kissinger diagnosed the situation precisely when he wrote to Nixon ahead of his trip to Moscow, Brezhnev "sees his relationship with you as legitimising and strengthening his own position at home. We may have an election in November; he acts as if he has one next week and every week thereafter."[11]

9. Conversation between Leonid Brezhnev and Walter J. Stoessel, March 5, 1974, RGANI: fond 80, opis 1, delo 807, list 32.

10. Memorandum by the President's Assistant for National Security Affairs (Kissinger) for the President's File, June 23, 1973, *Foreign Relations of United States, 1969–1976*, Volume XV, Document 131.

11. *Soviet-American Relations: The Detente Years, 1969–1972*, Douglas Selvage et al., eds., 780.

One thing in particular bothered Brezhnev. He had closely watched Nixon's performance in China in February 1972, and he was struck when Nixon announced in a toast during his dinner with Zhou Enlai that the two countries, China and the United States, "hold the future of the world in our hands."[12] Brezhnev repeatedly complained about this toast, and he wasn't even satisfied with Kissinger's explanation to the effect that Nixon simply had had too much to drink. The problem was that Nixon's words hinted at a very different picture of global politics than what Brezhnev fancied. In Brezhnev's view, as undoubtedly in the view of his predecessors Stalin and Khrushchev and his successors all the way to Gorbachev, it was the United States and the Soviet Union that held the future of the world in their hands. Brezhnev's entire foreign policy outlook was directed towards attaining this recognition for the USSR. As Brezhnev himself put it to Kissinger (who summarized his remarks for Nixon's benefit, "Look, I want to talk to you privately—nobody else, no notes . . . Look, you will be our partners, you and we are going to run the world."[13]

II

When Brezhnev spoke of running the world together with the United States, the part of the world he mainly had in mind was the Middle East. This was the testing ground for his idea of a US-Soviet condominium. The United States and the Soviet Union had long been making circles around one another in the region. Ever since Stalin had stirred up trouble in northern Iran and threatened Turkey, US policymakers had suspected that the long-term Soviet game was to subvert Western interests in the Middle East and to gain access to oil. The 1953 CIA-engineered coup in Iran ostensibly aimed at preventing Iran's slide into the Soviet orbit. Moscow's flirtation with Arab nationalism in Egypt, Syria, and Iraq had been a cause of concern for Western policymakers throughout the 1950s and the 1960s, though it appears clear in retrospect that for all the military aid the Soviets furnished to their clients, their actual influence was limited.

This was particularly the case with Egypt, which had suffered a humiliating defeat in the June 1967 war with Israel and presently itched to recover its lost territories in the Sinai. Brezhnev had provided arms to Cairo to rebuild its

---

12. "Text of Nixon Toast at Shanghai Dinner," *New York Times*, February 28, 1972.

13. As reported by Kissinger: Conversation Between President Nixon and his Assistant for National Security Affairs (Kissinger), May 11, 1973, *FRUS, 1969–1976*, Volume XV, Document 115.

shattered military but he was never sure that the Egyptians would even so much as consult him before putting those arms to use. He got on well enough with Gamal Abdul Nasser—who was willing at least to listen to Moscow's advice—but he was not sure of what to make of Nasser's successor, Anwar Sadat. After coming to power in 1970 in the wake of Nasser's death, Sadat, on the one hand, vowed his allegiance to the Soviets while, on the other hand, took actions that greatly annoyed the wary Brezhnev, including purging the allegedly pro-Soviet faction in the Egyptian leadership and expelling thousands of Soviet military advisers and experts from the country.

Above all, given Sadat's propensity to make militant proclamations, the Soviets could not be certain that he would not lash out at Israel, provoking a major war in the Middle East. If he did, would he not lose again, as the Arabs did in 1967? And if they lost, what would happen to Moscow's superpower prestige, given that the Soviets provided much of Egypt's military hardware? "We discuss the Middle Eastern problem at almost every meeting of the . . . Politburo," Brezhnev complained. "By their unthoughtful actions the Arabs could do themselves irreparable damage and deal a blow to our prestige, and we must not allow this."[14] The Soviets worried that Sadat would turn to the US if they failed to give him their best weapons and their strongest political backing. But they were also concerned that Sadat might lose unless he was supplied with what he asked for. Such entrapment was an uncomfortable position to be in, and Brezhnev worked hard to fix the problem by approaching the United States, which, he believed, could put pressure on *its* client Israel to allow Sadat to obtain through negotiations what he had until then failed to obtain by military force, especially the return of the territories lost in the Six Day War.

If the US-Soviet condominium was good for anything, it would have to work for this: avoiding a major war in the Middle East. In June 1973, Brezhnev made an effort to secure Nixon's agreement to some form of joint action. It happened during his visit to the United States, which marked the height of détente. Nixon stood in the Watergate's lengthening shadow but he was not yet as completely overwhelmed by the scandal as he would be later that year. The January 1973 Paris agreement ended US involvement in the Vietnam War, and so Brezhnev did not have to bend over backwards to keep his revolutionary

---

14. *Vstrechi i Peregovory Na Vysshem Urovne Rukovoditelei SSSR i Yugoslavii*, Volume 2, Miladin Milošević, V. P. Tarasov, and N. G. Tomilina, eds. (Moscow: Mezhdunarodnyi Fond 'Demokratiya,' 2017), 296.

clients appeased as he pursued better relations with Washington. Brezhnev himself was no longer the Brezhnev of the late-1960s, when he frequently had to defer to Kosygin on matters of foreign policy, nor yet the Brezhnev of the late 1970s, when his declining health reduced his scope for innovative policy. In 1973, Brezhnev was in his prime, and he revelled in the glorious trappings of Soviet-American summitry. "There are some people who keep throwing in this idea of there being two superpowers," he told Nixon during their first one-on-one in the Oval Office. "What, do they want the Soviet Union to become Guinea or some other little country?"[15]

Apart from glory, though, Brezhnev needed concrete results on the Middle East. He presented his case in a rather bizarre fashion, by suddenly calling for an unscheduled meeting with the president late in the evening on June 23, 1973, when the two were in San Clemente, at Nixon's residence in California. Nixon was taken aback by the unexpected demand (which he attributed to Brezhnev's attempt to separate him from his advisors, especially Kissinger). Nevertheless, the president agreed and heard Brezhnev out. The gist of the Soviet leader's proposal was that the Soviets would put pressure on the Arabs to moderate their hostility towards Israel, while the Americans would pressure the Israelis to withdraw to their 1967 borders. Then there would be peace in the Middle East, courtesy of the Soviet-US condominium. Only, Nixon wasn't buying it. As he quipped on one occasion, "We want Peace. They want the Middle East."[16] Brezhnev left frustrated and worried that war would break out at any moment.

The war began on October 6, 1973. The Soviets were forewarned, though not by their Egyptian client—Sadat kept his cards close to his chest until the last moment—but instead by their Syrian client Hafez al-Assad. But once the fighting began and it appeared that the Arabs were making unexpected gains against Israel both in Sinai and in the Golan Heights, Moscow's caution went right out of the window. Soviet arms were winning in an actual conflict, bringing Soviet superpower prestige to new heights. So, instead of putting pressure on Sadat to desist, the Soviet leaders feigned confusion and tried to fend off US pressure to put an end to the hostilities. "Is there an argument with the Soviets," asked the head of the CIA William Colby on the first day of war, "that

15. Conversation between Richard Nixon and Leonid Brezhnev, June 18, 1973, *White House Tapes*, No. 943, Richard M. Nixon Presidential Library and Museum.

16. Craig A. Daigle, "The Russians Are Going: Sadat, Nixon and the Soviet Presence in Egypt, 1970–1971," *Middle East Review of International Affairs* 8:1 (2004), 3.

their real interest lies with us and not with the crazy Arabs?"[17] Just weeks earlier, no one had had to make this argument—Brezhnev himself knew this better than anyone else—but now that the Arabs were winning, the Soviet leader seemed quite willing to let history take its course since it would raise Soviet standing with the Arabs and Soviet greatness as a superpower, even at the cost of undermining détente.

Part of the problem was that Sadat was a very difficult client, so when two days into the fighting Brezhnev quietly broached his opinion about a cease-fire-in-situ, the Egyptian president turned him down. It was only after the Arab offensive ran out of steam and the Israelis pushed back that Sadat evidenced any enthusiasm at all for negotiation. Sensing that the window of opportunity for the Arabs was closing fast—and that Israel soon would make a comeback—Brezhnev switched his tactic once again and invited Kissinger to Moscow to iron out a joint approach to the conflict. The urgent talks took place on October 20–21, even as the situation on the ground turned more and more dire for the Arabs. The two sides agreed to arrange for a cease-fire but to Brezhnev's chagrin, it appeared for a few days that the Americans were not putting any pressure on Israel to stop their offensive. With Egypt teetering on the brink of a military catastrophe, Brezhnev sent a letter to Nixon in the middle of the night on October 25, threatening unilateral Soviet intervention to rescue the Arabs. Brezhnev signed off on this desperate measure because he was under immense pressure from Sadat to do something. But what the general secretary did not quite expect was that the US would react by raising the readiness of its strategic forces to the alarming level of DEFCON 3.

This decision was Kissinger's bluff, a deliberate overreaction, which he would later blame on Nixon (who seems to have been informed only after the event). The Soviets backpedaled as fast as they could, and the gradual winding down of hostilities in the Middle East permitted a rapid de-escalation. In the weeks and months that followed, Sadat, having once again been defeated by the Israelis, but having proved himself a worthy adversary, engaged in a dialogue both with Tel Aviv and with Washington, turning his back on the powerful Soviet patron. Sadat had come to realize that only the United States could really "deliver" Israeli concessions, which, in fact, it helped do some years later at Camp David. In short order, the Soviets suffered another serious blow to their prestige in the Middle East and managed to lose an important client.

17. Minutes of Washington Special Actions Group Meeting, 1973–1976, *FRUS, 1969–1976*, Volume XXX, Document 110.

The episode illustrated the fragility of détente. As much as Brezhnev desired a Soviet-US condominium, he found it difficult to resist the temptation to undercut the United States where he could, and the same was also true of the United States. The Middle East was a grey area, a space where one could still make gains at the expense of the other. Winning and sustaining clients was important because it built up each side's bargaining power in this cooperative-competitive relationship. But, as Brezhnev knew all too well, clients had their own priorities that did not necessarily coincide with the agenda of their superpower patrons. Just as had occurred earlier during the Vietnam War when the Soviets had trouble convincing the North Vietnamese to listen to their advice, so Brezhnev discovered that Sadat could, and did, put détente at risk if doing so served his own political ends.

This tug-of-war in the Middle East had no real ideological content as far as the Soviets were concerned; instead, it had to do with perceptions of relative power and prestige. The fact that the Soviet leader was outmanoeuvred at almost every important turn by Kissinger should not blind us to the possibility that he would have done the same to Kissinger if only he had the ability. Co-running the world thus entailed watching each other for signs that the partner would stab you in the back, while also stabbing them in the back at the earliest opportunity.

III

To the extent that personal rapport between Brezhnev and Nixon mattered, Nixon's downfall in August 1974 signalled the beginning of détente's decline. Gerald Ford, although he promised to follow Nixon's policy, did not "click" with the general secretary in quite the same way. Kissinger stayed on but Brezhnev mistrusted him, a feeling that was accentuated by the way the US secretary of state kept the Soviets out of finding a negotiated solution to the Cyprus crisis, which overlapped with Nixon's exit and Ford's entry.

Cyprus, which first suffered a Greece-backed coup and then a Turkish invasion, seemed to Moscow to represent a wonderful opportunity for superpower cooperation in conflict management. Yet Kissinger thought otherwise and tried hard behind the scenes to undercut the Soviet proposal for an international conference.[18] It was in part his disappointment with US performance

---

18. Message from Secretary of State Kissinger to British Foreign Secretary Callaghan, 1973, *FRUS, 1969–1976*, Volume XXX, Document 110.

in the Cyprus crisis that prompted Brezhnev to write in a letter to the Soviet ambassador in Washington, Anatolii Dobrynin (which he never sent, but which reflects the Soviet leader's state of mind). "Don't you think that under such conditions, we must not only demonstrate our goodwill and readiness to develop relations with the US but also in some form let [the Americans] understand that we are not prepared to patiently stomach all unfriendly manifestations of US policy?"[19]

Brezhnev was annoyed by militant pronouncements emanating from the Ford administration, including from Ford himself. He also disliked the president's seeming unwillingness to stand up to the critics of détente in Congress, such as Senator Henry "Scoop" Jackson (D), whose name was then attached to a piece of legislation aimed at denying Moscow Most Favored Nation trade status. The Jackson-Vanik Amendment—which punished the Soviets for limits placed in the way of Jewish emigration—was especially frustrating for Brezhnev because it undermined what he hoped would be the real fruits of détente—a closer economic relationship, which would help address creeping Soviet stagnation. The Soviet leader accused Jackson of demagoguery and fumed at a supposedly ill-informed US public opinion. "Many laymen [in America] know very little about the Soviet Union. They have succumbed to internal propaganda and have become so lazy that they don't even want to read anything. They only watch TV, and that only if the programmes are interesting."[20]

This disappointment in Moscow with the state of Soviet-US relations occurred even while in some spheres détente continued to move forward, as if by inertia. The symbolic high point was the docking in space of the American and Soviet spacecraft—the Soyuz-Apollo—in July 1975. Two weeks later Ford and Brezhnev met in Helsinki at a conference that marked the conclusion of several years of hard negotiations on European security, and resulted in tacit acknowledgment of the two superpowers' respective spheres of influence. Ford faced domestic criticism for going (and so serving the ends of Soviet propaganda). Brezhnev had no problems of that kind back home, but he had another challenge—rapidly declining health. He barely struggled through his agenda in Helsinki and went on an extended vacation when he returned home, leaving Soviet foreign policy on autopilot.

19. Unsent letter from Leonid Brezhnev to Anatolii Dobrynin, August 28, 1974, RGANI: fond 80, opis 1, delo 811, list 26.

20. Conversation between Leonid Brezhnev and Egon Bahr, February 27, 1974. RGANI: fond 80, opis 1, delo 580, list 29.

It was in this context that Moscow became increasingly involved with events in Angola. The Portuguese had not quite left their former colony when the Angolans turned on each other, with three players vying for control. One of these—the People's Movement for the Liberation of Angola (MPLA)—enjoyed Soviet support, and in the fall of 1975 the Soviets, working with the Cubans, provided crucial military support to tilt the scales of the Angolan civil war in the MPLA's favor. Soviet involvement greatly annoyed Kissinger, who argued with Brezhnev that such open interventionism seriously endangered détente. "Don't mention that word to me," Brezhnev cut him off, referring to Angola. "We have nothing to do with that country. I cannot talk about that country."[21] That Brezhnev was lying is clear but what is less clear is why. Did he really not understand that by associating himself with the MPLA's cause he made it much more difficult for Ford to defend détente against his critics on the right and on the left?

What Kissinger did not perhaps fully appreciate was that Angola was not in any sense exceptional. After all, the Soviet experience of détente in the Middle East in 1973, and then in Cyprus in 1974, suggested that Moscow was involved in a struggle for influence with the United States. The Soviets inserting themselves into Angola was merely another episode of the superpower competition. If America had its clients, why should not the Soviet Union have clients too? But this overarching logic of Cold War rivalry obscures nuance. In Angola's case, much of the Soviet decision-making was actually at a level below Brezhnev's. While the incapacitated general secretary recuperated at his dacha, bureaucratic interests defined the Soviet response. The International Department of the Central Committee, which had long maintained contacts with the MPLA, came to play an outsized role—as did the Ministry of Defence, which had its own reasons for desiring to gain access to Angola's Atlantic coastline. Did any of these people worry about détente?

The archival record suggests that they did, though they were not as invested in better Soviet-American relations as the general secretary had been. In November 1975, the Soviet Politburo put pressure on the Cubans to moderate their enthusiasm for military actions in Angola in order to avoid a hostile US response.[22] In early December 1975, the Politburo reached out to the MPLA leadership to ask that it engage in dialogue with its rivals, because the deepening

21. Discussion between Henry Kissinger and Leonid Brezhnev, *FRUS, 1969–1976*, Volume XIX, Document 75.

22. Instructions for the Soviet Ambassador in Havana, November 27, 1975, RGANI: fond 3, opis 69, delo 1883, list 127–32.

crisis could "put in question the main policies of international détente." Interestingly, the approach was jointly authored by the Foreign Ministry, the International Department, the KGB, and the Ministry of Defence, and thus amounted to a policy consensus in Moscow. Of the above, only the Foreign Minister Andrei Gromyko was known for his concern for the future of détente.[23]

The big question is what would have happened if Brezhnev were still healthy enough to make his voice heard at the Politburo. Would he have curbed Soviet involvement, and put pressure on the Cubans, who depended heavily on Soviet arms and logistics, to pedal back? If the degree of trust between Soviet and American leaders were greater, would Brezhnev have been more open to Kissinger's pleas that the former's actions in Africa undermined the very foundations of détente? This is of course possible. What is clear, however, is that should he have chosen to work hand-in-hand with the US to diffuse the crisis in Angola, Brezhnev would have lost out in the eyes of the audiences that mattered to the Soviets, not least the Cubans but also other countries in Africa. There still remained a contradiction between being recognized as America's worthy partner and as the leader of the revolutionary world.

IV

In view of mounting tensions in Soviet-American relations (caused in part by Angola but also by a host of other issues, not least the fallout from the Jackson-Vanik Amendment), there were no regrets in Moscow when Gerald Ford failed in his 1976 election bid. His replacement in the White House, the former Georgia governor Jimmy Carter, had made some very critical remarks about the Soviet Union during his campaign, but Democratic emissaries who visited Moscow at the end of 1976 and early in 1977 reassured the Soviets that it was just for show.[24] Yet the Soviets were quickly disabused of any illusions they may have had when Carter, recently inaugurated, appeared to put human rights front and center of his policy. For example, in February 1977, Carter responded to a letter by the Soviet physicist-turned-dissident Andrei Sakharov, and a few weeks later the president received an exiled Soviet dissident, Vladimir Bukovsky, in the White House.

---

23. Memorandum from Andrei Gromyko, Boris Ponomarev, Yurii Andropov and Andrei Grechko to CC CPSU Politburo, December 3, 1975. RGANI: fond 3, opis 69, delo 1892, list 17.

24. "Anatolii Chernyaev's Diary," January 1, 1976, National Security Archive, https://nsarchive .gwu.edu/rus/text_files/Chernyaev/1976.pdf.

The Soviet leaders were predictably outraged and accused Carter of gross interference in their domestic affairs. The Republicans had proven to be unreliable partners at best but at least they never worried too much about such "silly things" (to quote from Kissinger's conversation with Ambassador Dobrynin) as human rights.[25] Carter, though, was really getting on the Kremlin's nerves. According to Carter's National Security Advisor Zbigniew Brzezinski, this was because the Soviets knew that human rights was a "compelling idea."[26] But Brzezinski misread the Kremlin's psychology. The reason for Soviet anger was that Carter's moral posturing undermined the idea of superpower equality treasured by the Soviets. After all, if one side deemed itself morally superior to the other, it thereby denied the other the recognition that this other thought it deserved. Even liberal Soviet commentators like Anatolii Chernyaev (who would go on to become Gorbachev's foreign policy aide and one of the architects of perestroika in foreign policy) scribbled in his diary that Carter's human rights campaign went overboard: "Carter . . . does not realize that in the eyes of serious Soviet people he looks like a petty provocateur."[27]

What made Carter appear particularly disingenuous to the Soviets was his administration's engagement with China. The same Brzezinski who chastised Moscow for human rights abuses travelled to Beijing in May 1978 to discuss the challenge "from the polar bear" that both countries faced. Beijing had in fact campaigned tirelessly to undercut détente, seeing it as directed against China.[28] In their interpretation, Nixon and Kissinger only reached out to China in the first place for leverage with Moscow. Before he died, Mao Zedong warned darkly that "some people wanted to turn the Soviet Union against China to protect themselves, just as Chamberlain and Daladier had tried to turn Germany against the Soviet Union."[29] Mao died in 1976 but his eventual successor Deng Xiaoping seemed to harbour similar sentiments, so Brzezinski's engagement with China (which resulted in full-fledged normalization in

25. Conversation between Anatoli Dobrynin and Henry Kissinger, November 23, 1979, Archive of Foreign Policy of the Russian Federation (AVPRF): fond 0129, opis 63, papka 482, delo 7, list 152.

26. Memorandum from Brzezinski to Jimmy Carter, April 1, 1977, *FRUS, 1977–1980*, Volume I, Document 32.

27. "Anatolii Chernyaev's Diary," 1977, National Security Archive, https://nsarchive.gwu.edu/media/22951/ocr.

28. Memorandum of conversation between Zbigniew Brzezinski and Deng Xiaoping, May 21, 1978, *FRUS, 1977–1980*, Volume XIII, Document 110.

29. Conversation between Edward Heath and Mao Zedong, May 25, 1974, FCO 21/1240, The National Archives, United Kingdom.

January 1979) could not help but trigger apprehension among the Soviet leaders. They imagined a military alliance between their worst enemy, China, and their one-time partner in the condominium that never was, the United States. This was a terrible geostrategic predicament, one offset by the hope that the Sino-American entente would not last. As Foreign Minister Gromyko put it (not entirely without basis), "You may be in a euphoric mood now about China but the time will come when you will be shedding tears."[30]

While the Soviets testily rejected US criticism of their human rights record and watched uneasily for signs of ever closer rapprochement or perhaps even a de facto military alliance between Beijing and Washington, the Cold War continued. The high point of tension in 1977–78 was the war in the Horn of Africa between Somalia (formerly a Soviet, at that point a potential American client) and Ethiopia (formerly an American, at that point a Soviet client). There was a brief period in the mid-1970s when the Soviet Union held both Somalia and Ethiopia as clients but the prospects of socialism in the Horn were undermined when it turned out that Somalian would-be Marxists and Ethiopian would-be Marxists could not peacefully coexist. Somalia launched an ill-thought-out military campaign against Ethiopia, which caused Moscow to side with Ethiopia, leading, within months, to Somalia's complete defeat on the battlefield.

Moscow's reasons for involvement in Somalia and then in Ethiopia were broadly similar to its earlier misadventure in Angola. Strategic reasons played a role (power projection in the Red Sea and the Gulf of Aden, and the Indian Ocean beyond, was certainly tempting to the military establishment). Ideological justifications were offered for helping fraternal regimes—first Somalia, then Ethiopia, then Ethiopia against Somalia. In the end, Moscow got bogged down in the Horn more through bureaucratic inertia than anything—this was especially noticeable with Brezhnev mostly out of the picture (for reasons of poor health). As before, Castro played a key role as a self-proclaimed strategist for socialism. It was Castro who first tried to mediate between Somalia's Siad Barre and Ethiopia's Mengistu Haile Mariam, only to conclude that the former was not a Marxist at all, that "socialism is just an outer shell that is supposed to make him more attractive. The party is there only to support his personal power."[31] These revelations about Siad Barre were duly passed on to the Soviets who then very much followed the Cubans' lead in providing military aid to the Ethiopians after Somalia invaded Ogaden.

---

30. Cable, US Embassy in Moscow to the Department of State, February 16, 1979, NLC 16-15-2-12-3, Jimmy Carter Presidential Library.

31. Westad, *The Global Cold War*, 274.

Soviet involvement in the Horn contributed to shifting perceptions in Washington. Coming in the wake of Angola, another successful Soviet intervention in Africa signalled Communism on the march. Brzezinski lobbied for stronger US support for Somalia and pressed the Somalis to speak out openly in support of Carter's human rights agenda, as if this could somehow change the nature of the atrocious tyranny in Mogadishu. The Somalian Ambassador in Washington Abdullahi Addou even met with Carter, and assured him that Siad Barre was inspired by Carter's human rights campaign.[32] Unfortunately, Addou's commitment to democracy proved short-lived; as soon as it became apparent that the Somalis were losing the war and that the US would not bail them out, he privately sought out Ambassador Dobrynin and offered to bring Somalia back into the Soviet camp.[33] The Soviets refused.

Even though it had been substantially derailed by the bickering over human rights, by the conflict in the Horn, and by what the Soviets perceived as a hostile Sino-American entente, there was some steam left to détente, or at least enough to deliver one final summit between Brezhnev and an American president. The occasion was the signing of the SALT-2 Treaty, an outcome of years of difficult arms control negotiations. The Kremlin attached considerable importance to SALT—both the first treaty, signed with Nixon in 1972, and its successor. Brezhnev of course had to reassure his military that on balance the Soviet Union emerged stronger from the talks. For him, it was part and parcel of a bigger idea of preserving world peace through Soviet-American cooperation. In June 1979, Brezhnev met Carter in Vienna to signal this new stage in détente. But there was no dialogue. The Soviet leader struggled through his text and at times seemed to have only a vague understanding of what he was reading. You could not build trust under such circumstances. You could not even have a normal conversation.

It was in this lamentable context that the Soviet leaders made one of their worst decisions of the Cold War—the decision to invade Afghanistan. One is struck in retrospect by some of the far-fetched explanations offered at the time by both US and Chinese policymakers concerning this Soviet blunder. Brzezinski imagined the Soviets working tirelessly to undercut the United States and its allies in what he termed the "arc of crisis" in the Middle East. The Chinese had an even more fanciful idea about Moscow's strategy, which they termed the

32. Conversation between Carter, Brzezinski, and Somalia's Ambassador Addou, June 16, 1977, *FRUS, 1977–1980*, Volume XVII, Document 20.

33. Conversation between Anatolii Dobrynin and Abdullahi Addou, February 23, 1979. AVPRF: fond 0129, opis 62, papka 474, delo 5, list 113.

"barbell theory." According to this theory, the Soviets were extending their gains in the Middle East and Southeast Asia (as a part of their grand design to control the warm seas), with the Malacca Straits playing the role of the "bar" that connected the two theatres. In one curious high-profile meeting, then-Chinese leader Hua Guofeng even took the time to tell US Vice President Walter Mondale about Peter the Great's Last Testament, whereby the tsar once commanded his successors to push south to the Indian Ocean.[34] This was done to show Moscow's expansive designs rooted in Russian imperialism (ironically, Peter the Great's Last Testament is a nineteenth-century forgery).

The reality was less dramatic but fully in line with the opportunism that characterised Soviet policy elsewhere in the Third World. The Soviets sensed an opportunity when, in 1973, Prime Minister of Afghanistan Mohammed Daoud Khan deposed King Zahir Shah and set himself up as the president of the new republic. Brezhnev privately called the coup in Afghanistan a "revolution," and described Daoud Khan as a "comrade." In meetings with emissaries from Kabul, the Soviet leader coached the Afghans to "be ruthless with the enemies of the revolution" and warned against "compromise."[35] Brezhnev was hardly oblivious to the fact that Daoud Khan was no Communist but, given Soviet setbacks elsewhere in the Middle East—including the loss of Sadat to the Americans and the growing clout of Iran (at the time America's close partner in the Middle East)—winning a client in Afghanistan looked like an attractive proposition. This only serves to underscore the inherent contradictions of the proposed Soviet-US condominium, even at the height of détente. The relationship, of course, had deteriorated significantly by the time Daoud Khan was himself deposed in April 1978 and the Communists came to power in Afghanistan.

There is no clear evidence that the Soviets assisted in the Communist takeover but they had no choice but to invest heavily in the regime once it established itself in Kabul. "In us, you have acquired a new brother who has neither clothes nor home nor bread," the leader of the People's Democratic Party of Afghanistan (PDPA), Muhammad Nur Taraki, told Brezhnev. "We pin all our hopes on you, as our elder brother."[36] This was a pattern that had repeated itself

34. Conversation between Walter Mondale and Hua Guofeng, August 28, 1979, *FRUS, 1977–1980*, Volume XIII, Document 266.

35. Conversation between Leonid Brezhnev and Mohammad Naim, September 11, 1973, RGANI: fond 80, opis 1, delo 458, list 74.

36. Conversation between Leonid Brezhnev and Aleksei Kosygin and a PDPA delegation led by Nur Muhammad Taraki and Hafizullah Amin, December 4–5, 1978, RGANI: fond 80, opis 1, delo 461, list 5–24.

year after year in various Third World theaters, invariably putting the Soviet leadership in a bind—would they respond positively to such entreaties and provide the political, economic, and military support to these self-proclaimed revolutionary regimes, even if that undermined détente? The balance became difficult to maintain once the key proponent of détente in the Soviet leadership, Brezhnev, became virtually incapacitated.

Détente was on life support in September 1979 when Hafizullah Amin, Afghanistan's Communist Prime Minister, toppled Taraki (and later had him murdered in prison). The Soviets were alarmed by this development but at first reconciled themselves to living with Amin. After all, Brezhnev claimed at the Politburo, Amin would still depend on Soviet economic and military aid.[37] Or would he?

Soviet intelligence was picking up signals of Amin's suspected flirtation with the United States. Fearful that Amin would become another "Sadat" who would deliver Afghanistan to the United States, and resigned to the sorry state of Soviet-US relations, the Soviets invaded Afghanistan, murdered Amin, and then stayed on to help their new puppet government survive. We know today that the decision had strategic underpinnings. Yurii Andropov (who played a key role in the fateful misadventure) cited the possibility that Amin would open Afghanistan to US intermediate-range ballistic missiles, or that the country would be used as a platform for spying on Soviet nuclear facilities, or even that Amin would attempt to destabilize Soviet Central Asia by exporting Islamic fundamentalism. It was Andropov, Defense Minister Dmitrii Ustinov, and Foreign Minister Andrei Gromyko (who at this point seems to have despaired in the fortunes of détente) who persuaded the ailing Brezhnev to endorse the intervention, dealing a fatal blow to détente.

V

By the late-1970s the Soviet Union was adrift. It had lost direction in foreign policy and involved itself in various Third World adventures through what Chernyaev once called "inertia of proletarian internationalism."[38] How much of it was proletarian internationalism and how much simply the logic of bureaucratic interests is difficult to say; ideas and inertia appeared mutually

---

37. Brezhnev's notes for presentation at the September 20, 1979, meeting of the Politburo, RGANI: fond 80, opis 1, delo 462, list 79.

38. Sergey Radchenko, *Unwanted Visionaries: The Soviet Failure in Asia at the End of the Cold War* (New York, NY: Oxford University Press, 2014), 119.

reinforcing. If Brezhnev knew that his treasured détente would get bogged down in open-ended adventures in support of self-proclaimed Third World revolutionaries, he would have thrown up his hands in despair. But by the late-1970s the general secretary was quite beyond such realization.

Brezhnev had seen better days. In 1972–75 he tried hard to reconfigure global politics by building a close relationship with the United States. He aimed at nothing less than ending the Cold War itself, a condition that, he thought, was merely a consequence of America's unwillingness to accept the Soviet Union as an equal. But, Brezhnev thought, the United States was finally coming around. Its defeat in the Vietnam War, and the considerable Soviet military might, seemed like persuasive arguments in favor of Brezhnev's vision of détente. In addition, there was the pressing civilizational factor—China's hostility. For now, it was only hostile towards Moscow, but Brezhnev spared no effort to persuade his American interlocutors that Beijing was a long-term threat to the West itself. Soviet-US summitry encouraged the general secretary, who relished such photo opportunities as evidence of American recognition of Soviet—and therefore his own—greatness. Détente thus became an important source of Soviet legitimacy—but not the only source.

Ever since the Cold War began, the Soviet leadership catered to distinct audiences. They wanted the USSR to appear not only as a coequal superpower vis-a-vis the United States but also as a revolutionary leader vis-a-vis the Communist world. The importance attributed to these different legitimacy discourses changed over time. Often they were in direct contradiction, as during the Vietnam War. But just as often the Soviets managed to pursue both on the understanding that fulfilment of their "revolutionary" responsibilities was merely an aspect of the increased Soviet stature as a superpower. Yet this condition introduced instability to détente. There was a temptation to undercut one's partner in the vaguely defined grey area that comprised much of the Third World. The instability was there already in the early-1970s, at the height of détente, though Brezhnev's personal commitment to the project helped take the edge off the intensity of this Soviet-American rivalry. Difficult clients complicated policy. Soviet friends in the Third World often had their own priorities that conflicted with the Soviet-American détente. Sometimes the Soviets ignored these priorities; more often, they had to take them into account.

Brezhnev tended to take a very personal approach to foreign policy. Nixon, he believed, shared his commitment to détente. Yet Brezhnev never developed an equally amicable relationship with Ford, never mind Carter. Since he did not understand how American politics worked, the Soviet leader concluded that the Watergate affair was basically an effort by Nixon's enemies to derail détente, and anti-Soviet rhetoric in Washington left him convinced that these enemies were winning the struggle over US foreign policy. Then came Carter's human rights campaign, which the Soviets thought was a deliberate effort to humiliate Moscow and further undermine détente. What sort of superpower equality could one speak of in such circumstances?

What the Soviets were unwilling to see, however, was how their own actions—from Angola, to the Horn, to Afghanistan—contributed to the deterioration of the Soviet-American relationship. Trying to be both America's partner in "running the world" and a revolutionary power with a far-flung clientele was a contradictory, even paradoxical strategy. Reaching accommodation with Washington in the context of a basically competitive relationship was an impossible highwire act. It ultimately hinged on America's acceptance of such a dual role for the USSR. Unfortunately for Brezhnev's hopes for a Soviet-American condominium, such acceptance was never in the cards.

CHAPTER 34

Arms Competition, Arms Control, and Strategies of Peacetime Competition from Fisher to Reagan

Thomas G. Mahnken

Arms races are often portrayed as the reflexive, almost unthinking, accumulation of weapons. Indeed, one popular metaphor from the Cold War was that of "apes on a treadmill." Similarly, attempts to limit the acquisition of armaments through arms control have frequently become unmoored from strategy. At times, however, both arms competition and arms control have served as elements of strategies for peacetime competition. This chapter examines strategies for peacetime competition across the twentieth century, focusing on the Anglo-German naval rivalry at the turn of the twentieth century and the strategic interaction between the United States and Soviet Union during the Cold War.

I

Strategy is about how to array limited resources in space and time in order to achieve one's aims against a competitor. Its essential elements are rationality (the existence of political objectives and a plan to achieve them) and interaction with a competitor who seeks to achieve different objectives, at the very least, if not to thwart one's ability to achieve one's aims.[1] As Edward Mead Earle noted, strategy is "an inherent element of statecraft at all times."[2] Strategy in peacetime has several distinguishing features. First, although military assets feature prominently in peacetime strategic activities such as arms racing and arms control, their role is to deter or dissuade rather than to defeat competitors. For example, governments in peacetime face the decision as to whether to reveal military capabilities in order to deter or influence a competitor, or to conceal them in order to preserve their effectiveness in a future conflict.[3] Strategic choices in peacetime must also contend with a fundamental and irreducible uncertainty about the character of a future conflict and the effectiveness of new ways of war. As Sir Michael Howard famously wrote, planning in peacetime is akin to navigating a ship through a thick fog of peace.[4] Moreover, statesmen and soldiers are generally more risk averse in peacetime than in war. As a result, they often shy away from actions that could be seen as provocative. Finally, it takes longer to determine the effects of one's strategy in peacetime than in wartime. Whereas the impacts of battlefield actions frequently manifest themselves in hours, days, weeks, or months, the consequences of peacetime actions may not become apparent for years or more.

Competition lies in the middle of a spectrum that is bounded by cooperation on one end and conflict on the other. Competition does not inexorably lead to conflict, nor does it preclude cooperation. Throughout history, states have developed strategies for competing with their rivals in peacetime, including: Athens and Sparta in the ancient world; France and Great Britain from the eighteenth to the nineteenth centuries; Germany and Great Britain in the nineteenth and twentieth centuries; the United States and Great Britain in the nineteenth and early twentieth centuries; the United States and Japan during the first half of the twentieth century; and the United States and the Soviet Union during the second half of the twentieth century. Some, such as the

---

1. See Thomas G. Mahnken, "Strategic Theory," in *Strategy in the Contemporary World*, Seventh Edition, John Baylis, James J. Wirtz, and Jeannie L. Johnson, eds. (Oxford: Oxford University Press, 2022), 58.

2. Edward Mead Earle, *Makers of Modern Strategy: Military Thought from Machiavelli to Hitler* (Princeton, NJ: Princeton University Press, 1943), viii.

3. Thomas G. Mahnken, *Selective Disclosure: A Strategic Approach to Long-Term Competition* (Washington, DC: Center for Strategic and Budgetary Assessments, 2020); Brendan Rittenhouse Green and Austin Long, "Conceal or Reveal? Managing Clandestine Military Capabilities in Peacetime Competition," *International Security* 44:3 (2019/20), 48–83.

4. Michael Howard, "Military Science in an Age of Peace," *Journal of the Royal United Services Institute for Defence Studies* 119:1 (1974), 4.

Anglo-American rivalry, ended peacefully, even amicably. Others, such as the Anglo-German competition, led to war. Still others, such as the US-Soviet competition, yielded conflicts on the periphery and an armed, sometimes uneasy, peace between the central actors.

Political and military leaders have adopted a variety of strategies for competing with their rivals in peacetime.[5] In some cases, they pursued a strategy of denial that sought to convince their adversaries that it was impossible to achieve their objectives. In other cases, leaders pursued strategies of cost imposition in an effort to convince a competitor's leadership that the costs of achieving its aims were so disproportionately high that accommodation would be more attractive than confrontation.[6] Such approaches may, for example, seek to dissuade or deter a competitor from engaging in actions that are disruptive or threatening by convincing them that they are too costly, ineffective, or will prove counter-productive. They may alternatively seek to channel a competitor into engaging in activities that are inoffensive or wasteful. In other cases, political and military leaders have attempted to attack their rivals' strategy by inducing them to question the assumptions guiding their strategy or even engage in self-defeating behavior. Finally, strategists have attempted to attack their competitors' political systems in an effort to exploit and influence factions within their political system.[7]

The history of arms competitions is as long as the history of strategy, going back at least to ancient Greece, when Athens's construction of its Long Walls alarmed its Spartan rivals.[8] However, it was in the nineteenth century, in an environment of accelerating technological change, that the topic of arms races assumed a prominent role in international affairs, and it was in the Cold War that arms races became a major topic in the field of strategic studies. Samuel Huntington defined an arms race as "a progressive, competitive peacetime increase in armaments by two states or coalitions of states resulting from

5. Bradford A. Lee, "Strategic Interaction: Theory and History for Practitioners," in *Competitive Strategies for the 21st Century: Theory, History, and Practice*, Thomas G. Mahnken, ed. (Stanford, CA: Stanford University Press, 2012), 28–32.

6. For an early articulation of this approach, see Thomas C. Schelling, "The Strategy of Inflicting Costs," in *Issues in Defense Economics*, Roland N. McKean, ed. (Cambridge: National Bureau of Economic Research, 1967).

7. Lee, "Strategic Interaction," 32–43.

8. Victor Davis Hanson, "The Strategic Thought of Themistocles," in *Successful Strategies: Triumphing in War and Peace from Antiquity to the Present*, Williamson Murray and Richard Hart Sinnreich, eds. (Cambridge: Cambridge University Press, 2014), 32.

conflicting purposes or mutual fears."[9] Subsequently, Colin Gray came to define an arms race as "two or more parties perceiving themselves to be in an adversary relationship, who are increasing or improving their armaments at a rapid rate and restructuring their respective military postures with a general attention to the past, current, and anticipated military and political behavior of the other parties."[10] An arms race thus has four elements. First, it involves at least two parties. Second, each competitor must develop its force structure with reference to its rival. Third, each side must compete with the other in terms of the quantity or the quality of their respective militaries. Finally, interactions must lead to a rapid increase in the quantity and/or the quality of weapons.

II

The Anglo-German naval arms race that preceded World War I offers an outstanding case study of the strategic use of an arms competition, and Admiral Sir John ("Jackie") Fisher's approach to it offers an example of a successful strategy for competition.[11]

The underlying cause of the Anglo-German naval competition was the rivalry between Great Britain and Imperial Germany in Europe and beyond. The proximate cause was the decision by Kaiser Wilhelm II's government—in particular, Rear Admiral Alfred Tirpitz, the state secretary at Germany's Imperial Navy Office—to expand the *Kriegsmarine* in a bid to rival the Royal Navy. Specifically, Tirpitz sought to build a German battle fleet that would equal the British fleet in size. Tirpitz calculated that such an approach would confine the competition with London to a scope that was both favorable and affordable to Berlin. Given Britain's need to project power globally, Tirpitz believed that a German fleet equal in size to Britain's would give Berlin local superiority over London in a future Anglo-German conflict. Moreover, because German ships would operate mainly in the North Sea, Berlin would not need to invest in costly design features for its warships that would have been needed to support global power projection. In addition, as a fleet designed primarily for political

---

9. Samuel P. Huntington, "Arms Races: Prerequisites and Results," *Public Policy* 8:1 (1958): 41.

10. Colin S. Gray, "The Arms Race Phenomenon," *World Politics* 24:1 (1971): 40.

11. Matthew S. Seligmann, "The Anglo-German Naval Race, 1898–1914," in *Arms Races in International Politics*, Thomas G. Mahnken, Joseph A. Maiolo, and David Stevenson, eds. (Oxford: Oxford University Press, 2016).

influence, Berlin could afford to maintain the Kriegsmarine in a state of reduced readiness and man it primarily with conscripts.[12]

Britain's response to the German challenge at sea was based on embracing
competition and devising a strategy that both imposed costs on Germany and
called into question the underlying assumptions of Tirpitz's strategy. Moreover, the British strategy for the Anglo-German arms competition rested on a
sound assessment of the relative strengths and weaknesses of Great Britain
and Imperial Germany. The main architect of Britain's strategy was Admiral
Sir John Fisher, who was appointed First Sea Lord in 1904 and held the position through 1910. Rather than competing with Germany on terms dictated by
Berlin and which served the intent of magnifying perceptions of Germany as
a sea power, Fisher sought to change the terms of the competition in ways that
were favorable to Britain. Fisher aimed to increase radically the "fighting efficiency" of the Royal Navy through major organizational reforms. Aside from
being a sensible response to tensions with Germany, the reforms magnified
Britain's qualitative superiority over the Kriegsmarine. The increase in the
Royal Navy's fighting efficiency in turn caused the German government to
change the Kriegsmarine's personnel policy by dramatically increasing its
cadre of long-service officers and men, with a concomitant increase in the
number of ships it kept in permanent active service. These changes came at
considerable cost and took time and effort to implement.

Fisher also sought to control the pace and scope of the competition by
continuously increasing the displacement and improving the design of the
Royal Navy's warships through a process he referred to as "plunging." Rather
than seeking to retard the growth of naval armaments, Fisher believed that it
was in Britain's interest to field progressively better and more advanced warships. Such a strategy was possible because of the tremendous competitive
advantage conferred on the Royal Navy by the scale, productive power, and
speed of construction of Britain's shipbuilding and maritime engineering industries. As Fisher summarized it:

> You see all your rivals' plans fully developed, their vessels started beyond
> recall, and then in each individual answer to each such rival vessel you
> plunge with a design that is 50 per cent [sic] better! knowing that your rapid
> shipbuilding and command of money will enable you to have your vessel
> fit to fight as soon if not sooner than the rival vessel.[13]

12. Seligmann, "The Anglo-German Naval Race," 23–24.
13. Seligmann, "The Anglo-German Naval Race," 28.

The initial embodiment of Fisher's strategy was the HMS *Dreadnought*, the world's first all-big-gun, single-caliber, turbine-powered battleship. Fisher conceived the design prior to his appointment as First Sea Lord in 1904 and moved to finalize it once in place. Laid down on October 2, 1905, and launched on February 10, 1906, the *Dreadnought* represented a major advance in battleship design—it was larger, faster, and more heavily armed than any previous warship. Indeed, all subsequent battleships would be known as "dreadnoughts" while those that preceded them would be relegated to being designated "pre-dreadnoughts."

The *Dreadnought* was, however, only the beginning of the strategy of "plunging," which saw Britain launch a series of ever larger and more capable battleships over successive years. Indeed, between the *Dreadnought* and the *Queen Elizabeth*, launched only eight years later, the displacement of battleships increased by 14,000 tons, making the now "super-dreadnoughts" of the *Queen Elizabeth* class nearly eighty percent heavier than the original *Dreadnought* and at least twice the displacement of any pre-dreadnought battleship.[14]

All this came at considerable expense. The *Queen Elizabeth* cost nearly seventy percent more than the *Dreadnought*. The growing size and power of their main armament further added to escalating costs. The strategy of plunging saw the British naval budget grow by over twenty-five percent between 1904 and 1914. The British government nonetheless judged the cost of the naval arms race that it had embraced to be affordable. The same was not true on the German side, where the British strategy of plunging threw Tirpitz's plans into disarray. Between 1905 and 1914, the German naval budget more than doubled. This growth was financially ruinous to the German Reich, which lacked the tax base to sustain such expenditures. Moreover, in 1911, the Second Moroccan Crisis shifted the German government's attention from threats at sea to those on land and on the need for greater spending on the army. From that point on, military spending would trump naval spending in Berlin.[15]

Britain's refusal to compete with Germany solely on the terms chosen by Tirpitz, and instead to move the competition to areas that were more favorable to Britain, such as war readiness, technological innovation, and design improvements, was a successful one. Moreover, Britain was better able to bear the costs

14. Seligmann, "The Anglo-German Naval Race," 30.
15. Seligmann, "The Anglo-German Naval Race," 31–32.

of competition. Germany could, however, have further changed the terms of competition away from Britain's strengths in battleship construction and toward an enduring British weakness: the vulnerability of the nation's food supplies. A German shift toward a strategy of trade interdiction would have posed a much greater threat to Britain than its construction of battleships. Fortunately for Britain, although the German Admiralty Staff favored such an approach, Tirpitz did not, and Germany continued to follow a self-defeating strategy.[16]

III

During the Cold War the study of arms races assumed a central place in the newly emerging field of strategic studies. Indeed, scholars writing during the Cold War devised a number of different explanations for the pattern of superpower interaction. One group emphasized external sources of arms competition. The most common, and simplistic, formulation was the "action-reaction" model of arms races. At its core, this model holds that the search for security, combined with uncertainty and worst-case estimates of a competitor's intentions and capabilities, will yield efforts to amass ever-greater stockpiles of weaponry. That is, exaggerated fears and overestimated threats will lead to the spiraling growth of armaments and arms spending. This tendency is abetted by the fact that plans for fielding weapons are often made before the appearance of the systems they are meant to counter.[17]

Central to action-reaction arms race theory is the concept of the security dilemma. As Robert Jervis noted in 1978, a security dilemma can be said to exist when "many of the means by which a state tries to increase its security decrease the security of others."[18] Countries that seek only security conclude that their adversary's motives are more malign than previously believed and act accordingly. The security dilemma is driven by uncertainty over whether a competitor is motivated by security concerns or by more expansive aims.[19] Jervis argued that the magnitude and nature of the security dilemma depend on the offense-defense balance and differentiation between offense and defense.

16. Seligmann, "The Anglo-German Naval Race," 38.

17. George W. Rathjens, The Future of the Strategic Arms Race: Options for the 1970s (Washington, DC: Carnegie Endowment, 1969), 25–26.

18. Robert Jervis, "Cooperation Under the Security Dilemma," World Politics 30:2 (1978): 169.

19. Charles L. Glaser, "The Security Dilemma Revisited," World Politics 50:1 (1997): 192.

Certainly, the action-reaction dynamic was an appealing model of US-Soviet strategic interaction, in part because of its elegant simplicity. Secretary of Defense Robert S. McNamara, for example, argued, "Whatever their intentions or our intentions, actions—or even realistically potential actions—on either side relating to the build-up of nuclear forces necessarily trigger reactions on the other side. It is precisely this action-reaction phenomenon that fuels the arms race."[20]

Despite its theoretical appeal, a number of scholars and practitioners, such as Andrew W. Marshall and Albert Wohlstetter, questioned the extent to which the action-reaction dynamic actually described or explained Soviet-American strategic interaction. Marshall enjoyed a full career at the RAND Corporation before coming to Washington, DC, to serve as the Director of Net Assessment at the National Security Council (briefly) and then at the Department of Defense (1973–2015). Marshall's thoughts on strategic interaction were shaped by his experience studying the Soviet Union at the RAND Corporation during the 1950s, where he had access to some of the most sensitive intelligence the United States possessed regarding its enemy. Such early, deep insight into Soviet decision-making was a rarity at the time. Working with his colleague Joseph E. Loftus, Marshall looked to the Soviet government's allocation of its scarce resources for insight into its strategy. As Marshall later wrote:

> [This research] highlighted efforts by Joseph Stalin to initiate several major programs to bridge the Soviet strategic offensive and defensive gaps during and immediately after World War II together with special organizations to manage them. The efforts needed substantial outlays of resources that suggested that the Soviet Union faced major challenges unlike the United States, and also that it was pursuing the competition with the United States in quite different ways.[21]

Overall, Marshall saw that Moscow poured a tremendous amount of its limited economic, industrial, and human resources into building nuclear weapons, ballistic missiles, and air defences, choices very different from those that the United States was making at the time.

20. Charles L. Glaser, "The Causes and Consequences of Arms Races," *Annual Review of Political Science* 3 (2000): 253.

21. Andrew W. Marshall, "The Origins of Net Assessment," in *Net Assessment and Military Strategy: Retrospective and Prospective Essays*, Thomas G. Mahnken, ed. (Amherst, NY: Cambria Press, 2020), 4.

Research on organizational behavior also shaped Marshalls views of competition. In particular, the work of Herbert A. Simon and James G. March, who studied how organizational preferences shaped strategic choices, influenced Marshall's thought and approach.[22] These influences collectively led to Marshall's view of competition with the Soviet Union that was very different from the action-reaction model. The United States and Soviet Union should not be thought of as unitary, rational actors who relentlessly and efficiently formulated and implemented well-articulated strategies, but rather as complex bureaucratic organizations that acted on imperfect information filtered through their organizational culture and misperceptions.

Marshall codified his thinking in a monograph entitled *Long-Term Competition with the Soviets: A Framework for Strategic Analysis,* published in 1972. His careful reconstruction of Soviet defence expenditures during the late-1960s revealed a much more loosely coupled interaction between the United States and the Soviet Union than that predicted by action-reaction theory. In his view, getting a better understanding of the dynamics of the US-Soviet competition would require a very different perspective, one that gave greater weight to the organizational context and constraints that the Soviets faced:

> If we really are to understand the nature of the competition, the nature of the interaction process, we will need to understand much better than we do now the decision making processes within both the US and Soviet political-military-industrial bureaucracies. We need an understanding of the processes that lead to the selection of specific R&D programs, to R&D budgets and their allocations, to procurement decisions, to the operation of the whole of the weapons system acquisition process. We would need to understand how the perceptions of what the other side is doing come about in various places within these complicated bureaucracies, and how these perceptions influence the behavior of the various organizations and the decision makers involved in the complex decision processes that drive evolution of the several defense programs involved.[23]

Marshall's monograph was part of a broader body of work that questioned the notion of a tightly coupled arms race. In another piece, his RAND colleague Albert Wohlstetter's analysis of US and Soviet defense spending and arms programs

---

22. Marshall, "The Origins of Net Assessment," 6.

23. Andrew W. Marshall, *Long-Term Competition with the Soviets: A Framework for Strategic Analysis* (Santa Monica, CA: RAND Corporation, 1972), 7.

during the first two decades of the Cold War showed only a partial connection between the actions of one side and those of the other. Wohlstetter found, for example, that US defense spending was not directly correlated to Soviet actions. Moreover, he showed that while in some cases the United States had overestimated Soviet arms acquisitions, in other cases it had substantially underestimated them.[24] Similarly, a highly classified history of the US-Soviet arms competition written by Ernest May, John Steinbruner, and Thomas Wolfe under the sponsorship of the US secretary of defense and with the benefit of access to a broad range of classified sources likewise concluded that, "budgets, forces, deployments, and policies of the United States . . . were products less of direct interaction with the Soviet Union than of the tension in the United States between dread of Communism on the one hand and the dread of deficit spending on the other."[25]

Over time, such insights were reflected in US strategy for competing with the Soviet Union. Beginning in the 1950s and stretching to the end of the Cold War, the US government—first unconsciously and then consciously—sought to use its approach to armaments to its competitive advantage.

One prominent effort to impose costs on the Soviet Union involved the US Air Force's pursuit of manned penetrating bombers against Soviet air defenses. During the early Cold War, US bombers planned to operate at high altitudes in order to remain safe from Soviet aircraft and surface-to-air missiles (SAMs). As the reach of Soviet air defenses increased in the late-1950s, however, the US Strategic Air Command adopted low-altitude attack tactics and eventually deployed aircraft, such as the FB-111 fighter-bomber and B-1 bomber, that were optimized for low-altitude attack and developed weapons, such as the *Hound Dog* air-to-surface missile (ASM) and Short Range Attack Missile (SRAM), that were designed to allow bombers to launch attacks outside the range of Soviet SAMs, as well as increasingly sophisticated electronic warfare suites. Such an approach yielded an advantage for US bombers that lasted for over two decades. When, beginning in the late-1970s, the Soviets began to field aircraft and SAMs with the ability to shoot down low-altitude bombers and cruise missiles, the United States changed the character of the competition again by deploying stealthy aircraft such as the F-117 attack aircraft and B-2 bomber that were designed to deny Soviet air defense radars the ability to

24. Albert Wohlstetter, "Is There a Strategic Arms Race?" *Foreign Policy* 15 (1974): 3–20; Albert Wohlstetter, "Rivals, but no 'Race,'" *Foreign Policy* 16 (1974): 48–81.

25. Ernest R. May, John D. Steinbruner, and Thomas W. Wolfe, *History of the Strategic Arms Competition, 1945–1972*, Part I (Washington, DC: Historical Office, Office of the Secretary of Defense, March 1981), 241.

identify and track them. Throughout most of the period, the United States was able to dictate the scope and pace of the competition to the Soviets, forcing the latter to respond to American moves while also retaining the initiative.

Such an approach inflicted a variety of costs upon the Soviet Union. First, the US Air Force's pursuit of manned penetrating bombers imposed monetary costs on the Soviet Union by forcing it to acquire air defenses against high-altitude bombers in the 1950s, low-altitude bombers beginning in the 1960s, stealthy bombers beginning in the 1980s, and electronic warfare throughout. Each of these moves made previous investments in air defense irrelevant or obsolete. According to one accounting, it cost the Soviet Union $120 billion to counter US manned penetrating bombers over the course of the Cold War.[26] The United States also forced the Soviet Union to bear technological costs by compelling the Soviet aerospace industry to invest first in look-down/shoot-down target acquisition systems to counter low-flying bombers and later in counter-stealth technologies against low-observable aircraft.

The United States bomber program confronted the Soviet leadership with a series of trade-offs. For example, resources devoted to the strategic air defense of the Soviet Union could not be allocated to other missions, particularly offensive missions. These resources included the deployment of more than 10,000 SAMs, tens of thousands of air defense artillery systems, and fifteen varieties of air defense interceptors. In addition, the Soviet Union built the MiG-25 *Foxbat* air defense interceptor to counter the XB-70 *Valkyrie* bomber, which the United States never actually deployed.[27]

The United States also pursued operational concepts that sought to attack the Soviet Union's strategy. For example, the "Offset Strategy" of the 1970s and 1980s, which included the development of AirLand Battle doctrine by the US Army and Air Force, combined American technological advantages with deep understanding of Soviet strategic and operational predilections, including the Soviet General Staff's need to choreograph operations and its concern over the security of the Soviet homeland, in order to shake the confidence of the Soviet leadership in its ability to carry out its preferred strategy.[28] The United

26. Caspar W. Weinberger, *Annual Report to the Congress, Fiscal Year 1988* (Washington, DC: Government Printing Office, 1987).

27. Thomas G. Mahnken, *Technology and the American Way of War Since 1945* (New York, NY: Columbia University Press, 2008), 163–64.

28. John A. Battilega, "Soviet Military Thought and the Competitive Strategies Initiative," in *Competitive Strategies for the 21st Century: Theory, History, and Practice*, Thomas G. Mahnken, ed. (Palo Alto, CA: Stanford University Press, 2012), 106–27.

States would effectively turn strengths of Soviet strategy—the use of highly scripted, echelon attacks that employed overwhelming mass to break through NATO defenses—into weaknesses, by using precision-guided munitions, deep-strike capabilities, and other innovations to inflict severe attrition on the Warsaw Pact forces before they could reach the front.

IV

Arms control represented yet another instrument for competing with the Soviet Union during the Cold War. In common with past great-power rivalries, the United States and the Soviet Union used arms control not only to further their own interests but also to limit unproductive or undesirable elements of the arms competition.

One of the key early theorists of arms control was Thomas C. Schelling, who saw arms control as an instrument of competition and a counterpart to military measures in preventing war. As he wrote with Morton Halperin in 1961, "cooperative arrangements with potential adversaries could have the same objectives as sensible military policies in reducing the likelihood of war."[29] They further suggested that arms control should seek to increase stability by focusing on constraining technology and modes of deployment that increased the possibility of war. The two men argued that, where mutual interest existed, strategies of cooperation could coexist with strategies of competition. As they wrote:

> While a nation's military force opposes the military force of potentially hostile nations, it must also collaborate, implicitly if not explicitly, in avoiding the kinds of crises in which withdrawal is intolerable for both sides, in avoiding false alarms and mistaken intentions, and in providing—along with its deterrent threat of resistance or retaliation in the event of unacceptable challenges—reassurance that restraint on the part of potential enemies will be matched by restraint on our own.

In their view, arms control would involve mutual restraint or collaboration to reduce the likelihood of war, the scope of war, or its consequences. Arms control was also seen as a way of "restraining and tranquilizing the arms race."[30]

---

29. Thomas C. Schelling and Morton H. Halperin, *Strategy and Arms Control* (McLean, VA: Pergamon-Brassey's, 1985), xi.

30. Schelling and Halperin, *Strategy and Arms Control*, 1, 32.

Schelling and Halperin argued that arms control might not be a way to reduce defense expenditures. Indeed, arms control might actually entail more rather than less spending if it involved a shift to forces that would reduce the ability of an aggressor to achieve a surprise attack as well as measures to make weapons less vulnerable, even in the face of such an attack.[31]

Central to the debate over arms control during the Cold War was the question of whether arms control was a tool of competition or could be used to reduce it. It appears that the Soviets viewed arms control as an instrument of competition that could lock in asymmetric advantages that they possessed. The record on the American side is mixed. The Reagan administration looked to the deployment of intermediate-range nuclear forces (INF) in Europe as a means of eliminating the entire class of missiles on both sides via negotiation. At other times, however, US administrations looked to arms control to provide a respite from competition. The Nixon administration clearly used arms control to reduce arms expenditures at a time when there was mounting pressure on the US defense budget. Nixon also saw arms control as a mechanism to enmesh the Soviet Union in a web of agreements that would help the United States gain Soviet assistance in extricating itself from Vietnam.

Throughout much of the Cold War, the strategic logic of arms control predominated. That is, arms control was seen as a way of avoiding some of the most nettlesome problems of the nuclear age, such as surprise attack or strategic instability. At other times, however, the arms control process arguably became divorced from its strategic rationale.

Early attempts at arms control, such as the 1946 Baruch Plan as well as negotiations over a nuclear test ban, were meant to lock in the United States' lead in nuclear weapons. However, Soviet leaders resisted becoming entangled in such negotiations and only agreed to the 1963 Limited Test-Ban Treaty after the Soviet Union had caught up to the United States in atmospheric nuclear testing.

At the same time, the Soviet Union embarked on a broad expansion of its nuclear arsenal. By the early-1970s, the Soviets had approached quantitative parity with the United States. In these circumstances, the United States embarked on a set of initiatives that sought to limit the size and shape of superpower nuclear arsenals. For example, the Johnson and Nixon administrations pursued a series of arms control negotiations with the Soviet Union that led to the 1972 Strategic Arms Limitations Treaty (SALT I) and Anti-Ballistic Missile (ABM) Treaty.

31. Schelling and Halperin, *Strategy and Arms Control*, 120, 12.

SALT I established quantitative limits on the further production of SLBMs and ICBM launchers, and locked in rough quantitative parity with the Soviet Union. SALT I was meant to prevent a quantitative arms race, a competition that would have favored the Soviet Union, while retaining options for the United States to exploit its technological advantages in microelectronics, precision manufacturing, and digital computing to generate a qualitative advantage.

In the face of congressional opposition to defense spending in general, and skepticism regarding ballistic missile defense in particular, the ABM Treaty similarly limited American and Soviet deployment of missile interceptors to two sites each, a level that Congress would reasonably fund. At the same time, the treaty's provisions allowed the United States to continue to develop and test advanced anti-missile technologies; it also preserved the option for Washington to restart the competition under more favorable future conditions.[32]

The next round of arms negotiations—SALT II—stretched on for seven years, from 1972 until 1979, when the negotiating teams were able to conclude a treaty that Jimmy Carter and Leonid Brezhnev signed in June. SALT II limited the total of both nations' nuclear forces to 2,250 delivery vehicles and placed a variety of other restrictions on deployed strategic nuclear forces, including MIRVs (multiple independently-targeted reentry vehicles). However, opposition to the treaty in the Senate arose almost immediately in reaction both to the treaty's verification provisions and also more broadly to Soviet behavior. The Soviet invasion of Afghanistan in December 1979 led Carter to withdraw the treaty from consideration.

Although much Cold War arms control had a strategic rationale, some initiatives lay largely outside the bounds of superpower competition and were aimed at the spread of nuclear weapons to new powers or domains. The Nuclear Nonproliferation Treaty, concluded in 1968, sought to prevent the spread of nuclear weapons, to promote the peaceful use of nuclear energy, and, ultimately, to achieve nuclear disarmament. The Outer Space Treaty, concluded in 1967, prohibits the deployment of nuclear weapons in space, while the Seabed Arms Control Treaty, concluded in 1971, bans the placement of nuclear weapons on the ocean floor. In addition, a number of states established nuclear-free zones via treaty, for example, the 1967 Treaty for the Prohibition

---

32. John D. Maurer, "The Forgotten Side of Arms Control: Enhancing U.S. Competitive Advantage, Offsetting Enemy Strengths," *War on the Rocks*, June 27, 2018.

of Nuclear Weapons in Latin America and the Caribbean (the Treaty of Tlateloco) and the 1985 South Pacific Nuclear Free Zone Treaty (the Treaty of Rarotonga).

V

The US strategy for competition with the Soviet Union—a strategy that involved both arms racing and arms controlling—culminated in the Reagan administration. Ronald Reagan and a handful of his close advisors formulated a coherent strategy toward the Soviet Union between 1981 and 1983 and implemented that strategy consistently throughout the remainder of his eight years in office.[33] The shifts that occurred over time resulted from the inevitable adjustments needed to implement the strategy in the face of bureaucratic, congressional, and allied constraints, as well as responses to changes in the strategic environment, particularly the emergence of Mikhail Gorbachev as leader of the Soviet Union. All told, Reagan's strategy combined elements of arms competition and arms reduction and played an important role in bringing the Cold War to a close both peacefully and on terms favorable to the United States and its allies.

The foundation of Reagan's strategy rested on a careful net assessment of relative Soviet and American strengths and weaknesses. To begin with, Reagan possessed an innate optimism about the United States and a commensurate pessimism about the Soviet Union. He thus weighed the balance between the two super powers differently than most others, including many in his own party. First, he rejected the notion that the Soviet Union was a permanent feature of the international system. Whereas for decades American policymakers had focused on how to live with Communism and had thus treated the Soviet Union as an equal, Reagan emphasized the transitory character of the Communist regime. As early as 1975, he had termed Communism "a temporary aberration which will one day disappear from the earth because it is contrary to human nature."[34] Such statements, often dismissed as rhetoric, in fact reflected the Reagan's deep convictions.

---

33. See the discussion in Thomas G. Mahnken, "The Reagan Administration's Strategy toward the Soviet Union," in *Successful Strategies*, Murray and Sinnreich, eds. (Cambridge: Cambridge University Press, 2014); Hal Brands, *Making the Unipolar Moment: U.S. Foreign Policy and the Rise of the Post-Cold War Order* (Ithaca, NY: Cornell University Press, 2016).

34. John Lewis Gaddis, *The Cold War: A New History* (New York, NY: Random House, 2005), 217.

Second, Reagan believed that the United States had much greater leverage over the Soviets than many others recognized. He saw the powerful American economy as a weapon that Washington could wield against Moscow. He also believed as early as 1977 that the United States could use the attraction of Western economic prosperity in effect to create de facto allies among Soviet citizens who wanted a better life for themselves and their children. Reagan became convinced that the Soviet economy "was a basket case, partly because of massive spending on armaments . . . I wondered how we as a nation could use these cracks in the Soviet system to accelerate the process of collapse."[35] The president also saw the Soviet regime as vulnerable in the realm of ideas.

Third, Reagan was willing to accept greater risk in standing up to the Soviets than the mainstream counseled. He did not shy away from confronting the Soviet leadership, either in word or in deed. Finally, and most fundamentally, he sought not to contain Soviet power but rather to transform the Soviet regime—to achieve a fundamental change in the character of the Soviet Union by pushing the Communist regime to confront its own weaknesses.[36]

The intellectual underpinnings of Reagan's strategy for competition can be found in a May 1981 memorandum written by National Security Council staffer and Harvard historian, Richard Pipes, entitled "A Reagan Soviet Policy."[37] It advanced four central propositions. The first was that Communism was inherently expansionist. That would change only when the Soviet regime collapsed or at least was thoroughly reformed. Second, economic difficulties and imperial overstretch confronted the Soviet system with a profound crisis. Third, the successors to Brezhnev were likely to be split into "conservative" and "reformist" factions. Fourth, and finally, Pipes argued that, "It is in the interest of the United States to promote the reformist tendencies in the USSR by a double-pronged strategy: *assisting pro-reform forces* inside the USSR and *raising for the Soviet Union the costs of its imperialism* elsewhere by a very determined strategy."[38]

This memorandum eventually informed National Security Decision Directive (NSDD) 75, "US Relations with the USSR," which Reagan signed on January 17, 1983. The directive stated that:

35. John Lewis Gaddis, *Strategies of Containment* (Oxford: Oxford University Press, 2005), 351.

36. Gaddis, *Strategies of Containment*, 354.

37. Richard Pipes, "A Reagan Soviet Policy," May 1981, Richard E. Pipes Files, Box 4, Ronald Reagan Presidential Library.

38. Pipes, "A Reagan Soviet Policy," 1. Emphasis in original.

US policy toward the Soviet Union will consist of three elements: external resistance to Soviet imperialism; internal pressure on the USSR to weaken the sources of Soviet imperialism; and negotiations to eliminate, on the basis of strict reciprocity, outstanding disagreements.[39]

NSDD 75 laid out three tasks to achieve these objectives: 1) "To contain and over time reverse Soviet expansionism by competing effectively on a sustained basis with the Soviet Union in all international arenas"; 2) "To promote, within the narrow limits available to us, the process of change in the Soviet Union toward a more pluralistic political and economic system in which the power of the privileged ruling elite is gradually reduced"; and 3) "To engage the Soviet Union in negotiations to attempt to reach agreements which protect and enhance US interests and which are consistent with the principle of strict reciprocity and mutual interest."[40]

The directive went on to outline a multi-dimensional strategy with military, economic, and political elements to exert both external and internal pressure on Moscow. It put particular emphasis on: 1) "sustaining steady, long-term growth in U.S. defense spending and capabilities"; 2) "creating a long-term Western consensus for dealing with the Soviet Union"; 3) "maintenance of a strategic relationship with China, and efforts to minimize opportunities for a Sino-Soviet rapprochement"; 4) "building and sustaining a major ideological/political offensive which, together with other efforts, will be designed to bring about evolutionary change of the Soviet system"; 5) "effective opposition to Moscow's efforts to consolidate its position in Afghanistan"; 6) "blocking the expansion of Soviet influence in the critical Middle East and Southwest Asia regions"; 7) "maintenance of international pressure on Moscow to permit a relaxation of the current repression in Poland and a longer-term increase in diversity and independence throughout Eastern Europe"; and 8) "neutralization and reduction of the threat to U.S. national security interests posed by the Soviet-Cuban relationship."[41]

During the first four years of the Reagan administration, the United States emphasized the first two objectives outlined in NSDD 75: containing and reversing Soviet expansionism by competing with the Soviets and promoting change within the Soviet Union. The emergence of Mikhail Gorbachev as the leader of the Soviet Union provided the occasion for Reagan to pursue the

39. NSDD 75, "U.S. Relations with the USSR," January 17, 1983, NSDD Digitized Reference Copies, Ronald Reagan Presidential Library, 1.

40. NSDD 75, "U.S. Relations with the USSR," 1.

41. NSDD 75, "U.S. Relations with the USSR," 8.

third objective: engaging the Soviets in negotiations to reach agreements to protect and enhance US interests. Both because of the pressure the United States had exerted on the Soviet Union and because of Gorbachev's recognition of the need to lessen tensions with the United States in order to implement much-needed domestic reforms, the Soviet leader agreed to the Intermediate-Range Nuclear Forces (INF) Treaty.

Formulating the strategy had involved forging a bureaucratic consensus behind a revised assessment of the US-Soviet balance and a more expansive set of political objectives. Implementing it required the Reagan administration to contend not only with bureaucratic opposition, but also with congressional and allied constraints.

One set of constraints involved congressional funding of the Reagan administration's initiatives. Although Congress provided a large-scale increase in defense expenditure, a number of programs, including the MX ICBM and the Strategic Defense Initiative, remained controversial.

Another set of constraints derived from America's allies, particularly those in Europe. On the one hand, a number of key European leaders, including Margaret Thatcher and Helmut Kohl, were supportive of the Reagan administration's strategy. Moreover, the deployment of US *Pershing II* medium-range ballistic missiles and *Gryphon* ground-launched cruise missiles in Western Europe in the face of Soviet intimidation was a key demonstration of allied resolve. On the other hand, Europeans were reluctant to give up the fruits of détente with the Soviet Union, including expanded East-West trade. As a result, American efforts to exert economic leverage over the Soviet Union by, for example, blocking the construction of the trans-Siberian oil and gas pipeline, triggered an acrimonious debate within Western Europe.[42]

The military competition with the Soviet Union was a central element of the Reagan strategy. NSDD 75 called for the United States to modernize its armed forces, with particular emphasis upon the development and acquisition of advanced technologies to provide leverage against the Soviet Union and to impose costs on the Soviet economy. In so doing, the US government exploited Soviet fears, reported by the CIA, of being outpaced technologically by America's military forces.[43] Significantly, NSDD 75 emphasized Soviet

---

42. Gordon Barrass, *The Great Cold War: A Journey Through the Hall of Mirrors* (Palo Alto, CA: Stanford University Press, 2009), 248, 283.

43. CIA Directorate of Intelligence, "The Soviet Defense Industry: Coping with the Military Technological Challenge," SOV 87–10035DX, July 1987, CIA Electronic Reading Room, iii.

perceptions of the military balance; US modernization was to be designed to ensure that "Soviet calculations of possible war outcomes under any contingency must always result in outcomes so unfavorable to the USSR that there would be no incentive for Soviet leaders to initiate an attack."[44]

The Reagan administration witnessed the wholesale modernization of US conventional and nuclear forces.[45] During the presidential transition, the Reagan team had planned a five percent real increase in defense spending. However, the Carter administration requested an increase of that magnitude during its last days in office. As a result, the incoming Reagan team pushed for a seven percent increase to emphasize that Reagan favored more defense than his predecessor.[46] In October 1981, Congress approved a defense expenditure of $1.5 trillion over five years, including the fielding of 100 MX (later *Peacekeeper*) intercontinental ballistic missiles, 6 *Ohio*-class ballistic missile submarines armed with 96 *Trident* D5 submarine launched ballistic missiles, 3,000 air-launched cruise missiles, and 100 B-1 bombers.

The United States also adopted a more aggressive operational posture, including naval and air exercises along the borders of the Soviet Union. US actions clearly alarmed the Soviet leadership. In May 1981, KGB Chairman Yuri Andropov became concerned that the United States was preparing for nuclear war with the Soviet Union. As a result, the Soviet leadership tasked the KGB and GRU to cooperate on Operation RYaN, an unprecedented effort to collect indicators of American preparations for nuclear war.[47]

In modernizing the US armed forces, the United States increasingly exploited its lead in the rapidly developing field of information technology. In 1975, the year that Microsoft was founded, the first personal computer (PC) hit the market; by 1981, annual PC sales in the United States topped one million.[48] The growth of information technology, in turn, spawned the development of new sensors and surveillance systems such as the Joint Surveillance Target Attack Radar System (JSTARS) aircraft, precision-guided munitions (PGMs) such as the Army Tactical Missile System (ATACMS) and the *Copperhead* artillery-launched PGM, and command-and-control networks to link them.

44. NSDD 75, "U.S. Relations with the USSR," 2.

45. See Mahnken, *Technology and the American Way of War*.

46. Michael Kramer, "Electoral Collage: The Budget Crunch," *New York Magazine*, Nov. 15, 1982, 31.

47. Barrass, *The Great Cold War*, 278.

48. Barrass, *The Great Cold War*, 249.

The Soviet General Staff was concerned about the development of advanced PGMs such as those being developed under the Defense Advanced Research Projects Agency's "Assault Breaker" program. The United States helped foster this perception by rigging advanced PGM tests to deceive the Soviets.[49] Soviet analysts saw PGMs as approaching nuclear weapons in effectiveness, while some saw the development of advanced conventional weaponry as presaging a revolution in warfare. In 1984, Marshal Nikolai Ogarkov, Chief of the General Staff, noted:

> Rapid changes in the development of conventional means of destruction and the emergence in the developed countries of automated reconnaissance-and-strike complexes, long-range high-accuracy terminally guided combat systems, unmanned flying machines, and qualitatively new electronic control systems make many types of weapons global and make it possible to sharply increase (by at least an order of magnitude) the destructive potential of conventional weapons, bringing them closer, so to speak, to weapons of mass destruction in terms of effectiveness.[50]

American developments demanded a response—one that the Soviet economy was manifestly unable to provide. In 1985, there were perhaps 50,000 PCs in the Soviet Union, compared to 30 million more advanced ones in the United States.[51] As Ogarkov told an American visitor, "In America, small children play with computers . . . For reasons you know well, we cannot make computers widely available in our society. We will never catch up with you in modern arms until we have an economic revolution. And the question is whether we can have an economic revolution without a political revolution."[52] In 1985, NATO mated emerging technologies with the doctrine of Follow-On Forces Attack (FOFA). The doctrine of FOFA envisioned using advanced sensors and strike systems to allow NATO forces to launch a counterattack deep into Poland. Two years later, to the consternation of the Soviets, NATO demonstrated this capability during an exercise dubbed Certain Strike.[53]

49. Barrass, *The Great Cold War*, 275.

50. Watts, *Long-Range Strike: Imperatives, Urgency and Options* (Washington, DC: Center for Strategic and Budgetary Assessments, 2005), 34.

51. Barrass, *The Great Cold War*, 317.

52. Barrass, *The Great Cold War*, 293.

53. Barrass, *The Great Cold War*, 338–39.

Reagan's announcement of the Strategic Defense Initiative (SDI) on 23 March 1983 marked an even more explicit bid to use US technology to compete with the Soviet Union. As he put it:

> Let us turn to the very strengths in technology that spawned our great industrial base and that have given us the quality of life we enjoy today.
>
> What if free people could live secure in the knowledge that their security did not rest upon the threat of instant U.S. retaliation to deter a Soviet attack, that we could intercept and destroy strategic ballistic missiles before they reached our own soil or that of our allies?
>
> I call upon the scientific community in our country, those who gave us nuclear weapons, to turn their great talents now to the cause of mankind and world peace, to give us the means of rendering these nuclear weapons impotent and obsolete.[54]

The US National Intelligence Council assessed that the Soviet Union would encounter difficulties in developing and deploying countermeasures to SDI. As one September 1983 memorandum put it:

> [The Soviets] are likely to encounter technical and manufacturing problems in developing and deploying more advanced systems. If they attempted to deploy new advanced systems not presently planned, while continuing their overall planned force modernization, significant additional levels of spending would be required. This would place substantial additional pressures on the Soviet economy and confront the leadership with difficult policy choices.[55]

In late 1983, in the midst of growing superpower tension, Soviet concern escalated further. NATO exercise Able Archer 83, which simulated a future war in Europe and included the use of nuclear weapons, heightened Soviet fears of a US nuclear attack.[56] The first report of the Soviet war scare reached the United States several months later, courtesy of Oleg Gordievsky, a Soviet KGB officer who was spying for the British Secret Intelligence Service.[57] The national intelligence officer for the Soviet Union and Eastern Europe, Fritz Ermarth,

54. Ronald Reagan, "Announcement of Strategic Defense Initiative," March 23, 1983, American Presidency Project.

55. NIC M 83, 10017, "Possible Soviet Responses to the US Strategic Defense Initiative," September 12, 1983, CIA Electronic Reading Room, viii.

56. Barrass, *The Great Cold War*, 278.

57. Barrass, *The Great Cold War*, 304.

concluded that, "We do not believe [Soviet activity] reflects authentic leadership fears of imminent conflict."[58] Subsequent information confirmed that the Soviets were concerned not that the United States was about to launch a war against the Soviet Union, but rather that the combination of Soviet economic and technological weakness with Reagan's policies were turning the correlation of forces against Moscow.[59] The war scare nonetheless highlighted the dangers of superpower miscalculation and induced greater caution in Washington.

The challenge of US advanced technology appears to have had a marked impact on Soviet leaders. In the words of Soviet Ambassador Anatoly Dobrynin, "[o]ur leadership was convinced that the great technical potential of the United States had scored again." Soviet leaders "treated Reagan's statement as a real threat."[60] The memoirs and recollections of policymakers in Moscow confirm that they took Reagan seriously. An expensive competition in ballistic missile defenses appeared particularly unattractive to Soviet leaders, who were aware of the country's economic difficulties. SDI also highlighted the Soviet Union's lag in computers and microelectronics.[61]

The announcement of SDI triggered a debate within the Soviet leadership over the wisdom of competing with the United States in space weaponry, as well as the form that competition should take. Indeed, it ultimately set up a situation in which Soviet leaders who favored a high-technology competition with the United States in space arms initially carried the day, only to be discredited by their inability to field advanced weapons. That is, SDI put in motion a chain of events that ultimately made the Soviet leadership aware that it could not compete with the United States in high-technology weaponry.[62]

The resource implications of responding to SDI became particularly apparent after Mikhail Gorbachev assumed control in 1985 and launched an effort to revive the lagging economy. As one 1987 CIA assessment put it:

58. SNIE 11-10-84/JX, "Implications of Recent Soviet Military-Political Activities," May 18, 1984, CIA Electronic Reading Room.

59. Fritz W. Ermarth, "Observations on the 'War Scare' of 1983 from an Intelligence Perch," November 6, 2003, *Parallel History Project on NATO and the Warsaw Pact*; Dima Adamsky, "The 1983 Nuclear Crisis: Lessons for Deterrence Theory and Practice," *Journal of Strategic Studies* 36:1 (2013): 4–41.

60. Jeremi Suri, "Explaining the End of the Cold War: A New Historical Consensus?," *Journal of Cold War Studies* 4:4 (2002): 65.

61. Suri, "Explaing the End of the Cold War," 66.

62. David E. Hoffman, *The Dead Hand: The Untold Story of the Cold War Arms Race and its Dangerous Legacy* (New York, NY: Doubleday, 2009).

The Soviets would find it difficult to mount a large response to SDI . . . without curtailing other military programs. Significantly expanding procurement of weapon systems based on existing technologies would strain the Soviets' already taut component supply base. Reliance on more complex technologies would cause still greater strain because many Soviet weapons programs projected to reach initial operational capability in the late 1990s will compete for the same resources.

The assessment went on to note that the demand for advanced technology would hit the Soviet economy just as Gorbachev was trying to modernize Soviet industry through accelerated investment in advanced technology for manufacturing. Moreover, Gorbachev's "modernization plans call for many of the same scarce, high-technology resources—including microelectronics and flexible manufacturing systems—that would be required for advanced BMD systems and countermeasures."[63]

The United States undertook several efforts to shape Soviet perceptions of the technological competition. One involved feeding deceptive information to the Soviets regarding the state of American military technology. In 1981, French intelligence recruited Colonel Vladimir I. Vetrov, a KGB officer assigned to collect intelligence on Western science and technology. Vetrov—dubbed "Farewell"—gave the French more than 4,000 documents that demonstrated Moscow's reliance on the theft of foreign science and technology to shore up the Soviet economy. The documents constituted a shopping list of the technologies the Soviets were seeking, information the French passed on to the Americans.[64] In early 1984, the CIA and Pentagon used their knowledge of Soviet requirements to begin feeding Moscow incomplete and misleading information. The disinformation campaign covered half a dozen sensitive military technologies that the Soviets were interested in, including stealth technology, ballistic missile defenses, and advanced tactical aircraft. The United States planted false information regarding development schedules, prototype performance, test results, production schedules, and operational performance.[65]

The Reagan administration's approach to the Soviet Union included not only arms competition, but also arms negotiation. Indeed, the INF Treaty was

63. SOV 87–10063X, "Soviet SDI Response Options: The Resource Dilemma," November 1987, CIA Reading Room, vi.

64. Gus W. Weiss, "The Farewell Dossier," *Studies in Intelligence* 39:5 (1996).

65. Peter Schweizer, *Victory: The Reagan Administration's Secret Strategy That Hastened the Collapse of the Soviet Union* (New York, NY: Atlantic Monthly Press, 1994), 189.

notable not only for the fact that it dealt with the threat to US allies in Europe and Asia posed by the Soviets by eliminating an entire class of missiles, but also that it shifted the remaining competition to ground more favorable to the United States. Whereas the INF Treaty scrapped Soviet and American intermediate-range ground-based missiles, it left intact air- and sea-launched weapons of similar ranges—areas where the US held a geographic and organizational advantage—untouched. Similarly, the Reagan administration's approach to strategic arms control emphasized limiting both the number and size of missiles, as a way of obsolescing the Soviet Union's considerable economic and technological investments in large, heavy missiles, an area in which they excelled, while also emphasizing American advantages in smaller, more accurate weapons. The Strategic Arms Reduction Treaty (START I), concluded during the George H.W. Bush administration in 1991, codified such an approach.[66]

VI

Successful strategies for competition have shared a handful of common features.[67] First, they were aimed at a particular adversary and accounted for the competitor's aims, resources, fears, and proclivities. Britain's strategy for competing with Germany was tailored to exploit Berlin's weaknesses, and the United States' approach to competing with the Soviet Union increasingly incorporated an understanding of Moscow's vulnerabilities and predilections.

Second, successful strategy has rested on the foundation of a solid understanding of the competitor. Such an understanding was indispensable for leaders to develop, implement, and assess the effectiveness of their strategy. Leaders needed an understanding of their own enduring strengths and weaknesses, and those of their competitors to ensure at least a reasonable chance that actions would elicit the desired response, or at least to narrow the range of potential responses.

The information requirements of successful strategy and the time needed to develop such expertise should not be underestimated. During the Cold War, the United States national security bureaucracy, to include the intelligence community, was almost singularly focused on the Soviet Union. The US government

---

66. Maurer, "The Forgotten Side of Arms Control."

67. Thomas G. Mahnken, "Frameworks for Examining Long-Term Strategic Competition Between Major Powers," in *The Gathering Pacific Storm*, Tai Ming Cheung and Thomas G. Mahnken, eds. (Amherst, NY: Cambria Press, 2018), 24–26.

and philanthropic foundations undertook a wide variety of programs to build intellectual capital regarding the Soviet Union.[68] The United States collected and translated Soviet military writings and made them widely available to the US officer corps.[69] Moreover, US intelligence organizations undertook a range of sometimes highly risky operations to gain deep insight into Soviet decision-making.[70] Despite all these efforts, it took decades for the United States to gain a deep and nuanced understanding of Soviet decision-making.

Both British and American strategies for competition took into account (and even exploited) the basic but often overlooked fact that both sides in a competition possess constrained resources. Indeed, the fact of limited resources—monetary, human, and technological—and the costs associated with them is central to strategy. Specifically, cost-imposing strategies have been most fruitfully pursued when strategists had an understanding of those constraints as well as ways to exacerbate them. These included bottlenecks within a state's defense sector, rivalries between various military organizations, as well as the tradeoff between defense and other forms of government spending. Effective strategies similarly took into account the basic fact that competitors are not unitary actors, but rather a collection of bureaucratic entities, each of which has its own preferences, proclivities, and culture, and this frequently leads to performance that diverges considerably from the optimal. Furthermore, strategies that matched the preferences and proclivities of one's own military to those of the competitor were more likely to be successful.

Fourth, successful strategies for competition exploited time, and made it a virtue. Strategists considered not only *what* actions they should take, but also *when*, with the latter timed to achieve the maximum effect. Finally, successful strategies accounted for interaction with competitors. Strategists realized that strategy does not involve imposing one's will upon an inanimate object, but rather a thinking competitor that is pursuing their own aims.

---

68. David C. Engerman, *Know Your Enemy: The Rise and Fall of America's Soviet Experts* (Oxford: Oxford University Press, 2009).

69. During the 1960s and 1970s, the US Air Force translated and published a series of Soviet doctrinal works. See A.A. Sidorenko, *The Offensive: A Soviet View* (Washington, DC: Government Printing Office, 1970).

70. Christopher Ford and David Rosenberg, *The Admirals' Advantage: U.S. Navy Operational Intelligence in World War II and the Cold War* (Annapolis, MD: US Naval Institute Press, 2005).

PART V

Strategy in the Post-Cold War World

CHAPTER 35

Dilemmas of Dominance

AMERICAN STRATEGY FROM
GEORGE H.W. BUSH TO BARACK OBAMA

Christopher J. Griffin

On March 6, 1991, George H.W. Bush addressed Congress on the recently concluded Gulf War and what he saw as "the very real prospect of a new world order." Bush foresaw a world in which "the principles of justice and fair play protect the weak against the strong . . . a world where the United Nations—freed from Cold War stalemate—is poised to fulfill the historic vision of its founders; a world in which freedom and respect for human rights find a home among all nations."[1] Bush's heady rhetoric was not without basis. The triumph over Iraq was a milestone in a period of geopolitical transformation that saw the collapse of Communism in Europe and the dissolution of the Soviet Union.

These momentous events followed a decade throughout which the Western political and economic model was on the march—before the Gulf War or final Soviet collapse. In a trend that political scientist Samuel Huntington described as "democracy's third wave," the number of global democracies had nearly doubled between the mid-1970s and 1991.[2] Francis Fukuyama, while serving on the State Department's policy planning staff in 1989, speculated that the "unabashed victory of economic and political liberalism" was bringing about

---

1. *Public Papers of the Presidents of the United States: George H.W. Bush (1991, Book I)*, 219–21, National Archives and Records Administration.
2. Samuel P. Huntington, "Democracy's Third Wave," *Journal of Democracy* 2:2 (1991): 12.

an "end of history" characterized by the "universalization of Western liberal democracy as the final form of human government."[3] More pointedly, journalist Charles Krauthammer observed in late 1990 that "now is the unipolar moment," in which the United States stood as "a single pole of world power."[4]

Three decades later, Krauthammer's coinage best describes the era that Bush shepherded and that shaped American policy choices for a quarter-century. Unipolarity was, as identified by Krauthammer, a matter of fact. It was the product of the wave of events that left the United States a solitary superpower, bolstered by the resilience of its Cold War-era alliances, an increasingly liberalized world economy, expanding democratization, and the implausibility of any near-term peer competitors.

The fact of unipolarity presented Bush and his successors with a fundamental, unexpected question: how should the United States exercise its newfound dominance in the international system? Over the quarter-century that followed, each administration would largely operate within the bounds of an approach first articulated by Secretary of Defense Richard Cheney and Chairman of the Joint Chiefs of Staff Colin Powell. The United States would seek to defend and expand the "zone of freedom" that had triumphed in the Cold War while the military pivoted from deterring global war with the Soviet Union to responding to regional crises.

This strategy was, in many respects, remarkably successful. There was no war among the major powers. The United States enjoyed a significant military edge over prospective adversaries. America's Cold War alliances were sustained and, in the case of NATO, enlarged. Global economic growth lifted more than a billion people around the world out of poverty.

The strategy fell short, however, in two critical regards. First, even Cheney and Powell's initial efforts were as much a response to budgetary pressures as a reckoning with new geopolitical realities. To the degree that strategy and resources were coherent during the post-Cold War era, it was because the latter dictated the former. More frequently, they were detached, leading to a strategy-resources mismatch during the relatively peaceful 1990s that metastasized into a dangerous strategic insolvency as new threats emerged.

Second, the US approach did not grapple with the inevitability that the unipolar moment would end. Although its authors in the George H.W. Bush administration anticipated that the unipolar moment would, of necessity, be

---

3. Francis Fukuyama, "The End of History?" *The National Interest* (Summer 1989): 16.
4. Charles Krauthammer, "The Unipolar Moment," *Foreign Affairs* 70:1 (1990/1991): 23–33.

transitory, later administrations came to accept it as a natural condition. American primacy emerged as a fact but was swiftly treated as an assumption that shaped other policy choices.

I

George H.W. Bush arrived in office at what he saw as a new and uncertain stage of the Cold War. Soviet Premier Mikhail Gorbachev had announced a combination of conventional and short-range nuclear force cuts in the winter of 1988–89 that Bush feared could "talk us into disarming without the Soviet Union having do to anything fundamental to its own military structure."[5] In response, Bush worked with Secretary of State James Baker and National Security Advisor Brent Scowcroft to escape Gorbachev's snares, reaching a solution that avoided a NATO crisis and paved the way to an eventual treaty on Conventional Forces in Europe with the Soviet Union.

The frenetic diplomacy of early 1989 characterized Bush's role as a "conservative manager" during a revolutionary time, acting through and reinforcing "pre-existing, Western institutions and structures" at each juncture.[6] This approach was largely the result of Bush's own temperament and long experience in governmental service. It also reflected his insight that the institutions that had allowed the United States to navigate the most dangerous junctures of the Cold War were best suited to both its final stages and whatever may follow. By preserving those institutions, Bush made possible the dominant position that the United States would enjoy in the years to come.

Bush's conversative management would define his approach to German reunification as well. In the year between the fall of the Berlin Wall on November 9, 1989, and the final reunification of Germany in October 1990, Bush and Baker worked against Soviet, French, and British resistance to ensure that Germany would emerge a unified state within the NATO alliance. In a February 1990 memorandum, Scowcroft succinctly captured this view and its implications for the future of NATO:

> We are entering the end-game of the Cold War. We must be impeccably prepared so that when the end-game is over, the North Atlantic Alliance

---

5. George Bush and Brent Scowcroft, *A World Transformed* (New York, NY: Vintage Books, 1999), 14.

6. Kristina Spohr, *Post Wall, Post Square: How Bush, Gorbachev, Kohl, and Deng Shaped the World After 1989* (New Haven, CT: Yale University Press, 2019), 6.

and the U.S. position in Europe remain the vital instruments of peace and stability that we inherited from our predecessors.[7]

Bush would be criticized throughout the period for excessive prudence in response to the collapse of European Communism, a point that he characterized as a refusal to "jump up and down" on the Berlin Wall. This public display of modesty, however, disguised an instinct for the jugular. When Bush and German Chancellor Helmut Kohl discussed the future status of Germany in February 1990, the president candidly described his view of stakes: "What worries me is talk that Germany must not stay in NATO. To hell with that! We prevailed, they didn't. We can't let the Soviets clutch victory from the jaws of defeat."[8] Bush indeed prevailed, and a unified Germany's inclusion in NATO left the Western alliance intact while the Warsaw Pact would dissolve the following spring.

If the resolution of the German question on American terms marked a decisive victory in the struggle to establish the post-Cold War order, the Gulf War demonstrated just how lopsided that order would be. Following Saddam Hussein's invasion of Kuwait on August 2, 1990, the Bush administration secured begrudging Soviet acquiescence to the war, organized a coalition of thirty-nine countries to wage it, and deployed more than half a million of its own service members to the region in a matter of months. After a forty-three-day air campaign and just 100 hours into the ground war, President Bush was able to announce a cease-fire after concluding that Kuwait was free and Iraqi forces had been defeated.

The Gulf War demonstrated the United States' unique ability to respond to global crises in the post-Cold War era. Even before it had crushed Iraqi forces, the United States' swift assemblage of a multinational coalition inspired Krauthammer's observation that America could make itself "a decisive player in any conflict in whatever part of the world it chooses to involve itself."[9] The war also raised the tantalizing possibility that the United Nations would no longer be subjected to a permanent US-Soviet deadlock on the Security Council, a development that inspired some of Bush's gauzier rhetoric on a "new world order." Bush and Scowcroft would later note the more practical benefits of seeking multilateral support for US military operations, which could at least facilitate securing overseas basing, while support from the United Nations

7. Hal Brands, *Making the Unipolar Moment: U.S. Foreign Policy and the Rise of the Post-Cold War Order* (Ithaca, NY: Cornell University Press, 2016), 290.

8. Bush and Scowcroft, *A World Transformed*, 253.

9. Krauthammer, "The Unipolar Moment," 24.

"could provide a cloak of acceptability to our efforts and mobilize world opinion behind the principles we wished to export."[10]

Moreover, the Gulf War was a showcase of the American military power
that would dominate the decades to follow. The United States' lift and logistics
capacity allowed it to project power into and sustain forces in the Middle East.
Once fighting commenced, the United States demonstrated the success of the
"second offset" strategy pursued by multiple late Cold War administrations,
which sought to overcome the Soviet Union's quantitative military advantages
in Europe with qualitative superiority. American forces were indeed superior
in every conceivable domain. Space-based communications, command-and-
control, and intelligence capabilities enabled operations. A combination of
stealth, precision, and electronic warfare allowed US aircraft to operate with
seeming impunity and devastating effect. Where US and Iraqi ground forces
met, an advantage in optics, munitions, and training proved decisive.[11] A
nearly 1,000-to-1 ratio of Iraqi to coalition casualties during the war showed
the devastating effect of US overmatch and instigated what would become a
long-running debate on whether Americans had unlocked a "revolution in
military affairs." The United States was poised to project military power in the
post-Cold War era, the only evident limitation being its willingness to do so.

II

As he managed the Cold War's endgame, President Bush proved reluctant to
prognosticate on the era to come and inarticulate when he tried. His vision
for a "new world order," for example, was couched in generalities. Clearer long-
term thinking emerged instead from the Defense Department, which was on
the hook for a widely anticipated "peace dividend" as the Cold War wound
down. In response to this budgetary reality, Chairman of the Joint Chiefs of
Staff Colin Powell and Paul Wolfowitz, Under Secretary of Defense for Policy,
each undertook reviews of US defense policy, strategy, force posture, and programs beginning in late 1989.

By early 1990, Powell had proposed the "Base Force," which would reorganize the military for regional conflicts in which the Soviet Union was not a
direct participant. This approach marked a significant departure from the Pentagon's decades-long preparations for global war with the Soviets, prioritizing

---

10. Bush and Scowcroft, *A World Transformed*, 490–91.
11. William J. Perry, "Desert Storm and Deterrence," *Foreign Affairs* 70:4 (1991).

instead the capacity for a global response to unexpected crises. The resultant plan emphasized maintaining overseas "presence" rather than "permanently stationed forces," while a larger US-based "contingency force" would be able to respond to emergencies as they arose. Under this approach, Powell anticipated that the United States would require a total military end strength of 1.6 million active duty service members, down from over 2.1 million at the time of his appointment.[12] In the face of demands for a peace dividend, Powell viewed the Base Force as "a floor below which the United States could not go and carry out its responsibilities as a superpower."[13]

Concurrently, Wolfowitz assigned a team working under I. Lewis "Scooter" Libby, Principal Under Secretary for Strategy and Resources, to undertake its own strategy review, resulting in a concept called "crisis response/reconstitution." Like the Joint Staff study under Powell, the civilian team focused on the need to respond to regional contingencies in a post-Cold War world. What distinguished the civilian effort was its contemplation of a wide range of underlying scenarios, from a future characterized by peaceful competition to a renewed Soviet threat. Because Wolfowitz was more skeptical than Powell that relations with the Soviet Union would continue to warm, his concept emphasized the need for a plan to "reconstitute" US global forces if the United States again faced the threat of global war.[14]

In June 1990, Secretary of Defense Richard Cheney packaged the two proposals. Wolfowitz's team had provided a clearer policy roadmap, while Powell had delivered the endorsement of his fellow chiefs of staff for his planned force cuts. President Bush rolled out the new strategy in a speech he delivered on August 2 at the Aspen Institute. In his remarks, Bush described "a world where the size of our forces will increasingly be shaped by the needs of regional contingencies and peacetime presence," concluding that, by 1995, the active military could be reduced by some twenty-five percent, as proposed by Powell. Concurrently, Bush noted that the new strategy would "guard against a major reversal in Soviet intentions by incorporating . . . the concept of reconstitution," which would retain the readiness to "generate wholly new forces."[15]

12. Lorna S. Jaffe, *The Development of the Base Force* (Washington, DC: Office of the Chairman of the Joint Chiefs of Staff, 1993), 17–26.

13. Jaffe, *The Development of the Base Force*, 21.

14. Jaffe, *The Development of the Base Force*, 32.

15. "Remarks at the Aspen Institute Symposium in Aspen, Colorado," August 2, 1990, George H.W. Bush Presidential Library, available at https://bush41library.tamu.edu/archives/public-papers/2128.

The president's remarks in Aspin were immediately overshadowed by Iraq's simultaneous invasion of Kuwait. The crisis provided the Pentagon with a brief reprieve from budgetary pressure, but also postponed further work on long-term strategy. The effort was picked up again in the development of the Defense Planning Guidance (DPG), a document that set forth the Pentagon's force planning and resource priorities. An initial draft was prepared in September 1991 before Zalmay Khalilzad, Assistant Deputy Under Secretary of Defense for Policy Planning, took the lead in writing a revised draft near the end of the year.

Written in the wake of victory over Iraq and the dissolution of the Soviet Union the year before, the February 1992 DPG draft argued that the United States' "first objective is to prevent the reemergence of a new rival, either on the territory of the former Soviet Union or elsewhere, that poses a threat on the order of that pose formerly by the Soviet Union." The draft identified a three-part strategy to avoid such a worst-case scenario. First, the United States should "show the leadership necessary to establish and protect a new order" that convinces potential competitors that they need not "aspire to a greater role or pursue a more aggressive posture to protect their legitimate interests." Second, in "non-defense areas, we must account sufficiently for the interests of the advanced industrial nations to discourage them from challenging our leadership." Third, the United States must "maintain the mechanisms for deterring potential competitors to even aspiring to a larger regional or global role."[16]

When the February draft of the DPG was leaked to the New York Times and Washington Post, furor ensued. The Times reported that the draft made the "case for a world dominated by one superpower" and articulated "the clearest rejection to date of collective internationalism" in favor of United States unilateral power.[17] The leak elicited criticism from both Congress, where Senator Joseph Biden called it "literally a Pax Americana" that "won't work," and the White House, where Scowcroft called the draft "nutty" and "kooky."[18] Despite the criticism, the draft DPG flowed directly from upon the strategy that President

16. All quotations from the draft guidance are from the version posted by the National Security Archive, "Document 3," February 18, 1992, available at https://nsarchive2.gwu.edu/nukevault/ebb245/doc03_extract_nytedit.pdf.

17. Patrick Tyler, "U.S. Strategy Plan Call for Ensuring No Rivals Develop," New York Times, March 8, 1992.

18. Zalmay Khalilzad, The Envoy: From Kabul to the White House, My Journey Through a Turbulent World (New York, NY: St. Martin's Press, 2016), 80.

Bush had articulated in August 1990. The most significant change was that the post-Soviet context dramatically elevated the implications of the DPG's "reconstitution" strategy. Cheney defended the draft strategy in an op-ed published in the *New York Times* and released a final version of the guidance retitled the Regional Defense Strategy (RDS) in January 1993.

The Regional Defense Strategy articulated the template for the United States' post-Cold War strategy. It committed the United States to "shaping an uncertain future so as to preserve and enhance the zone of peace" in the West. It described the necessity of working with the "states of the former Soviet Union in establishing democratic political systems and free markets so they too can join the democratic 'zone of peace.'" It emphasized that the United States must "preclude hostile, nondemocratic states from dominating regions of the world critical to us." Furthermore, it noted that the United States should "help preclude conflict by reducing sources of regional instability" and "limit violence should conflict occur."[19] The goals identified in the Regional Defense Strategy would largely define those outlined by future administrations.

Combined, the Base Force and the Regional Defense Strategy established what would become the standard, force-sizing criterion of the post-Cold War period, the "two-major regional contingency" (MRC) standard. The two-MRC concept rested on the essential proposition that, if the United States was engaged in conflict in one theater, a potential adversary would be tempted to initiate conflict elsewhere if it believed the United States could not respond. When presenting the Base Force concept to Congress near the end of the Bush administration, Powell testified that the Base Force would be able to accommodate one MRC "with great difficulty" but that two-MRC scenarios would put the force "at the breaking point." As a later analysis concluded, "Although the origins of the two-[MRC] standard were inauspicious, they would, with the [Bottom-Up Review] and [Quadrennial Defense Review], come to constitute high canon for defense planning."[20]

Finally, the team working under Wolfowitz introduced the concept of "reconstitution," which addressed a fundamental question as to how the United States should maintain its military overmatch if faced with "a new global threat

19. Dick Cheney, *Defense Strategy for the 1990s: The Regional Defense Strategy* (Washington, DC: The Pentagon, 1993), 3–4.

20. Eric V. Larson et al., *Defense Planning in a Decade of Change: Lessons from the Base Force, Bottom-Up Review, and Quadrennial Defense Review* (Santa Monica, CA: RAND, 2001), 13.

or some emergent alliance of hostile, nondemocratic regional powers."[21] The reconstitution strategy was derived, in the first instance, from the Pentagon civilians' skepticism that the Soviet threat had truly receded in the period 1989–90. That concern would evolve in the development of the draft DPG and RDS to reflect a concern about future, prospective adversaries, that would demand greater capacity than the Base Force could deliver. Cheney and his advisors had come to accept that a post-Cold War period had dawned and they described how the United States should posture itself if it should end.

III

"It's the economy, stupid." The poster in Bill Clinton's campaign headquarters starkly declared the candidate's agenda before the 1992 election. As a candidate, Clinton knew that the election would not be won over questions of foreign policy. As president, he would privately belittle the importance of grand strategy, arguing that his predecessors Franklin Roosevelt and Harry Truman had "just made it up as they went along."[22] Despite his lack of interest in the topic, however, Clinton sought to distinguish himself from Bush on two basic points.

First, Clinton placed a premium on human rights and democracy promotion. Clinton argued that Bush had prioritized "personal relationships with foreign leaders [over] how those leaders acquired and maintained their power."[23] This neo-Wilsonian tilt in Clinton's rhetoric was associated with Anthony Lake, who advised the campaign and would eventually be appointed as Clinton's first national security advisor. It also coopted congressional Democrats' attacks on Bush's rapprochement with the Chinese leadership following the Tiananmen Massacre of June 1989 as well as his opposition to independence movements within the collapsing Soviet Union in 1990–91. Although Clinton pledged to revoke China's most-favored nation (MFN) trading status and impose human rights sanctions, he punted the issue for a year before "de-linking" trade from human rights in 1994.

Second, Clinton doubled down on Bush's gauzy rhetoric about the United Nations, arguing that "multilateralism holds promise like never before" while

21. Cheney, *Defense Strategy for the 1990s*, 17.

22. Strobe Talbott, *The Russia Hand: A Memoir of Presidential Diplomacy* (New York, NY: Random House, 2002), 131.

23. "Excerpts from Speech by Clinton on U.S. Role," *New York Times*, October 2, 1992.

expressing support for a "new voluntary UN rapid deployment force."[24] This theme was most clearly articulated by Madeline Albright, who coined the term "assertive multilateralism," to describe the incoming administration's preference for working through the United Nations. This preference for multilateral action did not just echo Bush's view that UN support could provide a "cloak of legitimacy" for American action. It also offered "a relatively low-cost strategy for dealing with what were already considered low-priority issues."[25]

The Clinton administration's efforts to enlist multilateral support, however, quickly proved tough sledding. In December 1992, the outgoing Bush administration had deployed US military personnel to Somalia on a humanitarian assistance mission. The Clinton team worked at the United Nations to expand the mission to encompass what Albright described as "an unprecedented enterprise aimed at nothing less than the restoration of an entire country as a proud, functioning and viable member of the community of nations."[26]

The rapidly deteriorating situation in the Balkans proved even more confounding. The Bush administration had avoided entanglement in the conflicts that accompanied Yugoslavia's breakup. Instead, as events in the Balkans took their course, Europe was haunted by the dual specters of bloodletting on a scale unseen since 1945 and competing interests among NATO allies toward the conflict. For its part, the United Nations imposed an arms embargo in September 1991, which left Serbia, widely viewed as the aggressor in the conflict, with a significant military advantage. Fighting worsened after Clinton backed away from an early effort to intervene, leading French President Jacque Chirac to eventually observe that the position of leader of the free world was "vacant."[27]

Stung by criticism over his handling of foreign affairs, Clinton directed his foreign policy team to develop a coherent explanation for his approach to the world during the summer of 1993. Primary responsibility for the task fell on Lake, who coordinated a series of speeches by Secretary of State Warren Christopher, Albright, Clinton, and Lake himself leading up to the UN General Assembly meeting in late September.

24. "Excerpts from Clinton Speech on Foreign Policy Leadership," *New York Times*, August 14, 1992.

25. Jennifer Sterling-Folker, "Between a Rock and a Hard Place: Assertive Multilateralism and Post-Cold War U.S. Foreign Policy Making," in *After the End: Making U.S. Foreign Policy in the Post-Cold War World*, James M. Scott, ed. (Durham, NC: Duke University Press, 1998), 297.

26. John Bolton, "Wrong Turn in Somalia," *Foreign Affairs* 73:1 (1994): 62.

27. Elaine Sciolino, "Bosnia Policy Shaped by US Military Role," *New York Times*, July 29, 1996.

Of the speeches, Lake's provided the most compelling vision for the need for a strategy of "enlargement of the world's free community of market democracies" to replace the legacy of Cold War containment. Lake argued that current debates about Bosnia, Somalia, and "multilateralism" were "overdrawn," as none of those hot-button issues "by themselves define our broader strategy in the world."[28] Instead, he argued that the administration was pursing a four-part strategy that would: 1) strengthen the "core" of major market democracies "from which enlargement is spreading"; 2) "foster and consolidate new democracies and market economies" in the wake of Communism's collapse in Europe; 3) "counter the aggression" of "backlash states" like Iraq, Iran, and North Korea that are "hostile to democracy and markets"; and 4) pursue a humanitarian agenda that would both provide aid and help democracy and market economies "take root in regions of greatest humanitarian concern."[29] With but modest edits, these goals could have come directly from Cheney's Regional Defense Strategy.

Lake's remarks provided guidance for US relations with the other great powers. He noted that "our principal concerns should be" directed toward the first three items in the strategy, rather than the humanitarian crises that were dominating headlines.[30] He emphasized the importance of the conclusion of negotiations toward the World Trade Organization (WTO), the North American Free Trade Agreement (NAFTA), and a renewed role for NATO in the post-Cold War world. Lake discussed the importance of helping to consolidate democratic and market reforms in Russia and the other newly independent states, with the goal of turning them into "valued diplomatic and economic partners." These major emphases, however, were principally to be achieved through diplomacy and economic statecraft. The primary target for military strategy, in Lake's telling, was to prepare for the challenge posed by "backlash states" and humanitarian missions.

Responsibility for military strategy fell to Secretary of Defense Les Aspin, who was also charged with making defense-spending cuts of more than $100 billion beyond those that had been proposed by the Bush administration.[31]

28. Anthony Lake, "From Containment to Enlargement," Remarks Delivered at Johns Hopkins University School of Advanced International Studies, September 21, 1993, available at https://www.mtholyoke.edu/acad/intrel/lakedoc.html.

29. Anthony Lake, "From Containment to Enlargement."

30. Anthony Lake, "From Containment to Enlargement."

31. Eric Schmitt, "Plan for 'New' Military Doesn't Meet Savings Goal," *New York Times*, September 15, 1992.

Aspin brought to the task an approach he had developed while chairing the House Armed Services Committee, where he had proposed a Bottom-Up Review (BUR) as an alternative to the Base Force. Because the BUR focused on regional threats in the Middle East and the Korean Peninsula, an immediate question was whether to maintain a two-MRC standard, like that established in the Bush administration. Aspin proposed instead a "win-hold-win" strategy that would respond to simultaneous regional conflicts in sequence. In the face of congressional criticism and concerns expressed by allies, however, he relented, concluding that the US military must be capable of "fighting and winning two major regional conflicts that occur nearly simultaneously," given that "a potential aggressor in one region . . . [would] be tempted to take advantage if we are already engaged in halting aggression in another."[32]

The Bottom-Up Review also directed the United States to anticipate a larger role in humanitarian and peacekeeping operations, giving such activities the same footing as being prepared for major regional conflicts and peacetime oversees presence. The strategy noted, however, that "the military capabilities needed for these operations are largely those maintained for other purposes," such that they could be drawn from general purposes forces and provided specialized training and equipment as necessary.[33] As one study observed, the BUR gave "increased rhetorical and policy importance to U.S. participation in multilateral peace and humanitarian operations while setting the stage for an increased operational tempo and rate of deployment even as force reductions continued."[34]

One Cheney-era concept that the BUR dropped was "reconstitution" in anticipation of the prospect of a future near-peer aggressor. Instead, the BUR supposed that a force built on the two-MRC standard would provide a sufficient "hedge against the possibility that a future adversary might one day confront us with a larger-than-expected threat."[35] This change marked a step towards the adoption of American primacy as an assumption of policy rather than an objective. It is unsurprising that this exclusion was satisfactory to Powell, since Aspin's final report resulted in relatively modest cuts relative to the Base Force and the reconstitution concept that had been driven by the civilians

---

32. Les Aspin, *Report of the Bottom-Up Review* (Washington, DC: Department of Defense, 1993), 7.

33. Aspin, *Report of the Bottom-Up Review*, 8.

34. Larsen et al., *Defense Planning in a Decade of Change*, 42.

35. Aspin, *Report of the Bottom-Up Review*, 7.

working under Wolfowitz. In the end, Powell was satisfied to declare that the Base Force was a "linear ancestor" of the BUR on what he viewed as the most important matters.[36]

Despite Lake's protestations during his September speech about the debates over Somalia and Bosnia being "overdrawn," the botched raid on a Somali warlord on October 3 threw the Clinton administration's strategy rollout into disarray. The incident, which led to the deaths of nineteen soldiers, spurred deeper opposition to US participation in UN peacekeeping operations, and led the administration to formally decide that US personnel should never serve under a UN command. Aspin would resign by December, having served less than a year at the Pentagon.

The Bosnian conflict would provide redemption for the Clinton administration's strategy when the president finally accepted that muscular leadership would be necessary to both preserve the "core" of the market democracies and to respond to a worsening humanitarian disaster. The bloodletting in Bosnia worsened in 1995, punctuated by the Srebrenica massacre in July and the Sarajevo marketplace bombing in August. In response, the United States demanded negotiations and led massive NATO airstrikes. Under the capable management of Richard Holbrooke, the eventual negotiations resulted in the Dayton Accords, which ended the fighting and established a tenuous, multiethnic peace in Bosnia.

Success in Bosnia helped to springboard the Clinton administration's decision to move forward with the enlargement of NATO, which would eventually add the Czech Republic, Hungary, and Poland in 1999, while also initiating membership planning for another nine newly independent states. Secretary of State Warren Christopher emphasized the importance of one for the other, stating that while "Bosnia was unresolved, it was a cloud hanging over our heads"—"if NATO could not find a solution for Bosnia, then why think about enlarging it."[37] In 1999, the Clinton administration would again go to war in Europe, conducting a months-long aerial campaign against the Serbia's Slobodan Milosevic in response to his aggression against the enclave of Kosovo. Europe proved to be the model for the elements of "engagement and enlargement" that most closely mirrored the ambitions of the Regional Defense Strategy.

36. Colin L. Powell, *My American Journey* (New York, NY: Random House, 1995), 564.

37. James M. Goldgeier, *Not Whether But When: The U.S. Decision to Enlarge NATO* (Washington, DC: Brookings Institution Press, 1999), 98.

Through the latter 1990s, Asia would present its own distinct challenges. China never fit as neatly into Lake's categorization of countries as he may have hoped. In his remarks in 1993, Lake had discussed policy toward China in his discussion of "backlash states." This judgment would seem to be validated in 1995–96, when China attempted to intimidate Taiwan with a combination of military exercises and missile launches that "bracketed" the island's northern and southern ports. In response, the Clinton administration assembled the most powerful naval force in the western Pacific since the Vietnam War by deploying two carrier battle groups. The US move demonstrated its decisive military advantage in the mid-1990s, as Beijing was reported to be surprised to learn that one of the carriers had arrived from the Persian Gulf on short notice.

The Taiwan Strait Crisis marked not just the gravest crisis in US-China relations since the 1950s but also a dramatic transition in Washington's approach to Beijing. Having come to the brink of conflict, the Clinton administration would subsequently bet that the rise of an entrepreneurial middle class in an increasingly globally integrated China would compel China's leadership to liberalize. In a flurry of second-term diplomacy, Clinton and his Chinese counterpart Jiang Zemin described their desire to craft a "strategic partnership" and permanently settled the most-favored nation debate in order to facilitate Beijing's accession to the World Trade Organization. For its part, the Chinese military undertook a crash program to develop missiles and other capabilities that could deny US forces access to the western Pacific in the event of future conflict. The stakes of the respective efforts would only become apparent years later.

By the end of his administration, Clinton was acting with a degree of confidence best typified by his and Albright's frequent invocation of the concept of an "indispensable nation" to characterize America's role in the world. French Foreign Minister Hubert Vedrine coined the term "hyperpower" as an alternative, drawing attention to his view that the United States had grown too comfortable in its exercise of unilateralism across the globe.[38] Despite these successes, and the envy they induced, the Clinton administration's activism created its own challenges.

The frequency of US military interventions indicated a mismatch between US strategy and the resources available to it carry it out. Deployments to Somalia, Haiti, Bosnia, and Kosovo, along with operations to maintain the

---

38. Jane Perlez, "Suave Rival Has Words for the U.S.: En Garde," *New York Times*, September 20, 2000.

"Northern Watch" and "Southern Watch" no-fly zones in Iraq, placed a heavy burden on the Armed Forces at a time of diminishing resources. Since the post-BUR military expected that the forces for these missions would be drawn from those "maintained for other purposes," the military was undersized for both those missions and the larger two-MRC strategy. As the 1997 Quadrennial Defense Review noted, the Defense Department lacked the resources to maintain the current size of the force, its pace of overseas operations, and to procure new equipment to replace that purchased during the late Cold War buildup.[39]

In addition, US overseas operations had the pernicious effect of providing prospective adversaries with new insights into vulnerabilities in the American way of war. Throughout the 1990s, for example, Chinese analysts engaged in freewheeling debates about American efforts to capitalize on the "revolution in military affairs," the degree to which a first strike could disrupt the American model of expeditionary warfighting from theater logistics hubs, and specific vulnerabilities presented by US logistics, forward air bases, and aircraft carriers.[40] Meanwhile, terrorist leaders like al Qaeda's Osama bin Laden observed America's abrupt withdrawal from Somalia, causality-adverse military operations in the Balkans, and lackadaisical responses to attacks during the decade and concluded that Americans were too weak to mount a serious response to future provocations. Primacy carried a price, even if Americans did not realize that they were paying it at the time.

IV

Before the 2000 election, George W. Bush's views on foreign policy were characterized by his critique of the Clinton administration's "nation building" efforts, which he characterized as "endless and aimless deployments."[41] Pulling a page from Clinton's own 1992 playbook, Bush criticized the cozy relationship with Beijing, which he characterized as a "strategic competitor."[42] Although Bush's handling of relations with China was tested in spring 2001 when a Chinese

39. William Cohen, *Report of the Quadrennial Defense Review* (Washington, DC: Department of Defense, 1997), iv.

40. Michael Pillsbury, *China Debates the Future Security Environment* (Honolulu, HI: University Press of the Pacific, 2000), 285–95.

41. "Gov. Bush Vows Stronger Military, to 'Redefine War,'" *Chicago Tribune*, September 24, 2000.

42. Thomas W. Lippmann, "Bush Makes Clinton's China Policy an Issue," *Washington Post*, August 20, 2000.

fighter aircraft collided with an American reconnaissance plane, the incident was swiftly resolved. Through the rest of the year, the president focused his energies on tax cuts and education reform, the latter effort placing Bush at a Florida elementary school on the morning of September 11, 2001.

The attacks of September 11 recast both the Bush presidency and the entire post-Cold War period. The president and his top advisors believed that the attacks marked an epochal transition, a view he expressed several years later when he described the 1990s as "years of relative quiet, years of repose, years of sabbatical—and then there came a day of fire."[43]

The immediate aftermath of the attacks did not afford much time for reflection. In early October, the administration launched a campaign against al Qaeda and the Taliban regime in Afghanistan, all while undertaking a range of financial, intelligence, and judicial initiatives to strengthen counter-terror authorities. Throughout this period, Bush received dire warnings of possible al Qaeda plots involving the use of biological, chemical, or nuclear weapons. The prospect of a second wave of attacks weighed heavy and seemed validated by a series of anthrax-laced letters in the US postal system that fall. The initial, essentially reactive phase of the US response to the September 11 attacks was followed by swift and surprising success in Afghanistan, where a combination of US special operations forces, rebel fighters, and precision airstrikes routed the Taliban from all major cities by early December 2001.

In the months that followed, Bush used a series of speeches to explore the larger meaning of the global war on terror. These remarks would shape the administration's national security strategy, which would be primarily drafted by National Security Advisor Condoleezza Rice and Philip Zelikow, an academic and former colleague of Rice's during the George H.W. Bush administration. The thrust of these remarks, as well as the strategy that was released in September 2002, would both reflect and extend strategic concepts expressed by previous administrations.

First, Bush's rhetoric picked up concepts like the "zone of freedom" and "democratic enlargement" and took them into overdrive. He argued in December 2001 that the "vast majority of countries are now on the same side of a moral and ideological divide" as "a new threat to civilization is erasing old lines of rivalry and resentment between nations."[44] The National Security Strategy

43. George W. Bush, "Second Inaugural Address," January 20, 2005, available at https://georgewbush-whitehouse.archives.gov/news/releases/2005/01/20050120-1.html.

44. "Bush's Speech at the Citadel," *New York Times*, December 11, 2001.

would strike an even more epochal tone, arguing that "the international community has the best chance since the rise of the nation-state in the seventeenth century to build a world where the great powers compete in peace instead of continually prepare for war," as they were "united by common dangers of terrorist violence and chaos."[45] Bush would often be criticized for the Manichean nature of such pronouncements as "you are either with us, or you are with the terrorists," but he also offered the millenarian hope that great power relations would ascend to a new era of cooperation.

Second, Bush famously described North Korea, Iran, and Iraq as comprising an "axis of evil" that supported terror and sought weapons of mass destruction, warning that "America will not allow the world's most dangerous regimes to threaten us with the world's most destructive weapons."[46] The National Security Strategy expanded on Bush's rhetoric and described the circumstances under which preemptive military action would be legitimate in the future. It noted the need to "adapt the concept of imminent threat to the capabilities and objectives of today's adversaries," when "[r]ogue states and terrorists do not seek to attack us using conventional means." Under these circumstances, where "the enemies of civilization openly and actively seek the world's most destructive technologies, the United States cannot remain idle while dangers gather." Instead, the United States resolved "to act alone, if necessary, to exercise our right to self-defense by acting preemptively against such terrorists, to prevent them from doing harm against our people and our country."[47]

Third, Bush called for a "a peace that favors human liberty," a phrase that would reemerge in the National Security Strategy as a "balance of power that favors freedom," and eventually form the central theme of Bush's second inaugural address.[48] To achieve this end, the United States would maintain a military strong enough "to dissuade potential adversaries from pursuing a military build-up in hopes of surpassing, or equaling, the power of the United States."

45. George Bush, *The National Security Strategy of the United States* (Washington, DC: The White House, 2002), ii.

46. The White House, "President Delivers State of the Union Address," January 29, 2002, available at https://georgewbush-whitehouse.archives.gov/news/releases/2002/01/print/20020129-11.html.

47. Bush, *National Security Strategy*, 6, 15.

48. The White House, "President Bush Delivers Graduation Speech at West Point," June 1, 2002, available at https://georgewbush-whitehouse.archives.gov/news/releases/2002/06/20020601-3.html; Bush, *National Security Strategy*, iii.

As Bush had said at West Point during the summer of 2002, "America has, and intends to keep, strengths beyond challenge."[49]

Secretary of Defense Donald Rumsfeld was tasked with maintaining those strengths. Rumsfeld sought to implement Bush's campaign promise to "transform" the military by making it more "agile, lethal, rapidly deployable, and requir[ing] a minimum of logistical support." These proposals were an outgrowth of efforts to discern the lessons of the Gulf War a decade before and to maximize the benefits that US military technology afforded, particularly given advances in networking and precision munitions since that conflict. The Quadrennial Defense Review, completed in September 2001, emphasized the transformation agenda. Reflecting renewed optimism about American military might, the 2001 QDR had adopted the two-MRC force-sizing construct to not just defeat aggression in overlapping major conflicts but also to preserve the option for a decisive victory through "regime change or occupation."[50]

Victory in Afghanistan put a fine point on the prospects for future military operations. A combination of special operators on horseback and precision bombs had vanquished Taliban forces in the opening phases of the war. Although US-backed Afghan forces had failed to capture al Qaeda leader Osama bin Laden in late 2001, Afghanistan seemed surprisingly stable in the new year, with a minimal US footprint on the ground. As the Bush administration turned its gaze from Afghanistan to Iraq in 2001–2, the Afghan conflict suggested that it might be possible to achieve similar success without requiring the kind of large-scale commitment of troops as seen in the Persian Gulf War or a large-scale occupation to follow.

The invasion of Iraq in March 2003 put these hopes to the test. In just over a month, the invasion achieved the overthrow of the regime of Saddam Hussein. The conflict swiftly turned into a simmering guerilla campaign over the summer of that year, however, as former supporters of Saddam's regime launched an insurgent campaign against US forces, receiving support from Islamist fighters who flowed into the country. In early 2006, Iraq descended into a state of near civil war following the bombing of the al-Askari Mosque by Sunni extremists. US forces appeared incapable of mitigating, let alone solving, the sectarian bloodletting that was taking place in the country.

---

49. The White House, "President Bush Delivers Graduation Speech at West Point."

50. Donald Rumsfeld, *Quadrennial Defense Review Report* (Washington, DC: Department of Defense, 2001), 17.

The successful invasions of Afghanistan and Iraq had demonstrated that the United States was in a position to carry out Bush's National Security Strategy, but the wars themselves soon proved treacherous to its ambitions. As insurgencies bloomed in both conflicts, they would consume US deployments at a far greater rate than anything seen during the height of Clintonian activism in the preceding decade. Moreover, the Pentagon sought to use wartime budget growth to pursue ambitious modernization programs like the Army's "Future Combat Systems," but ultimately failed in the mid-2000s to either fund transformation or deliver urgently needed capabilities to forces in the Middle East. Robert Gates, who took over from Rumsfeld at the Pentagon in December 2006, would argue that this failure resulted from the military services' "preoccupation with planning, equipping, and training for future major wars with other nation-states, while assigning lesser priority to current conflicts and all other forms of conflict."[51]

Faced with a growing Iraq disaster in the winter of 2006–7, Bush made a series of decisions that would turn the war around, but at a high cost. Having been advised by members of his own party, the expert Iraq Study Group, and others to begin a drawdown of American forces from Iraq, Bush instead decided to "surge" more than 20,000 troops to the country in January 2007. This decision was informed by a combination of White House staff, outside experts such as retired General Jack Keane and Fred Kagan of the American Enterprise Institute, and officers in the theater who had adapted to the need to protect Iraqi civilians from the violence that was consuming their country. The result of these efforts was a dramatic reduction in violent attacks from the summer through the fall of 2007, which seemingly paved the way for a responsible transition to local governance and security.

The surge strategy saved the war, but the conflict in Iraq exacted a heavy toll across Bush's larger agenda. With an overwhelming share of military forces committed to the Iraq War, the president was compelled to pursue a degree of rapprochement in other critical theaters. North Korea was placated through a series of "Six Party Talks" in the period 2005–7. Though Iran would play a major role in supporting anti-American attacks throughout the Iraq War, as well as resume uranium enrichment, the administration did not offer any meaningful response. After learning that Syria was building an undeclared nuclear reactor with North Korean assistance in mid-2007, the administration demurred and allowed Israel to strike it instead. In August 2008, Russia

51. Robert M. Gates, *Duty: Memoirs of a Secretary at War* (New York, NY: Alfred A Knopf, 2014), 142.

invaded and partially dismembered Georgia. All the while, the situation in Afghanistan deteriorated, as the Taliban insurgency gained renewed strength. For all its ambition, the Bush strategy ultimately revealed the limitations of American power in the post-Cold War period.

V

Unlike like his predecessors in the post-Cold War period, Barack Obama campaigned with an emphasis on foreign policy amidst the ongoing Middle East conflicts. He had first achieved prominence when, as an Illinois state senator, he spoke at an anti-war rally in fall 2002, rejecting what he called "a rash war . . . based not on reason but on passion, not on principle but on politics." On the stump, he pledged to swiftly withdraw US forces from Iraq and focus instead on the conflict in Afghanistan, which he called "a war that we have to win."[52]

Obama's approach to the world was shaped by his view that the United States was dangerously overextended, especially following the 2008 financial crisis. He sought to improve US standing in the world through a program that paired engagement and retrenchment—improving relations with allies, making overtures to adversaries, and disentangling from the conflicts in the Middle East. Through a series of speeches on nuclear nonproliferation in Prague, on relations with the Arab world in Cairo, and on the US role in the world in Oslo, Obama sought to achieve a "new beginning" for the United States. He also believed that retrenchment from the Middle East would prepare the United States for the greater challenges, such as maintaining a constructive relationship with China even as Beijing's continued growth whetted its appetite for a more pronounced global role. In the early going of his presidency, Obama's agenda would be challenged on three major fronts.

First, through most of 2009, the president and his advisors debated how to implement his campaign pledge to resuscitate American efforts in Afghanistan. The previous year had seen the bloodiest fighting in the conflict's history, with every indication that neither the Afghan government nor the current scale of the American commitment were likely to reverse that trend. Informed by the success of the surge in Iraq, senior military advisors like Generals David Petraeus and Stanley McChrystal, the latter of whom Obama appointed to command the Afghan effort at the begin of the year, recommended a large-scale deployment suitable to

---

52. Barack Obama, *The Audacity of Hope: Thoughts on Reclaiming the American Dream* (New York, NY: Crown, 2006), 294.

a long-term, population-centric counterinsurgency campaign. Throughout the policy debate, however, Obama increasingly emphasized his desire for a near-term exit strategy, which he had established by the time of his announcement in December 2009 that the 30,000 troops surged to Afghanistan would begin to draw down after eighteen months. "I want the Afghan people to understand," Obama said, "America seeks an end to this era of war and suffering."[53] The outcome of the Afghan policy debate reflected Obama's growing commitment to retrenching America's global position, as reflected by Robert Gates's summary, "Obama simply wanted the 'bad' war in Iraq to be ended and, once in office, the US role in Afghanistan— the so-called good war—to be limited in scope [and] in duration."[54]

Second, in early 2011, widespread civil unrest in the Middle East presented Obama with a range of opportunities and crises. The swift downfall of Tunisia's Zine El Abidine Ben Ali and Egypt's Hosni Mubarak in January and February, respectively, offered the hope of a wave of "Arab Spring" of democratization in the region. Instead, an uprising against Libyan dictator Muammar al-Qaddafi swiftly turned violent. By mid-March, Qaddafi's forces were engaged in a bloody siege of Misrata and were bearing down on Benghazi, promising "no mercy" for the inhabitants of the country's second largest city. As Congress and European allies pressed for intervention, Obama devised a response that would meet his long-standing view that "it will almost always be in our strategic interest to act multilaterally rather than unilaterally" and that backing from the United Nations was a "force multiplier" for the United States.[55] The United States, joined by a combination of NATO and Arab partners, would conduct an air offensive that would halt Qaddafi's advance on Benghazi and other cities, before handing over primary responsibility for military operations in Libya to its partners. Just over a week after the operation began, Obama announced that "the lead in enforcing the no-fly zone and protecting civilians on the ground" had transitioned and that the United States would continue to provide the coalition with enabling capabilities such as intelligence.[56] The president's approach in Libya was dubbed by an anonymous staffer as "leading from behind," a term that Obama despised and that would become a common refrain of his critics.

53. Barak Obama, "The New Way Forward," December 1, 2009, available at https://obamawhitehouse.archives.gov/blog/2009/12/01/new-way-forward-presidents-address.

54. Gates, *Duty*, 569.

55. Obama, *The Audacity of Hope*, 310.

56. Barack Obama, "Remarks by the President to Address the Nation on Libya," March 28, 2011, available at https://obamawhitehouse.archives.gov/the-press-office/2011/03/28/remarks-President-address-nation-libya.

Third, the Obama administration trimmed future-oriented programs from the defense budget in a move that was followed by the far deeper cuts that resulted from the Budget Control Act of 2011 and sequestration. Dissatisfied with how the Pentagon balanced between investing for future, prospective state-on-state conflict and the ongoing irregular wars, between 2010 and 2011, Secretary Gates proposed the termination or curtailment of some thirty programs and identified $100 billion in proposed savings across the Defense Department.[57] He noted with satisfaction that the 2010 Quadrennial Defense Review placed "current conflicts at the top of our budgeting, policy, and program priorities," accepting additional risk against traditional challenges. Still, these initial steps paled in comparison to the draconian cuts required by the Budget Control Act (BCA). The sequestration provisions of the BCA would require $1 trillion in defense cuts over the course of a decade, a burden intended to be so unacceptable that Congress would be compelled to develop a prudent, alternative fiscal path. Congress failed, the sequestration cuts came into effect, and the military was forced to dramatically curtail training, maintenance, and programs while a series of stopgap bills were passed to allow temporary reprieves against BCA provisions.

The culminating influence of these three events led to the clearest official statement of US strategy during the Obama years—the 2012 Defense Strategic Review. Facing the reality of BCA-mandated defense cuts and in the wake of the withdrawal from Iraq in December 2011 and the drawdown from Afghanistan starting in June 2011, Obama stated that he sought to "clarify our interests in a fast-changing world." The policy described new priorities, including the need to focus on "the security and prosperity of the Asia Pacific," the view that the US posture in Europe should "evolve" now that "[m]ost European countries are now producers of security rather than consumers of it," and the determination that "U.S. forces will no longer be sized to conduct large-scale, prolonged stability operations."[58] In an era in which "the tide of war is receding," the review held, the United States would now be in a position to "focus on nation building at home," as Obama had declared the previous summer.[59]

57. Robert Gates, "Address at the American Enterprise Institute," May 24, 2011, available at https://www.americanrhetoric.com/speeches/robertgatesamericanenterpriseinstitute.htm.

58. Barack Obama, *Sustaining U.S. Global Leadership: Priorities for 21st Century Defense* (Washington, DC: Department of Defense, 2012), i-6.

59. Barack Obama, "Remarks by the President on the Way Forward in Afghanistan," June 22, 2011, https://obamawhitehouse.archives.gov/the-press-office/2011/06/22/remarks-president-way-forward-Afghanistan.

The Defense Strategic Review also had implications for the two long-standing questions that had shaped post-Cold War defense policy: the Pentagon's force-sizing concept and its readiness for a great power challenger. Although the document did not directly address the two-MRC construct, the decision to downsize land forces effectively conceded that the United States could not undertake one decisive campaign against a regional power, let alone two. Meanwhile, the shift in emphasis towards using sea and air power to deter China indicated a continued hope that future technology, rather than force size, would position the United States to defeat a revisionist competitor. Towards the end of the Obama administration, the "third offset strategy" developed by Deputy Secretary of Defense Bob Work would seek to build out the range of concepts and capabilities that such programs could provide, even in a period of reduced funding.[60]

As much as Obama wanted to pivot American energies from the Middle East, the escalating civil war in Syria forced the region back onto the agenda. Since early 2011, Bashar al-Assad had followed a deliberate strategy of gradual escalation against the Syrian people through two years of conflict. The means of Assad's violence escalated from the introduction of artillery, aerial bombardment, and Scud missiles in 2011 and 2012. The Assad regime began to employ chemical weapons in attacks throughout the spring of 2013, one year after Obama first warned that a "red line" for him would be if he saw "a whole bunch of chemical weapons moving around or being utilized."[61] When Assad's escalation culminatd in the Ghouta attack in August 2013, which claimed nearly 1,500 lives, Obama set in motion a plan to respond with retaliatory strikes against the Assad regime, with Secretary of State John Kerry tasked with making the primary argument for action. On August 31, however, the president swiftly changed tack, announcing that he would not act without congressional authorization.[62] As Congress debated the merits of action, Russia's Vladimir Putin swept in with a solution and brokered an agreement with Assad to voluntary surrender his chemical weapons stockpile.

60. Gian Gentile et al., *A History of the Third Offset: 2014–2018* (Santa Monica, CA: RAND, 2021), 33–40.

61. "Remarks by the President to the White House Press Corps," August 20, 2012, https://obamawhitehouse.archives.gov/the-press-office/2012/08/20/remarks-president-white-house-press-corps; "Government Assessment of the Syrian Government's Use of Chemical Weapons on August 21, 2013," https://obamawhitehouse.archives.gov/the-press-office/2013/08/30/government-assessment-syrian-government-s-use-chemical-weapons-august-21.

62. For Kerry's argument, see "Full Transcript: Secretary of State John Kerry's Remarks on Syria," *Washington Post*, August 30, 2013. For Obama's announcement, see "Statement by the President on Syria," August 31, 2013, https://obamawhitehouse.archives.gov/the-press-office/2013/08/31/statement-president-syria.

The Syria crisis would provide a defining view of the Obama national security strategy. Obama would later state that he was "very proud" of his handling of the crisis, which allowed him to break with the "playbook that comes out of the foreign-policy establishment."[63] Yet the denouement of the Syrian crisis seemed to open the flood gates to new challenges around the globe from state and non-state actors, alike.

Following a popular revolution against Ukrainian strongman Viktor Yanukovych in the spring of 2014, Russia invaded Ukraine and annexed the Crimea, starting a conflict that would last beyond the Obama presidency. That summer, the Islamic State of Iraq and Syria, a terrorist organization that was incubated by the civil war in Syria and exploited Iraqi instability following America's withdrawal, conquered much of northern Iraq and established a "caliphate" with its capital in Kabul. China also embarked on its large-scale island-building campaign in the South China Sea in 2014, literally creating new territory in disputed waters that it promptly militarized during Obama's final years. In response, the Obama administration coordinated sanctions on Moscow, deployed additional forces to Europe under the European Reassurance Initiative, launched new deployments to Syria and Iraq to fight ISIS, and initiated freedom of navigation operations in the South China Sea to contest China's growing territorial claims. Each move reflected Obama's rueful observation in the summer of 2014 that "it's harder to end wars than it is to begin them."[64]

Like its predecessor, the Obama administration pursued a bold theory of how the United States should exercise power in the world. Also like its predecessor, it was largely disappointed by the results. Obama left his successors a combination of crises and renewed great power competition.

VI

When Charles Krauthammer observed the dawning of the "unipolar moment," he also had the courtesy to describe the era's inevitable end when "the world will, in structure, resemble the pre-World War I era."[65] In many ways, Krauthammer's warning appeared to anticipate the world that would await the administrations of Donald Trump and Joseph Biden.

63. Jeffrey Goldberg, "The Obama Doctrine," *The Atlantic*, April 2016, https://www.theatlantic.com/magazine/archive/2016/04/the-obama-doctrine/471525/.

64. "Statement by the President on Afghanistan," May 27, 2014, https://obamawhitehouse.archives.gov/the-press-office/2014/05/27/statement-president-afghanistan.

65. Krauthammer, "The Unipolar Moment," 24.

Trump's December 2017 National Security Strategy recognized the "growing political, economic, and military competitions" the United States faced as a result of China and Russia's "challenge to American power," the determination of North Korea and Iran to "destabilize regions," and the efforts of terrorist and transnational criminal organizations to "harm Americans." Faced with "shrinking" advantages, the United States would require "sustained national commitment and attention" to meet these long-term challenges.[66] Released one month later, the 2018 National Defense Strategy likewise identified "the reemergence of long-term, strategic competition" by revisionist powers as the central challenge to US prosperity and security.[67] Despite his many differences with his immediate predecessor, Biden's March 2021 Interim National Security Strategic Guidance likewise pledged that the United States would be placed to "prevail in strategic competition with China or any other nation."[68]

Though the reemergence of great power competition marked the conclusion of the unipolar moment, the period left several lasting legacies. First, from 1989–2014, the United States sustained and expanded the "zone of freedom" that emerged victorious at the end of the Cold War. This was no small victory and left the West in as strong a position as could be hoped for at the dawn of a new era of competition. The efforts toward "enlargement," directed toward Russia and China, or through nation-building and occupation in the Middle East and the "backlash states," proved far less successful.

Second, the United States never settled on an appropriately sized military force for the scale of the challenges that it would face throughout the unipolar moment. The Base Force that emerged from the George H.W. Bush administration would bear, with modest adjustments, the weight of countless deployments, years-long conflicts, and the presence and shaping missions that were demanded of it by subsequent administrations. Throughout this quarter-century period, the Defense Department was forced to weigh trade-offs between force structure and modernization, failing to satisfy either imperative.

Third, the "reconstitution" strategy developed by the George H.W. Bush administration did not long outlast it. Rather, subsequent administrations

---

66. Donald Trump, *National Security Strategy of the United States of America*, December 2017, https://trumpwhitehouse.archives.gov/wp-content/uploads/2017/12/NSS-Final-12-18-2017-0905.pdf.

67. James Mattis, *Summary of the 2018 National Defense Strategy*, January 2018, https://dod.defense.gov/Portals/1/Documents/pubs/2018-National-Defense-Strategy-Summary.pdf.

68. Joseph R. Biden, *Interim National Security Strategic Guidance*, March 2021, https://www.whitehouse.gov/wp-content/uploads/2021/03/NSC-1v2.pdf.

placed their hope on the prospect of a revolution in military affairs, skipping a generation of weaponry, or a third offset to maintain US military overmatch. Many of the most ambitious modernization programs withered on the vine, while almost none matched the ambitions of the Pentagon. Meanwhile, America's adversaries studied US military operations to identify vulnerabilities that they could exploit in their modernization programs. The crises that marked the late Obama administration were as clear an indication to pursue a "reconstitution" policy as any to date, but the United States lacked both the budget and the programs in place to carry it out. In the unipolar era, the persistent gap between America's strategy and its resources had been problematic but manageable. In the far more contested world that emerged as that era ended, strategic insolvency threatened to carry a far higher price.

CHAPTER 36

The Two Marshals

NIKOLAI OGARKOV, ANDREW MARSHALL, AND THE REVOLUTION IN MILITARY AFFAIRS

Dmitry (Dima) Adamsky

Marshal is the most senior general officer rank. Requirements for promotion to this highest rank have varied over history and militaries, with one commonality—nomination typically has required some exceptional professional achievement. Allegorically speaking, this chapter explores the major contributions of two marshals of modern strategic thought—Marshal Nikolai Ogarkov, Chief of the Soviet General Staff (1977–84), and Andrew "Andy" Marshall, Director of the Office of Net Assessment in the Department of Defense (1973–2015). Ogarkov and Marshall came from opposing camps of the Cold War, but both dealt with one of the central concepts of modern strategy—the notion of revolution in military affairs, which would become a central feature in debates on the post-Cold War world. This chapter explores the impact of these two defense intellectuals, one Soviet and the other American, on conceptualizing and popularizing the concept of revolution in military affairs, as well as its practical and theoretical ramifications for academic communities and defense establishments worldwide.

By word and deed, Ogarkov and Marshall shaped the way professional circles today contemplate and execute military innovations. Arguably, individually and together, they stand behind three major concepts of the contemporary theory and practice of strategy.

First, both played a leading role in refining the notion of revolution in military affairs as an applied concept in the professional security lexicon and modern military thought. Second, Ogarkov and Marshall were pioneers in drawing the contours of modern warfare and the principles of operational art associated with it. Both defense intellectuals were leading figures in popularizing the two concepts that epitomize the ideal type of the present-day military machine: the reconnaissance-strike complex and network-centric warfare. Both ideas hold significant currency in modern military organizations and inform the primary logic behind force buildup, organizational structures, and concepts of operations worldwide. Finally, Ogarkov and Marshall were the intellectual fathers of the military innovations framework as an academic discipline and as an applied planning tool. This analytical lens, which derived from the ideas of military-technological revolution and revolution in military affairs, is used to explore the responses of defense establishments to the changing character of war.

The following sections unpack the above arguments. Additionally, this essay elaborates on two other conceptual legacies associated with Marshall and Ogarkov—the notions of competitive strategy and cross-domain coercion. By examining the two characters most closely associated with these ideas, this chapter offers an intellectual history of two of the main themes in modern strategy. If the influence of Ogarkov and Marshall is commonly accepted by defense scholars, this chapter uses the existing literature, as well as new sources and insights, to demonstrate the outsized influence these intellectuals had on contemporary military theory and practice.[1]

---

1. For examples see, Stephen Blank and Richard Weitz, *The Russian Military Today and Tomorrow: Essays in Memory of Mary Fitzgerald* (Carlisle Barracks, PA: US Army War College, 2010); Stephen Blank and Jacob Kipp, *The Soviet Military and the Future* (Westport, CT: Greenwood Press, 1992); Andrei Kokoshin, "Revoliutsiia v Voenom Dele I Problemy Sozdaniia Sovremennykh Vooruzhennykh Sil Rossii," *Mezhdunarodnye Otnosheniia I Mirovaia Politika* 25:1 (2009); Stephen Peter Rosen, "The Impact of the Office of Net Assessment on the American Military in the Matter of the Revolution in Military Affairs," *Journal of Strategic Studies* 33:4 (2010): 469–82; Andrea Gilli, "Net Assessment: Competition is for Losers," *NATO Defense College Policy Brief* 9 (May 2021); Niccolo Petrelli, "NATO, Strategy and Net Assessment," *NATO Defense College Policy Brief* 10 (May 2021); Andrew Krepinevich and Barry Watts, *The Last Warrior: Andrew Marshall and the Shaping of Modern American Defense Strategy* (New York, NY: Basic Books, 2015); Thomas Mahnken, ed., *Net Assessment and Military Strategy: Retrospective and Prospective Essays* (New York, NY: Cambria Press, 2020). See also Dmitry (Dima) Adamsky, "Through the Looking Glass: The Soviet Military-Technical Revolution and the American Revolution in Military Affairs," *Journal of Strategic Studies* 31:2 (2008): 257–94; Adamsky, *The Culture of Military Innovation: The Impact of Cultural Factors on the Revolution in Military Affairs in the U.S. Russia and Israel* (Stanford, CA: Stanford University Press, 2010); Adamsky, "The Art of Net Assessment and Uncovering Foreign Military Innovations: Learning from Andrew W. Marshall's Legacy," *Journal of Strategic Studies* 43:5 (2020): 611–44.

I

Revolution in military affairs (RMA) is a major military innovation in which new organizational structures, together with novel concepts of operations, usually but not always driven by new weaponry, change the conduct of warfare. While most revolutions are shaped by technological advances, more than such breakthroughs is required. RMA implies profound and multidimensional change in weapons, doctrine, organizational structures, and the culture of command and control that swiftly renders traditional forms of conflict obsolete.[2] Though technological advances are often necessary, RMA involves synergy among systems, doctrine, and organizational developments.[3]

Since the 1990s, international security experts and defense policy practitioners have been using the term "RMA" as a generic frame of reference for the changing character of war. To specify the innovation that has been unfolding since the end of the twentieth century and to indicate its scientific catalyst, experts have used the phrase information technology revolution in military affairs (IT-RMA). This relates to the transformation of contemporary conventional warfare brought on by the integration of precision-guided munitions with command, control, communications, and computers, as well as with a variety of reconnaissance, surveillance, and target acquisition systems.

In operational terms, IT-RMA has produced the means to strike with accuracy despite range, to penetrate defenses by stealth and using unmanned systems, and to communicate horizontally and vertically in order to exploit the impact of joint force.[4] Maneuvering on fronts with discernible lines and rear areas has become obsolete, and the number of platforms less important than the networks integrating them; fire projection has replaced massive maneuvering; sensor-to-shooter loops have been shortened; standoff and air power capabilities substitute for heavy ground units; small mobile forces operate over longer ranges with greater precision and lethality; and combat

---

2. Andrew W. Marshall, statement before the Subcommittee on Acquisition and Technology of the Senate Armed Services Committee, 104th Congress, Congressional Record (Washington, DC: US Government Printing Office, 1995); Max Boot, *War Made New: Technology, Warfare and the Course of History, 1500 to Today* (New York, NY: Gotham Books, 2006).

3. Barry D. Watts, *What Is the Revolution in Military Affairs?* (Arlington, VA: Northrop Grumman Analysis Center, 1995); Theodor W. Galdi, *Revolution in Military Affairs? Competing Concepts, Organizational Responses, Outstanding Issues* (Washington, DC: Congressional Research Service, 1995).

4. Michael G. Vickers and Robert C. Martinage, *The Revolution in War* (Washington, DC: Center for Strategic and Budgetary Assessments, 2004), 7.

planning aims at particular effects instead of attrition or the occupation of territory.[5] The origins of IT-RMA go back to the Cold War competition of learning in which the Soviet Union and US engaged, when the first generation of standoff, precision-guided munitions was introduced. Marshal Nikolai Ogarkov, then Chief of the Soviet General Staff, and Andrew W. Marshall, then Director of the Office of Net Assessment in the Pentagon, are the two individuals most closely identified with these concepts.

The inception of these notions and their post-Cold War diffusion worldwide came about in three steps. The first was the US "offset strategy" that produced the technological starting point for the innovation. During the 1970s, NATO began to contemplate employing qualitative technological advantages to neutralize the Warsaw Pact's overwhelming conventional quantitative superiority. The development of microprocessors, computers, lasers, and electronics enabled the production of smart weapons—land-, air-, and sea-launched precision-guided munitions, terminally guided to targets at standoff ranges through command, control, and automated reconnaissance and target acquisition systems. Deep over-horizon strikes, made possible by the novel technology, could break an enemy assault effectively without crossing the nuclear threshold. The concept was known as "Air-Land Battle" in the US and as "Follow-On Forces Attack" in NATO.[6] In theory, it was aimed at enabling the US and NATO to break a prospective Soviet conventional assault without crossing the nuclear threshold.

Initially, the offset strategy offered little more than the retention of a technological edge, and it did not alter the American paradigm of warfare. Scholars who have explored this historical episode argue that the US military developed technology and weaponry for nearly a decade without realizing its revolutionary implications. The techno-tactical focus of the majority of US defense analysts prevented them from recognizing anything of a revolutionary nature in this deep strike capability.[7]

Then came the Soviet input which characterized the innovation under scrutiny as revolutionary and offered a novel paradigm regarding the character of war. Historiography on both sides of the Atlantic associates this episode with Ogarkov, then Chief of the Soviet General Staff.

5. Eliot A. Cohen, "Change and Transformation in Military Affairs," *Journal of Strategic Studies* 27:3 (2004): 397–405.

6. Robert R. Tomes, *U.S. Defense Strategy from Vietnam to Operation Iraqi Freedom: Military Innovation and the New American War of War, 1973–2003* (New York, NY: Routledge, 2007).

7. MacGregor Knox and Williamson Murray, *The Dynamics of Military Revolution, 1300–2050* (Cambridge: Cambridge University Press, 2001).

Although the United States had laid the technological groundwork, it was Soviet rather than American theorists who considered the long-term consequences and multidimensional ramifications of this development. Beginning in the late-1970s, the Soviet military brass had followed closely what was happening in the US, particularly regarding weapons research, developments, and procurement driven by information technologies and related to Air-Land Battle and Follow-on Forces Attack. Their scrutiny of the Western military innovations led the Soviets to the conclusion that a discontinuity in the character of war might be emerging. In contrast to the West, which was focused on the narrow implications of the new weapons systems for a future war in Europe, the Soviets grasped this phenomenon as a "revolution in military affairs" or a "military technological revolution" (two terms that the Soviet scientific lexicon used interchangeably), and produced a large body of theoretical literature on the matter. In his programmatic professional articles, books, and internal documents, Ogarkov consistently argued that the recent developments could be a harbinger of a major change in military affairs and that information technology had begun revolutionizing warfare.[8]

Following Ogarkov's direction to uncover the concrete ramifications of this development for strategy and operations, there was a wave of intellectual activity within the Soviet military. By the mid-1980s, a significant corpus of insights on this matter and a relatively coherent picture of future war in the informational era was at the disposal of the Soviet defense establishment. Thus, without developing new weaponry or possessing advanced technologies, the Soviets were responsible for the seminal literature on how the military technical revolution has been changing the character of war. The Soviet theoreticians harnessed the technological superiority of the West as their point of departure in conceptualizing the innovation, predating by nearly a decade NATO efforts to think systematically about the same theme.[9] However, political, cultural, technological, and economic obstacles prevented the Soviet armed forces from bridging the gap between an idealized vision of military technological revolution and the actual capacity to realize it. It was not until the Russian operation in Syria, on which more momentarily, that Ogarkov's theory of victory would materialize in the Russian military.

Finally, the US acknowledged the emerging RMA and turned it into the linchpin of its defense transformation during the 1990s and 2000s. This

8. Adamsky, "Through the Looking Glass."
9. Adamsky, "Through the Looking Glass."

historic episode is mainly associated with Marshall in his role as Director of the Office of Net Assessment. Scholarship regards Marshall and his staff as among the first within the US defense establishment to acknowledge the accuracy of the Soviet views on the changing character of war and to promote the RMA concept.[10] Russian sources echo this claim, identifying Marshall as the luminary who fully grasped the nature of the Soviet vision and who founded the American version of RMA.[11] The story goes as follows. Towards the end of the Cold War, the insights from the Soviet exploration of the military technological revolution, especially those featuring in the classified professional periodicals, incrementally made their way to the West. There was growing interest in the Soviet vision, which offered a looking glass for US experts. By that time, as in the case of the British experimentation with armor in the mid-1920s, the US military had set the technological foundations for a revolution, but not the conceptual ones.[12]

In the early 1980s, only a small number of defense intellectuals perceived the advent of a major military innovation. Albert Wohlstetter was one of the first prominent figures to realize that the breakthroughs in microelectronics opened new vistas for force employment and political options. Aided by Marshall and a few others, Wohlstetter urged the (generally inert) defense establishment to consider the strategic implications of the growing family of capabilities and to re-conceptualize its vision of warfare.[13] Paradigmatic change began to happen. In 1987 the Commission on Integrated Long-Term Strategy, which Wohlstetter co-chaired with Fred C. Iklé, credited the Soviet Union with understanding the implications of standoff precision-guided munitions, space, stealth, radar, and targeting capabilities for modern warfare, claiming

10. Knox and Murray, *The Dynamics of Military Revolution*, 3.

11. Jacob W. Kipp, "The Russian Military and the Revolution in Military Affairs: A Case of the Oracle of Delphi or Cassandra?," paper delivered at the MORS Conference in Annapolis, Maryland, on June 6–8, 1995; Sergei Modestov, "Serii Kardinal Pentagona Andrew Marshall— ideolog novoi amerikanskoi revoliucii v voennom dele," *Nezavisimoe voennoe obozrenie* 4, December 14, 1995.

12. Knox and Murray, *Dynamics of Military Revolution*, 4; James Der Derian, *Virtuous War* (Boulder, CO: Westview Press, 2001), 29–32.

13. Andrew J. Bacevich, Jr., *The New American Militarism* (Oxford: Oxford University Press, 2005), 161–63; and Stephen Peter Rosen, "Net Assessment as an Analytical Concept," in *On Not Confusing Ourselves*, Andrew W. Marshall, J. J. Martin, and Henry S. Rowen, eds. (Boulder, CO: Westview Press, 1991), 283–84; Albert Wohlstetter, "The Political and Military Aims of Offensive and Defensive Innovation," in *Swords and Shields: NATO, the USSR, and New Choices for Long-Range Offense and Defense*, Fred S. Hoffman, Albert Wohlstetter, and David S. Yost, eds. (Lexington, KY: Lexington Books, 1987).

that the US lagged behind conceptually even as it was pushing ahead technologically.[14]

The Commission charged a working group, co-chaired by Marshall and Charles Wolf, to outline the probable contours of future military competition. The Commission's report stated that the Soviets and the Americans had identified roughly the same technologies—especially highly accurate, long-range systems—as being important for future war. However, the Soviets considered the technologies more systematically and envisioned a more distant future and in greater detail than the American experts. The working group concluded that the Soviets may have been correct in their assessment that the advent of new technologies would revolutionize warfare. If indeed this progression was the case, the transformation could affect some US force structures and command arrangements more profoundly than the introduction of nuclear weapons had nearly half a century earlier.[15]

From the late 1980s, Marshall replaced Wohlstetter as the leading proponent of exploring the emerging security environment. The Office of Net Assessment launched several studies and estimates of the Soviet visions of military technological revolution. The preliminary lessons from the Gulf War relating to the impact of information technologies on the design and execution of military operations further stimulated this research. Even so, the notions of RMA and IT-RMA remained an abstraction until Andrew Marshall and Andrew Krepinevich distributed a memorandum on the subject of military technological revolution.[16] This comprehensive review from 1992 is perhaps the best-known document that the Office of Net Assessment has ever produced. It postulated that Soviet claims since the late 1970s about the character of the emerging military regime had been correct. The net assessment argued that advanced technology, and especially informatics and precision-guided weaponry employed at extended ranges, were taking military art to the level of a revolution in warfare. Together with informational warfare, the assessment identified the reconnaissance-strike as a main feature of future battlefields.[17]

14. Krepinevich, *Military-Technical Revolution*, i–iv.

15. Notra Trulock III, "Emerging Technologies and Future War: A Soviet View," in *The Future Security Environment*, Andrew W. Marshall and Charles Wolf, Jr., eds. (Washington, DC: Department of Defense, October 1988).

16. Knox and Murray, *The Dynamics of Military Revolution*; Der Derian, *Virtuous War*.

17. Andrew W. Marshall, memorandum for the record, "Some Thoughts on Military Revolutions—Second Version," August 23, 1993, Office of Net Assessment, 2–4; Krepinevich, *Military-Technical Revolution*, iii–iv, 5–7; Vickers and Martinage, *Revolution in War*, 10–13;

The conclusions of this net assessment led to the most comprehensive reforms in the US defense establishment since the Vietnam War. Marshall's interest in the future of war and his specific explorations of the impact of information technology on military affairs inspired the "US defense transformation," a buzzword for the American military reform ongoing since the late 1990s. In a nutshell, this reform aimed to transform the US military and defense establishment along the lines of the IT-RMA vision outlined previously—to have an emphasis on accuracy, stealth, jointness, on networks over the platforms, on projection of fires over maneuver of the forces, on shortening sensor-to-shooter loops, on standoff and air power capabilities over heavy ground units, on small mobile forces operating over longer ranges with greater precision and lethality, and on combat effects instead of attrition.

The NATO campaign in Kosovo in 1999 further established the value of the information-era capabilities that the Gulf War had demonstrated. Since the mid-1990s, ideas that arose in the US have spread across the globe and the term "revolution in military affairs" has penetrated the professional lexicon. Operations in Iraq and Afghanistan demonstrated how the US fights the wars of the IT-RMA era.[18] As of this writing, the terms "RMA" and "IT-RMA" seldom feature verbatim in the current US professional discourse. Still, the conceptual legacy and spirit of Marshall's dictums clearly underlies the intent and predisposition of the US defense policy planners, even if not fully realized in ideal fashion.[19]

Michael Horowitz and Stephen Peter Rosen, "Evolution or Revolution?" *Journal of Strategic Studies* 3:6 (2005).

18. Chris C. Demchak, "Creating the Enemy: Global Diffusion of the Information Technology-Based Military Model," in *The Diffusion of Military Technology and Ideas*, Emily Goldman and Leslie Eliason, eds. (Stanford, CA: Stanford University Press, 2003); Keith Shimko, *The Iraq Wars and America's Military Revolution* (Cambridge: Cambridge University Press, 2010). The subsequent counterinsurgency campaigns turned into a fiasco and demonstrated the antithesis—the RMA of the other side. Itai Brun, "While You Are Busy Making Other Plans—The Other RMA," *Journal of Strategic Studies* 33:4 (2010): 535–65. These campaigns also illustrated the limitation of the IT-RMA against hybrid actors and supported the scholarly proposition about the continuity of the character of war in contemporary war. For elaboration, see Stephen Biddle, *Military Power: Explaining Victory and Defeat in Modern Battle* (Princeton, NJ: Princeton University Press, 2006).

19. This is not to argue that Marshall's professional philosophy has been materialized. Critical analysis of the cultural, mental, and organizational proclivities within the US defense establishment, even by those who claim they have been innovating, suggests the opposite. For discussion, see the essays in *Net Assessment and Military Strategy: Retrospective and Prospective Essays*, Mahnken, ed. (2020).

II

At the heart of the Soviet vision of future war on the operational level, which Ogarkov and his disciples promoted, was the notion of reconnaissance-strike complex. In the late 1970s, Soviet military theoreticians, encouraged by the dictum of the Chief of the General Staff to conceptualize the future battlefield in the precision era, introduced the term "reconnaissance-strike complex" to capture the essence of the changing character of war. In a nutshell, the vision argued that, in the information era, militaries would transform into a combined-arms system of systems, which links together intelligence, surveillance, and reconnaissance capabilities, command-and-control ($C2$) systems, and precision standoff fires. In the American concept of "Assault Breaker" and the capabilities associated with it, the Soviet military experts saw a harbinger of this emerging reality. The Soviet lexicon defined this phenomenon at the strategic-operational level as a reconnaissance-strike and at the operational-tactical level as a reconnaissance-fire complex. Air-Land Battle and Follow-on Forces Attack—the NATO innovations then gathering momentum in Europe—stimulated the imagination of the Soviet theoreticians, though these terms had a generic meaning for them, relating equally to one's own as well as to the enemy's battlefield architectures. The Soviet theory envisioned the future of war in the IT-RMA era as a clash of opposing reconnaissance-strike and reconnaissance-fire complexes.[20]

It took almost a decade for the US defense establishment to grasp the Soviet view on the character of military operations, which established the reconnaissance-strike complex as the dominant architecture of warfare.[21] By the early 1980s, the US defense community was already cognizant that the Soviet sources were discussing the development of so-called reconnaissance-strike organizations, out of concern for the threat posed by the comparable adversarial capabilities. (The frame of reference for the Soviets was the US "Assault Breaker" initiative—deep-striking, theater-level capability to engage with precision the follow-on Soviet echelons on the move.) American analysts correctly understood the Soviet vision of reconnaissance-strike organizations as consisting of an integrated triad of intelligence and target acquisition complexes, automated command and control elements, and long-range striking

---

20. Adamsky, *The Culture of Military Innovation*, 2010.

21. Jeffrey S. McKitrick, "The Revolution in Military Affairs," in *Battlefield of the Future: 21st Century Warfare Issues* (Maxwell Air Force Base, AL: Air University Press, 1995); Marshall, "Some Thoughts on Military Revolutions—Second Version."

systems. Further analysis of Soviet doctrine identified the Soviet assumption that the outcome of a future conflict would be determined by massed, conventional, precision-guided strikes and real-time reconnaissance rather than massed armor maneuvering.[22]

During the 1990s, Marshall and his acolytes used the Soviet notion of reconnaissance-strike complex as a starting point for their own contemplation of IT-RMA. The Americans reworked the concept and disseminated their understanding within the US defense establishment. Eventually, following several conceptual experiments, the US discourse came up with its own term to refer to the same phenomenon—network-centric warfare. The Soviet concept of reconnaissance-strike complex was its precursor. In a nutshell, both terms relate to the same system of systems that epitomizes the essence of warfare in the precision era. In the early 2000s, network-centric warfare—the quintessence of war in the information era—became one of the buzzwords associated with the US defense transformation. Since then, its ideal type has inspired and driven military innovations on both sides of the Atlantic, in the Middle East, and in Asia. Even if not all military organizations use these terms, states and non-state actors have been emulating, adopting, and adapting the main principles of operational art, organizational settings, and force buildup associated with the reconnaissance-strike complex and with network-centric warfare.[23]

Eventually, history came full circle. Andrew Marshall adopted the Soviet term reconnaissance-strike complex and used it as a frame of reference in formulating his own vision. The latter eventually metamorphosed into network-centric warfare—the US variation of the theme. This American term and concept then drew major attention in Russian expert circles. This was a concrete and applied interest; from the early 2000s, post-Soviet Russia began to rise from its geopolitical knees and to modernize its armed forces according to the network-centric vision. The Soviet Union, a pioneer in conceptualizing network-centric warfare, never actually materialized it. The post-Soviet reforms headed in this direction, but the flaws, which the Russian war in Georgia highlighted in 2008, were exactly along the axes of the reconnaissance-fire

22. Central Intelligence Agency, "Warsaw Pact Nonnuclear Threat to NATO Airbases in Central Europe," NIE 11/20-6-84, October 25, 1984; "Trends and Developments in Warsaw Pact Theater Forces, 1985–2000," NIE 11-14-85/D, September 1985, 9–13, 29–33; "Trends and Developments in Warsaw Pact Theater Forces and Doctrine Through the 1990s," NIE 11-14-89, February 1989.

23. Dmitry (Dima) Adamsky and Kjell Inge Bjerga, *Contemporary Military Innovations: Between Anticipation and Adaptation* (New York, NY: Routledge, 2012).

complexes: a deficit of precision-guided munitions; a low level of command, control, communications, computers, intelligence, surveillance, and reconnaissance; and a low capacity to wage network-centric combined arms warfare. Roughly since 2008, the Russian armed forces have embarked on a massive modernization comparable in logic and in scale to the US defense transformation, ongoing by then for more than a decade. The aim of this Russian reform has been to advance the conventional military as far as possible towards the ideal reconnaissance-strike complex.

Against the backdrop of this military transformation, the term "network-centric warfare" became part of the Russian professional lexicon, as both a frame of reference and a subject of systematic exploration. In the professional lexicon and discourse, for more than a decade, the term "network-centric warfare" somewhat eclipsed the reconnaissance-strike complex. However, following Russia's operation in Syria, which began in 2015, the Russian official and expert discourse, especially in the professional military periodicals, began to use both terms interchangeably. Similarly, when Western experts renewed their interest in Russian military modernization, they again started paying attention to the discourse on reconnaissance-strike complexes.[24]

The first fruits of the Russian military modernizations, which addressed the previously mentioned deficits of the 2008 war in Georgia, had matured by the time of the Russian intervention in Syria. In the reflections of Russian commentators, we frequently read and hear of the the Syrian operation as the first occasion in which the Russian military fought along the lines of the IT-RMA. The Russian General Staff saw the operation in Syria as a testing ground for almost all types of weapons and services, and more specifically for the use of intelligence, reconnaissance, surveillance, target acquisition, command, control, communications, and strike systems integrated into unified complexes on the operational and tactical levels. Unsurprisingly, the official and expert Russian discourses with regard to Syria are saturated with the terms "reconnaissance-strike" and "reconnaissance-fire complexes."[25]

No evidence is available regarding Ogarkov's and Marshall's take on the command-and-control culture and the procedures that the adoption of reconnaissance-strike complexes and network-centric warfare necessitates.

24. Roger McDermott and Tor Bukkvoll, "Tools of Future Wars—Russia Is Entering the Precision-Strike Regime," *Journal of Slavic Military Studies* 31:2 (2018): 191–213.

25. Russian sources often use the term "contours" instead of "complexes," but the meaning is the same.

One may speculate, however, that both men would have favored mission command and delegation of authority to the lower levels. This combat management style would bring out the maximum potential embodied in this system of systems. In recent years, the Russian Chief of the General Staff Valery Gerasimov has been much like Ogarkov in his recurring demands and prodding of the senior brass to explore the changing character of war. Gerasimov also has actively implemented Ogarkov's visions, refers to his theory of victory, and even uses professional terminology coined by his Soviet predecessor. Specifically, Gerasimov has advocated for the delegation of authority as well as for turning combat formations on the lower levels of command into self-synchronizing autonomous reconnaissance-fire complexes.

One may assume that Andrew Marshall would have been more likely than not to advocate a similar vision, partially reflected in the "power to the edge" vision that accompanied the penchant for network-centric warfare in the US armed forces in the early 2000s. Interestingly, an asymmetry is evident here, even though hypothetically the founding fathers of the concepts are in agreement. While in the Russian military there are indications of the adoption of this style of combat management, which runs counter to certain traditions of the Russian military, practices in the US military are going in a different direction. Evidence suggests that the employment of network-centric warfare and the weapon systems and procedures associated with it more often than not have inclined the US armed forces towards a more centralized style of management and away from the mission command culture.[26]

III

Exploration of the RMA phenomenon has left a significant imprint on the post-Cold War theory and practice of military strategy. This intellectual activity produced new terminology, a novel lexicon, and fresh frameworks of analysis. One of its most prominent byproducts has been the concept of military innovation: a sub-discipline in the strategic studies literature and a framework of reference for defense practitioners. In part, this concept grew out of the American IT-RMA discourse, and in part out of the Soviet approach to military futurology—a discipline in the pantheon of the Soviet-Russian military

---

26. On the evolution of mission command culture in the Western militaries, see Eitan Shamir, *Mission Command: The Pursuit of Mission Command in the U.S., British, and Israeli Armies* (Stanford, CA: Stanford University Press, 2011).

sciences exploring the future of war. One can trace the intellectual sources of the contemporary military innovation scholarship in Western academic circles to Nikolai Ogarkov and to Andrew Marshall.

The Soviet method of thinking about the future of war catalyzed the emergence of Western military innovation scholarship. As we have seen, the Soviet corpus of work on the future of war developed in the 1970s–80s incrementally became a looking glass for Western strategists and military planners during the 1990s. This body of knowledge had an additional impact. While most observers considered the Soviet literature on the military-technological revolution to be evidence of new technologies, Marshall and the experts from the Office of Net Assessment found something else.[27] In addition to knowledge on the emerging military regime, the Soviet insights offered Marshall a glimpse into a generic methodology for systematic thinking about the changing character of war. In particular, the Soviet case exemplified for Marshall the capacity to accurately diagnose, anticipate, and conceptualize the contours of future war (and to do so possessing neither the technology nor the weaponry).

The Soviet military theoreticians analyzed Western technological developments through the unique lenses of "forecasting and foreseeing in military affairs."[28] At that point, Western military thought did not possess an equivalent understanding, comparable in both sophistication and scale of institutionalization, to this sub-discipline of Soviet military science. In a nutshell, this was a method—and no less importantly, an organizational proclivity—to systematically examine new tools of war made possible by scientific-technological progress. The aim of this Soviet inquiry was to qualify the emerging technologies as either evolutionary or revolutionary in terms of weapon systems, concepts of operation, and organizational structures, and then to extrapolate the requirements with regard to force buildup, procurement policies, and doctrinal changes. Ideally, accurately anticipated trends in the future of war should inform the current planning of defense transformation, which the senior military brass initiates. Such examination was not only a traditional intellectual predisposition in Soviet (and Russian) military culture, but also an institutionalized endeavor of the defense bureaucracy, the signs of which are still visible in the post-Cold War era.[29]

---

27. Adamsky, "Through the Looking Glass."

28. *Metodologiia Predvideniia I Prognozirovaniia v Voennom Dele.*

29. The contemporary expression of this military tradition are the repeated calls that the Chief of the Russian General Staff Gerasimov made in his programmatic speeches to explore

The Soviet method of military forecasting and foreseeing in general, and in particular their method of anticipating RMAs, uncovering their ramifications, and figuring out the contours of future battlefields, was multidisciplinary. It combined qualitative and quantitative analytical tools and research practices, ranging from the humanities to the exact sciences. For example, the systematic exploration of military history (for the purpose of distilling generic principles of operations, trends in organizational dynamics, and stimulating hypothesis-generation about the emerging character of war) harmonically coexisted with formal modeling and advanced mathematical techniques.[30] This conceptual-organizational predisposition of the Soviet defense establishment resonated with the American Marshall, who had a long-standing interest in diagnostic analytical tools applicable to the problems of military strategy.

Since his time at the RAND Corporation assessing NATO-Warsaw Pact balances, Marshall had directed research on Soviet military theories, measures of effectiveness, and assessment methodologies. He became convinced that the Soviet approach differed from the common Western practices.[31] Among the main differences Marshall saw were the Soviet stress on revolutionary change (i.e., discontinuity), the deliberate quest to diagnose it, and their practice of studying the past in order to identify emerging dominant forms of warfare. Marshall thought it was reasonable to embrace the notion of discontinuity and the methodologies of diagnosing it. Such a stance, in his view, enabled one to consciously experience a change in the character of war. As Marshall described it:

> Usually, when one is situated in the middle of it, he is least aware of it. However, the earlier the military acknowledges the emergence of the change in the military regime, the more efficient defense management it will generate.[32]

The Soviet military technological revolution literature used the 1920s and 1930s as a frame of reference for pondering the emergence of discontinuity.

---

the changing character of war under the impact of modern technologies and to distill the ramifications for the art of strategy and military operations.

30. This multidisciplinary approach to military epistemology was symptomatic also of the Soviet and then Russian method of examining combat effectiveness and military balances, also known in the Russian lexicon as Correlation of Means and Forces.

31. Mahnken, *Technology and the American War of War*, 74–75; Watts, *What Is the Revolution in Military Affairs?*, 1–2.

32. Adamsky, *The Culture of Military Innovation*.

Similarly, Marshall often referred to the German and British interwar experiences to show that militaries often do not consciously think about revolutions and to encourage defense officials to pose the right questions regarding innovations.[33] The Soviet style also resonated with Marshall in not being technocentric. Emphasizing the long time frame and concentrating on the soft aspects (i.e., organizational cultures, structures, and operational concepts) versus focusing on new technology alone distinguished Marshall's approach from the overall technology-driven mentality of American strategic culture.[34] For Marshall, this was a competition of learning; superior technology was desirable, but the real contest was intellectual—to outperform the competitor in uncovering novel concepts of operation and the appropriate organizational settings for them.[35] Because the term "military revolution" gave too much weight to technology, Marshall and the Office of Net Assessment experts adopted, also from the Soviet lexicon, the term "revolution in military affairs."

Ogarkov, a bureaucrat-intellectual and a paragon of the previously mentioned Soviet approach, left a strong impression on Marshall. When the 1991 Gulf War proved the accuracy of Ogarkov's prognosis and validated the potential of the methods underlying Soviet military futurism, Marshall adapted, adopted, and advanced certain aspects of the Soviet tradition. He began moving and educating the US defense establishment towards adoption of a similar intellectual-bureaucratic predisposition. Marshall started to explore the subject in-depth. Viewing RMA as paradigmatic change, deliberately initiated and managed by the defense establishment, Marshall posed a set of questions: How do military organizations learn and innovate? What were the best and the worst historical practices in this matter? Why do some organizations do better than others in the competition of learning? How does the latter project onto combat effectiveness?

Starting in the early 1990s, the Office of Net Assessment commissioned historical studies to deal with these questions, and in particular to explore

33. This also corresponded with the Net Assessment credo—a focus on strategic diagnosis and not on policy prescription. McKitrick, "Adding to Net Assessment," 119; Williamson Murray, *Emerging Strategic Environment: Challenges of the Twenty-First Century* (Westport, CT: Praeger Publishers, 1999).

34. Watts, *Six Decades*, 77; Watts, *What Is the Revolution in Military Affairs?*, 6; Galdi, *Revolution in Military Affairs*, 9.

35. For framing strategy as a competition of learning between the opponents, see Yossi Baidatz, "Strategy as a Learning Process," *Markaz Middle East Politics and Policy*, November 29, 2016, Brookings Institution.

military innovations during the interwar years. Such outsourcing to academia, especially to historians, was not unprecedented; it carried on an earlier tradition of the Office to examine the distant past in order to better inform thinking about the emerging future. Marshall believed that the disciplined study of applied history could significantly improve one's thinking about the puzzles of defense policy, and of military affairs in particular.[36] Several of his efforts even predated the RMA period. In the 1970s, Marshall assembled several political scientists working with historical models and also military and diplomatic historians from leading American universities to examine how the bureaucracies of different nations in the distant and recent past dealt with estimates of strategic balances—a euphemism for the core mission of the Office of Net Assessment. In terms of the sociology of the field, a by-product of this activity was the emergence of a community of like-minded intellectuals in Western academia pursuing individual research agendas that pointed in a roughly similar direction.[37]

The most relevant predecessor with regard to the effort to explore RMA and military innovations broadly defined was the research into military effectiveness across different nations. This work involved multiple authors, was chaired by Williamson Murray and Alan Millett, and resulted in several volumes of academic publications in the late 1980s.[38] Eventually, it turned into a common practice of cooperation by historians on real-life strategic problems.[39] The successful completion of this project coincided with a spike in Marshall's interest in RMA. The approach replicated itself. Marshall assumed that "history could be useful in thinking about the implications of innovation," and that comparative historical research into particular cases of peacetime innovation could uncover how military organizations undergo paradigmatic change.[40] This time, the main research aim was to explore the technological, conceptual, operational, cultural, and organizational factors

36. Williamson Murray, "Contributions of Military Historians," in *Net Assessment and Military Strategy: Retrospective and Prospective Essays*, Thomas Mahnken, ed. (Amherst, NY: Cambria Press, 2020), 139–55.

37. Murray, "Contributions of Military Historians," in *Net Assessment and Military Strategy*, Mahnken, ed., 142–43.

38. Alan Millett and Williamson Murray, *Military Effectiveness* (Cambridge: Cambridge University Press, 2010), 3 Volumes.

39. Murray, "Contributions of Military Historians," 143–45.

40. Murray, "Contributions of Military Historians," 147.

that had driven and conditioned changes in how militaries envision future war and innovate towards it.[41] The endeavor resulted in a definitive academic text on the subject matter, followed by research that examined the flip side of the phenomenon—the enemy's response and theory of victory when adapting to this uncertainty.[42]

The support offered by the Office of Net Assessment stimulated academics—mainly American and British historians and political scientists—to embark on a systematic exploration of the subject of RMA throughout history.[43] Historical studies that the Office of Net Assessment commissioned found that "military institutions that developed organizational cultures where serious learning, study, and intellectual honesty lay at the heart" of professional preparation were the best equipped for the emerging military regimes. There were two consequences of this knowledge development endeavor. First, within the establishment, Marshall and Krepinevich recommended that institutions assign their best minds to considering future warfare. To that end, during the mid-1990s, the military services took part in roundtables and war-games that the Office of Net Assessment financed and ran.[44] Insights from these activities then informed various trends in the US "defense transformation" in the late 1990s–early 2000s.

In addition, in academia this impulse gave rise to a new discipline—military innovation studies. The discipline became a scholarly companion to the processes ongoing within the communities of practice. The two were interrelated: the research agenda of policy-oriented academic research, once published, produced the basis for the emergence of a new scholarly subfield. Path-breaking works by Stephen Peter Rosen, Murray, Millett, Knox, and Thomas Mahnken, to name just a few, exemplify the initial effort to frame the field and turn it into the academic (and policy-oriented) sub-discipline of

41. For examples, see Barry D. Watts and Williamson Murray, "Military Innovation in Peacetime," in *Military Innovation in the Interwar Period*, Williamson Murray and Allan R. Millett, eds. (New York, NY: Cambridge University Press, 1996), 369–415; Murray, "Contributions of Military Historians," 147; Geoffrey Parker, *The Military Revolution: Military Innovation and the Rise of the West, 1500–1800* (Cambridge: Cambridge University Press, 1988).

42. The definitive academic text is Watts and Murray, "Military Innovation in Peacetime." For the research on the flip side of the phenomenon see, Williamson Murray, *Military Adaptation in War: Fear of Change* (Cambridge: Cambridge University Press, 2011).

43. MacGregor Knox and Williamson Murray, *The Dynamics of Military Revolution, 1300–2050* (Cambridge: Cambridge University Press, 2001).

44. Galdi, *Revolution in Military Affairs?*, 9.

strategic or international security studies.[45] The titles of these works equally reflect the research interest of Marshall at the time, and the key terminology and main directions of the military innovations literature that have remained intact since then. The new field was interdisciplinary from the outset. It brought together international relations and political science scholars specializing in formal modeling and quantitative methods, as well as those employing qualitative, historical, anthropological, and sociological analyses of military organizations and the factors that shape them. Three leading scholarly periodicals—*International Security, Journal of Strategic Studies,* and *Security Studies*—turned into the main venues for military innovation research in Western academia.

The intellectual history of the military innovation literature in the Western strategic studies discipline has yet to be written. As of this writing, in-depth literature reviews by Adam Grissom and Stuart Griffin offer the most detailed accounts of the genealogy of the field.[46] There have been several waves of scholarship since the late 1990s, but not without analytical caveats and methodological challenges. However, the accounts by Grissom and Griffin clearly demonstrate that the topic has evolved beyond the generation of the founding fathers and has been consistently attracting significant numbers of new scholars to the field. Military innovations have become one of the main sub-fields of international security studies and among the most policy-relevant avenues of exploration. The research program of military innovation studies covers both soft and hard aspects of the phenomenon of defense transformations, and is not confined to the exploration of military technologies per se. It has also turned into a framework for uncovering and examining foreign military innovations, RMAs, of the other side. Thus, history came full circle again: Marshall was the conduit for certain postulates of Soviet thinking about the future of war, mainly associated with the Ogarkov era, into Western strategic theory and strategic studies.

45. Stephen Peter Rosen, *Winning the Next War* (Ithaca, NY: Cornell University Press, 2018). For the works of Murray, Millett, and Knox, see the sources previously cited in this chapter. Thomas Mahnken, *Uncovering Ways of War: U.S. Intelligence and Foreign Military Innovation, 1918–1941* (Ithaca, NY: Cornell University Press, 2009).

46. Adam Grissom, "The Future of Military Innovation Studies," *Journal of Strategic Studies* 29:5 (2006): 905–34. Stuart Griffin, "Military Innovation Studies: Multidisciplinary or Lacking Discipline?" *Journal of Strategic Studies* 40:1–2 (2017): 196–224.

IV

In addition to the notions of the RMAs and military innovations, one can trace back to Marshall and Ogarkov two other central concepts of modern strategy: the US idea of competitive strategies and the Russian idea of cross-domain coercion. While these two concepts are not directly related to the notion of military innovation and revolutions in military affairs, both are central to modern strategic thought, and both derive from the research endeavors and intellectual climate stimulated by IT-RMA.

Competitive strategy was one of the core professional products of the Office of Net Assessment, both during and after the Cold War. The concept was constantly polished and adjusted, based on lessons learned from interaction with the Soviet Union over a long time frame. Competitive strategy rests on the insights that net assessment offers. The latter is a term for the modeling of a dynamic and multidimensional competition between strategic antagonists. It is a holistic analytical framework that incorporates all the available social-ideational-cultural-organizational characteristics of both competitors, as well as trends in the strategic environment within which the competition occurs, in order to diagnose the intended and unintended first- and second-order consequences of the interaction over time. Although the goal of net assessment is to produce actionable insights, in essence, it is a diagnostic rather than prescriptive undertaking. The insights of net assessment—also a discipline that Marshall himself continually refined and promoted—are meant to serve as a basis for strategic planning and crafting competitive strategies.[47]

Competitive strategy is a long-lasting peacetime competition where the goal is to shape the opponent's strategic behavior in a way favorable to the initiator of the influence. It aims to maneuver an adversary's strategic investments away from threatening realms and capabilities and thus to produce a favorable correlation of means and forces. Competitive strategy seeks to diagnose and then exploit certain proclivities of the adversary. Analysis of the

---

47. For the central works on the net-assessment analytical technique, on the intellectual history of the Office of Net Assessment, and on Mr. Andrew Marshall's biography and his intellectual legacy, see Mahnken, ed., *Net Assessment and Military Strategy*; Thomas G. Mahnken, ed., *Competitive Strategies for the 21st Century: Theory, History, and Practice* (Stanford, CA: Stanford University Press, 2012); Krepinevich and Watts, *The Last Warrior: Andrew Marshall and the Shaping of the American Defense Strategy* (New York, NY: Basic Books, 2015); Paul Bracken, "Net Assessment: A Practical Guide," *Parameters* 36:1 (2006), 90–100; Philip A. Karber, *Net Assessment for SecDef: Future Implications from Early Formulations* (Washington, DC: Potomac Foundation, 2014).

adversary along the lines of net-assessment methodology makes it possible to highlight the cultural-organizational factors that shape strategic behavior, especially those inclinations which result in suboptimal, self-defeating, and counterproductive actions. In turn, accurate diagnosis of these proclivities can serve as a solid basis for planning how to maximize and exploit them. Competitive strategy is not an occasional undertaking but rather a permanent learning endeavor. It demands the constant identification of competitive advantages in a constantly changing game. It assumes constant assessment of the adversary, of the self, and of the environment within which interaction takes place.[48]

Competitive strategy is predominantly a peacetime endeavor, but it implies the use of military power. Development, acquisition, deployment, and exercising with military forces may shape competitors' choices in ways that favor one's objectives.[49] One of the best exemplars of this strategy in action is the American ability during the late Cold War to divert the allocation of Soviet resources away from offensive capabilities and towards far less threatening, mostly defensive means by building US air power in a certain way. The US strategists made a deliberate decision to produce and deploy new bombers, and by doing so, strengthened those voices within the Soviet defense establishment who argued for further investment in a formidable national air defense system. This shaped the Soviet strategic behavior during the peacetime competition in a way favorable to the US, since it prompted the Kremlin to invest huge funds not in the next generation of threatening offensive nuclear and conventional weapon systems, but in a relatively benign defensive capability. The aim was to impose "the maximum costs the Soviets would be willing to bear to modernize their AD [air defense]," but without forcing them to abandon this mission.[50] As of this writing, policymakers and defense planners continue to employ this analytical model mainly to inform their strategizing in the great power competition and when contemplating grand strategies. Next to RMA, the notion of competitive strategy is most closely associated with Andrew Marshall and the Office of Net Assessment. As of this writing, the concept features in the US national security discourse in reference to the long-term competition with China, Russia, and Iran.

48. Stephen Peter Rosen, "Competitive Strategies: Theoretical Foundations, Limits, and Extension," in *Competitive Strategies*, Manhken, ed.

49. Rosen, "Competitive Strategies."

50. Andrew Krepinevich and Robert Martinage, *Dissuasion Strategy* (Washington, DC: Center for Strategic and Budgetary Assessments, 2008), 15–16.

In turn, Ogarkov relates, albeit indirectly, to another notion of the contemporary Russian art of strategy—cross-domain coercion. This term is a euphemism for the current expression of the Russian art of military strategy. Dubbed "strategic deterrence" in the Russian professional discourse, cross-domain coercion is a form of integrated influence waged across several domains—nuclear, conventional, sub-conventional, and nonmilitary. Regardless of the means that take center stage at any given moment, cross-domain coercion operates under the aegis of the Russian nuclear and conventional arsenals and aims to manipulate the adversary's perception, to maneuver its decision-making process, and to influence its strategic behavior, while minimizing the scale of kinetic force used, at least as compared to the industrial warfare era. Current Russian operational art thus has a nuclear dimension that can only be understood in the context of a holistic coercion campaign, an integrated whole in which conventional, informational, nuclear, and nonmilitary capabilities can all be used in the pursuit of deterrence and compellence.

Ogarkov and his colleagues were most closely associated with the notion of RMA driven by the impact of information technologies. As described previously, they saw future military organizations as reconnaissance-strike complexes consisting of a family of advanced intelligence collection and target acquisition capabilities; formations employing long-range, standoff precision-guided munitions; and automated command, control, and communication systems linking the first two segments together. The Russian strategists envisioned future war as a clash of these complexes, which, as a matter of strategic choice, could be kept nonnuclear. The combat potentials encapsulated in these complexes made it feasible to achieve the political ends of war by nonnuclear means.[51] As compared to Ogarkov's contribution to the Soviet and contemporary Russian military modernizations, his influence on the conceptualization of deterrence has been underexplored.[52] One should not exaggerate and read too much into Ogarkov's writings, but his impact on contemporary Russian thinking on coercion strategy should not be overlooked.

51. Ogarkov promoted three interrelated arguments about the character of future war: that the prowess of advanced conventional RSCs would be comparable to the combat potentials of tactical-operational nuclear weapons; that these complexes blur the dividing line between the offensive and defensive modes of war, thus making this distinction obsolete; and that, on the battlefield, the precision strike into the entire operational-strategic depth underscores the maneuvering of fires and effects rather than of platforms and forces. Adamsky, *Culture of Military Innovation*.

52. The author owes the original idea to Michael Kofman.

Ogarkov's seminal works on a conventional theory of victory in the IT-RMA era provided a conceptual format for Russian thinking on escalation management as well as the relationship between nuclear and nonnuclear operations. One can trace back to Ogarkov the current Russian quest to craft a balanced military consisting of conventional general-purpose forces, capable of generating nonnuclear deterrence, and forces of strategic (nuclear) deterrence—even though the Soviet marshal did argue that the nuclear and conventional domains should be kept separate. Ogarkov was not talking about deterrence, but rather about a nuclear equalizer of conventional inferiority and about non-military forms of influence merged with conventional forces—the themes at the heart of deterrence *à la Russe* today. For the post-Soviet Russian military brass, however, Ogarkov's argument about the conventional reconnaissance–strike complex being comparable, in terms of the effects produced, to tactical-operational nuclear weapons, and thus capable of assuming some of their combat tasks, by extension implied why and how deterrence missions, previously associated only with nuclear capabilities, could extend to conventional weapon systems.[53]

Exploring the Russian approach to deterrence, Michael Kofman has traced the Russian calibrated approach to discrete levels of damage back to Ogarkov, and he may have a point. Ogarkov was turning away from the assumption that prolonged nuclear war is possible and survivable, and promoted instead the notion of a protracted conventional phase of war. He indeed emphasized conventional, entirely nonnuclear, strategic operations in the theater of military operations as one of the characteristics of the then-emerging military regime, and called for, albeit unsuccessfully, making the division between nuclear and conventional war the centerpiece of planning. Kofman took this interpretation of Ogarkov a step further, suggesting that the Soviet marshal saw tactical nuclear weapons as an intermediate escalation management tool in the transition from the conventional to the nuclear phase of war.[54] Research based on primary

---

53. Obviously, Ogarkov rejected limited nuclear war, as there was no conceptual place or empirical need to differentiate between regional and global nuclear engagements (a demand that would emerge in Russia in the 1990s). However, his vision of conventional battle alone achieving the political goals of war, and the notion of the strike into the entire operational-strategic depth without capturing the territory, were precursors to several aspects of modern Russian thinking about the operational art of deterrence. Michael Kofman, "The Ogarkov Reforms: The Soviet Inheritance behind Russia's Military Transformation," *Russian Military Analysis*, July 11, 2019.

54. Kofman, "The Ogarkov Reforms."

sources is required to support or refute this proposition; however, if this premise is correct, contemporary deterrence *à la Russe* should credit Ogarkov even more.

V

This chapter has explored the imprint left by Marshal Nikolai Ogarkov, Chief of the Soviet General Staff, and Andrew W. Marshall, Director of the Office of Net Assessment in the Pentagon, on the making of modern military strategy. Arguably, these two defense intellectuals shaped the way academics and practitioners of strategy today think about military innovations and the future of war. Specifically, Ogarkov and Marshall were the intellectual fathers of such concepts as "revolution in military affairs"—a euphemism for radical change in the character of war—"reconnaissance-strike complex"—a euphemism for the main battlefield architecture of the network-centric warfare era—and "military innovation studies"—a euphemism for the framework of exploration of defense transformations. All three concepts lie at the heart of national security discourse and defense policy worldwide and thus relate directly to the evolution of modern military strategy. The contributions of Marshall and Ogarkov to modern strategic thought go beyond those ideas, however. The notion of competitive strategy is an intellectual legacy of Marshall, and the notion of cross-domain coercion—the current Russian art of strategy—can be traced back to Ograkov. Thus, both men can also be credited with influencing how practitioners on both sides of the Atlantic today approach the operational art of coercion. In addition, the story about the imprint which Marshal and Ogarkov left on modern military thought demonstrates that paradigmatic changes in the way practitioners and theoreticians conceptualize various aspects of strategy often emanate from the competition of learning that crosses geopolitical lines. This intellectual action-reaction between strategic competitors and their cross-fertilization appears as a necessary condition for the emergence of new paradigms in strategic thought.

CHAPTER 37

Strategies of Counterinsurgency and Counter-Terrorism after 9/11

Carter Malkasian

Al-Qaʻedaʼs attacks on New York City and Washington, DC, on September 11, 2001, opened a new chapter in strategic thought. Previously considered a minor irritation, the attacks transformed terrorism into a real threat that presidents and world leaders could not ignore. The day after the attacks, the *New York Times* read:

> Every routine, every habit . . . was fractured yesterday. If a flight full of commuters can be turned into a missile of war, everything is dangerous. If four planes can be taken over simultaneously by suicidal hijackers, then we can never be quite sure again that any bad intention can be thwarted, no matter how irrational or loathsome . . . [it is] one of those moments in which history splits, and we define the world as "before" and "after."[1]

During the next year various Gallup polls showed between 50 percent and 85 percent of Americans worried a terrorist attack on the United States was likely or very likely.[2] The threat persisted over the next decade. Osama bin Laden was at large and new attacks and plots occurred against Europe and the United States.

---

1. Jack Lule, "Myth and Terror on the Editorial Page: The New York Times Responds to September 11, 2001," *Journalism & Mass Communication Quarterly* 79:2 (2002): 281.
2. Gallup, "Terrorism," accessed January 27, 2018, https://news.gallup.com/poll/4909/terrorism-united-states.aspx.

The threat of terrorism and a domestic political backlash to any attacks were a feature of American society from 2001 to 2021. The United States and its allies and partners were compelled to engage in wars in regions that had previously been peripheral. In October 2001, the United States entered Afghanistan. In March 2003, it invaded Iraq. The interventions confronted the United States and its allies and partners with armed resistance movements that practiced the tactics and techniques of insurgency and terrorism.[3]

How to defeat terrorism and insurgency became a pressing question for politicians, generals, scholars, and others thinking about strategy. Two concepts matured: counterinsurgency and counter-terrorism. Counterinsurgency followed the literature of the decolonization conflicts of the 1950s and 1960s and of Vietnam. General David Petraeus and a cadre of reformist officers revised the concept and instituted it in the US military, seen vividly in the counterinsurgency field manual, the 2007 surge in Iraq, and the 2009 surge in Afghanistan. Counter-terrorism was a newer concept. Refined by General Stanley McChrystal, it used special operations forces, strike aircraft, and drones to target insurgent as well as terrorist leaders. It was facilitated by evolving technology—precision weapons, unmanned systems, and intelligence collection platforms.

The political setting, culture, and identity of the countries where intervention took place mattered for strategy. The majority of military forces fighting insurgents and terrorists were made up of local peoples, such as Iraqis, Kurds, or Afghans. They shared a distinct set of methods, if no common strategic discourse, that influenced American and allied thinking. Strategy was defined by these local executors as well as by Western thinkers.

Over time, a new consensus emerged. Counterinsurgency proved too expensive for seemingly unending wars. Instead, counter-terrorism became preferred for fighting both insurgents and terrorists, largely determined by

---

3. A wide selection of sources explains counterinsurgency and counter-terrorism. For a general theoretical introduction, see Stathis Kalyvas, *The Logic of Violence in Civil War* (Cambridge: Cambridge University Press, 2006). On counterinsurgency, see John Nagl, *Learning to Eat Soup with a Knife* (Chicago, IL: University of Chicago Press, 2005); David Kilcullen, *The Accidental Guerrilla* (New York, NY: Oxford University Press, 2009); and *The U.S. Army-Marine Corps Counterinsurgency Field Manual* (Chicago, IL: University of Chicago Press, 2007). On counter-terrorism, see Stanley McChrystal, *My Share of the Task* (New York, NY: Penguin, 2013). On the Afghan and Iraq wars themselves, see Edmund Degen and Mark Reardon, *Modern War in an Ancient Land*, Volumes 1 and 2 (Washington, DC: Center of Military History, 2021); and Joel Rayburn and Frank Sobchak, *The US Army in the Iraq War*, Volumes 1 and 2 (Carlisle Barracks, PA: US Army War College Press, 2019).

President Barack Obama who sought a sustainable way to defend American interests. After 2014, small numbers of US and allied forces targeted insurgent leaders, advised local troops, and called in air strikes, relying heavily on partners, in Iraq, Afghanistan, Syria, and elsewhere. Thus, the wars of 2001 to 2021 represent a major development in strategic thought.

I

Insurgency was not new to strategy in 2001. A rich body of literature on insurgency and how to counter it had formed during the Cold War when France, Great Britain, and the United States had faced Communist and nationalist insurgencies in Algeria, Malaya, Kenya, Vietnam, Northern Ireland, El Salvador, Colombia, and a host of other countries.

The conundrum of insurgency was in identifying, locating, and removing insurgents. Since insurgents operated in small groups, wore civilian clothes, and hid among the people, government forces often found no enemy to fight. Normal conventional tactics consisting of massed units and concentrated firepower were ineffective. The concept developed to fight against insurgency was known as "counterinsurgency."

Cold War literature on counterinsurgency followed Mao's writings on guerrilla warfare in treating the people as the centerpiece of operations. Whereas Clausewitz favored destroying the enemy's military as the way to impose one's will, counterinsurgency subordinated destruction to protecting the people and turning them to the side of government. The literature was mostly composed by officers who had been in various conflicts across the globe. One of the most influential was Colonel David Galula, a French officer who served from 1956 to 1958 in the Algerian War of Independence. He wrote the easy-to-read *Counterinsurgency Warfare: Theory and Practice*, published in 1964. The main goal of counterinsurgency, Galula asserted, was to protect the people, not to kill insurgents. Military operations should concentrate predominately on "destroying or expelling from an area the main body of guerrilla forces, preventing their return, installing garrisons to protect the population, and tracking the guerrilla remnants."[4] Politics were primary. As Galula put it, "that the political power is the undisputed boss is a matter of both principle and

---

4. David Galula, *Counterinsurgency Warfare: Theory and Practice* (New York, NY: Praeger, 1964), 87.

practicality, and to defend it is a political affair."[5] Protecting the people and the primacy of politics would be two pillars of counterinsurgency.

British officers such as Frank Kitson and Gerald Templer (who famously coined the term "winning hearts and mind") expressed similar ideas, based upon experiences in Malaya, Kenya, and Britain's long colonial history in general. Another leading thinker was Robert Thompson, who wrote a series of books that encapsulated British tactics. The most famous was *Defeating Communist Insurgency*, published in 1966. Thompson described what it meant for politics to be primary. A government must have a clear political aim, function within the law, create an overall plan, and prioritize defeating political subversion.

Thompson also described what was known as an "oil spot" technique. Along with many others, he advised that government forces should first secure their base, usually meaning the cities and main towns, and then expand outward. The technique demanded lots of patrolling by small units on foot. Thompson characterized a process of "clear and hold":

> For clear operations . . . the first essential is to saturate it with joint military and police forces . . . "Clear" operations will, however, be a waste of time unless the government is ready to follow them up immediately with "hold" operations . . . The objects of a "hold" operation are to restore government authority in the area and to establish a firm security framework.[6]

A separate point of the British practice was minimum force. Heavy firepower or mechanized operations were recognized as prone to harming civilians or property, which could turn the people toward the insurgents. Minimizing the use of force was a virtue. British units retained these lessons as part of their collective experience and improved them during the long years in Northern Ireland, priding themselves on their record.

America's experience in the Vietnam War added to the body of Cold War literature on counterinsurgency. Even though General William Westmoreland, the US commander from 1964 to 1968, rejected counterinsurgency per se, the Special Forces, the Central Intelligence Agency, and the Marines introduced three innovations that would be remembered. First, Special Forces teams and Marine "combined action platoons" embedded with local forces in order to

---

5. Galula, *Counterinsurgency Warfare*, 89.

6. Robert Thompson, *Defeating Communist Insurgency* (New York, NY: Praeger, 1966), 111–12.

enable them to fight effectively, described in Bing West's classic *The Village*.[7] Second, the Civil Operations and Revolutionary Development Support (CORDS) program placed civilian advisory teams in the provinces and districts as a way to improve development and governance, described in Robert Komer's *Bureaucracy Does Its Thing*.[8] Third, the Phoenix program collected intelligence on insurgent leadership and operatives and then targeted and, when possible, killed them.

Overall, however, defeat caused the US military to disregard counterinsurgency. In the wake of Vietnam, no comprehensive doctrine was created. The haphazard manuals that were written neglected key tactics. The US Army and Marine Corps dived into perfecting maneuver and combined arms in order to fight a conventional war against the Soviet Union.

II

The wars in Iraq and Afghanistan rekindled interest in counterinsurgency. President George W Bush attacked Afghanistan in October 2001 because al-Qa'eda was located there and the Taliban government did not speedily surrender Osama bin Laden. The United States defeated the Taliban within two months and bin Laden fled to Pakistan. An insurgency lay dormant for the first few years. Not so in Iraq. Bush chose to invade in March 2003 over a faulty belief that Saddam Hussein, the Iraqi dictator, possessed weapons of mass destruction and had a relationship with al-Qa'eda. Again, the initial invasion was a smashing success but Sunni insurgents and the terrorist-insurgent network—al-Qa'eda in Iraq—were mounting major attacks before the year was out.

Bush's goal in both wars was winning, defined as the destruction of al-Qa'eda and the creation of "a functioning democracy" where "radicals would be marginalized." He was willing to stay for decades to do so.[9] A unifying ideal was the use of military force to create "free and open societies," as stated in the September 2002 Bush Doctrine.[10]

7. Bing West, *The Village* (New York, NY: Harper & Row, 1972).

8. Robert Komer, *Bureaucracy Does Its Thing* (Santa Monica, CA: RAND Corporation, 1972).

9. OEF Study Group: Interview of President George W. Bush, US Army Center for Military History, 2015.

10. *National Security Strategy* (Washington, DC: The White House, 2002).

In the early years, no uniform doctrine was implemented. Instead, commanders of various divisions, brigades, and battalions adapted on their own. In Mosul, Major General David Petraeus—who had a doctorate in international relations from Princeton University—employed an oil spot technique and worked with Sunni leaders to calm the city. In Anbar, Major General James Mattis focused his Marines on small-unit patrolling, formed his own combined action platoons, and famously gave his 1st Marine Division the motto, "First, do no harm. No better friend, no worse enemy." Colonel H R McMaster and other lower-level commanders enacted similar adaptations.

The writings of two military thinkers, Major John Nagl and Lieutenant-Colonel David Kilcullen, were widely read by US and allied military officers and civilian officials. Nagl had written his doctoral dissertation on counterinsurgency at Oxford University, under the supervision of Professor Robert O'Neill, who had been the intelligence officer of an Australian infantry battalion in Vietnam. The dissertation was published in 2002 as *Learning to Eat Soup with a Knife: Counterinsurgency Lessons from Malaya and Vietnam*. Nagl criticized the US Army for its body-count-centric approach in Vietnam and spread examples of how the British people-centric approach in Malaya had been superior:

> Defeating an insurgency by focusing on dividing the people from the insurgents, removing the support that they require to challenge the government effectively, is rather different from the direct [conventional] approach and in the long term is usually more effective. Once the local and regular armed units are cut off from their sources of supply, personnel, and, most importantly, intelligence, they wither on the vine or are easily coerced to surrender or [are] destroyed by the security forces with the aid of the local populace. Winning that support is the critical battle in counterinsurgency.[11]

David Kilcullen, an Australian officer with a doctorate in anthropology, served as an advisor to the US State Department and then the Defense Department, traveling to the various war zones and observing a range of operations. He condensed his foremost observations into a set of twenty-eight principles, modeled off T E Lawrence's twenty-seven articles of guerrilla warfare, and distributed it throughout the US military, entitled "Twenty-Eight Articles: Fundamentals of Company-level Counterinsurgency." His definition of counterinsurgency was "a competition with the insurgent for the right and the

11. Nagl, *Learning to Eat Soup with a Knife*, 28–29.

ability to win the hearts, minds, and the acquiescence of the population." Echoing Kitson and Thompson, Kilcullen advised companies to "know your turf . . . every village, road, field, population group, tribal leader and ancient grievance," to "be there . . . living in your sector, in close proximity to the population, rather than raiding into the area from remote, secure bases," and to "practice deterrent patrolling . . . one to two thirds of your force should be on patrol at any time, day or night." One of Kilcullen's unique additions was strategic communications. Accounting for the internet and media, he cautioned commanders that insurgents want to defeat them in "the court of global public opinion" and "to assume that the media will publicize everything they say or do." He called on commanders to build their own single, unifying narrative, based on nationalism, culture, and history, to undercut insurgent influence.[12]

The US military was also advising and building army, police, and special operations forces. Petraeus, Mattis, and Nagl recognized that Iraqi soldiers and police better understood the people and the local environment than did foreign forces; the people were consequently more comfortable giving them intelligence. Following the example of the Special Forces and the combined action platoons, embedding small teams of advisors with Iraq army battalions and later police units became commonplace.

The high point in counterinsurgency thinking was the famous counterinsurgency field manual (Field Manual 3–24), issued in December 2006. Under the guidance of Petraeus and Mattis, a team of military officers and civilian scholars, including Nagl and Kilcullen, wrote out the key principles of the past fifty years. The manual called for protecting the population over killing insurgents: "The cornerstone of any counterinsurgency effort is establishing security for the civilian populace."[13] Tactically, patrolling, outposting, and advising the local army and police were endorsed rather than seeking out insurgents for battle or sweeping through insurgent sanctuaries. The manual was famous for its nine tersely written "paradoxes," reminiscent of Sun Zi, such as:

> Sometimes, the more force is used, the less effective it is
> Some of the best weapons for counterinsurgents do not shoot
> Sometimes doing nothing is the best reaction.[14]

12. David Kilcullen, "Twenty-Eight Articles: Fundamentals of Company-level Counterinsurgency," *Military Review* 86:3 (2006): 103–8.

13. *The U.S. Army-Marine Corps Counterinsurgency Field Manual*, 42.

14. *The U.S. Army-Marine Corps Counterinsurgency Field Manual*, 47–50.

The manual especially stressed good governance: "The primary objective of any COIN [counterinsurgency] operation is to foster development of effective governance by a legitimate government."[15] Effective governance was defined ambitiously: a government in which leaders are supported by the majority of the population, corruption is low, rule of law is established, and economic and social development is progressing.

In line with the Cold War literature, the manual implied that, through adoption of the right tactics, an insurgency could be defeated. It repeatedly spoke in terms of "defeating" an insurgency rather than success being affected by political, cultural, social, and economic dynamics largely outside the control of a military force.

Since successes in Iraq to date had been associated with the large-scale deployment of US troops, Petraeus and other officers judged that a large number of US troops was necessary for effective counterinsurgency. A common guideline was a ratio of security forces to population of 1:50. The costs of such a deployment were often overlooked.

In January 2007, President George Bush decided to reinforce the 140,000 US personnel in Iraq with another 30,000 in what was known as the "surge." Winning remained Bush's goal:

> Victory in Iraq will bring . . . a functioning democracy that polices its territory, upholds the rule of law, respects fundamental human liberties, and answers to its people . . . it will be a country that fights terrorists instead of harboring them

US troops would stay until that goal was accomplished. The cost, Bush believed, was worth it. He remembered telling his team, "We must succeed. . . . If [the Iraqis] can't do it, we will . . . We have to make damn sure we do not fail."[16]

Bush appointed Petraeus commander of US forces in Iraq. Petraeus directed his troops to implement the fundamentals of counterinsurgency:

> Improving security for Iraq's population is . . . the over-riding objective of your strategy. Accomplishing this mission requires carrying out complex military operations and convincing the Iraqi people that we will not just "clear" their neighborhoods of the enemy, we will also stay and help "hold"

15. *The U.S. Army-Marine Corps Counterinsurgency Field Manual*, 37.
16. George W. Bush, *Decision Points* (New York, NY: Crown, 2010), 371.

the neighborhoods so that the "build" phase that many of their communities need can go forward.[17]

Counterinsurgency in Iraq was not solely the product of Petraeus and Western thinkers. Iraqis and their culture had an important hand in shaping the strategy and the thinking behind it from the bottom up. Nowhere is this more true than in the tribal movement intrinsically tied to the turnaround in Iraq.

The idea started in Anbar province. A few tribal leaders were upset that al-Qa'eda in Iraq was seizing their economic and political sources of power. In September 2006, Shaykh Abd al-Sittar al-Rishawi of Ramadi openly announced the formation of a tribal movement—*Sahawa al-Anbar*—opposed to al-Qa'eda in Iraq. Sittar, who read and wrote poorly, was hardly a great military thinker; rather, the idea was rooted in Iraqi tribal culture. Sittar and his fellow tribal leaders (*shaykhs*) were merely following tribal traditions in arming tribesmen to defend the tribe and pursuing *asabiyya*—an Arabic term that connotes tribal solidarity. Khamis al-Fahadawi, a tribal leader of standing, illustrated the ideal:

> I am not a politician. I am *shaykh* of 15,000 people. My people speak to me. The community speaks to me. I hear clearly what is happening. I hear from poor tribesmen to the most educated. I relay what the community says.[18]

Sittar and his tribal allies drafted a manifesto. The first point was to bring tribesmen into the army and police. The second point was to declare war on al-Qa'eda. The telling third point was to restore the respect due to tribal leaders.[19] The American commander in Ramadi, Colonel Sean MacFarland, exploited the opportunity this presented.

The tribesmen had their own ideas on how to fight. Instead of being standing units, tribal police and militias tended to gather when needed for operations, like minutemen. Instead of winning hearts and minds, Sittar put out word that the movement would hunt down and kill any outsiders in Ramadi. Rumors spread of executions and secret prisons. Instead of improving governance, the unelected Sittar and his allies created an eleven-point platform that undermined the government by calling for the dissolution of the elected provincial council, tribal oversight of the Iraqi security forces, and strengthening of the authority of tribal leaders.

17. General David Petraeus, Note to Troops, March 19, 2007.

18. Discussion with Khamis al-Fahadawi, Baghdad, April 2, 2017.

19. Gary W. Montgomery and Timothy S. McWilliams, "Interview 3: Sheikh Ahmad Bezia Fteikhan al-Rishawi," in *Al-Anbar Awakening*, Volume II, Gary W. Montgomery and Timothy S. McWilliams, eds. (Quantico, VA: Marine Corps University Press, 2009), 46–47.

With knowledge of their communities, the tribes combined with US soldiers and Marines to suppress insurgent activity in Anbar within a year in one of the most dramatic events of the war, referred to by MacFarland as a "tipping point."

The idea of an awakening spread. Tribal leaders from across the country learned what was happening in Anbar and wanted to secure their interests against al-Qa'eda in Iraq. Petraeus seized upon the idea. Under his direction, US forces directly paid Sunni tribes, resistance cells, and neighborhoods to form militias. Roughly 100,000 stood up. Dubbed the "Sons of Iraq," they helped turn the tide against al-Qa'eda in Iraq.

The magnitude of the "awakening" encouraged thinking that counterinsurgency could lead to complete victory. Petraeus told Congress that Anbar "is a model of what happens when local leaders and citizens decide to oppose al Qaeda and reject its Taliban-like ideology. While Anbar is unique . . . it does demonstrate the dramatic change in security that is possible with the support and participation of local citizens."[20] The ideas of disparate local actors and tribal culture consequently can be seen not simply as tied to recruitment of militias but as fundamental to US strategy.

By 2008, the Iraq surge had severely damaged the insurgency and had led to a dramatic drop in attacks and casualties.[21] Bush and much of Congress deemed the Iraq War to have been essentially won.

III

Apparent success in Iraq convinced Petraeus and many others that the same approach could succeed in Afghanistan where the government was struggling. "These standard general templates for campaign design, if you will, are adequate" to win in Afghanistan, Petraeus calculated in May 2009. The Taliban had launched a major offensive in 2006 and by 2009 were encroaching upon the cities and the capital of Kabul. "Clearly, the security situation in Afghanistan has deteriorated," Petraeus appraised, "markedly in 2008 and now into 2009. The Taliban has shown itself to be very resilient."[22]

20. David Petraeus, "Transcript of Iraq Hearing Statements," *CNN*, September 10, 2007, available at https://www.cnn.com/2007/POLITICS/09/10/patraeus.transcript/.

21. Stephen Biddle, Jeffrey Friedman, and Jacob Shapiro, "Testing the Surge," *International Security* 37:1 (2012): 7.

22. OEF Study Group: Interview with General David Petraeus, Combat Studies Institute, May 15, 2009.

Barack Obama succeeded Bush as president in January 2009. Having opposed the Iraq surge as a senator, Obama quickly approved 21,000 reinforcements to Afghanistan but questioned sending more. The big picture was on Obama's mind. Economic recession was at hand. Banks were crashing and the financial system was in danger. The Iraq surge had been expensive—$120 billion per year as well as the human cost at 1,200 Americans killed and 15,000 wounded, out of 4,431 killed and 31,994 wounded in Iraq overall. On a trip to Afghanistan shortly before the election, Obama had told Petraeus that it is "the job of the president to think broadly, not narrowly, and to weigh the costs and benefits of military action against everything else that went into making the country strong."[23] In the big picture, foreign policy was secondary to domestic policy.

An extensive debate ensued that pitted Petraeus (promoted to commander of Central Command) and General Stanley McChrystal (commander of US and allied forces in Afghanistan) against Obama.

Petraeus and McChrystal advocated for counterinsurgency and an Afghan surge. On August 30, 2009, McChrystal delivered a formal assessment of the situation in Afghanistan to the White House and the Pentagon. In it, he wrote:

> The key take away from this assessment is the urgent need for a significant change to our strategy . . . [the] new strategy must . . . be properly resourced and executed through an integrated civilian-military counterinsurgency campaign that earns the support of the Afghan people and provides them with a secure environment.

The assessment bluntly stated, "International Security Assistance Force [the US and allied command in Afghanistan] is not adequately executing the basics of COIN doctrine." In support of this strategy, a few days after submitting his assessment, McChrystal asked for 40,000 additional reinforcements.[24]

Obama doubted such a surge was the best way to defeat al-Qaʻeda, the true threat to the United States. In his judgment, completely defeating the Taliban would take too long and be too costly, untenable from both a domestic political and a strategic standpoint. At 40,000 additional troops, the cost of the Afghan War would be $889 billion over ten years. His fiscal stimulus package to get the United States out of the recession was roughly $800 billion over the same period. Obama told his staff, "This is not what I'm looking for. . . . I'm

23. Barack Obama, *A Promised Land* (New York, NY: Crown, 2020), 436.

24. Stanley McChrystal, "COMISAF's Initial Assessment (Unclassified)," *Washington Post*, September 21, 2009.

not doing 10 years. I'm not doing a long-term nation-building effort. I'm not spending a trillion dollars."[25] The war, Obama warned, could suck the oxygen out of everything else. With this wider matter at hand, Obama firmly opposed any open-ended commitment as incommensurate with US interests.

In the end, Obama pared down the goals and surged 33,000 reinforcements for a total of nearly 100,000 US troops in Afghanistan. He limited the goals to breaking Taliban momentum and enabling the Afghan government to stand on its own so that the United States could start pulling back the surge reinforcements in July 2011.

Just as American thinking in Iraq was shaped by Iraqis, so in Afghanistan was it shaped by Afghans. Minimum force had long been a principle of counterinsurgency, yet implemented inconsistently. Afghan President Hamid Karzai saw it as his duty to protect Afghan civilians from the American and Afghan militaries as much as from the Taliban. With Afghanistan's long history of resistance to occupation, the killing of Afghans endangered the legitimacy of any Afghan ruler. Repeated incidents of civilian casualties and unfulfilled promises to stop them angered Karzai. As early as 2006, he had cried on television over air strikes killing civilians. The next year, after air and artillery strikes allegedly killed one hundred civilians in one week, he called a press conference and denounced "careless" US and allied military operations: "Afghan life is not cheap and should not be treated as such. . . . The extreme use of force, the disproportionate use of force to a situation, and the lack of coordination with the Afghan government is causing these casualties."[26] Karzai told journalist Carlotta Gall, "I want an end to civilian casualties. As much as one may argue it's difficult, I don't accept that argument. . . . the war against terrorism is not in Afghan villages."[27]

Karzai's arguments convinced McChrystal. On July 2, 2009, the general issued a tactical directive that restrained the use of air strikes against homes except in self-defense or other prescribed conditions.[28] McChrystal wrote in his memoir:

I would ask soldiers and Marines to demonstrate what we soon termed "courageous restraint"—forgoing fires, particularly artillery and air strikes,

25. Bob Woodward, *Obama's Wars* (New York, NY: Simon & Schuster, 2010), 166–68, 251.

26. Barry Bearak, "Karzai Calls Coalition 'Careless,'" *New York Times*, June 24, 2007.

27. Carlotta Gall, "Afghan Leader Criticizes U.S. on Conduct of War," *New York Times*, April 26, 2008.

28. Stanley McChrystal, "Tactical Directive," *ISAF Headquarters*, July 6, 2009, available at https://www.nato.int/isaf/docu/official_texts/Tactical_Directive_090706.pdf.

when civilian casualties were likely . . . I was emphatic that fires could and should be used if the survival of our forces was directly threatened, but in cases where the only purpose was to kill insurgents, the protection of civilian lives and property took precedence.[29]

The directive caused a good deal of consternation within US ranks but, with some modification, stayed in place for the rest of the war.

Karzai was not the only source of Afghan influence upon strategy in Afghanistan. As in Iraq, various Afghan commanders and tribal leaders proposed forming tribal or community militias, though because of their own cultural experience rather than any interest in what had happened in Iraq. Special Forces, Army and Marine officers, as well as State Department political advisors in the provinces were exposed to Afghan ideas, sometimes from tribal leaders trying to help their villagers, sometimes from commanders with heavy-handed reputations. Asadullah Khalid, a governor, intelligence director, and minister of defense, counseled several US generals and organized tribal uprisings. Abdul Razziq, a border police commander and later police chief of Kandahar, had a similar impact. He announced to the press, "Right now we are providing training to the villagers. We have provided guns and bullets and we are supporting this."[30] US Special Forces Major Jim Gant was so moved by the advice of one Kunar tribal leader that he drafted a paper, entitled "One Tribe at a Time," about raising tribal militias as a means of pacifying the country. The paper made the rounds with Petraeus, McChrystal, and throughout Washington.

Like in Iraq, tribal militias were rooted in Afghan tribal culture. Tribal authority conflicted with government authority and with Taliban religious authority, described by anthropologist David Edwards as "deep-seated moral contradictions that press against each other like tectonic plates at geological fault lines below the surface of events."[31] Local tribesmen defending their villages as militia, traditionally known as *arbekai*, distinct from the government or the Taliban, fit tribal identity. "I stand for my own village. I do not stand for the government, or for the Taliban," stated Gul Mohammed, a tribal leader from Helmand.[32] Few of the Afghans, however, and especially not Karzai, thought tribal militias could win the war; Afghan tribes were too fractious. Tribal militias were merely a practical way to secure various villages.

29. McChrystal, *My Share of the Task*, 312.
30. "Afghan Villagers Rise up Against Taliban in the South," *AFP*, February 15, 2013.
31. David Edwards, *Heroes of the Age* (Berkeley, CA: University of California Press, 1996), 3, 4.
32. Discussion with Gul Mohammed, Marjah tribal leader, Kabul, February 24, 2014.

In 2009 and early 2010, a few tribal militias formed independently in Helmand, Kandahar, and a variety of other provinces. In early 2010, Brigadier General Scott Miller, US special operations component commander in Afghanistan, carefully implemented a new nationwide program, known as "Afghan local police," for Special Forces to work with villages in creating tribal militias. The program had been drafted by Miller's predecessor, Brigadier General Ed Reeder, and Dr. Seth Jones from the RAND Corporation.

Hoping to repeat Iraq's awakening, Petraeus secured Karzai's approval for the program in August 2010. The United States funded 30,000 local police. They enjoyed tactical successes in some provinces, were counterproductive in others, but overall, never sparked the dramatic momentum of the Anbar awakening. Nonetheless, working with local militias was etched into US thinking.

As Obama had wanted, the surge in Afghanistan broke Taliban momentum. What mattered more was the cost. When Obama reviewed the surge in spring 2011, it was clear that the whole affair was tremendously expensive, at a time when he was trying to reduce the deficit in the aftermath of the recession. Leon Panetta, Obama's first CIA director and later defense secretary, recalled:

> We were getting into a period where there were increasing budget constraints because of what was happening with the debt and with the deficit . . . You could see a building pressure that the budget was going . . . to be scaled back. And that the Congress was concerned about the cost of [war].[33]

Closer to the heart, the United States suffered 1,230 killed and over 12,500 wounded from 2009–11, the majority of its casualties for the whole war. Obama found the combined costs of the Afghan War, Iraq War, and the rest of the "war on terror" to be "staggering: almost a trillion dollars spent, more than three thousand U.S. troops killed, as many as ten times that number wounded."[34]

Hope for progress in Afghanistan was dim. The Afghan army and police were evaluated as dependent on the United States while the Taliban were still launching attacks, and could clearly recover from their setbacks. At the same time, the killing of bin Laden on May 1, 2011, removed the primary threat to the United States. According to a Gallup poll taken days after bin Laden's

---

33. OEF Study Group: Interview with former Defense Secretary Leon Panetta, undated.
34. Obama, *A Promised Land*, 314.

death, 59 percent of Americans believed that the US mission in Afghanistan had been accomplished.[35]

Weighing priorities and assessing progress convinced Obama that Afghanistan was a poor use of resources. His thinking moved beyond zeroing out the surge to reducing the entire US presence to as low as possible. In a series of decisions, Obama scheduled US military forces to withdraw from Afghanistan by the end of 2016. The withdrawal of US military forces from Iraq by the end of 2011 similarly went forward.

In the aftermath of the Afghan surge, counterinsurgency fell into disrepute. Chairman of the Joint Chiefs of Staff Martin Dempsey cautioned General John Allen, the new commander in Afghanistan, against thinking in counterinsurgency terms. Defense Secretary Bob Gates famously quipped, "In my opinion, any future defense secretary who advises the president to again send a big American land army into Asia or into the Middle East or Africa should have his head examined."[36] After the United States withdrew from Iraq in 2011, conventional wisdom was that the United States should get out of the intervention business entirely. In due course, Obama and his generals would lay out a new strategy.

IV

While counterinsurgency was being instituted, a separate concept was being developed, broadly known as "counter-terrorism," also known as "decapitation," "targeted killing," or "high-value targeting." While counterinsurgency focused on protecting the people, counter-terrorism focused on capturing or killing terrorist and insurgent leaders. In spite of its name, counter-terrorism was not just for fighting elusive terrorist organizations such as al-Qaʻeda. It was also applied against insurgent groups, such as the Taliban, with which terrorists were intertwined. The idea was that eliminating leaders could cripple a terrorist group or an insurgency.

US special operations forces were a sub-set of the US military. They included US Navy SEALs and US Army Special Forces and Rangers. When

---

35. Jeffrey Jones, "Americans More Positive on Afghanistan After bin Laden Death," *Gallup*, May 11, 2011, https://news.gallup.com/poll/147488/americans-positive-afghanistan-bin-laden-death.aspx.

36. Robert Gates, Speech at the United States Military Academy, February 25, 2011, available at https://www.stripes.com/news/text-of-secretary-of-defense-robert-gates-feb-25-2011-speech-at-west-point-1.136145.

terrorism ticked up during the 1960s and 1970s, special operations forces were assigned the mission of combating it. British SAS and Israeli special operations forces were specializing in the same mission and influenced their US counterparts.[37]

Counter-terrorism lacked the rich historical precedent and conceptual development of counterinsurgency. There was no comprehensive theory and the body of literature was thin. Early roots lay in the French model of detaining or killing insurgent leaders in Algeria and the Phoenix program (in which SEALs had taken part) in Vietnam.[38] Then, in the 1970s, certain units specialized in hostage rescue as airplane hijackings and kidnappings turned into a terrorist tactic. Special operations forces trained in rapid deployment, stealthy arrival, breaching a compound, room entry, communications, and precisely shooting all terrorists on site, collectively known as "direct action."[39]

William McRaven, an officer in the US Navy SEALs who would later lead counter-terrorism operations, sketched out some initial theory in the 1990s, published in his book, *Case Studies in Special Operations Warfare: Theory and Practice*. He described special operations as closely aligned to direct-action missions and as "conducted by forces specially trained, equipped, and supported for a specific target whose destruction, elimination, or rescue is a political or military imperative." The key to success was seizing the tactical initiative early in a mission and retaining it through bold individual action.[40] The notion of a few elite operators conducting direct-action missions against critical targets would be a starting point of counter-terrorism in Iraq and Afghanistan.

Civilian thinkers in the 1990s were writing about how to counter terrorism too. On the basis of Israel's experience against Hamas and Hezbollah, Bruce Hoffman at the RAND Corporation found that targeting mid-level leaders, financiers, and smugglers as well as senior leaders could effectively disrupt control, communications, operations, and long-term growth. Gordon McCormick, one of McRaven's professors at the Naval Postgraduate School, and John Arquilla explored how wide-ranging networks were an organizing principle of

37. Mark Moyar, *Oppose Any Foe: The Rise of America's Special Operations Forces* (New York, NY: Basic Books, 2017), 171–72.

38. Roger Trinquier, *Modern Warfare: A French View of Counterinsurgency* (New York, NY: Praeger, 1964).

39. Moyar, *Oppose Any Foe*, 157–58, 163.

40. William McRaven, *Case Studies in Special Operations Warfare: Theory and Practice* (New York, NY: Presidio Press, 1996), 1–5.

terrorist and insurgent groups and that the United States would have to build its own to counter them.[41] Their theories would influence US special operations in the 2000s.

During the 1980s and 1990s, technology advanced in ways that would enhance counter-terrorism. In Vietnam, air strikes were far too inaccurate to reliably kill insurgent leaders. By the 1990s, laser-guided precision bombs and Tomahawk cruise missiles could hit targets as small as a window. By the end of the decade, GPS satellite guidance systems could track a bomb against any programmed coordinate, down to a square meter. New unmanned, surveillance, and information technology was also coming online. Predator drones could fly hundreds of miles and then loiter over a target area for hours, observing possible enemy activity through onboard sensors and cameras. Certain versions carried Hellfire missiles. The fidelity of sensors and cameras improved dramatically over the next decade. Full motion video (FMV) could capture events happening in real time, providing a means of direct observation that previously had to be performed by human operatives under significant risk.[42] Communications also improved. Satellites allowed clear communication to anywhere on the battlefield and secure internet allowed near-instantaneous sharing of data across the force. Any unit could have large amounts of intelligence at its fingertips and be less dependent on higher headquarters for the information needed to act. Identifying, finding, and capturing or killing adversary leaders was simplified.

V

When September 11 happened, President Bush wanted bin Laden and the other members of al-Qaʻeda captured or killed. The initial US invasion of Afghanistan demonstrated how the combination of new technology and small teams of special operations forces could be lethal. After the Taliban were toppled in December 2001, Defense Secretary Rumsfeld passed guidance that counter-terrorism was the mission. Rumsfeld instructed the military in May 2002: "terrorists today are well-organized and well-financed; they are trying to get weapons of mass destruction and can impose tremendous damage on the United States. So finding them has become a Defense Department

41. John Arquilla and David Ronfeldt, *Networks and Netwars* (Santa Monica, CA: RAND Corporation, 2001).

42. Michael Flynn, Rich Juergens, and Thomas Cantrell, "Employing ISR: SOF Best Practices," *Joint Force Quarterly* 50:3 (2008): 59.

task."[43] His assistant secretary for special operations stated, "Once [Rumsfeld] fastened on the manhunt thing, he looked at that as the silver bullet against terrorism and he built a unit that can do manhunts."[44]

The campaign was global. Rumsfeld and Deputy Defense Secretary Paul Wolfowitz accepted that terrorists were a network that would have to be attacked at multiple points. Wolfowitz wrote to Rumsfeld in early 2002, "There are some distinct advantages to thinking about the war on terrorism as an attack on a network . . . The concept of networks is widely understood in this information age, and even more widely talked about." Defeating a network meant attacking repeatedly at multiple nodes. "Networks don't collapse through single-point failure. You don't decapitate networks. . . . Networks are defeated by a progressive weakening. Attack a network at many different points."[45]

Counter-terrorism was applied globally and especially intensively in Iraq and Afghanistan, where special operations teams established operating bases, sometimes alone, sometimes co-located with conventional forces. They gathered intelligence, surveilled areas of interest with drones, helicoptered to targeted locations, raided suspected homes and compounds, and called in air strikes on possible targets. During the first years of the wars, special operations units experimented with different techniques. Operations proceeded at a relatively slow tempo. Lieutenant General Stanley McChrystal, appointed to lead the Joint Special Operations Command (JSOC) in 2003, brought everything together.

McChrystal headquartered himself in Iraq where violence was escalating. Counter-terrorism operations at that point tended to focus on high-level leaders, carefully gathering intelligence before striking. The approach was deliberate and neglected technological advances. McChrystal critiqued his force as stovepiped. Teams in various cities toiled away on their own. Communication capacity was too small to quickly share information collected in one place that was crucial to somewhere else. Consequently, "the senders and receivers, in this case the forward team and its higher headquarters, had neither a shared picture of the enemy nor an ability to prosecute a common fight against it."[46] McChrystal decided to create an entirely new approach.

43. Donald Rumsfeld to Steve Cambone and General Myers, May 31, 2002, National Security Archive.

44. Moyar, *Oppose Any Foe*, 271.

45. Deputy Defense Secretary Paul Wolfowitz to Donald Rumsfeld, January 11, 2002, National Security Archive.

46. McChrystal, *My Share of the Task*, 105–6.

First, during 2004 and 2005, McChrystal reorganized his command from a set of independent units into a network. He connected surveillance, human and signals intelligence collection, analysis, and the different special operations units, which allowed him to find and strike targets rapidly. He brought together representatives from across the US government (CIA, DIA, NSA, FBI, and the National Geospatial-Intelligence Agency) in what was known as a Joint Interagency Task Force (JIATF) in order to leverage as much information as possible. Communications with higher headquarters improved while the various teams received greater intelligence and support assets. McChrystal wrote in his memoir:

> To transform ourselves from a traditional military unit into a network, we changed how we were organized and how we made decisions; we grew a new culture within proud and idiosyncratic communities; we continually added partners. In 2003 our "product" was our "shooters"—our ensemble of tactically unmatched strike forces. By the end . . . the command's formidable offering was its network—its ability to gel diverse talents into an organic unit that gathered information swiftly and acted accordingly.[47]

Decentralized decision-making allowed the teams to prosecute targets on their own without getting bogged in top-down process. Quoting Arquilla, McChrystal's mantra was, "It takes a network to defeat a network."[48] He liked to call his network a "team of teams."

Second, McChrystal instituted a specific targeting process, abbreviated as "F3EAD" for find, fix, finish, exploit, analyze, and disseminate. First developed by Gordon McCormick and special operations students, the process was: gathering intelligence to *find* a target; using surveillance assets such as drones to *fix* the target; executing a strike with a raid or missile from a drone or an aircraft to *finish* the target; interrogating a detainee or collecting materials such as computers left on site to *exploit* new evidence; *analyzing* that evidence; *disseminating* the analysis; and then starting the process all over again.

Third, McChrystal accelerated operational tempo. He aimed to disrupt terrorist and insurgent networks and to gather evidence through conducting as many strikes as possible to work the way up to the senior leaders, particularly to Abu Musab al-Zarqawi, then the leader of al-Qaʿeda in Iraq. In 2005, McChrystal broadened the target set in Iraq from mainly senior leaders to all leaders. The

47. McChrystal, *My Share of the Task*, 93.
48. McChrystal, *My Share of the Task*, 148.

logic was that low-level leaders might only be removed temporarily but in the meantime the organization would operate less effectively:

> I concluded there was no single person or place we could strike that would cause Al Qaeda to collapse; there was no coup de main option . . . We had to attack the organization head on as it sprouted up locally while also targeting its upper echelons of leadership. Doing so would deplete the organization of its entrenched expertise and institutional wisdom . . . If onlookers saw that the organization was losing—fleeing territory, hemorrhaging people—its brand would suffer.[49]

In August 2004, McChrystal's forces conducted eighteen raids. Two years later, in August 2006, they conducted 300.

New information, surveillance, and unmanned technology enabled McChrystal's approach. Interception of signals and exploitation of captured computers complemented traditional human intelligence collection.[50] Drones with cameras fixed and observed insurgent leadership, cued by other sources of intelligence.[51] Full motion video sensors on drones constantly tracked insurgent movements and developed patterns of life, allowing for a fuller picture of the insurgent networks and monitoring for civilian activity that operations could harm.[52]

McChrystal's approach worked. Raids and air strikes removed senior leaders, mid-level commanders, cell commanders, and IED layers. On June 7, 2007, his forces tracked down al-Zarqawi and killed him with an air strike. By 2009, McChrystal and his subordinates assessed that al-Qa'eda in Iraq no longer functioned in a cohesive manner. They also noted, however, that success had occurred hand in hand with the counterinsurgency approach of the surge and that continuous strikes were needed to keep al-Qa'eda in Iraq suppressed.

The Bush administration captured or killed terrorists beyond Iraq and Afghanistan. The global campaign was largely conducted by the CIA instead of McChrystal's special operations forces. As the production of Predator and Reaper drones expanded, Bush stepped up their use in 2008, though targeting processes remained deliberate in comparison to McChrystal's high-tempo strikes in Iraq.

49. McChrystal, *My Share of the Task*, 115.
50. Moyar, *Oppose Any Foe*, 277.
51. McChrystal, *My Share of the Task*, 177.
52. Flynn, Juergens, and Cantrell, *Employing ISR*, 57.

The possibility that counter-terrorism could manage the terrorist threat without the extended ground wars of Iraq and Afghanistan appealed to President Obama when he took office. A presidential directive in May 2009 prioritized the hunt for bin Laden. Obama wrote in his memoir:

> I viewed the elimination of bin Laden as critical to my goal of reorienting America's counterterrorism strategy. By losing our focus on the small band of terrorists who had actually planned and carried out 9/11 and instead defining the threat as an open-ended, all-encompassing "War on Terror," we'd fallen into what I believed was a strategic trap—one that had elevated al-Qaeda's prestige, rationalized the Iraq invasion, alienated much of the Muslim world, and warped almost a decade of U.S. foreign policy.[53]

John Brennan, Obama's counter-terrorism advisor, said that instead of a "hammer," America now relied on a "scalpel."[54]

Obama escalated the drone campaign in Pakistan. Strikes into Pakistan against terrorist leadership went from 36 in 2008, to 54 in 2009, and then to 122 in 2010.[55] They disrupted al-Qa'eda's North and South Waziristan safe havens. By one estimate, roughly 75 percent of al-Qa'eda leaders in Pakistan were wiped out.[56] Osama bin Laden wrote to a subordinate from his hideaway:

> Over the last two years, the problem of the spying war and spying aircraft benefited the enemy greatly and led to the killing of many jihadi cadres, leaders, and others. This is something that is concerning us and exhausting us.[57]

Operations also took place in Yemen and Somalia against al-Qa'eda affiliates.

The CIA had been tracking bin Laden himself for years. He had disappeared from sight after 2002. In 2010, the CIA found his hideaway, a walled compound in plain sight in Abbottabad, Pakistan, thirty-five miles north of Islamabad.

---

53. Obama, *A Promised Land*, 677.

54. Mark Mazzetti, *The Way of the Knife* (New York, NY: Scribe, 2013), 128, 129, 155.

55. New America Foundation, "The Drone War in Pakistan," https://www.newamerica.org/international-security/reports/americas-counterterrorism-wars/the-drone-war-in-pakistan/, accessed December 7, 2021.

56. Peter Bergen and Jennifer Rowland, "CIA Drone Strikes and the Taliban," in *Talibanistan*, Peter Bergen and Katherine Tiedemann, eds. (New York, NY: Oxford University Press, 2013), 229.

57. Osama bin Laden, "Summary on Situation in Afghanistan and Pakistan," Office of the Director of National Intelligence, trans., undated, https://www.dni.gov/files/documents/ubl/english/Summary%20on%20situation%20in%20Afghanistan%20and%20Pakistan.pdf.

Obama approved a daring helicopter raid by SEALs onto the compound, overseen by Admiral McRaven, that killed bin Laden on May 1, 2011. After his death, al-Qaʿeda was a shambles. Though planning to strike the United States persisted, the organization's cells hid in the Afghanistan-Pakistan border regions and other parts of the globe, occupied with regional conflicts rather than international terror.

The bin Laden raid was a stunning success for counter-terrorism. The Obama administration's 2011 national security strategy elevated special operations and drones as the means for suppressing terrorism. "I felt very good about our capabilities . . . both from an intelligence point of view as well as the ability to hit the targets we had to hit," CIA Director Panetta later stated, "gradually decapitating the lead guys did have an impact."[58] Cost-effective, counter-terrorism had become the preferred concept for fighting insurgencies and terrorism.

VI

At the end of 2011, Obama was drawing to a close America's wars in Iraq and Afghanistan. The terrorist threat to the United States appeared to be diminishing. In reality, al-Qaʿeda in Iraq was recovering in the absence of US counter-terrorism operations. Under a new leader, Abu Bakr al-Baghdadi, the group renamed itself the "Islamic State of Iraq and al-Sham [Syria]." In June 2014, the Islamic State swept up Mosul and Baghdadi proclaimed a caliphate. The group took over the northeastern third of Syria and spread to Afghanistan, Libya, Mali, and Nigeria. A spate of terrorist attacks rocked Europe. The rise of the Islamic State—abbreviated to "ISIL" or "ISIS"—returned intervention in broken countries to the center of US foreign policy. Post-bin Laden relief turned into renewed domestic concern over terrorism. The percentage of Americans who feared they could be a victim of a terrorist attack rebounded from 36 percent in 2011 to 51 percent in 2015.[59] Obama was forced to re-enter Iraq and eventually to suspend the withdrawal from Afghanistan.

Obama and his generals instituted a new "counter-ISIL" strategy which embodied the lessons of thirteen years of war. Obama refused to get dragged into another ground war in Iraq and ruled out the use of troops in combat. Senior

58. OEF Study Group: Interview with Former Defense Secretary Leon Panetta, undated.

59. "Terrorism," *Gallup*, December 8–9, 2015, https://news.gallup.com/poll/4909/terrorism-united-states.aspx.

military leaders—General Martin Dempsey, General Lloyd Austin, General Joseph Votel, and General Joseph Dunford—agreed. In their on-the-ground experience, sending tens of thousands of US ground troops would not be worth the cost. A lighter, more sustainable effort would be wiser.

Obama announced his counter-ISIL strategy to the American public on September 10, 2014. He set modest goals and explicitly applied counter-terrorism: "We will degrade and ultimately destroy ISIL through a comprehensive and sustained counter-terrorism strategy." The foremost component of the strategy was "a systematic campaign of airstrikes . . . hitting ISIL targets," which included both fighters and leadership.[60] The second component was partnering with the Iraqi government and other local forces fighting the Islamic State. US forces were to serve as advisors and trainers and support training, intelligence, and equipping. The third component consisted of global operations to target Islamic State operatives, cut off their funding, counter its ideology, and stem the flow of foreign fighters into and out of the Middle East. The strategy's timeline was, in Obama's words, "steady and relentless."[61] Secretary of State John Kerry estimated defeating the Islamic State would take three years.

The components of the strategy never changed but the means did. In order to train, advise, and coordinate air strikes across the broad Islamic State front, running from northwestern Syria to Mosul and on to Baghdad, Obama gradually raised the number of US troops from fewer than one thousand to more than seven thousand. He allowed Austin and Votel to position them at new bases and locations closer to the front line.

Air strikes also had to be escalated. During 2014 a relatively small number of 300 per month were being conducted, which paled in comparison to the previous campaigns in Iraq and Afghanistan. Votel commanded Special Operations Command and later Central Command and oversaw much of the campaign. Dunford was Chairman of the Joint Chiefs of Staff after September 2015. They realized that timely provision of air support was the difference between success and defeat for almost any partnered force. Initial White House restrictions designed to limit civilian casualties and mission creep

60. Barack Obama, "President Obama: We Will Degrade and Ultimately Destroy ISIL," *Obama White House*, December 10, 2014, https://obamawhitehouse.archives.gov/blog/2014/09/10/president-Obama-we-will-degrade-and-ultimately-destroy-isil.

61. Barack Obama, "Transcript: President Obama's Speech Outlining Strategy to Defeat Islamic State," *Washington Post*, September 10, 2014.

denied US special operations forces and advisors the flexibility needed for their partners to succeed. Votel worked out permissions for US commanders to have greater latitude to call in air strikes. Lieutenant General Charles Q Brown, who ran the air campaign, and US commanders on the ground worked out processes and procedures so that special operations forces and advisors could receive information quickly, either from drones or partnered forces on the ground, and then quickly clear and call in strikes.

Further technological advances eased execution of the new strategy. Smart phones, smart pads, and laptops that were simple for Iraqis and Syrian Kurds to use allowed for a greater flow of information than had been possible from 2003 to 2011. Advisors behind the frontline could see what was happening in real time. Easily transmitted GPS coordinates were especially valuable, circumventing the error-prone process of talking through an interpreter over a phone.[62]

By the end of the campaign, over a thousand strikes were being conducted per month as Iraqi and Syrian Kurdish forces battled into Mosul and Raqqa. Flexibility in calling in air strikes was the key to Obama's new strategy.[63]

To say that the strategy was purely counter-terrorism is inaccurate. Lessons from counterinsurgency survived in training, advising, and equipping Iraqi and Syrian forces. Votel called the approach "by, with, and through"—a familiar term from the earlier counterinsurgency campaigns—that he defined as "operations . . . led *by* our partners, state or nonstate, *with* enabling support from the United States . . . , and *through* US authorities and partner agreements." The advantage was that it was a "way of conducting military activities and operations with less direct combat employment of U.S. forces."[64]

The habit of working with tribes and militias was also felt. In Iraq, the United States worked closely with the Kurdish peshmerga, accepted the presence of tens of thousands of Shiʻa militia, and partially re-formed Sunni tribal militias. The most important of the local forces were the Syrian Kurds and their disciplined militia, the YPG (an acronym for *Yekineyen Parastina Gel*, or "People's Protection Units"). Led by the charismatic Mazloum Abdi, the YPG

62. William T. Eliason, "An Interview with General Joseph Votel," *Joint Force Quarterly* 89:2 (2018): 39.

63. Becca Wasser et al., *The Air War Against the Islamic State* (Santa Monica, CA: RAND Corporation, 2019), 41, 52–53, 115–16; Michael Gordon, *Degrade and Destroy* (New York: Macmillan, 2022).

64. Joseph Votel and Eero Keravuori, "The By-With-Through Operational Approach," *Joint Force Quarterly* 89:2 (2018): 40. Italics in original.

were close to the PKK (the Kurdistan Worker's Party), the long-standing Kurdish resistance organization in Turkey. The Syrian Kurds, who also fielded a large number of female fighters, attracted the attention of US special operations forces when they mounted a last-ditch defense of the town of Kobani on the Turkish border at the end of 2014. Frequently visiting Syria, Votel recognized the Kurdish leader Mazloum as "a fighter who was clearly thinking about the strategic aspects of the campaign" and "the right partner who could help us defeat ISIS."[65] At the end of 2015, Obama agreed to support 20,000 Kurds plus 3,000–5,000 Arab Sunnis in attacking Raqqa, the center of Islamic State power in Syria. Votel organized the advising and air support for the combined force, renamed the Syrian Defense Forces (SDF).

Local partners again had their own ideas on how to fight. Mazloum pursued historical Kurdish hopes for an autonomous homeland in northern Syria and so delayed moving directly on Raqqa in order to secure other towns near the border with Turkey. "This is our vision for Syria's political future: decentralized federalism, with religious freedom and respect for mutual differences," he stated.[66] In Iraq, Prime Minister Haider al-Abadi waited to advance on Mosul until towns of greater concern to Shi'a political power had been dealt with. In neither Syria nor Iraq was the use of force minimized. Governance was largely out of US hands. The Iraqi government remained highly sectarian. Furthermore, although the United States implemented measures to reduce civilian casualties, the Syrian Kurds and Iraqis needed air strikes to advance. Raqqa, Mosul, Ramadi, and other cities that had survived the 2003–11 war had barely a block left standing by the middle of 2017. Equally as disturbing, local forces in Iraq, especially Shi'a militias, were known to be guilty of extrajudicial killings and other atrocities. "When [we] rely on partners to do things, they're going to do it in [their own] way," Votel later said. "We're not going to like everything they do. It won't be exactly the way we'd do it, but that was the trade-off."[67]

Supported by thousands of US air strikes, Iraqi forces captured Mosul between November 2016 and July 2017. The Syrian Kurds captured Raqqa

65. Joseph Votel and Elizabeth Dent, "The Danger of Abandoning Our Partners," *The Atlantic*, October 8, 2019.

66. Mazloum Abdi, "If We Have to Choose Between Compromise and Genocide, We Will Choose Our People," *Foreign Policy*, October 13, 2019.

67. Brian Dodwell, Paul Cruickshank, and Kristina Hummel, "A View from the CT Foxhole: General (Ret) Joseph Votel, Former Commander, U.S. Central Command," *CTC Sentinel* 12:10 (2019): 12.

between June and October 2017, ending the major fighting against the Islamic State in Iraq and Syria. Islamic State remnants survived in the eastern reaches of the Syrian desert and in small cells in Iraq; Baghdadi was not killed until October 2019. A few thousand US forces remained in both countries. Votel, Dunford, and others advised Washington that US forces would need to stay in Syria and Iraq to prevent the Islamic State from re-emerging. As was the case in Afghanistan, the Iraqi army, Iraqi special operations forces, and Syrian Kurds showed little sign of being able to handle things on their own. Counter-terrorism, as McChrystal had noted, was not a path to total success but a way to disrupt and suppress a threat.

VII

The attacks of September 11, 2001 mark a breaking point for the study of strategic thought. The domestic political ramifications of the attacks forced US leaders to confront how to combat insurgents and terrorists in far-off countries, a question they had avoided since the Vietnam War. A niche field ascended to the mainstream of strategic thought. Over the ensuing decade, strategy changed. The nascent—and perhaps underdeveloped—concepts of the Cold War were revised. Counterinsurgency was attempted in Iraq and Afghanistan and ultimately lost out to counter-terrorism. Deploying large numbers of ground troops gave way to special operations forces, leadership targeting, drones, and high-tempo air strikes.

Why did strategy change? The explanation starts with technology. McChrystal and others capitalized upon technological advances to introduce new tactics and techniques that raised the effectiveness of counter-terrorism. Then, in the course of the wars, the United States and its allies went through a learning process. Years of combat experience revealed counterinsurgency to be an expensive way of solving the tactical dilemma of insurgency. As this became clear, shifting domestic politics of economics and terrorism drove a shift in strategy. The expense of counterinsurgency might have been acceptable in the early years of the war when fear of terrorist attack was high. It was less acceptable in the context of economic recession and ebbing fears of attack. Finally, individuals played a key role. The pivotal figure was Obama. It was Obama who realigned strategic goals with domestic political and economic imperatives and who recalibrated the ways and means to achieve those goals.

Strategy grew more militaristic in the process. Mao had centered his concept of insurgency around the people. Thompson, Galula, Nagl, Kilcullen,

Petraeus, and McChrystal followed in trace—structuring operations around protecting the population, the primacy of politics, and good governance. After 2011, strategy diverged from these characteristics. Targeting and killing the enemy took precedence. Obama based strategy less upon mobilizing the people and improving governance and more on eliminating insurgent leadership and providing the firepower for the host military and other local forces to prevail in battle.

The assessment that the insurgencies could not be defeated but had to be managed was perhaps the most dramatic change in strategic thought between 2001 and 2021. Years of war dispelled the conceit of the 2000s that America could win. Obama, Votel, Dunford, and others assessed that the political, social, and cultural challenges were too great for the United States to succeed or for host governments to survive on their own. The terrorist threat could only be suppressed as long as US military forces were present. Once removed, the government would regress and the threat would return. "This is term life insurance," Dunford articulated. "It's only good as long as you pay."[68] The virtue of counter-terrorism was sustainability. Forces could stay for years, until national security interests dictated otherwise—which they ultimately did.

As domestic politics shifted, even the relatively low cost of counter-terrorism could be too high. After Obama left office and the Islamic State lost Raqqa, the percentage of Americans who perceived terrorism to be a threat fell from 51 percent in 2015 to 36 percent in 2021. New emerging issues of climate change, the coronavirus pandemic, and the rise of China all polled as greater concerns.[69] Military presence in Iraq, Syria, and Afghanistan came under more and more question. President Trump nearly withdrew from Syria in 2018. President Joseph Biden actually did withdraw from Afghanistan in August 2021, accepting defeat because the terrorist threat no longer warranted the price of the strategy.

The response to insurgency after 2001 is not solely a story of the thinking of Americans, British, French, and Israelis. It is also a story of how Iraqis, Afghans, and Syrians shaped this thinking from the bottom up. They had no equivalent of Petraeus or McChrystal. Their influence came from an

---

68. Carter Malkasian, *The American War in Afghanistan: A History* (Oxford: Oxford University Press, 2021), 357.

69. "Terrorism," *Gallup*, https://news.gallup.com/poll/4909/terrorism-united-states.aspx, accessed January 27, 2018; "Most Important Problem," *Gallup*, https://news.gallup.com/poll/1675/most-important-problem.aspx, accessed December 7, 2021.

assortment of different actors and thinkers—Karzai, Sittar, Razziq, Mazloum, and countless tribal leaders, military officers, and politicians—sometimes serendipitously. They changed how Americans and their allies thought about and executed their strategy. Attention to civilian casualties, large-scale tribal mobilization, and confidence in strategic effectiveness owed more than a little to them. Preferences on tactics, governance reforms, and timelines yielded to their culture, identity, and politics. Local peoples adjusted the trajectory of Western strategic thought.

CHAPTER 38

Strategies of Jihad

FROM THE PROPHET MUHAMMAD
TO CONTEMPORARY TIMES

Ahmed S. Hashim

The word *jihad* is one of the most ominous and least understood in contemporary political discourse.[1] It is invariably associated with "holy war" or with terrorism in the popular imagination in the West.[2] For some anti-Islamic polemicists going as far back as the early interactions of Islam and Christianity, *jihad* as *violence* is the very essence of Islam.

What does jihad actually mean? Jihad is a broad term, which comes from the Arabic language root, *JHD* which is associated with "struggle," "striving," "exertion," or "effort." In this context, jihad generally may be associated with almost any activity by which Muslims strive to bring personal, political, social, and economic life into conformity with God's ordinances as revealed to man. The word "jihad" is frequently used in conjunction with the phrase *fi sabil Allah* ("in the path of God"). The full phrase in Arabic, *al-jihad fi sabil Allah*, means "struggling or striving for the sake of God," and this can be done in multiple ways, only one of which is associated with the waging of war.[3]

---

1. James Turner Johnson, *The Holy War Idea in Western and Islamic Traditions* (Philadelphia, PA: Pennsylvania State University Press, 1997), 21.

2. Rudolph Peters, *Jihad in Classical and Modern Islam: A Reader* (Princeton, NJ: Markus Wiener Publishers, 1996), vii.

3. Asma Afsaruddin, "Jihad and Martyrdom in Islamic Thought and History," *Oxford Research Encyclopedias*, March 2016, available at https://doi.org/10.1093/acrefore/9780199340378 .013.46.

What are the sources for Islam's thinking on war, and how is the word "jihad" used in relation to war? These include the *Quran*, the word of God directly revealed to the Prophet Muhammad during his period of prophecy and after; the *Sunnah*, the actions and behavior of the Prophet; and the *ahadith* or the written accounts of the *Sunnah*, which were assembled into sayings attributed to Muhammad. After Muhammad, the public declarations of his immediate successors were considered part of the sources of Muslim thinking about war. Islamic jurists, beginning in the Umayyad dynasty (661–750 CE) and continuing onto the Abbasids (750–1258 CE) produced the classical theory of jihad. These scholars built their theory on their understanding of what had been said and what had transpired in the past as well as on the geopolitical realities of their own times.

The Quran, however, is not a divine revelation on the strategy or philosophy of war. It speaks to many topics and its myriad principles regarding war are scattered in different verses or *suras*. War, in the Quran's view, is an integral part of human society; an evil institution but a necessary one; (Quran 2:216) "Fighting is ordained for you, while it is repugnant to you." The specific Quranic terms that are associated with military activity are *jihad, qital,* and *harb. Qital* is the term which specifically refers to "fighting" or "armed combat" and is an element of jihad in specific situations. *Harb* is the Arabic word for war in general. From early on in the trajectory of Islam, jihad came to be associated particularly with fighting or making war "in the path of God." Associated with jihad as warfare is the concept of martyrdom (*shahada*); in Islam, unlike in Christianity, martyrdom is inevitably understood to be dying in battle, either in the mission to expand the domains of the Muslim state— *ummah*—or in defense of the faith.

The association of jihad with war is a complicated issue. First, to reiterate, jihad is not the Arabic word for war; its association with war means exerting oneself or striving with the utmost effort in a war for the faith. Second, jihad is not an objective; one does not wage war for the sake of jihad. Third, it is a set of beliefs—a doctrine—laying out why to fight, whom to fight, and how to fight. Fourth, historically, jihad has been used in conjunction with the promotion of two key objectives: to expand the domains of Islam until the entire world comes under the faith or to protect Islam from assaults from within and without. Fifth, while military jihad was conducted by Muslim states and empires throughout much of history, even if it was merely a justification to hide the aggrandizement of rulers rather than the promotion of the faith, from modern to contemporary times, it has been promoted by *Islamist non-state actors,* be they insurgents, rebels, or militias fighting against domestic tyrants or foreign occupiers. Military jihad or "jihad of the sword" is thus a purposive activity, as this historical survey of the practice of jihad from Muhammad to contemporary times will show.

I

Most of the Arabian Peninsula is a "victim of *natura maligna.*"[4] Arabia is vast and inhospitable, and for the most part lacks fertile land. The environment had an impact on its political and social evolution.

The population of northern and central Arabia consisted of nomadic tribes—the Bedouin (*Badu*) and sedentary inhabitants (*hadari*) of the few existing towns. No centralized political authority existed in those parts of the Arabian Peninsula. "Political anarchy" reigned supreme, pushing the inhabitants to seek security within the confines of their respective tribes. The concept of *asabiyyah,* defined centuries later as the spirit of exclusivist clan cohesion and chauvinism, best described Arab tribal society.

The Bedouins were a suspicious lot. War or the threat of war was the normal condition. Two distinct forms of warfare existed among the pre-Islamic Arabs. The first, "real" war over substantive issues such as conquest of territory, was rare; Arab tribes generally did not have the manpower or resources to prosecute it. The second type, the *ghazw*—raid—was more prevalent. Ibn Khaldun referred to Bedouin warfare as the "technique of attack and withdrawal."[5] The primary purpose of raids was the brutal but largely non-bloody redistribution of limited material resources to supplement subsistence lifestyles. The *ghazw* itself was constrained by the low-level of military capabilities and technologies, paucity of manpower, and by cultural taboos on killing for fear of perpetual blood vendettas.

The few cities created stable political and socioeconomic structures that relied on trade to create wealth. In Mecca, the Qureish confederation dominated commercial traffic in Arabia and established trading links with the outside world. Most pre-Islamic Arabs were pagans and Mecca was the center for

---

4. P.M. Holt, Ann K.S. Lambton, and Bernard Lewis, eds., *The Cambridge History of Islam,* Volume 1A: *The Central Islamic Lands from Pre-Islamic Times to the First World War* (Cambridge: Cambridge University Press, 1970), 3.

5. Ibn Khaldun, *The Muqaddimah: An Introduction to History,* trans. Franz Rosenthal (Princeton, NJ: Princeton University Press, 1967), 421.

the various pagan deities that the Arabs worshipped. Arab tribes would come to Mecca to perform pilgrimage rituals around the *Kaabah*, an ancient cube shrine in the heart of the city. Commerce and religion were intricately linked, allowing the Qureish to become fabulously wealthy. An enormous gap emerged between the haves and the have-nots, and any old tribal feelings of solidarity with the less fortunate evaporated in the face of the elite's determination to hold on to their material gains.

Into this environment—later described by Muslims as the period of *jahili-yyah* or the time of "ignorance" of religion and the One God's purpose—was born Muhammad ibn Abdallah ibn Abd al-Muttalib ibn Hashim. His clan, the Hashims, were part of the Qureish confederation but had fallen on hard times. Muhammad's own early life did not begin auspiciously; orphaned at an early age, he was cared for by close relatives until maturity, when he became a trader and well-versed in commerce. His fortunes took a turn for the better when he married a rich widow.

II

Freed from the threat of poverty, Muhammad often partook of the opportunity to meditate on Mount Hira, above Mecca. There, Muhammad experienced visions and was instructed by the Archangel Gabriel—the Angel of Revelation—to recite the words of God that were being transmitted to him. Over the next several years, Muhammad experienced several revelations that announced him to be the "messenger" of a new religion, which were collected later as the Quran. The Quran revealed a monotheistic religion, Islam, which means surrender to the one God (*Allah*); a Muslim being a man or woman who has made that submission to the one God. Muhammad began preaching his monotheistic message in Mecca. That message—submission to the one true God, the creation of a community of believers who would treat their brothers and sisters as equals, and the institution of social justice—was not well received in the city whose well-to-do did not wish to do away with their lucrative deities or to redistribute their wealth. When Muhammad acquired a following among all social classes, the elite decided to crush the nascent movement.[6]

---

6. On Mohammad's life and military innovations, see W. Montgomery Watt, *Muhammad: Prophet and Statesman* (Oxford: Oxford University Press, 1961); Karen Armstrong, *Muhammad: A Biography of the Prophet* (New York, NY: HarperCollins, 1992); Russ Rodgers, *The Generalship*

This period of revelation was one of extreme vulnerability characterized by the persecution of Muhammad and his followers. Many of the Prophet's Companions urged retaliation. Muhammad refused, saying that he had been given an order only to preach. The Quran recognized the right to self-defence, but it maintained that the best course of action in this early period was for the Muslims to patiently bear the wrongdoing of others and to forgive those who caused them harm. This was justified on the basis that patience or *sabr* is a form of struggle, a jihad of the faithful. However, God did not intend that the adoption of nonviolent struggle meant passivity. In the face of grave oppression and injustice, passivity is immoral in the Quranic view.

Muhammad was a realist; armed struggle in the face of the overwhelming advantages of the ruling Qureish was not a viable option. Muhammad was exercising prudence in that period of weakness, but the consensus among scholars, given the yawning chasm between his message and the Qureish system, is that Muhammad recognized that in this confrontation between God and polytheism, only one side could ultimately triumph. Violence was going to be inevitable, but the situation in Mecca was not the time to engage in open confrontation.

However, remaining in Mecca was dangerous. The Muslims withdrew to the rival city of Yathrib, renamed Medinat al-Nabi or City of the Prophet. Muhammad's reputation as a negotiator facilitated the entry of the Muslim emigrants into Medina, where the various tribes were at loggerheads. This emigration—the *hijrah*—in 622 CE is a seminal event in the history of Islam. Muhammad and his followers did not flee merely to ensure their own personal safety in light of the threats in Mecca; it was a strategic retrenchment undertaken to allow them a sanctuary from which to build their power, to organize and gather resources, and to seek allies for the inevitable showdown. The move resulted in the creation of a more cohesive community based on faith—the *ummah*—the setting up of a state, and the formation of an armed contingent, ideologically motivated and willing to fight.

The Muslim community differed from that of the pre-Islamic Arabs. The Muslims fought for an ideology—a faith—and they fought in the disciplined ranks of a cohesive community united by that faith. But on what basis did they justify their fighting? The specific reasons for resorting to armed combat (*casus belli*) are mentioned in the Quran starting in the Medinan period. In

---

of Muhammad: Battles and Campaigns of the Prophet of Allah (Gainesville, FL: University Press of Florida, 2012).

the Medinan verse (Quran 22:39–40), unjust aggression against people and their expulsion from their homes and for affirmation of belief in one God is an explicit reason that makes *defensive* war permissible (Quran 22:39): "Those who have been attacked are permitted to take up arms because they have been wronged."

In Medina, Muhammad was also transformed into a military commander. He built sufficient manpower to engage in military action against his enemies. Jihad as war became an important strategy used by the nascent Muslim state. It started as a *defensive war* in accordance with Quranic injunctions. However, as the Muslim state under Muhammad grew in strength, jihad was transformed into an *offensive war* to defeat the Meccans, extirpate polytheism, and extend the sway of the faith. The Muslims introduced something almost unheard of in pre-Islamic Arab society: real war. Ibn Khaldun described this as the evolution from the "technique of attack and withdrawal" to the "advance in closed formation" among the Arabs. Fighting in "closed formation" is steadier and fiercer than fighting with the "technique of attack and withdrawal." Close quarter battle leads to greater casualties. Furthermore, in "closed formation," the lines of the soldiers are orderly and evenly arranged, *"like arrows or like rows of worshippers at prayers."*[7] Historian Malik Mufti pointed out that the political imperatives of the new religion "mandated a much higher degree of organization and discipline." Highlighting the bond between religious purpose and military deployment, Mufti cited Ibn Khaldun as noting that "the closed formation is the fighting technique most suitable for one willing to die."[8]

Economic warfare also played a significant role in Muhammad's jihad against Mecca. The nascent Muslim state in Medina used military raids to improve its economic position; the migrant Muslims from Mecca were financially dependent on the Muslims of Medina and these military expeditions were an important means to give them some economic independence. Economic independence would free the Muslims from being at the mercy of their Medinan benefactors and would allow them to create their own cohesive community.[9] The seizure of Meccan goods permitted the distribution of spoils

---

7. Ibn Khaldun, *The Muqaddimah: An Introduction to History*, 421. Emphasis in original. Various translations of this text are available—see, for instance, the Princeton University Press translation from 2015.

8. Malik Mufti, "The Art of Jihad," *History of Political Thought* 28:2 (2007): 195.

9. Marshall Hodgson, *The Venture of Islam: The Classical Age of Islam*, Volume 1 (Chicago, IL: Chicago University Press, 1974), 175.

among the warriors and their families to make up for the lack of formal pay. Economic warfare also served to lessen the economic superiority of the enemy, thus reducing its warfighting capabilities.

Muhammad triumphed over his Meccan enemies, and he marched into the city in early January 630 CE, or 8 years after the *Hijrah* to Medina (8 AH). Before his death, the Prophet dispatched military expeditions to different parts of the Arabian Peninsula in order to call the people to Islam. He initiated preparations for military expeditions beyond the Arabian Peninsula, allegedly to offer non-Muslims the choice of conversion to Islam, keeping their own faith and paying the tax on non-Muslims (*jizya*) as subjects of the Muslim state, or deciding the matter on the battlefield, that is, fighting.

III

After Muhammad's death in 632 CE, the Muslim state was led by four immediate successors—the *khulafah*—Abu Bakr, Umar, Usman, and Ali between 632 and 661 CE.[10] All four were known as the "Rightly Guided Caliphs." After defeating apostatizing Arab tribes, the first successor initiated raids into the extensive territories of the powerful Byzantine and Sasanian Empires to the northwest and northeast, respectively. Abu Bakr advised the Muslim soldiers not to kill women, priests, children, or the elderly; nor to mutilate or commit treacherous actions. They were advised not to cut down fruit trees nor burn houses and cornfields and to refrain from killing livestock. Despite Abu Bakr's injunctions to fight righteously, there was no elaborate doctrine of or strategy for jihad at that time; the advice was derived from the practices of the Prophet during the wars against the polytheists.

The raids set the stage for the impressive series of military campaigns and conquests—the *futuhat* or "openings" of adjacent lands. Under the caliphs Umar, Uthman, and Ali, the Arabs conquered Egypt, the Fertile Crescent, Iraq, and much of Iran.[11] Under the Umayyad dynasty, which ruled from Damascus and lasted from 661 CE to 750 CE, Muslim armies went on the offensive even further afield conquering vast swathes of territory. Historians have debated the motivations of the Muslim Arabs for erupting out of their

10. The singular is *khalifah*, from which comes caliph.

11. On these conquests, see Fred M. Donner, *The Early Islamic Conquests* (Princeton, NJ: Princeton University Press, 1981); Richard Bonney, *Jihad: From Qur'an to bin Laden* (New York, NY: Palgrave Macmillan, 2004).

homeland to engage in one of the most rapid conquests in history. Jihad to expand the sway of Islam was a potent weapon and provided the Arab forces with extraordinary unifying spiritual power, as did the promise of rewards of Heaven for those who fell in battle. Engaging in jihad for the sake of Islam largely accounts for the victories against the powerful Byzantine and Sasanian empires.

The quest for economic largesse cannot be discounted in the Arab conquests, although it was dressed up in the language of religion to legitimize the seizure of plunder. Given the economic poverty of their homeland, the idea of extra-peninsular expansion roused the Arabs to acquire the "spoils of war." The Quran itself promised Muslims that, if they went to war to defend Islam and extend its territories, they would get many spoils. *Ghanimah*—booty—provided the material motivation for Arab warriors to take part in jihad and to risk their lives; they knew also that if they fell in battle as martyrs their families would be looked after.

The Umayyad dynasty's expansion came to an end when the Muslims overextended themselves or were forced on the defensive. The Muslims then chose to consolidate their gains rather than to acquire more territory, while their Christian enemies, especially the Byzantines, generally proved loath to go on a counter-offensive to recover lost lands. Both the Byzantines and Muslims conducted annual campaigns along the frontiers, but these gradually became ritualized warfare designed to uphold the image of emperor and caliph, respectively; neither side was stirred mightily by religious motivation to conquer new territories, add new adherents, and convert or slay the unbeliever.[12]

Jihad doctrine was formulated in the latter stages of the Umayyad dynasty and more rigorously during the Abbasid dynasty. During the Umayyad period (661–750 CE), jurists based in Syria—the Umayyad center of power—promoted the view that offensive jihad was obligatory and that its prosecution was one of the caliph's chief tasks. This group's views stemmed from the fact that their Umayyad patrons were engaged in ceaseless frontier warfare with the Byzantines and there was a need to justify these frontier hostilities on a theological and legal basis even as expansion of the *ummah* stalled. Not everyone agreed with this argument; jurists not aligned with the powers that be believed that jihad was primarily defensive. In other words, the *ummah* merely needed to defend its gains against efforts to attack it.

12. Carole Hillenbrand, *The Crusades: Islamic Perspectives* (Edinburgh: Edinburgh University Press, 1999), 92–93.

The Umayyads' demise came at the hands of a major rebellion in 750 CE by the Abbasid family who were related to the Prophet Muhammad. The *ummah* with its capital in Baghdad constituted an advanced political and cultural civilization at the height of the Abbasids. It was then that jurists began the process of codifying classical Muslim law. They wanted to provide a solid framework within which the *ummah* might flourish, and it was within the overall context of the systemization of Islamic law that the religion's theory of international relations and the classical theory of jihad were elaborated.[13] As they set about their mission, the jurists had at their disposal a vast array of rules and norms scattered among disparate verses of the Quran, but which were not in chronological order, in the traditions of the doings and sayings—*Sunnah*—of the Prophet, which were assembled into the collections of sayings—*Hadith*—attributed to Him, in the public declarations of the Rightly Guided Caliphs, and finally in precedent based on the past wars conducted by the rulers and soldiers of Islam from the time of Muhammad to their own times. The classical theory of jihad established a number of norms.

Jihad as a military endeavor became defined as being obligatory for all able-bodied Muslims, in the same way as they are required to pray, make the pilgrimage, and give alms.[14] Muhammad bin al-Hasan al-Shaybani (749–805 CE), a leading jurist, reiterated that the object of jihad as war is the expansion of the domains of Islam. But offensive jihad—to expand the sway of Islam—is a collective, not individual, obligation on all Muslims. Collective obligation—*fard kifayah*—means that this duty of expanding the *ummah* is binding upon the community as a whole but not on every individual, as a single person. When a sufficient number of individuals from the community fulfill the duty of fighting to propagate the expansion of the faith, the rest will be exempt from waging war.[15]

The overall leadership of jihad belongs to the caliph or military commanders designated by him. It was the duty of the caliph to call for offensive jihad, to weigh its costs and benefits to the *ummah*, to issue the summons to jihad, and to lead it as overall commander. However, jihad becomes an individual obligation—*fard ayn*—when there is an aggression against or outright invasion

13. Hillenbrand, *The Crusades*, 94.

14. Hillenbrand, *The Crusades*, 95–96.

15. See, for instance, John Kelsay, "Al-Shaybani and the Islamic Law of War," *Journal of Military Ethics* 2:1 (2003): 63–75; Majid Khadurri, *The Islamic Law of War: Al-Shaybani's Siyar* (Baltimore, MD: Johns Hopkins University Press, 2002).

of Muslim territory; but at a time when the Muslims were on the offensive or holding their own against the infidels, defensive jihad was not a source of much debate.

Strictly speaking, Islam could not recognize any other polity according to the classical theory. An obligatory state of hostilities existed until the conversion or subjugation of all mankind. Thus, formally, jihad cannot be terminated until this objective is achieved. A legal peace treaty between the Muslims and non-Muslims is theoretically impossible. Though the purpose of jihad is to universally extend the sovereignty and dominion of Islam, this did not mean a state of incessant fighting and killing. The realities of the world at the time dictated the formalization of relations with the non-Muslim world and the codifications of conditions under which war was permissible or even prudent. The jurist Muhammad bin Idris al-Shafii (767–820 CE) divided the world into *dar al-islam* (the Abode of Islam) and *dar al-harb* (the Abode of War), which referred to non-Muslim territories, that is to say, those ruled by "infidels."[16] Al-Shafii allowed for a third set of possibilities—*dar al-ahd* (the Abode of Treaty) or *dar al-sulh* (the Abode of Reconciliation), concepts which allowed for Muslims and non-Muslims to enter into a wide-range of peaceful relations. Al-Shafii invented these concepts since they did not exist either in the Quran or in the hadith literature. At the time of Muhammad, the geographical extent and ambit of the Muslim state was limited. But the geopolitical realities of Shafii's times—the fact that the Abbasid Empire was part of a system of international relations within which other non-Muslim states existed and which one had to deal with, whether by means of diplomacy, trade, or war—dictated that Muslims recognize the existence of others and formulate norms for interaction with them. War could be suspended or ended by a peace treaty, however temporary, if the interests of the *ummah* so dictate, and diplomatic and economic relations were formalized.

The classical Muslim jurists also discussed in detail what has been referred to as *jus ad bellum* and *jus in bello*, principles in Western discussions of "Just War." The former pertains to justifications or reasons for waging war in the first place: just cause and possessing right intention—promotion and expansion of the faith—and must be declared by a proper authority, that is, by the caliph. *Jus in bello* pertains to how Muslim forces should conduct war: Should Muslim forces issue an invitation to an opposing force to submit to Islam before force

16. On Al-Shafi, see Asma Afsaruddin, "Jihad and Martyrdom in Islamic Thought and History," *Oxford Research Encyclopaedia—Religion*, March 2016.

is used? What are the rules of engagement? What are appropriate targets and tactics? What if the Muslim forces find themselves in a situation in which they must employ weapons and tactics that will result in the deaths of innocent civilians? What is the ultimate disposition of enemy prisoners of war? Are they to be killed, ransomed, or transported to the Abode of Islam as slaves? The jurists did not uniformly agree and the answers to these issues depended on the context and the situation; but ultimately many concluded that nothing should be done that is contrary to prosecuting the battle or war successfully or that puts Muslim forces in jeopardy.

The Abbasids too succumbed due to internal weaknesses and political and military pressures both from within and then from without the caliphate. Two major invasions of the *ummah* were to have a long-lasting impact on the concept and practice of jihad.

The Christians went on the offensive towards the end of the eleventh century. Byzantine Emperor Alexios I Komnenos (1081–1118 CE) set the stage for a confrontation between Christendom and the *ummah* when he asked Urban II, the pope of western Christendom, for help in thwarting the Muslims encroaching on Byzantine territories. On November 27, 1095, Urban II, went one better and gave one of the most influential speeches of the Middle Ages when he called on all Christians to go to war—*to wage a crusade*—against the Muslims to reclaim the Holy Land and promised absolution and remission of sins for all those who died in the service of Christ. Jerusalem was seized by the powerful Frankish knights. Eventually, groups of Western knights established four mini-states known as the Latin Kingdoms, essentially armed Christian settlements implanted within the heart of the *ummah*.

This Christian attack put the Muslims on the defensive for the first time and Islam's jurists struggled to adapt the classical theories that had been developed over the preceding decades. With the crusades, jurists reoriented their discussions away from offensive jihad to defensive jihad, a significant cognitive shift. Some Muslim jurists undertook detailed analyses of the Christian onslaught from a strategic perspective, exploring its goals, strategy, and strengths and weaknesses.

For jurist Abu al-Hasan Ali ibn Tahir al-Sulami (1039/1040–1106 CE) and others like him, the Christian assault in the Holy Land was a Christian jihad. It happened and was successful because the Muslims had neglected their duty of jihad to advance and protect the faith. Consequently, they then found themselves under direct threat. Al-Sulami implied a direct link between the martial spirit of jihad to advance or protect the faith and the presence (or lack thereof) of the spirit of jihad (i.e., religious cohesion) within the body politic.[17]

The strike into the Holy Land was the main effort of a three-pronged Christian offensive against Muslim lands. That it was done with the intention of promoting the Christian faith the Muslims jurists did not doubt, but they questioned whether it was being done strategically. Prior to the mobilization for the First Crusade, Christian offensives had been "nibbling" away at Muslim territories in Iberia and Sicily. Pope Urban's call for a crusade to retake the Holy Land from the Muslims could not have been promulgated without the pope's understanding and recognition of earlier Christian efforts in confronting the Muslims in the other two axes of attack.

These Muslim observers, al-Sulami included, initially assumed that the incumbent authorities—the caliph—would marshal the requisite forces and march out to meet the enemy. This did not happen. The Sunni caliph in Baghdad at the time, al-Mustaẓhir bi-Allah (1094–1118 CA) was expected to lead the resistance. Yet, al-Mustaẓhir was politically, militarily, and financially impotent. He had little legitimacy or authority left to order anybody around; most of his soldiers had absconded to serve under the various military freebooters and disparate chieftains roaming the increasingly decentralized territories of the *ummah*. The caliphate had little in the way of economic resources to wage wars against the crusaders. Al-Mustaẓhir ignored all the requests to intervene.

The incapability of the state to thwart the crusaders led to the conclusion that this "infidel" offensive required individual effort on the part of all Muslims to defend the *ummah*. To the consternation of the Muslim jurists observing the unfolding drama between Christendom and the *ummah*, the spirit of jihad was absent even within the Muslim population. The crusaders possessed the "ideological edge" over the Muslims.[18] Having dissected the lack of jihadi spirit—religious and ideological motivation—among Muslims, these contemporaneous scholars recognized that much work had to be done to rebuild that spirit among the people *before* any meaningful military response could occur.

Al-Sulami also pointed out that the crusaders were not invincible. Though they had been animated initially by religious zeal and spirit, those had dissipated as they settled into their conquests in the Holy Land. The crusaders were

17. See Nial Christie, *The Book of the Jihad of Ali ibn Tahir al-Sulami (d.1106): Text, Translation and Commentary* (London: Routledge, 2015).

18. Hillenbrand, *The Crusades*, 103.

over-extended, and their logistical problems could prove their downfall. The Muslims were more mobile, and they knew the land better than the invaders. It would only be a matter of time before these could be turned against the outsiders, but only if the Muslims could be roused spiritually, mobilized, and induced to wage a defensive jihad.

Due to internal dissension and weakness, it took the Muslims a half-century to organize a unified front against the crusaders. Eventually, after years of un-remitting defensive jihad by volunteers and irregulars, three commanders— Imad al-Din Zengi, his son Nur-al-Din, and Salah-al-Din (or Saladin)— prosecuted offensive jihad. The three men used the *ulama* (religious leaders) to diffuse a cohesive jihad spirit among the Muslim population. They pro-moted the achievement of political unity within the *ummah*. They then created effective armies and succeeded in whittling down crusader power before at-taining the paramount goal: recovery of Jerusalem from the crusaders in 1187.

The political climate changed drastically by the turn of the fourteenth century. The crusades, though still ongoing, had been replaced as the most urgent threat to the Islamic world by the Mongol invaders who sacked Bagh-dad and murdered the last Abbasid caliph, leading to the temporary extirpa-tion of the caliphate in 1258. The Mongols eventually settled in the region and converted to Islam. The conversion of the Mongols turned out to be a "prob-lematic" one: Were they really Muslims? The Mongols were lax in their ap-plication of Islam, and they made liberal use of their pre-Islamic polytheistic laws. For many jurists and scholars, it was precisely this kind of "internal rot" and lack of adherence to the faith that had dissipated the spirit of jihad among the *ummah* and which had led the *ummah* to internal chaos, leaving it vulner-able to external assault.

A prolific Syrian scholar, Ahmed Ibn Taymiyyah (1268–1328 CE), weighed in. He declared that, though the Mongols might have professed Islam, they did not follow all its prescriptions. Their practice of their non-Islamic customs and their imposition of non-Islamic laws made them *jahili*, in the sense of being deliberately and knowingly ignorant of the religion they professed. Thus, Mon-gol converts were pagans against whom jihad had to be waged. A tricky but significant issue arose: Who constituted the legitimate authority to "punish" the rulers if the rulers were themselves corrupt?[19] Ibn Taymiyyah provided the justification for rebellion against "unjust" rulers. Ibn Taymiyyah did not

---

19. John Kelsay, *Arguing the Just War in Islam* (Cambridge, MA: Harvard University Press, 2007), 121.

reserve his ire only for the wayward or so-called Muslim rulers; he vented his wrath on Muslim groups or sects that, in his view, had ventured out of Islam such as the Shia, Druze, and Nusairi sects.[20]

The Muslim world recovered from the Mongol onslaught. It subsequently witnessed an era of revival but never again as a unified *ummah*. By the sixteenth century, the Muslim world was divided into three empires: the Ottoman Empire (1300–1923) in the west and adjoining Europe; the Safavid Empire in Iran; and the Mughal Empire in northern India. The Turks practised jihad against their Christian foes to the west while the Ottoman sultan combined political and religious power in his person and declared the return of the caliphate. The Ottomans also used the ideology of jihad to legitimate their wars with the Shia Safavid dynasty (1501–1722) in Iran. Various sultans persuaded the *Sheikh al-Islam*, the chief religious scholar of the Ottoman Empire, to issue fatwas declaring the Shia Safavid shahs to be non-Muslims. Declaring Shias to be apostates neatly sidestepped the problem of declaring jihad against Muslims. Thus, jihad against the Safavids was not only legitimate; it was was also a religious duty.

IV

Beginning in the eighteenth century, the *ummah* was again in crisis. There was turmoil from within and pressures from without. Political, religious, and socioeconomic conditions within the *ummah* led to the emergence of revivalist and reformist movements seeking to rectify these conditions. Yet it was the external threat that starkly highlighted the decline of the *ummah*.

During the crusades, the Muslims had seen themselves as superior to the invading Christians, though the truth was not quite so clear. Both sides were materially equal to one another and neither side was more advanced than the other in very significant ways in terms of discipline, organization, or military technology. Ideologically, during the era of the crusades, the two competing religions excoriated one another, as they had been doing for centuries. Christians saw Islam as an imposter religion, while Muslims saw Christianity as an incomplete and twisted one.

Matters were different from the eighteenth century onwards. The Europeans were not the crusaders of yore. Though the modern European continued to see their religion as superior to Islam, religion was not the force behind

---

20. Kelsay, *Arguing the Just War in Islam*, 121.

post-Enlightenment Europe's intrusion into the *ummah*. More importantly, the Muslim world found itself in a position of material inferiority in almost all spheres vis-à-vis a rising Western civilization. The *ummah* began to know nothing but defeat in the military arena and was forced on the defensive. Due to tremendous intellectual, cultural, economic, political, and technological advancements, the West saw itself as a superior civilization. And if that was the case, then the West was justified in conducting a *mission civilisatrice*—"civilizing mission"—to bring the benefits thereof to savages.

Muslims under threat of colonial occupation justified their resistance as a defensive jihad against aggression aimed at seizing their lands, disrupting their ways of life, and threatening their religion.[21] Muslim empires such as the Ottoman and Iranian Qajars lost lands and their sovereignty was severely curtailed by Western powers. On the defensive, both empires issued calls for jihad against the "infidels" as a tool for mobilization of the populace, promotion of imperial cohesion, and motivation for their soldiery to fight.

Resistance was also launched by several non-state actors in the Muslim world who sought to establish just Islamic polities following the presumed achievement of victory. Islamic religious orders like those of Muhammad Ahmed al-Mahdi (1844–85 CE) in Sudan, Emir Abd al-Qadir al-Jazairi (1808–83 CE) in Algeria, and Imam Shamil (1797–1871 CE) in the Caucasus bitterly resisted foreign occupation. Jihad was an effort to repel the attack of infidels on Muslims and their territory—a defense of Islam in a time when the established orders had been subverted by foreigners or had collapsed due to foreign occupation.

V

When World War I broke out, the Ottoman Empire joined Germany's side. It then proclaimed a jihad against the Western powers, aimed at promoting dissent and insurrection among the Muslim populations of the British, French, and Russian empires. The Ottoman call for a jihad proved to be stillborn. The British outsmarted the Ottomans and helped the latter's Arab subjects, one of the largest population groups in the empire, to rise up and seek their own independence on the grounds of the right to self-determination.

The abolition of the Ottoman caliphate in 1923 by secular Turkish army officers roiled the Muslim world, but the most pressing issue was that the

---

21. Rudolph Peters, *Islam and Colonialism: The Doctrine of Jihad in Modern History* (The Hague: Mouton, 1979).

former Arab subjects of the Ottoman Empire found themselves under the control of Western powers. The Arabs were more politically conscious than they had been in the nineteenth century, and they recognized that they had exchanged one set of masters for another. What transpired next was an explosion of political expression vented on paper, as well as through popular demonstrations, revolutions, and insurgencies. Some of these insurgencies were framed as defensive jihads to kick out the foreigners who had taken over Muslim lands. However, secular intellectuals and politically modern elites framed them as wars of national liberation. The language of religion vanished from the lexicon of the secular parties of the secular left and right in the Islamic world. There was but one movement in the Middle East for which Islam remained the mobilizing ideology and jihad was a meaningful instrument of liberation: the Muslim Brotherhood, founded by the Egyptian Hasan al-Banna in 1928. The Brotherhood sought to enlist jihad as an instrument of liberation from the West. Its success would flow from its secular rivals' failure.

Multiple Muslim societies attained independence in the aftermath of World War II. The elites that took power styled themselves as modern, progressive, secular, and nationalist. Modern societies, dynamic economies, and powerful armies were the outcomes desired by these post-colonial elites. These "modern" elites promised much but delivered little except brutality, poverty, defeat in war, cronyism, and thievery. For many of the masses in Muslim states, secular-but-autocratic systems did not yield the promised opportunities. A profound malaise and sense of disenfranchisement began to grow.[22]

The distaste for Western secular ideologies and its related "materialist" lifestyles was articulated by the Egyptian Islamist thinker, Sayyid Qutb, a senior intellectual figure of the Muslim Brotherhood. Qutb asserted that Muslim societies were no longer Islamic but rather *jahili* societies: societies not living in ways that acknowledged the sovereignty of God (*hakimiyyat Allah*), under which the divine law, *Sharia*, would hold sway. The Islamic order stood in contrast to the imported (secular) man-made solutions—*hulul mustawridah*—of the West that had corrupted Muslim societies. Man-made political orders, such as secular-liberalism or Marxism, assert that sovereignty belongs to man. This was blasphemy according to Qutb, as God alone is sovereign. Political rulers who did not apply the rules of Islam are *kuffar* (non-believers), even if they claimed to be Muslims. The "wretched trifecta"—ignorance of

---

22. Nelly Lahoud, "The Evolution of Modern Jihadism," *Oxford Research Encyclopaedia*, August 31, 2016.

Islam, unbelief in Islam, and nonconformity to Islam—was what jihad must eradicate.[23]

While Qutb developed the contours of an ideological challenge to the incumbent regime and not a strategy of revolutionary jihad, he was sedition personified in the view of the Egyptian government, which executed him in 1966. A year later, the Arab defeat in the Six-Day War of 1967 against Israel reinforced Qutb's critique. The defeat was a catastrophe, something deeper than a "mere" battlefield reverse; it was a trenchant commentary of the sad state of the Arab polity, society, and psyche. The "modernizers" had been shown to be nothing but "corrupt, tin-pot dictatorships." Their countries' economies were a mess; they had not created a new "socialist man"; and they certainly had not built powerful modern armies.[24] Qutb had established the ideological context: what was wrong with the *ummah* and why. It was left to others—the men of action—to do something about it.

VI

From the 1970s, the formulation and prosecution of military jihad by radical Islamists took several distinct shapes. The strategies were different in many ways, reflecting ideological predispositions, varying degrees of popular support, the natures of the enemy, the geographic environments, and the geopolitical contexts. Nonetheless, their strategies had important commonalities.[25]

First, these Muslims believed that they were engaging in defensive jihad against their respective enemies, which meant that jihad was an individual obligation for all Muslims. Though many contemporary radical Islamists refute the classical distinction between offensive and defensive jihads, they do recognize that jihad in the contemporary era is a defensive one against what they see as unalloyed aggression against the *ummah*. From the radical Islamists' perspective, this is not the first time Muslim rulers have failed in their task of protecting the *ummah*. Furthermore, today the Muslim populace itself has strayed from Islam. It thus becomes incumbent on the activist and righteous

23. Anthony Tsontakis, "Revolution in the Eye of Sayyid Qutb," *The New Rambler*, February 2017.

24. Tsontakis, "Revolution in the Eye of Sayyid Qutb."

25. On the radical jihadists, see Shiraz Maher, *Salafi-Jihadism: The History of an Idea* (London: Hurst and Company, 2016); Jarret Brachman, *Global Jihadism: Theory and Practice* (London: Routledge, 2009).

Muslims—the "vanguard"—to respond in order to either implement Islam or fend off assaults from outside.

Second, the radical Islamists knew they could not rely on Muslim states for military jihad. The Muslim states were powerless and under the control of outsiders; their militaries were not effective. Rather, jihad was to be the instrument of liberation by a revolutionary vanguard who recognized that they would be weaker than their foes in almost all indices of power, and above all in military power. In this context, other measures had to be developed to counter the military superiority of the foe; these could include asymmetric attacks, the skillful use of terrain, intensive ideological preparation, and training to withstand the rigors of war.

Third, a key issue they all grappled with was: Who is the enemy? This depended on the political context, but Egyptian engineer-turned-Islamist activist Muhammad Abd al-Salam Faraj provided one of the earliest articulations of the purpose of contemporary defensive jihad. In his brief treatise *al-Farida al-Ghaibah* (*The Neglected Duty*) Faraj contended that the Muslim world of today was not an abode of Islam. Rather, the rulers of Muslim countries "were raised at the tables of imperialism" and served as "agents of imperialism." Faraj declared Muslim rulers to be the "near enemy" (*al-aduw al-qarib*) and argued that removing them ought to be the priority. Muslims must wage a defensive jihad against their own rulers; and since it was defensive it was the individual obligation—*fard ayn*—of every Muslim. Although the *invasion* of Islamic territory is what invokes defensive jihad according to the classical jihad theory, fighting the "near enemy" is resistance against a kind of insidious invasion and should take precedence over fighting against the "far enemy" (*al-aduw al-baid*)—specifically, Israel and Western countries supporting Muslim dictators.[26]

Within a number of Muslim countries, violent, radical, domestic groups followed Faraj's exhortation. Islamists rose up against the Algerian and Egyptian regimes in the 1990s and sought to do the same in Saudi Arabia in the early 2000s. All failed miserably. They rushed into precipitous action and alienated or failed to mobilize the populations to their side. Islamists engaged in jihad have always argued that a key element of their strategy of struggle against impious domestic regimes was to gain the populace. Yet these late twentieth-century groups' operational methods and tactics—wholesale

---

26. Johannes J.G. Jansen, *The Neglected Duty: The Creed of Sadat's Assassins and Islamic Resurgence in the Middle East* (New York, NY: Macmillan Press, 1986).

slaughter and the targeting of people's livelihoods—in fact turned the people against them. Finally, the rebel Islamist groups were dealing with regimes with enormous domestic security capabilities and whose determination to survive, and willingness to use brutality, exceeded their own.

In the 1980s and 1990s another kind of military jihad associated with national resistance against a foreign invader took place. This kind of military jihad was often referred to as the *muqawamah*—or "resistance." The term meant a war of national liberation framed in Islamic ideological garb as a defensive jihad.[27] In the Fertile Crescent, the fallout from the lengthy Lebanese civil war, which began in 1975, led to the collapse of the Lebanese state and instigated the awakening of a marginalized community—Lebanon's Twelver Shia. Tormented first by Palestinian groups and then by Israelis, Americans, and French intervention forces, a Shia radical Islamist group, Hezbollah—Party of God—introduced an innovative and bloody operational method to defensive jihad: suicide bombing. A series of suicide bombings universally known in the Islamist circles as martyrdom operations—*amaliyyat istishadiyyah*—bloodied the American and French contingents, which then withdrew; the same techniques were then used against the Israelis who themselves pulled out of Lebanon in 2000.

Suicide bombings elicited horror in the West and a variety of reactions in the Middle East. In the West, the prevailing and popular view was that suicide bombings were an intrinsic aspect of jihad. While Muslim jurists had opined about martyrdom operations centuries ago, they had been discussed in relation to a fighter deliberately *plunging* into the ranks of the enemy in battle and *possibly* dying in the process *at the hands of the enemy*, not as part of a deliberate death at one's own hands against innocent civilians. Given the non-existence of explosives in early Islamic military history, there was, of course, a structural impediment to earlier suicide *bombings* per se. Not so in the contemporary era when the phenomenon made its bloody appearance. Westerners saw it as terror, pure and simple. Muslims, both Sunnis and Shias, debated whether it was permissible, and, if it was, against whom it was permissible.

The most significant jihad of the twentieth century was the Afghan war of the 1980s. In December 1979, the Soviets occupied Afghanistan to support a weakening pro-Soviet Marxist government. This transformed low-level violent action against the Marxist regime into a full-fledged insurgency by the Afghans against the invaders and their puppets. This was consequential for two reasons.

27. Naim Qassem, *Hizbullah: The Story from Within* (London: Saqi, 2005), 34–49.

The influx of thousands of Muslim "foreign fighters" to fight alongside the Afghan *mujahidin* became the genesis of the global Islamist movement. The person behind the birth of this "foreign Muslim fighter" phenomenon was the Palestinian-born Abdallah Azzam (1941–89). In two works—*The Defence of the Muslim Lands* (1981) and *Join the Caravan* (1987)—Azzam elaborated a doctrine and strategy of jihad. In contrast to the orthodox Islamic view of different categories of jihad, Azzam recognized jihad as exclusively being that of the sword, that is, as exclusively military. Furthermore, jihad was not a collective duty (*fard kifayah*) but rather an individual duty (*fard ayn*). Because it was a defensive war against an invader, jihad was incumbent upon every Muslim—not just Afghans—for its prosecution; no permission was required from parents, creditors, or political authorities.[28]

Second, together with Saudi construction engineer-turned-Islamist, Usama bin Laden, Azzam founded the Service Bureau (*Maktab-al-Khadamat*) in Peshawar to facilitate the arrival of the "foreign fighters" and to coordinate their ideological preparation and training for combat. With Azzam's mysterious death in 1989, bin Laden rapidly emerged as the Islamist leader and founder of a movement called *al-Qaida al-Sulba*—the "Solid Base." The movement's adherents entered into prominence from the mid-1990s as followers of a particular ideological strand within Islam—*Salafi-Jihadism*.

The 1990s were a time of considerable turmoil in the Islamic world as well as in the wider international arena. Afghanistan succumbed to civil war following the withdrawal of the Soviets; a radical native Islamist movement known as the Taliban took over most of Afghanistan and implemented an austere Islamic system of rule. The unravelling of Yugoslavia led to a civil war in which tens of thousands of Muslims were killed. The downfall of the Soviet Union was viewed favorably by many Muslims, but its successor, Russia, crushed Muslim aspirations for self-determination. The most significant event followed Iraqi dictator Saddam Hussein's invasion of Kuwait in 1990: the invitation extended by the Saudi government to the United States to defend Saudi Arabia, home to two of Islam's holiest cities, against possible invasion by Iraq. The presence of "infidel" troops in the Arabian Peninsula caused consternation, both within mainstream and radical Islamist circles.

It was during these times that Salafi-Jihadism emerged. Contemporary Salafism is an unyielding and puritanical branch of Islam. At its root the term

28. See, besides Azzam's own works, Thomas Hegghammer, *The Caravan: Abdallah Azzam and the Rise of Global Jihad* (Cambridge: Cambridge University Press, 2020).

Salafiyyah derives from the Arabic word, *salaf*, literally meaning past. The term initially signified the pious forefathers (*al-salaf al-salih*) who represented the first three generations of Muslims, those who not only witnessed the rise of Islam but also applied the Prophetic model as the correct way of life. Salafism denotes the earliest and most accurate version of Islam, the one to which all Muslims must return.[29]

There are multiple Salafi movements, but Salafi-Jihadism in particular is based on a few core concepts.[30] For its adherents, the international modern order that divides the world into nation-states and which is dominated by America is totally illegitimate. This sets them off from other Islamist groups, which like Muslim states from the nineteenth century onwards had accepted (or at least adapted) to the international system, or merely railed against its "injustices," but still functioned within it. The Salafi-Jihadists' approach was a visceral rejection of the international system, one particularly reinforced by animosity toward Washington, which was increasingly viewed as the major enemy.

Jihad is a key component of the Salafi-Jihadism sub-strand of radical Islamism. Though classical jihad theory did not consider jihad of the sword to be one of the five pillars of Islam, for the Salafi-Jihadists it is the sixth pillar. They maintain an uncompromising commitment to jihad by military means, believing that it is the only way to rid Muslims of dictators and occupiers.

The Salafi-Jihadists have a defined concept of the "enemy." They draw on the concepts of *wala'* and *bara'* to define and delimit the parameters of friendship and enmity. *Wala'* refers to the loyalty or friendship that "true" Muslims must have toward those who love God and hate His enemies. *Bara'* refers to those from whom jihadists must dissociate because they have turned away from God. Finally, through jihad the Salafi-Jihadists believe that they will ultimately establish a global caliphate whose legitimacy is premised on God's Law, but as events were to show later, there was considerable divergence on the feasibility of, and need for, a caliphate.

The continued presence of the United States in Saudi Arabia *after* Saddam Hussein was defeated in 1991 as well as America's alleged depredations in the Muslim world from the 1990s onwards set the stage for the growth of al-Qaida. Bin Laden began the transformation to focus almost exclusively on the "far enemy"—the West—though he was initially conflicted, as reflected in the

29. Joas Wagemakers, "Salafism," *Oxford Research Encyclopaedia*, August 5, 2016.
30. Shiraz Mahir, *Salafi-Jihadism: The History of an Idea* (London: Penguin Books, 2016).

withering missive to the Saudi leadership castigating them for their weakness and failure to build a just and powerful Muslim entity. It increasingly seemed to bin Laden that the rulers of Muslim states—the "near enemy"—could not survive without the support of the "far enemy." If the "far enemy" is attacked so that it is compelled to withdraw support for the unjust and ungodly Muslim rulers, would that not constitute a series of steps towards establishing a just system within the *ummah*?

Al-Qaida formulated a jihad strategy to meet the challenges the *ummah* faced. Beginning in 1996, bin Laden launched an ideological and military assault on the United States. He infamously declared war on the United States and *its people*. He accused the United States of waging an offensive war on Muslims and supporting oppressive governments in Muslim countries. According to bin Laden, the Americans had launched the war; the *ummah* had no choice but to retaliate with a defensive jihad. The American people were culpable under the concept of "vicarious liability"; they had elected the government that waged war on Muslims, thus making them legitimate targets. This notion, which can also be described as the "democratization of responsibility," was shared by the other Salafi-Jihadists but not by the Muslim world writ large, or by its jurists who argued it contravened the limitations on targeting innocents.[31]

Al-Qaida launched a series of attacks, which it referred to as "raids," on US targets throughout the Middle East and beyond. The "raids" culminated in the massive attack on the twin towers in New York City and the Pentagon on September 11, 2001. That event was a strategic inflection point. The US became determined to root out al-Qaida and its host, the Taliban Emirate of Mullah Omar in Afghanistan. The US went into the country, setting off the longest war in American history, which ended in summer 2021 with defeat as the Taliban returned to power.

For al-Qaida the American invasion was of equal significance strategically. The Soviet invasion of Afghanistan had created the transnational phenomenon of Muslim "foreign fighters" waging jihad in a *specific place*. The focus on the United States as a target allowed bin Laden to further promote jihadist war as

---

31. On bin Laden's strategy, see Mohammad-Mahmoud Ould Mohamedou, *Understanding al-Qaeda: Changing War and Global Politics* (London: Pluto Press, 2011); Gilles Kepel and Jean-Pierre Mileli, eds., *Al-Qaeda in its Own Words* (Cambridge, MA: Belknap Press, 2008); Michael Ryan, *Decoding Al-Qaeda Strategy: The Deep Battle Against America* (New York, NY: Columbia University Press, 2013).

a transnational phenomenon. Since the US was "everywhere" in Muslim lands, it could be attacked in multiple locations. Rather than congregate in one *specific battlefield*, the "righteous" jihadist fighters could target the "far enemy," in *multiple battlespaces* throughout the region in a protracted war.

How the so-called raid on the United States fit into this strategy, the goal of which was to get America out of Muslim lands, is not clear, particularly since it led the US to reinforce its presence for another two decades. Whether there was an extensive debate of the pros and cons of striking the US among the leadership of al-Qaida cannot be easily confirmed. 9/11 lost the group Afghanistan as a sanctuary and al-Qaida subsequently decentralized and scattered to more peripheral regions. An interim strategic approach of "terrorist jihad" by autonomous groups or individuals—a form of Islamist "leaderless resistance"— was articulated by the al-Qaida strategist, Mustafa Setmariam Nasar—aka 'Abu Musab al-Suri—in his influential *Daawat al-muqawamah al-islamiyyah al-alamiyyah* or the Global Islamic Resistance Call.

The American invasion of Iraq in 2003, which destroyed Saddam Hussein's regime and sought to create a prosperous democratic state, was viewed by al-Suri as a "gift" to the jihadist movement. Iraq could be a solid platform from which to establish a sanctuary and conduct attacks on the Americans. That may have been the theory, but in reality, it did not go al-Qaida's way. Initially, the resistance to the American presence was initiated by disparate Sunni Arab groups. Styling themselves in most instances as the *muqawamah*—the resistance—these groups ranged from former regime elements to mainstream Islamists to nationalists and local Salafists.

The *muqawamah* could not transcend its limited popular appeal; it receded in importance as foreign Salafi-Jihadists from the Levant under Abu Musab al-Zarqawi (1966–2006), aka Ahmed Fadil al-Nazal al-Khalayleh, wreaked havoc in Iraq starting in 2004. Zarqawi had a definite conception of who his enemies were as well as a clearly articulated set of goals. Acknowledging the military weaknesses of the jihadists and the constraints on prosecuting a sophisticated insurgency, Zarqawi used Iraq's communal fissures as a weapon. He initiated a campaign of unbridled savagery against Sunnis, Kurds, and Shias. Zarqawi's military jihad by terror transformed suicide bombings—used on an industrial scale—into a bloody strategic weapon against civilians, Shia militias, and Sunni insurgents. He upended American designs by fomenting a civil war and the virtual collapse of the Iraqi state and society. Zarqawi's exploits won an ambiguous association with al-Qaida, which was initially impressed by his "achievements." Yet al-Qaida eventually turned away in disgust, due to the indiscriminate violence, which led to Zarqawi and his acolytes being referred to as *takfiris*—the excommunicators—because of their proclivity of excommunicating their Muslim foes first in order to justify their killing. Zarqawi was killed in 2006 and much of his group—by then known as the Islamic State of Iraq (ISI)—was decimated by 2010. Its leader after Zarqawi, Abu Umar al-Baghdadi, remarked after ISI's disastrous defeat that "there is no place left for us to make a stand even for a quarter of an hour."[32]

However, like a phoenix rising from the ashes, the Islamic State of Iraq returned in 2012. It began an offensive jihad based on practical principles derived from two distinct works. The first was its own *A Strategic Plan to Improve the Political Position of the Islamic State of Iraq*, written in 2010 at the time of immense difficulties. The stated *goal* was to establish an Islamic state and thwart the plan to establish to a Western political model in Iraq. The *key* to implementing this goal was to adopt clear strategic planning and appropriate operational methods. With the withdrawal of the modern "crusader" forces from Iraq, the focus would be targeting the population for "capture" or "submission," the elimination of political leaders (assassination), and the targeting for destruction of the domestic military, security, and police forces that the crusaders had built up.

The second work was al-Qaida's Abu Bakr Naji's (aka Muhammad Khalil al-Hakaymah) *The Management of Savagery*. It is noteworthy for its almost secular paean to unspeakable and savage violence as a rational instrument of policy. ISI's beheading of enemies, burning of captives, mass rape and enslavement of women, and wholesale slaughter of members of recalcitrant tribes in Syria and Iraq were designed to terrorize and break the will of the enemy—and were lifted from Naji's work. Naji emphasized extensive use of the media to highlight the necessity of jihad and to justify jihadist actions. He urged undertaking a series of attacks in vulnerable states against the enemy's vitals. This would force the incumbent regime to concentrate forces and thus leave peripheral regions unprotected. The "Muslim" forces could then move into these regions, which by then would be in "chaos," and proceed to establish an embryonic Islamic state.[33]

32. "Ubuwat al-nasifa: Ahamiyataha wa tariq istikhdamaha" (Explosive Devices: Importance and Ways to Use), *Al-Naba* 101:1439 (October 12, 2017): 8.

33. On ISI and ISIS, see Ahmed S. Hashim, *The Caliphate at War: Operational Realities and Innovations of Islamic State* (New York, NY: Oxford University Press, 2018); Abu Bakr Naji, *The Management of Savagery*, trans. Will McCants (Boston, MA: John Olin Institute for Strategic Studies, Harvard University, 2006).

ISI followed Naji's plan to some extent when it recovered in 2012 and after. It built sanctuaries and reconstructed its forces in the northern part of Iraq, where the government's hold was tenuous, and then sent the Iraqi military reeling from its northern bases. ISI did not merely terrorize the populace; its seizure of vast quantities of military equipment enabled it to create a quasi-conventional force structure with armor, artillery, and mechanized vehicles supplemented by the fearsome vehicle-borne improvised device (VBIED), and relatively proficient infantry. This force structure allowed ISI to seize territory for its political design of creating an Islamic State, which would take care of the needs of the population as well as implement God's law.

The movement's new leader, Abu Bakr al-Baghdadi, refused to acknowledge the "artificial" boundaries imposed by former colonial powers on Muslim territories and participated in the civil war in Syria. Though he renamed his movement the Islamic State of Iraq and Syria (ISIS) in April 2013, al-Baghdadi's primary ideological and material battlefield remained Iraq. On June 29, 2014, a senior member of ISIS proclaimed the return of the caliphate after an absence of almost a century. The new caliph, "Caliph Ibrahim," was none other than Abu Bakr al-Baghdadi. He called upon Muslims to undertake *hijrah* or emigration to help build the new polity so that it could persist and expand. Yet the rise and ferocious tactics of ISIS provoked another international intervention, and the caliphate's downfall in 2017 was even more precipitous and humiliating than that of its predecessor entity.

As early as 2016, ISIS "officials" were already preparing for the possibility that they would lose territory and large numbers of personnel. Defeat had been part of God's judgment on His "flock," and sometimes God's favor smiles on them and sometimes it does not. However, ISIS did not simply rely on the Divinity for explanations of setbacks; it took measures to remain militarily effective even after its defeat. The caliphate ended but the Islamic State went back "down the spectrum of violence" from a quasi-conventional force and continued the fight as a terrorist and insurgency force in scattered areas in Syria and Iraq, a model followed by its "franchises" in other parts of the world.

VII

The word "jihad" has been a controversial term in the Western world because it has been misunderstood. At the same time, it has been the source of much debate within the Muslim world itself due to its association with military action by non-state actor groups. Jihad does not mean war, nor does it mean holy war. It certainly does not mean terrorism, though it has been associated with terrorism, particularly since 9/11.

Jihad has many meanings and associations; only one of these associations is with war. Indeed, jihad has come to mean Islamic warfare in many ways, even though this is contentious. It can be considered the epitome of the Islamic way of war in the past as practised by formal Muslim states. The *ummah* has oscillated between two types of jihads historically: defensive and offensive depending on the geopolitical context. The formal integration of Muslim states into the Westphalian system of nation-states from the eighteenth century on proved to be a problem for the prosecution of jihad by Muslim states, which used it, nonetheless, in an instrumentalist sense when under attack. For contemporary Muslim states, jihad was never prosecuted as an approach to warfighting in the twentieth century.

Matters were very different as far as radical Islamist non-state movements and insurgencies from the nineteenth century through to the present. Contemporary jihadists have taken the classical notion of defensive jihad and modified it to fit their fight to redeem the *ummah*, which they see as being under unremitting assault from within and without. For them, the concept of jihad provides legitimacy for war against domestic and foreign opponents; jihad tells them whom to fight, why to fight, and how to fight.

CHAPTER 39

Xi Jinping and the Strategy of China's Restoration

Elizabeth Economy

Standing before the press corps in November 2012, newly selected General Secretary of the Chinese Communist Party (CCP) Xi Jinping raised the specter of "the great revival of the Chinese nation" and promised to "unite and lead" the Chinese people to realize the country's rejuvenation.[1] China's past glory as a world center of intellectual thought, culture, and innovation, as well as of economic and military power, is deeply imprinted in the consciousness of the Chinese people. It serves as a constant reminder of both how much the country has lost and how much must be regained. Xi is not the first Chinese leader to articulate the desire for the restoration of the country to a position of centrality on the global stage. Even before 1911, when the last remnant of imperial China, the Qing dynasty, collapsed, officials and scholars recognized that their government was failing and called for restoring the country to its earlier greatness. It is a call that every Chinese leader has echoed since that time.

Yet Xi Jinping stands apart from his predecessors in the scale and scope of his vision of rejuvenation and in his determination to realize that vision. At home, he seeks a China that is an economic, military, and innovation powerhouse, as well as a model of political and moral rectitude. On the global stage, Xi's rejuvenation signifies a transformed world order—one in which China has reclaimed its contested territories, is the dominant power in the Asia-Pacific,

---

1. "Full text: China's New Party Chief Xi Jinping's speech," *BBC News*, November 15, 2012, https://www.bbc.com/news/world-asia-china-20338586.

and defines the norms and values that are embedded in international institutions and arrangements. Xi is particularly skilled at creating a continuous historical narrative—fusing China's imperial past with its socialist present—thus enabling him to evoke a sense of nation and nationalism among the Chinese people that contemporary "socialist China" alone cannot elicit.

Xi's deadline for China's rejuvenation is 2049, the centenary of the founding of the People's Republic of China (PRC). He recognizes the challenge before him. As he stated in his speech before the Nineteenth Party Congress in October 2017, "The Great rejuvenation of the Chinese nation is no walk in the park or mere drum-beating and gong-clanging. . . . The entire party must be prepared to make ever more difficult and harder efforts."[2] However, Xi has also cultivated an air of inevitability around the eventual success of his ambition, advancing slogans such as "the East is rising, the West is declining."

There is ample evidence to support his confidence. Grand-scale initiatives, such as the Belt and Road Initiative (BRI), the reform of the People's Liberation Army (PLA), and the forcible integration of Hong Kong have drawn international attention and contributed to expanding China's global reach and standing. But Xi's rejuvenation vision embodies more than simply demonstrations of economic and military power. It seeks the revival of China's position as a center of global innovation, culture, and moral political leadership. In pursuing this vision, Xi understands his domestic and foreign policies as forming a seamless whole. Herein lies the central dilemma of Xi's strategy: his growing insistence on state control over elements that derive from individual creativity is eroding his ability to recapture a true essence of rejuvenation.

I

China's five-thousand-year history is punctuated by periods of great innovation in science and technology, the flowering of art and culture, and leadership in maritime trade and exploration. Unaware of other rival civilizations, ruling Chinese elites conceived of their country as the great middle kingdom. The country exerted significant influence globally through the attraction of its culture and religion, the power of its military and administrative controls, and the "manipulative" capabilities of its trade and diplomatic relations.[3]

2. Xi Jinping, Report at 19th CPC National Congress, *Xinhua*, November 3, 2017, http://www.xinhuanet.com/english/special/2017-11/03/c_136725942.htm.

3. Friso Stevens, "China's Long March to National Rejuvenation: Toward a Neo-Imperial Order in East Asia," *Asian Security* 17:1 (2021).

By the late Qing period, however, weak leadership and the failure of the country to keep pace with Western and Japanese scientific and military advances awakened a new sense of urgency among a broad range of Chinese scholars and officials. Qing Dynasty General Li Hongzhi, who attempted and ultimately failed to persuade the Qing leaders to modernize the military, noted in 1872 that China was experiencing "great changes not seen in three thousand years."[4] Both reform-oriented supporters of the Qing and those who opposed the dynasty urged the country's leaders to undertake a process of self-strengthening. They called for "restoring China to its original strength, surpassing foreigners," and becoming again the "leading power in the world" and the "Greatest country on earth."[5] They sought to recreate the "mighty accomplishments of [their] ancestors over the past five thousand years—in conquest, administration, expansion of national territory and the elevation of national prestige."[6] There was also an acknowledgment, however, that the world had already intruded in ways that would make such an effort extremely difficult.

China's rejuvenation narrative carries within it both extreme pride in China's historic greatness as well as the humiliation brought about by the country's exploitation by foreign powers. Chinese officials and citizens often reference the "hundred years of humiliation"—the period beginning with the first Opium War in the mid-nineteenth century and continuing to the end of World War II and the Japanese occupation of China in the mid-twentieth century, when China was forced to grant territorial concessions to Western powers and Japan. Successive Chinese leaders have relied on this sense of past humiliation to rally nationalist sentiment and to remind the Chinese people of the dangers of foreign influence. In September 1949, shortly after taking power and establishing the PRC, Mao Zedong stated, "The Chinese people have always been a great, courageous and industrious nation; it is only in modern times that they have fallen behind . . . [We] will no longer be a nation subject to insult and humiliation."[7]

4. "Featured Excerpt from 'The Long Game: China's Grand Strategy to Displace American Order,'" *China Leadership Monitor*, September 1, 2021, https://www.prcleader.org/dashi.

5. Hoo Tiang Boon, *China's Global Identity: Considering the Responsibilities of Great Power* (Washington, DC: Georgetown Press, 2018), 5–6.

6. Boon, *China's Global Identity*, 5–6.

7. Mao Zedong, "The Chinese People Have Stood Up: Opening Address at the First Plenary Session of the Chinese People's Political Consultative Conference 21 September 1949," as quoted in Victoria Tin-Bor Hui, "The China Dream: Revival of What Historical Greatness," *China*

Jiang Zemin, China's leader during 1989–2002, voiced a similar sentiment, blaming both the Qing dynasty rulers and the West for the country's humiliation: "After 1840, the invasion by Western imperialist powers reduced China to the status of semi-colonial and semi-feudal society and subjected the Chinese people to twofold repression by imperialism and feudalism."[8] During the first eighty-year period, 1840–1949, Jiang argued, the "feudal rulers surrendered the country's sovereign rights under humiliating terms, the whole society was thrown into utter chaos caused by wars, the country became impoverished and weak and the people lived in hunger and cold." Ultimately, Jiang continued, China was saved by the CCP: "In the second 80-year period, the Chinese people under the leadership of the Communist Party of China have got [sic] united and unprecedently organized, overcame numerous difficulties and won one victory after another in their revolutionary struggle."[9]

This humiliation narrative represents a potent source of legitimacy for China's leaders; it enables them to bind the Chinese people together and to establish a collective consciousness. As Seton Hall professor Wang Zheng describes:

> Chosen traumas and chosen glories are transferred to future generations through trans-generation transmissions of parent/teacher-child interactions and participation in ceremonies geared toward recalling past successes or traumas. This leads a group to incorporate the memory of traumatic events into its identity, so later generations share the suffering of past generations that was not personally experienced. . . . the mental trauma of past losses, defeat, and severe humiliation can become part of a groups identity and bind it closer together.[10]

Wang further argues that this notion of loss has played a critical role in the construction of the Chinese national identity and has even pushed the Chinese people to be "ready to sacrifice personal interests to serve the grand

---

Dreams: China's New Leadership and Future Impacts, Arthur Shuhfan Ding and Chih-shian Liou, eds. (Singapore: World Scientific Publishing Co, 2015), 8.

8. Jiang Zemin, Speech at the Meeting Celebrating the 80th Anniversary of the Founding of the Communist Party of China, Permanent Mission of the People's Republic of China to the United Nations Office at Geneva, http://www.china-un.ch/eng/zgbd/smwx/t85789.htm.

9. Jiang, Speech at the Meeting Celebrating the 80th Anniversary of the Founding of the Communist Party of China.

10. Zheng Wang, "The Chinese Dream: Concept and Context," *Journal of Chinese Political Science Association of Chinese Political Studies* 19 (2014): 3.

collective mission."[11] At the centenary of the founding of the CCP on July 1, 2021, Xi Jinping underscored this point:

> The Chinese nation is a great nation. With a history of more than 5,000 years, China has made indelible contributions to the progress of human civilization. After the Opium War of 1840, however, China was gradually reduced to a semi-colonial, semi-feudal society and suffered greater ravages than ever before. The country endured intense humiliation, the people were subjected to great pain, and the Chinese civilization was plunged into darkness. Since that time, national rejuvenation has been the greatest dream of the Chinese people and the Chinese nation.[12]

While the narrative of humiliation is well-defined, there is less clarity as to what constitutes a rejuvenated China. The country's history reflects dramatic swings in its governance at home and engagement with the outside world. At times, China's leaders encouraged scientific exploration, intellectual creativity, and openness to the outside world. During other periods, they burned books, destroyed the country's naval fleet, and effectively banned businesspeople from trading directly with the outside world.

While contemporary Chinese leaders have created a picture of a peaceful, benevolent, and well-ordered society, Notre Dame professor Victoria Tin-bor Hui has written eloquently on the tendency of the current rejuvenation narrative to ignore elements of China's real imperial history. Unlike what is portrayed in official narratives, she argues, China was not simultaneously economically, militarily, and politically strong. It also did not possess the global centrality or continuity of geography that have been attributed to it in contemporary Chinese historiography. In reality, "China established effective rule over the territorial space of today's China for only 81 years (1759–1840)."[13] She has catalogued scores of military incursions from the Han through the Qing dynasties that led to territorial expansion, further undermining the contemporary official narrative that China has always been peaceful and unified. Hui also notes that during many periods of unification, particularly during the Qin dynasty, wise and benevolent leaders were largely absent: peasants were treated brutally;

---

11. Wang, "The Chinese Dream," 4.

12. Xi Jinping, Speech on the CCP's 100th anniversary, *Nikkei Asia*, July 1, 2021, https://asia.nikkei.com/Politics/Full-text-of-Xi-Jinping-s-speech-on-the-CCP-s-100th-anniversary.

13. Victoria Tin-bor Hui, "The China Dream: Revival of What Historical Greatness?," in *China Dreams: China's New Leadership and Future Impacts*, Arthur S. Ding and Chih-Shian Liou, eds. (Singapore: New World Scientific, 2015), 12.

scholars were persecuted; and citizens were conscripted to expand the dynasty's territorial boundaries to the north and south.[14]

The lack of a fully articulated concept of rejuvenation has resulted in significant variation among modern Chinese leaders as to how they interpret and pursue the restoration of China. Sun Yat-sen, the revolutionary leader who helped overthrow the Qing dynasty, for example, rooted his conception of national rejuvenation in his "Three Principles of the People": national independence, people's livelihood, and people's rights. In practice, these principles translated into opposition to foreign imperialism, equal stature for China among other nations, democracy (including popular elections), wealth redistribution, and greater state involvement in the economy through the nationalization of core industries. His successor, Chiang Kai-shek, retained many elements of Sun's vision, such as the enhanced role of the state in the economy, but also sought to restore a "hierarchical Confucian core" and to exploit a "rising sense of national identity and nationalism" that grew from opposition to the Western imperialists.[15]

The ascension of Mao Zedong and the CCP to power in 1949 introduced a new dynamic into the official restoration narrative: the pursuit of socialism (and later Communism) as the ideal form of governance. China's centrality on the global stage was also reconceptualized as the epicenter of an international Communist revolution. The formal separation of the mainland from Taiwan in 1949 led Mao to stress the importance of unification with Taiwan as part of the country's rejuvenation, proposing a model of "one country-two systems," in which Taiwan would retain significant control over its domestic affairs and even military appointments, but would cede its foreign policy to the mainland.

In 1979, Mao's successor, Deng Xiaoping, retreated from Mao's vision of permanent revolution at home and support for revolution abroad and instead embraced a rejuvenation narrative that maintained the primacy of the CCP but focused on the practicalities of rebuilding the foundations of Chinese economic and military power through four modernizations: agriculture, industry, defense, and science and technology. On the heels of the normalization of relations with the United States in 1979, Deng welcomed foreign capital and ideas as part of the "reinvigoration of China," although he made it clear that foreign capital would cover only a small percentage of the Chinese economy and

---

14. Hui, "The China Dream," 26.
15. Friso Stevens, "China's Long March to National Rejuvenation."

would "by no means affect the socialist public ownership of the means of production."[16] Still, the process of rejuvenation included the rapid growth of the market and rising inequality. China also became party to many international institutions and arrangements, contributing to a widespread belief in the West that China was on a path toward political and economic liberalization.

Jiang Zemin deepened his predecessors' commitment to rejuvenation and suggested a soft target of 2049 for realizing the country's rejuvenation. In 1991 he claimed, "All endeavors by the Chinese people for the 100 years from the mid-twentieth century to the mid-twenty-first century are for the purpose of making our motherland strong, the people prosperous, and the nation immensely rejuvenated."[17] He stressed the importance of the private sector and high growth rates and began to elevate China's global economic presence by actively encouraging Chinese companies to "go out" in search of natural resources and by joining the World Trade Organization in 2001.

Jiang's vision was not fully embraced by his successor Hu Jintao, however. Like Jiang, Hu underscored the need for the Chinese people to take action in response to earlier humiliation by Western powers:

> China was bullied by foreign powers in modern times . . . A major reason for that was that China was chronically poor and weak during that period. Since then, the great rejuvenation of the Chinese nation has become the unswerving goal that each Chinese generation has striven to realize.[18]

However, Hu's vision for a rejuvenated China reflected the more egalitarian sensibilities of Sun Yat-sen and Mao Zedong. Hu equated rejuvenation with a "harmonious society." He sought, without success, to redress many of the social and economic inequalities, as well as other externalities, such as environmental pollution and degradation, that had resulted from the Deng and Jiang eras of largely unfettered economic growth.

While China's leaders all emphasized the centrality of economic development in their rejuvenation narratives, they also adopted noteworthy measures to bolster their political and military influence on the global stage. From the mid-1990s through the mid-2000s, Beijing established a set of regional organizations,

16. "Deng: A Third World War is Inevitable," *Washington Post*, September 1, 1980.

17. Zheng Wang, *Never Forget National Humiliation* (New York, NY: Columbia University Press, 2012), 130, as quoted in in Orville Schell and John DeLury, "Rejuvenation," Chinafile, July 2, 2013, https://www.chinafile.com/library/excerpts/rejuvenation-fu-xing.

18. Wang, *Never Forget National Humiliation*, 132.

including the Shanghai Five, which promoted political and security cooperation between itself, Russia, Kazakhstan, Kyrgyzstan, and Tajikistan (later expanded and renamed the Shanghai Cooperation Organization); ASEAN + 1, which advanced diplomatic and economic ties with Southeast Asian nations; and the Forum for China and Africa. These arrangements enabled China to play a leadership role in developing norms and values around issues of development and security.

China also dramatically enhanced its military capabilities over this same period. As early as 1977, Chinese leaders included military modernization as one of the four modernizations necessary to rejuvenate China's economy and position in the world. In 1993, in the wake of both the collapse of the Soviet Union and the US victory in the first Gulf War, Jiang Zemin articulated a new military strategy for the PLA that sought to acquire much more advanced weapons systems and combat capabilities, improve the education and quality of the People's Liberation Army (PLA), and focus greater attention on future "high technology" conflicts. Jiang's speech also marked the onset of over a decade in annual double-digit increases in China's military budget. The focus paid off. In the mid-2000s, Beijing stunned the world with a series of demonstrations of dramatically enhanced military capabilities, including destroying a Chinese satellite in space and surfacing a submarine near a US Navy aircraft carrier battle group in the East China Sea.

All Chinese leaders have reinforced the power of the humiliation narrative to strengthen the collective consciousness and nationalism of the Chinese people. They have differed in their understandings of rejuvenation and their paths to realizing it. While Xi Jinping is part of this tradition, he is nonetheless the first Chinese leader to fully articulate the elements of rejuvenation and to deeply entwine his leadership and legacy with the success of the country's restoration to great power status and centrality on the global stage.

II

The ascension of Xi to General Secretary of the CCP in 2012 and President of China in 2013 marked an inflection point in China's ambitions to realize the great rejuvenation of the Chinese nation. Xi argued that, while his predecessors had failed to realize the rejuvenation of the Chinese nation, he was prepared to assume the responsibility:

> Since then [the modern era], countless people with lofty ideals to realize the great revival of the Chinese nation rose to resist and fight, but failed one

time after another . . . Our responsibility . . . is to work for realizing the great revival of the Chinese nation in order to let the Chinese nation stand more firmly and powerfully among all nations around the world and make a greater contribution to mankind.[19]

During his visit to "The Road to Revival," exhibition, Xi made more explicit Jiang's timetable for rejuvenation:

> Our struggles in the over 170 years since the Opium War have created bright prospects for achieving the rejuvenation of the Chinese nation. We are now closer to this goal, and we are more confident and capable of achieving it than at any other time in history . . . The goal of building China into a modern socialist country that is prosperous, strong, democratic, culturally advanced and harmonious can be achieved by 2049, when the PRC marks its centenary; and the dream of the rejuvenation of the Chinese nation will then be realized.[20]

Over the course of his first six months in office, Xi delivered a series of speeches that reinforced the importance of China's rejuvenation as the dream and responsibility of all Chinese citizens. Moreover, he articulated a clear set of objectives: common prosperity; a robust CCP free of corruption; a clean environment; ethnic harmony; a strong social welfare system; a strong military; greater unity with Hong Kong, Macao, and Taiwan; continued economic development; and global leadership on innovation. While Xi's ultimate objective for China's domestic rejuvenation was "socialism with Chinese characteristics," he brilliantly constructed a narrative that wove together all of Chinese history—"5000 years of Chinese civilization, 170 years of modern history, and 60 years of CCP leadership"—with his contribution to the rejuvenation process: building socialism with Chinese characteristics.[21]

The Road to Revival exhibition was the perfect representation of Xi's reworking of Chinese history into one seamless narrative. As Ohio State University professor Kirk A. Denton has described, the exhibition portrayed the process of modernization and capitalist development that occurred under the leadership of the KMT (Kuomintang, the pre-revolutionary ruling political

---

19. Xi Jinping, "Achieving Rejuvenation is the Dream of the Chinese People," November 29, 2012, in *The Governance of China* (Beijing: Foreign Language Press, 2014), 37.

20. Xi Jinping, "Achieving Rejuvenation is the Dream of the Chinese People," 37.

21. Xi Jinping, "Address to the First Session of the 12th National People's Congress," March 17, 2013, as quoted in *The Governance of China*, 41–42.

party) as a positive period of development in the overall process of China's modernization, Mao was transformed from a "radical leftist" to a "modernizer," and the Great Leap Forward, which led to one of the greatest famines in world history, was revealed as a period of impressive infrastructure development. Even China's imperial past, long reviled, was described as one of greatness and glory that had been lost to Western and Japanese imperialism.[22] This recasting of the historical narrative enabled Xi to promote the infallibility of the CCP and to draw directly on the ideas, innovations, and culture of imperial China in ways that appealed to a wide cross-section of Chinese citizens.

While the "Great Rejuvenation of the Chinese Nation" refers to China's re-emergence as global great power, it involves equally the needs for domestic reform and rebirth. Xi Jinping's strategy to restore China's greatness, therefore, is not limited to a more expansive foreign policy but rather speaks directly to the historical concept of self-strengthening. For Xi that has translated into three interrelated efforts: the purification of the CCP and society by eliminating corruption and removing Western ideological influences; the rebalancing the Chinese economy away from Deng Xiaoping's reform, opening, and go-go economic growth; and the creating of a military capable of fighting and winning wars.

III

Xi Jinping's restoration vision hinges above all on a robust CPP at the forefront of the political system. As he noted in his speech on the hundredth anniversary of the CCP's founding:

> The more than 180-year-long modern history of the Chinese nation, the 100-year-long history of the Party, and the more than 70-year-long history of the People's Republic of China all provide ample evidence that without the Communist Party of China, there would be no new China and no national rejuvenation. The Party was chosen by history and the people. The leadership of the Party is the defining feature of socialism with Chinese characteristics and constitutes the greatest strength of this system. It is the foundation and lifeblood of the Party and the country, and the crux upon which the interests and wellbeing of all Chinese people depend.[23]

22. Kirk A. Denton, "China Dreams and the Road to Revival," *Origins* 8:3 (2014), available at https://origins.osu.edu/users/kirk-denton.

23. Xi Jinping, Speech on the CCP's 100th Anniversary.

The CCP that Xi inherited, however, was riven with corruption and devoid of an ideological center. It had become little more than a stepping-stone for personal political and economic advancement. Quoting the second-century BCE Confucian thinker Xunzi, Xi argued that if officials cultivate righteousness and morality in their actions and decisions, "a well-ordered state and society will naturally result."[24] University of Melbourne professor Delia Lin has noted that Xi's views draw on two separate intellectual traditions: Confucianism and Legalism. "Both Confucian and legalist governing principles reject the acknowledgement of individual desires to pursue self-interest—believing it to lead to nothing but selfishness and corruption. Nor do they trust individuals as autonomous moral agents." Legalism, she notes, emphasized "the absolute power and authority of the ruler and the uniform enforcement of punitive codes intended to curb corruption."[25] Xi enforced political rectitude within the CCP, therefore, by reviving the Maoist practice of self-criticism (which also has roots in Confucianism), as well as by launching a vast anti-corruption campaign that investigated almost three million Communist Party members.

Xi also called on the broader Chinese public to embrace a new sense of virtue and morality. He pushed the country's educational system to "not only pay attention to the cultivation of students' knowledge and skills but also guide students to establish a correct outlook on the world, life, and values and [to] focus on enhancing students' moral cultivation."[26] Students from primary school through college must now study "Xi Jinping Thought." According to the Ministry of Education, the objective is to "cultivate the builders and successors of socialism with an all-round moral, intellectual, physical and aesthetic grounding."[27]

China's State Council also issued explicit guidelines in 2019 to create a "person of the new era"—someone who has inherited the "red gene"; maintains positive content online; is civil, courteous, generous and honest; protects the environment; practices civilized dining; and follows Lei Feng (an early Communist-era

24. Xi Jinping, Speech on the CCP's 100th Anniversary.

25. Delia Lin, "Morality Politics Under Xi Jinping," *East Asia Forum*, August 1, 2019, available at https://www.eastasiaforum.org/2019/08/01/morality-politics-under-xi-jinping/.

26. Xiangzhen Tang and Xiaofei Fan, "Analysis on the Way of Integrating Xi Jinping's Educational Thought of 'Cultivating People by Virtue'," in "Teaching Paradigm of Ideological and Political Courses in Medical Colleges," *International Journal of Science* 6:7 (2019).

27. "China Schools: Xi Jinping Thought Introduced into Curriculum," *BBC News*, August 25, 2021, available at https://www.bbc.com/news/world-asia-58301575.

icon) in his selflessness.[28] Earlier guidelines published in 2001 during Jiang Ze-min's tenure also advocated "learning lessons from the successful moral construc-tion experiences and the achievements of advanced civilizations of all countries around the world."[29] The 2019 version, however, called for purifying the social and cultural environment and criticized people who "worship foreign things" and "harm the dignity of the country." The CCP is required to "establish a regular mechanism to punish immoral behavior and form a social atmosphere that nur-tures justice, dispels evil, punishes bad, and promotes good."[30]

Xi's vision of what constitutes a virtuous Chinese society has become in-creasingly restrictive over time. Under his rule, the country piloted a social credit system designed to evaluate the political and economic trustworthiness of Chinese citizens and reward and punish them accordingly. Xi banned "ef-feminate men" from appearing on television, limited children under eighteen years of age to three hours of online gaming per week and only on the week-ends (enforced through facial recognition), and called for eliminating "celeb-rity culture" and replacing it with "traditional Chinese culture, revolutionary culture, and advanced socialist culture."[31] China's National Radio and televi-sion administration issued supporting guidelines to prevent people with the "wrong politics, morals, or aesthetics" from working in the culture and enter-tainment industry.[32] In response, Tencent's microblog platform WeChat elimi-nated thousands of fan clubs and entertainment news sites and deleted scores of accounts belonging to LGBTQ college student groups.[33]

Most egregious, however, was the forced detention of more than one million Uygur and other Muslims into labor and reeducation camps in the Xinjiang

28. Eric Cheung, "Inherit the Red Gene: China Issues Xi-focused Morality Guidelines," *CNN*, October 30, 2019, available at https://www.cnn.com/2019/10/30/asia/china-morality-xi-jinping-intl-hnk/index.html.

29. Nathan Vanderklippe, "China's New Moral Guide Elevates Xi Over Mao, Urges National Pride Over Foreign Influence," *The Globe and Mail*, October 28, 2019, available at https://www.theglobeandmail.com/world/article-chinas-moral-guide-urges-national-pride-over-foreign-influence/.

30. Nathan Vanderklippe, "China's New Moral Guide Elevates Xi Over Mao."

31. "China Bans Effeminate Men from Tv," *The Associated Press*, September 2, 2021, https://www.npr.org/2021/09/02/1033687586/china-ban-effeminate-men-tv-official-morality.

32. Wanqing Zhang, "Chinese Director Speaks Out Against Culture Sector Crackdown," *Sixth Tone*, September 14, 2021, https://www.sixthtone.com/news/1008505/chinese-director-speaks-out-against-culture-sector-crackdown.

33. Joseph Brouwer, "Netizen Voices: LGBT Groups, #Metoo Activist Shuts Down by we-chat, weibo," *China Digital Times*, July 9, 2021, available at https://chinadigitaltimes.net/2021/07/netizen-voices-lgbt-groups-metoo-activist-shut-down-by-wechat-weibo/.

Uyghur Autonomous Region. These camps marked the most extreme manifestation of Xi's effort to eradicate traditional religious and cultural practices, such as banning veils, long beards, and religious education for minors, under the guise of anti-separatist and counter-terrorism activities.

Xi's campaign to create a virtuous Chinese society also reflects a clear rejection of Western culture. This is not new. During imperial times, China frequently vacillated between welcoming Western ideas and culture and sharply restricting them. Xi sought to eliminate Western textbooks from Chinese universities and schools, remove Western programming from prime-time television viewing, limit the number of foreign films permitted access to the Chinese people, and pass a law to cut the number of foreign non-governmental organizations (NGOs) in China from more than 7,000 to roughly 420 unique foreign NGOs.[34] The number of foreign journalists in China also fell precipitously: twenty were expelled in 2020 alone. The vice chairman of China's Foreign Affairs committee for the NPC, Fu Ying, in March 2014, asserted that the purpose of foreign journalists in China was to "overturn our system of government."[35]

Some Chinese openly championed these elements of China's rejuvenation. The nationalist blogger Li Guangman asserted:

> A monumental change is taking place in China . . . the economic, financial, cultural, and political spheres are undergoing a profound transformation—or one could say, a profound revolution. It marks a return from "capitalist cliques" to the people, a shift from capital-centered to people-centered. . . . a return to the original intent of the Chinese Communist party . . . and a return to the essence of socialism. It is a return to the revolutionary spirit, a return to heroism, a return to courage and righteousness. Current efforts to crack down on the arts, entertainment, film and television spheres are not nearly robust enough. We must use all the means at our disposal to strike down various forms of celebrity worship and fan culture, stamp out pretty-boy and sissyboy tendencies in our national character, and ensure that our arts, entertainment, film and television spheres are truly upright and upstanding.[36]

34. Jessica Batke, "The New Normal for Foreign NGOs in 2020," The China NGO Project, January 3, 2020, https://www.chinafile.com/ngo/analysis/new-normal-foreign-ngos-2020.

35. Peter Ford, "China Targets 'Hostile Foreign Forces' in Crescendo of Accusations," The Christian Science Monitor, November 9, 2015, https://www.csmonitor.com/World/Asia-Pacific/2014/1109/China-targets-hostile-foreign-forces-in-crescendo-of-accusations.

36. Cindy Carter, "Translation: Everyone Can Sense that a Profound Transformation is Underway," China Digital Times, August 31, 2021, https://chinadigitaltimes.net/2021/08/translation-everyone-can-sense-that-a-profound-transformation-is-underway/.

Other Chinese observers, however, were less supportive. Peking University politics professor Zhang Jian, for example, argued that the government was creating a "demonized west" to "buttress its legitimacy."[37] As China scholar Susan Shirk commented, "Xi is drawing a clear and hostile contrast between the Chinese system and the Western political values. He is creating an ideological conflict between Communist party values and foreign values . . . to mobilize commitment to the party."[38]

IV

The second pillar of Xi's domestic rejuvenation is a transformed economic relationship between the state, business, and society, as well as between China and the international community. During the fifteenth and sixteenth centuries, China was the largest economy in the world. It was renowned as a source of significant innovation, ranging from papermaking and printing to gunpowder and the compass. The earliest rockets and bristle toothbrushes originated in China. Recapturing that economic centrality and influence on the global stage has been a central element of Xi's rejuvenation effort. Already Xi has achieved his dual targets of eliminating absolute poverty and doubling per capita GDP during 2010–21. He also set forth that China will be a moderately prosperous country by 2035 and will have achieved "major breakthroughs in core technologies in key areas" that will "give China global leadership in innovation." By 2049, Xi's China will become a "fully developed, rich and powerful nation."[39]

Xi's strategy for China's economic revival has evolved over time. Initiatives such as "dual circulation" and Made in China 2025—a well-financed effort to dominate cutting-edge industries—reflect his belief that China, with its 1.3 billion people, the second largest economy in the world, and an impressive coterie of scientific and technological talent, can innovate, manufacture, and consume largely within itself. Much like his imperial predecessors, Xi wants to control foreigners' access to the Chinese economy, enabling only needed foreign capital and know-how to flow into the country and preventing foreign firms from dominating the Chinese market.

37. Ford, "China Targets 'Hostile Foreign Forces.'"
38. Ford, "China Targets 'Hostile Foreign Forces.'"
39. State Council Information Office of the PRC, "China's Epic Journey from Poverty to Prosperity," September 2021, available at https://news.cgtn.com/news/files/Full-Text-China's-Epic-Journey-from-Poverty-to-Prosperity.pdf.

Xi appeared initially supportive of China's entrepreneurial class, and particularly world-class tech firms, such as Alibaba and Tencent, which helped drive China's service economy and enhance the country's global stature. However, as he approached the Twentieth Party Congress in 2022, which marked his reselection as CCP general secretary for a third term, Xi adopted a more critical stance. The firms were too big; their CEOs too prominent; their influence on culture too great; and their control of individuals' capital too unregulated. China's economy had also become too unequal, with a Gini coefficient on par with that of the United States. In May 2020, Premier Li Keqiang shocked China and the world by announcing that 600 million Chinese earned approximately $140 per month—"not enough to rent a room" in a Chinese city.[40] Moreover, China's demographic challenge was accelerating. Despite relaxing restrictions on the one-child policy to permit three children, the country's birthrate continued to decline. The cost of education, child-care, and housing emerged frequently as reasons for young Chinese families' reluctance to have more than one child.

Xi's answer—"common prosperity"—signaled the end of the Deng model in which some individuals and regions were permitted to get rich first. A Maoist concept that first appeared in 1953 in the Party's newspaper, *The People's Daily*, common prosperity was aligned with socialism, while capitalism was described as a few people getting rich while the majority remained poor and destitute.[41] Xi first mentioned common prosperity in 2012, however, the term did not gain currency until 2021.

Xi called on the country's billionaires to share in their wealth. (He also levied heavy penalties on several of them for monopolistic behavior, cancelled firms' plans to undertake initial public offerings, and called on the CCP to take financial stakes in tech firms to exert greater political control.) Tech entrepreneurs and their companies quickly lined up to provide billions in charitable donations to contribute to wealth redistribution. Officials pledged to make education, healthcare, and housing more affordable. Some Chinese scholars view common prosperity as Xi's effort to take care of those who have been left behind over the past decades of rapid economic growth and to avoid the polarizing politics Western countries have experienced.[42] Other scholars, such as

40. Lily Zhao, "Chinese Prime Minister: 600 Million People Earn Less Than $145 a Month," World Socialist Web Site, August 19, 2020.

41. "A History of Common Prosperity," *China Newspeak*, August 27, 2021, available at https://chinamediaproject.org/2021/08/27/a-history-of-common-prosperity/.

42. Karishma Vaswani, "Changing China: How Xi's 'Common Prosperity' May Impact the World," *BBC News*, October 7, 2021, available at https://www.bbc.com/news/business-58784315.

City University researcher Ming Xia, however, view Xi's initiative as a cynical political ploy: a "piñata hung by Xi and his party-state" that "creates a target for people to vent their anger and frustration at the rich and venal."[43] Xi himself has described common prosperity as essential to the CCP's future. "Achieving common prosperity is not just an economic issue: it's a major political matter bearing on the party's foundation for rule."[44]

V

The third element of Xi's rejuvenation strategy is the transformation of the PLA into a modern military that is "ready for the fight, capable of combat, and sure to win."[45] The weakness of China's military—its failure to modernize alongside those of the West and Japan during late 1800s—was a central factor contributing to the country's century of humiliation and the Qing dynasty's collapse. In his July 1, 2021, speech to commemorate the hundredth anniversary of the founding of the CCP, Xi asserted that "the Chinese people will absolutely not allow any foreign force to bully, oppress or enslave us and anyone who attempts to do so will face broken heads and bloodshed in front of the iron Great Wall of the 1.4 billion Chinese people."[46] Xi has called on the PLA to "put all minds and energy on preparing for war" and to "maintain a state of high alert" and to be "absolutely loyal, absolutely pure, and absolutely reliable."[47]

At home, Xi played an active role in the "rebirth" of the Chinese military. Scores of senior military officials were removed from their positions as part of his ongoing anti-corruption campaign. Xi used his position as Chairman of the Central Military Commission to accelerate the process of military modernization in terms of both its organization and its capabilities. He modeled his new joint service theater commands on the US military, built the world's largest navy, and developed a conventional missile capability that rivaled that of the United States, among other initiatives.

43. Mercy A. Kuo, "China's Common Prosperity: The Maoism of Xi Jinping," *The Diplomat*, September 23, 2021, available at https://thediplomat.com/2021/09/chinas-common-prosperity-the-maoism-of-xi-jinping/.

44. Chris Buckley, Alexandra Stevenson, and Cao Li, "Warning of Income Gap, Xi Tells China's Tycoons to Share Wealth," *New York Times*, September 7, 2021.

45. "China Focus: 'Be Ready to Win Wars,' China's Xi orders PLA," *Xinhuanet*, January 8, 2017, available at http://www.xinhuanet.com//english/2017-08/01/c_136491455.htm.

46. Xi Jinping, Speech on the CCP's 100th Anniversary.

47. Ben Westcott, "Chinese President Xi Jinping Tells Troops to Focus on 'Preparing for War,'" *CNN*, October 14, 2020, available at https://www.cnn.com/2020/10/14/asia/xi-jinping-taiwan-us-esper-intl-hnk/index.html.

The breadth of Xi's ambition—and the progress China made in developing and deploying advanced weapons systems—stunned many outside observers. Much of China's military buildup over the course of Xi's first decade in power appeared dedicated to realizing Chinese regional objectives, for example, increasing the number and sophistication of missiles targeted toward Taiwan and strengthening the capabilities of its navy and coast guard to assert sovereignty in the South China Sea. However, during Xi's second five-year-term in office (2017–22), there was dramatic new evidence of more global ambitions. In 2019, Beijing revealed an intercontinental ballistic missile capable of hitting any target in the world, and in 2021, it tested a hypersonic missile that, according to experts, could strike the United States in thirty minutes. A new generation of anti-ship missiles, advanced radar capabilities, and the rapid expansion of its nuclear arsenal signaled China's determination to have a battle-ready military with global reach. While China had not indicated any interest in targeting the United States, its emphasis on new long-range capabilities was likely designed as a deterrent against US involvement in a Taiwan-based or other regional conflict.

The PLA has also been essential to Xi's strategy for reclaiming Chinese centrality on the global stage in a larger geopolitical context. Most notably, Beijing established its first military base in Djibouti in 2017. Although originally characterized as a military logistics base designed to assist in anti-piracy efforts, it has expanded to support an aircraft carrier and several nuclear-powered submarines.

This represented a dramatic shift from previous Chinese military strategy. Historically, the PRC had rejected stationing troops or building military bases abroad, but under Xi, Chinese scholars and PLA officials embraced the notion of overseas bases. Scholars Xue Guifang and Zheng Jie, for example, argued that, "As a growing economic power, it is natural and necessary for China to develop a limited number of overseas military bases to protect its international trade and overseas investments." They also suggested that China needed more bases in order to perform "out-of-area" and "international public goods" missions.[48] In the early stages of the COVID-19 pandemic (March–June 2020), for example, the PLA provided medical assistance to forty-six countries.[49] "For a

48. Xue Guifang and Zheng Jie, "China's Building of Overseas Military Bases: Rationale and Challenges," *China Quarterly of International Strategic Studies* 5:4 (2019): 493–510, available at https://www.worldscientific.com/doi/pdf/10.1142/S237774001950026X.

49. Merics, "The PLA's Mask Diplomacy," *China Global Security Tracker* 7 (August 3, 2020), available at https://merics.org/en/tracker/plas-mask-diplomacy.

truly great power," Xue and Zheng asserted, "ideally, its military should stand behind each step of its increasing responsibilities and expanding interests."[50] As of this writing, more Chinese military bases were under consideration in countries from Southeast Asia to the Middle East and Africa.

VI

The PLA's top military priority in the context of China's restoration strategy is not guarding overseas assets but rather securing territories that Beijing contests with other nations, such as Taiwan, the South China Sea, and the Diaoyu/Senkaku islands, among others. Taiwan is particularly important. Despite never having been formally governed by the PRC, Chinese leaders have all insisted that the PRC cannot be whole without Taiwan and that rejuvenation depends on unification. Sun Yat-sen was the first to assert the importance of unification: "If reunification can be achieved, the people of the whole country will enjoy a happy life; if it cannot be achieved, the people will suffer."[51] Deng Xiaoping conveyed a sense of urgency in his call for reunification, claiming in 1983 that his government would "complete the unfinished task for reunification left to us by our predecessors" and noting also that "People like us, who are advanced in years, want to see reunification as soon as possible."[52] Jiang Zemin asserted that "compatriots on both sides of the Taiwan Straits are all Chinese and are bound together by flesh and blood, and all of them, no matter what party or organization they belong to, ought to share the great goals of peaceful reunification and national reinvigoration." And in his speech commemorating the hundredth anniversary of the Xinhai revolution that triggered the overthrow of the Qing dynasty, Hu Jintao stated that the mainland and Taiwan should "heal wounds of the past and work together to achieve the great rejuvenation of the Chinese nation."[53]

Xi has repeatedly stated that unification with Taiwan is essential for the rejuvenation of the Chinese nation. He has attempted to isolate Taiwan by

50. Guifang and Jie, "China's Building of Overseas Military Bases: Rationale and Challenges," 495.

51. "Continue to Promote the Reunification of the Motherland," Embassy of the People's Republic of China in the United States of America, available at http://www.china-embassy.org/eng/zt/999999999/t36735.htm.

52. "An Idea for the Peaceful Reunification of the Chinese Mainland and Taiwan," June 26, 1983, available at http://en.people.cn/dengxp/vol3/text/c1120.html.

53. "China Calls for Peaceful Reunification with Taiwan," Outlook, October 9, 2011, available at https://www.outlookindia.com/newswire/story/china-calls-for-peaceful-reunification-with-taiwan/737680.

encouraging the island's few remaining diplomatic allies to recognize the mainland, blocking Taiwan's applications to participate in international organizations such as the World Health Assembly, adopting a threatening military posture toward Taiwan, meddling in its elections, and refusing to maintain cross-straits political dialogue since the election of Tsai Ing-wen as president. Additionally, in the fall of 2020, China released a film simulating an invasion of Taiwan.[54] In an October 2021 speech at the Great Hall of the People, Xi asserted that "Taiwan independence separatism is the biggest obstacle to achieving the reunification of the motherland, and the most serious hidden danger to national rejuvenation."[55] And in August 2022, in response to a visit to Taiwan by US Speaker of the House Nancy Pelosi, Xi authorized China's most significant military show of force in the Western Pacific in decades.

Xi has also identified the South China Sea as a core priority. China's claim to approximately eighty-to-ninety percent of the 3.5 million square kilometer sea is contested by Malaysia, the Philippines, Vietnam, Brunei, and Taiwan and was formally declared without legal basis in 2016 by the Permanent Court of Arbitration in the Hague. Nonetheless, Xi continued to press Beijing's claims by naming eighty new features—fifty-five of which were under water (most of which Vietnam claims within its EEZ or Exclusive Economic Zone)—deploying surveillance and research vessels within the EEZs of several of the claimants, and deploying fishing boats and the Chinese coast guard to reinforce Chinese claims. While Beijing's actions enhanced its physical presence in the region, they also alienated the other claimants and complicated its efforts by encouraging other countries, such as Australia, India, and Japan, as well as some European actors, to become involved in asserting freedom of navigation.

VII

In the midst of his speech before the Nineteenth Party Congress in October 2017, when he was reselected as general secretary of the CCP for his second five-year term, Xi uttered the phrase, "China has stood up, grown rich, and

---

54. "South China Sea, Island Exercise!" *CCTV Military*, October 10, 2020, available at https://mp.weixin.qq.com/s/eXWnAJmEa9tT4VRpC6TWtg.

55. Carlos Garcia and Yew Lun Tian, "China's Xi Vows 'Reunification' with Taiwan," *Reuters*, October 9, 2021, available at https://www.reuters.com/world/china/chinas-xi-says-reunification-with-taiwan-must-will-be-realised-2021-10-09/.

become strong." Later in that same speech, he added that the country was "moving toward center stage."[56]

Center stage is both a literal and figurative concept. Xi Jinping's flagship foreign policy initiative, the Belt and Road Initiative, positions the country as the figurative center of global trade and investment, as well as a physical center. In the design of the BRI, China's planners delineated three overland and three maritime corridors, all of which radiated out from China through to Asia, Europe, the Middle East, and Africa. Since its inception, the BRI has transformed China into the largest investor in many developing and middle-income economies and the largest lender in the world. The BRI began, in part, as an effort to export Chinese overcapacity in infrastructure-related sectors, such as construction and energy, and to connect the weaker regions of the country to external markets through ports, railroads, and highways.

The initiative quickly evolved, however, into a broader Chinese engagement in other countries' economies and political systems. A Digital Silk Road enabled Chinese technology companies—those responsible for fiber optic cables, satellites, and e-payments systems—to begin to define the world's digital infrastructure. Xi also established a health silk road that became a vehicle for China to export traditional Chinese medicine and medical devices as well as a polar silk road, along which China sought to make investments in, and establish partnerships with, Arctic countries to try to ensure its future access to the resources of the north. Although China portrayed the BRI as open to other countries, Chinese banks and firms dominated the financing, capital, and labor involved in the projects. Chinese officials have also used the BRI to gain acceptance for Chinese norms and values around Internet governance and human rights. China trains interested officials in BRI countries on how to manage the Internet, including how to censor it in real time, how to use technology to track opposition politicians, and how to draft cybersecurity regulations.

Xi's efforts to ensure centrality for China on the global stage extend to rule and norm-setting in international institutions. Chinese officials view as essential the creation of an international system that reflects their values, policy preferences, and technology standards. Xi has called for China to "lead in the reform of the global governance system," and senior Chinese foreign affairs officials have claimed that the United States supports a "so-called rules-based international order," whereas China and the international community support

---

56. See "Full Text of Xi Jinping's Report at 19th CPC National Congress," November 3, 2017, *Xinhua*, available at xinhuanet.com/english/special/2017–11/03/c_136725942.htm.

"the United Nations-centered international system and the international order underpinned by international law."[57] (Xi also has aligned closely with Russian President Vladimir Putin to advance this narrative. On the sidelines of the Winter Olympics in Beijing in 2022, the two leaders issued a joint statement reflecting their shared view of the international system around issues such as human rights and development.) What has emerged under Xi's leadership is a multilevel effort to take Chinese domestic values and norms, advance them through the BRI, and reinforce them in international institutions such as the United Nations as a means of cementing China's centrality.

VIII

The essence of China's restoration is found not in the country's economic and military power, but rather in its ability to attract other countries through its intellectual and cultural centrality. As Hu Jintao stated in 2007:

> Culture has become a more and more important source of national cohesion and creativity and a factor of growing significance in the competition in overall national strength . . . The great rejuvenation of the Chinese nation will definitely be accompanied by the thriving of Chinese culture.[58]

Xi's top theoretical advisor Wang Huning, who also served as an advisor to Hu, was an early proponent of the importance of soft power. In 1993, Wang published a paper on the topic that argued, "If a country has an admirable culture and ideological system, other countries will tend to follow it . . . It does not have to use its hard power which is expensive and less efficient."[59] Xi himself encouraged Party officials to "increase China's soft power, give a good Chinese narrative, and better communicate China's message to the world."[60]

57. "How it Happened: Transcript of the US-China Opening Remarks in Alaska," *Nikkei Asia*, March 19, 2021.

58. "Hu Urges Enhancing 'Soft Power' of Chinese Culture," *China Daily*, October 15, 2007, available at https://www.chinadaily.com.cn/china/2007-10/15/content_6226620.htm.

59. Wang Huning,"Culture as National Soft Power: Soft Power," *Journal of Fudan University*, March 1993, as quoted in Bonnie S. Glaser and Melissa E. Murphy, "Soft Power with Chinese Characteristics: The Ongoing Debate," in *Chinese Soft Power and Its Implications for the United States: Competition and Cooperation in the Developing World*, Carola McGiffert,ed. (Washington DC: Center for Strategic and International Studies, March 2009), available at https://csis-website-prod.s3.amazonaws.com/s3fs-public/legacy_files/files/media/csis/pubs/090310_chinesesoftpower__chap2.pdf.

60. Asit K. Biswas and Cecilia Tortajada, "China's Soft Power is on the Rise," *China Daily*, February 28, 2018.

Shanghai Jiaotong professor Wu You likewise argues that contemporary China has few ethnic or political values to offer to a world dominated by Western philosophies and that its cultural soft power is defined by traditional Confucian culture, with concepts such as moralism and humanism, virtue, propriety, and righteousness.[61] Beijing uses Confucianism, Wu argues, as a means of reminding regional countries of the cultural roots they share and thus increasing the country's influence. Yet she also concludes that China's soft power drive is ultimately limited by its top-down approach: "It is difficult for Chinese media to win over foreign audiences in a timely fashion due to the state-centric running model and strict control over news coverage."[62]

China's attempts to advance Chinese language and culture overseas through the establishment of Confucius Institutes (CIs) demonstrate the challenge of simply grafting an element of China's past glory onto its contemporary political system. While CIs were initially welcomed by many countries, Beijing's insistence on controlling the hiring, curriculum, and content of the CIs' offerings, as well as its insistence on secret contracts, challenged democratic norms of transparency and good governance. The result is that, by 2020, China had established only slightly more than half of its targeted 1,000 CIs.

In June 2021, Xi's call for Chinese officials to project an image of a China that is more "credible, loveable, and respectable" revealed the gap between his belief that China could control its image and the reality of a modern world in which Chinese actions were broadcast globally for the rest of the world to evaluate independently.[63] It was difficult to overcome images of China's Wolf Warrior diplomats' propagandistic attacks on other countries around the COVID-19 pandemic, the threats posed by Chinese warships to neighboring countries, the crackdown on Hong Kong, and its detention of more than one million Uighur-Muslims in Xinjiang in labor and reeducation camps. Instead of attracting international actors to China's model, Chinese actions contributed to dramatic new lows in global public opinion polls of China's image and the credibility of Xi Jinping himself.[64] And China's global standing only plummeted further during spring 2022, when the Chinese leadership implemented

61. Wu You, "The Rise of China with Cultural Soft Power in the Age of Globalization," *Journal of Literature and Art Studies* 8:5 (2018): 774.

62. Wu You, "The Rise of China with Cultural Soft Power in the Age of Globalization."

63. "Xi Jinping Calls for More 'Loveable' Image for China in Bid to Make Friends," *BBC News*, June 2, 2021.

64. Laura Silver, Kat Devlin, and Christine Huang, "Unfavorable Views of China Reach Historic Highs in Many Countries," Pew Research Center, October 6, 2020.

its "dynamic zero COVID" strategy, locking down hundreds of millions of people throughout the country and wreaking havoc on global supply chains.

IX

In September 2021, China's State Council released a White Paper entitled "China's Epic Journey from Poverty to Prosperity" that documented the country's achievements across the various dimensions of international power and influence. By many measures—economic standing, military power, the dominance of the CCP domestically, and Beijing's global reach—China's long road back to rejuvenation had achieved significant success.

Yet the risk that Xi's rejuvenation drive falls short is also significant. For China's rejuvenation to succeed fully, as Xi has defined success, the country must be more than simply recognized as a powerful and influential country. It must be accepted, respected, and even admired. As China defense analyst Daniel Tobin notes, China seeks international recognition not only for its achievements as a great power but also for its social system and development path.[65] Xi has claimed that China has a model of development that others can emulate.[66] Despite Xi's confidence in the China model, there is little evidence that countries are flocking to emulate it. Demographic challenges, the repression of the creative and entrepreneurial class, declining worker productivity, and skyrocketing rates of debt may ultimately act as a significant drag on future economic growth. The economic costs of China's "dynamic zero COVID" strategy, as well as the images of Chinese citizens being forcibly detained in quarantine centers, have also cast doubt on the viability of China's authoritarian approach. It will be difficult for China's model to gain traction globally if these types of challenges are not addressed.

In addition, while Xi's major foreign policy initiatives, such as the BRI and military gains in the South China Sea, have become part of the architecture of China's growing global economic and political influence, they also earned significant international criticism. Early accolades for the Belt and Road, for example, dissipated in the face of widespread concern and even protests in many

---

65. Daniel Tobin, "How Xi Jinping's 'New Era' Should Have Ended U.S. Debate on Beijing's Ambitions," Center for Strategic and International Studies Report (May 2020), available at https://www.csis.org/analysis/how-xi-jinpings-new-era-should-have-ended-us-debate-beijings-ambitions.

66. Xi Jinping, Report at 19th CPC National Congress.

host countries around Chinese financial, labor, and environmental practices. The BRI also triggered the United States, European Union, Japan, and Australia to increase their attention to and support for infrastructure projects globally, complicating Beijing's efforts. Moreover, beyond the declining levels of popularity China is experiencing globally, countries had begun to adopt significant economic and security measures to constrain Xi's ability to realize the full scope of his ambition. By 2021, Europe and the United States, as well as the Quad countries (America, Australia, India, and Japan), were rethinking global supply chains to ensure redundancy in the face of an unreliable China; they were also strengthening coordination in multilateral institutions. The United States, Australia, and the UK had even established a new defense pact to counter China's aggression in the Asia Pacific. Equally significant, China's decision to refrain from condemning Russia's invasion of Ukraine in February 2022, cemented an understanding in many political centers in Europe, North America, and Asia that China was at heart a revisionist power and raised alarm bells around the potential of a Chinese invasion of Taiwan. Previously non-aligned countries, such as Finland and Sweden, initiated discussions around joining NATO. In several respects, therefore, Xi's foreign policy choices have led other countries to adopt policies that ultimately undermine Xi's ability to realize his longer-term objectives, such as a new security order and the dissolution of the US-led alliance system.

Equally challenging for Xi is his effort to deliver the type of thought and cultural leadership that imperial China offered the rest of the world. While Xi continues to draw on the traditions of the past to bolster China's claims to intellectual and cultural centrality, he has little to offer from the China he leads today. The flowering of art, culture, intellectual thought, and even commerce that attracts citizens from other countries will require the CCP to relax not increase strictures in the education, media, innovation, and cultural spaces. China's persistently low-soft power rankings—and the lack of credibility accredited to Xi Jinping himself—reflect a potentially devastating vulnerability in Xi's restoration strategy. Ultimately, Xi Jinping and the rest of the Chinese leadership will likely need to decide whether to reform the way they govern to achieve their rejuvenation dream or to reform the definition of rejuvenation and simply declare success.

CHAPTER 40

Soleimani, Gerasimov, and Strategies of Irregular Warfare

Seth G. Jones

The grave of Major General Qassem Soleimani is situated in the Shrine of the Martyrs in his hometown of Kerman in southeastern Iran. It is unpretentious and boasts a bone-white marble slab, engraved with bright red tulips and an epitaph that lauds Soleimani as a "brave commander of anti-terrorist battles in West Asia" who was "targeted at Baghdad International Airport by the CENTCOM terrorist unit, and together with a group of his comrades achieved martyrdom." The simplicity of Soleimani's gravestone is emblematic of the Islamic martyr—humble and pure. It was designed to pay homage to Iran's best-known military leader in at least a generation. Since childhood, Soleimani had dreamed of becoming a chivalric warrior, or *javanmard*, for his country. On January 2, 2020, a US MQ-9A drone fired several Hellfire missiles at Soleimani's armored sports utility vehicle as it skirted down an access road at Baghdad International Airport, killing him and several others in his entourage, thus sealing his legacy as a martyr and *javanmard*.

Yet Soleimani was not a classic soldier who fought Iran's foes on a conventional battlefield. He was the quintessential irregular warrior. During his tenure as head of the Islamic Revolutionary Guard Corps-Quds Force (IRGC-QF), the paramilitary arm of Iran's military responsible for covert extraterritorial operations, Soleimani was aggressive and dynamic. Skilled in the art of subversion, he was inclined to flaunt it. "Mr. Trump, the gambler!" he once bragged in a 2018 Instagram post to US President Donald Trump. "Don't threaten our lives! You are well aware of our power and capabilities in the region. You know how powerful we are at asymmetrical warfare." Over the course of his lifetime, Soleimani expanded Iranian influence by aiding groups such as Lebanese Hezbollah, the Hashd-al-Shaabi (Popular Mobilization Forces) in Iraq, Ansar Allah (Houthis) in Yemen, and various militia forces in the Palestinian territory, Syria, Afghanistan, Pakistan, and other countries.

Much like Soleimani, Russian Chief of the General Staff Valery Gerasimov embraced irregular warfare as an important component of competition, including against adversaries like the United States with significant conventional and nuclear capabilities. Following the end of the Cold War, Gerasimov watched with alarm as US military and intelligence agencies conducted operations in the Balkans, Afghanistan, Iraq, and Libya. He also accused the US military and intelligence agencies of attempting to weaken or overthrow regimes during the various color revolutions. Based in part on US actions, Gerasimov concluded that "asymmetric actions have come into widespread use, enabling the nullification of an enemy's advantages in armed conflict."[1] Gerasimov supported the use of irregular methods to expand Russian power and weaken its main adversary (its *glavnyy protivnik*)—the United States. Russia seized the Ukrainian peninsula of Crimea without firing a shot in 2014; orchestrated an insurgency in eastern Ukraine that involved the use of proxy forces and extensive offensive cyber operations; leveraged Lebanese Hezbollah and other forces to retake Syrian territory against rebel groups; deployed clandestine private military companies to approximately three dozen countries across the globe; and waged a fierce disinformation and cyber campaign against the United States and its partners.

Soleimani and Gerasimov were quintessential strategists and practitioners of irregular warfare. Their countries established conventional militaries capable of fighting set-piece battles against adversaries, as demonstrated by Russia's February 2022 invasion of Ukraine. But Iran and Russia also directed considerable resources and attention to waging irregular warfare in response to US conventional and nuclear power; the enormous costs of a conventional and nuclear war against a major power like the United States, including economic destruction, large-scale casualties, and environmental and infrastructure

---

1. Валéрий Герáсимов [Valery Gerasimov], "Ценность науки в предвидении: Новые вызовы требуют переосмыслить формы и способы ведения боевых действий" ["The Value of Science Is in the Foresight: New Challenges Demand Rethinking the Forms and Methods of Carrying Out Combat Operations"], Военно-промышленный курьер [*Military-Industrial Courier*], February 26, 2013.

devastation; and the US vulnerability to irregular warfare. These factors created an impetus for leaders like Soleimani and Gerasimov to use irregular means to achieve strategic ends—particularly as a means of shifting the regional balance of power in their country's favor, weakening the United States, and undermining a US-dominated international order.

The irregular warfare methods practiced by Soleimani and Gerasimov were not new, but rather had a long tradition in the annals of warfare. And they will continue to be essential in the future.

I

The Chinese general and military strategist Sun Tzu wrote in his classic *The Art of War* that the acme of skill is to "subdue the enemy *without fighting.*"[2] Sun Tzu emphasized the importance of "moral influence," espionage, deception, and secret operations. "Where [the enemy] is strong, avoid him," Sun Tzu warned, and strike the adversary where it is weak and vulnerable.[3] The Roman general Quintus Fabius Maximus Verrucosus developed a strategy that focused on raids and harassment against a larger and better equipped Carthaginian army. During the Cold War, the towering US State Department diplomat and Russian expert George Kennan argued that essential tools of warfare "range from such overt actions as political alliances, economic measures . . . and 'white' propaganda to such covert operations as clandestine support of 'friendly' foreign elements, 'black' psychological warfare and even encouragement of underground resistance in hostile states." While conventional wars generally have a finite beginning and end, irregular warfare is a persistent reality of international politics—what Kennan called "the perpetual rhythm of struggle, in and out of war."[4]

Irregular warfare refers to activities short of conventional and nuclear warfare that are designed to expand a country's influence and legitimacy, as well as weaken its adversaries. Under its umbrella fall numerous tools of statecraft that governments can use to shift the balance of power in their favor: information operations (including psychological operations, disinformation, and propaganda), cyber operations, support to state and non-state partners, covert

2. Sun Tzu, *The Art of War*, trans., Samuel B. Griffith (New York, NY: Oxford University Press, 1971), 77. Emphasis added.

3. Sun Tzu, *The Art of War*, 67.

4. George F. Kennan, "Organizing Political Warfare," April 30, 1948, Woodrow Wilson Center, History and Public Policy Program Digital Archive.

action, and economic coercion, among others. Some of these tools—such as information operations, covert action, and cyber operations—can be used in conventional campaigns as well. They are simply a means to an end. In irregular warfare a country designs and uses these tools to undermine its adversaries as part of balance-of-power competition without engaging in set-piece battles. Other government officials and scholars have used different terms—political warfare, hybrid warfare, gray zone activity, asymmetric conflict, and the indirect approach—to capture some or all of these activities.

Irregular warfare is different from conventional warfare, nuclear warfare, and routine foreign policy. Conventional warfare—sometimes referred to as "regular" or "traditional" warfare—involves the use of a country's massed air force, army, navy, and other capabilities to defeat an adversary's armed forces in decisive battles; to seize territory, populations, and military forces; or to destroy an enemy's war-making capacity. Nuclear warfare involves the use—or threatened use—of strategic or tactical nuclear weapons against an adversary. Unlike conventional and nuclear warfare, irregular warfare is indirect because it involves leveraging clandestine units, partner forces, covert action, and economic instruments. Finally, irregular warfare is distinct from routine foreign policy, which can include diplomatic, humanitarian, intelligence, and other activities that have little or nothing to do with competition against adversaries. Much of routine foreign policy is not designed to weaken enemies as part of balance-of-power politics.

Some might object to using the term "warfare" to describe irregular operations, but that argument reflects a Western interpretation of warfare. Mao Zedong—founder of the People's Republic of China, Chairman of the Communist Party, and onetime guerrilla commander—wrote that irregular strategies are an essential component of warfare. "When guerrillas engage a stronger enemy," Mao wrote in *On Guerrilla Warfare*, "they withdraw when he advances; harass him when he stops; strike him when he is weary; pursue him when he withdraws."[5] Irregular strategies and tactics are a sine qua non of warfare, and countries generally use their own terms to describe irregular warfare.

Soleimani's Iran utilized *jang-e narm* (soft war), which includes activities like propaganda and disinformation against adversaries. Some Iranians have also utilized terms such as *jang-e gheir-e kelasik* (non-classic war). Russia has

5. Mao Zedong, *On Guerrilla Warfare*, trans. Samuel B. Griffith (Urbana, IL: University of Illinois Press, 2000), 46.

long embraced *aktivnyye meropriyatiya* (active measures), and includes under that category a range of tools from covert action to assassinations and disinformation. Major General Oleg Kalugin, the former head of foreign counterintelligence of the KGB's 1st Chief Directorate, described active measures as the "heart and soul of Soviet intelligence" that were used to "weaken the United States" and to "drive wedges in the Western community alliance of all sorts."[6] Russian leaders have also utilized such concepts as *gibridnaya voina* (hybrid war), *informatsionnoye protivoborstvo* (information confrontation), and *maskirovka* (denial and deception). "The important point," wrote US military historian Charles Bartles, "is that while the West considers these nonmilitary measures as ways of avoiding war, Russia considers these measures *as war*."[7] In addition, China has used terms like *san zhong zhanfa* (three warfares)—which includes media, psychological, and legal warfare—as part of balance-of-power competition. None of these components of China's three warfares involves the use of violence.

II

Among strategists of irregular warfare, few have been as influential as Qassem Soleimani. Born on March 11, 1957, in Rabor, a town in the southeastern Iranian province of Kerman, Soleimani was the middle child in a relatively poor family of five. In 1979, when Soleimani was in his early twenties, Iran experienced a convulsive revolution that overthrew Mohammad Reza Pahlavi and installed Grand Ayatollah Ruhollah Khomeini in his place. Khomeini's Iran centered around the doctrine of *velayat-e faqih*, or the Islamic system of clerical rule. Shia clergy—the *ulama*—governed the country as an Islamic republic and enforced conservative social values under a supreme clerical leader (the *faqih*) who provided guardianship (*velayat*) over the nation.

Energized by the Revolution but with no military experience, Soleimani joined the newly established Islamic Revolutionary Guard Corps (IRGC). Decades later he explained, "we were all young and wanted to serve the revolution in a way."[8] Khomeini had established the IRGC, or *sepah-e pasdaran-e*

6. Oleg Kalugin, "Inside the KGB: An Interview with Retired KGB Maj. Gen. Oleg Kalugin," interview by the Cold War Production Team, CNN, January 1998.

7. Charles K. Bartles, "Getting Gerasimov Right," *Military Review* 96:1 (2016): 30. Emphasis added.

8. "سردار قاسم سلیمانی گمنامی: خواسته شهیدان ما بود" ["Commander Qassemi: Anonymity Was the Wish of Our Martyrs"], روزنامه جمهوری اسلامی [*Jomhouri-ye Eslami*], June 7, 2005.

enqelab-e eslami, in 1979, shortly after the Revolution. He was suspicious of the loyalty of some officers in Iran's regular military, or Artesh. In addition, pro-clerical militants had been helpful in bringing down the Pahlavi regime, and Khomeini wanted to organize them under a single umbrella. The IRGC's devotion to Khomeini gave it substantial legitimacy, and it would become the lynchpin of Iranian irregular warfare as well as the epicenter of Soleimani's power.

In September 1980, Saddam Hussein's forces invaded Iran's Khuzestan Province, initiating a decade-long war between Iran and Iraq that Iranians frequently referred to as the "imposed war," or *jang-e tahmili*.[9] Soleimani eventually commanded the IRGC's Forty-First Division, which was nicknamed *Tharallah*—or Vengeance of God. During Operation Tariq al-Qods in late 1981, Soleimani was involved in heavy fighting around the Iranian city of Bostan. The Iranians used mass infantry assaults, or "human wave" attacks, which included kamikaze-style frontal assaults by large numbers of Iranian soldiers against dug-in Iraqi lines. While Iran lost more than twice as many soldiers as Iraq, Iranian forces eventually retook Bostan. Soleimani lost numerous friends during the brutal fighting, and the human wave attacks were a searing reminder of the risks for Iran of engaging in conventional warfare.

The Iran-Iraq War had a significant impact on Soleimani and the emergence of Iran's use of irregular warfare in several ways. First, Iran is encircled geographically by enemies. Many Iranians, including Soleimani, concluded that the Iran-Iraq war was primarily a Western—particularly an American—war. As an official IRGC history of the conflict claimed, "the war was financed and engineered by the US" because of "the severe threat that [the Iranian Revolution] posed to the predatory interests of world imperialism."[10] Many Iranians viewed Iraq as a puppet of the United States that was attempting to crush the 1979 Iranian Revolution on the latter's behalf.

Second, Iran's comparative advantage was unlikely to be in conventional warfare; Iranian leaders had to find an alternative. Iran's conventional military units did not perform well against Iraq's better-armed and better-prepared forces, and Iran's human wave infantry assaults were far too costly. Instead, Soleimani embraced irregular warfare—what some Iranians called *jang-e*

---

9. See, for example, سپاه پاسداران انقلاب اسلامی [Islamic Revolutionary Guard Corps], گذری بر دو سال جنگ [*A Glance at Two Years of War*] (Tehran: Political Office, 1982).

10. سپاه پاسداران انقلاب اسلامی [Islamic Revolutionary Guard Corps], گذری بر دو سال جنگ [*A Glance at Two Years of War*], 15.

gheir-e kelasik (non-classic war).[11] Iran adopted "Iran: Complete Regulations of the Islamic Republic of Iran Armed Forces," which focused on the need to mix conventional forces *and* irregular units to protect Iran.

Third, the IRGC aided anti-regime Shia groups in Iraq during the Iran-Iraq conflict—its first taste of irregular warfare—and saw its potential. Among the most important was Iranian support for the Badr Corps, the armed wing of Ayatollah Mohammad Baqir Hakim's Supreme Council for the Islamic Revolution in Iraq. During the war, the Badr Corps fell under the overall command of the IRGC and deployed to the Haj Omran area in northeastern Iraq. In Lebanon, the IRGC developed a close relationship with the Amal Movement and then with Lebanese Hezbollah, providing significant money, weapons, training, and strategic guidance over time to Hezbollah. Iran sent over a thousand IRGC advisers to the Bekaa Valley in Lebanon to build and run training camps that prepared Hezbollah fighters for war with Israel.

To expand and improve Iran's irregular warfare capabilities in countries like Lebanon and Iraq, Khomeini authorized the creation of the IRGC-Quds Force (or *sepah-e quds*) around 1988, led by Brigadier General Ahmad Vahidi. "Quds" is the Farsi term for Jerusalem, and the Quds Force became Iran's elite paramilitary arm for external operations. Its mandate included collecting intelligence; training and equipping partner forces; and orchestrating assassinations, bombings, and other operations outside of Iranian territory. A decade after its creation, IRGC chief Sayyid Yahya "Rahim" Safavi appointed Soleimani as chief of the Quds Force. In this position, Soleimani would eventually become the most influential military commander in Iran.

One of Soleimani's first major tests in irregular warfare was in Afghanistan in the 1990s. Iranian leaders had become alarmed as the Taliban overran northern Afghan cities. The Taliban was an extremist Sunni militant group whose ideology was deeply rooted in the Hanafi school of Islamic jurisprudence and hence a threat to Iran's Shia government. On August 8, 1998, Taliban forces executed nine Iranian diplomats and one Islamic Republic News Agency

---

11. See, for example, Brandon A. Pinkley, *Guarding History: The Islamic Revolutionary Guard Corps and the Memory of the Iran-Iraq War*, Special Historical Study 12 (Washington, DC: Joint History Office, Office of the Chairman of the Joint Chiefs of Staff, 2018). Also see various IRGC histories, such as حسین اردستانی [Hossein Ardestani], کتاب روی‌اروی‌ی استراتژی‌ها گنج ایران و عراق [*Confrontation of Strategies in the Iran-Iraq War*] (Tehran: Sepah Center for Sacred Defense Documents and Research, 1388 AH [2009 / 2010 CE]), 101–2; محمد درودیان [Muhammad Durudiyan], آغاز تا پایان: سال‌شمای تحلیلی [*Beginning to End: A Year-by-Year Analysis*] (Tehran: Sepah Center for War Studies and Research, 1383 AH [2004 / 2005 CE]), 44.

journalist in the northern Afghan city of Mazar-e-Sharif. In reponse, some in the Iranian government advocated invading Afghanistan in a conventional warfare campaign. In October 1998, nearly 200,000 regular Iranian troops massed along the border with Afghanistan, and the Taliban mobilized thousands of fighters to thwart an expected Iranian invasion. But Soleimani strongly opposed an Iranian invasion, arguing that the Soviets had lost roughly 15,000 soldiers during their war in Afghanistan, which was barely a decade old. It made more sense for Iran to adopt an irregular strategy, using his Quds Force and supporting Afghan resistance groups, particularly those under the Northern Alliance commander Ahmad Shah Massoud. Iran adopted Soleimani's approach.

Using Tajikistan as a base of operation, Soleimani and his Quds Force aided Massoud and his Jamiat-e Islami militia force. A picture taken around this time shows Soleimani standing to Massoud's left, with his hands folded in front.[12] Despite Iranian assistance, including Soleimani and his Quds Force, they failed to prevent the Taliban's take-over. By the summer of 2001, the Taliban controlled virtually all of Afghanistan, except for a small sliver of land northeast of Kabul in the Panshjir Valley. Then came September 11, 2001.

In the aftermath of the September 11 attacks, the United States conducted two major operations that benefited Iran. The first was the 2001 US-led overthrow of the Taliban regime, and the second was the 2003 US invasion of Iraq. In particular, the US overthrow of Saddam Hussein provided an opportunity for Iran to shift the balance of power in Iraq in its favor using irregular means. For Soleimani, irregular warfare was critical to achieve his country's national security objectives, including protecting the Iranian homeland from external threats and expanding Iranian power and influence outside of the country. Since the end of the Cold War, the United States had attacked governments on either side of Iran—Afghanistan and then Iraq—raising concerns about an American desire to eventually overthrow the Iranian government. After all, US President George W. Bush had labeled Iran a member of the "axis of evil," along with North Korea and Iraq, in his 2002 State of the Union address.

Irregular warfare was essential for several reasons. First, the United States and other Iranian adversaries—including Israel—enjoyed a significant advantage in conventional military power. Iran's aging inventory of conventional ground, air, and maritime capabilities lagged well behind the United States and other countries in the region. For example, the majority of Iran's aging air force

12. The photograph comes from Anisa Shaheed, "Who Is Soleimani's Successor Ismail Khan?," *Tolo News* (Afghanistan), January 5, 2020.

inventory consisted of US-supplied aircraft that predated the 1979 Revolution. Second, the United States had aleady proven vulnerable to irregular warfare. Iranian-linked groups had killed sixty-three people—including seventeen Americans—in April 1983 in Lebanon, 241 US soldiers in October 1983 in Lebanon, and nineteen US Air Force personnel in June 1996 in Saudi Arabia. Third, irregular warfare was an efficient way to fight without spending significant amounts of money, a commodity which Iran lacked in the face of devastating US and other Western economic sanctions.

Soleimani and the Quds Force designed an irregular strategy to expand Iran's influence in Iraq and weaken the United States by supporting Iraq's Shia militias, recruiting Iraqi government officials sympathetic to Iran, and targeting vulnerable US forces through improvised explosive devices and stand-off weapons, such as rockets and mortars. Within the borders of Iraq, Iran operated against the United States indirectly through Iraqi partner forces rather than directly through Iranian conventional forces. By 2005, US military casualties increased following a lethal campaign of improvised explosive devices from the Badr Corps and at least two other militias established with the help of Soleimani's Quds Force—Kataib Hezbollah, led by Abu Mahdi al-Muhandis, and Asaib Ahl al-Haq, led by Qais al-Khazali.

Among the most lethal Iranian IEDs were the explosively formed penetrators, or EFPs. They were specially engineered shaped charges that sent a slug of metal at near-hypersonic speeds through targets like armored vehicles, and then created a deadly spray of hot metal. EFPs killed 196 US troops and wounded another 816 US troops between July 2005 and December 2011, with the highest monthly totals in 2008.[13] Soleimani and his Quds Force were critical in transporting EFP components from Iran into Iraq. They also provided Iraqi militias with unmanned aerial vehicles, short-range ballistic missiles, artillery, anti-tank guided missiles, tanks, armored personnel carriers, and air-defense systems. With this assistance, Soleimani and his Quds Force increased their influence in Iraq by supporting local militias and targeting US soldiers through an irregular campaign.

Soleimani and his Quds Force expanded their involvement—and influence—when they came to the aid of Syrian President Bashar al-Assad, whose regime

---

13. US Department of Defense, "OIF EFP Detonations by Month: July 2005 to December 2011," undated, accessed on April 21, 2022, available at https://admin.govexec.com/media/gbc/docs/pdfs_edit/enclosure_tab_a_document_for_review_(150813_oif_efp_pull_no_summary)_(1).pdf.

had faced an insurgency since 2011. Within a couple of years, multiple Syrian cities fell to a mix of insurgent groups, such as the al-Qaeda-linked Jabhat al-Nusrah and the Islamic State. Among the most strategically important cities was Aleppo, which fell to insurgent groups in late 2012. Over the course of 2013 and 2014, Syrian regime forces encircled Aleppo in an attempt to asphyxiate insurgents in eastern parts of the city, but the Syrians didn't have sufficient firepower. Assad loyalists faced other threats as well, such as Islamic State forces that controlled some access routes into the city.

To help turn the tide in Aleppo, Soleimani reached out to Lebanese Hezbollah leader Hassan Nasrallah. Would he send additional Hezbollah fighters to Syria to aid the Assad regime? It was a difficult request. Nasrallah would have to risk the lives of Hezbollah fighters and face criticism for participating in a foreign war. Nasrallah eventually relented, deploying up to 8,000 fighters to participate in combat operations and to train, advise, and equip groups in Syria.

In a further effort to end rebel control of Aleppo, Soleimani established a joint operations center to help plan and execute the ground campaign. Soleimani's Quds Force trained and equipped approximately 55,000 forces that included Lebanese Hezbollah and foreign fighters from Iraq, Afghanistan, Pakistan, and other countries. When Moscow also intervened on Assad's behalf in 2015, these irregular forces gained the support of Russian air power. After months of Russian air strikes on rebel positions, two critical Shia villages near Aleppo—Nubl and Az Zahra—fell in February 2016, with the aid of Soleimani's Quds Force and Iranian-trained militias. In the spring of 2016, pro-Syrian forces stepped up their offensive to retake Aleppo, dubbed Operation Dawn of Victory. In July of the same year, Syrian forces and Iranian-backed militias cut off the Azzaz corridor, which had connected Aleppo to Turkey. Soleimani then lobbied for a final offensive. By late December 2016, the regime had regained full control of Aleppo City. The seizure of Aleppo was a pivotal battle in the Syrian civil war. With the opposition's strategic and symbolic stronghold retaken, pro-regime forces could now contain the remaining armed opposition to the greater Idlib.

With growing success in Syria, Soleimani's Quds Force aided non-state groups across the Middle East from Lebanon through Syria, Iraq, Iran, and Afghanistan—creating a 2,000-mile land bridge. Some Iranians referred to this broader region as *Wilayat Imam Ali* (the state or province of Imam Ali), in honor of Ali ibn Abi Talib, the cousin and son-in-law of the Prophet Muhammad. In addition, Soleimani's Quds Force trained forces and conducted operations in other countries, such as Yemen and Bahrain. By the time of his death in January 2020, Soleimani had provided aid to over 200,000 non-state actors across the Middle East. The Quds Force used these partners to control territory, influence politics, and move money, fighters, weapons, and other materials. In some cases, such as in Iraq, Soleimani's Quds Force was instrumental in helping retake territory from the Islamic State—including strategically-important cities such as Mosul.[14]

For all Soleimani's activities, however, locals did not always embrace Soleimani or his Quds Force. In Sunni areas of Iraq, for example, the population was disenfranchised by a government they believed was too closely aligned with Tehran. A leaked Iranian intelligence report from Iran's Ministry of Intelligence and Security, or MOIS, highlighted the destruction wrought by Quds Force-trained Shia militias at the expense of the local Sunni population. "In all the areas where the Popular Mobilization Forces go into action," it noted, "the Sunnis flee, abandoning their homes and property, and prefer to live in tents as refugees or reside in camps." The assessment concluded that actions by the Quds Force-linked militias alienated Iraq's Sunni population. "Destroying villages and houses, looting the Sunnis' property and livestock turned the sweetness of these successes" against the Islamic State into "bitterness."[15]

Some officers within Iran's MOIS directly blamed Soleimani for an overuse of Shia militias. They also accused him of being a self-promoter and using the campaign against the Islamic State to bolster his own political stock in Iran. One critical Iranian intelligence report condemned Soleimani for vainly "publishing pictures of himself on different social media sites."[16] Soleimani had an active social media presence, and videos and photographs of him became widespread as he toured battlefields in Iraq and Syria. Soleimani's overt activism created other challenges as well. Mass demonstrations engulfed Lebanon and Iraq in 2019, 2020, 2021, and 2022, with some protesters angry about growing Iranian influence in their countries.

Despite these drawbacks, Soleimani's legacy of a *javanmard* persisted following his death. Iran supported Lebanese Hezbollah in Lebanon, militia forces in Syria, the Hashd al-Shaabi in Iraq, the Taliban government and militias in

14. On these activities see, Seth Jones, *Three Dangerous Men: Russia, China, Iran, and the Rise of Irregular Warfare* (New York, NY: W. W. Norton, 2021).

15. Tim Arango, et al., "The Iran Cables: Secret Documents Show How Tehran Wields Power in Iraq," *New York Times*, November 19, 2019.

16. Arango, "The Iran Cables."

Afghanistan, Houthis in Yemen, and non-state actors in Palestinian territory, Pakistan, and other countries. Soleimani's successor, Ismail Qaani, continued to wage irregular warfare across the Middle East, South Asia, and other areas of the globe by training and equipping partner forces, conducting offensive cyber operations, and orchestrating clandestine activities to expand Iranian influence. But Soleimani and Iran were not alone. His focus on irregular warfare was shared by one of his main collaborators in the Syrian war—Russian Chief of the Army Staff, General Valery Gerasimov.

III

Gerasimov was born in the Russian city of Kazan on September 8, 1955. Supported by his father, Gerasimov attended Kazan Suvorov Military School and graduated in 1977. By that time, the prospects of a conventional and nuclear war with the United States had declined because of their unbearable costs—including fears of a nuclear holocaust. In response, the Soviet Union focused significant attention on "active measures" to compete with its rival superpower. These were designed to influence external populations using irregular means in ways that shifted the balance of power in favor of Moscow. As one former Warsaw Pact intelligence operative noted about active measures:

> Target No. 1 was the United States . . . The objective was to hurt the United States wherever and whenever it was possible, to weaken the positions of the United States and Western Europe, to create new rifts within the NATO Alliance, to weaken the position of the United States in developing countries, to cause new rifts between the United States and developing countries, to disinform the United States and the Western allies about the military strength of the Soviet bloc countries.[17]

In 1977, the Red Army sent Gerasimov to the Northern Group of Forces in Poland. He commanded a tank platoon and company, and served as chief of staff in the 80th Tank Regiment of the 90th Guards Tank Division. During these formative years, Gerasimov developed his views on warfare—including irregular warfare—by reading the works of numerous Russian thinkers, including

17. Statement of Ladislav Bittman, Former Deputy Chief of the Disinformation Department of the Czechoslovak Intelligence Service, "Soviet Covert Action (The Forgery Offensive): Hearings Before the Subcommittee on Oversight of the Permanent Select Committee on Intelligence," US House of Representatives (Washington, DC: US Government Printing Office, 1980), 43–44.

Georgy Isserson, Andrei Snesarev, Makhmut Akhmetovich Gareev, Alexander Suvorov, Konstantin Simonov, and Alexander Svechin.[18] After his time in Poland, Gerasimov served in the Far Eastern Military District and then attended the Malinovsky Military Armored Forces Academy in 1984. Following graduation in 1987, the Red Army sent Gerasimov to Estonia. It was a sobering experience, and Gerasimov watched as the Soviet empire collapsed. In 1993, the Russian army promoted Gerasimov to commander of the 144th Guards Motorized Rifle Division in the Baltic Military District. But, by the end of the year, Russian forces were gone from Estonia. In a humiliating setback for Gerasimov, he oversaw their withdrawal back to Russia.

With his country in tatters, the Russian army sent Gerasimov to the Russian Republic of Chechnya, where insurgents had declared independence from Russia and were engaged in a violent guerrilla war. It was Gerasimov's first combat tour. The war in Chechnya had an important influence on Gerasimov's views of irregular warfare as he faced guerrillas using irregular methods. Between 1994 and 1996, the Russian military fared poorly in Chechnya because of a combination of wildly optimistic planning, poor training for counterinsurgent warfare, low morale, and systemic alcohol and drug abuse among Russian soldiers. As Gerasimov admitted, "our personnel in the field, including commanders," were "sometimes woefully unprepared" because of a "lack of combat training; personnel being distracted from their training programs by other tasks; and failure to implement our combat training plans."[19]

Despite these challenges, Gerasimov became much more adept at fighting guerrillas. "I spent a lot of time in the field," he admitted. "I knew in great detail what was happening on the administrative border with Chechnya . . . No one had any illusions; we all knew that the Chechen boil would have to be punctured sooner or later."[20] Gerasimov's experience in Chechnya was, quite literally, trial by fire. At one point, insurgents ambushed his convoy near the Chechen border with Ingushetia, firing from close range with grenade launchers and

---

18. See, for example, Герасимов [Gerasimov], "Ценность науки в предвидении" ["The Value of Science Is in the Foresight"]; Валерий Герасимов [Valery Gerasimov], "Мир на гранях войны," ["World on the Brink of War"], Военно-промышленный курьер [*Military-Industrial Courier*], March 13, 2017.

19. Владимир Тихонов [Vladimir Tikhonov] interview with Валерии Герасимов [Valery Gerasimov], Военно-промышленный курьер [*Military-Industrial Courier*], May 25, 2005.

20. See the interview with Gerasimov in Наби Набиев [Nabi Nabiyev], "Горячие будни генерала Герасимова" ["Gen. Gerasimov's Busy Routine"], Красная звезда [*Red Star*], March 12, 2001.

small arms. Throughout his years in Chechnya, Gerasimov evolved into a principled commander who helped change the course of the war. Russian military and pro-Russian Chechen forces seized Grozny, the capital of Chechnya, in a siege that lasted from December 1999 to February 2000—eventually crushing most of the opposition through a punishing counterinsurgency campaign.

By that time, Gerasimov was one of Russia's bright, new generation of army leaders. Under President Vladimir Putin, who was appointed by Boris Yeltsin in December 1999, Russian leaders began a long journey to restore their country's greatness. To understand Russia's main enemy—the United States—Gerasimov closely studied US operations in Afghanistan and Iraq. He believed that the United States was shifting away from the "traditional" approach to warfare. Using only 350 special operations soldiers and 100 CIA paramilitary officers—all supported by US air power—the United States overthrew the Taliban regime in Afghanistan in a matter of weeks. Gerasimov believed the United States had developed a "new," more clandestine approach to waging war, an approach Gerasimov termed "concealed use of force."[21] Rather than using large numbers of conventional military forces to achieve political objectives, the United States utilized irregular methods.

According to Gerasimov, the United States conducted propaganda campaigns using information broadcast on television networks, the internet, social media, and even non-governmental organizations.[22] The goal was to incite political dissent from inside the other country. As the security situation deteriorated, the United States would then utilize irregular forces—special operations soldiers, intelligence units, local militias, and private military companies—as the main maneuver units. US air force and naval power were still important in this new way of warfare, but the clandestine approach, Gerasimov believed, allowed the United States to overthrow regimes using quasi-deniable means and local forces.

The 2011 US-led war in Libya had a particularly profound impact on Gerasimov's understanding of the evolving nature of war. Beginning in March 2011, US, French, and British aircraft conducted airstrikes against the regime of Muammar al-Qaddafi, and in support of Libyan insurgents. By August, Libyan

21. Valery Gerasimov, PowerPoint Slides, Moscow Conference on International Security, May 23, 2014. The slides were published in Anthony H. Cordesman, *Russia and the "Color Revolution": A Russian Military View of a World Destabilized by the U.S. and the West* (Washington, DC: Center for Strategic and International Studies, 2014), 11–25.

22. Bartles, "Getting Gerasimov Right."

militia forces—aided by US and other Western special operations and intelligence units—overran Qaddafi's headquarters, the Bab al-Aziziya, and overthrew the government. As the Arab Spring and the color revolutions spread throughout North Africa, the Middle East, and Eastern Europe, Gerasimov saw the hidden hand of the United States.[23] Russian leaders erroneously interpreted the Arab Spring and color revolutions as part of the US's new way of warfare: an attempt to increase US influence indirectly and discretely through clandestine means. According to Gerasimov, a color revolution is "a form of non-violent change of power in a country by outside manipulation of the protest potential of the population in conjunction with political, economic, humanitarian, and other non-military measures."[24] More than anything, however, what especially concerned Gerasimov was the speed of state collapse that the United States could apparently engineer.

By this time, Putin had elevated Gerasimov to Chief of the General Staff of the Russian Armed Forces. There is no equivalent position in the United States and Gerasimov had far more power than any flag officer in the US military. In an influential speech in May 2014 at the Russian Ministry of Defense's Moscow Conference on International Security, a gruff Gerasimov tore into the United States. Pointing to a map of the so-called color revolutions, he accused the United States of grossly irresponsible behavior by attempting to manipulate foreign governments and destabilize parts of the Middle East, Africa, Europe, and Asia through irregular means. The result, Gerasimov concluded, was that "forces were brought to power having mainly a pro-Western and anti-Russian orientation."[25] Gerasimov had long preached that there were no clear boundaries between war and peace in international politics, sounding a bit like George Kennan. "In the twenty-first century," Gerasimov wrote, "we have seen a tendency toward blurring the lines between the states of war and peace."[26]

23. Герасимов [Gerasimov], "Ценность науки в предвидении" ["The Value of Science Is in the Foresight"]; Валерий Герасимов [Valery Gerasimov], "По опыту Сирии," ["On the Syrian Experience"], Военно-промышленный курьер [*Military-Industrial Courier*], No. 44, March 9, 2016.

24. Gerasimov, PowerPoint Slides, May 23, 2014. Emphasis added.

25. Валерий Герасимов [Valery Gerasimov], "Военные опасности и военные угрозы Российской Федерации в современных условиях" ["Military Dangers and Military Threats of the Russian Federation in Modern Conditions"], Армейский Сборник [*Army Journal*], No. 5, April 16, 2015.

26. Герасимов [Gerasimov], "Ценность науки в предвидении" ["The Value of Science Is in the Foresight"].

Over the next decade, Russia sought to strengthen and expand its military power. Russia modernized its army, air force, and navy—including with the Project 955A Borey-A nuclear-powered ballistic-missile submarines, Su-57 fifth-generation fighters, and Avangard hypersonic glide vehicles. Russian military leaders also actively developed irregular strategies, capabilities, and organizational structures that complemented the country's conventional and nuclear power.

Gerasimov and other leaders focused on irregular warfare as an important component of Russia's efforts both to expand its own power and to weaken that of the United States for several reasons.

First, Gerasimov and other Russian leaders recognized that the United States had considerable conventional and nuclear power. For example, Gerasimov concluded that the war in Iraq was "characterized by a sharp increase in the [US] Air Force's contribution to the defeat of the Iraqi army, deep envelopments of defensive positions, and [the] delivery of the main strike bypassing defensive lines."[27] Based on the US's advances in precision strike capability and its evolution of conventional air, ground, and maritime capabilities, it would be difficult to defeat the United States in a conventional war. Moreover, any attempt to do so would risk escalation to nuclear war.

Second, Gerasimov saw the United States as vulnerable to irregular warfare. In Afghanistan, for instance, Gerasimov pointed out that the United States had failed to defeat a much weaker Taliban, whose strategies focused on such irregular techniques. The US failure had led to "growing terrorist activity" in the country and "a significant influx of drugs, weapons, and trained militants."[28]

Consequently, Russian leaders like Gerasimov attempted to expand Russian power and undermine the United States and its Western partners, particularly after losing substantial territory and influence following the collapse of the Soviet Union and the expansion of NATO and the European Union. Russian leaders viewed the US-led international order as a threat to Russia's core

27. Валéрий Герáсимов [Valery Gerasimov], "Влияние современного характера вооруженной борьбы на направленность строительства и развития Вооруженных Сил Российской Федерации. Приоритетные задачи военной науки в обеспечении обороны страны" ["The Influence of the Contemporary Nature of Armed Struggle on the Focus of the Construction and Development of the Armed Forces of the Russian Federation. Priority Tasks of Military Science in Safeguarding the Country's Defense"], Вестник Академии Военных Наук [*Journal of the Academy of Military Sciences*] 62:2 (2018): 18.

28. Валерии Герасимов [Valery Gerasimov], "ИГИЛ начался с 'Талибана'" ["ISIS Began with the 'Taliban'"], Военно-промышленный курьер [*Military-Industrial Courier*], October 12, 2015.

strategic objectives which included protecting the Russian homeland from foreign—particularly US—interference and subversion; maintaining the country's territorial integrity; expanding and sustaining Russia's core spheres of influence in Eastern Europe and Central Asia; increasing Russian political and economic power in other regions, such as the Middle East and Africa; and expanding Russian influence in international institutions, such as the Eurasian Economic Union, the Shanghai Cooperation Organization, and even the United Nations.

To achieve these strategic objectives, Gerasimov was instrumental in building Russia's irregular warfare capabilities. He established a new Russian Special Operations Command to conduct irregular warfare. "Having studied the formation, training, and use of the special operations forces of the leading countries of the world, the Defense Ministry's administration also began creating them," Gerasimov remarked. "An appropriate command has now been created to work on the plan."[29] With revamped special operations forces, Russia wasted little time using them in Ukraine.

Following protests in Ukraine that led to the 2014 overthrow of President Viktor Yanukovych's government, Russia seized the Ukrainian territory of Crimea through irregular means. Gerasimov and other Russian military leaders relied on special operations forces—not conventional units. On February 23, Russian Special Operations Command airlifted *spetsnaz* (elite infantry) units and Russian Airborne Forces (*Vozdushno-desantnye voyska Rossii,* or VDV) to the area. The next day, with help from Moscow, the city council in Sevastopol installed a Russian citizen as mayor. The Russians then moved quickly. On February 27, fifty members of the Russian Special Operations forces (*Komandovanie sil spetsial'nalnykh operatsii,* or KSO), disguised as local self-defense militia units, seized the Crimean Parliament and raised a Russian flag over the building. Later that night, Russian soldiers without markings surrounded Belbek Air Base, Ukraine's main military airport in Crimea. On February 28, Russian forces captured Simferopol's civilian airport, canceled all flights, and began airlifting VDV units into Crimea. On March 1 and 2, Russia brought reinforcements that quickly seized bases and military facilities.

Russia's take-over of Crimea was a success. In roughly two weeks—even faster than the US operations in Afghanistan and Iraq—Russia had used

---

29. "Special Operations Forces Created in Russian Armed Forces—General Staff," Interfax, March 6, 2013.

clandestine special operations and intelligence units to annex part of Ukraine. There were no major clashes between Russian and Ukrainian conventional forces. It was a textbook example of Sun Tzu's axiom, "To subdue the enemy without fighting is the acme of skill."[30] Gerasimov and other Russian leaders had fashioned their own version of irregular warfare—Russian style.

Following the annexation of Crimea, in March 2014, Russian intelligence and special operations forces stoked a wave of popular unrest—and eventually war—in eastern Ukraine. Six different *spetsnaz* brigades were involved in the Ukrainian operation in its early stages. Over the next several years, Russia continued to wage irregular warfare in eastern Ukraine. Gerasimov and other Russian leaders likely had several goals: punish Ukraine for its pro-Western shift by starting an insurgency in the east; deter a further deepening of relations between Kiev and the West, including possible Ukrainian membership in NATO and the European Union; send a message to other countries in Russia's sphere of influence that they would be targeted if they turned to the West; and deter further US and Western actions in Russia's periphery. Russian special operations forces—or "little green men," as they were called because they wore unmarked green army uniforms—provided training, weapons, money, and other assistance to local militia. They helped create and support separatist political parties and unions; aided paramilitary groups like the Russian Orthodox Army and the Night Wolves; and recruited Cossack, Chechen, Serbian, and Russian paramilitaries to fight in Ukraine.

In addition, Russia established an aggressive offensive cyber campaign. Russia had conducted a limited cyber campaign against the country of Georgia during the August 2008 war in the separatist region of South Ossetia. But Russian operations in Ukraine were a major escalation. GRU units—including Military Unit 74455, which was known within the GRU as the Main Center for Special Technologies (or GTsST)—orchestrated one of the world's most brazen offensive cyber campaigns by taking down multiple parts of Ukraine's critical infrastructure, including its electricity grid. Russian operatives planted several types of malware—including BlackEnergy, KillDisk, and Industroyer—in the computer systems of companies that supported Ukraine's electric power grid and against the Ukrainian government's State Treasury Service and Ministry of Finance. The Russians then used the malware to create blackouts across a wide swath of Ukraine's capital.[31]

30. Sun Tzu, *The Art of War*, 77.
31. See Jones, *Three Dangerous Men*.

Russia's overall campaign in eastern Ukraine was not a clear victory like Crimea, since Russian-backed forces failed to control significant territory. But the campaign was effective in creating a frozen conflict in eastern Ukraine, in which Moscow could dial up—or down—the intensity of war depending on political calculations. After Russian operations in eastern Ukraine and the Crimea, Gerasimov and other military leaders shifted their focus to Syria.

By 2015, Putin, Gerasimov, and other Russian officials had become alarmed at the deteriorating situation in Syria. The war had dramatically escalated over the previous four years. According to Russian intelligence assessments briefed to Gerasimov, there were up to 4,500 operatives from Russia and Central Asia in the ranks of the Islamic State and other terrorist groups in the Middle East—particularly in Syria—and a grand total of 60,000 terrorists.[32] Russian intelligence also concluded that Syrian government forces controlled a mere ten percent of Syrian territory.[33] In northern Syria, Kurdish forces had seized growing swaths of territory at the expense of the Assad regime. In southern and central Syria, the Islamic State also had enlarged its area of control and was conducting brutal attacks in the north and west. Finally, rebel groups such as Jabhat al-Nusrah had expanded their presence in northwestern and southwestern Syria, driving back Syrian government forces and threatening major population centers.

The situation seemed hopeless as cities like Hasaka, Raqqa, Aleppo, and even areas around Damascus fell to rebels. "It was a very difficult situation," recalled Gerasimov. "There was low morale and high fatigue, as well as a lack of ammunition, materiel, and other types of support."[34] For Moscow, Syria was not just any country. It had long been an important Russian partner, and its warm water port at Tartus could be helpful for Russia's regional ambitions and

32. Валерии Герасимов [Valery Gerasimov], "Вооруженные Силы Российской Федерации и борьба с международным терроризмом" ["The Armed Forces of the Russian Federation and the Fight Against International Terrorism"], V Московской конференции по международной безопасности [V Moscow Conference on International Security], April 27, 2016.

33. Віктор Баранёц [Victor Baranets], "Начальник Генштаба Вооруженных сил России генерал армии Валерий Герасимов: 'Мы переломили хребет ударным силам терроризма'" ["Chief of the General Staff of the Armed Forces of Russia Army General Valery Gerasimov: 'We Have Broken the Ridge of the Shock Forces of Terrorism'"], Комсомольская правда [*Komsomolskaya Pravda*], December 26, 2017.

34. Баранёц [Baranets], "Начальник Генштаба Вооруженных сил России генерал армии Валерий Герасимов" ["Chief of the General Staff of the Armed Forces of Russia Army General Valery Gerasimov"].

power projection into Europe, Africa, and the Middle East. But by 2015 Russian leaders were concerned that Washington was attempting to overthrow the Assad regime and replace it with a friendly government, much like the United States had done in Afghanistan, Iraq, and Libya—among others. Gerasimov criticized the United States for destabilizing Syria and establishing a terrorist sanctuary in the country. "The development of events in Syria according to the Libyan scenario would lead to the fact that a recently prosperous country would become a source of the spread of terrorist danger for the entire region," Gerasimov declared.[35] As a response to this growing threat, over the summer of 2015, Gerasimov helped oversee planning efforts involving Russian, Iranian, and Syrian political and military leaders. Russia then pre-positioned military forces in and near Syria.[36]

Unlike Moscow's campaign in Afghanistan in the 1980s, which had included 115,000 Soviet forces, Russian leaders adopted a smaller-footprint approach in Syria. Based on his assessment of recent wars, Gerasimov helped craft a light footprint strategy. Russia used well-directed air power from Su-24M and Su-24M2 frontline bombers, Su-25SM and Su-25UBM ground-attack aircraft, Su-30SM multirole fighters, and other aircraft, along with Russian naval vessels. The maneuver elements to retake territory included Syrian Army forces; Lebanese Hezbollah; additional Iranian-trained militias from Iraq, Afghanistan, Palestinian territory, and other countries; as well as Russian private military contractors like the Wagner Group. With Russia's support, the Syrian regime eventually regained control of virtually all the main cities in the country, except for pockets in such areas as Idlib Province.

Yet Syria was only one of many examples of Russia's embrace of irregular warfare. Increasingly, Russian military leaders saw irregular warfare as an important way to project and expand Russian power. As Gerasimov emphasized, "the methods of struggle are increasingly shifted towards the integrated use of political, economic, informational, and other non-military measures implemented with reliance on military forces."[37] After all, Russia is not a global

35. Герасимов [Gerasimov], "Вооруженные Силы Российской Федерации и борьба с международным терроризмом" ["The Armed Forces of the Russian Federation and the Fight Against International Terrorism"].

36. On Russian military preparations in Syria, see Валерий Половинкин [Valery Polovinkin], ed., Российское оружие в сирийском конфликте [*Russian Weapons in Syrian Conflict*] (Moscow: STATUS, 2016).

37. Герасимов [Gerasimov], "Ценность науки в предвидении" ["The Value of Science Is in the Foresight"].

superpower like the United States or China. Its gross domestic product was more than five times smaller than both the United States and China, according to 2020 estimates.[38] Its population was ten times smaller than China and more than twice as small as the United States in 2022.[39] Its defense budget was twelve times smaller than the United States and three times smaller than China, according to 2021 estimates.[40] Because of these limitations, Russia's irregular strategy included several components.

First, Russia utilized offensive cyber operations and electronic warfare to weaken its adversaries. These efforts were led by cells like the GRU's Military Unit 74455, which orchestrated a series of offensive cyber operations against the United States and other international targets—including the 2020 Olympics and Paralympics, scores of websites in 2019 in the country of Georgia, the 2018 Winter Olympics, and the 2017 French elections.[41] Russia placed malware, such as Triton and BlackEnergy, in critical US infrastructure, thus threatening power plants, electricity grids, communications networks, and financial systems in the American homeland. Other Russian intelligence agencies—especially the Foreign Intelligence Service, or SVR—played an important role as well. In 2020, for example, the SVR conducted an attack against dozens of US companies and government agencies by planting malware in a software update from SolarWinds, a company based in Texas that made network monitoring software. In addition, cyber hacking organizations, based in part in Russia, conducted numerous cyber attacks. In 2021, for example, hackers entered the networks of the US-based Colonial Pipeline—which provided nearly half of the US east coast's fuel, including gasoline, jet fuel, and diesel—and conducted a ransomware attack. In response, Colonial Pipeline temporarily closed

38. The data on gross domestic product (purchasing power parity) include: China, $22.5 trillion; United States, $20.5 trillion; Russia, $4.0 trillion (2020 estimates). Central Intelligence Agency, World Factbook, "Real GDP (Purchasing Power Parity)," 2021, https://www.cia.gov/the-world-factbook/field/real-gdp-purchasing-power-parity/country-comparison/.

39. The data on population include: China, 1.4 billion; United States, 335 million; Russia, 142 million (2022 estimates). Central Intelligence Agency, World Factbook, "Country Comparisons—Population," 2022, https://www.cia.gov/the-world-factbook/field/population/country-comparison/

40. The data on defense budgets include: China, $193 billion; United States, $738 billion; Russia, $61 billion (2020 estimates). International Institute for Strategic Studies, *The Military Balance*, Volume 21 (London: International Institute for Strategic Studies, 2022), 23.

41. Foreign and Commonwealth Office, *UK Exposes Series of Russian Cyber Attacks Against Olympic and Paralympic Games* (London: UK Foreign and Commonwealth Office, October 19, 2020); United States of America v. Yuriy Sergeyevich Andrienko, et al., United States District Court, Western District of Pennsylvania, Indictment, Criminal No. 20-316, October 15, 2020.

its operations and froze its information technology systems, causing massive lines of motorists at gas stations across the east coast of the United States.

Second, Russia conducted aggressive information and disinformation campaigns across the globe, reminiscent of the KGB's active measures during the Cold War. Some Russian government documents referred to these actions as *informatsionnaya bezopasnost* (information security), and they included influencing the thinking and, ultimately, the behavior of countries and their populations.[42] Russia attempted to influence the outcome of the 2016 and 2020 US presidential elections. Moscow also waged a broad disinformation campaign inside the United States, attempting to inflame social, racial, and political tensions through such issues as Black Lives Matter, COVID-19, the Me Too Movement, gun control, white supremacy, abortion, and immigration. These efforts were led by cells like the GRU's Military Unit 74455. With Gerasimov's involvement, Russian agencies also leveraged clandestine organizations to help conduct information operations, such as the Internet Research Agency (IRA), a Russian organization linked to Yevgeny Prigozhin, who was close to Putin and Russian intelligence. The Internet Research Agency created social media groups and accounts that falsely claimed to be affiliated with US political and grassroots organizations in order to influence US citizens. Russian intelligence agencies also conducted a wide range of disinformation campaigns, including falsely charging the United States with supporting the Islamic State and other terrorist organizations in countries like Syria and Afghanistan.

Third, Russia leveraged the GRU, SVR, KSO, and other clandestine units to conduct activities such as training foreign forces, directing combat operations, and orchestrating targeted assassinations. For example, Unit 29155 of the GRU, based at the headquarters of the 161st Special Purpose Specialist Training Center on the outskirts of Moscow, was linked to several incidents: the 2014 attack against a Czech ammunition depot; the poisoning of Bulgarian arms dealer Emilian Gebrev in 2015; a failed coup attempt in Montenegro in 2016; the poisoning in the United Kingdom of Sergei Skripal, a former GRU officer that defected to the British; providing aid to Taliban militants in Afghanistan to target foreign forces, including US troops; and the poisoning of Russian opposition leader Aleksei Navalny in 2020. Russian intelligence agencies also funded white supremacist and other far-right networks in the United

---

42. Совет Безопасности Российской Федерации [Security Council of the Russian Federation], Стратегия национальной безопасности Российской Федерации [National Strategy of the Russian Federation], July 2, 2021.

States and overseas—mostly through front groups—and spread white supremacist and other far-right propaganda on the internet and social media
through clandestine means. In addition, the GRU and SVR ran extensive campaigns to support political leaders in Europe—including far-right organizations like Italy's Lega Party and Austria's Freedom Party—in an effort to
weaken those countries and to undermine democracy more generally.

Fourth, Moscow expanded its use of private military companies like the
Wagner Group to approximately three dozen countries on four continents.
The Wagner Group and other private military organizations began operating
in countries such as Sudan, Libya, Ukraine, Syria, the Central African Republic, Mozambique, Madagascar, and Venezuela. Gerasimov had watched the
United States increasingly utilize private military companies in such campaigns as Iraq, Afghanistan, and Libya, and he supported the integration of
similar Russian companies into campaigns. The Wagner Group, led by Yevgeny
Prigozhin, was Russia's largest private military company. It conducted a variety
of missions overseas, providing services that included combat support, training, protective services, and site security. Russia's strategic aim with its use of
private military companies was relatively straightforward: to undermine US
power and increase Moscow's influence. The Russian strategy consisted of
using low-profile, deniable forces like militant groups and private military
companies that could do everything from providing foreign leaders with security to training, advising, and assisting partner security forces.

Despite Gerasimov's use of irregular warfare, Russian efforts were not always
successful. Russia's campaign in Ukraine failed to overthrow the pro-Western government and led to several embarrassing incidents, such as the July 2014 shoot-
down by Russian-backed rebels of Malaysian Airlines Flight 17 on its way from
Amsterdam to Kuala Lumpur. In addition, the United States and other Western
governments enacted sanctions against Russia for a wide range of irregular
activities—such as targeted assassinations, offensive cyber operations, and disinformation campaigns to influence US and other Western elections—that hurt
Russia's economy. Furthermore, the United States and European Union black-
listed a number of Russian companies, expelled Russian diplomats from their
countries, and enacted travel bans on Russian officials. Washington even barred
US banks from buying sovereign bonds from Russia's central bank, its national
wealth fund, and its Finance Ministry. The United States and other Western countries imposed additional sanctions following Russia's 2022 invasion of Ukraine.

Finally, Russia and Russian-backed organizations committed atrocities and
human rights abuses that triggered widespread international condemnation

and legal action. In 2021, for example, a group of UN experts publicly denounced the use of Russian private military companies—including Sewa Security Services, Lobaye Invest SARLU, and the Wagner Group—in the Central African Republic. The UN experts cited possible "grave" human rights abuses and violations of international humanitarian law, and they called for investigations into Russia's abuses.[43] In 2021, Human Rights Watch documented the cases of several dozen Libyans that were killed by landmines placed by Wagner Group employees.[44] In Syria, Russia blocked several international investigations into the Syrian government's use of chemical weapons against its own population. These problems were a stain on Russia's global image as well as a reflection of the limits of irregular warfare.

IV

The actions of Qassem Soleimani and Valery Gerasimov highlight an important way in which states have competed in the past—and will likely compete in the future. Major powers will continue to build conventional and nuclear capabilities, as well as prepare for conventional and nuclear war. The Russian invasion of Ukraine in 2022 illustrated that conventional warfare is not dead. But countries like Russia and Iran will also continue to develop irregular capabilities. For several reasons, irregular strategies and capabilities are likely to remain critical—and therefore a focus of the various international powers—in the coming years.

First, war among nuclear powers is likely to be prohibitively costly, especially among states that have a mutual second-strike capability, where no side in a conflict can launch a first strike that prevents retaliation from others. With a second-strike capability, there is a potential for massive destruction of cities, the death of hundreds of thousands of people, significant economic destruction, and long-term health implications. As Charles de Gaulle remarked in

43. "CAR: Experts Alarmed by the Government's Use of 'Russian Trainers,' Close Contacts with UN Peacekeepers," Human Rights Council, United Nations Office of the High Commissioner, March 31, 2021, available at https://www.ohchr.org/EN/NewsEvents/Pages/DisplayNews.aspx?NewsID=26961&LangID=E.

44. *Lawfare* (blog), "What Laws Constrain This Russian Private Military Company?" Zarko Perovic, posted March 23, 2021, https://www.lawfareblog.com/what-laws-constrain-russian-private-military-company; Samuel Ramani, "Russia's Strategic Transformation in Libya: A Winning Gambit?," RUSI Commentary, April 28, 2021, available at https://www.rusi.org/explore-our-research/publications/commentary/russias-strategic-transformation-libya-winning-gambit. RUSI is one of the top think tanks in the United Kingdom.

May 1960, "[After nuclear war, the] two sides would have neither powers, nor laws, nor cities, nor cultures, nor cradles, nor tombs."[45] In a joint statement decades later, US President Ronald Reagan and Soviet leader Mikhail Gorbachev agreed, concluding, "A nuclear war cannot be won and must never be fought."[46]

The costs of conventional war between nuclear powers are likely to be staggering as well—not least because they risk escalation to nuclear war. "Frontal engagements of large forces at the strategic and operational level are gradually becoming a thing of the past," wrote Gerasimov in highlighting the growing use of irregular methods.[47] According to one analysis, a US-China war could reduce China's gross domestic product (GDP) by as much as thirty-five percent and the US's GDP by as much as ten percent, thereby causing widespread economic destruction.[48] Both the United States and China in all likelihood would also suffer huge numbers of military and civilian deaths and risk large-scale destruction of their military forces. If war expanded to include their allies—as it did during World War I, World War II, and the Korean War—economic and casualty figures could skyrocket even further.

Many of these wars might take place in—or near—the homeland of competitors: in the Persian Gulf with Iran, in the Baltic countries with Russia, or in South China Sea or Taiwan Strait with China. As some wargames highlight, the United States and its partners could target air defense systems, communications headquarters, missile sites, and other military targets in or around Iranian, Russian, or Chinese territory, thereby risking escalation to nuclear war.[49] Based on these considerable costs and risks, leaders are likely to be deterred from engaging in conventional or nuclear war with other major powers—particularly with other nuclear powers. This is especially true for the US.

---

45. Robert Jervis, *The Meaning of the Nuclear Revolution: Statecraft and the Prospect of Armageddon* (Ithaca, NY: Cornell University Press, 1989), 1.

46. Jervis, *The Meaning of the Nuclear Revolution*, 1.

47. Герасимов [Gerasimov], "Ценность науки в предвидении" ["The Value of Science Is in the Foresight"].

48. David C. Gompert, Astrid Stuth Cevallos, and Cristina L. Garafola, *War with China: Thinking Through the Unthinkable* (Santa Monica, CA: RAND, 2016), xiv.

49. On games and scenarios, see, for example, John Gordon IV, et al., *Army First Capabilities for 2025 and Beyond* (Santa Monica, CA: RAND, 2019); Raphael S. Cohen, et al., *The Future of Warfare in 2030* (Santa Monica, CA: RAND, 2020); David Ochmanek et al., *U.S. Military Capabilities and Forces for a Dangerous World* (Santa Monica, CA: RAND, 2017); *War on the Rocks* (blog), "How Does the Next Great Power Conflict Play Out? Lessons from a Wargame," James Lacey, posted April 22, 2019; Gompert et al., *War with China*.

After all, the United States remains the world's dominant conventional and nuclear power. In 2020, its defense budget was (by some measures) roughly equivalent to the defense budgets of the next fifteen countries combined.[50] The US's land, air, naval, space, and cyber capabilities are formidable. For Russia, Iran, and even China, choosing to fight a conventional or nuclear war with the United States would be a risky and dangerous proposition indeed.

Second, irregular warfare has already proven to be successful in weakening target countries. As Gerasimov argued, irregular warfare can create "a state of complete chaos, political crisis, and economic collapse" in the target state.[51] Moreover, as Gerasimov and Soleimani both recognized, the United States and other Western states are vulnerable to irregular methods. The US military struggled against poorly equipped insurgent groups in Afghanistan, Iraq, Somalia, and other countries. Following the US withdrawal from Afghanistan in 2021, the Taliban—whom the United States had been fighting for two decades—overthrew the government of Ashraf Ghani in a matter of weeks. In addition, the United States and other democratic countries have politically divided societies, economies that are heavily digitalized and open, democratically elected governments, as well as a free press—all of which adversaries will attempt to manipulate through irregular means.

These realities create significant incentives for governments to engage in irregular warfare. Qassem Soleimani and Valery Gerasimov were scions of an age-old generation of clandestine warriors. They weren't the first, and they won't be the last. But their use of irregular warfare will be studied for generations as examples of how states can try to shift the balance of power in their favor, while remaining below the threshold of conventional and nuclear war.

50. International Institute for Strategic Studies, *The Military Balance* (London: International Institute for Strategic Studies, 2021), Volume 21, 23.

51. Валерии Герасимов [Valery Gerasimov], "По опыту Сирии," ["On the Syrian Experience"], Военно-промышленный курьер [*Military-Industrial Courier*], 44 (March 9, 2016).

CHAPTER 41

The Strength of Weakness

THE KIM DYNASTY AND NORTH KOREA'S STRATEGY FOR SURVIVAL

Sue Mi Terry

On June 25, 1950, North Korea's army invaded South Korea. This was a costly, almost catastrophic, blunder. After initial success, the North's forces were sent reeling back by United Nations troops under the command of General Douglas MacArthur. US and UN troops advanced almost to the Yalu River—the border between China and North Korea. The Northern regime was only saved by a massive and costly intervention by Chinese Communist "volunteers." Yet the North's survival in the succeeding decades was not due only to Chinese or Russian patronage. Indeed, the Kim family dynasty survived the collapse of the Soviet Union and the reform of the post-Mao Chinese economy while learning to manipulate its more powerful patrons.

It survived, moreover, even while economically underperforming its democratic opposite number, South Korea, by an ever-increasing margin. In 1960, North Korea was still an industrial powerhouse that was far ahead, militarily and economically, of its poorer southern cousin. Today, North Korea, which clings to a Marxist planned economy, is one of the poorest countries on the planet while free-market South Korea is one of the richest. South Korea has also gained the conventional military edge over the North, thanks to its technological advantage and its alliance with the United States, which retains the most powerful armed forces in the world.

Yet, despite decades of sanctions and setbacks that might have been expected to end the North Korean regime, it has survived—and the regime, if not ordinary people, has prospered. In the process, North Korea offers a master class in how a minnow can swim among whales. It shows how an economically weak and backward state can leverage its military, security, diplomatic, and intelligence resources to ensure the survival of a regime. North Korea has become a master of strategic Taekwondo. Just as Taekwondo masters employ fast kicks and punches to keep their opponents off-balance, so North Korea has learned how to use military provocations and brinkmanship tactics to wrong-foot its principal adversaries in Seoul, Washington, and Tokyo. The development of a formidable nuclear arsenal combined with missiles capable of hitting the continental United States has greatly heightened the North's leverage. Pyongyang has perfected the art of geopolitical blackmail, using its provocations and threats to extract concessions that enable the regime's survival.

While emphasizing its strength to its enemies, North Korea has leveraged its weakness with its principal outside supporter, the People's Republic of China. Beijing and Pyongyang have frequently been at odds, with China's more cautious and reformist rulers wishing that North Korea would do more to modernize its economy and to curtail military provocations that provide justification for the United States to enhance its military role in the region. But because Beijing does not want to risk a collapse of the North (which could bring refugees flooding into Chinese territory and US troops back to the Yalu River), it has never fully exercised its economic leverage on North Korea. Pyongyang has been able to get away with actions that irk its sponsors in Beijing because the Chinese government cannot run the risk of indefinitely cutting off fuel and other supplies to the North—steps that could lead to the Kim regime's downfall.

Meanwhile, the North Korean state was able to survive internally by employing ruthless Stalinist repression of its population. It employs coercive force and fear tactics through overlapping and stovepiped domestic intelligence and police agencies to control the population. The Kim family has also maintained tight control over the population through ideological indoctrination and the maintenance of a monopoly of information. Finally, and perhaps most importantly, the regime has been able to survive by securing the support, if not the loyalty, of the elites—powerbrokers or "shareholders" in the party, the military, and the government—by alternately rewarding them with power and prestige, or, if they step out of the line, by severely punishing them.

The North's wily, brutal, and unscrupulous strategy for survival did not emerge full-grown with the birth of the regime. It has taken three generations to gestate and perfect. This essay will examine the development of the North's survival strategy, both in regard to outside powers and its own population, under regime founder Kim Il Sung, who ruled from 1948 until his death in 1994; his son Kim Jong Il, who ruled from 1994 until his own death in 2011; and the first decade of the rule of his grandson Kim Jong Un, who has been in power since 2011. Together, these three men have managed to create and maintain the first and only hereditary, Confucian-Marxist dictatorship on the planet with a blend of a bizarre state religion, ideological indoctrination, repressive, totalitarian system, and the relentless pursuit of nuclear weapons and a brinkmanship strategy.

<h1 style="text-align:center">I</h1>

Immediately following the Korean War in 1953, North Korea, for all practical purposes, was a Soviet puppet state dependent on Moscow both politically and economically. The political elite of the North was fractious and far from what it is today—a Kim family dictatorship.

Kim Il Sung (birthname Kim Song Ju) was born on April 15, 1912, only two years after Japan formally colonized the Korean Peninsula. He was seven years old when he left North Korea and arrived in Manchuria with his family. He had humble roots. His father was an herbalist-turned-nationalist agitator who was incarcerated by the Japanese regime for his activism; his mother was a seamstress. Kim made his way to the Soviet Union and got drafted into the Soviet Army, where he became an officer. While there, he was able to cultivate Russian links and learned to speak Russian. In the 1930s and 1940s, he fought against the Japanese occupation of Korea as part of the Anti-Japan United Army, which had bases in northeast China, a region controlled by the Chinese Communist Party.

When Kim Il Sung returned to North Korea on October 10, 1945, after Japan's defeat, he was a relatively obscure figure, still only thirty-three years old, yet he received a hero's welcome under the auspices of the Red Army, which occupied the northern half of the peninsula. After intense jockeying among Korean nationalists, Kim was elected the first President of North Korea on September 9, 1948. He consolidated his power base during the Korean War and went on to methodically purge rival regime factions throughout the 1950s.

The beginning of a de-Stalinization campaign in the Soviet Union after Stalin's death in 1953 resulted in the steady deterioration of Sino-Soviet relations. That, in turn, gave Kim freedom to maneuver and to follow a more independent policy. Relying on the support of the "guerrilla faction"—veterans, like him, of anti-Japanese warfare in the 1930s—he outmaneuvered both the pro-China "Yanan" faction and the pro-Soviet faction while still maintaining support from both Moscow and Beijing; both Communist countries were afraid to stop supporting Kim for fear he would align with the other one. The last-ditch effort by the other factions to stop Kim's accumulation of power failed at the August 1956 Plenum of the Korean Workers Party Central Committee where he labeled his pro-Soviet and pro-Chinese rivals as "factionalists" who were tainted by foreign influence. All of his rivals were subsequently purged or exiled. Kim's final victory was celebrated in 1961 at the Fourth Congress of the Korean Workers Party, which was marked by unprecedented praise of him as the "Great Leader."

With Kim now firmly in charge, he stopped slavishly copying the Soviet model of Communism. Instead, Kim launched the policy of *Juche* (independence or self-reliance) which combined North Korean nationalism with a cult of personality. At home, Juche allowed him to establish complete control; abroad, it allowed him to carve out a measure of autonomy from Beijing and Moscow while still depending on their aid.

Based on Mao Zedong's efforts to "Sinify" Marxism-Leninism, Juche emphasized the superiority of all things Korean over all things foreign—and thus the superiority of Kim as the ruler of North Korea. By claiming that world civilization originated on the Korean Peninsula and that Koreans are a chosen people with "a historical mission to save humanity from capitalist materialism, consumerism, decadent culture and moral decay," as one scholar noted, Juche was important in elevating Kim's control and power.[1]

Christianity and all other religions were banned in North Korea but there are elements of Christianity in the Juche cult, which may be due to the fact that Kim's mother was a Christian. North Korea has a book called the "Great Leader's Tenets," like the Bible. It has "The Ten Great Principles of the Unitary Ideology System," like the Ten Commandments, which serve as the supreme law of the land. There is also an "Ode to the Great leader," like a hymnal. There are an estimated 450,000 Kim Il Sung Thought Academies or Revolutionary Research Centers, which are like churches.[2] Each North Korean citizen is

---

1. Han S. Park, *North Korea: Politics of Unconventional Wisdom* (Boulder, CO: Lynne Rienner, 2002), 47.

2. David R. Hawk, *Thank You, Father Kim Il Sung: Eyewitness Accounts of Severe Violations of Freedom of Thought, Conscience, and Religion in North Korea* (Washington, DC: US Commission

obliged to become a member of an organization or a league (child, youth, workers, laborers, farmers, women's league) and to attend weekly sessions for instruction, inspiration, and self- and mutual criticisms based on the Ten Principles.

Looming above all, of course, was the North Korean god, the "Great Leader" Kim Il Sung, and then the "son of god," the "Dear Leader," Kim Il Jong. Kim Il Sung's personality cult reached messianic proportions. There are over 30,000 statues of the Great Leader scattered across a nation about the size of Mississippi. There are also the Kim Il Sung Stadium, the Arch of Triumph modeled after the one in Paris (but bigger), and the Tower of Juche made of 25,500 white granite blocks, one for each day the Great Leader had lived by the time it was built in 1982. The North Korean calendar begins with Kim Il Sung's birth, hence 1912 is year one. Kim Il Sung's birthday is known as the "Day of Sun," for it marks the rise of the sun over the earth. Every North Korean adult is required to wear a badge of Kim Il Sung or Kim Jong Il on their bosoms. North Koreans are trained to consider portraits and badges of Kim Il Sung as more precious than one's own life or loved ones, even in calamities like fire and flood. About thirty percent of college education is devoted to the study of Kim Il Sung thought; each person is obliged to study the writings of Kim Il Sung on his own at least two hours a day. Other countries have had bizarre cults of personality—the Soviet Union under Stalin, China under Mao (and now Xi Jinping), Albania under Enver Hoxha, Libya under Muammar Qaddafi, Venezuela under Hugo Chavez, Iraq under Saddam Hussein—but none have gone quite as far as North Korea.

To snuff out any embers of free thought, the North Korean state since Kim's day has developed the most thorough system of control of any police state in the world; China is practically a liberal haven by comparison. All radio and TV channels receive only state broadcasts, foreign publications or videos are forbidden, and only a favored-few officials are allowed to leave the country. Informers and government agents permeate society. The Ministry of Public Security and the secret police, the State Security Department, arrest suspected enemies of the state. They are consigned to brutal political prison camps, the *kwanilso*, modeled after Soviet-style gulags, where inmates are subjected to back-breaking labor and Orwellian rituals of "self-criticism."

---

on International Religious Freedom, 2005), v, available at https://www.uscirf.gov/sites/default/files/resources/stories/pdf/nkwitnesses_wgraphics.pdf.

Crimes that can land one in the gulag include watching a South Korean film, attempting to travel to China, being in possession of a Bible, sitting on or defacing a picture of Kim, or simply being related to someone else who has committed a "political crime." Up to three generations of a family are routinely imprisoned for political crimes by one of its members. The UN reports that nearly thirty-six percent of political inmates are imprisoned due to "guilt-by-association." Under Kim Il Sung, the camps were estimated to hold 200,000 prisoners—a figure that today has fallen to between 80,000 and 120,000.[3] One prison camp in North Hamgyong Province is roughly three times the size of Washington, DC. Political prisoners are not told what "crimes" they have committed or how long they will be imprisoned.

North Korean society is defined by a hereditary caste system on the basis of perceived loyalty to the state. Every person is categorized at birth by their *Songbun*, or socio-political background. There are three main classifications— the "core," "wavering," and "hostile" classes—and fifty-one sub-categories; all are based on whether their families were loyal revolutionaries who resisted Japanese occupation (the core), landowners, capitalists, or collaborators of Japanese imperialism (hostile), or those in between who are neither actively hostile nor friendly (the waverers).[4] These classifications are inherited and determine all aspects of a person's life—where one would go to school, whom one would marry, where one would work, whether one would be assigned menial and heavy-labor jobs, receive better medical attention, or even obtain food. Whereas other countries have practiced discrimination based on race, religion, or other factors, in North Korea discrimination is based on one's perceived value as a friend or foe to the Kim regime. The system Kim created was totalitarian and brutal, but it was effective in consolidating his family's control and its essential elements remain unchanged to this day.

Meanwhile, when it came to external relations, Kim Il Sung developed a strategy of bullying, brinkmanship, and blackmail that kept Washington, Seoul, and Tokyo—his primary enemies—off guard while building up North Korea's military might. His ultimate goals were to evict US forces from South

3. Human Rights Council, "Report of the Commission of Inquiry on Human Rights in the Democratic People's Republic of Korea," United Nations, February 7, 2014, available at https://documents-dds-ny.un.org/doc/UNDOC/GEN/G14/108/66/PDF/G1410866.pdf?OpenElement.

4. Robert Collins, "Marked for Life: Songbun, North Korea's Social Classification System," Committee for Human Rights in North Korea, June 6, 2012, 7, available at https://www.hrnk.org/uploads/pdfs/HRNK_Songbun_Web.pdf.

Korea and unify the entire peninsula under his rule. In the meantime, by standing up to "capitalists" and "feudalists" abroad, Kim Il Sung heightened his aura of power and strength at home.

In the 1950s, Kim Il Sung was focused on consolidating power domestically. He was rattled, however, by the 1961 coup that brought Park Chung-hee, a pro-American, anti-Communist general, to power in South Korea. This caused Kim to launch a campaign of infiltration, subversion, and terror against the government in Seoul. His hope was to foment a revolution in the South to overthrow the Park government and then to merge North with South.

The North's secret offensive reached a peak on January 21, 1968, when Kim dispatched thirty-one commandos known as Unit 124 into the South in a failed attempt to infiltrate the South Korean presidential mansion, the Blue House, and kill President Park. These commandos, wearing South Korean military uniforms, came within 100 yards of the Blue House. A gunfight ensued. Twenty-nine North Korean commandos were killed along with two South Korean and four US soldiers. The Blue House raid was followed two days later by North Korea's capture of an American intelligence ship, the USS *Pueblo*, whose crew was held captive for nearly a year and only released following an American apology—swiftly rescinded—for spying on the North. The following year, on April 15, 1969, the North shot down a US reconnaissance plane, an EC-121, killing all thirty-one servicemen aboard, constituting the largest single loss of US aircrew during the Cold War era. Kim followed up with more attacks on South Korea. On September 17, 1969, North Korean infiltrators killed seven South Koreans near a small island called Wando, and on June 5, 1970, a South Korean airliner was hijacked to the North.

Meanwhile, the North built up its own military throughout the 1960s and 1970s. Defense spending rose from 4 percent of the national budget in 1959, to an annual average of 20 percent between 1960 to 1966, to an annual average of 30 percent between 1967 to 1971.[5] In the early 1960s, the Korean People's Army (KPA) had just 300,000 soldiers. By the late 1970s, the North had nearly a million men under arms (out of a total population of 17.5 million). That, writes one scholar, amounted to "total war mobilization on a permanent basis."[6]

While building up his conventional military strength, Kim also began pursuing nuclear weapons because he saw possession of the ultimate weapon as

---

5. Gavan McCormack, "Kim Country: Hard Times in North Korea," *New Left Review* 198 (1993): 35.

6. Nicholas Eberstadt, *The End of North Korea* (Washington, DC: AEI Press, 1999), 31.

essential for his regime's security—it would not only enhance regime prestige but also deter any US attack and potentially allow the North to force the South into unification. The germination of Kim's nuclear aspirations dates to the 1950s when North Korean scientists gained basic nuclear knowledge by cooperating with Soviet nuclear scientists and engineers. Kim's more serious nuclear development efforts began in earnest during the mid-1960s, when Moscow supplied North Korea with advanced nuclear reactor technology and infrastructure, including assisting with the construction of an eight-megawatt research reactor located near the town of Yongbyon starting in 1965. Kim expanded the North's nuclear program at a rapid rate in the 1970s and 1980s, as he began accumulating "sensitive nuclear technologies," including spent fuel reprocessing techniques, plutonium, and the development of facilities for the fabrication and conversion of uranium. He then built a significant nuclear complex, including the construction of a five-megawatt reactor at Yongbyon, in the 1970s and 1980s.

There was a brief thaw in South Korean-North Korean relations after the Nixon administration's opening to China in 1971. Seeing his major ally make nice with his major adversary made Kim nervous. As a result, in 1971–73, for the first time in its history, the North carried out direct, high-level talks with South Korea. But the rapprochement quickly fell apart and Kim went on the attack again. On August 15, 1974, a North Korean agent attempted to assassinate Park Chung-hee at the National Theater in Seoul as he was giving a speech. The shooter missed and killed the first lady, Yook Young-soo, instead.

By the mid-1970s, North Korea was losing the economic race with the South, which was emerging from abject poverty as one of the "tiger" economies of Asia. The South caught up with the more industrialized North on a per capita basis sometime in the mid-to-late 1970s, and then continued to pull further head. In response, Kim tried to stage a "great leap outward" by purchasing technology, capital equipment, and entire factories on credit from Western Europe and Japan. The North's plan was to pay for these imports with earnings from exports, but in the worldwide economic dislocation of the 1970s, characterized by high inflation and high energy prices, North Korea found itself unable to meet the fast-rising payments on its external debts. As a result, by 1976, North Korea's hard currency debt with Western creditors had reached $4.6 billion, about six times its annual hard currency exports.[7]

7. National Foreign Assessment Center, *Korea: The Economic Race between the North and the South* (Langley, VA: Central Intelligence Agency, 1978), 8.

South Korea was shaken by President Park's assassination in 1979 (the culprit was his own Korean Central Inteligence Agency, or KCIA, director) and another military coup the following year by General Chun Doo-hwan. Kim decided that he would not deal with Chun Doo-hwan's regime and again resorted to high-profile acts of terrorism in a renewed attempt to undermine an increasingly prosperous and stable South Korean state. On October 9, 1983, the North's agents attempted to kill Chun Doo-hwan with a bomb when he was on a state visit to Rangoon, Burma. Chun survived, but the blast killed twenty-one people, including four South Korean cabinet ministers and thirteen other South Korean officials. Four years later, on November 29, 1987, two Northern agents planted a powerful bomb aboard Korean Air Flight 858, killing all 115 people on board. Kim's aim was to dissuade the nations of the world from participating in the Seoul Olympics in 1988, but the Olympics went off without a hitch—thereby adding to South Korea's international standing. In 1987, the differences between the North and South became even more stark when South Korea held its first presidential election—an important milestone on its emergence as a democracy.

North Korea, meanwhile, was suffering under the strain of supporting a military that reached 1.25 million men by 1987—the world's fourth-largest force.[8] By the mid-1980s, North Korea had entered economic stagnation and decline. Free market reforms, of the kind that China began in 1979, were desperately needed—but they were not forthcoming because Kim did not want to risk undermining his hold on power. The collapse of the Soviet Union in 1991 further exacerbated the North's woes. By 1993, the North's imports from Russia were running at less than ten percent of the 1990 volume. The cutback made North Korea dependent on China for more than two-thirds of its imported energy, but China, no longer seeing itself in competition with Moscow for influence in the North, also scaled back aid. North Korea was forced to abruptly reduce its total petroleum consumption by between one-fourth and one-third.[9] The stage was set for food shortages and a terrible famine in the 1990s.

As North Korea sought a path out of international isolation and economic collapse, its nuclear program took on renewed importance, not only as a potential military deterrent and tool for regime survival and but also as a major source of leverage in Pyongyang's dealings with its adversaries in Washington,

8. Eberstadt, *The End of North Korea*, 35.
9. Eberstadt, *The End of North Korea*, 134.

Seoul, and Tokyo. In 1993, the North announced it was withdrawing from the Nuclear Non-Proliferation Treaty, creating its first nuclear crisis. When the North subsequently refused inspections of its facilities and kicked out International Atomic Energy Agency (IAEA) inspectors, the United States, for the first time since the Korean War, seriously contemplated military action. Secretary of Defense William Perry issued a warning that Washington was committed to stopping the North's nuclear weapons development, even if it meant "facing up to them in a way that could cause a catastrophic war."[10] The Pentagon stepped up a military buildup in and around the peninsula. Clinton administration war plans called for employing cruise missiles and F-117 stealth fighters to destroy the North's reprocessing plant at Yongbyon.

But the Clinton administration hesitated, just as have all its successors, to launch a preemptive strike on the North. A single airstrike, or even a series of strikes, would have only slowed down, not reversed, Pyongyang's nuclear progress. A full-scale war would almost certainly have meant North Korea's defeat, but the cost would have been prohibitive. North Korean shelling could have led to 250,000 casualties in Seoul alone, and some estimates put the total number of possible deaths at one million.[11]

The march towards conflict halted when, on June 15, 1994, former President Jimmy Carter went to North Korea to meet with Kim Il Sung and was able to start negotiations. Kim died from a massive heart attack less than three weeks after Carter left Pyongyang, but his successor and son, Kim Jong Il, continued the negotiations. The eventual result was the Agreed Framework signed on October 21, 1994, which stipulated that, under IAEA monitoring, Pyongyang would freeze the operation of, and later dismantle, its graphite-based nuclear reactors and ship its existing spent nuclear fuel out of the country. In return, the US agreed to supply 500,000 tons of heavy fuel oil annually and to organize an international consortium to build new nuclear reactors for the North based on a less-dangerous light water technology. (South Korea agreed to pick up the lion's share of the $4–$5 billion cost of manufacturing and providing the light-water reactors, with Japan putting up much of the rest.) The US was then supposed to gradually ease restrictions on trade, investment, and diplomatic contacts, leading to the eventual normalization of ties, security assurances, and

10. R. Jeffrey Smith, "Perry Sharply Warns North Korea," *Washington Post*, May 31, 1994.

11. Sue Mi Terry, "North Korea's Nuclear Family," *Foreign Affairs* 100:5 (2021), available at https://www.foreignaffairs.com/articles/north-korea/2021-08-24/north-koreas-nuclear-family.

the establishment of full diplomatic relations. The United States backed off the brink of war. But North Korea, it later emerged, had little interest in abiding by the terms of this agreement.

II

The Agreed Framework symbolized a brief era when some Westerners could imagine that the situation in North Korea was improving under a new ruler who would either prove more liberal than his father—or else would simply be overthrown now that the North Korean regime no longer enjoyed as much support from Moscow and Beijing. Those illusions would soon be shattered.

Kim Jong Il was likely born in 1941 in a Russian guerrilla camp in Khabarovsk, not in 1942 on Mount Paektu (a legendary and symbolic location in Korean culture) as his official biography claimed. His birth year was changed to 1942 to better align with 1912, the year of his father's birth. Kim did not have any of his father's military credentials or heroic guerilla exploits. His childhood was marked by tragedies—his mother died after complications from childbirth and his brother died when he was three. During the Korean War, Kim Jong Il moved to China with his younger sister, Kim Kyung Hui, and, by his own account, had a lonesome upbringing and a difficult relationship with his stepmother. Nevertheless, he enjoyed all the privileges that came with being the firstborn of the Great Leader. In the 1970s, Kim Il Sung started grooming Kim Jong Il as his successor.

Kim Jong Il lacked the gravitas, affability, or charisma of his father. But he had at his disposal all the same tools of repression to solidify his primacy in the succession struggle. He shrewdly exiled his half-brother, Kim Pyong Il, to faraway posts and smeared his uncle. He relentlessly attacked people who were deemed disloyal and planted doubts about their loyalty with his father. At the same time, he handed out privileged positions to the grown offspring of those in his father's inner circle to curry favor and legitimize the hereditary transfer of power. Kim continued his father's policies of terror, repression, propaganda, ideological indoctrination, and information blockade.

Kim Jong Il's ascent to power coincided with the famine years of 1995–98. Though the exact numbers are unknown, conservative estimates put excess mortality as a direct result of the famine at between 600,000 and 1 million people, or about 3–5 percent of the total population.[12] Through these arduous

---

12. Stephan Haggard and Marcus Noland, "Famine in North Korea Redux?," Working Paper Series, Peterson Institute for International Economics, 2008, 2.

years, Kim Jong Il was able to survive by maintaining elite support and by receiving foreign assistance. The international community responded to the North's famine with $2 billion in food aid over the course of the following decade.[13] Yet, rather than using foreign food aid to supplement his own commercial food imports, Kim used the aid as a substitute for them, cutting back on commercial food imports when more aid arrived, thus leaving his people short of the food they needed to survive. South Korea was particularly important in enabling the survival of the North Korean regime in the immediate aftermath of the food crisis. When progressive South Korean President Kim Dae-jung came to power in 1998, he launched a so-called Sunshine Policy of engaging North Korea through cooperation and aid. This policy was continued under Kim's successor, Roh Moo-hyun. Under the Sunshine Policy, Seoul pumped an additional $8 billion in economic assistance into the North over the course of a decade.[14]

As the North Korean people ate grass and tree bark, corpses piled up and abandoned or orphaned children roved the streets, Kim continued to spend resources on luxury items for regime loyalists in order to maintain their support. At the height of the great famine in 1995, Kim unveiled the Mt. Keumsoo Memorial palace, a mausoleum for Kim Il Sung that cost an estimated $800 million.[15] Kim spent millions of dollars more on birthday celebrations for his late father. The regime's other priority was the military. Kim reallocated food rations from civilians to the armed forces and continued to funnel scarce funds toward ballistic missiles and nuclear weapons along with other sophisticated military technology. In 1996, Kim Jong Il himself admitted that "the most urgent issue to be resolved at present is the grain problem . . . the food problem is creating a state anarchy," even as he directed resources toward regime survival rather than the survival of its people.[16]

Kim Jong Il's one major deviation from his father's policies was to prioritize the military above all else as a bulwark of the regime. Through the introduction

13. Stephan Haggard and Marcus Noland, "Aid to North Korea," Peterson Institute of International Economics, August 1, 2007, available at https://www.piie.com/commentary/op-eds/aid-north-korea.

14. Evan Ramstad, "Studies Ponder Reunification . . . Some Day," *Wall Street Journal*, November 22, 2010.

15. Namgung Min, "$800,000 Spent Preserving Kim Il Sung's Body," *Daily NK*, April 16, 2008, available at https://www.dailynk.com/english/800000-spent-preserving-kim-il-sun/.

16. Don Oberdorfer, *The Two Koreas: A Contemporary History* (New York, NY: Basic Books, 2001), 395.

of *Songun* or "military-first" politics, Kim Jong Il officially elevated the Korean People's Army (KPA) over the Korean Workers' Party to the top position within the regime. The Korean Workers' Party adopted the slogan, "The Military is the Party, the People, and the Nation."[17] In an inversion of classic Marxist-Leninist doctrine, the military first policy declared, "The gun barrel should be placed over the hammer and sickle." The military first approach was codified in 1998 in a revised constitution that granted the military the primary position in North Korean government and society.

According to Hwang Jang Yop, the author of Juche philosophy and the highest ranking North Korean defector to South Korea, the military first line was originally conceived as part of the compromise between the military leadership and Kim Jong Il. After Kim Il Sung's death, the army hierarchy accepted Kim Jong Il's ascendance to power in return for a greater role in the power structure and in policymaking. Starting around 1980, no senior military figure had been elevated to the Politburo. Once Kim Jong Il took over, he immediately started promoting senior military figures up the political hierarchy. Kim Jong Il in essence co-opted the military by bestowing on it policy influence and prestige, as well as a large share of the national budget (between twenty and thirty percent of GDP).[18]

While US leaders thought that a nuclear crisis had been averted in 1994 through diplomacy, Kim interpreted the crisis differently. From his perspective, it was North Korean military might that had forced the US to hesitate and not opt for preemptive military action. There was an element of truth to this view. After all, both South Korea and the United States were well aware that North Korean artillery dug in just north of the DMZ could pulverize the city of Seoul in the first hours of a crisis, potentially killing hundreds of thousands of people, including US service members. Seeing the deterrence provided by his military simply made Kim all the more determined to pursue nuclear weapons in spite of the Agreed Framework. Given the decline of North Korea's economy, the collapse of the Soviet bloc, and the reforms in China, this was the only card he had left to play. Like his father before him, Kim Jong Il was convinced that no other nation, not even a superpower such as the United

17. Kim Hakjoon, *Dynasty: The Hereditary Succession Politics of North Korea* (Stanford, CA: Shorenstein Asia-Pacific Research Center, 2015), 153.

18. Bureau of Arms Control, Verification and Compliance, "World Military Expenditures and Arms Transfers 2019," US Department of State, https://2017-2021.state.gov/world-military -expenditures-and-arms-transfers/index.html, accessed December 4, 2021.

States, would dare to attack, or even significantly undermine, a state armed with the ultimate weapon. Thus, far from stopping the nuclear weapons and ballistic missile programs he had inherited from his father, Kim Jong Il accelerated them.

We know now that, while the North froze its plutonium program in 1994 as part of the Agreed Framework, it began in earnest to pursue the enrichment of uranium instead. Pakistan, through its former top scientist, Abdul Qadeer Khan, supplied key data, stored on compact discs, concerning uranium enrichment in exchange for missile technology between 1990 and 1996, both before and after the signing of the Agreed Framework.[19] Exploiting cooperation with other rogue regimes was an important part of North Korea's survival strategy.

In October 2002, a visiting American delegation led by Assistant Secretary of State James Kelly confronted North Korean officials about the existence of a secret nuclear program, detected by US intelligence, which was based on uranium rather than plutonium. The North Koreans essentially admitted it, even though the covert uranium enrichment program was in violation of the North's agreements with Seoul and Washington. The George W. Bush administration responded by ending heavy fuel oil supplies to the North, and the IAEA adopted a resolution calling on the North to come clean on its secret uranium program. Kim, in turn, refueled and restarted the nuclear reactor, kicked out international monitors, removed seals on the facilities, disabled the monitoring cameras, and declared North Korea's withdrawal from the NPT (Nuclear Non-Proliferation Treaty) regime. In October 2006, the North conducted its first nuclear test.

By this point, the Bush administration was mired in two wars—in Iraq and Afghanistan—and had no desire to get embroiled in a third. In response to stinging criticism that his "hardline" policy of blowing up the Agreed Framework had led to the North testing its first nuclear weapon, President Bush made important concessions in the Six Party Talks, a series of multilateral negotiations held starting in 2003 and involving China, Japan, North Korea, Russia, South Korea, and the US. In September 2005, the six parties reached what was billed as a breakthrough with agreement on a Joint Statement in which all parties pledged to work toward the verifiable denuclearization of the Korean Peninsula and Pyongyang "abandoning all nuclear weapons and

---

19. "Khan 'Gave N Korea Centrifuges,'" *BBC*, August 24, 2005, http://news.bbc.co.uk/2/hi/south_asia/4180286.stm.

existing nuclear programs."[20] Despite the initial agreement, it would take over seventeen months before even the first steps of implementation were agreed upon.

To make progress with the North, the Bush administration made important concessions. For example, it abandoned an effective policy of financially squeezing the North Korean elites' cash flows. In September 2007, the US Treasury had imposed sanctions on Macau-based Banco Delta Asia, where the North reportedly kept $25 million, thereby blocking one of the regime's key sources of hard currency.[21] A North Korean official told a US diplomat that the US had finally found a way to hurt the Kim regime. Yet the Bush administration lifted the sanctions on Banco Delta Asia to entice North Korea back to the negotiating table where the Kim regime vowed to give up its nuclear weapons program. Unfortunately, after this leverage was traded away, the talks fell apart over verification: North Korea refused to allow IAEA inspectors access to its facilities.

In 2009, Kim Jong Il shifted away from the Six Party Talks altogether and towards a more concerted effort to develop the North's nuclear weapons capability. The North launched a long-range rocket in April and conducted a second nuclear test in May 2009. This merely confirmed that the possession of nuclear weapons had become a critical element of regime legitimacy and power.

III

When Kim Jong Il died in December 2011, and his son, the baby-faced, twenty-seven-year-old Kim Jong Un, came to power, many Korean watchers braced for regime instability. They questioned whether North Korean elites—many of them septuagenarians and octogenarians in a Confucian culture that values age and experience—would accept such a young man and a third hereditary succession. Some speculated that Kim Jong Un could become a figurehead and a "collective leadership" could emerge with people like Kim Kyung Hui, Kim Jong Il's trusted sister, and her husband Jang Song Taek, reputedly the second

20. US Department of State, "Joint Statement of the Fourth Round of the Six-Party Talks Beijing," September 19, 2005, available at https://2001-2009.state.gov/r/pa/prs/ps/2005/53490.htm.

21. David Lague and Donald Greenless, "Squeeze on Banco Delta Asia Hit North Korea Where It Hurt—Asia-Pacific—International Herald Tribune," *New York Times*, January 18, 2007.

most powerful man in North Korea, pulling the levers behind the scenes. Kim Jong Nam, Kim Jong Un's elder brother who was living overseas, speculated to a Japanese journalist that the new ruler would "just be a nominal figure" and "will not last long."[22]

At the time, the world knew little of Kim Jong Un. It was only in 2009—a year after Kim Jong Il's stroke and only two years before his death—that it started to become clear to outsiders that he had been tapped as the successor. In 2010, Kim Jong Un was appointed vice chairman of the Central Military Commission and made a member of the Party's Central Committee at a rare Party Congress. He was also made a four-star general despite never having served a day in the military. On October 10, 2010, on the sixty-fifth anniversary of the Korean Workers' Party, Kim Jong Un made his formal debut at a massive military parade, standing next to his father. One of the few sources of information about the new leader was Kenji Fujimoto, a pseudonym adopted by Kim Jong Il's sushi chef. The world learned from him that Kim Jong Un liked video games and basketball, and that he was a fan of Michael Jordan and Dennis Rodman—hardly the normal characteristics of a North Korean dictator.

To bolster Kim Jong Un's legitimacy, the regime presented him as a virtual reincarnation of his revered grandfather, right down to the same Mao suit, haircut, facial features, and even body size. On January 9, 2012, just two weeks after Kim Jong Il's death, North Korea released a documentary chronicling Kim Jong Un's supposed military exploits in a frenzied effort to build up his leadership credentials. The new ruler used every tool of totalitarianism to crush all potential opposition. Just like Kim Il Sung had done in his day, Kim Jong Un purged, executed, demoted, and marginalized all those who might compete with him for power. His victims included five of the "Gang of Seven," the senior party and military officials who had carried his father's coffin at the funeral. In his first two years, Kim ended up replacing half of the 218 party heads, ministers, and military officials.

Kim Jong Un proved to be even more ruthless than his father and grandfather. Just two years into his reign, Kim had his uncle, Jang Song Taek, publicly executed, reportedly by antiaircraft guns, on charges of plotting against him. Such an event was unprecedented, even in the bloody history of North

22. Jonathan Watts and Tania Branigan, "North Korea's Leader Will Not Last Long, Says Kim Jong-un's Brother," *The Guardian*, January 17, 2012, available at https://www.theguardian.com/world/2012/jan/17/north-korea-leader-not-long. See Tom Parry, "My Brother the Dictator Is a Big Joke—Book," *The Daily Mirror*, January 18, 2012.

Korea. Under Kim's father and grandfather, high-ranking officials were purged, exiled (and on occasions brought back into the fold after atonement in a re-education camp), or simply died of car "accidents." The high-profile execution of Jang spread fear among the elites as never before. Jang's execution signaled to the elites that their positions, and even their lives, were all linked to their loyalty to Kim and that no one was immune, not even a family member. In 2017, Kim reinforced that message by sending secret agents to kill his half-brother, Kim Jong Nam, at Kuala Lumpur Airport by employing VX nerve agent.

Many outsiders had hoped that Kim Jong Un might be a Deng Xiaoping- or Mikhail Gorbachev-style reformer. He briefly fed those hopes by shifting away from the *Songun*, or military-first policy of his father. In its place, Kim intro-duced the *Byungjin* policy devoted to the parallel development of the "econ-omy and nuclear weapons" at the same time. His message was that North Korea could have both butter and guns.

Kim displayed some interest in revving up the North's calcified economy. About six months after he came to power, North Korean state-run television showed footages of Mickey and Minnie Mouse and other Disney characters prancing around the stage while skimpily clad women played music in front of Kim, his young wife, Ri Sol Ju, and clapping generals. The Disney movies "Dumbo" and "Snow White" were projected on a jumbo screen. The appearance of these characters from the US, North Korea's mortal enemy, on a tightly con-trolled state television, was remarkable. Kim also funded lavish projects. He was seen riding roller coasters at the shiny amusement park he built, riding a ski lift at a new ski resort, and even galloping on a horse while he talked about the para-mount importance of raising living standards. He opened a dolphinarium and an extravagant water park, which includes a life-size plaster statue of his father.

Under Kim Jong Un's auspices, Pyongyang saw a construction boom, in-cluding impressive-looking apartment buildings. There were suddenly enough automobiles on its once-barren streets to employ car washers. Kim also granted state factories more autonomy over what they produced, including authority to find their own suppliers and customers, as long as they hit revenue targets. Families in collective farms were assigned to individual plots called *pojeon*. Once they met a state quota, they were allowed to keep and sell any surplus of their own.

Kim's most notable innovation was to allow private marketplaces. Scores of these markets called *Jangmadang* opened across the country, giving rise to a new of class of merchants and entrepreneurs (the so-called *donju* class) under the protection of Party officials. Between 2012 and 2021, the number of government-approved markets in North Korea doubled to 440, and satellite images showed them growing in most cities. They sold food, rice cookers, shoes, clothing, electronics, and other goods. Some also discreetly offered black-market goods such as foreign films and smartphones. People running stalls in the markets paid ten percent of the value of their sales to a state-controlled management office. The regime raked in about $70 million a year in market taxes and rental fees from merchants.[23] As the state economy failed and industry came grinding to halt because of a lack of electricity or raw goods, these markets became the lifeblood of North Korea. By 2021, some seventy-two percent of the population was making a living through market activity. An even higher percentage got its food from the markets.[24]

But this was the extent of Kim's reforms. He did not implement anything like what China did in the 1980s when it shifted to a "Market Leninist" policy. Chinese-style reform was not an option for Kim, because he feared it would invite regime instability. The North's economy remained limited by inadequate foreign investment and the absence of legal protections for private enterprise or procedures for contract enforcement. Proposals to set up special economic zones were not implemented. Foreign investors balked at North Korea's decrepit infrastructure and record of seizing assets from foreigners.

Rather than opening up to the outside world, Kim further tightened security. His efforts to stop refugees from leaving the country became even more draconian than under his father or grandfather. He cracked down on traders illegally smuggling in micro-storage SD cards, USB drives, and "notels," small DVD players which are a combination of notebook and televisions. While tightening his information blockade, Kim also enhanced efforts to guard against "ideological corruption." He ordered high schools across the country to teach a new course, eighty-one-hours long, devoted to him.[25] He continued the political caste system with zeal. His focus was on absolute control at all costs, cracking down on anything and everything that could challenge his rule.

In external relations, Kim's *Byungjin* policy was not all that different from *Songun*, the military-first policy of his father. Kim, in fact, accelerated the

23. Victor Cha and Lisa Collins, "The Markets: Private Economy and Capitalism in North Korea?" Beyond Parallel/CSIS, August 26, 2018, available at https://beyondparallel.csis.org/markets-private-economy-capitalism-north-korea/.

24. Cha and Collins, "The Markets."

25. "North Korea Requires Students to Take 81-Hour Course on Kim Jong-un," *KBS World*, November 25, 2014, available at http://world.kbs.co.kr/service/news_view.htm?lang=e&Seq_Code=106892.

North's development of nuclear weapons and ballistic missile delivery systems despite concluding a "Leap Day" accord with the Obama administration on February 29, 2012, in which the US promised aid in return for a freeze on North Korean nuclear and missile activities and a moratorium on nuclear and missile tests. A mere two weeks after signing the agreement Kim conducted a space launch banned by UN resolutions. Kim revised the constitution to codify North Korea's status as a nuclear armed state. In the meantime, Kim staged provocations such as the 2010 sinking of the South Korean naval ship *Cheonan* (killing forty-six sailors) and the shelling of a South Korean island in the Yellow Sea. The restrained response from South Korea and the United States encouraged him to keep pushing. (South Korean artillery did fire back on Yeonppyong Island but killed no one.) Prospects for negotiations with Washington dimmed further after Kim launched another, more successful, long-range rocket in December 2012. This was followed by a third nuclear test in February 2013 and the restarting of the Yongbyon nuclear complex. In 2017, North Korea successfully tested intercontinental ballistic missiles and conducted its largest nuclear test to date. Kim boasted that the North was now armed with a "powerful treasured sword" and told the world that it had perfected "the bomb."[26]

Tensions with the US spiraled throughout 2017 when President Donald Trump pursued the so-called maximum pressure policy and threatened to totally destroy North Korea in a rain of "fire and fury." There was even talk by the Trump administration of launching a preemptive strike to give Kim Jong Un "a bloody nose." Kim, in turn, called Trump a "rogue" and a "dotard" and released videos with simulated explosions of the US Capitol.[27] But as 2017 turned into 2018, Kim Jong Un abruptly turned from his own maximum pressure policy to maximum engagement with the United States and South Korea.

From Kim Jong Un's perspective, he had consolidated his rule. He had purged and assassinated all would-be rivals and threats to his power, real or imagined. During the first six years of his rule, he had relentlessly accelerated the North's nuclear and missile program and obtained a credible nuclear

26. Josh Smith, " 'Treasured Sword:' North Korea Seen as Reliant as Ever on Nuclear Arsenal as Talks Stall," *Reuters*, November 13, 2018, available at https://www.reuters.com/article/us-northkorea-missiles-nuclear-analysis/treasured-sword-north-korea-seen-as-reliant-as-ever-on-nuclear-arsenal-as-talks-stall-idUSKCN1NI132.

27. See, for instance, Erica Pardney, "The Trump Admin's 'Bloody Nose' Strategy to Strike North Korea," *Axios*, January 8, 2018.

deterrent. Now it was time for an image makeover to go from being seen by the world as a cruel, unpredictable, nuclear-armed tyrant to metamorphosizing into a warm, gracious, approachable statesman. He would now seek to shore up his rule by improving relations with the outside world with the eventual goal of securing international acceptance of the North as a legitimate nuclear weapons power.

Kim set the tone with the New Year's address in January 2018, which hinted at improving ties with South Korea. Then he dispatched his trusted and attractive younger sister, Kim Yo Jong, to South Korea to participate in the Winter Olympics, marking the first time since the Korean War that a member of the ruling Kim family had visited the South. The thaw at the Pyongchang Olympics soon led to Kim's first summit with South Korean President Moon Jae-in. At their first meeting, at the DMZ in April 2018, Kim even stepped into South Korean territory, the first time ever for a North Korean leader.

These meetings laid the groundwork for Kim to achieve one achievement that had eluded both his father and grandfather—a summit with a US president and all the prestige that such a meeting confers. Kim Jong Un met with Trump in June 2018 in Singapore. Two more meetings followed—in Hanoi in February 2019 and at the Demilitarized Zone in June 2019, where Trump became the first American president to set foot in North Korea. Trump was giddy. He declared that he and Kim "fell in love."[28] While these summits did not produce any tangible step toward denuclearization, they did serve to legitimize the hereditary ruler of North Korea as a world leader—and to strengthen his relationship with Beijing.

China has consistently supported the Kim dynasty in the hope of preserving a friendly nation on its northeastern border that would provide a buffer between China and the democratic, pro-American South Korea, where 28,500 American troops are stationed. But Xi Jinping had been unhappy with Kim Jong Un. The young ruler's nuclear and missile tests had fomented regional instability, his unwillingness to undertake market reforms were an implicit rebuke to China's more liberal economic policies, and his assassinations of Jang Song Taek (the North's main liaison to the Chinese regime) and Kim Jong Nam (who was living in Macau under Chinese protection) were seen as affronts to Beijing. Xi expressed his displeasure by cutting off oil shipments periodically, including, on one occasion, for three consecutive months. Beijing

28. Philip Rucker and Josh Dawsey, " 'We Fell in Love:' Trump and Kim Shower Praise, Stroke Egos on Path to Nuclear Negotiations," *Washington Post*, February 25, 2019.

also signed onto tougher UN sanctions with each nuclear test. By late 2017, Beijing had agreed to nine major United Nations Security Council resolutions that banned some ninety percent of North Korea's most lucrative exports, including coal, iron ore, seafood, and textiles. Beijing, perhaps spooked by Trump's fire and fury rhetoric, was finally doing its part to implement sanctions after years of dragging its feet.

But Kim and Trump's decision to hold summits changed all that. Xi Jinping didn't want to be sidelined. Xi would meet with Kim Jong Un four times, including visiting Pyongyang. Beijing returned to relaxing pressure on North Korea. (Kim's decision to close the border with China in January 2020 to prevent the spread of COVID-19, however, did more to exacerbate the economic situation in the North than sanctions ever managed to do.)

Kim furiously picked up the pace for the North's nuclear and missile modernization programs after the failure of the Hanoi summit—when he felt betrayed that Trump had not been willing to lift the majority of sanctions in return for a promise to stop work at one of the North's nuclear facilities (at Yongbyon). In an October 2020 parade marking the seventy-fifth anniversary of the Korean Workers' Party, Kim showed off a variety of North Korean technology including a new submarine-launched ballistic missile (the Pukusong 4) and a new ICBM dubbed the Hwasong 16—the largest, liquid-fueled, road-mobile ICBM in the world. By 2021, North Korea had missiles capable of hitting any point in the United States. It had also amassed up to sixty nuclear warheads and enough fissile material to build at least six additional bombs every year.[29] The available evidence suggested that Kim was moving onto the next step: placing multiple warheads on a single missile, which would frustrate US missile defenses.

In addition to improving the North's nuclear weapons and ballistic missiles, Kim continued to prioritize asymmetric technologies, particularly in cyber warfare. According to Kim, "Cyberwarfare [sic], along with nuclear weapons and missiles, is an 'all-purpose sword' that guarantees our military's capability to strike relentlessly."[30] South Korean press reports claimed that the Reconnaissance General Bureau (RGB), North Korea's agency for both traditional clandestine operations as well as cyber operations, had more than 6,000 cyber warriors. Its cyber unit 121, comprised of both an intelligence component and

29. Congressional Research Service, "North Korea's Nuclear Weapons and Missile Programs," December 13, 2021, https://sgp.fas.org/crs/nuke/IF10472.pdf.

30. David Sanger, David Kirkpatrick, and Nicole Perlroth, "The World Once Laughed at North Korea as a Cyberpower. No More," *New York Times*, October 15, 2017.

an attack component, was headquartered in Pyongyang but also had a bureau that conduct operations from within China. Unit 121 disrupted US and South Korean systems by infiltrating their computer networks, hacking to obtain intelligence, and planting viruses. North Korean hackers repeatedly penetrated US and South Korean computer networks. North Korea was suspected, for example, of staging a cyberattack in 2014 on Sony Pictures before the planned release of *The Interview*, a satirical movie about the assassination of Kim Jong Un. Cyberattacks were particularly attractive because of the low cost of entry and high yields, and they had the added benefit of difficulties and delay in attribution, creating plausible deniability.

Cyberattacks and other illicit activities were yet another way for Kim to stay in power. The regime was able to circumvent sanctions with the income generated by its criminality. It has a long record of illicit activities including smuggling cigarettes, counterfeiting currency, making and distributing narcotics like methamphetamines, and proliferating ballistic missiles to countries like Iran and Syria. Now add cybercrimes to the list. The UN Panel of Experts estimated in 2019 that the Kim regime had been able to generate $2 billion through cybercrime by stealing from banks and cryptocurrency exchanges. These funds were then funneled back into the nuclear program.[31]

IV

The North Korean state has repeatedly defied predictions of imminent demise. It didn't collapse after the death of Kim Il Sung in 1994 or the death of Kim Jong Il in 2011. More than a decade after Kim Jong Il's demise, Kim Jong Un remains entrenched in power.

The three Kims have built a system without equal. The world's sole Communist-Confucian hereditary dynasty rules the most militarized and tyrannized society on the globe. The crimes against humanity occurring in North Korea are unparalleled in the contemporary world—it is a repressive, totalitarian system that confines hundreds of thousands of its citizens in slave-labor camps while all others are kept in constant terror. It also a country that spends billions of dollars on armaments while at the same time many people literally starve. Living standards among the North Korean citizens are among the lowest

31. Michelle Nichols, "North Korea Took $2 Billion in Cyberattacks to Fund Weapons Program: U.N. Report," *Reuters*, August 5, 2019, https://www.reuters.com/article/us-northkorea -cyber-un/north-korea-took-2-billion-in-cyberattacks-to-fund-weapons-program-u-n-report -idUSKCN1UV1ZX.

in the world. (North Korea's GDP per capita, based on 2015 figures, is estimated by the Central Intelligence Agency as 216th in the world.)[32]

Yet, in spite of its failures to feed its own people, North Korea has shown an uncanny ability to survive. It has long outlived most other Communist regimes in the world—and it remains far more tightly regimented than the four other surviving Communist states: Cuba, China, Vietnam, and Laos. Other dictators, from Ceausescu to Qaddafi to Saddam Hussein, have been toppled and killed. Kim Jong Un remains alive and in power. The North's rulers have shown scant regard for the survival of their own people—but they have been supremely successful at ensuring their own survival.

The North Korean regime's strategy for survival has remained remarkably unchanged over more than seventy years. It is predicated on terror, repression, propaganda, ideological indoctrination, and information blockade. By maintaining an iron grip on North Korea's population, with a level of totalitarianism unseen since Stalin's heyday, three generations of Kims have been able to channel their country's scarce resources into expanding the military and the police state without fear of popular unrest. Meanwhile they have bought off the elites with luxury goods and privileges unavailable to the general population.

North Korea has not just survived but has been able to wield influence far beyond what its puny economy would suggest. North Korea's total GDP is comparable to Burkina Faso or Albania, yet it has become a nuclear-armed state and a player on the world stage. Its rulers have shown tremendous skill in managing relationships with far more powerful countries such as China, Russia, and the United States. Pyongyang's dealings with Washington and Seoul have been remarkably successful in keeping the regime's principal foes off balance. Although sorely provoked, neither South Korea nor the United States has been willing to risk another Korean war—even in the days before North Korea became a formidable nuclear power. From the US perspective, North Korea has always been a second-tier threat and never an existential one that would have justified running the immense risks needed to achieve total victory. US and South Korean leaders understandably have preferred to manage the threat rather than to eliminate it. North Korean leaders, in turn, have skillfully leveraged the fear they inspired in Washington and Seoul.

32. Central Intelligence Agency, "Real GDP Per Capita," *The World Factbook*, https://www.cia.gov/the-world-factbook/field/real-gdp-per-capita/country-comparison, accessed December 8, 2021.

The question for the long term is whether the Kim regime can continue to survive using the same strategies. The regime is hardly in imminent danger of collapse, but some cracks are starting to appear.

First, while all of Kim's purges and executions helped to strengthen his rule in the short term by terrorizing potential rivals, they may corrode long-term elite support of the regime. The elites know that if Kim can turn on his uncle and his brother, any of them could be the next to be killed. Second, Kim is hardly in the best of health. He is a heavy drinker and smoker with a family history of health problems from diabetes, high cholesterol, and heart ailments. If he were to drop dead suddenly, it is not clear who would succeed him since his own children are too young to take over. That could trigger turmoil and a power struggle that might destabilize the regime. Third, while Kim Jong Un was able to preserve the police state he inherited, high levels of corruption are eroding the strength of the security services. Fourth, while Kim maintained an information blockade, the regime had been unable to completely block the flow of outside information increasingly seeping into the North through borders with China and even South Korea; this is chipping away at regime myths and undermining the solidarity of the North Korean people. Fifth, and finally, North Korea remains burdened by a failing economy notwithstanding the relative success of private-sector markets. Economic reforms have been half-hearted and insufficient to reverse the economy's continuing decline.

While the popular uprisings that have toppled dictators in countries such as East Germany, Poland, Romania, the Philippines, Egypt, Libya, and Tunisia are unlikely in North Korea, they are still a reminder that sudden change is always possible. At some point, the North Korean control system could fail—but it is very difficult to determine when that might be. North Korea has proved to be a wily survivor. But it is unlikely that a regime that lacks the consent of the governed and that cannot deliver essential services or even provide food to all its citizens will last forever. Sooner or later the odds are that the North Korean regime will join other failed dictatorships on the dustbin of history—whether that happens in 10 years or 100.

CHAPTER 42

Strategies of Persistent Conflict

KABILA AND THE CONGO WARS

Jason K. Stearns

Wars are fought to be won. This seems to be a truth supported by popular culture and military history alike. Carl von Clausewitz's dictum that the objective of war is "the compulsory submission of the enemy to our will" finds expression in the strategies of most modern militaries.

But what if some wars are fought not to be won but as a means of governing, as an end in themselves? What if the parties fight each other on the battlefield, but are also locked in a sort of perverse symbiosis, in which none of them wants the war to end? This has increasingly become the case in the Democratic Republic of the Congo (DRC), as well as in other weak states. In these places, the political costs of conflict for the government are low; waging war becomes both a lifestyle and a fundamental tool of political survival, providing a means of managing dissent and doling out patronage.

In some ways this mode of violence resembles what Mary Kaldor famously, and controversially, has described as "new wars."[1] The lines between organized crime and armed groups are blurred, and financing for conflict has become

---

1. Mary Kaldor, *New and Old Wars: Organised Violence in a Global Era* (London: John Wiley & Sons, 2013). The "new wars" thesis has come under fire from scholars. Their main criticisms are that this form of warfare is not really new; that the distinction between criminal, identarian, and ideological motives does not hold up; and that the data does not support the claims about new wars. Mark Duffield, *Global Governance and the New Wars: The Merging of Development and Security* (London: Zed Books, 2014); Stathis Kalyvas, " 'New' and 'Old' Civil Wars: A Valid Distinction?," *World Politics* 54:1 (2001): 99–118; Mats Berdal, "How 'New' Are 'New Wars'?

transnational, spanning narcotics, diaspora remittances, and various forms of smuggling. There are few large, pitched battles, but the conflict is no less deadly for the local population. Most refugee and internally displaced people globally are arguably victims of this kind of warfare. In Colombia, the DRC, Myanmar, Syria, and other countries, much of the fighting is fragmented, with small irregular forces pitted against a weak state.

Many of these conflicts reveal a striking symbiosis between the government and its armed opponents. In all these cases, rebellion involves insurgents at the periphery interacting with political elites at the center of the state apparatus in a form of violent equilibrium.

Naturally, this understanding of war affects how we understand military strategy. It displaces the objective of fighting from victory on the battlefield—a definitive and achievable goal—to the management of political ambitions between different factions at the center of the state, more of a process than a finite solution. As such, it lies at the crossroads of the political, economic, and military spheres; conflict for belligerents is a means of governance, not a path to victory. In addition, it decenters and complicates agency. If conflict is systemic, exceeding the intentions of any of its participants, then military strategy is no longer something that is expressed in official documents and debated in war rooms; rather, there can be multiple, competing strategies developed in private by different factions of government and never expressed officially. The conflict in the DRC from 1996 until 2021 illustrates these dynamics, while also giving us insight into broader trends on the African continent.

I

The initial full-fledged war in the Congo (then Zaïre), which broke out around September 1996, followed the Clausewitzian model of trying to defeat the enemy and conquer territory. Three main factors set the stage for the war: a decrepit state that had been run into the ground over thirty-one years of clientelist rule by Mobutu Sese Seko; local power struggles in the eastern Congo that crystallized around notions over who had a right to Congolese citizenship; and regional tensions fueled by the presence of rebels from Angola, Rwanda, Burundi, and Uganda on Congolese soil.

Global Economic Change and the Study of Civil War," *Global Governance* 9:4 (2003): 477–502.

It was these rebel rear bases, especially those of the troops that had perpetrated the Rwandan genocide two years earlier, that triggered the First Congo War. Rwandan and Ugandan governments backed a small Congolese rebellion, the *Alliance des forces démocratiques pour la libération du Congo-Zaire* (AFDL), led by the mercurial Laurent-Désiré Kabila. While it is unclear whether this rebellion and its backers initially intended to overthrow Mobutu, this quickly became their goal after they broke up the rebel rear bases in the east. Garnering additional support from Ethiopia, Eritrea, Angola, and Tanzania, they toppled Mobutu in May 1997, putting Kabila in power.

Conquest of state power was initially also the goal during the Second Congo War, which lasted from August 1998 until June 2003. Triggered by a falling-out between President Kabila and his former Rwandan and Ugandan allies, by 1999 the war had ended up in a stalemate that divided the country into several main parts: the west controlled by Kabila's government and backed by Angola, Zimbabwe and Namibia; the east controlled by the Rwandan army and its rebel ally, the *Rassemblement congolais pour la démocratie* (RCD); and the north and northeast controlled by the Ugandan army and a variety of allied rebel groups, the most important of which was the *Mouvement de libération du Congo* (MLC).

It was during this stalemate of the second war that key dynamics began to transform the conflict and the strategies employed by most belligerents, from ones that saw conflict as a means to an end to treating conflict as an end in itself. The fighting shifted away from the frontlines towards remote, rural insurgency and counterinsurgency, particularly in the eastern Kivu and Ituri regions. The assorted belligerents became deeply invested in various forms of economic activity, a blend of racketeering, extortion, and taxation. This, combined with the rampant abuses of the local population, led to them losing most of their popular legitimacy.

Several shifts—military, political, and economic—are key in explaining why this was the case. The particular military situation played an important role. By the time the Lusaka cease-fire was signed in July 1999, it was clear that an outright military victory would be difficult, probably illusory, for all sides. The Rwandan and Ugandan advances had been stymied by the intervention of the much larger Angolan and Zimbabwean armies, who did not want to see Kinshasa fall to their regional rivals, but also did not want to suffer the casualties and financial losses that a conquest of the east would entail. Meanwhile, Western donors, upon whom the Ugandans and Rwandans were especially dependent, insisted upon a cease-fire. Following the blueprint for United

Nations peace processes at the time, diplomats pushed for peace talks, which they hoped would be followed by a power-sharing agreement and the reunification of the country. A United Nations peacekeeping mission was deployed in 1999, initially to monitor the cease-fire and then eventually to broker peace talks, further demobilization, monitor human rights, facilitate humanitarian aid, and protect civilians in imminent danger.

This blueprint for peace processes in the post-Cold War world has influenced the trajectories of conflicts, shaping belligerents' expectations. Some scholars go so far to argue that the penchant for power-sharing agreements by Western donors has inadvertently incentivized rebellions by making them an acceptable path to power and lowering the cost of insurgency.[2] While this finding is contested, it is clear that international norms against protracted military conflict have made it more difficult to achieve military victories. This is in part due to the influence of Western donors in the global periphery, where their aid funding and political support constitute important sources of support for governments.

At the same time, important economic and social developments were taking place in the Congo, shaping the contours of the conflict. By the early 1990s, the Zairian state monopoly on mining had been broken as parastatal companies crumbled and artisanal mining began to flourish. This was encouraged by structural adjustment packages drafted by international financial institutions, as well as by the search for foreign investment by a cash-strapped and collapsing Zairian government. The growth of artisanal mining lured large numbers of young migrant men to mining areas across the eastern Congo. New trade networks were established, linking cities such as Guangzhou and Dubai with Goma, Butembo, and Bukavu in the eastern Congo. First gold, then bulkier minerals such as tin and tantalum were shipped out of the region, while electronics, motor vehicles, and construction materials flowed in. When armed groups proliferated following the AFDL invasion, this burgeoning private sector quickly became a source of revenue through smuggling, protection rackets, and illegal taxation.

At the same time, the agricultural sector, where seventy percent of Congolese made a living, mostly in subsistence farming, faced a downturn.[3] The

2. Denis Tull and Andreas Mehler, "The Hidden Costs of Power-Sharing: Reproducing Insurgent Violence in Africa," *African Affairs* 104:416 (2005): 375–98. This is contested by Helga Malmin Binningsbø, "Power-Sharing and Postconflict Peace Periods," presentation at the 47th Annual Convention of the International Studies Association, San Diego, 2006.

3. USAID, "Agriculture and Food Security in the DR Congo," https://www.usaid.gov /democratic-republic-congo/agriculture-and-food-security, accessed November 2, 2021.

conflict-ridden east had previously been the country's breadbasket, exporting an array of agricultural products—beef, beans, potatoes, palm oil, and sugar—to the rest of the country and the region. The war made large-scale agricultural production almost impossible, cutting off trade routes to the rest of the country, pillaging livestock, and preventing investment. The economy became increasingly focused on the mining sector, which in turn became extremely militarized. Meanwhile, employment opportunities shrank for the youth, making armed insurgency more attractive.

This war economy was the most pronounced in the Kivus region, occupied largely by the Rwandan army and its allies, who oriented much of their military and administrative apparatus towards extraction. Traders had to give a portion of their profits to the Rwandan ruling party in exchange for access to lucrative trade routes and mining sites. Companies created by the Rwandan Patriotic Front, including some operated by the Rwandan Ministry of Defense, had preferential access to mining areas. This sector became particularly lucrative between June 2000 and July 2001, when the world market price for tantalum, a derivative of coltan, shot from $10 to $380 per kilo. Some researchers estimate that net profits made by Rwandan companies from coltan alone could have been as high as $150 million during this period, while other researchers estimate total profits from the minerals trade at $250 million per annum throughout the occupation.[4] While it is difficult to calculate a precise figure for this kind of clandestine activity, it is clear that for Rwanda, whose entire annual budget was $380 million at this time, such income made its expensive involvement in the Congo possible. President Kagame himself described his government's involvement in the Congo as "self-sustaining."[5]

II

The military stalemate was ended through a United Nations-led peace process that resulted in the formation of a transition government in which all major belligerents, as well as the political opposition and civil society, participated. The transition period lasted from 2003 to 2006 and was, in some ways, extremely

4. Stefaan Marysse and Catherine André, "Guerre et pillage économique en République démocratique du Congo," in L'Afrique des Grands Lacs, Annuaire 2000–2001, Filip Reyntjens and Stefaan Marysse, eds. (Paris: L'Harmattan, 2001); Bjørn Willum, "Foreign Aid to Rwanda: Purely Beneficial or Contributing to War?" PhD dissertation, Institute of Political Science, University of Copenhagen, 2001.

5. United Nations, "Report of the Panel of Experts," S/2001/357, April 12, 2001, 27.

successful. It reunited the country, drafted a new constitution, created new security services, and witnessed Congo's first democratic elections in over forty years.

Joseph Kabila, who had succeeded his father in 2001, emerged victorious, beating several former rebel leaders and political opposition leaders. For a variety of reasons, linked to choices made by the young president—he was just 29 when he ascended to the presidency—as well as systemic factors beyond his control, the younger Kabila presided over what came to amount to a strategy of disorder.

The official war had come to an end, confirmed by the transformation of the United Nations peacekeeping mission into a stabilization mission. And yet, violence persisted and even escalated, confined almost entirely to the provinces of North Kivu, South Kivu, Tanganyika, and Ituri in the eastern Congo. This "post-conflict" period further entrenched conflict dynamics as war-making became a means of survival for political leaders, a source of patronage for military commanders, and a way for local strongmen to bolster their power. At the center of these dynamics was the newly formed *Forces armées de la République démocratique du Congo* (FARDC), which had been cobbled together out of half a dozen former belligerents. Around 120,000 strong, FARDC was a patchwork of loyalty and patronage networks, and included former rebel and government soldiers with varying degrees of training, education, and experience. Under the terms of the peace deal, senior positions were appointed largely based on political considerations, not competency or merit.

Joseph Kabila was in a tenuous position. He was anxious to ensure the loyalty of the thousands of former rebels who had been integrated into the FARDC and were now based within striking distance of the capital. His predecessor and father, Laurent-Désiré Kabila, had after all been assassinated by a member of his own army in the presidential palace. State reform and stability were much less of a priority than his own personal survival; Kabila's army commanders and other security officials had a similar order of priorities.

The weakness of Kabila's own army and state institutions was perhaps the key factor. During the war, Joseph Kabila had relied largely on Angolan and Zimbabwean support on the battlefield and had not been able to forge a cohesive or committed army. Given the dominance of foreign militaries in his security services, he and his father had never been able to—or felt the need to—forge a loyal, competent military or intelligence apparatus. Instead, Kabila's army was a patchwork of competing patronage networks. Most experienced officers had been former members of Mobutu's army and had questionable loyalty. The officers who had fought alongside Joseph Kabila during the two wars had little training or cohesion.

These dangers shaped Kabila and his advisors' approach to the security sector. They concluded that it would be safer to manage a fragmented army in which they could cultivate independent networks of loyal officers, instead of trying to create a politically neutral and meritocratic army. A colonel who was in the general staff corps (*état-major général*) in Kinshasa at the time remembered:

> Our weaknesses today are the result of decisions we took in 2003. The goal then was not to create a strong army but, to a certain extent, the opposite: We were trying to defuse the strength of our former adversaries, to dismantle their networks and prevent them from becoming too strong. That was the goal, not security.[6]

This tendency was reinforced by events that took place during the transition, in particular a 2004–9 rebellion launched by former RCD officers and backed by the Rwandan government in the east of the country, a botched coup attempt in Kinshasa in 2004 by senior army officers close to Kabila, and fighting in the capital between the army and former-MLC troops in 2006.

The rebellion launched by RCD dissidents, in particular, had long-term consequences. Almost immediately in the wake of the reunification of the country, senior military RCD commanders, led by General Laurent Nkunda and coming mostly from the Tutsi ethnic community, defected and launched a dissidence around the trade hub of Goma, on the eastern edge of the Congo. In contrast to the many smaller insurgencies that were largely restricted to rural backwaters and the confines of a single ethnicity, the *Congrès national pour la défense du peuple* (CNDP) was able to briefly conquer the major town of Bukavu in 2004, threatened Goma between 2004 and 2008, and displaced hundreds of thousands of people. Given its backing by Rwanda, the Congolese government's archrival in the region—the rebellion was conceived, in part, by Rwandan generals and received sporadic backing from across the border—the CNDP was perceived as an existential threat by the Kinshasa government.

The Congolese government launched a large offensive against the insurgency, sending over ten thousand troops to the east. Yet with only a weak, fledgling army at their disposal, Kabila's generals decided to employ an array of militia to tie down the CNDP. This decision was both necessary and convenient for senior officers in the army, some of whom had close ties with local

---

6. Interview by the author in Kinshasa, August 21, 2013.

militias and were able to earn kickbacks from payments to these groups, as well as from some of the taxes that these groups extorted from traders, miners, and the local population. At the same time, pressures from local elites also fueled the conflict. Local strongmen such as Eugène Serufuli, the governor of North Kivu, saw the CNDP rebellion as a threat to their power base, and threw their weight behind armed groups.

Other unintended consequences of the peace process reinforced this tendency to use weakness and fragmentation as a means of governance, leading to the proliferation of armed groups across the eastern Congo. First, the merging of six different belligerents into the national army created many malcontents, some of whom then started new armed groups. The government failed to provide sufficient opportunities for many of the former combatants that it was merging into the FARDC. Even for a well-functioning and deep-pocketed state this would have been difficult, as tens of thousands of officers had to be kept happy and paid.

During this process, the government prioritized providing positions to those who had the greatest *capacité de nuisance* (potential to cause damage), as officials put it to me. Those individuals were often officers from remote rural militias, many of whom were called Mai-Mai, who lacked the connections or the required education to obtain good positions. Many of these officers returned to the bush and kept fighting; in some cases, the army supported some of them in operations against the CNDP, reinforcing these centrifugal dynamics.

Elections, which formed the core of the peace process, also inadvertently fed into armed-group politics. Some cynical politicians pushed the issue of citizenship for descendants of Rwandan immigrants into the limelight, using populist diatribes to garner voters' sympathies. This exacerbated the fears of Rwandophones, a small minority in the eastern Congo, and made it easier for armed groups rooted in those communities to mobilize. For other candidates, armed mobilization was an easy way to curry favor and intimidate opponents. Elections also created losers, some of whom then resorted to violence. With few safeguards to prevent armed groups from stepping into the electoral arena, some candidates—a small but important minority—sought alliances with various armed groups to bolster their own statures and intimidate opponents.

These dynamics set the security services on a trajectory that became difficult to escape. The weak and disorganized army and the proliferation of armed groups were the products of a path-dependent evolution; it was not a predetermined outcome. For many entrepreneurs of violence and their backers in the eastern Congo, the end of violence would imply an end to the way they have made a living over the past decades. For political elites and military commanders in Kinshasa, bringing an end to conflict would require cracking down on entrenched patronage networks in the security services, which would constitute a dangerous realignment of interests.

It is difficult to discern agency and responsibility in this trajectory. From interviews with Kabila's advisors, the president largely took a hands-off approach to security, except for immediate threats to his own personal security and that of the regime. "He made laissez-faire politics into a science," one of his former security advisors told me after having fallen out with Kabila. "He knows about everything that is happening, but he also never makes decisions, lets others stick their head out, pits people against each other."[7] This absence of leadership was part of his strategy—"he strategically did not have a strategy," as one African diplomat quipped to me—stoking confusion and division among his ranks.

This strategy was not just rooted in a cynical attempt to accrue power and revenue. After all, this could also have been done by centralizing power and using coercion and domination—not weakness and co-option—to conserve power. The reasons behind Kabila's decision-making lie both with his own personality—he was known to be a reclusive, uncertain leader—as well as with the history and political culture of the country. Kabila, as well as the key figures around him, drew from the playbook of Mobutu Sese Seko, who, after embarking on a nation-building exercise in the 1960s and early 1970s, had increasingly resorted to fragmentation and patronage to shore up his dictatorship.[8] "He was an expert in the politics of weakness," one of Kabila's former advisors told me.[9] In the late 1970s, faced with limited resources and becoming increasingly paranoid, Mobutu resorted to fragmentation, orchestrating the proliferation of ethnicity-based, vertical networks throughout the state. Fearing dissent in the army, he arrested or replaced dozens of officers based on their ethnicity or his suspicions of insubordination, promoting officers from his Équateur region of origin. He then allowed security services to proliferate, often in competition with each other. Many of the key figures—generals, security advisors, and politicians—around Joseph Kabila had grown up under Mobutu; some even served in key roles under the latter.

7. Interview by the author in Kinshasa, September 16, 2015.

8. Thomas Callaghy, *The State-Society Struggle: Zaire in Comparative Perspective* (New York, NY: Columbia University Press, 1984); Crawford Young and Thomas Turner, *The Rise and Decline of the Zairian State* (Madison, WI: University of Wisconsin Press, 1985).

9. Interview by the author in Kinshasa, July 8, 2014.

Over time, this system of fragmentation and clientelism became baked into the organization of the state, rendering it invested in the persistence of conflict. It can be observed in how members of the security services are paid—their compensation was structured in such a way that officers struggled to prosper in the absence of armed conflict. In 2014, more than ninety percent of senior officers' remuneration depended on legal or extralegal payments directly linked to military operations. For example, officers in command positions often received a *prime de commandement* worth up to $1,000 a month, and intelligence officers sometimes received a *fond secret de renseignement*, worth several hundred dollars a month, but only if they were conducting military operations. These payments were not statutory, and were made at the discretion of military officers, which reinforced their individual loyalty to those authorizing the payments.[10]

In addition, military operations came with opportunities for pillage, extortion, and the embezzlement of funds. The United Nations Group of Experts and other researchers have documented the involvement of both the national army and armed groups in the trade of minerals, the farming and trade of cannabis, the production of charcoal, cross-border smuggling, and poaching.[11] Examples are many. A UN report in 2008 estimated that local FARDC commanders in the eastern Congo were making $250,000 a month through taxation rackets. An NGO found that another general was receiving millions in cuts from a local gold mine. One commander of the Republican Guard sometimes even hired out units of the presidential guard to work for a private security company in South Africa, unbeknownst to President Kabila.[12] These sums dwarfed officers' salaries, which in 2018 peaked at around $150 a month for the highest ranks. In contrast, officers

10. These figures come from field research I conducted in the Congo between 2012 and 2016. See also, Jason Stearns, *The War That Doesn't Say Its Name: The Unending Conflict in the Congo* (Princeton, NJ: Princeton University Press, 2022).

11. See the various UN Group of Experts reports at https://www.un.org/sc/suborg/en /sanctions/1533/work-and-mandate/expert-reports; Ann Laudati, "Beyond Minerals: Broadening 'Economies of Violence' in Eastern Democratic Republic of Congo," *Review of African Political Economy* 40:135 (2013): 32–50; Judith Verweijen and Esther Marijnen, "The Counterinsurgency/Conservation Nexus: Guerrilla Livelihoods and the Dynamics of Conflict and Violence in the Virunga National Park, Democratic Republic of the Congo," *Journal of Peasant Studies* 45:2 (2018): 300–20; Michael Nest, Francois Grignon, and Emizet F. Kisangani, *The Democratic Republic of Congo: Economic Dimensions of War and Peace* (Boulder, CO: Lynne Rienner, 2006).

12. United Nations, "Final Report of the Group of Experts on the DRC Submitted in Accordance with Paragraph 18(d) of Security Council Resolution 1857 (2008)," S/2009/603, November 23, 2009, https://www.undocs.org/S/2009/603.

awaiting deployment are *à la disposition de la region militaire*—colloquially known as "dispo"—a label associated with indigence and humiliation.

As belligerents became increasingly invested in conflict, violence became a form of bargaining. Scholars have shown how, following the creation of the new Congolese army in 2003, discontent officers would defect in order to negotiate better positions inside the government, while senior government officials would back armed groups as a means of bolstering their own political stature.[13] Strongmen emerged in North and South Kivu who specialized in combining armed force with political popularity, including figures such as Eugène Serufuli, Justin Bitakwira, and Mbusa Nyamwisi. Congolese colloquially referred to this as the *phenomène pompier-pyromane* (fire-fighter-pyromaniac) or *maladie auto-immune*: strongmen starting a fire so that the government has to negotiate with them to put it out, or state officials backing militia that challenge their own government.

The Congolese government was not the only protagonist in this metastasis and entrenchment of the conflict. On the other side of the border, the Rwandan government, under the stern leadership of Paul Kagame, played a determining role. Its military commanders were deeply involved in the creation of both the CNDP and Mouvement du 23 Mars (M23) rebellions, in 2004 and 2012, respectively, dramatically undermining the stability of its neighbor.[14]

In contrast to its rhetoric at the time, Rwanda's government was under little threat from Rwandan rebels based in the eastern Congo. And while it did make significant profits from Congolese tin, tantalum, and gold mines, Rwanda would have arguably stood to benefit in equal measure if the Congo had become a stable country. Instead, here too, conflict became a means of governance, albeit in a very different way than in the Congo. Involvement in the eastern Congo reinforced the image of a besieged Rwanda and reminded domestic elites of the RPF's (Rwandan Patriotic Front) role as defender against genocidal forces, a key legitimizing discourse of the government. Bureaucratic dysfunction was also a factor. Decision-making was dominated by members of the security forces, was rarely the result of open internal debate, and was marked by a deep fear of internal military dissent.

---

13. Jason Stearns, Judith Verweijen, and Maria Eriksson Baaz, *The National Army and Armed Groups in the Eastern Congo: Untangling the Gordian Knot of Insecurity* (London: Rift Valley Institute, 2013).

14. Jason Stearns, *From CNDP to M23: The Evolution of an Armed Movement in Eastern Congo* (London: Rift Valley Institute, 2012).

Rwanda's continued intervention in the eastern Congo was thus a compromise between these competing imperatives. On the one hand, Rwanda wanted to retain influence. On the other, it knew that outright conquest of the state was no longer possible. This changing attitude was clear in interviews with belligerents. As the former Rwandan head of intelligence, Patrick Karegeya, told me after he had gone into exile:

> State power was everything to us. We grew up in the shadow of state oppression, we thought in order to bring about liberation we had to control the state. Which we did in Rwanda. But we then realized that the nature of power in the world was changing. We couldn't win a military victory in the Congo. But soon we realized we didn't need to. We could get what we wanted by waging covert operations, staying underground.[15]

III

The CNDP was eventually defeated, as was its successor rebellion, the M23. In both cases, diplomatic pressure from the international community on the Rwandan government played a critical role in forcing the groups to demobilize. In the case of the CNDP, despite overwhelming superiority in terms of troops and resources, the Congolese army struggled to gain the upper hand; it was, rather, CNDP military victories that forced donors and the United Nations to put pressure on Rwanda to reign in its Congolese allies. In the case of the M23, a similar dynamic played out with donors and the Rwandan government. In addition—and tellingly in terms of the theory laid out here—following an embarrassing string of defeats, the Congolese army was able to reform its units and mount an effective offensive, mostly by removing around a hundred senior officers who had encumbered its chain of command, siphoning off resources and issuing contradictory orders. This shows that, when security issues affected his legitimacy and survival, Kabila could indeed act; it was not merely a matter of state capacity. Once the M23 had been defeated, however, the impetus for reform stalled.

Meanwhile, other armed groups proliferated. By 2020 there were 120 armed groups in the eastern Congo, rendering a lasting and comprehensive solution to the conflict much more challenging. This conflict has had a devastating impact on the local population. In 2021, 5.5 million people were displaced in this region. According to polling conducted by the Harvard Humanitarian Initiative,

---

15. Interview by the author in Dar es Salaam, January 13, 2008.

fifty-seven percent of people there thought they were going to die as a result of the conflicts at some point between 2002 and 2014, nineteen percent had experienced a physical assault due to the conflict, and thirty-two percent had a member of their household killed.[16]

There are several reasons for this fragmentation. As the conflict has simmered on, local politicians and businesspeople have leveraged armed groups to promote their own interests, which some researchers have called "the democratization of militarized politics."[17] These elites have used armed groups to intervene in conflicts over land and local power, to intimidate opponents and to bolster their standing ahead of elections, and to further their hold over economic rackets. This has produced a centrifugal dynamic, leading to the splintering of groups. With little impetus from the national government to negotiate an end to conflict, armed groups that lack internal cohesion end up breaking up, furthering this dynamic.

The relative apathy of the government is perhaps the most striking element in these dynamics. Armed groups sprang up in large part because it was a possible and relatively low-risk way of making a living and achieving a modicum of dignity for an impoverished youth. The government invested little in army reform, and even a basic demobilization plan was on hold for years, largely due to inaction. In part this can be explained by the path-dependent events described previously: a weak government anxious for its own survival, confronted by a rebellion on its periphery, ended up using its army as a means of doling out patronage and coup-proofing the regime rather than ensuring security.

This account, however, does not explain why other considerations did not come to the fore. Why, for example, did violence not become an electoral issue, or even a pretext to suspend civil liberties and impose emergency rule, as it has in other countries?

Instability in the east was not a threat, in either political or economic terms, to the Kinshasa-based elites. Other than the CNDP, no armed group in the area could project power very far outside of its narrow ethnic confines, and the conflict was a thousand miles from the capital, separated by wide expanses, rainforest, and savannah. In addition, officials in government received so much revenue from other sources—in particular, major investments by large multinational mining companies—that they did not feel the need to extract rents

16. Patrick Vinck and Phuong Pham, "Searching for Lasting Peace Population-Based Survey on Perceptions and Attitudes about Peace, Security and Justice in Eastern Democratic Republic of the Congo," Harvard Humanitarian Initiative, 2014.

17. Judith Verweijen and Claude Iguma, *Understanding Armed Group Proliferation in the Eastern Congo* (Nairobi: Rift Valley Institute, 2015).

from the restive east, or to bring enough stability and infrastructure to attract large foreign investments there.

In the end, bringing stability to the eastern Congo was extremely peripheral to the survival of key decision-makers—politicians were not punished at the polls for their neglect of the east, nor was the fighting there a security threat to the country's capital a thousand miles away. "When I campaign in my constituency in Kinshasa, no one ever asks me about violence in the eastern Congo," one MP told me. Elected officials from Equateur, Kasai, and Bandundu provinces reported similar dynamics during my research.

This, in turn, raises the question of why the conflict did not become the basis for mobilization as did, for example, the holding of free and fair elections. After all, tens of thousands of people participated in high-risk protests against Joseph Kabila's government in 2015–18. In part, popular discourse molded perceptions of violence. Conflict in the eastern Congo was portrayed by media and politicians as inscrutable and tragic, but also normal. "Those people have always been at war," one parliamentarian from Kinshasa told me. "Nothing we can do will change that."[18] An analysis of articles written in two Kinshasa newspapers—*Le Potentiel* and *La Prospérité*—during the first part of the post-conflict escalation between 2003–13 shows that the conflict was largely framed as a Rwandan invasion, a battle over minerals by multinational companies, or as a quagmire of dozens of armed groups fighting for no clear reason. This framing placed an emphasis on the actions of rebels, usually without explaining the complex histories behind their motivations, instead of highlighting the inaction of the government. Articles were relatively infrequent—for example, in 2010 the popular daily *Le Potentiel* wrote an article on violence in the east roughly once a week, and only rarely on the front page.[19]

IV

Similar trends can be observed across the African continent, where other governments are accommodating, cohabitating with, and at times instrumentalizing conflicts. In contrast with past eras, there are few recent rebellions that aim to capture state power or to secede. Most of the insurgencies that aimed to topple governments petered out—the Democratic Forces for the Liberation

18. Interview by the author in Kinshasa, February 21, 2016.

19. This is based on a triage of keyword searches for "attaque," "violence," and "groupe armé" in the *Le Potentiel* archives through Nexis Uni. The results were sorted to retain only those that referred to specific attacks. Multiple articles on the same attacks were counted as one.

of Rwanda (FDLR) did not mount a serious attack on Rwanda between 2001 and 2021, and the various Burundian rebel groups based in the eastern Congo had splintered, as of this writing, to the point of near extinction. The complex insurgencies in Somalia, which featured a host of belligerents largely coalescing around clan identities or Al-Shabaab, resembled violent bargaining much more than attempts to overthrow the federal government.

One exception was the conflict in South Sudan, which began as a struggle for control of the state, but by 2020 had settled into a pattern in which violence was largely deployed as a means of bargaining at the center and extracting resources at the periphery. A similar situation prevailed with separatist insurgencies, although there were exceptions here as well. Groups like the Front for the Liberation of the Enclave of Cabinda (FLEC) and the Movement of Democratic Forces of Casamance (MFDC) had become inactive. Even the Tuareg insurgency in Mali, which began with separatist ambitions in the 1990s, had transformed, engaging in racketeering and bargaining with the central government.

Meanwhile, most of the insurgencies on the continent were repeat civil wars. Almost every single civil conflict on the continent at the time of this writing was taking place on top of the ruins—and, more importantly, on top of the social networks, worldviews, and grievances—of previous episodes of violence. This process has created entire social classes and networks invested in conflict, and armed mobilization has become an available and acceptable means of conducting politics. As one could see in the case of the Central African Republic and Chad, armed conflict had become a *métier*, an occupation, as Marielle Debos calls it.[20] Many of the armed groups in the Democratic Republic of the Congo, the Central African Republic, Nigeria, South Sudan, Sudan, and much of the Sahel did not aim at overthrowing the government or seceding. Rather, violence became an end in itself, a language of bargaining, a lifestyle, and a form of governance.

This does not imply a grand conspiracy to perpetuate conflict. It would be wrong to suggest, as one often hears among war-weary Congolese, that conflict is a strategy employed by Western powers, or sometimes by China, to weaken African states in order to extract minerals or other natural resources. It is more likely, as in the Congo, that the wars have reshaped societies, promoting actors with a vested interest in the conflict economy and whose goal is no longer to seize power but to carve out fiefdoms on the margins of the state.

20. Marielle Debos, *Living by the Gun in Chad: Combatants, Impunity and State Formation* (London: Zed Books Ltd., 2016).

Confirmation of this could be seen in the dramatic growth in the number of conflicts in Africa between non-state actors, which outnumbered those between the state and insurgencies. By 2019, there were twenty-four state-based conflicts and forty-two conflicts between non-state actors. This trend is compounded by a combination of apathy, opportunism, and pragmatism that has resulted in a government approach that shies away from cracking down on patronage networks or reforming the state and economy. Imposing stability and dismantling insurgents are often perceived by key decision-makers as too risky or not important enough. Violence thus becomes a means of governing as much as a means of protest or obtaining power, which means that ambiguities can be found throughout the conflicts in contemporary Africa. In Chad, outright aggression can alternate with camaraderie. As Marielle Debos has written, "Soldiers and rebels feel that they are divided by circumstances and divergent tactical choices rather than by irreconcilable identities or political stances." Similarly complicated relationships can be observed in the conflict in Guinea-Bissau, oscillating between friendship and enmity.[21]

A more difficult question to answer is: why? What has caused this new trend in African conflicts that produces violent bargains and involuted conflicts?

When surveying trends on the African continent over the past thirty years, the most obvious inference is the dramatic liberalization of societies, both in the economic and the political spheres. Contrary to the views of liberal democratic theorists, these trends did not produce greater stability. Instead, the wave of democracy sweeping across the continent after the end of the Cold War, along with the liberalization of African economies, produced a kind of hybrid political system that was able to accommodate low-level insurgencies.

At the same time, economies were liberalized, making it easier for armed groups and criminal gangs to capture rents, and while average incomes grew, so too did the number of poor people. Sub-Saharan Africa is home to over half the people in extreme poverty worldwide, with the extreme poor increasing from 276 million in 1990 to 413 million in 2015.[22] The size of the criminal economies has also grown. According to the United Nations, West African syndicates reap over $2 billion in annual profits from the cocaine trade alone;

21. Debos, *Living by the Gun in Chad*; Henrik Vigh, *Navigating Terrains of War: Youth and Soldiering in Guinea-Bissau* (Copenhagen: Berghahn Books, 2006).

22. Food and Agriculture Organization (FAO), *Ending Extreme Poverty in Rural Area* (Rome: FAO, 2018), 8.

an estimated \$3.5 billion is lost on the continent to cybercrime every year.[23] For relatively small economies, these are large amounts.

The introduction of multiparty democracy across most of Africa in the 1990s had an ambiguous impact on conflict dynamics, rendering them more peripheral but also integrating them into political and electoral dynamics. On the one hand, the advent of democratic competition drew would-be insurgents away from the battlefield and into electoral contention.[24] Meanwhile, the support for armed rebellion that had flowed during the Cold War—from apartheid South Africa, the United States, Cuba, and the Soviet Union—dried up, while large amounts of resources became available for political parties and elections. Norms changed as well. In its Constitutive Act of 2002, the African Union included an obligation to reject the unconstitutional change of a government.

It soon became clear, however, that democracy was far from incompatible with low-level conflicts, and in some cases even stoked unrest. Political elites could resort to backing armed groups to bolster their status, to intimidate rivals, or to extract resources. As this chapter makes clear, the Congo was a showcase for this, and militias in the Niger Delta played a similar role.[25] This latter case is instructive as the emergence of conflict was tightly interwoven with the transition to civilian rule in 1999. Some of the most important leaders of the largest militias there—the Niger Delta People's Volunteer Force (NDPVF) and the Movement for the Emancipation of the Niger Delta (MEND)—began their careers as enforcers for political parties in the Niger Delta. After the elections, these armed entrepreneurs branched out, continuing to provide protection to state officials and extracting rents from oil drilling and transport operations in the region. A similar trajectory can be seen elsewhere on the continent, with armed groups emerging in response to a particular need from political elites or local communities, but then becoming increasingly independent and self-interested.

23. United Nations Office on Drugs and Crime (UNODC), "The Transatlantic Cocaine Market," (Dakar: UNODC, 2011), 15; "Cybercrime Is Costing Africa's Businesses Billions," *Quartz*, June 12, 2018.

24. Scott Straus, "Wars Do End! Changing Patterns of Political Violence in Sub-Saharan Africa," *African Affairs* 111:443 (2012): 179–201.

25. Shola Omotola, "From Political Mercenarism to Militias: The Political Origin of the Niger Delta Militias," in *Fresh Dimensions on the Niger Delta Crisis of Nigeria*, Victor Ojakorotu, ed. (South Africa: JAPSS Press, 2009), 91; Judith Burdin Asuni, *Understanding the Armed Groups of the Niger Delta* (New York, NY: Council on Foreign Relations, 2009).

The opening up of a closed political system to electoral competition can also create instability as decisions are made around how public patronage is shared. Scholars have argued that democratization in Mali in the 1990s—much hailed by Western observers—was hijacked by national elites and regional "big men," feeding into cycles of insurgency.[26] Additionally, strongmen who are forced to democratize can use conflict and ethnicized governance to divide their opponents and stay in power. This was certainly the case during the final years of Mobutu, as it was in the various spates of ethnically tinged violence in Kenya's Rift Valley.[27]

Economic liberalization, which had begun with structural reforms in the early 1980s, also played a role, creating new sources of profit for armed groups and militia. The wars in Sierra Leone, Liberia, Angola, and later those in the Congo, Mali, and Libya showed how local actors could use transnational networks to obtain weapons, tax trade, and engage in commerce themselves. The structural adjustment reforms of the 1980s and 90s, intended to reduce the bloated state bureaucracies and create a more conducive environment for private enterprise, unintentionally furthered these dynamics by selling off state mining assets and reducing the capacity of the bureaucracy. The civil wars of Sierra Leone and Liberia were prime examples: the state apparatus was weakened, creating security and regulatory vacuums that criminal networks could exploit, all the while social safety nets were eroded.[28] It is not just the mediatized cases of "blood diamonds" in West Africa and "conflict coltan" in the Congo—in the Sahara, armed groups derived most of their profits from the trade in contraband cigarettes and human smuggling.

At the same time, structural adjustment programs hit rural peasants hard, leading to the concentration of agricultural capital and land in the hands of a small elite and creating increasing disparities between urban and rural areas.[29] More than ever, cities beckoned, promising consumerism and opportunity, but often resulting in sprawling slums and large numbers of subsistence

26. Morten Bøås and Liv Elin Torheim, "The Trouble in Mali—Corruption, Collusion, Resistance," *Third World Quarterly* 34:7 (2013): 1279–92.

27. Peter Geschiere and Francis Nyamnjoh, "Capitalism and Autochthony: The Seesaw of Mobility and Belonging," in *Millennial Capitalism and the Culture of Neoliberalism*, Jean Comaroff and John Comaroff, eds. (Durham, NC: Duke University Press, 2001), 159–90.

28. David Keen, "Liberalization and Conflict," *International Political Science Review* 26:1 (2005): 73–89.

29. Deborah Bryceson and Vali Jamal, eds., *Farewell to Farms: De-Agrarianisation and Employment in Africa* (London: Routledge, 2019).

farmers with shrinking farms.[30] However, whereas in previous generations urban intellectuals recruited among rural peasants, thus bridging the two spheres, many recent rebellions—those in Kordofan, Darfur, the Democratic Republic of the Congo, and increasingly in the Central African Republic and South Sudan, for example—feature armed groups hunkering down in rural areas with little intention of taking control of large towns. Armed rebellion has thus become both increasingly peripheral and better integrated into the logic of state governance.

Finally, international actors became complicit in this production of violence through a process of extraversion in which local elites draw on outside actors—in particular, donors, diplomats, and aid workers—to extract resources and bolster their status.[31] There have been different forms of this complicity. Tobias Hagmann, for example, has documented how Somali elites "regularly turned their participation in transitional governments into a resource appropriation tactic" from outside actors.[32] Similarly, anti-Islamist military backing from the United States became increasingly important as a source of financing for national armies. In Niger, US support to the army totaled fifteen percent of the military budget between 2012 and 2019, while Uganda benefited from military aid equivalent to a third of its military budget in 2016.[33] The United States was not the only source of such funding—the Burundian government obtained $13 million dollars a year by sending peacekeepers to the Central African Republic to serve in a United Nations force there, amounting to around twenty percent of its total military budget. Ironically, this support aims at stabilizing fragile states to prevent them from becoming rear bases for terrorist groups. However, by taking a militarized approach donors may be reinforcing that very logic of fragility.

The rising involvement of China in the coming years could reinforce these trends. The East Asian giant has invested enormous amounts in Africa, through bilateral loans, massive infrastructure deals, and by incentivizing its private sector to seek opportunities there. China is Africa's largest trade

30. William Masters et al., "Urbanization and Farm Size in Asia and Africa: Implications for Food Security and Agricultural Research," *Global Food Security* 2:3 (2013): 156–65.

31. Jean-François Bayart and Stephen Ellis, "Africa in the World: A History of Extraversion," *African Affairs* 99:395 (2000): 217–67.

32. Tobias Hagmann, *Stabilization, Extraversion and Political Settlements in Somalia* (Nairobi: Rift Valley Institute, 2016).

33. Zachariah Mampilly and Jason Stearns, "A New Direction for US Foreign Policy in Africa," *Dissent* 67:4 (2020): 107–17.

partner and invested over $2 billion on the continent between 2005 and 2020. Many of these investments and loans could further undermine accountability, especially if recipient countries decide to use the funds to shore up clientelist networks instead of strengthening their bureaucracies and security services.

V

This understanding of the Congolese conflict—of armed mobilization and military operations as a means of providing patronage and coup-proofing—has profound consequences for our understanding of strategy.

First and most fundamentally, the objective of fighting changes from defeating the enemy to broader political and economic goals. In the Congolese case, conflict is used as means to keep the military in check, to distribute patronage, and to extract profits by embezzling funds and through racketeering. This requires expanding our understanding of strategy from the military to the political and economic realms and from a goal-oriented to a process-oriented approach.

Second, it also requires a shift from an instrumental to a functionalist logic, decentering and complicating agency. Military strategy in this approach is not merely something devised by the commanders of battlefield operations. In the Congolese case, it is obvious that if one can speak of a strategy for military operations, it is one put together and dictated by a multitude of actors, ranging from government politicians to local commanders. After all, if conflict is systemic, exceeding the intentions of any of its participants, then it would be short-sighted to attribute too much importance to official strategy that has little impact on the behavior of units in the field.

The implications of these shifts in approaching conflict dynamics can seem counterintuitive. If we are to evaluate the success of the Congolese military strategy, we would have to ask ourselves whether it is achieving those goals, which can be utterly at odds with conventional strategic logic. What appears to an outsider to be a shambolic, disorganized military operation may be performing critical functions. Indeed, seen from Kinshasa, the Congolese military was successful at preventing any threats to civilian power, while allowing many security officials to enrich themselves.

These considerations are not confined to the Congo, nor are they of marginal importance in terms of global security dynamics. Most armed violence in the early twenty-first century takes place in weak states, in long-term conflicts with a high degrees of fragmentation in terms of their belligerents. The analysis developed here could apply, with modifications for local particularities and interests, to conflicts in Libya, Somalia, Syria, and Nigeria.

VI

It is perhaps strange to include this chapter in a volume on military strategy. The strategy described here is not expressed in any document, nor does it have a clear author or even authority behind it. Rather, it finds itself expressed in a system of conflict in which many belligerents participate but none is the ultimate master. The fundamental goal of the fighting becomes not to dismantle the rebellions or capture the state but to persist. Henry Kissinger famously said, referring to the leftist insurgencies the United States was facing in the 1970s, "The guerrilla wins if he doesn't lose." In this case, we could similarly argue, "The government wins if it doesn't lose."

The comparison that is perhaps most apt here is that with criminal networks such as the Sicilian mafia, or the various cartels that exercise enormous influence in Colombia, Mexico, Brazil, and other parts of Latin America. They are much wealthier organizations that operate in much greater secrecy than the armed groups described previously, with little intention of controlling large swaths of territory, but their objective is similar: not to overthrow the government, but to parasitize it, to evolve in symbiosis with it, all the while maximizing their own power and influence. This approach radically reframes the purpose and process of strategy in an era of globalization, when the sovereignty of nation states, especially those in the Global South, is being challenged by private enterprise, more powerful countries, security contractors, and humanitarian organizations.

CHAPTER 43

Strategy and Grand Strategy in New Domains

Joshua Rovner

What happens when military innovations open up new warfighting domains? How do strategists react when science and engineering breakthroughs create opportunities for combat in previously inaccessible places? Early modern advances in shipbuilding allowed great powers to project naval forces over vast oceans, clearing the path for ambitious imperial projects. Powered flight opened the skies to strategic bombing in the twentieth century, allowing combatants to leapfrog the front lines of conflict. More powerful rockets allowed states to send satellites into orbit, leading to speculation about organized violence in space. Techniques for exploiting the electromagnetic spectrum enabled states to obstruct and manipulate enemy communications. And most recently, states have turned their attention to cyberspace, where information operations might unlock the possibility of decisive victories at very low cost.

In all of these cases, military leaders invested in new tactics and procedures to optimize performance in future battles. They also grappled with deeper questions about force and politics, wondering whether traditional strategic ideas were still relevant in a world in which war looked very different.

The prospect of fighting in new domains has important effects on strategy and grand strategy. Strategy is a theory of victory, a logical story explaining how the use of force will help combatants achieve their political goals. Major military innovations have sometimes encouraged dreams of comprehensive victory on the cheap. For optimists, the ability to dominate a new domain renders the old ones unimportant, and allows for quick victories against defenseless enemies. It also suggests that a single service can win wars on its own, reducing the need for large and expensive armed forces that have to co-ordinate air, ground, and naval activities. Yet these same visions of victory also produce fears of catastrophic defeat. Military innovations inspire a race to operate effectively in new domains. Panic prevails when one's enemies get there first.

The intensity of these opposite impulses—fantasy and fear—attenuates over time. Practical realities let the air out of dreams of sure victory. Technical problems accumulate as states try to translate their warfighting visions into reality. What looked good on the drawing board is much more difficult in practice, especially given the presence of smart and motivated enemies. Using new capabilities also creates a great deal of wartime friction. The armed forces may not have the wherewithal to put new ideas into practice, especially if they discover that success requires coordination among services operating in different domains.

The emergence of new domains also affects grand strategy, which is a theory of security. A grand strategy tells a logical story about how states and non-state actors keep themselves safe. Some grand strategies are based on the premise that security is a function of keeping a low profile and thus avoiding conflict. These modest approaches do not demand much of the military beyond territorial defense. Other grand strategies, however, see security as a function of control. The surest way to enduring security is to maintain military dominance and political influence far beyond one's own territory. These ambitious grand strategies ask a lot. They require that the military project power across vast distances, and to be ready to fight against a variety of different challengers.

For great powers, the emergence of a new domain encourages ambition. The ability to control new space is often irresistible because military control promises both economic and security gains. If the military can guarantee freedom of movement in new domains, while inhibiting others' access, it can control natural resources and commercial routes. Control means setting the terms of international trade, opening new markets, and safeguarding the movement of money, goods, and people. It also implies the ability to set the terms of conflict by obstructing enemy communications and thereby forcing enemies into operational sclerosis. An enemy that cannot communicate, and cannot resupply its armed forces, cannot fight effectively for long. Such ideas have a very long pedigree. Great powers thought about the virtues of control when they set about building blue water capital ships, strategic bombers, space-based satellites, and cyberspace forces. The technologies changed but the underlying strategic logic did not.

Yet the desire to expand is often offset by logistical, organizational, and financial realities. Building platforms to operate in new domains is a terrific technological achievement, but those platforms cannot operate without a substantial supporting infrastructure. The logistics required to keep them operational in distant places are complex and prone to breakdown.

New domains may create grand strategic opportunities, but they also create organizational problems. Existing bureaucracies are usually ill-equipped to handle radically different operational needs. This is not because they are incompetent. It simply reflects the challenge of shifting institutionalized best practices onto a new domain. Bureaucracies are most efficient when they have well-honed standard operating procedures for managing clearly structured problems. Those procedures are unlikely to fit well in domains where problems are unstructured, and often not well understood.

One solution is bureaucratic restructuring, a process that usually pits traditionalists against reformers in a bruising internecine fight. Another solution is to create new bureaucracies altogether. Advocates for this approach, like those who called for independent air forces in the interwar period, argue that the only way to effectively exploit opportunities in a new domain is to create a service that lives there. Such calls provoke interagency contests for resources and authority. These contests do not always have a clean outcome. Rather than a rational organizational response in the service of grand strategy, the result is a ragged blend of reform and institution building, coupled with concessions to existing bureaucracies who are inclined to continue operating as before.

All of these efforts cost money. The combination of swollen logistics and organizational change is a heavy financial burden, and for many states it is too much. For these states, the temptation to add new domains to existing grand strategy is prohibitively expensive. For those with more resources, the costs may still restrict their activities, leading to a grand strategy that is far less than they had hoped for at the start.

This chapter explores these constraints in more detail. The first section describes how strategists envisioned warfighting in new domains, and why their visions proved illusory. The second section turns to grand strategy. Rather than focusing on new forms of combat, grand strategists thought about how projecting power in peacetime would leave them more secure. Their hopes also diminished over time, as the practical and political limits of power projection became clear.

I

New domains create opportunities to change the character of military operations. Confrontations among familiar adversaries in unfamiliar environments are inherently uncertain because the sources of combat effectiveness are largely hypothetical. Weak military powers see promise amidst that uncertainty, because their existing problems may become less relevant if military forces are able to take the fight to a place where they can exploit first-mover advantages. Strong powers, for their part, might sense an opportunity to consolidate their advantages by occupying new domains to surveil, encircle, and concentrate forces against their rivals. In so doing they could deny their rivals a sanctuary, defeating them in detail offshore, or safely delivering ground troops to previously unreachable locations.[1]

Beginning in the late Middle Ages, European commercial sailing vessels began their evolution into naval warships that could operate for extended periods outside their coastal waters. The high seas had previously been beyond the limit of naval technology; maritime conflicts were typically fought among narrow galleys near the shore. But a series of innovations made it possible to imagine large, self-sustaining battle fleets with enormous strategic potential. Capital ships outfitted with watertight side ports for cannon could deliver thundering volleys against enemy fleets, ports, and coastal cities. Engineers mounted cannon on wheeled carriages so they could absorb recoil on deck. Rudders replaced steering oars to control the movements of increasingly large and heavy vessels. And two eighteenth-century navigational innovations—the sextant and chronometer—gave ship captains the ability to pinpoint their latitude and longitude.[2]

Although a coherent body of naval theory did not really emerge until the second half of the nineteenth century, earlier observers did speculate about the unique possibilities of naval warfare. Lessons from antiquity seemed irrelevant, given the new suite of technologies that defined the age of sail. As Paul Hay du Chastelet wrote in 1668, "our usages are too different from practice in antiquity,

1. Enormous fifteenth-century "treasure ships" allowed the early Ming dynasty to send expeditionary forces far abroad. One such force defeated Ceylon and captured its king. Geoff Wade, "The Zheng He Voyages: A Reassessment," *Journal of the Malaysian Branch of the Royal Asiatic Society* 78:1 (2005): 37–58.

2. Alex Roland, *War and Technology: A Very Short Introduction* (Oxford: Oxford University Press, 2016), 48–49; and John Keegan, *The Price of Admiralty: The Evolution of Naval Warfare* (New York, NY: Penguin, 1988), xix–xxi.

and the invention of artillery has made all machines used then useless." Some thought naval battles of annihilation were unavoidable. "Combat does not cease," wrote Charles de la Rouvraye (1783–1836), "until one of the two [sides] is totally destroyed." Other contemporaneous French theorists focused on naval battles, notwithstanding the supposed French preference for commerce raiding.[3] British theorists, meanwhile, conceived of a grand "fleet in being" as a deterrent to continental great powers, who would not dare risk their smaller fleets. The Royal Navy did not typically go out in search of navies to destroy, but it was prepared to fight them, because the balance of risk would always be in their favor. If other countries refused to enter into fleet-on-fleet battles, Britain would fall back upon blockades and coastal shelling. In either case, the presence of a dominant fleet might create the chance for quick decisive victory over larger land powers.

Alfred Thayer Mahan popularized these ideas near the end of the nineteenth century. Mahan was an evangelist for building an American battle fleet, as opposed to one designed for coastal defense or commerce raiding. What mattered for Mahan was establishing command of the sea. Such command would allow the United States to control the pace of a conflict, and to apply pressure for surrender by strangling an enemy's economy. Seafaring nations could exert outsize warfighting power if they could achieve command—"that overbearing power of the sea which drives the enemy's flag from it, or allows it to appear only as a fugitive."[4] But this required a willingness to take great risks. For Mahan, the only sure path to command was "the defeat of the enemy's organized force—his battle fleet."[5] He conceded that blockades were also useful in pinning down rival navies, but this was a second-best solution. Better, if at all possible, was to destroy the enemy fleet rather than leave it as a threat in being. Commanders needed to risk battle whenever possible. If they hesitated, or thought more modestly about war on the sea, they would waste the peculiar strategic potential of naval operations. "A fleet is half beaten," Mahan warned, "when it goes into battle with one eye upon something other than fighting."[6]

3. Beatrice Heuser, *The Evolution of Strategy: Thinking War from Antiquity to the Present* (Cambridge: Cambridge University Press, 2010), 205–11.

4. Alfred Thayer Mahan, *The Influence of Seapower Upon History, 1660–1783* (Boston, MA: Little Brown, 1890), 138.

5. Alfred Thayer Mahan, *Naval Strategy Compared and Contrasted with the Principles and Practice of Military Operations on Land* (Boston, MA: Little, Brown, and Company, 1911), 176.

6. Mahan, *Naval Strategy*, 418.

Mahan is famous for his battle-centric approach to naval warfare, but his ideas built upon similar sentiments from the age of sail. Observers were inclined towards battle in this new domain because it implied a comprehensive victory; it was easier to imagine sinking a whole fleet than destroying a whole army. States could only afford so many capital-intensive capital ships, and they couldn't quickly rebuild navies the same way they could reinforce and replenish armies. Moreover, a decisive fleet-on-fleet engagement suggested lasting benefits, because the victory would control seaborne commerce in the aftermath of fighting, while simultaneously inhibiting the loser's ability to recover.

Consider Great Britain's extraordinary victory in the Seven Years' War (1756–63). Britain entered the key year of the war, 1759, deeply concerned about its prospects and genuinely frightened of a French invasion. A series of stunning victories that year turned the tide, however, culminating in the naval triumph at Quiberon Bay. The battle ended any French hopes of invading Great Britain, and ensured Royal Navy dominance. As a result of the war, Britain took Canada, Florida, Manila, islands in the West Indies, and territory in West Africa, while simultaneously ending French influence in India. As one historian concluded, the sequence of victories made 1759 "the year Great Britain became master of the world."[7]

Dramatic naval triumphs, however, were few and far between. Prosaic problems got in the way of the glorious vision of victory inspired by the clash at Quiberon Bay. The enormity of the oceans made it hard to locate and track enemy fleets, even with the benefit of rapidly improving navigational tools and techniques. And finding the ships was not enough. Decisive victory required tempting the enemy to give battle and keep fighting even when it was absorbing huge damage. This was inherently tricky as the ocean always permitted an escape route; there were no natural barriers to overcome. Willing combatants still faced the problem of arranging their fleets in such a way that they could bring their guns to bear. This was a delicate process given possible changes in the wind during the course of a battle. The ability to operate and fight at great distances encouraged dreams of massive fleet-on-fleet engagements with clear results, but few occurred during the first two centuries of the age of sail. Important battles usually occurred within sight of shore, and the outcomes were rarely decisive.[8]

7. Frank McLynn, *1759: The Year Britain Became Master of the World* (London: Penguin, 2004).

8. Keegan, *Price of Admiralty*, xxii–xxiii.

Steam power in the nineteenth century helped with some of these problems; electronic communications in the twentieth century helped with others. But increasingly sophisticated warships—the kind that might deliver on promises of decisive battles—were also increasingly expensive. This created a kind of paradox: the technologically advanced ships required to overcome the inherent constraints of the sea were too precious to risk. Battle fleets were huge concentrations of national wealth. The thought of losing them was deeply unsettling, and alternative approaches to naval strategy consequently rose in prominence. If decisive victories were possible, then so too were decisive losses, and naval theorists in the twentieth century set about thinking about ways of reducing the danger.[9]

At about the same time, strategists began imagining war in the coming era of air power. The exotic notion of fighting above and beyond the front led to a burst of theory. Attention to bombers intensified between the world wars as technology enabled aircraft capable of flying greater distances, leapfrogging front lines and national borders. And the domain itself—a sky that was open, vast, and permitted movement in any direction—provoked intense and lasting debates about what control of airspace meant for strategy on the ground. For the Italian writer Giulio Douhet, the most ardent proponent of strategic bombing in the interwar period, it changed strategy utterly. "Nothing man can do on the surface of the earth can interfere with a plane in flight," he argued, "moving freely in the third dimension." The implications forced a radical reconsideration about the nature of fighting. Range, geography, and natural defenses had always limited the potential for offensive action, but the advent of long-range bombers removed those constraints. Nor could civilians hope for refuge in a world in which rival great powers could target indefensible cities. The lines separating dueling armies from one another, and separating civilians from combatants, were disappearing.[10]

Bombing evangelists like Douhet believed command of the air would practically guarantee victory, but they envisioned a grisly process. Douhet imagined waves of bombers dropping explosives to create kindling, then incendiaries to start fires, and then chemical munitions to gas the firefighters arriving on scene. All of this was supposed to shatter civilian morale, and cause

9. Probably the most famous is Julian Corbett's "maritime strategy." Julian S. Corbett, *Some Principles of Maritime Strategy* (Annapolis, MD: US Naval Institute, 1988 [1911]).

10. Giulio Douhet, *The Command of the Air* (Washington, DC: Office of Air Force History, 1983 [1921]), 3–10, quoted at 9.

them to demand an end to the war.[11] Other air power advocates opted for less shocking strategic concepts. In the United States, officers at the Air Corps Tactical School explored the opportunities to bomb key targets that modern industrialized states relied upon for economic and military power. Closely interlocked economies had little slack, they believed, meaning that hitting key nodes in one part of the country would affect the enemy's whole war machine.[12]

Such optimism was tempered by the recognition that the air domain made everyone vulnerable. Failing to invest quickly in superior bombers, and in a dedicated air force, could lead to catastrophe. For Douhet, the "brutal and inescapable conclusion" was that "the strongest army we can deploy in the Alps and the strongest navy we can dispose on our seas will prove no effective defense against determined efforts of the enemy to bomb our cities."[13] Wealthy and powerful states could fall quickly, and no blessings of geography would save them. Just over a decade later, British Prime Minister Stanley Baldwin echoed this grim conclusion when he told Parliament, "The bomber will always get through."[14] As with earlier debates over the implications of blue water combat, hopes for quick decisive victory came hand-in-hand with fears of rapid defeat.

But the experience of the Second World War did not live up to expectations. Technology limitations and motivated defenders combined to limit the effectiveness of air campaigns. Hopes of rapid victory were replaced by grinding operations in which aircrews were often at greater risk than their targets.[15] Bombers struggled to locate targets, and bombs were notoriously inaccurate. Defenders proved adept at intercepting and destroying aircraft, using a combination of innovative tracking systems and organizational reforms to improve

11. Douhet, *Command of the Air*, 21. See also Stephen Budiansky, *Air Power: The Men, Machines, and Ideas That Revolutionized War, from Kitty Hawk to Iraq* (New York, NY: Penguin, 2005), 144.

12. Tami Davis Biddle, *Rhetoric and Reality in Air Warfare: The Evolution of British and American Ideas about Strategic Bombing, 1914–1945* (Princeton, NJ: Princeton University Press, 2004), 128–47; and Phil Haun, ed., *Lectures of the Air Corps Tactical School and American Strategic Bombing in World War II* (Lexington, KY: University of Kentucky Press, 2019).

13. Douhet, *Command of the Air*, 10.

14. Stanley Baldwin, comments in the House of Commons, November 10, 1932, available at https://api.parliament.uk/historic-hansard/commons/1932/nov/10/international-affairs.

15. William Emerson, "Operation Pointblank: A Tale of Bombers and Fighters," US Air Force Academy Harmon Memorial Lecture #4 (1962), available at https://www.usafa.edu/app/uploads/Harmon04.pdf.

performance.[16] Target populations proved resilient and adaptable, and target economies found workarounds to sustain production until late in the war. Historians have argued that the air campaigns did have important effects on the outcome of the war, but not in the ways that interwar theorists had expected, and not as soon as they had hoped.[17]

After World War II, the United States and the Soviet Union began investing in technologies that would allow them to exploit space for military purposes. Mastery of ballistic missile technology would make it possible to launch devastating nuclear strikes against which there was no reliable defense, and strategists began to think seriously about the implications for strategy and war.[18] That said, they did not spend much time thinking about warfighting in space, a notion that still evoked science fiction. Space might enable intercontinental missiles, wide-ranging surveillance, and communications among conventional military forces, but it was not seen as a likely arena for direct fighting. Perhaps for this reason, no leading space strategists emerged in the early years of the Cold War. No general strategic framework for outer space appeared in the following decades, and no theorist in particular defined the terms of debate.[19]

In the 1950s, the United States methodically invested in ballistic missile and satellite technologies, but it did so in order to enable nuclear attacks and intelligence coverage of its adversaries. Its goal was not to win in space, but rather to use space as a means for increasing military power on earth.[20] The Soviet Union did likewise, though it also viewed innovation as a source of terrific

16. Jon R. Lindsay, *Information Technology and Military Power* (Ithaca, NY: Cornell University Press, 2020), 71–108.

17. Two important additions to the debates are Philips Payson O'Brien, *How the War was Won: Air-Sea Power and Allied Victory in World War II* (Cambridge: Cambridge University Press, 2019); and Adam Tooze, *The Wages of Destruction: The Making and Breaking of the Nazi Economy* (New York, NY: Viking, 2007). Both conclude that bombing had significant effects on Germany's ability to wage war, but the results came only after years of hard experience.

18. Bernard S. Brodie, *Strategy in the Missile Age* (Santa Monica, CA: RAND, 1959).

19. Colin S. Gray, "The Influence of Space Power Upon History," *Comparative Strategy* 15:4 (1996): 293–308. For a recent attempt to provide such a framework, see Bleddyn E. Bowen, *War in Space: Strategy, Spacepower, Geopolitics* (Edinburgh: Edinburgh University Press, 2020). Bowen draws on Corbett's maritime logic to develop his theory, as does John J. Klein, *Space Warfare: Strategy, Principles and Policy* (London: Routledge, 2006).

20. The exception to this rule is the so-called high ground school of thought, which holds that "in the future, space forces will dominate terrestrial forces." But this idea did not emerge until late in the Cold War. Matthew Mowthorpe, *The Militarization and Weaponization of Space* (Lanham, MD: Lexington Books, 2004), 15.

propaganda value. It portrayed the success of *Sputnik*, the first orbiting satellite, as evidence of Soviet technological leadership.[21] Yet neither the Soviet Union nor the United States seemed to think about translating innovation in space technology into wartime victory on earth. Their hopes were more diffuse.

At the same time, both sides worried that space created particular wartime dangers. Mastery of satellite technology would improve military intelligence and improve coordination among sea, air, and land forces. But enemy anti-satellite missiles (ASATs) could put all that at risk. Paradoxically, the efficiency gains of exploiting space increased the possibility of catastrophic defeat; a small number of successful ASAT strikes could cripple wartime surveillance and communications. Such fears encouraged leaders to seek their own ASAT programs. President Kennedy authorized a ground-launched ASAT program based on existing IRBM (Intermediate-Range Ballistic Missile) technology. President Ford later ordered the Department of Defense to develop a new ASAT in response to analyses that the US satellite constellation was increasingly vulnerable. Neither of these efforts focused on hardening satellites against attack.[22] Instead, they suggested the possibility that future great power wars would start with reciprocal salvos against one another's orbiting platforms. If it was true that earthbound forces were utterly dependent on satellites, then future great power war was likely to start with a furious race to eliminate the opponent's satellites first. This would not guarantee victory because one's own satellites would still be vulnerable. But it would at least prevent disaster. What motivated action was the fear of sudden defeat, not the hope of decisive victory.

The emergence of space in this respect was different from other new domains. Bureaucratic politics, on the other hand, were not so different. Advocates of space power saw organizational opportunities, just as earlier advocates of sea power and air power had seen expanding domains as possibilities to grow navies and bomber fleets, respectively. So, while US policymakers were skeptical of warfighting in space, the Air Force viewed it as an extension of the atmosphere, and a domain in which it could naturally expand operations. In 1957, it inaugurated the X-20 Dyna-Soar concept, a prototype space plane that could destroy both ground targets and enemy satellites. Eisenhower rejected

21. Robert A. Divine, *The Sputnik Challenge: Eisenhower's Response to the Soviet Satellite* (Oxford: Oxford University Press, 1993).

22. Mowthorpe, *Militarization and Weaponization of Space*, 19–22.

the program. The Air Force reclassified X-20 as a research effort to keep it alive, but Kennedy cancelled it in 1963. Undaunted, the Air Force unveiled its concept for the Manned Orbital Laboratory, a space base under its control. The White House nixed this idea as well.[23] Ideas about militarizing space faded after the Outer Space Treaty in 1967, which reflected a general belief that conventional warfighting above the atmosphere was impractical.[24]

Cyberspace is the latest domain to inspire the familiar pattern of hope, fear, and resignation. In one sense it is quite different from the others, given that cyberspace is entirely artificial, a sprawling communications and data storage scheme built and maintained by human beings. Not everyone agrees that a man-made network of information systems counts as a warfighting domain. Some argue that characterizing cyberspace this way helps military officers comprehend the domain itself, while also shaping policy debates.[25] The notion that it is a military arena seems incongruous with the fact that the private sector dominates the infrastructure of cyberspace, and that private citizens are responsible for most of the information that flows through it.

Nor is it clear that "war" is the right way to describe cyberspace competition. In 1992, John Arquilla and David Ronfeldt wrote a milestone account of the strategic consequences of the information revolution. Advances in computing power foreshadowed changes in how military forces would fight and win wars. States would no longer settle their differences through wars of attrition or maneuver. Instead, they would battle over information, and the outcome would ultimately rest on which side could maintain control while enshrouding the other side in fog. This in turn suggested that states needed to reorganize their forces, reforming existing organizations or creating new ones to focus on managing information in cyberspace.[26]

23. Robert C. Harding, *Space Policy in Developing Countries* (Abingdon: Routledge, 2013), 53–54.

24. Roland, *War and Technology*, 97. Debates about "weaponizing" space returned in the late Cold War after President Reagan unveiled plans for a space-based missile defense system. This did not lead to a serious push to transform space into a genuine warfighting domain, though critics continue to warn about such a future. See, for example, Joan Johnson-Freese, *Space Warfare in the 21st Century: Arming the Heavens* (New York, NY: Routledge, 2017).

25. Jordan Branch, "What's in a Name? Metaphors and Cybersecurity," *International Organization* 75:1 (2021): 39–70; and Erick D. McCroskey and Charles A. Mock, "Operational Graphics for Cyberspace," *Joint Force Quarterly* 85 (2017): 42–49.

26. John Arquilla and David Ronfeldt, "Cyberwar is Coming!," in *In Athena's Camp: Preparing for the Next Conflict in the Information Age*, John Arquilla and David Ronfeldt, eds. (Santa Monica, CA: RAND, 1993).

Skeptics took aim at this argument. Chief among them was Thomas Rid, who argued that "cyberwar" was misleading. Following Clausewitz, Rid defined cyberwar as a "potentially lethal, instrumental, and political act of force conducted through malicious code."[27] He noted that in the two decades after Arquilla and Ronfeldt's seminal study, no cyberattacks had met any of those criteria. Cyberspace operations were adjuncts to traditional kinetic violence, or information operations that might enable lethal force. Critics also questioned the strategic assumptions underpinning the supposed cyber revolution, challenging popular fears that cyberspace favored the attacker and that cyber weapons were tools of the weak.[28] Others saw the domain as a natural venue for intelligence contests rather than military conflicts, given that the currency of cyberspace is not violence but information.[29]

Nonetheless, military services around the world have increasingly invested in cyber talent and capabilities. Optimistic strategists see possibilities for quick decisive victory. Well-executed cyberspace operations hold out the promise of corrupting enemy communications, thus forcing enemies into operational sclerosis. This scenario is especially appealing at the time of this writing given the complexity of war plans that require tight integration among sea, air, and land forces. Disrupting information flows disrupts enemy battlefield effectiveness. For states with aggregate military advantages, cyberattacks serve to buy time so they can bring superior forces to bear. For weaker states, cyberattacks help to level the playing field. If all goes well, gaining the advantage in this exotic new domain means dictating the scope and pace of military operations. It is not hard to understand why cyberspace is alluring to strategists, or why they have spent so much time developing doctrine for cyberspace operations.[30]

Like the natural warfighting domains, cyberspace also arouses fears of rapid defeat. Enemy attacks evoke nightmares of blank screens, lost ships, and suddenly inoperable systems. Even less dramatic attacks might badly impact military performance given the degree to which modern militaries rely on information technology systems. These systems have allowed them to coordinate activities

---

27. Thomas Rid, "Cyberwar Will Not Take Place," *Journal of Strategic Studies* 35:1 (2012): 5–32.

28. Jon R. Lindsay, "Stuxnet and the Limits of Cyber Warfare," *Security Studies* 2:3 (2013): 365–404.

29. Joshua Rovner, "What Is an Intelligence Contest?," *Texas National Security Review* 3:4 (2020): 114–20.

30. Joshua Rovner, "Warfighting in Cyberspace," in *Ten Years In: Implementing Strategic Approaches to Cyberspace*, Emily Goldman, Michael Warner, and Jacquelyn Schneider, eds. (Newport, RI: Naval War College, Newport Papers, 2021).

over vast distances, and to share granular information in near-real time. Losing that ability might force modern militaries to revert to a slower and costlier approach to fighting. Or it might simply cause them to lose.[31]

Other fears relate to how enemies might use cyberspace as a vector for propaganda and misinformation. The peculiar attributes of social media create an environment in which false information can spread quickly and easily. In addition, the ability to create "deep fakes" by manipulating audio and visual files might make it hard to understand basic facts about ongoing conflicts. This could complicate efforts to measure battlefield progress, interpret foreign signals, and maintain domestic support. War has always included a large dose of deception; cyberspace makes the problem much more complex and daunting.

Given the possible military implications, it is not surprising that militaries have invested in more cyberspace capabilities. Some have built new organizations dedicated to managing information and developing offensive and defensive warfighting concepts in the digital domain. Yet bureaucratic expansion creates problems of its own. Critics note that the traditional measures of military effectiveness make little sense in cyberspace, meaning that military officers might struggle to define what they mean by success. Critics also wonder if rigid military hierarchies can succeed in cyberspace in the first place, especially given the irreverent culture that characterizes the private sector hacker community. Recruiting and retaining irreverent hackers into the military, with all its rules and regulations, may prove difficult.[32]

This reflects a deeper problem: cyberspace is allergic to school solutions. The domain evolves constantly based on the preferences of users, the policies of firms and states, and the rules and norms that underpin international cyberspace governance. Security threats are likewise variable and changing, meaning that doctrinal solutions are likely to have a short shelf life. Institutionalized responses make sense when threats are stable and well structured, but this is not the case in cyberspace.[33] Similarly, the effectiveness of offensive

31. Jacqueline Schneider, *Digitally Enabled Warfare: The Capability-Vulnerability Paradox* (Washington, DC: Center for a New American Security, 2016). Nightmare scenarios are common in the literature on cybersecurity. Prominent analysts have used fiction to draw attention to the risks of catastrophic sudden defeat. Peter Singer and August Cole wrote the preface to the congressionally mandated *Report of the Cyber Solarium Commission* (2020), calling it "A Warning from Tomorrow." See also Eliott Ackerman and Adm. James Stavridis (ret.), *2034: A Novel of the Next World War* (New York, NY: Penguin, 2021).

32. Nina Kollars and Emma Moore, "Every Marine a Blue-Haired Quasi-Rifleperson?," *War on The Rocks*, August 21, 2019.

33. Lindsay, *Information Technology and Military Power*.

operations depends on the ability to exploit accesses to rival information networks. These accesses can be fickle and are prone to disappear for a number of reasons, including because of something as simple as periodic software updates. The upshot is that militaries cannot hold targets at risk the way they do in the physical world. This complicates traditional military planning, which translates operational best practices into institutionalized routines in order to maximize organizational efficiency. In this case, however, best practices are likely to be illusory and fleeting. Cyberspace field expedients might be required to operate given the technical realities of the domain, even if this means sacrificing a unified approach.

States are thus limited in their attempts to command the cyberspace domain, and early hopes about "information dominance" have given way to more modest aspirations.[34] Technological barriers are likely to prevent states from achieving rapid victory against reasonably competent state enemies. Societies are vulnerable to hackers because there are many lightly defended targets. Government networks are also vulnerable to intrusion. But gaining entry into foreign networks is not the same as executing successful operations against enemy military communications, and military organizations have obvious incentives to make their key networks secure and redundant. Rather than achieving victory by throwing enemy communications into disarray, Hollywood style, there are some indications that states are setting the bar much lower. Growing interest in the problems of protracted war suggests a different priority: not how to win quickly using exquisite cyberspace tools, but how to operate effectively in a degraded battlefield environment.[35]

Ideas about cyberspace echo the pattern in other new domains. Initial hopes of exploiting new battle spaces to achieve decisive results give rise to fears of catastrophic defeat. Over time, however, technical and organizational problems get in the way of attempts to dominate new domains. States become resigned to the limits of the possible; dreams and nightmares fade as the novelty wears off. When this occurs, strategists turn to integrating forces across domains rather than extolling the virtues of specialized military organizations.

---

34. Chris Dougherty, "Confronting Chaos: A New Concept for Information Advantage," *War on the Rocks*, September 9, 2021.

35. Recent commentary includes Hal Brands, "Win or Lose, U.S. War Against China or Russia Won't Be Short," *Bloomberg*, June 14, 2021; Andrew F. Krepenevich, Jr., *Protracted Great Power War: A Preliminary Assessment* (Washington, DC: Center for a New American Security, 2020); and Joshua Rovner, "Two Kinds of Catastrophe: Nuclear Escalation and Protracted War in Asia," *Journal of Strategic Studies* 40:5 (2017): 696–730.

II

Hope, fear, and resignation also describe the evolution of grand strategic thinking. The ability to project military force into new domains encourages ambition. Grand strategists often assume that economic rewards flow to those who can master these spaces, and prosperity will bring political power and enable lasting national security. It is not hard to understand the temptation, given the stakes. Indeed, expansion into new domains remains alluring even when the supporting infrastructure and technologies are immature. For some grand strategists, proof of concept is enough.

Yet states often fear that their rivals will beat them to the punch. They assume that competent adversaries will also sense the possibilities of power projection, and work quickly to establish their own presence in new domains. The desire to expand is related to the fear of missing out, and of finding oneself hemmed in by more aggressive competitors. In the worst case, states worry about becoming vulnerable to economic disruption or military encirclement. Such fears animated discussions the early days of blue water navies, bomber fleets, orbiting satellites, and cyberspace.

The term "grand strategy" did not exist in the age of sail, but observers made grandiose claims about sea command. Writing in 1593, Matthew Sutcliffe predicted that it would become a reliable refuge in times of trouble. "Those nations and cities that have the command of the sea, even if they are foiled on land, they can never be thoroughly vanquished, before they are beaten from the sea." His contemporary Francis Bacon believed that command of the sea meant freedom of action. It would give states the freedom to intervene in conflicts, or stay out, as it suited them. "He that commands the sea," Bacon concluded, "is at great liberty and may take as much or as little of the war as he will." Walter Raleigh saw the sea as the source of enduring prosperity and national strength. "Whosoever commandeth the sea commandeth trade; whosever commandeth trade commandeth the riches of the world." Controlling those riches meant money for larger navies, and the ability to exert influence anywhere those forces could reach. The Italian philosopher Tommaso Campanella (1568–1639) put the matter bluntly, "Whoever is lord of the sea is lord of the earth."[36]

European and Asian great powers soon set out to translate these dreams into reality. England and Holland built larger ships and larger fleets, as did the

36. All quoted in Heuser, *The Evolution of Strategy*, 201–7.

French, where Cardinal Richelieu expressed alarm that French power depended on imported gold and silver.[37] Without knowing it, they followed the example of the fifteenth-century Ming dynasty, which had sought to expand its military and political influence through enormous flotillas of "treasure ships" and smaller vessels.[38] In all of these cases, grand strategists assumed that controlling sea-lanes was necessary for regional and extra-regional maritime trade. They also believed that it would enable the expansion of land forces, which could be delivered abroad and thus compel distant rulers into favorable economic and political arrangements.

These dreams soon confronted reality. Elaborate sailing ships were marvels of engineering, but they could not operate effectively without a system of ports, shipyards, and storage facilities scattered around distant outposts. Organizing labor for these facilities—not to mention the ships themselves—was equally fraught. Efficient management of blue water logistics was not visibly achieved until the late eighteenth century, hundreds of years after blue water capital ships first appeared. In this case, as in others, the logistical burden was too much for most countries.

Even those who could afford it struggled mightily. The British Royal Navy was the gold standard by the late eighteenth century, but it took many decades to learn how to sustain the fleet. The rush to build more warships put massive strain on a limited number of dockyards to repair and maintain ships of all classes. The tradeoff between construction and upkeep became increasingly acute as the fleet grew, and labor disputes became more contentious.[39] The fleet itself was becoming more formidable, but more fragile as well. Capital ships were vulnerable to dry rot, for example, a pernicious problem that threatened their structural integrity. Technological solutions were available by the late eighteenth century, including a method to add a copper sheath to the bottom of warships to protect the hulls from saltwater corrosion and rot. But technical fixes required an efficient bureaucracy; this was no minor repair. Other bureaucratic reforms, such as more reliable storage systems for timber and other materials, took decades to implement. Economic volatility made

37. Heuser, *Evolution of Strategy*, 209.

38. Edward L. Dreyer, *Zheng He: China and the Oceans in the Early Ming Dynasty* (London: Pearson, 2006).

39. N.A.M. Rodger, *The Command of the Ocean: A Naval History of Britain, 1649–1815* (New York, NY: W.W. Norton, 2005), 368; and Roger Knight, "From Impressment to Task Work: Strikes and Disruption in the Royal Dockyards, 1688–1788," in *History of Work and Labor Relations in the Royal Dockyards*, Kenneth Lunn and Ann Day, eds. (London: Mansell, 1999).

things worse; cycles of boom and bust interfered with naval infrastructure spending that required many years to pay off.[40]

Several nineteenth-century great powers tried to compete in the race to build blue water navies, but they were often frustrated. For continental powers like France, Russia, and Germany, focusing on navies risked underinvesting in defense against continental rivals, and diverting them from more modest and sensible approaches to maritime grand strategy. Some scholars attribute their decision to pursue naval nationalism to a desire for domestic prestige.[41] There is certainly evidence for this argument. But the same leaders who indulged in naval nationalism were also most susceptible to the allure of sea command. Whatever the inspiration, their efforts to expand ultimately failed, or simply proved to be counterproductive distractions.

A similar story played out during the early history of air power. The proto-bombers and gas-filled airships of World War I were not capable of much damage, and they were notoriously inaccurate. Nonetheless, some theorists viewed air power as the centerpiece of great power grand strategy. Rapid innovations in the first decades of the twentieth century inspired astonishment and awe; even slow-moving airships were seen as instruments of domination.[42] In more concrete terms, control of airspace would allow states to hold their adversaries' key values at risk. The ability to credibly threaten cities and economic centers could be a powerful coercive tool, especially given widespread doubts about the practicality of air defense. The targets of bombing would surrender rather than die heroically.[43] States could thus ensure their security by maintaining dominant air forces. The most prominent early American air theorist, Billy Mitchell, declared that, in the "aeronautical era . . . the destinies of all people will be controlled through the air."[44]

Command of the air served as grand strategy for states in different circumstances. Great powers with modest aspirations could use it to deter their rivals

40. Nick Bunker, *An Empire on the Edge: How Britain Came to Fight America* (New York, NY: Vintage, 2015).

41. Robert S. Ross, "China's Naval Nationalism: Sources, Prospects, and the U.S. Response," *International Security* 34:2 (2009): 46–81.

42. Samuel Zilincik, "Technology is Awesome, But So What?! Exploring the Relevance of Technologically Inspired Awe to the Construction of Military Theories," *Journal of Strategic Studies* 45:2 (2021): 5–32.

43. B.H. Liddell Hart, *Paris, or The Future of War* (New York, NY: E.P. Dutton, 1925), 29–31.

44. William Mitchell, "Winged Defense," in *The Roots of Strategy*, David Jablonsky, ed.(Mechanicsburg, PA: Stackpole Books, 1999 [1925]), 423.

and surveil their frontiers. Great power empires, on the other hand, could use it to subdue uprisings in far-flung colonial possessions. This kind of air policing was appealing because it relied on technologies to reduce the need for large garrisons. Imperial officers counted on the idea that rebels unfamiliar with industrial technology would be utterly terrified by the appearance of manned aircraft armed with machine guns and bombs. All of this would make it easier and cheaper to maintain political control.

Yet there were practical and political limits to these dreams. The foreign victims of bombing raids were doubtlessly terrified on their first encounter with air power, but their fear declined as the novelty wore off. Targets learned how to camouflage themselves against overhead observers, and how to sound the alarm about incoming bombers.[45]

Great powers improved their air defenses during the interwar period. Innovation was slow and uneven, to be sure, but by the mid-1930s there were signs that altitude was not a permanent refuge. The idea that the bomber would not always get through suggested a lesser role for air power in grand strategy.[46] And critics of bombing became increasingly strident. They had genuine doubts about the utility of air power, and strong incentives to protect their organizational interests. Much as naval evangelists provoked army opposition, so too did air advocates raise the ire of other services that were not willing to concede that the air domain was key to success or failure in grand strategy. They certainly were not keen on seeing the establishment of independent air forces, over whom they would have little operational control.

Even in the interwar period, some skeptics of air power wondered about the actual results of bombing. Billy Mitchell famously staged a demonstration in which US bombers sunk a defunct German battleship, but critics argued that sinking a defenseless ship at anchor was hardly convincing. Real world British air policing was also hard to evaluate. It was not always clear that raids were doing much damage, or causing much consternation. Damage assessments were notoriously difficult and usually speculative given the limits of photo-reconnaissance and the fact that the raiders returned to base after their missions. Bureaucratic interests also colored these accounts; air advocates had obvious reasons to exaggerate the effects. For other observers, uncertainty

45. David E. Omissi, *Air Power and Colonial Control: The Royal Air Force, 1919–1939* (Manchester: Manchester University Press, 1990), 107–33.

46. See, for instance, John Ferris, "Fighter Defense before Fighter Command: The Rise of Strategic Air Defence in Great Britain, 1917–1934," *Journal of Military History* 63:4 (1999): 845–84.

prevailed. British Field Marshal Henry Wilson described RAF bombers as "appearing from God knows where, dropping their bombs on God knows what, and going off again God knows where."[47] The outcome of the First World War, ultimately decided through grinding campaigns of attrition, convinced most observers that, while air power would play a role in future grand strategy, it would not play the starring role that earlier theorists had imagined.

The Cold War witnessed expansion beyond the atmosphere, as scientists and engineers pushed the boundaries of propulsion and communications. Not surprisingly, advances in wartime rocketry led to postwar questions about grand strategy in space. Here the cycle of hope and fear was somewhat different, because leaders in Washington and Moscow did not seriously entertain visions of commanding space the way they could command terrestrial domains. Instead, they tended to think of space as a vector for missiles and an arena for surveillance. The vastness of space, and the massive technological hurdles involved in launching and maintaining satellites, made command a distant prospect. Nonetheless, the superpowers invested heavily in the technologies required to operate in space, and they watched their adversaries with alarm.

Success in space offered several grand strategic benefits. Maintaining a satellite constellation would enable persistent but unobtrusive intelligence coverage of key regions. US leaders in the Cold War sought reliable information about the balance of capabilities, which they could then use to adjust force structure as needed without panicking or overspending. Intelligence collection before the introduction of satellites was difficult and dangerous. Traditional espionage was inherently difficult in authoritarian countries like the Soviet Union, and overflights were vulnerable to air defenses. The revelation of spying also risked provoking a diplomatic crisis, as was the case after the Soviets shot down a US spy plane in 1960.[48] Little wonder, then, that presidents beginning with Eisenhower were so enthusiastic about satellite imagery.

Learning to operate in space also enabled power projection. Conventional militaries could travel further and faster when connected via a reliable space-based command and control net. Real time communications among far-flung forces gave leaders freedom of action in grand strategy. The ability to track and coordinate their movements implied the ability to shift them to new locations

---

47. As quoted in Budiansky, *Air Power*, 143.

48. Curtis Peebles, *Shadow Flights: American's Secret War Against the Soviet Union* (Novato, CA: Presidio Press, 2000).

as the need arose.[49] The danger, however, was that growing dependence on space created opportunities for weaker states. Anti-satellite weapons could disrupt US power projection. Weaker states need not build their own space infrastructure to frustrate their stronger rivals.[50]

Other risks have increased over time. The growing number of national and commercial satellites has sparked fears that accidents will leave behind dangerous clouds of orbiting fragments. More space junk means more risk to intelligence and military satellites. Repairing or replacing these platforms is a nontrivial problem, given their expense. States with an interest in competitive strategies, where relatively cheap investments provoke competitors into costly responses, may view space as an especially attractive domain.[51] The value proposition for grand strategy may change depending on the cost of defending against attack or accident. On the other hand, current space powers may try to maintain their position by investing in smaller and cheaper satellites, or by partnering with commercial satellite firms to spread out the cost and risk.

Public-private partnerships are perhaps most relevant for grand strategy in cyberspace, which is mostly owned and operated by the private sector. This complicates discussions of incorporating cyber operations into a broader theory of security. The fact that cyberspace is a synthetic domain, created by humans and not by nature, means that it is not neutral. Private actors who maintain networks care deeply about government actions, for better or worse, and they can take steps to enable or constrain state actors. This was not true for "new" domains in the past; the ocean didn't care about growing navies, and outer space didn't care about satellites.

Cyberspace is genuinely new. The other domains were visible long before they were passable, and scientists could study their properties long before militaries could explore them. The case of cyberspace is different because the domain emerged and grew alongside government interest in its security implications. Indeed, the US Department of Defense supported some of the

---

49. Analysts distinguish "militarization" from "weaponization." The former roughly describes space satellites that enable ground forces. Johnson-Freese, *Space as a Strategic Asset*, 82–140.

50. Bleddyn E. Bowen, "From the sea to outer space: The command of space as the foundation of spacepower theory," *Journal of Strategic Studies* 42:3–4 (2019): 532–56, at 542.

51. Thomas G. Mahnken, ed., *Competitive Strategies for the 21st Century: Theory, History, and Practice* (Stanford, CA: Stanford University Press, 2012). This logic may have played a role in the Strategic Defense Initiative during the Reagan administration. See Gregory G. Hildebrandt, "SDI and the Soviet Defense Burden," RAND Note N-2662-AF, September 1988.

critical early research and development that led to the creation of the modern internet.

States have mixed grand strategic incentives in cyberspace because the same information channels are used for intelligence activities, military communications, and economic exchange. The United States has long extolled the virtues of an open and reliable internet, in part because online commerce bolsters the US economy. At the same time, it has reportedly employed offensive cyberspace operations against rivals for a variety of purposes, including counter-proliferation, counter-terrorism, and election security. Critics warn that these activities will cause other states to restrict the free flow of information to reduce their own vulnerability to attack. If so, then the possible short-term national security benefits of cyber operations are in tension with long-term national economic interests.

How states weigh this tradeoff depends on their beliefs about grand strategy. Liberal approaches, for instance, rest on the premise that trade and international institutions promote international peace and national security. If this is true, then states should be reluctant to engage in clandestine behavior that creates cybersecurity dilemmas, and they should avoid attacks that undermine international trust. The risk/reward calculation also depends on their beliefs about the nature of the domain. If states believe that cyberspace is resilient, and that it can flourish despite active operations, then they will increase their activities. If they worry that cyberspace is fragile, and that states will increasingly raise barriers to information, then they will tend towards caution.[52]

Grand strategies in cyberspace depend on beliefs about whether the domain is a good venue for coercion. Some theories of cyberspace deterrence, for example, hold that adversaries will forego possible attacks if they fear retaliation in kind. If this is the case, then states can secure their interests in cyberspace simply by holding enemy networks at risk. But empirical studies of publicly known operations have concluded that coercion is especially difficult in cyberspace for several reasons. Victims are typically more tolerant of cyberattacks than of physical violence, and more wary of escalation; this takes some of the bite out of retaliatory threats. The characteristics of the domain itself also undermine coercion. Cyberspace only functions because of voluntary connections, and likely targets can always choose to disconnect. States already have different levels of exposure to the global internet, and some have taken

---

52. Joshua Rovner and Tyler Moore, "Does the Internet Need a Hegemon?," *Journal of Global Security Studies* 2:3 (2017): 184–203.

additional steps to bolster their national networks. These public displays are unsubtle signals of their ability to insulate themselves from offensive cyberspace operations, and their willingness to pay the costs.[53]

The United States has pursued an expansive grand strategy since the end of the Cold War. Not surprisingly, it has also expanded its activities in cyberspace, though official attitudes have changed. The fear of a "cyber Pearl Harbor" has been replaced by a generalized concern that weaker adversaries can erode US strength through persistent harassment. According to this logic, adversaries can conduct cyber operations against the United States without risking an armed response. The effects of these attacks might accumulate over time, however, in ways that put a dent in US military and economic advantages. In 2018, the Department of Defense declared its intention to "defend forward," by which it meant mitigating cyberspace threats by operating as close as possible to their point of origin. US Cyber Command operationalized this guidance through what it calls "persistent engagement," an approach which stresses the need for vigilance in a domain of continuous interaction with malicious actors.[54] None of this assumes that US adversaries will change their stripes. In fact, it assumes they are incorrigible. The resulting approach is thus more aggressive about confronting adversaries in cyberspace, but less ambitious about trying to influence their behavior.

The US approach has also self-consciously tried to integrate cyberspace operations with tools of statecraft in other domains. US Cyber Command has taken steps to improve coordination with the conventional military, in part to help overcome misperceptions about what cyberspace operations can achieve. The State Department has attempted to integrate its diplomatic efforts with other government agencies, reflecting the belief that a more consistent approach will strengthen its message. Domestically, a variety of interagency efforts have sought

53. Jon R. Lindsay and Erik Gartzke, "Coercion through Cyberspace: The Stability-Instability Paradox Revisited," in *Coercion: The Power to Hurt in International Politics*, Kelly M. Greenhill and Peter Krause, eds. (Oxford: Oxford University Press, 2018); Brandon Valeriano, Ryan C. Maness, and Benjamin Jensen, *Cyber Strategy: The Evolving Character of Power and Coercion* (Oxford: Oxford University Press, 2018); and Sarah Kreps and Jacquelyn Schneider, "Escalation Firebreaks in the Cyber, Conventional, and Nuclear Domains: Moving Beyond Effects-Based Logics," *Journal of Cybersecurity* 5:1 (2019): 1–11. On disconnecting, see Jane Wakefield, "Russia 'successfully tests' its unplugged internet," *BBC*, December 24, 2019, available at https://www.bbc.com/news/technology-50902496.

54. Paul M. Nakasone and Michael Sulmeyer, "How to Compete in Cyberspace," *Foreign Affairs* (online), August 25, 2020, available at https://www.foreignaffairs.com/articles/united-states/2020-08-25/cybersecurity.

to bridge intelligence, law enforcement, and military cyberspace activities. Most importantly, the government has sought to deepen its connections with the private sector, acknowledging the limits of what it can do alone. As was the case on the sea, in the air, and in space, a growing recognition of the limits of technology has encouraged grand strategy across domains.[55]

III

Military innovations open new warfighting domains. This is a mixed blessing. Projecting power into new spaces creates opportunities for enduring security by locking in economic and military advantages while simultaneously containing one's rivals. It also creates ways of winning quickly. Optimistic strategists foresee decisive triumphs over enemies whose capabilities are suddenly obsolete and vulnerable. All of this is good news.

The trouble is that adversaries are not potted plants. Strategists cannot expect that their rivals will overlook the opportunities found in new domains. Instead, they fear that other states will outpace them in the technological race to expand, reaping all the rewards. Such fears have animated historical responses to the opening of the oceans, air, space, and now cyberspace.

These hopes and fears fade over time. Technological, bureaucratic, and economic realities limit states' ability to dominate new domains. Great powers struggle not just with operating exotic new platforms, but also with building and maintaining the mundane infrastructure upon which they depend. Vast financial investments create intense political and organizational battles over resources, often with ragged conclusions that leave no one totally satisfied. States carry on in new domains, of course, but they struggle to achieve command.

---

55. For examples of inter-agency integration, see Gidget Fuentes, "CYBERCOM: Navy-Marine Integration Must Extend Across the Cyber Realm to Protect Weapons Systems, Data," *USNI News*, June 29, 2021, available at https://news.usni.org/2021/06/29/cybercom-navy-marine-integration-must-extend-across-the-cyber-realm-to-protect-weapons-systems-data; and Andy Ozment and Tom Atkin, "Critical Partnerships: DHS, DoD, and the National Response to Significant Cyber Incidents," September 23, 2016, available at https://dod.defense.gov/Portals/1/features/2015/0415_cyber-strategy/docs/DOD-DHS-Cyber_Article-2016-09-23-CLEAN.pdf. On the State Department, see Ferial Ara Saeed, "A State Department for the Digital Age," *War on the Rocks*, June 21, 2021. On public private integration see Justin Doubleday, "CISA Looks to Tie Together Public-Private Partnerships Through New Cyber Planning Office," *Federal News Network*, August 5, 2021, available at https://federalnewsnetwork.com/cybersecurity/2021/08/cisa-looks-to-tie-together-public-private-partnerships-through-new-cyber-planning-office/.

Peacetime success does not easily translate into wartime triumph. Gaining superiority in new domains is not the same as operating easily across them. A state that operates without much opposition will face increasing danger as it moves toward the fringes of its preferred domain. Even dominant great powers struggle for traction in these "contested zones," where technologically inferior but highly motivated enemies will find ways to undermine them.[56] Wartime clashes make fog and friction unavoidable. Disappointing wartime results on the high seas and at high altitudes reveal the limits of combat in new domains. We have not yet seen equivalent clashes in space or cyberspace, though the practical problems of hypothetical operations are already clear.

Still, a lot remains unclear. There are several questions that beg for more scrutiny among scholars and practitioners. When, for example, does a "new" domain stop being new? States might characterize a domain as new, for instance, until they commit forces to battle there. The experience of war may prove the best test of their ideas about combat across domains, and lessons there may put to rest some of their prewar expectations. Scholars might choose a different threshold. For example, they might set an arbitrary time period after states achieve initial operating capabilities for fighting in a new domain. States may behave differently over time, even if they do not confront enemies directly. By way of comparison, scholars of nuclear strategy have examined whether emerging nuclear powers become more cautious over time, after the initial flush of their technological breakthrough wears off.[57]

A second question is whether the pattern described previously is inevitable. It is not hard to understand the allure of new domains, or why strategists fall victim to false enthusiasm during periods of rapid innovation. Bureaucratic incentives and domestic politics also lead to exaggerated hopes and fears. Yet the experience of centuries ought to encourage intellectual modesty. There is a long list of prosaic problems that inhibit military effectiveness in new domains, as we know from hard experience. Will future strategists imagining war in new domains remember this list? Or will they just plow ahead?

These questions assume that there are still domains to be found. There might not be. The oceans, skies, and space are no longer novel spaces, so the

56. Barry R. Posen, "Command of the Commons: The Military Foundation of U.S. Hegemony," *International Security* 28:1 (2003): 5–46.

57. Michael Horowitz, "The Spread of Nuclear Weapons and International Conflict: Does Experience Matter?," *Journal of Conflict Resolution* 53:2 (2009): 234–47.

dilemmas that come with fighting in new domains might be of historical interest alone. On the other hand, there are still some spaces that remain theoretical. The deep sea remains extremely hazardous, for example, given the enormous pressures involved. Most of the sub-surface oceans remain unexplored. The moon is too, though it has been an object of enduring speculation by military dreamers. Space itself is hardly new, but the technologies for fighting in it are still immature. It has been explored but not exploited, and it has not witnessed combat. As a result, it does not exactly reflect the pattern of hope, fear, and resignation. For space strategists, resignation came early because the technological barriers were so high. The pattern will probably start over if and when those barriers start to fall. Indeed, recent technological advances (e.g., cheaper and reusable rockets) might explain why the debate about weaponizing space has intensified over the last two decades.

And it is possible that new man-made domains like cyberspace will emerge. Radically new technologies for storing and sharing information might make the current version of cyberspace obsolete. Forty years ago few predicted the growth of the internet. Twenty years ago few could have predicted the nature of social media today. A similarly unexpected change will force observers to reconsider their understanding of cyberspace, and the strategic implications that follow.

CHAPTER 44

A Revolution in Intelligence

Thomas Rid

The first twenty years of the twenty-first century were marked by a full-blown revolution in intelligence. That revolution is of historic proportions, ongoing, yet often underestimated, if not outright overlooked, by the uninitiated. Several elements drove a sea change in how information is collected in secret or put to effect under cover, ranging from the technical to the cultural, from the political to the historical, from tradecraft to diplomacy. The focus of this chapter will be on a neglected yet escalating and highly dynamic aspect of strategy and great power competition in the twenty-first century: the remarkable return and expansion of covert action that, in turn, was accompanied by, and later gave lift to, an entirely new form of counterintelligence. The resulting strategic interactions between two old yet digitally altered intelligence disciplines are sharper, faster, more dynamic, more granular, more asymmetric, more distributed, and more public than they were during the Cold War, or ever before.[1]

I

Traditional covert action persists, for instance the covert support of underground groups, political parties, or media organizations in contested places, or even paramilitary action including assassinations.[2] Even analog, low-tech

---

1. The author would like to thank Dmitri Alperovitch, Ben Buchanan, Alex Orleans, Hal Brands, and one unnamed reader for perceptive comments and suggestions.
2. For a typology of covert action, see Gregory Treverton, *Covert Action: The Limits of Intervention in the Postwar World* (New York, NY: Basic Books, 1987).

operations persist. Yet the apparent proliferation and prevalence of remotely executed, computer-enabled, hands-only-on-keyboard cases raises the question: has the rise of the internet enabled a new class of covert action? What characterizes these new operations? And how have governments started to counter these newly aggressive intelligence operations in the early twenty-first century?

Examples of computer-network enabled events that have all the trappings of covert intelligence activity abound. A list of recent cases would include the following entries: the 2007 distributed-denial-of-service (DDoS) attacks against Estonia; the late 2000s campaign known as Stuxnet; various wiping attacks against Iranian targets in 2011; the 2012 attack against Saudi Aramco and Rasgas; the neglected 2013 Britam Defence leak; the 2014 Sony Entertainment breach-and-leak; two remarkable blackouts in Kiev in 2015 and 2016, as well numerous other operations in Ukraine; the series of breach-and-leak operations against the US election in 2016; the mysterious series of Shadow Brokers leaks; the destructive attacks known as Wannacry and NotPetya in 2017; and many more, some of them subtle, others as yet not publicly discussed.

Yet covert action no longer stands alone. On closer inspection, digital covert action can only be understood in conjunction with—and in juxtaposition to—another new and partly related trend in twenty-first-century intelligence operations: the resurgence of public attribution of intelligence operations that go beyond classical espionage, including industrial espionage and adversarial covert action. Many publicly visible, network-enabled covert actions in the past two decades have been attributed, sometimes by governments, to other government-linked entities. These attributions were made with varying levels of confidence and certainty, from low confidence to full certainty—yet attributed they were, in many cases. One intelligence activity, in short, cannot be understood without the other—on two levels, for one reacts to the other, and one exposes and informs the other. The opposing practices are sharply different yet closely intertwined; they form the core of an intricate escalation in an observable intelligence contest, albeit an asymmetric escalation. Asymmetric because closed societies and authoritarian regimes tend to focus on covert action and neglect public counterintelligence—while the reverse tends to be the case for open societies and liberal democracies, although there are exceptions.[3]

---

3. "Covert action," historically, is an American (and British) term of art. Different intelligence establishments have used their own terminology over the decades, for instance "active

The argument, in short, is that the internet itself has enabled a set of surprisingly sharp, dialectic interactions between computer-enabled covert action and computer-enabled counterintelligence in ways that probably have no historical precedent. At the core of this dialectic is deniability. Covert action and public counterintelligence compete for *deniability*—the goal of the former is to take it and keep it, the goal of the latter is to take it away.

II

The novelty of digital covert action in the twenty-first century will come into sharper relief against the backdrop of established, twentieth-century covert action practices.

Covert action, sometimes called the "third way" between diplomacy and military force, is one of the most controversial policy instruments in the toolbox of governments.[4] Section 503 (e) of the National Security Act of 1947 defined covert action as "an activity or activities of the United States Government to influence political, economic, or military conditions abroad, where it is intended that the role of the United States Government will not be apparent or acknowledged publicly."[5] This definition, or versions of it, has weathered well over the decades. An internal CIA long-range plan for covert action from 1982 retained a similar understanding, describing covert action as "actions which are not attributable to the United States, and which are designed to influence foreign governments, organizations, persons, or events in support of US foreign policy."[6] Practically all definitions of covert action have one thing in common: a focus on deniability. Evading attribution is built into covert activity by design.

A pivotal element of the origin story of modern covert action lies in the early Soviet Union. The Cheka, the predecessor organization of the KGB, was born into an existential struggle, the Russian Revolution. Some of the Cheka's most formative operations were part of this struggle, most notably a sophisticated

measures" in the Soviet bloc. I am applying "covert action" globally for the term is conceptually productive and more precise than most alternatives. For a British view, see Rory Cormac, *Disrupt and Deny* (New York, NY: Oxford University Press, 2018), 4.

4. Roger George, *Intelligence in the National Security Enterprise* (Washington, DC: Georgetown University Press, 2020), 205.

5. US Government, *National Security Act of 1947*, 84.

6. Central Intelligence Agency, "CIA Long-Range Planning for 1985–1990, Phase 2—Covert Action Goals," May 12, 1982.

disinformation and deception operation known as the Trust.[7] Targeting exiled monarchist White Russians, the Trust shrewdly deceived them in an elaborate scheme that ran for years. In the West, by contrast, the practice of covert intelligence operations designed to achieve an effect came second, after simply collecting information without directly altering the target.

Postwar Western covert action was a reaction meant to counter Soviet subversion of Europe. Just weeks after the Truman administration launched the Marshall Plan, George Kennan, a charismatic US diplomat, drafted an influential memo entitled "The Inauguration of Organized Political Warfare." In it, Kennan suggested creating a central office to employ all the means at the nation's disposal "short of war." Kennan was on alert against Soviet expansionism. "Lenin," he wrote, "so synthesized the teachings of Marx and Clausewitz that the Kremlin's conduct of political warfare has become the most refined and effective of any in history."[8] Washington needed to up its own game in "political warfare."[9]

A few months later came NSC 10/2, a pivotal directive that authorized the CIA, less than a year after the agency's official creation, to expand from psychological operations to direct intervention. The core feature of such covert intervention was what is widely referred to as *plausible deniability*. The guidance spells out "covert operations" as referring to activities conducted or sponsored by this government against hostile foreign states or groups or in support of friendly foreign states or groups but which are so planned and executed that any US government responsibility for them is not evident to unauthorized persons and that, if uncovered, the US government can plausibly disclaim any responsibility.[10]

NSC 10/2 proceeded to list a wide range of covert activities, including propaganda, economic operations, sabotage, anti-sabotage, demolition, evacuation measures, as well as subversion in the form of assistance to underground resistance movements, guerrillas, and "refugee liberation groups." Some of the CIA's largest and most persistent covert action projects in the late 1940s and

7. Richard Spence, "Russia's Operatsiia Trest: A Reappraisal," *Global Intelligence Monthly* 1:4 (1999): 19.

8. George Kennan, "The Inauguration of Organized Political Warfare," History and Public Policy Program Digital Archive, April 30, 1948.

9. For details on the Trust, and American political warfare, see Thomas Rid, *Active Measures* (New York, NY: Farrar, Straus and Giroux, 2020) 18–32, 64.

10. NSC 10/2, June 18, 1948, Records of the National Security Council, RG 273, National Archives and Records Administration.

1950s would involve such refugee groups, with some of the most significant groups located in West Berlin, for instance the *Kampfgruppe gegen Unmenschlichkeit* (KgU). Effectively a small intelligence outfit, the KgU was designed to collect and aggressively disclose information about Soviet-zone prisoner abuses and Secret Police activity.[11]

The CIA was also particularly active in Chile between 1953 and 1973. The most prominent case is its interference in the 1964 election campaign on behalf of the Christian Democrat candidate, Eduardo Frei Montalva, in an attempt to prevent the victory of Salvador Allende, a Marxist candidate. The CIA spent $3 million in 1964, approximately $1 per Chilean voter (one well-placed Congressional staffer later pointed out that the US presidential candidates that same year—Johnson and Goldwater—together spent only about fifty cents per voter).[12] Frei won with fifty-six percent of the vote. Another, smaller project in Chile supported between one and five assets in *El Mercurio*, the main conservative paper. Those assets were tasked to write articles or opinion pieces supporting US foreign policy goals, for instance criticizing the USSR after the Warsaw Pact troops crushed the Prague Spring in 1968, or by suppressing detrimental news items about the Vietnam War.[13] The *El Mercurio* project had a peak rate of one CIA-guided editorial per day.[14] Another project in Chile—meant to influence the outcome of the 1970 election—instructed local collaborators to paint the slogan "*su paredón*" on two thousand walls across Santiago to evoke the memory of Communist firing squads.[15] Other US-funded posters in Santiago issued stark warnings that an Allende victory would portend the end of religious worship and family life in Chile.

Two larger historical trend lines stand out. First, covert action in the United States, and in allied intelligence agencies, has waned since the early 1960s in quantity. One internal CIA report from 1967, declassified in 2002, reveals the number of covert action projects undertaken in the early Cold War. The precise numbers were hard to come by even for the internal CIA analysts who prepared that report, as smaller "programs" sometimes merged into "projects" over time. The CIA counted 81 projects during the Truman administration

11. Rid, *Active Meausures*.

12. Treverton, *Covert Action*, 18.

13. Treverton, *Convert Action*, 15.

14. US Senate, "Covert Action in Chile 1963–1973," *Staff Report of the Select Committee to Study Governmental Operations with Respect to Intelligence Activities*, December 18, 1975, 22.

15. US Senate, "Covert Action in Chile 1963–1973," 22.

(from 1949–52), 170 under Eisenhower, 163 during the Kennedy years, and 142 under Johnson, until February 1967.[16] Thereafter the overall number of covert action projects continued to drop in a steep downward slope.

By the early 1970s, observed one CIA study of historical trends in covert action, the "adverse turn of events in Vietnam" had shifted public opinion on the appropriate role of US foreign policy objectives and America's wider role in world affairs. The "national trauma of Watergate" further accelerated introspection after 1972, the CIA memo argued. The use of covert action as a policy instrument had sharply declined by 1975, and "the Agency's covert action capabilities atrophied."[17] The covert infrastructure that was used to furnish the logistics for covert projects, such as dummy air transport companies, was sold off. By 1980, the CIA's entire covert action budget accounted for less than five percent of its overall budget.[18] The last decade of the Cold War temporarily reversed this trend, mostly due to the CIA's covert support for the Afghan resistance against Soviet occupation.

The second trend is related to the quantitative drop: projects changed in quality. Covert action, in a nutshell, became less aggressive. As the CIA assessed the future role of covert action in the early 1980s, the consensus emerged that projects should "play a narrower, more selective role" in the 1980s than they did in the 1950s and 1960s. In the early Cold War, the CIA had leaned into large, well-staffed front organizations, with only very few witting individuals at the top. One particularly remarkable one—codenamed LCCASSOCK—was a sizable publisher of magazines, booklets, and pamphlets in West Berlin, headed by Karl-Heinz Marbach, a former Wehrmacht U-Boot commander turned anti-Communist activist and influence agent. LCCASSOCK engaged in major forgeries, disinformation, and large-scale propaganda operations, and even developed commercial ambitions on its own. Throughout the 1960s, however, the CIA recognized that this type of covert activity was no longer sustainable. "The large counter-front organizations appropriate to the 50s and 60s will not be appropriate to the 80s and 90s," the CIA's long-range planning memo argued in 1982.[19] Some internal memos show an uncharacteristic sense of modesty and moderation in covert

16. Central Intelligence Agency, "Coordination and Approval of Covert Operations," February 23, 1967, 4.

17. Central Intelligence Agency, "CIA Long-Range Planning for 1985–1990," 1.

18. Treverton, *Covert Action*, 14.

19. Central Intelligence Agency, "CIA Long-Range Planning for 1985–1990," 1.

action programs. The long-range plan recommended that "policymakers be sensitized to and respectful of the limits of covert action."

The opposite trends appear to have played out in the Soviet Union. By the early 1980s, active measures had reached peak bureaucratic performance inside the KGB.[20] Soviet active measures had an annual budget between $3 billion and $4 billion, the CIA estimated.[21] Service A of the KGB was making a concerted effort to refine and distribute the covert disinformation methodology throughout the Eastern bloc intelligence establishment. In 1979, the head of Service A, Vladimir Ivanov, gave two secret briefings that have become available in a Bulgarian archive—"The Role and Place of Active Measures in Intelligence," and another briefing on the use of "influence agents."[22]

Ivanov noted that Service A was established in 1959.[23] The Communist Party then consolidated the new service within the KGB's First Chief Directorate. The agency was already running active measures at an impressive tempo by 1960, when US counterintelligence agencies started exposing its operations to Congress and the public. The KGB's pace picked up as more resources flowed into Service A. Sergei Kondrashev, who briefly headed the unit in 1968, estimated that he reviewed "three or four new proposals a day," which he recounted added up to "surely hundreds every year."[24] That figure counted only the USSR's operations. By 1979, the Soviet active measures community was thriving. One of the largest measures was codenamed MARS, and attempted to co-opt the wider peace movement in the West. Influence operations had steadily risen in importance within the KGB's foreign intelligence organization, and active measures had become so widespread that different parts of the Soviet intelligence and military establishment wanted to be part of the disinformation game. "Active measures have become too common and too successful," said Ivanov in 1979. "The divisions of the KGB have acquired a certain taste [for active measures], and many now insist they can prepare and conduct them on their own,"

20. The following four paragraphs draw on original work in Rid, *Active Measures*, Chapter 23.

21. House of Representatives Permanent Select Committee on Intelligence, *Soviet Active Measures*, July 13–14, 1982 (Washington, DC: Government Printing Office, 1982), 15, 221.

22. Vladimir P. Ivanov, "Роля и място на активните мероприятия в разузнаването," April 24, 1979, КГБ И ДС (Sofia: COMDOS Archive, 2010), 9, 3, 209, 45–54. Vladimir P. Ivanov, "Форми и методи на работа. Използването на агентура за влияние," беседа с др. В. П. Иванов на April 25, 1979, 5 юни 1979 г. (Sofia: COMDOS Archive, 2010), ф. НРС, пф. 9, оп 3, а.е. 209, л. 1–7.

23. Ivanov, "Роля и място на активните мероприятия в разузнаването."

24. Tennent Bagley and Sergei Kondrashev, *Spymaster* (New York, NY: Skyhorse, 2013), 187.

he recounted.[25] The First Chief Directorate insisted on strict centralization when planning and executing active measures. Vladimir Kryuchkov, head of the KGB's foreign intelligence arm since 1974, argued that active measures had taken "their rightful place in the overall enterprise of intelligence."[26]

But by the early 1980s, the West was also getting better at countering the most aggressive Soviet intelligence operations. Various congressional committees held hearings on Soviet active measures in the early 1980s, and both the CIA and the FBI provided a wealth of evidence to Congress in hearings and various highly publicized reports. The government's objectives were to raise awareness among the public and the press, and probably to render less useful some Soviet tactics through exposure.

When the Soviet Union fell and the internet rose, a historical trend was already firmly established: closed societies escalated influence operations, while open societies did the opposite.

Digital covert action is the art and science of crafting and administering effects that are enabled, at least in part, by some form of computer network operation in a manner consistent with ensuring some level of deniability. For example, breaching victims or victim networks, exfiltrating files, and then leaking the stolen material through the use of deceptive assets. Alternatively, it can be done by orchestrating an influence campaign that uses deceptive assets yet amplifies actual, existing grievances and cleavages in the target society. In continuity with their analog predecessors, a central purpose and design specification of such operations is the provision of deniability.

Computer network operations have a built-in temptation to make covert action more destructive, more aggressive, and to veer from subversion to sabotage. Three analog-digital contrasts stand out that may explain such an escalatory dynamic.

First, infrastructure costs are significantly lower online. In most cases, paramilitary covert operations historically involved a similar set of elements: providing funding and weaponry to groups or movements whose interests aligned with those of the United States, doing so in a way that was not easily traceable to the CIA, as well as advising and perhaps training the supported entities on how to operate. To achieve deniability, the CIA needed to procure both deniable military hardware and deniable infrastructure to move weapons systems across the globe. "In the early postwar years, weaponry manufactured by the Soviet Union and its allies, prized because it could most easily be denied as supplied by America, was hard to

25. Ivanov, "Роля и място на активните мероприятия в разузнаването."
26. Ivanov, "Роля и място на активните мероприятия в разузнаването."

come by," observed Gregory Treverton, a former Church Committee staffer.[27] By the early 1980s, the situation had changed. When the CIA began supporting the mujahideen in Afghanistan, the weaponry that the Americans provided to the holy warriors was initially almost all Soviet manufactured and thus "sterile."

The second major difference between covert action old and new is scalability. Infrastructure costs are not just lower, but rebuilding and repurposing infrastructure is also much faster when the infrastructure in question is remotely hosted on virtual machines with mostly generic settings, as opposed to an undercover logistics company with a base, aircraft hangers, maintenance, and local suppliers (the same logic, conversely, also reduces the impact of an attack, as defenders can rebuild much easier if only digital, and not physical, assets are damaged in an offensive operation). Finally, the personal risk to operators is much lower when they do not have to leave their offices at headquarters. All told, remote operations can be spun up faster, shut down faster, and approached with a higher tolerance for risk and experimentation.

Several time-tested aspects of intelligence work likely remain unaffected by technological progress. One is that collecting and influencing have a built-in tension, then and now. In most intelligence bureaucracies, espionage and covert action are done by the same entity. At the CIA, the Directorate of Operations—commonly referred to as the Clandestine Service—is in charge of both activities. In the Soviet and later Russian system, the collection and active measures appear to be integrated on a unit level in some organizations. One reason for this integration is that the same capabilities and networks—either networks of people or machines—can be used for either activity. It is this dual-use aspect that also drives the tension: the core values of espionage are patience, secrecy, perfection in operational security, and minimizing risks to assets—the core values of covert action, by contrast, are speed, publicity, pragmatic operational security (opsec), and taking risks. Achieving maximum results in covert action may come at the expense of collection—and vice versa.

III

"Counterintelligence is to intelligence as epistemology is to philosophy," observed Thomas Powers, a Pulitzer-winning author writing on intelligence.[28] When Powers wrote this pithy line in 1979, he intended to highlight a few

27. Treverton, *Covert Action*, 27.
28. Thomas Powers, *The Man Who Kept the Secrets: Richard Helms & the CIA* (New York, NY: Knopf, 1979), 284.

parallels between counterintelligence and the theory of knowledge. His comparison was about the value of skepticism, about showing one's work by making ways of knowing explicit. Three decades later Powers' aphorism began to acquire new layers of meaning. By the early 2010s, an entirely new type of counterintelligence activity had emerged: public, digital counterintelligence. This new form of counterintelligence was to intelligence as epistemology is to philosophy. Suddenly primary source artefacts became available to a larger community of researchers and investigators, and started to inform a more evidence-based and far less secretive debate. Artefacts of adversarial intelligence operations were now reviewed by peers, and presented, examined, analyzed, and reverse-engineered in conferences and work-in-progress meetings by a community of passionate investigators. The scrutiny of public debate improved and paradigms of what is possible in terms of attributing adversarial intelligence operations began to shift. A new theory of knowledge of public intelligence began to take shape.

A Cold War comparison reveals how drastic a change has occurred in the business of counterintelligence as a result of the rise of the internet in the 1990s.

Counterintelligence, as defined by Executive Order 12333, consists of:

> information gathered and activities conducted to identify, deceive, exploit, disrupt, or protect against espionage, other intelligence activities, sabotage, or assassinations conducted for or on behalf of foreign powers, organizations, or persons, or their agents, or international terrorist organizations or activities.[29]

Perhaps a simpler and more elegant definition is offered by William Johnson, a former CIA counterintelligence officer and author of an internal training manual. Counterintelligence, and the method it employs, wrote Johnson, is "aimed at frustrating the active efforts of adversary conspiratorial organizations to acquire secret or sensitive information belonging to the government that employs you."[30] Johnson's definition reflects both the defensive and offensive lines of effort inherent in counterintelligence.

One of the most insightful counterintelligence case studies of all time is the early 1990s mole hunt that resulted in the arrest of Aldrich Ames, one of the

---

29. US Government, "Executive Order 12333—United States Intelligence Activities," 1981, 200.

30. William Johnson, *Thwarting Enemies at Home and Abroad* (Washington, DC: Georgetown University Press, 2009), 2.

most damaging spies the Soviet Union ever ran inside the US government, in his case in the CIA. The investigation that uncovered Ames was triggered by the CIA's attempt to explain a series of debilitating losses of intelligence assets in the Soviet Union in 1985. Several Soviet spies working for the CIA were arrested and executed that year. The most authoritative account of the extraordinary investigation is *Circle of Treason*, a 2013 book by two core members of the counterintelligence team that identified Ames.[31] The book provides a glimpse into the wide range of techniques and methods used in high-profile counterintelligence investigations, as well as the painstaking clerical effort required to uncover suspicious behavior. One of the critical breakthroughs in the Ames investigation was a highly detailed and granular timeline of Ames's activity. When one of the CIA counterintelligence analysts entered the deposits into Ames's checking accounts into the tick-tock of Ames's activity log, the revealing pattern appeared:

May 17, 1985	—Ames lunches with Chuvakhin
May 18, 1985	—Ames deposits $9,000
Jul 5, 1985	—Ames lunches with Chuvakhin
Jul 5, 1985	—Ames deposits $5,000
July 31, 1985	—Ames lunches with Chuvakhin
July 31, 1985	—Ames deposits $8,500

Sergey Chuvakhin, a Soviet official Ames was officially meeting with, CIA-sanctioned, also turned out to be Ames's handler.

"Spy hunting takes experienced analysts, operations officers, technical specialists, lawyers, financial investigators, law enforcement officers, and psychologists, all working as a team," one CIA counterintelligence officer observed in 2009.[32]

IA's Counterintelligence Staff from 1954 to 1974 was led by James Angleton. In World War II, Angleton had worked for the secretive X-2 counterintelligence branch of the Office of Strategic Services (OSS) in London and Rome.[33] By the early 1960s, Angleton had become "a legend within the Agency," one classified study observed, "a brilliant, dedicated professional with

31. Sandra Grimes and Jeanne Vertefeuille, *Circle of Treason. A CIA Account of Traitor Aldrich Ames and the Men He Betrayed* (Annapolis, MD: Naval Institute Press, 2013).

32. John Ehrman, "Toward a Theory of CI," *Studies in Intelligence* 53:2 (2009).

33. Robin W. Winks, *Cloak and Gown: Scholars in the Secret War, 1939–1961* (New York, NY: William Morrow, 1987), 323.

counterintelligence experience unmatched in the Western world."[34] But Angleton was deeply flawed. By the early 1960s, he was "losing his sense of proportion and his ability to live with uncertainty," pointed out David Robarge, an eloquent CIA in-house historian.[35] In Angleton's counterintelligence-trained mind the line between conspiracy practice and conspiracy theory blurred. Soon he would come to tirelessly portray the KGB as an omnipotent agency that shrewdly implemented a vast conspiracy against the US government, involving faux defectors, penetrations, deception, and disinformation. CIA Director William Colby dismissed Angleton in 1974, just before Christmas. Embittered by his dismissal, Angleton continued to propagate his conspiracy theory to journalists and writers.[36] Angleton was a deeply polarizing and controversial figure in the US counterintelligence community—his legacy, even after his death in 1987, continued to divide, and divide bitterly.

Two KGB defectors had an outsize influence on counterintelligence in the 1960s and 1970s, and, via Angleton, on the study of counterintelligence since. The first was Anatole Golitsyn, chief of the KGB rezidentura in Helsinki, Finland, who defected to the United States in December 1961. The second was Yuri Nosenko, a KGB officer assigned to the UN disarmament conference in Geneva, who started spying for the CIA in June 1962, and defected to the United States in February 1964, in a highly publicized fashion.[37] Upon arrival, the CIA proceeded to assess Nosenko's bona fides—in an unusually prolonged process that eventually saw him held in solitary confinement for interrogation for approximately three years. Golitsyn offered to help the Counterintelligence Staff with assessing the bona fides of Nosenko. The CIA granted Golitsyn access to the interrogation documentation. On June 29, 1964, Angleton and two other CIA officers met with Golitsyn. "I have made a study of the documents and information which was provided to me about Nosenko and his interrogations," said Golitsyn. "I would like to make known my conclusions. . . . my conclusion is that he is not a bona fide defector. He is a provocateur, who is on

34. Robert Hathaway and Russell Jack Smith, *Richard Helms* (Washington, DC: Central Intelligence Agency History Staff, 1993), 102.

35. David Robarge, " 'Cunning Passages, Contrived Corridors:' Wandering in the Angletonian Wilderness," *Studies in Intelligence* 53:4 (2009), 4.

36. See "Draft Notes by TJG for Assassination Records Review Board," January 15, 1997.

37. Max Frankel, "Soviet Aide Sees Defector, Who Elects to Stay in U.S.," *New York Times*, February 15, 1964.

a mission for the KGB . . . to mislead."[38] Angleton in turn subscribed to Golitsyn's view that Nosenko was, in truth, not a defector, but rather a Soviet influence agent, dispatched by the KGB to inject disinformation into the FBI and the CIA.

Angleton is perhaps most widely known for describing the alleged Soviet disinformation via planted defectors as a "wilderness of mirrors," a term he lifted from a poem by T.S. Eliot.[39] Agency skeptics of Angleton derisively called his theory "the monster plot," which, a year after Angleton's dismissal, became the title of a harsh internal study of CIA counterintelligence.[40] Agency orthodoxy quickly turned against the Angleton school, and so would the public conversation. In 1980, *Wilderness of Mirrors* appeared, a book by the investigative journalist David Martin; it would become a classic of counterintelligence literature. One CIA review of Martin's book observed that it "exposed Golitsyn as an unimportant defector who caused more trouble than he was worth, suggested Nosenko was genuine, and punched many holes in the Angleton myth." The CIA history staff traced the outsize cultural impact of the former Chief of the Counterintelligence Staff.[41] One prominent and unyielding supporter of Angleton, himself a senior CIA officer, took "interested parties" deep into that wilderness of confusion and conspiracy theories as late as the mid-2010s, practically from his deathbed.[42]

Each of the US intelligence community's counterintelligence components is focused primarily on intelligence threats against their parent organizations. The CIA's Counterintelligence Staff, for instance, was historically focused on threats against the CIA, as the perennial Angleton debate illustrates. The Air Force Office of Special Investigations (OSI) is focused on the Air Force, the Defense Intelligence Agency (DIA) on the Department of Defense, and so on. The National Counterintelligence and Security Center (NCSC), a government outfit that traces its lineage to 2001, has a broader remit and a leadership

---

38. John Hart, "The Monster Plot: Counterintelligence in the Case of Yuriy Ivanovich Nosenko," CIA, December 1976. See also John Hart, "James J. Angleton, Anatoliy Golitsyn, and the 'Monster Plot:' Their Impact on the CIA Personnel and Operations," *Studies in Intelligence* 55:4 (2014): 47.

39. Cleveland Cram, *Of Moles and Molehunters: A Review of Counterintelligence Literature, 1977–92* (Washington, DC: Center for the Study of Intelligence, 1993).

40. Cram, *Of Moles and Molehunters*, 26.

41. See David Robarge, "Moles, Defectors, and Deceptions: James Angleton and CIA Counterintelligence," *Journal of Intelligence History* 3:2 (2003): 21–49.

42. Tennent H. (Pete) Bagley, "Ghosts of the Spy Wars: A Personal Reminder to Interested Parties," *International Journal of Intelligence and CounterIntelligence* 28:1 (2015): 1–37.

and support function for interagency counterintelligence coordination, and engages in public and private sector outreach, but the NCSC does not engage in field investigations.[43] The most central and important counterintelligence agency in the United States remains the FBI.

The FBI's Counterintelligence Division, from its beginnings and throughout the Cold War, was initially focused on countering Soviet intelligence operations, as the USSR posed the most formidable intelligence threat to the United States.[44] Probably the most popularly known FBI counterintelligence case is the unraveling of a group of Russian illegals, portrayed in the book *Russians Among Us*.[45] The FBI's remit includes finding, exposing, and countering industrial espionage; China is historically the most prominent and formidable foe.[46] Nicholas Eftimiades, an ex-DIA analyst with counterintelligence experience at the CIA and the State Department, published a classic study of Chinese intelligence operations in 1994, well before the at-scale onset of Chinese digital espionage. Eftimiades observed that China's collection operations, predominantly in industrial spying, "have increased to the point where agencies with counterintelligence responsibilities are overwhelmed by the sheer number of cases."[47] Chinese tradecraft, he added in an observation that carries over into the digital era, was not sophisticated, but quantity would compensate for this weakness. One of the most detailed case studies of an FBI investigation into industrial espionage is a recent book on the Chinese attempt to steal intellectual property on crop engineering from the corporate giants Monsanto and DuPont Pioneer.[48] By 2021, the FBI had put the price tag of industrial espionage at "hundreds of billions of dollars per year."[49] Soon after the end of the Cold War, the Chinese intelligence threat became dominant—but only in industrial, and perhaps political, espionage, so far not in covert action operations

43. National Counterintelligence and Security Center, "Strategic Plan 2018–2022," April 2018, available at https://web.archive.org/web/20200502204052/https://www.odni.gov/files/NCSC/documents/Regulations/2018-2022-NCSC-Strategic-Plan.pdf.

44. For a review of the FBI's Soviet-focused counterintelligence in the later Cold War, see Ron Kessler, *Spy vs Spy* (New York, NY: Scribner, 1988).

45. Gordon Corera, *Russians Among Us* (New York, NY: Harper, 2020).

46. See David Wise, *Tiger Trap: America's Secret Spy War with China* (New York, NY: Houghton Mifflin Harcourt, 2011).

47. Nicholas Eftimiades, *Chinese Intelligence Operations* (Annapolis, MD: Naval Institute Press, 1994), 6, 27.

48. Mara Hvistendahl, *The Scientist and the Spy* (New York, NY: Riverhead, 2020).

49. FBI, "Counterintelligence," https://web.archive.org/web/20211117104019/https://www.fbi.gov/investigate/counterintelligence, accessed December 16, 2021.

targeted at the United States (with the primary exception being those targeted at Chinese persons of interest residing in the United States).[50]

The FBI's counterintelligence remit goes beyond countering espionage. The Bureau is also in the business of investigating, exposing, and countering adversarial covert action in the United States, including active measures and disinformation campaigns such as election interference. A notable historical case is the FBI's investigation of the Soviet Union's attempted infiltration and support of the Peace Movement in the 1970s and early 1980s.[51]

The contrast between traditional counterintelligence in the twentieth century and digital counterintelligence practices in the twenty-first century could hardly be sharper. The former was highly secretive, cloistered in small teams and communities, and artefacts rarely became public, yet spy hunting received an excess amount of publicly, in the press, in nonfiction, and even in fiction and film. Moreover, it was often politicized, with a highly speculative character—twenty-first-century counterintelligence activity is characterized by the opposite attributes.

Digital counterintelligence is the art and science of finding, identifying, clustering, exposing, and possibly attributing adversarial intelligence operations, with the goal of frustrating such activity. Often, but not always, digital counterintelligence involves a public, or partly public, exposure of adversary operations, infrastructure, or other indicators. The counterintelligence action may counter both espionage and covert action. Such activity may have multiple overlapping goals, for instance to "burn" infrastructure on a tactical level, to remove deniability, or to deter an adversary on a strategic level. Among cybersecurity companies, "threat intelligence" teams, or alternatively named units, play an important role in placing or keeping a firm in a competitive market position—hence counterintelligence has become, to a significant extent, a sizable segment of a market-driven security industry. One of the first start-ups to recognize and shape this new market was iDefense, founded in May 1998 as Infrastructure Forum, Inc. In practice, however, one core driver of some of the most cutting-edge counterintelligence research is more mundane and more fundamental: curiosity and passion on the part of some of the world's most advanced malware reverse engineers and digital forensic investigators, be it in the for-profit or non-profit

---

50. See Sebastian Rotella and Kirsten Berg, "Operation Fox Hunt," *Pro Publica*, July 22, 2021.

51. J. L. Tierney, "Soviet Active Measures Relating to the U.S. Peace Movement," Federal Bureau of Investigation, March 9, 1983, available at https://archive.org/details/1983-FBI-active -measures-peace-movement.

sectors. These experts form a tight-knit community-of-practice that has even developed its own classification system—the Traffic Light Protocol.[52] The shared community spirit, coupled with the interest to "hunt" and protect against the most sophisticated adversaries, may lead threat intelligence teams of openly competing firms to privately share highly sensitive findings with each other.

The practice of public counterintelligence, notably, is not new, but is re-emerging in a reinvigorated form and with new articulations. The US intelligence community started publicly countering Soviet covert action, specifically a subset then known as "active measures." On June 2, 1961, Richard Helms, who had overseen the CIA's own covert operations, the Directorate of Plans, presented a wide range of examples and evidence to Congress in a hearing that exposed dozens of Eastern bloc covert measures against the United States and its allies. The CIA put an extraordinary amount of attention into preparing the documentation for this hearing, and authorized the publication of multiple appendixes with artefacts, 127 pages in total.[53] Indeed the hearing itself was a form of public counterintelligence. In later hearings in the 1980s, the CIA went even further. It revealed some of its investigative techniques, even having its own investigators and analysts testify on how the CIA built its attributive capabilities.

"Foreign intelligence services shrewdly use such U.S. organization boundaries to defeat American CI [counterintelligence] efforts," observed two former CIA counterintelligence officers in a 1988 article.[54] Indeed, just a few years later, the Russian officers behind Moonlight Maze, an operation entailing the massive theft of US classified information, selected as some of their most critical hop points machines inside the United States, specifically in a public library in Colorado. Some Department of Defense investigators assumed that the Russian intelligence officers suspected (accurately) that US counterintelligence agencies would have a harder time, for legal oversight reasons, tracing and watching an ongoing operation inside a public library.[55]

---

52. See First, "Traffic Light Protocol (TLP)," available at https://web.archive.org/web/20160918054223/https://www.first.org/tlp.

53. Richard Helms, *Communist Forgeries*, Hearing before the US Senate Judiciary Subcommittee to Investigate the Administration of the Internal Security Act and Other Security Laws (Washington, DC: Government Printing Office, 1961).

54. George Kalaris and Leonard Mccoy, "Counterintelligence for the 1990s," *International Journal of Intelligence and Counterintelligence* 2:2 (1988): 184.

55. Author interviews on the Moonlight Maze investigation, see Thomas Rid, *Rise of the Machines* (New York, NY: W.W. Norton, 2016).

Throughout the twentieth century, counterintelligence and covert action operators had skills and experiences that were not adequately valued by the market outside the government's intelligence community. Specifically trained and skilled individuals were, effectively, limited to one employer: their own government. Intelligence specialists worked in intelligence agencies, and counterintelligence specialists worked in counterintelligence agencies. No longer.

The field of digital counterintelligence—often called "threat intelligence" in the private cybersecurity sector since the early 2010s—is highly competitive, and indeed has transferred talent from the wider governmental intelligence community into the private sector—and occasionally back into government—since the late 1990s. This unique revolving door has injected more than just discipline, established methodologies, and organizational expertise into the private sector. When highly experienced analysts or subject area or regional experts make the move from, say, the NSA to Google, or from GCHQ (Government Communications Headquarters) to CrowdStrike, they bring with them privileged knowledge, and may know where to look for public or proprietary data and evidence that could help their new employers independently reconstruct findings and assessments on adversarial intelligence operations.

Governments simply no longer have a monopoly on counterintelligence. A large number of private firms have entered the business of exposing and defeating adversarial intelligence collection and covert action. One early example is Mandiant's landmark APT1 report, which exposed the industrial espionage activities of a Chinese PLA intelligence unit.[56] Google offers another early example. On September 5, 2014, the security team in Mountain View circulated a report entitled "Peering into the Aquarium" within the wider malware research community.[57] The title was a reference to Russia analysts in the intelligence business. "The aquarium" was a reference to the GRU's old headquarters building at the Khodinka airfield near Moscow. Google analyzed a set of tools, specifically Sofacy and X-Agent, that were used "by a sophisticated state-sponsored group targeting primarily former Soviet republics, NATO members, and other Western European countries."[58] The data that enabled

56. Mandiant, "APT1," 2013.

57. Neel Mehta, Billy Leonard, and Shane Huntley, "Peering into the Aquarium: Analysis of a Sophisticated Multi-Stage Malware Family," Google, September 5, 2014.

58. Mehta et al. *Peering into the Aquarium.*

Google's widely circulated analysis of ongoing GRU operations came from public and private submissions of malware samples to a malware repository and platform known as VirusTotal. Google's *Aquarium* report was only one particularly remarkable and early private sector analysis of what effectively was becoming a new form of counterintelligence activity, driven largely but not exclusively by investigators outside the traditional intelligence community.

Additionally, counterintelligence has evolved dramatically strictly within intelligence agencies. One long-standing feature of catching spies is the "normal and natural tension" between the intelligence collector and the counterintelligence officer, pointed out Richard Helms, a former CIA director, in 1984. What Helms was referring to is the intelligence collector's professional bias towards treating newly recruited human sources as genuine, and the counterintelligence officer's professional bias towards treating newly recruited human sources as suspect. The options were binary: succeed or fail to establish a source's bona fides, where failure meant abandoning the source. "I don't know any way to run an intelligence organization properly without this kind of tension," said Helms.[59] This normal tension may not have been removed entirely when machine implants are the sources, not humans; but the tension is no longer as "natural" as Helms suspected.

A remarkable yet not uncommon illustration is a phenomenon known as fourth party collection, a relatively recent term of art in signals intelligence. One undated internal NSA document, likely from the early 2010s, defines the concept as "4th party collection leverages CCNE access to provide foreign intelligence from foreign CNE victims." CNE is technical jargon for digital spying, or computer network exploitation. CCNE is shorthand for offensive digital counterintelligence, or "counter computer network exploitation." Fourth party collection, in plain English, is spying on spies spying.[60] The NSA unit in question was keen to stress that messing with an adversary's implants was not disruptive, or a form of attack, but rather that fourth party collection was a way to improve collection. "This is not a disruption or CNA activity," the NSA presentation explained, in all caps.

59. Richard Helms, Interviewed by Robert Hathaway, May 30, 1984, https://web.archive.org/web/20210323220904/https://www.cia.gov/readingroom/docs/5_30_oral.pdf.

60. See National Security Agency, "Fourth Party Opportunities," undated, https://web.archive.org/web/20200921163305/https://www.spiegel.de/media/f19becb4-0001-0014-0000-000000035684/media-35684.pdf, accessed October 29, 2022.

An example may help to illustrate this point. The NSA had "sustained collection" on a Chinese command-and-control node beginning in the summer of 2009. The Chinese intelligence actor—codenamed BYZANTINE RAPTOR by the US government—was collecting information on the United Nations. "NSA is able to tap into Chinese SIGINT collection," the agency stated. NSA's S2 UN target office subsequently issued three intelligence reports based on this fourth party collection effort, "all dealing with high-interest, high-profile current events."[61] Catching spies, in the digital context, no longer necessarily meant interrupting their work—catching spies could mean they might never notice somebody was making a clandestine copy of their work. In this case the line between the NSA's offensive and defensive missions—between collection and counterintelligence—had been crossed by design.

IV

The internet thus enhanced five interactions. *Deniability* itself offers the first interaction. Deniability is different from denial. Denial is the explicit refusal to claim responsibility for an action. One prominent example is the Kremlin's persistent practice of denying that Russian entities were behind the attempted interference in the 2016 election. Deniability is a subtler, more abstract, and more dynamic property.

At first glance deniability may appear as a diminishing asset. An actor may continue to deny yet lose deniability in relation to a specific action. A prominent example is the French government's initial denial of the sinking of the *Rainbow Warrior*, a Greenpeace ship, in New Zealand in July 1985. Only two months later, the evidence implicating the French government was so overwhelming that the French prime minister admitted to a covert DGSE (Directorate-General for External Security) operation to sink the ship.

Deniability, in simple terms, is determined by the structure of an action, by the intelligence that has become available on the action, and by the credibility of the actor in question. Deniability may quickly erode in response to new information becoming available. Deniability is also a non-binary property that in some cases may diminish but not be entirely reduced to zero. Even in the face of overwhelming evidence that entirely exposes a perpetrator, that

61. NSA/CSS Threat Operations Center, "NSA's Offensive and Defensive Missions: The Twain Have Met," *SIDToday*, April 26, 2011, https://edwardsnowden.com/2015/01/18/nsas-offensive-and-defensive-missions-the-twain-have-met/.

perpetrator's denial may still retain some appeal for specific groups or individuals in the target country, for political or psychological reasons. The most prominent example was Donald Trump's apparent inability to admit that Russian intelligence had attempted to interfere in the election that he legitimately won.

If the deniability of an action is either too low or too high, then deniability may disappear entirely and—counterintuitively—lose its value for the perpetrators either way. Diminished deniability implies a higher risk of consequences, for instance economic sanctions or international arrest warrants or diplomatic isolation. Excess deniability, on the other side, means an operation has no clear symbolic, strategic, or political value (beyond a potential tactical value), perhaps comparable to a natural event like a provably accidental explosion in a munitions factory, a lighting-caused fire, or a genuine traffic accident. One example is the infamous "Saudi Cables" leak, sourced from an advanced network breach at the Saudi Foreign Ministry, published on a mysterious website (wikisaleaks.com), and adopted as a Wikileaks leak—no noteworthy public attribution was ever achieved in this case.

Events with excess deniability may have direct effects, including intended effects, but no sufficiently clear political messages or threats attached to them as an indirect effect (although private messaging to targets should not be excluded, sometimes even on public channels). Public counterintelligence may therefore sometimes work, counterintuitively, in favor of the perpetrators, by keeping an operation's deniability in a productive range—not too high, and not too low.

V

The second interaction is related to *speed*. The faster a covert action is countered by contesting its deniability, the more effective the response will be. Yet an immediate tension will emerge. Investigating in detail what happened will take time, for instance the sifting of large volumes of log files and images, follow-on research into the full range of infrastructure used, the targeted analysis of large volumes of intelligence data, the issuing subpoenas and awaiting responses, and even the follow-on intelligence tasking to shed light an operation through targeted intelligence collection. In short, speed favors covert action whereas patience favors counterintelligence.

Yet there is a counteracting dynamic at work. The more successful an operation, the harder it will be to keep it covert in the long term. Deniability has a half-life, and the covert aspect of covert action is almost always temporary. Yet the half-life of an operation's secrecy is not a given constant like the half-life of a ra-dioactive isotope; it is a function of the resources that investigators invest in solving a case—and the resources that perpetrators invest in covering their footprints. These resources, in turn, are a function of the political stakes at play, on both sides.

Active measures and covert action operators tend to be pragmatists, not perfectionists. They tend to understand that an action may not remain covert for extended periods of time, for several reasons: firstly, its effects, by definition, are visible to the target, even if the target cannot immediately explain what is happening. An example is when Iranian enrichment centrifuges in Natanz no longer were spinning at the speeds they were programmed to do, and the engineers were struggling to understand what is going on, let alone to appreciate that they were the target of a sabotage campaign. Secondly, digital covert measures—and even digital clandestine intelligence operations—tend to leave behind digital forensic artefacts, from malware samples, on disk or in memory, to log files and command-and-control infrastructure. It is likely that investigators, often in the private sector, will notice such traces and act on them in one fashion or the other, for example by updating security products so they can detect the newly discovered, still unattributed threat, or by sharing the newly found indicators with partners, thus making full exposure more likely in the long run. Thirdly, especially large operations of historic proportion, particularly when considered successful, will tempt the operators, organizations, and political leaders to make information public after the fact, even if anonymously. Here again, Stuxnet is a useful example. US government sources anonymously gave information on the operation to investigative journalists, and engineers hinted at their roles on the sidelines of some technical conferences.

The most potent and common form of disclosure, in the long term, is to have the perpetrators speak for themselves. Intelligence agencies and intelligence officers speak for themselves in three primary ways. First, they can open their archives, in most cases only decades after the fact. Archival sources are some of the most detailed and reliable artefacts available. The second way in which intelligence officers speak for themselves is by writing or talking about their work. Such disclosures tend to be more detailed and revealing if the officers in question either defected to another country, where they can be debriefed more formally, or if their former employers no longer exist, for instance in the case of former Eastern bloc intelligence organizations. Finally, there is the less common unauthorized disclosure of intelligence documents through leaks. The Snowden leaks, for instance, enabled the detailed attribution of a range of Five Eyes intelligence operations that would have remained undiscovered and unattributed otherwise.

VI

The third interaction is related to the *public* aspect of both types of operations. The public counterintelligence response to a covert action will affect the countered action; the defense interacts with the offence. Put differently, the response to a covert action should neither fall significantly behind the visibility and impact of an offensive operation, nor should the response exceed the offensive act in visibility and impact. In the case of imbalance, in either direction, the offense likely has the advantage.

The textbook case for a covert action overshadowing the target's reaction is offered by Operations Plan 10–1. In the early 1960s, the KGB successfully penetrated the US Army Forces Courier Center at Orly Field, Paris, with a spy. The spy handed a large volume of photographs of secret US military documents to Moscow. Once he was exposed, the KGB decided to recycle some of the material in a series of leaks, amplified by forgeries. The highly controversial documents revealed US nuclear targeting in Western Europe, including in West Germany, as well as aggressive unconventional war plans for special forces to fight behind enemy lines in the case of a Red Army invasion of Western Europe. The US State Department counted twenty surfacings of these highly damaging leaks across Europe—yet failed to respond to the operation, arguably making it more effective as a result.[62]

A more recent illustration is the Shadow Brokers incident, one of the tactically most destructive leaks in intelligence history, which compromised sensitive hacking tools used by the US government. Yet the US government, at all levels, has studiously avoided acknowledging the incident, giving rise to the theory that the Shadow Brokers were perhaps one of the most sophisticated and effective covert actions ever to target the NSA.

A covert action, or the output of a covert action, can be highly visible and likely impactful, or it may lack impact, or alternatively it may be detected at an early stage before even any meaningful impact can be achieved. This problem is exacerbated by a new dynamic. The internet has lowered the risk threshold for covert action. Remote on-keyboard action is far less risky than traveling into foreign territory and planning or executing an operation on the ground, even a

---

62. For a detailed account, see Rid, *Active Measures*, Chapter 13.

simple one. The result is a higher prevalence of low-quality, low-impact attempts at covert action. This situation offers unique difficulties for investigators ahead of a revelation or "takedown," as the practice is known in social media companies. The takedown would often receive significant press coverage and attention on social media, and thus risk having a bigger effect, and more public visibility, than the revealed, "taken down" campaign itself. Several Facebook takedowns from 2018 to 2020 illustrate this asymmetry, especially in cases where Facebook removed campaigns in the "early stages." In the same cases, the removal or "dozens of fake accounts and pages" with low numbers of followers or impressions in turn created hundreds of press stories with high numbers of readers and impressions, thus creating an inevitable second-order effect that vastly outperformed the first-order effect.[63] Press interest in the subject of disinformation, paradoxically, resulted in more visibility for disinformation at the exposure stage.

VII

Attribution doesn't stop with the *who*; it also includes the *why* and the *so-what*. Identifying perpetrators, such as governments, agencies, units, contractors, or individuals, is one important step in public counterintelligence. Identifying intentions and goals that go into an operation, and the effectiveness in reaching these goals, is often more important—and harder. The so-called cyber kill chain is a seven-step conceptual model designed to analyze network intrusions, from reconnaissance all the way to action-on-target. What is missing in the model, however, and what cannot be gleaned from network forensics, is phase zero (planning) and phase eight (assessment). Attributing phase zero and phase eight is hard but crucial, for without doing so it is much more difficult to gauge an appropriate public counterintelligence response.

This specific attribution problem brings into sharp relief another counterintuitive interaction: the effect that is easiest to determine and to measure is the counterintelligence effect.

Both covert action and counterintelligence operate in a zone of epistemological ambiguity when it comes to assessing their effectiveness—and both offenders and defenders deal with this baked-in uncertainty. The internet has significantly increased this epistemological uncertainty. Assessing the

63. Barbra Ortutay, "Facebook Takedowns Reveal Sophistication of Russian Trolls," *AP News*, March 12, 2020.

effectiveness of the GRU operation to interfere in the US general election of 2016, for example, is inherently difficult for both the victim and for adversarial intelligence agencies. This lack of a "measurement device," as one Soviet bloc active measures defector put it to me in an interview, is a feature of disinformation operations as they attempt to exploit existing social or political divisions that would have continued to develop independently of an operation anyway. Assessing the effectiveness of the US public counterintelligence response is equally ambiguous for the US government—but not for, say, a specific GRU unit and its commanding officer.

Any public attribution claim with a counterintelligence purpose has two fundamentally different modes of communication that are, by definition, wrapped into one act, for instance the publication of a government press release or a law enforcement document such as an indictment. Those two modes of communication address two fundamentally different audiences: third-party audiences and the perpetrators themselves. The third-party audiences are primarily domestic, and only then an international audience of stakeholders, including third-party governments, third-party network defenders, as well as other actual and potential victims.

The primary target audience for any public attribution claim is the adversary. But the adversary, crucially, does not need to be convinced of the validity of the attribution claim—the perpetrators and their superiors already know the fact that they committed an operation that is now publicly revealed, albeit in a partly deniable way. For the adversary the question is how much of a campaign is revealed, how thoroughly and how accurately, how the revelation affects active assets still in use, how much the revelation reveals about the attributing entity's knowledge of an adversary's operations, and what the negative and positive aspects of the disclosure add up to. Attribution claims, especially detailed reports that include technical indicators, may not just burn capabilities, but also bind and tie down adversary resources in reactive counterintelligence investigations. The irony, of course, is that the recipients of successful counterintelligence measures will, in turn, try to keep that effect secret or deny it.

VIII

The final interaction is political, and related to the constitutional form of the governments engaged in either intelligence activity.

Deniable covert action, at its core, is an undemocratic tactic that is fundamentally incompatible with core values of accountability, openness, and transparency. It is no coincidence that the CIA's covert action activity declined amid the rise of more stringent congressional control and oversight of the intelligence establishment. Accountability comes at an operational price. The more ambitious an operation in its goals, the harder it will be for a democratically accountable intelligence agency to succeed in planning, funding, authorizing, and executing covert operations that rely, often to a significant extent, on deniability. The risk of subsequent exposure of successful covert operations is also significantly higher in an open democracy.

The resulting asymmetry in permissiveness for covert action between open and closed societies has had an invigorating effect on counterintelligence operations. Some Five Eyes countries especially have begun to expose, first and foremost although not exclusively, those types of intelligence operations that they themselves are not, or are no longer at the same level, engaged in: commercial espionage and aggressive covert action. By 2020 the US Department of Justice had indicted an entire range of adversarial cyber operators for engaging in intelligence operations other than classical, traditional political espionage.

The main ethical—and ultimately political—problem is the wide target set of many on-keyboard covert operations, which often resemble what used to be called active measures. Such operations may target entire political communities or subcultures, for instance by attempting to widen existing racial, cultural, or political divisions. But once the target set is narrowed to individual intelligence agencies—again counterintuitively—some covert action tactics become attractive as public counterintelligence tactics deployed by a growing number of liberal democracies.

The critical context here is the proliferation of entities and actors that take part in the public attribution process. By the early 2020s, it has become possible to reveal details about adversarial intelligence operations in creative ways, using the help—witting and unwitting—of an entire investigative counterintelligence community that has developed in the first two decades of this century.[64] Public attribution is enabled, in creative ways, through nongovernmental entities, first and foremost by cutting-edge cybersecurity companies, but also by educators, non-profit investigators, activists, and even hobbyists. It has become possible to feed investigative leads into this community in ways that are covert and, if necessary, deniable.

---

64. See, as an example, several presentations at the 2021 CYBERWARCON conference, held in Arlington, Virginia, on November 16, 2021, https://web.archive.org/web/20211020161336/https://www.cyberwarcon.com/2021-agenda.

Traditional counterintelligence investigations were predominantly defensive in nature, more reactive than proactive. However, the new and expanding practice of digital counterintelligence, perhaps paradoxically, offers liberal democracies and the wider investigative community a significant potential for deploying what effectively are offensive covert action tactics within the confines of countering and weakening adversarial intelligence organizations. Counterintelligence exposures range from the technical to the strategic, from identified to obscure, and from overt to covert.

The rise of a partly public counterintelligence community presents unprecedented challenges and opportunities to makers of modern strategy. Three dynamics stand out.

The first challenge for strategic decision-makers follows from the sharp contrast between open and closed systems. The foreign and security policy establishment in aggressive authoritarian regimes will follow a very different rulebook and ethical standards in comparison to their counterparts in open societies. Closed systems appear to escalate covertly—open systems tend to escalate overtly, for instance by exposing covert action. It serves the interest of open societies to emphasize and broadcast this ethical asymmetry in international affairs—and thus to defend and boost their own credibility against persistent attempted portrayals of moral equivalency.

The second challenge is closely related, and follows from contested evidentiary standards. Deniability is removed most effectively not just by pointing fingers at an adversarial intelligence agency in the abstract, but also by exposing operations in detail, and then by making fact-based attributive links, backed up by specific artifacts, evidence, and fingerprints. However, even the most convincing and orderly evidentiary chain will likely be contested, if not dismissed, by some adversaries, as well as by politically self-interested parties and conspiracy communities. The challenge for the strategic decision-maker is how to structure the cost-benefit calculation of disclosure, and to have a clear concept of the specific goals and target audiences for specific disclosures. The higher the stakes, and the more consequential an attribution claim, the more evidence is likely required.

The final challenge is the most vexing: assessing effects, a significant challenge for both victims and perpetrators. Both have a comparable evidentiary problem: covert action as well as public counterintelligence both aim to change adversary behavior. But explaining behaviors and collective decisions is fraught with difficulty, especially if a project was designed to exacerbate an organic, independent development, or if a target tries to conceal effects.

Assessing impact, or the lack thereof, may thus be extremely hard if not impossible. Closed systems will tend to overstate the effect of conspiracies, both real and imagined, both their own and those of others. Open societies, by contrast and by design, must culturally minimize the temptation of conspiracy narratives, and systematically err on the side of skepticism and scrupulously exercise evidence-driven caution. Intelligence officers and strategic decision-makers should lead by example. For collectively ascribing excess influence to the unknown and to the unexplained, in the absence of proper evidence, is a sign of a society closing.

CHAPTER 45

Grammar, Logic, and Grand Strategy

John Lewis Gaddis

With this third edition, *Makers of Modern Strategy* has come to resemble a comet, periodically revisiting and thereby illuminating the geopolitical system in which we live. The first of these volumes, edited by Edward Mead Earle, came out in 1943, two years before the militarily foreseeable end of an era of "world" wars that had begun twenty-nine years earlier. The second, under the editorship of Peter Paret, appeared in 1986, five years before the ideologically unforeseen conclusion of a four-and-a-half-decade "cold" war. This one arrives three decades into what we have come to know—quite unimaginatively—as the "post-Cold War era," and if the pattern holds it portends a future distinctly different, whether for better or for worse, from our own recent past. All three visitations, however, share an aspiration: that the long history of strategy may help us to anticipate what's to come.

History's most frequently acknowledged founders, Herodotus and Thucydides, lived in an age of oracles, and in some ways we still do. We consult think tanks, data bases, and artificial intelligences, but the languages through which they speak—even the names by which some of them go—echo those of Delphi. They pose *paradoxes*—puzzles more often than principles—requiring at least clarification, and, if the basis for action, navigation. For the purpose of a paradox is to turn opposites into single truths.[1]

---

1. See *Merriam-Webster*, s.v. "paradox," https://www.merriam-webster.com/dictionary/paradox, accessed April 21, 2022.

Chief among paradoxes, for historians, is the contrast between *timefulness*—fidelity, in narration, to how things were—and *timelessness*—patterns drawn from the past suggesting how things might in the future be. There's little hope of aligning these opposites through faith, luck, or independent variables. Historians have long believed that proficiency instead comes from experience, whether accumulated from life or absorbed through scholarship. *Strategy*, then, is alignment: the guide that points the way.

I

The foundational status of war in "strategy," Hal Brands has shown in his introduction to this edition, was more than understandable in its predecessors: wars, hot and cold, were why strategies were devised, applied, and, if necessary, modified. Everything else followed from them. Lawrence Freedman, however, has now broadened the focus. He sees a definitional progression, extending through the twentieth century, from war's "narrow confines" to "all aspects of human affairs." Strategy today is "a way of thinking, a habit of mind, an ability to assess vulnerabilities in situations, an appreciation of causes and effects, a capacity to link disparate activities in pursuit of a shared purpose."[2] What then, though, he asks, gets left out? What's to prevent strategy from becoming the intellectual equivalent of a French peasant soup, into which everything available gets tossed?[3]

The answer, I think, has to do with the adjective "grand," so often attached with so little explanation to the noun "strategy." There's not much that's grand about soup—until it's all that stands between would-be consumers and starvation. In those instances, what's in the pot, where it is, and who gets access to it become matters of life and death. Perhaps that's why Carl von Clausewitz, who witnessed the French retreat from Moscow in 1812, resisted absolute definitions. Instead, as Paret pointed out in the 1986 introduction to *Makers*, Clausewitz "varied the meaning of strategy according to the matter at hand."[4]

So do my students, not all of whom have read Clausewitz. Deciding where to get pizza may demand tough choices, they'll acknowledge, but only at the level of what they call "petite" strategy. What of the decisions made, though,

---

2. See Lawrence Freedman, "Strategy: History of an Idea," Chapter 1 in this volume. See also Matthew Kroenig, "Machiavelli and the Naissance of Modern Strategy," Chapter 4 in this volume.

3. Freedman, "Strategy." Freedman credits Williamson Murray with this useful metaphor.

4. "Introduction," in *Makers of Modern Strategy from Machiavelli to the Nuclear Age*, Peter Paret, ed. (Princeton, NJ: Princeton University Press, 1986), 3.

while they were still in high school, about which college or university to attend? Or are making now about what courses to take and majors to declare? Or will be making about what profession to enter after graduation? Or, at any of these points, about with whom to fall in or out of love? These are life-determining questions for young people, even if the lives affected are very few.

This suggests, then, that the "grandness" of strategy resides, not just in time and space, but also in the eye of the beholder, which is to say scale. Any situation in which small choices can have significant consequences falls within grandeur's range. Clausewitz knew this. His concept of *friction*—that what can go wrong sooner or later will—applies at all levels, from nails to horseshoes to horses to kings to kingdoms. His celebration of *coup d'oeil*—the assessment of complexity in the blink of an eye—implies seeing objects of all sizes in relation to one another. And his conception of war as a "paradoxical trinity"—the passions that cause combatants to risk their lives, the skill of their commanders, and the coherence of the objectives for which wars are fought—requires, as he put it, maintaining "a balance between these three tendencies, like an object suspended between three magnets."[5]

That makes strategy a three-body problem, the behavior of whose components is unpredictable. "[N]o theory can afford to leave any one of them out of account," Hew Strachan writes in his *Makers* essay on Clausewitz, but neither "can it fix relations between them because they are in perpetual flux."[6] Only retrospective narration can approximate what happened, but there's no assurance that it will happen that way again. How, then, can preparation for anything ever take place?

Clausewitz solved this problem by shifting theory's task from prediction to distillation. "Theory exists," he explained, "so that one need not start afresh each time sorting out the material and plowing through it, but will find it ready to hand and in good order." Its purpose is "to educate the mind of the future commander, or, more accurately, to guide him in his self-education, not to accompany him to the battlefield; just as a wise teacher guides and stimulates a young man's intellectual development, but is careful not to lead him by the

5. Carl von Clausewitz, *On War*, trans. and ed. Michael Howard and Peter Paret (Princeton, NJ: Princeton University Press, 1976), 89. I've discussed these points more fully in *On Grand Strategy* (New York, NY: Penguin, 2018), 200–5, 210.

6. Hew Strachan, "The Elusive Meaning and Enduring Relevance of Clausewitz," Chapter 5 of this volume. See also, on three-body problems, James Gleick, *Chaos: Making a New Science* (New York, NY: Viking, 1987), 43–45; and, as fiction, Cixin Liu, *The Three-Body Problem*, trans. Ken Liu (New York, NY: Tor Books, 2014).

hand for the rest of his life."[7] No youth has the time—and certainly not the temperament—to consider everything elders might wish to convey. But theory, conceived of as distillation, compresses what elders know into what youths need to know. That's what Clausewitz calls *training*: providing the skills and stamina needed to maintain poise under pressures the future will amply supply.

Poise, in Clausewitz, arises from the interdependence of what he calls *grammar* and *logic*. Grammar was the drill and discipline necessary in the armies he knew; today it's best thought of as the standard operating procedures of any large organization. These never exist, however, in isolation. All are subject to the actions of competitors, the workings of friction, the occurrence of accidents, the randomness of chance, and the inexpungible fear, however strongly suppressed, of simply ceasing to exist. When these things manifest themselves, grammars of groups give way to logics of individuals better chronicled by novelists than historians. " 'What men are these?' Rostov kept thinking, not believing his eyes. 'Can they be Frenchmen?. . . . Can it be they're running to me? . . . And why? To kill me? *Me*, whom everybody loves so?' "[8]

Training respects authority on the one hand, while on the other acknowledging the survival of common sense. When done well, it channels growth toward intended results. When done badly, it disappoints, and can even destroy. Either way, training is horticulture: the nurture and nudging of development. That in turn suggests a standard against which to assess results in strategy: "By these fruits, ye shall know them."[9]

II

No fruit can flourish in an unfavorable environment, and no strategy can either. The fitting of strategies to ecologies, therefore, must be the first linkage of grammar with logic, and Sun Zi's *The Art of War*, despite its difficulties, has long been the best guide. Sun himself, Toshi Yoshihara points out, probably

---

7. Clausewitz, *On War*, 141.

8. Leo Tolstoy, *War and Peace*, trans. Richard Pevear and Larissa Volokhonsky (New York, NY: Knopf, 2007), 189. Emphasis in original. The context is the Battle of Schöngrabern, in November 1805. For the grammar versus logic distinction, see Bernard Brodie, *War and Politics* (New York, NY: Macmillan, 1973).

9. Matthew 7:20, King James Version. For more on strategic horticulture, see Robert L. Beisner, *Dean Acheson: A Life in the Cold War* (New York, NY: Oxford University Press, 2006), 92; and John Lewis Gaddis, *George F. Kennan: An American Life* (New York, NY: Penguin, 2011), 495.

never existed: "his" book is an "anthology express[ing] the collective wisdom of faceless, nameless stewards of an emerging school of military thought in ancient China." Drawn from multiple viewpoints, it avoids single solutions. For many of its readers, it offers too many cherries from which to pick.[10]

But what if history itself speaks in multiple voices? What if comprehension requires the reconciliation of opposites? What if conclusions come shrouded in three-body opacity? *The Art of War* confronts these dilemmas much more directly than the individually authored writings of Herodotus, Thucydides, and their many successors. It defines what Yoshihara calls a "strategic culture"— an aggregation "of shared beliefs about the efficacy, role, and use of force . . . among members of a state's national security community." Because these "narratives of a remembered past" are "relatively stable over time," they may "exert a discernible influence on how contemporary statesmen and commanders think about and employ force."[11]

That has been the assumption behind all three *Makers of Modern Strategy* volumes. Contributors have identified strategic cultures within the times and places about which they've written, but with no clearer consensus than in *The Art of War* as to what the transferable components of these cultures might be. What follows is my own list, framed within Clausewitzian balancing of grammar and logic. For it's likely to be there, more than anywhere else in the study of strategy, that standards for success and failure lie.

First on my list is *ecological sensitivity*: an understanding that because everything relates to everything else, particularities across time, space, and scale can become uniformities. The ancient Greeks surely knew this. In resisting the Persian invasion of 480 BCE, they drew first on circumstances foreseen—winds, waters, and difficult terrain—but then also on opportunities unforeseen—the hungry lions that devoured load-bearing camels, the cryptic oracle at Delphi who praised "wooden walls," and the extreme overconfidence of Xerxes himself, who sent forth a fleet at Salamis manned by non-swimming rowers. That made the resulting Greek victory, with help from Herodotus, arguably the first demonstration of a home court advantage.

Other examples followed. Germanic tribes lured Roman legions into the Teutoburg forest in 9 CE, from where they never returned. The English invited the Spanish armada into their inhospitably eponymous channel in 1588, then

---

10. Toshi Yoshihara, "Sun Zi and the Search for a Timeless Logic of Strategy," Chapter 3 of this volume.

11. Yoshihara, "Sun Zi."

crippled its ships, leaving them at the mercy of winds, weather, and the much longer way home. George III sent armies across an ocean two centuries later to pursue rebels who had a continent into which to retreat. The Russians allowed Napoleon to take Moscow in 1812 as the first snowflakes of winter were beginning to fall. Woodrow Wilson and Franklin D. Roosevelt transformed geographical insulation from world wars into temporal preparation for them, ensuring maximum impact at minimal cost when the interventions finally did take place.[12]

All these events exemplify—even if none were inspired by—the Chinese concept of *shi*. This untranslatable term, Yoshihara explains, can apply to water rushing downstream, or boulders rolling down hills, or the lethal precision of predator's swoop, or the latent deadliness of a drawn crossbow. It implies turning inertia into "explosive power."[13] By animating improbabilities, it multiplies force, thereby reducing the need to use more. The closest analogue in English may be the concept of "leverage," which requires breadth in identifying potentials, ingenuity in applying them, and the timing needed to slip them through windows of opportunity before they close. There's nothing automatic, though, about any of these.

Breadth, for example, is at odds with specialization. That's why the ideas of Antoine-Henri Jomini and Alfred Thayer Mahan, experts respectively on land and sea warfare, never achieved the universality of Sun Zi or Clausewitz. By the time of Jomini's death in 1869, armies, employing railroads, were moving exponentially faster than those of Napoleon half a century earlier—or for that matter, those of Xerxes on the way to Salamis.[14] By the time Mahan died in 1914, navies had extended themselves above and below the surface of the sea, an unprecedented triple dimensionality. Both strategists knew of these innovations, but neither thought it necessary to revise their thinking. Their grammar was too narrow for new logics.[15]

Ingenuity, in turn, subverts conventionality. "It can't be done," it's frequently said, until it has been done, at which point it's often remembered as the only

---

12. I've discussed the examples in these two paragraphs at greater length in Gaddis, *On Grand Strategy*.

13. Yoshihara, "Sun Zi."

14. I owe this point to Sir Michael Howard, *Clausewitz: A Very Short Introduction* (New York, NY: Oxford University Press, 2002), 4. See also Antulio J. Echevarria II, "Jomini, Modern War, and Strategy: The Triumph of the Essential," Chapter 6 of this volume.

15. See John H. Maurer, "Alfred Thayer Mahan and the Strategy of Sea Power," Chapter 7 of this volume.

thing that could have been done. How could a faith that disdained the use of force have taken over the Roman Empire? How, a thousand years later, could a great queen have used virginity to balance great powers? How, three centuries after that, could the least-educated American president have become the most respected? And how, in the twentieth century, could unruly democracies have prevailed so consistently over disciplined autocracies? Mutations, we're often told, advance evolution. Surprises, in history, do much the same thing.

Finally, timetables aren't timing. Julius Caesar, Napoleon, Lenin, Hitler, and Lyndon B. Johnson all expected to live short lives.[16] They sought compulsively, therefore, to accelerate their ascents; they preferred flattening topographies to finding paths through them. The structures they built were impressive, even intimidating, but their foundations soon revealed cracks. Octavian/Augustus, Elizabeth I, Lincoln, and Roosevelt, in contrast, carefully tested topographies before proceeding. That required, at times, accepting delays, even appearances of inconsistency. These were, however, the adjustments to unconformities necessary for resilience and durability.

Success in strategy, Matthew Kroenig writes in his *Makers* essay on Machiavelli, comes from using "one's own skill to harness circumstances to one's own ends."[17] That suggests the necessity, in strategies as in ecologies, of balancing grammar with logic, for how else can suitability to situations be determined? Tightrope walkers have no choice but to do this: the path they're on precludes doubts. Strategists, however, must find their own way.

III

That brings up a second standard for strategic success, which is to *maintain credibility*: the expectation on the part of adversaries, allies, and constituencies, that promises made, even if extravagant, will be kept. Banks routinely lend beyond the value of their deposits, a grammar that creates its own logic as long as depositors don't all withdraw funds at the same time.[18] Great powers operate similarly: if called upon to honor all commitments extended, or to employ all deterrents deployed, their strategies, like overstretched banks,

16. See especially Brendan Simms, "Strategies of Geopolitical Revolution: Hitler and Stalin," Chapter 25 of this volume; and Robert A. Caro, *The Years of Lyndon Johnson: Means of Ascent* (New York, NY: Knopf, 1990).

17. Kroenig, "Machiavelli."

18. James Lacey's *Makers* essay, "Alexander Hamilton and the Financial Sinews of Strategy," Chapter 9 of this volume, provides a cogent account.

would quickly crash. But in the absence of such worst cases, credibility, like *shi*, can multiply power.

Upon what, though, does credibility depend? The answer for banks is clear enough: long lines outside locked doors are a bad sign. No such standard, however, exists for states. Their multiple audiences pull in different directions in crises, making credibility another three-body problem, or worse. There's no better illustration of this than that of Thucydides in his great *History of the Peloponnesian War*.

The Greeks, after their victories over the Persians, set up no central government. They developed instead a system of specialized city-states in which Sparta, a landed autocracy, and Athens, a maritime democracy, were contrasting exemplars. That made sense at the time because armies required obedient phalanxes, while navies depended on self-motivated rowers. Each city sought supremacy within its capability, so much so that the Athenians, if war came, were prepared to relinquish most of Attica to the Spartans. Athens itself, with its port, Piraeus, would become a *virtual* island, supplied by sea but enclosed on land within long walls. The Spartans became tigers and the Athenians sharks, each dominant in their own domain. Explosive power—their *shi*—would remain, supposedly, within separate spheres.

That was the grammar but it wasn't logic, however, for the spheres too easily assumed steady nerves. They provided no protection against what Walter Russell Mead calls "[s]torms of emotions, whether of gratitude, compassion or rage."[19] That became clear in the mid-430s BCE when, for obscure reasons, the citizens of Epidamnus, an obscure port in the Adriatic, began slaughtering one another. Those left alive appealed for help to Corinth and Corcyra, subordinates, respectively, of the Spartans and the Athenians, but those underlings passed the buck to their overlords, placing the credibility of both Athens and Sparta on the line.

The ensuing "debate" at Sparta, which took place in 432 BCE, became a vivisection of strategic cultures. The Athenians, Thucydides has the Corinthians complain, are "adventurous beyond their power, and daring beyond their judgment." They "take no rest themselves," and "give none to others." The Spartans respond "not by doing anything but by looking as if you would do something," thereby allowing "the power of an enemy [to reach] twice its original size." Neither recipient of these complaints responded convincingly, probably because those complaints were accurate. But that showed spheres not to be

19. Walter Russell Mead, "Thucydides, Polybius, and the Legacies of the Ancient World," Chapter 2 of this volume.

separate after all; one was expanding while the other was stagnant, for reasons so deeply embedded as to make remediation impossible. The result, Thucydides writes, was a collision of spheres: "The growth of the power of Athens, and the alarm which this inspired in Sparta, made war inevitable."[20]

The Spartans, as expected, invaded Attica in 431 BCE, and the Athenians, as planned, gathered their citizens within their walls. Even then, their leader Pericles promised, Athens would remain democratic; its defense would be engagement with the rest of the world, an openness more attractive than anything the grimly parochial Spartans might offer. But predictabilities and surprises soon subverted this strategy, as they had that of the Persians half a century earlier.

Landowners, as should have been foreseen, found it difficult to watch, from the Athenian walls, as Spartans torched their farms and vineyards. Openness, as couldn't have been anticipated, imported viruses along with commodities, and a lethal plague soon swept the city. Pericles's death from it coarsened politics and harshened the treatment of allies: defections to the Spartans began to seem to require preemption. That's why the supposedly enlightened Athenians told the previously neutral Melians in 416 BCE that, as "masters of the sea," they required obedience, not friendship, from all islands. Seeing none, the Athenians, in the interest of credibility, killed all the men on Melos, enslaved the women and children, and repopulated the place themselves.

At which point, in response to rumors that Segesta, a city eight hundred miles away in Sicily, might defect to the Syracusans, allies of the Spartans, the Athenian assembly voted to dispatch an *army* to prevent this possibility, even as Spartan phalanxes remained within a day's march of the Athenian long walls. The Sicilian "expedition" suffered a catastrophic defeat at the hands of the Syracusans and Spartans—who had now, at great cost, built a competent *navy*. This reversal of roles, Mead writes, left the victors in this war "almost as exhausted as the vanquished."[21] That opened the way for the conquest of all of Greece, at first by the Macedonians, but then eventually by Rome. The Greeks wound up destroying what they'd set out, so ingeniously, to defend.

It's common now to complain about "mission creep": the gradual expansion of objectives beyond original intent. Thucydides's *History* suggests, though, that "credibility creep"—the slow broadening of what's seen to be necessary to make commitments believable—is an older and more

---

20. Robert B. Strasser, ed., *The Landmark Thucydides: A Comprehensive Guide to the Peloponnesian War* (New York, NY: Simon and Schuster, 1996), 16, 39–40.

21. Mead, "Thucydides, Polybius, and the Legacies of the Ancient World."

troublesome problem. For when whatever might happen becomes a test of credibility, then capabilities must become infinite, or bluffs must become routine.[22] Neither is sustainable. Grammar and logic fuse, producing absurdity.

IV

The best safeguard against creep, then, is a third standard for success in strategy, which is *self-correction*. Tightrope walkers accomplish this by leveling long poles. Ships and airplanes stay afloat and aloft with gyroscopes. Markets depend on regulation, whether by visible or invisible hands. Strategists seek to retain the initiative—the freedom to choose where and when they'll deploy capabilities—but this requires stabilization: finding paths between detachments of grammar from logic on the one hand and, on the other, their unsustainable combination. Where, then, does this middle ground lie?

One answer might be with the passage of time. "Take time then in forming your resolution," Thucydides has the Athenians advising the Spartans, "do not be persuaded by the opinions and complaints of others, and so bring trouble on yourselves."[23] But the Greek city-states were young and foolish: they lacked the self-confidence to slow down and self-correct. Their lives as a consequence, like that of Achilles, were memorable but short. The Chinese, however, resisted haste, focusing instead, Yoshihara writes, on "the cool, dispassionate, and detailed evaluation of the security environment."[24] That may explain why so much of what we know about China today would have been recognizable at the time of the Peloponnesian War, even as Athenians and Spartans were trying so energetically to wipe each other out.[25]

China's leaders have, to be sure, wielded authority with wild inconsistency. At times, Elizabeth Economy points out, they "encouraged scientific exploration, intellectual creativity, and openness to the outside world." At others they "burned books, destroyed the country's naval fleet, and effectively banned businesspeople from trading directly with the outside world."[26] China's borders have been accordions, expanding and contracting as circumstances allowed.

22. I've lifted some phrasing here from Gaddis, *On Grand Strategy*, 60.

23. Strasser, ed., *The Landmark Thucydides*, 44.

24. Yoshihara, "Sun Zi."

25. See particularly, on language, Jing Tsu, *Kingdom of Characters: The Language Revolution That Made China Modern* (New York, NY: Riverhead Books, 2022), xi–xix.

26. Elizabeth Economy, "Xi Jinping and the Strategy of China's Restoration," Chapter 39 of this volume.

Ideology was and still is whatever rulers want it to be. But this long-standing capacity for self-correction—the Chinese would call it "self-criticism"—may nonetheless most clearly confirm its benefits.

Another path to stabilization has been diversity. We don't usually associate that term with empire; the words in our time have had different trajectories of approbation. For much longer, though, they were complementary because builders of empires lacked the administrative and military means to impose uniformity in all their territories.[27] Diversity offered an alternative, whether through the Romans' extension of near-universal citizenship, or European co-habitations with indigenous peoples, or elaborately staged delegations of authority by the British on the Indian subcontinent. Toleration, in these instances, became co-optation, a means of retaining power. Withdrawals of toleration, as in North America, could lead to revolutionary resistance.[28]

Religions stabilized themselves similarly, by learning to live with heresies. Popes stopped sending crusades to retake Jerusalem. "Jihad," Ahmed Hasim explains, came to include "almost any activity by which Muslims strive to bring personal, political, social, and economic life into conformity with God's ordinances as revealed to man."[29] And just as the "grandness" of strategy may rest in the eye of the beholder, so the Protestant Reformation firmly planted faiths in the souls of individual believers. That opened the way, after the Thirty Years' War, for a new system of secular states, which prized sovereignty in this world over salvation in the next.[30] And that in turn expanded the space between grammar and logic, making *balances of power* themselves objectives of strategy.

V

Security nowhere is totally free, but it costs more in some locations than in others. This doesn't automatically mean though, as is often assumed, that continental geography favors autocracy and that its maritime counterpart

27. See Greg Woolf, *Rome: An Empire's Story*, 218–22; also, for the larger pattern, Michael W. Doyle, *Empires* (Ithaca, NY: Cornell University Press, 1986).

28. A point freshly made by Andrew Roberts in *The Last King of America: The Misunderstood Reign of George III* (New York, NY: Viking, 2021).

29. Ahmed S. Hasim, "Strategies of Jihad: From the Prophet Muhammad to Contemporary Times," Chapter 38 of this volume.

30. See Henry Kissinger, *World Order* (New York, NY: Penguin, 2014), especially pp. 23–41; also Matt J. Schumann, "Generational Competition in a Multipolar World: William III and André-Hercule de Fleury," Chapter 12 in this volume.

encourages democracy.[31] The generalization works for the city-states of Sparta and Athens, but what about the empires they acquired? Or, for that matter, those of the Romans, Byzantines, Ottomans, Spanish, Dutch, French, British, or Japanese? It's safer to conclude that efforts to *alter* the nature of a state's power—to reshape, rather than to reflect, geography—tend to alarm spectators, but also to self-defeat perpetrators; there's evidence for this in whatever remains of Athenian army transports in Sicilian waters, in Philip II's wrecked hulks along English, Scottish, and Irish coastlines, and in the scuttled High Seas Fleet of the Kaiser William II at the bottom of Scapa Flow.[32]

Except that the United States *did* successfully reflect and reshape geography. Within its first century of independence, it went from being a beachhead on the edge of a great maritime empire to unquestioned domination of its own massive continent, while nonetheless maintaining, through even extreme internal disruptions, an increasingly raucous, if by no means corruption-free or equitably administered, democracy.[33] This was no shattering of ships, but of templates. And that suggests a fourth standard for strategic success, which is to *expect, even if only occasionally, the unexpected.*

It helped not to have strong neighbors. The British had pushed the French out of North America two decades before being pushed out themselves by rebellious subjects. Weakened by Napoleon in Europe and upheavals elsewhere in the Americas, the Spanish pruned back their empire to Caribbean islands. Native American resistance made the most of its circumstances, Kori Schake shows, but was unable to reverse the imported Americans' continuing expansion.[34] By the end of the 1840s, diplomacy (with Great Britain) and war (with Mexico) had extended the United States' boundaries westward to the Pacific and south to the Rio Grande, accomplishments then fortified by the inheritance, from civil war, of a world-class military-industrial complex—and, by 1869, a transcontinental railroad.

---

31. For more on the distinction, see Maurer, "Alfred Thayer Mahan and the Grand Strategy" of Sea Power"; S.C.M. Paine, "Japan Caught between Maritime and Continental Imperialism," Chapter 17 in this volume; and Gaddis, *On Grand Strategy*, 258–62.

32. See Graham Allison, *Destined for War: Can America and China Escape Thucydides' Trap?* (Boston, MA: Houghton Mifflin, 2017).

33. For a recent lively account, see Jon Grinspan, *The Age of Acrimony: How Americans Fought to Fix Their Democracy, 1865–1915* (New York, NY: Bloomsbury, 2021).

34. See Kori Schake, "Strategic Excellence: Tecumseh and the Shawnee Confederacy," Chapter 15 of this volume.

This wasn't so much creep as conquest: the fulfillment of a vision held by the nation's founders from its first moments. It had been John Adams himself, after all, who deemed the Declaration of Independence, which he had just signed, worthy of celebration "from one End of this Continent to the other from this Time forward forever more."[35] It fell to his son John Quincy Adams, however, in his capacity as secretary of state, to specify most clearly where the conquests should stop. Faced with calls to support Latin American and even Greek revolutionaries, the younger Adams announced, in his own 1821 Fourth of July commemoration, that the United States "goes not abroad in search of monsters to destroy. . . . She is the well-wisher to the freedom and independence of all," but "the champion and vindicator only of her own." For "by once enlisting under other banners . . . she would involve herself beyond the power of extrication."[36] She would abdicate the initiative, the preservation of which it is strategy's purpose to retain.

The United States, for well over a century, stuck to the Adams principle: it would determine for itself when credibility was at stake, unmoved, as Thucydides put it, "by the opinions and constraints of others." This meant keeping aspirations *within* capabilities, but with the expectation that continental expansion would in time *augment* capabilities. That was the logic behind the Adams-Onís Treaty of 1819 which, in setting a northern limit to Spanish (and, soon to be, Mexican) sovereignty on the Pacific, presumed an American sovereignty that wouldn't exist for another two decades. The Monroe Doctrine of 1823 did much the same thing: it ruled out further European colonization in the Western Hemisphere, while relying on the British navy to enforce that restriction until Americans themselves, decades later, had the power to do so. Credibility based itself, in these instances, on probability. They were the diplomatic equivalent of good banking.[37]

---

35. John Adams to Abigail Adams, July 3, 1776, in *Adams Family Papers: An Electronic Archive*, Massachusetts Historical Society (2022), available at https://www.masshist.org/publications/adams-papers/index.php/view/ADMS-04-02-02-0016#sn=66.

36. As quoted from John Quincy Adams, "Speech to the U.S. House of Representatives on Foreign Policy," July 4, 1821, in *Presidential Speeches: John Quincy Adams Presidency*, University of Virginia, Miller Center (2022), available at www.millercenter.org/president/jqadams/speeches/speech-3484. Charles Edel discusses the background in "John Quincy Adams and the Challenges of a Democratic Strategy," Chapter 14 in the present volume.

37. So much so that the *fear* of American intervention, after it became clear that the Union would prevail in the Civil War, was sufficient to bring about the abandonment, by his European sponsors, of the Emperor Maximilian of Mexico. A long-overdue modern account is Edward

Meanwhile, Americans just said "no" when other opportunities came their way. These included further annexations in Mexico, Central America, and the Caribbean, the appeals of which in the United States, after its near-breakup over African-American slavery, were now minimal. Racism wasn't a deterrent with respect to Canada but economic ties were, together with Great Britain's still formidable reputation as a naval power. And even after the British themselves, alarmed by the ambitions of a recently unified Germany, began encouraging the emergence of the United States as a counterweight, the American response was chiefly confined to completing *continental* expansion: the Spanish-American war of 1898, the acquisitions of Hawaii and Puerto Rico, and Theodore Roosevelt's decision to build the Panama Canal. Americans at the time, Robert Kagan points out, "did not act like a world power, and did not wish to be a world power."[38]

The United States' entry into World War I, for all of its importance in determining the outcome, didn't significantly alter the pattern. Woodrow Wilson allowed three years of neutrality before determining that American security was in fact on the line. He then used force with sufficient decisiveness to secure victory in half that time. Knowing how great a departure from tradition intervention had been, Wilson sought a postwar restoration of a balance of power in Europe requiring only minimal American management. His problem, though, was that victorious but vindictive allies insisted on an *imbalance* of power in their favor.[39] The League of Nations became Wilson's grammar for bridging that gap, but to critics at home it looked like a repudiation of logic: a delegation of responsibility to others certain, as Thucydides might have warned, to "bring trouble on yourselves."

The League's rejection, therefore, was not so much the shattering of a template, but rather a demonstration of how solidly entrenched American unilateralism still was. The only great power to have emerged from the war unweakened chose not to use its power. And the monsters duly took note.

Shawcross, *The Last Emperor of Mexico: The Dramatic Story of the Habsburg Archduke Who Created a Kingdom in the New World* (New York, NY: Basic Books, 2021).

38. Robert Kagan, "Woodrow Wilson and the Rise of Modern American Grand Strategy," Chapter 22 of this volume. Acquisition of the Philippines was a rule-proving exception. President William McKinley's decision to do so was controversial from the start, and President Franklin D. Roosevelt's 1935 promise of independence within a decade was one of the first for any imperial possession anywhere.

39. Kagan, "Woodrow Wilson."

VI

They were, in this instance, Adolf Hitler, Joseph Stalin, and the Japanese militarists, each of whom combined grievances to nurse with ambitions to feed. For Hitler and Stalin, Brendan Simms explains, the offenses were omissions. Germany's industrialization had expanded its population, Hitler believed, without providing it with the empire necessary to sustain both. Stalin, following Lenin, saw that Russia's empire of land, without industrialization, could never become the base for an international proletarian revolution. The Japanese, like the British, had industrialized an island, but had yet to secure an empire: opportunities lay, S.C.M. Paine writes, in both China and the western Pacific.

The outcome of World War I, each believed, had set them back: Germany through defeat; Russia through foreign intervention and civil war; and Japan through the peacemakers' racially motivated inattention. All held Britain chiefly responsible, but given that state's wartime exhaustion, none expected its power to grow much further. They did, however, respect and ultimately fear the rising power of the United States, even though few Americans at the time understood their own geopolitical criticality.[40]

All three malcontents—even the Soviet Union in the absence of formal diplomatic relations—had come to depend on American trade and investment, so the virus that originated on Wall Street in the fall of 1929 set them back yet again. The Great Depression drove the Japanese, in search of raw materials, to occupy Manchuria two years later. It reinforced Stalin's determination to achieve self-sufficiency whatever the costs. It collapsed what was left of democracy in Germany by bringing Hitler to power. But it also ensured the election, as President of the United States, of Franklin D. Roosevelt.

F.D.R. was not about to let grammar lose touch with logic, as had happened under Wilson. So the new president concentrated first on domestic recovery, without which credibility could hardly exist anywhere. Seeking congressional support, he refused to resist legislation strengthening neutrality: aggressors, he anticipated, would undo those restrictions for him. He had few illusions about authoritarian dangers, but he also saw in such systems a great weakness: their inherent inability to *share* authority with one another.

---

40. I've based this paragraph on Brendan Simms, "Strategies of Geopolitical Revolution: Hitler and Stalin," and S.C.M. Paine, "Japan Caught between Maritime and Continental Imperialism," Chapters 25 and 17, respectively, in the present volume.

That's why Roosevelt sought cooperation throughout his presidency with the Soviet Union. He saw in its lack of naval strength an absence of military threat to the United States; and because the USSR alone among the authoritarians lay between others, he foresaw that it might someday welcome assistance, and even provide it. These reasons led Roosevelt to recognize the USSR in 1933; to maintain an embassy in Moscow through Stalin's harshest purges; and, even after the signing of the Nazi-Soviet Pact in August 1939, to keep a door open for Stalin whenever he might choose to walk through it. Hitler's attack on June 22, 1941, vindicated these indulgences: the Soviet Union became from that moment, for Roosevelt, not a monster to destroy, but one to sustain.[41]

What followed was a triumph of grand strategic efficiency. Roosevelt brought two major wars fought on opposite sides of the earth to successful conclusions in only three and a half years, at a cost in American lives of only about two percent of all the combatants who'd fought in them. The United States combined its victory with an economy twice the size of what it had been in 1941, with the world's largest navy and air force, and with its first atomic bombs. This would never have been possible, though, without the sacrifices of the Soviet Union, whose wartime deaths came to *ninety times* those of the Americans.[42] That alone entitled it, Roosevelt believed, to postwar spheres of influence in Europe and northeastern Asia: a victory for one monster over two others. The trick would be to retain the support of Americans for their own spheres of influence in these regions given these very different outcomes from what they'd been led to believe they were fighting the war for.

The president hoped to solve this problem, Tami Davis Biddle writes, by "constrain[ing] Stalin within the boundaries of an international framework . . . that would also ease the American people into a sustained role in global politics."[43] That included the Atlantic Charter, the Bretton Woods economic agreements, and the United Nations; but the Soviet Union ignored the first, withdrew from the second, and soon vetoed the third into inactivity. To "constrain," however, can also mean to "contain," and by bringing the United States

41. I've developed the drift of these three paragraphs more fully in Gaddis, *On Grand Strategy*, 279–87; and in John Lewis Gaddis, *Russia, the Soviet Union, and the United States: An Interpretive History*, Second Edition (New York, NY: McGraw-Hill, 1990), 117–49.

42. John Lewis Gaddis, *The Cold War: A New History* (New York, NY: Penguin, 2005), 8–9; John A. Thompson, *A Sense of Power: The Roots of America's Global Role* (Ithaca, NY: Cornell University Press, 2015), 230.

43. Tami Davis Biddle, "Democratic Leaders and Strategies of Coalition Warfare: Churchill and Roosevelt in World War II," Chapter 23 of this volume.

out of the war with so much more power than it had going into it, Roosevelt bequeathed to his successors the ability to shift the verbs. We'll never know for sure whether he, had he lived, would have done the same. It is worth noting, though, that the second verb achieved what F.D.R. had hoped for from the first: there would be no American reversion to unilateralism after this war.

VII

Roosevelt's accomplishments suggest a fifth standard for success in strategy, which is the ability *to employ contradictions.* Authoritarians, in rising to power, *exploit* contradictions among their rivals: Lenin, Stalin, and Hitler all practiced this art skillfully. Once in power, however, dictators suppress criticism in order to remain where they are as long as possible. The constitution within which Roosevelt and his successors operated, however, legitimized challenges, whether through regular elections, separated authorities within government, or freedoms to criticize from outside it. So too did the systems of most postwar allies. How, then, did these unruly democracies, navigating these crosscurrents, maintain a steadier course toward common Cold War objectives than the disciplined autocracy that was now their principal rival?

One answer, Sergey Radchenko suggests, is that the Soviet Union wasn't really very disciplined, for by precluding term limits, it ensured erraticism in its leadership. The regime drifted from an initial confidence in the historically determined triumph of the international proletariat, through awkward attempts to speed the process by supporting national liberation movements, through costly arms and space races, through a quest for equal treatment in crises as they arose, to at last a forlorn search, under a zombie-like Brezhnev, for a "recognition of [Soviet] greatness by those greater still."[44] The USSR forgot, in the end, its own revolutionary beginnings.

A more general problem for authoritarians is that, while they seek uniformity, the world normally doesn't. Topographies, climates, cultures and faiths eventually evolve, but at rates far slower than dictators find desirable. Bulldozed ecologies tend to grow back, in ways disconcerting to the machine's operators. Democracies suffer less from this problem because they're more accustomed to disruptions. These most of the time build resilience: useful training for returning to compass headings after great storms.

---

44. Sergey Radchenko, "Strategies of Détente and Competition: Brezhnev and Moscow's Cold War," Chapter 33 of this volume.

Of which there have been, for the democracies, many. But despite distractions of "limited" wars, risks of technological overkill, and domestic coincidences of complacencies and injustices, Americans and their allies did manage repeated returns, during the Cold War, to the grand strategy of containment: the path between extremes of war and appeasement that would in time persuade adversaries to contain themselves, allowing *their* interests to change their most fundamental policies.[45]

One consequence was a *selective* convergence among authoritarians and democracies against dangers threatening both, one of which was great war itself. Most such conflicts in the past had had lovers, whether for reasons of conquest, redemption, revolution, vengeance, or character fortification. By the beginning of the twentieth century, nations not yet bloodied had come to be thought of by others, and even at times by themselves, as dangerously effete. The two world wars obliterated most of these illusions, and none survived, with significant consequence, into the Cold War.

Perhaps that was because World War II flattened so much more than wars fought previously. Perhaps bipolarity—the power distribution that emerged from the rubble—was more manageable than the multipolarities preceding it. Perhaps postwar leaders were more patient than their predecessors; none appear to have been driven by timetables. But surely the principal reason for the decline in bellicosity was the quantum jump in killing capacity demonstrated, with graphic specificity, over Hiroshima and Nagasaki in August 1945. Americans were looking for reasons *not* to use their atomic bombs ever again *before* their exclusive possession of them ended with the first Soviet test of such a device in 1949.[46]

Survival in the nuclear age came to depend less, then, on the balancing of grammar with logic than on their strict separation. Nuclear *doctrine* required making threats to use such weapons as convincing as possible: that seemed to be the only way to accomplish the offshore balancing of an onshore hegemon. But as Frank Gavin has shown, nuclear *practice* was to avoid any use of such

45. I've traced this process in *Strategies of Containment: A Critical Appraisal of American National Security Policy During the Cold War*, Revised and Expanded Edition (New York, NY: Oxford University Press, 2005).

46. I've made these points in further detail in John Lewis Gaddis, *The Long Peace: Inquiries into the History of the Cold War* (New York, NY: Oxford University Press, 1986), especially 106–15 and 216–32. See also, for further discussion, John Lewis Gaddis, Philip H. Gordon, Ernest R. May, and Jonathan Rosenberg, eds., *Cold War Statesmen Confront the Bomb: Nuclear Diplomacy since 1945* (New York, NY: Oxford University Press, 1999).

weapons in all situations, for no one knew how to use them without destroying what was to be saved and probably much else.[47] Technology inhibited violence instead of inciting it.

Something similar happened when the Americans and Soviets placed cameras on the satellites launched by rockets built to carry nuclear warheads. The reconnaissance revolution transformed transparency from a condition to be feared into one to be welcomed, even at times sought. Opacity, where still possible, risked appearing to be evasion. That made state-based surprise attacks close to impossible, while providing the reassurances needed for such arms control agreements as the Cold War superpowers, despite their continuing rivalry, were able to attain.

Situational surprises did still happen during the Cold War, but these arose more often from small power manipulations of superpowers than the other way around. The Korean War of 1950–53, the Taiwan Strait crises of 1954–55 and 1958, the Suez crisis of 1956, the Berlin crises of 1958–59 and 1961, the Cuban missile crisis of 1962, the Vietnam War of 1965–75, the Arab-Israeli wars of 1967 and 1973, the Angolan and Ethiopian crises of the late 1970s, and the Soviet Union's war in Afghanistan from 1979–88, all began—as had the Peloponnesian War—when underlings sucked in overlords: when tails, so to speak, wagged dogs.[48]

The greatest surprise of the Cold War, however, came with the way it ended. For the second time in the twentieth century, a great power chose *not* to use the power available to it; but beyond that, the comparison between the United States of 1919–20 and the Soviet Union of 1989–91 breaks down. For the Americans, in effect, *banked* their strength for future use, at times and under conditions they themselves would determine. The USSR had no choice but to end its existence once all of the states composing it seceded from it, not least Russia itself. That set off the greatest realignment of world politics since 1945, with the United States, for the moment, the only superpower left: a position from which it too would eventually recede, having failed to learn how to sustain preponderance in the absence of an adversary against whom to deploy it.

47. Francis J. Gavin, "The Elusive Nature of Nuclear Strategy," draft, Chapter 28 of this volume, 1–3; also, his *Nuclear Statecraft: History and Strategy in. the Atomic Age* (Ithaca NY: Cornell University Press, 2012).

48. See, on this point, Hal Brands and John Lewis Gaddis, "The New Cold War: America, China, and the Echoes of History," *Foreign Affairs* 100 (November/December 2021), 10–21.

VIII

"De quoi s'agit-il?" Marshal Ferdinand Foch used to ask his subordinates in World War I: *"What is it all about?"* That subtle student of geopolitics Bernard Brodie, too young to have contributed to the first *Makers* edition but no longer living when the second appeared, regarded Foch's question as "the single most important idea in all strategy."[49] If that's right, then it's a fitting final standard for evaluating successes and accounting for failures within that realm. For if you can't say where you're going, or what you're planning to do when you get there, then you're apt, whether as an individual or as the greatest of great powers, to lose your way.

During the Cold War, the United States sought to *balance* power in the international system, not to impose uniformity on it. The global scope of that strategy went well beyond the nineteenth-century continentalism of John Quincy Adams, but not beyond his insistence on keeping objectives within capabilities, even if that meant coexisting with monsters. To have searched for and sought to destroy such beasts, Adams argued in 1821, would have made Americans themselves monstrous in the eyes of the rest of the world. The admonition still made sense in 1949 when George F. Kennan, the principal architect of containment, resurrected it.[50] He would continue to quote it for the rest of his life.

For the Soviet Union was containment's useful monster. Whatever you thought of the United States, the behavior of Kremlin leaders from Stalin through Brezhnev and his immediate successors conveyed the impression of something worse. Georgi Arbatov, a top adviser to Mikhail Gorbachev, wasn't joking when he began warning American audiences in the late-1980s of his new boss's determination "to deprive you of an enemy." That would leave the United States "an outcast in the international community."[51]

Things never got that bad, but the prospect of an enemy-free world did worry the George H. W. Bush administration sufficiently for it to disavow a leaked 1992 document that proposed seeking such an objective.[52] Bush's successor, Bill Clinton, in turn, dealt with the possibility by moving in two directions at once. He sought, on the one hand, to forge a close personal relationship with

---

49. Brodie, *War and Politics*, 1.

50. Gaddis, *George F. Kennan*, 366.

51. Georgi Arbatov letter to the *New York Times*, December 8, 1987; Jean Davidson, "UCI Scientists Told Moscow's Aim is to Deprive U.S. of Foe," *Los Angeles Times*, December 12, 1988. Arbatov was the long-time head of the Moscow-based Institute for the Study of the USA and Canada.

52. See Eric Edelman, "The Strange Career of the 1992 Defense Planning Guidance," in *In Uncertain Times: American Foreign Policy after the Berlin Wall and 9/11*, Melvyn P. Leffler and Jeffrey W. Legro, eds. (Ithaca, NY: Cornell University Press, 2011), 63–77.

his boozy Russian counterpart Boris Yeltsin.[53] But, on the other, he also began the process of NATO expansion, apparently on the assumption that because the alliance had secured Europe against the Soviet Union, Russians would not object to its increasing proximity. After unsuccessful attempts to "bumper sticker" these initiatives as strategies of "engagement" and "enlargement," Clinton fell back upon the simpler claim that the United States was now the "indispensable" nation. "We stand tall and we see further than other countries into the future," Secretary of State Madeleine Albright explained in 1998, "and we see danger here to all of us."[54]

Dangers there were indeed, but "indispensability" failed to detect them. The September 11, 2001, attacks looked likely at first to force as great a departure from past strategies as had those of December 7, 1941. But the Roosevelt administration, knowing its enemies, decided within days what its responses would be and stuck to them. George W. Bush and his successors, conversely, indulged in mission meandering, an occupational hazard of indispensability. They went from ejecting the Taliban—the terrorists' host—from Afghanistan, to an invasion of Iraq in search of weapons of mass destruction that weren't there, to an effort to build democracy in that country without complete military control over it, to trying with no greater success to implant democracy in Afghanistan (again without military control), to seeking ultimately the Taliban's help in facilitating as abrupt an American exit from that country as the Americans had arranged for them two decades earlier. Foch might well have asked: "What was *that* all about?"

Meanwhile, Americans were tearing themselves apart. Domestic divisions had never been absent from the nation's history, but the early twentieth-century experiences of war, depression, and war again had mitigated them: for better or for worse, everyone seemed to be in the same boat. The 1960s, however, began a slow but steady unraveling of this cohesion, motivated only in part by global developments. This had progressed, by the second decade of the twenty-first century, to the point of speculation about a new civil war.[55] Rivals abroad—if not quite yet monsters—began to take note.

53. Talbott, *The Russia Hand*, pp. 7–10.

54. Madeleine Albright, interview by Matt Lauer, *The Today Show*, NBC-TV, February 19, 1998, https://1997-2001.state.gov/statements/1998/980219a.html. See also Strobe Talbott, *The Russia Hand: A Memoir of Presidential Diplomacy* (New York, NY: Random House, 2002), 130–34.

55. For a review of this literature, see Edward Luce, "Is America Heading For Civil War?," *Financial Times*, May 31, 2022. See also, for the historical and sociological background, Robert D. Putnam, *The Upswing: How America Came Together a Century Ago and How We Can Do It Again* (New York, NY: Simon & Schuster, 2020).

One was China, whose emergence from a century of humiliation the United States had facilitated, first as a counterweight to the Soviet Union, but then increasingly with the expectation that the internal embrace of market capitalism, together with the rising external tide of "globalization," would ease the "new" China into the post–Cold War liberal world order. What China really was showing, however, was that entrepreneurial enterprise could coexist with authoritarian rule, and that the ruling authoritarian, Xi Jinping, was less interested in liberalism than in shifting the international system to China's advantage. "Western" models, it turned out, didn't apply. China remained, as so often before in its long history, its own exemplar.

The other rival was Russia, which under the steely leadership of Vladimir Putin had emerged from its decade of humiliation under Yeltsin. Americans and their allies again misjudged what was happening. There were no modern models for a mystical messianic imperialism more characteristic of tsars than of commissars. That became clear on February 24, 2022, when Putin took it upon himself to correct Comrade Lenin's "mistake" of having acknowledged, within the new Union of Soviet Socialist Republics, a Ukrainian identity. The instrument was an unprovoked invasion, the first in Europe since Hitler launched his against the Soviet Union, then including Ukraine, eighty-one years earlier. That made Putin's monster status unimpeachable.

IX

The third decade of the twenty-first century has opened, then, with the strong evidence that the post–Cold War era has ended and that a new one—not yet named or defined—has begun. It seems likely to mean, for the United States, fewer friends and no shortage of enemies. Which may not be an entirely bad thing.

For strategies, in the absence of adversaries, become self-referential. They see systems as revolving around themselves, much as earlier astronomers believed that the sun revolved around the earth. The possibility of being part of something larger eludes them, and that can produce negligence, or arrogance, or both. Grammars in such systems lose their logic—the common sense that collisions with reality impose. Means no longer connect with ends.

The presence of adversaries, to be sure, poses its own dangers, and these require careful management. But that's what strategy is supposed to provide. It's the *balancing* of grammar with logic in worlds as they are, not in worlds hoped for. Aspirations always exceed capabilities: that asymmetry itself is the monster. But as a center of gravity and a safeguard against drift, it's a useful one.

INDEX

Names and Subjects

Chronological List of the More Important
Wars and Campaigns